This eighth and final volume of the UNESCO
General History of Africa examines the period
from 1935 to the present day. As liberation from
colonial rule progresses, the political, economic
and cultural dimensions of the continent are
analysed.

For Africa, 1935 marked the beginning of the
Second World War, with Mussolini's invasion of
Ethiopia. International conflict dominates the first
section of this volume, which describes crises in
the Horn and North Africa, and other regions
under the domination of the European powers.
The next three sections cover the ensuing Africa-
wide struggles for political sovereignty, from
1945 to independence; underdevelopment and
the fight for economic independence; and socio-
political change since independence, looking at
nation-building and changing political structures
and values. Section five deals with socio-cultural
change since 1935, from religion to literature,
language to philosophy, science and education.
The last two sections address the development of
pan-Africanism and the role of independent
Africa in world affairs. Acknowledging the
original irony that it was the imposition of
European imperialism that awakened African
consciousness, the volume points up the vital
and growing interrelation of Africa and the rest of
the globe.

The volume is illustrated with black and white
photographs, maps and figures. The text is fully
annotated and there is an extensive bibliography.

GENERAL HISTORY OF AFRICA · VIII

Africa since 1935

UNESCO General History of Africa

UNESCO would like to express its gratitude to the former Empress of Iran, to the Holy See and in particular to the Government of the Libyan Arab Jamahiriya for their generous financial contributions to the publication of the *General History of Africa*.

UNESCO International Scientific Committee for the Drafting of a General History of Africa

GENERAL HISTORY OF AFRICA · VIII

Africa since 1935

EDITOR ALI A. MAZRUI
ASSISTANT EDITOR C. WONDJI

HEINEMANN·CALIFORNIA·UNESCO

First published in 1993 by the
United Nations Educational, Scientific
and Cultural Organization,
7 Place de Fontenoy, 75700 Paris

and

Heinemann Educational
a division of Heinemann Publishers (Oxford) Ltd
Halley Court, Jordan Hill, Oxford OX2 8EJ
PMB 5205, Ibadan PO Box 54314, Nairobi
PO Box 10103, Village Post Office, Gaborone
FLORENCE   PRAGUE   MADRID
PARIS   ATHENS   BOLOGNA   MELBOURNE
SYDNEY   AUCKLAND   SINGAPORE   JOHANNESBURG
TOKYO   PORTSMOUTH NH (USA)   CHICAGO   SAO PAULO

First published 1993
in the United States of America by the
University of California Press
2120 Berkeley Way, Berkeley
California 94720, United States of America

© UNESCO 1993

Maps drawn by John Gilkes
Heinemann Educational   ISBN 0435 948148

UNESCO   ISBN 92–3–102758–1

University of California Press ISBN 0–520 03920–3
                             LCN 78–57321

Filmset in 11pt Monophoto Ehrhardt by
Selwood Systems, Midsomer Norton
Printed in Great Britain by
Richard Clay Ltd, Bungay, Suffolk

93 94 95 10 9 8 7 6 5 4 3 2 1

Contents

Key for maps

BAULE	Ethnic groups
ZAMBIA	States
FEZZĀN	Regions
S A H A R A	Natural regions
—.—.—.	International boundaries
●	Capital cities
Ubangui	Rivers

Additional information and keys are given on individual maps.

List of figures

List of plates

Acknowledgements for plates

© AFP Photo, Paris, 2.3, 3.1, 6.1, 7.4, 7.6, 20.7, 20.8, 24.2, 26.1, 27.2
© Agence Nationale de la photographie de presse et d'information, Algiers, 5.2
© al-Ahram, Cairo, 28.3
© Almasy, Paris, 12.1, 22.2
© APA, Photo by Ph. Khedoud, Paris, 13.2 (bottom)
© Archives CRDA, Paris, 7.3
© Archives Documentation française, Paris, photo by OFIC, 2.2
Archives of the Ecumenical Association of African Theologians, 17.1
© Associated Press, London, 29.1 (top left)
© Atelier R. Minnaert, Belgium, 30.3
© Camera Press, London, 4.2, 9.2, 10.5, 22.3 (top)
© CICIBA, Libreville, Gabon, 20.5
© Collection Musée de l'Homme, Paris, 20.9 (left), from the collection of the
     Musée d'ethnographie du Trocadéro in the 1920s
© College of Art, Ghana, photo by G. Owusu, 20.4 (bottom)
Editions du Seuil, Paris, 16.1
Embassy of the Federal Republic of Nigeria, Paris, 7.1
© Foundation Books Ltd, Nairobi, 16.4
© FRELIMO, 10.3
© Gamma, Photo by J. P. Bonnotte, Paris, 28.4
© Gamma, Photo by P. Giraud, Paris, 19.2 (top left)
© Gaumont Cinémathèque, Paris, 12.2
Gramma, Cuba, 28.2
© HOA QUI, Photo by P. Cassard, Paris, 17.2
© HOA QUI, Photo by M. Huet, Paris, 20.1
© Hulton-Deutsch Collection, London, 10.2, 10.4, 25.1, 25.3 (bottom left and
     bottom right), 27.3
© IDAF, London, 25.3 (top right)
© IMAPRESS, Paris, 16.5
© IMAPRESS, Photo by Kol al-Arab, Paris, 19.4 (top right)
Information Services Department, Government of Ghana, 5.3
© Keystone, Paris, 2.1, 6.2, 6.3, 24.1, 25.3 (top left), 30.2 (right)
League of Nations, Musée du Palais des Nations, Geneva, photo by L. Bianco,
     Geneva, 1.1
© Le Nouvel Afrique–Asie, Paris, 7.5, 16.3
Photo by J. L. Losi, Paris, 20.4 (top)
Photo by Makemba, ENFOTO Agency, Angola, 27.4
© Magnum, Paris, 1.2
© Magnum, Photo by Abbas, Paris, 28.1
© Magnum, Photo by M. Riboud, Paris, 16.2
© Magnum, Photo by S. Salgado Jr, Paris, 26.3
Photo by L. Mbuyamba, Libreville, Gabon, 26.2

Maison des Cultures du Monde, Paris, 20.6

© Moorland–Spingarn Research Center, Howard University, 23.1 (top right, bottom left and bottom right), 23.2

Photo by J. K. Muiruri, Nairobi, 13.2 (centre)

© Musée Royal de l'Afrique centrale, Tervuren, 8.1, 8.2

© Newslink Africa, London, 5.1, 9.3, 14.2 (top), 22.3 (bottom), 25.2

M. Ogundipe-Leslie, 19.5

Organization of African Unity, Addis Ababa, front cover

© Photothèque du Musée de l'Homme, Paris, 19.1

© Popperfoto, London, 6.4

Revue congolaise illustrée, 1959, No. 3, March, p. 25, 17.3

Photo by J. Scott, Paris, 21.1

L. S. Senghor, 19.2 (above right)

© SIPA Press, Paris, 11.1 (photo by ABC), 30.2 (left)

© SIPA Press, Photo by L. Chamussy, Paris, 19.6

© SIPA Press, Photo by Guner, Paris, 19.3

© SPADEM 1993, Paris, 20.9 (right), source: Musée de Grenoble, France

© Sygma, Photo by J. Langevin, Paris, 15.2

Photo by W. Tochtermann, 13.2 (top)

© Topham, London, 4.1, 7.2, 9.1, 9.4, 10.1, 13.1, 14.1, 14.2 (bottom), 22.1, 23.1 (top left), 23.3, 24.3

© UNESCO, Paris, 20.2 and 20.3 (photos by P. Migeat), 30.4 (MAB/PNUE), 30.5 (MAB)

© UNESCO, Photo by M. Claude, 29.2

© United Nations, 10.6 (UN Photo 146 221/T. Zagozdinski), 29.1 (top right, bottom left and bottom right), 29.3 (UN Photo 157267/J. Isaac), 30.1 (left and right, © UN, Photo by T. Chen)

© World Bank, Washington, DC, 11.2

© Xinhua News Agency, Beijing, 27.1

Preface

AMADOU-MAHTAR M'BOW

Director-General of UNESCO (1974–87)

For a long time, all kinds of myths and prejudices concealed the true history of Africa from the world at large. African societies were looked upon as societies that could have no history. In spite of important work done by such pioneers as Leo Frobenius, Maurice Delafosse and Arturo Labriola, as early as the first decades of this century, a great many non-African experts could not rid themselves of certain preconceptions and argued that the lack of written sources and documents made it impossible to engage in any scientific study of such societies.

Although the *Iliad* and *Odyssey* were rightly regarded as essential sources for the history of ancient Greece, African oral tradition, the collective memory of peoples which holds the thread of many events marking their lives, was rejected as worthless. In writing the history of a large part of Africa, the only sources used were from outside the continent, and the final product gave a picture not so much of the paths actually taken by the African peoples as of those that the authors thought they must have taken. Since the European Middle Ages were often used as a yardstick, modes of production, social relations and political institutions were visualized only by reference to the European past.

In fact, there was a refusal to see Africans as the creators of original cultures which flowered and survived over the centuries in patterns of their own making and which historians are unable to grasp unless they forgo their prejudices and rethink their approach.

Furthermore, the continent of Africa was hardly ever looked upon as a historical entity. On the contrary, emphasis was laid on everything likely to lend credence to the idea that a split had existed, from time immemorial, between a 'white Africa' and a 'black Africa', each unaware of the other's existence. The Sahara was often presented as an impenetrable space preventing any intermingling of ethnic groups and peoples or any exchange of goods, beliefs, customs and ideas between the societies that had grown up on either side of the desert. Hermetic frontiers were drawn between the civilizations and Ancient Egypt and Nubia and those of the peoples south of the Sahara.

It is true that the history of Africa north of the Sahara has been more closely linked with that of the Mediterranean basin than has the history of sub-Saharan Africa, but it is now widely recognized that the various civilizations of the African continent, for all their differing languages and cultures, represent, to a greater or lesser degree, the historial offshoots of a set of peoples and societies united by bonds centuries old.

Another phenomenon which did great disservice to the objective study of the African past was the appearance, with the slave trade and colonization, of racial stereotypes which bred contempt and lack of understanding and became so deep-rooted that they distorted even the basic concepts of historiography. From the time when the notions of 'white' and 'black' were used as generic labels by the colonialists, who were regarded as superior, the colonized Africans had to struggle against both economic and psychological enslavement. Africans were identifiable by the colour of their skin, they had become a kind of merchandise, they were earmarked for hard labour and eventually, in the minds of those dominating them, they came to symbolize an imaginary and allegedly inferior *Negro* race. This pattern of spurious identification relegated the history of the African peoples in many minds to the rank of ethno-history, in which appreciation of the historical and cultural facts was bound to be warped.

The situation has changed significantly since the end of the Second World War and in particular since the African countries became independent and began to take an active part in the life of the international community and in the mutual exchanges that are its *raison d'être*. An increasing number of historians has endeavoured to tackle the study of Africa with a more rigorous, objective and open-minded outlook by using – with all due precautions – actual African sources. In exercising their right to take the historical initiative, Africans themselves have felt a deep-seated need to re-establish the historical authenticity of their societies on solid foundations.

In this context, the importance of the eight-volume *General History of Africa*, which UNESCO is publishing, speaks for itself.

The experts from many countries working on this project began by laying down the theoretical and methodological basis for the *History*. They have been at pains to call in question the over-simplifications arising from a linear and restrictive conception of world history and to re-establish the true facts wherever necessary and possible. They have endeavoured to highlight the historical data that give a clearer picture of the evolution of the different peoples of Africa in their specific socio-cultural setting.

To tackle this huge task, made all the more complex and difficult by the vast range of sources and the fact that documents were widely scattered, UNESCO has had to proceed by stages. The first stage, from 1965 to 1969, was devoted to gathering documentation and planning the work. Operational assignments were conducted in the field and included campaigns to collect oral traditions, the creation of regional documentation centres for oral traditions, the collection of unpublished manuscripts in Arabic and Ajami (African languages written in Arabic script), the compilation of archival inventories and the preparation of a *Guide to the Sources of the History of Africa*, culled from the archives and libraries of the countries of Europe and later published in eleven volumes. In addition, meetings were organized to enable experts from Africa and other continents to discuss questions of methodology and lay down the broad lines for the project after careful examination of the available sources.

The second stage, which lasted from 1969 to 1971, was devoted to shaping the *History* and linking its different parts. The purpose of the international meetings of experts held in Paris in 1969 and Addis Ababa in 1970 was to study and define the problems involved in drafting and publishing the *History*; presentation in eight volumes, the principal edition in English, French and Arabic, translation into African languages such as Kiswahili, Hausa, Fulani, Yoruba or Lingala, prospective versions in German, Russian, Portuguese, Spanish and Chinese, as well as abridged editions designed for a wide African and international public.[1]

The third stage has involved actual drafting and publication. This began with the appointment of the 39-member International Scientific Committee, two-thirds African and one-third non-African, which assumes intellectual responsibility for the *History*.

The method used is interdisciplinary and is based on a multi-faceted approach and a wide variety of sources. The first among these is archaeology, which holds many of the keys to the history of African cultures and civilizations. Thanks to archaeology, it is now acknowledged that Africa was very probably the cradle of mankind and the scene – in the neolithic period – of one of the first technological revolutions in history. Archaeology has also shown that Egypt was the setting for one of the most brilliant ancient civilizations of the world. But another very important source is oral tradition, which, after being long despised, has now emerged as an invaluable instrument for discovering the history of Africa, making it possible to follow the movements of its different peoples in both space and time, to understand the African vision of the world from the inside and to grasp the original features of the values on which the cultures and institutions of the continent are based.

We are indebted to the International Scientific Committee in charge of this *General History of Africa*, and to its Rapporteur and the editors and authors of the various volumes and chapters, for having shed a new light on the African past in its authentic and all-encompassing form and

---

1. Volumes I and II have been published in Arabic, Spanish, Korean, Portuguese, Chinese and Italian; Volume IV and Volume VII in Arabic, Spanish and Portuguese. Volume I has been published in Kiswahili and Hausa and Volume II in Hausa.

for having avoided any dogmatism in the study of essential issues. Among these issues we might cite: the slave trade, that 'endlessly bleeding wound', which was responsible for one of the cruellest mass deportations in the history of mankind, which sapped the African continent of its life-blood while contributing significantly to the economic and commercial expansion of Europe; colonization, with all the effects it had on population, economics, psychology and culture; relations between Africa south of the Sahara and the Arab world; and, finally, the process of decolonization and nation-building which mobilized the intelligence and passion of people still alive and sometimes still active today. All these issues have been broached with a concern for honesty and rigour which is not the least of the *History*'s merits. By taking stock of our knowledge of Africa, putting forward a variety of viewpoints on African cultures and offering a new reading of history, the *History* has the signal advantage of showing up the light and shade and of openly portraying the differences of opinion that may exist between scholars.

By demonstrating the inadequacy of the methodological approaches which have long been used in research on Africa, this *History* calls for a new and careful study of the twofold problem areas of historiography and cultural identity, which are united by links of reciprocity. Like any historical work of value, the *History* paves the way for a great deal of further research on a variety of topics.

It is for this reason that the International Scientific Committee, in close collaboration with UNESCO, decided to embark on additional studies in an attempt to go deeper into a number of issues which will permit a clearer understanding of certain aspects of the African past. The findings being published in the series 'UNESCO Studies and Documents – General History of Africa'[2] will prove a useful supplement to the *History*, as will the works planned on aspects of national or subregional history.

The *General History* sheds light both on the historical unity of Africa and also its relations with the other continents, particularly the Americas and the Caribbean. For a long time, the creative manifestations of the descendants of Africans in the Americas were lumped together by some historians as a heterogeneous collection of *Africanisms*. Needless to say, this is not the attitude of the authors of the *History*, in which the resistance of the slaves shipped to America, the constant and massive participation of the descendants of Africans in the struggles for the initial independence

---

2. The following 11 volumes have already been published in this series: *The peopling of ancient Egypt and the deciphering of Meroitic script; The African slave trade from the fifteenth to the nineteenth century; Historical relations across the Indian Ocean; The historiography of Southern Africa; The decolonization of Africa: Southern Africa and the Horn of Africa; African ethnonyms and toponyms; Historical and socio-cultural relations between black Africa and the Arab world from 1935 to the present; The methodology of contemporary African History; The Educational Process and Historiography in Africa; Africa and the Second World War; Libya Antiqua.*

of America and in national liberation movements, are rightly perceived for what they were: vigorous assertions of identity, which helped forge the universal concept of mankind. Although the phenomenon may vary in different places, it is now quite clear that ways of feeling, thinking, dreaming and acting in certain nations of the western hemisphere have been marked by their African heritage. The cultural inheritance of Africa is visible everywhere, from the southern United States to northern Brazil, across the Caribbean and on the Pacific seaboard. In certain places it even underpins the cultural identity of some of the most important elements of the population.

The *History* also clearly brings out Africa's relations with southern Asia across the Indian Ocean and the African contributions to other civilizations through mutual exchanges.

I am convinced that the efforts of the peoples of Africa to conquer or strengthen their independence, secure their development and assert their cultural characteristics, must be rooted in historical awareness renewed, keenly felt and taken up by each succeeding generation.

My own background, the experience I gained as a teacher and as chairman, from the early days of independence, of the first commission set up to reform history and geography curricula in some of the countries of West and Central Africa, taught me how necessary it was for the education of young people and for the information of the public at large to have a history book produced by scholars with inside knowledge of the problems and hopes of Africa and with the ability to apprehend the continent in its entirety.

For all these reasons, UNESCO's goal will be to ensure that this *General History of Africa* is widely disseminated in a large number of languages and is used as a basis for producing children's books, school textbooks and radio and television programmes. Young people, whether schoolchildren or students, and adults in Africa and elsewhere will thus be able to form a truer picture of the African continent's past and the factors that explain it, as well as a fairer understanding of its cultural heritage and its contribution to the general progress of mankind. The *History* should thus contribute to improved international co-operation and stronger solidarity among peoples in their aspirations to justice, progress and peace. This is, at least, my most cherished hope.

It remains for me to express my deep gratitude to the members of the International Scientific Committee, the Rapporteur, the different volume editors, the authors and all those who have collaborated in this tremendous undertaking. The work they have accomplished and the contribution they have made plainly go to show how people from different backgrounds but all imbued with the same spirit of goodwill and enthusiasm in the service of universal truth can, within the international framework provided by UNESCO, bring to fruition a project of considerable scientific and cultural import. My thanks also go to the organizations and governments whose generosity has made it possible for UNESCO to publish this *History* in different languages and thus ensure that it will have the worldwide impact it deserves and thereby serve the international community as a whole.

Description of the project

Bethwell A. OGOT*

President, International Scientific Committee
for the Drafting of a General History of Africa (1978–83)

The General Conference of UNESCO at its sixteenth Session instructed the Director-General to undertake the drafting of a *General History of Africa*. The enormous task of implementing the project was entrusted to an International Scientific Committee which was established by the Executive Board in 1970. This Committee, under the Statutes adopted by the Executive Board of UNESCO in 1971, is composed of 39 members (two-thirds of whom are African and one-third non-African) serving in their personal capacity and appointed by the Director-General of UNESCO for the duration of the Committee's mandate.

The first task of the Committee was to define the principal characteristics of the work. These were defined at the first session of the Committee as follows:

(a) Although aiming at the highest possible scientific level, the history does not seek to be exhaustive and is a work of synthesis avoiding dogmatism. In many respects, it is a statement of problems showing the present state of knowledge and the main trends in research, and it does not hesitate to show divergencies of views where these exist. In this way, it prepares the ground for future work.

(b) Africa is considered in this work as a totality. The aim is to show the historical relationships between the various parts of the continent, too frequently subdivided in works published to date. Africa's historical connections with the other continents receive due attention, these connections being analysed in terms of mutual exchanges and multilateral influences, bringing out, in its appropriate light, Africa's contribution to the history of mankind.

(c) *The General History of Africa* is, in particular, a history of ideas and civilizations, societies and institutions. It is based on a wide variety of sources, including oral tradition and art forms.

* During the Sixth Plenary Session of the International Scientific Committee for the Drafting of a General History of Africa (Brazzaville, 1983), an election of the new Bureau was held and Professor Ogot was replaced by Professor Albert Adu Boahen.

(d) The *History* is viewed essentially from the inside. Although a scholarly work, it is also, in large measure, a faithful reflection of the way in which African authors view their own civilization. While prepared in an international framework and drawing to the full on the present stock of scientific knowledge, it should also be a vitally important element in the recognition of the African heritage and should bring out the factors making for unity in the continent. This effort to view things from within is the novel feature of the project and should, in addition to its scientific quality, give it great topical significance. By showing the true face of Africa, the *History* could, in an era absorbed in economic and technical struggles, offer a particular conception of human values.

The Committee has decided to present the work covering over three million years of African history in eight volumes, each containing about eight hundred pages of text with illustrations, photographs, maps and line drawings.

A chief editor, assisted if necessary by one or two assistant editors, is responsible for the preparation of each volume. The editors are elected by the Committee either from among its members or from outside by a two-thirds majority. They are responsible for preparing the volumes in accordance with the decisions and plans adopted by the Committee. On scientific matters, they are accountable to the Committee or, between two sessions of the Committee, to its Bureau for the contents of the volumes, the final version of the texts, the illustrations and, in general, for all scientific and technical aspects of the *History*. The Bureau ultimately approves the final manuscript. When it considers the manuscript ready for publication, it transmits it to the Director-General of UNESCO. Thus the Committee, or the Bureau between committee sessions, remains fully in charge of the project.

Each volume consists of some thirty chapters. Each chapter is the work of a principal author assisted, if necessary, by one or two collaborators. The authors are selected by the Committee on the basis of their *curricula vitae*. Preference is given to African authors, provided they have requisite qualifications. Special effort is also made to ensure, as far as possible, that all regions of the continent, as well as other regions having historical or cultural ties with Africa, are equitably represented among the authors.

When the editor of a volume has approved texts of chapters, they are then sent to all members of the Committee for criticism. In addition, the text of the volume editor is submitted for examination to a Reading Committee, set up within the International Scientific Committee on the basis of the members' fields of competence. The Reading Committee analyses the chapters from the standpoint of both substance and form. The Bureau then gives final approval to the manuscripts.

Such a seemingly long and involved procedure has proved necessary, since it provides the best possible guarantee of the scientific objectivity of the *General History of Africa*. There have, in fact, been instances when the Bureau has rejected manuscripts or insisted on major revisions or even reassigned the drafting of a chapter to another author. Occasionally, specialists in a particular period of history or in a particular question are consulted to put the finishing touches to a volume.

The work will be published first in a hard-cover edition in English, French and Arabic, and later in paperback editions in the same languages. An abridged version in English and French will serve as a basis for translation into African languages. The Committee has chosen Kiswahili and Hausa as the first African languages into which the work will be translated.

Also, every effort will be made to ensure publication of the *General History of Africa* in other languages of wide international currency such as Chinese, Portuguese, Russian, German, Italian, Spanish, Japanese, etc.

It is thus evident that this is a gigantic task which constitutes an immense challenge to African historians and to the scholarly community at large, as well as to UNESCO under whose auspices the work is being done. For the writing of a continental history of Africa, covering the last three million years, using the highest canons of scholarship and involving, as it must do, scholars drawn from diverse countries, cultures, ideologies and historical traditions, is surely a complex undertaking. It constitutes a continental, international and interdisciplinary project of great proportions.

In conclusion, I would like to underline the significance of this work for Africa and for the world. At a time when the peoples of Africa are striving towards unity and greater co-operation in shaping their individual destinies, a proper understanding of Africa's past, with an awareness of common ties among Africans and between Africa and other continents, should not only be a major contribution towards mutual understanding among the people of the earth, but also a source of knowledge of a cultural heritage that belongs to all mankind.

NOTE TO THE READER

Work on this volume was completed in 1989. For this reason, the significant changes which have taken place in the world since that date are not reflected in the text.

Introduction

Ali A. MAZRUI

For analytical purposes, this volume has divided Africa's history into cultural, economic and political domains. Our sense of *'cultural'* is not the narrow one of artistic experience but rather the wider one of values and traditions in society. We define the *economic* domain in terms of African production of goods and their distribution, as well as in terms of patterns of African consumption, and the pertinent modes of exchange.[1] We define Africa's *political* experience in relation to issues of power and control, and to the rules of participation in society.

Culturally, we have chapters which range from religion to literature. In *economics*, our concerns in this volume range from rural water-supply to the search for a new international economic order. Our *political* preoccupations include liberation struggles in Southern Africa, social revolutions in countries like Rwanda and Ethiopia, nation-building in Tanzania and political values in the Maghreb.

Why does our time span in this volume begin in 1935? For China the Second World War did not begin with Germany's invasion of Poland in 1939 but with Japan's invasion of China in 1937. Similarly, for Africa, the Second World War did not start in 1939 but began with Mussolini's invasion of Ethiopia in October 1935. We have devoted a whole section of the volume to this decade of international conflict (1935–45). We have also touched on the Second World War in subsequent chapters in the volume. We shall return to this theme of global conflict in relation to the Great Depression later in this Introduction.

Values, production and power

In the cultural field, this period of African history has witnessed an important phase in the Africanization of the imported religions of Christianity and Islam. Independent Christian churches were emerging with greater self-confidence, especially in Central and Southern Africa. And in places like Senegal, Islam was undergoing deeper Africanization under

---

1. For some of the economic debates, see World Bank, 1989a and United Nations Economic Commission for Africa, 1989.

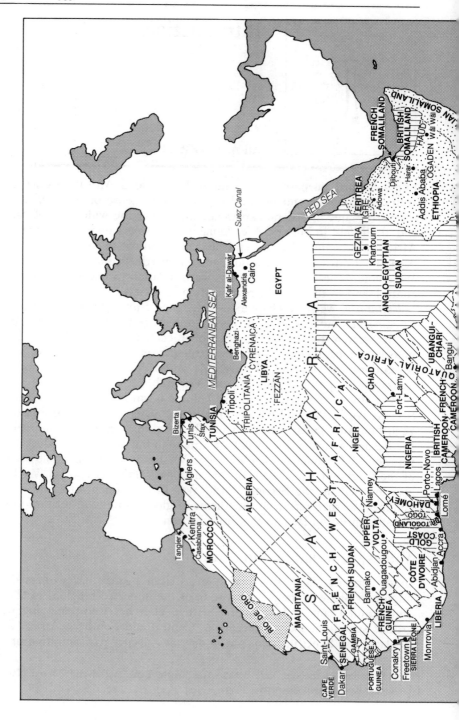

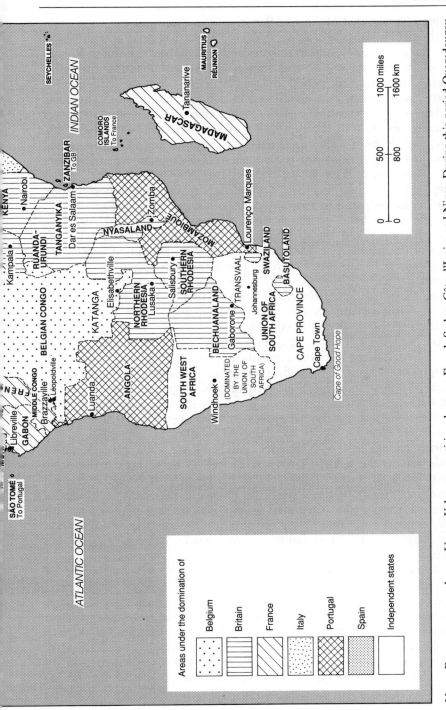

NOTE: Between 1932 and 1947 Upper Volta was partitioned among French Sudan, Côte d'Ivoire and Niger. During this period Ouagadougou was not the capital city.

FIG. 1.1 The political map of Africa in 1935 (*Source: adapted from J. Bartholomew, The Citizen's Atlas of the World, Bartholomew and Son Ltd, Edinburgh, 1935, pp. 122–3*)

3

local legacies like that of Amadu Bamba of the Mourides.

In the field of language, as we shall see, Africa has been up against the role of the imported European tongues and up against the Latin or Roman alphabet in relation to the codification of national tongues. Curiously enough, Africa in this period did not witness the same militancy in linguistic nationalism as it manifested in political nationalism. There has been less African resentment of the paramountcy of European languages than there has been of the supremacy of European political sovereignty. In fact, apart from Ethiopia, Somalia, Tanzania and Arabic-speaking Africa, linguistic nationalism is a much weaker emotion in Africa than, say, in post-colonial Asia. As we shall indicate later in the volume, Africa is prepared to tolerate linguistic dependency in this period more readily than it seems prepared to accommodate political neo-colonialism.

On the other hand, although often expressed in foreign languages, African literature and the theatre are inextricably intertwined with the politics of liberation. The *Theatre of Liberation* in this period is certainly more committed than the *Theatre of Development*. South African drama has been particularly concerned with liberation, as the volume will later indicate. Plays like *Sizwe Banzi is Dead* by Athol Fugard, John Kani and Winston Ntshona, and *Survival* by Workshop 71, started a whole new generation of the theatre of liberation.

Even Ngugi wa Thiong'o's populist play *Ngahiika Ndenda* ('I will marry when I want to') was arguably a play of liberation rather than development – liberation from class oppression (black against black) rather than racial oppression as in South Africa (white against black).

On balance, Africa in this period manifests linguistic dependency and literary nationalism. Foreign languages are used to express literary African self-reliance. Kenya's Ngugi wa Thiong'o signifies an attempt to merge linguistic nationalism with literary independence. His play *Ngahiika Ndenda* was in the Kikuyu language, as well as being against the post-colonial black African establishment in his country. If Ngugi attempted to combine literary nationalism with linguistic nationalism, Julius K. Nyerere of Tanzania has attempted to combine linguistic nationalism with literary dependency. Certainly a piece of theatre *seemingly* against liberation was Julius Nyerere's translation of Shakespeare's *Julius Caesar* into Kiswahili.

And yet Nyerere was calling upon Kiswahili to carry the burden of world culture – by carrying the weight of Shakespeare. In a sense, Nyerere's blow was in favour of development – linguistic development. In literature, preoccupation with Shakespeare seemed to be a negation of liberation. On the other hand, translating Western genius into an African language seemed to be an affirmation of development.

Nyerere's translation of *The Merchant of Venice* seemed also to go against liberation. And yet in a sense the translation was part of the theatre of development on two counts. The exercise amounted to the

4

promotion of Tanzania's *national* language for *international* purposes. Secondly, the choice of *The Merchant of Venice* was part of Tanzania's economic education against exploitation. Nyerere's whole *ujamaa* vision was a struggle against the 'Shylocks' of this world (more Gentile than Jewish). This was reinforced by Nyerere's translation of the concept of *The Merchant of Venice*. To him it signified *The Capitalist(s) of Venice* ('Mabepari wa Vanisi'). We shall return in subsequent chapters to the symbolism of the *Mwalimu* and the *Bard* in post-colonial culture.

In the economic field, this volume has concerned itself with the issues of poverty and underdevelopment at both the global and the micro-level. In the West, competition may be a capitalist prerogative at the level of the stock exchange. By contrast, in Africa competition is sometimes at the poverty level. In the forthcoming chapters we hope to reveal the wider global context of Africa's underdevelopment and indigence.[2]

One of the major questions for the 1990s is whether the worst days for Africa are over. There is already evidence, however inconclusive, to suggest that a decline has occurred in infant mortality in Africa from 40 to 24 per thousand. There is also evidence that Africa's life expectancy in this period has been rising from less than 40 years to towards 50 years.

On the issue of food production, there was evidence in 1986 of an increase in output of 3 per cent. This shift meant that food production had outstripped population growth in Africa for the first time in fifteen years. By the mid-1980s African farmers were beginning to be motivated by more rational African policies of agricultural returns. The wider context will be revealed in the economic chapters of this volume.[3]

With regard to the *political* stream of Africa's experience in this period, the major processes covered in the volume include:

(1) liberation;
(2) state formation; and
(3) nation-building.

There are chapters about liberation from European colonial rule proper, especially in the period up to the 1960s. Then there is coverage of the period of Africa's struggle against white-minority governments in countries like Zimbabwe. The volume will of course also discuss struggles in those African colonies which were intended to be part of metropolitan Europe (like Algeria and the Portuguese colonies). Finally, there will be analyses of post-colonial liberation from dependent relationships with the former imperial powers – the struggle against neo-colonialism.

In the post-colonial phase, a particularly significant process concerns the whole phenomenon of political succession within African states.

2. Consult J. Ravenhill (ed.), 1986; I am also grateful for stimulation to Wanjiku Kironjo of Kenya.
3. C. Bassett, 1987.

Occasionally, there has been *natural posthumous succession* – succession after a natural death. Examples include Moi's succession of Kenyatta and Chadli Bendjedid's succession of Boumedienne.

Then there is succession after assassination, political murder or ambiguous 'accident'. When al-Haji Shehu Shagari took power in 1979, three out of the six heads of government that Nigeria had had since independence had been killed: a 50 per cent 'regicide' rate. But since Shagari, the regicide rate has declined in Nigeria. There was no presidential assassination in Nigeria in the 1980s.

Far more recurrent in Africa has been political succession by a military coup. Well over seventy coups have taken place in Africa since independence, mainly north of the equator.

There is in addition political succession after a *civilian* coup (civilian succeeding civilian). In Uganda's experience this has included Obote's palace coup against President (King) Mutesa in 1966. Binaisa's succession to Lule in 1979 is another Ugandan coup with a civilian succeeding a civilian.

Then there has been political succession after *actual war*. One example is Lule's ascendancy after the *inter*-state war between Tanzania and Uganda (1978–9). Then there has been political succession after a *civil* war – Museveni's army in power in Uganda after Obote and Okello is the clearest example.

Next, there has been political succession after a popular uprising. Sudan has been exceptional in this regard. In 1964 an uprising spearheaded by civilians resulted in the collapse of the military regime of General Aboud. In 1985 Sudan repeated this style of democratic uprising – bringing down Nimeiri's regime and compelling the military to promise a restoration of democracy within a year. The promise was kept, though civilian rule did not last.

Cases of political succession after a voluntary military handover by soldiers to civilians include General Obasanjo's handover to civilians in Nigeria in 1979 and Flight-Lieutenant Jerry Rawlings's brief transfer of power to civilians in Ghana in the same year.

As for political succession after electoral defeat in Africa, Mauritius long remained almost the sole example. In most of this period of African history it has been extremely rare for an African government to be replaced through *electoral defeat*. The relevant chapters in this volume, especially Chapters 15 and 16, will explore some of the factors responsible for institutional fluidity in post-colonial Africa.

Meanwhile, however, precedents have been set for political succession after voluntary resignation or retirement. The clearest case in the first three decades of independence was the complete retirement of Senegal's President Léopold Sédar Senghor. In 1985 Julius K. Nyerere also became a case of stepping down from the highest office of state. But for a while Nyerere stopped short of abandoning his role in the national party, *Chama*

Cha Mapinduzi (CCM). Also ambivalent was Ahmadou Ahidjo's ostensible 'retirement' from state power in the United Republic of Cameroon a few years earlier.

In the relevant chapters we hope to demonstrate that the central political crises of Africa include the issue of how to make our nations more culturally coherent and how to make our states more politically legitimate and authoritative. Africa in this period is landed with artificial boundaries, ill-trained armies and excessively dependent economies. The political and economic chapters of this volume will address some of these problems, including the crucial issues of *human rights* in post-colonial Africa.

However, because of the special character of the twentieth century as a century of the truly *global* economy and of *global* politics for the first time in human experience, African history in this period can only be fully understood in the wider context of world history. What emerges from the story of this period is, in part, how Africa helped to re-humanize Europe, and how Europe helped to re-Africanize Africa. The history of decolonization in the twentieth century is one of the great dramas of the entire span of human history. Remarkable contradictions have been played out in the process.[4]

The years since 1935 especially are a period of history when the Western world has inadvertently reminded Africans of their *pan-African* identity. We know there would have been no *Nigerian* or *Kenyan* or *Ivorian* identity but for European colonialism. Europe is therefore the illegitimate parent of the national consciousness of Nigerians, Kenyans and Ivorians. But is Western imperialism also the illegitimate parent of pan-African consciousness? Our story in this volume is partly about the emergence of new identities and new aspirations among African peoples.

If class consciousness in Africa is partly the result of the intensification of capitalism, race consciousness in the continent has already been partly the result of the intensification of imperialism. Just as capitalist exploitation helps to make workers more collectively conscious of themselves *as workers*, so European imperialism over time has helped to make the colonized Africans more *collectively* conscious of themselves as a colonized people. It is in that sense that European imperialism helped the people of, say, Kikuyuland to recognize the Yoruba as 'fellow Africans' – and helped the people of Algeria to recognize the Zulu as continental compatriots.

---

4. We define 'decolonization' as the process through which colonial rule is ended, colonial institutions dismantled and colonial values and styles abandoned. Theoretically, the initiative for decolonization can be taken either by the imperial power or by the colonized people. In reality, decolonization is usually forced by the struggle of the oppressed.

7

Of course Africans in their own societies and sub-regions have long known and experienced the dignity of their own identity as Kikuyu, Amhara, Yoruba, Berber, Zulu and Maghreb Arabs without the help of Europe. But when in his book, *The Philosophy of the Revolution*, Gamāl 'Abd al-Nasser called upon Egyptians to remember that they were not only Arabs and Muslims but also *Africans*, he referred explicitly to the evidence of a shared struggle against alien rule with the rest of the continent. European imperialism had awakened a continental consciousness.

The Royal Imperial House of Ethiopia was rather slow in recognizing Ethiopia as an African country. For a long time Ethiopian rulers preferred to see themselves as part of the Middle East rather than Africa. But we begin this volume from 1935. When the Italians humiliated and occupied Ethiopia in 1935, the consequences were particularly poignant. The rest of Africa and the black world groaned in pain. The consequences have been extensively documented in some of the chapters of this volume.

PLATE 1.1 *Emperor Haile Selassie addressing the League of Nations on Italy's aggression against Ethiopia*

What has sometimes been forgotten is Ethiopia's self-discovery from 1935 onwards as being truly a part of the African condition. On the one hand, upon hearing the news of the Italian invasion, Kwame Nkrumah as a young man walked the streets of London, with angry tears running

8

down his cheeks. The bad news had been an additional stimulus to young Nkrumah's pan-African identity.

On the other hand, however, Emperor Haile Selassie was drawn into an experience to which other African rulers had already been subjected 30–50 years earlier – direct European occupation of their land and subjugation of their people. The emperor also witnessed the widespread African and black support for him and his people in the face of the Italian challenge. In those factors lay the beginnings of a new racial consciousness in the Royal House of Ethiopia – the shock of self-discovery as an African dynasty of an African people. Over time, Haile Selassie developed into one of the founding fathers, and in many ways *the* elder statesman, of post-colonial pan-Africanism. European imperial excesses had once again served as a growth medium for something far more positive than themselves. The splendour of a new pan-African identity had grown out of the squalor of European racism. This volume covers the critical transition from the squalor of European excesses to the splendour of Africa's self-discovery.

But what about the reverse impact of Africa upon the West? By fighting for its own independence, Africa was also helping to change the course of European and indeed global history. This volume is of course focusing upon historical developments within Africa itself. But since this is the period of Africa's maximum incorporation into the global system, and participation therein, it is important to remember that Africa was not merely a passive continent being acted upon by others. Africa's own actions have also helped to transform their fortunes. While Africa as a *continent* may indeed have been shocked into self-recognition under European pressure, Europe has been forced to learn some degree of international responsibility and democratic humility under the stress of an African challenge. The entire history of decolonization in the twentieth century is to be seen partly as a process under which the oppressed have learned more fully who they really are – and the oppressors have begun to learn the humility of humane global accountability. The story of Africa since 1935 is to be seen in the context of those major contradictions.

Who are the Africans?[5]

It was the poet-diplomat of Sierra Leone, Davidson Abioseh Nicol, who once wrote:

> You are not a country, Africa,
> You are a concept,
> Fashioned in our minds, each to each

5. This section is indebted to A. A. Mazrui, 1986, chs 1 and 5.

> To hide our separate fears,
> To dream our separate dreams.[6]

We shall return to this particular refrain later in the volume. Africa is indeed at once more than a country, and less than one! More than fifty territorial entities with artificial boundaries created by Europe have in the period covered in this volume called themselves 'nations'. All of them except the Republic of South Africa and Namibia had by the 1980s joined an international body called the Organization of African Unity (OAU). Yes, Africa is a *concept*, pregnant with the dreams of millions of people.

As we have intimated, it remains one of the great ironies of modern African history that it took European colonialism to remind Africans that they were Africans. Europe's greatest service to the people of Africa was not Western civilization, now under siege; or even Christianity, which is now on the defensive. Europe's supreme gift was the gift of African identity, bequeathed without grace or design – but a reality all the same. This has been particularly so in the twentieth century.

But how then did Europe pan-Africanize Africa? In what way is the sense of identity that Africans today have as Africans an outcome of their historical interaction with Europeans?

In fact, a number of inter-related processes were at work. We shall examine these more fully later in this volume. First and foremost was the triumph of European cartography and mapmaking in the scientific and intellectual history of the world. It was Europeans who named most of the great continents of the world, all the great oceans, many of the great rivers and lakes and most of the countries. Europe *positioned* the world so that we think of Europe as being above Africa rather than below it in the cosmos. Europe *timed* the world so that the Greenwich meridian chimed the universal hour. And Europe named the Tropics of Cancer and Capricorn. What is more, it was Europeans who usually decided where one continent on Planet Earth ended and another began. For Africa, Europeans decided that our continent ended at the Red Sea rather than at the Persian Gulf. Europeans may not have invented the name 'Africa', but they did play a decisive role in applying it to the continental landmass that we recognize today.

The second process through which Europe Africanized Africa was the process of racism in history. As indicated in previous volumes, this was particularly marked in the treatment of the black populations of the continent. The racially-inspired humiliation and degradation of black Africans across the centuries contributed to their mutual recognition of each other as 'fellow Africans'. Related to racism were imperialism and colonization. Again we shall show in later chapters that these generated

6. See D. A. Nicol, 1969.

a sufficient sense of shared African identity for the movement of pan-Africanism to take shape in this period. In the words of Julius K. Nyerere of Tanzania once again:

> Africans all over the continent, without a word being spoken either from one individual to another or from one African country to another, looked at the European, looked at one another, and knew that in relation to the European they were one.[7]

Black consciousness south of the Sahara is an aspect of the African identity – but black consciousness was itself born as a response to European racial arrogance. It attained a continental scale following the invasion of Ethiopia in 1935. As we shall see in later chapters, *negritude*, an intellectual and literary movement, was born out of the special cultural arrogance of French imperialism. It is against this background that Europe has pan-Africanized Africa. The period of history covered in this volume is particularly relevant in this process.

The era of global Africa

But in the twentieth century, African history is indeed intimately linked to global trends. We shall see later how Nyerere's translation of Shakespeare into Kiswahili was a literary example of the global connection. Chapter 29 on 'Africa and the United Nations' will politically dramatize this linkage. The period covered by this volume includes the dawn of the *nuclear age* and the emergence of the *space age* – two of the most dramatic shifts in our relationship with the universe. Later chapters will touch on these scientific trends. In looking at local and regional African experience in this volume, both writer and reader have to bear in mind the unique and 'cosmic' context of this period of human history. How has Africa been affected and conditioned by these immense technological break-throughs? In what ways has Africa contributed to those dramatic trans-formations in turn? We should bear in mind the global context of the regional processes covered in this volume.

Particularly relevant for both the re-humanization of Europe and the re-Africanization of Africa were two global cataclysms – the Great Depression and the Second World War. One of the great historical debates for Africa concerns which of the two impacted on African history the more deeply and the more fundamentally, and which re-humanized the West more.

The worst years of the Great Depression occurred in the period immediately preceding the years which are to be covered in this volume. The collapse of Wall Street was after all in 1929. But the 1930s generally

7. J. K. Nyerere, 1960, p. 149.

were part of the aftermath of that collapse – and some of the most ominous consequences of the depression (including the rise of Hitler) unfolded from the 1930s onwards.

Did the Great Depression hurt the Western world immediately but help Africa's liberation subsequently? Was the depression a catastrophe for Western capitalism but a future blessing for the colonies? If so, what was the precise nature of that equation? In what ways was Europe subsequently made more humane? Under what circumstances did Africa become more pan-African? Some of these issues will be made clearer in the relevant chapters.

But if every major global crisis is, by definition, partly African, have we reached a stage when every major *African* crisis is now partly global? In the period covered in this volume it is indeed true that every dramatic African convulsion stands a chance of being more widely internationalized. We shall explore in the relevant chapters the globalization of the Congo crisis (Léopoldville) in the early 1960s – with the violent death of two of the major political figures in the crisis, Patrice Lumumba and Dag Hammarskjöld. Some twenty years later the Chad crisis was increasingly internationalized – as more and more countries were either diplomatically or militarily involved. All this is quite apart from the diverse liberation wars in Southern Africa, each of which had a considerable international component. The evidence has been accumulating that just as there is a bit of Africa in every global emergency, there is a bit of the globe in every African tragedy.

The Suez war of 1956 was more difficult to categorize. Was it a global conflict which was fought out on African soil? Or was it an African conflict globalized? When Gamāl 'Abd al-Nasser nationalized the Suez Canal Company he unleashed both Northern forces of imperial power and Southern forces of liberation. The Suez crisis will feature in the relevant chapters of this volume as one of the great linkages between the fate of the world and the destiny of Africa.

But while in this volume we shall pay special attention to the internationalization of both the Suez war of 1956 and the Congo crisis of 1960–5, there is a sense in which the Nigerian civil war of 1967–70 was equally globalized, though in a different manner.

The Biafra war was indeed a 'world war in microcosm', without the nuclear factor! French support for Biafra counterbalanced British support for federal Nigeria. Israel's material support for Biafra counterbalanced Egyptian pilots for the federal airforce. South African and white Rhodesian support for Biafra counterbalanced the Organization of African Unity's concern for the territorial integrity of Nigeria. The Chinese also intervened for Biafra to counterbalance Soviet support for federal Nigeria. Indeed, the Soviet Union's strengthened intervention on the side of federal Nigeria coincided with Soviet intervention in Czechoslovakia on the side of an unfragmented socialist world. The Second World of socialism and the

Third World of underdevelopment were both embedded in the Brezhnev doctrine of proletarian internationalism.

The Czech government had previously obeyed a Moscow order to deliver Delphin jet fighters and other weapons to the Nigerians. But the Liberal Dubcek regime in Prague banned all arms sales to Nigeria in May 1968. Three months later the Warsaw Pact forces invaded Czechoslovakia – and a reversal of policy occurred concerning the ban on Delphins to the federal side.

The escalation of Soviet support for Nigeria was not due to Ojukwu's invasion of the mid-West or due to a counter-offensive into federal Nigeria. To the Soviets at that time the defence of socialism in the Second World had become almost indistinguishable from the defence of national unity in the Third World – from Vietnam to Nigeria.

And yet, although the Nigerian civil war came close to being a 'world war' in microcosm, we know that Uli Airport was its last frontier.

It is worth reflecting that the British Empire had once been an empire over which the sun never set – given that the Empire was scattered over all the time zones of the globe. But Biafra – in spite of its flag of the rising sun – was a republic over which the sun never really rose. Biafra died before its own dawn – in spite of Uli Airport, in spite of generating a 'world war' in microcosm. What it did demonstrate was Africa's incorporation into the wider world of global rivalries.

It also showed that an African identity born out of racial humiliation and foreign domination was bound to be fragile and uncertain. The shock of colonialism and imperialism had awakened Africans to the fact that in relation to the Western oppressors, Africans were *one*. But shared exploitation was not enough as a basis of enduring African solidarity. Uniting against the foreign oppressor was one thing; uniting for internal development was another. The earlier part of this period of history has demonstrated that Africans are effective when they unite for liberation. The later part of this era demonstrates that Africans are finding it hard to unite for political and economic development. Some of the chapters take a closer look at this dialectic between the pan-Africanism of liberation (basically a success story) and the pan-Africanism of integration and development (still basically an elusive dream). The whole dynamic between African identity and African development in this epoch is played out in the underlying politics of pan-Africanism. This volume is, in part, an introduction to that process.

Pan-Africanism in disarray

When the Organization of African Unity (OAU) was born in Addis Ababa in May 1963 the most important chair was perhaps an empty chair, the most important head of state was a dead president. This was Sylvanus Olympio, who had been assassinated in Togo earlier that year. His violent death symbolized the shape of things to come. This was the first killing of a head of state in post-colonial Africa – and the coup which followed was the first of its kind south of the Sahara. This volume will take note of this era of coups. The stage was set for a version of independence in Africa which was periodically rocked by violence and death.

Another theme that this volume explores is pan-Africanism with its objective of the attainment of African liberation and African unity, and the different approaches adopted for its attainment as exemplified in the policies and activities of Nkrumah and Nyerere, associated with those of the moderate Monrovia and the radical Casablanca groups. Put differently, one divide between radical and moderate pan-Africanism in the early 1960s concerned the issue of the geographical scale of African unity. The radical school was continental in ambition and was opposed to sub-regional integration; the moderate school accepted sub-regional experiments in pursuit of African unity. This was pan-Africanism's *horizontal divide* – a disagreement about how *wide* African unity should be.

On the other hand, the other disagreement concerned how *deep* African unity should be. This was the *vertical divide*. Should there be immediate political integration and the formation of a single country? Or should African states first aim for more modest (and 'shallower') forms of unity – like diplomatic co-ordination of foreign policies, or economic co-operation, or functional links in communication and shared utilities? As the chapters on pan-Africanism will indicate, the depth of the unity envisaged by the OAU when it was formed in 1963 and based in Addis Ababa was shallow, but the width of the unity was continental, encompassing both Arab and black states.

In 1966 and 1967 respectively, two separate events helped to change the nature of the divide between 'radical' and 'moderate' in pan-African politics. In February 1966 Kwame Nkrumah was overthrown in a military coup in Ghana. And the following year Julius Nyerere proclaimed his own radicalization by launching the Arusha Declaration of *Ujamaa na Kujitegemea* (Socialism and Self-reliance). From then on Julius Nyerere began to appear as one of the voices of radicalism on the African stage. Dar es Salaam became a more credible capital of a frontline state, a more credible headquarters of the OAU's liberation activities represented by the African Liberation Committee.

Yet by the time the OAU was celebrating its tenth anniversary in 1973, it looked as if radicalism was declining. Gamāl 'Abd al-Nasser had died in 1970. Nkrumah, in exile, also died not long after his Egyptian comrade-in-arms. Milton Obote had been overthrown by Idi Amīn. And countries like Kenya and Côte d'Ivoire* had moved substantially to the right in those ten years.

---

* Since 1985 the government of the country which was formerly entitled 'Ivory Coast' in English decided that its name would be 'Côte d'Ivoire' in all languages.

But, as this volume will later show, once again history came to the rescue of African radicalism precisely as the OAU began its second decade. Two critical events in 1974 contributed to this. One was the Ethiopian revolution, occurring around the very capital of the OAU. Sub-Saharan Africa's second-largest country in population was about to go Marxist–Leninist. Forty years after Ethiopia was victimized by Italian fascism the country was transformed for a while into an ally of Soviet communism.

But also in 1974 there occurred the *coup d'État* in the Portuguese capital, Lisbon. This resulted in a *coup de grace* to the Portuguese empire. Later chapters will demonstrate that this most ancient of all European empires in Africa rapidly disintegrated, leaving behind new radical members about to enter the politics of the OAU. Indeed, the issue of Angola's independence was for a while itself divisive – with the 'moderates' of Africa favouring a government of national unity consisting of all three liberation movements (MPLA, UNITA and FNLA) while the 'radicals' favoured the installation of the MPLA into power. It turned out that the FNLA was a paper tiger in any case, and UNITA was backed by the Republic of South Africa and the West. The majority of OAU members, including influential Nigeria which was sometimes classified as 'moderate', swung behind the MPLA. Angola, a new radical member, was soon to enter the ranks of the left within the OAU.

The independence of Zimbabwe five years later also favoured the left in the Organization. In other words, among the factors which favoured the radicals in the 1980s within the OAU was the simple fact that virtually every African country that attained independence from 1975 to 1980 had ideologically opted for a leftist orientation: that is, all the former Portuguese colonies, plus Zimbabwe.

Secondly, every genuine revolution in Africa is ideologically likely to be a move to the left. The most significant African revolution of the 1970s was the Ethiopian one. Somalia also moved substantially to the left of what it used to be in the 1960s. And Libya was truly radicalized under Muammar Kadhaffi.

On the other hand, military coups in Africa have been mixed in ideological orientation. The coups in Ghana and Burkina Faso in the 1980s were initially attempts to move leftwards ideologically, whereas the 1984 coup in Guinea (Conakry) was a move to the right.

On balance, the OAU as a whole had by the 1980s tilted somewhat to the left since its inception. The voting patterns concerning the status of the Ṣaḥrāwi Arab Democratic Republic (SADR) revealed a new left-of-centre coalition which had crystallized since 1974.

What of the future? Usually the future is not the proper focus of study for a historian. However, when we entitled the conclusion of this volume 'Towards the year 2000' we were implicitly recognizing that the history of the past can be used to estimate likely trends in the future. Namibia, now that it has become truly independent, will for a while probably be among the members of the left within the OAU. But radicalism and leftism in Southern Africa are fragile plants. When ostensibly radical countries like Mozambique begin to cooperate with the Republic of South Africa and to welcome Pretoria's economic enticements, a new look at the concepts of 'radical' and 'moderate' may be in order. After the political decline of Charles Njonjo, Kenya briefly adopted a tougher stance against South Africa than Mozambique. Which African country was more radical than which – even on the basic issue of *apartheid*?

In the 1960s Nkrumah was admonishing and denouncing Julius Nyerere for inviting British troops to deal with Tanzania's own military dissidents. In the 1980s Marxist Mozambique was in consultation with both the military and economic establishments of South Africa in a bid to control Mozambique's own dissidents.

Was Nkrumah turning in his own grave in the 1980s? Or was he more understanding of Mozambique than he once was when Julius Nyerere turned for British military assistance way back in 1964?

Perhaps only our ancestors, in their inscrutable wisdom, can answer such questions, as they continue to observe our antics from wherever they are. Kwame Nkrumah and Sékou Touré have now joined these ancestors, sitting side by side with Sylvanus Olympio at long last. Who said 'Death is an exercise in pan-Africanism'? Perhaps it is the most horizontal form of pan-Africanism, a kind of pan-Humanism, the great equalizer, the ultimate unifier: or is it? Africans have been pan-Africanized enough for liberation. But they have yet to be pan-Africanized enough for socio-economic development and political integration.

What about the pan-Africanization of *women*? Where does the 'female of the species' fit into the African equation? It is to this theme of gender that we must now turn.

On sovereignty and gender

In Chapter 19 on the development of modern African literature, attention is drawn to Léopold Senghor's poem 'Naked woman, black woman'. In the poem Africa *is* a woman – 'clad in your colour that is life, in your form that is beauty'.

And yet few chapters in this volume have chosen to describe explicitly the role of African women in the making of African history. Women's role in the struggle for independence, in general, has tended to be under-studied. However, there are times when historians – while aware of the role of women – prefer to present the story without reference to sexual differences. Most of our historians in this volume have presented the struggle for independence in terms of *people* rather than genders. Unfortunately, when the story is presented without reference to gender, there is often a hasty cultural presumption by observers that the only significant participants in the drama were men. Such a presumption is of course false.

The story of sovereignty in this volume can be seen in three stages: the stage of struggling for sovereignty (the fight for independence); the stage of exercising sovereignty (the use of state power); the stage of representing sovereignty abroad (the symbols of inter-state relationships). We hope to show in this volume that African women have been particularly significant in the first and final stages. As *combatants*, African women were part of the crusade for the empowerment of the continent. As *diplomats*, African women later represented the sovereignty which they had helped Africa to acquire in world affairs. But as *power-brokers*, African women seem to have been on the whole part of the periphery rather than at the centre of politics. Let us take each of these three phases of female participation in turn – beginning with the struggle for independence.

Although the slogan of African nationalism in the final decades of colonialism was sometimes couched in the sexist phrase of 'one *man*, one vote', African women rapidly learned to use the vote as part of the process of liberation. Much of the canvassing of the vote against Bishop Muzorewa's regime in Zimbabwe in 1979–80 was done by women. The white-settler establishment was taken by surprise by the election results partly because most Europeans underestimated the political activism of African women as the 'servants' visited each other from kitchen to kitchen.

More than a quarter of a century earlier, women in colonial Kenya had played a different role. There is little doubt that the 'Mau Mau' struggle in Kenya would have fizzled out much sooner if the Kikuyu, Meru and Embu women in the Central Province had not risked their lives to send in food and information to the male fighters in the Aberdaire forests.

There was also many an occasion during the Algerian war of independence when a particular nationalist operation depended on a woman revolutionary, shrouded in a traditional Islamic dress and veil, being able to penetrate the enemy lines. Indeed, if Franz Fanon's accounts are reliable, heavily-shrouded Muslim women were among the most crucial carriers of grenades at specific phases of the urban guerrilla war in Algeria.[8]

On balance, *internalized* liberation struggle within an African country at war has tended to involve more women than a liberation struggle in *exile*. In Southern Africa the internalization of struggle has been part of the intensification of struggle. And both internalization and intensification have meant greater involvement of women in at least supportive roles, and sometimes in actual combat roles. In Zimbabwe the liberation army of the Zimbabwe African National Union (ZANU) probably involved more women on the frontline than did the army of the Zimbabwe African People's Union (ZAPU).

8. See F. Fanon, 1963.

What is less clear is whether the balance between men and women in ZANU and ZAPU generally is partly due to cultural differences between the Shona (Robert Mugabe's ancestry) and the Ndebele (Joshua Nkomo's ancestry). Is the warrior tradition of the Ndebele (linked to Zulu culture) more purely masculine than the warrior tradition among the Shona? And did this difference affect women and how many of them were involved in armed struggle in each camp? This volume does not settle such debates. Inevitably contemporary history often raises more questions than it answers. But the warrior tradition is indeed addressed in Chapters 5 and 16. In any case, if women were more active in ZANLA (the army of ZANU) than in ZIPRA (the army of ZAPU) one additional explanation could have been *ideological*. Robert Mugabe's movement was to the left of Joshua Nkomo's.[9]

As for women in the Horn of Africa, the Islamized Somali, perhaps surprisingly, seem to be more sensitized to the role of women in combat than are the Christianized Amhara. Mogadishu does not have a tomb of the unknown warrior but it does have a statue of the martyred female warrior – a woman fatally wounded, and yet still fighting.

Legends abound in Mogadishu about Hawa Ismen 'Alī who stood up against the return of Italian colonialism after the Second World War, and paid with her own life in 1948. The Somalis being a particularly poetic African people, have celebrated the martyrdom of Hawa Ismen 'Alī in diverse rhythms. She was Somalia's Joan of Arc. She symbolized sacred patriotism with a female face.[10]

In the Muslim world as a whole, Somali women may well be *more* 'liberated' than average. In the Christian world as a whole, Ethiopian women may be *less* 'liberated' than average. But does that mean Somali women are, in *absolute* terms, more 'liberated' than Ethiopian women? By absolute standards, that is harder to assess. The two societies may be at the same level of public involvement of women. What is also possible is that in the early 1980s there were more Somali women in military uniform, proportionately, than there were Ethiopian. At least, in that period, Somalia seemed readier to enlist both genders in the armed forces than did Ethiopia.[11]

In South Africa the role of women in the struggle against racism has been wide-ranging. Women have joined movements of civil disobedience going back to the pioneering rebellious efforts of Mahatma Gandhi in Durban in 1906. Women were among the dead in both the martyrdom of Sharpeville (1960) and the martyrdom of Soweto (1976). Winnie

9. The author is indebted to the fieldwork done in preparation for a special Panorama programme, 'Searching for the New Zimbabwe', BBC Television, 1982.

10. The case of Hawa Ismen 'Alī is also discussed in Chapter 6 of this volume.

11. The author is indebted to the fieldwork done in preparation for the BBC/PBS television series, 1986.

Mandela became part of the vanguard against *apartheid*, carrying her imprisoned husband's torch of resistance for over a quarter of a century. Helen Suzman was part of the *parliamentary* opposition to *apartheid* for thirty-six years – stepping down only in 1989. Female movements against racism ranged from the historic Black Sash to the multi-racial alliance, Women Against Repression (WAR), rebelling against President F. W. de Klerk in 1989.

All this was quite apart from women under arms in the African National Congress (ANC) and the Pan-African Congress (PAC). This tradition of armed female comrades had precedents in FRELIMO during the struggle against the Portuguese.

In Angola under colonial rule, the role of women differed markedly among the three liberation movements – the MPLA, FNLA and UNITA.[12] The MPLA was both the most multi-racial of the movements and the most 'androgynous' in its regiments. Both its Marxism–Leninism and its multi-racialism favoured the greater participation of women as fighters.

FNLA was in some ways the most anachronistic of the three movements. It used marriage relationships as a basis of military alliances – beginning with Roberto Holden's own family ties with President Mobutu Sese Seko's establishment and the Bakongo.

Jonas Savimbi during the struggle against the Portuguese was to the left of Jonas Savimbi after Angola's independence. In other words, Savimbi and UNITA moved to the right when their enemy was not Portuguese imperialism but the MPLA, backed by the USSR and Cuba. In terms of his dependence on South Africa, his rightist tilt became dangerously reactionary. Savimbi came close to being an ally of *apartheid*.

And yet, by a curious twist of fate, as Savimbi moved to the right in political allegiance, he became more progressive in his use of women in the movement. He entrusted more leadership roles to women. Post-colonial Angola reduced Savimbi's chances of enlisting more *male* allies from distant ethnic groups – and increased his dependence on ethnic allies in his own Ovimbundu heartland, both male and female. The ethnic concentration of his constituency favoured an androgynous approach to struggle. It is also possible that his new international status made him more progressive towards women. At any rate UNITA used women in positions of responsibility more extensively after independence than before.

But when all is said and done, women all over Angola – like women elsewhere in Africa – were often the unsung heroines of the struggle for freedom. They made a bigger difference to the success of the whole enterprise than has often been realized.

Within this period of history, that struggle for freedom was itself a

12. MPLA (People's Liberation Movement for Angola); FNLA (National Liberation Front of Angola); UNITA (National Union for the Total Independence of Angola).

liberating experience even before its formal success on Independence Day. We have sought to show that in that fight for sovereignty, women were often *warriors* in their different ways. Let us now return to that other part of the equation – when, on attainment of sovereignty, women became at times the *voices* of Africa in world affairs.

It is worth remembering that Uganda appointed a woman foreign minister sooner than did the majority of Western countries – including the United States, Britain and France, none of which had entrusted the foreign ministry to a woman when Elizabeth Bagaya Nyabongo, the former Princess Elizabeth of Toro, became the voice of Uganda in world affairs. And when Angie E. Brooks of Liberia was elected president of the General Assembly of the United Nations in 1969, it was before any Western woman had risen to such prominence within the United Nations' system.[13]

In the 1970s and 1980s, Paris may have had more female ambassadors from Africa than it had female envoys from any other region outside Europe. African countries which had influential female diplomats stationed in Paris in the 1980s included Ghana, Liberia, Tanzania, Sierra Leone and Uganda. Indeed, Elizabeth Bagaya Nyabongo (Uganda's former foreign minister) would have been the *second* woman ambassador to France from Uganda and under President Y. Museveni had she not resigned from the diplomatic service in 1988. We shall return to this theme in Chapter 30.

The African National Congress of South Africa was for a while also represented by a woman (Mrs Dulcie September) in France – until she paid the supreme price for her patriotism. She was mysteriously assassinated in Paris in March 1988. She had been ANC representative to UNESCO, Switzerland and Luxemburg as well as France.

It is on such occasions that Léopold Senghor's poem fusing Africanity with womanhood acquires a particular poignancy. The female South African martyr in Paris became a brave symbol for the continent as a whole. The fact that she was born in 1935 gives her a particular relevance to this volume's period of history.

But in a sense Ambassador Dulcie September's sacrifice was also part of Africa's struggle to re-humanize 'the white man'. She was a martyr to that particular crusade. It is to this theme of Africa's re-humanization of Europeans that we must now return.

An African Gospel for Europe

There has been a strong tendency in modern historiography to regard Africa as a passive continent – a recipient of influences rather than a transmitter of the same. Insulting to both women and Africa, some have

13. We shall return to Ambassador Brooks's achievement in Chapter 30.

even gone as far as to call Africa 'the female continent' in the pejorative sense of passivity and penetrability. This was a far cry from Senghor's positive feminization of Africa.

The same event which one historian regards as an illustration of Africa under external influence could be viewed by another historian as an example of Africa's impact upon the outside world. This volume leans on the side of Africa as an *active* continent.

In recent decades, there has been Africa's role in redefining the ethics of racism in the world system. Africa, more than any other region of the world, has helped to make racism in any one country an issue of international concern. Under pressure from African states, it has become increasingly impossible for the Republic of South Africa to claim that *apartheid* is an issue of domestic jurisdiction. The volume will demonstrate that, under heavy pressure from both pre-independence African leaders and post-colonial African states, the struggle against institutionalized racism has been internationalized. People of African ancestry in the United States joined the struggle quite early. These African-Americans also helped to initiate the transformation of race relations in the Americas, as the relevant chapters will reveal.

This volume also shows that Africa has played a decisive role in stripping colonialism of its legitimacy under international morality and increasingly under the Law of Nations. For several centuries, rules of European statecraft and diplomatic history had made it perfectly legitimate for a European power to colonize and subjugate a non-Western society. Millions of people in Africa, Asia, and indeed the Americas, fell under European 'sovereignty' – and international law recognized and legitimized that 'sovereignty'. After all, international law was itself a child of European diplomatic history and statecraft. It was therefore saturated with European assumptions and prejudices as well as values and norms. It has taken the joint struggles of people of African and Asian ancestry to challenge some of these arrogant and ethnocentric assumptions of international law. If it was wrong for Hitler's Germany to occupy Poland or Belgium, why was it right for Disraeli's Britain to occupy the Nile valley? Africa and Asia have helped to revise the rules of international conduct in the second half of the twentieth century. The West has been encouraged to re-humanize itself.

But we shall see in this volume that Africa's struggles have had even wider consequences for our times. When the National Liberation Front (FLN) of Algeria was fighting for independence, it was not simply the future of Algeria which was at stake. It was also the future of Europe. The Fourth Republic of France came under severe stress as a result of the Algerian war. In 1958 France hovered on the brink of a civil war. The Fourth Republic collapsed under these pressures. Only one man could save France from widespread civil strife – General Charles de Gaulle. De Gaulle returned to power in Paris, insisted on a new

PLATE I.2   *On 11 December 1960, in Salembier, a district of the city of Algiers, young demonstrators for the first time managed to raise the green and white flag of the* Front de libération nationale *(FLN)*

22

constitution – and France's Fifth Republic was born. The entire history of France in the remainder of the twentieth century would have been vastly different had the Algerian war not destroyed the Fourth Republic and catapulted Charles de Gaulle back to supreme political power.

Indeed, a strong France under de Gaulle turned out to be also vital to the fortunes of the European Economic Community (EEC) in its early formative years: de Gaulle presided over those years of the European Common Market. De Gaulle's vision of the grandeur of France also led to a re-definition of the role of France in the North Atlantic Treaty Organization (NATO), and the removal of the United States' military bases from France. Paris decided to be *politically* integrated with NATO – rather than remain part and parcel of the alliance's *military* organization.

All these significant changes in the history of the Western world had for their catalyst the struggle of Algerian nationalists for the liberation of their country. While these African freedom-fighters were busy transforming the destiny of their own country, they were, perhaps unwittingly at the time, also participating in changing the course of history of the Western world. This is the kind of positive emphasis that underlies the perspective of this volume.

African nationalists in the Portuguese colonies of Angola, Mozambique, Guinea-Bissau, Cape Verde Islands and Sao Tome and Principe were also destined to alter the direction of Portugal's own history. It was the strain of the anti-colonial wars in those Portuguese dependencies which finally led to the military coup in Portugal in April 1974. This also marked the end of the era of fascism in the history of modern Portugal. The African nationalists of Angola, Mozambique and Guinea-Bissau helped to initiate both the democratization and the political modernization of Portugal. Portuguese political culture was as a result re-humanized.

In the case of Algeria's impact on French history, it is instructive to reflect on the reaction of Karl Marx and Friedrich Engels when the French were consolidating their hold on Algeria in the 1840s. These two European thinkers regarded French colonization of Algeria, in large measure, as a civilizing process. In Engels's own words:

> And the conquest of Algeria has already forced the Beys of Tunis and Tripoli and even the Emperor of Morocco, to enter upon the path of civilization. . . . And, after all, the modern bourgeois, with civilization, industry, order, and at least relative enlightenment following him, is preferable to the feudal lord or to the marauding robber, with the barbarian state of society to which they belong.[14]

If the French in the mid-nineteenth century helped to ignite the process of 'modernizing' Algeria, the Algerians in the mid-twentieth century, in turn, initiated the process of stabilizing France. An ancient debt was paid

14. F. Engels, 1849. See also A. A. Mazrui, 1986, ch. 15.

when the National Liberation Front (FLN) of Algeria helped to destroy the Fourth Republic of France with all its instability – and inaugurated the more solid Fifth Republic. Stripped of its empire, France was re-humanized.

The next phase for Africa as a whole is to roll back the curtain of Western *neo*-colonialism. This includes, on one side, reducing the power of the West upon Africa; and, on the other, it encompasses an effort to increase the power of Africa upon the West. Some of the economic chapters of this volume will clarify that strategy of counter-power.

In West Africa, Nigeria's most natural rival is not Libya, but France. Nigeria is by far the largest country in the region – with a population of a hundred million in 1980. This is larger than the population of all former French West Africa added together. Nigeria should be the natural leader of West Africa. And yet immense influence was still being exercised in West Africa in the 1980s by bureaucrats and business people from France.

Discussion on dependency in this volume will show that there was a need in West Africa to reduce French fiscal and economic control and to curtail the continuing French cultural and educational penetration of its former colonies. In the long run, Nigeria was destined to take the lead in the decolonization of its own region.

Quite early, France probably recognized Nigeria as a future rival for influence in West Africa. France attempted to assist the secession of Biafra in the Nigerian civil war of 1967–70 – in a futile bid to fragment Nigeria. When fragmentation finally failed, France then began an attempt at the greater penetration of Nigeria – through economic investment and joint projects. Making Nigeria itself dependent on France was one way of neutralizing Nigeria's potential rivalry in the future. Nigeria in the 1980s had yet to wake up fully to the challenge.

Great Britain was less of a rival to Nigeria in West Africa, partly because Britain invested far less money than France, utilized far fewer British personnel, and used no British troops at all in any of her former colonies. Nor was the British pound linked in any manner whatsoever with any of the currencies of the former British colonies – unlike the way the French Central Bank backed for so long the CFA franc in the former colonies. French influence in former French West Africa was therefore far greater than British influence in say, Ghana, or Sierra Leone, let alone Nigeria. The question for the 1990s is whether France will become less involved in Africa and become far more interested in the newly-transformed Eastern Europe, and in the more deeply integrated European Community after 1992. As a result, Nigeria may find it easier to exercise its influence in West Africa in the future.

On the basis of the data on mineral wealth and industrial potential covered in this volume, we are in a position to estimate that the second major power centre in Africa in the twenty-first century will probably be black-ruled South Africa. Following the probable racial war and the inevitable collapse of *apartheid*, black South Africans will inherit their birth-right. They will inherit the mineral wealth of one of the richest countries in the world – minerals which are indispensable for the economic well-being of the Western world.

Black South Africans will also inherit the most industrialized economy in Africa – built by their own black labour and by Western expertise. Thirdly, black South Africans may inherit a nuclear infrastructure – and become the black world's first nuclear power. Clearly, black South Africans, the most underprivileged blacks of the twentieth century, may become among the most privileged of the twenty-first century. The 'black untouchables' of today may well become the 'black Brahmins' of tomorrow.

A great Western novelist, Charles Dickens, once made the following suggestion:

> . . . think for a moment of the long chain of iron or gold, of thorns or flowers, that would never have bound you but for the formation of the first link on one memorable day.[15]

Africa has for so long experienced and moaned under the chain of iron: can the chain now be transformed into a necklace of gold? Africa has for so long suffered from a chain of thorns: is the garland of flowers at hand? This volume provides the data for calculating probabilities.

The lustre of the gold of South Africa should not dazzle us prematurely. The historic effort to loosen the chains of iron has had its successes – but we shall show in later chapters that the war is far from over. The struggle continues. To change the metaphor, the fallen angel is only beginning to rise again. This volume is about the last years of Africa's political damnation under colonialism. The volume is also about the dawn of Africa's salvation. Where the human species first began is where human freedom will at last be fulfilled.

At the beginning of Africa's story in this UNESCO series we saw a continent bequeath the human species to populate Planet Earth. At the end of Africa's story we shall now see a continent in the process of re-humanizing that species in moral terms. The years since 1935 have shocked Africans into a new depth of self-recognition. But by fighting for their own dignity, Africans have also shocked the rest of the world into a new approximation of global human identity. That is the story of this volume. Let it now unfold.

15. C. Dickens, 1975, p. 67. See also R. Smollan, 1987; and D. Killingray and R. Rathbone (eds), 1986.

SECTION I

Africa in a decade of world conflicts, 1935–45

2

The Horn and North Africa, 1935–45: crises and change

Tayeb CHENNTOUF

In the fourth and fifth decades of the twentieth century, the Horn and North Africa were, like other regions, shaken by two major upheavals – the world recession and the Second World War. The 1930s saw the beginning of a series of crises and changes deepened and accelerated by the war. In the post-war period, after many difficulties, new equilibria were established; they were at once threatened by political movements that had emerged from the war strengthened and more determined. Almost half a century later, as the archives are opened to historians, much has been written about this recent past in the correct belief that the years 1930–45 did indeed represent a turning point in contemporary history. Many questions of course remain unanswered or the subject of debate, but it is possible today to present an overview that indicates where gaps presently exist and the points that are still controversial.

The Horn and North Africa, 1935–40

From 1935 to 1940, economic and social crises arose.

Economy and society

The economies that had become sensitive to the international market were affected with differences in timing by the reversal of the world economic situation. Rapid population growth and urbanization, less dependent on the global economy, were affected by slower and older movements.

The greatest difficulties arise in determining the relative shares of the world economic crisis and its knock-on effects and the strictly endogenous difficulties of the local economies.

The economies of North Africa and the Horn had been integrated into world trade since at least the second half of the nineteenth century and their economies had, in varying degrees, been shaped by legislation prepared by the colonial powers; they thus proved to be sensitive to any international fluctuations. Any shift in trade had repercussions on local economies because of the importance of external trade, notably with the colonial powers, which increased during the inter-war period, and production in particular agricultural crops and minerals that constituted key elements in exports.

External trade directly felt the unfavourable economic climate and the crises of the French, British and Italian economies. The fall affected both imports and exports but the latter held up better to the fall which affected a small number of mineral and agricultural products traditionally exported to Europe. In Algeria, the value of imports fell by a half from 1929 to 1935. The collapse of Tunisian external trade was a result of the mineral and agricultural crisis. Exports halved in value between 1930 and 1935. Morocco's external trade weakened between 1929 and 1931 and then abruptly collapsed. In 1936, by value, exports were half what they had been in 1926 (1932 million francs as against 3800 million francs). The fluctuations in Libya's external trade were more limited because of its very weakness. External trade with Italy or other European countries in 1930 was extremely small. Even so, Libyan external trade fell from 482 million lira in 1925 to 366 million in 1934. This was a drop of 30 per cent not allowing for inflation.[1]

Since virtually all minerals were exported, the influence of the world market prevailed, with every fall in demand having repercussions on local production and leading to a mining crisis.

The mining crisis manifested itself first in Tunisia. The price of iron ore on the world market began to fall in 1928; in 1930 exports of the main mineral products fell abruptly: from 330 million francs in 1930 to 100 million in 1932.

In Morocco, the sale of phosphates declined in 1931, recording a sharp fall from 1.7 million tons in 1930 to 900000 tons in 1931. It stabilized subsequently, but remained low. In 1931 to 1932, every mining centre except the one at Djerada reduced its activities; the lead and zinc mines closed, manganese mining continued but at a low level.[2] In Algeria, the mining sector suffered a sharp fall in production. Iron-ore production fell 75 per cent between 1929 and 1932. The fall in phosphates of lime was about the same: production reached 920000 tons in 1925 – but by 1939 it had fallen to 400 tons. Other minerals followed the same pattern.[3]

In agriculture, some crops experienced a similar decline in production, since they too were essentially produced for export.

In Libya, the few products that the Italian settlers in Tripolitania could sell faced a slump in sales but this affected only a few products like cabbages.

Egyptian agriculture was affected by the catastrophic fall in the price of cotton on the world market. Farmers who had borrowed to develop

1. J. L. Miège, 1968, p. 186.
2. R. Galissot, 1964, p. 56.
3. A. Nouschi, 1962, p. 42.

irrigation or to purchase pumps found themselves unable to keep up their repayments. Small peasants were faced with the threat of losing their properties. The Sīdī government organized the stockpiling of cotton at state expense; in 1931 the Agricultural Credit Bank was established for small farmers. Signs of recovery appeared at the end of 1933; it encouraged the government to resume work on irrigation and drainage projects.

Algerian export crops (citrus fruits, cotton, oil, tobacco) experienced difficulties in finding markets especially in France; the measures adopted by the French Parliament temporarily deferred the question of the marketing of wine and protected wine-growing for a time. Conversely, given their role in agriculture and the economy, the fall in the price of cereals fuelled the agrarian crisis. The price of cereals fell on the world market from 1930 to 1935. Harvests were bad between 1929 and 1939 except for that of 1933–4; the worst harvests were in 1930–1 and 1935–6.[4]

For the most typical products of Tunisian agriculture (cereals, citrus fruits, olive oils) an initial fall in price occurred in 1928. The fall lasted from 1930–5 and even beyond, and was abrupt between 1932 and 1935. The fall was general for all agricultural export products, the lowest prices being in 1933. The crisis affected all farming activities and all regions: the incomes of farmers fell, threatening the situation of small peasants.

In Morocco, agricultural colonization was disrupted by the fall in prices. The price of wheat fell from 126.60 francs a quintal to 60 francs between 1930 and 1933; barley from 60 francs in 1930 to 23.20 francs in 1934. The harvests themselves were bad except for 1934. Between 1930 and 1933, farmers' incomes fell by 60 per cent.[5]

Compared to mining and agricultural activity for export, artisanal and industrial production was not affected by the world recession, at least directly. Indirectly, it accelerated a local crisis in Morocco and the other countries.

Tunisian handicrafts were already in crisis when the world recession appeared, disrupting it a little more: exports of woollen cloth declined between 1928 and 1932 by 82 per cent, whereas imports of woollen goods rose by 50 per cent; fez (*chechia*) exports fell continuously from 1932 to 1937: from 82 640 units to 26 491. In Tunis, almost 400 people were employed in coppersmithing; the number fell to barely 100 in 1932.

The Algerian craft industry evolved in the same way despite the adoption of recovery measures. Industrial activities that had begun during the First World War were devoted to activities derived from agriculture (flour-milling, oil-milling, brewing). They were import-substitution industries, and oriented towards the local market, employing 90 000 workers in 1936.

4. *ibid.*, p. 46.
5. R. Galissot, 1964, p. 67.

The significance of the crises

The world recession had repercussions in the sectors that were most closely involved in the world market. Indirectly, it worsened local crisis conditions in which the evolution of local economies played a determining role. The deterioration in the economic situation in the various countries was apparent even before the turnaround in the world economic situation was felt. In the same way, the improvement in the global economy did not automatically lead to a parallel improvement in Egypt and the Maghreb.

In Tunisia, while the world recession weakened, the local economic situation worsened because of the drought which made the harvest of 1935–6 disastrous. In 1939, the economy of Algeria had still not yet altogether recovered to its 1929 level.

The local economies were affected by a crisis whose origins were endogenous. In reality, there were several crises of varying and sometimes divergent significance. How long colonization had been underway and the scale of the economic transformations make it possible to distinguish various types of crisis.

In Libya, the economic difficulties were those of an agricultural development that was just beginning. In Morocco, the crisis came after a first stage of economic expansion and even euphoria. In Algeria and Tunisia, the crisis was that of the colonial economy itself whose foundations were shaken. In Egypt alone, despite the world recession, considerable economic progress continued to be made, making this country follow a path that was altogether an original one.

Libya became an Italian colony in 1916 but administration and development were seriously restricted until 1931 by continuing resistance. The Italian conquest cost the country heavy human and economic losses. Livestock, the principal wealth of Cyrenaica, were decimated; the number of sheep, goats, cattle, camels, horses and donkeys fell from 1 411 800 in 1910 to 978 000 in 1926 and 140 430 in 1933.[6] The country was depopulated and ruined by the time of the world recession. The 'traditional' economy had much more to do overcoming the difficulties consequent upon the Italian war of conquest than it had those of a world market to which it was hardly linked at all.

Italian agrarian colonization was confronted with a number of problems. Economic colonization as practised from 1911 to 1921 was abandoned in 1928 in favour of settlement colonization. The 1928 laws led to a first wave of immigration followed by a second launched by Mussolini himself after 1928. The agricultural land grants were intended for the settlement of Italian peasants recruited by the fascist organizations. Agrarian and settlement colonization was a double failure, both human and financial, of Italian fascist policy. The difficulties of agricultural enterprises in

6. J. Despois, 1935, p. 14.

Tripolitania and Cyrenaica were very similar to the crises met with by agrarian colonization in Algeria in the second half of the nineteenth century. In Libya, as in Algeria before it, agrarian colonization ran up against three obstacles: the lack of capital, the non-existence of an enlarged market and the absence of a work-force available for wage labour.

The crisis in Morocco, placed under a protectorate very late, had a different significance. After a first crisis of growth in 1924–5, expansion resumed until 1931. Between then and 1936, external trade diminished and speculative enterprises, particularly in construction, agriculture and mining, were affected. Industrial activities kept going although industrial growth fell. New activities developed: processing industries such as flour-mills kept going; sardine-canning factories flourished; the search for oil became productive; tobacco-processing factories came into operation in Casablanca and Kenitra; the vegetable horsehair industry continued to prosper.

Despite the difficulties, there was no decline in economic activity and even some slight growth. In total, while the growth of the years 1925–30 was lost, industrial activity held up to the crisis better and recovered.[7]

The Tunisian and Algerian crises were similar. The economic difficulties were less those of a colonization in its first stage than of colonial economies which had experienced deep transformations and periods of expansion.

In Tunisia, the world recession (1930–1) affected an agricultural under-production economy due to the drought of 1930 followed by floods in the centre and north in December 1931. The economic situation worsened in 1930 with losses of livestock in the south. The locust invasion followed the floods almost immediately; the agricultural harvest was bad because of heavy frosts and high winds.

Algeria represents the most complex example of difficulties of various origins. As in Tunisia there was a traditional type of crisis which affected essentially the Algerian population. It was aggravated by the crisis of the colonial sector masked and delayed by the measures adopted. The consequences of the world recession made themselves felt after the first local difficulties; the colonial sector was the first to be affected.

Although affected by the world recession the Egyptian economy made progress in two areas. The Misr group, which had appeared after the end of the First World War, continued its development by creating new industrial companies: shipping companies in 1932 and 1934, a cotton-spinning and weaving company in 1937 at Ḳafr al-Dawwar, and trading companies in 1940. The crisis of 1929–33 intensified the inflow of capital to the group and enabled it to strengthen its position in the Egyptian economy. It also benefited from changes in fiscal and customs legislation.

In 1930 Egypt recovered its fiscal autonomy and the right to collect customs duties on all imports. Until then, an international agreement

7. R. Galissot, 1964, p. 72.

prohibited Egypt from imposing customs tariffs. The last trade agreement with a foreign power having expired in 1930, a customs tariff was put into effect thanks to pressure by the Misr group and despite Great Britain. The decision marked an important turning-point for industrial development: textiles, food industries and light industries experienced expansion right up to the war. In the longer perspective, the beginnings of industrialization date from the 1930s.

In the Horn of Africa, as in Libya, the potential effects of the world recession were limited by the lack of economic change since the beginning of the century and integration into the circuits of world trade. The examples of Ethiopia and Somalia are even clearer than that of the Sudan.

In the latter country, the development of the railway network and the cultivation of Egyptian cotton made the economy sensitive to any international fluctuation. At the beginning of the twentieth century, Lord Kitchener built the strategic railway from the northern border to Khartoum. In 1905 it was linked to the Red Sea where Port Sudan was created at the same time as the town of Atbara at the junction. Later it was pushed as far as Sennār and reached Kordofān in the west in 1911. From 1924 a new line linked Sennār directly with Port Sudan to serve the cotton-growing areas.

The choice was for Egyptian long-staple cotton which was initially grown on non-irrigated lands. After the First World War, the Gezira Scheme, involving the irrigation of the whole of the eastern part of the Gezira by the Sennār dam, was launched. Other cultivation zones were created, notably on the Gash, a torrent that comes from Ethiopia and runs into the sands of Ķassala. In 1929, a convention was signed with Egypt on sharing the Nile waters.[8]

The extension of the rail network and cotton cultivation gave the Sudan an export product and greater monetarization of the economy. In the 1930s, cotton accounted for the bulk of exports. As in Egypt, the crisis had repercussions in the regions specializing in cotton-growing, affecting the producers directly. Indirectly, it affected Sudanese civil servants educated at Gordon College. Their wages were sharply cut in 1931, whereas those of their foreign colleagues were not affected. They took strike action and convened a congress which secured a compromise with the authorities.[9]

In Ethiopia, external trade was minimal at the beginning of the twentieth century: 8 000 000 thalers for the Shoa and Harar route, or 20 000 000 gold francs; for the whole country, external trade did not exceed 50 000 000 francs. Coffee, gold, ivory and skins were the main exports; cotton goods, weapons and ammunition were among the imports.

8. Collectif, 1966, p. 472.
9. J. Ki-Zerbo, 1972, p. 564.

The Djibouti railway had been under construction since 1903 and reached Addis Ababa in 1917. It made it possible to link the interior of the country with the seaports. In 1935, it made possible the export of 15 000 tons of coffee and 7000 tons of skins. Imports were even smaller.[10] However, the Ethiopian currency was seriously affected by the crisis.[11]

The population explosion and urbanization, already perceptible before 1930 in the statistics, known to a handful of experts, worried public opinion less than the world recession and were, in the short term, ignored by the administrations governing the protectorates and colonies. They were the result of an old and slow evolution and belong, by definition, to the 'long wave'. However, population increase and urban growth became massive after 1930 and became structural features of societies after 1930–45.

Population growth[12] took on the allure of a veritable explosion which was not peculiar to North Africa and the Horn. This is observable in other regions of Africa and contrasts with the tapering off of population growth in Europe.

The old population pattern lasted a long time, but its ending, which dates from the inter-war period, was spectacular. Until the middle of the twentieth century, birth and death rates remained high; famines and epidemics were receding, but they had not totally disappeared.

However, the population censuses carried out in the inter-war period show birth and death rates diverging: whereas the death rate was falling, the birth rate remained high. The example of Morocco clearly illustrates the changing demographic pattern: whereas the death rate fell considerably, the birth rates oscillated around 38 (average 1932–5) and 44 (average 1941–5) per thousand.[13] In northern Algeria, the birth rate was estimated at 38 per thousand between 1921 and 1925; it rose from 43 per thousand between 1926 and 1930 to 44 per thousand between 1931 and 1935 and fell back to 42 per thousand from 1936 to 1940. The death rate fell from about 19.8 per thousand in 1921–5 to about 16.6 per thousand between 1936 and 1940.[14]

The break in the old population pattern also occurred at different times in different countries. Libya and Morocco were close to the old population pattern; Egypt, Algeria and Tunisia already manifested a profoundly altered pattern. Libya, a lightly populated country, paid a high demographic price for its resistance to the Italian conquest. Guiseppe Volpi, appointed governor in 1921, decided to impose Italy's rights by force. The greatest loss of life occurred in Cyrenaica where military operation

10. Collectif, 1966, p. 482.
11. J. Ki-Zerbo, 1972, p. 462.
12. All population figures in the inter-war period are relative.
13. J. L. Miège, 1950, p. 55.
14. C. R. Ageron, 1979, vol. 2, pp. 471–2.

took place last. Changes in the population structure were much more a process of making up for the losses to get back to the pre-1916 level than a real growth. Morocco experienced the most rapid growth in the Maghreb: the birth rate was the highest in the region.

The Tunisian population (Muslims and Jews) increased by 25 per cent between 1936 and 1946. Estimated at 2 100 000 in 1926, it reached 3 200 000 in 1946.[15]

Population changes recorded in Algeria by the end of the nineteenth century became clearer and more marked. By the 1880s, the Algerian population had recovered its pre-1830 level with some slight growth. The demographic upheaval, barely perceptible in 1921, stood out very clearly in 1931. The population rose from 4 923 186 in 1921 to 6 201 144 in 1936, a growth rate of 1.53 per cent.[16]

The Egyptian population rose from 13 222 000 inhabitants in 1920 to 16 887 000 in 1940: an increase of 3 665 000, equivalent to an average annual increase of 183 000 persons. In 1945, the population was estimated at 18 460 000.[17]

Population growth was one of the factors in urban growth. In some towns, foreign inflow from the outside added to this, but the urban explosion was overwhelmingly the result of a rural exodus. The formation of shanty-towns shortly before the Second World War was the visible sign of the influx of rural dwellers to the medium and coastal towns.

Numerous factors pushed rural dwellers to move into the towns to look for work or to live on charity and assistance. Migrations that had previously been temporary became permanent with the arrival of families and their establishment on the outskirts of towns. In Morocco, Algeria and Tunisia, migratory movements extended overseas with the arrival in France of the first waves of immigrant workers.

The migratory movements began in Morocco even before the establishment of the protectorate. The crisis increased the number of departures to the towns after 1931; they were particularly numerous during 1937 because of the drought and typhus. The shanty-towns surrounding Casablanca had 85 000 inhabitants in 1932; Ben Msir at the same time had 3000–3500 shanties.[18] New shanty-towns were formed around Casablanca in 1935–6.

The migratory movements in Tunisia and Algeria were similar; shanty-towns came into existence at more or less the same date in both countries. The population of Tunis was growing by 1.04 per cent per annum between 1921 and 1936. The suburbs and outlying areas were growing at a rate of 2.61 per cent per annum during the same period. The

15. P. Sebag, 1951, p. 151; A. Raymond, 1955, p. 44.
16. A. Nouschi, 1962, p. 31.
17. F. J. Tomiche, 1974, p. 14.
18. R. Galissot, 1964, p. 73.

population of the countryside around Tunis rose from 172 000 in 1921 to 219 578 in 1936. The agricultural crisis precipitated the dismissal of workers who became unemployed and settled in the shanty-towns. Bizerta and Sfax experienced the same phenomenon.[19]

The least rapid urban growth was recorded in Libya where the oases remained the economic centres and were doubled in some cases by Italian administrative centres. The sole large town was Tripoli, whose population grew rapidly, whereas the centres of colonization were of very modest proportions.[20]

In Egypt, Cairo profited from the rural exodus much more than the towns in the Nile delta: the Egyptian capital grew from 570 000 inhabitants in 1890, to 865 000 in 1920 and 1 527 000 in 1940.[21]

Urban growth disrupted the old hierarchy among Moroccan towns more dramatically. Between 1931 and 1936 Casablanca became the city with the largest population (275 000 inhabitants in 1936 as against 163 000 in 1931). Marrakesh marked time (190 000 inhabitants in 1936) but towns with some commercial and industrial activity such as Rabat, Sale, Fez, Meknes, and Kenitra were the final destination of migratory currents.[22] In Algeria, the urban population, estimated at 508 235 in 1926, rose to 722 293 in 1936 and 1 129 482 in 1948.[23]

In the Horn of Africa, the population of the Sudan, estimated at 3 000 000 at the beginning of the century, reached 6 000 000 in 1939.[24] The most intense urbanization was recorded in Ethiopia between 1935 and 1940. After the conquest of the country, the Italians attempted to develop it economically by establishing areas of colonization. Major expenditures financed the establishment of settlers, the creation of industries and above all the construction of modern roads and buildings. Addis Ababa swelled to over 100 000 inhabitants in 1935.[25] Djibouti – which, following the building of the railway, replaced Zeiba as the outlet for Harar and Shoa – doubled its population, rising from 10 000 inhabitants in 1900 to 20 000 in 1940, which was almost half the population of the territory. In 1936, a port with a jetty was built there; the town spread beyond the salines as far as the Amnbouli oasis.[26]

19. M. Rouissi, 1977, p. 85.
20. J. Despois, 1935, pp. 103–104; R. Raneiro, 1982.
21. P. Léon, 1978, p. 479.
22. R. Galissot, 1964, p. 117.
23. C. R. Ageron, 1979, vol. 2, p. 473.
24. Collectif, 1966, p. 472.
25. *ibid.*, p. 482.
26. *ibid.*

Political crises

In the political domain, the various countries had been put under the control of European powers in the nineteenth and early twentieth centuries, except for Ethiopia which was so only in 1935. Their political evolution in the years preceding the Second World War was as varied as it was in the economic and social domain. Challenges to the status of colony or protectorate occurred through a series of political crises which culminated in the years 1936–7 and which were temporarily halted by the outbreak of the Second World War.

The evolution of Egypt and Libya

The political evolution of Egypt was in total contrast to that of Libya: the former won a considerable loosening of British control over its political life; the latter was integrated into Italian 'national territory'.

At the same time as the second wave of emigration of 'Ventemila',[27] fascist policy pursued the integration of Libya into Italian national territory. A fascist Grand Council decree was promulgated: the four coastal provinces of Tripoli, Misurāta, Benghazi and Dera became 'part of the national territory'. The territories of the Libyan Sahara retained their status as a colony. The local government retained its full autonomy, the governor-general having under his full and direct authority the four coastal provinces and the Sahara. In the administration, only junior positions were open to Libyans. 'Special citizenship' was valid only in Libya where it was granted to Libyans able to read and write.

In reality, the local population was excluded from administrative and political life. The sole political activity by Libyans was in Egypt. In 1923, Idrīs took refuge there, where a small colony of Libyans had formed. With British support, they engaged in anti-Italian propaganda.

Since the end of the First World War, Egyptian political life had been dominated by the complex interplay of the monarchy, the British representative and the political parties, notably the Wafd. Britain's concern with Italian propaganda in Egypt and their activity in Libya and Ethiopia made possible the signing of the 1936 treaty and the conclusion of the Montreux conventions of 1937.

The essential clauses of the treaty which was signed in London on 26 August can be summarized as follows: the independence of Egypt was reaffirmed and Britain in turn committed itself to defend Egypt against any aggression and, in the event of war, Egypt was obliged to offer Britain every facility on its territory; the occupation was terminated and ambassadors were to be exchanged; Britain undertook to support Egypt in its desire to suppress the capitulations and enter the League of Nations;

27. 'Ventemila': twenty thousand (Italian settlers).

38

no limit was put on the size of the Egyptian army, which was authorized to be stationed in the Sudan.

The treaty was valid for an unlimited period but was to be reviewed after 20 years. It represented progress compared to the unilateral act of 1929 but did not open up an era of true independence for the country. The British concessions were in fact minor and altogether formal. The security of lines of communication with the British empire was assured by British troops (limited to 10 000 soldiers) who were to leave the country and be stationed in the Canal Zone. British troops were authorized to occupy the whole country in the event of international tension or war. The *status quo* was retained in the Sudan.

As agreed in 1936, with London's support, the Montreux conference, which was held in April 1937, abolished the capitulations; the mixed courts would be gradually phased out over a period of twelve years. Thus the preferential regime enjoyed by the capitular powers was terminated, as were the consular courts and the mixed courts after a transitional period. All the powers and responsibilities of the consular and mixed courts devolved on national courts (the former native courts), with at their apex a court of appeal (after 1930) and an administrative tribunal or council of state (1946). Conversely, the personal status of Egyptians continued to come under religious courts.

The abolition of the capitulations made Egypt master of its financial legislation: in 1940, bilateral conventions signed with Britain and France put an end to the debt administration system. The signing of a similar agreement with Italy was rendered superfluous by the Second World War.

Despite the minimal nature of British concessions in the 1936 treaty, its signing and the withdrawal of British troops into the Canal Zone marked the triumph of the Wafd, and Nahhas Pasha for the first time was in a position to maintain himself in power for a reasonable length of time and the Wafd remained in power until the end of 1937. King Farouk enjoyed great popularity in the early years of his reign. Hoping to play the same political role as his father, he dismissed Nahhas Pasha and dissolved parliament. The 1938 elections were a serious setback for the Wafd weakened by its internal divisions and the criticisms provoked by its period in government.

The crisis of Franco-Maghrebi relations

In the three countries of the classical Maghreb (Algeria, Morocco, Tunisia) the coming to power of the Popular Front opened up the prospect of redefining relations with France. It was quickly followed by dis-illusionment: and, after the fall of the Popular Front government, repression. In fact, in the decade 1930–40, Franco-Maghrebi relations experienced their first serious crisis.

The League for Moroccan Action (*al-Kutla al-ʿAmal al-Watāni*), established in 1933, drew up a plan for reforms which roundly criticized the abuses consequent upon the protectorate regime and attempted, in a second part, to make a coherent doctrinal formulation around the principle of the inalienability of national sovereignty symbolized by Sultan Mohamed V. The Residency rejected the demands which were deemed incompatible with the French presence in Morocco and limited itself to implementing, belatedly, those that it felt were minor.

The formation of the Popular Front government, which was welcomed by the nationalists, made it possible to relaunch the demands through the despatch of a delegation to Paris and resort to mass action. The year 1937 was marked by agitation all over the country (Meknes, Marrakesh, Khemisset) which was severely put down. After the fall of the Blum government the repression worsened with the dissolution of the League for Moroccan Action (18 March 1937). At the end of the year, nationalism was leaderless. It had become increasingly radicalized and experienced a number of splits which were indicative of the debates going on inside it. Al-Wāzzani, competing with 'Allal al-Fasi, created a new party: the National Movement (*al-Ḥaraka al-Ḳawmiyya*); the section that continued to be led by 'Allal al-Fasi became the National Reform Party (*al-Ḥijb al-Waṭāni li-tahḳiḳ al-Matālib*). In the northern zone, an identical split gave birth to the Party of National Reforms led by 'Abd al-Khalik Tares and the Moroccan Unity Party led by Mekki al-Nāṣiri.

In Tunisia, after a period of repression, the Destūrians put a lot of hope in the Popular Front. The 'first Franco–Tunisian experiment' began: Habib Bourguiba presented the new party's programme in a note delivered to P. Vienot on 28 August 1936, in a speech in Tunis on 11 September, and in articles published in the newspaper *l'Action Tunisienne*.

P. Vienot's journey to Tunisia and his speech of 1 March 1937 marked a turning point. His journey was followed on 4 March by bloody incidents at the phosphate mine at Metlaoui. Indirectly, 'Abd al-'Azīz Ta'albi's return to Tunisia (5 July 1937) precipitated the deterioration of the situation.

In the short term, it gave a new impetus to the debates and struggles among the Destūrians. The Destūr, founded in the aftermath of the First World War, officially split at the Ḳsār Hellal congress (2 March 1934) into an Old Destūr and a Neo-Destūr in which Habib Bourguiba laboured to secure its position and disseminate its programme. Incidents continued to occur until the riot of 9 April 1938. The lifting of the state of siege on 18 August left a country in which the Neo-Destūr was leaderless but had become the voice of Tunisian nationalism. Even more than in the two neighbouring countries, the advent of the Popular Front raised great hopes in Algeria that demands would be met.

The elected representatives, the *'ulamā* and the communists, without the participation of the Etoile Nord-africaine, convened a Muslim Congress (7 March 1936) which drew up a 'Charter of Demands of the Muslim

Algerian People' which contained a series of demands for equality and respect for Muslim personal status.

The Blum government, which decided to meet some of the nationalists' demands, drafted a law to give the right to vote to the Algerian élite, on an individual basis and without their having to give up their Muslim personal status. Some 20 000–25 000 individuals would benefit from the proposed law which was denounced by Messali Ḥādj who wanted immediate independence. In fact, because of opposition from the settlers, the proposal was not examined by the National Assembly in 1937 or 1938 and remained a draft.

The atmosphere created by the Popular Front enabled the nationalist parties, for the first time, to achieve unity in demands and action. It enabled them to establish themselves in the towns and countryside above all by widely disseminating their ideas.

The political evolution of the Horn of Africa

The political evolution of the Horn of Africa was dominated by Anglo-Egyptian disputes in the Sudan and the Italian military intervention in Ethiopia.

The Sudanese political situation was complicated by the existence, at least formally, of the Anglo-Egyptian condominium. From the very beginnings of nationalism in the country, the question of relations with Egypt was the source of divisions among the nationalists.

Religious-based uprisings were harshly put down. The biggest of them was the one led by Wiad Halula in the Gezira. A follower of the *Mahdī*, he aimed at continuing his struggle by bringing his followers together and refusing to reply to a communication. After the assassination of two individuals, including the district commissioner, a military column quickly put an end to the attempt. The '*Mahdī*'s' successor was captured and hanged.

At the same time, national feeling was spreading in educated circles. The secret societies which came into being almost all advocated the end of the condominium and independence or union with Egypt. The best constituted of them was the White Flag Society founded in 1924 by an officer, 'Alī 'Abd al-Latīf, who opted for the freedom of the Sudan and the unity of the Nile valley.

In 1936, the agreement reached between Britain and Egypt restored to the latter rights that it had lost during political disturbances in Egypt and the Sudan. The Sudanese nationalists, not having been consulted, took up what they saw as a challenge. In 1938 a General Graduates' Congress was organized; it initially portrayed itself as a corporative and philanthropic organization in order to secure official recognition.

The Ethiopian war and its consequences

The Italian conquest of Ethiopia in 1935 brought about the disappearance of the last independent African state. It had a profound impact on African nationalists, and among black Americans; in the Horn of Africa, the consequences were direct and immediate. Italian expansion in north-east Africa had been halted in 1896 by the decisive victory of Emperor Menelik at Adowa. Italian aims were reactivated by fascism. The treaty of friendship only apparently masked colonial aims on Ethiopia, postponed until the Italian troops had dealt with the Sanūsiyya in Libya.

PLATE 2.1   *The advance of Italian troops in Abyssinia*

A frontier dispute in the Ogaden between Somaliland and Ethiopia served as a pretext for fascism. Skirmishes took place at Wāl Wāl. The Arbitration Commission appointed by the League of Nations failed in its mission. Britain and France supported Ethiopia but were not prepared to prevent Italian aggression. Mussolini's troops advanced along previously prepared routes from Adowa in the north and Mogadishu in the south-east. The fascist army of 400 000 men and with superior weaponry easily took Tigre whereas Gugsa had been bribed. Addis Ababa fell in 1936 after intense bombardments which destroyed towns, villages and flocks. The emperor had to take refuge in England.

Italy's East African empire became a reality for a few years. Ethiopia united with Eritrea and Somaliland constituted 'Africa Orientale Italiana'; the king of Italy took the title 'Emperor of Ethiopia'.

'Africa Orientale Italiana' included the coastal deserts and the Ethiopian highlands and had 12 000 000 inhabitants. It was subdivided into five large provinces each with a governor, the whole being headed by a viceroy. A large number of fascist troops maintained a police state; military operations were necessary in the south-west where resistance activities occurred.

War and peace, 1940–5

Except for Egypt, nationalist demands in 1937–8 met with intransigence from the colonial powers and repression. From 1940 to 1945, the evolution of the various countries was tied up with that of the war in which they were involved. In the political domain, the pre-war crises gave way to real changes; more powerful and more demanding nationalism appeared by 1943.

Countries at war

The First World War appeared as a conflict between Europeans that was happening in Europe. The Second World War transformed North Africa and the Horn into combat zones; military mobilization affected far more people; economies were directed towards the war effort. The end of military operations led to many economic and social difficulties.

Participation in the conflict
Between 1939 and 1945, the evolution of military operations and the participation in many forms of the various African countries was more important for the outcome of the conflict than it had been in 1914–18.

The various battle zones of the 'Africa War', from the Algerian–Tunisian frontier almost to Alexandria, were closely interconnected and involved prodigious efforts for three years. For the British, Egypt was a vital strategic zone. It was considered a key zone not only because of the existence of the Suez Canal but also as a hinge in the conduct of the war. Churchill felt that Egypt had to be defended as if it were Kent or Sussex. A first Italian attack from Libya, led by Graziani, was repulsed by Wavell in December 1940. The second attack made by the Afrika Korps led by Rommel was stopped by Auchinleck at al-'Alamein; on 23 January 1943 British troops entered Tripoli, while the Leclerc column – which had started out from Chad – arrived soon after and joined up with the Eighth Army.[28]

Italy also threatened Tunisia from Libya. The existence of a large Italian minority and old claims gave the country a special place in the

28. I. S. El-Hareir, 1985.

PLATE 2.2   *French soldiers in combat in the Tripolitania Desert*

war. The Anglo-American landing accelerated German designs in Tunisia. On 9 November 1942, a hundred German planes landed on al-'Awina airfield near Tunis with a thousand men. They entered Tunis without previous warning in the night of 13–14 November. The German occupation subsequently spread to all the large urban centres: Sfax, Sousse, Gabès.

The counter-offensive was waged by allied troops from Algeria where Anglo-American armies had landed – as also in Morocco. In November 1942 the British army began the Tunisian campaign with the crossing of the Algerian–Tunisian frontier. After a series of operations, the Allied High Command launched a general offensive on 22 April. The entry of the British into Tunis and the Americans into Bizerta in May marked the end of the Tunisian campaign.

In the Horn, as soon as they entered the war the Italians established in Ethiopia occupied two frontier towns in the Sudan (Kassala and Gallabāt) and the whole of British Somaliland, where there were virtually no troops.

In 1941, British troops reconquered the territories under Italian control. In Tigre, General Platt, starting out from the Sudan, won a victory at Keren; in Somaliland, General Cunningham set out from Kenya and reached Harar and then Addis Ababa. The two army corps met up on

44

the Amba Alaguir where the duke of Aosta surrendered. On 5 May 1941, Emperor Haile Selassie was able to return to the Ethiopian capital.

The countries of North Africa and the Horn, transformed into battle-fields, also supplied soldiers for the various European fronts. Up to the armistice, North Africa alone provided 216 000 men, including 123 000 Algerians. From 1943 to 1945, 385 000 men from North Africa, including 290 000 Algerians, Tunisians and Moroccans, took part in the liberation of France.[29] The army of Africa took part in the liberation of Corsica (September–October 1943), the Italian campaign (entry into Rome, 15 June 1944) and the Provence campaign (August 1944) and then moved northward to join up with the main body of the French army. In Cairo, where he had taken refuge, Idrīs approved the formation of battalions to wage a guerrilla war in the Djabal al-Akhdar as soon as the situation allowed. Britain, which asked for application of the 1936 treaty, did not expect real military assistance from Egypt. Diplomatic relations with Germany were broken as soon as war was declared, and with Italy on 12 June 1940; but the declaration of war on Germany and Japan came much later (26 February 1945).

In the Horn of Africa, a large Sudanese contingent took part with British troops in the reconquest of Ethiopia. Ethiopian refugees in the Sudan were organized militarily by General Wingate with the name 'Gideon Force', which penetrated into Gojam.

Along with the mobilization of men there was an economic policy to support the war effort. In October 1939 the Moroccan economy was declared a 'war economy'. The approach of war precipitated a rise in mineral prices creating a degree of prosperity. The Algerian and Tunisian economies also strengthened the economic front.

The Middle East Supply Centre, established in Cairo in the summer of 1941, was responsible with the regional resource mobilization office for reducing the dependence of the region on outside markets for imports by stepping up production and redirecting trade. Local industries were used to their full capacity for civilian and military needs.

The economic problems of peace
The war precipitated numerous economic and social difficulties. The disruption of transport had repercussions on external trade which collapsed, and the price rises increased the cost of living and the development of the black market. The demand induced by the war was responsible for some industrial growth that was called into question by the resumption in 1945 of commercial links with Europe.

The break in relations with France and Britain and the needs of the war, promoted – much more than in the past – the production of goods that had hitherto been imported. Egypt profited more than the other

29. P. Léon, 1978, p. 557.

countries from the new situation. The agricultural expansion of the 1920s and 30s was interrupted by the war but industrial activity remained at a high level and industry diversified to meet rising demand.

The increase in the size of the Egyptian army from 22 000 men in 1937 to 45 000 in 1945, and the wages paid by the Allies to the 20 000 civilians employed in the building and maintenance of military installations, increased the demand for manufactured goods; the markets of the region were open to Egyptian production.

Investment that had been directed towards the land and property now turned to industrial activities. The Middle East Supply Centre played a major role by giving technical advice to factory managers or helping them procure raw materials. Production of textiles, processed food, chemicals, glass, leather, cement, petroleum and machines expanded. New industries came into being: canneries, rubber products, jute, the making of tools and, above all, a wide variety of pharmaceutical and chemical products. Industrial output increased by 38 per cent between 1939 and 1945.[30]

In the Maghreb the war underlined the dependence in every domain on European economies.

Tunisia was deprived of its sources of production of raw materials and faced difficult economic problems. The impetus was given for the mining of lignite. To replace French products, the craft industries were revived where they had been replaced before the war by French imports of clothing, shoes and pottery.

Numerous enterprises were set up in Algeria from 1940 onwards to make up for imports that had become rare or unobtainable. Several large enterprises opened branches (factories and workshops): Lesieur oil mills set up a large oil refinery; near Oran, a pottery works and a glassworks were opened by Niedwiller and Saint-Gobain potteries. Lafarge cement enlarged their Algiers factory (Pointe Pescade) and built a second one near Oran (Saint Lucien).[31]

The Moroccan economy was forced to make similar efforts at local production faced with the fall in exports. The volume of industrial investment between 1940 and 1945 equalled that of the previous 27 years: during the years 1939–45, 53.3 per cent of capital was directed to industrial activities to develop already existing ones or build new ones. The Gouin soap and oil works opened a second oil refinery, and the Lesieur company came in in February 1942.[32]

The restoration of peace called import-substitution industrialization into question and brought about a halt to industrial growth. The economic and social situation was aggravated by demobilization, the ending of war industries and an unfavourable agricultural climate.

30. S. Radwan, 1974, p. 193.
31. A. Nouschi, 1962, p. 102.
32. R. Galissot, 1964, pp. 217–18.

The economic climate underwent profound changes at the end of hostilities. In every country, inflation led to very large price rises just when the French and British armies were laying off workers that they had employed during the war. Unemployment and under-employment were widespread.

The most pressing Egyptian problems were partly concealed by the voting of funds to help state workers and those laid off by the military administration. The most important problems were examined by inter-ministerial committees and commissions, a large number of which were set up in 1945–6. A Higher Labour Council met for the first time on 23 March 1945 to draw up a labour code. In order to mop up unemployment a five-year plan for large-scale works was granted £25 000 000 in 1945 to finance the opening of roads, the digging of irrigation canals, the draining of marshes, the laying on of drinking water in provincial towns, the building of schools and hospitals, etc. More than half a million *feddāns* of state lands were to be distributed to farmers on particularly advantageous terms. These measures proved in fact to be insufficient to put an end to the social unrest which was prolonged in some countries by bad harvests.

In Tunisia, after 1945, trade circuits resumed their pre-war pattern but the country was shaken for three successive years by famine. Following a persistent drought, catastrophic grain harvests, particularly in the centre and south, followed one after the other from 1944 to 1946. There were countless deaths among sheep and goats already weakened by the shortage of water and forage. Several tens of thousands of rural dwellers once again flocked northward to live by begging or work on public-works sites.[33]

Industrial growth
While a minority was able to get rich through various sorts of trafficking and the black market, the overwhelming majority of the population was subjected to harsh living conditions which continued in the post-war period. The European economies themselves were prey to difficulties and could be of no help despite the resumption of trade.

Moroccan external trade resumed in 1943: average imports rose from 936 000 tonnes before the war to 1 280 000 tonnes, and exports from 2 500 000 tonnes to 32 000 000 tonnes.[34] In every country, commercial flows resumed their pre-war pattern. The small amount of capital invested and the mediocre quality of their products made the enterprises set up during the war very fragile; several were obliged to close down. Algeria had the advantage of an industrialization plan. The war had shown the important role as a rear base played by the protectorates and colonies in

33. P. Sebag, 1951, pp. 163–4.
34. J. L. Miège, 1966, p. 115.

the outcome of military operations. The 'imperial ideology' promoted industrial plans with a third world-war seen as inevitable in mind. The structural problems of the Algerian economy were tackled in a speech by General Catroux in 1944. A 20-year programme was drawn up affecting every area: crafts, education, housing, public health, infrastructure, rehousing of Algerian farmers. After a rapid start, the five-year industrialization plan was abandoned.

Political changes

In 1948, the re-integration of North Africa and the Horn into the international division of labour put an end to the economic progress achieved during the war. It was not the same in the political arena where the war had the consequences of weakening France and Britain, while Italy was among the defeated. After a short interruption of political activity, the war favoured nationalism which moved to action in 1943 and in 1945–6 challenged the return to the *status quo ante* as colony or protectorate.

By 1939, nationalism, which had experienced a period of intense activity in the years 1936–7, had tempered its demands. It took advantage of the new situation created by the war to raise its head once again as soon as political life resumed – even before the end of the conflict.

From the eve of the war, the Algerian nationalist parties were directly or indirectly affected by measures of repression. The Algerian People's Party was banned on 26 September 1939; its leader (Messali Ḥādj) was again imprisoned in October with several other leaders; militants were sent to internment camps. On 28 April 1941, Messali Ḥādj and his companions were sentenced to forced labour or imprisonment by the Algiers military tribunal. The Algerian People's Party, disorganized, effectively disappeared from political life. The Communist Party was reduced to inactivity or underground activity as soon as war broke out. The *'ulamās'* press ceased appearing; Shaykh al-Ibrāhīmi was put under house arrest at Aflou during the winter of 1939–40 while Shaykh A. Ben Badis was not allowed to leave the city of Constantine without special authorization.[35]

The nationalists drew their own conclusions about what was initially an external conflict which gradually came closer; they seriously altered their attitudes and revised their perspectives. On the whole, and sometimes to the surprise of the 'metropoles', the nationalists, after a short period of wait and see, committed themselves to the Allied cause, issuing numerous statements to that effect and not opposing military mobilization.

They called for a rallying to the Allied cause and democracy. For

35. C. R. Ageron, 1979, vol. 2, p. 548.

Ferhat Abbas, 'if democratic France ceased to be powerful, our ideal of liberty would be buried forever'.[36] In a letter of 8 August 1942, Habib Bourguiba expressed his confidence in the victory of the Allies and his attachment to the democracies while 'leaving aside until after the war the problem of our independence'.[37] On 3 September 1939, the sultan of Morocco came out publicly in favour of France, to which he offered 'unalloyed help'. Several nationalists were called up into the French army or joined up voluntarily. Generally, mobilization took place amid 'an admirable order and discipline' (Le Beau).

As the conflict continued there was an almost imperceptible shift in the 'public mind' and the attitude of the nationalists. General Weygand, made governor-general of Algeria, noted that the population was 'undisciplined, rude, sometimes insolent'.[38] In 1940, taxpayers refused to pay their taxes. Several factors combined to lead to a resumption of and change in nationalist activity.

The outcome of the fighting in 1940 had immediate effects: France and Britain lost the capital of fear they had built up over almost a century by their power and prestige. The nationalists drew extra power and mobilization from their weakening and also drew all the consequences from the French divisions manifest in Algiers, Rabat and Tunis and from the Anglo-American landing.

When the armistice was signed they stressed the participation of their countries alongside the Allies in order to get their demands accepted. The Egyptian memorandum presented by the Wafd to the British ambassador at the end of the war recalled, in support of demands for reform, 'the inestimable help' given by Egypt to the Allies during the war. The statement made by Anthony Eden on 8 June 1942 to MPs explicitly referred to the contribution of Senoussi forces to the war which was being fought in Libya. On 18 June 1943, General de Gaulle hailed 'the faithful empire, the starting base for the recovery of the country'.[39]

Apart from a few very limited successes, Axis propaganda did not succeed in detaching the nationalists and public opinion from their commitment to the Allies. Mussolini's Islamic policy and fascist and Nazi propaganda failed utterly in the Maghreb countries; they had some impact in Egypt.[40]

The anti-colonialism of the great powers was on the contrary welcomed with a great deal of hope. Just as they had in 1918 Wilson's fourteen points, the nationalists hailed the Atlantic Charter (14 August 1941), the United Nations Declaration (1 January 1942) and the San Francisco

36. R. Le Tourneau, 1962, p. 335.
37. *ibid.*, p. 96.
38. Quoted by C. R. Ageron, 1979, vol. 2, p. 553.
39. S. Vacono, 1974, p. 52.
40. D. Grange, 1974 and 1976; J. Bessis, 1981, p. 403.

Charter. They relied on the positions taken by the great powers and interpreted their statements as meaning the emancipation of the colonial peoples.

Britain and France manoeuvered to retain their basic positions but the nationalists took advantage of the conditions created by the war to achieve their objectives.

Anglo-Egyptian difficulties derived from the 1936 treaty which Britain demanded should be applied. The Egyptian governments and opposition parties affirmed the principle of non-belligerence and sought to modify the treaty or even secure independence. In 1940, parliamentary circles demanded, immediately, substantial amendments to the treaty and the status of foreigners. The demands formulated by the Wafd in a memorandum handed to Sir Miles Lampson and dated 1 April 1940 were even more radical.[41]

The Libyan emigrés in Egypt organized a debate on the fate of their country after the end of the conflict (conferences in Alexandria on 23 October 1939 and Cairo on 9 August 1940). Assurances were sought from the British by Idrīs on the future independence of Libya. Anthony Eden's statement was circumspect about the future, simply promising that the Sanūsī in Cyrenaica would in no circumstances come under Italian rule again.

The French positions in Algeria, Tunisia and Morocco were less conciliatory. In the three countries, the pre-war crises resumed and were aggravated by a greater radicalization of demands. On 11 January 1944, the Moroccan sultan, encouraged by his meeting with Roosevelt in 1943 at Anpa, received, at the same time as the resident-general and the consuls-general of the United States and Britain, the 'Manifesto of the Istiklāl Party' signed by 58 representatives. It condemned the protectorate regime unreservedly and called for the 'complete national independence of Morocco under the auspices of His Majesty Sīdī Mohamed Ben Yūsuf' and 'the introduction of a democratic regime comparable to the system of government adopted by the Muslims in the east, guaranteeing the rights of all sections and all classes of Moroccan society and setting out the rights of each and all'.[42] In the towns, the slogan of independence mobilized the populations while the French representatives expressed their firm opposition. The situation deteriorated in the night of 28–9 January during which Ahmed Balafredj and M. L. Yāzidi were arrested in Rabat, and A. Ben Idrīs and H. Filāli in Fez. Incidents erupted in Rabat on 29 January and were put down by troops; the town of Fez was put under a state of siege at the beginning of February. The incidents continued all through the month, leaving at least forty dead and a hundred injured.

41. M. Colombe, 1951, pp. 100–1.
42. C. A. Julien, 1978, p. 190.

The accession on 19 January 1942 of Bey Mūnsif transformed the beylicate into 'a symbol' of Tunisian nationalism and gave birth to 'Mūnsifism'. In August 1942 Bey Mūnsif handed the resident-general for onward transmission to Vichy a memorandum in which he asked for major reforms, some of which affected the very structure of the protectorate. The attitude of Bey Mūnsif and the reforms that he wanted to secure led to the incident which brought him into conflict with Admiral Esteva on 12 October 1942. Following a second incident in the Council of Ministers (30 December 1942), he formed a new ministry. For the first time since 1882 a Tunisian ministry was formed without consultation with the resident-general. With his deposition (14 May 1943) and then his abdication (6 July), Mūnsif ceased to reign, Mūnsifism was born.[43] The Neo-Destūr took up the baton, issuing a proclamation entitled 'For a Franco-Tunisian bloc' and, in November 1944, drew up the 'Manifesto of the Tunisian Front' calling for internal self-government on a democratic basis and the formation of an assembly following a national consultation.

In Algeria, the disappearance of the political parties created a favourable situation for Ferhat Abbas who, on 10 April 1941, sent Marshal Petain a memorandum entitled 'The Algeria of tomorrow'. The Anglo-American landing gave a new fillip to his action while at the same time enabling him to make a serious shift in his political options. The first edition of the 'Manifesto of the Algerian People', dated 10 February 1945, was addressed to the United Nations and delivered to the governor-general. A second version, slightly toned down, was officially delivered to Peyronton on 31 March 1943. The essential principle of the right of the Algerian people to self-determination and the condemnation of colonialism was set out. The Addendum to the Manifesto called for the resurrection of the Algerian people through the formation of a 'democratic and liberal Algerian state' with 'a French right of oversight and military assistance from the Allies in the event of conflict'. Pending the end of hostilities, the Addendum suggested reforms that could be realized immediately.

In the Horn of Africa, after the military elimination of Italy, demands were addressed to Britain; these demands underwent changes in their form and content. Eritrea and Somalia were placed under military administration. In Ethiopia, the British also attempted to install a military administration for the duration of the war. Haile Selassie nevertheless succeeded in establishing his authority and safeguarding at least the formal independence of the country.

In the Sudan, in 1942, the General Graduates' Congress submitted to the government a list of 12 social and political grievances, demanding, among other things, recognition of the right to self-determination for the Sudanese at the end of hostilities, the definition of a Sudanese nationality, the creation of a representative Sudanese body to be responsible for

43. R. Le Tourneau, 1962, p. 105.

approving legislation for the country. The demands were rejected; the failure led to the formation of two groups in the Congress. The first led by the *al-Ashikkā'* (the blood brothers) was much the larger; it worked for a Sudanese government united with Egypt under the Egyptian crown. The second one, represented by the Umma Party (People's Party), demanded independence in friendship with Britain and Egypt. The two parties rapidly came to depend on two religious figures. The Umma Party lined up behind Sayyīd 'Abd al-Raḥmān al-Mahdī and the Ansar Brotherhood, the heirs of the *Mahdī* and intransigent on total independence. The Unionists were behind Sayyīd 'Alī al-Mirghāni and the Khaṭmiyya brotherhood.

In 1944, the Congress opposed the establishment of the Northern Consultative Council under the chairmanship of the governor-general with representation of the interests of the African and foreign communities. The members of the Congress feared that the exclusion of the south might mean that it was intended for separate independence or integration with Uganda. In addition, the Consultative Council, made up of officials and local chiefs, was considered to be unrepresentative and too dependent on the administration.

The problems in 1945–6

In every country, the Second World War caused an upheaval such that 'the relations between the colonial powers and the colonies could no longer be after the peril what they had been before it'. The conflict had direct repercussions in the Horn and Libya where the Italian defeat made change possible. Elsewhere, the colonial powers, conscious of the power of nationalism, feared the loss of countries placed under their tutelage. They showed themselves ready to make alterations which must nevertheless be within the framework of their supremacy and their interests.

The debate on the future status of Algeria and the neighbouring protectorates began in 1942; it was finally settled by the 1946 constitution. Nationalist activity resumed in the three Maghreb countries. In Morocco, where other political formations had come into being (Moroccan Communist Party, General Union of Confederated Trades Unions of Morocco, Democratic Independent Party), the Istiḳlāl exercised a hegemony. It had, even more than before the war, the direct or indirect backing of Sultan Sīdī Mohamed Ben Yūsuf. On 8 March 1945, it asked for the right for Morocco to sit in the United Nations and sent a report to the new resident-general, E. Labonne, without success. In August 1946, three of its representatives went to Paris where they held a press conference and made many contacts. Labonne responded to the slogan of independence by economic and social reforms without calling the protectorate into question.

In Tunisia the offensive began in June 1946 with the Kairouan incident, and the general strike launched at Sfax on 28 June by the UGTT. The

PLATE 2.3   *Sayyīd ʿAbd al-Raḥmān al-Mahdī about to set out for a tour of London, 15 July 1937*

Tunisian National Front was formed on 10 August through the coming together of all the Tunisian parties including the Communist Party. On 23 August, a congress of the main political movements was broken up by the police to the cry of 'Independence, independence'.

The most brutal confrontation was in Algeria where bloody 'incidents' erupted at Sétif on 8 May 1945. Demonstrations organized by the Friends of the Manifesto and Freedom turned into a riot, and repression continued over the following days causing a large number of deaths. In the short term, the events of 8 May 1945 led to a hardening of the attitudes of Europe and the French government, and to the radicalization of the nationalists. Many of them gave up any legal action to prepare for the armed struggle which seemed to them to be an inevitable outcome.

In 1943–4, several French statements (declaration by the CFLN of 8 December 1943, Constantine speech of 12 December 1943, Brazzaville conference of January–February 1944) held out the possibility of changes. Following the war, the 1946 constitution and the establishment of the French Union that it provided for in no way settled the question of relations between France and the Maghreb countries.

The terminology used transformed the protectorates into associated states defined in Chapter 6. They continued to be governed by 'the act that defines their relations with France' but they could however appoint representatives to the bodies of the French Union (High Council and Assembly). In fact, Tunisia and Morocco remained outside the French Union, retaining their status as protectorates without there being any revision of the treaties.

The Constituent Assembly took no decision about Algeria; the National Assembly several times discussed proposals introduced by Algerian deputies which rejected assimilation and demanded recognition of the Algerian personality in the framework either of an associated state or a republic or any other status which might be decided upon by an Algerian constituent assembly elected by universal suffrage. All the proposals were set aside and the question of Algeria deferred to the following year. The law called the Algerian Statute, tabled by the government, was adopted on 20 September 1947. It defined the political and administrative situation of Algeria; its political stance ruled out any risk of autonomy and left control with the European minority.[44]

The war had decisive consequences for Libya which was provisionally administered by the British and the French before international organizations took up the 'Libyan question'.[45]

The German and Italian defeat enabled the British and French to divide up the administration of the country: Cyrenaica and Tripolitania were entrusted to the British, the Fezzān to the French. A military

44. T. Chenntouf, 1969, p. 141.
45. P. Pichon, 1945, p. 318.

occupation regime was established but the USSR put forward a demand asserting its right to a share in the division of the former Italian colonies or at least their joint administration by the Allies. The Allies were unable to agree, so the question of Libya had to be put to the United Nations a year after the coming into effect of the treaty by which Italy renounced all its colonies. In principle, the UN had to pronounce by 15 September 1948.

Egyptian nationalism ran up against the position of Britain which nevertheless favoured the creation of the Arab League in the region.[46]

The time seemed to have come to obtain the complete independence of the country from Britain. The opposition parties did not wait for the end of hostilities to call on the government to take action. In July 1945, the Wafd gave the British ambassador a memorandum on Egypt's aspirations. Five months later, the Nūḵrashi Pasha government asked for the opening of negotiations. They were supported by the students and the press which were more radical (popular demonstrations in Cairo and Alexandria).

The Anglo-Egyptian talks led to a draft treaty in October 1946. It marked the extreme limits of British concessions but was very ill-received in Egypt where there were demonstrations and new clashes in Cairo. On 27 January 1947, Nūḵrashi Pasha, who was not in a position to impose the treaty on the country, decided to break off the talks with London and take the Egyptian question to the United Nations.

The creation of the Arab League
Despite this setback, Egypt played a central role in the creation of the Arab League. The desire for the unity of the Arab countries went back to the end of the First World War, it was voiced in the late 1930s and then again after 1942 with the encouragement of the British. Britain's aims and the Arabs' aims were different and two successive drafts were supported by Britain before the draft backed by Egypt was adopted. After the Alexandria Conference (25 September–10 October 1944), the charter of the Arab League was signed on 22 March 1945 at the end of the Cairo Conference by Egypt, Syria, Iraq, Lebanon, Transjordan, Saudi Arabia and Yemen. Any new independent Arab state had the right to join; the Palestinians were represented by Mūsā 'Alami. The principles of sovereignty and non-interference were reaffirmed and decisions taken by a majority bound only those states that accepted them. Cairo was made the headquarters of the League and its first secretary-general was an Egyptian theorist of Arab unity.

In the Horn of Africa, the consequences of the Italian defeat were the restoration of Ethiopian independence and resumption, with American aid, of the policy of modernization. In the Sudan, once again, the question

46. Documentation française, 1947.

55

of relations with Egypt dominated political life, while in Somaliland a nationalism transcending territorial and political fragmentation emerged.

Political demands were relaunched in the Sudan in 1946 on the occasion of Anglo-Egyptian talks for a review of the 1936 treaty. The two parties attempted a common approach and sent a delegation to meet the Egyptian government to discuss a programme for a democratic Sudanese government, united with Egypt and allied to Britain. After the negative response given to Egypt, the representatives of the Umma Party left the country. Britain, which hoped to maintain a military and economic presence in the Sudan, encouraged Sudanese self-government. The 1948 constitution was drawn up; it provided for a legislative assembly elected by universal suffrage and an executive council with Sudanese ministers. The Umma Party participated in the policy of self-government for the Sudan while the 'Ashikkā' Party boycotted the elections. Riots which it organized in the large towns were put down and its leader, Ismail el-Azhari was arrested. The Umma Party controlled the legislative assembly and enjoyed a majority in the executive council. However, by retaining the right of veto and a number of reserved matters, the governor-general kept close control of the political system.

In 1945, Ethiopia recovered its position as the sole independent African state. The resumption of the policy of modernization barely concealed a difficult economic and political situation. The country, which had 20 million inhabitants after the war, had a poor economic situation. Average national income in 1957 was US$30 according to United Nations statistics. The population was overwhelmingly rural and agriculture accounted for 75 per cent of production. Such progress as was recorded was in geological prospecting and hydro-electricity; processing industries like cement works grew rapidly. In the field of education, right after the war, new secondary schools opened in Addis Ababa with syllabuses and a teaching body based on the European model. Young Ethiopians were sent abroad to continue their studies.

The question of Eritrea remained in suspense until 1952. It was placed under British administration during and after the war. Its final fate was the object of several proposals at the United Nations but the region was integrated into Ethiopia with a large degree of autonomy through a federal arrangement.

The problem of territorial and political unity was even more acute in Somaliland. In 1946, the population was split between the northern province of Kenya, the provinces of the Haud and Ogaden in Ethiopia and French, Italian and British Somaliland.

The French Somali Coast became, after the elections, an overseas territory with a local assembly and parliamentary representation in Paris. The rest of Somaliland was administered by Britain. The Somali Youth League, formed after the war, drew its support from the towns. It called for the creation of a Greater Somalia which would embrace Italian

Somaliland, the Ogaden in Ethiopia, British Somaliland and French Somaliland. The proposal was supported by Britain but declined rapidly because of the attitude of the United Nations.

In the genesis of contemporary Africa, the crises and changes of the ten years between 1935 and 1945 were decisive; their consequences in some cases are still with us today. In a long perspective, two basic features of contemporary Africa became increasingly apparent during the decade: underdevelopment and nationalism. The pre-war and war years were in no way the starting point either of underdevelopment or of nationalism, whose origins are older and more complex, but both became apparent and the processes forming them accelerated.

Tropical and equatorial Africa under French, Portuguese and Spanish domination, 1935–45

3

Majhemout DIOP *in collaboration with*
David BIRMINGHAM, Ivan HRBEK,
Alfredo MARGARIDO *and*
Djibril Tamsir NIANE

Introduction

Tropical and equatorial Africa under French, Portuguese and Spanish domination stretched from the Cape Verde Islands in the Atlantic to Mozambique in the Indian Ocean. The French colonies formed a continuous block surrounding various British enclaves of greater or lesser size. The Portuguese colonies included three pieces of territory on the continent and two archipelagos, all far distant from one another. The southern Spanish colony of the area linked the mainland Rio Muni and the insular Fernando Poo, while the northern one controlled the Saharan coast.

The period between 1935 and 1945 has been called 'the golden age of colonization' and looked upon as the zenith of the colonial era, but these descriptions give a false impression of the real situation and this alleged 'golden age' ended during the great economic crisis of the 1930s.[1] What is closer to the truth is that the years 1935 to 1945 constituted 'the golden decade' of right-wing extremism in Europe. These were the years of the triumph and subsequent collapse of fascist ambition. The colonies of four European imperial powers were profoundly affected by these fascist trends in the core but in very complex ways. The empires of Italy, Portugal, Spain and France experienced the traumas of Europe at war with itself – but Africa was not a passive sufferer.

As indicated elsewhere in this volume, fascism in Italy resulted in the Italian invasion of Ethiopia and Africa's resistance to that aggression (1935–41). However, it is to the empires of Portugal, Spain and France that this chapter addresses itself.

Spain experienced in the mid-1930s a deeply divisive civil war. Portugal

---

1. 'Everywhere, colonialism is in open crisis', as A. Sarraut wrote (1931, p. 219), quoted by J. Suret-Canale, 1964, p. 567.

consolidated in this period a fascist political order which was to endure from the rise of Salazar in 1932 until De Spinola's military coup in Lisbon in 1974. France was occupied by a Nazi power in 1940 and the Vichy regime collaborated with fascism until France was liberated in 1944.

This chapter is partly about the nature of European imperialism in 'the golden decade' of European fascism. How were the empires of Portugal, France and Spain affected by the forces of right-wing extremism from 1935 to 1945?

In Portugal a right-wing dictatorship was stabilized in this period. It aggravated what was already a particularly repressive colonial policy. The divided trauma of France under the Vichy regime created fluctuating allegiances in the African empire. The triumph of General Franco in Spain changed Spanish colonial policy in Africa from a policy of neglect (under the monarchy) to a more vicious form of exploitation. The racist factor in Spanish imperialism became more pronounced after the Spanish civil war.

This chapter hopes to demonstrate that the fascist decade of 1935–45 had a greater impact on African nationalism than on the nature of European imperialism. While the colonial policies of France and the Iberian peninsula did change for the worse under fascist rulers like Salazar, Franco and the Vichy regime, the bigger change was in Africa's response to those policies. *The decade of 1935–45 was a greater turning point in the history of African liberation than in the history of European imperialism.* The fascist era was just a new *paragraph* in the story of Europe's empires; but the same decade inaugurated a whole new *chapter* in the annals of African nationalism.

But what was the nature of Africa's response to the fascist and imperial trends in this particular era? Africa's resistance had varied manifestations – political, military, economic and cultural. Politically, the decade 1935–45 witnessed the rise of modern nationalism, the emergence of new levels of political awareness, the beginnings of modern political organizations and the birth of such nationalist newspapers as *Courrier du Golfe du Bénin*.

Militarily, Africans participated as soldiers against the fascist dictators of Europe – though as colonial subjects, Africans were often exploited by both sides in European conflicts. There were times when Africans armed themselves against their own colonial masters as well.

Culturally, African resistance had religious manifestations from time to time. We shall later illustrate this religious tendency with the case of the Mourides in Senegal and the role of the followers of Shaykh Ḥamahūllāh in the Sahel region. Both movements began in an earlier period but they expanded in the decade 1935–45.

Islam was not the only religion which provided an African response to the era of fascism. Christianity and African traditional religion were also politicized from time to time. Particularly noteworthy was the 'androgynous' nature of indigenous creeds. Both priests and *priestesses* emerged to meet the pressures of social change. Under the economic difficulties of this fascist decade, the Joola (Dyola, Jola, Diola) of Basse-Casamance were briefly led by the priestess, Aline Sitoé, in a rebellion against the colonial order: yet again, African culture was provoked to meet the challenge of imperial injustice. We shall return to Aline Sitoé's rebellion later in the chapter.

As for Africa's economic resistance, this included the birth of modern trades unions and cooperative movements and Africa's insistence on a fairer share of the output of its own emerging economies.

The Second World War was particularly relevant as a catalyst of fundamental change. The Africa which emerged from the conflict was quite different from the mirage of tranquillity seen by the colonizers. From that perspective, the decade 1935–45 corresponded not to the zenith of colonialism but to the beginning of its decline.

But what was the nature of colonial rule during this period? How were the different European empires organized? What was the structure of imperialism? It is to these basic questions that we must first turn.

French colonial policy

The French possessions in this period were grouped into two federations of colonies and two mandated territories. French West Africa, with an area of 4 633 985 sq km included Senegal, French Sudan (now Mali), French Guinea, Upper Volta (now Burkina Faso), Côte d'Ivoire, Dahomey (now Benin), Niger and Mauritania; the federal capital was Dakar. French Equatorial Africa covered 2 510 000 sq km with Brazzaville as its capital, and embraced the colonies of the Middle Congo (now Congo), Chad, Ubangui-Chari (now Central African Republic) and Gabon. The two mandated territories were Cameroon (432 000 sq km) and Togo (57 000 sq km); these were possessions taken from Germany at the end of the First World War, divided between Britain and France, and placed under a mandate of the League of Nations.

The French colonial system was based on centralized direct administration. At the head of each group of territories was a governor-general, representing the minister for the colonies; the mandated territories were administered by a high commissioner of the Republic. Unlike the colonies, these latter were not liable to conscription and France was obliged to submit an annual report on its administration to the League of Nations.

For much of this decade, the governors-general and the high commissioners governed by orders that they issued on their own initiative or to give force to decrees issued by the president of the French Republic; they were assisted by a Council of Government that was purely advisory. The other members of this Council were senior officials who were directly dependent on the governor-general or high commissioner and were close collaborators, such as the secretary-general who acted for the governor when he was absent, the officer commanding the colonial troops, the public prosecutor and the directors-general of federal departments (finance, health, education). The governor-general had very wide powers: 'No law or decree emanating from Paris, even one adopted especially for the group of colonies involved, could come into force until it had been promulgated by order of the Governor-General'.[2] He not only had complete control of the administration, but was also the supreme commander of the army. He made appointments and dismissals as he wished. He was truly a proconsul.

In Dakar, Brazzaville, Lomé and Yaoundé, the governors-general and high commissioners were assisted by a series of bureaux carrying out general services. The most important ones were the Directorates of Political Affairs, Finance, Public Works, Education, Economic Affairs and Health. These departments enabled the governor-general to keep an eye on the administrative life of the colonies. Equatorial Africa, with only four territories and fewer means of communication, tended to be treated as a single colony. Quite often, the governor-general also acted as governor of the Middle Congo; he appointed delegates or senior commandants to Gabon, Chad and Ubangui-Chari.

At the head of each colony, there was a lieutenant-governor under the orders of the governor-general. He was assisted by a Council of Administration similar to the Council of Government. He was the head of the administration of the colony which included the specialized departments corresponding to the federal departments. Within the country, he had under him administrative officers known as *commandants de cercle*, or district officers, as each colony was divided into a varying number of territorial units known as *circonscriptions* or *cercles*; West Africa had about 100 and Equatorial Africa about 50. In Cameroon and Togo, the territory was divided into 60 to 70 and ten *circonscriptions* respectively.[3] The administration was linked at the bottom of the ladder to cantonal and village chiefs. In theory, it was former ruling families that performed these functions, but in reality chiefs were mere auxiliaries whose job it was to carry out the orders of the *commandant de cercle* and they were not always chosen from the relevant ruling families. Before 1914, the theoreticians of colonization had thought they could set up a network of officials at all levels, thus eliminating indigenous village intermediaries. This project was abandoned when posts were closed during the war.[4]

2. J. Suret-Canale, 1964, p. 388.

3. The name *cercles* prevailed in AOF (French West Africa) and Togo while in 1934 the 49 *circonscriptions* in AEF (French Equatorial Africa) were reduced to 20 and named *départements*; in Cameroon, the territory was divided into 15–20 regions including 60–70 sub-divisions. J. Suret-Canale, 1964, p. 391.

4. *ibid.*, p. 392.

The bureaucracy absorbed the majority of colonial administrators and, instead of serving in the field, they filled offices in the towns. In 1937, over half the 385 administrators were serving in towns. Bureaucratization spread to the districts and, instead of going on tour, administrators spent their time writing reports. Early administrators had been concerned to know 'their' country and even to write books. After the First World War, administrators were trained in the 'Ecole coloniale' and given a theoretical education. The result was fewer specialists and more interchangeable bureaucrats 'applying the same principles to Agades as to Sassandra without bothering about local reality'.[5]

The *commandant de cercle* was the principal representative of colonial power known to Africans. He was the local despot in a despotic system. He was at one and the same time the political chief, the administrative chief, the police chief, the chief prosecutor and the president of the indigenous court. He set the head tax, he controlled duties and levies, he demanded forced labour, he extracted export crops, he mobilized people for compulsory work and he imposed military service. He was judged for the profits he obtained for Europe and not for the services he offered to Africans. His concern was not to minister to the needs of the indigenous people but on the contrary to watch over the interests of chambers of commerce and large enterprises which could impose unorthodox methods on governors and administrators.

An administration that takes no account of the interests of its population may be liable to succumb to political oppression. The *commandant de cercle* and the canton chief caused profound traumas in rural areas. Collecting head taxes, recruiting soldiers and levying forced labour caused devastation in the countryside. Village chiefs became puppets and then the ruthless agents of exploitation. If they failed to levy tax, they were removed and imprisoned. If they were successful in colonial terms they were detested by the peasants who were their own people.

The advent of the French Popular Front government in June 1936 altered little in the colonial system. When confronted with strong right-wing tendencies all around, the socialist government did proclaim the need 'to extract the maximum social justice and human potential from the colonial system'.[6] It recommended a few reforms but failed to provide the means to carry them out. By the time the Popular Front fell, its modest reforming ideas had evoked no response in colonial Africa.

The fundamentally dirigiste structure of colonial administration devised a system of consultation which, although democratic in outward appearance, largely served to disguise its authoritarianism. The democratic system of *communes mixtes* (mixed communes), *communes indigènes* (native

5. *ibid.*, p. 394.
6. Minister for the Colonies, Marius Moutet, undated note, Archives nationales de France, Section Outre-mer, Aff. polit. PA 28/1/.

communes), *conseils de notables indigènes* (councils of native elders) and also the four urban communes of Senegal were systematically manipulated by the administration. Only a tiny minority of the population took part in consultations. The number of electors in the famous communes of Senegal (Saint-Louis, Dakar, Gorée, Rufisque) barely exceeded 10 000. In rural areas the council of elders prepared census campaigns and collected head tax by authority of the government and not as representatives of the people.

Portuguese colonial policy

Colonial policy in Portugal changed in 1930 while Antonio Salazar, the financial adviser to the military regime which had overthrown the liberal republic in 1926, was Minister for Colonial Affairs. One major step towards creating a semi-fascist civilian dictatorship called the 'New State' was to subordinate the economic interests of the colonies to the interests of Portugal itself. The crisis of the world depression and the loss of remittance from the overseas Portuguese in the Americas was partly met by a severe pruning of government services at home and partly by imposing a harsh new policy of wealth extraction from Africa. Neither the state nor private enterprise had resources to invest in Africa so that colonial exploitation was based on the simplest but hardest policies of forced labour, compulsory crop taxes and the sale of migrant-worker contracts to South Africa. Lisbon determined the overall conduct of colonial policy. The system was similar to the French one, with an administrative hierarchy from the governor-general down to the district heads, all subject to the laws and instructions decided on by the Lisbon government and endowed with powers similar to those of their French counterparts. Portuguese 'fascism', being autocratic and anti-democratic at home, further strengthened the draconian methods in the colonies.

Even before the fascist era, Portugal had commonly pursued a policy of segregation in Africa, especially after 1910, in which Africans were relegated to the bottom of the social hierarchy. As in the French areas, the local people had few rights and were liable to a forced labour regime which was almost a continuation of slavery. The Portuguese colonies were particularly marked by a lack of innovation and intensification of exploitation. Outside the capitals of Bissau, Luanda and Lourenço Marques and a few other towns where some industrial development occurred, the hinterlands remained the main areas of extortion of labour recruitment, partly through the white merchants who bought peasant crops.

The decade 1935–45 was thus marked in the Portuguese colonies by the economic crisis, by the hardening of the fascist regime and also by the Second World War.

In the Cape Verde Islands, the repercussions of the Great Depression

took the form of the return of several thousand migrant workers, repatriated by the USA. The newcomers brought to the country the money
they had saved in the New World. However, the archipelago was too
poor and many Cape Verdeans had once again to take the road into exile,
their preference naturally being for the countries of Latin America, until
such time as they could settle in the United States. Shortly before the
beginning of the Second World War, following the drought which struck
the islands, a current of migration began towards Dakar where the Cape
Verdeans took jobs as shoe-repairers, scrap-dealers and barbers while the
women became housemaids. A new drought in 1941–2 led to the death
of 20 000 people, out of a population of 180 000. During this time, the
Cape Verdeans were soon made aware that they were not fully-fledged
Portuguese, even though their country was not treated as a colony under
the *indigenat* system. In the Portuguese army, they could not even be
appointed corporal, despite the regulations. This army was stationed on
the islands during the war and although it had large food stocks, did
nothing to help the starving, who died with no help of any sort. An
ironical detail is that the construction of a concentration camp for the
enemies of the Salazar regime at Tarrafal after 1936 provided employment
to a good many of the inhabitants. Nevertheless, their situation as
Portuguese citizens, as well as their relatively high educational level,
enabled Cape Verdeans to look for jobs in Portuguese Guinea and Angola,
where some later played a special role in the liberation struggle.

The Cinderella of the Portuguese colonies during this decade, Guinea,
recorded little progress. The export of groundnuts grown by small farmers
rose only slowly because of continual soil erosion. On the other hand,
the attempts to introduce forced labour were undermined by the flight
of people to Senegal and French Guinea. The influence of Cape Verde –
always more important than that of Portugal – showed in the emigration
of Cape Verdeans not only as auxiliary servants of the administration but
also as small farmers or craftsmen.

In the Portuguese colonial system, the islands of Sao Tome and Principe
were the supreme example of plantation colonies; most of the cultivated
lands belonged to some 30 companies and the colonial administration was
simply their instrument, being concerned mainly with securing the
necessary manpower. This problem was aggravated under fascist conditions. The local population having no inclination to work on the
plantations, labour had to be imported from Angola and other colonies,
but with declining success: between 1920 and 1940, their numbers fell
from 40 000 to 30 000. At the same time, the natural fertility of the
formerly productive soils fell too, the result being a remarkable fall in
cocoa exports, followed by the loss of the islands' special position on the
world market for this product. It was a fine illustration of the inefficiency
of the Portuguese regime.

There was a similar situation in Angola and Mozambique: the fall in the prices of colonial products was deeply felt by all, particularly by the African smallholders, but also by the big planters. Portugal under Salazar lacked the means to develop the economy: it left investments to big companies with supranational capital, especially in mineral exploitation. In Mozambique, the bulk of the income was derived from the manpower sent each year in tens of thousands to South Africa to work in the gold-mines of the Rand.

The situation of colonial domination did not give Africans the least possibility of escaping the twin control of the administration and the settlers, who acted as one against the indigenous peoples. As early as 1933, the Minister for the Colonies, Armando Monteiro, had stressed the social importance of the colonies by suggesting that much of the unem-ployed white proletariat of Europe be moved to Africa to save Europe from labour unrest, and, at the same time, to ensure the 'whitening' of Portuguese Africa. It was fascist philosophy with a new face.

But this policy of immigration was hampered by the poverty of the settlers who had neither technical skills nor capital. They could only survive through the out-and-out exploitation of the indigenous peoples. Thus it was that they came to occupy the lowliest jobs, blocking Africans from access to offices, the administration and even factories. The colonial situation thus put up a powerful technical barrier between Africans and Europeans which strengthened and justified the colour bar.

To better secure its domination, the Salazar regime had to find allies. In 1939, the missionary agreement with the Vatican made possible the establishment of a missionary concordat in 1940: this made the Catholic missions an arm of the state in the education of the African population. The activities of the missions had no major or serious effects in Sao Tome and Principe and Cape Verde, but led to constant difficulties in Guinea where tradition, strengthened by the strong presence of Islam, resisted the attempt to 'Catholicize' the colony. The missions received some grants from the state, but the task that they had to perform – providing a minimal schooling – had to be paid for with the pennies obtained from believers.

Spanish colonial policy

In the Spanish colonies, the situation was scarcely more enlightened than in the Portuguese ones. Spain had no colonial policy adapted to tropical African territories. The old royal administration had long given preference to Cuba and later to Morocco. Before the Spanish civil war, equatorial Africa had no autonomous administrative existence and so lacked any political orientation of its own. The old monarchy's Africa policy was based on, at best, benign neglect.

The situation of the various parts of Spanish Guinea varied, given that the islands of Fernando Poo practised an essentially export-oriented agriculture, while mainland Rio Muni (now Equatorial Guinea) produced tropical woods. Agricultural policy in Fernando Poo led to the establishment of cocoa plantations – inspired by Portuguese colonization in Sao Tome – but was hampered by the refusal of the indigenous Bubi to work in them. Agricultural activity therefore depended on imported labour. After a 1930 scandal, and intervention by the League of Nations, the traffic in Kru workers from Liberia – a disguised form of slavery – was restricted and ultimately halted.

During the civil war in Spain, the Republican government and Franco's fascist insurgents confronted each other both in the Sahara and in Rio Muni. Once he had won power, Franco did make some budgetary changes in the administration of the colonies, thus giving Equatorial Guinea and Spanish Sahara financial autonomy. The Franco regime showed more interest in Guinea, leading to investment designed to extract profit from the colony and the imposition of a more oppressive and racist regime. The Spanish version of fascism was taking its toll in the colonies.

The Second World War

The Second World War broke the silence which shrouded colonial policy in the 1930s and threw Africa into a new turmoil. It accelerated the evolution of changing attitudes. It saw in particular the emergence of new policies in French Africa. Portuguese and Spanish domains came less to the fore since the Iberian peninsula did not participate directly.

French subjects in the colonies again became liable to recruitment and conscription. France had had a long tradition of using black troops, and during the First World War, African soldiers had fought alongside France on every front. After 1930, 15 000 men were recruited annually into the 'Tirailleurs sénégalais', a name used to describe all black soldiers in the French possessions whatever their origin. In 1939–40, an 80 000-strong contingent was sent to France and, between 1943 and 1945, another 100 000 crossed the sea to fight in Italy and beyond. This war effort was not limited to supplying soldiers. Black Africa had also to provide raw materials and staple foods secured from local populations in sometimes dramatic circumstances.

France in Africa was divided by the war. The armistice of 22 June 1940 ended the Third Republic. On its ruins, a fascist-type state was formed in Vichy headed by Marshal Pétain in collaboration with the Germans. His rival, General Charles de Gaulle, launched an appeal to continue the war alongside Great Britain under the name 'Free France'. It was precisely in black Africa that the confrontation between the Vichy regime and Free France took its most acute forms. West Africa and Governor-General Boisson declared loyalty to Vichy, while equatorial Africa, after much hovering, gradually sided with Félix Eboué. He was a black administrator from French Guiana and Governor of Chad. He announced his support for General de Gaulle, and gained support in Cameroon, the Congo and Ubangui-Chari. Gabon reversed its initial solidarity and was reconquered by Colonel Leclerc in a conflict between Vichyites and Gaullists. British and Gaullist attempts to seize Dakar failed and equatorial Africa became the main territorial base of Free France with Eboué as governor-general.

Neither of the French confederations prospered with the war effort. Restrictions cut them off from the centre, and the colonies received almost no manufactured goods except through a black market. In rural farming areas, peasants were forced to supply grains. In forest areas, it was the demand for rubber which desolated the countryside. Since hevea trees were not grown, people were obliged to go deep into the bush to seek vine-rubber. Many died victims of snakes and diseases. Meanwhile in the towns, ration cards were issued to Europeans and acculturated blacks 'living in the European manner'. Consumer goods came occasionally from neighbouring British colonies. Discrimination affected producers as well, and Africans were paid 2.6 francs per kg for their cocoa, while Europeans received 4.5 francs. Furthermore, whites were exempt from forced labour while whole black villages could be requisitioned to work at road-repairing or on the white-owned plantations.

By way of example, here are the obligations falling on an administrative circle in Guinea:

> The circle at present supplies: 490 labourers for the Conakry–Niger railway line; 80 labourers for the Baro plantation (Kankan circle); 80 labourers for the Delsol plantation; 15 labourers for the African banana plantation; 40 labourers for the Linkey banana plantations; 200 labourers for the Kankan public works; 100 labourers for charcoal-burning at Conakry; 100 labourers for road-repair work; making a total of 1105 workers. This is a heavy burden on the circle; there are many desertions, for the natives of the circle object to working for others even when paid and fed [sic], hence there are frequent complaints by the Conakry–Niger Railway Company and the planters. All deserters caught are sent to the court of first instance (Article 28 of the native penal code).[7]

In 1942, such extractions caused the Joola in Basse-Casamance to rebel. They were led by the priestess Aline Sitoé who protested that the commandant's agents were demanding from the peasants more rice than they actually produced. Troops were sent and several Joola were killed. Aline Sitoé was exiled to Timbuktu with her principal aides. She subsequently 'died' there.[8] Here, as elsewhere, production fell. Manpower

7. Archives de Kouroussa (Guinea), *Rapport politique de 25 août 1942*, quoted in J. Suret-Canale, 1964, pp. 580–1.
8. L. V. Thomas, 1958, vol. 1, p. 22 *et seq.*

was scarce because of recruitment and conscription and people fled to neighbouring British and Portuguese colonies to seek refuge from the agents of French colonization.

In Senegal, groundnut exports, which had reached 580 000 tonnes on the eve of the war, fell to 174 000 tonnes in 1941. *Navetane*, seasonal workers, had to be recruited in neighbouring French Guinea and French Sudan for production to rise to 429 000 tonnes in 1945.[9] The war had one fortunate side-effect on Senegal. This was the creation of a vegetable-oil factory as the prelude to modern industrialization. The French firm Lesieur obtained permission to build the oil works in Dakar and produced 40 000 tonnes in 1941. The government received requests from other industrialists for permission to open factories and, despite conservatism and red-tape, the ball was set rolling towards a new economic self-reliance. Thus, 'in spite of opposition by French industrialists, oil works developed in Senegal as a result of the shortage of fats inherent in the state of war and because of lack of transport'.[10] In the wetter countries along the coast some exports, such as bananas, collapsed while others, such as coffee and cotton, thrived. The purchasing power of Africans, however, was reduced by extremely low export prices and by high import prices.

Economic exploitation was accompanied in West Africa by a stiffening of colonial policy. The fascist-oriented Vichy regime suppressed all 'representative'-type institutions – the Colonial Council, the municipal councils, political parties, trades unions and representation in the French National Assembly. The penal code was made more repressive. The fascist regime also introduced new racist measures hitherto not witnessed. There were different rations for Africans and Europeans, different coaches for black travellers and white, even different prices according to one's racial category.

Political and social situation

During the decade 1935–45, there were, if not changes, at least signs heralding upheaval. The lethargy that marked the economy of the Portuguese and Spanish colonies went hand-in-hand with social conservatism. Social structures were hardly changed; urban life, the harbinger of change, was practically non-existent in the small territories. Bissau or La Praya were little more than big villages where old colonial quarters with a few whites or mixed-race people lived apart. Lourenço Marques and Luanda were quite different, but the thriving African urban life of the previous generation was muted. The rural areas had the highest level of colonial labour exploitation and produce extraction in almost the whole of Africa, but drew no benefit from it. In the islands of Sao Tome and

9. J. Suret-Canale, 1964, p. 592.
10. J. Fouquet, 1958, p. 125, quoted by J. Suret Canale, 1964, p. 594.

Fernando Poo, large plantations brought immigrant workers from the mainland under a system that did not disturb the order established by the colonizer.

In the French possessions, the signs of change were more perceptible. Even though the Popular Front government was short-lived and there was nothing radical about its colonial policy, it is nevertheless true that the coming to power of the socialists did have some effect on the life of the colonies. In the major towns like Dakar, Brazzaville or Cotonou, urban life experienced a degree of animation thanks to the *évolués* and the trades unions which had been legalized from 11 May 1937. While one cannot properly speak of a bourgeoisie in Senegal, traders, civil servants and a few rich merchants formed a category which was interested in the life of the colony. The workers there were numerous and organized enough to launch the railway workers' strike at Thiès in 1938.

Up to 1939, the rural areas lived the traditional patriarchal life without any great change; but everywhere the war effort tore aside the veil. A slow population drift began towards the major towns and capitals. Everywhere, this effort made the canton chiefs and *commandants de cercle* objects of hatred; the former were now perceived as wicked agents of colonialism. Thus many chiefly families were discredited, and the colonial authorities were forced to dismiss or even imprison chiefs who had lost influence and prestige in the eyes of their people. The calling into question of the traditional structures was initiated under cover of complaints against chiefs; the appearance of political leaders was to hasten this process.

The origins of some of the armed African resistance to French domination in this decade went back a long time. In the 1930s, the Moorish *ḳabīla* continued to send raiding parties (*ghazwā*) against the French forts and establishments in Mauritania. As if to make the point, the Riḳaybāt (Reguibat) launched attacks in 1931–3 and terrified the French, who were defeated at Kuntusi. It was only in 1935 that motorized troops from the Maghreb occupied Tindouf, the last point still unsubdued, thus making the first land link between Morocco and West Africa.[11]

In colonial Africa, the colonial peace and growth of trade favoured – against the colonizers' wishes – the expansion of Islam, at the same time as the missionaries were spreading Christianity. Two Islamic movements deserve special attention – Mouridism in Senegal and Hamallism in French Sudan – even though they had their roots in the previous period.

Mouridism linked to the Ḳādirīyya in Morocco was founded towards the end of the nineteenth century in Senegal by Shaykh Amadu Bamba, who was twice deported, once to Gabon (1895–1902) and once to Mauritania (1902–7). He was mainly active in Wolof country in Senegal, which was deeply affected by the upheavals of the conquest and the long

11. J. Suret-Canale, 1964, p. 530.

European presence. The founder was non-violent; without challenging the colonial regime, his doctrine demanded from his disciples absolute obedience to the leader and those mandated by him. Thus, a chain was established – a strict hierarchy; peasants and others living in the rural areas found patriarchal protection against the settlers who had replaced the traditional chiefs. Amadu Bamba asserted the sanctity of the labour of the believer in the service of the *marabout*. The authorities finally recognized that Mouridism was inoffensive. After Amadu Bamba's death in 1927, Touba, Mouridism's holy city, became a populous town 'where the peasant was called to work the land and produce groundnuts in large quantities. . . . Patriarchal collectivism was revived, sanctified by a religious bond. Hard work was demanded, and in exchange an assurance of eternal salvation and of present survival in a difficult world was given'.[12] Mouridism thus appears as an adaptation to the system imposed by the colonizer; after disagreements following the founder's death, the new brotherhood settled down comfortably in the colonial framework all the more easily because the Mouride chiefs were the biggest groundnut producers. In the 1930s, there was a veritable Mouride colonization of land in Djolof and Cayor where they founded crop villages, thus extending the groundnut-growing area. In 1936, there was a dispute between Mouride pioneers and Fulani clans in Baol: in spite of the verdict of the colonial court which recognized the Fulani as the legitimate owners of the land, the Mourides used force and destroyed the shepherds' villages. The administration let off the groundnut producers.

By 1945, there were an estimated 100 000 Mourides. They were producing one-third of Senegal's groundnuts. Touba had by now become a place of pilgrimage and attracted tens of thousands of pilgrims to visit Amadu Bamba's tomb and offer their gifts directly to the head of the brotherhood.

Hamallism came into existence at Nioro in present-day Mali in the Sahel. A mystic, Shaykh Ḥamallāh (actually Ḥamahūllāh) attracted thousands of disciples, and was the target of violent attacks from the established brotherhoods. Despite a few deviations, he was one of the leading propagators of the Tijjāniya in West Africa. At the same time, he fought for the dignity and identity of the peoples of Africa. The colonial authorities arrested him after incidents at Nioro in 1933, and interned him for two years. But the fights resumed between Hamallists and members of other brotherhoods. Even though these events looked like the result of theological differences, they concealed a profound disapproval, on the part of the Hamallists, of the position of colonial subjects and of those who had collaborated with the administration or remained passive. In 1940, supporters and opponents of Shaykh Ḥamallāh clashed over pasture rights; there were 400 casualties. The colonial government became

12. *ibid.*, p. 540; for a detailed study, see D. C. O'Brien, 1971.

alarmed and condemned the *marabout* to be deported, first to Algeria and then to France, where Shaykh Ḥamallāh died in January 1942.[13] An unanticipated consequence of this movement was the rectification of the border between Mauritania and French Sudan to the latter's loss, because of the desire to have the Hamallists in the Hōdh under a single administration.[14]

The first trade union movements and the new politics

As we have seen, it was in Senegal that the first political agitation appeared, in the Four Communes under Blaise Diagne, who had been under-secretary of state for the colonies in 1931, and a sponsor of the Colonial Exhibition in Paris, and who died in 1934.[15] There had been opposition to him in the 1920s from the 'Young Senegal' movement led by Tiécouta Diop. The opposition denounced colonial exploitation, of which Blaise Diagne was perceived as an agent; but the fact was that those backing this opposition would happily have settled for Diagne's position and jobs. These political struggles took place strictly within the confines of the Four Communes. Neither Diagne nor his opponents thought of the rest of Senegal, much less of West Africa. In 1928, Galandou Diouf, the mayor of Rufisque, Diagne's right-hand man, turned against him and stood against his patron. He was supported by the Dakar paper, *Périscope africain*. He was initially defeated, but in 1934, on Blaise Diagne's death, he was elected deputy to the National Assembly. No political programme really challenged the colonial system.

Dahomey, at this time, was another French colony with a significant middle class. There were many hand-printed newspapers. In 1936, a dozen of them had an ephemeral existence, of which the best-known were the *Voix du Dahomey*, *Courrier du Golfe du Bénin*, the *Phare du Dahomey*, and *L'Etoile du Dahomey*.

Even more significant was the rise of African economic resistance and the development of collective bargaining. The first African trades unions were formed in the 1930s after the promulgation of the decree of 20 March 1937 which introduced collective agreements and the election of staff delegates. The same year also appears as a turning-point because of the union-organized strikes in West Africa. French West Africa, and especially Senegal, had already had experience of this modern weapon of the labour movement in the second half of the nineteenth century, but it was in 1937–8 that strikes broke out on an unprecedented scale. The trades-union movement reached its peak with the railway workers' strike

13. V. Monteil, 1964, p. 128.
14. On Hammallism, see the excellent monograph by A. Traoré, 1983.
15. On Blaise Diagne and his policy, see UNESCO, *General History of Africa*, vol. VII, ch. 25, pp. 642–7.

at Thiès in 1938. Daily-paid workers on the Dakar–Niger railway protested energetically against their situation. The colonial government called in the army; six strikers died; 53 were wounded, but the strike ended in victory for the workers. This victory was marked by the government agreement that there would be no sanctions and no obstacles to the right of association, and that an inquiry would be set up to look into the demands and compensation for the families of the victims.

According to surveys by the Ministry for the Colonies, there were 33 strikes in French West Africa between 1937 and 1938: 13 in Dakar, three in provincial Senegal, two in French Sudan, seven in Guinea and eight in Ivory Coast. The most violent confrontation, with many deaths, occurred at Thiaroye in 1944. This trades-union activity mainly developed outside the parties, though under the aegis of the Popular Front government. In Senegal, however, the Senegalese Socialist Party was formed in 1935 by the lawyer Lamine Gueye who was fighting the deputy, Galandou Diouf, Diagne's successor. The French labour party also tried to put down roots in Senegal at this time, taking advantage of the rise of the Popular Front.[16] The war, however, put an end to such political ambitions in Africa.

The Brazzaville Conference

After the Allied landing in Morocco and the defeat of the armed forces of the Axis powers in North Africa, General de Gaulle installed his French Committee of National Liberation in Algeria in 1943. At least in the French empire the era of fascism was coming to an end. One after the other, the French African colonies slipped away from the Vichy regime and declared for General de Gaulle. In order to save the French empire and extract new resources from it, the Committee convened a conference at Brazzaville in January–February 1944. This conference determined the principles of post-war politics at a time when the coalition of anti-Hitler forces had almost defeated fascism.

The impact of this conference on the future of the colonies has been much exaggerated. Fascist excesses came to an end, but the conference did not aim to inaugurate a new era for the colonized subjects. On the contrary, it intended to make the colonial system more secure and preserve it from outside influences, especially American ones. It was called the Brazzaville 'French African Conference' – which throws light on the intentions of the organizers. General de Gaulle had understood that in order to continue to ask Africans for an ever-heavier war contribution, changes had to be promised. It was no longer possible to speak of liberty

16. In 1938, the Senegalese Socialist Party fused with the SFIO (*Section française de l'Internationale ouvrière*), the French socialist party.

PLATE 3.1   *The Brazzaville Conference, February 1944: centre left, Governor-General Félix Eboué; centre right, General Charles de Gaulle*

and democracy while denying Africans these fundamental rights. He declared:

> In French Africa, as in all other territories where men are living under our flag, there will be no real progress unless the inhabitants benefit from it, morally and materially, in their native land; unless they rise, stage by stage, to the level where they will be capable of participating, within their own country, in the management of their own affairs. It is France's duty to make sure that this comes to pass. Such is the goal towards which we are set. We do not close our eyes to the length of the successive stages.[17]

This statement by the head of Free France did not go so far as to proclaim the right of peoples to self-determination, even if there are hints of it, as in the phrase 'participating, within their own country, in the management of their own affairs'.

It should be observed that the Brazzaville Conference was above all a meeting of military men and senior officials. It was presided over by

17. *La Conférence africaine française*, 1944, p. 38, quoted by J. Suret-Canale, 1964, pp. 597–8.

Mr Pleven, the commissioner for the colonies; it brought together the governors-general of French West Africa, French Equatorial Africa and Madagascar, colonial notables, representatives of commerce and industry and the missions. Care was taken to exclude the communists. But the most significant fact was the total absence of African representatives. When purged of direct fascism, European colonialism was still racist.

The Brazzaville Conference set out as a principle:

> The aims of the work of colonization accomplished by France in the colonies *exclude any idea of autonomy, any possibility of evolution outside the French Empire: the constitution of self-government in the colonies, even in the distant future, is to be excluded.*[18]

Nothing could be clearer: since the principle of colonial sovereignty remains eternally untouchable, Africans can never hope to attain self-government or independence. The conference did, however, propose to endow the colonies with a federal assembly. Although it advocated respect for African custom, it was against the use of African languages in education.

It will simply be noted that the colonial authorities recognized the need for change, but that none of the participants in this conference could imagine the speed with which Africa was to erupt onto the international stage a few months after the end of the Second World War. Later, at the time of decolonization, the Brazzaville principles would become one of the most rigid obstacles preventing the French authorities from understanding what was really happening in Africa and the determination of the people to be rid of the colonial yoke. Not even its own trauma of occupation under the Nazis had succeeded in teaching France that imperialism was evil – at least, not yet.

Conclusion

How did fascist tendencies in Europe from 1935 to 1945 affect developments in the empires of France, Portugal and Spain? This chapter has sought to demonstrate that right-wing excesses in Europe only aggravated African problems and provoked an African response – but the basic nature of European colonialism had been racist and exploitative before the rise of European totalitarianism in the 1930s, and remained so after the demise of the fascist era.

On the whole, the impact of the decade 1935–45 was greater on African nationalism than on European colonial policies. European racism and imperial exploitation remained almost constant, but Africa became less and less ready to tolerate its own humiliation. New forms of African

18. *ibid.*, p. 45. The italicized section is printed in capital letters in the original; quoted by J. Suret-Canale, 1964, p. 599.

resistance were crystallizing in this period, including political movements, religious and cultural rebellions, new trade-union activism, readiness to go on strike, and the emergence of African political journalism.

The Second World War was particularly important as a catalyst. The war did *not* teach Europe to be less imperialist; but it did teach Africa to be more nationalistic. Greater political consciousness in Africa was stimulated by the war. The peasant masses, exhausted by the war effort, would listen particularly attentively to the leaders who were to emerge when the time came to elect black deputies to the French National Assembly. The colonial system became all the more intolerable because people had fought alongside the colonizer for liberty. The restlessness spread all through tropical Africa: upheavals, strikes, demonstrations and revolts revealed the character of the period that followed the war and which marked a sharp break from the lack of movement of the previous period. With the birth of political parties, such as F. Houphouët-Boigny's *Rassemblement démocratique africain* in 1946, tropical Africa entered abruptly into the cycle of liberation struggles, which began in the French colonies in 1945.[19] The Portuguese and Spanish colonies, lagging behind in their social and economic evolution, gradually awoke from their lethargy, but the fascist regimes in Europe had eliminated any possibility of political or trades-union organization, and had thus practically closed off every possibility of learning the art of politics. The awakening of the peoples of these colonies would come later, but with a suddenness that would shake the dictatorship in Portugal and contribute to the very liberation of the Portuguese people.

19. The RDA (*Rassemblement démocratique africain*) came into being at Bamako (French Sudan, present-day Mali) in October 1946. It was preceded by the Union Voltaïque, created in 1945, and the PDCI (*Parti démocratique de Côte d'Ivoire*), which came into being in April 1946.

Africa under British and Belgian domination, 1935–45

MICHAEL CROWDER*

Can British- and Belgian-dominated Africa be fruitfully examined together?

At the outset, the task of comparing British and Belgian rule in Africa might appear a difficult, if not eccentric, enterprise, so apparently different were they in character. At best one might, in the way of university examinations, compare and contrast British rule in Nigeria with that of Belgian rule in the Congo (now Zaire). But Britain controlled 16 territories in Africa during the period 1935–45, if we exclude South Africa, which was effectively independent after 1931, and Egypt, whose 'independence' was severely curtailed by the presence of British troops on its territory, particularly during the war. By contrast Belgium had only one enormous colony, the Congo, and the tiny mandated territory of Ruanda–Urundi (now Rwanda and Burundi) under its rule. After 1925 it was administered as part of the Congo just as the British mandated territory of the Togo was administered as part of the Gold Coast (now Ghana).

Unlike France, which maintained a largely uniform system of administration for its 14 tropical African colonies, Britain devised a variety of administrative systems for the government of its African dependencies with the result that generalization becomes extremely hazardous. These ranged from Southern Rhodesia (now Zimbabwe), where the white-settler community had gained control of its internal affairs since 1923, to the neighbouring Bechuanaland Protectorate (now Botswana) where *dikgosi*, or 'chiefs' in colonial parlance, had considerable control over the day-to-day government of their own people.[1]

The problems of generalizing about British rule in Africa are further compounded by the fact that within one territory several different systems of rule might be operating simultaneously. Thus Africans in the sparsely populated Bechuanaland Protectorate could be administered in any one

---

* Deceased in 1988. The author wished to thank J. F. Ade Ajayi and N. Parsons for their comments on the first drafts of this chapter.

1. For the methods employed by the British to administer their African subjects, see Lord Hailey, 1957, which is still invaluable.

of four ways depending on where they lived: indirect rule through a Tswana *kgosi* in the eight 'tribal' reserves; company rule in the Tati Concession; direct rule by a British magistrate in the Crown lands; and administration by settler justices of the peace in the various 'blocks' set aside for white farmers. In Nigeria, despite Sir Frederick Lugard's amalgamation of 1914, indirect rule in Northern and Southern Provinces of Nigeria involved in practice important differences, while the Northern Provinces successfully resisted central control by Lagos until the end of our period.[2]

The administration of the Belgian Congo was no more uniform than that of Nigeria, having to take into account the diversity of social structures to be found within its borders and the differing needs of the large plantations and mining concessions, where special devices had to be developed for the control of Africans converted overnight from peasant farmers to wage labourers. Clearly a system of administration established for peasants working on their own account would not be suitable for labourers working on the Lever Brothers' palm-oil plantations or the copper mines of Katanga. Indirect rule, Belgian-style, had no place either in the new urban agglomerations like Léopoldville (now Kinshasa), an administrative and small-scale industrial centre, or Elisabethville (now Lubumbashi), a mining-company town, both of which began to expand rapidly during the Second World War. In the apparently similar provinces of Ruanda and Urundi, differences emerged. In the latter 'the authority of the chiefs was never directly threatened by the administration. Some chiefs in fact managed to arrogate to themselves absolute powers in their provinces. Whether they paid or did not pay taxes was entirely up to them'.[3] In Ruanda, by contrast, Lemarchand shows that 'the cumbersome trinity of chiefs – land, cattle and army chiefs – was replaced by the rule of a single chief, with the result that the Crown became much more important than in Urundi'.[4] In the Belgian Congo large numbers of traditional chiefs had been removed and replaced by 'chiefs of the whites' in Governor-General Pierre Rykmans's memorable phrase. Yet the Belgians labelled their system of administration in both the Congo and their mandated territory as one of 'indirect rule'.

Over and above the many differences that can be distinguished between the administrations of the two colonial powers – let alone within their individual territories – from 1935 to 1945, both systems underwent considerable strains which were to have a profound impact not only on the patterns of colonial administration but on African responses to them. Major changes were caused by the Great Depression whose impact was felt throughout Africa after 1933. These were closely followed by the

2. See J. White, 1981.
3. R. Lemarchand, 1970, p. 70.
4. *ibid.*, p. 79.

Second World War which was to prove traumatic in a great variety of ways for both ruler and ruled in British and Belgian Africa, not least in the latter, where after the Nazi conquest of Belgium, the Congo became effectively an independent colony-state.

In dealing with the history of British and Belgian Africa during 1935–45, therefore, any attempt at neatly distinguishing between the administrative systems of the two powers and their respective strategies of exploitation has to be abandoned. Rather, it is necessary to sort the variety of administrative and developmental devices they both adopted into a spectrum of political and economic responses of ruler to ruled. The range of responses extended from a minimal devolution to the African of economic and political initiative, as in the case of Southern Rhodesia, to the very considerable African involvement in the political and economic process, at least by colonial standards of the day, that existed in the Gold Coast.

Although this approach is principally concerned with the colonial superstructures, an essential question is how the different types of administration, irrespective of whether they were British or Belgian, affected the lives of the Africans they controlled – socially, economically, politically and culturally. It is here that the two major world events that had such dramatic consequences for Africans – the World Depression and the World War – serve as tools for understanding the differing impacts of colonial rule and the differing responses to it. The Second World War, hitherto largely neglected in the historiography of the colonial period in Africa, has latterly begun to receive the attention it deserves.[5] It was, until recently, a commonly accepted thesis that the Second World War was a turning point in Africa's colonial history as a result of which the French and in particular the British seriously began to envisage the devolution of political power to their African subjects who, in turn, were moved by the war from a passive acceptance to an increasingly articulate rejection of the colonial dispensation.

Some scholars, however, now argue that the roots of the changes leading to 'decolonization' and the rapid transfer of power to Africans in the British, Belgian and French colonies lie in the Great Depression as much as in the war itself.[6] Before the war the collapse of the world market made it difficult for the colonial powers to deliver the goods to their subjects while the depression sapped their confidence in their imperial mission. Both within and outside the colonial offices of the various powers,

5. See in particular the special issue of the *Journal of African History*, vol. 26, part 4, 1985; also, D. Killingray and R. Rathbone, 1986.

6. French scholars have been particularly interested in the role of the depression in colonial African history. See in particular the special issue of the *Revue française d'histoire d'outre-mer*, vol. 63, nos 232–3, 1978. See also the *Journal of African History* (see fn. 5 above) where several papers compare the impact of the depression and the war in Africa.

reformers began to gain access to the formulation of policy before the outbreak of war. Rather than initiate reform, it is argued, the Second World War gave impetus to reforms already envisaged or undertaken. Thus in French-speaking Africa, the Brazzaville reforms had their roots in those introduced by the Popular Front government in 1937. Similarly, in British West Africa social and economic reform as envisaged by the Colonial Development and Welfare Act of 1940 and the constitutional reforms elaborated during the Second World War all had pre-war origins. Conversely, the Great Depression, by reducing drastically the purchasing power of both rural and urban Africans, led to increasing popular anti-colonial discontent, expressed in many areas by unrest, riots and demonstrations – the most spectacular of which, both from a political and economic point of view, was the Gold Coast cocoa hold-up of 1937.

Other scholars, who view the reforms introduced by the British Colonial Office not as an act of anticipation but of response to growing nationalist pressure, point to the importance of the 'Abyssinian crisis' of 1936 which outraged so many African intellectuals and heightened their demands for greater participation in their own affairs.

The spectrum of political and economic structures in British- and Belgian-dominated Africa

The colonial possessions of Britain and Belgium in the mid-1930s can each be placed on a spectrum ranging from one extreme, where the administration and the prevailing economic policies pursued were geared towards development of resources through the agency of white settlers, to the other, where Africans were seen as the principal agents of development.

In the white-settler colony, such as Southern Rhodesia or the Katanga province (now Shaba) of the Belgian Congo, the immigrant Europeans were perceived as the main agents for the exploitation of its resources, with Africans as adjuncts in the process: mere labourers for the whites who had dispossessed them of their land. For such colonies, the independent Union of South Africa, still closely associated with Britain as a Dominion in its Empire, served as a model to be emulated. As far as Southern Rhodesia was concerned it was well on its way to successful emulation of the South African model: already by 1934 settlers owned 49 million acres or just over 50 per cent of the land, with Africans living on a mere 28.5 million acres, much of which consisted of the agriculturally least viable areas of the colony.[7] As in South Africa, the areas inhabited by Europeans and Africans were strictly delimited by the Land

7. See R. Palmer, 1977, for further discussion of the impact of land alienation on Africans.

Apportionment Act of 1930, while the pass system for Africans was entrenched by the Natives Registration Act of 1936. Little regard was paid to the traditional status of the chiefs and effectively Africans were under a system of direct administration where chiefs were the corporals of the administration with few powers or initiatives of their own.

Northern Rhodesia (now Zambia) and Swaziland were both considered by the British government as pre-eminently white-settler territories, though they still had far to travel on the road followed by Southern Rhodesia. In the case of Northern Rhodesia, the white-settler population was much smaller than that of Southern Rhodesia and owned a much smaller proportion of the land: a mere 7258 sq miles compared with the 271 369 sq miles set aside for Africans. Furthermore, there were important white mining concerns on the Copper Belt whose interests did not always coincide with those of the white farmers. Politically the white settlers had much less influence than they did in Southern Rhodesia and were effectively limited to the line of the railway and to the white farming blocks. They had only a minority vote in executive and legislative councils which were dominated by officials. The majority of Africans were administered by British officials, who, for instance in the Barotseland Province, followed a policy of indirect rule not much different from that obtaining in Swaziland in the patchwork of African-owned land that was under the rule of the Paramount Chief Sobhuza II. In Swaziland, where the majority of the best land had been alienated to white farmers under dubious concessions granted by earlier Swazi rulers and equally dubious legislation enacted by early British administrators, attempts by Sobhuza to regain control of some of these lands failed in 1924.[8] Nevertheless, the contradictions in Britain's administration of its settler colonies were at their most acute in Swaziland.

If Kenya was in most British minds that thought about colonies pre-eminently a settler one, in fact the paramountcy of African interests had been proclaimed as early as 1923, albeit as a ploy against Indian demands for parity of representation in the legislative council with the white settlers. Nevertheless, the settlers by virtue of their position on the legislative council, with 11 elected seats, were able to put sufficient pressure on the colonial administration to ensure that policies inimical to their interests were not pursued until at least the mid-1930s. Only then, in the midst of the depression, did the administration prevent the wholesale restructuring of trade to protect the uncompetitive Kenya settler-farmers against the Kikuyu and Abuluyha maize-growers.[9] This was in contrast to Southern Rhodesia where the settlers established a monopoly over the local market and were able to arrange a bargain with the Northern Rhodesian copper mines to supply them with their high-

8. See H. Kuper, 1978, especially ch. 6.
9. D. Anderson and D. Throup, 1985, p. 328.

priced maize on condition that they guaranteed supplies of cheap migrant labour.[10] The doctrine of 'African paramountcy', as we shall see, came under renewed strain in the Second World War as the Kenyan administration had to make concessions to settler demands in pursuance of the war effort. But though from the point of view of the Kenyan Africans the doctrine of paramountcy of their interests must have appeared a hollow one, as they laboured under many of the disabilities of their Rhodesian counterparts, at least they had an edge over the Northern Rhodesian African. In Northern Rhodesian in the 1930s the future was still seen as one in which settler interests were paramount, while such a status had at least been formally denied the Kenya settlers.

Comparison between Northern Rhodesia and Kenya demonstrates just how difficult it is to place a colony exactly on this putative spectrum. In complete contrast with these settler colonies, were the four British colonies in West Africa – Nigeria, the Gold Coast, Sierra Leone and the Gambia – where there had never been any doubt as to whose interests were to be paramount. There the African was seen as the chief agent of production, albeit on the account of merchant capital, and consequently alienation of land to Europeans for farming was forbidden, whether on an individual basis or for company-owned plantations.[11] This was in fact the dominant policy in Uganda, itself a failed white-settler colony, and in the Anglo-Egyptian Sudan. Here again there were noteworthy exceptions to the rule. Mining interests were permitted to take over land for gold production in the Gold Coast, for iron and diamond mining in Sierra Leone, and for tin mining in Nigeria. In the Sudan, the administration sponsored the huge Gezira scheme, which involved the take-over of a million acres of land for the commercial cultivation of cotton. Similarly, in Nigeria the government took over land for coal mining to supply fuel for its railway system.[12]

In all these British West African colonies, the means of administration was indirect rule through the traditional rulers who became chief executives of local governments with responsibility for most of the business of a county council in Britain, with the difference that they were also responsible for the administration of justice in their own person. On the other hand, they were much more closely supervised by the agents of the central government than in Britain. Although the administrative officers were in theory advisers to the native authorities, as these units of local

10. *ibid.*
11. R. Shenton, 1986, has a very good discussion of the relationship of the merchant capitalists to the fortunes of the groundnut and cotton farmers in Northern Nigeria.
12. Technically, all land in Northern Nigeria belonged to the British administration, but in Southern Nigeria land was held to be in 'native occupation' and the administration limited itself to measures designed to control the alienation of land by Africans to non-Africans – though, of course, it did not include itself in this category! See Lord Hailey, 1957, pp. 731–5.

government were designated, in practice they often involved themselves in direct supervision of many aspects of their conduct. Nevertheless, the traditional rulers of these territories retained a great deal of initiative in the administration of their subjects and it is noteworthy that chiefs who ruled under the indirect system survived the independence settlement while those who were agents of direct rule largely disappeared as a class. Whatever the reason for this phenomenon, the white man impinged much less directly on the daily round of African life in territories administered under indirect rule. It would be a mistake, however, to consider that in these territories there were no elements of direct rule; when it came to implementing colony-wide measures, the chief was told what was to be done and rarely was he consulted as to the wisdom or otherwise of such measures as the construction of territorial roads and railways or the control of epidemics. Here the chief became as much an agent of the central administration as he was of the central government in French and Portuguese Africa, in all of whose territories rule was effectively direct.[13]

In between these two types of colonies – those on the one hand where the European was the main agent of production, and those on the other where the African was – were those colonies whose agricultural and mineral resources were exploited by companies, both large and small, which controlled the administration of the day-to-day lives of their African employees as well as those of their families. The prime example of this type of colony was the Belgian Congo with its large-scale plantations and its huge mining companies. Even so, the Congo contained large tracts of land that were not under the control of concession companies and within these areas, since the visit of Crown Prince Léopold in 1933, it had been declared official policy to keep agricultural lands exclusively in the hands of African farmers and to prepare them to become landowners in the more or less distant future.

In the areas outside company administration, the Congolese were under a form of rule not dissimilar from that of the French – although ostensibly it was modelled on British indirect rule. In the first place the Belgians tried to rationalize their chieftaincies by reducing their number to create more manageable units. Thus in 1917 there had been 6095 *chefferies* but by 1938 these had been reduced to 1212 with 340 *secteurs* which grouped together a number of small chieftaincies into councils over which one of the chiefs involved presided. This of course was a procedure that had been adopted in the so-called 'pagan areas' of Northern Nigeria and in Tanganyika (now Tanzania). Where Belgian differed from British 'indirect rule' was in the scant respect paid to tradition either in the appointment of chiefs or in the remodelling of the pre-colonial structures of the agencies of government. Although, when confronted by peoples who

13. The extent of interference by British administrators in the administration of one northern Nigerian emirate, Gombe, is brought out very effectively in I. A. Abba, 1985.

lacked centralized authority, as in parts of Eastern Nigeria, the British did create artificial 'Warrant Chiefs' who, because of their unpopularity, were replaced in the 1930s by councils which reflected as closely as possible the 'traditional' system of decision-making among the groups concerned. Belgian chiefs, on the other hand, were allowed little initiative of their own and were as closely supervised by their administrative officers as in the French system.[14] Even where the Belgian system differed radically from the French, for instance in the introduction of British-style native treasuries, the chief had very much less latitude in the control of expenditure than his counterpart in Nigeria. But even here, as Isa Alkali Abba warns, we must be wary of the orthodox view that 'indirect rule' in Northern Nigeria left considerable initiative to the emirs and district heads; his study of the district-head system in Gombe shows that they were closely supervised by the British administration.[15] Furthermore, the British by the 1930s had so restructured the system of local administration in the emirate that it bore little relationship to its pre-colonial counterpart, though it came to be accepted as 'traditional' by both the British and the people of Gombe.

Within the company concessions, whether it was a plantation or a mine, the life of the African worker was governed by the company for which he worked. The quality of their administration could vary widely. By the 1930s, the huge *Union minière* in Katanga – which by the mid-1930s was contributing nearly a third of the colonial state's revenue – had introduced a policy of labour stabilization which was to be copied by other mining and plantation companies in the Belgian Congo. The difficulties experienced with recruitment of suitable workers and their subsequent training led the *Union minière* to do all it could to keep its labour. Thus developed the policy of company paternalism for which the Congo was renowned: workers were offered three-year contracts; they were encouraged to bring their wives and children with them; housing was provided along with generous rations; medical services were provided for workers and their dependents; daily hours of work were limited to eight or nine, and workers were allowed four free days a month. Workers lived in a *cité des travailleurs* under the supervision of a company-appointed *chef de camp* who was responsible for settling disputes and listening to complaints. Africans were allowed little initiative in the management of their own affairs compared with the neighbouring Roan Antelope Mine at Luanshya in Northern Rhodesia. The management of the *Union minière* was interested in the 'complete control of employees' lives in order to increase copper output' and they therefore created what Bruce Fetter has described as an 'oppressive total institution'.[16]

14. See M. Crowder, 1970, pp. 320–50.
15. See fn. 13.
16. B. Fetter, 1976, p. 151.

On the tea estates in Nyasaland (now Malawi), workers under the *thangata* system, whereby tenants on European-owned land had to work unpaid for one month to pay tax and another to pay rent, considered themselves as 'mere slaves'.[17] In the inter-war years, the lives of the workers – including women and children – were controlled by the planters with minimal interference from the local representative of the British administration, though as Robin Palmer has shown workers indulged in effective day-to-day passive resistance in the form of loafing, absenteeism, desertion and so forth.[18]

Two groups of colonies represent special cases during our period although both manifested similarities to the three categories of colonial rule we have just described. The first comprised the three British High Commission Territories in South Africa whose long-term separate existence was always uncertain since their incorporation into the Union of South Africa was always a distinct possibility provided for in the South Africa Act of 1909.[19] As a result, British administration in these territories was ambivalent and without long-term goals since incorporation and the consequent abandonment of responsibility for these territories was always on the agenda. Conversely, African leaders both 'traditional' and 'modern' – and often the two were one and the same – were politicized from an early stage through their determination to stave off any prospect of incorporation into the hated Union. So symbiotic was their relationship with the Union that they were administered by the British high commissioner or chief British representative to the South African government. His administration was invariably conducted with an eye to the possible response of the South African government to events within these territories.

The other distinct group of territories was the former German colonies, mandated to Britain and Belgium after the First World War under League of Nations supervision. Here again there were few common features, either between Belgian and British administration of the mandates generally, or between the administration of the British mandates of Togo, Cameroons and Tanganyika. The only common thread was their supervision by the League of Nations, but in practice the British and Belgian governments were barely accountable to that world body for the conduct of the administration of their mandates. While the Permanent Mandates Commission of the League of Nations did keep watch over questions of infringement of the 'open-door' policy for international trade in its mandates and abuses in the administration of their inhabitants, it had no means of enforcing change or reform on the part of the mandatories. It

17. L. Vail, 1977, p. 365; and 1983, pp. 50–1.
18. R. Palmer, 1986, pp. 119–21.
19. South Africa Act, 1909: XI: New Provinces and Territories: Section 151. See G. W. Eybers, 1918, p. 554.

did not even conduct on-the-spot investigations of the territories for which it was responsible – as its successor, the United Nations, was to do. But the status of mandate did have some influence on the power exercising it. Thus, the Belgians were more protective of 'traditional' structures in Ruanda–Urundi than they were in the Congo; while in Tanganyika the British made it clear that this East African territory, which had been a settler one under the Germans, was to have a future in which Africans rather than immigrant Europeans would be the principal agents of development.

Tanganyika, the former German East Africa, alone of the mandates, was administered as a separate entity. The British mandated territory of Togo was integrated administratively with the Gold Coast, the northern sector of the Cameroons mandate formed an integral part of the Adamawa province of Northern Nigeria; and the Southern Cameroons was administered as a province of Southern Nigeria.[20] The Ruanda–Urundi Trusteeship, though treated as a distinct administrative entity by the Belgians in that it was not subject to the same policies as those promulgated in the Congo, came under the overall authority of the governor-general of the Belgian Congo.

It can be seen from the above that examination questions such as 'Were Africans better off under British or Belgian rule?' are difficult if not impossible to answer as there were so many varieties of rule subsumed under both systems. Thus the tin miner in Jos in Nigeria, the colony of African production *par excellence*, lived a considerably more oppressed life[21] than the Congolese farming on his own account or the worker for the paternalistic *Union Minière*. Nevertheless, in one respect there was a major difference between the Belgian and the British systems, whichever type of colonial administration prevailed. In the Belgian territories, Africans not only had no political rights, but during our period it was never envisaged that they should have them, even in a very remote future.

In the British African territories, with the exception of the Rhodesias and the high commission territories, the implicit if very long-term goal of colonial policy was the devolution of political responsibility to Africans. In 1922 the new constitution introduced in Nigeria had made provision for four elected African members on the legislative council. Even in Southern Rhodesia a limited number of Africans qualified for the vote, as they did up until 1936 in the Cape Province of the Union of South Africa. It is no coincidence that it was those British territories where Africans were earliest given a share of political power that were in the vanguard of the march to independence, and that these should have been the colonies in which Africans were the main agents of development. The

20. In 1939, the Southern Provinces were divided into Eastern and Western Provinces, with the Southern Cameroons being administered as one of the Eastern Provinces.
21. See B. Freund, 1981.

settler and mining-company presence proved a barrier throughout to political devolution, though as it turned out, with the exception of Southern Rhodesia, not a very great one. Kenya, after all, gained its independence a mere three years behind Nigeria. But the quality of independence clearly depended on the extent to which Africans had been given access to real forms of political power and education in the years preceding it. The fiasco of Congolese independence was the direct result of Belgium's failure to provide her African subjects with more than primary education and to offer them any opportunity of participating in the political processes of the colony, except very late in the day.

Whatever the variety of administration under which Africans lived and whatever its differing impact on their daily lives, three events took place during our period that affected both ruler and ruled in British- and Belgian-dominated Africa and served to highlight African responses to their rulers: the Great Depression, the 'Abyssinian crisis'[22] and the Second World War.

The Great Depression

The Great Depression that followed the Wall Street stock-market crash of 1929 had passed its peak by the beginning of our period, but its effects were to be felt well beyond it until the economic recovery stimulated by the Second World War. The impact of the depression varied from colony to colony, depending not only on the specific crops grown in particular regions, and the means by which they were cultivated, but also on how resilient subsistence agriculture or the industrial economy was. Similarly, the impact on mineral-based economies differed according to the mineral exported. While copper sales suffered drastically, gold experienced a boom. As a result, although generally all sub-Saharan territories experienced severe hardship as a result of the slump in world prices for primary products, South Africa secured its industrial base and laid the foundations of its economic hegemony over southern and central Africa.

As far as African peasant farmers engaged in the cultivation of crops for export were concerned, they now had to produce double or more the quantity in order to secure the same income. Groundnuts, which in 1929–30 were fetching £8 18s per ton, were by 1933–4 fetching only £2 13s per ton. The normal economic reaction to such a situation would be to reduce output in response to the lower price and concentrate on the cultivation of subsistence crops. But a number of factors militated against this.

First, in the Belgian Congo the administration ensured that there would be no economic demobilization, to use Emil Bustin's phrase,[23] by imposing

22. See UNESCO, *General History of Africa*, vol. VII, ch. 28.
23. E. Bustin, 1975, p. 101.

on the peasant compulsory production of crops both for export and domestic consumption, particularly for the mines, at prices fixed even below those obtaining on the market. Further, guaranteed supplies of cheap food for those workers who were retained during the worst years of the depression effectively reduced the cost of labour outside any reduction of wages and helped the large companies to survive.[24]

Secondly, in all the territories under consideration Africans paid direct tax during our period. Whereas before the slump indirect taxation had provided the bulk of revenue for their colonial administrations with the notable exception of the three high commission territories, direct taxation now played a much more critical role in the colonial budget. Despite the catastrophic fall in prices paid to peasants for their produce, they received no remission in their taxes. This meant that they had to produce more in order to pay them. In one instance in Northern Nigeria farmers were paying as much as 70 per cent of their cash income to the state.[25]

Thirdly, in colonies like the Belgian Congo where there was a large wage-earning workforce, its reduction in the face of the slump meant that many workers had to return to their villages and take up farming to pay their taxes. Indeed over 125 000 Congolese wage labourers lost their jobs between 1930 and 1932.

Fourthly, many Africans had become accustomed to purchasing imported goods which they did not treat as luxuries but as necessities – such as clothing, cooking utensils and school materials for their children – and were prepared to cultivate more land in order to be able to continue purchasing them. The net result was that in most cases output of export crops increased and in some cases doubled, even though total revenue from them may not have risen from its 1928–9 level by the eve of the Second World War.

By and large, the Africans who suffered least as a result of the depression were those least directly involved in the world capitalist economy, namely those concerned exclusively with subsistence farming. Already accustomed to paying taxes, they were otherwise only marginally involved in the cash economy. Demand for corn and yams did not fall,[26] while there was some revival in traditional industries. But for those who had become dependent on the sale of export crops to purchase part of their family's subsistence requirements, the depression hit hard.

The general effect of the depression on rural African producers was to instil in them discontent with a colonial system that hitherto, however marginally, had been paying them a price for their produce which, despite all the other exactions of the system, permitted many of them to improve their life-style. This trend was dramatically reversed in the 1930s and

24. B. Jewsiewicki, 1977, p. 328.
25. R. Shenton, 1986, p. 102.
26. See R. J. Gavin and W. Oyemakinde, 1980, pp. 506–7, for example.

began to prepare for the nationalist politicians a seed-bed of rural discontent which in the 1940s they were able to fertilize. The war, despite the boom in prices for primary products, only exacerbated this discontent because governments limited the benefits the cultivators received for their crops.

The effects of the world recession were acutely felt in the mining industry, particularly on the Katanga and the Northern Rhodesian copper belts, though in the case of the latter, it was more a question of laying-off workers on the construction work involved in opening up the mines. Prices for copper fell by 60 per cent between 1930 and 1932. The *Office central du travail au Katanga* (OCTK) all but gave up recruitment as a result, and became more concerned with the repatriation of laid-off workers whom the administration was loath to have doing nothing in the urban centres.[27] But even in the villages, in the words of the director of OCTK, most of the laid-off workers accepted 'traditional authority only with the greatest difficulty. It will take some time before they are re-adjusted to village life.'[28]

With the fall in prices for minerals there was a concomitant fall in wages for those who did not lose their jobs. The weekly income for workers in the Jos tin mines in Northern Nigeria fell from between six and seven shillings a week to three shillings and six pence. Although generally the mining industry began to recover in the mid-1930s it was not until the Second World War that its output reached pre-depression levels. The only exception was the gold-mining industry. In the Gold Coast, exports more than doubled between 1933 and 1938 in response to increased world demand accompanied by higher prices. In Tanganyika, gold came second in importance as an export to sisal; and in Kenya, a mini gold rush helped provide employment for some of the more marginalized white farmers who were put out of business by the depression.

It was the gold boom in South Africa that had the most dramatic effect on the British territories in Central and Southern Africa. Such was the demand for labour on the Rand and in the industries that sprang up in consequence of the boom that the Union government relaxed its ban on labour imports from north of 22°S, and recruited workers from as far north as Tanganyika. This provided jobs for many who would otherwise have had difficulty in paying their taxes and provided some income for their families in the form of remittances. The income derived from these remittances became vital for Basutoland (now Lesotho), which had few resources of its own other than its manpower, and for the Bechuanaland Protectorate, which was reeling under the weight restrictions imposed on

27. E. Bustin, 1975, pp. 116–17.
28. *ibid.*, p. 117.

importation of its cattle into the Union[29] and could now export labour from the large areas of the country lying north of 22°S.

For plantation workers, the effects of the depression were the same in whatever territory they worked: dismissal or reductions in their wages. Not all the migrant agricultural labour was employed by white farmers or expatriate plantation owners like Lever Brothers. In the Gold Coast, Western Nigeria and Uganda, a class of prosperous African petty capitalists had developed, and they too had either to lay off labour, reduce wages or stop expansion of acreage planted.[30] In the Gold Coast in particular, the prosperous cocoa farmers felt the pinch of the decline in cocoa prices, made more acute because it was a luxury commodity, and found greater difficulty in maintaining a life-style that had become heavily dependent on imported goods and oriented towards taking advantage of aspects of the Western way of life, particularly education, for which it became more difficult to pay.[31] In Uganda wages for agricultural labour in some cases more than halved between 1929 and 1934, particularly affecting Ruanda-Urundi whence a majority of migrants came.

The most badly affected by the depression – in that they had no alternative livelihood to fall back on – were the settler-farmers and expatriate employees of plantation and mining companies who were either unable to survive the fall in prices for their produce or were dismissed by their employers. Certain mining towns like Elisabethville had one in three of their European-style houses empty as a result. Farms in Kenya were either left fallow as their owners sought alternative employment or were sold off to larger-scale farmers more capable of surviving the economic hard times.

Commercial companies involved in the import and export trade were especially vulnerable to the economic situation in the 1930s. Many smaller houses went out of business or were taken over by more firmly established ones. Again, a large number of white as well as African employees were laid off and in the latter case many of these were literate clerks with few other openings commensurate with their talents, though some did find employment as teachers. Again, they swelled the ranks of potential recruits for the political parties that were to protest against the colonial regime. Those who went back to their villages brought with them new values. As early as 1929–30 in the Makoni district of Southern Rhodesia, Ranger notes that returning migrants from towns within the country as well as South Africa, 'embittered by the collapse of employment opportunity, brought with them the ideas of the South African National Congress and

29. See S. Ettinger, pp. 77–85.
30. See, for instance, G. Austin, 1987; J. D. Y. Peel, 1983, ch. 7; and J. J. Jorgensen, 1981, for the differing reactions to the impact of the depression by African petty capitalists.
31. D. Brokensha, 1966, pp. 37–8 and p. 238. The situation in the Gold Coast was made worse in the late 1930s when the cocoa trees were attacked by swollen-shoot disease.

the Industrial and Commercial Workers Union (ICU), and also of the Young Manyika Ethiopian Society, which some of them had formed in the towns to express regional aspirations and grievances'.[32] The few African businessmen who had survived on their own account into the 1930s found the depression difficult to weather and became even further disillusioned with a colonial regime which once they had supported.

One technique for survival employed by expatriate firms was the price-ring, the most notorious of which was the cocoa agreement between the British buyers of the Gold Coast cocoa crop which provoked the cocoa farmers' hold-up of 1937, followed by similar hold-ups in cocoa and palm-produce sales in Nigeria. In Uganda where the ginning industry represented one of the few substantial manufacturing industries in the region under consideration during this period, ginneries enjoyed a fixed minimum return per pound whereas it was the grower who bore the brunt of the drop in world prices. As the cotton-growers increased production to compensate for loss of revenue, so the ginneries, which did not increase in number, prospered.[33]

For all the colonial administrations, whether Belgian or British, the depression meant a fall in their revenues from import and export duties. The immediate response of the administrations was to lay off personnel since there could not be any saving on debt-servicing which for many of them was a major item in their budgets.[34] Africans who were dismissed were being forced out into a very inelastic labour market which could not absorb any further educated or partially educated Africans. The diminution in the ranks of European personnel in the administration was sufficiently dramatic to recall the exodus of expatriates that took place during the First World War.

The white exodus, however, did not evoke the belief on the part of Africans common in French West Africa during the First World War that the whites were leaving for good,[35] although the white population of the Congo was reduced from 25 700 in 1930 to 17 600 in 1934.[36] Reduction in personnel also resulted in the reduction of the services the admin-istration supplied to its African inhabitants, especially in the form of health, education and public works. Thus the colonial state, more than ever before, was perceived as bankrupt by those Africans – the educated

32. T. Ranger, 1983, p. 81.
33. J. J. Jorgensen, 1981, pp. 147–50.
34. Lord Hailey, 1938, pp. 1432–3. Excluding railways, Nyasaland devoted 15.8 per cent of its budget to debt-servicing in 1936–7; Northern Rhodesia, 16.2 per cent; Nigeria, 21.4 per cent. Some states had much lower percentages, however: Gold Coast, 3.7 per cent; Sierra Leone, 7.2 per cent. The percentage of the budget devoted to administration could be as high as 50 per cent (Gambia, Zanzibar) and as low as 29.3 per cent (Nigeria). The Belgian Congo spent nearly half its budget on debt-servicing in 1934 (p. 1454).
35. See M. Crowder and J. Osuntokun, 1986.
36. E. Bustin, 1975, p. 129.

élite – who in an earlier generation had so enthusiastically supported it as a means to plucking the fruits of Westernization.

While development had never been specifically on the agenda of the colonial powers, least of all as an obligation to their African subjects, much that we today would call developmental was undertaken by the local administrations in the form of road, railway, bridge and port construction – though of course they were mainly designed to facilitate the export of produce. The depression meant that many of these projects had to be axed or indefinitely postponed. Indeed, in most territories, public works did not regain the level of activity of the late 1920s until the Second World War. Nevertheless, the British Colonial Development Act of 1929, drawn up before the depression, was aimed at stimulating productive projects in the colonies, although these were to be selected with a view to the stimulus they would in turn provide for the home economy, particularly where jobs would be created. The amounts involved varied from territory to territory and were usually paltry. The major undertaking in our area was the opening of the Marampa iron mine in Sierra Leone at a cost of £264 000 and the Zambezi bridge.[37] The projects undertaken were not always beneficial to the colony concerned. Thus, as Vail has shown, the Zambezi bridge was built not with the interests of Nyasaland in mind but to provide orders for a stagnating British iron and steel industry. The net result for Nyasaland was that it was saddled with an enormous debt burden which prompted the authorities to permit recruitment of Africans for work in Southern Rhodesia and South Africa.[38] The sums made available by the Colonial Development Act of 1929 were minute in the context of the revenue lost by the colonies in the slump.

The depression laid bare the bankruptcy of colonial policy in such a way that at least some of those involved in its implentation – like Sir Philip Mitchell, governor of Uganda from 1935 to 1940 – did not suffer from the myopia which seems to have affected the perception of later viewers of the colonial record. His confidential briefing to European colonial officials in 1939 put the situation starkly:

> If, resolutely shutting our minds to the effects of habit or the perhaps still lingering romance of the primitive and picturesque, we look at modern East Africa as it really is, the picture is disturbing.
>
> Poverty is widespread and the people suffer from a great number of diseases, and generally from malnutrition as well.
>
> Employment for wages often means worse housing and food, while the wages themselves are low, and the level of effort and efficiency poor.

37. See D. J. Morgan, 1980, vol. 2, for the general background; also S. Constantine, 1984.
38. L. Vail, 1975.

> Education is still rudimentary and inefficient except for the favoured
> few . . . less than 5 per cent of the population attain the standard
> which is compulsory for every child in the United Kingdom.[39]

And so at the very time that African protests against the conduct of
colonial rule, heightened by the depression, were gathering momentum,
similar criticisms were being raised by government officials and by
politicians in Britain not only in the press and in parliament but in the
corridors of the Colonial Office itself.[40] A parallel development did not,
however, take place in Belgium, although it did in France.[41]

The impact of the Second World War on British- and Belgian-dominated Africa

The British and Belgian territories had led almost entirely separate
existences during the depression years. What contact there had been was
limited to issues of common borders and migrant labour between the
Belgian territories and their British-ruled neighbours in East and Central
Africa: Sudan, Uganda, Tanganyika and Northern Rhodesia. During the
Second World War the destinies of the two sets of colonies were to be
united, as they had been during the first, as once again Britain and
Belgium faced a common adversary in Germany. Belgium was overrun
by the Germans in May 1940 so that her Congo colony became the locus
of her independent existence, just as French Equatorial Africa did for
Free France. By contrast with French Equatorial Africa, however, the
Belgian Congo operated as an effectively independent colony-state with
the Belgian government-in-exile in London able to exert relatively little
control over its administration or economic policies. Indeed the Belgian
government-in-exile depended on the Congo for 85 per cent of its
funding.[42] Britain, of course, survived intact and the government was able
to maintain as strong a control of her colonial dependencies as during
peace time. But her fortunes became intimately intertwined with those
of her African colonies on whom she depended for troops and carriers
for her army, and agricultural products and minerals for her factories.
This was particularly so after the fall of the European colonial empires
in South-east Asia to the Japanese, which dealt a major blow to Britain's
prestige in the eyes of her colonial subjects.

It was this loss of the major source of tin, rubber and palm produce
that was to link the role of the Belgian Congo with that of the British
dependencies as together they became providers of these vital commodities

39. Sir P. Mitchell, 1939, p. 29.
40. R. D. Pearce, 1982.
41. Fondation Louis de Brouckerie, Institut Emile Vandervelde, n.d., p. 20 ff.
42. Académie royale des sciences d'outre-mer, 1983, p. 12.

for the Anglo-American war effort. Even before the Japanese victory in South-east Asia, there had been a major re-orientation of the trade of the Congo, with 85 per cent of her exports going to 'Britain, the United States, Rhodesia and South Africa in 1941 as against only 5 per cent in 1939'.[43] Because of its very importance to the Allied cause, the wartime administration of the Belgian Congo was at pains to safeguard its autonomy with respect both to the Allies and the Belgian government in London, and to preserve its economic independence by insisting on keeping open commercial relations with those clients who paid best.[44] The impact of the demands of the Allies on the Belgian Congo for commodities previously obtained from South-east Asia was dramatic: tin production rose from 2750 tonnes in 1939 to 17 300 tonnes in 1945; rubber from 1142 tonnes in 1939 to 11 337 tonnes in 1944; palm-oil from 89 947 tonnes to 144 271 tonnes.[45] There were corresponding increases in other essential products such as zinc, cassiterite, coal, copper and timber. Similar increases in output were registered in British dependencies. Indeed, as Raymond Dummett has shown, Africa's mineral exports were indispensable for the ultimate Allied victory. In particular, the manufacture of the atom bomb, which brought the war against Japan to an abrupt end, was dependent on uranium supplies from the Belgian Congo.[46]

Such increases in production were not achieved without imposing strains on the labour resources of the colonies involved. In the first place, all the British territories were being tapped as a source of troops as well as labourers. In the Bechuanaland Protectorate, for instance, 10 000 men were recruited for the African Pioneer Corps out of a total population estimated at less than 250 000. This represented an unusually high extraction of adult males from the agricultural and industrial workforce, but in all colonies where recruiting, voluntary or forced, was undertaken, heavy burdens were placed on those left behind as demands for increased production of food, rubber, timber and minerals were coupled with the requirements of public-works projects connected with the war effort and the increasing demand for labour in factories established, particularly in the Belgian Congo, to produce materials no longer available in Europe.

The methods used to ensure production of the required increases of strategic raw materials varied from colony to colony. In the Belgian Congo, which contributed relatively few men to the Allied armies – a Congolese unit joined the expeditionary force which liberated Ethiopia from the Italians, while men were incorporated in South African and Rhodesian units – the civilian population was mobilized in an almost military fashion to increase production. Peasants were pressed into forced

43. A. Lederer, 1983, p. 134.
44. J.-C. Williame, 1983.
45. R. Anstey, 1977, p. 144.
46. R. Dummett, 1985, p. 392.

labour on the roads or detailed to collect wild rubber. Crops were requisitioned. Long before the war, it had been a cardinal point of Belgian policy in the Congo that male Africans living in 'customary society' should perform 60 days of obligatory labour – paid or unpaid – for their local community. This included the construction and maintenance of roads, and the production of subsistence and cash crops. This policy, which had been formalized in the decree of December 1933 and used to combat the effects of the depression, was now employed even more vigorously to prosecute the war. If Belgium could not fight, at least she could provide the wherewithal for the Allies to do so. By 1944 the maximum number of days devoted to obligatory labour had increased to 120. Those who failed to perform this work were brought before the *tribunals de police* so that the judicial arm of the state was employed to assist the administration to enforce its policy of increased production.[47] The main agents of this policy were, of course, the chiefs, whose unpopularity was thereby further increased. Overall, the increased burdens imposed on the peasants in the Congo during the war were, in the words of Jean Stengers, 'considérables et parfois très durs'.[48]

In British Africa compulsory production was less widely used. The chief examples were the use of forced labour in the Nigerian tin mines,[49] and the conscription of workers for the sisal plantations of Tanganyika after the fall of the Philippines and Indonesia to the Japanese in order to meet demands for binder twine from America[50] and from white farmers in Kenya who thus, as Arthur Creech-Jones protested at the time, 'secured, under the cloak of war emergency, another concession at the expense of Africans'.[51] But much of the recruitment of soldiers and military labour was, if theoretically voluntary, in practice often compulsory. Again the chiefs were the principal agents for recruitment. Where they had to use compulsion to ensure the numbers requested by the administration their unpopularity increased *pari passu*. One of the reasons for the unpopularity of Tshekedi Khama that led to his rejection by the Bangwato in 1949, after nearly a quarter of a century as their ruler, was the role he played in recruitment for the British.[52] And yet, as David Kiyaga-Mulindwa has shown, this was undertaken with the best of motives – by delivering up all the men the British required into a military unit entirely separate from the South African army, he and his fellow chiefs hoped to create a sense of indebtedness to the Botswana on the

47. R. Anstey, 1977, p. 147.
48. J. Stengers, 1983, p. 11.
49. See M. Crowder, 1980, p. 495, for the furore this caused in Parliament.
50. J. Iliffe, 1979, p. 343.
51. Quoted in R. Smyth, 1985, p. 241.
52. See M. Crowder, 1985a; also N. Parsons, 1985.

PLATE 4.1   *A heavy anti-aircraft defence gun manned by East African gunners during the Second World War, 3 December 1945*

part of the British which would ensure their never being handed over to South Africa.[53]

A major difference in the mobilization by the British and the Belgians of their African populations relates to their approach. The Belgians, who envisaged no future political role for educated Africans in the administration of the colonial state, were not at particular pains to *enlist* as distinct from *require* their support. In the British African colonies, even in the white-dominated ones like Northern Rhodesia,[54] considerable efforts were made to persuade the African to participate in the war effort whether by volunteering for military service, by increasing production, or by giving contributions to wartime funds in return for promises of improvement in economic, social and political conditions after the war. Africans were told by poster and over the radio, through mobile cinema shows and information bureaus, that they were partners with their colonial masters in the fight for democracy and that a brave new post-war world awaited them.[55] Colonial civil servants thus 'found themselves thrust into the

53. D. Kiyaga-Mulindwa, 1984.
54. R. Smyth, 1984, pp. 345–58.
55. See J. Cary, 1944.

95

unfamiliar role of propagandists for empire. They went out into the market place employing all the media channels to woo public opinion'.[56]

The new Colonial Development and Welfare Act, though it made available only £5 million a year for the whole empire, was enacted at the very beginning of the war and marked an important departure in Britain's attitude towards the management of her colonies: development should now be undertaken not with an eye focused on the benefits it would bring the donor country but with respect to the immediate needs of the colony concerned; perhaps just as important, the colonial government should provide funds for the social welfare of the people whether in the form of increased educational services or hospitals; and, probably most significant of all, the old principle that colonies should pay for themselves was finally abandoned.[57] Within the Colonial Office and in the Cabinet itself, debate had begun about the political future of the colonies, though it was not until after the war that a definite programme of 'decolonization' was fixed upon. During the war there was uncertainty as to who should be the eventual inheritors of power: the native authorities, or the educated élite, or a mixture of both. Certainly there was no timetable as to when power, in whatever form, should be transferred to Africans. Nevertheless, in the West African colonies, promises were made of political reform and significantly these, though very minor as it turned out, were elaborated in both Nigeria and the Gold Coast during the war, in each case reflecting the uncertainties as to whom power should in the long term be transferred to.[58]

In the Congo, no such promises were made by the administration. Even though the colony state was effectively independent during the war, and was economically involved with the British and Americans, it maintained the same rigid control of the African population as it had done when it was under the direct control of the Belgian colonial office. No concession was made to the idea of a political role for the African in the life of the colony, despite the growing signs of unrest and discontent that manifested themselves during the war.[59] As Stengers points out, for the Congo the war was not 'une période de transformations majeures. A aucun point de vue, dans l'évolution du Congo elle n'a representé un tournant'.[60] After the war the former pattern of colonial rule under central control was reimposed. And for the immediate post-war years the Congo

56. R. Smyth, 1984, p. 76.
57. This was certainly the view of one colonial governor – Sir Bernard Bourdillon: see J. White, 1981, pp. 233–4. See also, S. Constantine, 1984, ch. 9.
58. See J. Flint, 1983, pp. 389–411, also the reply by R. D. Pearce, 1984, pp. 77–93, for an interesting discussion about the debates on the future of the African colonies in the Colonial Office during the war, with particular reference to whether or not plans for decolonization were envisaged at that time.
59. R. Anstey, 1977, p. 157.
60. J. Stengers, 1983, p. 11.

became as vital for the reconstruction of the shattered Belgium as it had been for provisioning the Allied victory. As Anstey put it, the 'economic and administrative policies of the war years were essentially developments of existing practice rather than new departures; continuity is also the hallmark of the post-war period'.[61] It was not until after 1950 that Belgium began to contribute substantially to the economic and social development of the Congo.

The impact of the war in the British African dependencies was very different. Generally the new concept of the obligation of the British government for the economic and social welfare of the colonies, itself a child of the depression, was nurtured during the war. Plans for the development of institutions of higher education in the African colonies were drawn up during the war, as were those for the development of trades unions. Money was set aside for colonial research: a Colonial Products Research Council, a Colonial Social Science Research Council, a Medical Research Committee, and a Committee on Colonial Agricultural, Animal Health and Forestry Research were established.

These tentative reforms were undertaken by Britain partly under pressure from her American allies who were not prepared to fight a war on her behalf merely to preserve her empire, partly in response to calls for reform both within and outside the Colonial Office, and partly to avoid a repetition of the disturbances in the West Indies in 1940 caused by the prevailing scandalous economic and social conditions. What became clear very soon after the war, particularly in West Africa, was that the tentative programme of reform launched during the war was far from adequate. The war, despite the economic recovery that came in its wake, exacerbated rather than mollified the rural and urban discontent of the 1930s. Farmers did not gain the full benefit of the revival in prices paid for their export crops since these were controlled by the administration during the war and the difference was held, in the case of Britain, in sterling balances in London that helped finance the purchase of war materials from the United States. Thus in Tanganyika sisal was sold at less than half the price paid for it by the Americans and Iliffe has calculated that the British exchequer thereby gained £11 million before price control was ended.[62]

In Kenya, the white farmers had a revival in their fortunes, particularly after the Japanese occupation of the Allies' Far Eastern colonies. Guaranteed prices were paid to them by the government for maize, and schemes of financial assistance were introduced for flax, rye and wheat as well. The guaranteed prices were often as much as twice as high as those available to African farmers, who nevertheless experienced a boom which encouraged them to put more land under cultivation. This further

61. R. Anstey, 1977, p. 159.
62. J. Iliffe, 1979, p. 344.

exacerbated the potential conflict of interests between the two groups of farmers.[63]

While African farmers did not reap full or, in the case of compulsory cultivation, any benefit from the increase in the world market price, they had to pay higher prices for imported goods which were in short supply partly because of shortage of shipping space. The result was inflation that hit both rural and urban workers. In Tanganyika prices nearly doubled during the war and an enquiry undertaken in Dar es Salaam in 1942 reckoned that 'some 87 per cent of Government employees . . . are in receipt of a wage on which they cannot possibly subsist without getting into debt'.[64] The number of urban workers had increased substantially as industries were established to provide substitutes for unobtainable imports, and as construction projects were undertaken to improve the communications route from West Africa to North Africa which became vital for the North African campaign or for the provisioning and refuelling of shipping on its way to India and the Burma campaign. In the Belgian Congo the exodus from the rural areas was stimulated by the war as Africans sought to escape the unrestrained recruitment policies of the government and its heavy quotas on agricultural production.[65]

The growth of an urban proletariat was not accompanied by a comparable expansion of accommodation and many of them lived in shanty towns in intolerable conditions. These and inflation made them ripe for political indoctrination and strike action. There were numerous strikes for higher pay in British Africa during the war. Even in the much more tightly controlled Belgian Congo, workers of the *Union Minière* struck over the decline in their living standards in 1941 and they were only forced back to work after the army was brought in and seventy strikers were killed.[66]

The war heightened the expectations of the educated élite, some of whom now found themselves incorporated into the colonial administrative and business structure as British officials and managers left for the front. In particular they were inspired by the Atlantic Charter signed in 1941 by Franklin D. Roosevelt and Winston Churchill with its affirmation of 'the right of all people to choose the form of government in which they live' and their expressed desire to see 'sovereign rights and self-government restored to those who have been forcibly deprived of them'. The subsequent denial by the British prime minister that the charter applied to his country's African territories merely served to heighten nationalist frustration with the colonial regime. Here, there was of course a dramatic

63. D. Anderson and D. Throup, 1985, p. 335 ff.
64. *Report of enquiry into wages and cost of living of low-grade African Government Employees in Dar es Salaam*, September 1942, cited in J. Iliffe, 1979, p. 354.
65. R. Anstey, 1977, p. 173.
66. B. Fetter, 1976, p. 173.

contrast with Belgian Africa, which just did not have such an educated élite, since the highest level of education available for most Africans was the primary school, with further education being limited to the Catholic seminary.

It was not only the expectations of the élite that were heightened by the war. Soldiers who had been taken from rural farms to fight in Burma or work as labourers in the Middle East or Italy learnt new skills and trades; many were taught to read and write; large numbers of them expanded their horizons as they sojourned in India where the nationalists were demanding that the British should quit their country, or in Italy where they saw the immense destruction one group of white men could visit on another. When they returned to their countries they did so with ambitions for themselves and their children that were utterly different from those they had when they first stood before the recruiting officer. In the Belgian Congo aspirations engendered abroad were dampened by a strictly controlled system of administration where there was no political outlet available to Africans. Even so, the war witnessed the first protest by educated Africans against the colonial regime when black non-commissioned officers enlisted their support in a poorly organized and easily suppressed conspiracy against the Belgians in Elisabethville.[67] But in those colonies like the Gold Coast and Nigeria where the new aspirations of the returned soldiers had avenues of expression open to them, they became supporters, if not leaders, of the political parties which were now demanding self-government.

Conclusion: British- and Belgian-dominated Africa on the eve of the struggle for independence

In 1935 the possibility that most of British and Belgian Africa would be independent within a quarter of a century was not even entertained. The colonial administration in Britain talked in terms of a minimum of three generations, the Belgians in terms of at least a hundred years as the earliest independence could even be conceived of. Not even the most optimistic political leader in West Africa would have envisaged 1960 let alone 1957 as a realistic target date. Indeed, in the 1930s independence was not a word that appeared prominently in the vocabulary of African politicians. By 1945 in much of British Africa, if not Belgian, independence now seemed a realistic though still distant goal. The possibility of the Gold Coast becoming independent was being raised in the Colonial Office though it was considered that it was 'unlikely to be achieved in much less than a generation'.[68] The decade 1935–45, then, is a crucial one in

67. *ibid.*

68. *Constitutional Development in Africa*, memo. drafted by A. Cohen, Public Record Office, London, CO847/36/47238, cited in J. P. Hargreaves, 1985, p. 438.

PLATE 4.2 *Independence Day, Swaziland: Chief Sobhuza II, 'The Lion of Swaziland', inspects his troops*

colonial history, and the debate will no doubt continue as to what brought about that change. The Great Depression and the Second World War had a profound effect on the attitudes of both colonized and colonizer. But certain developments had been taking place even before the Great Depression – and certainly before the impact of the Second World War.

In the first place, the original investment of education in Africa, particularly in British Africa, at the end of the nineteenth and beginning of the twentieth century was starting to bear fruit in the growth of a politically conscious élite and there was a direct correlation between the size of the educated élite as a proportion of the population of a colony and the growth of an effective nationalist movement. Thus the rich Belgian Congo, where educational opportunities for Africans were minimal, lagged behind the impoverished neighbouring Anglo-Egyptian Sudan (now Sudan) where schools of law, engineering, veterinary science and agriculture, and medicine had all been opened before the war. Secondly, whatever the system of colonial exploitation employed by the colonial power concerned, by the mid-1930s most Africans were directly involved in the colonial economy in one form or another and few were unaffected by the policies of the colonial masters.

The Great Depression and the Second World War in their different ways both heightened the élite's perceptions of the injustices of the colonial system – in particular with regard to their participation in it by first denying them that participation and then by providing them with greater opportunities for doing so. Similarly, the Great Depression and the Second World War both heightened awareness of the farmers and the nascent proletariat of the colonial state through the hardships that the colonial economy could inflict and the opportunities it could present and frustrate. Together these left the colonial powers confronted by a very different Africa from that of the early 1930s. The British were prepared to accommodate themselves to these changes when they recognized them as having taken place; the Belgians were not, with consequences of disastrous magnitude.

The struggle for political sovereignty: from 1945 to independence

Seek ye first the political kingdom

5

ALI A. MAZRUI

'Seek ye first the political kingdom, and all things shall be added unto you.'[1] When he said that, Kwame Nkrumah was convinced that political independence was the key to all other improvements in the African condition. Underlying the statement was a philosophy about the primacy of politics in human affairs – a radically different philosophy from *economic* determinism. Had Nkrumah been a thorough-going Marxist he would have been tempted to proclaim 'Seek ye first the *economic* kingdom – and all else will be added unto it.'

And yet, in a colonial situation, Kwame Nkrumah's political primacy was at least partially right. Colonial Africa did initially have to seek political sovereignty before anything else could be added unto it. What Nkrumah overlooked was a simple distinction in the science of logic – the distinction between what was a *sufficient condition* and what was a *necessary condition*. Political sovereignty (or 'the political kingdom') was indeed a necessary condition before Africa could fulfil or realize any of her other fundamental aspirations. But by itself political sovereignty was not enough – it was not a sufficient condition. It was simply not true that 'all else would be added unto it'.

By the 1980s, in Nkrumah's own country, Ghana, the conditions seemed to testify to an opposite conclusion from what Nkrumah had in mind. Ghana's situation in the early 1980s seemed cruelly to proclaim: 'Seek ye first the political kingdom – and all else will be *subtracted* from it'. The economy was worse than it was on attainment of political sovereignty; the educational system had deteriorated; roads had disintegrated, railways rusted, telephones had gone silent and the rest of the infrastructure was in decay. A Ghanaian diaspora had come into being – many of the most gifted Ghanaians had scattered to the four corners of the world. Ghanaian cocoa was masquerading as Ivorian in search of greater returns. If there had indeed been a wager between Ghana's founder-president, Nkrumah, and the Côte d'Ivoire's founder-president, Houphouët-Boigny, concerning the value of their contrasting models, the

1. K. Nkrumah, 1957, p. 164.

Ivorian seemed to have won. His were the credentials of diluting political sovereignty for the sake of higher economic returns.

If Nkrumah was right that Africa should first seek the political kingdom, and wrong in his assumption that it was a sufficient condition for 'all else' to be added unto it, what is likely to be the judgement of history on the two parts of Nkrumah's imperative? What is the balance sheet in the search for the political kingdom? What is the likely outcome in the struggle for 'all else' to be added to the African condition? These are some of the questions to be addressed in this chapter.

Nationalism re-born

The struggle for the political kingdom – or for political sovereignty – in colonial Africa had four phases which sometimes empirically overlapped, but were nevertheless analytically distinct. There was first the phase of pre-Second World War élite agitation for greater autonomy. There was then the phase of popular involvement in the struggle against Nazism and fascism. There was, thirdly, non-violent popular struggle for full independence after the Second World War. Finally, there was armed engagement for the political kingdom – the guerrilla wars against white minority governments especially from the 1960s onwards. The chronological outcome of all these different struggles is summarized in Table 5.1 (pp. 108–11).

Some of the earliest forms of élite organization were through cultural bodies and special-interest groups. In the period between the two world wars a variety of ethnic and kinship unions developed in different colonies – partly inspired by a sense of solidarity among migrant workers in cities, and partly because of the wider sense of African alienation in conditions of colonial exploitation. The range of kinship organizations which emerged was from the Kikuyu Central Association in East Africa to the Urhobo Renascent Convention in West Africa. In Muslim Africa the cultural organizations were sometimes linked to religion rather than ethnicity. In 1935, for example, Shaykh 'Abd al-Ḥamid Badis in Algeria formed the Association of '*Ulamā*, partly in defence of Islam in a colonial situation.

There were other forms of restlessness during the inter-war years. For example, in May 1935 there were African strikes and riots on the copper belt in Northern Rhodesia. And in Nigeria a variety of special-interest groups began to organize themselves. In Lagos alone this enthusiasm for organization resulted in the following explosion of associations:[2]

Lagos Fishermen's Association	1937
Alakoro Union Women's Trading Co.	1939
Farina Women Sellers' Union	1940
Lagos Wholesale Butchers' Union	1938

2. See J. S. Coleman, 1963, pp. 212–13.

Taxi Drivers' Association	1938
Lagos Canoe Transport Union	1938
Lagos Night Soil Removers' Union	1942
Lagos Union of Auctioneers	1932
Palm Wine Sellers' Association	1942

Other cultural and élite organizations among Africans and people of African ancestry were formed abroad. Pan-Africanism was also entering a new phase. Léopold Sédar Senghor and Aimé Césaire founded *L'étudiant noir* in France. And Kwame Nkrumah, Jomo Kenyatta and W. E. B. DuBois were active pan-Africanists in Britain and the United States.

But although many of these early movements were basically élite organizations, and many of the interest-group associations were primarily urban, the beginnings of mass politics were at hand in the inter-war years. Habib Bourguiba organized a civil disobedience campaign in Tunisia which resulted in riots in Tunis. Bourguiba and others were court-martialled. Their party (Neo-Destūr) was officially dissolved but continued underground.

Although the techniques used against imperialism at this stage were primarily non-violent and agitational, one of the exceptions was the Ethiopian struggle against Italian occupation. In February 1937, grenades were thrown at the Viceroy in Addis Ababa. In 1939 Ethiopian resistance managed to hold down 56 Italian battalions for a while. Native freedom-fighters maintained the struggle until they were joined by a small British force in 1940. In March 1941, Britain invaded Ethiopia with the agreement of Emperor Haile Selassie.

As the Second World War unfolded, Africa as a whole had to choose between imperialism under bourgeois liberalism and imperialism under the new menace of Nazism and fascism. The dilemma became particularly acute in the French colonies – since France itself was occupied and was split. As far back as 1938 France had recruited 20 000 troops from French West Africa (AOF) of whom 7000 had been sent to France in addition to 18 000 *tirailleurs* in AOF and 29 000 already in France and North Africa.

Dakar as the capital of AOF was initially under the Vichy regime. In June 1940, 130 000 troops were recruited in AOF – the Germans treating them with cruelty and contempt. In September 1940, there was an Anglo-French expedition to take Dakar, but this failed. However, in the previous month Niger and Chad had declared in favour of Charles de Gaulle and the French Resistance. In December 1942, French West Africa finally joined the Allies against the Nazi menace.

African participation in the Second World War was of course extensive all over the continent. Was Africa's involvement a case of collaboration with the existing colonial powers? Or should it be seen as a special phase of Africa's anti-colonial struggle?

TABLE 5.1. *Chronology of African independence*

State	Date of independence	Colonial power	Notes
Ethiopia	Ancient	—	Italian occupation 1935–41.
Liberia	26.7.1847	—	Private colony 1822–47.
South Africa	31.5.1910	Britain	(*Suid Afrika*) Union of four colonies, Cape Colony, Natal, Orange River Colony (*Oranje Vrij Staat*) and Transvaal (*Zuid Afrikaansche Republick*), the last two of which had been independent republics to 31.5.1902. The Union became a republic outside the British Commonwealth 31.5.1961. White minority rule. Unrecognized 'independent' homelands: Transkei 26.10.1976 Bophutatswana 6.12.1977 Venda 13.9.1979 Ciskei 4.12.1981
Egypt	28.2.1922	Britain	United with Syria as United Arab Republic (UAR) from 1.2.1958 to 28.9.1961. Federated with Kingdom of Yemen from 8.3.1958 to 26.12.1961. Name of UAR retained by Egypt until 2.9.1971.
Libya	24.12.1951	Italy	British (Tripolitania and Cyrenaica) and French (Fezzān) administration 1943–51.
Ethiopia (Eritrea)	11.9.1952	Italy	British administration 1941–52. Federation of Eritrea and Ethiopia 1952. Full union 14.11.1962.
Ethiopia (Ogaden)	1955		Italian occupation 1936–41. British administration 1941–55.
Sudan	1.1.1956	Britain Egypt	Anglo-Egyptian condominium.
Morocco	2.3.1956	France	(*Maroc*)
Tunisia	20.3.1956	France	(*Tunisie*)
Morocco (part)	7.4.1956	Spain	(*Marruecos*) Spanish northern zone.
Morocco (part)	29.10.1956		International zone (Tangier).
Ghana	6.3.1957	Britain	(Gold Coast) including British Togoland (UN trust), part of former German colony of Togo.

State	Date of independence	Colonial power	Notes
Morocco (part)	27.4.1958	Spain	(*Marruecos*) Spanish southern zone.
Guinea	2.10.1958	France	(*Guinée Française*)
Cameroon	1.1.1960	France	(*Cameroun*) UN trust. Larger part of former German colony of *Kamerun*.
Togo	27.4.1960	France	UN trust. Larger part of former German colony of Togo.
Senegal	20.6.1960 (20.8.1960)	France	Independent initially as 'Federation of Mali' with former French Soudan (Mali). Federation broke up after two months. Joined with the Gambia as Confederation of Senegambia from 1.1.1982.
Mali	20.6.1960 (22.9.1960)	France	(*Soudan Français*) Independent initially as 'Federation of Mali' with Senegal. Federation broke up after two months.
Madagascar	26.6.1960	France	(Malagasy; *République Malgache*)
Zaire	30.6.1960	Belgium	Congo Free State (*Etat Indépendant du Congo*) 2.5.1885 to 18.11.1908 when it became the Belgian Congo (*Congo Belge, Belgisch Congo*). Name changed from Congo on 27.10.1971.
Somalia	1.7.1960	Italy Britain	UN trust. Union of two colonies. British Somaliland independent prior to union from 26.6.1960.
Benin	1.8.1960	France	Name changed from Dahomey on 30.11.1975.
Niger	3.8.1960	France	
Burkina Faso	5.8.1960	France	Name changed from Upper Volta (*Haute Volta*) on 4.8.1984.
Côte d'Ivoire	7.8.1960	France	
Chad	11.8.1960	France	(*Tchad*)
Central African Republic (CAR)	13.8.1960	France	(*Oubangui-Chari, République Centrafricaine*) Central African Empire from 4.12.1976 to 20.9.1979.
Congo (Brazzaville)	15.8.1960	France	(*Moyen Congo*)
Gabon	17.8.1960	France	
Nigeria	1.10.1960	Britain	

State	Date of independence	Colonial power	Notes
Mauritania	28.11.1960	France	(*Mauritanie*)
Sierra Leone	27.4.1961	Britain	
Nigeria (British Cameroon North)	1.6.1961	Britain	UN trust. Part of former German colony of *Kamerun*. Plebiscite 11/12.2.1961.
Cameroon (British Cameroon South)	1.10.1961	Britain	UN trust. Part of former German colony of *Kamerun*. Plebiscite 11/12.2.1961. Union with Cameroon as United Republic of Cameroon.
Tanzania	9.12.1961	Britain	(Tanganyika) UN trust. Greater part of former German colony of *Deutsche Ostafrika*. Name changed to Tanzania following union with Zanzibar 27.4.1964.
Burundi	1.7.1962	Belgium ⎫	UN trust. Ruanda-Urundi, divided at independence, was smaller part of former German colony of
Rwanda	1.7.1962	Belgium ⎭	*Deutsche Ostafrika*.
Algeria	3.7.1962	France	(*Algérie*)
Uganda	9.10.1962	Britain	
Tanzania (Zanzibar)	10.12.1963	Britain	Union with Tanganyika as Tanzania 27.4.1964.
Kenya	12.12.1963	Britain	
Malawi	6.7.1964	Britain	(Nyasaland) Federated with Rhodesias 1.10.1953 to 31.12.1963.
Zambia	24.10.1964	Britain	(Northern Rhodesia) Federated with Nyasaland and Southern Rhodesia 1.10.1953 to 31.12.1963.
Gambia	18.2.1965	Britain	Joined with Senegal as Confederation Senegambia from 1.1.1982.
Botswana	30.9.1966	Britain	(Bechuanaland)
Lesotho	4.10.1966	Britain	(Basutoland)
Mauritius	12.3.1968	Britain	
Swaziland	6.9.1968	Britain	
Equatorial Guinea	12.10.1968	Spain	Comprises *Rio Muni* and *Macias Nguema Biyogo* (*Fernando Poo*).
Morocco (Ifni)	30.6.1969	Spain	(*Territorio de Ifni*)
Guinea-Bissau	10.9.1974	Portugal	*Guine-Bissau* formerly *Guine Portuguesa*.
Mozambique	25.6.1975	Portugal	(*Moçambique*)
Cape Verde	5.7.1975	Portugal	(*Cabo Verde*)

State	Date of independence	Colonial power	Notes
Comoros	6.7.1975	France	(*Archipel des Comores*) Excluding island of Mayotte which remains a French Overseas Territory (*Territoire d'Outre-Mer*).
St Thomas and Prince Islands	12.7.1975	Portugal	(*São Tomé e Principe*)
Angola	11.11.1975	Portugal	(Including Cabinda)
Western Sahara	28.2.1975	Spain	(*Rio de Oro* and *Seguit el Hamra*) on Spanish withdrawal seized by Morocco. Occupation disputed by POLISARIO, formed 10.5.1973.
Seychelles	26.6.1976	Britain	
Djibouti	27.6.1977	France	(*Territoire français des Afars et des Issas* formerly *Côte Française des Somalis*)
Zimbabwe	18.4.1980	Britain	(Rhodesia, formerly Southern Rhodesia) UDI in effect from 11.11.1965 to 12.12.1979. Federated with Northern Rhodesia and Nyasaland 1.10.1953 to 31.12.1963.
Namibia	21.3.1990	South Africa	(South West Africa) UN trust. Former German colony of *Deutsche Südwestafrika*. South Africa in dispute with UN.

Source: I. L. L. Griffiths, *An Atlas of African Affairs*, 1989, Routledge, Chapman and Hall Inc, New York; and Routledge, London, pp. 182–5. Updated by UNESCO as far as the date of Namibia's independence is concerned.

Footnote by the Volume Editor: Although continental Africa is now wholly independent, a number of islands and small enclaves are still dependent territories. These include Madeira (under Portugal), Canary Islands and Spanish North Africa (under Spain), St Helena with Ascension and Tristan da Cunha (under Britain), Mayotte and French Indian Ocean Islands (under France). Reunion is an Overseas Department of France and Socotra is part of Yemen.

It is true that there was widespread ambivalence in Africa about the Second World War. But on the whole the philosophy which prevailed favoured the 'devils' which Africans already knew (especially Britain and Free France) rather than the new devils of Nazism and fascism.

And those Africans who had experienced pre-Nazi German rule (like Tanganyikans and Togolese) knew that the Germans were among the most brutal of imperial powers in Africa's experience. Hitler's demand for the return of German colonies in 1936 had caused widespread consternation in those parts of Africa previously ruled by Germany. For example, the Tanganyika League was formed in 1938 – with its head-quarters in Nairobi – to resist the return of Tanganyika to German rule. White residents and black people were united in their opposition. During the war against the Axis (1939–45), 87 000 Tanganyikan Africans served on the side of the Allies to prevent the return of the Germans.

It is against this background of 'choosing between devils' that African participation in the Second World War must be seen. Africa's involvement was not a process of collaboration with imperialism but was a commitment against a worse form of hegemony. To that extent, Africa's involvement in the war was, paradoxically, part and parcel of Africa's struggle against foreign exploitation and in search of human dignity.

Indeed, the war itself played a part in weakening imperial powers on both sides of the conflict. France had been humiliated by the Germans. The French defeat helped to destroy the myth of France's own imperial invincibility. Britain was impoverished and exhausted by the war – and lost her will to hold on to too big an empire. Within little more than two years after the end of the global conflict, Britain was forced to let go of 'the brightest jewel in the British crown' – her Indian empire. The war also helped to raise even higher the global roles of the United States and the Soviet Union – which from then onwards overshadowed imperial Europe. In their own different ways the new superpowers began to put pressures on European colonial pioneers to dismantle their empires. (The superpowers had different imperial designs of their own for the post-war years.)

The birth of the United Nations in 1945 also contributed to the process of decolonization worldwide. As the world body became more truly representative of the human race, colonialism became less and less legitimate. Almost every new member of the United Nations following India's independence was a voice against the old systems of empire. And the Trusteeship Council of the world body became a major lobby against colonialism at large.

The very rationale of the war as a struggle against tyranny and conquest seemed to be incompatible with colonialism: after all, colonialism was itself a form of tyranny and conquest. When Winston Churchill and Franklin D. Roosevelt signed the Atlantic Charter in August 1941, they were not only denouncing injustice in Europe – though Churchill was more obsessed with Europe. Even without realizing it, they were also signing the death warrant of the whole idea of 'legitimate colonialism' for the rest of the twentieth century.

But the Africans themselves were the most important force against colonialism in Africa as they gradually became better organized, more articulate in their demands, and ultimately better armed for the struggle.

A number of different traditions of African resistance are discernible in this period. There was the *warrior tradition*, the *djihād tradition*, the tradition of *Christianity in revolt* and the related tradition of *non-violent mobilization*. Finally, there was the tradition of *guerrilla warfare*. Let us take a closer look at each of these strategies of resistance, bearing in mind also that they were sometimes used to reinforce each other rather than as separate techniques of war.

The warrior tradition of resistance

This concept is linked to the Dar es Salaam School of African History and its emphasis on 'primary resistance'. The Dar es Salaam School used the term 'primary' in a chronological sense to mean resistance at the very time of European penetration and conquest. After all, many African societies had decided not to take the colonial advance 'lying down' – but to fight it as it encroached. Resistance ranged from the Asante wars to the Matabele uprising. These are struggles which have been covered in earlier volumes of the UNESCO *General History of Africa*.

But there is another sense of 'primary resistance'. In this second sense, what is 'primary' is not necessarily what took place *earlier* in time, but what is more deeply rooted in the indigenous warrior tradition. This is a *cultural* meaning of 'primary' rather than a chronological one. The Mau Mau freedom-fighters challenged the British as late as the 1950s – but on the basis of Kikuyu values of warriorhood and related religious beliefs, with all the symbolism of indigenous combat cultures, including elaborate oathing ceremonies. The movement was 'primary' in this cultural sense.

A similar kind of primordial symbolism was later discerned – in more subtle forms – in the liberation struggles in Southern Africa. Spirit possession was not unknown among the guerrillas. And Basil Davidson has drawn our attention to the fact that an oath taken by guerrillas in the names of the great spirits of Chaminuka and Nehanda used to form part of the continuities of struggle.[3]

In the days before independence, Nathan Shamuyarira also drew our attention to the indigenous tone of Zimbabwe's struggle:

> In rural areas meetings become political gatherings and more . . .
> the past heritage was revived through prayers and traditional singing,

3. B. Davidson, 1969, p. 255.

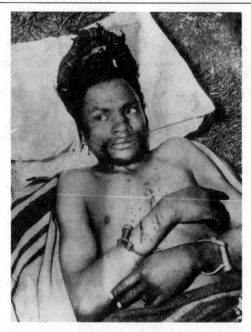

PLATE 5.1   *Dedan Kimathi, hero of the Mau Mau War for Independence, captured on 21 October 1956 and later executed*

ancestral spirits were evoked to guide and lead the new nation. Christianity and civilization took a back seat and new forms of worship and new attitudes were thrust forward dramatically.[4]

Joshua Nkomo, the Zimbabwe freedom-fighter, was met at Salisbury airport in 1962 by a survivor of the 1896–9 resistance. Nkomo had just arrived from abroad. The older man presented Nkomo with a spirit axe to symbolize martial succession and the transmission of the warrior torch.[5]

As the armed struggle gathered momentum some of the campaign zones were named after senior spirit mediums. Indeed, some of the mediums actually operated in the guerrilla camps. The link between the warrior and the prophet was permitted to persist in the struggle for Southern Africa. The ancestral warrior tradition had found a new incarnation in a modern struggle.

But African resistance was sometimes inspired by other cultures at work in Africa – including especially the force of Islam. It is to this other culture that we must now turn.

4. N. M. Shamuyarira, 1965, pp. 68–9; see also T. O. Ranger and J. Weller, 1975.
5. N. M. Shamuyarira, 1965; T. O. Ranger and J. Weller, 1975.

The *djihād* tradition in African resistance

Earlier volumes of the UNESCO *General History of Africa* have already indicated how the *djihād* tradition (meaning 'struggle in the Path of God') was mobilized in the resistance to imperial penetration by the Sultanate of Sokoto in Nigeria, by the Mahdīyya movement in Eastern Sudan and by the sacralized nationalism of Sayed Muḥammad 'Abdallāh Ḥassan (the astonishingly *sane* 'Mullah').

The Mahdīyya spirit persisted in Sudan and played a role against both British imperialism and Egyptian expansionism. The Mahdīyya techniques changed over time but a basic anti-imperial tendency continued to be a feature of the movement.

In Algeria, the tendency to refer to the indigenous population as 'Muslim' reinforced the link between Islam and nationalism. Racialist laws made by the Vichy regime in the summer of 1942 created a new form of *apartheid* in Algeria from which French Algeria never fully recovered. 'Muslims' were denied the use of markets, cinemas and bathing beaches at the same time as Europeans. At its worst, this Francophone *apartheid* even forbade 'Muslims' to sit next to Europeans.

When Algeria was 'rescued' from the Vichy excesses, improvements for the indigenous people were only cosmetic. Indeed, the year the Second World War ended was also one of the worst years of French repression in Algeria. In May 1945 a nationalist procession of Muslims in Setif clashed with the police. Riots broke out both in Setif and Kabylie. Repression by the French army and police resulted in some 10 000 deaths of Algerian Muslims. The spirit of the *djihād* tradition could only be re-kindled by this scale of martyrdom. By 1954 the National Liberation Front of Algeria was ready to inherit the *djihād* torch from the nineteenth-century Algerian hero, 'Abd al-Ḳādir al-Jazairi. The new Algerian revolution had started.

The Egyptian revolution of 1952 established a different kind of linkage with Islam. Gamāl 'Abd al-Nasser, the leader of the revolution, interpreted Egypt as the centre of three circles – the circles of Islam, the Arab world and Africa. The struggle against imperialism was therefore to be seen in the context of the three forces of Islamic resistance, Arab nationalism and pan-Africanism.

And yet al-Nasser was cautious about what he regarded as the more 'extreme' forms of Islamic fundamentalism – especially the movement known as the Muslim Brotherhood. He outlawed the movement and imprisoned some of its leaders. In an age of increasingly competitive ideologies, Islam was indeed a potential ally in the struggle against imperialism – but also a potential danger to political stability among Egyptians themselves.

Gamāl 'Abd al-Nasser's own preference was for the political mobilization of pan-Arabism against both Zionism and Western imperialism.

PLATE 5.2   *Forced assembly of people arrested after the uprising of 8 May 1945 in Algeria*

Although his pan-Arabism had a military arm in the struggle against Israel, the central force of the Egyptian revolution lay in non-violent mass mobilization. Al-Nasser's refusal to permit the execution of King Farouk, and his henchmen in 1952 was part of al-Nasser's vision that 'a revolution born of blood will die in blood'.

Other African nationalists were much more directly influenced by the Indian leader, Mahatma Mohandas Gandhi. It was all part of the wider strategy of *non-violent political mobilization*, distinct from and yet simultaneously reinforcing the forces of the warrior tradition and the legacy of the *djihād*.

The tradition of radical Christianity

Islam was not the only religion which rebelled against colonial rule. Even more ironical was the revolt of Christianity against Western imperialism. Outside North Africa and the Nile valley, Christianity had arrived in Africa in partnership with European colonialism. In the nineteenth century it was sometimes missionary groups which persuaded their own European governments to colonize Africa. This was particularly true of the colonization of East Africa. The moral justification advanced by missionaries in European capitals was the suppression of the Arab slave trade and the spread of the Christian gospel. Imperial reluctance was sometimes swept aside by missionary zeal and moral enthusiasm.

The partnership between European imperialism and Christian mission deeply affected educational policies in the colonies. The division of labour between Church and state in the task of 'educating the natives' varied from colony to colony – but there was little doubt about the political partnership between organized Christianity and the state. Indeed, the immediate aim of colonial education was for a while to produce Africans who were 'fit to become either schoolmasters or religion teachers'. Kwame Nkrumah's own initial aspirations included the ambition to become a Catholic priest.[6]

Considering this partnership between European colonization and Christian mission, it was the more surprising that missionary schools produced some of the earliest African nationalists of the modern variety. The partnership between Christianity and colonialism turned out to be a dialectic almost in the classical Hegelian sense of *contradiction* at the level of the *idea*. The missionary schools helped to promote not just Christian spiritual ideas but also Western secular ideologies. African radical nationalists who emerged from Christian missionary schools included such towering figures as Julius K. Nyerere, Tom Mboya, Eduardo Mondlane, Robert Mugabe, Léopold Sédar Senghor as well as Kwame Nkrumah.

All these were relatively secular figures arising out of a religious womb. Indeed, Kwame Nkrumah said of himself: 'I am a Marxist-Leninist and a non-denominational Christian – and I see no contradiction in that'.[7]

However, European Christianity did not only produce secular African rebels, it also produced African *religious* rebels against the Euro-Christian order. Among the most successful in this historical period was Simon Kimbangu. His followers argued that if God wanted to send a message to the black people, would he have chosen a white messenger? Kimbangu's message sought to reduce the role of the cross in Christianity – a 'dangerous equivalent of the graven image'. Kimbangu's Africanization of Christianity in a matrilineal society also permitted female leadership in the Church well before the rise of feminist Western assertiveness in mainstream European churches.

Simon Kimbangu paid a heavy price for his religious–cultural crusades. The Belgians arrested him in the Congo and locked him up. Simon Kimbangu spent almost as much time in a Belgian cage as Jesus Christ spent on earth: for some 30 years Kimbangu languished behind bars.[8]

By the 1980s the Kimbangu Church had not only transcended colonialism, it had established enough international credibility to have become the first African denomination to be admitted to the World Council of

---

6. See K. Nkrumah, 1957.
7. *ibid.*
8. See also Chapter 17 below, and UNESCO, *General History of Africa*, vol. VII.

Churches. By the 1980s the Kimbangu Church was some four million strong. It is worth remembering that such a figure constituted a bigger following than Jesus Christ had in the first three centuries of the Christian era.

As will be shown in Chapter 17, the whole phenomenon of separatist and millenarian churches during the colonial period was part of Africa's struggle to recover identity and defend its cultural dignity. Some movements were more moderate than others, but all of them have to be seen in the context of Africa's revolt against racism and foreign domination in the religious and secular spheres.

What about the role of *mainstream* Christian churches in the history of anti-imperialism? Was the Christian contribution to decolonization limited to secular products of missionary schools (like Nkrumah and Mugabe) and separatist religious movements (like that of Simon Kimbangu)?

It is true that the mainstream Western churches were slow to join the struggle against racism and imperialism in Africa. But individual members of those churches stood up against oppression from quite early. And later, Africa's first Nobel laureates were devout Christians in revolt against racism – Chief Albert Luthuli and Bishop (now Archbishop) Desmond Tutu, both of South Africa. Even the Dutch Reformed Church of South Africa eventually produced some of the most eloquent voices against *apartheid*. Perhaps the most eloquent of all was the moral oratory of the Reverend Alan Boesak, especially from the mid-1970s onwards. Much earlier, Hastings Banda, an elder of the Church of Scotland, led Nyasaland to independence as the new Republic of Malawi.

In the light of these developments, we may reaffirm that the Christian contribution to decolonization took three main forms – first, through secular products of mission schools (the Nkrumahist tradition); secondly, through Christian separatism (the Kimbanguist tradition); and, thirdly, through the radicalization of mainstream Christian leadership (like the tradition of Archbishop Desmond Tutu).

The strategy of non-violent political mobilization

It was between 1906 and 1908 that a civil-disobedience campaign was launched in South Africa under the leadership of Mahatma Mohandas Gandhi, directed against laws in the Transvaal which required Indians to carry registration certificates. The movement did initiate a distinct tradition of resistance in South Africa and beyond. By the 1950s the African and Indian Congresses in South Africa were trying to coordinate the efforts of Africans, Indians and 'Coloureds' in a mass campaign against the pass laws, the Group Areas Act on racial segregation, and the Bantu Authorities Act designed to promote the 're-tribalization' of Africans. The campaign was a success as an exercise in relative solidarity among

PLATE 5.3   *Kwame Nkrumah on the eve of Ghanaian independence, at the Old Polo Ground,*
5 March 1957

the oppressed – but a failure in terms of its actual objectives against the oppressors.

Kwame Nkrumah in West Africa had also been fascinated by the ideas of Mahatma Mohandas Gandhi. His strategy of 'Positive Action' for greater freedom in the Gold Coast was directly inspired by Gandhian strategies of *Satyagraha* (soul force).[9]

Also a self-conscious disciple of Gandhi during the colonial period was Kenneth Kaunda. Kaunda admitted that in the racial and colonial conditions of Northern Rhodesia, violence was a tempting strategy of desperation for those denied alternative means of redress. But Kaunda insisted on the need for passive resistance or civil disobedience:

> I could not lend myself to take part in any [violent] campaigns. *I reject absolutely violence in any of its forms as a solution to our problem.*[10]

African opposition to armed struggle was also evident at the All-Africa Peoples' Conference held in independent Ghana in 1958. The Algerians – who were at the time locked in an armed struggle against France – found it difficult to get pan-African endorsement of their struggle at the Accra conference. A combination of Gandhism and Francophilia among some of the participants was responsible for this rebuff of Algerian freedom-fighters.

On the whole, the 1950s constituted the last decade of Gandhian strategies of liberation in Africa. After Algeria's independence in 1962 it became increasingly clear that the most difficult areas to liberate peacefully were going to be those which were either under Portuguese rule or under entrenched white minority rule. In neither category were Gandhian methods of civil disobedience likely to succeed. On the contrary, such tactics would only result in ruthless suppression and even massacre of unarmed civilians. The massacre of Sharpeville in March 1960 had already driven that lesson home. Almost exactly a year later the new rebellion against the Portuguese in Angola began to unfold. The age of full armed liberation struggle had arrived in Southern Africa. It is to this modern tradition of armed struggle that we now turn.

The strategy of armed liberation

The most international of all strategies of decolonization in Africa have been those which have required sophisticated modern weapons. The warrior tradition (like the one which was at work in the Mau Mau war) could be based primarily on local self-reliance and home-made weapons. The *djihād* tradition was more linked to international forces (in this case Islamic) – but within Africa, the *djihād* was still relatively domesticated.

9. See K. Nkrumah, 1957.
10. K. Kaunda and C. Morris, 1960, emphasis as in the original.

The strategy of Christian radicalism and of non-violent political mobilization, even when influenced by Gandhi, was ultimately a national process within individual colonial territories.

But when we look at more modernized versions of armed struggle – in the Portuguese colonies and Southern Africa, as well as in Algeria – we are dealing with highly internationalized conflict. Many external countries have been involved in these confrontations in ways which have ranged from contributing funds or weapons to actual participation with troops. If the Soviet Union and its allies had not been involved in the struggles in Southern Africa, African liberation there could have been delayed by at least another generation. The sophisticated weapons used by Africans in Southern Africa – including surface-to-air missiles in the Zimbabwe war – came overwhelmingly from socialist countries abroad. As for the active participation of Cuban troops in the struggle to defend Angola's sovereignty, this marked the strongest level of external support in an African war of liberation.

But external participation was not only on the side of liberation-fighters; it was also on the side of the colonial and racist oppressors. The North Atlantic Treaty Organization was for a long time, directly or indirectly, subsidizing Portuguese repressive stubbornness in its colonies. NATO weapons were used against African liberation-fighters.

A particularly symbolic comparison of external support would be a comparison between Cuba and Israel in their respective involvement in Southern Africa, especially from the 1970s onwards. Both countries were then pariah states in their respective regions – Cuba as the pariah of the Western hemisphere and Israel of the Middle East. Each country was closely allied to a superpower – Cuba to the Soviet Union and Israel to the United States. Both Cuba and Israel had been involved before in conflicts with global implications – John F. Kennedy came close to a nuclear war in the Cuban missile crisis of 1962; President Richard Nixon ordered a worldwide nuclear alert in defence of Israel during the Middle East October war of 1973. Both Cuba and Israel were small countries which attained considerable global visibility; also, both had been involved in nearby conflicts among their neighbours.

But although the two countries did share a number of characteristics, their respective roles in Southern Africa were in sharp contrast. Cuba helped train black freedom-fighters; Israel instructed South Africa's armed forces in counter-insurgency. Cuba provided extension services to Angolan farmers; Israel helped South Africa's nuclear programme, including the development of its nuclear bomb.[11] In March 1987 it became increasingly a matter of public knowledge that Israel had maintained other areas of extensive military collaboration with the Republic of South Africa, in spite of the United Nations' ban on arms deals with the Pretoria regime.

11. For South Africa's nuclear programme, see R. W. Walters, 1987.

To summarize the comparison between Cuba and the Jewish state, while Israel had been a *de facto* ally of white supremacy, Castro's Cuba had been involved in black liberation.

On the whole, armed struggle in Southern Africa has worked well so far. Against the Portuguese, it was a war of attrition which finally resulted in a coup in Portugal in April 1974 – and the speedy collapse of the Portuguese empire soon after. In Zimbabwe it culminated in independence in 1980, and in Namibia in 1990.

But will 'all else' be added to the 'political kingdom' in South Africa when it is finally achieved? Political sovereignty has certainly not necessarily led on to other achievements elsewhere in Africa. As we have indicated earlier, political independence was a necessary condition but by no means a sufficient condition for a fuller realization of African aspirations. In economically ravaged countries like Ghana, and in politically devastated countries like Uganda, it would be truer to articulate, as we indicated, a more pessimistic imperative:

> *Seek ye first the political kingdom, and all else will be subtracted from it.*

But here we must pause and reflect. Kwame Nkrumah is on record as having said that the freedom of Ghana would be meaningless if it was not accompanied by the freedom of the whole of Africa. By 'the political kingdom' did he really mean just the independence of each separate African country? Or did Ghana's supreme pan-Africanist mean instead the full liberation of the African continent as a whole?

In the context of Kwame Nkrumah's political philosophy as a whole, it seems more probable that he meant the following incremental stages:

(1) *The independence of each African country will help the independence of the next one, a stage-by-stage approach to political decolonization.*
(2) *Only when the whole of Africa is decolonized will the 'political kingdom' of the whole continent stand a chance of having 'all else' added unto it.*

If the first shots have indeed been fired in the struggle for South Africa as the last bastion of white-minority rule, it is this final stage of the quest for the 'political kingdom' that we must now examine more fully. Underlying the struggle is the changing relationship between racism and capitalism in Africa's experience.

Revolution and the political kingdom

A central feature of this phase is that the alliance between racism and capitalism in South Africa may be on the verge of breaking up. Are capitalism and *apartheid* on a collision course? Yet while the break-up of the alliance may wound *apartheid* mortally, capitalism in South Africa may still remain intact when the struggle is all over. The political kingdom may *not* have socialism added unto it.

If what we have witnessed in South Africa in the 1980s has been a revolution in its infancy, how quickly are we to expect the maturation of the revolution? How near is victory?

The optimist will see similarities with either the Ethiopian revolution of 1974 or the Iranian revolution of 1979 – both of which began with demonstrations in the streets and built up to a climax. Pre-revolutionary Iran and Ethiopia were each an alliance of domestic feudalism and international capitalism. In a sense, those two regimes of Iran and Ethiopia had lasted many hundreds of years – and yet they were overthrown in a few months of demonstrations. The alliance between domestic feudalism and international capitalism collapsed speedily.

As compared with the Shah and Haile Selassie, *apartheid* will last a few years longer – but racial supremacy is not invincible either. It will be overthrown – but neither by street demonstrations nor by external African armies. *Apartheid* can only fall as a result of *organized struggle from within*. External African armies may be organized but they are not from within. Street demonstrations are from within but they are not yet a case of organized struggle. African states can support and nourish and arm the internal liberation-fighters. Demonstrations can make the townships ungovernable. But without internal guerrilla fighters and saboteurs, the struggle cannot triumph.

But will international economic sanctions bring about the fundamental change? We should distinguish between *expressive* sanctions or boycott and *instrumental* sanctions or boycott. Expressive boycott is a moral judgement, but instrumental boycott is intended to be a political tool. International sanctions will not in themselves lead to 'one man, one vote'. Expressive boycotts will boost up the morale of the oppressed. Western instrumental boycotts may help liberalize the regime – but they will fall short of 'one man, one vote'. Armed struggle from within will still have to be the core of the revolution.

But what about South Africa's nuclear weapons? Will not they protect the *apartheid* regime? A quarter of a century ago, Kwame Nkrumah warned Africa about the two swords hanging over it – the sword of racism and the sword of nuclear power in hostile hands. At that time the French were testing their atomic devices in the Sahara. And so there was nuclear desecration of Africa in the north, and racial rape of Africa in the south. Later on France helped Israel to develop its own nuclear capability at Demona. In turn, Israel subsequently helped South Africa develop its own nuclear weapons. But will they make any difference to the fate of *apartheid*? The answer is 'No' – or, more correctly, only a very small difference.

South Africa's nuclear status can be used to intimidate neighbouring states or warn off countries like Nigeria. But South Africa cannot use nuclear weapons in the streets of Soweto. The use of nuclear weapons *within* South Africa will cause one of the regime's two nightmares: not the nightmare of 'More blacks are coming', but the nightmare of 'More whites are leaving'.

But if *apartheid* will not be saved by nuclear weapons, will it be saved by its alliance with capitalism? In fact, that alliance is already under severe stress. When racism begins to interfere too much with the laws of supply and demand, capitalism begins to feel betrayed. Alternatively, when economic racism becomes inefficient, capitalism feels uneasy. It happened in the days of the slave trade. Capitalism once prospered on slavery. And then as technology became more efficient, slave labour made less sense than wage labour. And so England, the leading slaving power of the eighteenth century, became the leading abolitionist power of the nineteenth. Similarly, an alliance between capitalism and *apartheid* has made good (if narrow) economic sense until recently. Why is that alliance now under stress? Capitalism may now gain by the demise of *apartheid*.

First, black purchasing power is now ready to expand dramatically if the system was economically more equitable. Secondly, black skills have reached new levels and could make the productive forces more efficient. Thirdly, a better educational and training system for blacks could rapidly transform South Africa into a black Australia – rich and highly industrialized. Fourthly, opposition to *apartheid* is creating instability which is unhealthy for capitalism. Fifthly, instability in turn creates uncertainty about the future – capitalist investment is a form of calculated planning which needs some degree of predictability.

Then there is the fact that escalating repression in South Africa alienates important sections of public opinion in the Western world – and these outraged groups begin to put pressure on business firms and chain stores. Western businesses which have disinvested include IBM, General Motors, Barclays Bank, Coca-Cola and Kodak. Many institutions had previously closed their accounts with Barclays Bank. Nigeria led the way a few years ago.

Then there is fear in business circles that prolonged struggle against racism could become a struggle against capitalism – as the activists get radicalized (as happened in Angola, Mozambique and, to some extent, Zimbabwe). Sooner or later capitalism has to cut its losses – and break its bonds with *apartheid*. Capitalism has to protect its interests in a changing situation.

But what is the future of capitalism in South Africa once *apartheid* is defeated? Can we be sure that socialism will be added to the political kingdom? For better or worse, victory against *apartheid* will not necessarily mean victory against capitalism. There is after all a degree of capitalist development which, when reached, makes capitalism almost irreversible.

Karl Marx thought that capitalism was a stage of development lower than socialism. When capitalist development reaches its peak, it would result in a socialist revolution. But more recent history demonstrates that there is a stage of capitalist development beyond which a communist revolution is almost impossible – unless imposed from without. The USA and most Western European countries have reached such a stage.

But what would make a communist revolution impossible in an advanced industrial capitalist country? Marx's prediction of increasing enlargement of the proletariat has not happened in the leading capitalist countries. What has happened is increasing enlargement of the bourgeoisie. Marx's prediction of increasing misery has not materialized. The workers have not got poorer – but richer. And the very poorest are not workers at all (lumpen militariat at best). Western workers have a lot more to lose than their 'chain' – they have cars, business shares, TV sets, boats, and so on. Class consciousness has not prevailed over national consciousness. On the contrary, anti-communism is linked to working-class Western patriotism. Marx underestimated capitalism's capacity to co-opt, convert and corrupt others in its own support. Prosperous capitalism can do just that.

But has South Africa reached the stage of irreversible capitalism – the stage which most Western countries have reached? The evidence suggests that it has not. And therefore under black rule South Africa stands an even greater chance of either continuing as a capitalist system (but without racism) or embarking on a socialist path of development.

Is there no hope of socialism being added to South Africa's political kingdom? If there is a chance, what in South Africa are the predisposing factors in favour of socialism after black majority rule? First, radicalization through prolonged struggle could turn black South Africa socialist. Secondly, class polarization as an off-shoot of racial polarization could help to socialize post-*apartheid* South Africa. Thirdly, a high degree of urbanization in South Africa is an asset for modern socialism. Fourthly, an enlarged black proletariat alongside an arrested embourgeoisement should help the cause of building socialism. Fifthly, the white man's prophecy that every black nationalist is a Marxist could at long last fulfil itself. As for the atomic bomb, South Africa under black majority rule may well become the first black nuclear power by the end of the twentieth century.

The political kingdom in South Africa may have more 'added unto it' than almost anywhere else in Africa. The high level of industrialization built by black labour and Western technology, the enormous mineral wealth endowed by nature, the discipline arising out of prolonged African struggle for justice, and the new credentials of nuclear status, these are all bound to enhance considerably the meaning of South Africa's political kingdom under majority rule before the end of this century.

Yet only when all Africa's wealth is truly under Africa's sovereign control – from the Cape to Cairo, from Dar es Salaam to Dakar – will we be able to assess more definitively Kwame Nkrumah's immortal imperative:

> *Seek ye first the political kingdom and all things shall be added unto you.*

North Africa and the Horn

Ivan HRBEK*

At the end of the Second World War no country of the region was free from foreign political and military control. Even in the formally independent states such as Ethiopia and Egypt, there was a strong British military presence which exercised influence on political life. A further feature of the post-war period was the demise of Italy as a colonial power. All its former colonies – Somalia, Eritrea and Libya – were conquered during the war by the Allies and remained under British – and in the case of Fezzān in Libya, also French – military occupation. Their future had to be decided at an international level.

The Maghreb

Although in the three Maghreb countries under French domination, the defeat of France in 1940 had seriously weakened its position of authority, all the post-war French governments did their utmost to regain their hold; they even introduced a more oppressive regime after a war which was claimed to have been fought to liberate people from foreign domination. It was that rigid attitude that led to the disastrous colonial war in French Indochina (now Vietnam) whose people did not see any justice in the French claim to re-occupy a colony which they virtually had lost to the Japanese. Although in 1954 the military catastrophe at Dien-Bien-Phu led the French government to the conference table at Geneva where France bid farewell to its South-Asian colonial empire, the French politicians – like the Bourbons – did not learn the lessons of history.[1] True, some cosmetic reforms were undertaken in the three Maghreb countries but the colonial situation of dependence, exploitation, lack of political liberties, and a special dose of French cultural arrogance in addition, remained unchanged. In Chapter 2 we saw how the French colonial administration reacted against the wave of national protests in the last years of the war and in its aftermath.

---

* Deceased in 1993.
   1. On the history of the post-war Maghreb, R. Le Tourneau, 1962; and S. Amin, 1965; 1970a and 1970b.

Morocco

Each of the three countries had to go through its own version of martyrdom before it attained independence. A fresh impetus to the Moroccan nationalist movement was given by a speech of Sultan Mohamed ibn Yūsuf – later King Mohamed V – in Tangier in April 1947.[2] The speech referred to the brilliant future of his country, its unalienable rights and its fidelity to Islam and the Arab world. Although the French general resident expected to hear some words of recognition and gratitude to France, no such compliments were heard. From that time on the Sultan became the focus as well as the leading figure in the struggle for independence. There followed a wave of anti-colonial demonstrations and strikes. The strikes, which occurred between 1947 and 1952, showed that the working class had become well-organized and fully integrated into the nationalistic movement.

During his visit to Paris in October 1950, the Sultan asked the French government for political and economic autonomy, the widening of the constitutional and political rights for the Sharifian government and the general revision of Franco-Moroccan relations, but without success. At that stage the six independent Arab states asked the United Nations to put the Moroccan question on the agenda of the Sixth General Assembly in 1951 and though they repeated their proposal in the following year, the colonial powers refused even to discuss the lawful claim of Morocco for independence.

Recognizing the Sultan's role as paramount, the French decided in 1953 to dethrone him; for that purpose they used the influence of the powerful Pasha of Marrakesh, Thāmī al-Glāwī, among the feudal leaders of some Berber *ḳabīla*s as well as the influence of a few religious leaders. On 14 August 1953, that group – without any legal basis in Islamic or Moroccan law[3] – declared Mohamed ibn Yūsuf unworthy of the throne and proclaimed his cousin, Mohamed ibn 'Arafa, an old man without any political background, the new Sultan. The conspiracy – engineered by the Residence, French *colons* in Morocco and high financial circles in Paris – did not attain its expected results: after the Sultan's deportation to Corsica and later to Madagascar, the whole country rose almost unanimously against the colonialists.

National struggle took diverse forms. The Istiḳlāl Party founded an underground '*Organisation secrète*'. The most important among other similar groups was the left-wing 'Black Crescent'. The strikes and street demonstrations in urban centres became more numerous; the Moroccans

2. On the Moroccan independence struggle, see A. al-Fāsī, 1954; A. Ayache, 1956; D. E. Ashford, 1961; J. L. Miège, 1950; and J. Waterbury, 1970 and 1975.

3. On the legal incompetence of al-Glāwī as an owner of brothels, see the penetrating essay by L. Massignon, 1962, pp. 250–64.

began to boycott French products; people refused to attend Friday prayers where homage was expected in the name of the French-appointed sultan. In the Rīf and the Middle Atlas, a 'Liberation Army' was formed by the Berber rural population and started to attack French military posts and barracks. The years 1954 and 1955 marked a high tide in the Moroccan independence struggle.

When during 1955 the general violence increased, and the police and the counter-revolutionary groups of the French *colons* proved, with all their terrorism, incapable of stemming the liberation movement – which in turn was united in its unanimous demand for the return of the legitimate sultan – the French government was forced to change its policy towards Morocco. In the meantime, the war in Algeria became a serious problem and the fresh experience of the defeat in Vietnam demonstrated the inability of the French army to cope with the wide popular movement. In August 1955 the first negotiations with various representatives of Morocco's political life, including Istiḳlāl, were opened in Aix-les-Bains, and General Catroux was sent to Madagascar to arrange for the return of the sultan. Events then moved quickly: Mohamed ibn 'Arafa was obliged to abdicate and al-Glāwī, being abandoned by his masters, issued in October an unexpected proclamation of loyalty to Muḥammad ibn Yūsuf.

After a few weeks' stay in France where the terms for ending the protectorate were negotiated, Muḥammad ibn Yūsuf – from 1957, King Mohamed V – returned triumphantly to his homeland on 26 November 1955, acclaimed by millions of his subjects as they rallied in Rabat. Sīdī Bekkāi then formed the first independent Moroccan government which completed the negotiations with the French. The independence of Morocco was proclaimed on 2 March 1956.

A month later, on 7 April, the Spanish protectorate over the northern zone was abolished and the region integrated into the Kingdom of Morocco; in July of the same year, the international zone of Tangier followed suit. Thus all the parts of pre-colonial Morocco were united in one state with the exception of the Spanish enclaves of Ifni, Mellila and Ceuta. Whereas Ifni was reintegrated in 1968, the latter two remained for a time under foreign domination and were the subject of reiterated claims by Morocco to the Madrid government.

Tunisia

The independence of Morocco was soon followed by that of Tunisia. There was a certain parallelism between the course of the liberation struggle in the two countries. Both were conditioned by the same colonial power, disrupted by the presence of an influential French community and, last but not least, influenced by the international situation.[4] On the

4. See H. Bourguiba, 1954; D. L. Ling, 1967; A. Kassab, 1976.

other hand, the dissimilarities were not negligible either. There was early participation by the trades unions – led by a brilliant organizer, Farhāt Hāshed. There followed the gradual steps from partial participation of the Tunisians in government to internal autonomy. But there was also a serious split in the leadership of the Neo-Destūr Party between Habib Bourguiba and Ṣalāḥ ben Yūsuf and the relative passivity of the bey, the formal head of the state.

After the founding of the Tunisian National Front in August 1947 the pressure on the French was intensified through many demonstrations and strikes in which the call for improved living conditions was accompanied by the demand for political independence. The years between 1945 and 1955 witnessed also the worsening of the general standard of living among the masses; some parts of the country suffered from famine. In 1949, after Bourguiba's return from voluntary exile (1945–9), the Neo-Destūr leadership took a major step forward and elaborated a strategy for the Tunisian independence struggle. Although the achievement of full independence was the rallying point for all Tunisians, Bourguiba – aware of the strength of the French opposition to immediate Tunisian independence – was prepared to compromise tactically and to gain his goal gradually. At first the French agreed to negotiate about the question of partial internal autonomy, and in August 1950 a new government under Muḥammad Chenik was formed, composed of an equal number of French and Tunisian ministers. But whereas the French considered this the final concession which would allow them to retain control of the country, the Neo-Destūr Party soon increased its demands. A new crisis exploded in 1951 when France rejected the demand for a Tunisian parliament. That rejection was due more to the pressure of the French settlers than to the French political will in Paris. This particular feature – the settlers' influence on French colonial policy during the Fourth Republic – was a recurring theme in all Maghreb countries. Its consequences were in every case most tragic for the oppressed people and, in the long run, catastrophic even for the white settlers themselves. At the beginning of 1952, France stopped further negotiations with Tunisian nationalists, banned the Neo-Destūr party congress and arrested both the radical Bourguiba and the moderate Chenik, together with many others. A few, among them Ṣalāḥ ben Yūsuf, the second strong man of the Neo-Destūr Party, escaped to Cairo. At the end of the same year, the trades-union leader Farhāt Hāshed was assassinated, probably by the settlers' secret terrorist organization, the Red Hand.

In spite of hardened French repression, demonstrations and strikes continued in towns. During the first quarter of 1954, general discontent with colonial rule spread to rural districts. For the first time in modern Tunisian history, the peasants formed themselves into armed groups, the *fellaghas*, to attack European colonists, to sabotage communications (cutting wires, derailing trains) and to fight smaller French units. These activities were not restricted to outlying districts. On the contrary, they

PLATE 6.1   *The Neo-Destūr Congress, November 1955: centre, Habib Bourguiba*

concentrated on Cape Bon peninsula and the northern part of the country. Settler farms had to be protected by tanks; mass mopping-up operations by the French police and army failed to stop the insurrection.

In the middle of the increasingly difficult situation, there came the shock of the French defeat of Dien-Bien-Phu (7 May 1954) and the French governmental crisis from which the Mendès-France government emerged. New policy-makers decided to reopen negotiations with Tunisian nationalists: Bourguiba and others were hurriedly set free and later returned to Tunisia. The French offered Tunisia internal autonomy, retaining for themselves control over the armed forces and foreign policy. Protracted negotiations were concluded as late as June 1955. Tunisia won internal autonomy but at the price of binding itself to safeguarding French interests and to retaining a close relationship with France. France continued to control foreign policy, defence and even internal security. That Franco-Tunisian Convention fell far short of the aspirations of the Tunisian people, but Bourguiba as a veteran politician knew that under the then-prevailing conditions it was impossible to gain more by nego-tiations from France, and so he and the majority of the Neo-Destūr Party agreed with it. The alternative view was represented by the left-wing group led by Ṣalāḥ ben Yūsuf who after his return from Cairo advocated the continuation of the armed struggle as a means of forcing France to recognize the full independence of Tunisia. In the ensuing clash, Bour-guiba was able to win the majority of the Neo-Destūr members. At the party congress in November 1955, Ṣalāḥ ben Yūsuf was expelled from the party for his opposition to the Convention. Although the party congress expressed the view that the Tunisian people would continue its struggle until the achievement of full independence, the compromise of June 1955 and the expulsion of ben Yūsuf signalled that from then on the party would follow a moderate policy, rather than a radical one.

In any case, the period of 'internal autonomy' did not last long. Under the impact of the events in Morocco and more so of the beginning of the Algerian war, France was ready to negotiate, in order to salvage as much as possible of its interests, both economic and strategic. After a month of negotiations in Paris a protocol recognizing full Tunisian sovereignty was signed on 20 March 1956: after 75 years of colonial rule, Tunisia re-entered the community of free nations of the world.

The Algerian war[5]

As already pointed out, the liberation process in Morocco and Tunisia was accelerated by the outbreak of the war in Algeria: one of the bitterest

5. The most important works among the abundant literature on this theme are: F. Abbas, 1962; A. Nouschi, 1962; M. Lacheraf, 1963; G. C. Gordon, 1966; Y. Courrière, 1968–72; J. C. L. Vatin, 1974; C. R. Ageron, 1979; M. Kaddache, n.d.; A. K. Saadallah, 1981.

and longest anti-colonial wars ever waged in Africa. It owed these qualities both to the stubbornness of the French to retain the country and to the determination of the Algerian people to achieve liberty. In the case of Morocco and Tunisia it was possible for some French governments to compromise and to respond positively, even if belatedly and reluctantly, to the nationalists' demands. But to follow a similar policy in Algeria was for a long time out of the question for any French politician of any political colour. The dogma of 'Algérie française' was neither contested nor even subjected to any critical consideration – it would have been close to sacrilege to deny that 'Algeria is France. . . . Who among you would hesitate to use all means in order to save France?'[6] That myth was based on the presence of nearly one million French settlers (the so-called *Pieds noirs*, Black legs), on heavy investment of French capital in agriculture and mining, and on the disproportionate influence of the Algerian lobby in French political life. The myth that Algeria was French was given a new impetus by the discovery of oil and natural gas in the Sahara in the 1950s. For the first time in its history, France had oil wealth in considerable quantity on its own territory. The vision of being able at last to have an independent oil policy considerably coloured French decisions during the war of Algerian independence.

The history of Algeria between 1947, the year of adoption of the Algerian Statute, and 1 November 1954, the date of the outbreak of the war, is a lesson on how a colonial administration, while solemnly adhering to democratic principles, can at the same time circumvent them. It was also a lesson in the futility of a moderate policy with such an adversary in a situation of steadily worsening misery and economic and social inequality.

In 1954 the area of cultivable land in European hands represented 23 per cent of the total, but it was to be found in the most fertile areas. That proportion should be compared with the demographic growth: between 1936 and 1954 the number of Muslim Algerians rose from 6.3 to 8.7 million, whereas the number of Europeans only rose from 946 000 to one million. Two-thirds of the Algerians lived in a subsistence economy, forming not an independent peasantry but semi-proletarians. The annual income of an Algerian employed in agriculture averaged 22 000 old francs, in contrast with 260 000 old francs for a European. In the countryside there were about one million unemployed or underemployed – resulting in out-migration to the urban centres or to France. In 1957 about 300 000 Algerians – that is, every seventh adult – worked in France.

6. F. Mitterrand, November 1954. The socialist, François Mitterrand, was at that time Minister of the Interior in the Mendès-France government.

TABLE 6.1 *The distribution of income in Algeria in 1955*[7]

	Population		Income	Percentage share of the national
	(millions)	*(%)*	*(million francs)*	*income*
Non-Muslims	1.0	10	298 000	47
Muslims				
rural	5.3	55	117 000	18
non-rural	3.4	35	222 000	35
Total	9.7	100	637 000	100

The economic and social inequality was also reflected in the political sphere. The Algerian Assembly comprised 120 members, half of them French, half Muslim Algerians. The administration took care to ensure that the majority of Algerians elected were those whose loyalty to colonial rule was beyond doubt. And so all elections were cleverly rigged. No wonder the Assembly neither represented Algerian public opinion nor discussed such serious national problems as the vote for Muslim women, the teaching of Arabic in schools, and Islamic cults.[8]

All manifestations of Algerian nationalism, even the most moderate demands for civil and political equality, were suppressed and repressed. The two main nationalist parties, the *Union démocratique du manifeste algérien* (UDMA) led by Ferhat Abbas, and the *Mouvement pour le triomphe des libertés democratiques* (MTLD) led by the veteran Messali Ḥādj, were as yet not prepared to abandon their policies of negotiation. The former made vain attempts to persuade the French to accept the autonomous but associated Algerian Republic, whereas for the latter the recognition of Algerian sovereignty was the prime condition.

When these policies failed, both parties went through crises: UDMA lost support among the better-off urban classes and the MTLD increasingly came under the personal leadership of the erratic Messali Ḥādj. It lost its popular appeal and began to take a typical *petit-bourgeois* line. The Communist Party of Algeria, supported mostly by the poorer classes of the European population, did not show much enthusiasm for the Algerian nationalist cause.

In 1953–4 the MTLD split into three factions: the 'Messalists' who supported unconditionally the old leader (deported in 1952 to France), the 'Centralists' who wanted more power to be given to the collective Central Committee, and the *Comité révolutionnaire d'unité et d'action*

7. S. Amin, 1970b, p. 61.
8. T. Chenntouf, 1969.

PLATE 6.2 *Ferhat Abbas addressing a mass meeting in Casablanca, 9 July 1961, in the presence of King Hassan II*

(CRUA) preaching insurrection and revolution as the only means for achieving independence when all constitutional and legal roads proved ineffectual. CRUA was made up of one-time members of the *Organisation spéciale* (OS), an offshoot of the MTLD founded in 1947. The nine 'historical chiefs' of the Algerian revolution – Aït Aḥmed, Mohamed Boudiaf, Ben Boulaid, Aḥmed Ben Bella, Mourad Didouche, Rabah Bīṭāt, Larbī ben MʿHīdī, Belkāsem Krīm and Mohamed Khider – decided to start armed insurrection on 1 November 1954. For this purpose the whole country was divided into five military districts (*wilāyas*) each of them under a commander-in-chief. At the same time, three leading members went to Cairo to assure the aid of Egypt in arms, money and propaganda.

In the first phase, the *Armée de libération nationale* (ALN) amounted to no more than 2000–3000 men, armed with rifles and knives. The first actions took place in the Aurès Mountains and in Kabylie, but by the summer of 1955 action had spread to eastern and central Algeria. Most of the ALN fighters were peasants, but successively they were joined by members of the urban classes as it became clear that the French – that is, the colonial administration, the army and the European colonists – were not making any distinction between those who were fighting and those who remained passive – French reprisals were falling on all Muslim Algerians indiscriminately. Although the French gradually increased their armed forces in Algeria from the initial 56 000 men to an impressive half a million in 1960, they were unable to defeat the will of the Algerians for independence.

The armed struggle had finally ended with the spirit of moderation that had characterized the preceding period. By its call to the masses, the new struggle aroused their latent patriotism and turned them into active fighters. In the course of the war, the French myth of the non-existence of the Algerian nation finally crumbled, and with it the illusion inherited from the early twentieth century that with the police force and a strong army it would be possible to maintain a nation in French colonial subjugation for ever. More and more Algerians joined the ALN which at the height of the fighting totalled some 130 000 members in the guerrilla groups. Equally important was the support given to the fighters by the civil population.

As early as May 1955 the *Front de libération nationale* (FLN) was founded as a supreme political organization of the Algerian people. The majority of Algerian political parties and groupings were successively dissolved and their adherents entered the FLN. An exception was Messali Ḥādj who founded his own party and bitterly opposed the FLN in such a way that he joined the camp of the French collaborators. The Algerian Communist Party did not enter the FLN as it would have meant its dissolution, but from 1956 onwards it co-operated and subordinated its guerrilla groups to the central command of the ALN.

In August 1956 the FLN held its first congress in the Soumman valley in Kabylie; about 200 delegates discussed actual political and organizational problems as well as the prospects and future of Algeria. A radical line was taken: independence was not enough; the establishment of a socialist order with fundamental agrarian reform was needed. The congress again reiterated the Arab and Muslim character of the Algerian nation and its full right to self-determination.

The Algerian problem now took on a new, international dimension. The Arab, Asian and socialist countries supported Algerian independence in the UN and many of the progressive Arab regimes aided with weapons, military instructions and finance. Most prominent among them was Egypt – and in the Suez crisis of October 1956 one of the French goals was the overthrow of President al-Nasser because of his support of the Algerian revolution.

In France itself, the Algerian war had a more radical influence. Opinion was divided between the progressive elements, who wanted to end the new 'dirty' war which had followed so soon after that in Vietnam, and the right-wing groups, who wished to escalate the war until the French achieved victory. The weak governments of the Fourth Republic, afraid of being accused of treason if they even contemplated negotiations with the 'rebels', were incapable of doing anything but give more and more power to the generals on the spot. The strategy employed by the French military consisted of three main elements: the 'regrouping' of villages, intended to destroy the FLN's network of support; the psychological warfare of terror to isolate the FLN from the majority of the people; and then the erection of a wire barrier on the Tunisian and Moroccan frontiers to stop supplies coming from the neighbouring countries.

The 'regrouping' affected hundreds of thousands of peasants and uprooted them from their lands and their traditions without providing any alternative way of life. The regrouped villages became concentration camps and their inhabitants became vagrants. Their normal productive work practically ceased.[9] The terror reached its height in 1957 with the 'battle for Algiers', an attempt by the ALN to implant itself more deeply in the city. The French answered with a merciless campaign of persecution, jailing and torture, which indeed destroyed the ALN organization in the city, left a legacy of hatred and aroused a wave of indignation both in France and in the whole world where the methods of the French paratroops were compared with those of the Gestapo in Nazi Germany. In the same year of 1957 the Algerian–Tunisian border was sealed by a continuous electrically-charged wire barricade; it meant the total isolation of the Algerian guerrilla fighters from the outside world. But none of these measures succeeded in breaking the fighting spirit. The guerrilla operations continued even if on a smaller scale than before, and armed resistance lasted to the very end.

The political crisis in France caused by the Algerian war was precipitated in May 1958 by the revolt of the French senior officers in Algeria who demanded the arrival of General de Gaulle, considered as the man who would be able to finish the war to the French advantage. The last government of the Fourth Republic abdicated and de Gaulle took over. Two main political forces were behind him: the financial oligarchy and the French colonists in Algeria, supported by the officers. Gradually it became manifest that the interests of those groups were divergent and that de Gaulle had his own political concepts in mind (the increasing role of France in Europe, the establishment of a new relationship with the Third World, and so on). In fact, his aims were closer to the interests of the French financial and industrial oligarchy than to the interests of the colonists in Algeria, who clung to the obsolete colonialism of 'Algeria of papa'. But it took de Gaulle some time to evolve a more positive policy towards the Algerians and the war continued as before. The last attempt to win the Algerians back to the French side was the 'Constantine plan' announced by de Gaulle in 1958: it proposed to rewaken the traditional countryside and to industrialize Algeria. But like many other projects of the time, the plan proposed was to prove a

9. A quarter of a million of these people preferred to flee from the country to Morocco and Tunisia; from these the reserves of the ALN were then recruited.

PLATE 6.3 *On 20 September 1959, Messali Ḥādj approved General Charles de Gaulle's declaration on Algeria*

parody.[10] Its consequences would have been to bring major advantages to the French colonists but only very minor ones to the Algerians. The agrarian 'reform' would have affected only about 250 000 hectares, leaving on one side the fundamental problem of the 2.7 million hectares owned by the colonists.

In answer to the changes in France, the FLN proclaimed in September 1958 the formation of the government-in-exile, the GPRA (*Gouvernement provisoire de la République algérienne*), whose first leader was Ferhat Abbas. In 1961, the leadership of the government was taken over by the more

10. S. Amin, 1970b, p. 125.

radical Yūsuf Ben Khedda. The provisional government was recognized *de jure* by all Arab and many Asian countries and *de facto* by the socialist states.

When neither military actions nor the Constantine plan achieved the expected results, de Gaulle's government at last decided to negotiate. When it became known what was about to begin, the fascists in Algiers rose in revolt in January 1960; after the 'Week of the Barricades' it collapsed. In March of the same year de Gaulle for the first time employed the magic slogan '*Algérie algérienne*' throwing away – after more than one hundred years – the myth that 'Algeria is as French as Brittany'. The negotiations were opened in the middle of the year but soon broke down over many crucial problems. Important was the fact that the French recognized the FLN and the GPRA as partners. The talks were the first political victory of the Algerians, and others were soon to follow.

In April 1961 the 'ultras' in Algeria tried one last throw in the 'Generals' Plot' led by four high-ranking generals. It failed but the ultras decided to continue their fight for the preservation of *Algérie française* through the terrorism of the OAS (*Organisation armée secrète*).

The ensuing negotiations were protracted and hard; one main obstacle was the French insistence on the separation of the Sahara, with its oil wealth, from the territory of Algeria. Nevertheless, the firm refusal of the FLN to allow this, forced France to a compromise. In March the Evian protocol, announcing a cease-fire and proclaiming that the future of Algeria would be decided by a referendum, was signed. Organized on 1 July 1962, the referendum resulted in a vote of 99.7 per cent for independence.

The last months of colonial rule as well as the first weeks after independence were marked by the rampant sabotage of OAS fascists who in their powerless fury killed, destroyed and burned. By their acts they also killed all chances for the European minority to remain in independent Algeria as provided in the Evian protocol. There followed a mass exodus of colonists: by the end of July about half a million left for France and by the end of the year fewer than 20 per cent of the Europeans remained in Algeria. On the one hand, the mass and abrupt departure of the colonists – including almost all the technicians in the country – caused the young republic many initial difficulties; on the other hand, it largely simplified the ethnic and social structure of Algeria and spared it otherwise inevitable racial conflicts.

The proclamation of Algeria's independence brought to an end the period of French colonialism in the Maghreb. The cost of liberation was heavy: it is estimated that nearly one million Algerians lost their lives; another two million were uprooted; ten thousand houses and buildings were destroyed during the war, and subsequently by OAS terrorism. No other African nation paid such a high and tragic price for its independence. But by their heroic fight, the Algerians objectively aided the political struggle in the other French colonies. The Algerian war made clear to the French public and their political leaders the futility of the old colonial system, and forced them to recognize the right of every nation to self-determination.

Libya[11]

In Chapter 2 we left Libya in 1948, still under military occupation, awaiting the decision of the UN as to its future fate. Britain and France were already established in the country. There now came the USA with the establishment of a great air-base at Wheelus Field near Tripoli. All three Western powers now had vested interests in Libya and were rather reluctant to leave the country. It is therefore no wonder that Western interests soon clashed both with the wishes of the Libyan people and with the policy of the Arab, Asian and socialist countries. The British took the initiative with the Bevin–Sforza plan envisaging a British trusteeship in Cyrenaica, an Italian one in Tripolitania (where the majority of the Italian settlers lived), and a French one in Fezzān. Against that attempt to divide the country into three parts, the USSR advocated a global collective trusteeship by the UN. The Libyan people expressed their opposition to the Bevin–Sforza plan by huge demonstrations; in Tripoli more than 40 000 Libyans took part in them. The UN General Assembly rejected the plan in May 1949. In November 1949, the USSR proposed immediate independence for Libya, the evacuation of foreign troops in three months and the closing of the foreign military bases. The proposal was not accepted; the UN then voted that Libya as a whole should be constituted as an independent and sovereign state not later than 1 January 1952.

These international aspects should not be interpreted as meaning that independence came to the Libyan people as a gift from the UN. On the contrary, it was the expansion of the Libyan anti-colonial struggle that made world opinion aware of the Libyan question and then forced the hand of the UN. This patriotic movement worked under very difficult conditions, caused partly by history and partly by unequal social structures in diverse parts of the country. The problems were compounded by the British policy of exploiting the situation to disrupt the national liberation movement. From the beginning the British preferred the head of the Sanūsiyya order, Muḥammad Idrīs – who, in 1947, returned to Cyrenaica from his Egyptian exile – as their chosen candidate for fulfilling a major role in Libyan politics. His known conservative attitudes aroused opposition among the Tripolitan nationalist bourgeoisie who wanted a democratic regime, the unification of the whole of Libya, close

11. For Libyan history in the pre-revolution period see E. E. Evans-Pritchard, 1949; I. R. Khalidi, 1956; M. Khadduri, 1963b; J. Norman, 1963b; N. I. Proshin, 1975.

co-operation with the already independent Arab states and the evacuation of foreign troops. The Tripolitan opposition was afraid that Idrīs would try to introduce the Sanūsī theocratic feudal system into Tripolitania; its leaders were also aware of his close collaboration with the British. Idrīs from his side distrusted the Tripolitan liberal bourgeoisie with its republican ideals and for some time preferred to be an absolute ruler in Cyrenaica than to share power with them over the whole of Libya.

That dissonance was cleverly exploited by Britain to protract negotiations about Libyan independence. In June 1949 Cyrenaica was proclaimed independent under Emir Idrīs: the constitution elaborated by the British safeguarded the emir's almost unlimited power, and established a parliament, half of whose members were to be nominated by the emir. The new regime did not correspond to the wishes of the progressive part of the Cyrenaican population who wanted more political participation. Strikes and demonstrations were suppressed by the emir with the help of British troops.

But in spite of the clearly reactionary character of the Idrīs regime, and in spite of the serious misgivings of the Tripolitanian politicians, it soon became clear that full Libyan independence could be attained only through unification under the leadership of Idrīs. In the years 1949–51 protracted and difficult negotiations were undertaken between both parties. Since the main aim of the Tripolitan leaders of the national liberation movement was independence and unity, they finally accepted a compromise. Under British pressure and in accordance with the wishes of Idrīs, Libya became a federation of three provinces – Tripolitania, Cyrenaica and Fezzān – with great provincial autonomy at the expense of a rather weak central government. On 24 December 1951, the independence of the Kingdom of Libya was proclaimed; the former emir of Cyrenaica and the head of the Sanūsīyya order, King Muḥammad Idrīs I al-Sanūsī, became the first ruler.

Libya entered independence with a heavy colonial legacy, and with the legacy of wartime destruction and the presence of foreign troops. In economy and social structure, it belonged with the most underdeveloped countries of North Africa; in agriculture, the patriarchal feudal relations were dominant and a high percentage of the inhabitants still led a nomadic or semi-nomadic way of life. Industry was nearly non-existent; crafts were produced only for the local market. The Libyan bourgeoisie and proletariat were numerically weak and badly organized. The majority of the banks, wholesale shops and plantations, as well as foreign trade, were in the hands of non-Libyans. The educational level was low, more than 85 per cent of the Libyans being illiterate.

The prospects were rather dim; a UN Commission in 1951 underlined the fact that Libya was 'without mineral resources or oil' (!) as until that time oil prospecting had shown only negative results.

The activities of the surviving political organizations in Tripolitania soon aroused the suspicion of the ruling group of feudal chiefs, comprador bourgeoisie, Sanūsī leaders and members of the royal family. In 1952 all political parties were banned and other organizations, like trades unions and youth clubs, were strictly controlled.

The general disappointment that long-awaited independence had not brought improved conditions led to an increase in mass demonstrations and protests, but with only negligible results. The Western powers used the economic difficulties of the new state to conclude 'aid agreements' with it. This meant new dependency. The United States, Britain and France obtained the right to maintain their military and air bases on Libyan territory, and also an open door for foreign capital. In 1957 the share of foreign capital in the Libyan economy was already 75 per cent. Both the economy and administration were virtually run by foreign advisers and the Libyan government proclaimed that it would confiscate neither the land of 15 000 Italian settlers still remaining in the country nor the property of the Italian commercial companies.

Between 1953 and 1956 the prospecting for oil showed surprising results and in the following years Libya granted concessions for oil extraction to various American, British, French and Italian companies under the proviso of 50–50 sharing of net profit. At the beginning of 1960 commercial extraction on 15 oil-fields began, and in the next few years both the number of fields and the production increased rapidly; pipe-lines were built to the coast and oil harbours to facilitate transport.[12]

The oil boom proved to be an ambiguous gift: on the one hand, Libya became in a very short time one of the richest countries in Africa with increasing per capita income and abundant capital for development projects, but on the other hand the economy, being based on one single product, became dependent on world market fluctuations. Instead of giving Libya a freer hand, the boom made its government even more subservient to foreign interests. Although the oil production offered many jobs for Libyans, it was as unskilled labour only and it did not bring about any pronounced changes in the social structure. There was, of course, a partial exodus of the rural population to the oil-fields and towns; the skilled labour was supplied by the immigrants from other Arab countries so that a true Libyan working class was slow to develop. The boom was followed by inflation, felt mostly by the peasants, nomads and poorer classes. True, the government increased expenditure on the social services, health and education – but these lagged behind the needs of the population. Even worse, no real policy was elaborated for the diversification of the economy, nor were investments in industry and agriculture contemplated. It is not an exaggeration to say that the royal regime was at a loss to know what to do with the cornucopia that so unexpectedly showered on the country.

12. See Libyan Oil, 1972.

After 12 years of experimentation with a costly and ineffective system, the federal structure was abolished in 1963; the three autonomous provinces ceased to exist and Libya became a unitary state. In foreign policy, the close alliance with the Western powers continued, although there emerged a tendency to take a more independent position on some Arab issues. The passivity of the regime during the June 1967 war led to a lot of protests and demonstrations which forced the government to join the short-lived oil boycott and later to offer aid to Egypt and Jordan. The demonstrations were signs of the growing impact of Arab nationalism among the Libyan bourgeoisie and intelligentsia. In spite of the increasing discontent of those groups with the regime's internal and foreign policy there existed in Libya no civilian organized body capable of overthrowing the government, either peacefully or by violent means, and then inaugurating a policy more adequate to the opportunities offered by the oil wealth.

It thus fell to a group of army officers led by Captain Muammar Kadhaffi to effect a bloodless take-over of power on 1 September 1969, during a visit abroad by Idrīs I. Inspired by the ideas of pan-Arabism, Arab socialism and Islam, the new leadership inaugurated a political, social and economic revolution that was soon to change all facets of Libyan life.

Egypt

After the breaking-off of the Anglo-Egyptian talks in January 1947, Egypt decided to take the question of its relations with Great Britain to the United Nations. If the Egyptians really hoped to win their case in this international body, they were disappointed; after several sessions of the Security Council in which only the USSR, Poland and Syria backed the Egyptian demands, and the USA recommended a renewal of direct negotiations, no resolution was adopted and the Egyptian question was postponed indefinitely.

In mass anti-British demonstrations, strikes and other manifestations, the Egyptians showed their discontent with both the British presence in the country and the Egyptian government's inability to overcome the impasse.

At this juncture the Palestine problem – which later lay at the root of several Arab–Israeli wars, as well as of many internal crises in the Arab world – appeared for the first time on the international scene. It would go beyond the scope and purpose of this chapter to try to discuss the complicated history of the Zionist colonization of Palestine, British policy during the Mandate, and Arab reactions between the wars and in the immediate after-war period. Stripped to bare facts, the problem was the colonization – against the will of the autochthonous population – of Palestine by people of European origin determined to make the territory their permanent home on the grounds that 2000 years ago Palestine had belonged to their forefathers. It is beyond doubt that the Zionist idea of founding the state of Israel would not have been realized without the backing of the imperialist powers, first of Great Britain, later of the USA, both of whom pursued their own political aims in the region.[13]

The creation of the state of Israel and the failure of the armed intervention of the Arab League (Egypt, Jordan, Syria, Iraq and Lebanon) on behalf of the Palestinians by the end of 1978 shocked the Arab world. This failure was attributed to the crisis of the system of political power in the Arab world. In Egypt, as well as in some other independent Arab countries, it was the army and its junior ranks who in the course of the war for the first time realized the failures, corruption and incompetence of the regimes of the ruling big bourgeoisie and the landlords. Among other groups and classes the defeat led to the intensification of the struggle for total independence and definitive liberation from foreign tutelage.

In the Egyptian elections of January 1950, the Wafd Party again came to power; by freeing a number of political detainees it gained a lot of sympathy but was unable to solve the economic crisis and to stop soaring prices and unemployment, or to calm general unrest.[14] A wave of demonstrations and strikes combined anti-British slogans with social and economic demands. Under these pressures, the Egyptian government started new negotiations with Britain, demanding the evacuation of 85 000 troops – instead of 10 000, as stipulated in the 1936 treaty – from the Suez Canal Zone not later than 1952, and the unification of Sudan and Egypt. When Britain showed unwillingness, the Egyptian parliament on 15 October 1951 abrogated unilaterally both the 1936 treaty and the 1899 Agreement on Condominium in the Sudan. At the same time, fighting commandos began guerrilla warfare in the Canal Zone, which was answered by British troops with reprisals that cost hundreds of lives.[15]

Suddenly, on 25 January 1952 the accumulated anger exploded: hundreds of thousands of Egyptians went into the streets of Cairo demanding a total boycott of the British, the sending of the Egyptian army to the Canal Zone, and the conclusion of a friendship treaty with the USSR. The initial normal demonstration then turned into mob frenzy by instigation of provocateurs directed from the royal palace; some elements began to loot, to commit arson and to assassinate Europeans and well-to-do Egyptians. Although human losses were small, the material damage was estimated

13. On the Palestinian question, the conflict between the Arabs and Israel, as well as on the international aspects, an enormous literature exists; see the bibliography by R. M. De Vore, 1977; the best short introductions are the books by M. Rodinson, 1968a and 1968b.

14. See M. Colombe, 1951; N. Tomiche, 1966; J. Berque, 1968; P. J. Vatikiotis, 1969; H. Mahmoud, 1970 and 1973.

15. On Anglo-Egyptian relations, see J. Marlowe, 1954 and E. Monroe, 1963.

in several millions of pounds, over 700 buildings (villas, hotels, cabarets, banks, shops) having been destroyed.

The Wafdist government fell but none of the succeeding governments in the remaining period before the revolution – despite severe measures against the strikers and demonstrators – achieved full control over events.

The internal crisis, the defeat in Palestine and the failure in dealings with Britain, discredited the entire regime of political parties and monarchy. No political organization within or outside the established system was capable of doing anything to improve the deteriorating general situation. The initiative came from the Free Officers, an organization of middle-rank officers among whom the leading role was played by Lieutenant-Colonel Gamāl 'Abd al-Nasser who became known generally as al-Nāṣir, or al-Nasser. Their experience during the Palestinian war – the supply of faulty arms, in which members of the palace clique were implicated – turned them into enemies of the monarchical regime with its farcical parliament and democracy for pashas and landlords, with its corruption and inability to solve the most pressing problems. On 23 July 1952, the Free Officers supported by part of the army occupied the important places in Cairo, without bloodshed, seized power and on 26 July forced King Farouk to abdicate. Although at that time the officers did not propose any concrete programme – and it seems that none existed – the Egyptian people welcomed enthusiastically the departure of the king, the symbol of everything that was rotten in Egyptian society.[16]

The full significance of the 1952 revolution was at first not recognized in Egypt itself, the Arab world or abroad. It was considered generally as a military take-over similar to those in Syria or to the Latin American *pronunciamentos*. It took some time before the anti-feudal and anti-imperialist character of the revolution became apparent. The first agrarian reform in 1952 which confiscated the royal domains and limited land ownership in any family to 200 *feddāns*, affected merely 10 per cent of the arable land and could not solve the basic problems of the Egyptian village. But even so it signified the first step in curbing the power of the feudal class which had for long dominated Egyptian political life. The old political parties including the Wafd, which was initially favoured by some members of the Revolutionary Council, were dissolved at the end of 1952 since they refused to collaborate. In June 1953 the Revolutionary Command Council abolished the monarchy and Egypt was declared a republic, General Naguib becoming its first president. After two thousand years of foreign rule – since the time of the Ptolemais dynasty – Egypt was once again governed by a native Egyptian as the head of the state.[17]

16. Three leading figures of the revolution published their accounts: G. 'Abd al-Nasser, 1954; M. Naguib, 1955; A. al-Sadat, 1957. See also J. and S. Lacouture, 1962; A. Abdel-Malek, 1962; and C. Issawi, 1963.

17. The Ptolemais were followed by Romans, Byzantines, Arabs and various Turkish, or Kurdish, dynasties; the dynasty of Muḥammad 'Alī was of Albanian origin.

Within the Revolutionary Council two groupings crystallized: one led by al-Nasser advocated more radical policies in internal as well as in foreign policy, whereas the group of Naguib considered that the aim of the officers was already achieved and wanted to return to civilian government. In his conservative policy, which stressed Islam, Naguib was supported by the Muslim Brotherhood. The struggle for power continued during most of 1954 but when in October a member of the Muslim Brotherhood attempted to kill al-Nasser, its leaders and several thousands of its supporters were arrested. On 14 November 1954, General Naguib, accused amongst other things of being involved in the Muslim Brotherhood conspiracy, was relieved of the office of president and placed under house arrest. Gamāl 'Abd al-Nasser became the acting head of state.

In those first years, the foreign policy of the Revolutionary Council concentrated on two issues: the Sudan and the Suez Canal. The Anglo-Egyptian agreement signed in February 1953 ended the Condominium and offered the Sudanese the choice between independence or union with Egypt; at that time the unity of the Nile valley was much closer to the hearts of the Free Officers than Arab unity, and Egypt expected that the Sudan would choose union with Egypt. Only when Sudanese politicians, disappointed by the overthrow of Naguib and the suppression of the political parties, decided against the union, did al-Nasser launch a more active Arab policy.

After protracted negotiations an agreement on Suez was signed in October 1954; the British promised to withdraw their troops from the Canal Zone within 20 months. The agreement recognized the international importance of the Suez Canal but at the same time it described it as an integral part of Egypt.

Under al-Nasser, Egypt began to play a more important role in world affairs. To the three circles described by al-Nasser as forming the environment in which Egypt was involved – the Islamic, the African and the Arab – a fourth was added: the 'non-aligned' nations. This was the result of al-Nasser's participation in the Bandung Conference in 1955 where for the first time he came into contact with other Third-World leaders like Nehru, Sukarno and others. Egypt also led the opposition of certain Arab states to the Baghdad Pact which was seen as an attempt to conserve the vanishing influence of the West in the region.[18]

During 1955 tension with Israel continued to be high and there were many raids and counter-raids across the border of the Ghaza Strip. When Egypt, alarmed by the incessant flow of weapons to Israel, asked the Western countries for similar aid, its demands fell on deaf ears. In September 1955, al-Nasser announced an arms deal with Czechoslovakia which was to supply large quantities of military equipment including

18. See E. Lengyel, 1957.

tanks and aircraft in return for cotton and rice. This move to free Egypt from a unilateral dependency on Western arsenals was acclaimed by most of the Arab and Asian states but aroused a wave of hysteria in the West and deepened the distrust and aversion to the Egyptian regime headed by al-Nasser.

The immediate effect of this move was the refusal of Britain, the United States and the World Bank to finance the High Dam project at Aswān. The aim of the project was to increase cultivable land and generate electricity for industrialization, in the hope of solving the country's increasing population problems. President al-Nasser's reply to this was his announcement on 26 July 1956 that the Suez Canal Company had been nationalized and that revenue from the Canal would be used to finance the Aswān High Dam. The share-holders were to be compensated. Britain, France and the United States protested strongly against the action and furious propaganda was launched against Egypt, especially against President al-Nasser, who was depicted as a new Hitler.[19] Various diplomatic manoeuvres to force Egypt to renounce its rights and to accept international control under another label failed. In October, Israel, Britain and France after reaching a secret agreement among themselves invaded Egypt. The common goal of all three aggressors was the overthrow of al-Nasser and his regime as well as making Egypt a dependent semi-colony again.

The Israeli forces crossed into Sinai on 24 October and advanced towards the Suez Canal; the Anglo-French air operation against Egypt began on 31 October, but the paratroops and seaborne forces landed in the Port Said area only on 5 November. In the meantime, the USSR and the United States proposed in the UN Security Council resolutions calling for immediate Israeli withdrawal – but these were vetoed by Britain and France. Later, the UN General Assembly called for a general cease-fire and ending of hostilities. The common pressure of the USA and the USSR then forced Britain and France to cease hostilities at midnight on 6 November. In the following month the aggressors' troops were withdrawn from the Canal Zone to be followed later by the Israeli evacuation of the Sinai peninsula and the Ghaza Strip.[20]

Thus Britain's last attempt to employ 'gun-boat diplomacy' in order to regain its former supremacy in the region ended in a total failure. For Britain and France it meant a further loss of influence not only in the Arab region but in the whole Third World. On the other hand, Egypt

19. The Western mass media intentionally confused the issue by stating that Egypt unilaterally nationalized the international waterway whereas in fact the Suez Canal had always been an integral part of Egyptian territory and Egyptian sovereign rights to it were never in doubt. By nationalizing the Suez Canal Company, Egypt was within its sovereign rights and in no way violated the international character of the Canal as a waterway.

20. On the Suez crisis and conflict see A. Nutting, 1967; and K. Love, 1969.

PLATE 6.4   *The ruins of Port Said, in the Canal Zone, that bore the brunt of the Suez war in 1956*

and President al-Nasser became symbols of a new attitude to the imperialists: for the first time in history a former colony did not retreat before threats but offered a spirited resistance causing acute embarrassment to the Western powers and even internal political crisis in both Britain and France. The colonial and newly independent nations appreciated both al-Nasser's bold move in nationalizing the Suez Canal Company and his resistance to armed aggression. It had been clearly demonstrated that imperialism was not as strong as it used to be and that, by exploiting its weakness, it would be possible for the oppressed nations in Africa and elsewhere to achieve their independence.

The Sudan

The post-war history of the Sudan – still called Anglo-Egypt despite the minimal Egyptian participation in its administration – was marked by three principal issues: the struggle for independence, the relationship with Egypt and the emergence of the southern problem.[21]

21. See J. S. R. Duncan, 1957; P. M. Holt, 1961; M. 'Abd al-Raḥmān, 1969.

Even after the 1948 constitution was proclaimed which provided for a legislative assembly elected by universal suffrage and an executive with Sudanese ministers, the British governor-general retained the right of veto and many other powers. The British preferred the Umma Party led by the grandson of the *Mahdī* whose anti-Egyptian attitude and conservative inclination were more convenient than the policy of the Ashikkā' Party which insisted on close union with Egypt under the slogan of 'Unity of the Nile valley' and whose membership was recruited from the more progressive segment of Sudanese society.

The 1952 revolution in Egypt was positively accepted in the Sudan at first, partly because the unpopular King Farouk was deposed, partly because General Naguib had close links with the country, his mother being Sudanese. In November 1953 the new National Unionist Party, the successor of the pro-Egyptian Ashikkā', won the elections. In its programme the party emphasized the liquidation of colonial rule in the shortest possible time; the deposing of General Naguib in Egypt and the negative attitude of al-Nasser to the multi-party political system had adverse effects even among the former adherents of the union. In December the respective leaders of the most powerful religious orders, the Anṣārs (pro-British) and the Khaṭmiyya (pro-Egyptian), both of which commanded a large following, declared that they were prepared to collaborate for the achievement of total independence for the Sudan. Notwithstanding strong Egyptian pressures, even the National Unionist Party now steered towards independence without any ties with Egypt.

On 19 December 1955, the Sudanese parliament declared that the Sudan was to become an independent republic; then, on 1 January 1956 independence was officially and solemnly proclaimed.

The problem of the southern Sudan, which was to bedevil Sudanese history for several decades, emerged shortly before independence:[22] in August 1955 the Equatoria Corps of the Sudanese army revolted against the gradual take-over of the administration and command posts by the northerners. Although the mutineers soon surrendered, disorder had by that time spread through the southern provinces and many northerners lost their lives. The crisis was the consequence of the British policy to develop the south in strict separation from the north under the pretext that the Muslim Sudanese would subjugate the unsophisticated southerners and subject them to slavery as they did in the last century. Proselytizing Islam was forbidden; Christian (mostly Catholic) missions were encouraged. In the missionary schools only English was used, whereas in the north Arabic was the vehicle of teaching and soon became the official language.

Thus there evolved two totally separate and mutually alien regions. The British, of course, did not invent the cultural and social distinctions

22. See J. Oduho and W. Deng, 1963; and M. O. Beshir, 1968.

between the Muslim Arabic-speaking northerners and the Nilotic or Central Sudanic southerners of traditional religion – but they did everything to perpetuate those differences and to sow deep distrust. During the early colonial period there were some indications that the relationship between the northerners and the southerners could have developed in a friendly way: the leader of the first national movement, the White Flag League, was ʿAbd al-Latīf, a Dinka (Jieng) from the south, and among his followers were people from both regions. Similarly, when in 1924 the Egyptian troops were forced by the British to evacuate the Sudan, the Sudanese officers and cadets, the majority of whom came from the south, mutinied in protest, paying for their gesture of solidarity with many dead.[23] It was after these events that the British colonial administration made the isolation between north and south even stricter.

The northerners were not guiltless in the deterioration of relations: when they began in 1954–5 to take over the administration of the southern provinces from the British, they started hastily to introduce Arabic as the official language, paying no attention to the differences in cultural background and to the grievances of local people and their political leaders. It was from both the previous colonial policy and mutual incomprehension that the tragic conflict arose.

The Horn of Africa

The war of resistance, the Second World War, and the Italian occupation caused enormous losses to Ethiopia: more than 760 000 Ethiopians lost their lives, 525 000 dwellings were destroyed, nearly 14 million cattle perished. In all, the total material losses have been calculated at £180 million.[24] The defeat of the Italians did not mean that the country automatically recovered its independence and sovereignty. Great Britain only reluctantly allowed the reinstallation of the Ethiopian administrative machinery, which until the end of the war and some time afterwards was fully controlled by the British Occupied Enemy Territory Administration (OETA), run from Nairobi and headed by Sir Phillip Mitchell, an ex-governor of Uganda. For some time the British even nursed plans to establish a kind of protectorate over the whole of former Italian East Africa.[25] Although in the 1942 Anglo-Ethiopian Agreement the freedom and independence of Ethiopia were declared, its various articles and more so the accompanying military convention preserved and legitimated a very substantial degree of British control. Some parts of Ethiopian territory like Ogaden, the Haud and large stretches adjacent to French, British and

23. See UNESCO, *General History of Africa*, vol. VII, ch. 23, pp. 589–92.
24. R. K. Pankhurst, 1955, pp. 548–9.
25. L. Mosley, 1964, p. 275.

Italian Somaliland were to remain under British military administration indefinitely.

It took two more years of negotiations to reach at the end of 1944 a new agreement which abolished the unequal character of the previous one and resulted in the decolonization of the greater part of Ethiopia except for Ogaden and the Reserved Area which remained under British military administration. It was not until 1954 that those regions were returned to full Ethiopian jurisdiction and British troops were withdrawn.[26]

Under the British military occupation that lasted until 1951 there emerged in Eritrea a number of political parties which reflected the complicated ethnic and religious situation. The Christian Tigre from the plateau founded the Unionist Party supported by the Ethiopian government and church; it advocated a total union with Ethiopia. A Christian minority, afraid of Amhara supremacy, adhered to the Liberal Progressive Party, seeking the establishment of an independent Eritrea. The Muslim League followed a similar programme and both these parties (together with some smaller ones) formed the Independence Bloc, later re-named Democratic Bloc.

The Fifth UN General Assembly in 1950 adopted the resolution about the creation of a federation between Ethiopia and Eritrea; the latter was endowed with its own constitution, legislative assembly and government. Foreign affairs, defence, finance and international communication were to be the responsibility of the federal government.[27]

In March 1952 the first parliamentary elections were held: Muslim and Christian parties remained in equilibrum. In September of the same year the last British administrator handed over the administration of Eritrea to the Ethiopian crown. The federation meant victory for the Unionist Party which also became the ruling party in the government. Many leaders of the Independence Bloc left the country and went into exile (mostly to Cairo) where they continued to propagate the idea of Eritrean independence.

From the start there evolved an anomalous situation. Eritrea – with its political parties, elected parliament and a more progressive constitution – contrasted sharply with the political order in Ethiopia where the emperor still controlled all reins of power. Haile Selassie from the very start looked with suspicion on Eritrea and soon began systematically to abolish one democratic institution after another: in the 1956 elections no political parties were permitted to present candidates; in 1958 the Eritrean flag was abolished; in 1959 the Ethiopian codex was introduced; in 1960 the Eritrean parliament – already purged of open opponents to the union with Ethiopia – changed the 'Eritrean government' into 'Eritrean administration'. That process found its logical conclusion in 1962 when the

26. See R. K. Pankhurst, 1981.
27. See G. K. N. Trevaskis, 1960; L. E. S. Pankhurst and R. K. Pankhurst, 1953.

Eritrean assembly voted first for the abolition of federal status and then for its own dissolution. Eritrea became an integral part of the Ethiopian empire. The seeds of future conflict were thus sown at that time, particularly when further opposition leaders went into exile and when in the country itself armed guerrilla groups began the fight against the Ethiopian administration and troops, thus creating another grave problem for Ethiopia.[28]

When their attempts to recreate a British-controlled former Italian East Africa proved unrealistic, the British became ardent partisans of the pan-Somali idea and proposed in 1946 a unification of all the Somalilands.[29] Naturally, the Ethiopians and the French were strongly opposed to the plan for a British trusteeship over all the Somalis and the project failed – but it helps to explain why Britain occupied the Ogaden for such a long time. However, it was during the period of the temporary unification of all the Somalis under British administration that pan-Somalism, as the most prominent component of Somali nationalistic ideology, took root among the young intelligentsia.[30]

All these issues were connected with the liquidation of the Italian colonial empire. In the peace treaty of 1947 Italy renounced the ownership of its colonies but this did not mean that it had abandoned the idea of regaining them by some other means. The Italians aspired, as in Tripolitania, to be given at least the trusteeship over Somalia. In 1948–9 when the question was discussed in the UN, a wave of popular demonstrations in Mogadishu and elsewhere arose against the return of the Italians in any form. Women organized by the Somali Youth League (SYL) participated actively in the independence struggle and in January 1948 one of them, Hawa Ismen 'Alī was killed as the first woman martyr of the Somali national liberation movement. Although the anti-Italian feelings of the people were manifest even to various UN commissions, the three Western powers favoured the trusteeship under Italy while the Soviet Union supported a collective four-power control. On 21 November 1949, the General Assembly decided to entrust Somalia for ten years to Italian trusteeship under UN tutelage. The immediate independence hoped for by the people of Somalia was thus postponed for a whole decade.

Although the SYL remained the leading political party, a position acquired during the British occupation, other parties founded on a clan

28. On the post-war history of Ethiopia, see R. Greenfield, 1965; J. Doresse, 1970; H. G. Marcus, 1972; P. Gilkes, 1975.

29. See S. Touval, 1963; I. M. Lewis, 1965.

30. Also, it should not be forgotten that in Italian schools in Somalia the period of *risorgimento*, i.e. of Italian unification in the nineteenth century, was explained as the most glorious part of national history. It was natural and easy for the young Somalis to draw a comparison between their present situation and that of the Italians in the past as both were confronted with a multi-national empire the overthrow of which, together with the liberation of compatriots, was considered to be progressive from all points of view.

basis had already emerged during that period. One major effect of Italy's return was the proliferation of political parties so that by March 1954, at the time of the first municipal election, there were 21 of them as against eight in 1950. This mirrored to a high degree the clan-based structure of Somali society. Although the clan-based parties accepted officially national-ist and pan-Somali goals in their programmes, they nevertheless remained attached to the defence and promulgation of their own particular inter-ests.[31] The first three years of the decade were marked by Italian–SYL hostility as the party claimed more participation in administration and organized many anti-Italian demonstrations. Between the municipal elec-tion in 1954 in which the SYL confirmed its lead, and 1960, the former hostile attitude of the Italians towards the SYL changed as it became clear that after independence it would be the leading party and the Italians did not wish to antagonize it unnecessarily. In the first general election to the legislative assembly in February 1956 the SYL again won the majority of votes. The new assembly was given full statutory powers in domestic affairs and the first Somali government under Abdillahi Ise was formed. Nevertheless the head of the Italian Trust Administration retained the right of absolute veto and jurisdiction over military and foreign affairs and Italian councillors were attached to the Somali ministers. As SYL power increased and independence approached, these developments led to tensions and splits inside the party which, although claiming a pan-Somali policy, was ridden with conflict between its Darood and Hawiye members.

Political development in the British Somaliland Protectorate lagged behind that of Somalia.[32] Britain did not permit any political party representation, recognizing only representation on clan lines. The legis-lative council was established as late as 1957 and the franchise was extremely limited before 1960. The few political parties founded before 1950, the Somali National League (SNL) and the Somali Youth League (SYL), although sometimes persecuted by the colonial administration, developed only minimal activity. Under the impetus of the 1954 agreement which transferred the Somali-inhabited Haud and Reserved Area to Ethiopia, a new nationalist fervour was aroused. Massive demonstrations occurred throughout the protectorate and a national convention called the National United Front (NUF) was organized. It launched a vigorous campaign with the objective of recovering the Haud and of obtaining independence. Although the Haud campaign did not succeed, the issue of independence in the near future became the main concern of all parties. All of them also shared the aim of unification with Somalia. Under the growing nationalist pressure, the legislative council was reformed early in 1959 to include 12 elected Somali members; a year later the reform

31. See A. A. Castagno, 1966, pp. 512–59.
32. See I. M. Lewis, 1965, pp. 148–55.

being considered insufficient, a new constitution with fuller Somali representation and providing for ministerial responsibility was introduced. The pace of events was accelerated by the approach of the date for Somalian independence. Already in 1959 the delegates from all political parties in Somaliland had participated in Mogadishu in the formation of the National Pan-Somali Movement; in April 1960 all elected members of the new legislative council passed a resolution calling for independence by 1 July 1960 and unification with Somalia. A delegation went to Mogadishu where an agreement was reached about the future united republic. British Somaliland then became fully independent on 26 June 1960 and five days later Somalia followed suit; the two territories then immediately became united on the previously agreed basis.

The tiny French colony called until 1967 *Côte française des Somalis*, and afterwards *Territoire français des Afars et des Issas* (TFAI), possessed in French eyes the multiple assets of a good harbour, an excellent strategic position and the head of the only Ethiopian railway.[33] France was therefore strongly opposed to growing local demands for independence even long after the majority of the continent became free. The existence in the country of two distinct and numerically almost even ethnic groups, with a slight preponderance of Somalis, gave the colonial administration a good pretext to postpone independence indefinitely;[34] it seized every opportunity to exacerbate the rivalry. The nomadic Afar (also called Danakil) were systematically favoured against the more urbanized Somali. That policy was partly successful but it should be mentioned that before 1958 the two principal rivals on the political scene, Maḥmud Harbi and Hassan Gouled were both of Issa Somali origin and their following was recruited from both ethnic groups. They differed in their political opinions – Harbi being a supporter of unification with independent Somalia, his opponent of a closer union with France. The first elections in 1957 brought victory for Harbi who became vice-president of the Council of Ministers; his pan-Somali inclination soon made him unacceptable to the French and in 1958 he was forced to flee abroad. The de Gaulle referendum of 1958, which attracted only a minority of voters, resulted, as in all French African territories except Guinea, in further adherence to the French community. But whereas the intermediate period before independence lasted for only two years in other Francophone countries, the people of the *Territoire français des Afars et des Issas* had to wait for nearly 20 years before achieving their independence.

During those years the political leadership fell to the Afar supported by the French administration; the leading Somali politicians were mostly

33. See V. Thompson and R. Adloff, 1968; P. Oberlé, 1971; and R. Saint-Véran, 1977.
34. See the commentary of *Le Monde*, 26 April 1964, that 'The administration reckons, not groundlessly, that that rivalry between the Afar and Somali is the best guarantee of stability': quoted in *Politika Frantsii v Azii i v Afrike*, 1965, p. 175.

in exile and the only officially recognized Somali party, *Ligue populaire africaine pour l'indépendance* (LPAI) did not emerge until 1972. More radicalism was shown by the underground *Front de la libération de la Côte des Somalis* (FLCS) with headquarters in Mogadishu. In 1967 a new referendum for an 'enlarged autonomy' was held in the territory; in the new government, the Afar party – *L'Union nationale pour l'indépendance* (UNI) – led by 'Alī Arif Bourhan retained the dominant position under the slogan 'Unity and progress within the French community'.

After the Ethiopian revolution in 1974 the liberation movement gathered momentum. Open guerrilla actions against the French took place, organized by the FLCS, and the demands for independence were now voiced not only by the LPAI but within the ruling party, too. The issue of the country's independence came before the UN General Assembly in 1975, when a resolution of immediate granting of independence to the TFAI was adopted.

In March 1977 the Somali-dominated LPAI and FLCS and some of 'Alī Arif's former supporters formed the coalition *Rassemblement populaire pour l'indépendance* (RPI) under the leadership of Hassan Gouled. It won the combined elections and referendum and Gouled was elected president of the Council heading a government of ten ministers, half of them Afar.

Finally, on 26 June 1977, the territory at last became fully independent, under the neutral title of the Republic of Djibouti. It was the last of the continental African countries north of the equator to become independent – attaining its sovereignty even later than the majority of Southern African territories. The Republic of Djibouti became the forty-ninth Member of the Organization of African Unity and the twenty-second of the Arab League.

The ideologies of the liberation struggle

During the period under discussion – and, indeed, during all the colonial period – three main ideologies were present in the Arab countries of North Africa: Islam, nationalism and socialism. Their respective influence and impact were uneven at different times and places mirroring the changing social and political situation. Nevertheless, it could be maintained that the leading ideology in the region during the decisive stage of the anti-colonial struggle was Arab nationalism, tinged in various countries with variable doses either of Islam and socialism or both.[35]

Let us at first examine the role Islam played in the decisive years of the national liberation movement. Islam had the advantage of being the oldest traditional ideology in the whole Arab region; it permeated the life of the great majority of the population, sensitizing their world view and attitudes towards actual political and social issues. Religious convictions

35. A. Abdel-Malek, 1969, 1980; A. Laroui, 1967.

have always dominated the thinking of the peasant and middle and lower urban classes and at various stages provided fuel for the struggle against feudalism and foreign oppression. Islam often played an important role in mobilizing the masses and in a number of Arab countries Muslim *'ulamā'* have participated in campaigns against colonialism together with the people, or have even led them. That was the case in Algeria where the 'Society of the Algerian *'ulamā''* and other groups did valuable work to prepare the ground for the liberation struggle and after 1954 took active part in the armed conflict. The national liberation movements against imperialism have often assumed the religious form of defending Arab–Muslim culture threatened by the invasion of Western culture and its values, sometimes diametrically opposed to the Muslim way of life and Islamic ethics.

In the late 1940s and early 1950s the religious organizations whose passionate reassertion of fundamental Islamic beliefs, values and standards responded far more closely to the feeling of the suppressed lower classes, became more active. They protested against both the Westernized ruling classes and imperialism.

The most active among them was the Muslim Brotherhood – *al-Ikhwān al-Muslimīn*.[36] Founded in 1927 by Ḥassan al-Bannā (1906–49), an Egyptian teacher, the movement grew steadily, gaining by its various non-political, mostly humanitarian and social activities, large membership. Although claiming Islamic goals the movement was not strictly pan-Islamic but rather an offshoot of Egyptian nationalism and its original programme aimed at the reform of the Egyptian society only. It offered rather simple and in many ways nebulous prescriptions for social reform based on Islamic ethics and a strict adherence to the *sharīʿa*, and it protested vigorously against the secularizing tendency of liberal national-ists. In the period between the end of the war and the advent of the military regime, the Muslim Brethren began to play a major and stormy role in Egyptian politics. Some groups within the organization sought to relieve their frustration by acts of individual terror aimed at the politicians and later on at the British occupation troops in the Suez Canal Zone. Many times officially denounced by the al-Azhar *'ulamā'*,[37] debarred by assassination or execution of their leaders – under both monarchy and military regime – the Brotherhood continues still to exist and to retain, if not increase, its influence among Egyptian *petite-bourgeoisie*, unemployed intelligentsia and junior ranks of the civil service. In the period under discussion the Brotherhood remained restricted to Egypt but later its branches or similar movements began to emerge in other Islamic and Arab countries. On the ideological field as well as in the fight to win the

36. On this movement, see R. P. Mitchell, 1969; I. M. Ḥusaynī, 1952.

37. The *'ulamā'* accused the Brotherhood of having 'crossed the limits fixed by God in revelation between good and evil'; see P. Rondot, 1958, vol. 1, p. 253.

support of the masses, these fundamentalist movements are the most serious rivals to both the nationalists and the socialists.

In the Arab nationalist movement there emerged two tendencies, sometimes complementary, sometimes competing: the pan-Arabic and particular (local) nationalistic trends existed side by side in most Arab countries, but their intensity was conditioned by actual conditions.[38] The anti-colonial struggle in the inter-war period rather strengthened local nationalism; in North Africa particularly, pan-Arab ideology did not play any outstanding role and was limited to some groups of the intelligentsia. It developed there much later than in the eastern part of the Arab world and found rather weak response. Only the Algerian liberation war brought changes – but restricted, however, to the Maghreb countries only.

Neither Arab nationalism nor the idea of Arab unity became an important element in Egyptian policy. The Egyptian national movement was oriented towards achieving full sovereignty and liberation from any vestiges of British rule. Its efforts were concentrated on unification with the Sudan, to realize the 'Unity of the Nile valley', this idea being closer to Egypt's aspirations than that of Arab unity. Even for the military regime, the union with the Sudan remained until 1955 one of the central political issues.[39]

The pan-Arab idea which emerged during the First World War in the Asiatic part of the Arab world was for a long time even ridiculed by many Egyptian politicians and rejected by the majority of the intelligentsia.[40] Nevertheless, many pan-Arab theoreticians, among them the influential Sāṭiʿ al-Ḥusrī, emphasized Egypt's leading role in the anticipated process of unification.[41]

Nationalism in the Arab countries expressed itself primarily as a reaction against foreign rule, and not as an expression of the economic growth of the local bourgeoisie; thus in the inter-war period it integrated groups which in Europe usually remained aloof from nationalism: religious clergy and feudal landlords. During and after the Second World War, parallel to the expansion of the bourgeoisie, the influence of these groups diminished and Islam became more a moral than a political factor.

In the structure and content of Arab nationalism, Islam forms an integral and important part: the spread of Islam is the most glorious part of Arab history and their most valuable contribution to universal history. Arab culture and civilization were formed by Islam and the Islamic way

38. S. G. Haim, 1962; J. Berque, 1960 and 1964; M. Khadduri, 1970; a bibliography until 1959 is given by F. Qubain, 1960.

39. A. Abdel-Malek, 1969.

40. Even the General-Secretary of the League of the Arab States, ʿAbd al-Raḥmān ʿAzzām, proclaimed in 1950: 'Firstly we are Egyptians, secondly Arabs and thirdly Muslims': see S. G. Haim, 1962, pp. 52–3.

41. H. Z. Nuseibeh, 1956.

of life bears many specific features of its Arab origin. Thus, Arab nationalists emphasize the importance of Islam and Islamic ethics for Arab nationalism, calling them 'the Arab high ideals'.

The attitude of Muslim orthodoxy and traditionalists towards Arab nationalism has been negative and even the concept of a special unity between the Arabs and Islam was attacked. According to the traditionalists, Arab nationalism was destroying the unity of Islam by depriving it of its universal character and by contributing to the false idea that Islam is primarily an Arab religion. Every Muslim should be proud first of his being a member of a supra-national community (*umma*) – and thereby having achieved a higher stage in the evolution of mankind than individual nations.[42]

Moreover, there are profound theological objections against nationalism – a genuine Muslim should be loyal only to God and the Islamic *umma* whereas the nationalists put the Arab nation as the highest ideal. On the other hand, Arab nationalists made attempts to integrate Islam into their ideology and programmes but more as a cultural and social factor than as a pure religion. Those attempts have not been entirely successful and an ideological uncertainty about the role Islam has to play in Arab nationalism prevails. The nationalists had to reckon with the adherence of the Arab masses to the Islamic religion whereas the Islamic orthodox groups, theoretically averse to any kind of nationalism, had to reckon with the reality that in the majority of Arab countries the leadership of the anti-colonial movement remained firmly in the hands of the nationalists.[43]

Although in the post-war period the pan-Arabic aims of nationalistic ideology in many Arab countries were proclaimed even louder than in the preceding period, the actual anti-colonial movement was ideologically based and politically organized on concrete local – Egyptian, Sudanese, Tunisian, and so on – nationalism. As already pointed out, the Egyptians especially remained for a long time quite impermeable to pan-Arabism and their actions against Britain were inspired by the old slogan of early nationalists – Egypt for the Egyptians.

The disparity between pan-Arab nationalism and local nationalism deepened after the war. The local national movements were more concrete and sure in their aims and methods – being closely linked with the social and economic situation, which was underestimated by the theoreticians of pan-Arabism who often lived in a realm of wishful thinking. They contented themselves mostly with nebulous ideas about the glorious future of the unified Arab nation but did not pay much attention to the economic and social conditions necessary for its emergence.

The people in the Arab countries in North Africa fought against

42. See M. Berger, 1962.
43. B. Dodge, 1965, pp. 94–119.

colonial rule neither for the restitution of an ideal Islamic state nor for some uncertain pan-Arab unity. Both the leaders and the masses realized that their fight was a struggle against the enemy who occupied their fatherland, and who selfishly oppressed its people politically, economically and culturally. National independence was to be achieved by and for the society living on the territory; that was the first goal to attain and it was for those practical reasons that the local nationalism in the Arab countries prevailed over the ideas of pan-Arabism, not to speak of pan-Islamism, as the rallying ideology of the anti-colonial struggle.

Thus the specific nationalism remained the predominant force both in politics and ideology. A characteristic feature of post-war anti-imperialist Arab nationalism was the deepening of its social content; nationalism confined itself not only to solving the national problem but put forward a social programme as well.

Socialist ideas had already been known in the Arab countries of North Africa for a long time but were restricted to the narrow circles of the intelligentsia and – with the exception of Algeria at a later stage – did not feature in the nationalist programmes. The communist parties in Egypt and in the Sudan worked in illegality whereas in the Maghreb states their membership was, even after the war, predominantly European.[44] Thus neither those parties nor the working class were able to become preponderant in the national-liberation movement.[45] A Moroccan Marxist, 'Azīz Belal, notes the main causes of this phenomenon: the numerical weakness of the workers due to industrial underdevelopment; illiteracy, the survival of traditional values, the lack of class consciousness; and the initial failure of the Arab Marxist movement to adapt to the socio-cultural and psycho-sociological context prevailing in the Arab world. Marxist parties appeared initially more as progressive ideal movements with 'European colouration', ill-adapted to national realities, and not as exponents of 'national thought' and the struggle for national affirmation.[46]

But at the same time, the victory of the USSR in the Second World War and its success in changing underdeveloped Russia into an industrial power, attracted many Arab nationalists to socialism. There emerged various kinds of Arab socialism; this socialism adopted many social and economic teachings of Marxism but refused to subscribe to the Marxist world view with its atheism and internationalism.

In most variants of Arab socialism, capitalism is rejected not as a mode of production but only certain stages of its development – capitalist liberalism or *laissez-faire* attitudes. Socialism is interpreted not as a class outlook of the exploited, but rather as a set of technical and organizational

44. M. S. Agwani, 1969.
45. See A. Abdel-Malek, 1966.
46. A. Belal, 1972, pp. 21–2.

methods for ensuring progress which are linked mainly with the activities of the government and with an expansion of its economic functions.

Socialist slogans were pressed into the service of Arab nationalism. One of the founders of the Ba'th Party, Michel Aflaq, once said bluntly that socialism was just an appendage to the nationalist platform.[47] Essentially that approach is common to many ideologies of the national liberation movements. Since their representatives came to socialist slogans in the course of the struggle to win and assert political independence, they are inclined to understand socialism merely as a means of achieving national objectives and reconstruction.[48] In such situations, socialism is the other face of nationalism.

47. 'To us, socialism is a tool relating to our national needs and conditions, and consequently it cannot be a fundamental philosophy or outlook dominating our life . . . The Arab nationalist realizes that socialism is the best way to revive his nationalism and his nation'; quoted in S. A. Hanna and G. H. Gardner, 1969, p. 300.

48. See O. V. Martyshin, 1978, p. 100.

West Africa 1945–60

Jean SURET-CANALE *and* A. Adu BOAHEN

Introduction

The end of the Second World War and the victory of the Allies could not fail to raise immense hopes in the peoples of Africa subjected to colonial domination. The defeat of fascism was the defeat of a doctrine which was based on racism, the exaltation of brute force and the denial of the right of peoples to self-determination; it was, implicitly, the condemnation of colonialism whose principles – or practice – rested on similar bases. Already in 1941, the Atlantic Charter had placed among the Allies' war aims 'the right of all peoples to choose the form of government under which they will live'. In the minds of the signatories, that was supposed only to apply to Europe; but the African peoples seized on it and demanded this right for themselves. In a memo entitled 'The Charter and British West Africa', Azikiwe of Nigeria demanded immediate reforms and representative government. G. E. Moore, a member of the legislative council in Ghana also in a speech in 1943 claimed that if it was 'the right of all peoples to choose the form of government under which they live it was a right to which the Africans share', while in the same year the Sherbro paramount chief, Albert George Caulker, demanded that after the war the colonial authorities would surrender sovereign power to the people of Sierra Leone in the spirit of the charter.[1] Having taken part in the war in the name of these principles, providing both men and supplies (at least the French and British colonies), the peoples of West Africa were thus to challenge the colonial regime.

The awakening of radical political forces in West Africa was assisted by other factors. The first was the anti-colonialism of the two great victors of the allied coalition, the USSR and the United States, even if it rested on very different motivations. The second was the rise of the forces of the left in France and Great Britain signified by Socialist–Communist majority in the French Constituent Assembly of 1945 and the accession to power of Labour in Great Britain.

---

1. P. O. Esedebe, 1971, p. 24; A. A. Boahen, 1986, pp. 141–2; A. A. Mazrui and M. Tidy, 1984, pp. 13–14.

The Second World War affected the political situation in West Africa in other ways which have been discussed elsewhere but which must be touched upon here briefly. First, the compulsory recruitment of so many Africans for the war greatly aroused the anger of all classes of Africans – especially wives, mothers and grandmothers who could not bear to see their husbands, sons and grandsons being torn from them. Many of the Africans who were left behind suffered almost as much as those who went to war – but of course in a different way. Secondly, those Africans who saw active service in Burma and India came into contact with the independence movements in these areas. The ensuing experience not only broadened their political horizons but also exposed them to the anti-colonial strategies and tactics being applied at the time, some of which they would not hesitate to apply on their return home. Thirdly, these soldiers returned home after the war full of hopes of great rewards in the form of compensation, gratuities, employment and so on, which never materialized. This disappointment drove them into the ranks of the nationalists and some of them even became active leaders of the masses themselves. In all these ways, the war greatly strengthened anti-colonial and nationalist sentiments in West Africa.

Economic and social changes

The desire for a better and a different life manifested itself in the years 1945–8 at times in an explosive manner because of the economic and political regime imposed during the war. This was marked by the excesses of the 'War effort' such as forced labour and compulsory deliveries of products, the shortage and sharp price rises leading to the 'black market' combined with wage freezes, and the authoritarian methods of the traditional rulers and the colonial authorities, all of which became intolerable when peace returned. In this context, the élites' desire to secure recognition of their rights and their entitlement to play an economic and political role rested on a profound popular movement in which economic demands were closely associated with anti-colonial demands such as the abolition of forced labour and racial discrimination and the granting of political rights.

This apparent unity concealed divergences that were already reappearing by the late 1940s, and did so especially after independence. For some bourgeois or would-be bourgeois strata, the goal was limited to taking the place occupied by the Europeans; for the masses, the desire for national liberation was inseparable from a desire for social liberation. Some leaders among the élite (the minority that had received a European-type education) made themselves the spokesmen of these popular desires. Following this path to the end assumed, to use Amilcar Cabral's celebrated formula, these people agreeing to 'commit class suicide' and this route was not the one usually chosen.[2]

In the years following the end of the war, the shortages continued, and the first 'plans' implemented in the colonies aimed at developing their role as suppliers of raw materials. These aims were later slightly modified, but remained centred on the development of primary production, and on associated essential capital investment such as in ports, airports, roads and power stations. Economic needs for a sufficiently skilled and healthy labour force and popular aspirations also worked together to produce an effect in health, education, and other sectors.

The economic backwardness of West Africa, where the colonial predatory economy (*économie de traite*) persisted, aggravated by the war years, made essential a contribution to investment by the colonial powers, which had not generally been made before the war. The word and the myth of 'aid' made its appearance. In the framework of the predatory economy, which lasted until the late 1950s, agricultural export crops developed, but so did the mining industries, which had been virtually non-existent before 1949–51 in the French domain. Manufacturing industries began to develop – mainly in the ports, which doubled as capitals – in the form of import-substitution or the initial processing of exportable goods.

Socially, more elementary schools were established during the period while a University College was opened at Ibadan in Nigeria and Legon in Ghana. Urbanization was also given a great boost as unemployed school-leavers left the rural areas in ever increasing numbers after the war and moved into the towns in search of jobs and entertainment. Moreover, after the war an increasing number of West Africans, educated and trained abroad as lawyers, doctors and engineers (but mainly the first), began to return home, especially in British West Africa.

The result of all these changes was a steady increase in the number of the professional bourgeoisie of lawyers, doctors, university graduates, civil servants and middle-level African businessmen and transport owners, and of a working class of teachers, mechanics, drivers, miners, railway-workers, store-keepers and small African businessmen; above all, it led to an increasing number of unemployed school-leavers concentrated in the few towns which served either as the capital, administrative or mining centres. In the rural areas, where the mass of the African people still reside, there was also a steady increase in the numbers of cocoa-farmers, groundnut-planters, coffee-growers and labourers especially in Ghana, Nigeria and the Côte d'Ivoire. Compared with the French and Portuguese territories which surrounded them, the four British colonies were notably more developed. Economically, they had a more complex railway network while their agricultural and mineral production was much higher. Socially and culturally, the population of Nigeria alone was larger than that of all the

2. A. Cabral, 1975.

French colonies put together, while they could boast of the already century-old existence of an Anglicized élite (lawyers, clergymen, teachers) and an African press that was almost a century old, too.

It is against this background that we should examine the phenomenal political changes that occurred in West Africa during the decade and right after the Second World War. These changes were indeed striking for – just as it took about two decades from 1880 for the European imperial powers to partition and occupy Africa – it took the same time for most African countries to regain their political independence and sovereignty after the war. During the period under review, of the 15 Western African colonies, 11 had regained their political sovereignty by 1960 of whom as many as nine did so in the single year of 1960, the next two between 1961 and 1965, and the last two in 1973 and 1974 respectively. Of these colonies, four were British – Nigeria, Ghana, Sierra Leone and the Gambia; nine were French – Dahomey (now Benin), Guinea, Côte d'Ivoire, Mali, Mauritania, Niger, Senegal, Togo and Upper Volta; and the rest were Portuguese – Cape Verde and Guinea-Bissau. Of the British colonies, Ghana was the first to win her battle for the overthrow of colonialism followed by Nigeria, then Sierra Leone and finally the Gambia. Of the French colonies, Guinea led in 1958 followed by the rest, all of which regained their sovereignty in the single year of 1960. The last of the Western Africa colonies to overthrow colonialism were the Portuguese colonies of Cape Verde and Guinea-Bissau.

These bare facts pose a number of rather intriguing and interesting questions. The first of these is why was colonialism virtually ended in Western Africa in the decade and half after the Second World War? Secondly, why was a British colony the first to regain her independence – not only in West Africa but throughout Africa south of the Sahara – and why was this colony Ghana? Thirdly, why did Guinea lead in French West Africa, and why did all the remaining French colonies gain their independence in the same year of 1960? The final question is why were the Portuguese colonies the last set of colonies to regain their independence? These are the questions that this chapter seeks to answer, beginning first with British, then French and finally Portuguese West Africa.

British West Africa

The liquidation of colonialism from British West Africa within two decades after the Second World War was the outcome of three main factors which are more or less equally true of all the other colonies. The first and easily the most important factor was what Mazrui and Tidy have termed 'the great upsurge of African nationalism'[3] during the period

3. A. A. Mazrui and M. Tidy, 1984, p. 1.

under review; the second was the nature, objectives and activities of the political parties and nationalist movements that were launched; and the third was the actions as well as reactions and responses of the British colonial power to the activities and demands of the African nationalists and their supporters.

As has been amply demonstrated in Volume VII of this *History*, African nationalist or anti-colonial activities started from the very beginning of the imposition of the colonial system on Africa and grew in intensity and complexity with the years.[4] African nationalism or anti-colonialism reached its xenophobic height during the decade following the end of the Second World War due to a number of factors. The first of them – which has been dealt with in the Introduction – was the impact of the war itself and the disappointment generated by the British government's attitude to the Atlantic Charter.[5]

The second factor, which not only greatly stimulated but also radicalized nationalist activities in British West Africa in particular, was the Pan-African Congress which was held in Manchester in 1945. This congress is discussed in Chapter 25 below, but some aspects which are of relevance here must be highlighted. Though there have been many pan-African congresses since 1900,[6] this one was unique and epoch-making in a number of ways. To begin with, it was the first of these congresses in which Africans, such as Kwame Nkrumah of Ghana, played a leading role in its planning and running, and in which a far greater number of Africans attended. Among them were Obafemi Awolowo, H. O. Davies and Jaja Wachuku of Nigeria; J. E. Taylor, Ako Adjei and Dr R. G. Armattoe of Ghana; Jomo Kenyatta of Kenya; and Hastings Banda of Malawi. Secondly, it was this congress that for the first time not only called for 'complete and absolute independence' and a unified Africa with a socialist economy but also outlined the strategies to be applied. 'If the Western World is still determined to rule mankind by force' asserted one of the resolutions, 'then Africans, as a last resort, may have to appeal to force in the effort to achieve Freedom even if force destroys them and the world'. Another resolution, couched in Marxist terminology, also called on colonial workers, farmers and intellectuals to unite and form effective organizations to fight against imperialist exploitation and for independence, and recommended the use of such methods as strikes, boycotts and positive action, as well as other non-violent strategies.[7] But what is particularly significant about this congress is that most of the Africans who were present soon returned to their respective countries and in the spirit of those resolutions launched or joined the ongoing

4. UNESCO, *General History of Africa*, vol. VII, chs 3–10.
5. P. O. Esedebe, 1971, p. 24.
6. See UNESCO, *General History of Africa*, vol. VII, ch. 29.
7. P. Gifford and W. R. Louis, 1982, pp. 57–87; A. A. Boahen, 1986, pp. 142–3.

campaigns for independence, the most notable of them being Nkrumah of Ghana, Awolowo of Nigeria, Kenyatta of Kenya and Banda of Malawi. It is important to note that no African from French, Portuguese or Belgian Africa attended this epoch-making congress.

PLATE 7.1   *Obafemi Awolowo of Nigeria, leader of the Action Group Party, founded in 1950*

However, the factor that made the greatest contribution to the great upsurge of nationalism was the sense of anger, disappointment and frustration generated by the deteriorating economic and social conditions as well as the inadequate reforms introduced by the colonial powers in general and the British in particular after the war. The period immediately after the war was marked by acute shortages and prohibitive prices of consumer goods for which the colonial governments were held responsible.

166

It was partly this frustration and anger which found expression in the strikes of workers in Nigeria between 1945 and 1948, and the demonstration by ex-servicemen followed by the boycott and looting of European goods in Ghana in 1948, activities in which all the classes listed above were involved[8] and which further strengthened and diffused anti-colonialism. On the social front, the decision of the British colonial power to establish only a single university for the whole of British West Africa instead of one in each colony as recommended by a majority of its own Commission further exacerbated feelings. Nor did the constitutional changes that were introduced after the war in any way meet with the aspirations of the educated élite in particular throughout British West Africa. This is evident from an analysis of the constitutions introduced into Nigeria, Ghana and Sierra Leone in 1946, 1946 and 1947 respectively.[9] The common denominator of these constitutions is that though they all introduced unofficial African majorities in the legislative assemblies, a majority of the new members were to be either nominated by the governors or elected by the traditional rulers. In both Sierra Leone and Nigeria, these new proposals also meant the domination of the northern parts of the countries over the southern and more Westernized areas. As would be expected, these new constitutions aroused the anger of the educated élite in all the British West African colonies and further intensified their resolve to bring about an end to the colonial system.

Besides the intensification and radicalization of nationalism in British West Africa, the other factor which accounts for the overthrow of the colonial system was the nature and objectives of the political parties that emerged after the Second World War and the strategies that they adopted. This factor is of crucial importance because it explains why Ghana rather than, say, Nigeria was the first British colony to attain independence, and secondly why in the rest of the colonies it was the northern rather than the more sophisticated southern parts that came to dominate and are still dominating the political scene.

A whole host of political parties emerged in Africa in general and in British West Africa in particular during the first decade after the end of the Second World War.[10] These included the United Gold Coast Convention (UGCC), the Convention People's Party (CPP) and the Northern People's Party formed in Ghana in 1947, 1949 and 1954 respectively; the National Council for Nigerian Citizens (NCNC), the Action Group (AG) and the Northern People's Congress (NPC) in Nigeria in 1944, 1950 and 1951 respectively; the National Council of Sierra Leone (NCSL) and the Sierra Leone People's Party (SLPP) in 1950 and 1951 respectively; and finally

8. D. Austin, 1964, pp. 49–84.

9. C. M. Fyle, 1981, pp. 138–9; O. Ikime, 1980, pp. 524–8; D. Austin, 1964, pp. 84–92.

10. T. Hodgkins, 1961, pp. 179–209.

the United Party and the People's Progressive Party (PPP) in the Gambia in 1951 and 1959 respectively. It was under the leadership of these parties that the battle for independence was won. The question then is why did these post-Second-World-War political parties and movements succeed while those in the period before failed.

The first answer is the nature of the parties, associations and clubs of the post-war period. Unlike those of the pre-war period, these parties were not élitist parties confined only to the educated élite and to the urban centres but they were, by-and-large, mass parties with following in the urban as well as the rural areas. They had the support, to varying degrees, of the ex-servicemen, the trade union congresses, students, women's organizations, farmers, traders, traditional rulers, and so on. Because of this support, these post-war parties could not be ignored or written off by the colonial authorities as the former parties were. The role of the trade unions, to be discussed below, should be emphasized here, for whereas in Ghana the Trades Union Congress (TUC) gave its full support to the CPP and played a leading role in its campaigning, in Nigeria and the other colonies either because of its weakness or its divisions reflecting the regional divisions, the TUC was not a major participant. Secondly, unlike the former groups, these parties were not run on a part-time basis but were well-organized parties with offices, slogans and modern equipment such as propaganda vans, loudspeakers and presses – and, above all, they had full-time officers at national, regional and local levels. They were able therefore to put their views across and extend them to the remotest parts of their regions or countries with a consequent increase in their membership and strength. Thirdly, unlike the former parties, some of the parties were ready to use any strategies, peaceful or violent, constitutional or unconstitutional, local and international to achieve their ends. The peaceful and constitutional strategies included mass rallies, newspaper campaigns, participation in the many elections, some of which were insisted on by the colonial powers, and appeals to international bodies such as the United Nations Organization and anti-colonial governments such as the United States of America and the Soviet Union. The violent and unconstitutional methods included boycotts, strikes, looting and attacks on colonial institutions and commercial establishments. Fourthly, most of the leaders of these parties were extremely charismatic and demagogic, which enabled them to capture and hold a mass following – the greatest of them being Kwame Nkrumah of Ghana and Azikiwe and Awolowo of Nigeria. Finally, and the most important of all, their objectives and slogans were very radical because they both reflected and provided blueprints for the resolution of social issues and were therefore very irresistible for the masses; the call was for 'Self-government now' or 'Self-government step-by-step' – but not, as in the 1930s, for a reform of colonialism. Of all the parties that emerged in British West Africa, if not in the whole of Africa, there was none that

PLATE 7.2 *Dr Nnamdi Azikiwe, governor-general of Nigeria, with the Duke of Devonshire in London, 10 July 1961*

was better-organized, better-disciplined, more dynamic and radical and enjoyed more charismatic and demagogic leadership than the Convention People's Party of Ghana – thanks principally to its founder and leader, Kwame Nkrumah. It was obviously this unique status of the CPP that partly explains not only why it gained the ascendency in Ghana but also why Ghana was the first British colony south of the Sahara to win the battle for independence.

However, structurally and in terms of mass following, the parties differed in many important respects and it is these differences that further explain not only the timing of the end of the independence struggle but also the leadership of the independent country. In the first place, while some of these parties were truly national parties with branches and a following in all the regions of the country, others were essentially ethnically based and regional parties. This difference was the outcome primarily of the strength or weakness of the ethnic and religious polarization in the country. Thus, in Ghana where this polarization was very weak, two of the three parties, the UGCC and the CPP, were truly national parties with branches and support in all the regions of the country. In Nigeria and the other two British colonies where ethnic and Muslim–Christian polarization and confrontation were deep and bitter, the parties were essentially regional parties. Thus the NCNC, AG and NPC of Nigeria were typologically and essentially Igbo, Yoruba and Fulbe–Hausa ethnically based and regional parties, dominant in the former Eastern, Western and Northern regions respectively. In Sierra Leone, the NCSL was the party of the Creoles in the south, while the SLPP was in reality the party of the Protectorate in the north though it enjoyed the support of a few Creoles. Indeed, the latter party was formed specifically to oppose the former.[11] Similarly, in the Gambia, while the United Party was like the NCSL of Sierra Leone a party of the 'Colony', the PPP was essentially that of the Protectorate.[12] Thus, while the parties of Ghana readily agreed on the issue of independence as well as the date for it, both issues became subjects of bitter controversy among the parties in the other colonies. In Nigeria, for instance, while as early as 1951 the NCNC and AG agreed that Nigeria should be independent in 1956, the NPC vigorously opposed it with the slogan 'Self-government as soon as practicable', and it was not until 1959 that all the parties agreed on the fateful year of 1960. In Sierra Leone, too, it was not until 1959 that consensus was reached on the date for independence. Is it surprising, then, that Ghana was first to break the independence tape, to be followed three years later by Nigeria, and four years later by Sierra Leone? Moreover, because in all the colonies other than Ghana, the northern or protectorate section was more heavily populated than the southern section, the outcome of the inter-party wrangling was the political domination of the latter by the former. Since in nearly all the cases, the southerners were economically, and in terms of Western education and modernization, more advanced than the northerners, this political outcome not only strengthened and deepened regionalism but it also led to a legacy of anger, impatience and frustration on the part of the southerners which has not been entirely eliminated to this day.

There is yet a third factor to be taken into account in explaining the outcome of the independence struggle in British West Africa and this was the attitude of the British colonial power to the demands and activities of the nationalist parties and organizations. Had the latter been met with

11. P. O. Esedebe, 1971, p. 24; C. M. Fyle, 1981, pp. 138–9.
12. T. Hodgkins, 1961, p. 188.

hostility and suppressed with brutality, as happened in Madagascar in the late 1940s, and, as will be seen below, in French West Africa and in Portuguese Africa, there is no doubt that independence would not have been achieved when it was, nor would power have been handed over to the nationalists as it was. From their long experience with nationalist struggles and demands stretching as far back as the eighteenth century in the United States, Canada and Australia, and culminating with the events in the 1940s in Asia in general and India in particular, and of the rising intensity of the African nationalist tide, the British had accepted the principle of self-government as the inevitable end of all colonies. By the early 1950s, if not late 1940s, both the Conservative and Labour parties as well as a majority of even the main expatriate firms operating in the West African colonies, or, as Fieldhouse puts it, a majority of 'the official as well as the unofficial mind' had come round to that view with respect to those colonies.[13] What had not been agreed upon was the period of apprenticeship or 'preparation' for self-government. While some thought in terms of a period of 50 years, others even deemed that unrealistic. Nor, contrary to what scholars like Flint and Pearce have been arguing,[14] did the British draw up any programme for so-called decolonization. On the contrary, from the late 1940s onwards they rather reacted to the initiatives and pressures being exerted on them by the nationalist activities and demands in Africa. Some minutes taken by the officials in the Colonial Office, then debating the issues of indirect rule and of the constitutional changes to be introduced into the British colonies after the war, are very relevant here. Having secretly toured the colonies, Hailey submitted a report to the Colonial Office in 1942 in which he reported *inter alia*:

> There are forces both at home and *in the dependencies* [author's emphasis] which will exert increasing pressure for the extension of political institutions making for self-government, and the fuller association of Africans in them. The strength of this pressure is likely to be largely enhanced as the result of the war. Unless we have a clear view of the constitutional form in which self-government is to be expressed, the answer to this pressure will be ill-coordinated, and may lead to the adoption of measures which we may afterwards wish to recall.[15]

Supporting Hailey's advocacy of the change of the system of so-called indirect rule, the Colonial Office legal adviser, Sir H. G. Bushe, also minuted 'On the other side of the picture there appears in an ever-growing progression the educated African, and he views with extreme

13. D. K. Fieldhouse, 1986, pp. 3–12.
14. J. Flint, 1983; R. D. Pearce, 1984.
15. Quoted in P. Gifford and W. R. Louis, 1982, pp. 250–1.

distaste the primitive, inefficient and in many cases corrupt institutions of indirect rule. If, like the white man, he needs no more than worship them he might be content. Unfortunately, however, he finds that unlike the white man, he has to subject himself to them'. Not only did the assistant under-secretary, Sir Arthur Dawse, accept this view but he also went on to state:

> I think that the truth of Sir G. Bushe's remark . . . is becoming increasingly realized. It is absurd to erect what is an ephemeral expedient into a sacrosanct principle. *Things are moving so fast in Africa* [author's emphasis] that the doctrinaire adherents of the indirect rule principle may find themselves out-moded, much quicker than anyone would have thought possible a few years ago.[16]

What is clearly revealed by these minutes is that the Colonial Office was acting in response to or in anticipation of African nationalists' demands, and it is this which makes the terms 'decolonization' and 'transfer of power' now being increasingly used by Eurocentric historians so misleading and so unacceptable.

Confronted, then, with growing African nationalist activities which reached their intensity from the mid-1950s onwards, and free from any lobbying or opposition from any white settlers – as was the case in Eastern and Southern Africa – the British, unlike the French in the 1940s or the Portuguese, decided not to resist the nationalists. Rather, they opted to abandon their hitherto close allies and tools, the traditional ruling élite, and to concede to or bargain with the nationalists in each country, allowing the agreement or lack of it among them over such issues as independence itself, the nature of the independence constitution, revenue allocation, and so on, to determine the timing and outcome of the negotiations. Furthermore, unlike the French and the Portuguese, the British resorted mainly to peaceful and constitutional means in West Africa – though the use of force or violence was not entirely ruled out, as was evident in the shooting incident in Ghana in 1948 or the imprisonment of Nkrumah and many of his followers in the early 1950s, or the suppression of the strike in 1955 and the anti-chieftaincy agitation in 1955–6 in Sierra Leone in which 100 people were killed.

It was because nearly all the parties in Ghana as well as a clear majority of Ghanaians – as is evident from the outcome of the elections of 1951 and 1956 which were won by Nkrumah and his party – had reached a consensus on those issues that the British fixed the date of 5 March 1957 for the independence of Ghana. And it was because, after a series of constitutional conferences both locally and in Britain, all the parties in Nigeria and Sierra Leone agreed on the independence issues at stake in the late 1950s that Britain conceded their claims for independence. It

16. Quoted in J. Flint, 1983, p. 395.

should be emphasized that, contrary to the recent claims of some Euro-centric historians, the initiative in the struggle for independence lay with the West Africans themselves and not with the Colonial Office, the British parliament or British public opinion.

French West Africa and Togo

If the British did not decide the timing of the outcome of the struggle for independence in their West African colonies, the French certainly did. This is clearly borne out by the fact that while all the British West African colonies became independent at different times stretching from 1957 to 1965, with the exception of Guinea and Djibouti, all the French colonies on the African continent became independent in the same year, 1960! Why then this rather interesting outcome in French West Africa? Here again the answers lie in the nature of the nationalist demands and activities, the nature of the political parties that emerged and, above all and most decisively, the reactions and responses of France and particularly of one single individual, namely General de Gaulle, to these activities.

Whereas British West Africa was made up of four distinct units, French West Africa, consisting until 1958 of a 'federation' of eight colonies – termed Overseas Territories after 1946 – formed a single administrative unit under the authority of a governor-general who, in 1946, was renamed high commissioner (*Haut-Commissaire de la République*). The French part of the Togo, a trusteeship territory, had a separate status.

Less populated and less well developed, French West Africa was behind in all areas compared to British West Africa. Outside the three full communes of Senegal, namely Dakar, Rufisque and St Louis, whose inhabitants, black and white alike, were French citizens and could therefore participate in politics and elections, the colonial regime had excluded most forms of political life from the colonial 'subjects'. In addition, both the public and the private sectors had to face competition even for low-level employment from 'poor white' settlers who did not exist in British West Africa.

The end of the war led to strong reactions, for the reasons mentioned above, but also as a result of a sudden transformation of political status. The French Africa Conference held at Brazzaville from 30 January to 8 February 1944 which had brought together, before the liberation of France, governors and settlers, in no way opened the door to any sort of 'decolonization' as legend has it. On the contrary, it rather excluded 'any idea of autonomy, any possibility of evolution outside the French imperial bloc' and specified that the 'constitution of "self-government" in the colonies, even in the distant future, is to be excluded'.[17] It limited itself to promising, for an indeterminate future, a possible 'participation' by

17. La Conférence africaine française, 1944. This part is printed in capitals in the text.

Africans in the management of their own affairs. These remarks were taken literally by the Africans which subsequently provoked the ire of the settlers, as being intolerable.

In 1945, the rise of the forces of the left had consequences in Africa. For the first time, in October 1945, a small minority of the subjects – which for French West Africa consisted of 117000 out of 16 million inhabitants – were to elect deputies to the French Constituent Assembly. This, along with the settlers, formed the 'First College' of electors and received a disproportionate representation in relation to their numerical importance. French West Africa was given five deputies – that is one for 5000 people, as against one for 60000–70000 in France. Through this colonial representation, General de Gaulle hoped to compensate for the predictable large vote for the left in France. The settlers were sure supporters; the ex-subjects would vote as the administration wanted. But things did not turn out that way: the election within the framework of the 'Second College' picked as deputies those who had campaigned for the end of the colonial regime. In Senegal – where the winning candidate from the First College, which was dominated by Africans, was the lawyer Lamine Gueye, a veteran of politics in the 'three communes'; and that from the Second College, the young *agrégé de grammaire* Léopold Sédar Senghor – the two winners joined the socialist party, *Section française de l'Internationale ouvrière* (SFIO); the winner from Guinea, Yacine Diallo, and Dahomey, Sourou Migan Apithy, affiliated with the socialist group. Félix Houphouët-Boigny, elected from the Côte d'Ivoire, and Fily Dabo Sissoko, elected from Soudan–Niger, joined the communist group in the Assembly.

Assimilation and persistence of the colonial regime

The first Constituent Assembly had a left-wing majority made up of the socialists and communists to which most of the indigenous members elected from overseas affiliated. The constitution, of which the deputy from Senegal, Senghor, along with Pierre Cot, had been one of the drafters, integrated the former colonies into the Republic and introduced the expression '*French Union*' but left the door open for an evolution towards independence. The Constituent Assembly also adopted the law of 11 April 1946 (the so-called Houphouët-Boigny law) abolishing forced labour, and the law of 7 May 1946 (the so-called Lamine Gueye law) granting French citizenship to all the colonial ex-'subjects'. Other measures abolished the much-hated *indigénat*, which allowed the administration to impose penal sanctions on 'subjects', and established freedom of the press and association.

This constitution provoked a violent campaign of opposition from the right, represented in the government by the Social-Christian Popular Republican Movement (*Mouvement républicain populaire* – MRP), in which the Catholic Church, the Radical-Socialist Party, the settlers and de Gaulle himself (who had in the meantime resigned as head of the government) took part. The constitution was rejected in a referendum, and, in the second Constituent Assembly elected in June 1946, the left no longer had a majority. Compared with the previous one, the constitution of October 1946 – which became that of the Fourth Republic – contained major retreats. The abolition of forced labour and the granting of citizenship were not called into question as the settlers would have liked. However, the text of the constitution eliminated any possibility of evolution towards independence and left the door open to the maintenance of the 'dual college' and special representation for the settlers.

Why did the African deputies accept the 'assimilationism' of the two constitutions and did they all really accept it? Assimilationism had, it is true, deep roots – especially in Senegal. But above all, the African deputies feared, in the federalism advocated by the right, 'self-government' on the South African model. This would have given power to the settlers whom they hoped on the contrary to be able to fight with the support of a 'left-wing' central government. But this hope was not realized.

The development of parties

It was in this 'assimilationist' context that political parties came into being in French West Africa. But it should be emphasized that unlike their counterparts in the British colonies, these parties were associated with French parties, sometimes as their direct scions. This was the case with the Socialist Party, whose Senegalese Federation dominated political life in Senegal up to 1948. After 1947, the Rally of the French People (*Rassemblement du peuple français* – RPF), created by de Gaulle, gained support mainly among Europeans and became identified as the extreme settler party. In 1949, under the auspices of the MRP, which then held the Overseas France portfolio, a parliamentary group was formed known as the Overseas Independents, closely linked to the MRP but based on electoral committees rather than on one or several parties (except for Senghor's African Convention in Senegal).

The Communist Party, whose principles ruled out the creation of overseas branches, had limited itself in the period 1944–50 to inspiring *Groupes d'études communistes* (GEC), with the aim of uniting Frenchmen and Africans to create purely local 'anticolonialist front' parties or movements called 'Democratic' or 'Progressive' – such as the Democratic Party of the Côte d'Ivoire, the Niger Progressive Party, and so on.

Faced with the counter-attack launched during the summer of 1946, a number of African deputies called for a conference of all political parties (*Rassemblement*) in Bamako in October 1946. The socialist Minister of Overseas France, Marius Moutet, gave instructions that this was to be prevented at all costs. He pressurized the socialist deputies who had

PLATE 7.3 *The RDA (Rassemblement démocratique africain) Congress in Bamako, 1946: centre, Félix Houphouët-Boigny; left, Gabriel d'Arboussier*

signed the call for the rally not to attend, while the delegates from French Equatorial Africa were unable to get there. The congress, however, took place as planned and resulted in the establishment, under the leadership of Houphouët-Boigny, of the *Rassemblement démocratique africain* (African Democratic Rally, or RDA), federating local African parties on the basis of the anti-colonial struggle. Its deputies (seven in the National Assembly in November 1946) affiliated with communist groups in the various assemblies.

The Cold War and the attempts at colonial restoration

The presence of African deputies in the French assemblies had scarcely any influence on the local administration. The constitution had envisaged first the establishment of local assemblies or 'general councils' and then in 1952 'territorial assemblies'. However, except in Senegal, the elections were made by the 'dual college' with a separate and excessive representation for the settlers. There was also an assembly at the federal level, the 'Grand Council' elected indirectly by the territorial assemblies.

Yet, the governor-general and governors retained all their powers intact while the powers of the assemblies were limited to a consultative role and the approval of the budget, which was largely predetermined by the 'mandatory expenditure'.

The removal of the communist ministers in France in May 1947 and the beginning of the Cold War were accompanied by what amounted to a policy of colonial restoration evidenced by the war of reconquest in Indochina, the repression of the nationalist movement in Madagascar, and so on. In French West Africa, the policy of repression was focused on the Côte d'Ivoire, the stronghold of the RDA, which, around 1950, had 850 000 members there out of a population of 2.3 million. The leader of the *Parti démocratique de Côte d'Ivoire* (PDCI, an RDA section), Félix Houphouët-Boigny, an African doctor from a reigning family in Baule country, a former *chef de canton* and a big planter, had in 1944 been the founder of the *Syndicat agricole africain*, bringing together African coffee- and cocoa-planters. At the time they were locked in bitter conflict with the settlers, who had inherited exorbitant privileges from the Vichy regime – such as preferential buying prices and monopoly of the workforce, supplied by forced labour, and of equipment. The Ivorian agricultural bourgeoisie which he represented defended its class interest by demanding the abolition of racist privileges and the abolition of forced labour which would give it access to the labour hitherto reserved for whites. But, in so doing, it was *ipso facto* defending the interests of the masses oppressed by the colonial regime, and awakened a profound mass movement of which the PDCI was the expression.

In order to reduce the 'weight' of the Côte d'Ivoire, the Territory of Upper Volta, which was suppressed in 1932 and mostly annexed to the Côte d'Ivoire, was restored in 1947. Then, at the end of 1948, Governor Péchoux was sent with the mission of 'breaking' the RDA. In 1949 and 1950, he resorted to violence and 'combing operations' (*ratissages*), during which villages were burned down and peasants murdered. An increasing number of bloody incidents occurred which were always attributed to the RDA. Among the victims was Senator Victor Biaka Boda, who 'disappeared'. Later, a few of his charred bones were found, along with his gold signet-ring. Almost all the territorial and local leaders were arrested, except for the deputies Houphouët-Boigny and Ouezzin Coulibaly.

As a result of these brutal and oppressive measures, Houphouët-Boigny gave in. Following contacts with François Mitterrand, a member of the same group (*Union démocratique et socialiste de la Résistance* – UDSR) as René Pléven, the minister of Overseas France, he decided at the end of 1950 to disaffiliate from the communist groups, drop the radical demands, and join the government. Thus, he voted for military supplies for the war in Indochina. To the militants and members of the RDA, this about-turn was at first presented as a 'tactical withdrawal' in order to put an end to the repression. The general-secretary of the RDA, Gabriel d'Arboussier, and the Senegal and Niger sections refused to follow this change of course while the others, and notably those in Guinea and French Sudan, resigned themselves to it so as not to break the unity of the movement.

Popular pressure and the move to independence

Despite Houphouët-Boigny's about-turn, popular pressure persisted. Trade union action and strikes directed against the persistent measures of racial discrimination in wages, status, right to work, and so on, developed after 1951. In Guinea, the *Parti démocratique de Guinée* (RDA), led by the trade unionist Sékou Touré, extended its support in the countryside by waging the fight against chieftaincy, a cog in the colonial administration. In French Sudan, the *Union soudanaise* (RDA), led by Mamadou Konate and Modibo Keita, continued its resistance. The deterioration of the international situation and of the French colonial situation signified by the French defeat at Dien-Bien-Phu in Indochina, the independence of Tunisia and Morocco, and the beginning of the liberation war in Algeria obliged the French government to make a sacrifice and forestall the demand for total independence. The *loi-cadre* drawn up in 1956 by the socialist minister of Overseas France, Gaston Defferre, without the least consultation with the deputies or with the African assemblies, came into force in 1957. It granted the Overseas Territories 'semi-autonomy', with a 'council of government' presided over by the governor, with an African vice-president chosen from among the majority in the assembly as his deputy. But nothing similar was set up at the federal level. The French government, which had hitherto stressed centralization in the government-general, was preparing to break up the federations that were 'too big economically, administratively and politically'.[18] The aim was to associate and compromise the African political leaders with colonial policy, without giving them real responsibilities.

The *loi-cadre* could not stand in the way of the desire for independence expressed clearly for the first time by a new Marxist-oriented party, the *Parti africain de l'indépendance*, based mainly among students who had returned home from France. Independence was further popularized both in France and Africa by students of the *Fédération des étudiants d'Afrique noire en France* (FEANF)[19] and the *Union générale des étudiants d'Afrique occidentale* (UGEAO). The desire for unity – after the failure of a merger with the RDA – led the groups deriving from the Overseas Independents

18. P. H. Teitgen, former prime minister of the French Overseas Territories, quoted in F. Ansprenger, 1961, p. 245.

19. For a detailed and interesting discussion of the role of African student movements in the political and social evolution of Africa from 1900 to 1975, see UNESCO, (forthcoming).

and the Socialist Party to merge into the *Parti du regroupement africain* (PRA). At its congress at Cotonou in July 1958, the PRA adopted a motion demanding immediate independence.

Meanwhile, in May 1958, General de Gaulle had returned to power and buried the Fourth Republic. The new constitution which he had prepared – and which was to be approved in a referendum on 28 September 1958 in France and the overseas territories and *départements* – took a further step by granting autonomy to the territories, which became republics with an elected president replacing the governor. The 'French Union' was replaced by the 'French Community'; but the French government retained a whole series of essential powers, and independence was explicitly presented as being incompatible with membership of the French Community.

De Gaulle submitted his new proposals to a vote in French Africa and the colonial administration succeeded in securing a 'yes' vote even in Niger, whose government, headed by the trades-unionist Bakary Djibo, had called for a 'no' vote, except in Guinea, where the 'no' vote totalled more than 80 per cent of the votes and which proclaimed its independence on 2 October. This choice sounded the death-knell of the French Community in the short run, despite Houphouët-Boigny's fierce opposition. By causing the disappearance of French West Africa (FWA) as a political unit, the constitution had sanctioned the 'balkanization' of French Africa. Senegal and French Sudan attempted to oppose it by creating a 'Federation of Mali', which initially included Upper Volta and Dahomey, but they soon left under Ivorian pressure. Reduced by two members, the Federation of Mali asked for its independence in September 1959 and France had to resign itself to granting it on 20 June 1960, at the price of an amendment to the constitution. The other states followed and their independence was proclaimed during August (for Dahomey on 1 August; Niger on 3 August; Upper Volta on 5 August; Côte d'Ivoire on 7 August), but Mauritania's not until 28 November 1960.

Togo, because of its status, had followed a path of its own. The *Comité d'unité togolaise* (CUT), led since 1946 by Sylvanus Olympio, and the Juvento (Juventus Togo), created in 1951, had been calling for unity and independence since that date. Unity was ruled out by the referendum of 9 May 1956 in British Togo, which voted by a majority of 58 per cent for annexation to Ghana. Independence (*Ablode*) remained the slogan, despite the election-rigging which enabled the French administration to ensure a majority for its supporters until 1958. The dual college was abolished in 1952, and a 'council of government' with five elected members out of nine was created in 1955. In July 1956, Togo was given the status of an 'Autonomous Republic'. The CUT won the elections held in 1958, and independence was proclaimed on 27 April 1960, with Sylvanus Olympio as first president.

PLATE 7.4 *Sylvanus Olympio, president of Togo, proclaims his country's independence, 27 April 1960*

It should be obvious from the above that unlike the situation in British West Africa, the outcome and timing of independence in French West Africa was really determined by the French government rather than the African nationalists. In the first place, had the French government been as tolerant to the political parties that emerged – especially the RDA and later the *Parti africain de l'indépendence* (PAI) – as the British were to theirs, the French West African colonies would probably have achieved independence before the British colonies. But sticking to the illusionary idea of the French Union and later the French Community, they completely ruled out any idea of total independence until the accession to power of Charles de Gaulle in 1958. And even then it was because Guinea called de Gaulle's bluff, coupled with the political developments taking place in the neighbouring Anglophone West African countries that de Gaulle and his advisers accepted the inevitable and virtually handed independence on a platter to almost all the French colonies in Africa in that fateful year of 1960 (the exceptions were Djibouti and the Indian Ocean islands, whose independence came later).

The labour movement and the trades unions

The persistence of the *économie de traite* (predatory economy) and the preponderance of smallholdings explain why, despite the advances of industry and services between 1946 and 1960, the working class remained relatively small in West Africa. For FWA and Togo there were only 245 538 wage-earners in 1947 and 412 810 in 1957, excluding civil servants and domestic servants, which represented only 2 per cent of the population in 1957. The proportion would be a little higher if civil servants, whose importance in the trade union movement was out of all proportion to their number, were included. The administrative 'élite', including teachers and government doctors, played a major role in the trade union movement and often provided its leaders.

In the British territories, trade unionism was transformed in the tradition of the British Trades Union Congress (TUC), often with the blessing of the administration and in a spirit of collaboration with the administration and employers. Nevertheless, they found it hard not to get caught up in the nationalist movement. In certain cases they were in fact the prime movers – for example, the railway unionists of Sekondi Takoradi in the Gold Coast, in the 1940s.

In Ghana, the TUC soon established close ties with the CPP: in January 1950, it was to back the CPP's 'positive action' campaign that the TUC launched the general strike.

In Nigeria, the close alliance between the Nigerian Trade Union Congress and the NCNC was not sustained after 1951. The Nigerian trade union movement remained marked by its fragmentation and division into rival bodies; radical elements never played a sustained major role in it.

In the French territories, the trades unions were in the beginning, and remained until 1957, mostly affiliated to the French *Confédération générale du travail* (CGT) – the General Confederation of Labour – while enjoying considerable *de facto* autonomy under the leadership of a *Comité de coordination des unions de syndicats confédérés de l'AOF*. Many CGT union leaders were at the same time political leaders with the RDA, even after 1950 – for example, Sékou Touré in Guinea and Bakary Djibo in Niger. The *Fédération des cheminots de l'AOF* (railway union) was autonomous, but left its member unions free to affiliate as they wished. Thus in 1947, the Abidjan–Niger Railway Union of Côte d'Ivoire was affiliated to the CGT while the Benin–Niger railway union of Dahomey joined the *Confédération française et démocratique du travail* (CFDT), which it left in 1948 following pressure from French leaders of the Catholic unions to get them to abandon the strike. The Catholic unions, affiliated to the *Confédération française des travailleurs chrétiens* (CFTC) were in a small minority and only existed where the influence of the missions was felt, such as in Dahomey and coastal Guinea. The split in the trade union movement in France in 1948 had little influence in Africa since the African unions remained almost all with the CGT; *Force ouvrière*, the breakaway confederation, had an almost wholly European membership.

To the extent that the union struggle was directed essentially against the colonial administration and European employers, and its demands were aimed principally at eliminating racial discrimination in the areas of wages, status and social rights, this struggle was part and parcel of the general anti-colonial struggle and received the support of the whole African population. This was the case with the strike by African railway workers in Senegal in 1947–8, which could not have lasted five months without this linkage and in which the intransigence of the administration sought to break the union movement. The administration failed, however, and had to go back on its decision to sack the strikers. The strike movements of 1952, 1953 and 1955 for the adoption of the Overseas Labour Code had the same features, as did those after the passage of the Code through parliament, for its implementation.

It was only in 1956 that, on the initiative of Sékou Touré, a *Confédération générale du travail africain* (General Confederation of African Labour) was established. It received a cool welcome as it appeared to be under the remote control of the leadership of the RDA. The colonial administration attempted to remove the unions from the influence of the CGT and get them to collaborate with the administration. The CGT then took the initiative of calling for the formation of an independent African central trade union organization bringing all the unions together. This appeal initially gained universal approval among the CGT, CGTA, autonomous railwaymen and Catholic unions except for the *Force ouvrière*. The Catholic unions, however, went back almost at once on their decision by creating a *Confédération africaine des travailleurs croyants* (African Confederation of Believing Workers, CATC), a formula which they felt would enable them to attract Muslims. The call for a centralized union finally took concrete shape with the holding in Cotonou in January 1957 of the congress which created the *Union générale des travailleurs d'Afrique noire* (General Union of Workers of Black Africa, UGTAN) under the leadership of Sékou Touré. The UGTAN did not survive independence, each state having moved quickly to remove the national central trade union organization from any external influence.

The role of cultural and religious movements

The assertion of the African personality inherent in the anti-colonial struggle was bound to take on a cultural dimension. Paradoxically, and for reasons that have to do with both the colonial heritage and the material conditions flowing from it, this assertion took mainly a literary form and did so in the language of the colonizer. It was a new phenomenon in itself to the extent that, before 1946, this form of expression had been extremely limited and channelled into forms acceptable to the colonial regime.[20]

In Paris in 1947, the review *Présence Africaine* was launched by Alioune Diop, a Senegalese university graduate converted to Catholicism, temporarily a socialist senator from Senegal. This review, around which the *Société africaine de culture* was formed, was not politically aligned, but its assertion of an African cultural personality was in itself a challenge to the colonial ideology and fact of colonialism. It was in the same year that L. S. Senghor, a politician as well as a poet, published his first collection of poems. Subsequently, he developed the concept of *negritude*, borrowed from a formula launched in 1932 by West Indian writers and remodelled by Jean-Paul Sartre. This concept was at once strongly challenged by the revolutionary school led by Gabriel d'Arboussier in 1949.

In contrast to this cultural self-assertion, which did not call into question the established order, a militant, vigorously anti-colonial poetry began to appear in the years 1947–50, in the columns of the Dakar weekly, *Réveil*, the organ of the RDA, written by such poets as Bernard B. Dadié, Jean Malonga and Keita Fodeba. The last-named continued this activity in 1950 by founding the *Ballets africains* which took his name, creating a new form of cultural expression on an African foundation. Recordings of poems by Keita Fodeba accompanied on the guitar by Kante Faceli were banned in FWA as subversive.

David Diop continued this trend in the 1950s, and it was also in the 1950s that there appeared through the novel, in a less 'militant' but equally critical form, a satire of colonial reality. Among these new novelists were Mongo Beti, Ferdinand Oyono of Cameroon and Sembene Ousmane of Senegal, plus the already-mentioned Bernard B. Dadié as the leading writers. Their elder, the Senegalese Abdoulaye Sadji, who was writing before 1940 but was only published later, limited himself to criticizing manners and customs. Camara Laye was more equivocal: his folkloric and idyllic work entirely ignores the reality of colonialism.

This anti-colonial stance can be found in Ghana in the writings of George Awoonor and de Graft-Johnson and, to a much lesser extent, before 1960, in Nigeria, where the work of Amos Tutuola remained folkloric and the so-called Onitsha popular literature was more moralizing than political.

Like cultural movements, religious movements both reflected social and political changes and, sometimes, actively accompanied them. The development of communication encouraged the advance of universalist religions at the expense of local creeds; Islam, less compromised than the Christian sects with the colonial regime, was the chief beneficiary of this. While the Senegalese Muslim brotherhoods, long under a cloud of suspicion, were now integrated into the colonial order, new ones came

20. See Chapter 19 for a wider discussion of literary trends.

under suspicion. This was the case in French Sudan (now Mali) with Hamalism, in itself apolitical, which was driven closer to the anti-colonialist movement (in this case the RDA) by persecution.

The Catholic Church, the one most involved, at least in the French possessions, in the colonial system, continued to be associated with the most colonialist elements until the early 1950s. It denounced the RDA as an agent of 'atheistic communism', whereas most of the leaders of the RDA were practising Muslims or Catholics!

The change came late, with the encyclical *Evangeli praecones* of 2 June 1953. Faced with the rise of nationalism, the Catholic Church felt the need to modify the 'colonial structures of the missions', such as the division of the territory into 'fiefdoms' by the Congregations and slowness about promoting an indigenous clergy. In French Africa, the episcopal hierarchy was introduced in November 1955. While the Anglican Church had long had coloured bishops, it was only in 1956 that the first African bishops were promoted in Dahomey and Upper Volta (now Burkina Faso) and only in 1957 in Ghana for the Catholic Church.

Portuguese West Africa: Guinea-Bissau and the Cape Verde Islands

While all the British and French colonies in West Africa had achieved their independence by 1965, it was not until 1973 and 1974 that Guinea–Bissau and the Cape Verde Islands as well as the other two Portuguese African colonies, Angola and Mozambique, succeeded in overthrowing Portuguese colonialism. Furthermore, while the struggles for independence in all the other West African colonies were by and large peaceful, taking the form of round-table conferences and inter-party wranglings, in Portuguese Africa it was a violent, bloody and protracted affair assuming the dimensions of wars of liberation. The key to the explanation of these unique features of the anti-colonial struggle in Portuguese Africa lies in the principles and practices of Portuguese colonialism as well as in the nature of the nationalist movements that emerged.

Portugal, like France, from the very beginning considered its colonies (as has been amply demonstrated in volume VII) not as colonies but rather as overseas provinces of Portugal. While the French abandoned this erroneous and unrealistic policy in the 1950s, Portugal stuck to it – and with increasing fanaticism and delusion – until the very end, in the face of and despite the increasing tide of African nationalism. Thus, while France abandoned its repressive and violent reactions of the 1940s and resorted to peaceful negotiations and even the ballot box, the Portuguese maintained the policy of keeping their empire intact through any and every means.

Another aspect of Portuguese colonialism was the state in which her colonies in Africa in general and those in West Africa in particular were by the 1950s. Because of the features peculiar to Portuguese colonialism (a 'sub-imperialism', itself dependent on outside powers since the eighteenth century) and to the fascism that had been ruling Portugal since 1926, the Portuguese colonies lagged considerably behind neighbouring countries in West Africa. They had no capital investment, no railway, no roads and a primitive *économie de traite* (predatory economy) in the hands of a monopoly, that of the *Companhia União Fabril* (CUF). Officially regarded as 'Portuguese provinces' since 1930, these two colonies bore the stigmata of the most backward colonialism. Behind a façade of 'assimilationism' was concealed the most brutal discrimination. In the *Provincia de Guine* of the 1950s, out of half a million inhabitants and after 'five centuries of Portuguese presence', 8320 individuals (including 2263 whites and 4568 of mixed race) enjoyed political rights – which in any case were purely formal – with the status of 'civilized'. Only 1478 Africans – 0.3 per cent of the population – enjoyed this status: the white man, even if illiterate, which was common among the Portuguese, was 'civilized' *ipso facto*; the black man had to know how to read and write Portuguese, be a practising Catholic and be in the colonizer's good books.

In the Cape Verde Islands, overpopulated and ravaged by periodic famines, 20 000 died in 1940–3 and 30 000 in 1944–8 – out of a population of fewer than 150 000 at the time. The population, which had originally come from the mainland, was wholly 'assimilated' and Portugal drew on it for subordinate colonial officials for the other colonies in Africa. With very limited educational facilities at the secondary and none at the tertiary levels, there was none of that upper-middle class or bourgeoisie class which would also have provided leadership and inspiration. And with the Portuguese determined and ready to suppress any anti-colonial agitation with the most extreme of means, it was not until the late 1950s that political parties began to emerge in Portuguese Africa.

On 19 October 1956, an agronomist of Cape Verdian origin but born in Guinea, Amilcar Cabral, with his five companions, created the *Partido Africano da Independencia da Guiné e Cabo Verde* (PAIGC) in Bissau. From 1956 to 1959, its activity was concentrated in the towns, and it used peaceful means. However, when the illegal strike of dock-workers it organized in August 1959 was brutally suppressed with more than 50 dock-workers killed and many wounded, the PAIGC decided to abandon its peaceful methods in favour of armed struggle. It therefore not only shifted its activities from the towns to the bush but also there devised a new policy and political programme, the politics of liberation, calculated to win the masses of the countryside who were then apathetic towards independence or building a new nation. As Cabral told his cadres, 'Keep always in your mind that the people are not fighting for ideas, for the things in anyone's head. They are fighting to win material benefits, to live better and in peace, to see their lives go forward, to guarantee the future of their children', therefore that they must 'practise revolutionary democracy . . . hold frequent meetings . . . hide nothing from the masses of our people . . . tell no lies . . . claim no easy victories'.[21] Between 1961 and 1963, his young militants, who were mainly 25 years of age or even younger, worked clandestinely in the villages, teaching the people that their local grievances could only be solved by working and fighting to get rid of the entire Portuguese colonial system.

PLATE 7.5 *Armed women soldiers of the PAIGC (Partido Africano da Independencia da Guiné e Cabo Verde)*

It was only after this education and organization that the PAIGC launched its armed struggle in 1963. Beginning first with 'small guerrilla groups in favourable zones of bush or forest', they next developed them into 'large units but also non-localized units, available for rapid movements over long distances, and capable of fighting wherever they were sent'.[22] Actively supported and helped by the rural people, these mobile groups increased in size and strength, learned the use of all sorts of weapons, including even long-range missiles, even though they were mostly illiterate. Whenever they liberated any area, they launched their politics of liberation. On the one hand, they expelled all colonial officials and traders, abolished all colonial taxes and exactions, and ended forced labour and the compulsory growing of crops. On the other, the more positive side, they introduced a new trading system and established bush schools and clinics

21. Quoted by B. Davidson, 1980, pp. 10–11.
22. *ibid.*, pp. 13–14.

186

where there were none before, staffed with teachers and nurses from men and women often trained in Europe or in Cuba. What was even more important, the PAIGC introduced true democracy into the liberated areas. The people were encouraged to elect representative committees which were assigned the responsibilities of local government. Cabral summed up the strategy employed against the Portuguese as follows:

> In order to dominate a given zone, the enemy is obliged to disperse his forces. In dispersing his forces, he weakens himself and we can defeat him. Then in order to defend himself against us, he has to concentrate his forces. When he does that, we can occupy the zones that he leaves free and work in them politically so as to hinder his return there.[23]

Using these tactics as well as their politics of liberation and assisted by some people from the Cape Verde Islands, some African countries and above all the USSR and Cuba, the PAIGC made steady progress. In spite of the huge increase in the number of Portuguese soldiers from 1000 in 1961 to more than 30 000 in 1967, the PAIGC could not be stopped by the Portuguese. Despite the active financial and military support for Portugal of all the major Western powers as well as the other members of NATO, by 1967 the PAIGC had gained control of two-thirds of Guinea. Although the Portuguese subsequently increased the strength of their army there, they failed to defeat the Africans, and not even the callous assassination of Amilcar Cabral in January 1973 could reverse the tide rolling in favour of liberation. On 24 September 1973, the PAIGC proclaimed the independence of Guinea-Bissau. It should be pointed out that the humiliation and demoralization suffered by the Portuguese army not only in Guinea-Bissau but also in Angola and Mozambique, coupled with the ideas of liberation with which the Portuguese soldiers became infused in Africa, led to the overthrow of the oppressive Salazar regime in Portugal itself by some young officers of the Portuguese army in April 1974. It was the new regime which not only confirmed Guinea-Bissau's independence but also conceded independence to both Angola and Mozambique in 1975.

The PAIGC called for the union of Guinea and the Cape Verde Islands because of the origins of their populations. The geographical conditions of the islands ruled out a resistance of the same type as in Guinea – an attempted uprising at Praia, in 1962, ended in failure – but after the fall of Portuguese fascism the hitherto underground organization of the PAIGC took control of the country's destiny. It was Cabral's successor as secretary-general of the PAIGC, Artistides Pereira, who negotiated independence in September 1974 and became the first president of the Republic of Cape Verde.

23. *ibid.*, p. 14.

Liberia

By 1945, though one of only four independent states in Africa theoretically in control of its own destiny, Liberia had in practice become a neo-colony of the United States. The administration and resources of the country were entirely dominated by the relatively small Americo-Liberian community of the coastal districts of the country while the overwhelming majority of its citizens who lived in the interior were discriminated against, looked down upon and made to feel completely isolated and exploited by the small ruling oligarchy.

External, Liberia – like the rest of the then independent states of Africa – was not in contact with the rising tide of anti-colonialism around it nor did it make any effort to provide leadership of any kind to the aspiring colonial states in Africa. Economically, the country was on the verge of bankruptcy by 1945 and, to quote Mazrui and Tidy, 'remained tied to the apron-strings of the United States, subject to a mightier economic imperialism than could be imposed in Africa by European colonial powers'.[24] Fortunately, this rather grim situation underwent some far-reaching changes due to the efforts of one man, William Vacanarat Shadrach Tubman, who became president in 1944 and remained in power till his death in 1971.[25]

Adopting an open-door economic policy and anxious to break the stranglehold of the Firestone Rubber Company on its economy, Tubman succeeded in attracting foreign investors, mainly from the United States, whose number rose from one in 1925, to 25 by 1960 and 38 by 1966.[26] This resulted in the diversification of economic activities from solely rubber planting and manufacturing to the building of artificial harbours at Monrovia, iron-mining at Bomi Hills in the Nimba mountains and other areas, and light manufacturing industries such as the production of cement. By 1966, the export value of iron ore was $112 million as compared to $30 million of rubber. By 1978, Liberia had become the leading producer and exporter of iron ore in Africa. All this led to the construction of a growing network of roads which greatly accelerated the opening up of the interior. According to Liebenow, this development brought 'a radical transformation in the way of life of tribesmen, who until recently were rigidly wedded to subsistence economies and able to afford few of the material luxuries of westernization'.[27] Tubman also began to divert the trade of Liberia from exclusively American channels into others. Here again, some success was attained, and Liberian exports to the United States fell from 90 per cent in 1950 to about 60 per cent in

24. A. A. Mazrui and M. Tidy, 1984, p. 29.
25. J. G. Liebenow, 1969, p. 73.
26. J. B. Webster and A. A. Boahen, 1980, p. 373.
27. J. G. Liebenow, 1969, p. 79.

PLATE 7.6   *William Tubman, president of Liberia (photographed in September 1956)*

the mid-1970s; and imports fell from about 70 per cent to less than 50 per cent in the same period.

While Tubman adopted an open-door policy in the economic field, he pursued the policy of integration and national unification in the political and social fields, with the primary objective of eliminating the centuries-old cleavage and confrontation between the American–Liberian oligarchy and the indigenous mass of people. As he stated:

> We must destroy all ideologies that tend to divide us. Americo-Liberianism must be forgotten and all of us must register a new era of justice, equality, fair dealing and equal opportunity for every one from every part of the country, regardless of tribe, clan, element, creed or economic status.

He himself set the example by taking an African name, wearing African dress and encouraging and promoting indigenous art and dancing. He brought the educated indigenous Liberians more and more into the local government system and by 1966, according to one authority, they had virtually taken over the running of their offices in the provinces. Those who were incompetent and corrupt were dismissed, even some of his close relatives. Furthermore, he extended legislative representation and suffrage to the indigenous people while the membership of the House of Representatives was increased to allow more of the interior people to enter the House. He also steadily appointed qualified indigenous people to appropriate offices. Socially, greater educational facilities were provided for the interior people, especially with the opening of the Cuttington College by the Episcopal Church with the assistance of the Methodist and Lutheran missions at Gbarnga, more than a hundred miles inland, while elementary schools were established in other districts by the Lutherans, Methodists and Episcopalians.

It should be obvious from the above that a great deal was accomplished in Liberia during the period under review. However, by 1960, all was not yet well. Life in the country was still dominated by the Americo-Liberian élite, while the policy of integration and national unification had really not been pushed far enough. Though the economy had improved significantly and had grown, this growth had occurred without real development, while the grip of international capitalism had become even tighter with mineral resources being exploited primarily to the advantage of foreign investors. In short, Liberia had by 1960 still a long way to go even to catch up with the achievements of some of the newly independent states of Africa. Unfortunately, during the next two decades neither Tubman nor his successor succeeded in really forcing through the changes needed, the result being the military *coup d'Etat* of 12–13 April 1980 which marks the end of an era, the era of the True Whig Party.

Conclusion

The period 1945 to 1960 was indeed a turning-point in the history of West Africa in particular and Africa south of the Sahara in general. Beginning from a position where colonialism seemed impregnable and destined to last for ever, it ended a mere 15 years later with its liquidation from not only a major part of West Africa but also from substantial parts of Central and Eastern Africa. It is equally evident from the analysis above that in the case of British West Africa and Portuguese Africa, the initiative throughout lay with the Africans themselves. This was even true of French Africa until de Gaulle's accession to power. It is also true that the pace in West Africa was set throughout by the British colonies in general and Ghana under Nkrumah in particular, and in French Africa by Guinea under Sékou Touré. Not only did Ghana's victory inspire her neighbours from 1957 onwards but, together with that of Guinea, inspired and accelerated the independence revolution throughout the whole of Africa south of the Sahara. But for the courageous and defiant stand of Sékou Touré with the full support of the workers and the students, French Africa would have emerged quite differently from what it is today. Indeed, the role of students and the trade unions in the independence struggle in French Africa, in particular, is now being recognized. Another significant feature of the independence struggle is that it marks a transfer of power not to the traditional ruling élite, as the British in particular had piously envisaged, but rather to the middle-class nationalists and, in some countries such as Ghana, not even to the upper but rather the lower strata of that class – the class of 'verandah boys', standard-seven school-leavers, junior civil servants, teachers and small traders. Finally, the independence struggle had a significant impact on Europe, which is also now being acknowledged. De Gaulle's accession to power and the overthrow of the fascist and racist dictatorship of Salazar in Portugal were the direct by-products of the anti-colonial struggle in Asia in general and in North-western Africa in particular, and these by-products, as Ali Mazrui has shown, have also changed the course of European history since the 1950s.

Finally, to conclude this chapter as we began, the independence struggle grew out of a world which had seen the defeat of fascism and Nazism, both based on racism and the denial of human rights and liberty. The successful outcome of the struggle therefore raised great hopes and expectations in Africa. How far, then, have these hopes and expectations been realized? Subsequent chapters in this volume will attempt to address this question.

Equatorial West Africa

ELIKIA M'BOKOLO

How many paradoxes were strewn over the long 'combat course' of the decolonization process for equatorial Africa! How many misunderstandings, too, lay in wait, and how many disappointments when the seemingly hardest and most decisive stages were passed!

First to fall under the colonial yoke, equatorial Africa was also one of the last parts of the continent to win free from it. Portugal's crafty seizure of the Kongo kingdom and Angola dates right back to the period of the 'discoveries'. And when modern colonial imperialism came to flourish in the late nineteenth century, it was consolidated in the Congo basin with the setting up in 1885, at the close of the Berlin Conference, of that curious legal construction and inexhaustible source of profit known as the 'Congo Free State'. On the other hand, the emancipation of the region was not to be completed until 1975 – 15 years after the great wave of accessions to independence.

Marked by unheard-of cruelties in the early days of colonization, equatorial Africa was to invent a wide variety of methods, techniques and ideologies to win its freedom. The turn of the last century is rightly remembered everywhere as the most distressing period. Anti-colonial protest 'blossomed here in a hundred flowers'[1] and was made apparent in all sorts of ways – peasant insurrections, politico-religious Messianism, political and parliamentary agitation, urban revolts and strikes, people's liberation wars.

Then the misunderstandings. Seldom have colonial powers been so reluctant to release their prey. Brazzaville, for instance, a symbol of freedom during the war, was in 1944 the scene of one of the most skilful moves in French colonialism, for the authorities – meeting in the 'capital of Free France' – while stating their firm intention to make far-reaching changes in colonial practices, decided 'to rule out any idea of autonomy, any possibility of development outside the French empire bloc [or] of instituting self-government in the colonies, even in the distant future'.[2]

---

1. Adapted from Mao Zedong's rallying-call: 'Let a hundred flowers blossom'; M. Zedong, 1966, p. 126.
2. For further details, see E. M'Bokolo, 1982, pp. 190–3.

Seldom, too, have peoples felt so sorely balked of their victories and their hopes: scarcely had independence been won, therefore, when they rose again to overthrow Abbé Fulbert Youlou's regime in Brazzaville and plunge the Congo (Zaire) into a terrible civil war, that lasted from 1960 to 1965.[3]

Post-war disturbances and uncertainties

The post-war years were marked throughout Central Africa by great popular excitement and, in some regions, by real political agitation.

Seen from the outside, of course, Central Africa still appeared to be the *'empire du silence'*, to borrow the title of a book by O. P. Gilbert dealing with the Belgian Congo.[4] For example, no Central Africans were present at the Fifth Pan-African Congress held in Manchester in October 1945, and it was an intellectual from British Togoland, Dr Raphaël Armattoe, who reviewed the economic, social and political situation obtaining in the Belgian, French and Portuguese colonies in that region.[5] But the silence only seemed to be such. The war years had in fact proved to be a time of particular distress (see Chapter 3). Everywhere more and more had to be produced and the colonial authorities did not hesitate to revert to the most brutal methods which had been employed at the end of the nineteenth century. The war effort bore particularly hard on French Equatorial Africa and the Belgian Congo. Moreover, those Africans who had taken part, voluntarily or under compulsion, in the military operations had had an opportunity of discovering new horizons and absorbing novel ideas – those from French Equatorial Africa in North Africa and Europe, those from the Belgian Congo in Ethiopia, Madagascar and Burma.

The new climate was obvious to all in the towns, where the impoverished masses of the industrial proletariat, the downtrodden workers and the dissatisfied and impatient 'educated' African classes already represented a real political force.[6] Revolutionary and reformist ideas from the outside world easily made their way in and found a sympathetic

3. F. Youlou (1917–72), ordained priest in 1946, entered politics in 1956 when he was elected mayor of Brazzaville. He became prime minister in 1958, then president in 1960, only to be overthrown in 1963, following a popular uprising in Brazzaville known as the 'Glorious Three' [days] on 13–15 August 1963.

4. O. P. Gilbert, 1947.

5. I. Geiss, 1974, p. 405.

6. There is far from general agreement among specialists on Africa regarding the issue of social classes, and this is not the place to add to the debate. Suffice it to say, quoting Engels, that the term 'proletariat' is used here to mean the class of modern wage labourers who, having no means of production of their own, are reduced to selling their labour to live. (See the note by F. Engels in the 1888 English edn. of the *Manifesto of the Communist Party*; K. Marx and F. Engels, 1955, p. 21.) The subproletariat comprised all those – for the most part recent urban immigrants – who had not yet found stable employment as wage-earners in industry.

audience in these strata of society. Angola received, mainly from Brazil, a great amount of literature about the Second World War, fascism and the national liberation struggles.[7] In the trust territories – the Cameroons, Ruanda–Urundi – public attention concentrated mainly on the principle of the right of peoples to self-determination, laid down in the Atlantic Charter, the United Nations Declaration and the United Nations Charter. In Brazzaville, Libreville and perhaps also in Bangui and smaller centres, communist study-groups were set up under the leadership of Europeans who were active members of the French Communist Party.[8] It may be mentioned, incidentally, that the first political parties to be set up legally at this time in French Equatorial Africa clearly showed their allegiance to the parties of France: in the Middle Congo even before the Second World War there was a local branch of the SFIO (the French Section of the Socialist International) led by Jacques Opangault, while the Congolese Progressive Party, founded in 1946 by Jean Félix-Tchicaya, became after the Bamako Congress (October 1946) a member of the RDA (*Rassemblement démocratique africain*), which was itself closely connected with the French Communist Party. The main Gabonese party, Jean Aubame's UDSG (*Union démocratique et sociale gabonaise*) obviously tried to keep very close to the French UDSR (*Union démocratique et socialiste de la résistance*) led by François Mitterrand. Only the MESAN (*Mouvement d'évolution sociale de l'Afrique noire*), founded in 1949 by Barthélémy Boganda in Ubangui-Chari, was entirely independent of the parties in France, although its ideas were largely based on those of the Christian Democrats. In Angola, colonial domination combined with the Salazar dictatorship prohibited the legal constitution of political parties. It was as underground formations and on the initiative of the Portuguese Communist Party that three revolutionary movements led by young intellectuals were set up in Luanda round about 1948: the *Comité Federal Angolano do Partido Communista Português*, the *Comissão de Luta das Juventudes contra o Imperialismo Colonial em Angola*, and the *Angola Negra*.[9]

The most significant activities in urban areas were, however, attributable to the local efforts of the Africans themselves. In Angola, several very active groups which were formed in the inter-war period were to maintain their pressure after 1945: the *Liga Nacional Angolana* and the

7. J. Marcum, 1969, p. 23.

8. Interviews with Paul Lomani-Tshibamba, Kinshasa, September 1981. Paul Lomani-Tshibamba (or Tchibamba), 1914–85, lived until the age of six in Brazzaville, where his father was a customs officer. His articles in *La Voix du Congolais* and his book *Ngando* got him into numerous difficulties with the Belgian colonial authorities and he went into exile in Brazzaville (December 1949–July 1961) where he became a French citizen and for ten years edited *Liaison*, French Equatorial Africa's first intellectual review. See P. Hazoumé and P. Lomani-Tshibamba, n.d.

9. J. Marcum, 1969, pp. 26–7.

ANANGOLA (*Associação Regional dos Naturais de Angola*), both particularly influential among the Luanda *mestizos*. The former worked
mainly for economic and social reforms, while the latter concentrated on
cultural action. In 1948, under the auspices of the ANANGOLA, a young
poet, Viriato Francisco Clemente da Cruz, founded a literary movement
whose members began to publish great numbers of anti-establishment
poems in the review *Mensagem*. This poetry from the *muceques*, or poor
districts of Luanda, was for long to represent the principal form of
social criticism and nationalist demands.[10] In the Belgian Congo, violent
revolutionary movements came to the fore as early as 1944: the very
serious unrest which was smouldering among the urban garrisons broke
out on 20 February in the Luluabourg mutiny. The revolt was crushed
but some of the mutineers managed to escape, to Katanga and Sankuru
among other places, where they planted the seeds of further insurrection.
Another mutiny broke out almost at the same time in Jadotville, while
in Elisabethville the colonial administration managed only just in time to
get wind of 'plotting among intellectuals' with the object of securing, in
line with the Atlantic Charter, 'freedom of speech and of the press',
'individual freedom, with the abolition of the chain and the whip, which
reduce us to the condition of beasts of burden', freedom of movement,
'provision of the education required for the intellectual progress of the
native population' and the right to political representation.[11] This violent
radical trend was to continue in the ensuing years, with the strike of
dockers in the seaport of Matadi in November 1945, marked by rioting
and bloodshed (seven deaths according to official figures).

At the same time, another, moderate and reformist trend gained ground
among the 'educated' population of the Belgian Congo. As early as March
1944, the 'educated' inhabitants of Luluabourg, taking advantage of the
dismay caused by the mutiny of the garrison, presented to the district
commissioner a memorandum demanding first and foremost 'that the
government recognize the existence of a social class of educated natives,
for the members of that class are convinced that they deserve a special
status, or at least special protection from the government, which will keep
them safe from certain measures or certain types of treatment which may
be applied to people who have "remained ignorant and backward"'.[12]
From then on, the claim for 'special status' polarized the energies of the
educated native population. It appears in most of the articles published
in the very important review, *La Voix du Congolais*, founded in January
1945, and in particular in the famous article '*Quelle sera notre place dans
le monde de demain?*' ('What will our place be in tomorrow's world?') by
Paul Lomani-Tshibamba, who suffered a long exile in Brazzaville as a

10. J. Marcum, 1969, pp. 22–6; R. Pélissier, 1978, pp. 240–3.
11. Memorandum quoted by J.-L. Vellut, 1983, pp. 504–6.
12. M. Makombo, 1977, p. 838.

result of it.[13] The UNISCO (*Union des intérêts sociaux congolais*), set up in 1945, took up the same theme. And in 1947 the senatorial mission sent to the Congo by the Belgian government received the same complaints from the educated inhabitants of Léopoldville and Paulis.

In the Cameroons, it was mainly the French part and the south that suffered from the effects of the war – shortage of staple commodities, requisition of labour for the plantations, for the development of the Douala–Yaoundé–Abong highway, for the working of the rutile and gold mines, and for rubber-tapping. The hesitations of Governor Nicolas and the reactionary conservatism of the colonists were the root causes of very serious clashes. In August 1945 the town of Douala was the venue for the 'Colonial States General', attended by delegates of the colonists of French Equatorial Africa, French West Africa and Madagascar, which attacked all the constructive aspects of the Brazzaville Conference and rejected *en bloc* all the proposed reforms.[14] On the other hand, in July 1945, a trades-union confederation, bringing together all the workers' organizations, had been set up and from the outset encountered combined opposition from the colonial administration, the Catholic clergy and the colonists belonging to the Chamber of Commerce and the ASCOCAM (*Association des colons du Cameroun*). The inevitable clash between these antagonistic forces occurred in September 1945 with the railwaymen's strike and the Douala riots. In the course of those riots, the railwaymen had support from the best-organized members of the working class – the very poorly-paid hired workers – and from the worst-exploited. Governor Nicholas authorized the European colonists to arm and to maintain law and order from 24 September to 9 October, thus legitimating a full-scale massacre. The judicial repression which followed was no less severe. In consequence it was not until 1948 that the first modern mass party was formed. This party, the UPC (*Union des populations du Cameroun*), was the creation of the trade unionist Ruben Um Nyobe and his lieutenants, Félix Moumié, Ernest Ouandié and Abel Kingue. Though affiliated to the RDA, the UPC, through its newspaper *La Voix du Cameroun*, launched a much more radical slogan than those of the RDA – 'Unification and immediate independence'. Appealing strongly to the working classes, the UPC gained a footing mainly among the lower strata of the urban population (in Douala and Yaoundé) and among the Basa and Bamileke in the southern half of the country.[15]

Little is yet known about the state of mind of the rural population, for want of sufficient research. What seems to have prevailed everywhere is an attitude of passive resistance to the representatives and symbols of colonization – administrators, missionaries, agents of commercial and

13. Reproduced in M. Makombo, 1977, pp. 842–53; see also fn. 8, above.
14. J. Suret-Canale, 1972, pp. 44–50.
15. R. A. Joseph, 1977, pp. 39–99.

agricultural companies. This was the case, in particular, in the regions in which Messianic and syncretic movements had developed between the two world wars. In the Belgian Congo, for instance, the Kongo populations remained faithful to the teachings of Simon Kimbangu (1881?–1951) despite the removal of the Prophet and his internment from 1921 onwards in Katanga, where he was to die. So too, as soon as it was founded in 1950, the Abako (*Association des Bakongo*) won the immediate, spontaneous, mass support of the population. In the Middle Congo, a similar movement had grown up under the name of Amicalism, or Matsouanism, started by André Matsoua. After Matsoua's death in 1942 and the terrible repression launched against his supporters, the Lari populations, who had been most receptive to his message, turned in on themselves and refused to take part in any way in elections or in modern political life up to 1956.

In places where Messianic movements did not spring up, there are plenty of signs of the opposition of the rural populations. In Gabon, for instance, the governor, who was worried by the growth of political interest in the towns, wanted to use the rural population and the customary chiefs against the town-dwellers. The first Pahouin Congress, convened for this purpose at Mitzik, 26–8 February 1947, backfired on the colonial administration: not only was it critical in its attitude towards the colonial power but by popular vote it recognized Léon M'Ba, the spokesman of the town-dwellers, as sole *N'Zoe Fang* (Chief of the Fang). This was the first indication of the alliance between townspeople and countrypeople which was to make the nationalist movements of Central Africa so strong during the 1950s.[16]

Economic growth, social change and social tensions

The decade that followed the Second World War was marked by a good overall world situation, the effects of which were felt in Central Africa. The colonial powers, in the process of rebuilding their economies, called still more on their empires. This led to quite remarkable and in some cases spectacular growth in the territories as a whole, though the colonial imperialist set-up designed for exploitation was not questioned in any way. In view of the inevitable discrepancies and inequalities in development, associated with the natural resources then known and the economic policies adopted, several types of growth and organizational structure have to be distinguished.

Most of the colonies had predominantly agricultural economies up to the time of independence. The development of capitalistic production relations was very slow and insignificant except in the zones that were settled by European colonists, who confiscated the land and reduced the expropriated peasants to the status of permanent or temporary agricultural

16. G. Balandier, 1963, pp. 198–203.

workers. The colonies were tied in with the international capitalist system through what has been described as '*l'économie de traite*' (predatory economy), that is to say, the linking up of a hegemonic commercial capitalist economy, dominated by the colonizers, with non-capitalist agricultural economies. In these circumstances, the territories concerned were confined almost exclusively to relations with the respective colonial powers.

Small territories regarded as poor in mineral resources, such as Equatorial Guinea, the Sao Tome and Principe Islands, Rwanda and Burundi lent themselves best to this type of economic exploitation. Only the Sao Tome and Principe Islands had a plantation (*roças*) economy, dominated by European absentee landlords (*roceiros*) of large estates worked by contractual labour imported in great numbers from Cape Verde, Angola and Mozambique. Elsewhere production was in the hands of small farmers and their families.[17] Coffee, cocoa, bananas and oil-seeds were the principal exports from Sao Tome, Principe and Equatorial Guinea. In the last-named colony, these products were purchased by the Spaniards at high prices (double the world market price for cocoa, for example). Represented as generosity on the part of the Spaniards, this price system was actually due to Spain's desire to avoid the drain of foreign currency that would have resulted from the purchase of these products outside its empire. Rwanda and Burundi were in a special situation owing to the very high density of their population. The efforts made by the farmers finally got the better of the famines, the last of which occurred in Rwanda in the 1916–31 period, and even produced exportable surpluses of Arabica coffee and tea.

This agricultural economy was also to be found in the larger territories – the Cameroons, French Equatorial Africa and Angola. The active prospecting that the colonial companies had engaged in since the end of the war had not yet located any significant mineral resources except in Angola. A distinct improvement was brought about in the situation of French Equatorial Africa, which had been neglected by the state – 'the Cinderella of the French Empire' was M. Devèze's apt term for it[18] – and literally bled white, if we may put it so, by the concessionary companies. Following the schemes put forward at the Brazzaville Conference, a ten-year plan was drawn up, to be financed by the Overseas Territories Investment and Development Fund, FIDES (*Fonds d'investissement et de développement économique et social des territoires d'Outre Mer*). Between 1947 and 1956, French Equatorial Africa received 51 344m CFA francs, which were used mainly for the development of infrastructure.[19] Foreign trade therefore continued to draw on the agricultural sector (wood in Gabon and the

17. R. Pélissier, 1979, pp. 211–27.
18. M. Devèze, 1948, p. 1.
19. E. M'Bokolo, 1982, p. 195.

Middle Congo, cotton and coffee in Ubangui-Chari). The FIDES was also active in Cameroon: although agriculture remained the basis of the economy (cocoa, 50 per cent of the country's exports; bananas and coffee, 20 per cent, in 1955), small industry began to develop, based on the production of aluminium (the Edéa hydro-electric and metallurgical complex owned by *Alucam*, in which the French company Péchiney–Ugine had a dominant 82 per cent interest) and on the processing of fats. At the time of independence, this emerging industry already represented 10 per cent of the national product.[20] A similar process was under way in Angola. Agriculture was still the principal source of foreign currency thanks to coffee (40 per cent of exports in 1962: the second-highest production in Africa, after that of the Côte d'Ivoire) and to various natural products (sugar-cane, oil-seeds, cotton, wood). But the mining industry was steadily developing: besides diamonds, already mined before the war, iron and oil were mined after 1945. Portugal was, of course, anxious to remain the first to benefit by this tardy development: in 1960, Portugal supplied 50 per cent of Angola's imports and the setting up of a common market for the *escudo* zone in 1962 consolidated this integration still further.

In Angola itself, the European sectors of the economy gained most from growth. White immigration increased significantly after the war; moreover, the number of Europeans living in Angola rose from 44 083 in 1940 to 78 826 in 1950, 172 529 in 1960, 290 000 in 1970 and about 335 000 in 1974.[21] Many of these people, of course, were originally from the lower classes – tradesmen, agricultural workers, small farmers; ignorant and illiterate and accordingly lacking in ambition and initiative. For them Angola was a land of unhoped-for material success. In the 1959–64 six-year plan, three-quarters of the investments were accordingly allocated to the development of sectors controlled by the colonists. After the war, a measure of economic internationalization[22] began to occur and was to develop further after 1962, with the investment of British, American and South African capital and increased trade with all the OECD countries.

In contrast to these predominantly agricultural countries, only the Belgian Congo had an economy that had already come fully into the

20. R. A. Joseph, 1977, pp. 111–18.
21. G. J. Bender, 1978, p. 229.
22. The process known as 'internationalization' differs from 'dependence'. 'Dependence' refers to the particular process whereby African countries became part of the international capitalist economy. Beginning as early as the sixteenth century in parts of Central Africa, it became widespread during the colonial era. The economy of a colony was, therefore, first and foremost a dependent economy. In the context of the favoured relations between the colony and the colonial power, this dependence was defined in relation to such a power. In a few exceptional cases, the colonial power found itself obliged – for one reason or another – to yield to other capitalist countries in matters of investment and trade: a process here referred to as 'internationalization'.

industrial age. As early as 1930, the Congolese economy showed the predominant features which were to remain the same right up to independence: extraversion and disarticulation; concentration on particular sectors (mining and transport – 70 per cent of capital investments) and regions (dynamic role of the mining provinces of Kasai and Katanga); capital investments in the colony controlled by a very few financial groups (75 per cent of the capital being owned by four groups – *Société Générale*, *Empain*, *Cominière* and *Brufina* – including 60 per cent by the *Société Générale* alone); active participation by the colonial state in the economic sector, both directly (through its own companies, particularly in the transport sector, and through its interests in the private sector) and indirectly (through the authoritarian mobilization of manpower).

The growth of the Congolese economy, brought to a sudden halt by the economic crisis of the 1930s, started off again with increased vigour as a result of the Second World War and, after 1945, of the overall international situation and that of the colony itself. A phase in which the colonial economy was built up, was succeeded by what I have already suggested calling the 'phase of extended reproduction of the production structure'.[23] This phase was marked by three outstanding features:

(1) a very substantial growth of the mining sector (index 100 in 1950; 175 in 1959), enabling the big colonial firms to reach the stage of self-maintained growth as a result of the reinvestment of a fairly small part of their rising profits and to increase the real wages of the African workers;[24]

(2) an appreciable development of the domestic market as a result of a general improvement in wages (Africans earned 5000 Fr. on the average in 1945 and 18 000 Fr. in 1952; Europeans earned 260 000 Fr. in 1945 and 450 000 Fr. in 1958),[25] since the state, industries and plantations, prompted by social and political considerations, followed the example of the mining sector, combined with a definite increase in farmers' incomes; and

(3) the development of the industrial sector (index 100 in 1950, and 260 in 1956), some industries being closely associated with the export sector (mines and plantations), while others were replacing imports, and still others, which had made a hesitant appearance prior to 1930, were experiencing spectacular growth which triggered off development in many areas (food, tobacco, textile and building industries).

In 1958 cash-crop agriculture represented only 44.6 per cent of the gross domestic product, whereas mining represented 19.8 per cent, industry for

23. E. M'Bokolo, 1981a, p. 5.
24. J.-L. Lacroix, 1966, p. 22.
25. F. Bézy *et al.*, 1981, p. 38.

export 18.8 per cent and industry for the home market 16.8 per cent.[26] Despite these achievements, the Congolese economy retained all the features imposed on it by the colonial regime – constant recourse to compulsion and very great inequalities between Africans and Europeans. In 1958, while Africans represented 99 per cent of the total population of the colony, they controlled only 5 per cent of capital investment and accounted for only 55 per cent of wages, 69 per cent of consumption and 12 per cent of private savings.[27]

The social changes accompanying these economic changes are, of course, too numerous for them all to be even briefly mentioned here. The economy is, in any case, not the only factor involved in change: the general development of schools and of government departments must also be taken into account. The very extent of these changes suggests that, besides the always uncomfortable experience of a reclassification of individuals in the new social registers imposed by colonization, the situation contains all the elements of a real crisis.[28]

One of the most spectacular signs of this crisis was the drift to the towns, which provided evidence of the old familiar crisis of agrarian societies while at the same time triggering the new crisis of urban societies. Urbanization was particularly rapid in the Belgian Congo, where the proportion of town-dwellers increased from 8.8 per cent in 1938 to 14.8 per cent in 1945 and 24 per cent in 1955.[29] Less sudden elsewhere, it was no less uncontrolled, leading everywhere to the formation of a working-class proletariat and, even more, a huge mass of exploited workers,[30] which increased dramatically after the reversal of overall economic conditions in the mid-1950s. In Angola, for instance, in 1960 one African out of three lived in a makeshift dwelling in a town or its outskirts. The *senzala* or 'native quarter' of Lobito had a population of 20 000 in 1954, but there was only one tap with running water for 1200 people, and in the two primary schools in these districts there were only 250 places in all.[31] The *muceques* or shore-side shanty towns of Luanda were still more wretched.

In French Equatorial Africa, the proletarianization of the population, which was not very noticeable before the war because of the economic system in force, speeded up after 1945. Generally speaking, the number of wage-earners rapidly increased since, according to official estimates, there were 108 600 in 1947; 189 500 in 1949; 193 000 in 1950; 155 000 in

26. J.-L. Lacroix, 1966, p. 31.
27. F. Bézy *et al.*, 1981, p. 11.
28. For the Belgian Congo, see the analysis by M. Merlier, 1962, pp. 89–103, 145–64 and 231–49.
29. *ibid.*, p. 147
30. See fn. 6, above.
31. I. B. Kaké and E. M'Bokolo, 1979, p. 111.

1952 and 1953; 135 600 in 1954; and 190 000 in 1958.[32] The variations in these figures show just how vulnerable this social category is, affected as it is by the slightest veering of the overall situation. In these figures, manual workers and labourers are by far the largest group: in 1949 there were 39 150 'semi-skilled workers and labourers' and 142 500 unskilled workers; in 1958 these figures had dropped to 34 600 and 98 500 respectively. There was considerable unemployment: 16 000 of the 33 000 male adults living in Brazzaville were unemployed in 1956. In the urban centres of the Cameroons and the Belgian Congo, the picture was the same.

The drift to the towns, while bringing them manpower, also drained the country areas of their work-force and of their most dynamic elements, the young people. But conditions in the agrarian societies varied greatly from one region to another. There was, for instance, no comparison between the relative affluence of the Beti-Bulu cocoa-planters and the increasing poverty of the Basa farming community in Cameroon.[33] Similarly, in French Equatorial Africa about 1952, the average annual income of the majority of farmers fluctuated between no more than 1800 and 2100 CFA francs, whereas that of an industrial worker was in the region of 36 000 francs.[34] Only a few fortunately-situated regions were better off: the Woleu-Ntem region in Gabon, owing to the cultivation of cocoa, and above all the southern Congo, where the farmers could regularly dispose of what they produced to an exceptionally dense network of towns (the Pointe-Noire–Dolisie–Jacob–Brazzaville axis), with many small shop-keepers taking their produce and a good transport system (roads, Congo–Ocean railway). So far as the Belgian Congo was concerned, a fraction of the farming community (about 2500 families in 1952) advanced from the stage of small-scale commercial production to that of small-scale agrarian capitalism, particularly in the Lower Congo, the Kasai and Kivu: many had benefited from the measures taken by the colonial power to bring into being 'indigenous farming communities' (making private individual ownership of the land easier, providing financial and technical assistance).[35]

The last major aspect, with lasting consequences, of this process of social change was the formation of a small black bourgeoisie.[36] In some cases, the inequalities of economic development and educational policy resulted in the lower middle classes being drawn mainly from certain regions. For instance, in the seaboard countries, where relations with Europeans dated back a long way in the coastal districts, it was in fact the people from the coast, educated in mission schools or state schools, who largely supplied the lower middle class of salaried officials and clerks.

32. E. M'Bokolo, 1981b, p. 401.
33. R. A. Joseph, 1977, pp. 124–41.
34. E. M'Bokolo, 1981b, pp. 398–403.
35. E. M'Bokolo, 1981a, pp. 10–11; F. Bézy *et al.*, 1981, pp. 41–5.
36. For a general account and case-studies, see E. M'Bokolo, 1981a and 1981b.

This was the case with the Duala in Cameroon, the Myene from the Gabonese coast, the Vili of Loango and the blacks and *mestizos* of Luanda and Lobito (Angola). In the Belgian Congo, there was a similar disparity to the advantage of the southern savannahs (Bas-Congo, Kwango, Kwilu and Kasai in particular) as compared with the northern forest areas (the Oriental and Equateur provinces, especially the latter). In any case, the vocabulary of the period reflected the advent of this new class: the terms 'literate' and 'educated', which were very fashionable in the 1940s, were replaced by expressions with more precise sociological connotations and a richer sociological content: 'middle classes', 'ruling class', 'bourgeoisie', and so on. It is by no means certain that the colonial authorities actually created this class. At all events, they tried to use it as a moderating element at a time of rising political tensions. It is in this sense that the recommendation that the colonists of the Belgian Congo made to the colonial government is to be interpreted:

> An educated native class must be organized, who will endorse the ideals and principles of our Western civilization and, with equal standing, will be our equals in rights and obligations; fewer in numbers than the native population at large, but powerful and influential, they will be the allies that we need to find among the indigenous communities. These middle classes will be the black bourgeoisie that is beginning to emerge everywhere, which we must help to grow rich and to become organized and which, like bourgeois everywhere in the world, will be against any sort of upheaval either from within or from without. There will no longer be any race differences but, as in all the countries of the world, there will simply be class differences, the classes remaining open to all.[37]

Figures from which the real weight of this class can be measured are not yet available for all the countries concerned. In the Belgian Congo, where the services of the colonial power made quite sound estimates, some sources reckoned that, in 1958, there were 176 600 people out of a total population of 13 million belonging to these middle classes, comprising 31 642 'white-collar workers', 110 220 skilled and semi-skilled workers, 2335 foremen, 1430 members of the liberal professions, 19 710 shopkeepers and 11 259 self-employed craftsmen. Other estimates, however, put the figure at 300 000.[38] On perusal of these figures, nevertheless, it will be noted that the proportion of employees, possessed of the knowledge and skills dispensed by the colonial schools, greatly outweighed that of the entrepreneurs, whose initiative found no scope in the constricted and discriminatory system of colonization. These key personnel were to lead the independence movements. The conclusions already reached with

37. A 'confidential' note, published in 1959 and cited by M. Makombo, 1977, p. 187.
38. E. M'Bokolo, 1981a, p. 3.

regard to the Belgian Congo and French Equatorial Africa are no doubt significant with regard to the whole of equatorial Africa. Table 8.1, showing the occupational background of politicians in French Equatorial Africa (AEF), demonstrates the undeniable predominance of the lower middle class.

Colonial practices: continuity and breaks with the past

As soon as the war finished, the clearest thinkers among the colonizers appreciated that a new age had begun. In the Belgian Congo, for instance, where there had not as yet been any question of decolonization, the governor-general, Pierre Ryckmans (1934–46), wrote in 1946: 'The days of colonialism are over'.[39] This remark was echoed in French Equatorial Africa six years later in an important speech by Governor Paul Chauvet to the Grand Council:

> Whether we like it or not, these educated people will have gradually to take over from the old élites and customary authorities. If they do not do so with us and under our supervision, they will inevitably do so without us and in opposition to us.[40]

These statements recognized shrewdly enough the structural transformations that had occurred in local societies and the irreversible changes that had come about in the psychology, attitudes and aspirations of the community and of individuals. New policies adapted to this situation were, however, worked out piecemeal, with each colonial power taking action in terms of its own traditions, the internationally recognized status of the territory under its domination, the local balance of strength and what it believed to be the opinion of the 'natives'.

The policy followed by the French in French Equatorial Africa was in keeping with its overall African policy, though with undeniable particularities. French Equatorial Africa had the advantage of the 'great emancipation laws'[41] passed by the Fourth Republic in its early days: abolition of forced labour; recognition of trades unions and setting up of an inspectorate of labour; abolition of indigenous rights of citizenship and granting of French citizenship to Africans without detriment to their personal status in their own countries; institution of local assemblies in Gabon, Middle Congo and Ubangui-Chari and of a Grand Council in Brazzaville, while French Equatorial Africa also sent several parliamentary representatives to the French National Assembly and the Council of the French Union. Despite the fact that the majority of Africans did not have the vote and that the electorate was divided into two colleges up to

39. *ibid.*, p. 6.
40. E. M'Bokolo, 1981b, p. 400.
41. Phrase used by P. Aujoulat, 1958, p. 263.

TABLE 8.1   *Politicians in French Equatorial Africa, occupational background*

	French Equatorial Africa		Middle Congo
	1952	*1957*	*1946–60*
Europeans			
Businessmen	32	28	12
Planters, timbermen	13	3	1
Civil servants	18	10	8
Liberal professions	6	7	2
Journalists	–	3	4
Unspecified	–	1	1
Africans			
Physicians (Dakar Medical School)	–	6	2
Primary-school teachers	10	34	25
Nurses	9	20	5
Senior administrative personnel	1	7	3
Clerks and administrative employees	33	36	18
Technicians	1	8	5
Secretaries of chiefs	–	2	–
Chiefs and prominent members of the population	18	14	4
Persons employed in the private sector	13	19	25
Workers	–	2	5
Shopkeepers, restaurant-keepers	9	13	10
Planters, timbermen	8	11	4
Journalists	–	1	1
Other self-employed persons	1	1	1
Ex-servicemen	3	3	1
Clergymen, priests	1	2	4
Students	–	–	1
No occupation	–	–	1
Unspecified	–	2	14
Total	176	233	157

Note: In the case of French Equatorial Africa this covers members of the National Assembly and of the Council of the French Union, members of the Grand Council and of the territorial councils (1952) with the addition, for 1957, of the mayors and deputy mayors of the fully-fledged communes and members of government councils. In the case of the Middle Congo, the sample also includes unsuccessful candidates in election to these bodies and party leaders.

Sources: Annuaire politique de l'AEF (1952 and 1957); J. M. Wagret, 1963, pp. 233–47; and E. M'Bokolo, 1981b, p. 400.

1956, effective political life began: political parties came into being and the parliamentary elections of 1946 and 1951 and the territorial elections of 1947 and 1952 gave rise to far-reaching democratic discussions among the different sections of opinion.

These advances were not, however, achieved without difficulty and resistance. The colonists, of whom there were relatively large numbers in Gabon and Ubangui-Chari and who were efficiently defended by the chambers of commerce, were violently against the new policy. In 1946, the Bangui Chamber of Commerce had no hesitation about protesting formally to the governor-general in Brazzaville that:

> The measures just adopted are appropriate only for populations less backward than those of French Equatorial Africa. The abolition of forced labour is clearly interpreted here as legal recognition of the right to do nothing. . . . A swift drop in cotton production is to be feared. . . . No one who knows these countries can believe that an enactment will be enough to bring about a sudden change in the mentality of the black man.[42]

The administration itself, in which there were still many 'old colonials', was in no hurry to put the new measures into practice and continued to increase the humiliations imposed on both the people at large and the élites. These included the covert maintenance of forced labour; harassment of politicians thought to be over-independent, in particular the deputy for Ubangui-Chari, Barthélémy Boganda, who was sentenced in 1951 for 'incitement to riotous assembly' and threatened with loss of rights; and support for moderates, like those who, in the Middle Congo, founded a short-lived section of the Gaullist RPF (*Rassemblement du peuple français*).[43]

In the Belgian Congo, the legendary paternalism of the colonial authority continued to be the backbone of policy in regard to the Africans. Until the mid-1950s, this policy was the joint product of three structural systems – the colonial administration, the big firms and the Catholic missions – so closely connected by such manifold and inextricably interwoven ties that they were dubbed, together, the 'colonial trinity'.[44] We have already referred to the relations between the state and the leading companies, including the 'companies of 1906', the *Union minière du Haut-Katanga*, *Forminière* and the BCK (Bas-Congo–Katanga railway) which dominated the economy of the colony. The Catholic missions, for their part, continued to enjoy the benefit of the agreement signed in 1906 between Léopold II and the Vatican. The weight they carried in the colony was considerable, as attested by the 1958 figures: 669 mission stations; 6000 European missionaries, assisted by 386 brothers and 745

42. Quoted by P. Kalck, 1973, p. 475.
43. E. M'Bokolo, 1982, pp. 198–200.
44. C. Young, 1965, pp. 10–32.

sisters of the teaching and nursing orders; 25 560 black catechists. The chief prelates of the colony, Mgr Roelens and Mgr de Hemptine, were the busiest architects of the colonial ideology, while the missionaries were over-represented in the 'Colonial Council' which, from Brussels, master-minded the framing and application of colonial policy. The influence of the missions was further increased by the existence of many associations of former pupils which continued to keep a firm hold on the modern élites well after their school-days were over. One of the main associations of this kind, the ADAPES (*Association des anciens élèves des Pères de Scheut*), which was founded in 1925, had some 15 000 members in 1950.[45] The missionaries kept very closely in touch with the work of these associations since, in the absence of parties, which were prohibited by law, they really served as a laboratory in which most of the future leaders of the national movement were produced.

Following the disturbances of 1944–5 and the demands made by the 'educated natives', the colonial authority conceded a few reforms. These reforms, which disregarded the political aspect of post-war agitation, changed only minor aspects of life and society: recognition of trade unions; establishment of bodies for contact between employers and their black workers (indigenous works councils, local committees of indigenous workers, participation in regional and provincial commissions concerned with indigenous labour and social progress); setting up of a welfare fund; and, in particular, the granting of 'civic merit' cards and the system of registration which enabled card-holders (1557 'civic merit' and 768 'registered' cards in 1958), after humiliating probationary tests, to enjoy certain privileges reserved for Europeans.[46] Nothing fundamental was otherwise changed despite the appointment of black representatives to the provincial councils and the government. The Belgians continued to apply their maxim 'No élites, no trouble!'. It was not until 1952 that a black man from the Congo was authorized for the first time to attend a Belgian university.

The regimes established by the Portuguese in Angola and Sao Tome and Principe and by the Spaniards in Equatorial Guinea fell between the Belgian and the French practice, for while people were theoretically treated on the same footing, there was in fact no move away from narrow paternalism and the *status quo* in any respect. The official doctrine of the Portuguese, first expressed in 1912, proclaimed that 'Angola must be considered a Portuguese nation rather than a colony'.[47] Salazar's *Estado Novo* was to reaffirm this in the 1930 Colonial Act and the constitution of 1933. The act distinguished between the 'non-assimilated' and the 'assimilated'. The latter, who enjoyed all the rights pertaining to

45. M. Makombo, 1977, p. 54.
46. *ibid.*, pp. 83–135.
47. I. B. Kaké and E. M'Bokolo, 1979, p. 78.

Portuguese citizenship, in particular the right to vote, were required, among other obligations, to be able to read and write Portuguese, to give up the communal way of life, to be loyal to the state and, if they were *mestizos*, to have been born in wedlock. The number of *assimilados* remained very small; there were 91 548 (24 221 Africans, 23 244 *mestizos*, 44 083 whites) out of 3 737 947 inhabitants, including 3 665 000 blacks in 1940; and 135 250 (30 089 blacks, 26 335 *mestizos*, 78 826 whites) out of 4 145 163 inhabitants, including 4 037 000 blacks in 1950.[48] While all whites and 90 per cent of the *mestizos* had the status of *assimilados*, that privilege was extended to barely 1 per cent of the blacks. The other 99 per cent were *indigenatos* and therefore subjected, among other things, to forced labour since, under the terms of the Labour Code of 1899, blacks were 'under a legal and moral obligation to earn by their work the means of subsistence and of improving their social condition'.[49] The Spanish *patronato de indigenas* system was little better. Devised in 1904 and reformulated in 1938, it was based on the conviction that blacks were morally, mentally and legally under age. Hence, a long series of restrictions, such as the rule that blacks could not without authorization engage in transactions involving more than 2000 pesetas. Emancipation cards were issued by the Curadoria but, despite the fact that almost everyone received basic schooling, the number issued remained very small.

The situation of the mandated territories was clarified and in theory improved after the end of the war, with the founding of the United Nations which, though taking over from the League of Nations, did not simply carry on with the mandate system unchanged. The territories formerly held under mandate became 'trust territories' and Article 76 of the United Nations Charter provided that the powers concerned should 'promote . . . their progressive development towards self-government or independence'. By means of the 'visiting missions', UN supervision was more closely exercised and open encouragement was given to the sending of petitions or delegations by Africans. But the pace and pattern of actual change varied from one territory to another. In Cameroon, the French part received the social and political reforms granted by France to the whole of its part of Africa; but progress towards autonomy was slower there than in Togo, which was made an 'autonomous republic under trusteeship' by the basic law of 23 June 1956, while Cameroon had to await a vote to this effect by a majority of its legislative assembly on 28 January 1957.[50] In Western Cameroon, which was administered by the United Kingdom, the change took a long time to materialize since the British had joined the territory with Nigeria and it was not until 1954, when a federal government was established in Nigeria, that there was any

48. G. J. Bender, 1978, p. 151.
49. I. B. Kaké and E. M'Bokolo, 1979, p. 78.
50. R. A. Joseph, 1977, pp. 171–201.

clear prospect of internal autonomy.[51] In their 'trust territories' the Belgians carried on their pre-war policy, the avowed objective of which was to 'rationalize' and 'modernize' political structures by regrouping chieftaincies, turning traditional leaders into civil servants and democratizing the councils of the kings of Rwanda and Burundi. The effect of these often somewhat clumsy measures was to increase the tension in both countries between the Tutsi and the Hutu.[52]

Progress towards independence

The diversity noted in the political practices of the colonial powers was echoed in the ways in which independence was gained. For while in three cases – French Equatorial Africa, Spanish Guinea and the Belgian 'trust territories' – decolonization was effected amicably, following more or less arduous political bargaining, in the two cases of Cameroon and Angola it took a war of liberation to force the colonial powers to negotiate. The Belgian Congo represents an intermediate situation, with decolonization negotiated between the opposing political forces, though the negotiations were possible only as a sequel to scattered uprisings which were prevented from turning into a full-blown revolutionary war by the actual opening of the discussions.

In French Equatorial Africa, the gradual move towards independence was controlled throughout by the French authorities, the main local parties in most cases merely following the process as onlookers.[53] This was due to the sociological features of the local political formations, drawn mainly from among clerical workers and civil servants; in short all the categories of the emerging lower middle class, which succeeded only to a very limited extent in mobilizing the masses. The only notable exception was the MESAN, founded in Ubangui-Chari by Barthélémy Boganda. The 'educated natives' had misgivings about that party, which earned them among the public at large the scathing nickname of *mboundjou voko* ('white Negroes'). Drawing its leaders and active party members from among lower-paid employees, the urban masses and the farming population in the bush, the MESAN was obliged to provide itself with a relatively elaborate ideology, particularly in the economic and social fields, where at a very early stage it proposed the formation of co-operatives.[54] The African parties of equatorial Africa nevertheless enjoyed real popular support, partly on account of their affiliation (except in the case of the MESAN) to the RDA, whose alliance with the French Communist Party

51. T. Eyongetah and R. Brain, 1974, pp. 123–42.
52. R. Lemarchand, 1970, pp. 118–79 and 315–23.
53. See E. M'Bokolo, 1981b and 1982, for further details.
54. See P. Kalck, 1977.

was regarded as the surest sign of a progressive attitude,[55] and partly because of the particularly reactionary line taken by the French colonists, who long demanded nothing but the maintenance of quite outdated structures and practices.

The high commissioner Paul Chauvet, whose government (1951–8) covered this crucial period, was adroit enough to take the most appropriate steps to break 'White racism . . . still as deplorable and dangerous for the maintenance of law and order'[56] and to win over the African élites. These measures included banning the familiar '*tu*' habitually used by Europeans when addressing blacks, inviting prominent Africans as a matter of course to official and private ceremonies, liberally awarding study grants, and systematically recruiting young people with secondary and higher education for local positions of responsibility in French Equatorial Africa. As a result, when the basic law was passed in 1956, the African élites enthusiastically accepted political autonomy but without any hostility towards France and without any desire to break the structural relationship with the former colonial power. In August 1958, a few weeks before the Gaullist referendum instituting the 'Community', on which they recommended an affirmative vote, these élites sent a long petition to General de Gaulle in which they extolled the 'civilizing work' of France in French Equatorial Africa and the principle of 'independence in freely accepted interdependence' for the former colonies. They reserved the right ultimately to call for independence, essentially because, they said, they 'suffered from an inferiority complex *vis-à-vis* the former British colonies which had become independent States'.[57] One of the essential questions then was whether, after independence, the federal institutions would or would not be maintained. Barthélémy Boganda became the most ardent, and at once the most perceptive and the most visionary advocate of the federalist scheme. As the president of the Grand Council of French Equatorial Africa, he proposed more than a very close federation between the four former French colonies. That federation, under the name of the 'Central African Republic', was to be the first step towards what he called 'the United States of Latin (or Central) Africa', including also the Belgian Congo, Cameroon, Angola, Rwanda and Burundi. The scheme came to nothing largely because of Gabon, which reacted in the same way as the

55. The RDA was less strong and its policy more fluctuating in French Equatorial Africa than in French West Africa. Its firmest allies were the *Parti progressiste tchadien* of Gabriel Lisette (Chad) and the *Mouvement mixte gabonais* of Léon M'Ba (Gabon). Founded in 1946, these two parties from the outset formed sections of the RDA. In the Congo, the RDA had as its section the *Parti progressiste congolais* led by Jean Félix-Tchicaya from 1946–57 and, from 1957 on, the *Union démocratique de défense des intérêts africains* led by Abbé Fulbert Youlou. Concerning Cameroon, see note 65, below.

56. These views, expressed in 1954, thus related to an evil recognized very late; see E. M'Bokolo, 1982, p. 203.

57. Petition published in full in *Marchés Tropicaux du Monde*, 6 September 1958.

Côte d'Ivoire in West Africa had done a short time previously and as Kenya in East Africa was later to do: being the least poor country, Gabon was afraid of having to shoulder the financial burden of the future federation. Boganda's death in a mysterious plane crash on 29 April 1959 sounded the death-knell of all the federalists' hopes. The territories of French Equatorial Africa consequently advanced separately towards independence.[58]

The later independence of Equatorial Guinea and that of Sao Tome and Principe also came about under the fairly close supervision of the colonial powers, Spain and Portugal. In Equatorial Guinea, nationalist demands first began to be voiced in 1950, when the *Cruzada Nacional de Liberación* was founded. Led by Acacio Mañe, a planter from the Bata region, its members comprised the agents of the colonial administration, in particular the teachers who, since 1945, had been calling in vain for an improvement in their salaries. Spain's sole response was to maintain a stone-walling, repressive attitude, designed to preserve the *status quo*. After Spain joined the UN in 1955, it was the subject of repeated attacks by the Afro-Asian group, but was protected by the veto constantly exercised by the United States of America. A terrible wave of repression culminated in the assassination of the two most prominent nationalist leaders, Acacio Mañe (1958) and Enrique Nvó (1959); hundreds of Guineans fled into exile in Gabon and Cameroon. As a result, the two major parties formed in 1959, the MONALIGE (*Mouvement national de libération de la Guinée Equatoriale*) and the IPGE (*Idée populaire de Guinée Equatoriale*), had their most active officers and rank-and-file supporters abroad, particularly in Cameroon. The establishment of these bases abroad also helped, incidentally, to foster the annexationist claims of certain Nigerian and Cameroonian parties on the Rio Muni and in Fernando Poo. After 1960, the support given by the newly independent states to the Guinean parties proved decisive. Faced in addition by growing social unrest, particularly on the part of civil servants, Spain gradually gave way. In 1963, it recognized the political parties, before conceding self-rule in 1964. The constitutional conference which met in 1967–8 agreed to the need to grant independence, which was proclaimed on 12 October 1968.

The accession to independence of the major Central African states stimulated in turn the process of emancipation of Sao Tome and Principe, where the first major mass movement to emerge had been put down harshly in 1960. In 1964, the OAU recognized the Liberation Committee of Sao Tome and Principe, which eight years later was transformed into the MLSTP (the Liberation Movement of Sao Tome and Principe). After the bloodless coup of 25 April 1974 (the 'Revolution of the Carnations'),

58. The Congo on 15 August 1960; Gabon on 17 August 1960; and the Central African Republic on 13 August 1960.

Portugal negotiated a timetable of emancipation with the MLSTP, and independence was proclaimed a year later, on 12 July 1975.

In Rwanda and Burundi, at that time united under the name of Ruanda–Urundi, the United Nations, as the trusteeship authority, played its role to the full. The complications which marked the final colonial decade saw growing ethnic tensions that colonial practice had inevitably encouraged and was unable to contain.[59] In Rwanda, the educated Hutu élites took advantage of the change in attitude of the Catholic missionaries about 1955 to launch an attack on the Tutsi, who not only made up the political aristocracy but had also been systematically placed by the Belgians in responsible religious and administrative posts. The Catholic newspaper, *Kinyamateka*, which had been published in Kinyarwanda since 1933, became their mouthpiece after Grégoire Kayibanda (Hutu) succeeded Alexis Kagame (Tutsi) as editor-in-chief in 1957. He made 'Hamitic neo-feudalism' his favourite target. In March 1957, shortly before the arrival of the UN 'visiting mission', nine Hutu intellectuals published a forceful and widely noticed *Manifesto of the Bahutu, Note on the social aspect of the indigenous racial problem in Ruanda*.[60] Its content, which was hostile to the 'political, economic, social and cultural monopoly of the Tutsi' and favourable to the 'genuine advancement of the Bahutu', supplied the ideology of the parties then coming into being, APROSOMA (Association for the Social Promotion of the Masses) and PARMEHUTU (Party of the Hutu Emancipation Movement). The Tutsi reacted by clinging on to their privileges, which gave rise to the very serious clashes that took place in November 1959, sparked off by the Hutu (with 200–270 killed, over 1200 arrests and some 7000 other disaster victims). These ethnic tensions were no less real in Burundi but did not there erupt into violence. The political parties, founded from 1958 onwards, were formed along ideological rather than ethnic lines. This at least is what was overtly suggested by their names: the Party of Unity and National Progress (UPRONA, with its motto 'God, King, Burundi'), the Association of Burundi Democratic Progressives, the Rural Democratic Party, and the African National Union of Ruanda–Urundi, founded by expatriates returning from Tanganyika and modelled on TANU.

It was not until 10 November 1959 that the Belgian government, affected by events in the Congo, specified the stages which were to lead the two trust territories to emancipation.[61] Far from easing the tension, this statement by the Belgian government merely whipped up passions

59. R. Lemarchand, 1970, pp. 118–96 and 324–42.
60. This group was coordinated by Grégoire Kayibanda. For the text of the *Manifesto* and a full list of its authors, see *Ruanda Politique, 1958–1960*, 1960, pp. 20–9. The expression 'Hamitic neo-feudalism', very much in vogue at the time, was popularized by the sociologist Jacques Maquet.
61. Rwanda and Burundi, 1 July 1962.

in Rwanda. The period from November 1959 to July 1962 was marked by very serious clashes, particularly at the time of the June 1960 and August 1961 elections, each leaving scores of dead and driving thousands into exile. An additional complication came from the Belgian government, which, breaking with its traditional policy, started systematically backing the Hutu, while the United Nations was torn between these contradictory positions. The local government elections of June–July 1960 were a triumph for the Hutu (with 2390 seats out of 3125 for PARMEHUTU and 233 for APROSOMA) and a crushing defeat for the Tutsi RADER Party (*Rassemblement démocratique ruandais*, 209) and UNAR (*Union nationale ruandaise*). The government formed in the following October reflected that ratio with six Hutu and two Belgian ministers out of the total of eight). On 20 January 1961, the Belgian government, prompted by the United Nations General Assembly, decided to postpone indefinitely the elections scheduled for 28 January. The people's response was the 'Gitarama *coup d'Etat*' carried out on that same 28 January: the elected communal representatives, accompanied by some 25 000 people, met at Gitarama and proclaimed the deposition of Mwami Kigeri V (who had already left Rwanda in May 1960), the establishment of the republic, the

PLATE 8.1   *Mwami Kigeri V, the last king of Rwanda*

immediate election of a government and a head of state, and the adoption of a constitution. The general elections, which were held in September 1961 under UN supervision, subsequently legitimized the *coup d'Etat*. Upon independence, Rwanda separated from Burundi, where the Belgian government was glad indeed not to have to contend with ethnic tensions. This did not prevent the administrators on the spot from increasingly engaging in delaying tactics. At the local government elections in 1960, for example, UPRONA, which was feared for its uncompromising nationalism, was in all probability sabotaged and won 19 per cent of the seats. But it won a sweeping victory in the general parliamentary elections of September 1961 (with 56 seats out of 62) held under UN supervision. Internal autonomy was granted by the Belgians in December 1961 and a United Nations commission prepared the way for independence but did not succeed in preserving the union between Rwanda and Burundi, which had been desired by the UN but was unanimously rejected by the governments of the countries concerned.

In the Congo, once the violent uprisings of the immediate post-war period were over, the need to become organized was felt still more acutely. But political parties were still banned. The Congolese consequently adopted two specific forms of organization which were to have lasting effects on the country's political and social future: the associations of former pupils and the traditional societies. Those associations, already long established, such as ADAPES (*Association des anciens élèves des Pères de Scheut*), ASSANEF (*Association des anciens élèves des Frères des écoles chrétiennes*) or the *Cercle Saint-Benoît* of Elisabethville (Lubumbashi), then entered their golden age: the young Congolese élites, thus kept under the constant patronage of the missionaries, contracted the very bad habit of approaching the consideration of society – and later of policy – by proxy, handing the whole business over to obliging advisers. The colonial authorities also tolerated the existence of ethnic cultural associations, which were essentially inoffensive to them since their membership was limited and they maintained or accentuated divisions among the Congolese. New associations of this kind included ABAKO (*Association des Bakongo*) and the *Lulua-Frères*. Colonial practice nevertheless ran into serious difficulties from about 1955 onwards, when the secular policy of the new minister for the colonies, Auguste Buisseret, broke the alliance between state and Church, causing the latter to criticize the colonial undertaking, albeit in moderate terms. The language dispute between Flemings and Walloons also spread to the Congo and so brought the divisions among the colonizers to public notice.

The African élites nevertheless continued to believe in the colonialist ideology and, in particular, in the doctrine, still formulated as a promise, of Belgian–Congolese community, as can be seen from the book written by Patrice Lumumba at that time, *Le Congo terre d'avenir est-il menacé?* (Is the Congo, land of the future, threatened?). It was a relatively obscure academic, Professor A. A. J. Van Bilsen, who, no doubt involuntarily, set the debate going again and prompted some Africans to adopt radical positions, by publishing the very soon famous *Plan de trente ans pour l'émancipation politique de l'Afrique belge* (Thirty-year plan for the political emancipation of Belgian Africa) in December 1955–January 1956.[62] The Congolese immediately responded by two manifestos: that of the Catholic group, *Conscience africaine*, which accepted the statement of the problem and the timetable set out in the *Plan*; and that of ABAKO, from then on led by the former seminarist Joseph Kasavubu, which bluntly concluded that 'Since the time has come, emancipation must be granted forthwith rather than delayed for another thirty years'.[63] The colonial government made the concession of organizing local elections in December 1957 in the major cities. But by skilfully imposing restrictions on these elections in the indigenous districts, it saw that the Congolese were left engaged in a profitless debate in which they had to fight among themselves and not against the colonizers, the effect of which was to accentuate ethnic divisions. Political parties nevertheless began to emerge on that occasion. In October 1958, Patrice Lumumba founded the *Mouvement national congolais* (MNC), which was the only major party that had a truly national base. Among the people at large, the social crisis, which had been simmering since the situation drastically worsened about 1957, exploded in the insurrection of the African quarters of Léopoldville (Kinshasa), 4–7 January 1959. Despite the severe repression, colonial rule collapsed.

The Belgian authorities, who had never seriously contemplated de-colonizing their empire, hastily improvised and pushed through the emancipation of the Belgian Congo. A 'round-table' conference held in Brussels in January 1960 set the date of independence at 30 June of that same year. The Congolese élites were nevertheless sharply divided on many points: less on the future structure of society than on the form of the state and the policy line of the regime. On these bases – and largely without regard for the people's aspirations – regionalists and nationalists, federalists and unitarians, moderates and radicals confronted one another. The solution adopted, a shaky compromise, did no more than temporarily stave off major conflicts. The head of state, Joseph Kasavubu, represented the regionalist, federalist and moderate trends, while the head of the government, Patrice Lumumba, embodied the nationalistic, unitarian, radical and pan-African aspirations. The inevitable conflict broke out immediately after independence, giving rise to frustration among the people at large and a very long civil war.

In Cameroon and Angola, wars of liberation brought home to the colonial powers the necessity of granting independence.

The UPC (*Union des populations du Cameroun*) incited and spearheaded

---

62. The text of the *Plan* can be found in A. A. J. Van Bilsen, n.d., pp. 164–202.
63. These two manifestos are reproduced in *Congo 1959*, pp. 9–21.

PLATE 8.2   *From left to right: Joseph Kasavubu, president of Congo, Prime Minister Patrice Lumumba, and King Baudouin of Belgium, in Léopoldville, Congo, June 1960*

PLATE 8.3   *Three of the leaders of the UPC (Union des populations du Cameroun): from left to right, Ernest Ouandié, Félix Roland Moumié and Abel Kingue*

the national struggle in Cameroon.[64] The French administration was unsuccessful in its efforts to encourage the emergence of rival formations, which were both short-lived: a *Bloc démocratique camerounais*, holding Christian-Democrat views, founded in 1951, and a *Union socialiste camerounaise*, which came into being in 1953. The UPC was a front rather than a monolithic party, as regards both its membership (intellectuals, trades-unionists, downtrodden workers in the towns, poor farmers from the Sanaga region, well-to-do Bamileke planters and shop-keepers) and its ideology, since the doctrine of its founder, Um Nyobe, was mainly nationalistic, while that of Félix Moumié and Ernest Ouandié was Marxist-inspired.[65] The party was also able to broaden its following through its close links with the *Union des syndicats confédérés*, close to the French *Confédération générale du travail* (CGT), and its own 'mass organizations', the *Union des femmes du Cameroun* (UDFC) and the *Jeunesses démocratiques du Cameroun* (JDC) in particular. The setbacks suffered by French colonialism in 1954, with the defeat at Dien-Bien-Phu and the outbreak of the Algerian revolution, prompted the UPC to launch a vast offensive the following year, which culminated in the 'bloody week' of 22–30 May 1955. The repression was severe, the number of dead being put officially at 25, though in fact five times as many were killed. The UPC and its subsidiary organizations were dissolved,[66] but they continued none-the-less, with Um Nyobe taking to the bush 'like Mao Tse-tung and Ho Chi Minh', while Félix Moumié was active in arousing international opinion. The small moderate parties that the legal action of the UPC had prevented from developing took advantage of its dissolution, winning the 1956 elections, which the UPC had called upon people to boycott. Cameroon, which was promoted to the status of an 'autonomous republic under trusteeship' in 1957, then had a government headed by Mbida with Ahmadou Ahidjo as vice-president. In the same year, Ahidjo founded the *Union camerounaise*, to which several regional parties rallied but which kept its hard core in the north, from which he came. The UPC, which had been pronounced dead, sharply reminded people of its existence by launching a fresh insurrection in September 1957, first in the Sanaga coastal area and subsequently in the Bamileke region. France was called upon to intervene and 11 months of 'pacification' were needed before Um Nyobe was arrested and executed. The security situation then seemed good enough for a proclamation of independence (1 January 1960). But

64. R. A. Joseph, 1977, pp. 171–331; see also J. F. Bayart, 1979, pp. 54–108, and Mongo Beti, 1972.

65. After the break between the RDA and the French Communist Party in October 1950, relations between the UPC and the RDA became purely nominal. However, the UPC was not excluded from the RDA until 2 July 1955, at the meeting of the RDA Coordinating Committee. See R. A. Joseph, 1977, pp. 186–8 and 190–2.

66. The RDA also took the opportunity to repudiate the UPC and break all ties with it.

the UPC's underground resistance groups were still active in the Bamileke region, and attacks even took place frequently in Douala and Yaoundé. Furthermore, the legal opposition was active, since the new constitution, put to a referendum, was accepted by 800 000 voters but rejected by another 530 000. It took the intervention of five French battalions, the assassination of Félix Moumié in 1960, and a plot discovered at just the right time in 1962, to reduce the underground resistance and get rid of the legal opposition. But the end of the civil war was not proclaimed until 1972 and the compulsory pass for travel between towns was abolished only in 1975. Meanwhile the reunification with the southern part of the British Cameroons had taken place. The Cameroon National Democratic Party of John Ngu Foncha won the 1959 elections in the south of the British territory and got the United Nations to organize a referendum in February 1961 throughout the British trust territory. The north then voted to unite with Nigeria while the south opted for reunification with the former French Cameroons. This was made official by the constitution of 1 October 1961 establishing the Federal Republic of Cameroon.[67]

In Angola, the post-war movements were quickly muzzled: the newspaper *Mensagem*, with its highly nationalistic motto '*Vamos descobrir Angola*' ('Let us discover Angola'), was banned, along with the ANAGOLA, which published it, and the other cultural and political associations. In Portugal itself, however, a number of young intellectuals, many of them close to the Communist Party, such as Mario de Andrade, Francisco Tenreiro and Agostinho Neto, kept the nationalist flame alive. These various underground groups gradually grew into true political parties: the UPNA (Union of the Peoples of North Angola), founded in 1954, subsequently becoming the UPA (Union of the Angolan Peoples) and later the FLNA (National Liberation Front of Angola); the MPLA (People's Liberation Movement of Angola), set up in 1956 by activists, many of whom came from the Angolan Communist Party and from the Party of the Struggle of the Africans of Angola.[68] The first serious disturbances broke out in 1959 and 1960, following the convulsions of the emancipation process in the Belgian Congo, where many Angolan emigrants or exiles were living. The very violent repression resulted in mass arrests, admirably described in the fine short story by Luandino Vieira, *The True Life of Domingo Xavier*. In 1961, rebellion erupted in several places: at Luanda on 4 February; at the Congo (Zaire) border in the north on 5 March; and in the Baixa de Cassange at about the same

67. T. Eyongetah and R. Brain, 1974, pp. 128–66.
68. As they were clandestine, the number of these parties, apparently large, is uncertain and their early history much disputed; see, for example, J. Marcum, 1969, pp. 27–30 for the MPLA, and R. Pélissier, 1978, pp. 259–96 for the FNLA and the 'ethnic-nationalist' groups. J. Marcum (pp. 347–9) gives a deliberately incomplete but representative and clear table of the main nationalist movements between 1944 and 1962.

time. The Portuguese reacted with extreme violence and their repression left a great many victims: between 30 000 and 50 000 dead, and 150 000–200 000 Angolans, mostly from the north-west (Bakongo), forced into exile in the Congo (now Zaire) in the space of a few months.[69] Following this setback the military front became stabilized: while the Portuguese army was getting bogged down in the economically and financially ruinous[70] repression of an interminable guerrilla war, the differences between the nationalist movements grew and were even brought out into the open for all to see. Despite the growing support for Portugal from its NATO allies,[71] however, this war, added to those in Guinea-Bissau and Mozambique, eventually undermined the Portuguese economy and Portuguese society and created a political malaise which exploded into the bloodless coup of 25 April 1974, 'the Revolution of the Carnations'. This broke the stalemate, since the Armed Forces Movement, now wielding power in Portugal, was determined to speed up the process of decolonization.

Among the Portuguese imperial possessions, however, the case of Angola was particularly complex. What was to be done about the 335 000 Portuguese, including some 172 000 colonists, a third of whom had been born in the colony and for whom the Portuguese economy, far less advanced than those of its European neighbours, could not provide jobs? To which African movement should power be transferred? The three that existed were deeply divided and the differences in their membership, sociological composition and ideological standpoints were compounded by ethnic tensions. Led by the lower middle classes of the towns, the FLNA and UNITA (National Union for the Total Independence of Angola, founded in 1966 by FLNA dissidents) had gained a footing mainly in rural areas and along distinctly ethnic lines, the former appearing as the spokesman of the Kongo and the latter as that of the Ovimbundu. With its much broader social coverage and firmer roots in the towns, the MPLA alone had a national base. Furthermore, the country's resources in agriculture, mining and oil – the latter concentrated in Cabinda and the source of a strong local identity – aroused the cupidity of the great powers. It was only on 15 January 1975 that the Alvor Agreement, signed between the three movements and the Portuguese government, fixed the date for independence.[72] But disagreements immediately re-emerged. From February to July 1975, the 'Battle for Luanda', won by the MPLA, enabled the MPLA to drive its rivals out of the capital. Independence

69. For a full account, see R. Pélissier, 1978, pp. 301–664.
70. See M. de Andrade and M. Ollivier, 1971.
71. J. Marcum, 1969, pp. 181–90; M. de Andrade and M. Ollivier, 1971, pp. 93–122.
72. 11 November 1975 – i.e. at roughly the same time as Mozambique (25 June 1975) and Sao Tome and Principe (12 July 1975), but later than Guinea-Bissau (24 September 1973).

was proclaimed on the scheduled date, but in the greatest confusion – at Luanda by the MPLA and at Huambo by the FLNA and UNITA. Civil war took over from the war of liberation. The OAU, which was divided (22 voting in favour of the MPLA and 22 against, with Ethiopia and Uganda abstaining), was a passive spectator of the fratricidal struggle. After a series of military successes (January–March 1976), the MPLA made the People's Republic of Angola a member of the OAU (11 February 1976) and of the United Nations (November 1976). But several regions were still outside the control of the central authorities.

The struggle for political sovereignty in Eastern Africa, 1945 to independence

Michael TWADDLE *in collaboration with*
Lucile RABEARIMANANA *and*
Isaria N. KIMAMBO

'Eastern Africa' for the purposes of this chapter includes not only the former British-ruled colonies of Kenya, Uganda, Tanzania (then the separate territories of Tanganyika and Zanzibar), Malawi (then Nyasaland), and Zambia (then Northern Rhodesia), but the great island of Madagascar previously administered by France along with the Comoro Islands and Reunion, and also the islands of Mauritius and the Seychelles formerly governed by Britain. During the Second World War, Kenya became the centre of Britain's East African empire, especially after the fall of Singapore to the Japanese, and differences between the 'haves' and the 'have-nots' increased dramatically as the country's importance as a source of raw materials and food for Britain's wartime effort increased. These growing internal differences were to be a crucial cause of the single most important example of anti-colonial insurgency to erupt anywhere in tropical Africa against British colonial rule: the Mau Mau rebellion. But five years before that particular rebellion broke, the French colonial presence on the great island of Madagascar suffered a shock – also intimately influenced by the global crisis of the Second World War – in the shape of the insurrection of March 1947.

Madagascar[1]

There had been organized resistance in Madagascar to French colonization from its very beginning, and some southern areas of Madagascar did not lay down their arms until some ten years later. Before the First World War a secret nationalist society was founded in Tananarive, the *Vi Vato*

1. This section is based upon an initial draft by M. Twaddle, one based upon original research by L. Rabearimanana, and a final precis and revision by M. Twaddle: the views expressed are essentially those of L. Rabearimanana. The section depends primarily upon J. Tronchon, 1983; L. Rabearimanana, 1980a and 1980b; R. Litalien, 1975; C. Cadoux, 1969; P. Boiteau, 1982; A. Spacensky, 1970; and R. W. Rabemananjara, 1952.

Sakelika or VVS, the Malagasy initials for 'iron-rock-greenstem'.[2] In the inter-war period, the national movement concerned itself mainly with demanding equality of rights between Malagasy subjects and French citizens. The French were prepared to offer full citizenship rights to selected Malagasies much more generously than was then customary in neighbouring British colonies on the African mainland. However, as the survival of VVS and its transformation after the Second World War along with other secret associations into something politically much more serious indicates, while French assimilative policy succeeded temporarily in creating a pliable Malagasy collaborating élite, as a long-term strategy it failed. Indeed, French colonialism in Madagascar stimulated cultural nationalism amongst the indigenous people paralleled in intensity in British-ruled areas on the African mainland perhaps only amongst Mau Mau insurgents in Kenya. But the French were not working purely by themselves in this endeavour; they were unwittingly building upon the earlier cultural renaissance of nineteenth-century Madagascar discussed in Chapter 10 of Volume VII. It was the Second World War, however, that enabled élite nationalism in Madagascar to fuse with mass discontent.

This happened for several reasons. Global war was a traumatic experience affecting all European colonies in Africa, but on Madagascar the traumas of war were further radicalized by the indignities of defeat. In 1940 the French administration there declared for Vichy, and immediately Madagascar became a target for the British and the Free French. In 1942 the great island was successfully invaded and, while governor-generalship of Madagascar was handed over to a Gaullist nominee, the British in fact remained on Madagascar until 1946. This was deeply damaging to French colonial prestige. Amongst ordinary islanders, post-Vichy rhetoric also clashed with the hard facts of post-Vichy life. All European colonies in Africa suffered from shortages of imported goods during the Second World War and the consequent inflation, and Madagascar's position as an occupied island after 1942 created further problems of foreign exchange. In 1943–4 there was a serious famine. The price of rice, the staple food, went sky-high. The *Office du Riz* became extremely unpopular, some farmers paying enormous prices to buy back food they themselves had grown and earlier sold at lower prices. While there was much talk about a better deal for colonies after the Atlantic Charter of 1941 and the Brazzaville Conference of 1944, it was easy for nationalist leaders on the great island to argue persuasively after the war that 'colonization was simply exploitation'.[3]

---

2. *Vi vato*: i.e. iron and stone, symbols of the purity and steadfastness desired for the organization by its founders, combined with the fact that the society is divided into *sakelika*, i.e. branch or section: thus the acronym VVS. See UNESCO, *General History of Africa*, vol. VII, pp. 221–48.

3. Quoted by J. Tronchon, 1983, p. 125.

Admittedly, immediately after the war the hated *indigénat* system of forced labour was abolished, and political representation in Paris accorded to Madagascar along with other French colonies. In this the French were far more generous than their British counterparts in Eastern Africa (it is difficult to conceive of Jomo Kenyatta, for example, being elected to London at this time as a parliamentary representative for Kenya!). However, while prepared to go further within the more generous traditions of a Greater France, there was a point beyond which metropolitan Frenchmen became exceedingly intransigent compared with British – the point of total independence, which the British had already accepted. And it was independence which Malagasy delegates to the French parliament demanded after the Second World War. The Saintenay–Ho Chi Minh Accord of March 1946, which 'recognized the Democratic Vietnam Republic as a free state, having its own government, parliament, army and finances, as part of the Federation of Indo-China within the French Union', prompted the two Malagasy deputies to Paris also to table a bill making Madagascar into 'a free state', having its own government, parliament, army and finances, within the French Union.[4] The bill was immediately attacked as 'anti-constitutional' and lost during the dissolution of the first constituent assembly. But it was a precedent. It was also an example of French intransigence which convinced many Malagasy nationalists that all the reforms of the immediate post-war period were really a fraud, a mere 'patching-up' (*'replâtrage'*) of earlier French colonialism.[5]

The local context and the international situation following the Second World War therefore led to a decisive stepping-up of nationalist demands, and from 1945 until 1960 the nationalists campaigned for independence. This ambition was not confined to the politicians of Tananarive or other cities but spread into the heart of the country and the coastal regions and was shared by both upper- and lower-income groups. Above all, it found expression in a political party: the *Mouvement démocratique pour la rénovation malgache* (MDRM).

The MDRM had come into being in Paris in February 1946, under the leadership of the two deputies elected to the French National Assembly in 1945 by the second electoral college – that is, by the indigenous voters in Madagascar, voting rights being dependent upon a property qualification at this time. Nonetheless, the MDRM spread rapidly throughout Madagascar in urban and rural areas and among all social classes. Its success was principally due to its programme being presented as immediately realizable. However, a rift developed gradually between the rank-and-file and the MDRM leadership as the deputies started talking about a 'free

4. N. Heseltine, 1971, p. 174; J. Tronchon, 1983, p. 127.
5. J. Tronchon, 1983, p. 129; '*L'Union française n'était donc qu'un "replâtrage" de l'empire colonial français*'.

state' within the French Union, as already noted. This caused some MDRM militants to join secret societies – the JINY[6] and the Malagasy national party (PANAMA). These were organized by the nationalists who were convinced that France would not easily grant independence, thereby making its achievement by force inevitable. Nevertheless, this did not prevent the MDRM from achieving increasing electoral success through-out the island, which caused concern to the leading figures in the coastal areas attached to France and to the existing regime. In July 1946 they founded the *Parti des déshérités de Madagascar* (PADESM).

The PADESM drew its members from the leading citizens of the coastal areas and it opposed the MDRM most vigorously. It deliberately identified the MDRM with the Hova, in other words with most of the people living closest to Tananarive, and made its appeal to the seventeen other ethnic groups of Madagascar, excluding the Hova. It recruited members on an ethnic basis. The French administration, worried about the rise of Malagasy nationalism in its MDRM form, made haste to give its active support to the PADESM.

In late 1946, following the election of three deputies to the legislative assembly, all of whom were from the MDRM, measures began to be taken against the party. Newspapers were curtailed. MDRM members and leaders were arrested on the flimsiest excuses. Also throwing them-selves into the fray, French settlers in the coastal areas ill-treated workers belonging to the MDRM and had no scruples about harassing its local leaders. The provincial elections of January–February 1947 thus took place in an explosive atmosphere. Tension was further increased by the colonial authorities' interference in the proceedings. Nonetheless, despite this, most of the elected provincial councillors came from the MDRM. Conflicts between differing shades of political opinion became fiercer. Rumours of an imminent uprising abounded. When it actually occurred, on 29 March 1947, the French authorities and the Malagasy people in general were only half surprised.

On 29 March uprisings occurred in the eastern part of the island, in Moremanga, Manakara and elsewhere. However, in cities like Tananarive, Fianarantsoa and Diego Suarez the movement was ineffectual. But in the eastern upland region insurrection spread rapidly, the rebels continuing to gain ground until July 1947 and controlling a large part of the Tanala and Bezzabozano area. However, because of difficulties of communication between them and the fact that they were surrounded, the insurgents were forced into a more defensive position after August. The uprising was only finally suppressed by French colonial troops in November 1948, well over a year later.

---

6. The Jiny is a night bird. The fact that its name was given to a secret society founded during the war clearly indicates a determination to escape surveillance by the French authorities.

There were many reasons for the uprising in Madagascar in 1947, among them the experiences of wartime which not only increased the sufferings of the people but also persuaded Malagasy nationalists that independence could be demanded and obtained for the island with foreign (especially British and American) help.[7] The principal explanation, however, was the unstoppable growth of the desire for independence amongst an ever-increasing number of Malagasy people after the Second World War, and their membership of the MDRM.

The political success achieved by this political party, and the uneasiness its success aroused in French colonial officials were such that, at the start of the insurrection, French officials declared that the MDRM was behind it. This belief was also shared by the French settlers and the PADESM. The inhabitants of the Tananarive area, the Hova, too were attacked as being behind the insurrection; only the Hova really wanted independence, so it was believed, and the insurgency in the coastal areas was simply the means by which power was to be seized. This flew in the face of the facts, and disregarded the yearning for independence that by now was widespread amongst Malagasies from every social and ethnic background. Many white settlers in rural areas now took the law into their own hands. Immediately the insurrection erupted, however, MDRM deputies declared that they could not be held responsible for either the preparation or the outbreak of unrest. Similarly, nationalist newspapers defended the Hova people and pointed out that they had always served the cause of colonization, too. They were also quick to point out how attached Malagasies were to French culture.[8]

A spirit of repression quickly spread throughout Madagascar soon after the insurrection began. The leaders and even ordinary members of the MDRM were arrested, and the party itself was dissolved on 10 May 1947. In addition, all other parties (including the PADESM) were proscribed. Court hearings were held throughout the island. The Tananarive trial of November 1948, the most notorious of all, resulted in six death sentences, two of them for former MDRM deputies Joseph Raseta and Joseph Ravoahangy, and several terms of hard labour for life.

Who was really behind the insurrection? The colonial administration, French settlers and the PADESM all believed that it was the MDRM. MDRM members themselves, and French supporters of the party in France, considered the events of 1947–8 to have been due to provocation by a colonial administration bent on doing everything it could to get rid of that troublesome party. On the other hand, the view of those actually involved in the insurrection, as recorded by the historian Jacques

---

7. J. Tronchon dwells at length on the causes of the insurrection. C. Guérin du Marteray's unpublished thesis (Nice, 1977) on the longer-term causes of the insurrection is also valuable for insight into the severe character of colonial exploitation in Madagascar.

8. See L. Rabearimanana, 1980a, p. 143.

Tronchon, was that it was a genuine nationalist movement that arose out of the firm resolve of some Malagasies to throw the French out of Madagascar – Malagasies, moreover, who were convinced that only armed struggle would enable them to achieve this end.

It is commonly held that Malagasy nationalism was stamped out by this colonialist repression, which caused the death of close to 100 000 Malagasies,[9] but this is untrue. The insurrection of 1947 was a bitter failure, but Malagasy nationalists did not give in. Even between 1948 and 1956, a period when repression was especially harsh, the ambition to achieve independence persisted and found expression principally in newspaper articles published in the capital. They demanded, not only that the country should be granted the desired status, but also that an amnesty should be declared for the numerous victims of post-insurrection repression.

Those demanding the status of 'free state' were few in the immediate aftermath of the insurrection, but as the local political situation became calmer and the French regime less repressive an increasing number of Malagasies supported it. France's setbacks elsewhere within the French Union – in Vietnam and North Africa especially – also contributed to renewed boldness by Malagasy nationalists. The most spectacular support now given to Malagasy nationalism was undoubtedly that of the Roman Catholic hierarchy, which in November 1953 officially recognized the legitimacy of popular demands for independence. This declaration was followed by direct support for the nationalist movement, given to the moderate wing of it so as to frustrate its communist sympathizers. Increasingly thereafter the nationalist movement followed a haphazard course. There was no single unifying organization. Politicians were divided more by personal rivalries than by ideological differences. However, in 1956 the situation changed again as an outcome of the war in Vietnam, the beginnings of the national liberation struggle in Algeria, the influence of the 1955 Bandung Conference, and the coming to power of a socialist government in France. It was after the 'framework law', passed as a result of these influences, that a number of differing political parties were founded locally.

Prominent among the moderate parties founded at this time was the *Parti social démocrate* (PSD), established in Majunga in December 1956 by Philibert Tsiranana and André Resampa. It spread first to the western and northern parts of Madagascar and soon had sections all over the island thanks to the goodwill of a colonial administration ready to help a left-wing offshoot of the PADESM and the satisfaction with the institutional changes introduced by the 'framework law'. There was also Antoine Zafimahova's *Union démocrate et sociale de Madagascar* (UDSM)

9. This is the figure given by High Commissioner de Chevigne at a press conference in 1949.

whose following was in the south-east and the Fianarantsoa area. It was a party with very moderate political demands, mostly concerned with the social measures needed in coastal areas.

Between 1956 and 1960 there was a broad political spectrum in Madagascar. This made inter-party rivalry more violent, and election campaigns more heated. The formation of the Rev. R. Andrianamanjato's AKFM (*Ankotonny Kongreiny Fahaleovantenan Madagasikara*) in 1958 as one of the most radical parties increased the inter-party militancy of the period.[10] The local colonial authorities constantly said that they had no intention of interfering in elections, but nonetheless irregularities were widely committed by lower-level French officials, while those thinking of voting communist were threatened with excommunication. Nationalists nonetheless won a majority of seats in a few places such as Tananarive, Tamatave, Diego Suarez and Talear. At the provincial elections in March 1957, however, they lost ground. Responsibility for this can unquestionably be attributed to the French colonial administration, religious authorities and white settlers; but disunity amongst nationalists themselves also contributed to their downfall.

When General de Gaulle organized a referendum on continued membership of the French Community in September 1958, the 'ayes' triumphed in Madagascar. The 'nays' were in a majority in the capital and well-represented in Tamatave and Diego Suarez also, but the pressure brought to bear by the French administration and moderate politicians was so great that the advocates of complete independence from France were defeated. In June 1960, when Madagascar finally became independent, the party which gained most from it was the *Parti social démocrate* of Philibert Tsiranana. Those who had fought for complete independence from France earlier now found themselves in the parties of opposition, amongst them the *Parti du congrès de l'indépendance*[11] and the *Mouvement national pour l'indépendance de Madagascar*.[12]

To evaluate fully the struggle for political sovereignty in Madagascar requires a more detailed picture within which not only the respective strengths and weaknesses of Malagasy nationalism and French colonialism may be examined adequately, but also one within which their successive interactions may be analysed intelligently. Here, despite some useful work,[13] much further research needs to be undertaken in Madagascar as

10. In the inter-war period, the AKFM had been associated with the Communist Party in France, and during the Second World War both parties were suppressed. The 1958 AKFM, though radical, tried to avoid being called a Marxist party. See V. M. Thompson and R. Adloff, 1965, p. 87 and p. 105.

11. This party is commonly called AKFM after the initials of its Malagasy name.

12. This party was founded in November 1958 by Monja Jaona. Originally based in the south, it subsequently spread throughout the country.

13. In addition to the sources already cited, there has been research on the Jiny secret society, conducted at the University of Tananarive. See also, R. Archer, n.d.

well as on the immediately adjacent African mainland and islands.

Forces for change in British-ruled areas

Immediately after the Second World War, Britain had a Labour government committed to sweeping socialist reforms at home as well as change in the colonies. Like their socialist and communist counterparts in France at this time, the British Labour Party saw no contradiction between these two objectives.[14] In retrospect, matters appear differently. The sheer scale of the economic and social plans for post-war development in East and Central Africa have been described by two British historians as amounting to a 'second colonial occupation' of the area,[15] and can be seen to have had a far more disruptive effect upon the stability of British colonial rule there than the token representation of one or two Africans in local legislative assemblies of which British politicians made so much at the time. For, while the British in East and Central Africa did not have the problems of defeat and loss of prestige to cope with that the French encountered in Madagascar, they too had problems of economic devastation at home as a consequence of the Second World War. East and Central Africa, therefore, had considerable importance for Britain's post-war economic recovery, in bridging the dollar gap through the sale of colonial produce and raw materials on the world market.[16]

Uganda[17]

Uganda in 1945 differed from Madagascar in several ways. Besides being a land-locked territory rather than an island, it was governed not only by a victorious European colonial power but also one whose policy had been to preserve rather than to destroy the leading pre-colonial polity within its borders, the Buganda kingdom. Uganda and Buganda were of course not geographically the same, there being several smaller kingdoms and peoples in the western section of the Uganda Protectorate, not to mention the many kingless societies in the north and east of the territory. But the British in Uganda had based their rule upon Buganda, recognizing its quasi-autonomy and introducing an unusual form of quasi-freehold land tenure through the Uganda Agreement of 1900, and they based their administration of many other areas of the Uganda Protectorate upon Buganda intermediaries.

Ugandan nationalism as it developed in reaction to British colonialism had therefore what seemed to be a contradictory character, sometimes

14. See D. Goldsworthy, 1971.
15. D. A. Low and J. M. Lonsdale, 1976, p. 12.
16. See M. Cowen, 1984, pp. 63–75.
17. C. Gertzel, 1976, provides fuller narrative and references.

identifying with the greater glory and autonomy of the Buganda kingdom, at other times reflecting the multifarious grievances of ethnic groups occupying other areas of the British protectorate. Wartime rhetoric about defending the rights of oppressed nationalities in Europe, like the Poles, served to enhance the force of these ethnic demands for a status comparable to Buganda. But the greatest impact of the Second World War upon Uganda probably lay less in the ideological fillip given to local cultural nationalism than in the more obviously material grievances to which global conflict gave rise in both urban and rural areas.

To understand fully these tensions within Uganda in the 1940s, one has to take into account the various interest groups which were created by the colonial system itself. They reflected the fragmented character of the élite – or the petite-bourgeoisie – in Uganda. Its three main fragments had particular interests which tended to be in harmony only over the short run and, in terms of forming nationalist struggle, also tended to be complicated by ethnic and religious divisions. The first fragment consisted of the civil servants whose main grievance was racial discrimination in pay scales when compared with their British and Asian counterparts. The second group was that of cash-crop farmers who were full of resentment against cotton-ginners (who were mainly Asians) and state marketing boards for creaming off a substantial part of their surplus product. The third fragment consisted of the traders who were demanding an end to state-protected monopoly privileges granted to certain Asian and British companies. Over and above these fragments of the petit-bourgeois class, were the urban workers who were demanding higher pay. All these interests coalesced in the historic mass opposition to colonial order in the 1940s.[18]

In January 1945 there were serious riots in several Ugandan towns over low wages and rising costs of living caused by wartime inflation. Tensions associated with the austerity programme, introduced by the Buganda provincial government during the 1930s depression, also led to the assassination of its chief minister later in 1945 as well as further complicating the riots earlier in the year. The British response to these disturbances was repression which proved severe enough to arouse widespread sympathy for those detained unjustly, but which was insufficient to destroy their political credibility to any serious extent because – unlike in Madagascar after the 1947–8 disturbances – these particular political detainees were released comparatively speedily. In 1949 many of them were associated with further disturbances in the Buganda kingdom, caused mainly by excessively low prices paid to local cotton-growers compared with those that the British Treasury was benefiting from on the world market, and in 1952 many were associated also with the founding of the

18. For more detailed information, see M. Mamdani, 1976, ch. 7; D. W. Nabudere, 1980, ch. 8.

Uganda National Congress (UNC) by Milton Obote and its policy of 'self-government now'.

The formation of the UNC was the first attempt to create a nationalist movement (with mass support) uniting many sections of the élite in Uganda. Yet, although leadership came from Buganda, the UNC gained strength in regions of Uganda where there was a cash-crop-growing peasantry but which had no significant segment of rich farmers (*kulak* formation), such as in Teso, Bukedi, Lango and Acholi. The main leaders were traders, teachers and civil servants. But in 1955 territorial nationalism in Uganda received a paradoxical setback. Andrew Cohen, the new socialist governor who has been seen by some historians as the architect of political independence for Britain's West African colonies,[19] quarrelled with the *Kabaka* of Buganda over the future development of Uganda as a unitary state; the *Kabaka* was deported to Britain; and overnight the *Kabaka* became the hero of anti-colonial resistance in Uganda rather than (as during the 1949 riots) one of its local allies. The Buganda farming élite turned to the UNC in large numbers between 1953 and 1955, when the restoration of the *Kabaka* made the alliance between different interests in the UNC disintegrate and gave birth to *Kabaka Yekka* ('the king alone') as the main political organization of Buganda.

But what kind of nationalist hero was Mutesa II to become – one for Uganda as a whole, or only for the Buganda kingdom which had enjoyed a specially privileged position within the Uganda Protectorate through the 1900 Agreement? The Uganda Peoples' Congress (UPC) was formed partly as successor to the UNC. Although it tried to reunite the nationalist forces this aim was never to be achieved. In 1962, when Uganda finally attained independence from Britain as a single entity under the prime ministership of Milton Obote, it did so under a coalition government between the royalist *Kabaka Yekka* movement and the UPC of Milton Obote. The UPC had received almost all its electoral support from outside Buganda – even before Buganda started electing its own MPs to the Uganda National Assembly indirectly through the Buganda Lukiko. It was an uneasy alliance and in 1966–7 Obote called in the Ugandan armed forces to integrate Buganda forcibly into national politics. Before Obote agreed to Buganda's demands for indirect elections in 1962, however, Uganda had briefly enjoyed a government in 1961–2 under the control of the Democratic Party (DP) of Benedicto Kiwanuka.

The formation of the DP can be seen as an attempt to organize certain groups which fell outside the existing forums. The rich farmers in Buganda had successfully organized themselves under the traditionalist KY; the traders had rallied under the UNC/UPC succession. Other social forces at national level that had felt left out were to be mobilized by the expansion of DP which had originally started in Buganda using a religious

19. R. Robinson, 1980, pp. 50–72.

PLATE 9.1   *King Mutesa II, the* Kabaka *of Buganda, in exile in London*

base. Historically, Catholic chiefs had found themselves with less privileges in Buganda and, using this religious base, they started the organization. But the religious ideology was mainly used as a rallying point in trying to create a rival nationalist movement, attracting civil servants and other educated élite who found themselves left out of the Protestant-dominated UPC. DP support came from both inside and outside the Buganda kingdom in geographical terms. Furthermore, despite its ideological starting point, the DP may be said to have made a considerable effort in creating a pan-Ugandan political movement. It has enjoyed considerable support from trade unions besides the Catholic Church.[20] In the final pre-independence elections of 1962, the DP came second to the KY–UPC coalition.[21] On the whole, however, the rise of nationalism in Uganda does display ideological and regional divisions which made it difficult for

20. See S. Karugire, 1980, pp. 144–69; M. Twaddle, 1978, pp. 255–66; and D. A. Low, 1971.
21. See D. Rothchild and M. Rogin, 1966, pp. 337–440.

the *petite-bourgeoisie* to emerge as an integrated and unified class in fighting against colonialism, unlike what happened in neighbouring Tanganyika.

Tanganyika[22]

If wartime inflation and artificially-low producer prices laid the ground-work for mass nationalism in Uganda after 1945, and ineffectual British repression of Ganda intellectuals thereafter enabled Ganda nationalism to first fuse with popular discontent and then fatally divide it along ethnic lines, in Tanganyika it was massive intervention by Britain in the organization of African agriculture which led to the first widespread local protests against British colonial rule. The first effect of these protests was to encourage the trend Dr John Iliffe called 'tribal aggregation'.[23] Colonial policies had led to socio-economic change that 'accentuated regional differentiation and rivalry' among educated groups for faster development within their ethnic areas. As a result, a number of ethnic-based associations were formed which in turn were used to articulate opposition to unpopular policies. In some areas the process led to successful demand for paramount chiefs to strengthen ethnic unity, as was the case of the Chagga in the north-eastern part of the country. But the effect of this ethnic aggregation movement was to weaken the territorial organization, the Tanganyika African Association (TAA). Having started in the late 1920s as a welfare organization of civil servants,[24] during the 1930s TAA stimulated the formation of provincial branches and, from time to time, the central organization was to be strengthened by their vitality.

In the post-war period, the country-wide protests organized on ethnic lines tended to weaken the territorial organization of TAA but, ironically, the protests against colonial policies were to become one of the pillars on which the territorial organization was to be revitalized and eventually on which a strong political party, the Tanganyika African National Union (TANU) was to be built. The revitalization stimulus came from the Lake Province, an area of Tanganyika roughly equal to Nyasaland but providing approximately half the value of Tanganyika's total agricultural exports. In this province, as in many other areas, post-war British reforms in local government made it, in one scholar's words, 'easier to impose unwelcome agricultural policies from above than for the participation in democratic institutions from below'.[25] Widespread popular protest erupted in the

22. This section is based principally upon J. Iliffe, 1979, and R. C. Pratt, 1976. On UTP, see A. Ross, 1977, pp. 519–35 and 1981.
23. J. Iliffe, 1979, p. 487.
24. See UNESCO, *General History of Africa*, vol. VII, pp. 671–2.
25. A. Maguire, 1970, p. 643.

PLATE 9.2   *Julius K. Nyerere, president of TANU (the Tanganyika African National Union)*

province and the provincial branch of the TAA was quick in taking up the grievances, thus linking the urban welfare association with articulation of rural problems. This was the beginning of the transformation of the TAA into a political movement. The Lake Province branch did three remarkable things: it penetrated the countryside; it articulated the attack on the colonial regime, and finally, it demanded strengthening of the central organization and convening of a national conference. Among the well-known prominent leaders of this revival were M. Bomani, B. Munanka and S. Kandoro.

In the central office in Dar es Salaam, the immediate post-war activities had come from a combined effort of civil servants and educated townsmen who had fought in Burma during the war. But by late 1952 the momentum had faded as articulate leaders had been transferred from Dar es Salaam and the association seemed to have no president and held no meetings. The Lake Province leaders had even considered transferring the headquarters to Mwanza. It was at this point that a new leader appeared on the scene to coordinate the revitalization efforts, and within two years TAA had transformed itself to a formidable political party which adopted the name Tanganyika African National Union (TANU) on 7 July 1954.

TANU took over power from Britain in 1961. Its effective founder, apart from the Lakes Province branch, was a teacher from one of the smallest ethnic groups in the territory, Julius Nyerere. Returning from studies in Britain in 1952, Nyerere has been described as 'racially sensitive' at this time – he 'hated foreign rule', John Iliffe tells us, 'feared Conservative (Party) complicity with settler ambitions, and knew that Africa was moving towards conflict and liberation'.[26] It was also his achievement to make maximum use of Tanganyika's international status as a trust territory of the United Nations in order to hasten its decolonization.

In 1946 Britain had been unhappy about the terms under which its former mandate in Tanganyika under the League of Nations had been transformed into a UN trusteeship territory. Anti-colonialism was already a powerful sentiment at the United Nations, and it proved a most effective platform upon which Tanganyikan grievances could be publicized. The Meru land case,[27] which involved the removal of about 3000 Wameru from Engare Nanyuki to give place to European settlers, demonstrated this in 1952, but three years later, within a year of the TAA's transformation into TANU, not only had Nyerere's prestige been raised considerably by a visit to New York but paid-up membership of TANU shot up too. In 1956 Edward Twining, the very unsocialist governor of Tanganyika, persuaded most of the unofficial members of the legislative council (all of whom were of course nominated, not elected, at this time) to form a rival political party, the United Tanganyika Party (UTP). But the UTP soon faded into *Utupu*, 'nothingness' in Kiswahili. In September 1960, TANU won 70 of the 71 seats in the first contest for the legislative council in which it was electorally possible for Africans to win a majority. Nyerere immediately became chief minister of an internally self-governing Tanganyika, and in December 1961 it became the first British dependency in East and Central Africa to attain full independence.

Explanations for the speed with which Tanganyika gained full independence – before both Kenya and Uganda – customarily include the leadership qualities of Nyerere; the organizational vitality of TANU (originating as a trans-ethnic urban voluntary association and developing very differently thereafter from both the Uganda National Congress and its various Ugandan successors on the one hand, and all its counterparts in Kenya, which basically were all tactical coalitions of ethnically-based notables); the absence of major regional cleavages in Tanganyika; its status as a UN trust territory; and the dramatic change in the strategic importance attached to Tanganyika as well as Kenya when the Suez imbroglio of 1956 led Britain to reappraise very radically its defence commitments east of Suez. In other words, a mixture of local nationalist assertion *and* conscious political disengagement on the British side, customarily serve

26. J. Iliffe, 1979, p. 509.
27. See *ibid.*, p. 500; K. Japhet and S. Japhet, 1967.

as explanation for Tanganyikan independence, scholars differing only over the precise balance of factors within differing paradigms. Nonetheless, whatever particular framework of interpretation is adopted, crucially important too in speeding up the British retreat from formal empire throughout East and Central Africa was the Mau Mau rebellion in Kenya.

Kenya[28]

Unlike the French in Madagascar, the British in Kenya at the close of the Second World War did not feel at all insecure. They had won the war. There were therefore to be no unnecessary political reforms in Kenya. Admittedly, there was to be token African representation in the Kenya Legislative Council – of Eliud Mathu from 1944, the first African to be nominated to Legco anywhere in British-ruled East and Central Africa; but there was to be no idea whatsoever of telling white settlers how to behave as regards labour recruitment (the outlawing of the *indigenat* recruitment system, by contrast, sharpened settler attacks upon the MDRM in Madagascar). To be sure, development was in the air, and the British administration in Kenya did have considerable plans for improvements in *African* agriculture, but the white settlers were expected to help with this rather than have their own ways unduly disturbed.

Indeed, the white settlers of Kenya had never had it so good. Besides producer prices boosted by Kenya's wartime role as supplier to the Middle East as well as to troops nearer to hand, Nairobi had been the nodal point of production and distribution throughout Britain's East African empire and white settlers were entrenched in innumerable committees. So powerful indeed did white settlers seem to be in post-war Kenya that Sessional Paper 210, which increased unofficial representation in the Kenyan Legco by providing for the election of an additional member by the whole council, became symbolic with élite Africans of a scheme to give Europeans a *permanent* working majority there.

Shortly after the Mau Mau emergency itself was declared in October 1952, the Kenya African Union (KAU) wrote to the British Colonial Secretary, arguing that:

> Much of the present trouble is due to the fact that Africans are not adequately associated with the machinery of Government to make them feel that they are a real part or partners in the Government of the country. This has the two-fold effect of denying to the Government the benefit of considered African opinion in the making of Government policy; and on the other hand of creating an

28. This section is indebted to the pioneering account by C. G. Rosberg and J. Nottingham, 1966; see also J. Spencer, 1985, and D. Throup, 1985, pp. 399–433. Also helpful are A. Clayton, 1976; F. Furedi, 1974; and the special issue of the *Kenya Historical Review*, 1977, dealing with the Mau Mau.

PLATE 9.3 *Jomo Kenyatta, president of KAU (the Kenya African Union), photographed in 1946–7*

impression in the minds of the people that the Government, because of its composition, does not work in the interests of Africans. During the last thirty years, while the requests of the European community have been conceded, the requests of the African community have been consistently ignored. This has led the ordinary African to believe that only if he has a government of his own can he benefit and not otherwise.[29]

However, by this time the principal officers of the KAU had all been detained on account of their suspected complicity in organizing the Mau Mau. In retrospect, this does not seem to have been any more the case in Kenya than in Madagascar. Indeed, if anything, the gap between the African nationalist élite and the men of violence seems to have been much greater in Kenya. Originally founded as an extra-parliamentary support group for Eliud Mathu in 1944, the KAU quickly proved to be very moderate. Jomo Kenyatta became its president in 1947, a year after his return from self-imposed exile in Britain and, briefly, in the Soviet Union. But Kenyatta was

29. Quoted by R. Frost, 1978, p. 213, and forming part of a memo from the provisional committee of the KAU, signed by W. Odede and J. Z. Murumbi.

now no Bolshevik. The British might remain intensely suspicious of him, but by October 1952 Kenyatta, along with most other KAU notables had been repudiated by the men organizing Mau Mau oathing.

Who these people were it is still difficult to say with certainty, and the whole question of the organization of the Mau Mau is still a matter of political controversy in Kenya. That many of them were younger men associated with trade union activity and with Nairobi seems clear. That Mau Mau itself was a violent conspiracy to oust the British as well as to regain control of 'stolen lands' also seems clear. There were oathing campaigns amongst the Kikuyu people throughout the post-war period, but it was not until 1951 that the violence associated with oathing seems to have got out of hand: riots against *rinderpest* regulations as well as compulsory terracing in that year, followed by arson against white-settler farms, the maiming of their cattle and, at the start of October 1952, the murder of the leading Kikuyu loyalist, Chief Waruhiu, by armed gunmen in broad daylight. From subsequent memoirs published by Mau Mau insurgents we know that preparations were being made for eventual armed revolt in the forests by thefts of arms. But it is probably the declaration of a state of emergency at the end of October 1952 by a newly-arrived British governor, acting under white-settler pressure, that caused the Mau Mau to go off at half-cock.

In terms of sheer territory taken over, Mau Mau insurgents were less impressive than their earlier counterparts in Madagascar, who within a few months had taken over a sixth of the island. Very few Mau Mau fighters had been equivalents of *anciens combattants* during the Second World War; no whole townships were seized; no significant stretches of cultivated land were ever completely controlled; and fewer European civilians were killed by insurgents throughout the whole Mau Mau emergency than died through traffic accidents in Nairobi during this period. Admittedly many Africans died, and many scholars today consider that the Mau Mau was principally a Kikuyu civil war; but even most of these murders took place *after* the British security forces launched their counter-insurgency campaign, *after* they had started detaining Mau Mau suspects without trial, and *after* compulsory villagization had been intro-duced in order to separate forest fighters from rural as well as urban supporters.

What, then, was the Mau Mau? On present evidence it seems to have been a number of separate things, sometimes overlapping, at other times going off in different directions: a squatters' revolt; resistance against enforced agricultural improvement policies; a cultural revival; an internal war; and an anti-colonial movement that echoed earlier primary resistance against the imposition of British colonial rule half a century earlier.[30]

30. R. Buijtenhuijs, 1982, provides a review of contrasting interpretations. See also D. Throup, 1985, 1987; T. Kanogo, 1987.

PLATE 9.4 *Langata Detention Camp set up by the British during their anti-Mau Mau operations, April 1954*

To begin with, the Mau Mau was a squatters' revolt. When white settlers first established farms in the White Highlands of Kenya in the early twentieth century they were frequently assisted by Africans who exchanged their labour services for herding and cultivation rights, but with the economic boom that began at the end of the 1930s many white farmers became increasingly specialized and mechanized and as a result threw many squatters off their farms. Some ex-squatters were settled by the colonial administration at Olenguruone in the Rift Valley, but at the end of the 1940s many of these were expelled for disobeying agricultural instructions. And it was at Olenguruone that secret oathing was widely employed as a form of popular solidarity and resistance.

Oathing also erupted in the Kikuyu Reserve, where land consolidation was also proceeding apace as a result of population growth as well as the continuing boom in commodity prices; the Kikuyu Reserve being unusual in white-settled Africa in being comparatively central as regards roads and railways for an African reserve, and in having good soils. 'It was this double peculiarity of the Kikuyu', comments John Lonsdale, 'land consolidation at home and a farm tenantry outside, which determined that they, and they only, would be the seat of a violent agrarian revolt which not only set Africans against whites, but Kikuyu against Kikuyu too'.[31]

In Nairobi, by 1952 a city of nearly 100 000 people, and in other urban areas of upland Kenya such as Nakuru were other Africans, frequently called 'spivs' in British documents of the time, who provided passive support and supplies for the forest fighters until Operation Anvil in 1954 completely cleared them out of Nairobi. It has been suggested that this alliance of workers and peasants against imperialism provides evidence of a growing proletarian consciousness in colonial Kenya,[32] but such evidence as there is from contemporary Mau Mau hymns and subsequent memoirs suggests more a protest by recently displaced peasants against proletarianization than proletarian consciousness itself.

On yet another level, the Mau Mau must be seen as cultural assertion. But here we must be careful. The British colonial government saw oathing and opposition to terracing as back-looking conservatism, when it did not consider these things to have been deliberately provoked by 'agitators' such Jomo Kenyatta. Oathing was obviously loaded with 'culture'. To be sure, some of the most bizarre evidence about the cultural aspects of the Mau Mau comes from Europeans of the time concerned sometimes to project their own fantasies onto Africans themselves.[33] Nonetheless,

31. J. Lonsdale, 1982, p. 6.

32. R. Buijtenhuijs, 1982, pp. 157–62. A leading advocate of this view is S. Stichter, 1982.

33. R. Buijtenhuijs, 1982, p. 104, quotes the comment of D. L. Barnett: 'We feed our own "needs" for the obscene and the orgiastic when we read deep meanings into the oathing abnormalities of the Kenya peasant revolt'.

through all the Mau Mau oathing ran certain irreducible cultural elements which appear to have acted as effectively as deterrents to recruitment of activists amongst non-Kikuyu as they assisted it amongst Kikuyu. In Mau Mau hymns too there were cultural elements which have led Professor Ogot to argue that 'because of their exclusiveness they cannot be regarded as the national freedom songs which every Kenyan youth can sing with pride and conviction'.[34]

Finally, the Mau Mau must be seen as an anti-colonial movement, albeit a regionally paradoxical one. The areas of Kikuyuland most affected by colonial penetration and 'stolen lands', namely Kiambu and its environs, were ones displaying the least overt support for the insurgents, while other areas away from Nairobi like Nyeri and Fort Hall proved much more militant though much less disrupted by either British colonialism or white settlers. But Robert Buijtenhuijs points out that Fort Hall and Nyeri were also areas of Kikuyuland where the British colonial entry at the start of this century was very brutal. Kiambu by comparison was pacified much more gently.[35] If this is so, Ali Mazrui may well also be right to call the Mau Mau 'the first major resurrection of the warrior tradition in recent East African history'.[36]

Nevertheless, resurrection or regression, what most concerned British politicians in the 1950s was the difficulty of keeping such a tumultuous area under colonial control. The British probably overestimated the actual military threat posed by the Mau Mau rebels, as well as underestimating the extent to which the British reaction itself would lead to mayhem and murder in which 'private property was left to the care of thieves and Providence'.[37] But violence was violence, and the sheer expense of continuing to support white settlers could not be continued indefinitely within the British political tradition.[38] And so it was that, after the Conservative Party won its third election in a row in Britain in 1959, Iain Macleod was appointed colonial secretary and the Mau Mau emergency was ended and a constitutional conference arranged.

This conference led to a 65-member legislative assembly in Kenya, 33 of them elected from open seats. The KAU was resurrected as KANU (the Kenya African National Union) and won 67 per cent of the votes in the ensuing election with a still-detained Jomo Kenyatta as the national president, Odinga as vice-president, and Mboya as general secretary. KANU was opposed by KADU (the Kenya African Democratic Union), formed by an alliance of coastal politicians and up-country notables from

34. B. A. Ogot, 1977, p. 286.
35. R. Buijtenhuijs, 1982, pp. 200–1.
36. A. A. Mazrui, 1975b, p. 77.
37. E. N. Wanyoike, 1974, p. 190.
38. See the comment of the British colonial secretary of the time, Lord Chandos, 1964, p. 397.

the smaller ethnic groups. However, it was not until after his release from detention (August 1961), a second Lancaster House conference, and a landslide victory for KANU in the May 1963 general election, that Kenyatta became prime minister and, six months later, leader of a fully independent country.[39]

At independence in Kenya, many white farmers were bought out by a massive British-funded aid scheme. Sometimes in retrospect this has been considered a neo-colonial masterstroke, consciously designed together with earlier measures like the Swynnerton Plan to create a pro-British black bourgeoisie in post-colonial Kenya. Certainly the British *tried* to create such groups in several British African colonies, but the African middle classes tended to produce leaders of revolt as well as supporters of the *status quo*. For Kenya this tendency is graphically illustrated by the complaint of the white-settler politician, Michael Blundell, that 'go-ahead better farmers' there had a paradoxical tendency to vote for 'the more extreme and radical candidates . . . [with views] quite contrary to their own interests as property owners' and, when asked why, said that such candidates were 'the only people capable of dealing with the British colonial system'.[40] A black middle class *was* built up in colonial Kenya, but its origins must be sought much further back in time than the 1950s. It was in the early colonial-government employment and farm income;[41] and anti-colonial nationalism in Kenya was a much more complicated phenomenon than simply political action by an emergent black bourgeoisie acting independently of both the wider and the local context.

Nyasaland and Northern Rhodesia[42]

In Nyasaland (now Malawi) and Northern Rhodesia (now Zambia), increased British interference in African agriculture aroused considerable unrest in the immediate post-war period,[43] but it was the imposition of the Central African Federation (CAF) in 1953 which caused a really explosive political convergence of élite nationalism and mass discontent in both these British-administered territories.

Why did the imposition of federation cause so much African discontent? For years the white settlers of Southern Rhodesia – self-governing, it should be remembered, since 1923 – had toyed with the idea of 'amal-

39. G. Bennett and C. Rosberg, 1961, pp. 21–2.
40. Sir M. Blundell, 1964, p. 208.
41. Several papers of M. Cowen, published and unpublished, are of crucial importance here; see, for example, M. Cowen, 1981. See also the synthesis by G. Kitching, 1980.
42. This section is indebted to several authors, most notably P. Gifford, 1982; R. Tangri, 1975, pp. 254–81; and J. Van Donge, 1985, pp. 265–77.
43. R. Tangri, 1975, p. 262. The case study analysed by J. Van Donge suggests that this unrest is best understood by seeing the nationalist movement as 'a rapidly shifting set of alliances being determined by the wider political setting'.

gamation' with Northern Rhodesia and Nyasaland; both then administered by the British Colonial Office along with Kenya, Uganda and Tanganyika; and both with European minorities living in them. Immediately after the Second World War the new socialist government in Britain vetoed amalgamation but looked more favourably upon 'federation' as an aid to economic development as well as possibly creating a political buffer against infiltration by Afrikaners from South Africa. However, protests from élite nationalist associations such as the Nyasaland African Congress (founded 1944) and its Northern Rhodesian counterpart (founded 1948), and others, were sufficient to stop anything actually being done before October 1951, when a British Conservative government came to power in London.

This government was much more closely tied to business interests and white settlers favouring federation. The federal idea was also supported by civil servants (such as Andrew Cohen, before he went to Uganda and deported the *Kabaka*) for more bureaucratic and developmental reasons. In 1953, federation was finally imposed upon both Nyasaland and Northern Rhodesia despite considerable local African protest.[44] In Southern Rhodesia, needless to say, it was welcomed by the white electorate there because of the economic potentialities of Northern Rhodesian copper.

For a time, African resistance to the Central African Federation was muted after its actual imposition. In Northern Rhodesia the influential African mine-workers' union ignored the 'two days of prayer' called, Gandhian-fashion, by Congress, and Congress itself suffered from leadership disputes which were never resolved. Finally in 1958 Kenneth Kaunda broke away to form what later became the United National Independence Party (UNIP). A year before, however, the CAF authorities had gone too far, attempting to entrench white privilege further by establishing a new federal citizenship which Nyasaland Africans, for example, could purchase for £5 and by signing away their existing rights as persons 'protected' by the British Colonial Office. Two electoral rolls were envisaged, the only clear thing about their otherwise complicated provisions being that Africans, as the poorest citizens materially, would have enjoyed the worst benefits under it politically.

There were now political storms. In mid-1958, Hastings Banda, a medical doctor who had acted for the Nyasaland Congress in London before going off to work in Ghana, returned as candidate for the Nyasaland African Congress presidency. Upon confirmation, there began a campaign of non-cooperation which culminated in full independence from Britain six years later. A state of emergency was declared in 1959, and under Operation Sunrise, Banda and 200 other Congress activists were detained. The commotion caused by these arrests and the associated violence and use of white troops from Southern Rhodesia led to the appointment of a commission of inquiry by the British government in London.

44. P. Gifford, 1982, provides fuller details.

The Devlin Commission embarrassed both the local governor and the authorities in Britain. 'Nyasaland is – no doubt temporarily – a police state', in which it was unsafe for anybody publicly to express support for the Congress leaders, Devlin reported. Devlin also said that most of the violence that occurred during this particular emergency (in which 52 Africans had been killed) was the result of government activity.[45]

The British colonial secretary and Nyasaland governor of the time both said that Devlin was misleading. Harold Macmillan, the British prime minister, was evidently not so sure and subsequently despatched another fact-finding commission to Central Africa, the Monckton Commission. Few Africans would talk to it, certainly neither of the two African Congresses in Nyasaland and Northern Rhodesia. Some 'moderate' Africans did talk, however, and on the basis of their comments Monckton reported that opposition to federation throughout Northern Rhodesia and Nyasaland was 'almost pathological . . . widespread, sincere and of long-standing'. He advised that 'immediate political advances' be made there in order both to promote 'true partnership' and greater economic development.[46] Nyasaland might be a comparatively unimportant economic backwater for Britain, but Northern Rhodesia was crucial for Britain's copper supplies.

Before Monckton left for Central Africa, Harold Macmillan had appointed Iain Macleod as colonial secretary. Macleod, who was a skilled bridge-player, devised some extremely complicated electoral arrangements for both Nyasaland and Northern Rhodesia as well as for Kenya. The political results of these were, for Malawi (as Nyasaland was henceforth to be called), a Congress victory in all the seats it fought in the 1961 election and, after a further conference, full independence in July 1964; and, for Zambia (as Northern Rhodesia now became), a victory shared between UNIP and the rump of the former Northern Rhodesian Congress in the elections of late 1962 and, after the first election under full adult suffrage in 1963, 55 out of 65 main-roll seats for UNIP, and full independence in October 1964.

Zanzibar

Zanzibar is a much smaller island than Madagascar, with just under 300 000 people on Zanzibar Island and Pemba in 1958. During the nineteenth century, Zanzibar had been the centre of an extensive trading network in the East African interior under an Omani dynasty. In 1890 Zanzibar passed under British colonial protection, and in December 1963 it passed out of it. A month later there was an unexpected and bloody revolution, designed, so its principal instigator said shortly afterwards,

45. *Report of the Nyasaland Commission of Inquiry*, 1959.
46. *Report of the Advisory Commission*, 1960.

'to liberate the African people of Zanzibar from the yoke of Arab colonialism'.[47]

Racial opposition between African and Arab on Zanzibar was partly a hangover from the slave trade of the nineteenth century, partly the result of British stereotyping during the colonial period, partly a consequence of capitalist penetration of the clove industry which created an Arab landlord class and an African underclass as well as further entrenching local Asian financiers.[48] After the Second World War these racial categories were given enhanced political meaning by British reforms in local government (which because of the smallness of Zanzibar assumed correspondingly greater territorial significance) and the onset of independence.

More a by-product of political developments on the East African mainland than of any urgent desire for it on Zanzibar itself, the onset of independence prompted the Arab landlord class – through the Arab-dominated Zanzibar National Party (ZNP) – to seek to remove British overrule before the African underclass became mobilized sufficiently to seize power for itself through the Afro-Shrazi Party (ASP) led by Abeid Karume, president of the local African Association since 1953. The smallness of Zanzibar and the face-to-face character of its politics lent a complexity and violence to this struggle that still have to be fully disentangled.[49] Nonetheless, by December 1963 it looked as if the trick had worked. The ZNP and its allies in the Zanzibar and Pemba Peoples' Party (ZPPP) – a pro-Arab splinter group from the ASP – together gained more seats than the ASP in the immediate pre-independence elections, and together took Zanzibar into full independence from Britain on 10 December 1963. But then came the revolution of 12 January 1964.

While recognizing the election tricks under which the ASP with its majority votes was prevented from getting majority seats, scholars have given two explanations of what happened on the revolution night, both of which reveal acceptance of the ASP's alleged inability to organize the upheaval. First, they see the split of the Umma Party under Abdul Raḥmān Muḥammad Babu from the ZNP to join the ASP as an asset to the latter. They insist that the Umma Party may well have been planning their own *coup* against the ZNP had it not been proscribed just a week before the so-called Okello's Revolution. For it was from members of the Umma Party that the ASP obtained organizational ideas for the revolution.[50] Secondly, the real catalyst for the revolution was the Uganda-born John Okello 'who used a small personally-enlisted force, in which Umma supporters were prominent, to topple the vulnerable ruling

47. *Uganda Argus*, 4 April 1964.
48. See F. Cooper, 1980.
49. See M. F. Lofchie, 1965; and A. Clayton, 1981.
50. See the two perceptive articles by K. Kyle: 1964a and 1964b; and M. F. Lofchie, 1967, pp. 36–42.

regime'.[51] John Okello himself has tended even to claim the whole credit for the revolution. As an independent house-painter in Pemba, he was able to step in and organize local policemen – who were disgruntled by the replacement of their British superiors by Arab officers at independence – into the stormtroopers who successfully seized power in Zanzibar town during the night of 11–12 January 1964.[52]

Perhaps the facts about the Zanzibar revolution are still too contemporary to be available to researchers. A lot of the information is still confidential and the participants, most of whom are still active in politics, are unlikely to disclose all the facts. Nevertheless, recent research is beginning to reveal that Okello's claims were probably somewhat overstated.[53] It is now more evident that the events of the revolution night were more closely supervised by Abeid Karume, the ASP president, and his Committee of Fourteen than previously recognized. According to this view, Okello was deliberately used by the ASP within the Committee as one of the coordinating members. His main asset was his powerful voice which was used in making announcements. But his personal claims soon made him unacceptable to the party leadership and he had to leave Zanzibar. It is claimed that Okello was eventually lured away from Zanzibar on 20 February and never allowed to return. By then, Karume had managed to form Zanzibar into a one-party state under the ASP and was in a position to negotiate amalgamation with Tanganyika to form the United Republic of Tanzania on 26 April 1964.

New states and old colonies

Political independence in Eastern Africa was intimately connected with the development of nationalism in colonies established as a result of the nineteenth-century European scramble for landed territory. Sometimes this nationalism was that of some pre-colonial territorial entity like Madagascar or Zanzibar. More frequently it was the conscious creation of nationalists organizing an anti-colonial movement within the arbitrarily defined boundaries of some European colony like Tanganyika for, as Nyerere has remarked:

> until we were colonized this 'nation' did not exist, different laws operated among the constituent tribes and there was conflict between them. It was the colonial power which imposed a common law and maintained it by force, until the growth of the independence movement put the flesh of an emotional unity on the skeleton of legal unity.[54]

51. A. Smith, 1976, p. 211.
52. Okello's own account was published in 1967.
53. See B. F. Mrima and W. Mattoke, 1980; and A. Sheriff and E. Ferguson, 1991.
54. J. K. Nyerere, 1967a, p. 271.

During actual independence struggles there was also frequently a pan-African dimension, especially after Ghanaian independence in 1957: evidenced by such things as the clear inspiration both Kenneth Kaunda and Hastings Banda received for their fight against the Central African Federation by attendance at the Accra All-African Peoples' Conference in 1959;[55] or in the ultimately abortive attempt to create from below an East African Federation by Uganda, Kenya and Tanzania during the early 1960s.[56] On Zanzibar there were traces of pan-Arabism too.[57] And, insofar as all these territories were British-ruled, independence struggles were also affected by the examples of previous movements towards self-government within the British Commonwealth, of India and Pakistan as well as Canada and Australia.

But with France, the framework was different. With France there was a longing for a greater France progressively transforming dominance into equality by administrative integration into the metropole. In Madagascar after the Second World War, too little was offered too soon after the Vichy defeat for the policy to be accepted without insurrection. But the old colony of Reunion was another matter.

Reunion[58]

Originally Reunion had been settled by French seamen and African slaves in the seventeenth century. During subsequent centuries it developed as a sugar colony, with further influxes of African slaves during the early nineteenth century and then, for another third of a century, of indentured labourers from India. By 1946, three-quarters of the island's cultivable surface was devoted to sugar, and the local communist party was as eager as the French Communist Party to attack the local plantocracy by fully incorporating it into the French state and thereby raising poorer people's living standards as well. Living standards did rise in the next quarter of a century, but not as much as in France itself. The economic stagnation which had afflicted this volcanic outcrop 700 km east of Madagascar ever since the Napoleonic Wars, was however ended when Reunion (along with the French West Indian colonies of Martinique, Guadeloupe and Guyana) was turned into an overseas *département* in 1946.

Thenceforth, Reunion became a very different model of decolonization for the still British-ruled islands of the Seychelles and Mauritius to consider alongside the various mainland models already discussed. However, with the triumph of the Gaullists in France in 1958, local communists switched to a policy of autonomy for Reunion; and should this policy

55. R. I. Rotberg, 1966, p. 292.
56. See J. S. Nye, Jr, 1966. Much more work needs to be done on this subject.
57. See A. Clayton, 1981, p. 40 and p. 46.
58. On Reunion, I am indebted to J. Houbert, 1980, pp. 145–71 and 325–47; and M. Robert, 1976.

ever turn into a popular Reunionnais demand for full independence from France, pressure may well arise for Reunion to follow the more customary path to national sovereignty within the international system.

Comoro Islands[59]

Ethnographically, the Comoro Islands are more akin to Zanzibar and other areas of the East African Coast than to the Creole and cosmopolitan inhabitants of Reunion, Mauritius and the Seychelles. They are Kiswahili-speaking. Mayotte became a French colonial possession by purchase (from a local sultan) in 1841, and the rest followed during the European scramble for colonies at the end of the century. During the colonial period, the Comorian islands were not a focus of any great French interest. Anti-colonial nationalism did not really arise there until 1968, when French paratroopers and legionaries brutally suppressed a school strike and people came onto the streets to demonstrate. The first political parties were then formed and, as a by-product of political turbulence in nearby Madagascar shortly afterwards – following the overthrow of the Tsiranana government, the subsequent ending of French military bases on Madagascar and the nationalization of leading French companies there – a popular demand arose for full independence for the Comoro Islands too.

The French held their customary referendum, but as the island of Mayotte (the least Islamized and most influenced by Christian Malagasies) voted against the general trend of other islands in the group and demanded continuing ties to France, another set of referendums were held, this time island by island. All the islands apart from Mayotte declared UDI[60] from France in July 1975. Mayotte alone continues to call itself French.

Mauritius and the Seychelles[61]

Mauritius, like Reunion, lies several hundred miles off the east coast of Madagascar and developed as a classic sugar-growing colony during the nineteenth century, with former slaves from Africa and then indentured labourers from India doing most of the work on the island while a Creole French–Mauritian plantocracy enjoyed most of the profits. Like other 'old colonies' growing sugar in the West Indies as well as in the Indian Ocean, Mauritius was badly hit by the Great Depression of the 1930s, which left a bitter legacy of strikes and labour unrest. Politics in post-1945 Mauritius were mostly preoccupied with the rights of workers on

59. This account is derived principally from H. Chagnoux and A. Haribu, 1980; and T. Flobert, 1976.

60. UDI: Unilateral Declaration of Independence.

61. On Mauritius and the Seychelles, I am indebted to J. Houbert, 1980; and L. Favoureu, 1970, which has a good bibliography.

the sugar plantations and in the docks, as against those of the plantocracy, with self-government from Britain being very much a secondary issue for some time. Indeed, in the light of Reunion after 1946, closer association with Britain seemed a much more attractive objective to work towards. That, however, was never really on the agenda. The struggle in Mauritius was therefore for the best terms possible in the light of Britain's efforts during the 1960s to enter the European Economic Community at the very same time that Mauritius itself was moving towards independence.

Independence was won in 1968 by the Mauritian Labour Party, most consistently nationalist of all the parties representing the predominantly Hindu proletariat of the island. There was, however, another catch. In 1965 certain islands associated hitherto with Mauritius or the Seychelles were amputated by Britain and grouped into the British Indian Ocean Territory, a new oceanic colony which shortly afterwards became the setting for an American nuclear-submarine base at Diego Garcia. Mauritian independence was clearly conditional upon acceptance of this set of amputations.[62]

Independence for the Seychelles was also delayed for a time by strategic considerations associated with a tracking station as well as Diego Garcia. But, to begin with, neither the Seychelles Peoples United Party (SPUP) of Albert René nor the Seychelles Democratic Party (SDP) of James Mancham were primarily concerned with independence from Britain. Rather it was control of government positions and policy in a desperately poor small island colony that formed their major preoccupation, and it was only when a quarrel arose between the SDP and the British over control of the island police before full independence, and the designation of the SPUP as a national liberation movement by the OAU, that independence became a serious issue. Eventually Mancham allied with René to gain the independence that Britain, newly eager to divest itself of all its remaining colonies as quickly as possible, was only too willing to grant to the Seychelles in 1976.

Colonialism had thus turned full circle since the eighteenth century. At that time island colonies such as the Seychelles, Mauritius and Reunion were crucial links in an essentially maritime set of European empires. Then, with the invention of the steam combustion engine, came the conquest of the great land masses such as sub-Saharan Africa and Westerners became the masters of land-based and densely populated tropical empires too. The global crisis of the Second World War undermined many of these empires, and what the war itself did not do, over-ambitious colonial development projects, 'uncaptured peasantries' and nationalist parties finished off within a generation. But with the advent of the thermonuclear age, oceanic colonialism has again come into its own, with a much more ominous importance.

62. See J. Madeley, 1982.

Southern Africa since 1945

David CHANAIWA

Introduction

In 1935 Southern Africa was already the most *economically* important part of Africa in a global perspective. In the last third of the twentieth century Southern Africa has also increasingly become the most *strategically* important sub-region of Africa at the same time. The *economic* pre-eminence arose primarily out of mineral wealth, vital for the West's industrial civilization. There was also large-scale agriculture and local industrialization. The *strategic* pre-eminence has been a combination of the wealth of the region and the rising importance of the Cape route for sea-traffic between Asia and the Western world, including the traffic of oil-tankers from the Gulf.

But there has been a third superlative which has profoundly affected the history of the sub-region. This third vital force has been *race*. A part of Africa which has been richest in mineral wealth (see Figure 10.1), and increasingly critical in strategic location, has also been the most deeply affected by the issue of race relations in this period of world history.[1]

This chapter is about that interplay between *economy*, *strategy* and *race* in the fate of Southern Africa. But each of these forces in turn has involved sub-themes. In the economic domain, the story of Southern Africa is partly about *land*, especially the struggle for the best and most fertile land. The story is also about *labour*, both voluntary and forced – both sedentary and migrant. Thirdly, the economic history of Southern Africa is of course also about *extractive capital* – in the sense of capital primarily derived from, or related to, mining activities. We shall address these three economic sub-themes, and how they have affected this particular period of Southern African history.

The strategic importance of Southern Africa and the area's location

---

1. For a general introduction to the history of Southern Africa in this period, see E. H. Brookes, 1968; B. Davidson *et al.*, 1976; W. R. Duggan, 1973; J. Duffy, 1962; G. M. Gerhart, 1979; R. H. Green *et al.*, 1981; R. Gibson, 1972; P. Keatley, 1963; C. R. Hill, 1964; and R. P. Stevens, 1967.

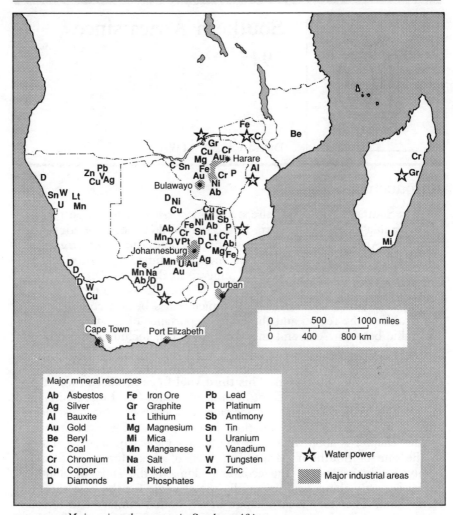

FIG. 10.1   *Major mineral resources in Southern Africa*

also have their sub-themes for our subsequent consideration. What should be remembered is that if there is any part of Africa for which the Western world would be prepared to go to war to ensure Western access to its resources, that part is indeed Southern Africa and Zaire. The strategic importance of these areas rests on a combination of *economic* and *geopolitical* factors.[2]

2. For further details, see D. Chanaiwa, 1976a; M. Morrell, 1971; C. Kadalie, 1971; W. M. Macmillan, 1963 and 1970; and T. Karis and G. M. Carter, 1977.

As for the issue of *race* in Southern Africa, the sub-region is the last great battlefield of racial confrontation on the continent.[3] But underlying the story of a sub-region of Africa is a global saga – the strange history of the reincarnation of political evil. On the one hand, the years 1935 to 1945 marked a successful global struggle against fascism and racial repression in Europe. On the other hand, the year 1948 marked the *rise* of a new version of fascism and racial repression in Africa – a version called *apartheid*. The defeat of Hitler and Mussolini in the first half of the 1940s was indeed a major blow against 'Aryan supremacy' and genocidal policies in Europe. The triumph of the National Party in South Africa in 1948, by contrast, was a victory for 'white supremacy' and for potential genocide in the southern portion of Africa. Hitlerism was being reincarnated on African soil. 'The Fuehrer is dead; Long live the Fuehrer!'

Needless to say, Africans were not going to take this with resignation. There is a sense in which the final armed crusade against 'fascism' and 'Nazism' is today being waged in Southern Africa. In that sense, the struggle against *apartheid* is part of the unfinished business of the Second World War. This chapter is partly about that moral crusade, in all its political and religious forms.[4]

This chapter has also been designed to provide historical perspectives of the political economy of European colonialism and African responses in Southern Africa.[5] A major theme will be the historical relationship and mutual interdependence between the economic bases, interests and classes and the political ideologies, structures and institutions of colonial Southern Africa.

Background to the age of *apartheid*

In both South Africa and Southern Rhodesia, the overriding issue was the European struggle to maintain economic monopoly over land, minerals, jobs and social services, and to repress African competition and nationalism. In particular, white rural bourgeoisie and urban working classes looked up to settler political vigilance and state capitalism to protect their racialist economic privileges against real and imaginary African competition.[6]

On the one hand, settler farmers wanted the state to make laws that would eliminate any competition with Africans over land, minerals, agricultural produce and extension services, while simultaneously assur-

---

3. D. D. T. Jabavu, 1920. See also P. Duignan and L. H. Gann, 1973; and G. S. P. Freeman-Grenville, 1973.

4. For details of separate churches and Ethiopianism, see B. Sundkler, 1961; also D. Chanaiwa, 1980, pp. 9–39.

5. See P. Duignan and L. H. Gann, 1973.

6. See, for example, G. Arrighi, 1970, pp. 393–426.

ing them of cheap African labour. On the other hand, white miners, technicians, drivers, civil servants and professionals wanted the state to make laws that would eliminate any competition with African workers, perpetuate the scarcity of skills and increase their wages, collective bargaining and political strength; while simultaneously subsidizing their high standard of living by passing the tax burden to the Africans.

By the 1930s, both settler states had passed an array of segregationist laws, such as the Natives' Land Act, the Group Areas Act and the Industrial Conciliation Act of South Africa and the Land Apportionment Act, the Industrial Conciliation Act, The Natives Registration Act, and the Masters and Servants Act of Southern Rhodesia, for the purposes of:

(1) expropriating African land and minerals;
(2) procuring cheap African labour;
(3) controlling the deployment and movement of African labourers; and
(4) eliminating inter-racial competition.

The Industrial Conciliation Acts of both South Africa and Southern Rhodesia were labour-relations laws covering all industries, sectors and workers of the economy. But they did not recognize African trade unions nor African workers as employees. Instead, they authorized industrial councils consisting of white employers and workers to negotiate on wages, conditions of work and benefits on behalf of the Africans. Africans were not allowed into apprenticeship programmes, and had no right to strike or to collective bargaining. Under the Workmen's Compensation Acts of both countries, Africans were excluded from retirement benefits, hospitalization schemes and occupational-safety measures.

Thus, in the political economy of Southern Africa, whites did not vote as capitalists, farmers, employers or proletarians but as whites. White workers formed all-white railway-workers' and mine-workers' unions as well as labour political parties. All high-paying, skilled and supervisory jobs were reserved for whites. There were numerous statutory para-statal marketing boards for milk, meat, maize, tobacco, cotton, minerals, and so on for whites which deliberately boycotted African products in order to eliminate competition from African farmers and manufacturers.

The division of the countries into European and African lands was systematically designed to destroy the African's resources and ability to maintain self-sufficiency, by restricting him to barren rural reserves and urban locations. Through the deliberate process of peasantization, ghettoization and, thus, impoverishment, the settlers created the necessary underdevelopment and dependency to force the Africans to work for the white men just to survive.

By the eve of the Second World War, there was in existence a well-established centre–periphery, interdependent relationship between the settler colonies and the British high commission territories of Basutoland,

Bechuanaland and Swaziland; the British protectorates of Northern Rhodesia and Nyasaland; and the Portuguese colonies of Angola and, especially, Mozambique. By both politico-economic designing and geographical location, Basutoland, Bechuanaland and Swaziland were economically the first peripheral 'bantustans' of South Africa.[7]

Basutoland was completely surrounded by South Africa; it had a tiny European population consisting primarily of government officials, traders and missionaries; and it had a peasant agriculture and animal husbandry on eroded land. Bechuanaland was essentially an expanse of desert dependent on cattle-ranching and migrant labour. Swaziland was the most viable of the three territories because of its fertile soils, rich mineral deposits of iron ore, asbestos and tin, and corporate development in forestry and irrigation. But much of the rich land had been alienated to Europeans.

The Portuguese colony of Mozambique was economically dependent on an export-oriented agricultural plantation economy of state farms and private estates; on customs duties and tariffs obtained from the Rhodesian use of the road, railway and port of Beira and the South African use of the port of Lourenço Marques; and from labour.[8] The British protectorate of Nyasaland was the beautiful 'Cinderella of the protectorates', but was also poor and overpopulated. Most Europeans there were government officials, traders and missionaries, and they totalled a mere 2000 in 1937. There was no settler need for land and cheap African labour; so there were neither African reserves nor pass laws. Northern Rhodesia was dependent on a single-industry, export-oriented mining economy centred on the Copper Belt. The few Europeans there were primarily mining technicians, government officials, traders and missionaries, without the intention of permanent settlement. However, due to the possibility of inter-racial rivalry for jobs and services, there were, to a lesser extent than in South Africa and Southern Rhodesia, African reserves, pass laws and the importation of migrant labour from Nyasaland, Tanganyika and the Belgian Congo.

Migrant labour

Undoubtedly, there were various causes that led thousands of African males and females to leave their homelands for labour migration to the mines, farms and factories of South Africa and Southern Rhodesia.[9] The

7. For the historical relationship of Botswana, Lesotho and Swaziland with South Africa, see R. P. Stevens, 1967; J. E. Spence, 1964, pp. 221–46; and *Migrant Labour in Africa South of the Sahara*, 1961.

8. *Migrant Labour in Africa South of the Sahara*, 1961; J. Duffy, 1962; J. Sykes, 1971; C. F. Spence, 1951; and L. B. Serapiao and M. A. El-Khawas, 1979.

9. *Migrant Labour in Africa South of the Sahara*, 1961.

most common and universal explanation is, of course, economic motivation, deriving from the general underdevelopment, unemployment, low standard of living and the poverty of the countries of origin, when compared to the economic boom and development, to high employment opportunities, high standard of living and the social thrills of the countries of destination. But in Southern Africa, the migrant-labour system was one of the most highly regulated forms of inter-territorial relations.

There were in Basutoland, Bechuanaland, Swaziland, Mozambique, Angola and Nyasaland numerous recruitment agents who deliberately enticed the illiterate peasants with advance payments and goods and with glamorous advertisements of urban life in South Africa and Southern Rhodesia. There were transit camps in the out-migrating countries where the job-seekers were housed, fed, interviewed, examined, attested and then escorted to the mines, farms and factories. After 12–18 months of work, the migrant labourer was provided with the same transport services for repatriation. There also were economic incentives for the labour-exporting colonies in the form of licensing, passport and attestation fees, as well as in deferred payments and hut tax, all of which earned foreign currency.

The Portuguese in Mozambique actually used brutal force in recruiting Africans for migrant labour.[10] To facilitate this naked exploitation of the Africans, the Portuguese signed the Mozambique Convention (1928) with South Africa, and the Tete Agreement (1934) with Southern Rhodesia.[11]

It is difficult to estimate the total number of men, women and children who were involved and affected by the migrant-labour system in the countries of origin and destination. At its peak, South Africa employed around 600 000 and Southern Rhodesia around 250 000 migrant workers annually. Nyasaland led the list with over 280 000, followed by Mozambique with around 220 000, Basutoland with 210 000, Botswana 60 000, Zambia around 40 000 and Swaziland 30 000 official emigrants annually. These official figures do not take into account the people who died in the transit camps and, especially, the many who entered South Africa and Southern Rhodesia through unorganized, clandestine routes and methods.

The migrant-labour system has had very significant impacts on Southern Africa. On the one hand, it gave the sub-region distinct and common cultural–historical development and character. On the other hand, it led to the intensification of the centre–periphery dependency of out-migrating countries on the countries of destination. In the countries of origin, there were general social disorganizations characterized by broken families, illegitimate children, divorce, and underdevelopment due

10. *ibid.*; also, J. Duffy, 1962; and J. E. Spence, 1964.
11. *Migrant Labour in Africa South of the Sahara*, 1961.

to the lack of balance in the population caused by the continued absence of a large number of able-bodied men.

Thus, on the eve of formal *apartheid*, Southern Africa was already characterized by the politics of inequality, racism, exploitation and oppression; by mass poverty in the midst of minority affluence and supremacy. The coalition of white workers and the rural bourgeoisie were already entrenched in Southern Rhodesia.

In South Africa the coalition of white workers and the rural bourgeoisie, consisting mainly of Afrikaaners, had formed the Nationalist Party[12] to challenge the United Party of the urban white bourgeoisie, the professionals and international capitalists, most of whom were English-speaking. English–Afrikaaner differences over the most effective methods of maintaining white supremacy over the Africans culminated in the election victory of the Nationalist Party under Dr Malan in 1948.

Simultaneously, African responses to colonialism in Southern Africa were characterized by political parties such as the African National Congress of South Africa and Southern Rhodesia; by self-help, self-reliant welfare organizations; by trades unions such as the Industrial and Commercial Workers Union of South Africa and Southern Rhodesia; and by separatist and Ethiopianist churches.[13]

The leaders of the African political parties were mission-educated, Christian élites who were deeply committed to the ideology of individualism, capitalism, non-racialism, non-violence and universalism. Their major objective was 'Equal rights for all civilized men, irrespective of race and colour'; their means were constitutional resolutions, delegations, telegrams, sermons, pamphlets and assemblies; and their allies were white liberals and missionaries. They erroneously perceived settler colonialism mainly as a humanistic tragedy instead of a worldly, deliberately orchestrated racio-economic system. In South Africa in particular, they misjudged the political rivalry between English and Afrikaaner colonists as a clash over humanity and, therefore, overlooked their underlying ideological consensus on white supremacy.

African trade-unionists, on the other hand, were preoccupied with bread-and-butter issues of wages, conditions of work, housing, racial discrimination, and the right to strike and to collective bargaining. In spite of the legal injunctions, African workers went on strike to force resolution of their grievances. Some mission-educated preachers and laymen broke away because of the racism and paternalistic authoritarianism of white missionaries, and set up their own separatist churches along the same Christian doctrine and liturgy.

12. S. Trapido, 1970; W. R. Duggan, 1973; W. M. Macmillan, 1963; G. Carter, 1959; T. D. Moodie, 1975; and J. H. P. Serfontein, 1979.
13. See, for example, D. Chanaiwa, 1976a; C. Kadalie, 1971; P. Walshe, 1971; and E. Feit, 1967.

Another set of African preachers and laymen not only broke away from the missionaries, but also Africanized Christianity to include such elements as:

(1) polygamous marriages;
(2) communalism;
(3) puritanism on matters of drinking, smoking, dancing and dress; and
(4) general condemnation and boycott of Western culture and values.

This religious movement is known as Ethiopianism,[14] and the followers are generally called *Vapositori*.

On the other hand, the 1948 general election between Smuts's United Party and Dr Malan's Nationalist Party in South Africa was fought on economic issues, on the Black Peril and on pro-British and pro-dominion *versus* pro-Nazi and pro-republican sentiments. Malan and his Nationalist Party won and, therefore, instituted official *apartheid* and republicanism. South Africa withdrew from the Commonwealth and declared itself a republic in 1961.

Economically, the Second World War had brought a new era of economic growth and boom, following the depression and stagnation of the 1930s. The military and economic destabilization of Europe and the Japanese occupation of European colonies in Asia created insatiable demands for:

(1) raw materials of food, textiles, minerals, and timber;
(2) manufactured goods for military supplies and provisions; and
(3) training, refuelling and recovery facilities in tropical Africa.

With its established infrastructure in South Africa and Southern Rhodesia, its migrant-labour system and favourable climate, Southern Africa was most capable of meeting the new demands.

While the war brought economic growth, wealth and employment, it also led to new class formations and, therefore, rivalries. Among the whites of South Africa and Southern Rhodesia, the war increased the role of international capitalism, represented by Anglo-American, Tanganyika Concessions, the British South Africa Company, Lonhro and many others, which had not only intensified mining operations in South Africa, Rhodesia and Katanga, but also had expanded into agro-business with sugar and fruit estates, cattle ranches and forestry. The war changed the urban manufacturing sector from the small-scale to a large-scale, syndicated and automated industry and increased the socio-economic role of the urban bourgeoisie against that of the traditional rural bourgeoisie.

The white urban bourgeoisie was then also manufacturing local, low-cost, import-substitute goods such as mean-meal, sugar, oils, clothes,

14. B. Sundkler, 1961.

shoes, sweets, bread and jam for the emerging African middle class, the urban proletariat and rural peasants. Unlike the rural bourgeoisie which was export-oriented, the urban bourgeoisie was interested in skilled African labour and in African purchasing power. There was the possibility of an effective alliance between the urban white bourgeoisie, the African middle class, and the African urban proletariat against the traditional alliance of the rural white bourgeoisie and the white working class.

Among Africans, the war increased the numbers and significance of the emerging African middle class consisting of businessmen, professionals, teachers, preachers, as well as owner-manager farmers, carpenters and builders. This class was still responsive to urbanism, Westernism, constitutionalism and non-racialism. The war also created a larger urban proletariat class of workers and war veterans who were then more politically conscious and more pressing for better wages, working conditions, benefits, collective bargaining and basic human rights. Given the lack of social security, workers' compensation, and retirement benefits, however, the urban proletariat maintained close ties with their rural relatives as an insurance against sickness, loss of job and old age. The vast majority of the Africans still were rural, subsistence-level peasants.

Southern Africa from 1948 to 1960

The winds of change

The post-war decade in Southern Africa was dominated by the conflict and change brought about by the militant confrontation between African and European nationalisms. The advent of what has been called orthodox African nationalism was a continental post-war phenomenon. From the Cape to Cairo, Africans were demanding the end of foreign rule, racism and imperialism, and the implementation of political independence based on majority rule, universal suffrage and parliamentary democracy. They were forming mass-based organizations that included the urban proletariat and rural peasants, and using the tactics of civil demonstrations, boycotts and strikes. They were espousing the doctrines of pan-Africanism and negritude, and were advocating a United States of Africa.

In Southern Africa, the dominant African organization was the African National Congress (ANC) whose most eloquent and popular spokesman was the Nobel Peace Prize winner, Chief Albert Luthuli.[15] The ANC still stood for the same objectives and means it had espoused during the inter-war period, but was more militant in its demands and demonstrations. It was, however, being challenged by more militant African members of the South African Communist Party and the ANC Youth League. The Youth League was formed in 1943 by Aton Muziwakhe Lembede and it consisted

15. See, for example, P. Walshe, 1971; and A. Luthuli, 1962.

of Africans who had become disillusioned with the ANC's alliance with white liberals and with the lack of clear commitment to majority rule and universal suffrage.

In 1949 the ANC formed a Congress Alliance with Indians, coloureds and white liberals and, together, they formulated a Nation Building Programme. In 1952 the ANC and its allies organized a nationwide Defiance Campaign during which 8500 people were arrested. In 1955, a Congress of the People, representing Africans, coloureds, Indians and whites adopted a 'Freedom Charter for the Democratic South Africa of the Future' which advocated a free, united and non-racial South Africa and a bill of basic human rights.

In the face of black unity and militancy, the Nationalist government decided to apply repressive and reactionary measures such as prohibition of meetings, police surveillance and harassment, banning of political parties, and the torture, banishment and imprisonment of individuals. With the tacit support of the United Party and the Progressive Party, the all-white parliament passed successive repressive laws such as:

(1) the Group Areas Act of 1950 which required the classification of all South Africans by race;
(2) the Supression of Communism Act (1950) which categorized any person or organization that criticized *apartheid* or advocated non-racialism and civil liberties as a communist. The Communist Party itself was also banned in 1950;
(3) the Native Labour (Settlement of Disputes) Act (1953) which legally abolished the rights of freedom of association and collective bargaining for African workers;
(4) the Criminal Law Amendment Act (1953) which made it an offence to protest or support any campaign against any law; and
(5) the Mines and Works Act (1956) which prohibited Africans from doing skilled work in the mines.

When it became clear that repressive laws and police violence alone were failing to break up African determination, the Nationalist government under Prime Minister Verwoerd appointed the Toulinson Commission (1954) to seek alternative means. The Commission recommended the notorious bantustan policy which led to the Bantu Self-government Act and the Bantu Investment Corporation of 1959. Under the Act, Africans were divided into black homelands corresponding to the traditional ethnic groups of the Zulu, Sotho, Xhosa, Tswana, Tonga and Venda in which they were to develop separately under some measure of self-government. Matters of defence, internal security, foreign affairs and the budget were controlled by white South Africa though the administrator.

The bantustan policy was basically a 'divide and rule' technique designed to balkanize African nationalism and to buy time while consolidating white supremacy. The idea was to revive and revitalize ethnic

258

rivalries of the Mfecane era by reversing the unifying factors of pan-Africanism, education, intermarriages, urbanization and nationalism. Simultaneously any redundant worker and any political 'agitator' would be banished to his/her respective bantustan. Legally, all Africans in 'white' South Africa became temporary sojourners, without title to civil liberties and property ownership. Squatter and tenant-labour problems as well as personal disputes and housing shortages were resolved by forced resettlement in the bantustans.

The bantustan policy failed to destroy African nationalism. It also further divided South Africa itself by creating new factions among the ethnic and racial groups. It created a new type of leadership and nationalism in the bantustans. Some of the leaders, especially Chiefs Kaiser Matanzima of the Transkei and Gatsha Buthelezi of the Kwa Zulu bantustan, achieved national and international fame. They became interested in complete independence which white South Africa could not afford to grant. Economically, the bantustans turned out to be modern versions of the old African reserves, characterized by overpopulation, over-stocking, erosion, underdevelopment, unemployment, poverty and despair, and leaving the young males with no alternative but to offer themselves to the white man for low-paid jobs.

As Nelson Mandela had stated in his presidential address at the ANC convention of September 1953, there was going to be 'No easy walk to freedom' for the Africans of South Africa. Another peaceful demonstration of 1956 led to the famous Treason Trial of 156 leaders which dragged on until March 1961. As with most protracted and complex historical struggles, the ANC leadership began to differ over the correct and most effective means of confronting white violence and repression, and, as a result, the Pan African Congress (PAC) was born in April 1959.

As stated in the *Africanist* by Robert Mangaliso Sobukwe, the founding president, the PAC regarded South Africa as an African country and was committed to the overthrow of white domination and to pan-Africanism. It was opposed to multi-racialism and to white leadership because it regarded all whites 'as shareholders in the South Africa Oppressors Company (Pty) Ltd'. Simultaneously, the all-African Federation of Free African Trades Unions of South Africa (FEFATUSA) was also formed due to the disillusionment with the multi-racial South African Congress of Trades Unions which supported the ANC. On the whole, the ANC and PAC drew their membership from the same middle class, proletariat and peasant groups on an individual basis. But the students and progressive intellectuals tended to join the PAC.

The PAC declared 1960 as the 'Year of destiny, positive action, African independence and self-determination', and for its inaugural issue it chose a 'Positive, decisive campaign against the Pass Laws', beginning on 21 March 1960. According to the instructions issued by Sobukwe in the PAC circular, *Calling the Nation*, African males in every city and village

PLATE 10.1   *Robert Sobukwe, president-founder of the PAC (Pan-African Congress), photographed in 1963*

were to leave their passes at home, join demonstrations and, if arrested, offer 'no bail, no defence, no fine'. The circular demanded total abolition of the passes and a national minimum wage of £35.

The campaign, which took place in several locations throughout South Africa, ended in the tragedy of the Sharpeville Massacre where a line of white policemen, armed with guns and tear gas, opened fire upon an 'unarmed, amiable, well-mannered and unaggressive' crowd of between 10 000 and 20 000, killing 72 and wounding 186 others – including 40 women and eight children.

Predictably, the government blamed communist conspirators for the demonstrations, and banned the PAC and ANC. Nelson Mandela, Walter Sisulu and others in the ANC formed an underground movement called *Umkonto we Sizwe* (the Spear of the Nation) centred at Rivonia near Johannesburg which was raided in 1963 and, after the famous Rivonia Trial, the leaders were imprisoned for life at Robben Island. The PAC also organized another underground movement called POQO and it too was soon destroyed. The PAC and ANC were forced to go underground and operate from outside South Africa, while the only meaningful internal

PLATE 10.2   *The Sharpeville Massacre, South Africa, 28 March 1960*

African opposition came from Steve Biko and the Black Consciousness Movement.

The Federation of Rhodesia and Nyasaland

Southern Rhodesia, Northern Rhodesia and Nyasaland were federated for ten years from 1953 to 1963, from an admixture of factors and interested groups.[16] The British government wanted the federation to counter the anti-British, republican sentiments and *apartheid* of the Afrikaaners in South Africa by a neighbouring pro-British and multi-racial domination. British and South African international capitalists wanted the federation as an alternative area of investment to escape possible nationalization by the Afrikaaners. The English-speaking, white minorities of the two Rhodesias and Nyasaland, having ruled out the possibility of joining Afrikaaner-dominated South Africa, wanted the federation to contain African nationalism in Southern Rhodesia and prevent the impending independence of the Protectorates of Northern Rhodesia and Nyasaland, which they perceived in terms of creeping communism and nationalization.

Africans of Northern Rhodesia and Nyasaland generally were opposed to the federation because they realized that it would lead to the dominance of the settler colonialism of Southern Rhodesia, and therefore rob them of their protectorate status and independence. Africans of Southern Rhodesia generally had mixed feelings about the federation because they thought that the avowed federation policy of multi-racial partnership would possibly ameliorate settler colonialism and racism in their own country.

The federation consisted of the federal and three territorial assemblies; matters dealing with African affairs, such as housing, pass laws and lower education, were reserved for territorial assemblies. African interests in the federation were represented by a multi-racial African Affairs Board.

As an entity, the federation was characterized by remarkable post-war economic development, with tremendous foreign investment and white immigration. Between 1946 and 1960, the white population in Southern Rhodesia, Northern Rhodesia and Nyasaland rose from 82 000 to 223 000, and from 22 000 to 76 000, and 2400 to 9000 respectively. The federation built the world-famous Kariba dam for hydro-electricity, the University of Rhodesia and Nyasaland, several technical colleges and greatly expanded the communication systems.

But the economic bonanza was in sharp contrast to the African feelings of betrayal and, therefore, disillusionment because most of the wealth, jobs and wages were going to whites while the colonialist and racialist laws were continuing. In retrospect, the federation was moribund because of the incompatibility between settler colonialism and multi-racial part-

16. See, for example, P. Keatley, 1963; D. Chanaiwa, 1976b; and L. Bowman, 1973.

nership. Through concerted effort, the Nyasaland African National Congress under Dr Hastings Banda, the Northern Rhodesian African Congress under Harry Nkumbula and Kenneth Kaunda, and the Southern Rhodesia African National Congress under Joshua Nkomo, Ndabaningi Sithole and Robert Mugabe soon mobilized strong African opposition against the federation. The British appointed the Monckton Commission which inquired into the federation and concluded that 'partnership was a sham'. In 1963 the federation was dissolved and Nyasaland and Northern Rhodesia became independent Malawi (1963) and Zambia (1964) respectively.[17]

In Southern Rhodesia the post-war urban white bourgeoisie had attempted to contain militant African nationalism of the urban African proletariat and rural peasants by partial incorporation and assimilation of the emergent African middle class, through the policy of partnership, voting rights determined by educational and property qualifications, and preferential treatment in areas of education, housing, health, businesses and farming. The urban bourgeoisie failed because its assimilationist strategy came too late and offered too little. When the African middle class joined forces with the masses, the white urban bourgeoisie became vulnerable to the political opposition of the white rural bourgeoisie and the white working class who rallied behind the Dominion Party and played upon the racio-economic interests of the white electorate.

In frustration, the urban bourgeoisie decided to destroy African nationalism and to stay in power by appeasing the whites.[18] As in South Africa, the white parliament passed successive repressive laws, such as the notorious Law and Order (Emergency Powers) Maintenance Act. In 1957 Prime Minister Garfield Todd was ousted because he was considered 'negrophile'. In 1959 Prime Minister Edgar Whitehead conducted an Operation Sunrise raid, imprisoned 500 officials of the African National Congress, and banned the party. Africans formed the National Democratic Party (NDP) on 1 January 1960 under the same constitution, tactics and leadership.

In a last-ditch attempt to placate African nationalism, the British government, the settler government and African leaders agreed on the 1961 constitution which advocated a legislative assembly of 50 white and 15 African members, a cumbersome A- and B-roll voting mechanism, a constitutional council and a bill of rights. The African leaders, however, had to withdraw their support because of formidable opposition by the masses. A massive 'Build-a-Nation' and 'Claim-your-Vote' campaign by the Whitehead government failed to break up African opposition to the constitution. Consequently, the NDP was banned on 9 December 1961.

17. P. Keatley, 1963.
18. See, for example, L. Bowman, 1973; D. Chanaiwa, 1976b; G. Arrighi, 1970; and E. Mlambo, 1972.

In the 1962 general election the United Federal Party urban bourgeoisie was defeated by the Dominion Party (rural bourgeoisie and working class) led by Winston Field. The Dominion Party was renamed the Rhodesia Front and Field was replaced by Ian Douglas Smith.

The Africans formed the Zimbabwe African Peoples Union (ZAPU) – under the same NDP constitution, leadership and tactics – which was banned on 19 September 1962. The period between September 1962 and June 1963 was characterized by the leaderlessness, confusion and frustration which resulted in the formation of the Zimbabwe African National Union (ZANU). Briefly, the causes of the ZAPU–ZANU split, like that of the ANC–PAC, were:

(1) the long-range frustration over the lack of progress towards independence;
(2) the inevitable scape-goating syndrome;
(3) the differences over non-violence *versus* armed struggle, and internal struggle *versus* government-in-exile; and
(4) a general disillusionment with the leadership, especially Nkomo's.

Simply put, the Nkomo faction at that stage was inclined to be more cautious, non-violent, and pro-government-in-exile, while the Sithole–Mugabe faction wanted a more radical, underground struggle.

Between August 1963 and August 1964, ZANU and ZAPU were engaged in a fierce membership drive which was accompanied by violence and intimidation on both opponents and neutrals. Predictably, the Smith regime, which was preparing for its Unilateral Declaration of Independence (UDI) from Britain, took full advantage of the fratricide to further divide the Africans and to turn the colony into a police state. On 26 August 1964, both ZANU and ZAPU were banned and both leaderships were put under detention which lasted until December 1974. Like the ANC and PAC, ZANU and ZAPU were forced to go underground and into exile in Zambia, Malawi and Tanzania where they began the armed struggle under the acting leadership of Herbert Chitepo and James Chikerema respectively. The Smith regime moved swiftly with an all-white referendum on UDI in November 1964, a general election in May 1965 and UDI on 11 November 1965.

Mozambique

The post-war period in Mozambique was characterized by a vigorous Portuguese drive to turn the colony into a settler economy similar to South Africa and Southern Rhodesia. Politically, Portugal had no intention of ever granting independence to its colonies. Instead, it wanted to draw them into a complex relationship with itself. It propogated the myth of a new *missao civilizado*, under which Portugal was allegedly a unitary, universal state without colonies. Mozambique was supposedly a province and the Africans were Portuguese citizens.[19]

Economically, Portugal wanted to take advantage of the post-war economic boom in its colonies to solve its own problems of unemployment, overpopulation and need for raw materials and markets. Mozambique continued to prosper after the war. Railways, roads and hydro-electric dams like Cabora Bassa were being built. Colonies consumed 25–30 per cent of Portuguese exports and contributed 20–25 per cent of Portugal's national revenues.

Portugal's strategy was to intensify European settlement in both Angola and Mozambique. On an average, 4000–7000 Portuguese were exported for resettlement annually. The settler populations of Angola and Mozambique jumped from 44 000 to 250 000 and 27 000 to 130 000 respectively between 1940 and 1960.

Consequently, Angola and Mozambique increasingly resembled the settler colonies of South Africa and Southern Rhodesia, except for the historical constraints of the lack of sufficient capital for investment, ineffective colonial administration and economic dependency on the British capitalists. The bulk of the settlers were illiterate peasants or from the unemployed proletariat, and were not known for their cultural or racial tolerance. The resettlement scheme, therefore, led to the intensification of racism and the exploitation of African labour.[20]

As a result, the first political parties were formed in exile. Mozambique started off with the National Democratic Union of Mozambique (UDENAMO) under Adelino Gwambe which was formed in Salisbury (Harare) in 1960 and the Mozambique African National Union (MANU) under C. Mahal which was formed in Mombasa, Kenya, in 1961. In June 1962, UDENAMO and MANU combined into the Front for the Liberation of Mozambique (FRELIMO) under Dr Eduardo Chivanbo Mondlane. Beginning with the formation of these political parties in Angola and Mozambique and following the banning of the ANC and PAC in South Africa and of ZANU and ZAPU in Rhodesia, there was a transformation from orthodox nationalism to the liberation movement, and from militant demonstrations to armed struggle, which we shall discuss later.

High commission territories

One of the major concerns of Africans in post-war Basutoland, Bechuanaland and Swaziland was their constitutional status, especially their possible transfer to the Union of South Africa. The 1956 Tomlinson Commission on bantustan policy actually included the high commission

19. See, for example, L. B. Serapiao and M. A. El-Khawas, 1979; J. Sykes, 1971; T. M. Okuma, 1962; D. Barneet and R. Harvey, 1972.

20. For further details, see International Labour Organization, 1962.

PLATE 10.3 *Dr Eduardo Chivanbo Mondlane (in the centre), founder and first president of FRELIMO (the* Frente de Libertação de Moçambique), *photographed in 1962*

territories among the proposed bantustans. Another issue was the dual role between the resident commissioners and traditional kings. The third question was on the nature and functions of district councils and hereditary chiefs. Then there was the perennial problem of economic development and migrant labour.

Through concerted opposition by Africans and the British disappointment with Afrikaaner republicanism, the territories were never transferred to South Africa. The remaining domestic issues were resolved constitutionally. Administrative proclamations, constitutional conferences, national referendums, or orders-in-council changed the traditional kings into constitutional monarchs, and made district councils the primary organs of local governments.

In Swaziland a Constitutional Committee report of 1963 was rejected by the people, and after another constitutional conference in London, the country was first granted self-government in 1966 and then independence in 1969. For Basutoland, there were constitutional negotiations in London in 1958 and in Maseru in 1959, followed by orders-in-council in 1960 which led to self-government consisting of an executive council, a national legislative council of 80 members and elective district councils. On 4

PLATE 10.4   *Seretse Khama, exiled chief of the Bamangwato (Bechuanaland) with his English wife, Ruth Williams, and their 20-month-old daughter, England, March 1952*

October 1966 the territory became independent Lesotho.

The post-war constitutional history of Bechuanaland was complicated because of two issues. The first was the conflict between the high commissioner, who wanted to exercise more power over the appointments of chiefs and over local government, and Tshekedi Khama, the Ngwato paramount chief, who wanted to preserve his traditional powers and culture. On the basis of the Native Administration Proclamation of 1943, the high commissioner appointed the African and European advisory councils, and thereby injected racism into local politics.

The second issue was the lengthy dispute (1949–56) over the marriage of Seretse Khama, the heir-designate, to an English woman which led to his forced exile in England and his permanent banishment from the chieftainship for him and his heirs. The high commissioner was under pressure from *apartheid* South Africa which did not want a black ruler married to a white woman as a neighbour.

After 1956 the territory resumed its normal constitutional course. The two advisory councils were joined into a joint advisory council, there was a legislative council in 1960; and the first political party – the Bechuanaland Peoples' Party – was formed in 1960. After the Lobatsi Conference of 1963 led to self-government, the territory became independent Botswana on 30 September 1966.

Southern Africa from the 1960s to the 1980s: the armed struggle

The dominant theme of Southern African history of the 1960s and 1970s was the revolutionary tide of liberation movements and the armed struggle in the settler colonies of South Africa, Rhodesia, Mozambique, Angola and Namibia.[21] By then Africans had finally accepted the failure of middle-class liberalism and orthodox nationalism, and of militant demonstrations in the face of settler power and intransigence. Furthermore, historical hindsight derived from the disappointing performance of most independent African states had taught Africans about the futility of political decolonization and independence without accompanying economic and cultural emancipation.

It had become clear that true independence in a settler-colonialist and multi-ethnic society like South Africa and Rhodesia would require structural dismantling of the existing institutions, as well as the modes of production, ownership and class formations. It would necessitate a proletarian economic democracy of mass-controlled resources, means and goals of production, distribution and services, in order to satisfy basic human needs, end economic exploitation and insecurity, and promote social justice.

Liberation movements, therefore, were rooted in a comprehensive, emancipatory ideology, the dominant components of which were:

(1) an uncompromising commitment to anti-imperialism, anti-colonialism, anti-racism and sometimes anti-capitalism, as well as to national self-determination, to pan-Africanism, non-alignment and basic human rights;

(2) a bias towards the urban proletariat, rural peasants and progressive intellectuals who were perceived as the vital revolutionary vanguard in the liberation process;

(3) the adoption of, in some cases, scientific socialism along Marxist–Leninist principles in the areas of economic production, distribution, consumption and social relationships; and

(4) the prevention of external links of dependency and subordination and the promotion of militant solidarity with the other liberation movements and oppressed peoples of the world.

21. See, for example, E. Mlambo, 1972; T. M. Okuma, 1962; N. Mandela, 1965; B. S. Biko, 1972; G. M. Gerhart, 1979; and UNESCO, 1981b.

The protracted armed struggle was launched around 1964. Internally, the liberation movements received political and material support from the urban and rural masses, and from progressive intellectuals, civil servants and businessmen. Externally, they obtained diplomatic and material support mainly from the Liberation Committee of the Organization of African Unity (OAU), from non-aligned nations and from the USSR, China and other socialist countries; as well as from the Scandinavian countries and humanitarian and solidarity groups in the Western world. The movements themselves co-operated and assisted each other with joint intelligence networks and military operations. The operational bases and training camps were located in the frontline states of Tanzania, Zambia and, later, Angola and Mozambique.

Conversely, the white settlers of South Africa, Rhodesia, Angola and Mozambique obtained diplomatic and material support from Western governments, mainly the United States, Britain, France and West Germany. Regionally, South African, Rhodesian and Portuguese forces assisted each other with joint intelligence and anti-guerrilla operations. The Portuguese and Rhodesian governments placed the Africans in operational zones into strategic concentration camps which they euphemistically called 'protected villages', in order to isolate and starve the freedom-fighters.

The first successes of the armed struggle were in the Portuguese colonies. In Angola, the MPLA gained control of a large territory around Luanda; the UPA was operating in the north from Kinshasa; and UNITA in the east from Zambia. In Mozambique, FRELIMO gained effective control of the northern districts of Tete, Niassa and Cabo Delgado. In defence, the Portuguese intensified the 'protected-village' system and resorted to brutal methods of torture, massacres, banishments and assassinations. For example, Dr Mondlane was assassinated in February 1969. He was succeeded by Samora Machel.

Despite the massive support from Western governments, the colonial wars soon became too burdensome for Portugal. By the late 1960s, Portugal was spending nearly half its annual budget on colonial wars, and although the conservatives, senior army officers and financiers wanted to continue the wars, the general public had given up. General Antonio de Spinola wrote a book, *Portugal and the Future*, which advocated the end of Portuguese colonialism in Africa. Then on 25 April 1974, the army overthrew the government of President Caetano and installed Spinola as head of the *junta*.

The liberation struggle had forced the Portuguese to look inwardly and critically at their own economic underdevelopment and dependency and at the political dictatorship of Salazar and his successor, Caetano. The new interest in domestic issues and the increasing deaths and expenses from the wars, left the Portuguese with no option but to negotiate for the quickest end to colonialism. On 8 September 1974, they signed the

Lusaka Agreement with the liberation movements, which set up interim self-governments for Angola and Mozambique and established the mechanisms for conducting general elections. In 1975 Angola and Mozambique became independent under the MPLA and FRELIMO respectively.

The independence of Angola and Mozambique had an irreversible effect on the armed struggle in Southern Africa, especially in Rhodesia and Namibia. It stabbed the settlers of South Africa and Rhodesia and their Western allies in the back and left them diplomatically and militarily vulnerable. They were no longer insulated by Mozambique and Angola. The United States' foreign policy on Southern Africa, which, as stated in the National Security Memorandum 39 of 1969, was designed to support and promote white-minority regimes, was suddenly invalidated. Ian Smith, the prime minister of Rhodesia, who previously had sworn that Africans would not obtain independence in a thousand years, had to reckon with impending African rule in his lifetime. The Western powers had to change their pro-white policy to one of *détente* with the frontline states, while promoting for a while pro-West and neo-colonialist African regimes in Rhodesia and Namibia. The settlers were pressured to negotiate with African leaders for internal settlements.

Meanwhile, independent Angola and Mozambique provided the liberation movements of Rhodesia, South Africa and Namibia with tremendous advantages in the form of their proven legacy of military organization and tactics. The two former Portuguese colonies also placed their former bases and training camps at the disposal of their oppressed neighbours. With the frontline hospitality of Angola, Mozambique, Botswana, Tanzania and Zambia, ZANU, ZAPU, the South West Africa People's Organization (SWAPO), the ANC and PAC were able to intensify the armed struggle.

For ten years (1964–74), the Zimbabwean freedom-fighters had waged the armed struggle from Tanzania and Zambia, under their acting leaders – Chitepo for ZANU and Chikerema and, later, J. Z. Moyo, for ZAPU. The target was the illegal UDI of Smith and his fellow cowboys. Britain had not recognized the UDI and had persuaded members of the United Nations to apply economic sanctions in the hope of forcing Smith into a negotiated internal settlement. The sanctions had not been effective because the settlers had found allies in South Africa and the Western world who assisted in breaking them. Meanwhile Britain had sponsored several 'peace talks' with both Smith and the moderate elements among the African and white bourgeoisie.

Internally, the United African National Council (UANC) had been formed under the leadership of Bishop Abel Muzorewa in response to the power vacuum and the British-sponsored peace talks. The UANC was the replica of the past orthodox nationalist organizations like the NDP, aiming at decolonization through militant demonstrations. The goals and tactics of the UANC were, of course, tailored to the internal realities of settler power and repressive laws, and some internal followers of ZANU and ZAPU also belonged to the UANC.

The independence of Mozambique gave new hope and vigour to ZANU, ZAPU and the UANC, and made Smith receptive to a negotiated settlement.[22] Under pressure from South Africa, Britain and the United States, Smith agreed to release the detained African leaders for constitutional talks in a train stationed over the bridge at Victoria Falls in 1974. Following the abortive conference, Nkomo, Sithole, Mugabe and Muzorewa attempted to form a common organization under the umbrella of the UANC and the leadership of Bishop Muzorewa which never materialized. Then Nkomo and Mugabe formed a common Patriotic Front which intensified the armed struggle with ZAPU operating from Zambia and ZANU from Mozambique.

The Victoria Falls conference was followed by other abortive constitutional conferences in Geneva, Salisbury and Malta on the ways and means of transferring power from the white minority to the African majority. Then, after three months of negotiations, Smith, Muzorewa, Sithole and a traditional chief called Jeremiah Chirau, agreed upon the Internal Settlement on 3 March 1978, the terms of which were:

(1) an African majority rule based on universal adult suffrage of citizens of 18 years and above;
(2) an Independence Day on 31 December 1978;
(3) removal of racialist legislation;
(4) a bill of rights;
(5) a 100-member parliament of which 72 would be Africans and 28 whites; and
(6) a transitional government consisting of an executive council and a ministerial council in which Africans and Europeans would share power equally.

The Patriotic Front boycotted the negotiations, denounced the Internal Settlement as 'a political and legal swindle', and continued the armed struggle against the Smith–Muzorewa government.

The deadlock was finally resolved at the Lancaster House Conference of 1979 at which Smith, Muzorewa and the Patriotic Front agreed to the Lancaster House Constitution which set the terms for a British-monitored general election, for a parliament of 80 Africans and 20 whites, for a bill of rights, universal suffrage and independence in 1980. At the election, ZANU–Patriotic Front won 57 seats, ZAPU won 20 seats, the UANC won 3 and ZANU–Sithole failed to win a single seat. Robert Mugabe, president of ZANU–PF, formed his government with him as prime minister and Reverend Canaan Banana as president. On 18 April 1980, the former colony of Rhodesia became the independent state of Zimbabwe.

22. UNESCO, 1981b.

PLATE 10.5 *From left to right: Sally Mugabe, Prime Minister Robert Mugabe, President Rev. Canaan Banana and Vice-President Simon Muzenda, photographed in 1980, the year of Zimbabwe's independence*

The problem of Namibia

Namibia has had a very complicated constitutional history.[23] Under European colonialism, it started off as the German colony of South-West Africa until 1920, when it became a mandated territory of the League of Nations to be administered by Britain. Britain delegated the responsibility of administration to the then pro-British Union of South Africa. When South Africa became an Afrikaaner-dominated republic, it continued to rule Namibia practically as its own province. The *apartheid* laws and practices of South Africa were applied to Namibia.

Economically, Namibia became South Africa's captive source of raw materials and migrant labour. The Namibian economy consisted of:

(1) mining (diamonds, uranium, copper, zinc and lead);
(2) agriculture (cattle and sheep); and
(3) fishing.

More importantly, it is typically a neo-colonialist, externally-oriented economy based on a selective exploitation of natural resources for export.

23. For example, see R. H. Green *et al.*, 1981.

Over 90 per cent of domestic production (100 per cent for minerals, 99 per cent for fish, 100 per cent for karakul and 90 per cent for cattle) is for export. The bulk of the exports go to South Africa for processing, or through South Africa for re-exporting. Furthermore, ownership of the means of production, as well as the top management and the technicians, are foreign. Mining is dominated by the South African-based Anglo-American Corporation, the American-based Metal Climax–Newmont at Tsumeb and the British trans-national corporation, RTZ, at Rossing uranium mine.

Legally, Namibia became a trustee territory of the United Nations, which succeeded the League of Nations. The UN General Assembly resolved in 1966 that South Africa's occupation and rule over Namibia were illegal. The UN Security Council passed the same resolution in 1969 and, after a protracted trial, the International Court of Justice ruled in favour of the United Nations in 1971. The UN then established the United Nations Council for Namibia as the *de jure* governing authority, and acknowledged SWAPO as the 'authentic representative of the Namibian people'. But, for economic, political and military reasons, South Africa refused to leave Namibia in defiance of the world community. Thus, *de facto* power remained in the hands of South African police, soldiers and administrators.

The independence of Angola and Mozambique radically changed the course of the armed struggle in Namibia and South Africa. Being afraid that Angola and Mozambique would be used as springboards for carrying out the armed struggle, South Africa decided to destabilize the newly independent states by providing arms, training and mercenaries to UNITA under Savimbi in Angola and to the so-called Mozambique National Resistance Movement. In Namibia, South Africa pursued a dual strategy of intensified exploitation of natural resources, especially minerals, and consolidation of a pro-South African puppet leader and government.

Under South African sponsorship, the white Republic Party led by Dirk Mudge and the South West African National Party consisting of anti-SWAPO puppet chiefs, bourgeoisie and their followers, held a conference at Turnhalle in Windhoek. The participants formed the Democratic Turnhalle Alliance under the leadership of Mudge and agreed on peripheral reforms designed to remove only petty *apartheid*.

Like most reformist developments in colonial situations, the Democratic Turnhalle Alliance came too late and offered too little. It was denounced by SWAPO, the frontline states, the OAU and the UN. The United Nations initiated its own plan which advocated a cease-fire, a UN peace-keeping mission, and a UN-monitored general election leading to the independence of Namibia. Furthermore, Angola brought in Cuban troops which assisted its forces in resisting Savimbi and South Africa; and the US Congress temporarily refused to continue financing American mercenaries in Angola.

PLATE 10.6 *A SWAPO (the South West Africa People's Organization) detachment on patrol*

For a while South Africa rejected the UN plan because it still wanted a puppet government and its soldiers in Namibia, and it insisted on keeping the port of Walvis Bay as leverage over independent Namibia. With the connivance of the United States, Britain, France, West Germany and Canada, who constituted themselves into the so-called Western Contact Group, South Africa adopted the strategy of appearing to be interested in a settlement in order to deflect international criticism, while consolidating its neo-colonialist plan in Namibia. In December 1978, South Africa sponsored the election of 50 puppet members of the Constituent Assembly under martial law during which the entire internal leadership of SWAPO was arrested. Consequently, the Namibian conflict became a multi-pronged struggle with SWAPO, the frontline states, the OAU and the UN on one side, and South Africa, the Turnhalle Alliance and the Western Contact Group on the other. However, by 1989, the independence of Namibia and the electoral victory of SWAPO seemed certain. Namibia's political dawn was at last about to break.

South Africa

Following Sharpeville and withdrawal from the Commonwealth, the Nationalist Party moved swiftly to consolidate the *apartheid* system and to turn South Africa into a fully-fledged police state, by passing additional repressive and racialist laws. For example, in May 1963, it passed the General Law Amendment Act which authorized policemen to detain a person *incommunicado* for 90 renewable days. The Criminal Procedure Amendment Act of 1965 authorized policemen to detain a court witness *incommunicado* for 180 renewable days. The Prohibition of Political Interference Act of 1968 made it illegal for any political party to have inter-racial membership. The Liberal Party decided to disband, while the Progressive Party complied with the law.

In spite of South Africa being a police state, with its arsenal of weapons, soldiers, tear gas and police dogs, the liberation struggle actually intensified. Internally, the struggle was spearheaded by students and trades-unionists. One of these students was Steve Biko, a medical student at Natal University, who experienced profound frustration and disillusionment with the racialist politics of the multi-racial National Union of South African Students (NUSAS). He wrote *Black Souls in White Skins* which was a PAC-type treatise on multi-racialism and white liberalism.[24] In July 1969, Biko became the founding-president of the South African Students Organization (SASO), because black students wanted to 'do things for themselves and all by themselves'.

Biko and SASO finally brought home the pan-Africanism of George Padmore and Kwame Nkrumah, the negritude of Léopold Senghor and Aimé Césaire, the revolutionary philosophy of Franz Fanon, Malcolm X and Amilcar Cabral, and the socialism of Sékou Touré and Julius Nyerere to the African masses of South Africa. Their ideology, which became known as Black Consciousness, exposed the weakness of the orthodox African nationalism of the past and popularized the liberation movements and the armed struggle.

The Black Consciousness Movement resulted in a student–worker alliance among SASO, the Black Allied Workers' Union, the Black People's Convention (BPC), and the Soweto Students Representative Council. Together, these organizations revived the pre-Sharpeville tactics of militant demonstrations. When industrial strikes became widespread and forceful, the government used the Anti-Terrorism Act of 1967 to arrest Biko and the executives of SASO and BPC. Biko died in detention on 12 September 1977, having been mortally beaten and tortured by the police.

24. For further details, see B. S. Biko, 1972; G. M. Gerhart, 1979; and T. Thoahlane, 1975.

Nevertheless, both organized and spontaneous opposition continued the struggle against *apartheid* inside South Africa. From June to December of 1976, a tide of demonstrations and strikes rocked the cities of South Africa, exemplified by the students' riots in Soweto at which the police killed 23 people and wounded 200 others. In the same year the Azanian African People's Organization (AZAPO) was formed for effective political mobilization.

Predictably, the Nationalist government responded with stern police action and bannings. On 19 October 1977, SASO and 16 other organizations, including the BPC and the Soweto Students Representative Council, were banned. The African newspaper, *The World*, was banned and its editor, Percy Qoboza, was imprisoned. In November, the whites held their general election and the Nationalist Party was returned with an even greater majority. But the liberation *versus* repression cycle inside South Africa, and the armed struggle waged by the ANC and the PAC with the support of the frontline states, the OUA, the UN and the vast majority of the world community continued with greater intensity into the 1980s. By the election of 1989 white consensus in South Africa was beginning to crack from both the right and the left. Afrikaanerdom was less of a monolith than it had ever been.

Global strategy and regional geopolitics

In this period of African history, three primarily external conflicts helped to boost the strategic value of Southern Africa. These were, first, the Second World War; secondly, the Cold War between the Western world and the Soviet alliance; and, thirdly, the Arab–Israeli conflict.

The industrial value of the minerals of Southern Africa for Britain and its empire rose to new levels of importance under the challenge of the Axis during the Second World War. Strategic metals vital for the factories of the Commonwealth and its allies were at stake. At the beginning of the war there was some anxiety about Italy's capacity to strike southwards from the Horn of Africa, capture the important eastern seaport of Mombasa, and then endanger traffic to and from the mineral transit points of Southern Africa. But Italy during the Second World War turned out to be a paper tiger from quite early. Mombasa was only briefly imperilled.

The second external military threat to Southern Africa was potentially from African colonies whose European imperial powers were under Nazi occupation. Madagascar, for example, was for a while under 'hostile' neo-Vichy control. In was not until May 1942 that the British invaded the island – and General Charles de Gaulle's authority was at last recognized.

The third external military threat was potentially from Japanese battleships or war planes. But the level of technology in the 1940s necessitated more refuelling stops than were accessible to the Japanese for such long-distance adventures, though the resources of Southern Africa were profoundly tempting to the mineral-poor Japan.

But in many ways the most important threat to Commonwealth control of South Africa was *internal*. It was within the Union of South Africa – in the form of considerable Nazi sympathies among the Boers. Almost immediately after Britain declared war on Hitler's Germany, Hertzog attempted to have South Africa declare itself neutral. The parliamentary motion was defeated by 80 votes to 67. On 5 September, Smuts formed a coalition government – and declared war on Germany. In February 1941 riots broke out after a pro-Nazi *Ossewabrandug* meeting in Johannesburg.

But there were enough Afrikaaners in agreement with English-speaking whites to ensure support for the Allies. Major harbour improvements in Table Bay were undertaken soon after the declaration of war. In the previous year the South African Air Force had been enlarged – and preparations for munitions factories in Pretoria were initiated.

In July 1940, Smuts broadcast to Britain and the United States about an 'international society of free nations'. And in August, General Smuts was gazetted field-marshal. In July 1943, Smuts won the general election in South Africa. The pro-Nazi forces in the country were temporarily subdued. For the rest of the Second World War, the strategic worth of Southern Africa for the industrial democracies was protected.

The world war closed with the dropping of atomic bombs on Hiroshima and Nagasaki. A new strategic value was now added to Central and Southern Africa – the presence of uranium. For a while Zaire was the most important source of uranium in the southern hemisphere – and prospecting for other sources further south was soon under way. The nuclear age had dawned upon the world – and Central and Southern Africa were part of the new era, for better or for worse. The strategic calculus of the area had become more complex.

Meanwhile, a new and more pervasive rivalry had descended upon the post-war world – the Cold War between the Western powers and the Soviet alliance. It is to this second conflict affecting the strategic value of Southern Africa that we must now turn. The Soviet Union had of course been an ally of the Commonwealth and the United States in the Second World War. While the paranoia about 'communism' in Southern Africa was basically unabated even during the global conflict, the open denunciation of the Soviet Union was temporarily muted from about 1942 to 1945.

Once the Cold War got under way following the end of the Second World War, both anti-communism and hostility to the Soviet Union resumed their ascendancy in Southern African politics. By February 1956 the Pretoria government was ready to close down Soviet consulates in the Union of South Africa. The tendency to equate domestic communism with 'treason' became a feature of the paranoia of the regimes in Southern Africa. In South Africa this resulted in a number of highly publicized 'treason trials' and trials against communism. These included the mass 'treason' trials of anti-*apartheid* Africans, Asians and Europeans. We have also referred earlier to the celebrated martyrdom of Nelson Mandela; and in March 1966 Abram Fischer, Queen's Counsel, was tried for communism in Pretoria and sentenced to life-imprisonment.

But as the Soviet Union was losing even its symbolic presence in Southern Africa, it was soon gaining a new diplomatic status north of the Zambezi. One African country after another – newly independent – established diplomatic relations with the USSR. The Soviet diplomatic presence in the continent in this period started to move relentlessly southwards. By the middle of the 1960s, the Soviet Union was represented in Lusaka – becoming part of the 'frontline'. By the middle of the 1970s, the Soviet diplomatic presence had moved even further south – and gained a higher profile than ever before. Maputo and Luanda became for a while two of the staunchest African friends of the USSR – and self-proclaimed Marxist–Leninist republics, however tentative. From a Western point of view, the strategic importance of Southern Africa as a whole was under a new challenge.

The strategic rivalry between East and West was at its most dramatic over the issue of the Soviet and Cuban presence in Angola. The war between the governing MPLA and UNITA under Jonas Savimbi was internationalized – as Cuba and the Soviet Union supported the ruling party and South Africa and the United States subsidized and attempted to strengthen UNITA. The fortunes of Namibia were caught in between – especially when South Africa and the United States declared Namibia's independence to be dependent upon the withdrawal of Cuban troops from Angola. The ruling party, the MPLA, regarded that condition as a challenge to its sovereignty. And the South-West African People's Organization (SWAPO) naturally insisted that Namibia's right to self-determination could not be held hostage to superpower politics in neighbouring Angola. Throughout most of the 1980s a stalemate continued between the issue of Namibia's independence, on one side, and, on the other side, the strategic chess-game between the Soviet Union and the United States, played out in Southern Africa. It was Mikhail Gorbachev's policies of *perestroika* and the policy of defusing regional conflicts, combined with the persistence of Chester Crocker of the United States, which finally helped the parties to reach agreement in 1988–9.

The political economy of location

So far we have discussed the Second World War and the post-war rivalry between East and West as two supreme conflicts which have highlighted the strategic value of Southern Africa. But there has been a third area of conflict which has had a similar impact on the significance of Southern Africa. This third area of international dispute is the Arab–Israeli conflict.

By a strange twist of destiny, Israel and the *apartheid* regime of the National Party of South Africa were born in the same year – 1948. As the Zionist state was coming into being in the Middle East, the Afrikaaners were taking over power in South Africa. The historical interaction between these two troubled regions of the world was to be long-lasting and sustained.

Part of the strategic interplay between the two regions arose from the fact that well endowed in underground riches as Southern Africa was, there was one subterranean wealth which the region more or less lacked – *petroleum*. And yet oil was precisely the wealth which the Middle East had in abundance. This geological accident was to play a remarkable role in the strategic interaction between the two regions.

Related to the geopolitics of oil is the fact that the Suez Canal and the Cape of Good Hope have been for a long time alternative routes for the oil traffic and other central commodities of international trade, especially between Asia and the Western world. Some of the minerals of Southern Africa needed the Suez Canal to reach many of the Mediterranean seaports. And some of the oil of the Middle East needed the Cape route to reach the Western world at large.

Under ideal conditions this complementarity would have served both regions well. What has periodically disturbed the equilibrium has in fact been the Arab–Israeli conflict and its wider global implications.

The first major shock came in 1956 with Egypt's nationalization of the Suez Canal Company. The Western world regarded the move as a major threat to the international traffic through the canal – including the all-important traffic in oil. The Suez crisis later exploded into the tripartite invasion of Egypt by Israel, Britain and France. President al-Nasser deliberately blocked the canal by sinking junks and dilapidated boats. The canal was well and truly incapacitated.

Perhaps for the first time in the twentieth century, the Cape route resumed supremacy in the calculations of the international trade of the Western world. The shock of Suez also resulted in long-term planning in favour of giant oil-tankers more suited to the Cape route than to the narrower Suez lifeline.

It is true that shortly after the Suez war, Egypt obtained the help of the United Nations for clearing the canal. But in reality the shock of the Suez war was to tilt the balance of reliable seaworthiness in favour of the Cape route for decades to come. This calculation was reaffirmed by the repercussions of the Six-Day Arab–Israeli War of June 1967. The Suez Canal was once again incapacitated – this time for a longer duration. The strategic value of the alternative Cape route for the oil-tankers and other international traffic was once again dramatically enhanced.

But the politics of the Middle East and of Southern Africa had other areas of interaction. With the death of al-Nasser in Egypt, and the rise of Henry Kissinger as power-broker in the early 1970s, the Soviet Union sustained setbacks in the Arab world. Particularly serious was Egypt's move to the right under Anwar al-Sadat and the increasing deradicalization of Sudan under Gaafar Nimeiri.

This had repercussions in Southern Africa. The decline of Soviet influence in North Africa in the early 1970s was a major motive behind the Soviet Union's bid for greater influence in Southern Africa from the mid-1970s onwards. The game of strategic compensation between the superpowers was at work. It was not as crude as the exchange of Soviet patronage of Somalia for American patronage of Ethiopia within the same period. But there is little doubt that Soviet setbacks in North Africa were part of the story of Soviet determination to establish a foothold in Southern Africa. The strategic stakes of Southern Africa were of course further enhanced by superpower rivalry.

The final factor to be borne in mind in the interaction between the Middle East and Southern Africa concerns Afro-Arab political solidarity. A minimum political alliance involves *sharing enemies*. In relations between black Africa and the Arab world, solidarity has entailed declaring *apartheid* and Zionism as joint foes. In the course of the 1970s, opposition to Afrikaaner nationalism and opposition to Zionist nationalism became joint political forces in the politics of both the United Nations and the Organization of African Unity. There were two dramatic diplomatic manifestations of opposition to Zionism. One was the almost complete African diplomatic break with Israel, especially in 1973. The other was the successful passing of a United Nations resolution in the General Assembly declaring Zionism as a form of racism in 1976. The *quid pro quo* in Afro-Arab relations involved continuing Arab support in all areas of the struggle against *apartheid*. Some rightist African countries also expected the bonus of Arab money for their own domestic development. The more leftist regimes in Africa regarded it as adequate that Africans should support the crusade against Zionism in exchange for Arab support in the liberation war against *apartheid*. The strategic equilibrium between South Africa and the Middle East was once again affected by the wider realities of international politics. But when Egypt under al-Sadat signed the Camp David accords and recognized Israel, the united Afro-Arab front against Israel was weakened to some extent. Yet Israel's friendship with South Africa remained relatively strong.

Conclusion

We have sought to demonstrate in this chapter that the three forces which have affected Southern Africa in this period of African history have been *economy*, *strategy* and *race*. On the economic side we have scrutinized the politics of *land*, *labour*, and the *extractive capital* of minerals. On the strategic side we have investigated the impact of the Second World War, the repercussions of the Cold War between East and West, and the strategic interplay between the Middle East and Southern Africa in relation to the Arab–Israeli conflict.

And yet the most politicized aspect of the Southern-African experience has been the transient problem – the racial tensions of the sub-region. The range of racial experience in Southern Africa has been from the colour politics of the Federation of Rhodesia and Nyasaland to the controversial marriage of Seretse Khama and Ruth Williams, and from the political culture of *mulattos* in Mozambique to the political economy of 'bantustans' in South Africa. Racism in Southern Africa in this period has permeated every factory, defined every policy, affected every school, penetrated every religion, and disturbed the peace of mind of every family.

In the final analysis, Southern Africa may well be the last great battleground of the human struggle against the more blatant forms of racism. The economic and strategic value of the sub-region is a long-term asset, but the racial malaise is probably a temporary liability.

A prophecy has already been proclaimed that the most disadvantaged blacks of the twentieth century may well become among the most privileged of the twenty-first. The people of Southern Africa – the 'untouchables' of much of this period of African history – stand a chance of becoming Africa's economic 'brahmins' of tomorrow.[25] It will be up to them to respond to this unique opportunity.

25. See Chapter 1 above; also R. W. Walters, 1987.

The repercussions of the Cold War between East and West, and the changbe might "between the Middle East and Sequmentation for a relation to the Arab-Israeli conflict

SECTION III

Underdevelopment and the struggle for economic independence

Economic changes in Africa in the world context*

Catherine COQUERY-VIDROVITCH

The crisis of the 1930s not only upset the economy of the West, by emphasizing the crucial role to be played henceforth by the United States, but it also marked a decisive turning-point in the sense that economic phenomena took on a global dimension. From then on, everything that happened at the centre had repercussions all over the periphery, usually through a strengthening of the economic ascendancy of the West.

The Second World War revealed the strategic importance of the continent of Africa which had become a key, and hastened the spread of the concept of the right to self-determination among the colonized peoples.

The euphoria of post-war reconstruction, with its plethora of infrastructure investment conducive to industrialization, and the world crisis that followed the Korean War (1951–2) and the Suez crisis (1956), were followed in turn by a more difficult restructuring stage punctuated by decolonization. The general recovery of the mid-1960s gave a momentary impression of a 'miracle', but the drastic reversal of the situation that followed in the 1970s brought about a further crisis in North–South relations, whose outcome is not yet foreseeable.

Coming out of the Great Depression

The 1930s crisis, which represented a major upheaval for the economy of the West, gave the signal for a fundamental restructuring of the world economy.

The cushioning role of the colonial system

The restructuring began with a defensive strategy, with colonial protectionism being momentarily strengthened.

France had not waited for the crisis to occur before introducing, in 1928, a colonial 'Customs Union' that facilitated falling back on the empire: this involved reciprocal exemption from duty between the colonies and the mother country and the application of at least the same customs tariffs to foreign goods.[1] The same thing happened in Great Britain where,

---

* Chapter written in 1986.
1. Law of 30 March 1928. See K. Hoffher, 1939, p. 55.

after the First World War, the determination at all costs to get the pound sterling back on to the gold standard (1925) had led to a deflation that left Britain vulnerable to competition from those countries whose currencies had depreciated. The result was disastrous for growth: between 1913 and 1937 its exports fell by 30 per cent, a much greater rate than the contraction in world trade. Britain fell back on the Commonwealth (which from then on held over 50 per cent of British total foreign investments); and this reflected a state of crisis, which was borne out by recourse to the defensive protectionism Great Britain had always hitherto rejected: through the Imperial Economic Conference held at Ottawa in 1932, it clutched at the 'lifeline of empire trade'. Salazar's Portugal for its part had in 1933 adopted the course of colonial corporatism tightly controlled by the state, and in 1937 extended to the colonies the social and economic organization of the mother country. Based on authoritarian planning and the organization of state corporations and compulsory producers' associations (or *gremios*), this was designed to direct and control production and regulate foreign trade.[2]

Empires were all the more at the mercy of the economic context because their credit markets were quite uncontrolled: total freedom of transfers to and from the mother country meant that the colonies were open to capital transfers, currency operations and dealings in stocks and shares. The more open a colony was to the Western world, the more it was affected by the international financial implications of the crisis – this was particularly the case in Morocco, which because of its protectorate status carried on less than 50 per cent of its trade with France (as against 70–89 per cent for Algeria, roughly as much for Tunisia and French West Africa, and even more for Madagascar).

But the financial crisis itself, so acute in the West, had a limited impact in the Maghreb and in tropical Africa because the credit market was still in its infancy. The colonies most closely linked to the mother country were the ones that stood up best to the depression. 'Falling back on the Empire' played its cushioning role to the full, in both directions: the mother countries absorbed relatively easily primary products that in most cases represented only a small proportion of world output and, in return, the overseas territories served as the mother country's outlet for its least competitive products, such as textiles, iron and steel. This was apparent in France with the introduction in 1931 of a policy of major public works financed by loans raised at home, which ensured that the products of the steel industry were disposed of in the colonies despite being more expensive than elsewhere. This approach above all made it possible to support the most archaic (and hence the most depressed) sectors of the economy – chief among them being the textile industry, which turned to the colonial market on a large scale. France, which in 1913 was selling

2. See M. Cahen, 1984, pp. 10–13.

18 000 tonnes of cotton goods to Africa (including Madagascar), had almost doubled that figure by 1936 (34 000 tonnes). It was the same for Great Britain, whose manufactured goods the outside world had less and less need of, while it needed more and more foreign foodstuffs: in 1935 the balance of payments surplus disappeared, and a regular structural deficit became an established feature. This was a decisive turning-point in British economic history. Although, thanks to devaluation, which had become inevitable, the British economy recovered between 1931 and 1939 rather sooner than elsewhere, it was at the cost of a system of controls, quotas and 'empire preferences' which reduced competition and hence tended to increase rather than diminish the country's technical back-wardness.[3]

Recovery and the world system

The 1930s crisis ushered in the *planned economy*. This was the inner meaning of the *New Deal* in the United States and the *Front populaire* in France (to say nothing of Salazar's colonial corporatism). For Africa, the result was an acceleration of the penetration of capitalism, which brought these 'colonial reserves' into the realm of contemporary imperialism.

The accent overseas was on the need for *economic reforms* based on productive investments, particularly in energy and mining; starting with the short-lived recovery of 1936–8, efforts were stepped up, particularly after the interlude of the Second World War, by the implementation of these new trends, and many grandiose projects of this type were to be counted. They mostly fell victim to their disproportionate size and unsuitability to the environment. A typical example on the French side was the investment in the *Office du Niger*, which was first set up in 1931 and was taken up and expanded under the Economic and Social Investment Development Fund (FIDES) after 1946.

Social reforms designed to produce a modernized work-force were also introduced. The colonial practice of *forced labour* tended to give way to the establishment of a free labour market, in the form of the payment of wages in exchange for the labour of an admittedly overexploited but voluntary work-force.[4] Here the 'Belgian paternalism' exemplified by the labour policy of the *Union Minière du Haut Katanga* is a case in point: the company, which provided workers and their families with employment, schooling, recreational facilities and a standard of living far less under-privileged than elsewhere, ended up by acting as 'chief, father and maternal uncle' all rolled into one, in exchange, of course, for total submission.[5]

3. See C. Coquery-Vidrovitch, 1976b.
4. International Labour Office, 1931.
5. B. Fetter, 1973.

The official abolition of forced labour (in 1946 in French Africa) certainly seems to have been the culmination of this restructuring process, which had given a flying start to new cash crops such as coffee, cocoa and timber and had made forced labour obsolete. This was in the context in which the mechanism of worker migration had been set in motion once and for all, boosted as it was both by the impoverishment of the rural areas and by the growing boom in the labour market.

In the light of the above, the subdivision of the stages of African dependence varies widely from one area to another according to how longstanding the colony was, whether or not capital had been invested early on, and so on. By and large, the development of South Africa can be regarded as being nearly a century ahead of that of West Africa, and the intensive accumulation of capital in Zaire (Belgian Congo) at least a generation ahead. Nevertheless, even for South Africa, it was also in the 1930s that there was a change of regime, from the usual type of *colonial-imperialist* exploitation (mainly British) to a type of white *national-capitalist* exploitation. The latter became established politically in the 1920s, but only carried the day economically with the gold boom of the 1930s.

The South African gold boom, which was triggered off in 1933, made it possible for the country not only to counteract the effects of the world economic crisis but also to stimulate the restructuring of the economy by promoting the expansion of the industrial sector in the towns. The number of firms rose from 6500 to 10 000 between 1933 and 1946; industrial production increased by 140 per cent between 1933 and 1939 (and by as much again during the Second World War) and GNP tripled. The main problem, which was once again racial, became that of a rapidly expanding black urban proletariat; the number of Africans employed in the towns doubled between 1933 and 1939. In 1946, one African in four in South Africa was living in a city and blacks outnumbered whites in the towns.[6]

Tropical Africa and even North Africa had not yet reached this stage. But there also the impact of the Great Depression took the form of a deep internal social crisis: for though the colonial economies – that is, the interests of expatriate firms – on the whole got through the Great Depression more easily than their counterparts in the mother countries, the downtrodden peasants were the main victims of the upheavals taking place on all sides.

A set of specific processes now came into play: the impoverishment of the countryside, the beginning of the flight to the towns and, thirdly, rapid differentiation into social classes. On the one hand, a small section of the indigenous population became 'well-off'; on the other, the lot of indigenous workers deteriorated in relative terms, collapsing by comparison with that of the European work-force. This introduction of

6. See, among others, R. Cohen, 1979; and D. O'Meara, 1974.

'unequal exchange' led, at the international level, to an accelerated flow of profits to the mother country, and points to the emergence of the typical features of present-day underdevelopment.

The Second World War

With the Second World War, the continent of Africa became a major prize contended for by the world powers and was briefly split between the British-held area and the ambitions of Germany and Italy.

The ambitions of the Axis countries[7]

Italy claimed the Mediterranean area as its sphere of influence. The 1937 Munich Agreement between Hitler and Mussolini abandoned southern Europe and, further afield, North Africa to Mussolini. Italy had already colonized Libya, and Italian troops had been in occupation of Haile Selassie's Ethiopia since 1936. Together with Somalia, which had been Italian since 1885, and Eritrea, which had been under Italian rule since 1890, the conquest of Abyssinia was expected to ensure the formation of an Italian East Africa (Fig. 11.1). Mussolini meant to link this with North Africa, hence his designs on Egypt, which brought about the conclusion of the 1936 Anglo-Egyptian Treaty by way of reaction, and on Tunisia, at the expense of France.

However, the realization of Italy's claims presupposed complete victory over Britain and the consent of Italy's German partner, but these designs conflicted with those of Germany itself, not to mention the demands of Vichy France and Spain.

The Third Reich's interest in Africa had started long before the war. Towards the end of the 1930s, a precise statistical survey had been carried out by German industrialists and the government bureau of statistics. The German authorities noted that in 1938 Africa held the first place on the world market for cotton, groundnuts and palm nuts, second place for cocoa, tea, tobacco and bananas, and an exceptional position in respect of its mining output (diamonds, gold, cobalt, vanadium, uranium and phosphates). Lastly, Africa possessed 40 per cent of the world's reserves of hydraulic energy.[8] Germany realized how little profit its trade was making out of the wealth of Africa; hence the idea of a planned economy in a great German Empire, in which Africa was seen as 'Europe's natural, historic area of influence . . . Consequently, its most important parts (mainly French Equatorial Africa, the Belgian Congo and South-West

---

7. This section was drafted after consultation of the following works: J. Bessis, 1982; A. Kum'a N'Dumbe III, 1980; R. H. Romero, 1986, pp. 213–18; and UNESCO, 1985b.

8. See M. Schmitt, 1942.

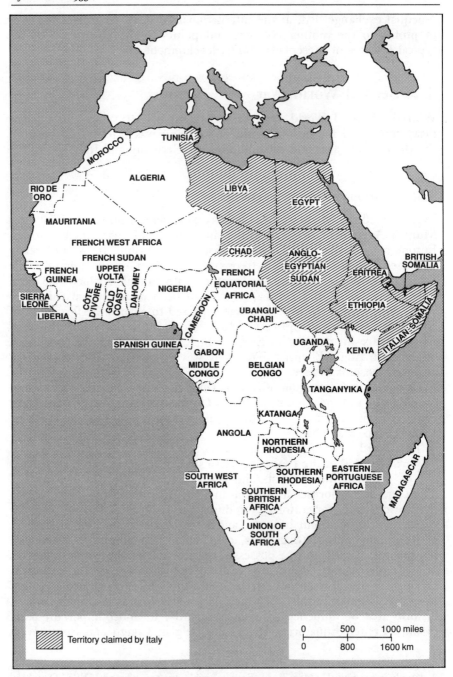

FIG. 11.1 *Italy's territorial claims in Africa (1940 plans) (Source: adapted from A. Kum'a N'Dumbe III*, Hitler voulait l'Afrique, *Editions l'Harmattan, Paris, 1980)*

Africa) would have to be brought directly or indirectly under German control'.[9]

After the defeat of France in 1940 various projects for the 're-colonization' of Africa south of the Sahara were accordingly tabled by either business circles or the Ministry of Foreign Affairs.

America's reaction

North Africa was coveted at one and the same time by the Germans, who wanted to set up military bases there, by the Italians and also by the Spaniards, who wanted to extend their colonial possessions. Vichy France did its best to obtain some assurance; but until the end of the war North Africa remained very much a disputed area between all the powers.

This is why the president of the United States, in his message to Pétain, justified his country's entry into the war, with the consequential landing of American troops in North Africa, in the following terms:

> Today, with covetous eyes on the empire that France has so laboriously built up, Germany and Italy plan to invade and occupy French North Africa in order to implement their plans for the domination and conquest of this whole continent . . . It is of course obvious that an invasion and occupation of French North Africa and French West Africa would represent for the United States and the American republics the gravest of threats to their security . . .[10]

Above all, the war decisively established America's economic supremacy. It triggered off an unprecedented industrial mobilization in the United States. Even before Pearl Harbor, the machinery of a planned economy – introducing price and wage controls – had already been set in place. Between 1934 and 1944 this made possible the creation of new jobs for some 9 million unemployed. Industry, 40 per cent of which was given over to military objectives, took a technological leap forward; for example, substitute products such as synthetic rubber were developed.

On the international scene, the key intervention technique used by the Americans was known as *lend-lease*, which consisted of providing the Allies with a variety of goods, subsequent repayment for which was negotiated on very liberal terms, without there being any question of war-debts. This system was accordingly prompted less by economic necessity than by strategic considerations.

9. J. Rohrbach (Director of the Colonial Department), 1940, p. 10.
10. Telegram of 8 November 1942 from Roosevelt to Pétain, quoted by A. Kum'a N'Dumbe III, 1980, p. 111.

The Commonwealth bastion[11]

Great Britain based her war effort largely on the Commonwealth, which it made a 'sterling area' (with the exception of Canada and Newfoundland). This was institutionalized in 1939–40 and covered almost one-third of all world trade. Full exchange control in dealings with countries outside the area was exercised by London. Hence, this self-contained economic Commonwealth defrayed the bulk of the military expenditure incurred in local currencies. That enabled it to pay its dollar reserves into a common pool managed by London which, in exchange, credited the member countries with 'sterling balances' that were not convertible into currencies outside the area. The system was primarily geared to guaranteeing imperial 'self-sufficiency' in respect of foodstuffs and raw materials.

Colonial economic policies

The Second World War was of decisive importance for black Africa. Unlike the previous war, it did not merely step up the pressure on the colonies through more intensive production and forced labour in the name of the 'war effort', or make use of their manpower (about 160 000 men were recruited in French West Africa between 1914 and 1918, and as many again in North Africa, but only half this number was mobilized by the French between 1943 and 1945; on the other hand, the strength of the British West African Frontier Force rose from 8000 to 146 000: over 160 000 Kenyans were enlisted as porters, and East Africa as a whole lost nearly 50 000 men). The war speeded up the spread of an anti-colonial mentality in Europe and Africa which soon made obsolete a regime that had formely been regarded as sacrosanct.[12]

After having been widely employed outside the continent, African troops brought back home with them the new ideas which they had gleaned from their contacts with Europeans and Asians. The superiority of the white man was dispelled once and for all; the African élite was quick to grasp the advantage offered by Soviet or American anti-colonialist propaganda. At the same time, however, the continent's economic role was reinforced. Owing to supply difficulties, the Allies were compelled to step up local production of strategic materials, such as iron from Sierra Leone and tin from Nigeria, and above all to develop processing industries. Between 1938 and 1946, British West Africa's foreign trade doubled, from £44 million to £86 million.[13] The idea of considering granting the Africans political, economic and social rewards for the effort they had made during

11. See D. J. Morgan, 1980; also E. R. Wicker, 1958, pp. 170–92.
12. UNESCO, 1985b.
13. M. Crowder, 1968, pp. 481–513.

the war came to take root. That effort had been mobilized through the interventionist economic approach of the mother countries, which represented the only way of providing support for a strict policy of investment and industrialization.

British policy: the Colonial Development and Welfare Act (1940)

When the war broke out, the British set up bodies for overseeing the large firms. These were the forerunners of the marketing boards, whose reserves were expected to offset the risks entailed by a fall in the purchasing prices paid to producers in the event of production rising.

In particular, they broadened the scope of the 1929 Colonial Development Act, which had for the first time sought to distinguish between 'development work' and 'ordinary administrative work', which was alone financed out of a colony's normal revenue. Apart from 'physical-development' schemes, the former already included public health (with the aim of ensuring an efficient work-force) and initiatives in the educational field.

Despite the limited sums made available between 1930 and 1940, 30 per cent of all funds went into transfer infrastructure, 16 per cent into health and 10 per cent into water-supply systems. Yet neither scientific research nor agricultural development ever received more than 7 per cent of the total.

The 1940 Act provided for credits at the still very modest level of £50 million for the following ten years (though they rose to £120 million in 1945). It widened the scope of development, which became 'planned development' and was organized with the backing of a sizeable administrative structure geared to both planning and implementation.

Nevertheless, planning was delayed by shortage of staff, which had been mobilized for the war. Yet the key point had been reached: the principle was officially proclaimed that *laissez-faire* policies were no longer acceptable where the colonies were concerned.

French planning policy: from Vichy to the Free France

Despite political differences, the French attitude was altogether similar. Colonial economic planning, which was unquestionably in the wind, was not a new idea. It had already been put forward in 1934, in the middle of the crisis, by the *Conférence économique de la France métropolitaine et d'outre-mer*; this introduced the idea of the state's role not only in financing but also in planning. Supplementing the already-acknowledged principle of developing infrastructure was the more novel one of stimulating industry by setting up a *Comité des industries de l'Empire*. Nevertheless, the idea of not competing with interests in the mother country was still firmly entrenched.

At the time of the *Front populaire*, colonial economists had taken up the question again. They suggested a consistent economic programme that was both modernist and reformist and was based on a 'planned

293

economy in the public interest', as opposed to exclusively private enterprise under free competition. For the first time, the need was stressed
for developing productive activities in the colonies, first of all *domestically*,
thereby giving rise to an industry-oriented approach as part of an
'economic decentralization' that would 'develop' the territories – a newer
term than the 'improvement' hitherto advocated.[14] However, the *Front
populaire* colonial programme ran out of time, and the colonial empire
accordingly entered the war more or less as it had been since it was first
set up.

It was under the Vichy government that a team of 'technocrats' went
to work. In the middle of the Second World War, they drew up the first
French economic plans – including one for the colonies. Admittedly, the
Ten-Year Plan (1942–52), which was never actually ratified by the
country's own government, made only modest provision for the colonies,
amounting to only 84 billion francs or 11.8 per cent of the total. In any
case, this was a purely notional figure, since the state was required to
intervene only if private enterprise was unable to cope (only 40 per cent
of the work was regarded as profitable).[15]

Although the intention was not to set up productive capacity in the
colonies that would be liable to compete with the mother country
(industrial investment overseas, including the Maghreb, represented only
7.5 per cent of that for metropolitan France), as a matter of 'imperial
solidarity' the problem was posed in a new way:

> The colonies and the mother country form a *community* . . . Since
> the colonies are bound to gain access to modern technology, their
> industries will develop either with our support or . . . against us,
> which is to be avoided.[16]

The prime aim was to protect the foreign trade of the French empire by
guaranteeing it markets outside occupied France. The African Economic
Conference held in Vichy in 1942 accordingly decided to set up the
Thomson–Houston Radio and Electrical Appliance Company in North
Africa, to treat French and colonial vegetable oil mills on an equal footing,
and to institute a co-ordinating committee for the textile industries of
the French empire.

Thus Vichy's modernism stemmed from the thinking of an administrative élite which had taken advantage of the exceptional circumstances
of the war to draft, in close collaboration with business circles converted
to industrialization, a plan that was to remain after the war the framework
of an ambitious colonial economic policy.[17]

14. L. Mérat (Adviser to Marius Moutet, Minister for the Colonies), 1936.
15. See C. Coquery-Vidrovitch, 1979, pp. 69–94.
16. P. Le Cacheux, n.d., p. 58.
17. See J. Marseille, 1984, pp. 340–2.

From the post-war years to the period of decolonization

At the end of the war, the mother countries set out to incorporate Africa into the international capitalist system. The instruments of 'acculturation' were now within the reach of the new élites; and it was finally accepted by all that Africa was getting ready to open itself up to the rest of the world.

Internal crises and conflicts

But this opening-up did not move off all that smoothly. After five years of relative commercial isolation, the re-establishment of peacetime relations with the West brought about violent internal economic and social traumas.

The standard of living had declined dramatically. In addition to the wage-freezing during the war, import prices had rocketed following wartime inflation in Europe. On the French side, the creation of the colonial or CFA franc with a value double that of the French franc (which correspondingly increased the value of raw-material exports) was not enough to offset the high cost of imported consumer goods[18] and in retaliation for its settlers' lukewarm support for the Free French, North Africa did not enjoy the benefit of this measure.

An urban sub-proletariat was coming into being all over Africa, swollen by the influx of jobless people driven out of the rural areas by the war effort, with its forced labour, compulsory crops and heavy taxation: they consisted of ill-paid workers, rootless individuals from here, there and everywhere, and the unemployed. Temporary accommodation became permanent, with hardly any roads, public services or sanitation.

Until then, the colonial authorities had been careful to check the formation of any working class, whether black or white, especially in the mining areas and the ports. The war broke down this 'empire of silence'. Disturbances broke out in many different places; and because of the severity and repressive nature of the administration, they mainly took the form of the 'spontaneous' uncontrolled outbursts. The towns became the prime focus of the clashes. In 1944, the first sign was the uprising at Thiaroye (Senegal) which was sparked off in the camp of a colonial infantry regiment awaiting demobilization.[19]

In 1945, a riot in Douala brought together the trades unions and the sub-proletariat.[20] In 1947, a populist 'agitator', Lamine Kaba, held the town of Kankan, in Guinea, for 48 hours.[21]

18. 1 CFA franc = 1.70 FF in 1946–7, and 2 FF the following year as a result of the French devaluation.
19. M. Echenberg, 1978, pp. 109–28.
20. R. A. Joseph, 1974, pp. 669–87.
21. J. Suret-Canale, 1972, vol. 3, pp. 14, 18 and 27.

During the same period, major insurrections broke out in the Algerian *département* of Constantine in 1945 and in Madagascar in 1947, along with strikes in Abidjan and Dakar and disturbances in Elisabethville and Brazzaville, where 'abject poverty' was rife. There were also strikes in Nairobi and Accra coinciding with the return of Kwame Nkrumah, not to mention the wholesale stoppage of work by miners on the Rand in 1946.

African trades-unionism was thus moving from inter-racial class consciousness to nationalist rebellion. While the severe repressive measures meted out helped to give a political complexion to these movements, they also drove some of them back into traditional forms of resistance represented by such messianic movements as Kibanguism, Matswanism and Hamallism. Thus an explosive mixture was being formed by groups cut off from the mainstream in both towns and rural areas. This gave rise, in the 1950s, to the rebellion fomented by the *Union des populations du Cameroun* (UPC) in Cameroon and to the Mau Mau insurrection in Kenya.

The situation in the West

The period from 1946 to 1971 was by and large one of rapid economic recovery especially in the first stage before the recession that followed the end of the Korean War (1951–2).

The revival was backed by American aid grounded in anti-communism and the reconstruction of the pillars of capitalism, first of all in Europe. This strategy hinged on two main programmes: the Marshall Plan, introduced in 1947, which was the sequel to lend-lease and part of which France managed to use for the promotion of its empire; and the Atlantic Pact concluded in 1949. The International Bank for Reconstruction and Development (IBRD) and the International Monetary Fund (IMF) were established to regulate the economy of the non-communist world. The outcome was under the impetus of a state-controlled sector, ever swifter modernization, driven forward by nationalizations and technological and biogenetic revolutions. All this led to increased interdependence among the industrialized countries: each nation became more sensitive to the situation of its neighbours. It is true that African countries derived some benefit from 'technology transfers' and the expatriation of a number of industrial plants on the look-out for cheap raw materials and/or labour. But the main feature was an accentuation of both solidarity and dependence: on highly export-oriented multi-national corporations, and on countries producing raw materials, above all energy, and especially imported hydrocarbons – whence the scale of the oil shock of 1973.

PLATE 11.1 *OPEC (the Organization of Petroleum Exporting Countries) meeting in Vienna, 21 November 1973*

Colonial economic policies

The new turning was taken almost before the war was over: the Brazzaville Conference was held in the French empire in 1944 and was followed in 1946 by the abolition of forced labour and the creation of FIDES (Economic and Social Investment Development Fund) to finance investment in black Africa and Madagascar. An attempt was also made to launch the industrialization of Algeria with a grandiose 'Constantine Plan' that was interrupted by the war of liberation. The British Colonial Development Fund was reorganized in 1945, followed by the independence of India in 1947. The result in Africa was an upsurge in industrialization, with emphasis being placed on transport infrastructure and increased production for the mother countries. France in particular broke new ground in the planning field. The first plan (Monnet Plan, 1946–52) included the overseas territories: it focused mainly on reconstruction, with the stress on *capital investment*, modernization and industrialization, and gave importance to mining and energy production (with the first hydro-electric schemes for Africa). The second plan (Hirsch Plan, 1954–7) included a separate capital investment plan for the French Union: it aimed at *productive development* designed to identify in the colonies the new resources needed to speed up their integration with the home economy.[22]

22. *Commissariat général au plan*, 1954 and 1955; Ministry of Overseas, 1954; Ministry of Cooperation, n.d.

In constant-value terms, French investment in Africa, accentuated by the transfer of the colonial interests lost in Indo-China, was at its height during this period, peaking in 1951–2 (Fig. 11.2); between 1950 and 1954, imported capital goods accounted for over half the gross fixed-capital investment. The main channel was public investment (70 per cent to over 80 per cent of the total in French Equatorial Africa and Cameroon); the same was true even in French West Africa, despite the relatively higher contribution from the territories' domestic budgets.[23]

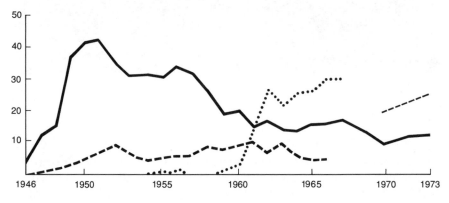

FIG. 11.2 *The financing of capital investment in French-speaking black Africa and Madagascar, 1946–73, in billions of 1960 constant CFA francs (Source: C. Coquery-Vidrovitch,* 'L'imperialisme français en Afrique noire: idéologie impériale et politique d'équipement, 1924–75', Relations internationales, 7, 1976, pp. 261–82)

Great Britain adopted a more flexible type of planning, refusing to direct everything by remote control from London for two main reasons: first, because it was absorbed in the immense task of reconstruction at home and, secondly, because excessive centralization ran counter to the principles of a process leading towards earlier self-government.

The Fund was therefore broken down, with an Office for Development and Reconstruction for each territory. The plan for Nigeria, for example, stood at £55m, of which £13m were provided by the Colonial Development and Welfare Fund. Though regarded as quite inadequate by the élite, such an amount would have been unthinkable a few years before. Above all, it was difficult to implement, not so much on account of the

23. C. Coquery-Vidrovitch, 1976a, pp. 261–82, and 1982, pp. 237–52.

shortage of funds as of the shortage of capital goods, since Great Britain was unable to provide the materials needed (particularly steel). British aid was far more differentiated than French aid: half the total funds (1946–58) went into social investments (education, health, water supply and housing), 20 per cent into agriculture and (unlike France) only 20 per cent into transport infrastructure. Nevertheless, productive effort was also sharply focused on the raw materials necessary to the mother country, whence the particular emphasis on oilseeds of which there was an acute shortage in the post-war West. In every case, the dominant ideology of industrialization as the key to development ran up against the over-ambitious scale of the projects, shortage of staff and ignorance of local ecological constraints. The failure of the large-scale groundnut schemes (the British Tanganyika Scheme[24] and the *Compagnie générale des oléagineux tropicaux* in Senegal) still symbolizes these obstacles.

Planning and industrialization were not the preserve only of the liberal mother countries. With quite another aim – to maintain its grip on the colonies at all costs – Salazar's Portugal took similar action: the first six-year plan goes back to 1953. Portugal had little capital, but American banks took an interest in its African colonies early on, through shared interests with South Africa. Great Britain and the United States had long been Portuguese Africa's main customers after the mother country; though American interests only became important with early attempts to find oil (1948 in Mozambique and 1957 in Angola), and above all with the beginning of Angola's and Mozambique's wars of liberation. It was in fact only then – that is, in the 1960s – that Portuguese colonial possessions began to 'modernize' rapidly.

In the Belgian Congo, after a very Eurocentric first plan (1950–60), it was only at the end of the colonial period that the administration drew up an economic and social expansion plan based on a new strategy:[25] it laid emphasis particularly on peasant agriculture and greater government intervention in the industrial sector, the aim being to process the country's raw materials locally, avoid imports and increase employment. It remained a dead letter, however. After Mobutu had come to power and the presidential authority had become extremely centralized, a planning department came into being that was initially remarkably competent. But the 'brains trust' of advisers did not manage to stay, and the gap between plans and their execution remained as wide as ever. The 1979 plan, supported by massive foreign financial aid, had only a very limited success; for the state had not the means to implement a plan and still less to get the private sector to fall in with it. In Zaire as elsewhere the main reason for this is still the lack of a real political will to plan, which is the prime feature of a nation's determination to develop.

24. J. S. Hogendorn and K. M. Scott, 1981, pp. 81–115.
25. See F. Bezy *et al.*, 1981.

Decolonization in black Africa

This took place in the context both of a temporary slowing-down in growth, accentuated by the crises of 1951–2 and 1956 (Suez) and also by the repeated American recessions of 1953–4, 1957–8 and 1960–1.

The short but acute recession that followed the 1951–2 world crisis came at a time when dominance–dependence relationships were being radically questioned. It marked the beginning of the decolonization process in black Africa which from then on was accepted and even advocated by the business circles concerned, particularly in France: it thus appears that political decolonization which, in Algeria, ran directly counter to French nationalist traditions had been preceded in the mother country by a strictly pragmatic economic decolonization. From the 1950s onwards, the downturn in the underlying trend of the profits curve (Fig. 11.3), which had been growing steadily since the beginning of the century, makes it possible to explain the parallel rise of a current of nationalistic anti-colonialism which was early on expressed by the specialized economic press as part of a conservative approach which favoured decolonization on the grounds of the rationality of sound economic management. The big firms such as the *Société commerciale de l'Ouest africain* (SCOA), the *Compagnie française de l'Afrique occidentale* and Unilever therefore observed a prudent neutrality: since the regime was no longer in a position to guarantee special profit margins (and was even liable to reduce them to nought by political action if there were to be a war of liberation), new working relations were called for.

The main currents of opinion opposed to the loosening of the mother country's grip had been expressed elsewhere before (in the case of France, at the time of the Indo-Chinese and Algerian wars). In black Africa, both French and British colonial officials were aware of the escalating cost of aid, and soon came up against the difficulty of mobilizing both the necessary local potential and work-force without seeking the help of local political leaders, who for their part were aspiring to take over the running of operations without breaking with the mother country.[26]

Independence brought the African states into the field of competition of international imperialism; and this meant a revision of operating policy, which hastened both the intensification and the internationalization of capital. The decisive step for industrializing tropical Africa, often with advanced technology, was taken at this time (mining in Gabon, Guinea and Nigeria and manufacturing industry elsewhere).

26. See J. Marseille, 1984.

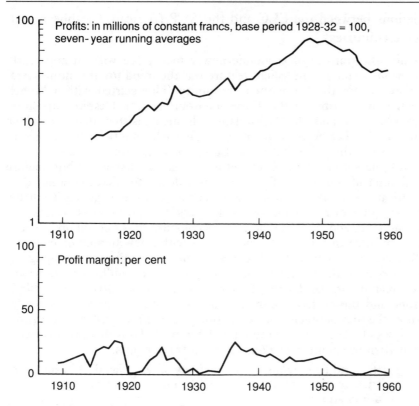

FIG. 11.3 *SCOA's profits, 1910–60 (Source: C. Coquery-Vidrovitch, 'L' impact des intérêts coloniaux: SCOA et CFAO dans l'ouest africain, 1910–1965', Journal of African History, 16, 1975, pp. 595–621)*

Independence

The new states had to contend with the disjointed structures of under-developed economies on inherited colonial lines, with production geared for export and with a very limited domestic market. Now independence came at a bad moment, when the price of raw-material exports, their main source of income, was perceptibly falling, causing a marked deterioration in the terms of trade. Public revenue and expenditure suffered accordingly, while at the same time an unprecedented population explosion was gathering speed. This inevitably affected the growth of *per capita* GDP (Table 11.3, p. 315).

But worldwide growth soon recovered in the second half of the decade, and for a while it seemed as though the 'miracle' whereby underdevelopment was conquered had come true in a few cases (Côte d'Ivoire, for example).

Relations between the EEC and the ACP (African, Caribbean and Pacific countries)[27]

Initially, the transfer of economic power took place without apparently too serious a shock. The salient feature was the trend towards multilateral relations within the European Community. This started with a French initiative at the time of the Treaty of Rome (1957). Despite opposition from Germany and the Netherlands, France insisted that the whole Common Market be opened up to the French and Belgian colonies in Africa. Since the existence of the European Community was, of course, unthinkable without France, the latter got its way, barely a month before the signing of the treaty. This was less a desire for decolonization than a political action, aimed initially at favouring Europe by giving it reliable extra supplies of raw materials as the period of post-war shortages was drawing to an end, whereas the African colonies, thus opened up to wider trade and investment, were to be content with a few limited objectives.

In fact, the system was to prove a flexible mechanism encouraging the transition from tight colonial links to a network of multilateral relations. The Preamble to the Treaty of Rome affirms 'the solidarity which binds Europe and the overseas countries', and the desire of member states 'to ensure the development of their prosperity, in accordance with the principles of the Charter of the United Nations'. Thus the way was paved for an African common market, based on three points:

(1) the gradual opening of the markets of 'associated' African countries to the exports of all EEC member states, without discrimination;

(2) the opening of EEC markets to the produce of the associated countries, under special preferential arrangements; and

(3) the inauguration of an economic and social investment programme in the overseas countries, financed by the EDF (European Development Fund).

Initially, the gains were more theoretical than real; opening up to the whole of Europe went slowly, but the diversification of markets had become possible, especially since tariffs were reduced more quickly than was provided for in the treaty. The associates' entry into the EEC had been negotiated by the mother countries, but at the beginning of the 1960s no questions were asked – least of all by the new states, who confined themselves to confirming their acceptance of the commitments the mother countries had made on their behalf – about the advantages arising out of the special multilateral relationship: that was left to Yaoundé I and II (1963 and 1969) and then to Lomé I, II and III (1975, 1980 and 1986).

27. See C. Cosgrove-Twitchett, 1978; F. Long, 1980; and C. Coquery-Vidrovitch, 1988b, pp. 105–34.

For the African states the objective was to re-negotiate advantages at least equal to those guaranteed by the Treaty of Rome. They needed help from the EEC in transforming their economies, particularly in the industrial sector. They wanted to negotiate on a footing of parity and equal representation, and to obtain an export-price stabilization programme. But Europe, now rebuilt and confident of having organized its own self-sufficiency, was not too keen to grant further advantages. It only agreed to preferential tariffs on tropical products, but without shutting itself off from Asian and American markets.

The Lomé Conventions, in particular, marked a major turning-point in European policy: the number of partners rose from 18 states (17 of them French-speaking) to 46 (including 21 Commonwealth countries), and later to 69. The new aim was, starting with the ACP (African, Caribbean and Pacific) countries, to cover all co-operative relationships with the Third-World countries 'in a spirit of international solidarity'. From then on, the problem went far beyond the case of the former mother countries alone. The setting up in 1975 of STABEX, which to some extent stabilized commodity prices, especially of agricultural produce (plus iron), within the limits of available funds – in 1980, $138 million out of $261 million recoverable – and then in 1980 of SYSMIN, intended in principle to play a similar role for mining products, began to lend an air of reality to demands for a 'new international economic order', which had been called for by all the underdeveloped countries since the UNCTAD Conference in 1974.

By virtue of their economic characteristics, the African states accordingly joined the ranks of Third-World – and particularly Fourth-World – countries: underprivileged countries mostly without either minerals or oil.

The crisis of the 1970s and African poverty

Once again, the blow suffered by the centre of the system is entailing a recasting of the structural features of dependence in the periphery. The countries of black Africa, which include two-thirds of the world's 25 poorest countries, hold even fewer trump cards in the North–South confrontation than those of North Africa. Buffeted as they are by natural catastrophes such as drought, the dubious legacy of the precolonial and colonial past, and the constraints of the world market, those countries are first calling for a new international economic order, a prerequisite for any internal restructuring, whereas their partners from the North are making 'internal structural adjustment' a prerequisite for any further assistance. With very few exceptions, such as Namibia and Zimbabwe, black Africa seems to be struck in a rut: Africa as a whole is the continent attracting the lowest volume of foreign investment and it accounted for

TABLE 11.1   *Direct foreign investment in the continent of Africa, 1965–83*

	Annual average value of flows in $bn				Percentage of total			
	1965–9	1970–4	1975–9	1980–3	1965–9	1970–4	1975–9	1980–3
Industrial countries	5.2	11.0	18.4	31.3	79	86	72	63
Africa	0.2	0.6	1	1.4	3	5	4	3

Source: World Bank, 1985, p. 126. For all the developing countries taken together, the nominal value of direct investment grew during the period by 10 per cent a year, but the real value remained virtually unchanged.

only 3 per cent of the world total between 1965 and 1983 (Table 11.1). Virtually all sub-Saharan countries, apart from Zaire, Ethiopia and Nigeria, have a relatively small population, often ranging between 2 and 8 million inhabitants, with a very low purchasing power. There are few oil-producing countries, and what few there are, are not very important. No country can compare with Libya, except Nigeria. The production of Gabon, Angola and Congo hovers around the 10 million tonne mark. The oil resources of Côte d'Ivoire, Cameroon, Ghana, Benin and other countries are still no more than forecasts. The oil companies, especially following the recent fall in oil prices, tend to regard the oil deposits south of the Sahara as being in the nature of a 'reserve' to be drawn in the event of need, and exposed to political risks.

The early 1980s saw a disturbing worsening of the situation, accelerated by the drought which between 1983 and 1985 affected over 20 countries and some 35 million people. At present, the fall in *per capita* income and unchecked domestic deficits are such that public savings, which were still 15 per cent (of GDP) ten years ago, have fallen to the extremely low rate of 6 per cent. At the same time, the net flow of outside capital is falling dangerously.[28]

Despite an increase in debt reschedulings (14 countries had to have recourse to this in 1984–5), the proportion of export earnings devoted to debt repayment rose from an average of 18 per cent in 1980 to 26 per cent two years later and to 38 per cent for the poorest countries. Neither the present and no doubt transient boom in coffee prices nor the fall in oil prices will right a situation whose seriousness was again, in 1985, illustrated by a fall of nearly 3 per cent in GNP per head of population.

What is to be done? The first thing is to stop financing dubious large-scale projects whose only impact is political. Though these schemes are getting rarer, such a measure is easier said than done, for it depends not only on awareness by the African governments but also, and perhaps above all, on the many donors, who must co-ordinate their actions so as

28. World Bank, 1986, quoted in *Le Monde*, 15 April 1986.

to avoid waste and agree to fit them into programmes laid down by the Africans themselves.

A modest growth hypothesis would just about make it possible to reverse the declining trend in sub-Saharan Africa; this would entail, according to the World Bank, no less than $35.2 billion a year in external resources to cover debt-servicing and ensure a minimum quantum of imports. The equation is simple: estimating in 1985 export earnings at $20 billion a year, the lightening of the debt burden by periodical rescheduling at $2.3 billion, and the combined inflows from concessional aid, multilateral credits, and loans and investments at market rates at $9.5 billion, there is still a shortfall of $2.5 billion. The combined efforts of institutions such as the World Bank, the IMF and the regional development banks should produce an extra $1 billion. Hence, $1.5 billion remained to be found, representing a 20 per cent increase in the bilateral aid programmes currently envisaged between 1985 and 1990.

As a working hypothesis, the above calculation puts the ball right back into the court of the industrial countries. However, the better able Africa is to solve its own difficulties, the less dependent Africans will be on emergency aid, which is sometimes vital but whose destabilizing effects have been amply illustrated in recent years.

To round off this depressing picture, it should be added that almost one half of the world's refugees are Africans.

The new forms of imperialism

It is therefore understandable that in Lagos in April 1980 the secretary-general of the Organization of African Unity, the Togolese Edem Kodjo, shouted: 'Africa is dying . . . there seems to us no future in the future'.[29]

The main feature of contemporary Africa is more than ever its dependence on the West. This dependence is, of course, due to poverty; but also to the recent colonial past, which has brought about a very special relationship with the former mother countries.

This dependence is undoubtedly the West's doing; but it is also an internal, accepted, interiorized feature because culturally-speaking the model is still European. Thus in terms of cumulative investment, France is only third (with 16 per cent of the total), behind Great Britain (39 per cent) and the United States (21 per cent); but it is at present the leading net exporter of capital to Africa, and overall (though the Federal Republic of Germany is hard on its heels) remains Africa's prime trading partner and main supplier of technical assistance. Contrary to a widely-held belief, penetration by the United States is still relatively limited. Admittedly, with nearly 15 per cent in North Africa, 45 per cent in tropical Africa and 40 per cent in South Africa, American investment is fairly evenly

29. Quoted by *l'Express*, 14–20 March 1981.

distributed over the whole continent, whereas France's is mainly in the north and Great Britain's in the south. But apart from oil (57.5 per cent of capital invested in 1976) and mining (19.2 per cent), its impact is still small (only 9.3 per cent in the industrial sector).

The result is that the Western model of economic and social development is put forward as the only positive explanation of the movement of universal history; the keystone of the system is the *idea of progress*, but diminished by being identified only with scientific and technological progress; development is reduced to catching up with the West through 'modernization' – that is, through ever-closer integration into the Western market.

This is what gives rise to the model of economic success, and likewise that of the analysis of social classes. Local revolutionary Marxists (whose Western training initially directed their attention to the Soviet model) are nonplussed by the difficulty of advocating the doctrine of the pre-eminence of the working class in countries where it hardly existed. Only Tanzania has sought to define a socialism rooted in home-grown values and potentials.

This dependence has another consequence common to all the countries and peoples of black Africa: a deep *social distortion* between the masses and the 'élites'. The élite (only some 5 per cent of the population on average) aspires to Western living-standards. But this consumption model (at least four times higher than for the ordinary citizen) is just what the hinterland is incapable of supporting. The very fact of integrating the privileged minority into the world system presupposes the marginalization of the masses in the form of a rural or urban sub-proletariat; instead of concentrating, in a very narrow domestic market, on the distribution of very cheap consumer goods, the tastes of the social minority require that trade be outward-oriented and reduce the economy to a subordinate, fragmented appendage of the international market.

In this context, the injection of capital and the transfer of technology take place mainly for the benefit of certain national oligarchies or multi-national corporations. For instance, Zaire's GECAMINES, which, in principle, controls the production of copper and other non-ferrous metals and is the country's leading enterprise as far as foreign exchange and tax earnings are concerned, has, in fact, contracted out the processing and marketing of its copper to two firms controlled by the *Société générale de Belgique*. Broadly-speaking, the main banks, which exercise control over foreign investments in conjunction with the government departments responsible for finance and diplomacy in the countries of the North have, as their essential motivation, the making of a profit from their operations, whatever their repercussions may be locally, upstream or downstream.

Results on the ground are not insignificant. But they are mediocre as far as the domestic market is concerned. The most striking factor is thus the constant decline in savings, which has become more marked since the

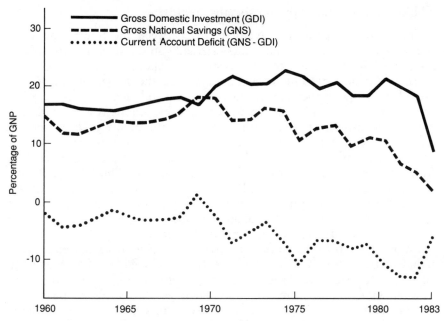

FIG. 11.4 *Investment and savings in Africa, 1960–83, excluding oil-exporting countries (Source:* World Development Report, *World Bank, Washington, D.C., 1985, p. 49)*

early 1980s (Fig. 11.4). The deficit on current account, coupled with the low inflows of foreign investment, makes it imperative to resort to borrowing, but such a course only adds to the debt-servicing problem (Table 11.2).

TABLE 11.2 *Evolution of the debt burden in low-income Africa, 1970–84*

	1970	1974	1976	1978	1980	1981	1982	1983	1984
Ratio of debt to GNP	17.5	23.5	27.7	26.9	39.8	43.4	47.7	52.0	54.5
Ratio of debt to exports	75.2	99.5	135.3	162.3	175.8	216.5	260.5	279.5	278.1
Debt service ratio	6.1	8.6	8.5	9.6	12.5	13.8	15.7	16.5	19.9

Source: World Bank, 1985, p. 24.

Furthermore, favouritism and corruption often give rise to systems in which the state is run as if it were the property of its leaders: those managing the economy and those managing the state seem to be concerned only with sharing out the national cake – for their own benefit and their respective regional clientèles.

The economic policy of the socialist countries

In the triangular pattern of relationships between the South, the West and the East, the third partner stands virtually on the sidelines. In African eyes, the 'North' chiefly means Western Europe. It was only with the Moscow Economic Conference in 1952 that the Russians decided to extend the scope of their financial, commercial and technical co-operation beyond the Eastern bloc. In 1956, Khrushchev promised to provide the newly-decolonized countries with Soviet aid without any *quid pro quo*. On the other hand, Vice-President Nixon made several visits to Africa; an African desk was set up in the State Department, and the leading American foundations provided funding for work on Third-World issues.

This is because policy in regard to Africa very quickly became enmeshed within the context of the 'Cold War', and continued until only recently to be marked by imperative strategic considerations, as evidenced by the massive Soviet interventions in Angola, Mozambique and Ethiopia.

China, in its turn, came onto the scene, often in a bid to counter the action of the Soviet Union, as in the case of Somalia;[30] she undeniably offers an alternative to Africans responsive to the original nature of the Chinese experiment. Some features, such as the emphasis placed on the peasantry and agriculture, particularly reflect African conditions. Independent of ideological considerations, many African states thus take advantage of Chinese expertise in everything to do with rice.

The role of international organizations

Although international organizations are unwieldy machines that are often looked upon as being excessively bureaucratic, they nevertheless perform a real job. In the first place, they have amassed an enormous quantity of technical and scientific studies and reports, not to mention the action in which they have engaged in the field in combating illiteracy (UNESCO), epidemics (WHO), drought and hunger (FAO), and so on. Those organizations are supported by the United Nations Development Programme (UNDP), the World Bank and the International Monetary Fund (IMF), whose priorities are determined by the sacrosanct criterion of profitability, a criterion not easily accepted by the beneficiaries of their action, especially in UNESCO's fields of competence (education, science and above all culture). This is why the United Nations has endeavoured to promote a new body, the International Fund for Agricultural Development (IFAD), with a view to 'increasing food production and improving the nutritional level of the poorest populations'. The Fund placed emphasis on the food crops grown in local communities and on the rechannelling of agricultural credit to small-scale farmers, for whom, failing the existence of a mortgage

30. See J. Herzog, 1979.

PLATE 11.2   *Bernardo Vieira, president of Guinea-Bissau, meets with M. A. Qureshi, senior vice-president of the World Bank, in October 1988*

or other collateral, the lender accepts the venture as being viable. In an endeavour to avoid ruinous expenditure on bureaucracy, IFAD intends to make as much use as possible of the channels of existing institutions. It has thus opened up a new approach, in the face of an unavoidable observation: it is impossible to find a narrowly economic answer to problems that are eminently social in character, such as malnutrition, hunger, health and employment in the continent of Africa.

The reaction of Africans

The Africans' first reactions to international pressure were *non-alignment* and the establishment and strengthening of relations with the developing regions of the world, with the Arabs, the Asians, Latin Americans and the peoples of the Caribbean, which are fully discussed in Chapter 28. This stemmed from the profound conviction, born of experience, that underdeveloped countries can exert very little influence on the outcome of the North's problems, in either the Western or Eastern blocs, whether within those blocs or in the event of conflicts between them.

Non-alignment actually came into being at the time of the Cold War and the most acrimonious confrontations between East and West. Set up

309

on the initiative of three undisputed leaders, Tito, Nehru and al-Nasser, it quite soon became the rallying point of all Third-World countries: at the 1979 Havana Conference they numbered 95. In Africa, non-alignment developed early on because of the failure of the Afro-Asian movement following the 1955 Bandung Conference. It was explicitly written into the Charter of the OAU (1963). But the criterion for non-alignment – 'to follow an independent policy based on peaceful coexistence' – is vague enough to be interpreted flexibly; and this, by satisfying everybody, crucially weakens its meaning because it is enforced more and more slackly – thus the prohibition on concluding a bilateral military alliance with a great power is now as little-observed on the Western side as on the Eastern.[31]

But what remains is a general grievance against the 'North'. It originated in UNCTAD, the Conference on Trade and Development set up by the United Nations in 1964 under pressure from the developing countries. At that time, it was attended by nearly 150 states, 77 of which – since known as the 'Group of 77', though they had become 96 by 1971 and 122 by 1982 – constitute the joint mouthpiece of the Third-World countries in opposition to 'Group B' composed of the industrial states. Their proceedings led in 1974 to a Declaration and Common Programme, calling for the unjust order of the present international division of labour to be replaced by a 'new economic order based on equity, sovereign equality, interdependence, common interest and co-operation between all States'.

Needless to say, since then the North–South dialogue has by no means lived up to expectations, and the African partners are bitterly disappointed. The establishment of industrial 'free zones', like the one at Dakar, enables EEC countries in particular to protect their exports. The main demand of the ACP countries is still for an inflation-indexed increase in the price of their raw-material exports. This is the thing that would enable them to finance the massive importation of advanced technologies needed for the next stage in their industrialization. Then, perhaps, like some Asian countries, they would be able freely to take advantage of the combination of suitable natural resources and plentiful cheap labour to export large quantities of manufactured goods to the developed countries. We are a long way from that.

Self-reliance for Africa, in the shape of a vast integrated pan-African entity for which Kwame Nkrumah strived so hard, is still only a pious hope, despite the many bilateral or multilateral economic agreements within the continent (Fig. 11.5). These are still hampered by a two-fold obstacle: on the one hand, the powerful push–pull effect, both to and from the industrialized countries and, on the other hand, intra-African political rivalries, which prevent the drive towards unity from being fully

31. See E. Berg, 1980.

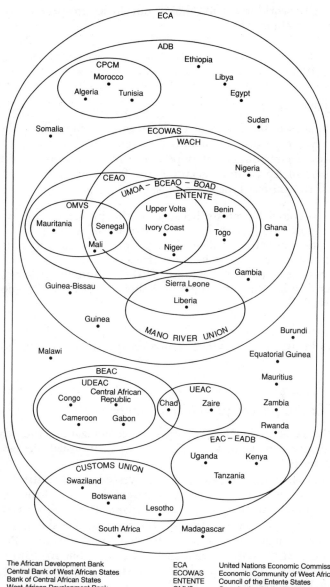

ADB	The African Development Bank	ECA	United Nations Economic Commission for Africa
BCEAO	Central Bank of West African States	ECOWAS	Economic Community of West African States
BEAC	Bank of Central African States	ENTENTE	Council of the Entente States
BOAD	West African Development Bank	OMVS	Organization for the Development of the Senegal River
CEAO	West African Economic Community	UDEAC	Central African Customs and Economic Union
CPCM	Maghreb Permanent Consultative Committee	UEAC	Union of Central African States
EAC	East African Community	UMOA	West African Monetary Union
EADB	East African Development Bank	WACH	West African Clearing House

FIG. 11.5 *Regional and sub-regional organizations for co-operation and integration in Africa (Source: UNCTAD, TD/B/609/Add.I, vol. III, 1976, pp. xi–xii)*

effective. The world recession holds out little prospect of significant progress in the short term.

New factors

South Africa

One of the keys to the future of the African economy will be the way in which the South African problem is resolved. Until very recently, South Africa was the embodiment of imperialism in the region. As the West's strategic base in Africa and a secure home for its investments, it was the focus of all the various types of protest:[32]

> (1) anti-colonial protests because of the intolerable dependence it imposed on Namibia and the Africans of Azania;
> (2) anti-imperialist protests, because of the economic and military sovereignty it symbolizes in Africa; and
> (3) anti-racist protests, because of the iniquitous *apartheid* regime enshrining the unacceptable belief that whites are superior to blacks.

The fact that Western imperialism is 'ditching' the Afrikaner nationalist is likely to bring about a radical change in the situation in a short space of time.

The rise of the proletariat and trade unionism

Despite the great nationalist upsurge of decolonization, there has been no real subsequent large-scale identification of social demands with political determination.

In Portuguese Africa, industrialization pressed ahead relatively strongly from the 1960s onwards, both in the mines of Angola and the main ports of Mozambique; but the risk of proletarianization was curbed by the setting up of national corporative unions reserved for skilled (educated) workers. These mainly worked to the benefit of the new Portuguese immigrants. 'Native' status was abolished in 1961, but Africans ineligible for union membership were nevertheless restricted to carefully supervised 'professional associations for natives'.[33]

In French-speaking black Africa, railway and civil-service trades unions became relatively powerful. But the idea of *assimilation*, which was not really consistent with the struggle of the working class, was deep-rooted

32. C. Coquery-Vidrovitch, 1986, pp. 347–67.
33. M. Cahen, 1984, pp. 10–13.

312

both in political circles and among workers with a foothold in the money economy. The French political and trades-union tradition as regards the colonies, including the CGT (*Confédération générale du travail*) and the Communist Party, reinforced this tendency to confine working-class demands to the traditional framework of economic and social trades-unionism.

In English-speaking Africa, the reformist traditions of the trades unions put wage negotiations firmly before violent action. The example of Nigeria is particularly illuminating: each wave of strikes led to arbitration by a committee of inquiry, which usually ended in wage increases. Even so, it is questionable whether it is possible to speak in terms of a 'labour aristocracy'. Nigerian industrial workers are undoubtedly proletarians. Not far from Lagos, tens of thousands of workers are concentrated around some 50 factories; they work in various high-capital-investment and high-productivity sectors. The workers are experienced and organized, but professional mobility is non-existent and wages soon reach the top of the scale. The workers are capable of taking industrial action for a specific local concession and are quite ready to speak of imperialist exploitation in general and the flagrant inequalities of Nigerian society, but their *petit-bourgeois* ambition is eventually to become small independent businessmen. Their strategy is one of reaching an accommodation with the existing system, reinforced in general by the fact that many political regimes have put trades unions under state control.[34] This situation is almost universal in North Africa, paralysing workers' self-expression despite the fact that their numbers are high.

Here again, the decisive impetus may come from South Africa, which is now dominated by the major social fact that the urban and mining proletariats make up the vast majority of the African population.[35] This observation, obvious in the case of blacks, is also true, although to a lesser degree, for coloured (13 500 employers for 700 000 workers) and Indians (17 000 for 160 000). In South Africa it is the peasantry and the middle classes that are now dependent on the working class and not the other way round. Admittedly, since the explosion of strikes in Durban in 1973 and the renewed agitation of the 1980s, the violence of the repression has so far managed to contain workers' uprisings. But the quite recent setting-up (again in Durban) of a Trades Union Federation encompassing nearly all trades-union organizations has now produced a political and economic pressure group that could become decisive: the African National Congress has already drawn a lesson from this by including the workers' basic demands in its charter for freedom.

---

34. On the entire sub-Saharan working-class evolution in English and French-speaking regions, see C. Coquery-Vidrovitch, 1988c, chs 12 and 13.

35. See D. Dutoit, 1981.

The demographic and urban revolution

The increase in population that began at the end of the nineteenth century in North Africa but got underway in black Africa only in the 1930s, has everywhere since the Second World War and still more since independence turned into an unprecedented explosion. The 'demographic transition' stage is unlikely to be reached before about 2015.

This fact is a major feature of Africa's contemporary economy; but its long-term implications cannot be precisely gauged because population growth and economic growth may react on each other in contradictory ways depending on other political, social and cultural variables.

In the short term, the situation is agonizing. Despite real growth in GDP (though this has slowed down greatly since 1973) growth in GDP per head of population shows a lasting fall (Table 11.3). But though there are at present overpopulated areas (especially given the low profitability of farming), the continent as a whole is far from being overpopulated. In the long term, population growth has economic advantages that have been experienced elsewhere, though none of these parameters has operated yet in Africa, where economic development has so far undoubtedly been less successful than in the rest of the world.[36] Population growth makes it possible to widen the domestic market and increase production and economies of scale; it speeds up the replacement of generations of illiterate workers by educated young people readier to adapt to the modernization of farming methods and industrial employment.

At present what is more significant is the spectacular trend-reversal Africa is experiencing as between town and country. From 1950 to 1980 total African population growth led to a tripling of the population (from 219 to 560 million), and nearly two-thirds of this growth took place in the country-side (still 85 per cent of the population in 1950; barely 60 per cent by 1980, but still over 70 per cent in black Africa). However, over the same period, the urban population increased almost five-fold (from 32 to 133 million), which is the highest rate of urban growth in the world.[37] The result will be, around the year 2000, a population that not only will have doubled in 23 years but will have become predominantly urban (55 per cent), and nearly two-thirds of total growth will be in the towns. It should be noted, however, that these forecasts do not take account of such post-1980 trends as the slow-down in urban growth and the dreadful depletion due to AIDS. The second half of the twentieth century will have seen the urban population of Africa increase ten-fold, for the same push and pull reasons as in other continents: poverty in the countryside, landlessness and social marginalization on the one hand; the mirage of money, freedom and the Western model in the towns on the other hand.

36. See E. Boserup, 1985.
37. See United Nations, 1981.

TABLE 11.3 *Population, gross national product (GNP), gross domestic product (GDP) and average annual per capita growth rate, 1965–95*

	Population (m)	1980 GNP ($bn)	GDP ($bn)	GNP per capita ($)		Average annual per capita growth rate of GDP and GNP (%) 1965–73	1973–80	1981	1982	1983	1984[b]	1980–5[a]	Forecasts 1985–95 Low[a]	High[a]
AFRICA														
Low-income countries	197	52	53	270	GDP	3.9	2.7	1.7	0.7	0.7	1.6	1.4	2.8	3.2
					GNP per capita	1.3	−0.1	−1.7	−2.6	−2.6	−1.5	−1.7	−0.5	−0.1
Middle-income oil-importers														
North Africa and Middle East	31	25	24	830	GDP	5.6	7.1	0.7	6.2	1.5	1.2			
					GNP per capita	3.5	4.3	−2.5	2.6	0.5	−1.3			
Sub-Saharan Africa	780	26	27	330	GDP	5.1	3.6	6.9	−1.0	−1.8	−2.1			
					GNP per capita	2	0.5	4.1	−4.8	−5.4	−5.4			
INDUSTRIAL COUNTRIES (market economy)	714	7477	7444	10480	GDP	4.7	2.8	1.4	−0.3	2.6	4.8	2.3	2.5	4.3
					GNP per capita	3.7	2.1	0.7	−1.0	1.5	4.3	1.8	2	3.7

[a] Mean percentage of annual variation.
[b] Forecast.
Source: World Bank, 1985, pp. 138, 148, 149.

The pressure of numbers is not spread equally over each of the 55 states of Africa, whether those with the highest populations, such as Nigeria (90 million) or Ethiopia (31 million); the largest, such as Zaire or Sudan; the least densely populated, such as Mauritania, Niger or Gabon; or Rwanda and Burundi, which remain densely-populated small rural states. But the majority of African countries are feeling the full impact of an unprecedented wave of urbanization.

Today, African cities are the focal point for political and social confrontation and the melting-pot for new forms of adaptation to the 'modern' world which are difficult to categorize and are roughly covered by the trite but vague term 'the informal sector'. Attention has been rightly drawn to the extraordinary capacity for adaptation, evidence of real ingenuity, shown by small producers in this informal sector; so far from being stagnant and unproductive, this sector is probably capable of producing structural changes by revolutionizing the jobs available to the urban and rural masses.

In the short term, however, the situation is likely to be much gloomier: all the signs point to an ever-growing influx of idle hands in the towns, compelled to use increasingly fragile stratagems to eke out an existence in a labour market that is virtually stationary or growing infinitely more slowly. The absorption of workers through the development of the modern sector is illusory in countries where the population growth rate is over 2.5 per cent. For newcomers on the labour market to be fitted into industrial society there would need to be paid jobs for 50 per cent of the active population, whereas in most cases the percentage is barely 10–20.

There in a nutshell is the tragedy of Third-World towns, which are evolving in a very different way from the industrial centres of nineteenth-century Europe. When all is said and done, it is a matter of sharing out increasingly inadequate opportunities in terms of work (and hence of resources and markets) among a fast-growing and increasingly-deprived mass of people. Hence the formulation of the pessimistic economic concept of urban *involution* – the virtual impossibility of escaping from a vicious circle of poverty except by emigration.

The point to be remembered from now on is that the turbulent flood of uncontrolled or ill-controlled urban growth is bound to become, in black Africa as elsewhere, the main vector of possible upheavals. From now on the towns are where people, employment and organizational structures are concentrated; economic and cultural influences are brought to bear, and political power is determined: in short, where tomorrow's decisive social pressures are destined to be deployed.

Agriculture and rural development since 1935

Maxwell OWUSU

Introduction

Agricultural policy and rural development in Africa have been distorted in a variety of ways by the whole legacy of the colonial experience. Rural effort and output have been hampered by a number of biases in policy and process.

The bias which has been discussed the most is the *export bias* in African agriculture. This chapter will examine the nature of this distortion in production. The emphasis on cultivating crops for export has sometimes resulted in *dessert and beverage economies* – economies which are based on crops like tea, coffee, sugar and cocoa for the dessert confectionaries of the Western world, while the African people themselves are short of such basic foods as grain, meat and root crops. The export bias in African agriculture was created during the colonial era, sometimes under white-settler control in places like Algeria and Kenya. But the bias has persisted in post-colonial Africa partly because of the need for foreign exchange with which to import other products.

At its worst, Africa produces what it does not consume – and consumes what it does not produce. Within the agricultural sector on its own that generalization may not be fully valid, since the continent does produce much (but by no means all) of the food it consumes. But the trend has been towards importing a larger and larger percentage of the food needed by the continent.

A number of factors are responsible for the expanding need for food imports. These factors include expanding population (more mouths to feed), changing consumption patterns (more wheat and rice being consumed than before), the deteriorating infrastructure for agricultural production (shortage of spare parts and decaying roads), and inadequate incentives for local farmers either to produce more of the old food crops (such as maize and root crops) or to start producing the new crops (rice and wheat).

The cash crops are still the royal family of African agriculture – attracting a disproportionate share of attention, reverence and resources. The export bias in rural development is still triumphant.

The second perfidious distortion in African agriculture is the *urban bias*. At a more general level, this has been a policy which has subordinated the needs of rural folk to the requirements of the city-dwellers. In per capita terms, the cities have had a bigger share of the revenues of the state than the countryside. This has been true of hospitals and schools, roads and railways, electricity and gas supplies, housing projects and other facilities.

In terms of actual agricultural policy, a major consequence of the urban bias has been the tendency for African governments to subsidize the city consumer rather than the farmer. Many African governments have become virtual prisoners of this policy even when under external pressure from the World Bank or, more often, the International Monetary Fund (IMF). The IMF has often championed a switch of emphasis from subsidizing the consumer to motivating the farmer. But removal of food subsidies has sometimes resulted in bloody riots in cities as different as Tunis and Ndola, Cairo and Monrovia. Food subsidies in Africa tend to hurt farmers and benefit consumers. Essentially they are part of the urban bias in Africa's agricultural priorities.

But the urban bias has been served by other factors as well. As we shall later indicate in this chapter, the entire colonial educational system seemed almost designed to produce *rural misfits*. Peasants themselves felt betrayed if their educated offspring did *not* turn their backs on country life on the farm. Education was supposed to be a process of liberation from physical work, especially from farm labour. Some of the best minds of Africa were systematically insulated from productive effort in the countryside. Educated Africans – born in the villages – were irresistibly diverted to the lure of city life. It was in such ways that the African school was conscripted to wage war against African agriculture. This was one of the most pernicious aspects of the urban bias in Africa's development.

Sometimes the bias took the form of seeking foreign aid for local cultivation of a crop like wheat, consumed mainly by city folk. One of the more dramatic examples of this kind of urban bias was the agreement between Canada and Tanzania to produce wheat under conditions of advanced technology not far from the snows of Kilimanjaro. It may be true that 'man does not live by bread alone', but in that part of Tanzania man did not live by bread at all. And yet a major project was brought to fruition by the Canadians. The Hannan plains yielded an impressive tonnage of wheat – destined for the distant bread-eaters of the towns of Tanzania. Locally in the plains there was 'heavy cost – partly human and partly ecological'. The human cost was borne by the pastoral Barabeg people, who were pushed away to worse pastures than ever as a result of the wheat project. The ecological cost was borne by the soil of the place – volcanic and exposed to more torrential downpours than the prairies of Alberta. The result of the Canadian wheat project in the Hannan plains of Tanzania has been devastating soil erosion. Once again, the urban bias in Africa's strategies of development had carried significant casualties in its wake.

We shall see later that the third distortion of colonial agriculture concerned *the role of the state*. Para-statal bodies in agriculture have, paradoxically, prospered under both colonial bureaucracies and post-colonial socialist and other experiments. Government intervention in the production of cash crops has been particularly marked. The cultivation of basic foods outside the subsistence sector has also felt the nearness of the state. In the post-colonial era, marketing boards for agricultural produce have tended to expand dramatically in terms of personnel – and to deteriorate in efficiency. Marketing boards became one more area of 'jobs for the boys'.

One major casualty of over-bureaucratization of agriculture was inevitably the farmer. The farmer subsidized the bureaucracy – the reverse of European strategies of government subsidies for the farmer. The over-blown para-statal bodies in Africa have indeed eaten away into the farmer's profit margin – and may have undermined the farmer's motivation as a producer.

President Ibrahim Babangida's decision to dissolve Nigeria's marketing boards in 1987 no doubt had political reasons, as well as economic ones. But the economic ones certainly included the quest for greater efficiency and the desire to improve both the profit margin and the overall incentives for the farmer. Symbolically, the dissolution of marketing boards was also a form of decolonization – a case of the government reducing the size of its own para-statal bureaucracies. We shall return to some of these themes later in the chapter.

The fourth major distortion in the legacy of colonial agriculture was the *male bias*. Much of traditional African agriculture had involved women. Indeed, women were often the majority of the farmers in African societies. The colonial impact did not end the numerical preponderance of women, but it did contribute to their marginalization. In the traditional setting, women had considerable say in determining the value of commodities. With the coming of the cash economy, women could still be the main determinants of *prices* for the local market in the hustle and bustle of conventional bargaining and exchange. But a number of colonial changes helped to shift the balance in favour of the *men*, especially in determining the *value* of agricultural produce. One factor consisted precisely of the marketing boards, which in personnel were overwhelmingly male. The buffer institutions between the producer and the consumer were a masculine preserve which marginalized women in the allocation of value to agricultural produce.

A related aspect concerns the internationalization of African economies. The traditional local economies gave women considerable leverage in the processes of exchange. But as soon as African economies demanded distant contacts with buyers in Japan, Europe and the Americas, the boards of directors of African firms consisted overwhelmingly of men.

The modernization of agriculture has also increased the role of *credit* facilities for the purchase of seeds, fertilizers, equipment and for the construction of storage facilities. The expanding role of credit, in both the colonial and post-colonial periods, has often resulted in the expanding role of men. Partly because of indigenous constraints on women owning land, and partly because of more universal banking prejudices concerning the credit-worthiness of women, monetized agriculture in Africa has contributed to the marginalization of the female cultivator.

The very promotion of cash crops helped the male bias in African agriculture. African women were often in control of the cultivation of yam, cassava and maize. But in the cultivation of tobacco in Southern Rhodesia, or sugar in Uganda, or sisal in Tanganyika female expertise began to give way to masculine calculation and planning. Admittedly, female labour was still needed even in cash crops. Tea-picking in Karicho, Kenya, is overwhelmingly done by women. On the other hand, tobacco work in Zimbabwe and rubber-tapping in Liberia are overwhelmingly male jobs. On balance, cash-crop cultivation has tilted the balance in favour of male labour.

What is at least as significant is the *managerial* shift in favour of men on issues of cash crops. Decision-making about traditional food production allowed for a much bigger female role than decision-making about cash crops. Production, processing, pricing and export functions in cash crops have basically been taken over by men.

These then are four of the major distortions which the colonial aftermath has inflicted on African agriculture and on patterns of African development. This chapter examines the basic trends in the agricultural history of this period in the context of this colonial legacy and its distortions. Pre-eminent among them are the export priority, the urban emphasis, the state focus, and the primacy of the male. But the chapter will also draw attention to the other forces affecting the pace and direction of African agriculture.

African peasant production and plantations

It has been estimated that 60 to 95 per cent of the labour force of African countries are engaged in *subsistence* (farming and pastoral) or cash-crop agriculture or both. At least 80 per cent of the half a billion Africans make their living from agriculture with much of the planting, weeding, harvesting, simple processing and marketing being done by women.[1]

1. CIDA (Canadian International Development Agency), 1984, p. 12.

PLATE 12.1 *Woman agricultural worker, Morocco*

In a comparative estimate of the relative importance of subsistence agriculture in underdeveloped countries, Abercrombie points out that in Africa, *exports* account for a higher proportion of total agricultural production than in the Near or Far East, but domestic market sales were less in Africa than in the former two regions.[2] This is consistent with the well-known fact that colonialism drastically re-oriented the African rural sector toward export cash-crop production and overseas, as opposed to *internal* markets.

In Algeria, Kenya, Angola and Mozambique, the settler plantation as a dominant form has more or less died with independence. However, in Kenya and particularly in Tanzania, sisal, coffee, tea, tobacco, pyrethrum and rubber plantations were still employing, in the 1960s, about one-third of the total labour force. On Zanzibar, the clove and coconut plantations owned by Arabs and Indians are still important. In Zambia, a great part of commercial agricultural production is still provided by hundreds of settler farms spread along major railway lines.

Plantations are noted for their research and efficient production when properly managed and capitalized. However, they have not contributed much to the alleviation of rural poverty in Africa, nor have they promoted equity-oriented national developments, as the example of the Firestone Tire and Rubber Company of Liberia shows.[3]

After the Second World War, farming by public corporations, a new development of plantation agriculture, emerged in a number of West African countries. There are some indications that multi-national agro-business will become increasingly an important form of agricultural production in some African countries.[4]

Agricultural and settlement schemes and co-operatives

One of the first major and successful settlement schemes in colonial Africa was, of course, the large-scale, irrigated and mechanized Gezira project in the Sudan for the production of cotton for *export*, already discussed in Volume VII. The project began full-scale operation in 1925 and until 1950, when the management was taken over by the Sudan Gezira Board – a government organization – it was operated on a partnership basis between the government, African tenant cultivators and two commercial companies acting as managers. Considered 'the backbone of the Sudan economy' it involved in 1958 about 26 000 Sudanese tenant farmers.[5]

One of the most grandiose and disastrous of such schemes was the East African Groundnut Scheme undertaken by the British Overseas Food Corporation in 1946.

2. K. C. Abercrombie, 1961.
3. R. L. Curry, 1971; G. L. Beckford, 1972.
4. C. Windstrand and S. Amin, 1975.
5. UNESCO, *General History of Africa*, vol. VII, pp. 455–6; D. H. Reader, 1964, p. 34.

Elsewhere in Africa, colonial governments faced with the problems of overpopulation, pressure on land, soil erosion and exhaustion due to land over-exploitation caused by colonial measures, resettled Africans under improved agricultural conditions, as occurred in the Eastern Province of Northern Rhodesia.[6] The French in French West and Equatorial Africa and the Belgians in the Congo established many *paysannat* settlement schemes aimed at improving the stabilizing peasant cultivation and at developing commercial crops.

At the close of the colonial period, a large number of marketing, servicing and credit co-operatives were operating to handle problems of supply and the distribution of farm products among smallholder farmers. The evolution of cocoa-growing in Ghana and Nigeria and coffee in Tanzania by Africans was greatly advanced by co-operatives which among other things provided marketing, storage, pulping, transport and credit facilities (Table 12.1). In French West Africa, the *Société indigène de prévoyance* helped to educate farmers in better cultivation methods.

Since independence in many parts of Africa, governments and public corporations have been intervening in agricultural development along modern capitalist (and a few along socialist) lines, as government-controlled co-operatives have mushroomed everywhere. New settlement and irrigation schemes have been established to promote agricultural transformation and rural development. They have varied greatly in size, aims, methods and results from small pilot projects intended to test the adaptability of agricultural machinery and new techniques in African ecological and agronomic conditions, to large-scale commercial ventures such as the Aswan High Dam of Egypt which has resettled 180 000 fishermen and farmers in Aswan, and has made possible perennial irrigation and has tripled land use.[7]

Tanzania initiated the *ujamaa* villagization project to regroup the dispersed rural population in order to make various improved agricultural and other services easily accessible to farmers on a collective basis.[8] In the early days of independence, one of the most popular modes for the development of settlement schemes in East and West Africa was that of the Israeli *moshav*, which involved small-scale individual farms with centralized services for cultivation, marketing and social welfare. In 1959 in Western Nigeria farm-settlement programmes were consciously based on the *moshav* model. In Tanzania, Kenya and Ghana, Israeli advisers played a crucial role in the planning of settlement schemes.[9]

In several countries, mechanized farming schemes to bring larger areas under cultivation and to achieve higher levels of productivity were

6. W. Allan, 1965.
7. *The Economist*, 25 May–1 June 1984, p. 42.
8. J. Nyerere, 1967b.
9. L. Cliffe and G. Cunningham, 1973.

TABLE 12.1   *Number and volume of trade of consumer and marketing
societies in selected territories, 1954 and 1957*

Territory*	Number[a]		Trade (value in £1000s)	
	1954	1957	1954	1957
Consumer societies				
Northern Rhodesia (Zambia)	24	21	490	2 020
Nyasaland (Malawi)	16	12	36	124
Kenya	17	17	3 787	4 510
Tanganyika (Tanzania)	4	5	26	35
Uganda	11	5	128	53
Zanzibar (Part of Tanzania)	2	2	2	9
Gold Coast (Ghana)	16	6[b]	–	27[b]
Nigeria	50	37	41	500
Sierra Leone	2	1	–	16
Marketing societies				
Northern Rhodesia (Zambia)	80	138	3 638	4 578
Nyasaland (Malawi)	48	70	68	83
Kenya	297	425	12 264	18 491
Tanganyika (Tanzania)	231	462	7 830	10 360
Uganda	991	1 373	2 619	4 112
Zanzibar (Part of Tanzania)	1	2	–	c
Gold Coast (Ghana)	363	376[b]	6 059	7 457
Nigeria	538	1 105	2 188	4 331
Sierra Leone	133	216	138	218

* Present-day name given in brackets.
[a] At end of year.
[b] 1955.
[c] Less than £1000.

Source: Co-operative Information Circular for the Colonial Territories, November 1955,
January 1957, February 1958 and March 1959 (issued by the Co-operative Union Ltd,
Manchester, England).

established; in Western Nigeria, agricultural resettlement programmes
were implemented to counteract the drift of school-leavers to towns;[10]
while in Kenya, the 'Million Acre' settlement scheme was meant to
redistribute European farms to landless African farmers. According to
Chambers, very few of the settlement schemes in Africa involved the
establishment of communal forms of land tenure.[11] Since the 1970s, with
the assistance of the World Bank and other development agencies, such

10. D. Olatunbosun, 1967.
11. R. Chambers, 1969.

as UNAID and CIDA (the Canadian International Development Agency), a host of poverty-oriented integrated rural development programmes have been initiated throughout Africa, including irrigation works, livestock development, soil and water conservation, credit, infrastructure development – all designed to increase agricultural output and rural incomes to alleviate rural poverty, both absolute and relative.[12]

Agricultural produce marketing and the price mechanism

The dualistic colonial and neo-colonial character of African agriculture and rural development is nowhere more evident than in the system of marketing of agricultural produce and the prices peasant farmers face in the principal markets, which determines their income and hence partly their standard of living.

Since the Great Depression and especially the Second World War, colonial governments, in assuming a new initiative for economic and social development in their African territories and, with the attainment of political independence, *centralist* African governments, in their pursuit of a policy of import-substitution industrialization involving the establishment of local food processing and other industries, have systematically intervened in the market for agricultural commodities – export crops as well as basic foodstuffs for domestic consumption.

Among the mandated objectives of such official intervention in produce marketing by marketing boards have been the stabilization of producer prices and hence of incomes of peasant farmers and the use of surpluses for the benefit of peasant farming communities, and the general development of African countries. Marketing remains one of the major bottlenecks to successful agricultural development in Africa.

The problem of marketing stems in part from the colonial legacy where pre-independence departments of agriculture and the marketing boards and marketing agencies which were created expended their greatest energies on export crops for external markets.[13] As a result of this, the market sector of the rural economy in the majority of African countries has tended to depend for most of its cash earnings on the conditions of supply and demand in the overseas markets in industrialized core countries, and on officially fixed and controlled prices.

Apart from the effects of official controls, the inherited pattern of marketing and price movements is influenced by several other factors which include notably poor physical infrastructural facilities (in many countries in Africa, agricultural products are still transported to the

12. See R. L. Ayres, 1983.
13. See, for example, S. La-Anyane, 1970 and 1971.

market by head loads, hand-pulled carts, canoes, bicycles and camels), poor storage and inefficient harvesting, processing and packaging facilities, limited or poor access to credit and capital, low and uncertain crop yields, poor market and price information associated with poor communication, extension and other institutional networks.

The institutional and infrastructural networks inherited from the colonial period by African states were for the most part created to facilitate the colonial export–import trade – that is, to connect areas of plantation and cash crops to the cash-crop-producing centres for sale. In 1957, a quarter of all exports from tropical Africa originated, according to some estimates, from within 161 km of the coast, and of agricultural exports a much higher proportion were drawn from this zone.[14]

The infrastructure and institutionalized framework were not designed to facilitate the sale of locally produced commodities for the domestic market. For instance, no durable road network criss-crossing the country-side was constructed to transport bulky (low value per unit weight) foodstuffs produced on remote and scattered farms to urban market centres. Adequate transport and storage facilities to preserve foodstuffs in transit do not exist in most tropical African countries, so that a high proportion of surpluses spoil. The FAO (Food and Agricultural Organization) estimates post-harvest losses of cereal crops at 10 per cent and losses for fruits and vegetables at 30–50 per cent. This compares unfavourably with losses in the industrialized countries of 2–3 per cent. Those reaching the urban market thus tend to be relatively expensive in spite of price controls, contributing to the high cost of living for urban consumers.[15]

In many African countries, problems of unreliable markets both for producers and consumers, fluctuating and differential prices of basic food crops exist – in spite of, even because of, the high degree of official state control exerted over the marketing of foodstuffs. And state control was supposed to *stabilize* prices and make them uniform. Low farm-gate prices that obtain as a result of government intervention, coupled with price uncertainties, often compel farmers to produce primarily for their subsistence needs. Young school-leavers, especially in West Africa, get discouraged about taking up farming as an occupation, thus contributing to labour shortages on farms.

Increasingly, the African smallholder producer produces simultaneously *for export*, for the domestic markets (peripheral markets, mining townships, urban markets) and for subsistence, the last being dominant in many African countries. This fact partly accounts for changes in the volume of domestic food supply.

14. D. Grigg, 1970, p. 81.
15. See FAO, 1977.

Marketing boards, co-operatives and price control

Since the 1930s, three principal methods have been adopted for solving nearly all marketing problems in Africa, namely marketing boards and agencies, co-operative marketing and price controls. In East, Central, South and North Africa, where European settler-farmers were dominant, the production and marketing of high-value agricultural products were controlled by a system of legal or quasi-legal monopolies from which Africans were excluded. In Kenya, for example, the quasi-co-operative Kenya Farmers Association purchased and sold grain and distributed seeds, and so on, and built up a near-monopoly of grain-milling, while the Kenya Co-operative Creameries controlled and secured the profitable domestic markets for dairy products and bacon by a system of protective tariffs, coupled with legislation to fix prices in the pre- and post-war years. In Algeria, by a 1947 French decree, most of the highly profitable *colon* agricultural production (wine, cereals, vegetables, fruit, tobacco, cotton, figs, olives, sugar beet) was marketed through 449 co-operatives – notably the *Office algérien interprofessionnel de céréales* (OAIC) and the *Coopérative d'achat des fabricants algériens* (CAFTA) which were heavily subsidized by settler and metropolitan government and credit agencies, such as the *Caisse algérienne de crédit agricole mutuel* (CACAM).[16] Elsewhere in colonial Africa, before the Second World War, the export trade in agricultural produce was dominated by expatriate companies which in West Africa employed local (African) middlemen – in some countries they included Lebanese and Syrians, and in East Africa, Asians – to purchase from the farmers and transport to the chain of stores and sheds of the companies. The largest of these companies in British Africa was the United Africa group.

In African countries like Uganda, Ghana and Nigeria where African small-scale peasant agriculture was the basis of development, there existed African co-operative societies mostly for the principal export of cash crops, but their annual share of the crop as a percentage of the total crop for the pre- and post-war periods tended to be small. For instance, in 1939–40, in the Gold Coast (now Ghana), then the world's leading producer of cocoa, there were 395 co-operative societies with a total membership of 10 282. The societies handled 3971 tons of cocoa that year, a mere 2.2 per cent of the total Gold Coast crop. But nearly 98 per cent of the total output was controlled by 13 expatriate firms. By 1952–3, co-operative cocoa had increased to only 19.2 per cent of the total Gold Coast crop (Tables 12.2 and 12.3 for details). By the end of colonial rule, a very high proportion of all the major agricultural exports from British territories in Africa – including practically all exports produced by Africans – was handled by state export monopolies, namely marketing

16. See T. L. Blair, 1970.

TABLE 12.2 *Progress of Gold Coast co-operative societies*

Year	Number of societies	Total membership	Tons of cocoa	Co-operative cocoa as a percentage of total Gold-Coast crop
1939–40	395	10 282	3 971	2.2
1940–1	285	6 539	6 736	2.8
1941–2	265	6 375	9 924	4.0
1942–3	253	6 149	9 446	4.6
1943–4[a]	254	6 439	12 420	6.3
1944–5[b]	150	6 102	16 765	7.3
1945–6	97	6 712	14 604	7.0
1946–7[c]	106	7 948	14 451	7.5
1947–8	134	11 919	21 942	10.6
1948–9	160	13 133	27 720	10.1
1949–50	179	14 612	29 468	11.6
1950–1	199	16 355	31 617	12.1
1951–2	225	18 398	28 818	13.7
1952–3	291	26 287	47 423	19.2

[a] Department of Co-operation established in 1944.
[b] Gold Coast Co-operative Federation formed in November 1944
[c] Gold Coast Co-operative Bank Ltd registered in October 1946.

Source: J. C. DeGraft-Johnson, 1958, p. 78.

TABLE 12.3 *Progress of Nigerian cocoa co-operative societies*

Year	Number of societies	Total membership	Tons of cocoa	Co-operative cocoa as a percentage of total Nigerian crop
1939–40	138	9 346	5 915	5.24
1946–7	242	18 594	13 253	11.95
1947–8	283	20 585	11 090	14.68
1948–9	276	19 404	12 918	11.96
1949–50	309	21 299	9 697	9.65
1950–1	319	19 529	10 908	9.01

Source: J. C. DeGraft-Johnson, 1958, p. 95.

boards, which controlled the purchase and sale of the controlled commodities. A similar development occurred in much of Francophone Africa.[17]

The marketing boards accumulated large surplus balances which

17. See R. Dumont, 1966; R. H. Bates, 1981; and P. T. Bauer, 1981, for detailed discussions of marketing boards and agencies.

resulted from high world demand and prices for commodities, especially in the late 1940s and 1950s. Between 1940 and 1962, at least £700m was withheld from the producers in the form of marketing-board surpluses and high export taxes. These levies, which fell mostly on small-scale peasant producers, represented on average between one-third and one-half of the commercial value of the output. The heavy taxation of producers of cash crops imposed by marketing boards in colonial and post-colonial Africa has 'inhibited the spread of cash crops, the accumulation of private capital, and the development of a prosperous peasantry and an independent middle class'.[18] Again after independence, the large sums accruing to African governments and their agencies through the state export monopolies promoted large-scale political and administrative corruption as these sums were divested for national *urban-based* development and the control of these funds became a major prize of political power, as West African examples clearly demonstrate.[19]

Since the export surpluses of Uganda and West Africa were held in sterling during the colonial period, this represented an enforced transfer of resources from the colonies to Britain.

Apart from state intervention in the marketing of export crops, African governments have directly intervened in the marketing of staple foodstuffs, with profound effects on the marketing of export produce and foodstuffs. In countries like Ghana, Zambia, the countries of the Sahel, Tanzania and Kenya, the governmental role of food marketing has greatly increased. For example, between 1971 and 1976 the Tanzanian government, through its monopsonistic marketing agencies, offered to farmers prices for the main cereals that ranged from one-fifth to one-half of the then-current world prices.[20] Thus these government marketing agencies – legalized monopsonies – buy produce at officially-fixed, lower prices and sell food products through price-controlled marketing outlets in town. In several African countries, many agricultural products are subject to official price controls.

To maintain lower consumer food prices in *urban* markets, the marketing agencies import food, thus in effect competing with local producers in supplying the urban market, thereby lowering the price obtained by the farmers for their products, a policy which tends to worsen rural poverty. The imports are subsidized by overvalued exchange rates which lower the perceived price of imported food supplies, especially when the domestic price exceeds the world price. Increasingly, since the 1970s, the policy of African governments of subsidizing basic food prices has made food imports a major item in the balance of payments of several African countries. Since the militancy of organized urban workers has been known

18. P. T. Bauer, 1981, p. 180.
19. See, for example, V. Le Vine, 1975.
20. R. H. Bates, 1981, pp. 39, 85.

to topple African governments following demonstrations and food riots associated with high food prices and cost of living, governments have developed a vested interest in keeping food prices low, despite the detrimental effects of official price controls and in spite of the fact that the policing of the marketing and distribution of food crops has been costly and largely unsuccessful.[21] The major results of official food-prices policies include falling domestic food production and the growth and spread of illicit marketing and smuggling as a means by which producers evade or counter the marketing monopoly of state agencies and seek to increase their returns on what they produce, even though the government may have heavily subsidized the inputs – fertilizers, seeds, mechanical equipment and credit for farmers' use. Smuggling of both food and export crops (the prices for which are also fixed by marketing boards) to neighbouring countries where they usually fetch better prices has reached massive proportions which in several countries armed border patrols and border guards are unable to eliminate and/or check. Notable examples are the cocoa, kola nuts, and foodstuffs smuggled from Ghana to Côte d'Ivoire and Togo, the food and cash-crop smuggling which goes on from Guinea to Sierra Leone, from Nigeria to Benin, and from Tanzania to Zambia and Kenya.

Moreover, the marketing of nearly all agricultural products still encounters serious problems in most countries of Africa. Though on the whole the well-established cash or export crops handled by the marketing boards tend to be more efficiently marketed, after the physical take-over of such produce by the boards, than the marketing of food crops, both face similar problems. The problems we have noted include those associated with the pattern of production itself – such as the scattered, wide spatial distribution of farms and producers, making them not easily accessible, and the technical marketing problems of storage, transportation and physical facilities and information – making produce-marketing very costly and risky. However, foodstuff-marketing has its own special problems. First, it is characterized by a large number of buyers and sellers, linked by a host of middlemen with a very complex system of distribution and arbitrage – not to mention the producers who often sell directly to consumers on farms and by road. At least six distinct categories of distributors have been identified in Africa – namely, farm-gate middlemen; non-commissioned agents; commissioned agents; co-operative agents; wholesalers; and retailers – all of them at one time or another carrying out various marketing functions either as individual entrepreneurs or in association with others.[22] While wholesalers tend to be oligopolists and ologopsonists in dealing with retailers and consumers, retailers generally function within a highly competitive structure. Prices therefore tend to

21. See M. Owusu, 1972.
22. Q. B. O. Anthonio, 1973, pp. 251–2.

a great extent to be market-determined, though price fluctuations stem-ming from high transportation costs, high losses from poor and ineffective storage, the high degree of risks involved and haggling are common.[23] It is worth pointing out that the bulk of the marketed food production in Africa is distributed through 'unofficial' marketing channels. The overwhelming problems that exist in the marketing of local foodstuffs and the inflationary tendencies in the domestic urban market for foodstuffs common in many African states are themselves reflections of the dualistic and underdeveloped economies African governments inherited from the colonial period, characterized by the dominance of non-market subsistence activities and peripheral markets.[24]

Ecological and social constraints on agricultural production 1960–80

Broadly, the principal ecological (physical environmental) constraints which significantly account for the poor performance of African agriculture and for the worsening of rural poverty observed between 1960 and 1980 have included the following: cyclical droughts – such as the Sahel drought of 1968–74, the advance of the desert, soil degradation and deforestation. Some of these are the direct result of misguided colonial economic and land policies. Other constraints are the abject poverty, poor health, disease, malnutrition, illiteracy and under-employment of the farming population; all characteristic features of underdeveloped economies. Mass migration of the male adult work-force from rural to urban-industrial and service centres leading to uncertainties and fluctuations in agricultural labour supply; an education system that encourages the youth to seek non-farm employment; traditional values, beliefs and cultural practices; land-use and land-tenure practices, rapid population growth and pressure on land; civil strife and political instability have all been major social constraints on agricultural production. For instance, during the 1970s, refugees, mostly farmers and pastoralists, fleeing across national frontiers as a result of liberation struggles, *coups d'Etat* and civil wars, rose from 750 000 to over 5 million – accounting for nearly half of all refugees world-wide.[25]

Between 1960 and 1980, the population of tropical Africa increased by 63 per cent to a total of 344 million. During the 1970s, the average increase was 2.7 per cent per annum in Africa as a whole. Most of this population growth has been concentrated in rural areas, creating severe pressures on land in parts of Kenya, Ethiopia, Rwanda, Tanzania and

23. V. C. Uchendu, 1967, pp. 37–50.
24. See R. H. Bates, 1981; J. Heyer *et al.*, 1981; P. Bohannan and G. Dalton, 1965, pp. 1–32, on African economies and markets.
25. United States Committee for Refugees, 1981.

Egypt. Only a few of these ecological and social constraints can be discussed here because of limitations of space.

Between 1960 and 1980, a comparison of 35 African countries, occupying a variety of ecological and mini-climatic zones, on the basis of their agricultural production trends in relation to population yields a paradoxical picture: a handful of countries such as Swaziland (middle-income), Côte d'Ivoire (middle-income), Cameroon (middle-income), Burundi (low-income), Rwanda (low-income) and Malawi (low-income), greatly increased both their total agricultural and food output per capita; a number of them, such as Botswana (middle-income) and Sudan (low-income), managed to raise their production above the level of population growth; and the great majority of tropical African countries, notably Ghana (middle-income), Nigeria (middle-income), Congo (middle-income), Chad (low-income), and Tanzania (low-income), experienced stagnation or even a decrease in agricultural production.[26]

For some African countries, particularly the countries of the Sahel – Mauritania, Mali, Chad, Senegal, Gambia, Upper Volta, Niger – the new agrarian crisis associated with a rapid succession of unanticipated droughts from 1968 to 1974 and during 1977–8 accounts in great part for the decline in the growth rate of agricultural production (crops and livestock); for the stagnation of agricultural exports and the shares in world trade for several commodities; for the rapid growth of commercial imports of food grains – wheat and rice – and for the increase in food aid and for aid dependency (Table 12.4).[27]

Ecological constraints: natural and man-made

Most of Africa's soils are naturally thin, delicate, deficient in organic materials and moderately fertile and require careful management. It has been suggested that the pace of environmental destruction and desertification in Africa has been accelerated rather than retarded by the introduction, especially in the humid tropics, of advanced farming technology in colonial and post-colonial periods.[28]

Specialists agree that the African climate is becoming increasingly variable, a fact which limits the choice of crops or livestock production, contributes to radical environmental deterioration, especially in the arid and semi-arid belts, and makes long-term planning of agricultural productivity extremely difficult. It is estimated that approximately 55 per cent of Africa is threatened by the desert's advance (Fig. 12.1) and 45 per cent is subject to severe drought.[29] Thus over half the continent and

26. See J. Hinderink and J. J. Sterkenburg, 1983; and the World Bank, 1982, for detailed discussions.

27. See Accelerated Development, 1983, pp. 46–50 and Table 6.

28. J. Omo-Fadaka, 1978, p. 48.

29. S. Galal, 1977; FAO, 1977.

TABLE 12.4 *Percentage value of wheat and food imports for selected countries in West Africa, 1968–78*

Country	Year	Food as percentage of total commodity imports	Wheat as percentage of total food imports	Country	Year	Food as percentage of total commodity imports	Wheat as percentage of total food imports
Nigeria	1968	7.4	24.1	Mali	1968	18.0	18.0
	1969	8.3	41.2		1969	14.2	14.2
	1970	7.6	26.6		1970	26.9	26.9
	1971	8.1	23.5		1971	25.6	25.6
	1972	9.6	23.5		1972	20.2	20.2
	1973	10.3	29.5		1973	no data	no data
	1974	8.9	32.8		1974	54.3	54.3
	1975	8.0	18.4		1975	19.4	19.4
	1976	8.5	22.1		1976	16.4	16.4
	1977	10.5	12.9				
Côte d'Ivoire	1968	12.5	14.5	Upper Volta	1968	18.7	18.7
	1969	11.7	11.4		1969	16.9	16.9
	1970	12.6	15.5		1970	17.3	17.3
	1971	12.4	5.6		1971	17.6	17.6
	1972	14.1	10.7		1972	19.1	19.1
	1973	17.5	10.5		1973	22.4	22.4
	1974	14.8	6.4		1974	31.0	31.0
	1975	12.0	8.8		1975	17.4	17.4
	1976	10.8	14.3				
	1977	11.7	12.3	Niger	1968	8.4	15.9
	1978	11.3	11.3		1969	9.4	10.4
Sierra Leone	1968	17.5	10.3		1970	10.6	25.6
	1969	16.4	12.0		1971	9.6	15.7
	1970	21.5	12.5		1972	12.6	7.1
	1971	19.2	13.4		1973	15.6	9.6
	1972	17.5	14.8		1974	17.9	5.2
	1973	24.0	18.0		1975	9.3	7.6
	1974	22.3	13.5		1976	6.4	6.2
Senegal	1968	34.8	9.0				
	1969	31.6	11.9	Chad	1968	10.3	39.4
	1970	26.1	16.9		1969	16.3	14.2
	1971	29.2	14.5		1970	15.7	10.9
	1972	25.7	11.8		1971	15.6	15.2
	1973	34.1	11.0		1972	20.9	12.5
	1974	26.7	8.5		1973	24.7	15.3
	1975	22.0	16.8		1974	20.7	15.5

Source: D. E. Vermeer, 1983, pp. 74–83; reprinted with permission of the Helen Dwight Reid Educational Foundation; published by Heldref Publications, 4000 Albermarle St, N.W., Washington, D.C. 20016.

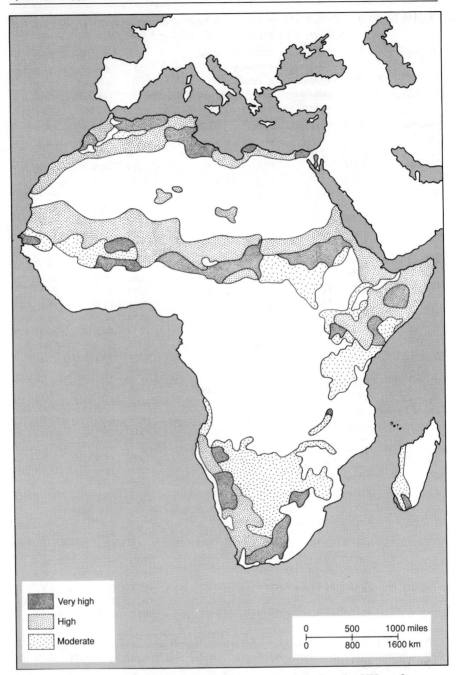

FIG. 12.1 *The risk of desert advance in Africa as recorded after the UN conference on desertification, 1977 (Source: adapted from UNEP, Studies, 1981, Vol. 2, p. 7)*

approximately one-quarter of the population, mostly in the rural areas, is threatened.[30] About 10 million sq km in a total of 21 countries is tsetse-fly-infested and therefore cannot sustain livestock (Fig. 12.2 on page 338).[31] The negative implications of this development for agricultural production are obvious.

Throughout Africa most of the farming population (outside the European, company or state modern large-scale mechanized farms) are engaged in *rainfed* agriculture. In North Africa irrigated agriculture is

TABLE 12.5   *Land use in North Africa*

Country	Cultivated area including fallow land (in 1000 ha)			
	Total	Rainfed	Irrigated	Rainfed as a percentage of the total
Algeria	7000	6750	250	96.40
Egypt	2650	10	2640	0.03
Libya	2520	2395	125	95.00
Morocco	7040	6590	450	93.60
Mauritania	263	260	3	98.90
Somalia	960	800	160	83.30
Sudan	7800	6240	1560	80.00
Tunisia	3500	3360	140	96.00

Source: A. Arar, 1980, p. 13.

dominant only in Egypt (Table 12.5). The African environment is generally not favourable to the development of irrigation because of inadequate water supplies and good soils and salinization. Only about one-third of the continent receives over 1000 mm of rain a year. In Africa, north of the Sahara, 90 per cent of the rainfall occurs between October and May; south of the Sahara, rainfall is concentrated in the summer months. About one-third of the continent gets under 250 mm of rain a year. Well-watered areas make up only about 25 per cent of tropical Africa. The unreliability and poor distribution of rainfall over the year, along with high temperatures and evaporation, severely limit the type of crops and livestock, if any, which can successfully be raised. In East Africa, for example, it has been estimated that 760 mm is the minimum annual requirement for successful cereal production, and that a farmer can expect one crop failure in every three years.[32]

30. UNEP, 1981.
31. C. Ayari, 1983.
32. D. Grigg, 1970.

In Algeria, a combination of overstocking and drought led to a severe reduction of livestock from 8 million head to 2 million in 1945 following a few years of drought.[33] Again during the drought of 1968–74 it is estimated that by December 1972, Mauritania had lost about 1.6 million cattle (80 per cent of its total). Before the 1968–74 drought, exports of livestock and livestock products (meat and hides) accounted for about half the total export income for some countries in the Sahel – exports which naturally suffered during the drought years. In some parts of the Sahel livestock numbers fell by 90 per cent.[34]

PLATE 12.2   *Drought in Algeria in 1947: sheep at an empty water trough*

According to estimates, in the early 1960s, there were about 1 million pastoralists, 12 million cattle, 25 million sheep and goats and 1 million camels in the Sahel. The massive destruction of livestock in the Sahel during the drought years forced thousands of nomads, along with peasants existing symbiotically whose economic base has been utterly ruined, to flee to urban centres, compounding problems of poverty and unemployment in these areas.

It must be pointed out that the spread of settled farming, partly encouraged by the development of cash crops for export, has accentuated

33. J. Omo-Fadaka, 1978.
34. N. Twose, 1984, p. 1115.

the traditional competition for land and water between pastoralists and settled farmers, compressing pastoralists and their herds into even smaller areas in the Sahel. The crucial flexibility of the traditional methods designed to cope with the cyclical patterns of good and bad years of rain, and allowing skilful local migration or judiciously selling off surplus livestock, has become extremely limited, forcing a decline of pastoralism. The installation of an increasing number of water holes on pasture lands for various flocks by various national and international agencies between 1960 and 1980, especially in West Africa, has led to overgrazing, widespread trampling and soil erosion.

Another set of constraints in the African environment affecting crop and livestock production are the famous enemies – rodents, birds (such as the keleo-kelea), insects (notably locusts) and the cryptogramic virus diseases. In the well-watered humid tropics the presence of tsetse fly prevents the raising of cattle and the development of mixed farming (Fig. 12.2). The amount of damage caused to crops and livestock varies with the insect or disease and zone in question, but as we have seen it is generally significant.

Apart from unbalanced diet and hunger, one should mention bacterial and parasitic diseases (WHO – World Health Organization – has identified 12 main ones), including malaria, influenza and dysentery, which have a debilitating effect upon human energy and economic productivity.[35]

Social constraints on production

Among the leading social constraints on agricultural production in Africa are the *cultural* practices of African farmers. In North Africa, the traditional practices of dry farming – deep ploughing, frequent disc cultivations and fallow rotation which occupies about 40–50 per cent of arable land for an average of 15–18 months – tend to lead to the degradation of the soil structure and poor yields. In much of Africa, fragmentation and the small size of holdings (the average seems rarely to exceed 10 hectares, in many areas the norm is less than 2 hectares) associated with land-tenure practices have made the application, *where appropriate*, of improved practices which could bring about increase in productivity almost impossible.

The communal or family ownership of both land and cattle is a factor making improvement in methods of cattle and land management problematic.[36] It prevents, for instance, selective breeding and renders the control of disease rather difficult. The African attitude to cattle is often cited as a factor contributing to low productivity. Many African

35. See P. Richards, 1983, for an intelligent critical review of ecological constraints on African agriculture.
36. G. Kay, 1965.

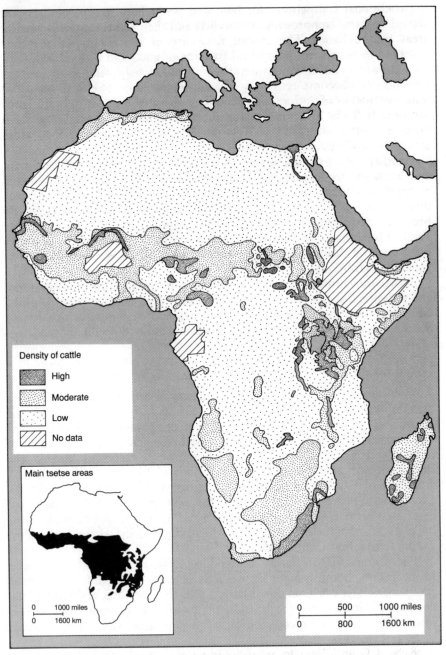

FIG. 12.2 *The distribution of cattle in Africa, with an inset map showing the main tsetse areas (Source: adapted from R. S. Harrison-Church et al.,* Africa and its Islands, *Longman, London, 1971, p. 91)*

338

communities are generally still more concerned about the size rather than the quality of the herd. A large herd enhances social status, prestige and wealth and pays the bride price.

In much of Africa, especially West Africa, pure communal tenure has been modified or has disappeared as a result of commercialization of agriculture. But despite its traditional advantages – shifting cultivation and rotational bush fallowing – the dominant type of farming in tropical Africa is becoming less and less efficient, particularly where population density exceeds the critical threshold of 60 per sq km of usable land.[37] At this critical level, soil fertility is difficult to sustain because of shortened fallows and the opportunity to raise productivity is hence decreased. The reduction in fallows associated with pressure on land is leading to rapid soil exhaustion and declining yield in many parts of Africa.

Again, where land is communal and can only be acquired from a local chief, as is the case in many parts of tropical Africa, it may be difficult for non-members of the appropriate kin group to acquire land. This may prevent the exploitation of unsettled or unused land when the potential farmers are 'strangers' or outsiders.

Throughout Africa, as the anthropological evidence shows, religious beliefs and practices may be inimical to sustained increase in agricultural productivity. In many parts of West Africa, for example, agricultural work, including fishing, is forbidden on certain days in deference to certain spirits.[38]

The negative attitudes of the non-farming community to farming is largely responsible for the lack of progress in African agriculture as a whole. In most African countries, mainly because of colonial education which stressed (and still does) academic subjects and a reward structure which has favoured urban employment, very little respect is accorded farming as an occupation and farmers by the rest of contemporary African society. In most areas of Africa, farmers encourage their educated sons and daughters not to take up farming.[39] The result has been that individuals who would perhaps prove more efficient and more successful in the development of the agricultural industry and therefore in the improvement in the quality of life in rural areas are not attracted to farming. Tanzania is one of a few African countries which has been making a serious effort to integrate schooling and agriculture in the countryside.[40]

There is a close relationship between education and agricultural development especially as reflected in the provision of extension services

---

37. D. Grigg, 1970.
38. See J. C. de Wilde, 1967, vol. II, for examples.
39. See, for example, N. O. Addo, 1974.
40. See J. K. Nyerere, 1968c.

to educate farmers in new practices.[41] However, in many parts of tropical Africa, many of the older illiterate farmers are inherently convinced that their traditional farming practices are in most cases better and more rewarding and that they are more knowledgeable about farming than young educated agricultural officers and extension workers, yet their professional knowledge and expertise is frequently undervalued by donor agencies and government extension officers. Their belief has often been confirmed by several cases of field disasters resulting from recommendations made by extension officers.[42]

It is noteworthy that African farmers, though mostly illiterate, traditional and ageing, have as a whole been willing to accept and apply innovations when they make better sense. During the post-war period, they have accepted new production methods, new (improved) crops and modern inputs, new processes of cropping and storage and new marketing systems. But most of these changes instead of leading to improvements in the quality of life of peasants have rather deepened rural poverty. This suggests that one of the most critical constraints to agricultural productivity in Africa is rural socio-economic inequality and peasant exploitation.

Agriculture and class disparities in post-colonial Africa

Whatever the exact nature and dynamics of 'social classes' in rural Africa in the post-colonial period,[43] the subject deserves systematic ongoing research – the extent of poverty and prosperity among the peasantry and within peasant communities at any given time has varied a great deal from country to country and from region to region (for example, North Africa as compared with tropical Africa or with *apartheid* South Africa).

The origins of accumulation and rural inequities

The development of rural inequality and rural class disparities in Africa have continued to be shaped by the *politics* of agriculture in general.[44] Political patronage, the pricing and marketing policy of state marketing boards (discussed above) may subsidize and hence enrich large capitalist farming, as has been the case in Kenya and Southern Africa, or may exploit smallholder producers by reducing their income.[45] Trans-national

41. D. Grigg, 1970, p. 152.

42. See S. La-Anyane, 1970 and 1971; J. Heyer *et al.*, 1981 and P. Richards, 1983, for critical discussion of the problems of innovating agricultural practices.

43. See, for example, P. C. Lloyd, 1974; A. Manghezi, 1976; G. Kitching, 1980; R. Stavenhagen, 1975; P. Waterman, 1983; L. Cliffe, 1976.

44. J. Barker, 1984; G. Dharam and S. Radwan, 1983.

45. C. Leys, 1975; M. Morris, 1976.

agro-industrial capitalist firms, international agencies (such as the World Bank) and government boards may dictate – often to the detriment of a vast majority of smallholders – the conditions and terms on which peasant smallholders can cultivate or sell export or industrial crops.[46] Illustrative examples of these are 'group' farms (Uganda); 'block' farms (Tanzania); contract-tenant and 'outgrower' production (Sudan); collective villages (Mozambique, Tanzania) and large centrally-managed settlement schemes found throughout Africa which directly compete with smallholder production for high-potential land, water and pasturage.

Not only has capitalist penetration and commodity production led to the rise of a small but growing group of rural capitalists,[47] but it has simultaneously generated an on-going process of peasantization and proletarianization in rural Africa.[48] In Central and South Africa, the need for a substantial and guaranteed labour force for expanding mines, settler estates and plantations produced land, labour and fiscal legislation which has created and institutionalized a large, low-wage impoverished rural proletariat of farm workers and tenant and male-migrant seasonal labourers (Fig. 12.3), many of whom are landless.[49] In West Africa and parts of East Africa, the development of African commercial export agriculture (cocoa, coffee, tea), has long stimulated a similar rise of seasonal migrant agricultural wage-labourers.[50] In Nigeria, the petroleum extraction enclaves have attracted peasants from neighbouring villages who abandon their farms for unskilled and semi-skilled daily-wage industrial employment.[51]

Thus regional disparities of economic development reflected in the geographical concentration of the means of production related to both the uneven regional natural-resource endowment and to the strong export orientation of colonial and neo-colonial African economies, and the fact that frequently the distribution and location of colonial and post-colonial agricultural, commercial and industrial enterprises has had little bearing either on social-equity considerations or on the current or future needs of rural African populations, have all directly contributed to the different forms of rural inequality and rural class formation in much of Africa.

In areas where semi-feudal forms of land-tenure or landlordism have prevailed, as in parts of North, West and East Africa (but with exceptions such as post-revolution Ethiopia), commodity production has transformed powerful landlords overnight into wealthy capitalist farmers who use their political connection and influence to dispossess the poor, indebted and

---

46. C. Windstrand and S. Amin, 1975; S. Bernstein, 1978; M. S. Halfani and J. Barker, 1984; J. Loxley, 1984; L. Freeman, 1984.
47. P. Hill, 1970.
48. G. Arrighi and J. S. Saul, 1973; K. Post, 1977.
49. M. Morris, 1976; G. H. T. Kimble, 1960.
50. See, for example, A. L. Mabogunje, 1972; P. Hill, 1970; R. Stavenhagen, 1975.
51. E. Chikwendu, 1983.

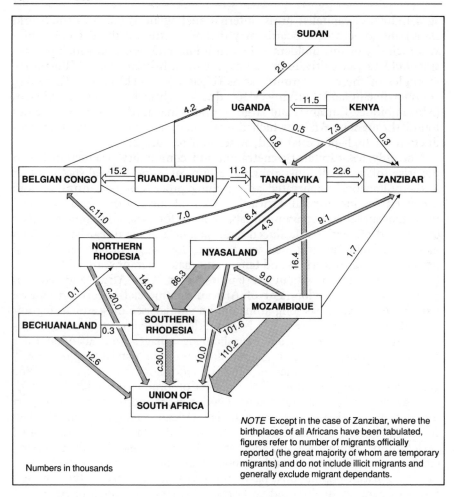

FIG. 12.3 *Patterns of international labour migration in Africa, 1946–52 (Source: G. H. T. Kimble,* Tropical Africa: Vol. 1, Land and Livelihood, *Twentieth Century Fund, New York, 1960, p. 584)*

defenceless tenant farmers and sharecroppers of their land, thus creating a huge class of landless and exploited agricultural labourers.[52] High-value cash-crop production and male labour migration as a dominant form of capitalist penetration have had a profound and negative impact on the sexual division of agricultural labour and have seriously undermined the traditional household economy in which men and women shared tasks, especially in Southern and East Africa, by imposing an unequal and heavy

52. See A. Richards, 1982, on Egypt, for example.

TABLE 12.6   *Division of labour between men and women in rural Africa*

Task	Percentage of total labour	
	Men[a]	Women[a]
Land clearing	95	5
Turning the soil	70	30
Planting	50	50
Hoeing and weeding	30	70
Harvesting	40	60
Transporting crops from farm to home	20	80
Storing crops	20	80
Processing food crops	10	90
Marketing excess crops	40	60
Trimming tree crops	90	10
Carrying water and fuel	10	90
Caring for domestic animals	50	50
Hunting	90	10
Feeding and caring for children, men and aged	5	95

[a]With or without some help from children.

Source: ILO, 1985, p. 120.

burden on women agricultural producers, driven to work longer hours (Table 12.6) without male help, and leading to the 'feminization of poverty' in rural areas, deepening gender stratification.[53] Women's jobs and incomes are also threatened in other ways – home-brewed traditional beer, for example, is in some African countries now facing competition from the products of modern large-scale breweries.[54]

Class and planned rural poverty

Since independence African governments, socialist and non-socialist oriented, have in co-operation with international agencies (UNFAO, USAID, CIDA, the World Bank, and so on) and foreign governments embarked upon a variety of agricultural and rural development projects as part of their national development plans.

The part played by foreign aid in the provision of investment capital and advice in planned agricultural and rural change has been tremendous.[55] For instance, under McNamara, the World Bank between 1973 and 1980 provided $2.4 billion out of about $5 billion in aid flows into African

53. G. Gran, 1983; B. Brown, 1983.
54. R. Dauber and M. L. Cain, 1980.
55. R. E. Clute, 1982.

agriculture.[56] But on the whole, as studies have shown, agricultural credit and institutional support have been concentrated largely on export crops, and international and state assistance in the form of inputs, credits and marketing has largely been seized by a few rich peasants – large 'progressive' farmers, who are already privileged. It is significant, for example, that hardly any of the many World Bank projects in Africa were designed to reach the growing impoverished rural landless, the tenant farmers, sharecroppers or squatters.[57]

Some countries, including Algeria, Morocco, Ethiopia, Egypt, Tanzania and Zimbabwe, have adopted measures with the objective of reducing or eliminating rural inequities and exploitation.[58] Some of these measures have been socialized agriculture (Tanzania, Mozambique, Ethiopia, Algeria, Ghana); land-tenure changes; land redistribution; and the abolition of sharecropping, landlordism, rural-debt payments, and so on (Morocco, Algeria, Tunisia, Ethiopia, Egypt, Kenya).

In many countries state farm enterprises have collapsed (as in Ghana), socialized agriculture has been an economic disaster (Tanzania, Ghana, Mozambique), co-operatives have been weakened by excessive bureaucratic or state control, and in many areas of Africa peasant agricultural production has declined. In countries like Chad, Ethiopia, Eritrea, Mozambique and Angola, civil war continues to disrupt peasant agriculture, undermining any immediate hope for increased food self-sufficiency and the alleviation of mass rural hunger and starvation.

At the heart of the various policy measures designed by African governments and international agencies to improve agriculture and rural welfare has been a concern for exercising control over the peasants' productive process, and for the extraction of the peasants' marketed surplus by privileged, powerful public and private agencies and groups.[59]

The privileged and powerful individuals and groups in rural Africa vary from country to country with respect to their social origins, their incomes, standard of living, farm size, size of annual crop yield and so on. Everywhere, the commercial farming class is internally differentiated, and in some countries, like Ghana, Nigeria, Côte d'Ivoire, Uganda and Kenya, the differentiation is very marked. However, throughout Africa, two broad rural classes are distinguishable, namely the richer peasants (and cattle-ranchers) – the exploiting classes – and the poorer peasants (and pastoralists) – the exploited classes.[60] The richer peasants consist of

56. World Bank, 1981, p. 47.
57. C. Payer, 1982; R. L. Ayres, 1983.
58. For Algeria, see K. Pfeifer, 1981, and T. L. Blair, 1970; for Morocco, see Z. Daoud, 1981; for Ethiopia, see R. Lefort, 1983; for Egypt, see A. Richards, 1982; for Tanzania, see I. G. Shivji, 1976; J. K. Nyerere, 1967b; B. M. de Gennaro, 1981; and for Zimbabwe, A. Astrow, 1983.
59. J. Heyer *et al.*, 1981.
60. K. Nkrumah, 1966; G. Kitching, 1980.

the large landowners and producers of cash crops (such as cocoa, coffee and tea), who may include government officials, military officers and big business people with ready access to credit and funds to invest (North and East Africa) or traders, traditional chiefs and religious leaders, who have easy access to new technology, credit and services and to the ruling class in regional and national capitals.

The poorer peasants (and pastoralists) may be tenant sharecroppers, debt farmers of the richer peasants, or landless rural labourers. It is noteworthy that in a 1977 government Integrated Rural Survey in Kenya (a middle-income richer African state) over 40 per cent of smallholder farming families had incomes scarcely sufficient to provide for basic necessities of life. The Kenyan government was forced to admit that not all groups shared *equitably* in Kenya's economic development, and identified five target groups as needing special attention, including small farmers, pastoralists, the landless and squatters – about a third of the Kenyan population.[61]

In 1971, the annual rural per capita income in Kenya was estimated at only $58, which was slightly above the conditions of absolute poverty – an annual per capita income equivalent to $50 or less. Rural incomes in most African countries remain abysmally low, and the general quality of rural life, as measured by the percentage of the population with reasonable access to a safe water supply or waste-disposal facilities, is very poor. In Africa only 21 per cent of the rural population had access to such a water supply and only 28 per cent to waste-disposal facilities.[62] Survey after survey in several countries has shown that class and income disparities are growing. In Zambia half to two-thirds of rural households have 'incomes that are so far below official wages that malnutrition and seasonal famine is a constant fear and too frequent a reality'. Seventy out of every hundred Africans are either destitute or on the verge of poverty.

Throughout rural Africa, sharp class inequities and peasant exploitation continue,[63] worsened by the world recession and the oil crisis of the 1970s, the decline in world commodity prices, foreign exchange constraints of African governments, natural disasters and political instability. The alleviation of rural poverty in Africa definitely requires a new international economic order and a radical redistribution of power which would truly permit the rural masses genuine control over decisions affecting their livelihood and socio-economic well-being.

61. See P. D. Little, 1983, pp. 91–108.
62. WHO, 1976.
63. See, for instance, Z. Daoud, 1981, pp. 27–33, on Morocco; and T. L. Blair, 1970, on Algeria.

345

African agriculture in the world economy since 1935: from dependent colonies to dependent neo-colonies

African countries entered the global capitalist economy mostly as colonies of rival European imperialist powers. Colonial policies of economic development through international trade relied on an international division of labour based on a doctrine of comparative advantage. The exploitative doctrine forced African countries to devote their resources to the production of primary products for export and to use their export earnings to import manufactured goods and any deficit food requirements from abroad. This in effect legitimized the dependence of African economies on monocultures, and their export orientation.

Over 80 per cent of exports from developing Africa consist of primary products such as coffee, cocoa, tea, tobacco, sugar, groundnuts and cotton, and minerals such as petroleum, copper and phosphate rock.[64]

At the time of the First World War, compared with commodity exports from Latin America and Asia, Africa's exports were negligible, though palm oil and cocoa were already important African export crops. By 1935, according to one estimate, Africa was producing 65 per cent of the total world commercial production of palm oil coming from the *colonies*; 63 per cent of groundnuts; 90 per cent of olive oil; 54 per cent of sesame; 56 per cent of cotton; 87 per cent of wool, and 88 per cent of cocoa (Table 12.7). Africa's agricultural exports began to rise in the inter-war period, and for a number of commodities increased at an even faster rate after the Second World War (Tables 12.8–12.15). Africa's share of total world commodity exports rose from 8 per cent in 1938 to 10 per cent in 1948 and 14 per cent in 1965.[65] Thus at the time of independence many African countries had become important world suppliers of several primary products.

Though Africa is dominant in the world production of strategic minerals (Fig. 12.4), the continent remains principally an agricultural producer (Figure 12.5). Africa continues to produce about two-thirds of the total world production of palm oil, sisal and cocoa. Since the war, Africa's share in the world market for coffee – produced by 21 African countries – has tripled, and in the 1970s accounted for about 30 per cent of the world total.[66]

The rate of expansion of African agricultural production in the 1950s and 1960s was particularly high for cocoa, coffee, tea, bananas, groundnuts and cotton. This rapid expansion was made possible by the development of infrastructure by colonial and post-colonial governments, the supply of government-subsidized modern inputs, such as insecticides, chemical

64. C. Ayari, 1983, pp. 8–11.
65. W. A. Lewis, 1969.
66. A. M. Kamarck, 1972.

TABLE 12.7 *Colonial commercial production of raw materials and foodstuffs expressed as a percentage of world commercial production*

Commodity Raw materials 1934 or latest available data)	Percentage of world commercial production (colonial)	Principal sources of colonial commercial production with their production expressed as a percentage of world production in African territories	African territories' commercial production as percentage of world commercial colonial production
Palm oil	98.8[b]	Nigeria (42.9), Belgian Congo (13.9), French West Africa (6.1), Angola (1.2).	65.0
Tin ore[a]	56.9[d]	Nigeria (4.4), Belgian Congo (3.7).	14.0
Phosphates	52.0	French North Africa (34.6), French Equatorial Africa (7.2).	80.0
Graphite	46.0	Madagascar (7.5).	16.3
Groundnuts	28.5[b]	French West Africa (13.2), Nigeria (4.8).	63.0
Copper[a]	21.3[d]	Northern Rhodesia (12.3), Belgian Congo (8.6).	98.0
Manganese ore	13.7	Nigeria (12.4)[e]	90.5
Chrome ore	12.3[b]	Southern Rhodesia (8.6).	70.0
Olive oil	12.9[h]	French North Africa (11.2), Libya (?0.4).	90.0
Sesame	8.0[f]	Sudan (2.2), Congo (?0.8), Nigeria (1.3).	54.0
Gold	9.2[b]	Southern Rhodesia (2.8), Gold Coast (1.3), Congo (1.4).	60.0
Asbestos	9.5[g]	Southern Rhodesia (9.0).	95.0
Cotton[j]	2.5[f]	Uganda (0.9), Sudan (0.5).	56.0
Wool	2.3[b]	French North Africa (2.0).	87.0
Zinc[a]	1.9[d]	Northern Rhodesia (1.4).	74.0
Foodstuffs 1933			
Cocoa	74.0[b]	Gold Coast (40.6), Nigeria (11.3), French West Africa (6.8), French Cameroons (2.8), British Togo (1.9), French Togo (1.1), British Cameroons (0.6).	88.0
Maize[e]	24.1[d]	French West Africa (5.9)	24.0
Citrus fruits[e]	9.7[b]	Algeria (1.0).	10.0
Tobacco	4.8[b]	Nyasaland (0.3).[k]	0.6
Coffee	7.6[b]	British East Africa (0.7), Madagascar (0.6).	17.0

[a]Metal content. [b]1933. [d]1934. [e]Net exports. [f]1933–4.
[g]1931. [h]1934–5. [j]Ginned.
[k]A considerable amount of tobacco is now being grown in the Rhodesias (now Zambia and Zimbabwe).

Since these figures were compiled, for the year 1934, there has been, owing to rising prices, increased production of many raw materials, notably of tin, rubber, copper, gold and zinc. If, therefore, a table for 1936 could be compiled, there might be material differences in the percentage of world production provided by individual colonies.

Source: The Colonial Problem. A Report by a Study Group of members of the Royal Institute of International Affairs, 1937, p. 290.

TABLE 12.8   *Africa's share of world palm-products production*

Year	Oil equivalent (in 1000 tonnes)	Percentage of world production
1954	920	77
1955	870	78
1956	940	79
1957	900	79
1958	940	80
1959	930	81
1960	920	79

Source: FAO, 1961a, p. 115.

TABLE 12.9   *Africa's share of world coffee production*

Year	Thousand tonnes	Percentage of world production
1934–38 (average)	140	6
1948–52 (average)	280	13
1954	390	16
1955	510	18
1956	510	20
1957	540	17
1958	610	17
1959	670	15
1960	730	18

Source: FAO, 1961b, pp. 145 and 161.

fertilizers and disease-resistant seedlings, and by improved production techniques, good rainfall and the rapid spread of commercial agriculture – all at the expense of food production. In 1966 the contribution of agriculture to the gross domestic product (GDP) in African countries was as high as 53.9 per cent for West Africa and 41.2 per cent for East Africa (see Tables 12.2 and 12.6).

But despite the rapid growth, the value of agricultural exports declined. Between 1953–4 and 1971–2 the commodity terms of trade declined from 126 (1953) to 86 (1971) or from 138 (1954) to 84 (1972). The terms of trade dropped significantly for 23 out of 28 commodities indexed by UNCTAD (United Nations Conference on Trade and Development), many of them major sources of foreign exchange for African countries.[67] For example, in 1954–5, Ghana's production of cocoa was 210 000 tonnes, nearly half of Africa's total, and her export earning from cocoa was £85.5

67. UNCTAD, 1976; A. G. Frank, 1980.

TABLE 12.10 *Africa's share of world groundnut production*

Year	Unshelled weight (in thousand tonnes)	Percentage of world production
1948–52 (average)	2440	26
1957	4100	30
1958	3630	26
1959	3520	29
1960	4080	29

Source: FAO, 1961a, p. 118.

TABLE 12.11 *Africa's share of world cocoa production*

Year	Thousand tonnes	Percentage of world production
1934–8 (average)	490	66
1948–52 (average)	500	66
1954	490	60
1955	530	64
1956	580	64
1957	460	60
1958	570	62
1959	660	65
1960	840	76

Source: FAO, 1961b, pp. 145 and 161.

million. In 1964–5, with an estimated crop of 590 000 tonnes, the estimated external earning dropped to about £77 million![68] The fact is that prices of primary commodities, which are controlled not by producers but by the consumers – the industrial countries – are subject to wide swings. The wide fluctuations in price are hardly offset by increasing the quantities produced – as the case of cocoa mentioned above illustrates.

Since the foreign exchange needed by most African governments for development derives from taxing exports in one way or another, export price fluctuations directly lead to fluctuations in total receipts from year to year. Between 1950 and 1965, for instance, the fluctuations in price for sisal, Tanzania's principal foreign-exchange earner, averaged over 26 per cent,[69] making implementation of development plans extremely difficult. The low income elasticity of demand for most of the primary products of African countries as compared with manufactures of industrial countries exacerbates the problem. A fairly constant relationship exists

68. K. Nkrumah, 1966, p. 10.
69. A. M. Kamarck, 1972.

TABLE 12.12   *Africa's share of world natural-rubber production*

Year	Thousand tonnes	Percentage of world production
1934–8 (average)	10	1.0
1948–52 (average)	60	3.6
1957	115	5.8
1958	125	6.3
1959	145	7.1
1960	145	7.1

Source: FAO, 1961a, p. 146.

TABLE 12.13   *Africa's share of world sisal production*

Year	Thousand tonnes	Percentage of world production
1934–8 (average)	160	62
1948–52 (average)	225	70
1954	290	69
1955	300	65
1956	310	63
1957	325	65
1958	350	68
1959	370	64
1960	375	64

Source: FAO, 1961a, p. 145.

between world industrial production and world trade in primary commodities, with the former growing at a faster rate than the latter. In other words, the terms of Africa's incorporation into the global capitalist market since colonial days have up till now condemned Africa to the production of agricultural export commodities of little or no immediate use in Africa, which promotes African underdevelopment, and which by its very nature also promotes hunger and starvation as subsistence output is neglected in favour of export production.

The colonial pattern of the flow of trade between Africa and the world has not radically changed, as the trade-bloc patterns between Africa and industrialized capitalist countries show. Trade with Western Europe – that is, with the former colonial powers – is still the most important for Africa. Indeed nearly two-thirds of Africa's total trade is with Western Europe; about 12 per cent with the United States; 10 per cent with other African countries; and 10 per cent with Eastern Europe. Indeed, no other Third-World primary-producing area is so heavily dependent on trade

TABLE 12.14   *Africa's share of world cotton production*

Year	Thousand tonnes	Percentage of world production
1934–8 (average)	651	11.3
1947–51 (average)	627	11.9
1956	787	11.0
1957	813	12.0
1958	962	13.5
1959	953	12.5
1960	876	11.9

Source: Commonwealth Economic Committee, 1961, Table 31. Reproduced with the permission of the Controller of Her Britannic Majesty's Stationery Office.

TABLE 12.15   *Africa's share of world sugar production*

Year	Thousand tonnes	Percentage of world production
1934–8[a]	1100	7.4
1948–52[a]	1560	7.9
1956[b]	2230	8.9
1958[c]	2555	8.8
1959[c]	2675	9.0
1960[c]	2400	7.6

Sources: [a] FAO, 1956, p. 73.
  [b] FAO, 1958, p. 71.
  [c] FAO, 1961a, p. 73.

with Western Europe,[70] a point worth remembering when considering the obstacles facing the demands by the Third World for a new international economic order.

The virtual collapse during the late 1960s, 1970s and 1980s of the agricultural sector, especially in tropical Africa – on which about 80 per cent of African population depends and which is the main source of foreign exchange and public revenues for a majority of African countries – has been aided and abetted by the deep and prolonged world recession and imported inflation, related sluggish world demand and severely depressed prices for most groups of export commodities, unfavourable exchange-rate movements, increasing debt burden, the decline of agricultural-export subsidies by principal trading (industrial) countries, and restrictions on imports of agricultural and other labour-intensive products from African (and Third-World) countries. It has also been exacerbated by

70. A. M. Kamarck, 1972, pp. 93–124.

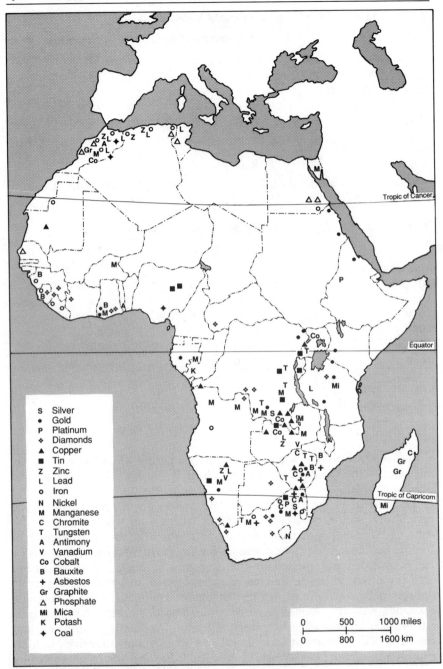

FIG. 12.4 *Major mineral workings in Africa (Source: adapted from R. S. Harrison–Church et al, Africa and its Islands, Longman, London, 1971, p. 99)*

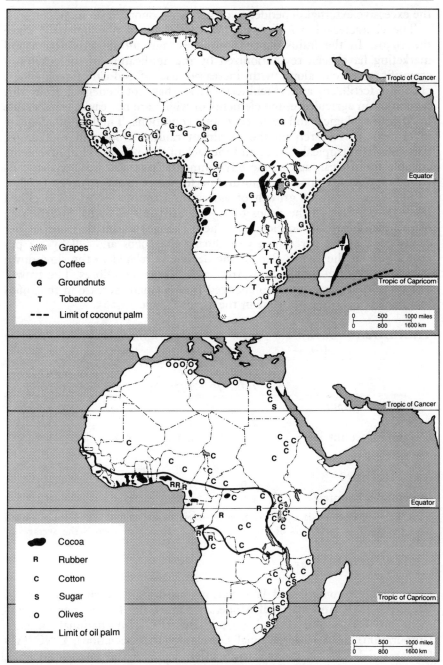

FIG. 12.5 *The distribution of cash crops in Africa (Source: adapted from R. S. Harrison-Church* et al, Africa and its Islands, *Longman, London, 1971, p. 87)*

353

the excessive external dependence of African economies on monocultures.

The character of world agriculture has changed phenomenally since the 1950s. In the industrialized countries, agricultural production and marketing have been revolutionized by the application of the results of scientific research, along with increased use of industrial technology, chemical fertilizers and machinery. Africa has not benefited from this revolution in agriculture, the elements of which are not easily transferable to African ecological and socio-economic conditions. The lack of adequate investment in research on the dominant rainfed crops and root crops, particularly in tropical Africa, and the lack of technological improvements suitable for African agronomic environments have also been major contributors to Africa's poor agricultural performance in the 1970s and 1980s.

The annual rate of growth of agricultural output in Africa declined from 2.7 per cent in the 1960s to 1.3 per cent in the 1970s, but the rate of population growth accelerated. These changes meant that output per capita grew at 0.2 per cent a year during the 1960s and fell by 1.4 per cent a year in the 1970s. Part of the decline is related to the slow-down in production of non-food crops, tropical beverages and fibres. The growth of food output per capita also changed from a small increase in the 1960s to a decline of −1.1 per cent in the 1970s (Table 12.16).

TABLE 12.16   *Percentage growth rates of agriculture and food output in Africa*

	Total		Per capita	
	1960–70	*1970–80*	*1960–70*	*1970–80*
Agricultural output				
Africa	2.7	1.3	0.2	− 1.4
Developing countries	2.8	2.7	0.3	0.3
Food output				
Africa	2.6	1.6	0.1	− 1.1
Developing countries	2.9	2.8	0.4	0.4

NOTES: Production data are weighted by world export unit prices. Decade growth rates are based on midpoints of five-year averages, except that 1970 is the average for 1969–71.

Source: FAO, 1982a, p. 41.

Since the Second World War, various institutions, such as the World Bank, the IMF (International Monetary Fund), GATT (General Agreement on Tariffs and Trade) (1948), the IFC (International Finance Corporation), IDA (International Development Association), UNCTAD (1964) and STABEX (1975), to mention some of the most influential, have been established in part to regulate trade in commodities (GATT), or to provide some form of external economic aid to poor countries. This is provided indirectly through increasing their share of the market for given commodities; their participation in commodity agreements negotiated periodically which distribute market shares to signatories and stabilize fluctuations in price and/or provide a higher average price than would result from uncontrolled market forces (for example, the recent international coffee agreements); a system of general tariff preferences in a growing market, *à la* UNCTAD, to promote manufacturing in developing countries; and 'compensatory' or 'supplementary' finance to offset fluctuations or unanticipated shortfalls from expected export earnings.[71] Direct aid from the World Bank and the IMF is in the form of long-term and short-term loans.

All these are aimed at providing some relief, *not cure*, for Third-World primary producers who continue to suffer severely from the ill-effects of the cyclical fluctuations in the economies of the industrialized countries. They are, in other words, aimed at perpetuating neo-colonialism, 'paying the raw material exporting countries for remaining exporters of raw materials rather than turning to higher levels of processing, or ... becoming more self-reliant'.[72]

It is estimated that Third-World producers obtain not more than 15 per cent of the value of their export commodities, as paid for by the consumers – industrial countries. As long as Third-World producers (of whom Africans constitute some of the poorest) remain price-takers rather than price-setters (price-setting is the privilege of the consuming nations); continue to have scarcely any control over processing, shipping and marketing, which are monopolized by the trans-national corporations of industrial countries; and continue to be discriminated against by a pattern of protection in the industrialized countries, which directly contravenes GATT rules – that is, as long as the crisis of the old international economic order survives in its present form – Third-World countries, particularly African countries, have little hope of climbing out of their mass poverty. For instance, according to World Bank estimates, if the dominant industrialized countries – especially the 24 OECD member countries, which constitute the major export markets for African countries – were to eliminate all tariff and non-tariff barriers on imports from developing countries, these countries could add some 33 billion to their foreign-exchange earnings.[73]

It is in terms of these considerations outlined above that the urgent demands of the Third-World countries for the establishment of a new international economic order – which would restructure trade, production, monetary system, surplus allocation and decision-making, and thus

71. For example, STABEX; see O. H. Kokole, 1981, on STABEX, pp. 441–59.
72. J. Galtung, 1976, p. 40.
73. J. F. Rweyemamu, 1978, p. 36.

eliminate the gross inequities and discrimination against Third-World countries – should be assessed and supported.[74]

It has been pointed out that the existing terms of international trade tend to deteriorate for the exporters, notably Africa, of primary commodities and agricultural products, as against those of manufacturers; that is, the terms of trade tend to deteriorate for poor as against rich countries. To reverse these abuses, Third-World countries are asking for the stabilization and enhancement of international prices for the primary products exported by them, either through fairer and more comprehensive international commodity agreements or, if necessary, by exploiting the potential commodity power of producers, as was demonstrated in 1973–4 and 1979–80 by OPEC (Organization of Petroleum Exporting Countries). The establishment of the UN Conference on Trade and Development (UNCTAD) in 1964 and its ICP is designed to prevent the effects of the failure of international markets to be fair to the primary-commodity exports of Third-World countries. A Common Fund was established by UNCTAD as a means of financing ICP. Though accepted in principle by Western industrial countries, they are yet to ratify it.

Meanwhile, following the Plans of Action adopted by the OAU Special Economic Summit held in Lagos, Nigeria, in 1980,[75] African governments are made to accept full responsibility for Africa's agrarian crisis, for not according the necessary priority over the years to agriculture – especially food production for domestic consumption – both in the allocation of scarce resources, and in paying sufficient and systematic attention to policies for promotion through the provision of adequate incentives of productivity and general improvement of rural life. African governments should have the courage to implement the programme of action designed to ensure a beneficial income-distribution impact on the rural poor, and a radical reduction, if not total elimination, of the widening gaps in income and standard of living between the rich and the poor in rural areas. In the decades ahead, this will mean the reversal of the flow of massive investments away from urban areas and into the rural areas of Africa in the form of rural industries, the provision of health posts and clinics, good all-weather feeder roads, better sanitation and so on. Poor farmers should be guaranteed access to credit and new, improved, appropriate farming technology. This, after all, would be a fair and reasonable return of a portion of the enormous taxes that are appropriated by the state from the farming population.

74. See W. Brandt, 1980.
75. See International Institute for Labour Studies, 1982.

13

Industrial development and urban growth, 1935–80

Pierre KIPRÉ

Introduction

This chapter sets out to show that industrial development in Africa inherited a heavy burden as a result of the unbalanced relations existing between the continent under colonial rule and dominant Europe. It is difficult now to turn that heritage to Africa's advantage on account of a host of objective and subjective inhibiting factors and impediments that are both internal and external in origin. Thereafter, against the background of the present-day urban explosion, it attempts to highlight some of the reasons why the *industrialization and urban growth* of Africa are not synchronous, or are only seldom so. This has the effect of further tilting the social imbalances that are among the factors preventing genuine economic development.

The questions we shall examine one by one will accordingly be: industrialization policies in Africa since the 1930s; the main features of industrial development in terms of both production and consumption; and the part played by industrialization in the process of urban growth.

Industrialization policies in Africa from 1930–5 to 1980

Patterns of industrial development in Africa, at least from the 1930s to 1980s, were bound up with the implementation of industrialization policies that had been more or less well thought out; overall, they bore some relationship to the nature of external economic relations and to the general goals of the continent's economic development. While the former changed little, the latter brought out the contrast between the colonial period and the post-colonial era, having regard to the ambiguous status of countries that were theoretically independent but whose economies were subject to external control.

In terms of industrial development, it can be seen from an analysis of policies and actual trends over the period from 1935 to 1980 that modern-style industry in Africa was initially fostered in the mining sector, followed by different levels of agricultural processing. The continent's role was seen as being that of a supplier of primary commodities in their more or less raw state. When manufacturing appeared at a later date, the idea was to bring light industrial output closer to its African customers.

Colonial policies from 1930 to 1960–5

Although colonial economic policies displayed the same features everywhere, in that they were designed to exploit the colonies primarily for the benefit of the metropolitan countries against the background of a capitalist system operating on a worldwide scale, the individual colonial powers, under pressure from colonial business interests, evolved specific policies for their own empires, in some cases right down to the local level. Hence, industrial development did not occupy the same place in these policies in every instance. Despite their differences and similarities, three main cases call for brief consideration: these are the examples of the British, French and Belgian areas of influence in Africa.

Industrial policy in British Africa
The works on the economic history of Africa provide little evidence of a comprehensive industrial policy on the part of the relevant authorities in London or in their colonial territories in Africa. Official development policy in British Africa can best be grasped, especially for the period before the Second World War, from the sectoral measures taken or, more often, from the approach adopted in local situations.

Believing as it did in free trade, the Colonial Office in London was a strong supporter of entrepreneurship in the colonies; it held to the doctrine that the main task of the state was to ensure freedom of movement and the protection of businessmen in the colonies. As a result, until the Second World War, industry remained basically the province of private enterprise, without the authorities becoming involved in the mobilization of capital. Since the colonial powers had been hard hit by the economic crisis from 1930 onwards, a policy of falling back on the empire was advocated by the Imperial Conference in Ottawa in 1932. That policy was applied in British Africa over the period from 1935 to 1939. However, it was not accompanied by official measures geared to attracting some of the free-floating capital of the time to Africa for its industrial development, despite the creation of the Colonial Development Fund in 1929. A second period started to take shape during the war years from 1939 to 1945, and gathered strength especially after the victory. This saw the discreet intervention of the state, which passed the Colonial Development and Welfare Act in 1940.

It was only after the war that Britain started to take a serious interest in the industrial future of its African territories. The idea was to mobilize imperial funds to assist in the 'modernization' of the colonies. The commissions of inquiry set up for the purpose stressed the need for official incentives for industrial activity in British black Africa. However, it was generally acknowledged that the setting up of a genuine capital-goods industry (except in Southern Rhodesia) was a pipe-dream. All that was needed was to promote a consumer-goods industry adapted to local income levels and needs. It was not meant to be an export industry, except for primary commodities, and the influence of British interests, especially in the settler colonies like Kenya and Southern Rhodesia, was expected to be paramount. In this regard, the case of Southern Rhodesia, a settler colony *par excellence*, is revealing. Close as it was to South Africa, and largely dominated by the business circles that had been instrumental in its creation, this colony had, from 1946–7 onwards, an industrial policy that was more systematically in line with the concerns of the British settlers living there, who were anxious to soften the impact of South African competition.

In sum, industrial policy in British Africa during the colonial period remained broadly inspired by the classical pattern whereby Africa supplied industrial raw materials and consumed large amounts of imported manufactured goods, the whole exercise being conducted through a form of capitalism purged of all idealism and all direct intervention by the state.

The French colonial areas
For many years until the beginning of the 1930s, the industrial development of the colonies and protectorates in Africa had not been an issue in official circles. In line with the Sarraut doctrine on the 'development of the colonies', industry was a matter for the private sector alone. It was not until the crisis of 1930 that the topic came to be raised in those circles. In 1934, the 'Economic Conference of Metropolitan and Overseas France' for the first time specifically and clearly set out the new thinking on the subject. Stressing the role of the state in the process of industrialization in the colonies, this conference introduced the concept of 'industrial impetus' in the colonies. The idea was not to create or develop a colonial industry that would compete with that of the metropole, but merely to set up, in the vicinity of the production regions, industries 'making it possible to enhance unusable raw materials'.

In business circles, the modernist current favourable to the idea of industrializing the colonies to some degree (P. Bernard, L. P. Morard, Maspétiol, and so on) was gaining ground. Its influence can be seen in the draft Ten-Year Plan (1942–52) drawn up by the Vichy regime, which even envisaged the promotion of semi-finished products from the *in situ* processing of raw materials.

In 1944, the Brazzaville Conference proposed that the industrialization of French Africa should 'as a general rule, be carried out by private enterprise'. However, it made a recommendation to the effect that the colonial administration should contribute to the success of such ventures by defraying the cost of pilot factories, supporting vital industries that 'appear to be incapable of paying their way', and by creating testing and

359

research centres 'made available to industrialists for studies or quality controls'. This line of thinking marked a breakthrough in the traditional outlook of colonial business circles, which were attached to the colonial predatory economy (*économie de traite*). It also broke with the fear of possible competition with metropolitan industrial output.

The establishment, in 1947, of FIDES (*Fonds d'investissement pour le développement économique et social* – Investment Fund for Economic and Social Development) was designed to give substance to official policy. The need to reconstruct the metropole, the enormous magnitude of the needs of the colonies and protectorates – industry there was only in an embryo state in 1946 – and the priority given to strategic expenditure on transport and infrastructure against the background of the Cold War in the 1950s soon showed up the modest scale of those public investments and the reticence displayed by the private sector.

In 1960, despite significant progress compared with the situation in 1935,[1] the French-governed areas were still severely under-industrialized and had not been prospected sufficiently even to become suppliers of industrial raw materials. Only commercial agriculture offered a few products of that type (coffee, cocoa, groundnuts, cotton). As in the British colonial areas, industry was by no means one of the typical activities of these colonies.

Belgian policy in the Congo

In 1935, as indeed since 1908, Belgium remained generally faithful to the heritage left by King Léopold II of always working hand-in-hand with big business for the development of the Congo.

It was mainly in the industrial sector, and especially in mining, that the state chose to work in partnership with business circles. Its involvement, which was more clearly spelt out in the mining legislation adopted in 1935, took the form of the ownership of a significant shareholding in most of the mining companies. The close 'linkage' between private enterprises and the state until 1956–7 left little room for an industrial development policy guided by the aim of establishing the colony's industrial independence.

Between 1935 and 1960, however, it should be noted that the restrictions imposed by the 1939–45 war seem to have fostered the timid establishment of a local consumer industry, as in the British and French areas. In the 1950s, in a bid both to cater for an increase in African and European consumption – there were between 25 000 and 30 000 Europeans – and

1. Over the period 1946–58, industrial investment was 27.6 per cent of total private investment – as against 13 per cent for 1900–40. In 1942, capital investment in industry accounted for only 0.01 per cent of the works carried out with borrowed funds in French black Africa since 1935. In the Maghreb, the situation was much the same, although industrialization began there at an earlier date.

to take account of the major interests of Belgian industry, this consumer industry received the bare modicum of public encouragement necessary for its share of the local market to rise from 30 per cent in 1950 to 44 per cent in 1958. This made the Belgian Congo on the eve of independence one of the continent's most 'industrialized' colonies.

To conclude on the subject of the industrial policies of the colonial powers between 1935 and 1960–5, it can be seen that they all produced the same results: in the first place, respect for the doctrine that the colony should never compete with metropolitan industry and the continuing maintenance of metropolitan control through the movement of capital and patterns of technological dependence; secondly, and above all from the time of the Second World War, the creation of a light industry that just about satisfied the needs of the domestic market for consumer goods. Even in instances where a strong mining industry existed – which was in varying degrees the case, depending on the colonial areas concerned – it was the policy never to encourage a true industrial framework in the colony that would threaten the metropolitan monopoly.

Does this mean that the 'colonial pact' was a permanent feature? To some extent, it was, provided that it is understood as being the manifestation of an international division of industrial labour to which the colonial authorities subscribed. The case of the 'semi-colonies ' in Africa is a partial illustration of this development between 1935 and 1960, depending on the country.

Industrial policy in the 'semi-colonies'; the cases of Egypt, Liberia and South Africa

A few countries in Africa that were already independent in 1935 were theoretically in command of their industrial development policy before the Second World War. Apart from the period from 1935 to 1941, when Ethiopia was occupied by Mussolini's Italy, the governments of these countries each drew up their own industrial development policy. Indeed, the impact of external interests, local collusion with those interests in some instances, the volume of resources available and the strategic issues with which the evolution and future of these countries were bound up, all severely limited the room for manoeuvre of the governments and influenced those industrial policies. We shall mention briefly three cases: Egypt prior to al-Nasser, Liberia and South Africa: each reveals a certain level of dependence of their industrial policy in the mid-twentieth century.

The Egyptian example from 1930 to 1952
In the 1930s, two features marked the place occupied by industry in the Egyptian economy: the fact that the industrialization process was already long-established and the considerable influence of external interests, coupled with the country's overall debt.

On the first point, recent studies have shown that, in the follow-up to the Westernization movement begun by Muḥammad ʿAlī, it was primarily in the 1890s that modern industrialization got under way. With the crisis of 1929, the decline in foreign investment and the adoption of a vague protectionist policy prompted the emergence of new features in Egyptian industry. Owing to its limited financial and technological resources, local capital turned towards import-substitution industry, geared to meeting the demand for consumer goods and intermediate goods.

The Second World War accentuated these trends as a result of the sharp drop in European imports. However, between 1945 and 1954, this evolution did not prevent the country from resorting to foreign capital, at least for the extension of manufacturing ventures.[2] The Egyptian governments of King Farouk, beholden as they were to their foreign creditors, had to tread very carefully when drafting and following up an industrial policy that was resolutely favourable to the national middle class. Hence, it is understandable that in the case of the European colonies and because such an industrialization policy posed little threat to the vital interests of European capitalism, import-substitution industry should have developed in Egypt between 1930 and 1954. The deliberate policy pursued by President al-Nasser after 1956 marked a break with the industrial policy of Farouk's Egypt.

Liberia
The oldest republic in black Africa had been in a period of financial difficulties since the beginning of the century and by 1935 it was ruined and virtually bankrupt, so much so that the European chanceries considered placing the country under a League of Nations mandate. After 1945, under the presidency of William Tubman, private investment, chiefly with American capital, took off again. It was directed towards the exploitation of the country's mineral wealth in the form of high-grade iron ore from Mount Nimba and of bauxite, and was offered considerable incentive by a policy very largely designed to grant all sorts of privileges to foreign enterprises.

This industrial policy long remained subject to two constraints: first, the need to set up the minimum amount of infrastructure required to hold out any hope of industrial development; and, secondly, the need to cater for the demand for manufactured consumer goods from a population of African American origin living virtually in a world of its own. At the beginning of the 1960s, Liberia was just starting to move towards the setting-up of a small consumer-goods industry in the shape of brickworks, a soap factory, breweries, and so on, under the very limited control of the local middle class, which had no control at all over the mining industry.

2. See C. Issawi, 1982, p. 72.

South Africa

In contrast to Liberia, and to a greater degree than Egypt on account of its fabulous mineral wealth, South Africa in 1935 was intent on making the most of the 1929 depression to equip itself with a true industrial base. The already long-standing application of a policy of discrimination in industrial employment was an added factor that was not unconnected with the results obtained.

The revolution in the mining industry which began in the 1860s had made it possible from a very early date to build a basic infrastructure before the 1920s. Despite a decline in mining production between the end of the First World War and 1921–2, industrial growth was relatively buoyant as a result of the operation of the goldfields. At the end of the 1920s, a new industrial policy began to take shape: in a bid to curb undue dependence on the production of precious metals, there was a move to diversify the industrial sectors. The Great Depression provided the opportunity for stepping up this trend, if need be with state participation. Until the Second World War, industry continued its growth[3] and was easily able to adapt to the fall in imports of manufactured goods.

However, although local investment was encouraged – its share of the mining industry rose from 15 to 40 per cent – the financial impact of foreign interests (above all British, but also American from the 1920s onwards) was still very significant in 1945. In the post-war period, there was a further growth in the hold exerted by foreign capital over the fast-growing manufacturing industry.

While the country's industry was geared to import-substitution catering for the consumer needs of the black population, it was also, in the wider context, an industry producing intermediate goods, and even capital goods, with the support of foreign capital, which was anxious to take advantage of local raw materials and to circumvent a customs-tariff policy that had been growing increasingly protectionist since the 1930s.

The outcome was that, by 1945, South Africa had already emerged as the leading industrial power on the continent, thanks to a repressive social policy and also to its natural advantages. However, this situation, which went back to the 1930s, was the result of a purposeful industrial policy, firmly based on the promotion of a diversified local industry. That policy was increasingly sustained by foreign capital, in some instances in partnership with local capital, although not in others.

Although the connection with such a policy is by no means obvious, the industrial development policies of independent Africa have, to varying degrees, followed a similar pattern.

---

3. Between 1939 and 1945, the value of manufacturing output increased by 116 per cent at current prices. See D. H. Houghton, 1971, p. 36.

'Industrializing nationalism' and the industrial policies of independent states

General considerations

It was less against the industrial policies of the colonial powers than against economic exploitation in general that the 'fathers of African independence' directed their main criticism, especially after the Second World War. However, in the early 1950s, the idea gained ground that the economic development of the colonies also entailed 'gradual industrial development'. At the time, everybody realized that it would take time to attain the goal of industrialization and that the support and assistance of the former colonial powers and foreign capital would also be needed. However, that attitude gradually came to be compounded by another idea, particularly at a time when political demands were beginning to prove successful. This was that industrial development was not merely one of the habitual tasks of the state, but was a mandatory condition of sovereignty and genuine national independence, as Kwame Nkrumah was already asserting in 1945.[4]

These were the foundations of 'industrializing nationalism' in Africa which developed with African political independence. In every instance, it involved a more clear-cut industrial policy than at the time of colonial or semi-colonial rule. But over and above the experiences and statements of intent, the industrial policies of the independent states have to be split into two broad categories, leaving aside the particular case of South Africa, especially after 1948. On the one hand, there were the 'non-capitalist' policies and, on the other, the policies of countries with a 'free-enterprise' economy.

The policies of countries opting for a 'non-capitalist economy'

Nkrumah's Ghana and Boumedienne's Algeria opted for an industrial policy on the 'socialist' model.

In 1957, Nkrumah's Ghana entered the post-colonial era with a rudimentary economy. Although he had been leading his country since 1951, Kwame Nkrumah had to make allowance for the domestic balance of power and he did not really begin to put his ideas on industrial development into practice until after 1959, with the adoption of Ghana's Second Five-Year Plan. In this view, the basic objective was to carry through an 'economic revolution' which would gradually make it possible to break with capitalism; this revolution entailed the widespread industrialization of the country carried out mainly by the state as the owner of the bulk of the means of production in local industry. The private sector could continue to exist; but the effort of will by the state should, in due course, ensure that the public sector would occupy pride of place.

4. See the first edn of K. Nkrumah, 1945 (republished in 1962).

Nkrumah also defended the idea of systematic vocational training and the planning of the industrial development effort. The Second Five-Year Plan (1959–63) and the First Seven-Year Plan (1964–70) illustrate this industrial strategy quite clearly, in that 72 per cent of the budget credits in 1959–63 and 61 per cent in 1964–70 were earmarked for industry as against 38 per cent in 1951–7 (the period of the First Development Plan). By 1965, 10–12 per cent of all industrial production was coming from a public sector that had virtually not existed prior to 1961.

The fall of Nkrumah in 1966 and the successive changes of regimes and economic options made it impossible to pursue this policy, which had largely drawn its inspiration from the anti-capitalism and radical nationalism of Kwame Nkrumah.

Algeria emerged from the colonial period with an industrial sector that accounted for only a very small proportion of GNP. Neither the application of the policy of imports without state protection, which had been in effect since 1943–5, nor the implementation of the much-vaunted 'Constantine Plan' of 1954, which, in the industrial sector, was mainly instrumental in initiating oil-exploitation policy, had really had any significant effect on the country's progress towards industrialization. The industrial sector was still very weak in 1962 and largely under French control, despite the Evian Agreements.

Before independence, the FLN was already developing theses heralding what we have called 'industrializing nationalism'. G. D. de Bernis recalls this very aptly when he says that 'Industrialization was to be achieved through the creation of cooperatives working for heavy industry'.[5] This meant that the state was to play a pre-eminent role as a deliberate act of policy; the socialist model was to be adopted through the creation of co-operatives; and heavy industry was to be established. These were the main thrusts of a doctrine which Algeria was to put into effect, especially from Boumedienne's time onwards.

The country had considerable natural advantages: it had iron and, above all, oil, and it was the rise in the price of oil that was to provide the resources for embarking on a systematic policy. On the basis of these FLN theses, three broad lines prevailed, especially after 1969: the investment of state resources, with or without nationalization, in giant enterprises (often turnkey projects) with a significant knock-on effect on the structuring of an industrial economy; the maximum enhancement of natural resources and the decentralization of industrial plants in an endeavour to foster the integration of regions that had been left to their own devices during the colonial period, and hence combat regional imbalances in industry.

But the policy of priority for 'industrializing' industries did not rule out state support for the private sector, which was geared to the production

5. See G. D. de Bernis, 1975, p. 26.

of consumer goods. This was the last broad thrust of this industrial development policy which was pursued, with correctives here and there irrespective of the limits, after the death of Houari Boumedienne.

As to the question whether the cases of Ghana and Algeria are special, it could be answered that they are perhaps not altogether special, for the deliberate 'industrializing' approach, the idea of planning without the accompanying anti-capitalist and socialistic discourse and the important place occupied by the public sector in industry were to be found in the policies of a number of new states with a 'free-enterprise' economy.

The policies of countries opting for a 'free-enterprise' economy: Côte d'Ivoire and Nigeria

Despite a weak industrial base at the time of independence, and although the years 1955–60 were among the most intense periods of African nationalism, several countries in Africa refused to ascribe their under-industrialization to the strategies of international capitalism since the colonial era. They opted for free-enterprise capitalism in the economic field; their evolution towards an industrial economy was to be consonant with market forces. But an analysis of their individual policies reveals a number of nuances and even differences, some of which are illustrated by the cases of Côte d'Ivoire and Nigeria.

In 1960, Côte d'Ivoire, an agricultural country where the colonial-style trading economy flourished as it did in neighbouring Ghana, had very little industry, despite a positive external trade balance. In 1959, the decision had deliberately been taken to remain within the framework of a market economy. In the case of industry, while it was recognized that there was a need for more conspicuous development, it was decided to let the burden be borne primarily by the private sector and above all by calling on foreign capital. This was at the origin of one of the earliest investment codes on the continent to grant highly favourable terms to foreign enterprises (cf. the law of 3 September 1959), in the form of a variety of tax exemptions, the repatriation of profits, guarantees against nationalization or social demands, and other facilities.

Owing to the low level of industrial potential at the outset – there was little known natural wealth and vocational skills were of a low standard – and in order to respect the industrial strategy adopted prior to 1960, emphasis was placed in the first instance on a policy of producing substitutes for imports of mass-consumer goods. The state was much more concerned with its policy of diversifying and increasing agricultural production (especially of agricultural primary commodities), and it hardly intervened in this sector. However, as Mohammed Diawara, the then minister of planning and industry, recognized in 1972, this policy resulted in securing 'substantial profits for the entrepreneurs, but not always for the community'.[6] The incentives offered to export industries and to enterprises expecting to benefit from the 'manpower' factor, but above all the policy of promoting domestic investment in this area of activity from 1970 onwards, were then aimed at giving fresh impetus to industrial development.

Lastly, the third broad thrust featuring in the 1976–80 Five-Year Plan was directed at the enhancement of local resources chiefly through the promotion of export-oriented agro-industry. In this case, the state intervened directly through state-owned companies producing palm oil, sugar, cotton and other commodities, in the name of a theory of 'state capitalism' by way of a transition to 'conventional capitalism'. Pending the emergence of a national middle class, the state would ensure that the country participated in industrial investment and would later sell off its shares to Ivorians capable of pursuing the effort. The entrepreneur-state was only intended to perform that role as a temporary measure.

Alongside this Ivorian policy which some analysts praised as being 'the Ivorian miracle' or strongly, criticized by labelling it as 'growth without development', there was the case of Nigeria. In Nigeria, there was much the same free-enterprise stance based on a policy of increased diversification and decentralization of industrial production, and a more active role for the private sector, especially after the civil war from 1967 to 1970. Indeed, in 1960, industry was a negligible quantity in the Nigerian economy and received only a small share of the planned investment (7.66 per cent of that investment in the 1955–60 Five-Year Plan). Between 1960 and 1967, borne along by its free-enterprise options and its recourse to foreign capital, the federal government scarcely intervened, except mainly to provide incentives to the oil industry. The political crisis of 1966 and the civil war of 1967–70 narrowed down the state's margin of manoeuvre even further.

The end of the civil war and the need to build up the economy again after its disruption by that crisis, coupled with the oil-price rises between 1973 and 1980 and the resulting increase in the revenue of the federal and state governments, provided the basis for a more far-reaching industrial development policy. This was centred on three main themes: the selective liberalization of imports of industrial goods which, by providing greater facilities for the import of raw materials and machinery, made it possible to support and protect the increasingly sophisticated import-substitution industry; the more or less direct support by the state for the capital-goods industry, as awareness grew of the considerable dependence on technology as a consequence of the progress made by import-substitution industry; and lastly, at the same time as it provided incentives for the processing of local raw materials, the so-called 'Nigerianization' policy

6. See *Colloque international de Dakar sur le développement industriel africain*, 1972, p. 133.

gave nationals priority in particular sectors of activity and government contracts, and offered facilities for forming partnerships with foreign capital. Nigeria was to be a 'giant' of African industry.

In sum, whether it be in states declaring themselves to be 'socialist' or in 'free-enterprise' economies, industrial development policies in independent Africa display one feature in common, in that they all set out to wage an effective struggle against the under-industrialization of the colonial era in order to ensure a degree of industrial self-sufficiency. But Africa in the 1960s, 1970s and 1980s was starting from too far behind and was saddled with a variety of handicaps, not the least of which were the strategies evolved outside the continent to maintain or preserve an international division of labour that was progressively imposed on Africa, especially under cover of the years of economic crisis from 1930 to 1935 and from 1973 to 1980. An analysis of the features of African industry since 1935 reveals its structural weaknesses and vulnerability, in spite of the efforts of the post-colonial period.

General features of industrial development in Africa, 1935–80

The evolution of industrial production and of industry's share in the GDP of African countries shows quite clearly two main periods: the first from 1935 to 1960–5 and the second from 1960 to 1980. In order to see each of these periods in finer detail, due account has to be taken of local structural crises and the results achieved by the sub-regional or territorial industrial policies already mentioned.

Embryonic industrialization before 1960–5

Whether it be the level of production, the rate of industrial growth or the share of industry in the African economy before 1960–5, the modern industrialization of the continent had scarcely begun.

The evolution of production and the industrial growth rate

The statistical data by country or colonial area for the period 1935–60 are irregular, sometimes unreliable, and often piecemeal. Hence it is not possible to obtain a continuous overall picture of the scale of production and the industrial growth rate of the entire continent. At first sight, however, the available figures point to a positive evolution of industrial

TABLE 13.1   *Indices of industrial production for certain countries, 1939–59/60*

Country	1939	1945	1950	1954	1960
Egypt	49	67	98	106	161
Belgian Congo	30	58	100	190	235
Nigeria	–	–	100	147	278
South Africa	–	35	–	57	71

NOTES: Base 100 set at 1950–2; for South Africa, base 100 set at 1963, and indices are for the years 1948, 1953 and 1958.

Sources: S. Radwan, 1981, p. 200; J. L. Lacroix, 1966, pp. 295–6; U. E. Okeke, 1985, pp. 36–7 (reproduced by permission of *African Review of Business and Technology*, formerly known as *African Technical Review*) and United Nations, 1970.

production, with the post-war period marking a distinct acceleration. Table 13.1 relates to three countries that were relatively 'industrialized' at the time; it shows a distinct progression in 1960 compared with the situation in 1939, while the 1950s were the period when production virtually doubled.

However, these figures are deceptive for in absolute terms they relate to industry on a very modest scale. Except in South Africa (with a figure of more than £75 million already by 1938, excluding the mining sector), the value of industrial production in most countries in 1960 seldom exceeded US$200 m (Egypt). It stood at $160 million in Nigeria, $128 million in the Belgian Congo, $120 million in Southern Rhodesia, $94.7 million in Ghana and barely $140 million for the whole of French black Africa (French West Africa, French Central Africa, Madagascar, Cameroon and Togo). In the Maghreb, the level was not much higher, even counting mining production.

The industrial growth rates, very uneven from sector to sector (mines, consumer goods, intermediate goods), show that the industrial policies then being implemented were virtually ineffective. Apart from mining, they were relatively mediocre (between 0.5 and 3 per cent depending on the country and year) and in some instances there was a lengthy period of stagnation (for example, in North Africa between 1948 and 1954).

The share of industry in the African economy
The place occupied by industry is an even more eloquent pointer to the level of industrialization of the continent at that time.

Despite differences in estimates, all the studies carried out acknowledge that industrial activity still played a very minor role in Africa in the late 1950s. Indeed, to a greater extent than Table 13.2 shows, it was even altogether marginal in many countries (2.6 per cent in Dahomey, 3 per cent in Tanganyika, 4 per cent in Togo). It was primarily agriculture,

369

TABLE 13.2 *Percentage share of industry in the national income of selected African countries, 1956–60*

Year	Belgian Congo	FWA	Nigeria	Rhodesia–Nyasaland[b]
1956	8.0[a]	2.0	2.0	11.0
1960	14.0	5.5	4.5	16.0

[a] Figure for 1958.
[b] Southern Rhodesia only for 1960.

Sources: United Nations, 1959, p. 15; P. Kilby, 1975, p. 472; United Nations, 1970.

often using rather rudimentary methods, that was the main driving force behind the economy in cases where there was absolutely no mining industry at all. Some writers[7] have sought to relate this fact to the number of European settlers. In point of fact, this is not at all relevant. In the Maghreb, for example, despite a long-established and large French-settler population, the share of industry in the GDP of that part of the continent was not any more substantial. In Algeria, in 1962 – on the eve of independence – industry accounted for only 9.36 per cent of GDP (23.8 per cent including the mining industry). Industry was of little importance in the colonial economy except in its primary form, such as mining, and it employed few workers, as we shall see. This was certainly not because production methods were more highly automated than anywhere else, but it was rather the mark of under-industrialization.

All this explains Africa's modest share in world production – except for raw materials – and in the consumption of manufactured goods.

Africa's place in world production and consumption
The image of Africa as a major supplier of industrial raw materials was not something new in 1935 – quite the contrary, for that image already dated from the distant past. The place occupied by South Africa in the world production of precious metals, the proven quality of the iron-ore deposits in Liberia, with their 65 per cent metal content, the industrial production of bauxite in Guinea and copper in the Congo or Northern Rhodesia, even before those countries became independent, all lent credence to that idea as far as the period from 1935 to 1965 is concerned.

However, apart from a few mineral raw materials – precious metals in South Africa, phosphates in Morocco and non-ferrous metals elsewhere – there had still been too little prospecting activity for Africa to occupy a leading place in this sector. While more extensive prospecting was carried out after 1945, the colonial home countries or the dominant powers (such as Great Britain in Egypt and Libya, France in Egypt, or the United

7. J. D. Durand's (1967) estimates are merely an extrapolation from previous estimates, such as those of W. F. Wilcox (1931). As such, they have to be treated with caution.

States in Liberia) imposed a virtual monopoly on such mineral production, exclusively in favour of metropolitan companies at least until the mid-1950s.

The production of industrial raw materials was thus largely subordinated to the interests and strategies worked out by metropolitan capital which regulated its development. For example, oil production in North Africa (Egypt, Libya, Algeria, Tunisia and Morocco) rose from 7 million barrels in 1940 (almost entirely from Egypt) to 17 million barrels in 1950 (out of which Egypt accounted for 94 per cent) and 91 million barrels in 1960 (72.5 per cent for Algeria and 26.4 per cent for Egypt), representing less than 1 per cent of the production of the Middle East. In Algeria, the search for oil only really got under way after 1957 (541.6 million fr. being spent over the years from 1952 to 1956 compared with 679 million fr. in 1958 and 917 million fr. in 1962).

Africa thus occupied a position in the production of industrial raw materials that was incommensurate with its natural potential. But what is more, in manufacturing industry, Africa's share of world production was marginal. This accounts for the very large proportion of manufactured goods in African imports. The breakdown of these imported manufactured goods shows how much most countries depended on the outside world for their consumption (Table 13.3). Thus, in the best cases (the Belgian Congo, for example), black Africa, excluding South Africa, was in the 1950s, some 70–75 per cent dependent on the outside world for consumer goods. In the case of capital goods, it was virtually 100 per cent dependent. This situation did not change until between 1960 and 1965, depending on the country.

TABLE 13.3 *Percentage breakdown of Egypt's imports of manufactured goods, 1945–60*

	1945	*1952*	*1957*	*1960*
Consumer goods	43.3	34.9	54.3	22.1
Intermediate goods	40.7	36.7	27.7	44.3
Capital goods	16.0	28.4	18.0	33.6

Source: S. Radwan, 1981, p. 216.

The post-colonial era in Africa accordingly started out under a major handicap: people had become accustomed to consuming manufactured goods while the African economy was still largely in the pre-industrial age. It was, as we saw above, a challenge which had to be taken up by the 'fathers of independence'.

Post-colonial developments, 1960/65–80

Advances in production and consumption
Whether one looks at the production of industrial raw materials or of
manufactured goods, there can be no doubt that industry in Africa made
progress in quantitative terms between 1960 and 1980. However, this
progress was uneven in terms of both time and space (Table 13.4). This
at times spectacular increase in industrial production (for example, it
amounted to 400 per cent in Egypt between 1956 and 1971) brings out
two main features. On the one hand, in many countries there was a
significant growth in the production of industrial raw materials – of oil,
of course, but also of strategic ores and metals. On the other hand, there
was a widespread growth of consumer-goods industries to cater for
domestic demand, but also with the aim of winning foreign markets
both through intra-African trade and by exporting to the industrialized
countries, especially in the case of the products of agro-industry from
countries like Côte d'Ivoire.

TABLE 13.4   *Indices for African exports of manufactured goods, 1970–8*

Geographical and trading areas	1970	1973	1977	1978
North Africa	39	65	128	163
of which,				
Maghreb	26	58	140	183
Members of ECOWAS	46	78	–	–
of which,				
Côte d'Ivoire	25	56	132	122
South Africa	49	85	157	–

NOTE: Base 100 set at 1976.

Source: UNCTAD, 1980, pp. 108–29.

Even so, while the diversification of production was still scarcely in its
infancy in many countries, it was already well under way in others like
Egypt, South Africa and Algeria. However, this African industry
accounted for only a small proportion of the consumption of manufactured
goods, which was growing at a much faster rate: in 1978, imports of
manufactured goods represented over 60 per cent of the total imports of
most countries on the continent (including South Africa), whereas exports
of manufactured goods generally amounted to less than 10 per cent of all
exports.

Export figures grew not only for energy products but also as a result
of the demand generated for finished or semi-finished goods. Hence, there
was some progress, although this was by comparison with the period of

PLATE 13.1   *Cotton textile factory at Mahana, northern Egypt*

TABLE 13.5   *Structure of manufacturing industry in Nigeria, 1958–78 (in percentages)*

	1958	1963	1965	1972	1975	1978
Consumer goods	92.3	90.6	84.2	93.3	90.9	80.9
Producer goods	7.7	9.4	15.8	6.7	9.1	19.1

Source: P. N. C. Okiglo, quoted by U. E. Okeke, 1985, p. 46.

early industrialization rather than in relation to the ever-growing needs. Since a capital-goods industry was a rare feature or was virtually non-existent in some countries, the idea of what constitutes progress in this sector has to be severely qualified. Even so, industry could no longer be said to be a negligible quantity in the national economies.

The share of industry in the post-colonial economy
Despite shortcomings in the statistical data in many countries, notably as regards the precise areas covered by the traditional-crafts sector and by modern industry, the share of industry in GNP has risen steadily since the late 1950s. In the former European colonies – in instances where a measure of relative political stability allowed it – the post-colonial period even made it possible to step up the process, and thereby enabled a number of small-scale industries to be integrated into the world market.

However, apart from the fact that the tempo varied from country to country (Table 13.6), this was often the result of the more rapid growth of local processing industries even though, in overall terms, the share of industry seems to have grown faster than that of agriculture in many countries. The idea that the outcome of this growth in industry's share in GDP amounted to genuine industrialization accordingly needs to be treated with caution.

TABLE 13.6   *Evolution of the percentage share of industry in the GDP of three countries, 1960–74*

Years	Nigeria	Algeria	Côte d'Ivoire
1960	4.5	–	5.3
1963	7.8	23.8	–
1965	8.6	25.0	19.0
1968	13.1	29.0	23.8

Sources: Government of Côte d'Ivoire, 1976 (the last figure is that for 1970); *Comptes économiques, 1963–1968*, quoted by G. D. de Bernis, 1975, p. 52; Nigerian Federal Office of Statistics, quoted by U. E. Okeke, 1985, p. 37.

Africa in world industrial production: the limits of 'industrializing nationalism'
between 1960–5 and 1980

It has to be asked whether independent Africa can be said to have occupied a stronger position in manufacturing in 1980, as it emerged from a period that had been particularly marked by a deliberate drive for industrialization. It is difficult to change everything in some 15 to 20 years of independence, and Africa then accounted for only 0.9 per cent of the world manufacture of finished goods. At the same time, there can be no doubt that its share in the production of industrial raw materials was greater than before 1960–5. Hence, all things considered, Africa was still the planet's least industrialized continent and to judge from the analysis of world trade flows, it was a continent that was mainly a supplier of industrial raw materials to the industrialized countries of Europe and America. Thus, in 1980 it was still the underdeveloped continent *par excellence*.

Such a situation raises the question of identifying the limits of what we have called 'industrializing nationalism' as both the continuation and instrument of the policy of independence. Neither 'anti-capitalist' nor 'free-enterprise' policies have so far succeeded in breaking the vicious circle of the continent's economic dependence and under-industrialization. In an endeavour to explain that fact, the arguments put forward have been both political (such as misguided decisions in a climate of chronic political instability that frightens off private investors) or technical (such as low standards of vocational training, for example, or the low level of domestic savings that cannot be properly or readily channelled into industrial development). Other arguments will be needed to fill out these analyses. We feel that many of the 'fathers of independence' did not pay sufficient heed to the structural vulnerability of African industry as it emerged from the colonial era. This vulnerability had increased by 1980.

The vulnerability of industrial development

Among other, probably more secondary aspects, this vulnerability is bound up with four factors: the absolute dependence on foreign investment; the illusions entertained about a possible transfer of technology by the trans-national corporations operating on the continent; low productivity in what is above all a primary-industrial sector; and the low level of integration of industrial enterprises in a market that is severely inhibited by under-population and generally low incomes.

Industrial investment in Africa: dependence on the outside world since 1935
No one can deny the considerable place occupied by the outside world in the modern industrialization of the African continent, at least since 1935. Until recently it even accounted for the bulk of the capital invested in industry in the form of direct public investment (or of indirect public

investment with foreign 'assistance') or else of private investment or investment through the international lending agencies. In the case of French-speaking black Africa, especially before 1960, the metropolitan country (public investment) and the French private sector accounted for 95–8 per cent of all industrial investment, while in the economy of the Belgian Congo, the share of foreign (especially Belgian) holdings and interests in 1958 was 95 per cent (and almost 100 per cent in industry).

Above all in the mid-1960s, recourse to public capital and the nationalization of private (very often non-African) enterprises and the so-called 'indigenization' policy in industry (like the 1974 and 1977 decrees in Nigeria), were instrumental in reducing the influence of outside interests in industrial investment. In reality, however, since foreign capital had to be attracted for financing new industrial projects, whether by indirect means or some other device, dependence on the outside world was still largely an unavoidable fact of life. It is this dependence that explains the main trends that industry has taken in most countries.

Indeed, already back in the 1930s and right up to 1950, the bulk of industrial investment went into the mining industry which, together with plantations, was more profitable for European enterprises than manufacturing industry. According to J. Marseille,[8] the yield from French colonial enterprises in 1938 was 5.6 per cent for industry as against 24.9 per cent for mines and 15.2 per cent for plantations; in 1954, the figures were 6 per cent for industry, 9.7 per cent for plantations and 8.6 per cent for mines. With varying shades of difference, similar trends could be found in other instances, as a result of the main goals pursued by the industrial holding companies of Europe or America.

Today, the situation has changed little except in particular cases: in 1965, 67.18 per cent of the investment approved in the states of French-speaking black Africa for the period 1965–70 was allocated to the mining industry; in 1976, an examination of the various development plans of these same countries showed that the range was between 60 and 75 per cent.

Did this situation arise from the need for those countries to secure a minimum volume of resources for financing a more sophisticated industrial sector? That may well be true, but it was above all the outcome of the strategies dictated mainly by trans-national corporations regardless of the countries' wishes.

The role of trans-national corporations since the Second World War and illusions about the transfer of technology

Before the Second World War, the trans-national corporations were not very active in Africa, other than in the mining sector. It was between 1946 and 1955 that the main ventures came to be established, either as

8. J. Marseille, 1984.

a result of restructuring exercises based on the take-over of large colonial trading companies or through direct, though hesitant, action. However, it was only after most of the countries had gained their independence that these companies were more clearly perceived as having become established in a big way, either by increasing the number of intermediate branches or primary firms or else by setting up 'national' subsidiaries. Among the factors that made this development possible after the early 1960s were the terms offered by the new states' investment codes and the desire to minimize production costs by moving closer to the raw-material-producing regions with their cheap labour supply. We have already shown that, in the case of South Africa, there was also a need to circumvent a body of regulations that had become decidedly protectionist from the mid-1930s onwards. Up to 1980, the same situation prevailed in most of the independent countries of black Africa. The growth of the multi-nationals' industrial activities was governed by the need for them to secure markets and the protectionist measures taken by the state offered them that guarantee.

But, in addition to the fact that most of these enterprises concentrated on import-substitution and mining, they were by no means the main channels for the transfer of industrial technology to the African countries: their contribution to vocational training was infinitely less than that of the states or even that of smaller enterprises. The technology used in their production units was strictly confined to the plants belonging to the parent company and had to be used in accordance with its instructions. In Côte d'Ivoire, as in the case of many other African countries, there was neither 'any widening of the conditions of supply through the production of new goods promoting new industrial sectors nor any introduction of new manufacturing techniques leading to the increased productivity of labour'. All this had a further adverse effect on the already low or relatively low (in such countries as South Africa and Egypt) productivity that is one of the features of African industry.

This has been one of the main grounds for disappointment with the role played by the multi-nationals, compounding as it has done the trans-national strategies of these enterprises which, by disregarding international boundaries and 'national' industrial development policies, perpetuate the vulnerability of industry and may even weaken it further.

Industrial integration and the relative failure of the pan-African organizations
It has now become commonplace to speak of the very limited size of the markets of the individual African countries: the main reasons for this are the under-population of vast areas of the continent and above all the low income levels. It was in a bid to make up for this handicap that the idea of more far-reaching economic integration and more effective har-monization of industrial policies began to gain ground at the end of the 1960s. The increase in the number of sub-regional or pan-African

organizations was also consistent with that goal. Some new ventures even saw the light of day (such as CIMAO – Cement Company of West Africa – which was set up in 1974 to develop Togolese clinker with the participation of Côte d'Ivoire and Ghana), and the Lagos Plan of Action (1979) put forward by the OAU strengthened these views.

It has to be recognized, however, that a number of impediments stood in the way of such a policy of harmonization and industrial integration, such as sensitivity over exercising sovereignty in economic matters, the extremely wide differences in regard to financial policies and industrial strategies, the absence of an industrial-technology policy based on the needs of populations having to contend with the challenges of under-development, and so on. In short, the failure of inter-African organizations, such as the OAU, ECA (Economic Commission for Africa), ECOWAS (Economic Community of West African States) and UDEAC (*Union douanière des états de l'Afrique centrale*), in this area is clear for all to see.

One of the factors in the weakness of African industry in 1980 lay in its inability to withstand competition from imported goods, other than under the protection of government subsidies or high customs duties. Since African industry was less well organized (despite exceptional cases of industrial enterprises in some countries) and was marked by low productivity, it still could not, without running major financial risks, move on to the stage of exports except through so-called intercontinental co-operation agreements – such as the EEC (European Economic Community)/ACP (Africa/Caribbean/Pacific) conventions – whose financial or commercial advantages in respect of primary commodities or goods produced by import-substitution industries did not really make up for the drawbacks inherent in the continent's main role of 'supplier' of industrial raw materials.

What is more – and this would tend to be borne out by a detailed analysis of every one of the attempts at industrial integration – modern industry in Africa did not bring out the sectoral linkage between its different component parts, owing to its total dependence on foreign capital and intermediate goods. It was accordingly difficult to establish a complementary relationship between geographical sectors, with a view to their integration. From the industrial standpoint, the fact that the individual countries were constantly taking the independent initiative of stepping up their trade outside the continent, whether this involved capital, mining products or agricultural raw materials, was the corollary of such a situation. This accounted for the vulnerability of African industry, since it was unable, by its own means, to cope with a balance-of-payments crisis or a decline in investment from outside Africa.

Lastly, the fact that links between industry (both capital goods and processing) and agriculture were weak, when they should have enhanced industrial performance and broadened the agricultural base, resulted in

African industrial output being less competitive than non-African goods, even within the individual countries themselves.

The circle of dependence and under-industrialization was still there in 1980.

The above comments call for considerable qualification, however. Since 1935, if not earlier, the industrial geography of the African continent has shown two broad types of imbalances that are historically linked in the case of many countries, namely the imbalances between geographical sectors that were industrialized long ago and geographical sectors that were initially mainly agricultural and were only latecomers to industrial activity, and the imbalances, especially within the individual countries, between the port areas through which goods transit and areas of industrial production. These imbalances have significant effects on spatial organization and land-use planning, as well as on the industrial policy pursued.

TABLE 13.7 *Geographical concentration of industries in French-speaking Africa in 1970*

Urban centres and countries	Percentage of enterprises	Percentage of industrial investment	Percentage of industrial employment	Percentage of turnover
Dakar (Senegal)	75.0	79.6	81.8	80.9
Abidjan (Côte d'Ivoire)	69.5	62.2	46.5	68.5
Bouaké (Côte d'Ivoire)	5.6	7.1	9.2	7.6
Douala (Cameroon)	51.8	44.9	44.7	61.7
Yaoundé (Cameroon)	10.2	6.5	4.9	6.4
Pointe-Noire (Congo)	36.1	32.4	25.5	27.6
Brazzaville (Congo)	40.9	20.1	25.9	28.9
Libreville and Port-Gentil (Gabon)	75.0	81.1	81.1	93.7
Cotonou (Benin)	69.0	80.4	78.1	71.4
Lomé (Togo)	85.0	90.0	96.8	87.6
Niamey (Niger)	45.0	56.4	50.3	17.3
Ouaga and Bobo (Burkina Faso)	89.0	55.7	73.5	65.6
Bamako (Mali)	53.0	17.0	?	?
Ségou (Mali)	10.0	23.0	?	?

Source: J. Suret-Canale, 1987, vol. 2, pp. 482–3.

The pattern of industrial location in 1935 and 1980 shows five sub-regional groupings which are distinguished by the age and extent of the industrial fabric, the level to which the installations are integrated and their variety. These are the Egypt–Maghreb grouping; the East–Central grouping; the Southern sub-region; Central–West Africa; and West Africa. By way of conclusion to this review of the general features of industrial development, it should be mentioned that the inadequate industrialization of Africa reinforced the nature of the continent's underdevelopment and dependence in 1980, despite undeniable progress since 1935. The forms assumed by industrial development created, or helped to accentuate, imbalances which contemporary urban patterns reflect very imperfectly, as we shall see below.

Industrialization – a secondary factor in urbanization in Africa between 1935 and 1980

The history of the continent's urbanization shows that there have been 'generations of cities'. These differ according to whether they are related to the time when they were founded – that is, whether they are pre-colonial or colonial settlements, or new cities dating from the post-colonial era – or to the prime function they fulfil as ports, trading stations, mining settlements or administrative centres. History has already shown that the twentieth century is a period when there can be said to have been an 'urban revolution' in Africa.

However, regardless of whether the issue is one of the relationship between the evolution of the industrial population and urban growth or of the patterns of urbanization since 1935, it would be going too far to establish a direct link between the two phenomena in the case of Africa, even though in some instances, urban growth has contributed to industrial development to some extent, as in the case of the mining towns of Tarkwa in Ghana, Ndola in Zambia and Mwadui in Tanzania or the townships of Mauritania, Niger and South Africa.

Urban growth since 1935 and the evolution of the industrial population

There is often some inconsistency in the figures used for estimating both the total urban population and the proportion of the active population engaged in manufacturing production. This is as much a problem of methodology (varying criteria are used to identify what constitutes a *town* and different statistical approaches are used) as a problem of documentation (sometimes incomplete censuses are available for different years). As a result, it is difficult to determine precisely the real scale of urban growth and the proportion of that growth accounted for by 'the industrial population'. We shall often have to be content with estimates.

Statistical data on population and urban growth from 1935 to 1980
Before the Second World War, which was the pre-statistical period *par excellence*, urban-population estimates are far from reliable. Little interest was taken in systematically counting that population throughout the country. Only a few territories were interested in doing so and those were mainly in North Africa and Southern Africa. Hence it is known that the urban population of South Africa rose from 25.1 per cent of the country's total population in 1921 to 31.4 per cent in 1935 and 38.4 per cent in 1946. In North Africa, the growth in the urban population was equally striking: in Egypt, which had 13 million inhabitants in 1920 and 16 million in 1938, the urban population had risen from 6.3 to 9 million by the eve of the Second World War. In the countries of the Maghreb, the urban population was likewise growing apace.

Elsewhere, figures are less readily available. Even so, to take the example of French West Africa before 1939, in several of the colonial outposts founded by France in a number of pre-colonial towns useful to the colonists, the population not only levelled out but, especially in territories such as Côte d'Ivoire, had, in fact, been rising since 1923–5.[9] In the neighbouring Gold Coast and in Nigeria prior to 1935, the increase in the urban population can be seen from the censuses conducted at the time: for example, the population in Gold Coast towns of at least 5000 inhabitants rose from 5 per cent in 1921 to 9.3 per cent in 1931.

After the Second World War, the figures become more accurate and we have a clearer picture of the population explosion in African towns right up to 1980. For the continent as a whole, it is estimated that the urban population rose from 31.8 million in 1950 to 49.5 million in 1960 and 132.9 million in 1980, with an average annual rate of increase of 4.8

TABLE 13.8   *The urban population as a percentage of the total population of Africa, 1950–80*

	1950	*1960*	*1970*	*1975*	*1980*
Eastern Africa	5.50	7.54	10.69	13.20	16.14
Middle Africa	14.57	18.10	25.16	29.66	34.37
Northern Africa	24.51	29.77	36.61	40.12	43.83
Southern Africa	37.27	41.70	43.76	44.81	46.49
Western Africa	10.15	13.48	17.27	19.58	22.29
TOTAL AFRICA	14.54	18.15	22.85	25.67	28.85

Source: United Nations, 1981, p. 159.

9. See P. Kipré, 1985.

per cent between 1950 and 1980. The pace was stepped up primarily from 1960 onwards.[10]

Not every country or every town was affected to the same extent. Indeed, despite its very rapid growth, the proportion of the urban population in the total population of Africa was still relatively low, although it was higher in some parts of the continent (the Maghreb, for example) (Table 13.8).

It has to be asked whether the occupational distribution of the population, and above all that of the towns, makes it possible to establish a correlation between the population working in industry and the urban population.

Trends in the occupational distribution of the urban population
The figures are even more fragmentary in this case. However, by extrapolating the available figures, a number of features can be identified.

In the 1930s, if the active population employed in the mining industry is excluded, the proportion of the urban population working in industry rose above 20 per cent only in the case of South Africa. Everywhere else, only a very small proportion of town-dwellers was employed in factory work: in 1938, 1.58 per cent of the Egyptian urban population worked in industrial enterprises with more than five employees, while in French West Africa the proportion was below 1 per cent in the period immediately after the end of the Second World War.

Later, especially after 1950, the proportion of city-dwellers employed in the secondary sector (not including traditional crafts) increased relatively quickly, but it was always well below the rate of urban growth (Table 13.9). In the case of Algeria, for example, the country recorded a striking growth of urban industrial employment between 1970 and 1980 (from 117 000 jobs in 1967, it rose to 347 000 in 1977 and 400 000 in 1980). However, it can be seen that, with an annual average growth rate of 4.3 per cent between 1966 and 1977, the country's urban population rose from 4.16 million in 1966 to 6.57 million in 1977. Industry continued to lag far behind service activities and the tertiary sector in general.

As Table 13.9 shows, the relationship between urbanization and industrialization is far from obvious: there is a tendency for this relationship to diminish between 1950 and 1970, thereby clearly showing that the two phenomena were not synchronous during the period under review.

The African urban population began to increase steadily even before the continent had really embarked on developing an industrial economy. In the years 1965–80, the attraction of a job in industry could serve as the pretext for migrating to the towns. At the same time, however, improvements in preventive medicine encouraged the natural growth of the towns, while the very considerable rural exodus after the Second

10. See United Nations, 1981.

TABLE 13.9 *Relationship between urbanization of the population and industrialization of the labour force, 1950–70 (in percentages)*

	Eastern Africa	Middle Africa	Northern Africa	Southern Africa	Western Africa
1950					
Industrial manpower (1)	3.66	5.87	10.44	24.56	6.10
Urban population (2)	5.50	14.57	24.51	37.27	10.15
Ratio (1/2)	66.54	40.29	42.59	65.90	60.10
1970					
Industrial manpower (1)	6.32	9.54	15.75	26.35	11.30
Urban population (2)	10.69	25.16	36.61	43.76	17.27
Ratio (1/2)	59.12	37.92	43.02	60.21	65.43

Source: United Nations, 1981, p. 19.

World War was triggered off not so much by competition between the secondary sector and agriculture as indeed by the actual crisis in agriculture, which was finding itself increasingly ill-equipped to cope with the money economy.

Modern industrial employment is not the only temptation of such a money economy; in broader terms, it lies in the desire for a regular cash income and in the collective and individual ability to withstand the decline in the terms of trade for agricultural produce. This was particularly true of countries like Algeria, Kenya and Southern Rhodesia, where European settlement gave rise to land pressures among African communities from a very early date, as well as those countries hard hit by ecological calamities like those of the Sahel and Ethiopia, where the question was merely one of struggling to eke out an existence. The main factor accounting for urban growth, at least from 1935 onwards, was more the crisis in African agriculture than the prospect of finding industrial employment in urban areas.

With minor sub-regional or local differences, the same mechanisms can be found at work everywhere in Africa, although they differ in intensity and follow differing patterns, depending on whether we are dealing with the colonial period, at least from the 1930s onwards, or the post-colonial period (at least between 1960–5 and 1980).

Patterns of urbanization and urban growth in the colonial period

From 1935 to 1960–5 in the case of all the dependent African countries, and from 1935 to 1980 at least in the case of South Africa, colonial labour policies and the functions performed by urban areas in the colonial economy were both instrumental in setting in motion a pattern of urbanization that was quite different from that of the pre-colonial period. This gradually altered the actual manner in which urban areas were developed.

Colonial labour policies and trends in African migration
Before the crisis of 1930, colonial labour policies can all be epitomized as consisting of the wholesale mobilization of manpower for the development of the natural wealth controlled by the colonialists in the shape of mines, plantations, forests, and so on. There was scant concern with promoting a higher level of skills among the labour force; on the contrary, the idea was to make up for the relatively low level of capital investment by an input of labour which gave rise to a variety of abuses. At the same time, the pressure of taxation and the development of a wage-labour force, which was very slow in some territories, were further powerful factors at work in this policy.

In some instances, the crisis of 1930 hastened the process, while in others it broke down the precarious balance between the manpower resources of the rural areas and the requirements of labour policy. In 1935, labour policy paid little heed to this crisis in the rural areas, which drove thousands of peasants on to the road and into the towns. It was the starting point of the rural-exodus phenomenon that is still going on to this day. For example, the population of Cairo rose from 800 000 in the mid-1920s to 1 400 000 in 1938. The increasing overcrowding in the towns was compounded by growing poverty. Claude Liauzu has shown in the case of Tunisia that the urban population was growing faster than production (starting from a base of 100 in 1925–9, the population index rose to 122 in 1935–9 and to 136 in 1940–4, while the production index stood at 106 in 1935–9 and had fallen to 65 in 1940–4.[11] During this same period, urban unemployment became a structural feature in Tunisia.[12] The same conclusions have recently been reached in studies of the towns of the Maghreb and former French West Africa.

In South Africa, it was the migration of white farmers ruined by the crisis, as well as of their African workers, and the controls on the African population leaving the reserves that were responsible for the increase in the urban population. In this connection, however, it should be pointed out that the policy of residential segregation, that had been slowly evolved since about 1910, fostered a policy whereby the African population was debarred from the towns but not from entering the mines. Moreover, by as early as 1935, Portugal had already introduced in Mozambique and Southern Angola a 'temporary-contract labour system' for African workers sent to the South African mines. Except in South Africa where, after

11. C. Liauzu, 1978.
12. *ibid.*

1948, the policy of *apartheid* underscored the trends already visible before 1935, the years from 1945 to 1960–5 represented a period when the authoritarian labour policy was slackened. Stress was laid to a greater degree on allowing the unskilled labour force to move about more freely.

The urban centres of the 1950s were towns that were sometimes the focal point for small-scale light industry, but were more frequently trading towns at nodal points fostering the development of various services such as domestic servants and labourers. They accordingly acted as reception centres for an overwhelmingly rural population that was being progressively uprooted: in 1954, 50 per cent of all non-agricultural occupations in Algeria were in trade, construction and a variety of services. Employment of this type was very often only of a temporary nature (47 per cent in Algeria in 1954) and had to cater for an urban population that was growing to an ever-increasing extent as a result of a surplus of rural migrants (in the Maghreb, this surplus accounted for 44–53 per cent of the population increment before 1960), in instances where those migrants were not leaving Africa altogether (the number of Algerians in France rose by 180 000 between 1947 and 1955).

Urban growth in Africa between 1935 and 1960 was thus fuelled by a rural exodus born of the crisis in the rural areas rather than being the outcome of industrial development. It is this situation which accounts for the emergence, from 1930–5 onwards and especially after 1945, of the squatter-settlement phenomenon in the urban centres of the continent.

The pattern of urban development and the beginnings of 'squatter' settlements
In 1935, Africa already displayed a variety of different situations as regards the pattern of urban development. Since at least the beginning of the twentieth century, two main cases were to be found: on the one hand, there were ancient pre-European towns, numerous in North Africa, Sahelian West Africa, Ethiopia and Yorubaland (Fig. 13.1); while on the other hand, there were the towns created by the colonialists, in some instances, although not always, from pre-colonial African villages. Depending on the case, the patterns of new development in the towns were marked by the more or less obvious imprint of government authority that was typically European in essence (in the case of the colonies) or else had merely undergone European influence (in the case of the North African protectorates).

In 1935, the state (the colonial power or the local government) was the main agency responsible for the creation of more-or-less planned areas that were allocated to the inhabitants for building purposes (dwellings or work-places). As a result of the role played by the state in this regard, living space had already started to show signs of social segregation in most towns and it also pointed to the nature of the ties of political and economic dependence by which the African population was bound. In North Africa, for example, the *medinas* and *souks* came to be increasingly

385

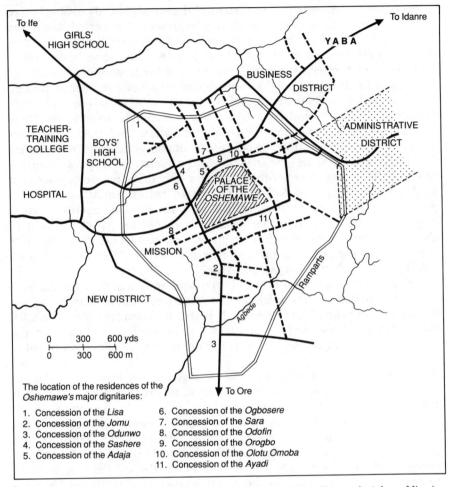

To Ife

GIRLS' HIGH SCHOOL

To Idanre

YABA

BUSINESS DISTRICT

TEACHER-TRAINING COLLEGE

BOYS' HIGH SCHOOL

ADMINISTRATIVE DISTRICT

HOSPITAL

PALACE OF THE OSHEMAWE

MISSION

NEW DISTRICT

Ramparts

Agbede

To Ore

0   300   600 yds
0   300   600 m

The location of the residences of the *Oshemawe's* major dignitaries:

1. Concession of the *Lisa*
2. Concession of the *Jomu*
3. Concession of the *Odunwo*
4. Concession of the *Sashere*
5. Concession of the *Adaja*
6. Concession of the *Ogbosere*
7. Concession of the *Sara*
8. Concession of the *Odofin*
9. Concession of the *Orogbo*
10. Concession of the *Olotu Omoba*
11. Concession of the *Ayadi*

FIG. 13.1 *A pre-colonial city: Ondo (Source: C. Camara, 'Une ville précoloniale au Nigeria: Ondo',* Cahiers d'études africaines, *No. 51, vol. XIII, 1973, p. 431, Mouton, Paris, The Hague);* © Ecole des hautes études en sciences sociales, *Paris*

contrasted with the new residential quarters for Europeans and a section of the indigenous population belonging to the higher and more-or-less 'Europeanized' social classes. In black Africa, especially in those urban areas created by the colonialists, the contrast was even more marked between the 'European towns' and the 'African townships' and was evidence of a segregation that was both racial and social.

Since the early years of the century, this had become systematic policy in South Africa. However, as a result of the crisis of 1930, the situation was made even worse by urban growth that, as we have already seen, was largely fuelled by the exodus of impoverished country-dwellers into the towns. These new town-dwellers, unable as they were to pay the rising rents or the cost of urban property, and not earning enough to purchase building materials such as cement, corrugated sheeting or tiles, were compelled to go and crowd into the *medinas* and *souks*. Increasingly by the early 1930s, it was the unplanned urban areas outside the state's control, such as rubbish dumps, marshes, disused cemeteries and so on, that were sought out by these town-dwellers to build their homes out of anything that came to hand. In Tunis, where the French term *bidonville* for squatter settlement or shanty-town was used for the first time in 1931 (in an article by Dr Materi in the *Voix du Tunisien* of 6 November 1931), the number of such shanty-dwellers thus rose from 2000 in 1935, to 5000 in 1938 and 10000 in 1941; by the beginning of the war, Tunis was ringed by squatter settlements. It was also between 1935 and 1945 that squatter settlements began to appear in Abidjan, Accra, Lagos and Douala. In British East Africa (Nairobi, for instance) or Central Africa, and above all in South Africa, successive Land Laws and the 1923 Native Urban Areas Act were instrumental in enforcing the colour bar, but they failed to prevent the progressive spread of the townships by the late 1920s onwards. The official doctrine was based on the fact that 'the Africans were not by nature town dwellers and they had not yet made a success of city life', as the Native Affairs Commission put it in 1921.

After 1945, the squatter-settlement phenomenon took on greater proportions and little-by-little, above all in the 1950s, spread to virtually every town on the continent. Each crisis in the colonial economy, each period of drought or failed harvests (1945–6, 1951–3) brought its quota of country-dwellers to the towns and their rising rents. Despite efforts to produce new, planned urban layouts or to cater more effectively for the growing demand for decent housing, the colonial powers and the national authorities never succeeded in controlling the 'squatterization' of African towns that has now become a permanent feature of the urban scene in Africa.

The question is whether there was any change in the patterns of urban growth and its effects with the relinquishing of the colonial ties.

Urban growth and its effects since independence

In the first 20 years of African independence, there were no fundamental changes in the causes and effects of the rural exodus or in the gap between urban growth and urban employment, or indeed in the patterns of urban development, in spite of the more acute awareness of the phenomena involved and a greater determination to solve the problems they posed.

PLATE 13.2   *Squatter settlements: above, in Lagos; centre, Mathare Valley in Nairobi; below, Belcourt in Algiers*

The crisis in African agriculture and the acceleration of the rural exodus
In the 1960s, if the superficial effects of political instability in some of the countries of Africa are disregarded, African agriculture can be said to have largely withstood the population drain to the towns, subject to minor variations from one country to another.

However, since the beginning of the 1970s, drought and poor harvests have led to a succession of bad years (1972–4, 1979–81) and famines, mainly in Sahelian and Sudanic Africa stretching from Senegal to the Horn of Africa. The unsuitability of the farming methods used and the somewhat rash agricultural policies adopted also explain why, by 1980, there were few African countries where foodstuffs accounted for less than 10 per cent of their total imports. The crisis in agriculture was thus even more acute and was the impetus behind the massive rural exodus to an even greater extent than before 1960. In Algeria, for example, the urban population nearly doubled between 1966 and 1977, rising from 3 700 00 to 6 800 000; the urbanization rate rose from 25 per cent in 1954 to 41 per cent in 1977, with the annual growth rate averaging 4.3 per cent between 1966 and 1977. In Côte d'Ivoire too, the same phenomenon can be observed, with annual growth rates varying from 6 to 9 per cent for towns with 100 000 inhabitants and 11 per cent for Abidjan.

An even more revealing pointer to the important role of the crisis in the countryside was the urban growth in Sahelian Africa, where the urban population was growing at rates ranging between 3.5 and 5 per cent, as a result of a surplus in the balance of migration between towns and countryside, with the balance invariably working out in favour, of course, of the towns. The population of Ziguinchor, an old colonial and trading town in Casamance (Senegal), had barely doubled between 1951 (15 700 inhabitants) and 1960 (31 000 inhabitants).[13] However, owing to the crisis in the groundnut sector, which grew worse just at a time when monetary needs were rising, notwithstanding the crisis of an urban economy dominated by trade and lacking any industrial base, the urban growth rate rose sharply to reach 8 per cent a year after 1961. The population rose to 40 000 in 1966 and 70 000 in 1971. It was composed primarily of young people who had severed their roots in the rural areas, and was largely underemployed (structural unemployment). It was compelled to survive by finding accommodation that was as cheap as possible. The same situation arose in Rufisque, which had had a growth rate of 6–6.5 per cent a year since 1968–70. Here, as in numerous African towns, there was an unprecedented surge in 'spontaneous housing' after independence.

Spontaneous housing and urban development: the spread of slums
The existence of squatter settlements around or within African towns, which has now become a common feature, appears to have increased after

13. See P. X. Trincaz, 1984; and A. Dubresson, 1979.

1960. Describing Mathare Valley, one of the most famous squatter settlements in Nairobi, Wa–Githumo had this to say in 1983:

> Obviously, there are many slums in Nairobi; Mathare Valley is the largest and represents one of the classic examples of the slums which have become a citadel of poverty, underdevelopment and other manifestations of human sufferings. Rat-ridden shanties, sheds, stalls and other slum-type shelters in Mathare are either rented or owner-occupied, either legal or illegal. Hundreds of thousands of families live in over-crowded, unsanitary and substandard shelters.[14]

This description of Mathare Valley is not so far removed from that which V. S. Naipaul gave in 1980 of some areas of Kinshasa in *The Return of Eva Peron:*

> Where does the sense of responsibility, society, the state, begin? A city of two million, with almost no transport, with no industries (save for those assembly plants, sited, as in so many 'developing' countries, on the road from the airport to the capital), a city detached from the rest of the country . . . It doesn't have to work; it can be allowed to look after itself . . . when it is hot the gutters smell; in the rain the streets are flooded. And the unregulated city spreads . . .

These descriptions raise the key problem of urban policies in post-colonial Africa, as well as that of the solutions to the urban housing crisis dreamed up by town-dwellers. To a greater extent than in the colonial period – and this tends to be borne out by the surveys being carried out in Côte d'Ivoire – the 'candidates' for spontaneous housing were not only newcomers but also a high proportion of long-standing inhabitants: outsiders or local people ruined by economic crises, the unemployed, social and other marginals, people on the fringes of the market economy and the new consumer society, were all to be found there, living from hand to mouth, sometimes by dealing in wooden shacks or waste materials.

Faced as they were with this situation, the authorities can be said to have become aware of it at a relatively early date (see the 'developmentalist' ideology in the official speeches in the period immediately after independence). However, the solutions and the facilities needed to put them into effect came too late. Urban planning agencies and city master-plans only made their appearance and grew in number in the 1970s in most African countries, at least in those cases where the colonial powers, which had been primarily concerned with the big cities, had left nothing behind them. By 1980, the very limited resources available for development had not yet enabled the state to come to grips with a phenomenon that was becoming increasingly entrenched.

14. See Wa-Githumo, 1983, pp. 126–48.

The so-called 'informal' sector, which may represent the sole means of survival in African towns, especially in black Africa, became the main form of urban economic activity for the bulk of the population – to a greater degree than industry was capable of becoming. Studies of this aspect of the urban economy are still very recent, but they already show the marvels of ingenuity to which many town-dwellers on the continent are driven in order to survive in present-day African towns, on the fringes of the industrial economy that was still not sufficiently developed in the Africa of 1980.

Not all countries on the continent, nor indeed all African cities, were in the same predicament or were affected in the same way. There were sub-regional differences. There were contrasting situations between those countries with high earnings from oil or agricultural commodities, which were accordingly capable of financing their industrial development and of thereby increasing the scope for urban employment, and those countries that had to contend with a more serious economic crisis and were therefore less able in 1980 to exercise control over all the parameters of economic development. But these were more differences in the degree of under-development than differences in kind. Although Africa was moving very fast towards greater urbanization in 1980, there were very few countries on the continent that could be described as industrialized.

General conclusion

If, despite all we have said above and by comparison with the precolonial period, it were nevertheless necessary to speak in terms of an 'industrial revolution' in Africa, it would have to be made clear immediately that it was a revolution that was having to contend with difficulties in the worst possible conditions at least from 1935 onwards, on account of the unfavourable international situation, the control and increasingly inhibiting influence exerted by trans-national corporations standing in the way of genuine industrialization, and the sluggishness inherited from the state of colonial dependence and perpetuated by the muddle or errors of post-colonial industrial policies. Not the least of the impediments was the fact that the towns were growing faster than industry. It might almost be asked – and this is what some well-meaning people are asking today – whether any useful purpose is served by industrializing a continent that is barely able to feed itself.

Yet the industrial development of Africa is a necessity, indeed an obligation, both for its own sake and for the sake of the rest of the world. For itself, it is a way of laying the foundations for a self-directed economy and of fitting itself out with technological resources suited to its real development. It is also a way of creating, through the improved linkage of agriculture and industry, the conditions for the more rational deployment and mobilization of manpower. It may also afford it the opportunity of providing itself with the means of imparting a new and authentic lease of life to African cultures, strongly marked as they still are by their pre-scientific features.

For the rest of the world, the point is that, by exercising more effective control over its immense potential, Africa should make that potential available to all the nations of the world rather than for merely serving the purposes of a handful of individuals or trans-national enterprises; the contradiction between 'dependent economy' and 'self-directed economy' must be overcome.

The question is how this can be achieved at a lower political, economic and social cost than at present. Perhaps the answer chiefly lies in:

(1) genuine inter-African co-operation and the increased integration of industrial utilities and policies (the outlook should be less towards the seaboard than towards the interior of the continent);

(2) less ostentatious industrial choices (giant turnkey factories are primarily geared to producing goods for export outside Africa); and

(3) investment designed to accommodate technological innovation to the true needs of the peoples of Africa.

Comparative strategies of economic decolonization[1] in Africa

Adebayo ADEDEJI

As soon as their countries became independent, African governments were genuinely desirous of improving the standard of living of their people by increasing their incomes and providing essential social services and infrastructural facilities. All were virtually convinced that the most rational way to bring about these changes was through economic planning. Indeed, before African independence, the development literature had featured debates as to whether or not to plan. However, in immediate post-independence Africa, these debates were won hands-down by the planners as post-independence governments came out soon after the demise of colonial rule with a plan document responding to the perceived development needs of the country and its people. But these plans, which were more often than not prepared by foreigners with relatively little experience of the countries concerned, were 'lacking in real control, political support or potential for implementation'.[2] It is therefore not surprising that at least during the first independence decade, the decisions as to the grand areas of development strategy or ideology were not normally within the province of the planners. We must look elsewhere for the pursuit of major strategic changes of direction. However, except in the case of very few countries, concrete evidence is hard to come by of a clearly articulated and coherent strategy of economic decolonization – in contrast to that of political decolonization to which all African countries subscribe and which is pursued vigorously.

Yet, it should have been clear to all, even in those early days of independence, that Africa marching toward the future hand-in-hand with its colonial economic inheritance has no dignified future at all. Indeed, if the truth must be told, the economic crisis that has engulfed the continent since the second half of the 1970s has been largely the cumulative result of the continued operation of the African economies within the framework of the inherited colonial economic legacy. Unfortunately, it has taken the

---

1. We define 'decolonization' as the dismantling of colonial institutions and the minimization of foreign control and power. Decolonization is not a gift from the imperial powers: it needs the initiative of the oppressed.
2. G. K. Helleiner, 1972, p. 333.

first few decades after independence to realize that as long as Africa continues to nibble at the colonial economic system so long will it continue to fail to achieve any breakthrough in socio-economic engineering and so long, indeed, will it continue to be 'part of the lowest caste in the international (economic) hierarchy' with its 'place at the bottom of that hierarchy continuing to threaten to be rigid'.[3] Without doubt, effective strategies for the economic decolonization of Africa are a necessary condition for achieving high rates of growth and diversification and an increasing measure of self-reliance and self-sustainment.

Unfortunately, for virtually all of Africa and for the overwhelming majority of its citizens, the rapid economic transformation which had been hoped for on independence, failed to materialize. Instead, the African economy moved from one crisis to another; the revolution of rising expectations gave way to the revolution of rising frustrations with the consequent waves of military revolts and political upheavals in different parts of the continent. Why did Africa fail to achieve the economic promise of independence? Where did it go wrong? To answer these questions in any scientific manner, we must first and foremost begin with an analysis of the economic strategies pursued by independent African countries in the early 1960s.

Toward a socialist strategy of decolonization

As we have already pointed out, post-independence development plans in Africa failed to articulate a coherent development strategy or ideology. More often than not, they concentrated on the major classical and neo-classical economic parameters: increase in gross domestic product; increased investments and mobilization of savings; provision of social overhead capital; expansion of social services; foreign aid and private foreign investment and incentives for attracting the latter. Many of them – implicitly, if not expressly – endorsed the inherited colonial economic policies and strategies.

For example, the first development plan[4] of post-independence Côte d'Ivoire which covered the period 1960 to 1970 considered essential the maintenance and even the increase in the flow of foreign factor inputs on the grounds that national investment resources were insufficient and that the Ivorian economy lacked know-how. One of the plan's principal objectives was the diversification of agricultural production for export, thereby intensifying the external dependence of the economy. The plan gave the state a pivotal role in the control of the development process. And while this Ivorian model was found in many newly-independent countries of Africa, most of the former French colonies went further and

3. A. A. Mazrui, 1977, pp. 17–18.
4. Côte d'Ivoire, Government of, 1967.

took measures to strengthen their economic links with France. Thus, for example, while the other African countries established independent monetary institutions, all former French colonies, except Mali and Guinea, retained monetary links with France in a common monetary zone.

In contrast to this neo-colonial development strategy, a few African countries embarked, immediately after independence, on policies and programmes which they considered would decolonize their economies. But most of these countries associated economic decolonization with the desire to direct their societies towards *socialist* goals. Although the term socialism was given different connotation and qualifications such as 'African socialism',[5] 'democratic and cooperative socialism',[6] 'neo-Desturian socialism',[7] or 'realistic and common-sense socialism',[8] the social and economic content was very similar. Unlike the countries following a liberal neo-colonial economic strategy, the objective of these countries was not only to increase the level of well-being of the population but also to achieve fundamental change in the very structure of society and in the colonial economic structure by developing the domestic processing of primary products and by pursuing an import-substitution industrialization strategy.

One of the remarkable features of these early socialist experiments was *the rejection of any massive expropriation of foreign or private property*. In fact, the various governments were more anxious to emphasize the creation of new capacity rather than nationalization as the spring-board of their socialist dreams. But one country which differed markedly from this approach was Mali. While countries such as Ghana accepted a mixed economy as a transitional stage in the construction of a socialist society, Mali set out to put under direct state control and monopoly most of the modern sector, particularly the foreign-trade sector. This latter step was particularly important from Mali's perspective since the control of foreign trade was seen as a key instrument in controlling the commodity-export surplus. Following Marxist economic theory, Malian planners saw in the foreign trade companies the conduit through which surplus value was exported; and while the other ex-French colonies signed a monetary agreement with France, giving them a common currency guaranteed by the French treasury, Mali created its own independent currency, the Mali franc.

Algeria, after its independence in 1962 following a long and bloody war of liberation, also chose a socialist path to development. In the words of the Algerian liberation leader and first prime minister, Ben Bella:

5. Ghana, Government of, 1964, p. 15.
6. Mali, Government of, n.d., p. 6.
7. Tunisia, Government of, 1962, p. 8.
8. Madagascar, Government of, 1964, p. 9.

> We are adopting the economic analysis of Marxism because we think
> it is the only one of value for the development of our country, but
> without espousing its ideology, because our action is guided by
> Algerians who are Muslims and Arabs.[9]

In a way, this choice was imposed on post-independence Algeria as the
country was faced with a void caused by the mass exodus of the European
population who abandoned farms, factories and real estate. The abandoned
property was taken over spontaneously by Algerian farm labourers,
workers and population. Thus was established the unique feature of
Algeria's economic structure: the self-managed agricultural sector. These
self-managed farms became collective organizations run by workers'
assemblies which elected the administrators. The occupation was soon
legalized by nationalization which covered practically all the former
European farms – or around 2.3 million ha producing 65 per cent of total
cereal production. The nationalization process was progressively extended
to the manufacturing, mining and petroleum sectors, so that by the end
of the 1960s the public sector – excluding self-managed firms – represented
more than a third of total output.

All these several species of socialism have, of course, multiple objectives.
These are:

(1) economic decolonization;
(2) pervasive state intervention in the development and control of
the economy;
(3) a striving for the equalization of economic and social opportunities; and,
(4) limitation of the role of the private sector and of private investment and property.

But on this last point, there appears to be an ambivalence in the attitude
of some governments. Many did not want to abolish private property and
investment. Rather, they sought to control it and to harmonize the efforts
of the private sector with those of the public sector in order to achieve
the social and economic objectives. As the *Ghana Seven Year Development
Plan 1963/64–1969/70* vividly puts it, 'any suggestion that vigorous
state and private sectors within the same economy are incompatible is
unacceptable. Ghana's policies will be so designed to obtain maximum
contribution from each sector towards the overall growth of the economy'.[10]

It was, however, in Tanzania that socialism was given the most articulate
expression as the basis for overcoming poverty, reducing the country's
external dependence and reorganizing fundamentally production, power

9. Translated from *Le Monde*, 23 January 1965; a speech made to the *Union générale
des travailleurs algériens.*
10. Ghana, Government of, 1964, p. 3.

and social relations within Tanzanian society. True enough, Tanzania, immediately after independence in 1961, followed the liberal development strategy being pursued by other African countries with, of course, some variations on the theme. It emphasized production for export. It actively searched for foreign factor inputs, particularly foreign aid, and concentrated on the rapid expansion of infrastructure. But unlike most other African countries, Tanzania began to expand the ideology of self-reliance. However, until the Arusha Declaration of 1967, Tanzania was following the path of other African states. As Joel Samoff has succinctly put it:

> To the socialists, it became increasingly clear that Tanzania was following the path of other African states. There were many more schools and hospitals, a number of senior positions had been Africanized, there were some beginnings of local industry, substantially improved minimum-wage rates had been established, and the economy was expanding. But so were dependence and the inherited external orientation of the Tanzanian political economy. An analysis of the failure of the liberal hope led to and informed the Arusha Declaration of 1967.[11]

Thus the failure of the liberal hope which had guided policy from 1961 to 1967 unmasked socialism. It brought about an institutionalized pervasive socialism and a whole series of institutional changes. A one-party system was formally adopted, along with the commitment to increase democratic participation within the new framework. Above all, a radical development strategy was promulgated. Its main features were the nationalization of major economic institutions, particularly banks, insurance business, foreign trade and manufacturing enterprises and large agricultural estates; restrictions on consumption by the affluent bourgeoisie principally through the imposition of progressive taxation; decolonization of the school curriculum; greater attention to economic diversification and industrialization; and a well-publicized commitment to self-reliance.[12]

But the most radical aspect of the new socialism of Tanzania was the ideology of *ujamaa vijijini* or village socialism which was based on the policy of self-reliance. Socialism was to be based on the traditional values of the village, emphasizing the group and mutual support in contradistinction to the individualistic and exploitative values of capitalism. The leadership code which emphasized moral values, hard work, austerity, self-denial and dedication to the community forbade the cadres from engaging in private business and from owning more than one house. By this measure, incomes from rent were eliminated and the nationalization measures were extended even to small businesses. By the mid-1980s, over 80 per cent of economic activity was in the public sector.

11. J. Samoff, 1981, p. 289.
12. See J. K. Nyerere, 1968a, and also J. Samoff, 1981, p. 289.

But in spite of its radicalism, Tanzania has remained as dependent on foreign assistance for financing its development as ever. Economic decolonization has continued to elude it. Self-reliance has become a will-o'-the-wisp. But even more seriously the economy had for years ceased to grow; on the contrary it had for some years stagnated with recurring negative rates of growth. The cumulative effect of all this is that Tanzania has been classified by the United Nations as among the least-developed of the developing countries (LDCs) – one of 27 such least-developed countries in Africa. Yet, ironically, Reginald Green could in 1977 assert that 'the transition to socialism in Tanzania could be said to be nearly accomplished'.[13]

In Senegal, the African socialism formulated by prime minister Mamadou Dia (1957–62) and Léopold Senghor stressed building a socialist society based on traditional communitarian values and through the development of the co-operative movement and the regrouping of Senegalese villages into self-governing rural communes. Thus, both Dia and Senghor envisaged that village-based multifunctional co-operatives would constitute the basic economic unit of an agrarian socialist society in Senegal. Needless to say, Senegal is as ever a classic example of a dependent economy, and in spite of more than 25 years of independence, most of its foreign trade is still with France, which for years has also been supplying over two-thirds of Senegal's public development capital and nearly all its foreign technical and financial assistance needs. French investors provide more than four-fifths of the country's private capital, while the French treasury for years was covering Senegal's foreign-trade deficits.

However, Senegal's African socialism has had very significant impacts. First, it has discouraged the emergence of large-scale capitalist enterprises in the countryside and has fostered the development of rural co-operative structures. Secondly, African socialism has been used to justify massive state intervention in regulating and controlling key sectors of the Senegalese economy. Thirdly, Senegalese socialism welcomed foreign capital and private capital. This is not altogether surprising as Senghor has been a great advocate of Euro-African, or even Euro-Arab–African, dialogue. It was therefore easy for his socialist government to collaborate with foreign capital and the Senegalese private sector. And not surprisingly, the economic dependence of the country has persisted.

Sectoral strategies for economic decolonization

A sectoral analysis of the early post-independence macro-development strategies and policies pursued by African governments will give us more insight into the efforts at economic decolonization. Our focus will be

13. R. H. Green, 1977, p. 24.

the two directly-productive sectors of agriculture and industry and the indigenization policy of bringing the modern sector of the African economy under African control.

In colonial Africa, two distinct structural agricultural models may be said to have existed. One is traditional subsistence agriculture which constituted both a way of life and an economy in which disposal of produce by sale was incidental, depending on the availability of marketable surpluses and the need for cash to pay for imported commodities and taxes imposed by the government. The other is modern commercial agriculture which was entirely within the money economy. In certain African countries, these two types of agriculture were represented by the co-existence of African farming – which was predominantly traditional and subsistence – and non-African farming, which was dominated by the expatriate settler community which predominantly produced for export on a large-scale plantation basis. In some parts, particularly in West Africa, this dual classification does not hold as the peasant farmers also dominate the export-crop production.

Invariably, production for export was favoured by the colonial government because it was the most important source of foreign-exchange earnings and of public revenue. Even today, in countries which are neither oil exporters nor mineral exporters, export crops account for as much as 80 per cent of foreign-exchange earnings and public revenue. Technical inputs, such as high-yielding seedlings, fertilizers, credit facilities, research support and extension services, were not available to food-crop farmers. Almost all of the products of modern agriculture were marketed through agricultural co-operatives. During the Second World War years and immediate post-war years, these developed into marketing boards or *caisses de stabilisation* in French-speaking countries, which were given the monopolistic power of being the sole buyers and exporters of these commodities with the authority to fix the producer prices every farming season. In the settler colonies in Eastern and Southern Africa, colonial policy forbade the indigenous farmers from growing export crops in order to protect white settlers from competition. Indeed, the foundation of excessive external dependence of the African economy rests upon this dichotomy. It was the beginning of the dualistic monocrop economy where a fairly advanced, largely foreign-owned modern export sector existed side-by-side with a large, low-productivity subsistence sector in which the majority of the population were engaged. Colonial Africa emerged into independence with an economy that devoted a considerable proportion of its resources to the production of export commodities for which there was little domestic demand and depended on extra-African countries for the supply of its basic needs, even including most of its food requirements. Such an evolution had nothing to do with the theory of comparative advantage. It was only the cumulative consequences of imperial policy that looked to the colonies for the supply of raw materials.

399

Under such circumstances, what decolonization strategy was pursued after independence in the field of agriculture? To what extent did the governments of independent Africa attempt to change the colonial framework of their agricultural sector, with its over-emphasis on export production and with its excessive focus on foreign-exchange earning? As Ali Mazrui wrote, 'a new juju has cast its spell [on Africa], mesmerizing the ambitions, titillating the greedy, spellbinding the acquisitive. The new juju is called foreign exchange, the availability of convertible currency as a form of international power.'[14] Regrettable as it is, it is not surprising in such circumstances that independent Africa pursued, more vigorously than ever before, the development of export-crop production. Scant attention continued to be paid to food production. Thus, between 1960 and 1965, while export crops registered a global 23.3 per cent increase, food crops expanded by only 6.7 per cent. Right from the beginning of independence, African governments appeared to have ignored the advice that 'the most certain way to promote industrialization . . . is to lay the foundation it requires by taking vigorous measures to raise food production per person engaged in agriculture'.[15] Indeed, as Fig. 14.1 graphically demonstrates, per capita food production continued its downward trend throughout the 1970s and the early 1980s.

The poor performance of the food sector is indeed symptomatic of the overall poor performance of the agricultural sector. On the whole, this sector has persistently lagged behind and performance has worsened progressively since independence. For example, between 1971 and 1980, agricultural production increased at an annual average rate of 1.7 per cent compared with 2.1 per cent in the 1960s. The reasons for this deteriorating performance are apparent from Table 14.1. African governments have not been backing their avowed agricultural development strategy with adequate allocation of public resources. Available data indicate that on a per capita basis, public expenditure in agriculture has been declining in real terms in all the sub-regions, the sharpest decline being in Central Africa, which also has the lowest internal capital flow per capita for its agricultural population.

Worse still has been the fact that the extremely limited resources available for investment in agriculture have been invariably unwisely and uneconomically spent. There has been too great a reliance on heavy capital investment and over-capitalization through extensive mechanization. Most public projects have built into them very expensive welfare provisions with little thought given to the capacities and needs of the African farmer. Although between 80 and 90 per cent of the agricultural producers are small-scale peasant farmers – the majority of whom especially among the food-growers are women – yet they are starved of vital agricultural inputs.

14. A. A. Mazrui, 1980a, p. 65.
15. A. Lewis, 1953.

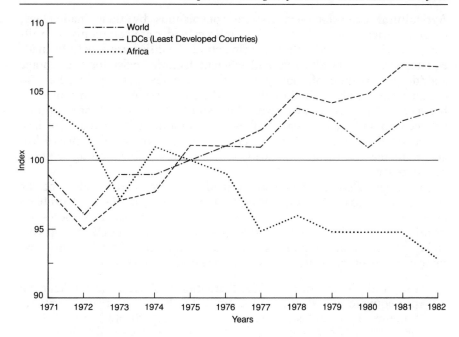

FIG. 14.1. *Trends in per capita food production: the world, the LDCs and Africa (base 1974–6) (Source: FAO*, Production Yearbook, *FAO, Rome, 1982)*

TABLE 14.1 *Average annual growth rates of total public expenditure for all sectors and for the agricultural sector, at constant prices*

Area of Africa	All sectors					Agriculture				
	1979	*1980*	*1981*	*1982*	*Average 1979–82*	*1979*	*1980*	*1981*	*1982*	*Average 1979–82*
North	6.1	4.0	−6.0	3.6	1.8	−6.3	2.2	−0.3	−5.8	−2.6
West	9.1	−15.7	−18.4	−1.7	−7.3	−10.4	18.9	−5.4	8.0	2.1
Central West	20.3	−3.0	3.1	−8.8	2.4	68.7	−7.5	−34.2	−34.5	−9.5
Central	–	–	–	–	–	−13.5	−48.6	10.0	39.1	−0.2
East and Southern	14.5	−3.9	−11.0	−18.7	−5.5	27.0	4.9	−1.1	−30.7	−2.2

NOTE: The data in the table are based on 24 countries.

Source: FAO, 1983.

Agricultural extension services are conspicuous by their inadequacy; modern varieties of seeds, fertilizers and pesticides are commonly unavailable; feeder roads and other infrastructural facilities are woefully inadequate; virtually no effective and efficient facilities exist for the storage and/or preservation of food grains; there are few systematic efforts to organize the supply of food items from the countryside to urban centres or between different rural areas, with the result that a very high proportion – between 20 and 45 per cent – of the food produced is wasted from lack of access to markets; and producer price policy, by keeping prices low and reducing the income of farmers, has adverse effects on agricultural productivity.

The *Lagos Plan of Action* underlined this systematic neglect of the smallholder peasant farmer, stating that 'at the root of the food problem in Africa is the fact that member States have not accorded the necessary priority to agriculture, both in the allocation of resources and in giving sufficient attention to policies for the promotion of productivity and improvement of rural life'.[16] The plan went on to add that

> for an improvement in the food situation in Africa, the fundamental prerequisite is a strong political will to channel a greatly increased volume of resources to agriculture, to carry through essential re-orientation of social systems, to apply policies that will induce small farmers and members of agricultural cooperatives to achieve higher levels of productivity, and to set up effective machineries for the formulation of relevant programmes and for their execution.[17]

As for the industrial sector, *industrialization was seen by the newly-independent African countries as a major instrument for decolonizing their economies.* Manufacturing activities had been discouraged by the colonial governments who saw the role of the African economies as being supportive of those of the colonial powers to whom they supplied raw materials and for whose manufactured goods they provided captive markets. As is shown in Table 14.2, manufacturing activities accounted, at independence in 1960, for only 7.6 per cent of the GDP, compared to 12 per cent in South-east Asia, 13 per cent in the Middle East, and 22 per cent in Latin America. Pre-independence industrial activities were limited to the processing and semi-processing of agricultural and forest products and minerals, and to the production of light consumer goods. Consequently, after independence, the governments paid special attention to the development of manufacturing industry.

However, the general pattern for establishing manufacturing industries was very much on an *ad hoc* basis without any plan for linkages within sectors or with other sectors of the economy. Appropriate strategies

16. Organization of African Unity, 1981.
17. *ibid.*, p. 11, para. 18.

TABLE 14.2 *Sectoral composition of GDP at constant 1970 prices, in percentages*

Countries	Agri-culture	Manu-facturing	Elec-tricity	Min-ing	Con-struction	Com-merce	Trans-port	Public adminis-tration	Other
Major oil-exporting									
1960	43.1	5.5	1.3	3.8	8.4	19.3	5.5	7.5	5.6
1970	30.2	5.2	0.7	18.5	6.3	24.8	3.2	8.3	2.8
1980	16.3	6.4	0.9	8.6	14.3	24.2	6.6	19.5	3.2
Non-oil-exporting									
1960	42.4	8.6	1.4	4.6	4.0	15.5	5.9	8.9	8.7
1970	35.1	11.7	1.4	5.4	4.7	17.7	6.2	9.4	8.4
1980	27.7	12.4	1.7	5.1	5.4	19.2	7.2	12.8	8.5
Least-developed									
1960	59.2	5.3	1.4	0.8	4.6	15.4	4.3	7.8	1.2
1970	50.6	8.7	1.1	0.9	3.8	17.5	5.0	7.0	5.4
1980	44.2	8.1	1.3	1.3	4.2	17.7	6.9	10.0	6.3
Developing Africa									
1960	42.6	7.6	1.3	4.4	5.4	16.7	5.8	8.4	7.8
1970	33.4	9.5	1.2	9.8	5.2	20.1	5.2	9.0	6.6
1980	22.8	9.8	1.3	6.6	9.3	21.4	6.9	15.7	6.2

NOTE: Sectoral growth for 1960–70 is based on data for 39 countries of developing Africa for which data are available, while for 1970–80 sectoral as well as overall GDP growth are based on all the 50 African developing countries.

Source: ECA Secretariat.

for making industry contribute significantly to economic and social development were lacking. Right from the start, industries were set up in partnership with foreign enterprises or under total foreign ownership which operated them primarily for their own interest. Virtually all the factor inputs and the raw materials were imported. Thus industrialization opened another dependency door in Africa. Instead of becoming a major source of foreign-exchange savings and, possibly, earnings, industry became the principal source of foreign-exchange leakages.

Although, as will be seen from Table 14.3, the manufacturing sector developed faster than any other sector except mining, commerce and public administration in the 1960s, and a little faster than the GDP in the 1970s; the industrial sector even today is still partly a small foreign enclave and partly a small urban enclave in a vast sea of rural backwardness. Relative to world manufacturing output, Africa had a share of manufacturing

TABLE 14.3   *Average annual growth at constant 1970 prices, in percentages*

Countries	Agri-culture	Manu-facturing	Elec-tricity	Min-ing	Con-struction	Com-merce	Trans-port	Public adminis-tration	Other	GDP
Major oil-exporting										
1960–70	5.6	8.8	3.1	28.3	6.3	12.2	3.5	10.6	1.8	9.4
1970–80	1.4	10.1	6.6	1.1	11.4	5.8	8.3	11.2	4.8	7.9
1960–80										8.7
Non-oil-exporting										
1960–70	6.5	12.0	8.9	10.2	10.2	10.0	9.0	9.1	11.1	4.3
1970–80	1.2	4.2	5.4	3.1	5.1	4.4	5.1	6.8	3.8	3.8
1960–80										4.0
Least-developed										
1960–70	− 3.6	15.4	8.9	5.2	12.6	12.2	9.9	13.6	12.8	4.8
1970–80	1.7	2.4	10.5	7.3	17.1	7.6	16.1	17.5	9.6	3.1
1960–80										4.0
Developing Africa										
1960–70	3.7	7.1	4.6	17.3	6.3	9.1	5.1	7.2	4.3	5.8
1970–80	1.3	5.5	4.2	7.3	4.1	3.2	6.4	6.9	6.2	5.2
1960–80										5.6

NOTE: Sectoral growth for 1960–70 is based on data for 39 countries of developing Africa for which data are available, while for 1970–80 sectoral as well as overall GDP growth are based on all 50 African developing countries.

Source: ECA Secretariat.

value added of only 0.9 per cent in 1980 compared to a share of 2.7 per cent and 6 per cent for South-east Asia and Latin America respectively. Thus, by 1980 Africa was still the least-industrialized region of the world. As indicated in the *ECA and Africa's Development 1983–2008: A Preliminary Perspective Study*,

> except for the production of a narrow range of intermediate goods, the sector is characterized by light industries producing consumer goods and by a crude and relatively weak degree of processing and semi-processing of mineral and agricultural raw materials, mainly for export. Further, the existing production structure is based on small size plants with little in terms of economies of scale. Heavy industries are rudimentary and have been attempted coherently in only a few countries. Therefore, the production of capital goods has remained marginal and as a result, Africa remains one of the world's major importers of capital goods with imported equipment and

machinery accounting for over 35 percent of the total annual investment of the region.[18]

Thus, although post-independence African governments saw industrialization as having six major objectives, viz:

(1) the satisfaction of the basic needs of the population;
(2) the exploitation of local natural resources;
(3) the creation of jobs;
(4) the establishment of a base for developing other economic sectors;
(5) the creation of the basis for assimilating and promoting technological progress; and
(6) the modernization of society,[19]

regrettably none of these have been realized during the past two or three decades. Rather,

> because of the heterogeneous character of the manufacturing industry in Africa, their interminable need for subsidies in one form or another, the considerable dependence of many of them on imported factor inputs and their failure as a whole to mitigate unemployment or to provide a dynamic thrust to the African economy, the industrial sector has become a crisis sector and the crisis of industrial stagnation should now be added to the growing list of crises affecting our poor beleaguered continent.[20]

Consequently the failure of the industrialization strategy together with the cumulative neglect of agriculture has no doubt accounted for the intensification of Africa's economic dependence.

The strategy of indigenization

We shall conclude our analysis of the major sectoral approaches to economic decolonization by evaluating *the economic indigenization strategy* pursued by many African governments in the late 1960s and 1970s. As pointed out in *The Indigenization of African Economies*,

> the economy of the typical African state by the time of independence consisted of three levels: Europeans at the top, commanding the large industries, major mercantile concerns and plantation farming; Asians and Lebanese in the middle, controlling medium-level industrial activities and wholesaling as well as the larger retail outfits; and, Africans at the bottom, engaged in peasant farming, petty trading and labour services.[21]

18. Economic Commission for Africa, 1983, p. 11.
19. Organization of African Unity, 1981, p. 20.
20. A. Adedeji, 1984, p. 5.
21. A. Adedeji, 1981, p. 29.

The situation in the civil service was not much different either. Africans were in the clerical and messengerial classes, while the Asians were in the executive, middle-level technical grades, with Europeans in top-level administrative and professional classes. Although better in British West Africa (particularly in Nigeria and Ghana), this situation was the order of the day at the time of independence in British East and Southern Africa and in the French, Belgian and Portuguese territories. Indeed, many of these countries came to nationhood with only a handful of indigenous college graduates and a couple of hundred high-school graduates.

Consequently, a priority for independent African countries was the Africanization of their civil services. It has been estimated that in 1958, the number of European civil servants in Africa was about 100 000.[22] This figure, which does not include university personnel, missionaries, Europeans hired by local authorities and UN personnel, gives an idea of the magnitude of the Africanization of the civil services in purely quantitative terms. It was not simply the exchange of Africans for non-Africans. The Africanization of the civil services was seen as the process of transforming the inherited colonial type of public service into indigenous public services.

In a way, the Africanization or indigenization of the key sectors of the national economies is an extension of the very successful Africanization of the public services. The indigenization policy assumes many forms. At one extreme is nationalization, which is the wholesale take-over of enterprises; and at the other extreme is the government policy of linking and supervising the extent of expatriate participation in various activities. As Leslie L. Rood indicated,

> most of the takings of foreign property in Africa fall into one of three categories: the nationalization of large extractive industries owned by multi-national corporations; the nationalization of small branch enterprises of multi-national corporations, typically banking, insurance, and petroleum distribution; and, the indigenization of small- and medium-sized enterprises owned by alien residents. However, there are some takings which do not fall neatly into these categories: nationalization in the socialist countries has included manufacturing, buildings and plantations; and indigenization in the free-enterprise countries has touched some fairly large European-owned companies. Each kind of taking can be blunt or sophisticated, compensated or uncompensated, voluntary or compulsory.[23]

According to a United Nations study,[24] between 1960 and 1974, there were more nationalizations and take-overs in sub-Saharan Africa than in

22. N. A. Shaath, 1975, p. 99.
23. L. L. Rood, 1976, pp. 430–1.
24. United Nations Secretary-General, 1974.

other regions. Of the 875 cases of nationalization in 62 countries of the world reported during this period, 340 (or 39 per cent) were in black Africa. The region led in all categories of industry except petroleum, and the total values of the indigenized enterprises ran into several billions of US dollars.[25]

As the case-studies on the impact of indigenization on the economies of Egypt, Ethiopia, Ghana, Kenya, Nigeria, Senegal, Tanzania, Zambia, and the Southern African countries of Botswana, Lesotho and Swaziland clearly indicate, while some measure of control has passed into African hands, the dominance of foreign capital, expertise, technology and entrepreneurship is still there in all African countries.[26] The indigenization policy has therefore had very limited success. But

> how successful can the indigenization policy be in a country whose economy is stagnated? How much can a country overburdened by external debt attempt to indigenize its economy? A country that is overly dependent on external trade and on a vulnerably narrow spectrum of primary export commodities, and where there is a sharp bifurcation between the traditional and modern sectors of the economy with a circumscribed and fractured industrial base, cannot truly be indigenized. Africa must therefore see indigenization not merely as the taking over of ongoing expatriate concerns, but as a challenge to transform its present colonial economy to an authentically self-reliant African economy with an internally-generated and self-sustaining process of development.[27]

The strategy of intra-African penetration and pan-African integration

As already indicated, the partition of Africa and the granting of political independence occurred with complete disregard for history, culture, economic and political viability. Thus, at independence Africa was a patchwork of a large number of minuscule states. Furthermore, the nature of the colonial legacy was such that contiguous political units existed as separate and isolated entities with minimum structural links between them. African states were consciously structured to produce primarily for, and trade exclusively with, their respective colonial powers. The national markets that resulted were too small and fragmented for industrial products.

Under the circumstances, the pursuit of national goals of economic decolonization was seen to be dependent on a strategy of regional economic

---

25. It is estimated that some $4bn of the property of US nationals alone was nationalized world-wide in the period 1960–73; this suggests the magnitude of the total values involved.

26. A. Adedeji, 1981, pp. 45–327.

27. *ibid.*, p. 389.

integration and the establishment of multi-national institutions to promote development and undertake joint co-operative efforts.

As a matter of fact, regional economic co-operation and integration were recognized as essential components of strategies of economic decolonization long before the attainment of political independence. They actually started off as aspects of the pan-Africanist movement which aimed at the unification of African forces against imperialism and colonial domination. Thus, one of the earliest calls for economic integration was made at the Fifth Pan-African Congress held in Manchester, England, in 1945, when, with great foresight, the congress recommended the establishment of a West African Economic Union as a means of combating the exploitation of the economic resources of the West African territories and for ensuring the participation of the indigenous people in the industrial development of West Africa. The Bandung Declaration of 1955 also made reference to the need for economic co-operation among African countries.

Because of this link with pan-Africanism, strategies for regional integration adopted in the early post-independence period favoured all-embracing regional organizations. Thus, in 1958, the First Conference of Independent African States, which was held in Accra, Ghana, resolved to set up an Economic and Research Committee within each country and a Joint Economic Research Committee composed of representatives of all independent African countries. Their task was to consolidate the economic development policies of the states, promote trade and a common industrial policy, and co-ordinate economic planning among the different states with a view to achieving an all-African economic co-operation arrangement. Later, in 1960, the independent African states of that time recommended the creation of an African Council for Economic Co-operation, an African Development Bank and an African Commercial Bank. It was recommended that a system of preferential tariffs among independent African countries should be established. It was largely as a result of this collective fervour for economic integration that the Monrovia, Casablanca, Brazzaville, and Maghreb groups were formed. These in turn made various recommendations for the creation of an African Common Market, an African Payments Union and an African Bank for Economic Development.

But the actual establishment of all-embracing multi-purpose regional organizations encountered various obstacles. Foremost amongst these was the newness of the states which made it difficult for national leaders to divest themselves of their newly acquired authority in favour of collective decision-making. The lack of adequate interstate infrastructure, particularly transport and communications links, also circumscribed intrastate trade and movement. A third obstacle arose from the differences in political ideologies adopted by the emergent states. There were also the strong bilateral links with the former colonial powers which continued to militate strongly against intra-African connections.

No all-embracing multi-purpose regional organization existed before

408

the formation of the United Nations Economic Commission for Africa (ECA) in April 1958. Five years later, the Organization of African Unity (OAU) was established. The ECA was entrusted right from its inception with the primary task of initiating, facilitating and participating in the economic development of Africa, including its social aspects; and for monitoring and strengthening the economic relations among African countries and territories and with other countries of the world. The objectives of the OAU were principally political, but they do include the co-ordination and intensification of co-operation to achieve a better life for the peoples of Africa; eradication of all forms of colonialism; and promotion of international co-operation. While both organizations were requested to co-operate very closely with each other, the primary responsibility for promoting economic co-operation and integration in Africa rests with the ECA.

Early in the 1960s, the ECA realized that the most viable approach to regional integration was one that was gradual and embraced narrower geographical areas as opposed to an all-embracing continental arrangement. The African region was therefore divided into four sub-regions: Eastern and Southern, Central, West, and North Africa. Sub-regional offices were established in each of these four sub-regions. Their main function was to provide backstop services that would facilitate collective decisions and actions at the grassroots level by undertaking relevant studies, participating in the programming and implementation of multi-national projects and provision of on-the-spot technical assistance on a continuous basis. However, the sub-regional offices were soon found to be not as effective as expected in getting African states to form co-operation arrangements; first, because they were plagued by a dearth of resources, and secondly, because there were no provisions to ensure the participation of governments in the activities and work programmes of the offices. To enhance the ECA's role as a catalyst for regional integration, United Nations Development Advisory Teams (UNDATs) were created to improve the operational capability of the sub-regional offices. It was, however, soon realized that what was needed was not simply advisory bodies, but more operational instruments for the promotion of economic co-operation. The UNDATs were therefore replaced in 1977 by the Multi-national Programming and Operational Centres (MULPOCs). Today, there are five MULPOCs in the various sub-regions of the continent (Fig. 14.2). Their operation holds great promise for the future of regional economic integration in Africa.

At present, there are several economic communities organized along sub-regional lines and at various stages of integration (Fig. 14.3). In West Africa, the Economic Community of West African States (ECOWAS) exists (Fig. 14.4) and embraces the membership of other communities, such as the West African Economic Community (CEAO), the Council for the Entente and the Mano River Union. In Central Africa, the latest

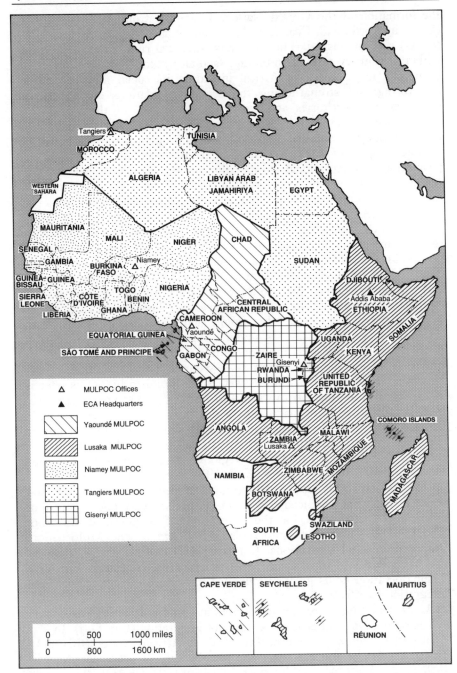

FIG. 14.2 *MULPOC regional groupings in Africa (Source: adapted from Economic Commission for Africa, Addis Ababa)*

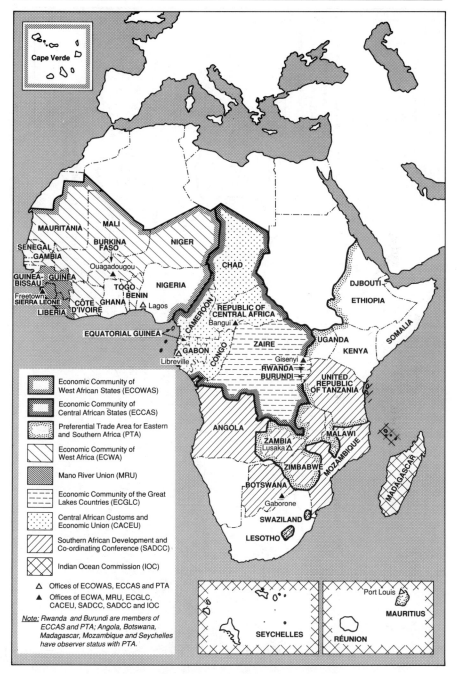

FIG. 14.3 *Regional economic groupings in Africa (Source: adapted from Economic Commission for Africa, Addis Ababa)*

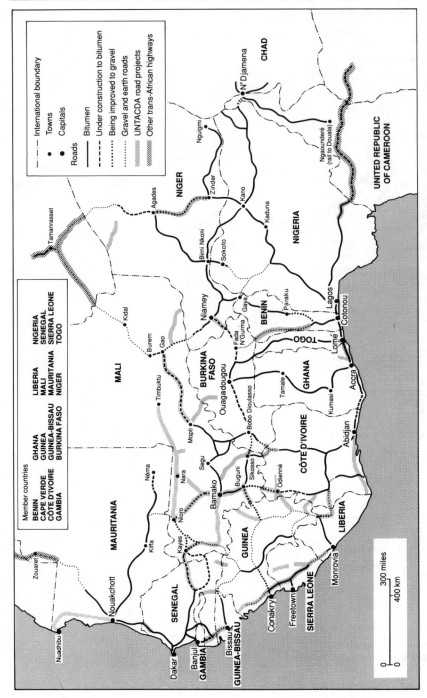

FIG. 14.4 *Trans-West African Highways Master Plan, ECA/ECOWAS (Source: adapted from a map provided by the Economic Commission for Africa, Addis Ababa)*

of the economic communities established by the ECA in 1983 – the Economic Community of Central African States – has brought together the five states that constitute the *Union douanière des Etats d'Afrique Centrale* (UDEAC), namely the Central African Republic, Congo, Chad, Gabon, and the United Republic of Cameroon, into what will eventually become a Central African Common Market. The Economic Community of the Great Lakes Countries (CEPGL – *Communauté économique des pays des Grands Lacs*) comprising Burundi, Rwanda and Zaire has also been established. In East Africa, the East Africa Economic Community established in 1967 between Kenya, Uganda and Tanzania has since collapsed (July 1977). The ECA, using its MULPOC for Eastern and Southern Africa, succeeded in establishing the Eastern and Southern African Preferential Trade Area with provisions not only for the liberalization of trade, but also for co-operation and inter-country specialization in the development of basic and strategic industries, the production of food crops and livestock, the development of science and technology, the exploitation and utilization of natural resources, human resources development and the creation of transport and telecommunications networks (Fig. 14.5). In North Africa, a Permanent Consultative Committee was established in 1964 between Libya, Morocco and Tunisia.

Cutting across the membership of these multi-purpose organizations are about 130 inter-governmental, multi-sectoral economic organizations that are meant to promote technical and economic co-operation in Africa. In addition, there are institutionalized conferences of ministers and officials in a number of specific areas.

Despite their multiplicity, the effectiveness of many of these organizations in promoting co-operation is yet to be proved. Intra-African penetration has been constrained by, first and foremost, the inadequacies in understanding the objectives and modalities of economic co-operation. Far too often, assumptions which are obtained in advanced countries, but which are untrue as far as developing African countries are concerned, have been brought to bear on the formation and operation of economic groupings in Africa. These assumptions include the existence of many units of production, each producing and selling a relatively small share of the national output; an economy operating at near full employment with plants expected to operate at the margin so that new investment is also marginal compared to current productive capacity; an ample supply of highly-motivated entrepreneurs with an extensive knowledge of markets for financing inputs and products who are capable of exploring new economic opportunities as they arise at home and abroad; and the benefits of co-operation which are usually distributed fairly among the co-operating countries because the capacity to derive benefits from co-operation are fairly equitably distributed.[28]

28. Economic Commission for Africa, 1976, p. 50.

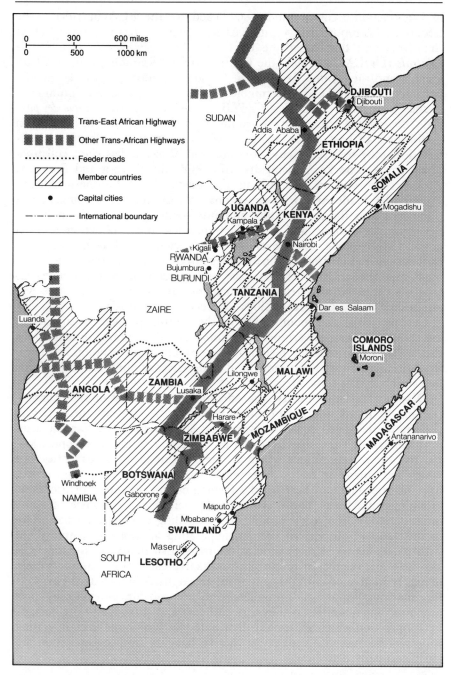

FIG. 14.5 *Eastern and Southern Africa Preferential Trade Area: Highway Master Plan (Source: adapted from a map provided by the Economic Commission for Africa, Addis Ababa)*

Conditions obtaining in Africa are by contrast characterized by:

(1) an inadequate supply of competent entrepreneurs in both the public and private sectors;
(2) scarcity of skilled manpower;
(3) limited familiarity with the sources of raw material supply;
(4) limited range of choice of technology;
(5) limited inter-industry integration; and
(6) limited domestic markets in relation to plant sizes.

Given these conditions, the objectives and modes of co-operation should differ fundamentally from those co-operation arrangements organized amongst the industrialized countries.

In other words, economic co-operation arrangements in Africa should not be oriented solely to trade facilitation but to production as well. Co-operation should lead to the creation and utilization of new productive capacity, especially in the production of goods and services for use as further inputs for other industries or consumption.[29] To achieve this, it will be necessary to integrate national economies and to reorient consumption and production patterns towards satisfying domestic requirements and to promote national self-reliance. But often, the various sectors in an African economy are only tenuously linked.

Another major problem has been that of reaching acceptable formulae and procedures for sharing the costs and benefits of economic co-operation. Of particular importance in this respect has been the concern of participating states over the possibility of loss of income from export and import taxes as a result of trade-liberalization measures implicit in common-market arrangements.

This problem is closely linked with considerations of equity and of balance within economic groupings whereby certain countries have progressed at slower rates than they would have done outside the groupings. The formulation of generally acceptable equalization measures to redress the imbalance has however constituted one of the most intractable problems facing economic groupings, since such measures usually must cover 'not only losses of revenues on duties forgone but also benefits from the imponderable unquantifiable "dynamic" factors such as improvements in the efficiency of the country's factors of production attributable to economic integration, operation of external economies, expanded employment'.[30]

Another obstacle to effective economic co-operation in Africa has been the over-consciousness on the part of many African countries of their national sovereignty. Too often, the political leadership has been reluctant to surrender national sovereignty over crucial areas of economic policy.

29. For further development of this point, see A. Adedeji, 1976.
30. *ibid.*, p. 45.

The inadequacy of infrastructure and the absence of appropriate institutional frameworks to promote economic co-operation have also constituted real constraints on regional co-operative efforts. The most critical gaps include the lack of modern transport and communications links among member states; the absence of intra-African clearing-house arrangements and of common currency and payments arrangements; and the absence of multi-national development institutions with the capacity for project identification, preparation, investment promotion and consultancy services. In this connection, the setting up by the ECA of the West African Payments and Clearing House, and the Central African Payments and Clearing Arrangements, and by the PTA of a PTA Clearing and Payments Arrangements should help considerably. The United Nations Transport and Communications Decade for Africa, initiated by the ECA, has started to lay the foundation for networks of transport and communications at regional and sub-regional levels.

Growing differences, such as between socialist and capitalist states, in political ideology and economic orientations have also taken their toll on co-operative arrangements. Under the prevailing circumstances, the critical issue has been how to devise institutional mechanisms that would minimize conflict and maximize the area of co-operation.

A final source of constraint has been the ambivalence in attitudes towards economic co-operation. Apparently, political initiatives and declared collective goodwill have too often not been matched by practical action. There is also the tendency for actions at the national level to be completely at variance with declarations made in international fora.

Spurred by the Final Act of Lagos which was one of the outcomes of the African Economic Summit held on 28 and 29 April 1980, in Lagos, by which the heads of state and government committed themselves to the setting up of an African Economic Community by the year 2000, the ECA, in collaboration with the OAU, has been intensifying its effort to streamline and strengthen existing regional economic groupings and to establish others in the regions where they do not exist, so as to cover the continent as a whole. With the signing on 21 October 1983 of the treaty establishing the Central African Economic Community by ten member states of Central Africa, there have now emerged in sub-Saharan Africa three major regional economic co-operation arrangements which will become the main instrument for pushing forward the strategy of intra-African penetration and providing the framework for pan-African integration. They are

    (1) the 16 member states of the Economic Community of West African States (ECOWAS), whose establishment preceded the Final Act of Lagos by five years;

    (2) the Preferential Trade Area of Eastern and Southern Africa (PTA), which is expected to have 22 member states and which came into existence in December 1981; and

(3) the ten-nation Economic Community of Central African States (ECCAS).

Deteriorating African economic conditions, the persistence of neo-colonial economic systems and of economic dependence

In spite of all the various strategies for economic decolonization pursued by African governments both at macro and sectoral levels, the African economy has still retained its colonial pre-independence structure (Table 14.4) and has made a rather insignificant positive impact on the living conditions of the people. The strategies were unsuccessful in engineering the expected socio-economic transformation; at best, they only achieved marginal structural changes.

Between 1960 and 1980, the combined GDP of African countries about tripled, reaching in 1980 some US$86 billion (at constant 1980 factor cost) which implies an annual growth of 5.6 per cent on the average (see Table 14.2). In per capita terms, average incomes rose from US$133 in 1960 to US$243 (or US$740 at 1983 prices). While this rise looks impressive, in relative terms the 1980 regional average income is only 7.6 per cent of the US$9684 average current income for the industrial countries, underscoring the magnitude of African underdevelopment. Growth performance has been unstable and sometimes erratic. The facts that agriculture is the most dominant sector and that African economies are open to the vagaries of climate and international trade, help to explain most of this instability and relatively modest growth. Thus, the up-swing in GDP growth during 1965–70 was due essentially to the record performance in agriculture and the improved demand for exports. Similarly, the slowing down of growth to 4.5 per cent during the subsequent five years was again due primarily to the unprecedented fall in the growth of agricultural production to 1.4 per cent a year and the recessionary conditions following the quadrupling of oil prices in 1973–4 which stifled demand for the region's exports, which grew by a mere 0.5 per cent a year in real terms. The slight recovery in the 1975–80 period, however, followed primarily from the picking up of demand for non-petroleum products after a short period of adjustment to the costlier energy regime in the developed countries. But the situation took a dramatic sharp down-turn immediately afterwards with the new rises in oil prices and the cumulative impact of an assortment of problems, ranging from protracted droughts to falling export demand and prices to unprecedented foreign-exchange squeezes. In 1981, regional growth plummeted to a negative rate of − 3.0 per cent (at 1980 prices), its first in recent history. All in all, GDP growth in the 1960s at 5.8 per cent was slightly better than the average of 5.2 per cent a year achieved during the 1970s.

TABLE 14.4 *Monoculturalism in African economies*

Country	Main export commodity	Contribution to total exports (%)			Contribution to public services (%)			Contribution to GDP (%)			Contribution to capital formation (%)		
		1960	1970	1980	1960	1970	1980	1960	1970	1980	1960	1970	1980
Algeria	Petroleum	–	67.5	91.6	–	50.1	–	–	18.8	381.9	–	10.7	332.5
Botswana	Diamonds	–	14.7	60.8	–	16.5	89.8	–	4.1	40.0	–	9.2	300.0
Congo	Petroleum	–	10.5	77.9	–	4.7	128.7	–	1.4	41.4	–	3.1	615.4
Côte d'Ivoire	Wood	–	52.3	11.6	–	23.7	19.1	10.4	6.5	1.3	15.5	19.5	91.1
	Cocoa	22.4	20.5	25.2	–	26.4	25.7	7.0	8.1	9.6	45.3	19.2	95.0
	Coffee	48.5	33.2	20.5	–	42.6	20.9	15.2	13.1	9.8	98.4	13.2	77.1
Egypt	Wood	16.3	17.9	15.1	–	23.2	15.4	5.2	7.1	6.7	33.9	5.0	56.7
	Petroleum	–	4.6	57.8	–	2.2	15.0	–	0.6	1.8	–	3.6	31.1
Ethiopia	Cotton	66.1	44.6	13.9	–	21.0	3.6	9.9	5.6	1.9	59.7	14.6	12.3
	Coffee	49.0	59.3	64.1	–	38.9	47.4	1.6	4.1	7.0	13.4	32.6	96.3
Gabon	Petroleum	21.4	34.3	62.3	–	–	–	9.0	17.6	–	20.4	19.6	–
	Manganese	–	8.5	6.6	–	–	–	–	4.4	4.4	–	12.3	41.4
Gambia	Groundnuts	–	95.1	54.1	–	190.0	35.8	–	29.8	8.1	–	191.6	53.1
Ghana	Cocoa	57.3	64.2	56.2	–	68.6	–	22.2	14.1	12.6	96.7	93.7	220.1
Kenya	Petroleum products	–	15.4	31.5	–	20.7	26.0	–	3.3	7.2	–	13.4	88.4
	Coffee	–	20.5	21.0	–	27.5	17.3	–	4.3	4.8	–	17.7	58.8
	Tea	–	12.1	11.2	–	16.3	9.3	–	2.6	2.6	–	10.5	32.5
Liberia	Iron ore	41.9	70.1	52.7	–	221.9	153.4	128.1	39.5	30.6	115.3	169.7	208.3
Libya	Petroleum	–	99.7	99.9	–	228.0	–	–	78.4	61.9	–	410.5	850.6
Malawi	Tobacco	–	33.4	43.9	–	43.0	52.9	–	6.7	11.4	–	13.9	107.0
Mali	Groundnuts	–	14.5	2.3	–	14.0	–	–	1.6	–	–	8.6	7.5
	Cotton	–	21.0	48.1	–	20.5	–	–	2.4	7.1	–	10.7	157.6
Mauritania	Iron ore	–	84.8	77.8	–	48.0	–	–	39.5	23.6	–	163.5	247.9
Mauritius	Sugar	22.0	91.6	67.0	–	149.1	125.3	29.8	38.5	30.6	67.9	243.1	653.2
Morocco	Phosphates	23.7	23.1	31.2	–	16.6	17.2	5.1	3.4	5.3	45.7	13.5	557.9
Niger	Uranium	–	–	74.3	–	–	–	–	–	5.6	–	–	–

Country	Main export commodity	Contribution to total exports (%)			Contribution to public services (%)			Contribution to GDP (%)			Contribution to capital formation (%)		
		1960	1970	1980	1960	1970	1980	1960	1970	1980	1960	1970	1980
Nigeria	Cocoa	20.6	15.0	9.0	–	19.7	–	3.1	1.8	–	27.1	192.9	6.0
	Groundnuts	–	–	–	–	–	–	–	–	–	–	–	–
Senegal	Petroleum	2.7	57.6	95.3	–	110.2	–	0.4	7.1	–	3.9	596.0	615.1
	Groundnuts	83.9	37.7	13.3	–	40.3	–	16.5	7.1	8.3	155.7	69.8	40.1
	Phosphates	1.6	7.8	16.4	–	8.5	–	0.3	1.6	2.8	3.3	1.5	49.7
	Petroleum products	–	3.1	18.7	–	3.3	–	–	0.6	3.3	–	–	37.0
Sierra Leone	Iron ore	14.0	11.9	–	–	18.4	–	38.2	3.1	–	69.0	18.6	–
	Diamonds	55.6	62.5	53.3	–	96.6	63.3	112.2	16.4	10.2	275.0	76.1	100.0
Sudan	Cotton	52.2	61.3	44.9	–	32.0	21.8	9.5	9.9	1.8	10.5	10.1	62.9
Togo	Phosphates	–	24.5	39.6	–	46.5	–	–	5.6	13.7	–	35.1	125.2
Tunisia	Petroleum	–	24.4	50.7	–	–	40.3	–	3.6	15.0	–	–	141.6
	Phosphates	17.7	20.3	3.0	–	–	5.6	3.1	3.0	2.1	15.0	15.3	19.4
Uganda	Coffee	36.9	50.4	98.7	–	85.2	31.0	8.5	11.9	8.9	91.3	81.6	372.0
	Cotton	32.3	17.4	1.2	–	29.4	82.1	7.4	4.1	–	80.0	27.8	4.6
United Republic of Cameroon	Petroleum	–	–	–	–	–	–	–	–	–	–	–	–
	Cocoa	–	23.8	21.3	–	34.8	27.5	7.2	5.4	4.2	51.8	27.0	47.0
	Coffee	–	22.8	21.7	–	33.4	25.4	4.1	5.2	6.3	36.7	25.9	48.5
	Wood	–	6.5	11.3	–	9.5	14.7	–	1.5	2.3	–	7.6	25.1
United Republic of Tanzania	Coffee	13.1	17.4	23.4	–	19.6	–	3.9	3.8	8.2	31.5	15.1	36.4
Zaire	Copper	63.6	–	43.3	–	80.7	51.4	–	35.4	18.7	–	106.5	49.5
	Cobalt	22.4	–	21.2	–	7.5	25.2	–	3.3	6.2	–	9.8	24.2
Zambia	Copper	–	95.2	91.3	–	149.0	132.1	–	63.5	79.5	–	196.4	446.0
Zimbabwe	Tobacco	–	–	13.5	–	–	–	–	–	3.6	–	–	76.4

Source: ICA Secretariat, IMF, *International Financing Statistics:* Yearbook 1982 and 1983 and Vol. 37, No. 5 (May 1984).

The search for a new national, regional and international economic order

It had become crystal clear to most African states by the beginning of the 1970s that if Africa was to get out of its low-level economic trap and lay the foundation for any significant process in economic decolonization, new national, regional and international economic strategies had to be formulated and rigorously pursued. Such strategies, at the national level, involve the installation of a new economic order based on the firm principles of self-reliance and self-sustainment; at the African regional level, on the concentration of efforts leading to the achievement of an increasing measure of collective self-reliance among African states; and at the international level, on the establishment of a new international economic order.

In this search for a more effective and realistic strategy for economic decolonization, the place of honour must be accorded to the ECA's *Africa's Strategy for Development in the 1970s* which its Conference of Ministers adopted in February 1971[31] and to the OAU's *African Declaration on Cooperation, Development and Economic Independence* adopted by the Assembly of Heads of State and Government at the tenth anniversary of the organization in May 1973.[32] But before the ECA and OAU declarations could be put into operational forms, the world was confronted with a decision of fundamental importance which was to have devastating impact on the economic and political relations between the industrialized countries and the Third World.

The announcement by the Shah of Iran, on 23 December 1973, that henceforth a barrel of light crude oil would sell for US$11.65 rather than the then prevailing price of US$5.04 shook the international economy, at least for some time, to its very foundations. This single decision of the Organization of Petroleum Exporting Countries (OPEC) was hailed as a critical point in history for it enabled some OPEC member states, such as Algeria, to take advantage of the opportunity to pursue the strategy of counter-penetration of the industrialized countries by leading the demand for the establishment of a new international economic order (NIEO). The OPEC action was seen as a practical illustration of what the developing world could do.

The sixth special session of the General Assembly of the United Nations in 1974 thus provided an opportunity for Third-World solidarity in their demand for a new international economic order. However, the impact of the oil-price rise on the fragile economies of oil-importing African countries, particularly on their foreign accounts and their pro-

31. E/CN/14/493/Rev.3 of 6 February 1971.
32. CM/ST.12 (xxi).

duction costs, led to disillusion among them, especially as the OPEC example had failed to create a model for correcting the prices of other raw materials. Other primary commodities continue to be priced on free international markets which are, more often than not, subjected to severe fluctuations both in demand and price and where multi-national corporations invariably have the upper hand. In spite of all the attempts which have been made and continue to be made for the cartelization of other export commodities and minerals, the economic fundamentals are unfavourable. The industrialized countries which import these commodities have open to them many possibilities for substitutes which amount to a form of countervailing power against producer cartels. Consequently, all that was made of the OPEC successful price coup was to use it as the springboard for intensifying Third-World agitation for a new international economic order which concentrated on seven issues. These are

(1) commodity stabilization;
(2) discrete treatment of Third-World debts;
(3) restructuring of international trade and removal of protectionist policies in the industrialized North to Third-World countries;
(4) halting the reverse resource flows from poor to rich countries and increasing Official Development Assistance (ODA) to 0.7 per cent of the GNP of the industrialized economies;
(5) easy access to Western technology;
(6) redeployment of world industrial production capability in favour of Third-World countries; and
(7) the reform of the international monetary and financial system, i.e. the World Bank and the International Monetary Fund.[33]

Although Africa joined hands with the rest of the Third World for a NIEO, and indeed played a leading role in the various abortive negotiations, it was soon increasingly realized that the most economically backward and underdeveloped region in the world, Africa and particularly sub-Saharan Africa, would not be able to participate on an equal and equitable basis in any NIEO should it ever emerge, unless it first put its own economies in order at the national level and at the regional level and adopted a truly economic decolonization strategy.

It is for this reason that the Economic Commission for Africa (ECA) deemed it necessary to initiate a series of actions from the second half of 1975, which led to the eventual adoption of the *Development Strategy for Africa for the Third United Nations Development Decade*[34] and the *Lagos*

33. A. Adedeji, 1983, p. 7.
34. ECA Resolution 332 (xiv) contained in document E/CN.14/INF/109/Rev. 1. This ECA Resolution later became known as the Monrovia Strategy, following its adoption in July 1979 by the Assembly of Heads of State and Government of the OAU.

Plan of Action for the Economic Development of Africa 1980–2000.[35] The theoretical and intellectual foundation of both was, of course, the basic document adopted by the ECA in 1976 entitled the *Revised Framework of Principles for the Implementation of the New International Economic Order in Africa, 1976–1981–1985*[36] which challenged conventional wisdom in the field of development economics as it applied to the African economy and systematically exposed the inappropriateness of the different strategies being pursued for bringing about the economic decolonization of Africa and its transformation into a self-reliant and internally-self-generating and self-sustaining dynamic economy. After noting that the available pool of knowledge and experience of how economies grow and how socio-economic changes can be managed was limited, the ECA argued in the *Revised Framework* that because economic policy-making in Africa took the form, in most cases, 'of successive responses to diagnoses of social and economic ills originating outside the region, both the diagnoses and prescriptions were greatly influenced not only by a firm belief in the efficacy of international trade and associated economic relations as an engine of desirable economic growth and social change but also by strong adherence to a particular interpretation of the genesis of international trade'.[37] The ECA also put into doubt the

conventional linear thinking by which economic growth is regarded as a semi-mystical process, the outcome of which is measured by increases or decreases in the GDP or GNP and which is the result of a semi-mystical input called investment which consists mainly of resources received by means of foreign exchange. In such a conventional approach, the role of indigenous factor inputs is hardly examined or, if examined at all, is not given a central role in the development process. Because of national or multinational programmes for the production of such indigenous factor inputs, we have had to rely heavily on foreign exchange as a means of commanding these factor inputs. Hence the vital importance of our monoproduce exports, and the net flow of foreign private investment and our willingness to 'beg' for foreign aid and loans to supplement these two. Of course, our greatest weakness as a people is the lack of any visualization by our political, social, and community leaders and by our captains of industry as to what they would like to see our countries become individually and as a group in, say, twenty-five years from now. It is this image of one's self in the future that is a condition of policy-making and strategy design in every developed or semi-developed country. Without it, no reliable path towards the future can be followed either by individuals, communities, countries,

35. Economic Commission for Africa, 1981.
36. Economic Commission for Africa, 1976.
37. *ibid.*, pp. 6–7.

or groups of countries. And it becomes easy to go astray or be led astray.[38]

The *Lagos Plan of Action* was therefore seen by the ECA, which had prepared the Monrovia Strategy three years after the adoption of the *Revised Framework*, as Africa's economic Magna Carta and as the basis for the economic decolonization of the continent. Both the *Strategy* and the *Plan* focus on the achievement of an increasing measure of self-reliance and self-sustainment. The one means the internationalization of the forces of demand which determine the direction of development and economic-growth processes and patterns of output; increasing substitution of factor inputs derived from within the African economy for those derived from outside; and increasing the participation of the mass of the people in the production and consumption of the social product. The other – that is, increasing self-sustainment – means the deliberate installation of the patterns and processes of development and economic growth in which different components mutually support and reinforce each other so that when related to the internationalization of the forces determining demand and supply, the whole system develops its own internal dynamics.[39]

Only a development strategy which is based on the principles of self-reliance and self-sustainment can bring about a complete departure from the colonial economic past of Africa and lead the continent along the path of normative development. Such a strategy, being inward-looking rather than externally-oriented, does not make a sacred cow of foreign-exchange earnings and therefore does not attach excessive importance to foreign trade as the basis for initiating development, particularly the type of foreign trade with which Africa has been engaged both before and since independence. The development strategy espoused in both the Monrovia Strategy and the *Lagos Plan of Action* accordingly puts the domestic market, including African sub-regional and regional markets, rather than external foreign markets at the heart of the development effort.[40] The challenge which therefore faces Africa is to put into operational terms at the national, sub-regional and regional levels the essence of both the Monrovia Strategy and the *Lagos Plan of Action*. It is only by doing so that economic decolonization can become realizable.

But decolonization may require more than reducing alien power on African economies. It is likely to require increased *African* power on the world economy. African resources can be more than just a basis of dependency. They can become the foundations of Africa's counter-leverage on the global system. In this quest for counter-power, solidarity with other developing countries is more vital than ever.

38. A. Adedeji, 1983, p. 9.
39. *ibid.*, p. 10.
40. *ibid.*, p. 11.

Strategies of solidarity and counter-power[41]

Two forms of solidarity are critical for Africa and the Third World if the global system is to change in favour of the disadvantaged and of final decolonization.

Organic solidarity concerns South–South linkages designed to increase mutual dependence between and among African or Third-World countries themselves. *Strategic solidarity* concerns co-operation among Third-World countries in their struggle to extract concessions from the industrialized North. Organic solidarity concerns the aspiration to promote greater integration between Third-World economies. Strategic solidarity aspires to decrease the South's dependent integration into *Northern* economies. The focus of organic solidarity is primarily a South–South economic marriage. The focus of strategic solidarity is either a North–South divorce, a new marriage settlement or a new social contract between North and South. The terms of the North–South bond have to be re-negotiated.

We start also from the additional basic observation that economic flows are in any case far deeper between North and South than between South and South. On the whole, Southerners do far greater trade with the North than with each other, and have more extensive relations of production with industrialized states than with fellow developing countries. But those economic relations between North and South are distorted by a tradition of dependency involving unequal partnership. The structural links give undue advantage and leverage to the North – and leave the South vulnerable and exploitable.

What then is the way out? How can these two forms of solidarity help to ameliorate the Third World's predicament of dependency and its persistent economic vulnerability?

One of the more neglected areas of co-operation is humanpower and humanpower training. A start has been made in humanpower exchange between some Third-World countries and in the field of humanpower training across Third-World boundaries. But the importance of this area has been grossly underestimated.

It is not often realized that the most obstinate line of demarcation between North and South is not income (criteria of wealth) but technology (criteria of skill). The entire international system of stratification has come to be based *not* on 'who owns what' but on 'who *knows* what'. Libya and Saudi Arabia may have a higher per capita income than some of the members of the European Economic Community, but Libya and Saudi Arabia are well below Western Europe in skills of production and economic organization. Indeed, members of OPEC do not even have adequate skills to control or drill their own oil.

41. This section has been drafted by A. A. Mazrui, and is indebted to his previous work on counter-penetration, including that for the FAO. See also A. A. Mazrui, 1986.

Nowhere is this demonstrated more clearly than in Southern Africa and the Middle East. Some five million whites in South Africa have been able to hold to ransom a black population in the region ten times their own. They have held neighbouring blacks to ransom both economically and militarily. The main explanation is not simply because South Africa is rich, but because that wealth has been extracted through African labour and *European* expertise. South Africa's neighbours have African labour too. Some of them are also rich in minerals. What the blacks have lacked indigenously is the superior technology of production and the accompanying culture of efficient organization.

The Middle East is a clearer and more staggering illustration of the power of skill over income. At least since the 1970s, much of the Arab world has become significantly richer than Israel in sheer income. Indeed, the Israeli economy would have suffered complete collapse but for the infusion of billions of dollars from the United States and from world Jewry. And yet, in spite of being out-numbered and out-wealthed, the Israelis have retained the upper hand militarily against the Arabs. The supremacy of skill over income and numbers has been dramatically illustrated in one Middle-East war after another.

In both South Africa and Israel the cultural variable is critical. Had Israel consisted entirely of Middle-Eastern Jews, the Arabs would have won every war. Indeed, it would not have been necessary to have more than the 1948 war. After all, Middle-Eastern Jews are not very different from their Arab neighbours in culture and skill. In a war against fellow Middle-Easterners, the numerical preponderance of the Arabs would have triumphed against Jews long before the numerical advantage was reinforced by Arab petro-wealth.

What has made the Israelis militarily pre-eminent is not the Jewishness of 80 per cent of the total population, but the Europeanness of less than half of that Jewish sector. It is the European and Western Jews who have provided the technological foundations of Israel's regional hegemony.

If then the ultimate basis of international stratification is indeed skill rather than income, what is Africa to do in order to ameliorate the consequences of its technological underdevelopment?

The more obvious answer is for Africa to obtain the know-how from the Northern hemisphere as rapidly as possible. But there are difficulties. Countries of the Northern hemisphere are often all too eager to transfer certain forms of technology, especially through trans-national corporations, but the South's need for certain technological transfers only helps to deepen relationships of dependency between the two hemispheres.

On the other hand, there are other areas of technology which the North is not at all keen to transfer. Pre-eminent among the taboos is the transfer of certain branches of nuclear physics and technology. The computer is part of the phenomenon of dependency through technology transfer; the nuclear plant or reactor is a symbol of dependency through technological monopoly by the North. The trans-national corporations are often instruments of Northern penetration of the South through technological transfer; nuclear power, on the other hand, is a symbol of Northern hegemony through technological monopoly.

The dual strategy for Africa and the Third World is both to learn from the North and to share expertise among each other. Those aspects of technology which are being freely transferred by the North should be 'decolonized' and stripped of their dependency implications as fast as possible. Those aspects of technology which are deliberately monopolized by the North should be subjected to Southern industrial espionage in a bid to break the monopoly.

A new international economic order would be void without a new international technological order. Africa needs strategies of solidarity to realize both. But although *the power of skill* is at the moment still overwhelmingly in the hands of the North, there are other areas of power which the South possesses but which the South has under-utilized.

OPEC is an illustration of *producer power*. From 1973 to 1983, OPEC grossly under-utilized its leverage. Instead of using that golden decade to put pressure on the North for fundamental adjustments in the patterns and rules of the world economy, OPEC concentrated almost exclusively on the prices game, a game of short-term maximization of returns.

There is a crying need for other 'producer cartels', no matter how weak in the short run. Cobalt has more promise as a mineral of leverage than copper, and would involve fewer countries. Experimentation in a cobalt cartel could pay off if Zaire asserted itself a little more decisively as an independent power. After all, Zaire has the credentials of being the Saudi Arabia of cobalt when the market improves in the years ahead.

The Third World has also under-utilized its *consumer power*, regionally specific and patchy as it is. The Middle East and African countries like Nigeria are especially important as consumers of Western civil and military hardware, technology and household products. Occasionally Nigeria or individual Middle-Eastern countries flex their muscles and threaten to cancel trade contracts or to refuse to renew them. But such muscles are flexed usually for relatively minor issues – like protesting against the television film *Death of a Princess* or when an Arab or African delegation is diplomatically snubbed by a Western power. The consumer power of Africa and the Middle East could be used as leverage for more fundamental changes in the exchange patterns between North and South.

The fourth form of power currently under-utilized by the South is *debtor power*. Julius Nyerere of Tanzania, upon being elected chairman of the Organization of African Unity in November 1984, identified development, debt and drought as the three leading concerns of the current African condition. Of course, African debts are modest as compared with those of Latin America, but Nyerere identified debt as a source of power and not merely as a source of weakness. At the first press conference

426

after his election, Nyerere lamented that the Third World was not utilizing the threat of defaulting more efficiently to induce Western banks to make more fundamental concessions to the indebted.[42]

In reality, Tanzania would still be vulnerable unless there was substantial strategic solidarity among both African and Latin-American countries. The utilization of debtor power requires considerable consensus among the indebted. The Western banks have evolved a kind of organic solidarity of their own as well as mechanisms of almost continual consultation. The creditors of the North are united – but the debtors of the South are in disarray. Africa and Latin America need to explore the possibility of creating a strategic solidarity of the dispossessed and the indebted – to help induce the creditors of the North to make concessions on such issues as rates of interest, schedules of payment, methods of payment, and the conditions for a moratorium or even total debt relief where needed. Fundamental as all these areas of strategic solidarity are, they are no substitute for organic solidarity in terms of greater trade, investment and other interactions among Third-World countries themselves. Here, the least developed countries (LDCs) are caught up in one of several con-tradictions. In their relations with the North, the LDCs need to diversify their economies. But in their relations with each other, the LDCs need to specialize in order to increase mutual complementarity. Uganda could revive its cotton industry and sell the fibre to Kenya to process into a textile industry. This specialization would help the two countries develop in the direction of complementary specialization. But the imperatives of Uganda's relations with the world economy as a whole dictate diver-sification of Uganda's industry rather than specialization. This is an acute dilemma which Third-World countries need to resolve as a matter of urgency. They need to find a suitable balance between diversification for North–South relations and specialization in South–South trade.

Related to this is the imperative of finding alternative methods of payment in South–South trade. The principle of using Northern cur-rencies for South–South trade has been very stressful. The bogey of 'foreign exchange' has bedevilled Southern economies. Tanzania, Zambia and Zimbabwe have been exploring possibilities of reviving *barter* as a basis of at least some aspect of their economic relations. Nigeria, in the 1980s, has experimented with 'counter-trade' – exchanging oil for manufactured goods. The new detente between Kenya and Tanzania also envisages areas of barter trade between the two countries in the years ahead. And if Uganda's cotton did feed Kenya's textile industry more systematically in the future, it would not be unrealistic for Kenya to pay back Uganda in shirts and processed military uniforms, rather than in hard foreign exchange.

42. The *Voice of America's* African Service broadcast a recording of both Nyerere's speech and his press conference; one such broadcast was on 24 November 1984.

Another area of organic solidarity among Third-World countries concerns the issue of sharing *energy*. There have been years when Kenya has needed to get a third of its electricity from the dam at Jinja in Uganda. Uganda is still a major supplier of power to Kenya.

PLATE 14.1 *Jinja Dam in Uganda*

The Akosombo Dam on the Volta River in Ghana was also designed to be a major *regional* supplier of electricity in West Africa. Unfortunately, the level of water has been so low that far from supplying power to neighbours, Ghana has periodically had to ration power domestically. Ghana has sometimes needed electrical co-operation from the Côte d'Ivoire. Southern African dams like Kariba have had more successful regional roles. They all symbolize a kind of pan-Africanism of energy – organic solidarity through interlocking structures of hydro-electric power.

An integrated European steel complex once served as midwife to the birth of the European Economic Community (EEC). Indeed, the integrated steel industry was envisaged as an insurance against any future fratricidal war in Europe. If European steel production was interlocked, industrial interdependence was at hand – and separate military aggression in the future would therefore be less likely.

In the same spirit, interlocking electrical systems between Third-World countries should deepen mutual dependence – and create incentives for co-operation in other areas.

The struggle for a more integrated Africa has encountered many setbacks – from the collapse of the East African Community of Kenya, Uganda and Tanzania to the substantial drying-up of the Akosombo Dam.

An experiment worthy of Africa's attention and study is South-east Asia. The struggle for a more integrated South-east Asia is more of a success story – as the Association of South-east Asian Nations (ASEAN) has emerged as a major economic and diplomatic force in the affairs of the region. The struggle for a more integrated Arab world is a mixed story – ranging from the positive promise of the Gulf Cooperation Council to the negative internecine squabbles of Arab politics. Libya and Egypt are often close to conflict.

In Latin America, regional integration is also a mixed record. Central America in the 1980s was tense under the clouds of war. On the other hand, Chile and Argentina – through the mediation of the Vatican – diffused the sensitive issue of the Beagle Channel. Economic co-operation has had its ups and downs throughout the region, but the ideal of greater integration is still a live flame. Africa should watch this distant political laboratory with fascination.

The Northern hemisphere, as a whole, has been divided between two economic blocs which coincided with the ideological divide. The split was of course between the socialist world of COMECON (Council for Mutual Economic Assistance/CMEA), and the capitalist world of the North Atlantic Treaty Organization (NATO) and the European Community.

Africa, as a Southern region, on the other hand, is still in multiple fragments. It is now in search of the elusive secret of putting the fragments together. It is in search of the secret genius of cohesion.

Strategies of solidarity are but the means to an end. The goal is distant and difficult – but Africa's reach should exceed its grasp, or what's a heaven for?

Philosophers have distinguished between negative freedom (freedom from control) and positive freedom (freedom to participate). When African slaves were 'emancipated' in the Americas they were at best given negative freedom (freedom from ownership by others). One hundred years later,

PLATE 14.2   *Above: Akosombo Dam in Ghana; below: Great Kariba Dam in Zimbabwe*

Africans in the *diaspora* are still looking for positive freedom (freedom to participate effectively).

Similarly, *negative decolonization* is like emancipation from slavery – freedom from being owned by others. But real *positive decolonization* will only arrive when Africans are effective participants in the world economy and have commensurate share in global power. It is indeed not enough to reduce alien power on our economies – vital as that stage is. It is urgent that we seek ways of increasing African power on the world economy at the same time. Africans must move from being pawns in the games of others to becoming true players on the chessboard of global destiny.

SECTION IV

Socio-political change since independence

Nation-building and changing political structures

J. Isawa ELAIGWU

in collaboration with

Ali A. MAZRUI

Africa's supreme political struggle in the post-colonial era can be reduced to two paramount longings – a striving to give greater coherence to African *nationhood*, and a striving to lend greater stability to African *statehood*. The crisis of nationhood is a crisis of flawed collective *identity*. The crisis of statehood is a crisis of unstable *authority*. The two dramas are inter-related but each has a logic of its own. Most independent African countries are colonially-created *states* struggling to become more coherent nations. A country like Somalia, on the other hand, is an indigenous *nation* struggling to become a more stable and more inclusive state. But because nationhood and statehood in the twentieth century are inter-related, both categories of countries continue to experience the twin crises of identity and authority in the post-colonial era.

In many ways the greatest threat to national identity in independent Africa is the legacy of artificial boundaries created by the colonial powers. The greatest question mark hanging over stable statehood has often been the standing army, which was also a creation of colonial rule. Most African societies before colonialism created armies only when needed in times of conflict. They did not have regiments permanently under arms, whether there was conflict or not. They did not have brigades consuming a large proportion of the resources of the country. What colonialism created was a military machine with an imported technology of destruction well ahead of the rest of the infrastructure. Both African nationhood and African statehood have been under pressure from the twin forces of artificial boundaries and unstable civil–military relations.

However, in terms of planning for indigenous leadership, a central dilemma for colonial policy-makers had been whether to maintain the authority of traditional leaders and rulers or to cultivate a cadre of Western or semi-Westernized intelligentsia. The British genuinely grappled with that dilemma and never really resolved it, even in their own minds. Their ideology of 'indirect rule' favoured traditional leaders where it was applied, especially in Northern Nigeria. But from the 1930s onwards, colonial policy-makers in the British tradition were also engaged in 'colonial development and welfare' – which included the expansion of secondary

435

and tertiary education in the Western style. A larger Westernized élite was in the process of being created.

In the French colonies, the balance was more clearly in favour of creating a Gallicized intelligentsia at the expense of traditional rulers. But even in the French empire there were contradictions. The *marabouts*, in colonial West Africa, retained considerable authority; and the monarchy in 'protectorate' Morocco retained considerable power in spite of periodic confrontations with the French overlords.

On the whole, the central dilemma of African authority during the colonial period remained between indigenous traditional credentials of legitimacy and the new credentials of Western education. On the other hand, the central dilemma of authority after independence has been between the Westernized civilian intelligentsia and the post-colonial armed forces. During the colonial period, traditional rulers were on the defensive as they faced the challenge of the Westernized intelligentsia. Since independence, the Western-educated leaders have been on the defensive as they face the challenge of the military.

Of course, the debate about traditional rulers is far from dead yet, especially in countries like Nigeria and post-Amīn Uganda where indigenous monarchical traditions have refused to be completely extinguished. But on the whole, the divide between traditional rulers and Westernized leaders is a declining confrontation – whereas the divide between Westernized civilians and the armed forces threatens to be an indefinite contest for power.

In post-colonial Ghana every civilian ruler has been a Westernized university graduate, usually with a doctorate of a kind (Nkrumah, Busia and Limann). But the pendulum has then swung towards the soldiers as alternative rulers, usually less Westernized. Other African countries have also illustrated this pendular tendency between Westernized civilians and military rulers. Uganda's civilian rulers have included a product of Makerere College (Milton Obote), a former principal of Makerere College (Y. K. Lule), and the country's first Queen's Counsel (QC) in the British tradition (Godfrey Binaisa).

But some of Uganda's rulers have combined different credentials. Sir Edward Mutesa as the first president was both a traditional king and a Westernized African. Yoweri Museveni is both a soldier and a university graduate. The picture is not neatly in the proverbial 'black and white'. But in general it can indeed be re-affirmed that while the choice of African leaders during colonial rule was between traditional ones and the newly Westernized intelligentsia, the choice of leaders after independence has been between Westernized civilians and professional soldiers under modern arms.

But underlying all these tensions are the historic twin processes of nation-building and state-formation in twentieth-century Africa. Our emphasis in this chapter is on the post-colonial phase. But Africa's

<small>PLATE 15.1</small>   *King Mutesa II, the last* Kabaka *of Buganda, in military uniform*

problems after independence have been merely a continuation of its history before independence. And if nation-building and state-formation are central to our understanding of political Africa, let us be sure to understand the concepts of 'nation' and 'state' themselves.

Nation and state: towards definitions

The concept of a *nation* may refer to at least three categories of human groups. First, it may refer to 'a stable, historically developed community of people with a territory, economic life, distinctive culture, and language in common'. Secondly, it may refer to 'the people of a territory united under a single government; county; state'. Thirdly, a nation may refer to 'a people or tribe'.[1]

Often scholars in attempting to define the concept of *nation* make distinctions between objective and subjective properties of a nation. Among such objective indicators of a nation often mentioned are: language, history, territory, culture (at times including religion), political organization and economic life. The subjective indicators include a common

1. D. B. Guralnik, 1970, p. 946.

437

sense of identity and commitment or loyalty to the group. These psychological variables do not render themselves easy to measure. M. G. Smith, however, did a good job of combining both the objective and subjective variables when he defined a nation as

> . . . usually a single inclusive group whose members – or the majority of them – share common traditions, institutions, history, and ethnic identity.[2]

By our first definition, a nation may refer to the Igbo, Yoruba, or Hausa-Fulbe in Nigeria; the Kikuyu or Luo in Kenya, the Hutu in Burundi; or the Tswana in Botswana. For our purposes, however, the operational definition of a nation is the second one, which states that a nation is 'the people of a territory united under a single government', country, or state. By this definition, we should be talking about Nigeria, Kenya, Burundi and Botswana as *nations* – not about the various 'nations' within the nation-state or state-nation.

Much of the literature on nation-building refers to this process 'whereby people transfer their commitment and loyalty from smaller tribes, villages or petty principalities to the larger central political system'.[3] From their own experiences, Western writers also create the notion that state- and nation-building processes are two separate processes which eventually lead to the establishment of a nation-state. Implied in this view is that the development of a nation-state is the highest point in the process of state- and nation-building. Thus, in Western experience, the *nation* is normally established before the state, and the nation-state forms the end product of their processes. In essence, the process of nation-building is the cultivation by a people over time of political 'attitudes, beliefs and values – the development of a political culture'.[4] The emphasis in nation-building is thus on the 'congruity of cultural and political identities'.[5] It is a 'trend toward cultural homogeneity (nationhood)'.[6]

For us the process of nation-building does not involve the *transfer* of 'commitments and loyalties' from narrow or parochial levels of ethnic groups to a larger political unit such as Nigeria. That you are an Igbo, a Yoruba, or a Kikuyu, is a matter of identity. You cannot transfer it. You cannot cease being an Igbo or a Hausa or a Kikuyu simply because you so declare. For us it involves the widening (rather than transfer) of horizons of identity of parochial units to include larger units such as the state.

2. M. G. Smith, 1971, p. 32.
3. G. Almond and B. Powell, 1966, p. 36; see also L. Pye, 1962.
4. G. Almond and B. Powell, 1966, pp. 33–6; M. G. Smith, 1971, pp. 30–3.
5. This does not make sense in developing or Third-World states. For a good discussion of this, see S. Rokkan, 1973.
6. A. A. Mazrui and M. Tidy, 1984, p. 373.

By nation-building we refer to two dimensions of identity. One is closely linked to state-building. We refer to the progressive acceptance by members of the polity of the *legitimacy* of a central government, and identification with the central government as a symbol of the nation. This is the *vertical* dimension of nation-building – that is, that you not only have a *state*, but that people accept the authority of the state (and not merely its coercive power) and see its government as the symbol of their political community. Hence, secessionist bids in Nigeria, Ethiopia, the Sudan and Zaire were challenges to the authority of the central government and a denial of a shared sense of identity. The end of the civil war in Nigeria not only indicated the renewed acceptance of the Nigerian state by its citizens, but also an acceptance by Nigerians that the central government should be the symbol of an emerging Nigerian nation.

On the horizontal dimension, nation-building involves the acceptance of other members of the civic body as equal fellow-members of a 'corporate' nation – a recognition of the rights of other members to a share of common history, resources, values and other aspects of the state – buttressed by a sense of belonging to one political community. It involves the feeling that all members of the polity are entitled to a share of the sweet and the bitter in the process of political development – not only the sweet. Nation-building, therefore, is the widespread acceptance of the process of state-building; it is the creation of a political community that gives a fuller meaning to the life of the state.

Both processes of state- and nation-building can take place concurrently, and often do overlap. For many ex-colonial African states, the state has preceded the nation. Many groups of peoples were arbitrarily sandwiched into a territorial unit, which then formed a geopolitical entity called the state. To many of the peoples of these states, there was no identification with the state as a symbol of a people, a political community. In fact, most of these groups became exposed to one another in the terminal colonial period, as the colonial masters folded their political umbrellas and rolled their flags.[7]

For these peoples there was no sharing of common 'values, beliefs, and attitudes' among the peoples of new states that would have created a political culture. In addition, emerging mainly after the 1960s, the periods of state-building for many African states have been short. As experiments in state-building go on, so also have experiments in nation-building.

---

7. Thus, writing to the Nigerian head of state for the creation within Nigeria of a separate state (from the former Benue-Plateau State), the Plateau Students' Association (1974, p. 2) stated:

> The Tiv and Idoma have social set-ups, completely distinct from that shared by the various groups on the Plateau. There have been no cultural ties between our people of Southern Benue. History has it that we in fact never knew of their existence until recently.

These add to the strains on the capabilities of the political systems in all African states. Rajni Kothari was correct when he observed that in the Third World, 'the concept of nation itself tends to draw less from cultural and linguistic notions which were the origins of national consciousness in Europe and more from a transcendent notion of statehood which coincides with nationhood.'[8]

Furthermore, as Sheldon Gellar persuasively argued, the processes of state- and nation-building have witnessed the development of 'state-nations' which recognize the paradox of national integration, that is, 'diversity in unity' and not only 'unity in diversity'.[9] The process of nation-building could thus entail the creation of 'state-nations' as well as 'nation-states' as end products.

PLATE 15.2   *The Second Summit of the Maghreb Countries, Marrakesh, 15–16 February 1989; from left to right: President Ben Ali of Tunisia, President Muammar Kadhaffi of Libya, King Hassan II of Morocco, President Chadli Bendjedid of Algeria and President Ould Sid 'Ahmed Taya of Mauritania*

Does nation-building necessarily involve homogenization of cultural and political identities? As Clifford Geertz observed, any attempt at simple replacement of primordial ties and identifications by civil ones is 'sheer

8. R. Kothari, 1973, p. 104.
9. S. Gellar, 1972, pp. 40–1; see also M. Rejai and C. Enloe, 1969.

impossibility'.[10] The compromise is to be found, he contends, in 'adjustments between them', so that the processes of government can proceed
'fully without threatening the cultural framework of personal identity'.
Whatever discontinuities occur as a result of this would, therefore, 'not
radically distort political functioning'. Perhaps Ali Mazrui and Michael
Tidy are correct in suggesting that what nation-building implies is
'substantial cultural homogeneity' to enable the sense of nationhood to
stick.[11]

It may be argued, therefore, as Edmund Burke wrote, that 'the love of
the whole'

> is not extinguished by . . . subordinate partiality. . . . to be attached
> to the subdivision, to love the little platoon we belong to in society,
> is just the principle . . . of public affections.[12]

Perhaps it is the degree of attachment to the sub-national loyalties which
may threaten the whole. The process of nation-building consciously
attempts to widen the horizons of sub-national loyalties to coincide with
state boundaries, and ultimately partialize the level of commitment to the
parochial groups.

Finally, we should hasten to argue that the processes of *nation-building*
in African *states* have been punctuated by conflicts and crises. Given the
diversity of the groups involved in this process, conflict is inevitable. It
is not just the conflicts, but the intensity of the conflicts without
threatening the consensual values on which the association is grafted, that
are important in the process of nation-building. As Ali Mazrui has
suggested, 'an accumulated experience of resolving conflicts between
antithetical forces is, after all, one of the great indices of national
integration'.[13] After all Lewis Coser has argued that conflicts may be
positively functional to group solidarity.[14]

For our purposes, 'changing political structures' refer to political
institutions inherited and the amendments to these and/or new institutions
introduced to assist African states to build a nation, after their independence in the 1960s.

From colonial models to independence constitutions

In addition to indirect rule, the British established *legislative councils* in
their colonies. The membership of these changed in composition from

10. C. Geertz, 1963, p. 155; see also M. Fortes and E. E. Evans-Pritchard, 1940, and
P. Brown, 1970, for another typology.
11. A. A. Mazrui and M. Tidy, 1984, p. 373.
12. Quoted in S. Huntington, 1968, p. 30.
13. A. A. Mazrui, 1969a, p. 105; see also A. A. Mazrui and M. Tidy, 1984, p. 12;
J. F. A. Ajayi, 1968, p. 194; and I. L. Markovitz, 1977, p. 47.
14. L. Coser, 1956, p. 188.

predominantly white administrators to Africans and from appointed members to elected members, towards the terminal stage of colonialism. The process was gradually democratized as prospects for self-government and independence became greater.

In the last years of colonial rule, the British transferred to their territories the 'Westminster' model of government – in Nigeria, Sudan, Kenya, Uganda, Zimbabwe, Tanganyika, Ghana and others. Except in a few cases such as Tanzania, this model encouraged multi-partyism and electoral competition among such parties. As prospects for independence came closer in these territories, semblances of 'parliaments' (very often bicameral) began to emerge and Africans began a period of tutelage in the operation of the cabinet system as some elected members became ministers. Similarly, the British often bequeathed federal structures (which they did not have at home) to their colonies.

In this terminal colonial period, the prospect of independence brought together many ethnic groups or 'cultural nations' to compete for political power, now to be bequeathed to the new state. Very often the competitive setting led to a new parochialism based on awareness of one another in a competitive setting. Thus political élites often withdrew into their ethnic or geo-ethnic or regional platforms to mobilize support for such competition. The Northern People's Congress (NPC) and the Action Group (AG) in Nigeria; the National Liberation Movement (NLM), the Northern People's Party (NPP), and Togoland Congress Party (TCP) in Ghana; the ABAKO, the *Confédération des associations tribales du Katanga* (CONAKAT) in Zaire; and the *Kabaka Yekka* (KY) Party and the Democratic Party (DP) in Uganda, are only a few examples of these parties. All these were providing a setting for the politics of the post-colonial era. Some of these parties, such as CONAKAT, were even sponsored by business concerns in the colony or by the colonial authority itself in order to dilute support for national parties. The seeds of future dependency were being sown.

There were, however, territory-wide political parties which in mobilizing the masses for political action, tried as much as possible to transcend parochial horizons of loyalty and commitments. As noted in an earlier chapter, among such political parties was the National Council for Nigeria and Cameroons (NCNC – later 'for Nigerian Citizens' after Western Cameroon opted out of Nigeria). The NCNC later staged a retreat from being a nationwide party and gave the semblance of being a regional party.

We have noted that in Guinea the *Parti démocratique de la Guinée* (PDG) under Sékou Touré mobilized various ethnic groups and trades unions into an effective national institution for participation. Not only did this party organization drive underground other ethnic associations and parties, it effectively mobilized the Guinea people against French rule. We know that the 'No' vote to de Gaulle's referendum of 1958 came as a shock to the French after the pro-France campaigns of de Gaulle. In fact, the attempt to transcend ethnicity is amply illustrated by the ability of the PDG to get five of its leaders selected in the 1956 'municipal elections outside their regions of origin'.[15] Sékou Touré's ancestry also created some form of traditional legitimacy for him, though with some risk of alienating other ethnic groups.[16]

Senghor's *Bloc démocratique sénégalais* (BDS) transcended ethnic loyalties and mobilized Senegalese people for independence. It is even more interesting that Senghor, a Christian in a predominantly Muslim country, could so effectively woo prominent Muslim religious leaders, or *marabouts*, to his side. These people were very important in Senghor's victory over his opponent Lamine Gueye. More than anything else, Senghor's experience illustrates an effective if inchoate process of nation-building before independence. This Roman Catholic ruled a country which was over 80 per cent Muslim – a great ecumenical achievement.

Senghor's experience was in a way similar to that of Julius Nyerere of Tanzania. He not only hailed from a small ethnic group (the Wazanaki), but found himself operating as a Christian in a country with a Muslim plurality. But Nyerere had neither the large and autonomous sub-state 'nations' nor the linguistic problems of Nigeria. Tanzania is a poly-ethnic but not a multi-national state in the sense that Nigeria is, and it has Kiswahili as a country-wide language which provides an umbrella over other differences. Julius Nyerere helped to establish the Tanganyika African National Union (TANU) in 1954. This sole party led Tanganyika to independence without much opposition, ruling the country until it expanded into *Chama cha Mapinduzi* (CCM) in 1977.

In other areas, such as Uganda, pluralism did create problems, as we stated earlier. Though an essentially pan-ethnic party, Milton Obote's Uganda People's Congress (UPC) found that it had to go into alliance with the *Kabaka Yekka* (KY) to form a government at independence. The duality of the *kabaka*'s role as the king of Buganda and the ceremonial president of Uganda did create problems of nation-building and symbolism of nationhood. Kenyatta's Kenya created a mobilization organ, the Kenya African Union (KAU) and later the Kenya African National Union (KANU). Essentially ethnic, it was dominated by the Kikuyu and the Luo in an uneasy alliance. On the eve of independence, the fear of a one-party-state under Kikuyu–Luo dominance had led to the formation of the Kenya African Democratic Union (KADU) which was also pan-ethnic. But KANU won the 1961 elections to the legislative council, and fought for Kenyatta's release from prison. The 1963 elections swept Kenyatta to power as prime minister, and independence came in December, 1963.

15. A. A. Mazrui and M. Tidy, 1984, p. 90.
16. Sékou Touré was the grandson of the Samori Touré, the Mande king.

The Zairean experience was more turbulent. Lumumba's party, *Mouvement national congolais* (MNC) was a pan-ethnic political party. A nationalist and pan-Africanist, Lumumba was able to mobilize the Zairois (or Congolese) to press for independence. His main opposition parties were more parochial in their bases of appeal. ABAKO, for example, pushed for separation and the formation of a Congo state which could later on merge with French Congo (later Congo, Brazzaville.)[17] The CONAKAT, under Moïse Tshombe, opted for secession. This situation led to a civil war immediately after independence. Lumumba's was an uphill task – to unite a country which was constantly threatened by foreigners and Zairois alike. It is ironic that after independence Mobutu found it necessary to use Lumumba's name as one of the symbols of nation-building. Thus, what Lumumba could not do while alive, Mobutu was trying to do in (deceased) Lumumba's name.

Not all nationalist reactions, in the last years of colonialism, ended up in peaceful concession of independence by colonial authorities. In Angola, Zimbabwe, Mozambique, Guinea-Bissau and Algeria, there were armed struggles. The *Partido Africano para a Independência de Guiné e Cabo Verde* (PAIGC) in Guinea-Bissau was able to effectively mobilize the people for anti-colonial struggle. In fact the Guinea-Bissau *nation* was born before the *state* – a rare occurrence in Africa. Nation-building became a condition here for the attainment of a state. Angola, immediately after the precipitate withdrawal of the Portuguese, was embroiled in a civil war among the *Movimento Popular de Libertação de Angola* (MPLA) under Agostinho Neto, the *Frente Nacional de Libertação de Angola* (FNLA) under the leadership of Roberto Holden, and the *União Nacional para a Independência total de Angola* (UNITA), led by Jonas Savimbi. With the backing of the Organization of African Unity (OAU), the MPLA government of Agostinho Neto was recognized as the legitimate government of Angola.

Elsewhere in Southern Africa, the white-settler element created problems of decolonization for the British. Here, racism and ethnicity played an important part. Kamuzu Banda's Malawi Congress Party (MCP) was able to mobilize Africans against racism and colonialism in Malawi. He succeeded in getting an independent Nyasaland, baptized as Malawi.

In Zimbabwe the struggle was as much a fight against racism as colonialism. In the process, the ethnic cleavages between the Shona and Ndebele played an important part. South Africa continued its *apartheid* policy in spite of Macmillan's 'wind of change' speech there, and held on to its usurped authority over Namibia.

At independence, therefore, a number of features were discernible in the new states. Traditional African religion and Islam survived colonial

17. A. A. Mazrui and M. Tidy, 1984, p. 96; see also C. Young, 1965, p. 659.

rule, and Christianity attained greater saliency in Africa's triple religions – traditional, Islamic and Christian. These had consequences for communal stability and nation-building after independence.

Traditional leadership and authority survived colonial rule and their roles differed between Francophone and Anglophone states. Traditional authority attained higher political saliency in Anglophone than in Francophone states. This had consequences (as the experiences of Nigeria and Uganda later illustrated) not only for state-building but also nation-building.

Western education became a passport to the modernizing sector of society. More than that, Western education created a new African élite, which, at different levels and given their colonial experiences, suffered from cultural schizophrenia.[18]

Political parties emerged in Africa, and with few exceptions such as Tanzania (and given its peculiar nature, Guinea-Bissau), colonial authorities encouraged multi-partism. Often this encouragement emanated from the desire to divide the ranks of nationalist movements or from the desire of these colonial authorities to transfer to the colonies their model of 'democracy' at home. Thus all colonial authorities, apart from Portugal, bequeathed to African states parliamentary systems along with multi-partism.

Similarly, European laws were imposed at territorial level to govern or regulate the behaviour of colonized peoples. The Francophone and Anglophone countries not only inherited these laws but also the judicial institutions of the imperial country. No wonder Nigeria still operates the English Common Law as the core of its legal system.

Colonial bureaucracies were inherited by the new political élite. These bureaucracies were essentially colonial structures of administration for the maintenance of law and order, and for extraction of resources. How have these changed? What new goals have been set for them?

Finally, the forms of government bequeathed to the élites on independence had their own contradictions. While Britain is unitary in spite of its cultural pluralism, it often bequeathed federal or quasi-federal institutions to its ex-colonies. Nigeria, Kenya, Ghana,[19] the Federation of Rhodesia and Nyasaland and Uganda's amorphous and contradictory federal-unitary relations between sub-national units and the centre are examples.

If de Gaulle's France had operated a federal colonial West and Equatorial Africa, de Gaulle never favoured federalism and even worked against it. As he once said:

18. See A. A. Mazrui, 1978, p. 392.
19. This was challenged and effectively changed by Nkrumah's CPP. Ghana became a unitary government.

It is not certain that the concept of a federation, which replaces in certain areas to a certain extent the concept of colonization, is always very good and very practical, and particularly in Africa – but not only in Africa, for in fact, that consists in automatically putting together very different peoples, sometimes very different indeed, and who, in consequence do not like it at all. One sees this in Canada, one sees this in Rhodesia, in Malaysia, in Cyprus, and one sees it in Nigeria . . .[20]

Most Francophone states inherited unitary governments except for Cameroon, which tried federalism for a brief period after its absorption of Western Cameroons from Nigeria. The Senegal–Sudan (Mali) federation attempt failed.

Let us now turn to how African leaders coped with the problems of creating *nations* out of the *states* inherited from colonial rule.

Integrative processes and changing political structures

On attaining independence, the leaders of Africa's new states found that they had to grapple with basic challenges of nationhood and statehood – that is, the challenges of political development. These challenges included

(1) centralization of political *authority*, often referred to as the process of state-building;
(2) creating *unity* among heterogenous groups in their polity, often referred to as the process of *nation-building*;
(3) providing avenues for political *participation*; and
(4) distributing scarce but allocatable resources.[21]

If earlier developers such as Britain and the United States had had the luxury of treating these challenges sequentially, African states found that that technique had become a luxury. The technological revolution which also entailed a communication revolution had not only created a smaller globe, thus denying these states the relative isolation within which to tackle these problems, but had made simultaneous solutions to these challenges a political imperative. Thus new leaders who took over the reins of government soon found their decision-making units overloaded with demands and expectations but with few capabilities and resources to meet them.

The first shock was that those political leaders, especially those in British Africa who had undergone a period of dyarchy with colonial rulers, soon found that the new parliamentary system they were to implement did not give them as much power as it gave to their predecessors. Thus, if the colonial governor-general combined legislative and

20. C. de Gaulle, 1968, p. 1186.
21. This is the Social Science Research Council position. See L. Binder *et al.*, 1971.

executive powers, the new system had checks and balances and division of functions between the executive, the legislature and the judiciary. Schooled in authoritarian colonial political culture, it was not easy making a transition to parliamentary democracy with values of participation, accommodation of political opponents, and the spirit of tolerance.

Did the new political élites actually try to change the inherited political structures such that they could build a 'nation' out of the state they were now leading? Using the *inheritance* model,[22] what did the heirs of the colonial legacy do with the inherited political structures in the nation-building process?

By our inheritance model, the colonial authorities bequeathed to indigenous political élites a central government with control over instruments of coercion and maintenance of law and order, such as the police, the army, and the legal system. The bureaucracy which they inherited was not only the largest employer, it was to be the main engine of growth. The government also had the greatest economic resources in the state.

Given these legacies, were the new élites able to dissociate themselves from the colonial structures in order to achieve new goals? To a large extent Sheldon Gellar was correct in observing that

> Since the control over the colonial territorial centre and its resources was the main prize of pre-independence politics, there was little desire to diminish this prize. On the contrary the main goal for inheritance elites after independence was precisely the consolidation and expansion of state authority.[23]

There was hardly any effort at making substantial changes in the inherited institutions for purposes of nation-building. In any case the multi-national and poly-ethnic structures of these countries did not change overnight because they had attained independence. The heterogeneity of these states was also part of the legacy of colonial rule. New states in Africa, except in the very few cases we have mentioned earlier, hardly coincided with the boundaries of old nations, empires and kingdoms. For the new leaders, nation-building was really a long-term goal. More immediate was the desire to consolidate the powers of the centre they had inherited and penetrate the periphery more effectively – that is, state-building. Actually, when political élites speak of nation-building, they

> make it clear that strengthening the centre, either through the state and/or the party, comes first in their order of priorities since the state and/or party is perceived as the principal instrument for creating a national consciousness.[24]

22. This model was used by S. Gellar, 1972, pp. 384–426.
23. *ibid.*, p. 398.
24. H. Bienen, 1974, p. 215.

Given these circumstances, therefore, it was more in the interest of the inheritance élites to retain the colonial political structures which were not, in the first place, established for nation-building purposes. Continuity in institutions provided relative predictability and security for the leaders. Where there were changes, reformist (rather than revolutionary) options were chosen.

It was hardly surprising, then, that gradually the central bureaucracy in post-colonial African societies expanded rapidly. The structures not only remained essentially as those established by the colonialists, their goals hardly changed. Francophone West African states, as well as Ghana, Nigeria, Kenya and Uganda, illustrate such expansions in the bureaucracy at the expense of political parties. This was mainly because bureaucracies were seen as institutions for political control. With regard to Kenya, as Henry Bienen has clearly illustrated, the civil service provided more opportunities for participation and representation than the political party, KANU.[25] Kenya's regional administration is reputedly strong and centralized under the office of the president.

The Nigerian bureaucracy expanded rapidly after independence but hardly showed any signs of other forms of change. The general orders, which governed the behaviour of the civil service, were written under the colonial regime and for a long time had perquisites which Europeans inserted for themselves such as 'bush allowance', 'horse allowance', and so on.

In essence only in a few states such as Tanzania were there attempts to set new goals for the state bureaucracy. Nyerere within the context of his Arusha Declaration envisaged a new role for the bureaucracy – to 'enable the Central Government to give guidance and assistance to local people, as well as check on their work, while it reduces the amount of red tape and bureaucracy which is, at present, in danger of strangling our people's enthusiasm.'[26]

In most of Africa, the influence of the bureaucracy increased but it was not always clear that their roles had changed. If colonial rule saw the bureaucracy as an instrument for maintaining law and order as well as for exploitation, inheritance élites did not go much beyond this to include welfare of the people as a goal. In some states, such as Nigeria, it took various successors to inheritance élites to get the bureaucracy to intervene in essential areas of the private sector which affected the lives of the people.[27] This was something Tanzania had embarked upon much earlier.

25. *ibid.*
26. J. K. Nyerere, 1972, p. 2.
27. Nigeria, Federal Republic of, 1972; see also P. Collins, 1983, pp. 412–14.
This is the decree aimed at indigenization of the economy, thus giving the bureaucracy additional powers of intervention in the private sector in order to protect the interest of Nigerians. It took 12 years before such an action could be taken.

Perhaps, it is pertinent at this point to note that, because of the European colonial policies described earlier, and the differences in administrative styles, Francophone state bureaucracies were generally more dependent on the ex-colonial power than the Anglophone state bureaucracies which had been used to a relatively higher degree of autonomy.

The currencies of the new states also reflected the caution on the part of the inheritance élites in effecting changes. Much of Francophone Africa still operates in the franc currency zone, while many Anglophone states operate in the sterling zone. Nigeria only left the sterling zone in 1973, while Tanzania, Kenya and Uganda still use the word 'shilling' as a currency denomination.

The pluralism of African countries extended to language – as indicated in the chapter on language and social change. The Francophone states, of course, use French as the official language, while most Anglophone states still use English as the official language. In East Africa Kiswahili has been adopted as an official language in Kenya, Tanzania and, for a while, Uganda. It is hoped that Kiswahili will turn out to be a unifying force in these countries in the future. The introduction of Arabic as Sudan's official language was resisted in vain by the southern Sudanese. But English has a role in southern Sudan. Liberia adopted English as the official language, while Ethiopia uses Amharic for the same purpose. Angola, Guinea-Bissau, Cape Verde, Sao Tome and Principe and Mozambique use Portuguese as the official language. The dangers of introducing a national language had dissuaded inheritance élites from effecting changes. For most of them, in any case, it was not a priority.

The educational system was hardly changed in content in either Francophone or Anglophone states. However, as indicated in the chapter on education and social change, there was an expansion of the school systems. These schools were not used for purposes of socialization of youths for nation-building. Thus Shakespearean literature and British and Commonwealth history featured prominently in Anglophone African educational curricula. In Nigeria (and this was true for most Anglophone states) many adults who studied for the General Certificate of Education examination registered for subjects such as 'British Constitution', even though they hardly understood their own nation's constitution. If the Gauls were presented in France's empire as the ancestors of Francophone Africans, it was not the priority of the inheritance élite of some states to focus on changes in the content of education. In any case, French colonial education as a tool in cultural imperialism was even more thorough and effective than British or Belgian education.

Traditional institutions had been really weakened by colonial rule. However, in Nigeria and Uganda traditional rulers played an active role in politics and administration. In Uganda, the *kabaka* (or king of the Baganda) became the president of the country (1963) as a whole in almost the same way as Lesotho's king ascended to political heights even in the new

449

political set-up. In Northern Nigeria, the emirs wielded substantial power through the native-authority systems inherited from colonial rulers but which did not undergo any real changes until the advent of military rule. In Tanzania, while chieftaincy was legally abolished, chiefs still existed and operated albeit at a very low-key level. Guinea abolished chieftaincy as a reactionary institution after independence; so did Rwanda.[28]

In the French empire, the French had done an effective job of relegating chiefs to political obscurity for the inheritance élites. But in Swaziland a traditional leader, King Sobhuza, wielded executive authority for decades in a country of about half a million people.

Reactions to traditional institutions in independent African states have been varied, but at least three basic patterns are easily identified. First, is the reaction of inheritance élites, some of whom had roots in traditional royalty, to define and limit the powers of the chiefs in politics and administration, as in Nigeria before 1966. The second reaction, as in Nkrumah's Ghana, relegates the chiefs to political obscurity but concedes to them advisory powers. The third is one which sees no place for them in the new political set-up, as in Guinea or Rwanda.[29] However, traditional institutions have persisted (if on the defensive and in decline) and still have to be dealt with today by either military and/or civilian regimes. Their political resilience is to be found in the nature of African community life in rural areas. Traditional rulers represent one of the continuities in Africa's political history. Nigeria's first Republic maintained regional houses of chiefs – a demonstration of their saliency in politics.[30] Today Nigeria operates traditional councils at sub-national state levels. These councils are essentially advisory in matters such as chieftaincy, culture and local government. The tension between traditionalists and the Westernized is now overshadowed by the divide between the military and Westernized civilians.

Ideology and political systems

Generally because of the fragility of authority in African states, most inheritance élites preferred unitary systems of government. In Ghana, Nkrumah succeeded in getting a unitary constitution for the country and so the regional legislatures disappeared. In mobilizing against federal or quasi-federal institutions in Ghana, Nkrumah was trying to overcome any threats of aggressive regionalism in the country. Kenya at independence was laden with regional legislatures under the *majimbo* constitution. Kenyatta did his best to weaken and kill regional administration and

28. L. Rubin and B. Weinstein, 1974, pp. 213–14.
29. *ibid.*
30. All the three regions, except the Eastern Region, had houses of chiefs after independence.

legislature. As Kenyatta told the National Assembly in 1964, 'The majority of the voters in Kenya agree with KANU that the constitution was too rigid, expensive, and unworkable.'[31] He gradually reduced the powers of the regions such that they had 'no executive authority or legislative competence in any matter'. Local governments were brought directly under central-government control and the public service was centralized.

In the same vein, Kenya moved away from the parliamentary system as it had been inherited at independence. As the minister of justice and constitutional affairs, Mr Tom Mboya, told the same parliament:

> The historical process by which, in other lands, Heads of State, whether Kings or Presidents have become figureheads, are no part of our African tradition. So in this respect, we politely reject the Westminster model. The man we choose for our President will be the leader of our nation and the leader of our Government; and this, Sir, is what our people understand.[32]

Thus, Kenya not only had a unitary constitution by the time it became a republic, it shifted to an executive presidential system in which the president was also to be an elected member of the parliament. Even Kenya's institutional adjustment, as we have seen, buttresses our earlier contention that inheritance élites' priorities after independence were the consolidation of the colonial state and central government that had been bequeathed to them. If regionalism had been overcome, echoes of ethnicity were still being heard on the political horizon.

Unlike Kenya, Nigeria operated a federal system of government, originally based on three regions. The aggressive ethno-regional politics of Nigeria led to the emergence of strong regions under powerful regional premiers, and a weak centre in the context of a parliamentary system. Unlike Kenya, Nigeria did not go presidential after becoming a republic. Centrifugal forces were so powerful in the country, that Balewa, the first prime minister after independence, remained a weakened leader of a fragile central government. Nigeria's federal system was popularly described as one in which '*regional tails wagged the federal dog*'. Threats of secession by regions in the period 1950–66 were rife in the polity. Nigeria's inheritance élite found it very difficult to centralize authority and/or consolidate the inherited state.[33]

Francophone states remained unitary in their governments except for Cameroon, which turned federal with the incorporation of Western Cameroon into that state. With the ghost of French colonial presence

31. Kenya, Republic of, *Official Report*, House of Representatives, First Parliament, Second Session, vol. II, part II, 14 August 1964, cols 1707–10, in C. Gertzel *et al.*, 1972, p. 193.
32. *ibid.*, p. 195.
33. See J. I. Elaigwu, 1979, pp. 155–81, for some discussion of this.

behind the inheritance élites, the consolidation of their dependent state did not seem to be as much of a problem as in Anglophone states which had had a history of autonomy for sub-national units.

Another experiment at federalism was the quasi-federal association between Zanzibar and Tanganyika, thus transforming the country into Tanzania under the TANU political party.

Generally, African inheritance leaders preferred the unitary system which assisted in the consolidation of their power base. In addition, federalism is expensive to operate.

Ideologically, it is possible to identify some 'radical' African states and 'moderate' African states in terms of their choice of paths of economic development. As William Foltz correctly pointed out, ideologies were important in African mobilization for development. However,

> these ideologies should not be seen in classic 'left–right' terms; the distinction between those states hewing to some explicitly socialist policy and those favouring a more capitalist mode of development rather concerns alternate means of achieving similar ends of political control.[34]

Thus, while Tanzania, Mozambique and Guinea-Conakry preferred to go 'socialist', Nigeria, Kenya and the Côte d'Ivoire opted for the 'capitalist' route of development. Of all African states, Tanzania under TANU and later CCM leadership seems to have ventured further into structural reorganization in order to achieve the declared ideological objectives of the *ujamaa* villages and the Arusha Declaration.[35]

Of course, other African leaders had espoused their own philosophies of the state. Obote's *Common Man's Charter*, Sékou Touré's *National Democracy*, and Senghor's *Négritude* are all examples of the philosophical positions of these leaders. But few of these leaders really empirically mobilized the populace to achieve their dreams of the state.[36]

To what extent did the political parties, which really were the indigenous institutions of political participation and mobilization, perform effectively? To what extent were these institutions used for political integration? Sheldon Gellar was persuasive in assuming that

> to the extent that the party was an indigenous institution whose functioning depended largely upon the organizational skills of its leaders and energies of its followers, it was less tied to colonial institutions and norms and therefore could be used as a more popular agent for promoting a post-colonial national identity than could the state.[37]

34. W. J. Foltz, 1973, p. 365.
35. See J. K. Nyerere, 1967b and 1968b; and United Republic of Tanzania, 1967a and 1967b.
36. See G. C. Mutiiso and S. W. Rohio, 1975.
37. S. Gellar, 1972, p. 401.

In some states, especially the relatively 'radical' single-party states, the value of political parties as mobilizational instruments of nation-building heightened after independence. Tanzania's TANU, Guinea-Bissau's PAIGC, and the PDG of Guinea are examples of single-party states in which the parties served as vehicles for relative dissociation from ex-colonial rulers and for effecting changes in inherited political structures.

In many states, the trend has been in the direction of one-party state or one-party-dominant state – for example, KANU in Kenya, the CPP in Ghana, the *Union démocratique voltaïque* in Upper Volta (now Burkina Faso), the *Union soudanaise* in Mali, the *Parti démocratique de la Côte d'Ivoire* (PDCI) in Côte d'Ivoire (as from 1957), and the Malawi Congress Party (as from 1966). In Senegal, the *Union progressiste sénégalaise* (UPS) has been the dominant party in the state. In Cameroon, the *Union nationale camerounaise* became the only party as from 1966. The politics of consolidation of the inherited state often entailed killing opposition parties, sometimes through legislation, and at other times, through different mechanisms of political overkill. Many of these parties, unlike the ones in the 'radical' states, were dormant between elections. Some of them became increasingly personalized with the rise of authoritarian executives in the context of political insecurity and centrifugal social forces in the state.

Thus by 1966 the trend was in the direction of single-party states or single-party-dominant states. Some of these parties, as in Kenya, have managed to contain ethnic conflicts. Others hardly changed the polity or mobilized the people, but virtually became bureaucratic institutions of control and penetration of the periphery.

Yet in countries such as Nigeria, Zaire, civilian Ghana after Nkrumah, and Uganda, which have had multi-party systems under civilian rule, the conflicts generated by parochial parties had provided an opportunity for military interventions.

Increasingly, political parties in such systems ceased to become organs for articulating and aggregating the interests of the masses. Nor did they provide alternative political élites for ruling the countries. As political parties decayed, so also did electoral competitive processes and the inherited functional legislative institutions. In place of parties arose strong individual executives – such as Nkrumah, Sékou Touré, Houphoüet-Boigny, Kaunda, Kenyatta, Banda, Ahidjo and others – whose political parties always won elections.

However, in the context of nation-building, it seems that single-party states, such as Tanzania, Guinea-Bissau, Guinea-Conakry under Sékou Touré, Côte d'Ivoire, Kenya and Cameroon, have had a better record of creating a semblance of unity in their countries than multi-party states. Multi-party states, such as Nigeria, Zaire and Uganda, found it difficult to curb the parochial nationalisms of the various 'nations' within them. Does this recommend the single-party system for Africa? It is hard to say as the records of some single-parties, such as in Burkina Faso (formerly

453

Upper Volta), Mali and Nkrumah's Ghana, did not prevent military interventions. It must, however, be conceded that in Nkrumah's Ghana, aggressive ethnicity was not really a feature of the polity. Does Mugabe's push for a one-party state entail an attempt to contain ethnicity?

Part of the problem of nation-building inherited by African élites was cultural sub-nationalism. Nigeria experienced a bitter civil war (1967–70) as a climax of its inter-ethnic strife. Uganda's inter-ethnic squabbles have succeeded in immobilizing every leader except Amīn, whose dispensation of misery among Ugandan people united most Ugandans against him. The communal conflicts in Zaire exploded into a civil war (1960–65) which led to military intervention and the ascendancy of General Mobutu. Chad is ridden with different types of communal instability – religious, racial, ethnic and ideological – all mixed up in a complex form. Sudan was engaged in a civil war from 1955 to 1972; it has again relapsed into civil war. Angola had a civil war from 1975–6 after independence. The conflict continued, with the rebel UNITA forces, led by Savimbi, controlling substantial parts of the country, until a cease-fire was signed on 31 May 1991. Ethiopia had one or more civil wars from 1961 to 1991. Prospects for reconciliation improved after the flight from the country of Mengistu Haile Mariam in 1991.

All the above are manifestations of ethnic, racial and sometimes religious strife which bedevilled the capabilities of the inheritance élites. After independence, aggressive domestic communal and parochial nationalisms emerged which, during the anti-colonial nationalist period, had been submerged. Thus the capacity of the inheritance élites to build a nation out of a state was often inhibited or complicated by cultural sub-nationalism. In their reaction, the leaders opted for an immediate process of consolidation of state power before embarking on the arduous process of nation-building. In some cases ethnic and racial differences were reinforced by class distinctions – as the cases of Burundi and Rwanda illustrate in the relation between the ruling Tutsi and the ruled Hutu.

To summarize then, post-colonial Africa showed relative continuity of political structures inherited from colonial regimes. There have been very few attempts at changing political institutions fundamentally, for purposes of nation-building. However, Western parliamentary institutions gradually failed as political parties and legislatures declined in their importance and as elective processes decayed. Authoritarian executives emerged and compounded problems of political succession. But what led to the spate of military interventions in African politics and how did the military react to existing political structures in the context of nation-building?

The pendulum of civil–military relations

Since the Egyptian army overthrew King Farouk in 1952, military coups have spread across Africa – from the Sudanese coup of 1958, in Zaire

(1965), Dahomey or Benin Republic (December 1965), Central African Republic (January 1966), Nigeria (January 1966) and Ghana (February 1966) to the piecemeal supplanting of Emperor Haile Selassie of Ethiopia in 1974 and the overthrow of Moktar Ould Daddah in 1978. More recently, there have been coups in Ghana (December 1981), Nigeria (December 1983) and Mauritania (1984). By the mid-1980s, Africa had had more than 70 military coups (Table 15.1).

Why have there been military coups in Africa? What are the causes of constant extensions of the boundaries of the barracks into the political arena? It is possible to identify at least four broad reasons for military implosions into the African political arena.[38] First are causes which are basically *ecological* or societal (that is, from the socio-political and economic environment). Among such reasons are cleavages in the socio-political structure (ethnicity, class, and so on), leadership controversy, political ineptitude of leaders, economic malaise and 'praetorian' traits in the society. The second broad cause of military intervention in politics has its roots in *intra-military* or *socio-military* sources (that is, those factors within the military which encourage the military to attempt coups and/or those factors within the society which gate-crash through the boundaries of the barracks). These include the level of professionalism of the military, civilian intervention in decidedly military matters, political use of a supposedly apolitical army, tensions in barracks, rival military or para-military units used by the political leader, defeat in war and generational cleavage.

The third source of military coups in Africa is *extra-societal* or *international* (factors within the international environment which give momentum to coups within the nation-state). Among these are cross-national contagious effects of coups from one country to another, training sources of the officer corps, externally instigated subversion and more direct external intervention (especially when an ex-colonial master intervenes with its own troops).

Finally, we may look at other causes of coups which may be classified under *miscellaneous*. These include personality conflicts between the military chief and the supreme political leader, problems of development overwhelming the capability of leaders, institutional transfer and inchoate socialization processes of the military in the value of civilian supremacy.

After intervention, the military find themselves laden with the same problems that the civilian regimes had experienced. The problems of state- and nation-building, as well as economic development, stare them in the face. Africa's experience shows that, depending on the country and the socio-political context, the military play *guardianship*, *reformist* or *radical* roles.[39]

38. See J. I. Elaigwu, 1981, pp. 17–38.
39. C. E. Welch Jr and A. K. Smith, 1974, pp. 55–70.

TABLE 15.1   *Government changes in Africa, 1962–92*

Country	Colonial name	Date of independence	Capital city	Leaders since independence	Coups
Algeria	Algeria	1962	Algiers	Ahmed Ben Bella, 1962–5 Col. Houari Boumedienne, 1965–78 Chadli Bendjedid, 1978–92 Mohamed Boudiaf, 1992 'Ali Kai, 1992–	1965
Angola	Angola	1975	Luanda	Dr Agostinho Neto, 1975–9 José Eduardo dos Santos, 1979–	
Benin	Dahomey	1960	Porto-Novo (officially) Cotonou (in practice)	Hubert Maga, 1960–3 Gen. Christophe Soglo, 1963–4 Sourou-Migan Apithy (Pres.), Justin Ahomadegbe (Vice Pres.), 1964–5 Tahirou Congacou, 1965 Gen. Soglo, 1965–7 Lt. Col. Alphonse Alley (Pres.), 1967–8 Dr Emile Zinsou, 1968–9 Maj. Kouandete, 1969 Hubert Maga, 1970 Sourou-Migan Apithy, 1971 Justin Ahomadegbe, 1972 Maj. (later Lt.-Gen.) Matthieu Kerekou, 1972–91 Nicéphore Soglo, 1991–	1963 1965 1965 1967 1969 1972
Botswana	Bechuanaland	1966	Gaborone	Sir Seretse Khama, 1966–80 Dr Quett Masire, 1980–	
Burkina Faso (since 1984)	Upper Volta	1960	Ouagadougou	Maurice Yameogo, 1960–6 Lt.-Col. (later Gen.) Sangoule Lamizana, 1966–80 Col. Saye Zerbo, 1980–2 Maj. Jean-Baptiste Ouedraogo, 1982–3 Capt. Thomas Sankara, 1983–7 Capt. Blaise Compaoré, 1987–	1966 1980 1982 1983 1987
Burundi	Part of Rwanda-Urundi	1962	Bujumbura	Mwami Mwambutsa IV, 1962–5 Col. Michel Micombero, 1966–76 Lt.-Col. Jean-Baptiste Bagaza, 1976–87 Maj. Pierre Buyoya, 1987–	1966 1976 1987
Cameroon	French Cameroon and British Cameroon	1960	Yaoundé	Ahmadou Ahidjo, 1960–82 Paul Biya, 1982–	
Cape Verde	Cape Verde Islands	1975	Praia	Aristides Pereira, 1975–91 Antonio Mascarenhas Monteiro, 1991–	
Central African Republic	Ubangui-Chari	1960	Bangui	David Dacko, 1960–6 Lt.-Col. (later Emperor) Jean-Bedel Bokassa, 1966–79	1966

456

Country	Colonial name	Date of independence	Capital city	Leaders since independence	Coups
				David Dacko, 1979–81	1979
				Gen. André Kolingba, 1981–	1981
Chad	Chad	1960	N'Djamena	François Ngarta Tombalbaye, 1960–75	
				Maj.-Gen. Félix Malloum, 1975–9	1975
				Goukouni Oueddei, 1979–82	1979
				Hissène Habré, 1982–90	1982
				Idriss Deby, 1990–	1990
Comoros	Comoros	1975	Moroni	Ahmed Abdallah, 1975	
				Ali Soilih, 1975–8	1975
				Ahmed Abdallah and Mohamed Ahmed (co-Presidents), 1978–89	1978
				Said Mohamed Djohar, 1989–	
Congo	Congo	1960	Brazzaville	Abbé Fulbert Youlou, 1960–3	
				Alphonse Massemba-Debat, 1963–8	
				Capt. (later Maj.) Marien Ngouabi, 1968–77	1968
				Col. Joachim Yhombi-Opango, 1977–9	
				Col. (later Gen.) Denis Sassou-Nguesso, 1979–91	
				Gen. Denis Sassou-Nguesso (Pres.), 1991–2	
				PM: André Milongo, 1991–2	
				Pascal Lissouba (Pres.), 1992–	
Côte d'Ivoire	Côte d'Ivoire	1960	Abidjan	Félix Houphouët-Boigny, 1960–	
Djibouti	French Somaliland then Afars and Issas	1977	Djibouti	Hassan Gouled, 1977	
				Hassan Gouled Aptidon, 1977–	
Egypt	Egypt	1922	Cairo	King Farouk, 1937–52	
				Gen. Muhammad Naguib, 1952–4	1952
				Lt.-Col. Gamāl 'Abd al-Nasser, 1954–70	
				Muhammad Anwar al-Sadat, 1970–81	
				Hosni Mubarak, 1981–	
Equatorial Guinea	Fernando Poo and Rio Muni	1968	Malabo	Francisco Macias Nguema, 1968–79	
				Lt.-Col. (later Brig.-Gen.) Teodoro Obiang Nguema Mbasogo, 1979–	1979
Ethiopia	Ethiopia	1st century of the Christian era	Addis-Ababa	Emperor Haile Selassie, 1932–74	
				Gen. Aman Andom, 1974	1974
				Gen. Teferi Bante, 1974–7	
				Lt.-Col. Mengitsu Haile Mariam, 1977–91	
				Ato Meles Zenawi, 1991–	
Gabon	Gabon	1960	Libreville	Leon M'Ba, 1960–7	

457

Country	Colonial name	Date of independence	Capital city	Leaders since independence	Coups
				Albert-Bernard (later Omar) Bongo, 1967–	
The Gambia	Gambia	1965	Banjul	Sir Dawda Kairaba Jawara, 1965–	
Ghana	Gold Coast	1957	Accra	Kwame Nkrumah, 1957–66	
				Lt.-Gen. J. A. Ankrah, 1966–9	1966
				Brig.-Gen. A. A. Afrifa, 1969	
				Dr Kofi Busia, 1969–72	
				Col. (later Gen.) I. K. Acheampong, 1972–8	1972
				Lt.-Gen. Frederick Akuffo, 1978–9	1978
				Flight-Lt. Jerry J. Rawlings, 1979	1979
				Dr Hilla Limann, 1979–81	
				Flight-Lt. Jerry J. Rawlings, 1981–	1981
Guinea	French Guinea	1958	Conakry	Ahmed Sékou Touré, 1958–84	
				Gen. Lansana Conté, 1984–	1984
Guinea-Bissau	Portuguese Guinea	1973	Bissau	Luis de Almeida Cabral, 1973–80	
				Maj. João Bernardo Nino Vieira, 1980–	1980
Kenya	Kenya	1963	Nairobi	Jomo Kenyatta, 1963–78	
				Daniel T. Arap Moi, 1978–	
Lesotho	Basutoland	1966	Maseru	Chief Leabua Jonathan, 1966	
				King Moshoeshoe II, 1966–90	dethroned
				King Letsie III, 1990–	
Liberia	—	1847	Monrovia	William V. S. Tubman, 1944–71	
				William R. Tolbert Jnr, 1971–80	
				Master-Sgt. (later Gen.) Samuel K. Doe, 1980–90	1980
				Prof. Amos Sawyer, 1990–	
Libya	Italian provinces of Cyrenaica, Tripolitania and Fezzān	1951	Tripoli	King Idrīs, 1951–69	
				Col. Muammar Kadhaffi, 1969–	1969
Madagascar	Madagascar	1960	Tananarive	Philibert Tsirinana, 1960–72	
				Gen. Gabriel Ramanantsoa, 1972–5	1972
				Col. Richard Ratsimandrava, 1975	
				Lt.-Cdr. (later Admiral) Didier Ratsiraka, 1975–	
Malawi	Nyasaland	1964	Lilongwe	Dr Hastings Kamuzu Banda, 1964–	
Mali	French Soudan	1960	Bamako	Modibo Keita, 1960–8	
				Lt. (later Gen.) Moussa Traoré, 1968–91	1968
				Lt.-Col. Amadou Toumani Touré, 1991–2	1991
				Alpha Oumar Konare 1992–	

Country	Colonial name	Date of independence	Capital city	Leaders since independence	Coups
Mauritania	Mauritania	1960	Nouakchott	Moktar Ould Daddah, 1960–78 Lt.-Col. Mustapha Ould Mohamed Salek, 1978–9 Lt.-Col. Ahmed Ould Bouceif, 1979 Lt.-Col. Mohamed Khouna Ould Haidalla, 1979–84 Col. Maaouya Ould Sid 'Ahmed Taya, 1984–	1978 1984
Mauritius	Mauritius	1968	Port-Louis	PMs: Sir Seewosagur Ramgoolam, 1968–82 Aneerood Jugnauth, 1982–92 Cassam Uteem (Pres.), 1992– PM: Aneerood Jugnauth, 1992–	
Morocco	Morocco	1956	Rabat	King Mohamed V, 1956–61 King Hassan II, 1961–	
Mozambique	Mozambique	1975	Maputo	Samora Machel, 1975–86 Joaquim Alberto Chissano, 1986–	
Namibia	South-West Africa	1990	Windhoek	*de jure*: The UN Council for Namibia *de facto*: South Africa Sam Nujoma, 1990–	
Niger	Niger	1960	Niamey	Hamani Diori, 1960–74 Lt.-Col. Seyni Kountche, 1974–87 Brig. Ali Saibou, 1987–	1974
Nigeria	Nigeria	1960	Lagos (from 1991 Abuja)	Dr Nnamdi Azikiwe (Pres.) and Sir Abubakar Tafawa Balewa (PM), 1960–6 Gen. J. T. A. Aguiyi-Ironsi, 1966 Lt.-Col. (later Gen.) Yakubu Gowon, 1966–75 Gen. Murtala Muhammed, 1975–6 Gen. Olusegun Obasanjo, 1976–9 Shehu Shagari, 1979–83 Maj.-Gen. M. Buhari, 1983–5 Gen. Ibrahim Babangida, 1985–	 1966 1966 1975 1983 1985
Réunion	Réunion	French Overseas Dep.	St Denis	President of France	
Rwanda	Part of Ruanda-Urundi	1962	Kigali	Grégoire Kayibanda, 1962–73 Maj.-Gen. Juvenal Habyarimana, 1973–	1973
Sao Tome and Principe	Sao Tome and Principe	1975	Sao Tome	Manuel Pinto da Costa, 1975–91 PM: Miguel Trovoada, 1975–8 Miguel Trovoada, 1991–	
Senegal	Senegal	1960	Dakar	Léopold Sédar Senghor, 1960–80 Abdou Diouf, 1981–	

Country	Colonial name	Date of inde-pendence	Capital city	Leaders since independence	Coups
Seychelles	Seychelles Islands	1976	Victoria	James Mancham, 1976–7 France-Albert René, 1977–	1977
Sierra Leone	Sierra Leone	1961	Freetown	Sir Milton Margai, 1961–4 Sir Albert Margai, 1964–7 Siaka Stevens, 1967 Brig.-Gen. David Lansana, 1967–8 Brig.-Gen. Andrew Juxon-Smith, 1968– Siaka Stevens, 1968–85 Gen. Joseph Saidu Momoh, 1985–92 Capt. Valentine Strasser, 1992–	1967 1968 1992

Somali Democratic Republic	Italian Somaliland and British Somaliland	1960	Mogadishu	Aden Abdulle Osman (Pres.), 1960–7
				PMs: Abdi Rashid Ali Shirmarke,
				   1960–4
				    Abdi Razaq Hussen, 1964–7
				Abdi Rashid Ali Shirmarke (Pres.),
				   1967–9
				PM: Mohamed Haji Ibrahim Igal,
				   1967–9
				Maj.-Gen. Mohamed Siad Barre,
				   1969–90
				Ali Mahdi Mohamed, 1990–
					1969

South Africa	Union of South Africa (1910–61)	1910	Pretoria (administra-tive) and Cape Town (legislative)	Jan Smuts, 1939–48 D. F. Malan, 1948–54 J. G. Strijdom, 1954–8 Dr Hendrik Verwoerd, 1958–66 B. J. Vorster, 1966–78 P. W. Botha, 1978–89 F. W. de Klerk, 1989–	

Sudan	Anglo–Egyptian Sudan	1956	Khartoum	Ismail el-Azhari, 1956
				Abdallah Khalil, 1956–8
				Gen. Ibrahim Aboud, 1958–64
				Sayed Sir el-Khatim el-Khalifa, 1964–5
				Mohamed Ahmed Mahgoub, 1965–9
				Col. (later Gen.) Gaffar Mohamed
				Nimeiri, 1969–85
				Gen. Abdulrahman Swareldarhab,
				   1985–6
				Ahmed Ali Al-Marghani 1986–9
				Lt.-Gen. Omer Hassan Ahmed el-
				   Bashir, 1989–
					1958
					1964
					
					1969
					
					1989

Swaziland	Swaziland	1968	Mbabane	King Sobhuza II, 1921–82
				Queen Mother Indlovukazi Dzeliwe,
				   1982
				Queen Regent Indlovukazi Ntombi,
				   1983–6
				King Mswati III, 1986–	

Country	Colonial name	Date of independence	Capital city	Leaders since independence	Coups
Tanzania	Tanganyika and Zanzibar	1961 1963	Dar es Salaam (being transferred to Dodoma)	Julius K. Nyerere, 1961–85; Ali Hassan Mwinyi, 1985–	
Togo	Togo	1960	Lomé	Sylvanus Olympio, 1960–3 Nicolas Grunitzky, 1963–7 Lt.-Col. (later Gen.) Etienne Gnassingbe Eyadema, 1967–91 Gen. Etienne Gnassingbe Eyadema (Pres.), 1991– PM: Joseph Kokou Koffigoh, 1991–	1963 1967
Tunisia	Tunisia	1956	Tunis	Habib Bourguiba, 1956–87 Zine El-Abidine Ben Ali, 1987–	
Uganda	Uganda	1962	Kampala	Milton Obote, 1962 King Mutesa II, 1963–6 PM: Milton Obote, 1963–6 Milton Obote (Pres.), 1966–71 Gen. (later Field Marshal) Idi Amīn Dada, 1971–9 Yusufu Lule, 1979 Godfrey Binaisa, 1979–80 Paulo Muwanga, 1980 Milton Obote, 1980–5 Tito Okello, 1985–6 Lt.-Gen. Yoweri K. Museveni, 1986–	1966 1971 1980 1985 1986
Western Sahara	Spanish Sahara	(1975)	El Aaiun	In dispute between the Polisario and Morocco	
Zaire	Belgian Congo	1960	Kinshasa	Joseph Kasavubu (Pres.), 1960–5 PMs: Patrice Lumumba, 1960 Joseph Ileo, 1960–1 Cyrille Adoula, 1961–4 Moïse Tshombe, 1964–5 Evariste Kimba, 1965 Gen. (later Field-Marsh.) Mobutu Sese Seko, 1965–92 Field-Marsh. Mobutu Sese Seko (Pres.), 1992– PM: Etienne Tshisekedi, 1992–	1960 1965
Zambia	Northern Rhodesia	1964	Lusaka	Kenneth D. Kaunda, 1964–91 Frederick J. Chiluba, 1991–	
Zimbabwe	Southern Rhodesia	1980	Harare	President Rev. Canaan Banana, 1980–7 Robert G. Mugabe, 1987–	

Source: A. A. Mazrui and M. Tidy, 1984; and updated by UNESCO, 1992.

461

The *guardian* role is when the military regime's major preoccupation is the maintenance of law and order rather than introducing social changes. Very often this emanates from the general political climate that the military inherited. There is a high reliance on coercion. The *reformist* regime is concerned mainly with 'creating national identity and promoting orderly economic development'.[40] The *radical* regime often acts as 'the linkage of interest between military officers who are essentially of the middle and lower classes, and the masses, who previously had been unintegrated into the national political life'.[41] Often a regime can also move from radical, through reformist, to guardianship role in time – or take a reverse direction of change.

We suggest that the Mobutu regime in Zaire has been essentially guardian in its role, even though it has taken some actions in a reformist direction. The military regimes in Ghana, Republic of Benin, Mauritania, Burundi and Rwanda are examples of these regimes for which political stability is the key objective. Coercion contains sub-nationalism. Often these regimes consolidate the state they inherited rather than reform it. Nation-building is not necessarily part of their package of action.

Reformist regimes in Africa include Nigerian military regimes which not only built a federal state with a strong centre but undertook institutional engineering in the creation of 12 and 19 states. They also carried out a number of laudable economic programmes at the height of the oil boom and embarked on indigenization of the economy. Their local government reforms during 1968–76 basically eroded the political powers of traditional leaders. The civil war and its lessons seem to have put Nigeria at the inchoate stage of nation-building – the ethnic, geo-ethnic and religious differences still simmer on the surface. Mobutu may be credited with pulling Zaire out of its chaos. He has survived the various Shaba attempts, but one must concede to him that he has engaged in state-building in Zaire. This has stretched out to the point of carrying out institutionalization of political processes to the level of personalization of these processes. In his attempts at nation-building, he has used Lumumba's name and embarked on a crusade of authenticity.

Some military regimes gave a verisimilitude of radicalism on coming to power. These often tapered off to reformist and guardianship roles. Thus the Egyptian and Algerian military, on coming to power, embarked on land reforms and espoused Arab socialism. In Ethiopia the military regime, as in Egypt, took over from an aristocratic class and made attempts at land reform. It even launched the 'Zematcha' programme and sent students, professionals and others to the rural areas to assist in its socialist programmes. In both areas, the radicalism hardly lasted. Egypt and Ethiopia have both formed parties to enable them to mobilize the

40. *ibid.*, p. 63.
41. *ibid.*, p. 65.

population. But it is clear that the Ethiopian regime is fast moving towards a guardianship role. While the Idi Amīn regime was hardly reformist, it took an action which could, in a way, be regarded as revolutionary – that is, the 'de-Indianization' of the Ugandan economy. But he hardly created any tangible economic structures to indigenize the economy.

Generally military regimes have been more effective in state-building than in nation-building in Africa. They are better at asserting authority than consolidating identity. The military leaders often suffer from the same problems of ethnicity, class, race and religion as their civilian predecessors. A few military leaders have tried to assume the national-hero position as symbols of nation-building – Gowon and Murtala in Nigeria, al-Nasser in Egypt, Kadhaffi in Libya and Mobutu's attempts in Zaire. While in some African countries the records of the military are no better than those of the civilian leaders, in others, their records have been better, and generalizations can be deceptive. But neither the military nor the civilian regimes have been able adequately to mobilize the people for nation-building except for a few states where the leaders have used ideology and single-party structures for nation-building purposes.

Thus, in Africa, parliamentary institutions and political parties have constantly been dismantled by the military. The state bureaucracy has been the most persistent institution in the fragile authority base of Africa's leaders. They have provided institutional continuity from colonial, through inheritance élite regimes, military regimes, and back to civilian regimes after military withdrawal from the political arena (where this happens). Generally, the boundaries between the barracks and the political arena are often so thin that the alternation of government between the military and civilian élites is likely to continue for a while.

Human rights and the ancestors

Caught up in all these conflicts in post-colonial Africa have been human rights. But here we must distinguish between *fundamental* human rights and *instrumental* human rights. Government by consent, for example, is a fundamental human right – an end. But the right to vote is an *instrumental* right – the means for achieving government by consent.

There is considerable consensus in post-colonial Africa about fundamental human rights. Most African societies were traditionally based on some doctrine of 'government by consent'. But whose consent? Some societies believed in the consent not only of the living, but also of the dead, and of those yet to be born. Under traditional conditions the elders were supposed to be well-informed about the ancestors and to have acquired their wisdom through cultural continuity, custom and tradition. Policies which were in gross violation of custom and tradition were supposed to be devoid of the consent of the dead. Policies which did not make allowances for the survival and happiness of children were supposed to be bereft of the consent of future generations. It was the duty of the living to estimate the wishes of the dead and of those yet to be born – and to act accordingly. 'Government by consent' was not a voting day once every four, five, or six years. It was a constant receptivity to generations of both the past and the future. It was partly in this light that Julius Nyerere reminded us of 'elders sitting under the tree, talking until they agreed'. It was a doctrine similar to the Islamic idea that the *Umma*, the Community of Islam, would never agree on *error*. Absolute consensus was a link between the present and both the past and the future. Consensus was a guide to the true general will, to the truth:

> We have no more need of being taught democracy than we have of being taught socialism. . . . Both are rooted in our past, in the traditional society which produced us.[42]

But in reality the imperial Western world had introduced Africa to a new concept of democracy, a new principle of 'government by consent'. A general election became the *instrumental* right for achieving government by consent. It was no longer enough for 'elders to sit under a tree and talk until they agreed'.

Elections under the Western model had to be *competitive*. The shift from a culture of *consensus* to a culture of *competition* in post-colonial Africa has proved to be devastating for human rights. Most African societies have shown that they need time to learn the secret of preventing high-stake political competition from becoming high-stake political conflict. The result has been rigged elections, harassment of opposition parties, suppression of dissidents, and persecution of dissenting opinions in the media and elsewhere. Human rights suffered in Africa when fundamental human rights were re-defined to exclude the rights of tradition (ancestors) and the rights of posterity (children of tomorrow). Human rights also suffered when instrumental rights were excessively based on neo-Western principles of 'winner takes all' in periodic general elections. From the point of view of human rights, it was unfortunate that the basic debate in Africa shifted from a dilemma between traditionalists and Westernized élites to a dilemma between Westernized civilians and soldiers equipped with Western weapons. The later confrontation has been more damaging to human rights. The worst violations in the 1970s occurred in places like Uganda under Idi Amīn, the Central African Empire under Jean Bedel Bokassa, and Equatorial Guinea under Francisco Macias Nguema.

Rights and duties – if they are to be respected – need to be rooted in tradition and continuity. If nation-building suffers from inadequate cultural coherence in national identities in Africa, so do human rights. The cultural interruptions in post-colonial Africa are not merely between one

42. J. Nyerere, 1962.

464

ethnic group and another (as in Nigeria), not just between one race and another (as in South Africa), not just between one generation and another (as in Ethiopia), but at least as fundamental is the break between today and yesterday everywhere in Africa. All these cultural interruptions are part of the background to repression, suppression and torture in post-colonial Africa. *Apartheid* in South Africa is only one elaborate case of denial of human rights. There are other kinds of violations in black Africa itself.

What is the way out? One solution is a pan-African system of monitoring and enforcing performance in human rights, continent-wide. We need an African equivalent not only of Amnesty International but of the European Commission for Human Rights. We need an institution manned by Africans to inform Africans about their own moral performance in the public domain. But in due course Africa also needs a pan-African system within which aggrieved citizens are able to accuse their own governments of violations of human rights. The Charter of the Organization of African Unity and the Banjul Declaration on Human Rights and People's Rights[43] (the charter was adopted in June 1981 and came into force on 21 October 1986, when it was ratified by a clear majority[44]) was an important step towards Africa's monitoring and enforcement of human rights in the decades to come. To that extent it must also be seen as part of both nation-building and state-formation in post-colonial Africa.

Conclusion

In this chapter we have argued that state- and nation-building experiences are not new to Africa. Pre-colonial states and empires have had to cope with these challenges. However, most of the current states do not correspond with these pre-colonial nations. In many cases, strange bed-fellows have found themselves in a state in the throes of the European scramble for colonies in Africa. The colonial authorities created certain institutions in these territories which later attained independence and thus became sovereign states. Nation-building, therefore, has meant attempts at the horizontal integration of these 'strange' bedfellows in the new state in order to create a 'nation', a political community to which the people now owe their allegiance, loyalty and commitment.

We noted, however, that there were problems of institutional change for the inheritance élites. Colonial structures and even pre-colonial political structures (such as chieftaincy) persisted and at times made the process of state-building difficult. In addition, because of the vested interests of

43. For an interesting discussion of the charter, see E. Kannyo, 1984, pp. 128–76.
44. *Keesing's Contemporary Archives: Record of World Events*, 1986, vol. 32, no. 11, p. 34729.

the post-colonial élites in the consolidation of the inherited power centre, the leaders could not embark on institutional or structural changes.

Except in few areas, inherited colonial structures even decayed. Thus, except in a few states – such as Tanzania, Guinea-Conakry and Guinea-Bissau – which used ideology and single-party structures to mobilize the populace towards nation-building, political parties declined in their political saliency. Even in countries where single parties have been useful in state-building – such as Zambia, Malawi, Cameroon and Côte d'Ivoire – they more or less became bureaucratic instruments of penetration and control (that is, of state-building) rather than instruments of nation-building.

Generally, with the decline of political parties (and political acrimony was worse in multi-party states), so also competitive electoral processes and parliamentary institutions declined. Military intervention in some states put the death knell on some of these structures. The most perennial of these structures has been the state bureaucracy which has survived regimes of all kinds.

In spite of the few structural changes made in African states in order to mobilize people for nation-building, the efforts have been tedious and have often been punctuated by setbacks or failures. We identified a number of factors which contribute to the failure of nation-building in Africa. Among these is the legacy of colonial administration. Ali Mazrui and Michael Tidy were perhaps correct to assert that in the context of nation-building in the current state, French assimilation was more positively functional than the British 'dual mandate'.[45] The assimilation policy, the centralized technique of administration, imposed relative uniformity of French cultural and political values in these states. Francophone states may suffer more from dependency on ex-colonial masters, but the nature of their colonization provided a basis for less complicated efforts towards cultural homogeneity than in Anglophone states.

Anglophone states experienced British racial arrogance and its attendant cultural and administrative autonomy. These have created a basis for more sovereign *states*. But in creating sovereign states, indirect rule preserved traditional institutions and structures which crystallized primordial identities, thus making nation-building a more difficult task in Anglophone than in Francophone states. Lest we be misunderstood, nation-building in both Francophone and Anglophone Africa (and in any state) is a difficult political enterprise in any case.

The prevalence or survival of pre-colonial primordial identities – ethnicity, religion and race – all in a modern competitive setting, make nation-building more difficult. While Islam is a unifying element in Senegal, Guinea and Mali, both Islam and Christianity have divisive

45. A. A. Mazrui and M. Tidy, 1984, p. 373.

consequences in Nigeria. The problem with sub-cultural nationalism based on primordial identity is that

> rightly or wrongly, each dismissal from a cabinet, each military coup, tends to get interpreted in these terms; even where ethnic identification has played little part, the actors often feel such forces are the real key to the interpretation of events.[46]

If pre-colonial chieftaincy institutions have survived all regimes, especially in Anglophone states, if these institutions have been obstacles to state-building, they have been real obstacles also to the process of nation-building, as Nigerian and Ugandan experiences have illustrated. They have served as focal points for the regimentation of parochial nationalism.

Only recently have some African states started reorganizing their educational systems. Yet, education (and its embedded socialization function) is crucial to nation-building. Related to it is the role of ideology and political education. Only a few African states have used ideology for nation-building purposes. Ideologies are useful instruments for dissociating a state from colonial institutional structures and more African states may take note of this. If nothing else ideology, well sold to the masses, prepares people for action and transcends parochial loyalties.

Finally, let us conclude this chapter by suggesting that most African leaders have been more concerned with changing political structures for the consolidation of their power base than for nation-building. Since both state- and nation-building processes for African states are simultaneous, unless more efforts are made to change and adopt those political structures which would enhance nation-building processes, even state-building processes in some states would remain fragile. The quests for greater coherence in nationhood and more stable authority in statehood continue to be the paramount political imperatives of post-colonial Africa.

46. J. Goody, 1973, p. 353.

Nation-building and changing political values

Joseph KI-ZERBO, Ali A. MAZRUI *and*

Christophe WONDJI *in collaboration with*

A. Adu BOAHEN

Introduction

Two familiar dialectics have conditioned political values in Africa during the period since 1935 – the dialectic between collectivism and individualism, on one side, and the dialectic between pluralism and nationalism, on the other. Older traditions of collectivism have sometimes clashed with newer forms of individualism; principles of pluralism have interacted with the values of nationalism.

As we shall elaborate later, thinkers like Julius K. Nyerere of Tanzania and Tom Mboya of Kenya identified traditional collectivism as a potential foundation for modern forms of socialism. Mboya put it as follows:

> Socialism . . . is a continuing tradition among our people. . . . It is an attitude towards people practised in our societies and did not need to be codified into a scientific theory in order to find existence.[1]

Sékou Touré used traditional collectivism to deny almost all forms of *individualism* in post-colonial Guinea.

> Africa is fundamentally communocractic. The collective life and social solidarity give it a basis of humanism which many peoples will envy. These human qualities also mean that an individual cannot imagine organising his life outside that of his family, village or clan. . . . Intellectuals or artists, thinkers or researchers, their ability is valid only if it coincides with the life of the people, it is integrated into the activity, thinking and hopes of the populace.[2]

Sékou Touré used traditional collectivism against both individualism and pluralism. The collectivist ideas also became part of the rationalization of the one-party state in Guinea and elsewhere in post-colonial Africa.

We have shown elsewhere how, in his *Philosophy of the Revolution*, Gamāl 'Abd al-Nasser married nationalism to Egypt's three overlapping circles – the Arab, Muslim and African circles, within each of which

1. T. Mboya, 1963a.
2. Cited in C. Wauthier, 1966, pp. 173–4.

468

Egypt was a crucial actor. Al-Nasser's ideology was collectivist and nationalist, but fundamentally anti-pluralist and distrustful of individualism.

What were the *phases* in the history of ideology in Africa in this era since 1935? Is it possible to sub-periodize this era into distinct ideological phases?

The heyday of *compatibility* between nationalism and pluralism in most of English-speaking and French-speaking Africa were approximately the last years of colonial rule (1945–60). Those were the years when African nationalism – partly as a strategy of fighting colonialism – expressed itself in such liberal slogans as 'One man, one vote', multi-party democracy, the free press and opposition to detention without trial. Far from nationalism and pluralism being in conflict, they were in strategic and tactical alliance. Leaders like Kenneth Kaunda, Hastings Banda, Habib Bourguiba and Léopold Senghor were at once great nationalists and great liberal democrats in the concluding years of colonial rule. In the fight against British and French imperialism, it made good sense in any case to invoke Western liberal values against the West itself. Such slogans did not work against *Portuguese* colonialism.

After independence, many African countries witnessed the decline of both nationalism and liberal democracy (1965–85). Collectivism was invoked by one-party ideologues and by socialists – and pluralism and individualism were in decline. Indeed, even nationalism was in decline in the 1960s and 1970s almost everywhere but in Southern Africa. The heavy hand of authoritarianism and pseudo-collectivism stifled much of Africa well into the 1980s. Senegal, the Gambia, Mauritius and Botswana were among the very few exceptions. We shall return to such exceptions later.

Then came the liberal revival of the *late 1980s* and *early 1990s* from Algeria to Mozambique – with renewed popular demands for multi-party democracy and agitation for greater privatization of the economy. Both military regimes and one-party states found themselves on the defensive. Pluralism was in the air – and African public opinion was becoming truly activist. This chapter will address these themes more fully. Is the collectivist ethos under challenge? Is a liberal revival under way in Africa?

In addition to the twin-dialectic of collectivism *versus* individualism and pluralism *versus* nationalism, political values in Africa have been conditioned by what Kwame Nkrumah called '*Consciencism*' – the interplay between indigenous tradition, Islam and Euro-Christian culture. Does liberal democracy in Nigeria favour Muslims? Does Islam in Algeria favour liberal democracy? In the first two republics of Nigeria, Muslims captured the leadership (First Republic under Abubakar Tafawa Balewa and Second Republic under al-Haji Shehu Shagari). In Algeria more recently, on the other hand, the fear of the Islamic opposition forced the FLN regime to seek allies among non-Islamic opponents – and speeded up democratization. In Nigeria's first two republics pluralism favoured Islam; in Algeria more recently Islam has favoured pluralism, in effect if not by intent.

Let us look more closely at some of these sub-themes of political values and nationhood in Africa's experience.

Nation-building and political values

The increasing success of the demand of liberalism all over the world in 1989–90, and especially in Africa, brings into sharp perspective the problem of the political values that underlie the action engaged in by African leaders over the past few decades. Virtually every country of the continent has agreed to implement structural-adjustment programmes 'proposed' by international financial institutions. Was there a liberal revival in Africa in the concluding years of the twentieth century? In addition, there has been the spectacular renunciation of the values and institutions of Marxism–Leninism by other countries (Benin, Mozambique, Ethiopia, and so on), which shows that those values had not really taken root in the political class and even less in civil society. Once again, African countries seem to be faced with the choice between several value systems, or rather, as at the beginning of colonization, they are being obliged to make their policies in a context of implicit values which are not always frankly articulated. Colonialism dismantled the vast majority of African political institutions and with them the related values. But some indigenous values outlived the institutions, while structures spared by the colonizer or preserved by the colonized continued to generate autochthonous values. The anti-colonial struggle, particularly before and after the Second World War, was also a debate and a struggle between political values. What was at stake was the resumption of control over the ends and motivations of political action.

That is why the winning of independence in the 1960s was, in the area of political values, the critical moment of more or less relevant choices, lack of choice or deferred choices, the results of which are unfolding as the century draws to an end.

As countries became independent, the issue was the building of states and national communities, building economies able to satisfy the needs of the people and weaving a network of inter-African and international relations that would help to realize the global political options, while at the same time transforming the values that underlie international transactions. Formidable obstacles stood in the way of this project: national integration conflicted with certain ethnic or pseudo-ethnic interests, while African integration was thwarted by 'micro-national' ambitions. Furthermore, societal projects aiming to ensure the socio-economic progress of the majority of the population clashed with certain 'negative' values of pre-colonial societies and the colonial system.

Faced with this web of vicious circles, African leaders initially either chose to manage the neo-colonial *status quo* or opted for the total transformation of African and international socio-political values. Nevertheless, by the end of the 1980s, we find them almost all professing similar or analogous values, either because of the objective structures that impinge on them or because of changes in values occurring outside being reflected in African attitudes. All African countries are the home of often similar pre-colonial and colonial political traditions. They have a double heritage of political values. These values provide benchmarks for analysis and action, motivating ideas and ideals that systematically enlighten and orient individual and collective choices.

But values are not transcendent entities frozen outside time. Political values produce history, but they are also produced, influenced and transformed by history. That is why the questions that arise here are the following: What are the constant features and the changes in African political values since 1935? What are the contradictory levers of the work of nation-building from the independence struggles to the final decade of the twentieth century? What values underpin the events, institutions and ideologies marking that evolution?

From colonial rule to political pluralism in the independence struggles

The colonial system was built on a semi-coherent body of political values. Lord Lugard expressed it well in his book *The Dual Mandate in Tropical Africa*.[3] These two mandates, of civilization and of exploitation, are carriers of explicit and implicit values. For Lugard, the best political institution to reconcile them was indirect rule. On the other hand, under colonizing countries with assimilationist aims such as France and Portugal, the imposition of colonialist political values was more flagrant.[4] After the Second World War, African demands for self-government and independence were stepped up in all colonial territories, creating or promoting two sets of political values destined for a great future: the values of pluralism and the values of nationalism.

The legacy of pluralism

Even in the national liberation movements, pluralism was the basis, at least initially – for example, in Angola, Southern Rhodesia and Mozambique. But it is above all in the cases of *peaceful evolution* towards independence that the value of political pluralism was expressed most forcefully on the

3. Lugard, Lord, 1922.
4. See R. F. Betts, 1985, pp. 312–31.

basis of the liberalism professed in the metropole by the colonial powers, and resting on the principle of the freedom of the individual in every domain. Liberal ideology thus provided an arsenal of legal formulae and political methods to African leaders fighting against colonialism; it was on the basis of the very principles and values ideologically proclaimed by the colonizer that intellectuals in the colonies claimed equal rights and later independence for the colonies, often with the support of opposition groups in the metropole.

In *North Africa*, except for Algeria which established presidentialism and the single party from independence in 1962, pluralism prevailed: as in Egypt with the 1923 constitution up to the time of the Free Officers' *coup d'Etat* in 1952. Similarly, the constitution which put an end to the French protectorate in Tunisia in 1955 was essentially liberal. Furthermore, the Neo-Destūr agenda was to reform social institutions in accordance with the Western liberal code: abolition of polygamy, civil law, and the granting of voting and eligibility rights to women. Morocco under Mohamed V (1956–61) was a compromise between the traditional monarchy and parliamentary institutions. But after proclaiming liberal values as norms for the rebuilding of society, the states of North Africa were to turn their backs on liberalism after periods of varying lengths.

In *Africa south of the Sahara* dozens of parties and movements, legal and otherwise, proliferated in black Africa between 1945 and 1960 on the basis of the values of Western pluralism, which was far and away the dominant model. This was true of both Anglophone and Francophone countries. In the Gold Coast, the political movement led by J. B. Danquah in 1947, the United Gold Coast Convention, had not been in existence for more than two years when Kwame Nkrumah broke away from it to form the Convention People's Party (CPP). In Nigeria, the constitutions granted in 1945 and 1948 permitted the burgeoning of a dynamic press inspired by youth associations, trades unions and parties centred on the country's main regions. In Sierra Leone and the Gambia, liberal pluralism set the 'Creoles' of the 'colony' against the majority indigenous peoples of the protectorates in the hinterlands. In the British Central African Federation, long and tortuous three-sided negotiations were conducted between the Africans, divided among several parties, the white settlers, themselves sometimes divided, and the government in London.

In the *Francophone territories*, there was the same proliferation of political parties and movements between 1935 and 1960, mainly after the end of the Second World War. Assimilation, here written into the political structures themselves, took African elected representatives into the parliamentary bodies of France, in Paris or Versailles, and still further steeped political leaders in the political values prevailing in the French system. Political *apparentements* or associations did not function on their own at the beginning. Thus the Communist Study Groups (*Groupes d'études communistes*, GEC) were extremely active in many African cities. In

PLATE 16.1   *Franz Fanon, French writer born in Martinique*

Senegal, these French GECs devoted to training for the benefit of the RDA were overtaken by African activists belonging to the French Socialist Party (*Parti socialiste français*, SFIO).

In short, before independence, the political values advocated in African countries constituted a cultural transfer under the cover of the notorious 'civilizing mission'. This transfer ignored endogenous democratic features, thus seriously compromising the internal organic adjustment between political society and civil society. Nevertheless, the transfer of Western political ideals to Africa, especially when the values of Marxist socialism were mixed up in them, was bound to accelerate the dynamic of nation-building and first of all the struggle for African independence.

The political values of pluralism in Africa between 1945 and 1960 enabled minority progressive parties, whether Marxist (like the *Parti africain de l'indépendance*, PAI) or not (as in the case of the *Mouvement de libération nationale*, MLN)[5] to make their voices heard and play a vanguard role in carrying along the moderate or conservative parties closer to the colonial administration. Moreover, while the colonial powers

5. *Libérons l'Afrique*, MLN Manifesto, 1958.

themselves doggedly defended the vast material interests they had invested in Africa, they were bound sooner or later, whether they liked it or not, to accept the demands of African nationalists or else repudiate their own domestic ideological values.

The values of nationalism

At the same time as the values of democratic pluralism were being conveyed by the liberal political institutions borrowed from Europe and in dialectical interaction with them, the values associated with nationalism were growing in Africa, particularly from armed resistance movements and struggles but also in areas where the colonial system evolved peacefully. It was above all in these violent struggles that the values of African nationalism were most highly developed. In reality, these armed struggles were not explosions that simply came out of nowhere; they were the historical continuation of the struggles and resistance movements that arose in Africa against invasion and rule by colonizers.

T. O. Ranger has stressed the connections between the nationalist movements in sub-Saharan Africa and the many-sided resistance movements opposing foreign rule. The activists of Julius Nyerere's party saw themselves as the direct heirs of the Maji Maji movements which fought German imperialism during 1904–6; and the leader of TANU (Tanganyika African National Union) himself declared: 'Our new nation was built on the ashes of Maji Maji'.[6] In Zimbabwe too, the nationalists invoked the memory of the anti-colonial revolt of 1896–7, and they restored to a place of honour the concept of *Chimurenga* (armed resistance) which was the expression of African patriotism at the time. In South Africa, even Nelson Mandela sought his inspiration in the story of 'the wars the ancestors fought to defend the homeland which are the glory and pride of the whole African nation'. In addition to the heritage of armed and political resistance movements, the legacy of religious-type cultural resistance was also used. In Kenya, the militants of KANU (Kenya African National Union) drew on the ideological legacy of the *Mumbi* cult and *Dini Ya Musambwa* cult between the two world wars and in 1947. Through historical memory, the liberation struggle was thus linked to a mobilizing past in which the struggle found its legitimacy.

More generally still, the need to assert by force the right of exploited people to resist the domination of the colonizers restored to a place of honour the 'value' of *violence as a therapeutic agent of historical progress*. The whole context pointed in that direction: the exaltation of militarism during the world wars, the exactions of the colonial forces engaged in so-called 'pacification', the use of blacks recruited *en masse* for the wars of colonial reconquest in Indochina, Algeria, Madagascar and elsewhere. If

6. T. O. Ranger, 1968a, p. 636.

we add to that the uniform, the pensions and the standard of living of ex-soldiers, we can see how the warrior myth was formidably stimulated in popular imagery.

Furthermore, the anti-colonial wars were sometimes fought on the very sites of exploits accomplished by the ancestors in their confrontations with the foreigner: for example, when the Algerian FLN established its sanctuaries in the Aurès mountains in Kabylie or in the Chouf. Likewise, the special name of Houari Boumedienne is taken from the names of two saints of Algerian Islam: Houari and Bou Médin.[7] Habib Bourguiba was to be styled 'the Supreme Combatant' (*le Combattant Suprême*), Jomo Kenyatta 'the Flaming Spear of Kenya', Houphouët-Boigny 'the Ram who defends his People' (*le Bélier défenseur du peuple*), Kwame Nkrumah 'the Osagyefo', the victorious general, and Amilcar Cabral 'Abdel Jessi', the sabre-bearing justiciar.

The values of militant nationalism were further fuelled by *Marxist–Leninist theory*, which attributed to all forms of violence the status of demiurge of history and which makes imperialism the highest stage of capitalism. The colonized continents, with Africa in the forefront, thus became the 'soft underbelly' through which mortal blows could be dealt to the world capitalist system. Such were the messages of the Third International (Moscow, 1919) and the Congress of Oppressed Peoples (Baku, 1920).

Nationalism and the wider culture

Apart from the armed struggles or struggles directly engaged in political action, Africans have cultivated the values of nationalism in a particular historical context, but in forms that are sometimes original, sometimes merely imitative.

The *ideology of the nation-state* was, along with capitalist imperialism, one of the twin pillars of colonial conquest; and African borders, for example, were simply a projection of the European borders of the time. Although this ideology has given Europe and the world both local wars and worldwide holocausts, it is the 'values' of the European nation-state that were bequeathed to colonized territories at the time of their independence.

Another important aspect of nationalism is *religion* whose role is crucial. The Mahdist uprising against foreign rule in the late nineteenth century was largely inspired by the values of a religious-based nationalism. In 1899 a Mahdī appeared too among the Somali against the British and Italians: he was Muḥammad 'Abdallāh Ḥassan, nicknamed by imperialists as 'the mad Mullah'. In West Africa, revivalist and Mahdist movements erupted sporadically, echoing the numerous resistance movements of

7. See the article on Boumedienne in M. Mourre, 1978, vol. 1, p. 619.

Muslim leaders such as <u>Sh</u>ay<u>kh</u> Amadu Bamba (Senegal) and <u>Sh</u>ay<u>kh</u> Ḥamallāh (Mali and Mauritania). But the values of rejection of any submission to an external authority were also abundantly illustrated by the leaders of African traditional religion. Thus, the leaders of the Maji Maji rebellion in Tanganyika sought to fight the Germans between 1905 and 1907 using holy water to protect themselves against bullets. Another dramatic example is provided by the revolt, in 1947, of all the south-east and east of the island of Madagascar. The rebels also believed bullets could not harm them because they were protected by magic. The suppression of this uprising was horrific. It, too, is considered by the Malagasies as a significant step on the road to independence, even though the whole of the island did not take part.

Another element often close to language and religion that marks nationalism is *ethnicity*. This concept must, however, be handled with the greatest care because of its highly equivocal content. Thus the Mau Mau movement in Kenya (1952–60) was a struggle emerging from the quest for land disputed among the peoples of central Kenya and against the seizure of the best agricultural land by Europeans. But it was also a battle for political and cultural liberation. The symbolic rituals initially used by the guerrilla fighters were borrowed from the religious heritage of the Kikuyu and related ethnic groups (Meru and Embu): for example, in the oath-taking ceremonies, designed to make a sacred commitment that would discourage any idea of betrayal. Similarly, Mugabe's army in Southern Rhodesia two decades later was made up mainly of Shona but the aims of the movement made it a liberating struggle for the whole of Zimbabwe. In short, any resistance by the Shona, Ndebele or Fon of Dahomey, the Asante or Samo of Burkina Faso, or the Wolof or Joola (Diola) of Senegal was both an act to protect the ethnic group and a struggle for wider interests and values of a nationalistic character. It is precisely the colonial intrusion itself which, by upsetting this earlier map, broke the coincidence between 'national' and 'ethnic' identities.

The other fundamental dimension of the nation-state is obviously *territory*; but unlike European countries and pre-colonial Africa, where the shaping of the 'national' space by peoples and states was the result of a centuries-long effort, the borders of the modern African states were drawn by the conquering zeal of a handful of foreigners in one or two decades. Yet some territories federated under colonial rule in British East Africa or French West Africa were broken up. Moreover, in their struggle for independence, African nationalists were often aiming not at the emancipation of a particular territory but at putting an end to the submission of African peoples. The values of nationalism were almost always closely associated with the values of African unity as indissolubly linked elements.

Finally, and here we touch on an aspect of the contents of African nationalism at once more ambiguous but also more fundamental, that pertaining to *'race'* and *civilization*. The French statesman René Pleven said that: 'To colonize is to spread civilization in space'. Colonization, an eminently economic act, was thus also a cultural phenomenon. As a result, decolonization was bound in some way to be a cultural conflict. There had to be a decision on the relative weights to be given to the values of the autochthonous heritage and the cultural principles purveyed by the colonizers. As early as the end of the nineteenth century, the movement of cultural awakening in the Arab-Muslim world (*nahda*) and the black renaissance movement in America (the Negro renaissance) had to face this problem. As regards *Negro-African civilization*, two movements of ideas symbolize this effort, which goes from African Personality and pan-Africanism to Negritude, the intellectual focus created around the review *Présence Africaine* and its editor, Alioune Diop.

The fundamental question had in fact come from E. W. Blyden in *Christianity, Islam and the Negro Race* (1887), where he proposed a synthesis of the values of the Western Sudan and those of the Christian West and later advocated racial consciousness and pride among blacks of the continent and those in the *diaspora*. This contributed to the inauguration of the pan-Africanist movement. Negritude belongs in this current with its project of a 'civilization of the universal'.

In the first half of the century, as was indicated in Volume VII, the leadership of the pan-African movement was in fact held by people of African ancestry in the western hemisphere; that is to say, in the Americas, especially in the United States and the Caribbean. People like Marcus Garvey of Jamaica, George Padmore of Trinidad and W. E. B. DuBois of the United States were among the founding fathers of pan-Africanism. From 1900 on there were pan-African meetings to emphasize racial solidarity, and organize for the struggle against discrimination and in pursuit of racial dignity for black peoples both in Africa and in the Western world.

As we indicated elsewhere in this volume, it was not until 1945 that the leadership of the pan-African movement passed from blacks of the Americas to blacks of Africa. This was the fifth Pan-African Congress held in Manchester, England, in 1945. Two of those who were present there later became founding fathers of newly independent countries. These were, as related in other chapters, Kwame Nkrumah of Ghana and Jomo Kenyatta of Kenya. The Africans at the conference were still slightly overshadowed by some of the giants of black nationalism from the Americas, but nevertheless 1945 signifies the re-Africanization of pan-Africanism, the passing of the torch from *diaspora* people of African ancestry abroad to citizens of African countries. Twelve years later, Kwame Nkrumah headed the first government of independent Ghana, which was itself the first black African country to be liberated from European colonial rule, and pan-Africanism took a more militant form, which will be discussed later.

In *North Africa*, the problems of the general orientation of the countries and the values that were to inspire this orientation lay between the Koranic or Islamic path of nationalism and the liberal or modernizing one, with intermediate reformist positions in favour of individualism combined with Islam.

Hence, in the late nineteenth century, the Egyptian Muḥammad 'Abduh, who had disciples in the Maghreb ('Allal al-Fasi), led a movement for a return to the sources of the Ḳur'ān or *salafiyya* without totally rejecting contributions from outside or the progression towards representative institutions. His fellow scholar, A. Razeq, stressing the essentially political nature of the caliphate, accepted the principle of the separation of the spiritual and temporal powers. Later, in the 1930s, Taha Hussein could be seen as resolutely defending liberal modernism, presented moreover as the continuation of Mediterranean Hellenistic civilization. But extreme positions are also to be noted, such as those of the Muslim Brothers opposed to any reformism and of the socialists in their dire hostility to bourgeois liberal modernism. Writers and artists championed individual creativity.

The acceleration of the historical process towards independence occurred at a time when neither in North Africa nor in sub-Saharan Africa had an integrated body of social thought succeeded in taking on board the exogenous values of Western modernism in an autonomous thought anchored in the endogenous cultural heritages; for the maturing of ideologies is more sluggish than events. This lack of a global philosophy of national culture and liberation was to weigh heavily in the subsequent global evolution of African countries.

In short, the period from 1935 to independence was chiefly marked by two great political values – pluralism and nationalism – but beneath an older cultural tension between collectivism and individualism. In a way, these two ideologies were mutually reinforcing; but their limits were soon revealed and they began in the 1960s to give way to other values.

Political values since independence

With the winning of independence by African countries, a period opened which might have led to an explosion of original and positive values mixing with the best of pre-colonial experience and exogenous contributions, building on deliberate choices. But most of the time, there was a spectacular withering away of the values of pluralism. Both endogenous and exogenous indications and behaviours were mobilized to this end. But when this process culminated in personal power, it also sounded the death knell of the values associated with nationalism and pluralism.

In the beginning, if we look at the mottoes, anthems and flags adopted by the new independent states, we can see the values that they wanted to achieve. *State mottoes*, concise words which strike people because they appear to have the character of categorical imperatives, invoke such fundamental collectivist values as 'Unity, Peace and Development'; 'One people, One goal, One faith' (Senegal), 'Union, Discipline, Work' (Côte d'Ivoire), 'Unity and Faith, Peace and Progress' (Nigeria), 'Unity, Freedom, Work' (Zimbabwe), 'Peace, Work, Homeland' (Cameroon) and 'Freedom and Justice' (Ghana). National anthems exalt collective struggle, unity and African and universal brotherhood (the Senegalese anthem), or recall the honour of the ancestors, freedom and unity (Cameroonian and Nigerian anthems). *The colours of flags and emblems* or national arms refer above all to symbolic animals: the lion of Senegal, the elephant of Côte d'Ivoire, the eagle of Nigeria, the leopard of Zaire, the mysterious bird that flies over the ruins of Zimbabwe. The colours of national flags show the predominance of green, which may symbolize plant resources, Islam or hope in the future. Common too are red, for the blood of martyrs, the heroism of struggles or the revolution, and yellow (the gold of mines, the African sun). When it features (which is rarely), white is the colour of peace and unity. Finally, black identifies the race or has an Islamic referent.

In sum, four ideological messages are dominant in this dense discourse of emblems and symbols: the assertion of an identity, the quest for development, the desire for unity, and the call for freedom and social justice. All this shows continuity with the immediate pre-independence values. Much of it reaffirms collective freedom.

New political ideologies

Beside these mottoes, anthems and emblems, some of the new African leaders formulated their own ideologies. Among them are al-Nasser, Nkrumah, Senghor, Bourguiba, Sékou Touré, Nyerere, Amilcar Cabral and Kaunda. From the *Philosophy of the Egyptian Revolution* (1954) to the National Charter (1962), Gamāl 'Abd al-Nasser of Egypt accentuated his abandonment of Western liberal values in favour of pan-Arabism, Islam, Arab socialism, pan-Africanism and charismatic presidential power. The National Charter vigorously denounces the charade of Western-type democracy which operates in the interests of ruling feudal and capitalist groups, but welcomes socialism which guarantees economic democracy and collective liberty to the masses. It describes socialism as 'the path that leads to this social liberty',[8] hence the necessity for the people to own the instruments of production and direct the surplus of this production through a plan. Nasserite ideology was both pro-socialist and anti-Marxist.

8. For further details, see the texts assembled by A. Abdel-Malek, 1980, and J. P. Charnay, 1966, pp. 225–46.

On the other hand, Arab socialism also expressed itself through the single party and categorically rejects atheism as the absolute anti-value, together with the dictatorship of the proletariat. It advocates the assimilation of classes into the democratic power of the whole people, whose confidence legitimizes and inspires the leaders.

Furthermore, Arab socialism postulates the imperative of Arab unity. This option brought al-Nasser close to the supporters of the Ba'th like the Syrian Michel Aflaq, for whom the real issue is 'how are we to give our nation back its soul, to ensure that the Arab and the nation as a whole recover a positive, active, determined and correct attitude to life, consisting for the individual Arab in a mastery of his destiny?' Whence the imperative need for a Ba'th revolution of which 'socialism is the body and unity that soul'; this resurgence (*ba'th*) will have to rely on the people, the sole force capable of realizing unity.

The key ideas of Nasserism and Ba'thism – socialist democracy, theistic socialism, authentic values of Islam (fraternity, defence of the community), Arab unity and recourse to the people – were to spread all over North Africa.

In *Algeria*, a peasant-based and Islamic revolutionary socialism, emerging from a long and bloody liberation struggle, attempted to combine the

PLATE 16.2 *Ahmed Ben Bella's arrival in Algeria on 5 July 1962, Algerian Independence Day*

political values of nationalism and self-management under the aegis of Ben Bella and, after 1976, an FLN that had now become the single party whose leading role was to confirm socialist democracy, while Islam became the state religion.[9]

In *Tunisia* there emerged a co-operationist-type Neo-Destūrian socialism linking the notions of profit and capital accumulation with those of public enterprises and state participation. According to the theoretician and advocate A. Ben Ṣalāḥ, what was needed was to exorcise the horrors of the class struggle through a revolution 'in minds more than in structures' with a view to securing acceptance of the sacrifices required for economic take-off.[10]

In *Libya* the overthrow of the monarchy in 1969 was followed by the establishment of an Arab socialist republic based on nationalization and pan-Arabism. In his *Green Book* (1976), Kadhaffi undertook a systematic demolition of the liberal thesis, seeking in Islam a third way between capitalism and socialism, both deemed to have failed. Representative democracy, he says, is just a circus; the referendum is an imposture, hence the recourse to the direct democracy of popular committees and congresses (*Jamahiriyyah*) that are traditional in inspiration.[11]

In sub-Saharan Africa, Kwame Nkrumah in his *Consciencism* (1964) formulated one of the most important doctrines of decolonization and development for Africa. He wrote that

> The way out is certainly not to regurgitate all Islamic and Euro-colonial influences in a futile attempt to recreate a past that cannot be resurrected. The way out is only forward to a higher and reconciled form of society in which the quintessence of the human purpose of traditional African society reasserts itself in a modern context.[12]

Consciencism is, therefore, an attempt at synthesis which, like the Nasserist project, combines the values of anti-imperialist nationalism, technological and scientific modernization and the African and Islamic heritage, all by way of socialism and African unity.

Julius Nyerere also stresses above all the African legacy of collectivist values of which the key one is communal solidarity. 'Africa', he says, 'has no lesson in socialism to learn from Europe; it would rather have something to teach'. Such a socialism is above all an attitude which consists in 'everyone being concerned for the welfare of others'.[13] *Ujamaa* is 'the community bound together by affection and solidarity among its

9. J. P. Charnay, 1966, p. 245.
10. Texts by A. Ben Ṣalāḥ, in A. Abdel-Malek, 1980, pp. 255–8.
11. Text by M. Kadhaffi, in A. Abdel-Malek, 1980, pp. 337–41.
12. K. Nkrumah, cited by Y. Benot, 1969, p. 394.
13. J. Nyerere, 1963b, p. 8.

members who work to enrich the common heritage and through this work
to satisfy their personal needs'. If it was Nkrumah who did the most to
integrate the values involved, it is perhaps Nyerere who has done the
most to promote the development and critical and creative exploration of
the African heritage of values. Thus to those who fear that the value of
solidarity might stifle the spirit of individual initiative and the imperative
of work, he replies by saying that the solidarity of all implies that all
must work. If there exists a duty of hospitality, the individual beneficiary
also has the duty to join in communal work. This leads to an emphasis
on the values of 'African socialism' which must animate both civil society
and political society.

PLATE 16.3   *Amilcar Cabral of Guinea-Bissau, president of the PAIGC, on the East Front*

Through the discipline of Marxism–Leninism, Amilcar Cabral, the
founder of the PAIGC in Guinea-Bissau and Cape Verde, also tried to
integrate the values of socialism and nationalism. He thought that only
such an organic association would make it possible to give the aspirations
of the people a proper place in the political arena through people's power,
and in the socio-economic and cultural sphere, thanks to social justice
and the fact of being rooted in the values and civilization of ordinary

people. Such a societal project had been initiated in the zones liberated by the liberation war in Guinea-Bissau.

Finally, Léopold Sédar Senghor, a follower of African socialism, while acknowledging the usefulness of the conceptual framework offered by Marxism, refuses to accept an ideology enthralling the class struggle and atheism. 'Thus', he writes, 'while using Marx's method to analyse the economic and social situation of Senegal and Black Africa in the grip of capitalism, we may legitimately give our religious and cultural values their natural place in our spiritual life.'[14]

It is quite evident that all these ideas which came under the general classification of African socialism were very much influenced by Islam, Marxist–Leninism and African traditional values.

What sort of regimes then emerged in Africa during the post-colonial period in the light of all these old and new ideologies?

The post-colonial regimes of Africa

In all about five types of regimes have emerged in Africa in the post-colonial era. First were the socialist regimes founded by those leaders whose ideas have already been discussed. The move was led by al-Nasser in 1952 when he dissolved all the parties in Egypt and set up the Arab Socialist Union – a state party, or rather a state agency for political control of the masses.[15] This precedent was widely copied in Africa under a variety of labels: rally, movement, front, convention, congress, union, and so on. But they were one and all socio-political and ideological apparatuses functioning as systems to monopolize communication between the membership and the grass-roots. Kwame Nkrumah also converted Ghana into a one-party socialist regime in 1964 after suppressing ethnic, regionalist and religious organizations. So also did Sékou Touré of Guinea, Modibo Keita of Mali and Julius Nyerere of Tanzania in the 1950s. In Mozambique, in 1974, FRELIMO was also established as the sole party, the instrument of incorporating rural society into the project for creating a nation through the state apparatus. Amilcar Cabral of Guinea-Bissau and Agostinho Neto of Angola also aligned their countries with socialist countries at least for a while.

The second type of regime is the military. Regimes of this type, whose number varies from year to year, have already been discussed in Chapter 15. Suffice it to state here that they are the regimes in which the civilian rulers have been replaced by soldiers through military *coup d'Etat*. These abrupt incursions, of which there have been dozens, imply new political values: the imposition of consensus by force of arms and the repudiation of the rule of law.

14. L. S. Senghor, 1971, p. 58.
15. P. Wanyande, 1987, p. 71.

The third type is the *apartheid* regime found fortunately only in South Africa. We do not intend to discuss this regime here except to state that it is an extreme case of the theorization and implementation of monstrous political 'values': inequality, segregation and bloody racism. Even religion has been called in to help justify the *status quo*. For decades the presence of this regime has led the frontline states in Southern Africa to widespread violence that has taken many forms: ethnic wars, state wars or liberation wars (Namibia), revolts by bandits and mercenaries, *coups d'Etat*, massive forced migration, acts of sabotage, and so on. *Apartheid* has prevented nation-building in many countries.

The fourth type of regime is the conservative regime. Regimes of this type, professing belief in and respect for the capitalist approach to development and nation-building, have abandoned their concomitant liberal and democratic aspects in favour of the one-party system or a dominant one-party system and autocracy. These regimes constitute a high proportion of African states and include Côte d'Ivoire, Sierra Leone, Senegal (until 1978), Cameroon, Kenya, Zambia, Zaire, Malawi and Gabon. One of their fundamental values is 'modernization', that is, the race for extroverted growth. Sixty to eighty per cent of export earnings come from the sale of one, two or three agricultural or mineral products. State capitalism syphons off vast resources into the public coffers at the mercy of the political class. The scramble for money pervades all motivation, attitudes and behaviour. Power and wealth have become communicating vessels. The sense of public service and the sense of responsibility are shaken in all these states; individuals are deprived of certain rights and associated values. Similarly the poor classes, deprived of the fruit of growth, do not have the right to express themselves, for that would endanger the stability necessary for a development incidentally not guaranteed.

These are ideal conditions for the unbridled accumulation of capital at the expense of a defenceless lumpenproletariat: a 'hybrid political system', declared the Zaireian bishops' conference on 15 March 1990 in its contribution to the 'national consultation on the general situation of the country'. The system, the bishops continued, 'draws from liberalism the advantages offered to a minority by the enjoyment of private property and borrows from totalitarianism the methods of winning and retaining power'.[16] The incoherence of calculated contradiction transformed into a perverse political 'value' is at the root of the African sickness in that it accumulated all the negative aspects of three systems: the African heritage, capitalist liberalism and the Marxism–Leninism of the old Eastern bloc countries.

Finally, there are the regimes that have stuck to the liberal values of pluralism and parliamentary democracy. Unfortunately, they constitute

16. *Jeune Afrique*, No. 1527, 9 April 1990.

the smallest group, five in all: namely, the Gambia, Botswana, Senegal, Namibia and Mauritius. It is only in these countries that competitive political elections are still allowed and opposition parties operate unhindered. It is true that in these countries the economic situation is only a little brighter than elsewhere. But as will be seen in other chapters, it simply shows that all African countries are subject to the same structural limitations. However, with regard to political values the situation is qualitatively different, given the existence of an independent press, an autonomous judicial system with legal guarantees, the relative separation of powers, open if not absolutely free elections, freedom of movement and assembly and so on.

Pan-Africanism and non-alignment

Besides the new ideologies and regimes that have emerged in post-colonial Africa two other themes have also become part-and-parcel of the political values of Africa. These are a more radical and Africanized form of pan-Africanism and non-alignment. Both themes will be discussed in Chapters 24, 25 and 28 below. Suffice it to state here, first, that though the leadership of the pan-African movement passed from blacks of the Americas to blacks of Africa at the fifth Pan-African Congress held in Manchester in 1945, it was not until after the attainment of independence by Ghana in 1957 that pan-Africanism as an operational movement was transferred from America and Europe to the African continent itself. This was signified by the two conferences which the new leader of Ghana, Kwame Nkrumah, who was one of the joint secretaries of the Manchester Conference, organized in Accra in 1958. These were the conference of the heads of the then-independent African states and the All-African People's Conference. It was also from that time that the focus of territory entered the universe of pan-Africanism. From then on, pan-Africanism now assumed two dimensions, the trans-Saharan variety of pan-Africanism and the trans-Atlantic variety of pan-Africanism, one urging unity based on the mystique of the African territorial continent and the other the mystique of the black race. Ideologically, pan-Africanism also now emphasized two themes, the pan-Africanism of liberation and the pan-Africanism of integration – both of which will be discussed later.

The second new ideology that became part of the world-view of African states, especially in the realm of external and global relations, was that of non-alignment. Again, the comment that should be made at this stage is that no principle of foreign policy in the second half of the twentieth century has had a greater impact on relations between small countries and big powers than non-alignment. The concept has changed in meaning and operational implications since its inception in the 1950s, but it continues to affect significantly the diplomatic orientation of a majority of states in the developing world. Kwame Nkrumah and Gamāl 'Abd

485

al-Nasser were among the African founding-fathers of non-alignment. Originally, the movement served as a solidarity of protest and for modernization in East–West relations. But ever since the 1970s, especially from the Algerian summit of September 1973, there has been a change of focus to a more pronounced emphasis on attaining a basic restructuring of the global system in the direction of greater equity in North–South relations.

The new political trends in Africa

It was not in the realm of non-alignment and global relations that new trends began to emerge in the 1970s but also in the internal political situation in Africa. These trends are signified first by the collapse of the socialist regimes in Africa, secondly, by the change-over from military to civilian regimes signified by the temporary return of both Ghana and Nigeria to civilian rule in the late 1970s, and, above all, in the movement back from one-party and autocratic rule to the former values of liberal democracy and multi-partyism.

Failure of the socialist model

As has been indicated already, the socialist model which was a combination of Marxist–Leninism, Islamic socialism and traditional African values became extremely popular in the early decades of independence and was adopted by countries like Egypt, Guinea, Ghana, Mali, Tanzania, Mozambique and Angola. But without a single exception, that model has been dropped by all these countries, a process which began in Egypt with al-Nasser and continued with the fall of Nkrumah in Ghana and Modibo Keita in Mali in the 1960s. The interesting question is how this failure of socialism in Africa can be accounted for.

It should be pointed out immediately that this failure has nothing to do with the collapse of communism in the Soviet Union and Eastern Europe in the 1980s. As has been pointed out already, the process began in Africa in the 1960s. What that Eastern European collapse has done has been merely to accelerate the African process. It seems that in Africa the failure of socialism has been due to the fact that while the intellectual climate for socialism has been quite good, the sociological and material soil has not proved fertile enough for socialism. The intellectual climate for socialism became favourable in the early decades of independence first, because many African nationalists had conceptually come to associate capitalism with imperialism and colonialism, and the progressive African leaders therefore became 'socialists' because they were nationalists. Secondly, as the capitalist approach to development in the early years of independence proved inadequate, some African leaders tended to look to the socialist path as an alternative strategy of social and economic improvements and transformation.

The third factor which predisposed many Africans in favour of socialism was the rampant corruption that soon appeared among the post-colonial rulers of the continent. It is true that corruption is by no means a peculiarity of capitalism and is not unknown in socialist countries. It was, nevertheless, felt that social discipline could at times be more difficult to uphold in conditions of *laissez-faire* economic behaviour than in conditions of relatively centralized planning and supervision. The fourth factor was the widespread belief that traditional African culture was basically collectivist, and therefore 'socialist'. This was certainly the contention of African leaders like Senghor, Nyerere and Mboya. Above all, African regimes which were planning to go the one-party-state route were particularly tantalized by socialist symbolism. After all, the centralizing tendencies of socialism could help justify a one-party monopoly of power.

PLATE 16.4 *Tom Mboya of Kenya, former trade union leader and minister of economic planning, assassinated in 1969*

It was for all these reasons that the intellectual climate looked more broadly favourable to socialism. Indeed, most African governments soon after independence paid some kind of lip-service to socialism, while those countries already listed adopted it not only ideologically but operationally.

But all these countries have failed because of the barrenness of the sociological soil for socialism in spite of the suitability of the intellectual climate. The first unfavourable sociological factor was, and is still, the fact that ethnicity in Africa is far stronger than class consciousness. Most Africans are members of their ethnic group first and members of a particular social class second. When the chips are down, the Luo and the Yoruba workers are more likely to identify with the Luo and Yoruba bourgeoisie in Kenya and Nigeria respectively than they are with fellow peasants, as the experience of both Jaramogi Oginga Odinga and Chief Obafemi Awolowo clearly signified. Oginga Odinga attempted to form a radical socialist party. He soon discovered his supporters were not the disadvantaged of Kenya but almost exclusively Luo. Similarly, despite Chief Obafemi Awolowo's socialist rhetoric in both the first and second Republics of Nigeria, he soon discovered that he was a hero not of the working class of Nigeria as a whole but of nearly all classes of Yorubaland. On balance, it can be legitimately argued that whenever there has been near confrontation and competition between the forces of ethnicity on one side and the forces of class–consciousness on the other, ethnicity has almost invariably triumphed in Africa.

The second unfavourable sociological factor is the strength of cultural élites in Africa as against economic classes as such. Owing to the weakness of economic classes, the only class that could have brought about the socialist revolution in Africa was the élite. Unfortunately, the élite was composed entirely of highly Westernized Africans who acquired their power not through the possession of wealth but the possession of Western education and verbal skills. Thus, even when this élite became revolutionary, they could not bring about the socialist revolution since, as Karl Marx had expected, it was the least-advantaged class in the most advanced societies – and not the best-advantaged class which the Westernized African élite was – that could bring about the revolution. Even those Africans who went to the Soviet Union or China had to be Westernized first since the works of Marx, Engels, Lenin and Mao have not been translated into indigenous African languages like Kiswahili or Yoruba. It is a socio-linguistic impossibility for an African to be a sophisticated Marxist without being at the same time substantially Westernized. The nature of élite formation in Africa can therefore be counted definitely as an aspect of the uncongenial sociological soil that socialism had to confront in African conditions.

A third factor of this barrenness of the soil concerns Africa's organizational capabilities in the present historical phase. Many hastily assume that a tradition of collectivism in a traditional setting is a relevant preparation for organized collective efforts in a modern setting. Unfortunately, much of the evidence points the other way. Collective effort based on custom and tradition and kinship ties leaves Africa unprepared

488

for the kind of organized collectivism which needs to be based on command rather than ritual. If socialism requires a rational, efficient command-structure which is not based on custom, ethnic empathy or ritual, the present stage of social change in the African experience is still inhospitable to socialist transformation.

The fourth aspect of the infertility of Africa's sociological soil for the socialist plant would take us back to issues of historical continuity. Many African economies have already been deeply integrated into a world economy dominated by the West. African countries which go socialist domestically find that they are still integrated in the world capitalist system. The rules of that system are overwhelmingly derived from principles evolved in the history of capitalism. In international trade, countries seek to maximize their return and acquire profit. The rules of business and exchange at the international level, the banking system which underpins those exchanges, the actual currencies used in money markets and in meeting balance of payments, are all products of the capitalist experience. Countries like Vietnam, Angola and even Cuba, discover soon enough that their best economic salvation is to gain international legitimacy by Western standards. Vietnam and Cuba may fail in gaining their legitimacy, but it is part of their ambition to begin receiving Western benefaction and to have easy access to Western markets for their goods, and Western currency markets as well.

What all this once again means is that Third-World countries can make their internal domestic arrangements socialist while remaining deeply integrated in the international capitalist system at the same time. It has also been argued that a country like Tanzania is today more dependent on the world capitalist system than it was before it inaugurated its neo-socialist experiment under the Arusha Declaration in 1967.

This then is the configuration of factors which on one side reveals that Africa is ready for socialism intellectually and, on the other side, warns us that the material conditions for genuine socialist experimentation in Africa are not yet at hand. The intellectual climate is promising; the sociological soil is forbidding.

Return to liberal democratic values

In addition to the demise of socialist values in Africa, there has also been a steady return to the former liberal democratic values of the early years of independence. There are liberal democratic movements now in a majority of African states demanding an end to one-party and military rule, the return to a multi-party system and competitive political elections, and the restoration of basic human rights, in particular freedom of association and of the mass media, and freedom from arbitrary arrest and detention. Other demands are for social justice and accountability, and for privatization, free-market forces and decentralization and for the participation of all classes in the decision-making and developmental processes. Even former stalwarts of the one-party system and the socialist model of development such as Nyerere have joined the new band-wagon. And that this new movement is achieving success is evident from the granting of multi-partyism and free elections by such leaders as Mobutu of Zaire, Houphouët-Boigny of Côte d'Ivoire and Kerekou of Benin. There followed open competitive elections in Benin, Cape Verde, Sao Tome and Principe, Gabon and Senegal, all of which decided to join the small group of democratic countries in Africa. Once more, one cannot help but demand an explanation of this very welcome turn of events.

Again, one should hasten to add that these developments are neither of recent origin nor have they been touched off by the *glasnost* and *perestroika* of Gorbachev or the pressure of international financial institutions such as the World Bank and the IMF or by aid-donors such as the United States, Britain and France. In some African countries such as Ghana, Nigeria, Côte d'Ivoire and Kenya, the demand for democracy and civilian rule began as early as the late 1960s and 1970s following the introduction of the one-party system or military dictatorships. Surely, everybody is aware of the Mwakenya movement in Kenya and the arrest and detention of the novelist Ngugi and some members of parliament and other intellectuals in Kenya in the 1970s, and of the anti-Union government movement in Ghana in the 1970s, led by the People's Movement for Freedom and Justice against the military rule of Col. I. K. Acheampong, which demanded the restoration of civilian rule and parliamentary democracy based on the multi-party system. What the fall of communism in Eastern Europe and the Soviet Union and the pressures of the IMF and the industrial countries of the West are doing is to compel African leaders to concede to the demands of these movements instead of arbitrarily and brutally suppressing them, as had been the case in the 1970s and early 1980s. The real reason for the rise of these movements is the simple fact that by the 1970s not only the socialist regimes but also the one-party systems had failed to deliver the goods, namely development and nation-building.

It should be emphasized that two key arguments that were advanced in the late 1950s and 1960s for the introduction of the one-party democracies were the imperative of national unity over-and-above classes or ethnic groups and the demand for development. Thus Julius Nyerere contended:

> Now that the colonialists have left, there is no longer any division between the rulers on the one hand and the ruled on the other . . . Multi-partyism is a luxury that we in Africa cannot afford. We have too little time and there is too much to do to allow ourselves such an idle pastime.[17]

17. J. K. Nyerere, 1970a, p. 48.

Madeira Keita of Mali also argued that the single party, the concentrated structure of the nation, is 'the crucible in which the peasant and the urban-dweller meet'.[18]

'Continuous development', wrote F. Tombalbaye (Chad), 'requires the commitment of all to an objective agreed upon together, as well as the coming together of all energies; and, as mobilizer, the single party, will play a key role in the area'.[19]

PLATE 16.5 *Ahmed Sékou Touré, president of the Republic of Guinea, 1958–84*

'If the party identifies itself with the people', Sékou Touré maintained, 'it is obvious that the State must also identify itself with the party so as to form the unbreakable trilogy: people, party and state'. Thus 'no reason of party can or should prevail over the reason and interest of the people, just as no reason of state can prevail over the party line'.[20] The 1982 constitution in Guinea provided that 'revolutionary power . . . is exercised by the people organized in the Democratic Party of Guinea, the party-state, on the basis of democratic centralism'; all organs of power are organs of this party-state and 'judges shall be elected by party bodies at all levels'. This was also the language of the leaders of Togo, Cameroon,

18. M. Keita, cited by L. Sylla, 1977, p. 260.
19. F. Tombalbaye, 1977, cited by L. Sylla, 1977, p. 260.
20. A. Sékou Touré, 1977, cited by L. Sylla, 1977, pp. 245–7.

491

Zimbabwe and Zaire. In the latter country, the president's party was 'the only state institution'.[21] Collectivism had become a political monopoly.

However, after decades of this system, neither national unity nor development had been achieved in those African countries. On the contrary, it was obvious by the late 1970s that the few democratic countries like Mauritius and Botswana had done significantly better in terms of economic development, political stability and nation-building. What had in fact happened in all these countries was surely the suppression of the basic human rights, blatant autocracy, widespread corruption, nepotism and the domination of all aspects of the society by the state apparatus and the monopoly of the resources and wealth of the state by the party leaders or the military oligarchies and their clients. On the contrary, it is now being increasingly realized that while pluralism has not been a panacea for political ills, it does facilitate the attainment of one of the highest political values, namely, freedom. For in the end, as many Africans are now asking, why talk of development and unity as absolute values? Development for whom? Unity for whom? What is development for those who are not apparatchiks of the party? Herein lies the heart of the democratic revolution sweeping through Africa in the early 1990s. What Africans are demanding, then, is a return not only to liberal democratic values but also to those values embodied in and symbolized by their national mottoes, anthems and flags: national unity, development, freedom and social justice.

Towards a new capitalist ethic

However, in its present push for the liberal and democratic mode of development, should Africa go the whole hog of privatization and the free-market approach of the West? In the light of past experience, Africa should exercise some caution here and introduce some modification. In the first place, Africans have all seen how strong ethnicity with its concomitant nepotism still is in Africa, and if they adopt this approach, is there not the likelihood of the whole market being cornered or monopolized by an ethnic group or two? Should Africa therefore not introduce some ethnic 'anti-trust legislation' to prevent or break up 'ethnic monopolies' like say those of the Igbo or the Kikuyu in Nigeria and Kenya respectively in the early years of independence?

The second important lesson is how the prestige motive in African economic behaviour has encouraged ostentatious consumption and self-indulgent 'aristocratic' and monarchical exhibitionism. The Mercedes-Benz has continued to be a symbol of Africa's ostentatious indulgence – but in places in Nigeria the expensive fleet of cars sometimes went with

21. P. F. Gonidec, 1983, p. 72.

a palace or two, sometimes a private plane and a helicopter, and a loud way of life, all for a single family!

While the profit motive in classical economic theory was supposed to lean toward greater *production*, the prestige motive in contemporary African economic behaviour leans towards greater *consumption*. What is more, the consumer products commanding the most prestige are often imported and require foreign exchange. Privatization on its own does not make an African economy produce more. The prestige motive operates both privately and at the state level, ominously eating away into the resources of the country.

When Westerners call upon African countries to privatize, they are expecting the profit motive to be given a free play. But in fact, the problem in most of Africa is not simply how to liberate and activate the *profit motive*, but also how to control and restrain the *prestige motive*. Arguably the latter crusade is even more urgent than the former.

Indeed, the ultimate crusade may well turn out to be how to tap the prestige motive in such a way that it serves the goals of production and not merely the appetites of consumption. Should Africa not then make creativity more prestigious than acquisition? Should Africa not make production more prestigious than possession? Should Africans not take a closer look at the problems of *incentives* in Africa? How can we be more precisely sensitized to the *African* equilibrium between prestige and profit?

A third major *private* constraint on the market (after ethnic nepotism and the prestige motive) is the general problem of bribery and corruption prevalent in post-colonial Africa. Corruption can clog up procedures and substantially paralyse production and distribution. Again corruption can be both in the public sector and in the private; it can be bureaucratic or omnipresent. Privatization of the economy may simply mean the *privatization of corruption* – and sometimes this is more contagious in the wider society than the corruption of officials and bureaucrats.

Capitalism has come to Africa without the 'Protestant ethic' of work and frugality. Economically Protestantism was not against the acquisitive instinct; it was distrustful of the instinct to consume, especially indulgently. As a Puritan saying put it at the time of the Reformation, 'You may labour to be rich for God, though not for the flesh and sin'. Wealth was regarded as unethical only insofar as it was a temptation to idleness and sinful indulgence. The acquisition of wealth was only dangerous if it eroded the twin disciplines of *work* and *frugality* in the name of God.

Capitalism arrived in Africa with the imperative of acquisition without the discipline of work and frugality. The white man himself in Africa set a dangerous example. He never washed his own clothes, or cooked his own food, or polished his own shoes, or made his own bed, or cleaned his own room, or even poured his own gin and tonic! The luxurious aristocratic life of white settlers as they played masters to African servants was detrimental to the spirit of the capitalism the white man himself had

493

arrived with. Africa's own prestige motive – which had been sociable in its original versions – now was transformed by the aristocratic life-styles imported by the white man. Africa's prestige motive was given the colonial incarnation of expensive European consumer culture complete with huge houses, domestic servants and 'garden boys'.

If the ideology of entrepreneurship simply means acquisitiveness, this has now arrived in a big way in much of Africa. Indeed, those who do not take advantage of their opportunities to become wealthy, and to help their kinfolk, are sometimes despised.

The challenge is partly about the means used to acquire wealth. Is the wealth *created* or simply obtained? Acquiring wealth from a prosperous farm is a creative process. Acquiring wealth as either a middle-man on behalf of external interests or through corruption may not be creative at all. Can we transform the acquisitive instinct in Africa into something more directly productive?

But if the *means* of acquiring wealth need to be creative, the *ends* of acquiring wealth also need to be healthy. Ostentatious consumption is not usually among the healthier ends of economic success. In short, the African ideology of entrepreneurship needs a fundamental reform of both the means and the ends of the pursuit of wealth in society. Until that happens, privatization of African economies – far from being the best way of achieving a healthy and free market – may itself be detrimental to the market-place. For those who are sufficiently attentive, the African experience demonstrates that privatization is not necessarily the best protection for the free market in all cultures. Other social, moral and legal safeguards are often necessary.

Conclusion: a chronology of ideology

History is partly a struggle to identify trends. Particularly elusive are trends in the history of ideas and values. Nevertheless, what can we make of the years since 1935 in Africa's experience? What have been the trends in values and ideas?

At the general level, we have identified the more familiar dialectic between collectivism and individualism in Africa's ideological history. We have also identified the dialectic between pluralism and nationalism – encompassing issues as diverse as democracy and pan-Africanism, the state and ethnicity.

This chapter has also addressed what Nkrumah designated as *consciencism* – the interplay between indigenous culture, Islam and Euro–Christian civilization. Edward Wilmot Blyden had preceded Nkrumah in this vision of the triad. Ali Mazrui developed it further in his television series, *The Africans: A Triple Heritage*, and in Mazrui's companion book of the same title.

494

But on the *ground* in Africa are there definite trends identifiable as *sub-periods* in the era since 1935? We have already referred to the golden age of the alliance between pluralism and nationalism – the period of the last years of colonial rule. African nationalists used liberal and pluralistic rhetoric against their own Western masters. Liberal slogans served the nationalist cause.

In the 1960s most of Africa experienced a turn towards authoritarianism. One-party systems, military coups and presidential autocracy were on the increase throughout much of this first decade of Africa's independence. Many regimes claimed to be socialist in the 1960s – even when they followed the capitalist path. Jomo Kenyatta's senior ministers like Tom Mboya talked enthusiastically about 'African socialism' in the early years of Kenya's independence.

Claims about 'Arab socialism' were also strong in parts of North Africa. The 1960s were Gamāl 'Abd al-Nasser's last decade in power. He spent those years partly consolidating 'socialist' changes in Egypt and partly pursuing vigorous pan-Arab, pan-African and non-aligned policies in world affairs. Al-Nasser died in 1970.

Ahmed Ben Bella was overthrown in Algeria in 1965, but the succeeding regime of Houari Boumedienne continued the politics of state socialism which had characterized the earlier rhetoric of the Algerian revolution. Muammar Kadhaffi overthrew King Idrīs in 1969 – and before long Kadhaffi initiated a version of Libyan welfare socialism which Kadhaffi subsequently called 'the Third Way'.

What was missing throughout the 1960s was an open declaration of Marxism–Leninism as official ideology, almost anywhere in Africa. The 1960s were, in general, the years of enthusiasm for socialism but with a cautious attitude towards Marxism–Leninism. Indeed, regimes like that of al-Nasser in Egypt were both strongly pro-socialist and anti-Marxist at the same time. Many Egyptian communists were imprisoned by al-Nasser.

Gaffar Nimeiri in the Sudan began his 1969 coup in strong alliance with Sudanese communists. But the alliance did not last long. The partners turned against each other. Nimeiri triumphed.

Politically fragmented Nigeria did not develop a nationally popular ideology. But left-wing tendencies were discernible not only on campuses but also in Chief Obafemi Awolowo. Communism was almost totally absent.

It was not until the 1970s that Marxism–Leninism attained a high profile on Africa's continental landscape. Two factors in the 1970s were crucial – first, social revolutions in countries like Ethiopia and the Malagasy Republic and, secondly, the collapse of the Portuguese empire. The 1974 Ethiopian upheaval was perhaps the most far-reaching social revolution in Africa in the second half of the twentieth century. The regime which succeeded Haile Selassie eventually declared itself Marxist–

Leninist. Francophone countries like the Malagasy Republic, the Congo and Benin also moved in a Marxist–Leninist direction – though some more in rhetoric than in substance.

With the collapse of the Portuguese empire, Marxism–Leninism acquired additional visibility elsewhere. Both Angola and Mozambique declared themselves as Marxist–Leninist states and Guinea-Bissau flirted with the radical ideology for a while.

Is the golden age of Marxism–Leninism in Africa from the 1970s to the late 1980s? Certainly by the late 1980s countries like Mozambique, Benin and the Congo were moving away from Marxist–Leninist rhetoric at the governmental level. Some were to give up the labels of being Marxist–Leninist states altogether before long. By the late 1980s and early 1990s was pluralism re-asserting itself in Africa? Was a liberal revival under way? As we indicated, many countries even returned to multi-party constitutions and competitive elections. What could not be predicted with certainty was the durability of these new pluralistic tendencies. Would they at least characterize the remaining few years of the twentieth century? It remains to be seen.

A final historical puzzle concerns the relationship between the precise nature of colonial policy, on the one hand, and the post-colonial ideological consequences, on the other. Virtually no country on the African continent previously ruled by the United Kingdom has declared itself a Marxist–Leninist state. On the other hand, virtually *every* country previously ruled by Portugal has at least experimented with Marxism–Leninism or actually adopted it as official ideology. Countries previously ruled by France lie somewhere between the Anglophone paradigm (no Marxism–Leninism) and the Lusophone paradigm (widespread Marxism–Leninism). Francophone Africa is ideologically diverse. To what extent were the different colonial policies of the three imperial powers responsible for the post-colonial ideological differences between their former colonies? For example, was the greater oppression of Portuguese colonial rule responsible for the greater ideological radicalization of its colonial victims? Some historical puzzles in Africa's experience have no easy answers, but comparative repression may be part of the background.

In any case, the post-colonial ideological differences between Anglophone, Lusophone and Francophone countries may turn out to be very short-lived. The values and ideas which come with colonial rule may turn out to be far more temporary than the underlying cultural continuities of indigenous Africa.

Colonial rule enclosed together people who had previously lived separately – and divided people who were once united. Ethnic tensions are conflicts of values. They have also partly become the greatest threat both to Africa's stability and to African democracy. The answer lies in purposeful national integration and a shared experience in ideas and values. Africa is in search of a creative ideology.

When multiple cultures confront each other within the same national boundaries, their relationship can be at varying degrees of social depth. The minimum stage of relationship is that of *co-existence* – when two or more cultural communities barely know about each other. Each may have its own conservative paradigm of thought, grounded on ethnic exclusivity. Indigenous traditionalism can reign supreme at this level.

The second degree of relationship is that of *contact* – when two or more groups either begin to trade with each other, or participate jointly in the job-market, or become members of the same political party, or listen to each other's music. Above all the contact must include sharing ideas and evolving shared priorities. Ancient traditions of the elder, the warrior and the sage may interact between ethnic cultures.

The third degree of inter-ethnic relationship is that of *competition* – when these contacts result in rivalry for resources, for power, or for social and economic opportunities. Debates about ideology and policy are part-and-parcel of this competitive stage of nation-building. Capitalism may conflict with socialism in the political arena. Individualism may be on the defensive against collectivism.

The fourth relationship between two or more ethnic cultures is that of *conquest* – when one of the ideologies or cultures begins to get the upper hand. One ideology, for example, may become more influential than others. Or the newly-dominant system of values may successfully claim a disproportionate share of power, resources or socio-economic opportunities. Nepotism could prevail even under socialism. Pluralism maybe stifled by political hegemony and monopoly of power.

The fifth stage of relationship between cultures is that of *compromise*. This is a stage when the competing ideologies, political values and traditions find a *modus vivendi*, an acceptable formula of conflict-resolution and a viable basis of social partnership. Individualism may be reconciled with collectivism; pluralism with nationalism.

The sixth stage of relationship is that of *coalescence* – when the values and identities of the political groups begin to merge, and their boundaries become less and less distinct. The cultures, values and ideologies, and even languages, intermingle, and a larger sense of identity starts to emerge. That enlarged identity could be national consciousness. Ethnicity merges with national consciousness. A national ideology may be evolving.

In some African countries ideological divisions are also affected by *international relations* and by *economic factors*. But it should be borne in mind that diplomacy and economics are often integrative as well as divisive. The balance varies from society to society. Non-alignment can consolidate a sense of national identity at home.

The struggle for national integration and state-building in Africa has only just begun. Ideological intercourse and cultural interaction are part-and-parcel of the evolution of nationhood and the consolidation of collective identity in the post-colonial era.

This social trend will have to include the creative contributions of Africa's thinkers and intellectuals allowed to operate in freedom. The more innovative aspects of individualism may truly enter into an alliance with the more humanistic aspects of collectivism. Only then will state and nation in Africa, instead of destroying each other, be able to engage at last in a process of mutual construction and enrichment.

SECTION V

Socio-cultural change since 1935

Religion and social evolution

Tshishiku TSHIBANGU
in collaboration with
J. F. Ade AJAYI *and* **Lemin SANNEH**

Introduction

> Our society is not the ancient society but a new society broadened by Euro-Christian and Islamic influences. So, a new ideology is necessary, an ideology that can be stated in a philosophical definition, but which is at the same time an ideology which does not abandon Africa's original and human principles . . . an ideology whose aims will be to contain the African experience of the Islamic and Euro-Christian presence as well as the experience of African traditional society.[1]

Religion, it has been said, impregnates the entire texture of individual and commercial life in Africa. The African is 'profoundly, incurably a believer, a religious person'. To him, religion is not just a set of beliefs but a way of life, the basis of culture, identity and moral values. Religion is an essential part of the tradition that helps to promote both social stability and creative innovation.[2] It is therefore not surprising that in his agenda for social transformation and in the search for a new ideology to guide that transformation, Nkrumah saw in religion a resource to be utilized as well as a problem to be contained. He sees African society as rooted in traditional religion and broadened by Euro-Christian and Islamic influences. As a resource, he sees the new ideology as a 'gestation' of the three religious traditions in Africa. And yet if 'social harmony' is to result, the religious factor has to be constrained: the new ideology should be one that 'can be stated in a philosophical definition' – that is to say, in secular terms without abandoning the basic values of African traditional religion or the African historical experience of both Islam and Christianity.

The problem of religion in African social transformation arises from both the strength and the plurality of religion. Traditional African religion was, among other things, a vehicle for exploring the forces of nature and for systematizing new knowledge both of the human and the physical

---

1. K. Nkrumah, 1964, pp. 93–7.
2. See Présence Africaine, 1972; V. Mulago, 1980; M. Glélé, 1981.

environment. In the search for understanding and coping with the many aspects of nature, the African recognized several divinities and established many cults. Traditional African religion was non-proselytizing and open-ended. It was tolerant of religious innovation as a manifestation of new knowledge, always hoping to interpret and internalize the new knowledge within the traditional cosmology. Thus, in time, both Christianity and Islam developed within Africa, initially in a symbiotic relationship with traditional religion. But both Christianity and Islam are proselytizing religions, claiming exclusive revelation of the Truth, fiercely competitive and intolerant of co-existing with other religions, particularly each with the other. In their competition, ancient Christianity was rubbed out in North Africa and the Nile valley, except among the Copts of Egypt and in Ethiopia. Periodic movements of reform and religious purification produced a continuum from situations where Islam and Christianity were interpreted in traditional African cosmology to those in which Islam and Christianity provided the cosmology but which was indigenized within African social thought. Thus, plurality of religion became an essential feature of African society, but there was also what Nkrumah called a distinct 'African experience of Islamic and Euro-Christian presence'.

The widespread activities of Christian missions in Africa in the nineteenth century in the wake of colonialism complicated the religious situation. The degree of indigenization of Christianity and Islam in the past had depended on the autonomy of the people both socially and politically. With the loss of autonomy under colonialism, traditional African religion became identified in the mind of many Africans with an Africa that had failed and had been subjugated. Many people began to proclaim adherence to Christianity or Islam as representing new developments, progress and the future, without necessarily abandoning the old cosmology or basic religious beliefs. Western education, sponsored largely by the Christian missions, became the vehicle both for the African aspiration for new knowledge and the technology of Europe, and for alienation from traditional culture.

Thus, the problem that faced Nkrumah and other leaders of the period of decolonization was how to achieve social transformation and create a new society in the face of the strength of religious beliefs and yet of divided commitments to different religious views of society. What role should traditional religion play? How far could a person be a faithful Muslim or Christian and still be a good African? The conflict of values and ideologies produced trauma in the private lives of individuals and communities that has been the subject of several novels. It is the crises in the public sector occasioned by the religious factor that has interested historians: the role of the different religious traditions in the struggles for liberation in Kenya and Zimbabwe, in Morocco and Algeria, in Senegal, Zaire and Zambia; the religious factor in the competition of various groups for sharing political and economic power, the control of education or control over foreign policy and foreign relations; the struggle between various religious groups seeking autonomy within a state aiming for exclusive monopoly of power, or minority religious groups resisting a dominant one seeking to impose its own faith as the national religion, the only basis of values, and of access to political and economic resources of the state.[3]

Accurate statistics are notoriously difficult to come by,[4] partly because national censuses are either out-of-date or non-existent, partly because claims of rival statistics are an important part of the competition for power, partly also because there is genuine doubt as to when some who claim to be adherents of Islam or Christianity have effectively ceased to belong to the traditional religion, and when they may have reverted back to it. By 1935, it does appear that roughly 80 per cent of the total African population were divided roughly equally between Islam and Christianity, with Islam probably having a slightly larger share. Since then, both Islam and Christianity have made rival claims of further advances at the expense of African traditional religion, though more recently the widespread revival of traditional religion has been reported. Countries in Southern and Central Africa which used to return figures of almost total affiliation to Christianity are discovering substantial survival or revival of traditional beliefs.

Equally important is the national distribution of religious adherents (Fig. 17.1). There are countries with wholly or almost wholly Islamic populations where Islam has been declared the state religion, whether or not the *shariʿa* is enforced. These include Morocco, Tunisia, Algeria, Libya, Somalia, the Comoro Islands and Mauritania. Egypt is predominantly Muslim but with a significant Christian minority group of less than 10 per cent, and so is Senegal. There are several countries where the balance between Christianity and Islam is a major political issue. These include the Sudan, Ethiopia, Chad, Nigeria, Cameroon and Tanzania. Some of these officially declare in their constitutions that the state is 'neutral' or 'secular' in relation to religion. In practice, all the leaders of Africa belong to an élite that has been educated within schools and religious structures that are either Christian or Islamic. While proclaiming the need for reviving traditional African values and principles, few leaders, irrespective of private beliefs and practices, have dared to alienate the religious susceptibilities of the Christians or Muslims by openly embracing traditional religion.

3. For a sample of sources, see E. Fashole-Luke *et al.*, 1978; A. Hastings, 1979; M. O. Beshir, 1968; A. F. Walls, 1978; Gatta Gali Ngothe, 1985; D. Ndogo Bidyogo, 1977.

4. Compare, for example, the two very different sets of statistics for Uganda, 1977, in *Pro Mundi Vita* (Brussels), 1985, and M. Glélé, 1981.

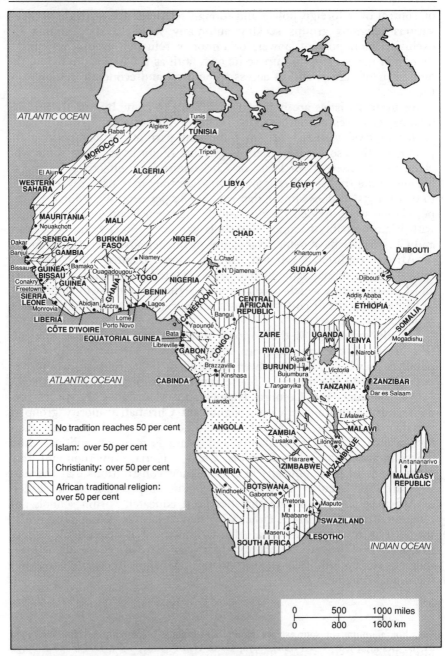

FIG. 17.1 *Distribution of Christianity, Islam and African traditional religion in Africa, where each religion claims 50 per cent or more of the country's population (Source: adapted from* The World Almanac and Book of Facts, *World Almanac of Books and Facts, New York, 1991,* © Pharos Books, 1990)

The continuing relevance of traditional religion

The importance of traditional African religion[5] goes well beyond what the statistical affiliation figure of 20 per cent of the total African population may suggest. For many Christians and Muslims, the basis of moral values still derives more from the old cosmology than from the new beliefs: there is still respect for ancestors as in the pouring of libations, belief in the continuing involvement of ancestors in the life of their successors, belief in the forces of good and evil which can be manipulated by direct access to the divinities through prayer and sacrifice, belief in the efficacy of charms and amulets to ward off evil, and so on. Belief in spirits and witches in social relationships remains a major factor beyond the avowed adherents of traditional religion. Even where such beliefs and practices cease to be held as matters of religion, they are still observed as custom, tradition and part of the cultural heritage. Thus the solidarity of many an extended family or clan or community still revolves round some beliefs in ancestral spirits, venerated periodically by rituals conducted by priests set apart for the purpose.

There is a vast area of African life which both Islam and Christianity have invaded but have not succeeded in completely displacing. This is the area of health and healing. The concept of health in traditional African society was very broad, including well-being in day-to-day life, success on the farm or in whatever craft or other venture one was engaged, in the health of the children, their happiness in the choice of life partners, and so on. Physical ailment is only a symptom of ill health which could arise from the anger of some malevolent force which itself could be because of some misdeed or lack of healthy relationship with one's neighbours or with some ancestor or some divinities. Securing good health meant that the healer would inquire into these varieties of relationships and, through prayer or sacrifice or both, put right whatever was amiss. In addition, the physical ailment was then treated with herbs or incantation if necessary. Many a Christian and Muslim continued to patronize traditional healers and diviners. Many Muslim teachers practice as medical consultants, making charms and amulets for clients who operate within the framework of the traditional healing systems. Much of the current revival of traditional religion is associated with the greater official recognition of the continued importance of the traditional healing systems in the delivery of health care. Official recognition has lessened the necessity for clandestine cover of the continued patronage of traditional healing systems even by the highly-placed Westernized élite.

Similarly, there is today a wider appreciation of the value of the oral traditions of Africa, hitherto nourished by traditional religion, but now studied for their spiritual, literary, philosophical and humanistic qualities

5. Présence Africaine, 1972; M. Glélé, 1981.

independent of religious beliefs. Only a fraction of this has yet been committed to writing or embodied in scholarly dissertations. The accumulated wisdom of several generations of Africans is to be found in these oral sources. The Western-educated élite, by cutting themselves off from this rich source which is the root of their culture, suffer a great deficiency in their mental development and their creativity. Much of the balance and the dignity of villagers regarded as illiterates comes from continuity with these rich cultural traditions. Of particular importance is the heritage of scientific knowledge in agriculture and health care which is embodied in these traditions, developed over the centuries through acute observation, experimentation and practice. Much of this knowledge has been transmitted through the training of priests and diviners which, in many places, has remained meticulous and rigorous. It involves much botanical, zoological, pharmacological and mathematical knowledge, the properties of plants and animals, complex calculations of probabilities, the power of words, and numbers.[6] While these could be detached from traditional religion, there is no doubt that it is association with religious beliefs that has kept alive these systems of knowledge and ideas which form the bulk of the African claim to distinctive culture and contribution to the world pool of ideas. And this body of ideas must have a part to play in re-educating the intellectual leaders of Africa as a basis for any renaissance and revival of creative efforts.

This is not to deny that for many Africans, African religion as a body of religious ideas has an autonomous value of its own.[7] It is ironic that while Western-educated Africans were abandoning the religion even without knowing anything about it, many in the New World in Cuba, Brazil, Haïti and other places were deliberately choosing it in preference to Christianity and Islam because of its deep spiritual qualities. Many people have thus achieved a stable synthesis between the spiritual values of Christianity and African traditional religion. This New-World appreciation has itself played a part in the revival of interest in African traditional religion among the Western-educated élite in Africa.

Until recently, the adherents of traditional religion have, as a body, made few demands on the state in the group struggle for power or the control of education or economic resources. Yet the leaders frequently evoked the cultural resources of traditional religion in the process of decolonization, not only in the ubiquitous dance troupes and festivals of arts, but more seriously in the search for an African ideology, theology or philosophy and the source of African renaissance and creativity. Some traditional rulers, even when they are personally Christian or Muslim,

6. Various scholars are beginning to draw attention to knowledge in agricultural sciences and health sciences. For the mathematics of the Yoruba divining system, see O. Lange, 1985.
7. See A. Hampaté Bà, 1972; K. Mabika, 1965; C. A. Diop, 1957.

are beginning to consider it necessary to emphasize the religious foundation of the pre-colonial polities in their struggle against total eclipse in the post-colonial socio-political order. So also associations of traditional healers[8] are drawing attention to the need for allocation of state resources for developing the traditional healing systems that, as we have shown, have remained so important.

Christianity, decolonization and development

Christianity illustrates best the contradictory role of religion in the social transformation of Africa as both a resource and a problem. On the resource side, there was no doubt that Christianity had been welcome and had grown because of its direct involvement in the development of Africa.[9] Its role in the promotion of Western education at different levels – elementary, secondary, teacher-training, and sometimes also technical and tertiary – was at the heart of African development. Throughout Africa, except in the predominantly Muslim areas, the colonial powers were usually satisfied to leave the missionaries in charge of education in return for some financial support from taxes. The missionaries had extended their interest in Western education to the study of African languages, the elaboration of orthographies, initial linguistic studies, and the translation of the Bible and other religious works to initiate a new literary tradition in African languages and promote literacy. The Christian missions also dominated the book trade, printing and publishing, bookshops and libraries. They played a similar pioneering role in the introduction of Western-type health care in the establishment of hospitals and clinics. Thus, a great attraction of Christianity was in its essential pioneering effort in progressive measures, and encouraging the transition of its members from traditional society into the modernizing world which was set as the goal of colonization, but which colonial policies did little to realize.

At the same time, Christianity had grown up in close collaboration with colonialism while Islam and traditional religion were more distant and sometimes hostile. The European and American missionaries who maintained a rigid hold on the churches they had created were closer in their thought and attitudes to the colonial officials and European settlers than to their African colleagues, assistants and parishioners. By 1935, many missionaries did not believe that Africans could hold positions of responsibility in the Church comparable to positions they had held in the nineteenth century prior to the establishment of colonial rule. The Church

8. M. Last and G. Chavunduka, 1986.
9. J. Mbiti, 1962; R. Sastre, 1962.

establishments were thus part of the colonial structures that African independence movements were trying to decolonize.[10]

Most of the leaders were products of Western education, but they were nonetheless most conscious of the extent to which their education had involved a degree of mental colonization, enforced subordination to Western ideas, and alienation from the roots of African culture. They had first to transcend these constraints and, benefiting from missionary work on African languages, renew their contact with African thought and values, and use these to create the vision of a new African society. Thus, decolonization had to begin with the Church, not only to transform its structures and replace European leadership with African, but also to seek indigenization of its form and content without losing the essence of Christian values. This task of indigenizing the Christian Church was tackled by both Catholics and Protestants, but it was widely recognized that the issues involved went beyond the question of control, content and form of the Christian churches. It concerned the whole development strategy, Nkrumah's search for an ideology of social transformation, the adaptation of Western science and technology, the search for an African philosophy, and a definition of the identity of the African in the modern world.

One of the most influential documents on the question of the indigenization of the Church was the collective work of African leaders of the Catholic Church published in 1956 and setting out the various issues involved: *Des prêtres noirs s'interrogent* (Black priests ask themselves questions). At the same time, the African Society for Culture based in Paris and led by Alioune Diop, saw the issue as the most crucial part of the debate about negritude. Diop used the journal *Présence Africaine* to conduct a lively debate on African religious thought, and specifically even theological research. Thus when the Second Congress of Black Writers and Artists was convened in Rome in 1959, a sub-committee of African theologians and philosophers was established. In 1962, at the time of the Second Vatican Congress, Alioune Diop canvassed the opinion of African Christian intellectuals and, in 1963, published a special issue of the journal on the work of the Vatican Congress entitled *Personnalité africaine et catholicisme*. Diop was also the moving spirit in the three international symposia, in Abidjan in 1961 on 'Religions in Africa' in general, in 1970 in Cotonou on 'African Religions as a Source of Values of Civilization', and in Abidjan in September 1977 on 'The Catholic Church Festival and Black Civilization'. The Colloquium of the World Festival of Black and African Art and Civilization (FESTAC) in 1977 also had an important section on religion.[11]

10. A. Hastings, 1979.
11. See *Bulletin de Théologie Africaine* edited at Kinshasa in French, English and Portuguese. On FESTAC, see M. Amoda, 1978.

PLATE 17.1   *On the occasion of a meeting in Cairo with Third-World theologians, members of the Ecumenical Association of African Theologians paid a visit to Pope Shenouda III, Patriarch of the Coptic Church of Egypt*

The search for models for the indigenization of the Christian Church in Africa went on not only within Catholicism but also within the Protestant churches as well. What is more, both Catholics and Protestants realized that the issues involved were in no way sectarian and there have been efforts to work together not only at a pan-African but also at an ecumenical level. Notable in this regard was the meeting of African theologians convened in Ibadan in 1969 by the World Council of Churches. Several institutes, such as the Kinshasa Centre of African Religions, have tried to reflect this pan-African ecumenism both in their journal (*Cahiers des religions africaines*) and their symposia on Christianity and African Religions (1978); Christianity and African Forms of Spiritual Life (1983); and African Mediations of the Sacred Rites and Religious Language (1986). All these have encouraged the formation of the Ecumenical Association of African Theologians (*Association œcuménique des théologiens africains* – AOTA). In all these, three trends have been discernible in the approach to the question of African theology.

(1) Initially, the approach was to explore the theology of traditional African religion in its various forms: the nature and attributes of the supreme being; the nature and meaning of sacrifice; the

509

role of prayer and religious rituals. Distinct from the efforts of usually-European agnostic anthropologists and ethnologists, these were studies by African theologians and Christian leaders who saw traditional African religion as preparatory to the Christian gospel, and were exploring it for spiritual values which could be used to bring home more clearly to Africans the gospel message.

(2) Others rejected that approach and made a distinction between the theology of traditional African religion and African theology as such. They are wary about suggesting a dialogue between the Christian theology and the theology of traditional African religion. They see African theology as the thought of African Christian theologians, deriving from the Bible, interpreted in the light of African historical experience and reality, and in dialogue with Christian theology in other non-Western parts of the world.

(3) There is also emerging a black theology or liberation theology, specifically in South Africa, drawing its inspiration from biblical faith expressed in the languages and categories of Africa, as well as the experience and reflections of the oppressed peoples struggling for liberation, such as blacks in North America and marginalized groups in Latin America.[12]

Side by side with this search for a new theology, there has also been the effort to organize and structure the liturgy, and develop a system of sacramental rites that, while being faithful to the received Christian formulae, takes account of the African reality. For example, what role could African musical styles and musical instruments play? How could Christian rites of baptism, marriage and burial take account of African family institutions in which the naming of a new child is a family affair; marriage is not just a union of the bride and bridegroom but a union of their two families, and burial ceremonies have various family dimensions and implications. The missionaries saw clearly enough that if the Christian Church were not to lose its social and political significance, Africanization of the personnel in the leadership of the Church must keep pace with, or even move ahead of, that of the institutions of the state. It was important that the spokesmen of the Church in the ensuing struggle for political and economic power, the control of education, the shaping of the structures of the state, and so on, should be Africans. And these new leaders of the Church could not but contribute their views to the political search for the African personality, identity and authenticity.

Islam and modernization

Unlike Christianity which was an ally of colonialism, Muslim states gave the colonial powers some of the most determined resistance. Yet, in spite

12. V. Y. Mudimbe, 1985.

of continued suspicion and occasional hostility, Islam benefited from the colonial presence. The colonial powers were most suspicious of, and continued to monitor cautiously, the international connections of Islam, especially with well-known anti-imperialist centres such as Cairo. They controlled the movement of would-be scholars seeking education, and even the pilgrimage in the Middle East. But at home, they found that collaboration with quiescent Muslim communities could be of advantage both to the colonial powers and the Muslims. Islam, it has been shown, benefited from the degree of urbanization and increased mobility encouraged by the railways, motor roads and demand for migrant labour. While the colonial powers were hostile to many institutions of traditional religion, they encouraged elementary Islamic education in the Ḳur'ānic schools; they enacted laws protecting Muslims in the free practice of their religion, including the provisions of the *sharī'a* in the regulation of civil law among Muslim communities. They placed restrictions on the access of Christian missionaries in Muslim areas. Many African communities who had previously resisted the spread of Islam, considered it more honourable after the colonial conquest to join Islam than the religion of the conquerors. But even with such people who became Muslim as an act of passive resistance, there often developed a remarkable degree of collaboration with the colonial authorities. The most notable example was the Wolof whom the pre-colonial *djihād* movements had failed to convert but who came out of the colonial period thoroughly Islamized.[13]

This remarkable achievement was in no small measure due to the work of Shaykh Amadu Bamba,[14] founder of the *ṣūfī* order called the Mourides. The success of his evangelical work among the Wolof benefited from the combination of religious belief and economic prosperity in the cultivation of groundnuts for export. He himself became a highly respected figure in the colonial period and was decorated for his services in recruiting troops for the French army to serve in France during the First World War. The success and continued importance of the Mourides in contemporary Senegal illustrates one way in which Islam, through the spiritual values of mysticism, has accommodated itself within African society and culture as a vital religious force.

Thus, in the process of decolonization, Muslims did not face the same problems of colonial structures and cultural alienation that faced Christians. That initially they regarded independence as an 'Ambiguous Adventure'[15] was because of their hostility to Western education under the control of Christian missionaries and the fear that this had given an unfair advantage to the Christians. While in North Africa there was a

13. L. Sanneh, 1986.
14. See F. Dumond, 1975; M. Klein, 1968; D. C. O'Brien, 1971; and L. Brenner, 1984.
15. C. A. Kane, 1962.

PLATE 17.2 *Shaykh Amadu Bamba, head of the Mourides of Senegal, with his* talibe

continuous evolution of nationalist ideas, Muslims in West Africa to begin with tended to be lukewarm in the nationalist movements. They had stood outside the mainstream of the pan-African movement which was inspired from the New World through European Christian circles. It was one of the contributions of al-Nasser that he became the point of juncture of pan-Arabism, pan-Islamism and pan-Africanism. His influence helped to pull West African Muslim leaders into the mainstream of the nationalist movement.

For 50 years, in several African countries, Islam has made advances toward modernism, particularly by launching an educational system that branched out from the purely traditional paths. First, there was the Aḥmadiyya movement, outside the mainstream of Islamic orthodoxy, combining Western education with Islamic and Arabic studies. The Aḥmadiyya were important in Nigeria and Sierra Leone. Then the *Wahhabis*, within the Wahhabiyya reform movement, developed after the Second World War, formed two important action groups: the *Subbanu al-Muslim*, leading the movement for educational reform, and the *Union culturelle musulmane* (Moslem Cultural Union), now an international organization concerned with all Islamic affairs, including politics.[16]

The expansion of the Wahhabiyya reform movement coincided with the appearance of the *Rassemblement démocratique africain* – RDA (Democratic

16. L. Kaba, 1974; H. M. Amiji, 1984.

African Union), the most important movement for decolonization in French West Africa. Many Wahhabi, acting individually, rallied to the RDA, their chief political aim being to establish a democratic state based on Koranic teaching of liberty, equality and *idjmā'* or 'consensus'. Their conviction of the need for a radical reform of society, their firm opposition to the colonial order and to Westernization, and their openness beyond ethnic barriers, all allowed them to co-operate with African leaders who had more secular views. Islam therefore appeared as a force for independence, unification and the transformation of society. As Ken Post put it:

> In areas where Islam has long been established, in northern Cameroon, northern Nigeria, Niger, Mali, Guinea, Senegal and Mauritania, it has profoundly affected the process of élite-formation produced by the social changes of colonial rule. In some of them it offered an alternative cultural tradition, and even indigenous political systems, and provided ways of obtaining power and influence other than the purely modern ones.[17]

On the east coast of Africa, ideas on the transformation of society developed through reformist newspapers such as *Al-Islah* (Reform), which began to appear in Mombasa, Kenya, in 1932. To counter the attraction and influence of Islamic anti-imperialistic and nationalistic messages that spread from Cairo and other places, the British colonial government at the end of the 1940s and during the 1950s encouraged the setting up of the East African Muslim Welfare Association under the patronage of His Highness Aga Khan III and of the Sultan of Zanzibar. Similarly, they helped to finance the establishment of the Mombasa Institute of Moslem Education (MIOME). This institution served all of East Africa, and many young African Muslims were able to receive a modern education at secondary and post-secondary level, in an Islamic cultural and religious environment.[18]

Historians and ideologists have emphasized that conditions existed in Africa for the establishment and development of an Islamic socialism. According to Mustafa as-Sibaci,[19] society at the time of the Prophet Muḥammad and of the first four caliphs was socialist in character, and these leaders are considered to be founders of the first socialist community. Elsewhere in black Africa some have insisted that pre-colonial African society was also socialist in character. 'The sense of solidarity within the community between the members of the same group, and also the collective right to ownership of land, are seen as the most important

17. K. Post, 1964, p. 52.
18. H. M. Amiji, 1984, p. 115.
19. M. as-Sibaci, n.d.

elements of socialism in primitive Islamic society and of that of African precolonial society'.[20]

In fact, Islamic socialism is the official ideology in North Africa of countries such as Egypt, Algeria and Libya; that of the majority party in power in Tunisia is specifically termed 'Destūrian socialism'. It is also practised in Somalia. The statesman Mamadou Dia advocated it in Senegal, and argues for it in his book, *Islam, sociétés africaines et culture industrielle* (Islam, African societies and industrial culture).[21]

There is increasing reflection on the doctrinal principles of research for lines of action that favour the psycho-social liberation and the promotion of women within Islam. This is particularly necessary on the social plane, because of the problem of the status of women in a regime of polygamy, a regime that is generally officially recognized and inscribed in the family law of African states that are influenced by Muslim doctrines.[22]

The problems of indigenizing Islam in depth arise only in relation to black Africa. Here, one must establish that Islam is stricter than Christianity, for example as regards admitting adaptations of its ritual system. With some delimitation of detail only, imposed by local conditions and particularly climate, black Muslims carry out all the essential obligations called the five pillars of Islam: the profession of faith in one God and in his Prophet Muḥammad; daily prayers, carried out five times; the *Ramāḍān* fast, which has connotations of mortification, purification and solidarity with the poor; the required giving of alms; the pilgrimage to Mecca, to be accomplished at least once in a lifetime.

Can one then legitimately speak in Africa of a true 'Africanization' of Islam? Amadou Hampaté Bà is categorical on this subject:

> There cannot be a black Islam any more than a black Christianity or a black Judaism. What there is is the principal Islam, the only one that must be studied. Naturally, as my master Tyerno Bokar the sage of Bandiagara told me, it may happen and happens quite frequently that in islamizing itself, a country adopts one of the multicoloured tones that the gigantic triangular prism of Islam may offer, breaking up the divine white truth whose light Islam diffuses.[23]

However, African Islam shows none the less characteristic currents and tendencies according to the moral and social problems of local situations. This is the explanation for the emphasis on brotherhoods, particularly in West Africa. And we have already mentioned the reformist current that is well known through the procedures of the Moslem Cultural Union

20. J. M. Abun-Nasr, 1979, p. 120.
21. M. Dia, 1975; R. Milon, 1962.
22. See, for example, A. Boudhiba, 1975.
23. Statement made at the *Colloque sur les Religions*, Présence Africaine, 1961.

founded in 1953. On the decidedly 'progressive' orientations of this movement, Vincent Monteil says: 'It favours all that expresses the African personality – despite some of its Bamako members who wanted to destroy the masks and the statuettes. So it admits songs, dances and Negro art. It insists on the necessary distinction, on religious matters, between dogma and cult on one side, and social relationships on the other.' The latter in his opinion may be accommodated. Some people even think that fasting may be given freedom of choice, that the number of daily prayers could be reduced to two, or even dropped, because 'work is the true prayer'. What count are morals, conduct and social behaviour. As to polygamy, 'there will necessarily be evolution, linked to the education of girls and to the emancipation of women'.[24]

The development of Islam in contemporary Africa must also have been influenced by the socio-political reality in most African countries of co-existing with Christianity and traditional African religion. While formal dialogue with traditional religion is unacceptable, there have been interesting attempts to establish, in religious and doctrinal centres, high-level dialogue with Christianity. One such centre was opened in Tunis in 1977 under the leadership of Professor A. Boudhiba.[25] In Senegal, at the Bopp Centre,[26] there is an effort to achieve Muslim–Christian co-operation in community development. In spite of fierce competition which seems to characterize religious rivalries, especially among the élite, generally there is a good deal of actual co-operation and genuine dialogue at the more popular village level.

One of the most important results of the process of decolonization has been the transcending of the bounds of localism imposed on Islam by colonialism, and the re-emphasizing of the universal and international aspects of Islam. Contacts with the Middle East through the pilgrimage, pan-Islamic movement and exchange of scholars have been revived and greatly expanded. Thus major movements in the Middle East – such as the *Shi'ite* fundamentalism of Khomeini's Iran and Kadhaffi radical revolutionary ideology – have had their impact on Africa. It is never certain, however, to what extent such localized anti-modernist radical movements in popular Islam, such as Maitatsine in Northern Nigeria, can be attributed to international influences. However, through its international links, Islam makes a definite contribution to the general socio-economic development of Africa thanks to the financial support made to different countries by the oil-producing Arab states of North Africa and of the Gulf.[27]

'Religion', says Hatim M. Amiji, 'plays an important role in the granting

24. V. Monteil, 1964.
25. *Centre de rencontres islamo–chrétiennes.*
26. D. El-Hadjdj Badara, 1979.
27. A. A. Mazrui, 1975c; H. M. Amiji, 1984.

of aid to Africa'. But observers of Afro-Arab relations have noticed that almost all the Arab aid went to African beneficiaries who are connected with Islam. This link between economic aid and religious obedience corresponds to a precise political objective on the part of the Arab donors, which has been officially recognized by the Kuwaiti Minister of Finance, who said in 1974: 'The major portion of our international financial aid will be placed at the service of Arab countries and to assist the Moslem countries, particularly in Africa'.

However, since then Arab aid has been diversified and has gone to African states of differing political tendencies, Muslim or non-Muslim. And one should note among the Arab institutions for multilateral aid the Arab Bank for the Economic Development of Africa (*Banque arabe pour le développement économique de l'Afrique* – BADEA), and the Special Fund for Africa set up by OPEC, as well as the Fund for Arab–African Technical Assistance which is attached to the Economic Council of the Arab League.

Independent African churches and African identity

Although they have existed from the beginning of this century and even from the end of the last century, the movements of independent churches, including various kinds of sects, either messianist or millenarian, have expanded greatly since the 1960s. In 1967, they totalled 15 500 000 according to the specialist D. B. Barrett. In 1970 there existed 6000 strictly independent African organizations, with congregations of 16 million. Today, in 1987, there must be about 10 000 independent churches and sects, totalling some 33 million faithful.[28]

Although these churches and sects are spreading throughout Africa, the greatest concentration is found in South Africa with 3000, in Nigeria with 800, in Zaire which has more than 600, in Ghana with about 400 at the present time, and in Kenya 180. One of the most important of these independent churches is the Church of Christ on Earth, founded by the prophet Simon Kimbangu. This Church alone estimates having about three million followers spread in several communities besides Zaire, particularly in the Congo Popular Republic, in Angola, in Rwanda and in Burundi.

These independent churches and sects have been classified into five categories by H. W. Turner.[29] The first category comprises politico-messianic movements – that is, groups essentially aiming at cultural and political liberation. One of the oldest of these movements is the United Native African Church of Nigeria, already active in 1891. Harrisism (from William Wade Harris), active in the Côte d'Ivoire, in Liberia and in

28. D. B. Barrett, 1982, p. 815.
29. H. W. Turner, 1968, p. 178.

PLATE 17.3   *Simon Kimbangu of the Belgian Congo (now Zaire), banished to prison in Elisabethville (now Lubumbashi)*

Ghana, is classified within this group. Another church along the same lines is that called the *Aroti* or 'dreamers', which fought as early as 1934 in Kenya for liberation from British domination. This group of movements insists on the need to develop an African Christianity, culturally integrated into Africa.

A second category is that of the movements called neo-traditionalist. In this group, for example, there is the organization known as *Dini Ya Musambwa*, that is 'religion of the ancestors'. In Nigeria, Godianism may be mentioned. This places at its centre the 'God of Africa', who is said to have revealed himself for the first time in Egypt several thousand years ago.

517

The third category is that of the syncretic cults. These cults include a mixture of borrowings from African traditional beliefs and practices and from Christian beliefs and practices. The group includes the *Bwiti* cult from Gabon and the *Deima* cult from the Côte d'Ivoire.

Other movements declare themselves to be monotheist or Hebraist, in the sense that they completely reject all traditional religions and are turned towards monotheism as revealed in the Old Testament.

The fifth category groups the prophetic and healing churches. These proclaim themselves to be Christian, believing in Jesus Christ as the 'Saviour' and placing great weight on the revelations of the Holy Spirit; for this reason they are often also known as 'Churches of the Holy Spirit'. Among these the best-known are those with the name of Sion, which are implanted especially in South Africa and in the surrounding countries.

It used to be emphasized that the historic and circumstantial origins of these movements are related purely to the colonial situation, and linked on the political, cultural and social plane with the African struggle for independence. This point of view is well expressed by Baëta when he says:

> The entire phenomenon of the prophetic and separatist churches has been very closely linked with the conflict between the European governments and the dominated peoples. In practically all analyses of these churches, from the first movements in central Africa and southern Africa to the contemporary movements among the Bakongo of the Belgian Congo and French Equatorial Africa, their importance has been noted and pointed out everywhere . . . In Southern Africa, Sundkler attributes their appearance to the total lack of all other opportunity for black citizens to express their political or even social opinions.[30]

According to this view, the extension and proliferation of these independent churches were greatly stimulated by the availability to African Christians of the translations of Holy Scriptures in the different African languages. 'These translations', wrote J. R. Leferink, 'gave Africans the possibility of comparing the Christianity presented by the churches founded by missionaries, and the message they read in the Scriptures. This comparison gave them the consoling impression that from then on, God spoke to them in their own language and was close to them. They like very much to *feel* him present and not simply to know that he is present.'[31]

Summing up, a specialist states that the sects are the fruit of a double movement of disappointment and enthusiasm:

30. C. G. Baëta, 1962, pp. 3–4; N. I. Ndiokwere, 1981, pp. 16–20.
31. J. R. Leferink, 1985.

In different terms and through different practices, the sects offer a reply to the frustration that many feel faced by the model of society and of the church during a particular epoch. The sects are an indicator and a challenge. Behind their multicoloured movements can be seen a claim of the senses, an immense thirst for betterment, freedom and salvation, lived in the socio-cultural conditions of the present time.[32]

It is now generally agreed[33] that this emphasis on the resistance, protest and proto-nationalist aspects takes too limited a view of the value of these independent African Church movements. It has distracted from the more positive and creative aspects of the churches, in the effort to develop an African theology that finds accommodation between African spiritual values and the inspiration of the Christian Bible. The churches could be viewed as centres for the re-evaluation of African religions and theology, in renewing the themes of humanism, sanctity of life and solidarity. Perhaps more important than the protest value of the churches was also the preservation of the African cosmology within the scope of Christian teaching. This made it possible for the urban poor and rural villagers to join the churches in large numbers, to abandon the old divinities of traditional religion, and to make sense of colonialism and its version of modernism without the trauma of having to abandon the essence of their world view. In particular, the traditional view of healing and deliverance through faith which the mission churches were unable to provide was what attracted most people to these churches. The churches offered their members security against the traditional forces of evil, sorcery and witchcraft in particular. In the urban areas, they offered a framework of security, solidarity and hospitality, aspects of welfare which the colonial system could not provide. They provided scope for the traditional patronage of artistic talent in the drama of ritual, and the music, both vocal and instrumental, that traditional religion had provided. But above all, it was the churches that kept alive the traditional healing systems within the Christian idiom until their social value began again to be publicly appreciated.

It can be said that generally the emergence of the multiple and complex messianistic movements in African societies both before and after independence was a reply to socio-economic requirements, and to the search for new spiritual paths in these societies.

Seeking a new global balance in society, Africans felt the need to reconstruct their former religious systems, which used to give them all the elements that satisfied their global situation. Imported religious systems seeming to be ill-adapted and inadequate, they produced new

32. R. De Haes, 1982.
33. T. O. Ranger, 1986.

systems that brought new values and new motivations.[34] On these grounds, these new religious movements questioned contemporary African societies in transition, but especially official Christianity and official Islam. But can it be said that they point the way towards eventual resolution of the plurality of religion in Africa?

Conclusion

(1) The religious factor, manifested in different forms, is undeniably influential in the historic development of Africa, where it plays a very important role.

(2) It is important to be aware of this role, to be able to discern its advantages as a resource to be used and encouraged, and, on the other hand, as a problem to be contained, so as to condemn the negative effects of a religiosity that is contrary to the true meaning and requirements of African development.

(3) African traditional religion, eroded though it is by the spread of Islam and of Christianity, is still alive and still has its own humanistic and spiritual principles, which have supported successive African generations for thousands of years. When given rational, scientific and philosophical criticism, these principles can be validly accepted and lived by contemporary African man, whether he has become Christian or Moslem, or has opted for a rationalist spiritual path. However, it must be noted that still too often, a certain African mentality that is superstitious, magical and mystical in character and therefore irrational, causes blockages in the processes of constructive thought and action towards effective progress within African society.

(4) The Christian and Muslim religions have already deeply influenced the history of the African continent, particularly over the last 50 years. For example, the influence of Islamization as of Christianization is clearly visible in the working out of African law. This is particularly so in the case of family law, and also certain civil laws which are impregnated with Islamic or Christian principles, according to whether they refer to countries predominantly Islamic or Christian. They indicate present sociocultural tendencies, and play a major role in the development of Africa, both in the orientation of thought and also in the establishment and development of social and economic infrastructures, the bases of the general development of Africa. From the point of view of African identity, it is logical that in Africa both Christianity and Islam undergo at least a minimal process of 'inculturation', especially concerning doctrinal or ritual

34. E. De Rosny, 1983.

expressions compatible with the basic requirements of these religions, imported by history into the bosom of African society.

(5) The spread of African brotherhoods in relationship with Islam, or the independent churches, sects, messianisms and other Christiano-African syncretisms, causes one to reflect on the questions these pose to the religions that were historically constituted and hierarchically controlled – as, in fact, was African society itself. These movements reveal the faults and shortcomings in the principles of social organization; they draw attention to spiritual aspirations and psycho-social needs that are not entirely satisfied by the existing political and economic systems.

So, the religious factor, adequately perceived, analysed and criticized, and correctly planned, can still contribute to the harmonious social transformation and total development of Africa at this end of the twentieth century.

Language and social change

Alfa I. SOW *and*
Mohamed H. ABDULAZIZ

The most salient features of this period have been the consolidation of traditional colonialism and racism, with their far-reaching language and cultural policies; the struggle of the African peoples for self-determination and independence; the emergence of neo-colonialism, which has altered the language and cultural situation; and the incipient African awareness of the importance of preserving and developing national cultures and languages.

The period can be divided into three parts:

(1) 1935 to 1960, when African languages were being confronted with the danger of assimilation;
(2) 1960 to 1982, when a new language and cultural policy was being shaped; and
(3) on the horizon of the year 2000: important challenges as from 1982.

African languages and the danger of assimilation: 1935–60

The colonial powers, each acting according to its inclination, its chosen course of action, its interests at the time, and its ability to enlist differing numbers of middle-grade administrators to run its empire, either engaged in a straightforward policy of linguistic, educational and cultural assimilation or else adopted a selective and more subtle approach. For instance, the French colonial administration, with its centralizing bent, set out to integrate the Africans into its education system, which it looked upon as being universally valid. On the other hand, the pragmatic British stood resolutely aloof from the 'natives' and introduced the use of African languages in the early years of primary schooling, especially for such subjects as history and geography, religious instruction, natural history, and so on. In reality, this practice paved the way for the learning of English.

522

Assimilation as the aspiration of a whole era

Until quite recently, assimilation was a goal much sought after by the Africans themselves and it came to be rejected only at a later stage, from 1954 onwards.

In a paper entitled 'Traditional cultures and social changes', Amadou Hampaté Bà had this to say:

> When the European colonialists went into action [in the cultural field] they did not meet with any fierce instinct of social preservation on the part of autochthones, who were already well-accustomed to adapting themselves to conversions imposed on them by the trend of history. They seemed to be mere nonentities, following meekly along like Panurge's sheep.[1]

However, the colonial system was organizing itself and tightening its grip on Africa at a time when the world was being shaken to its foundations and colonial empires were being toppled by two world wars within the space of 21 years, by the triumph of the Socialist Revolution in October 1917, by the concept of the 'right of peoples to decide their own fate', and by the movements aimed at liberating the colonized peoples. At a time when the far-reaching social and political changes of the twentieth century had already been set in motion, Africa was still being exposed to a serious threat to its cultural identity. The authentic values of the past that had withstood the test of time were being decried, ridiculed and debased in the face of the new values imported by the European civilizations. Confrontations arose between the more and less 'advanced' members of the population or between those who were deemed to be 'assimilated' and the 'natives'. For many Africans, assimilation came to be regarded as a legitimate demand or as a moral ideal to which they sincerely aspired. Hence, the new ambitions of the colonized subjects took the form of wanting to live like the colonialists, dress like them, eat and drink like them, speak and be housed like them, and laugh and get angry like them, in short to have the same religious, moral and cultural yardsticks.

Colonization: a blow dealt by fate

While some colonial administrators and technical personnel learnt 'native languages' primarily in the hope of understanding the Africans and penetrating their innermost secrets, after the First World War and its ensuing social and cultural upheavals, Africans who were in a position to do so sent their children to the 'white men's schools' back in the colonial home country, so that they could study the real knowledge which the

1. UNESCO, 1975a, p. 48.

whites imparted to their own children, discover the reasons for their power and their victory and, 'things being what they were', live on good terms with them.

There are a host of examples of this attitude in the African-language literature of the period, both oral and written in Arabic script (the so-called *Ajami* literature).

The wish to gain an insight into the other side's secrets, so as not to be deceived, became an increasingly widespread aim and a lasting obsession on both sides. With few exceptions, however, those detached observers on the African side were completely overwhelmed and won over, so that they eventually allowed themselves to be transformed and drawn into the system.

European colonization was accepted practically everywhere as being a blow dealt by fate. An assimilationist trend emerged in the literature of the period, sometimes at the instigation of the colonial administrators themselves. This trend contributed to the demoralization of Africans by calling on them to co-operate loyally with the colonialists, and to assist them both in the war effort and in mobilizing forced labour and conscripts, house and feed their agents, provide them with the workers they needed to make roads, lay railways and build bridges spanning rivers, as well as pay the income tax and other taxes which they levied on the population. This defeatist current, which was often encouraged by leading traditional figures, extolled the colonial order, the sense of security, which it had established, and the major discoveries and marvels of the 'white man's century', such as motor vehicles, aircraft, radio, railways, motor roads and so on.

However, a minority and usually anonymous counter-movement made its voice heard in the name of ancestral values and age-old tradition. Setting out as it did to be the conscience of the people, this minority denounced the loyalist faction and its standard-bearers and became the spokesman of the colonized peoples, whose emancipation it presented as an irreversible process, especially after the victories of Lebanon and Syria and the independence of the peoples of Indochina, followed by the uprising in Algeria in 1954.

Literature as a fall-back value

African-language oral and *Ajami* literature derided 'those who ape the white man' and those 'who speak the white man's language without understanding it', and cursed women 'who shamelessly take off their clothes and talk like the soldiers they hope to attract'. As critical bystanders, some of the cultural élites described the major upheavals taking place in their writings and warned African societies of the danger of surrendering their fundamental values and of thereby losing their personalities.

The sense of helplessness felt by those élites, with their traditional upbringing, who had to contend with the grave perils of the time, found expression in their literary and artistic works and in the proverbs and songs which they composed or inspired. For example, a Muslim poet from the Futa Jalon, in Guinea, writing in Fulfulde, described the 'woes of our century' in the following words:

> Misfortune is upon us: the times have changed,
> Lawlessness is spreading and the law is retreating,
> Tradition has vanished and heresy has appeared,
> Morals have declined and selfishness is the rule,
> Kinship has yielded to the quest for pleasure,
> Compassion has been banished; adultery is rife
> And its offspring is legion,
> Truth is forsaken,
> Education suffers and hypocrisy is rampant,
> Wealth abounds and discord is rampant,
> Theft is rampant, looting is rampant,
> Lying is rampant: Satan has triumphed!
> Their evil hearts are more poisonous than venom,
> Their sole concern is to amass wealth
> And women and jewellery,
> They have chosen this world and abandoned the other,
> Those who deny or ignore the truth are on the increase,
> Conflict and sin are on the increase,
> We must escape,
> But there is nowhere to flee, nowhere to stay,
> Caught as we are in the clutches of this vast world.[2]

The African peoples accordingly rediscovered their identity in their languages and literatures, which continued to provide close and indissoluble links with the lost past and the vanished generations by still conveying the ancestral moral values and representing particularly precious fall-back values. However, even those values were affected by the changes occurring.

Enrichment of the vocabulary and vehicular languages

As a result of contacts with Islam and with Arab and Asian traders, especially from Iran, as well as of contacts with European languages and Christianity, all the African languages considerably enriched their vocabulary and a whole wealth of religious, technological, scientific and cultural terms still bear witness to the economic and social developments over that 25-year period.

2. A. I. Sow, 1966, p. 136.

Euro-African languages, such as Creole and pidgin, developed and became genuine black African languages in some of the countries and cities of the Atlantic seaboard, such as Cape Verde, Guinea-Bissau, the Gambia, Sierra Leone and Cameroon. The Creole languages of Gambia and Cameroon and the *krio* of Sierra Leone borrowed a large number of words from English, and the *crioulo* of Cape Verde and Guinea-Bissau likewise borrowed from Portuguese. In the cases where such languages exist, their basic phonological, syntactical and semantic features are African, even though their vocabulary, which is a reflection of a particular power relationship, is borrowed to a considerable degree from European languages. In some countries, such as Mauritius, Creole is the most widespread and popular means of linguistic communication.

With the encouragement of the colonial powers, Kiswahili, Lingala, Bambara and Hausa all underwent remarkable growth as inter-ethnic vehicular languages that were widely used in the armies and police forces of the German, English, Belgian or French administrations.

Furthermore, from the late 1920s, there were, among the colonial technical personnel and senior administrators, specialists who pointed to the dangers of assimilation and who made out a case for engaging in far-reaching research on Africa and its inhabitants and called for an in-depth study of African languages and literatures.

A cleverly engineered development

Thus it was that in June 1926, the inaugural meeting of the International Institute of African Languages and Civilizations was held in London, attended by delegates from South Africa, Germany, Belgium, Egypt, the United States, France, Great Britain, Italy and Sweden. This new institution was defined as being a body designed to gather information of all kinds on the languages, civilizations and particular problems of Africa, and to act as a liaison office between specialists on those subjects. It set out to 'link science to practical experience by showing how the discoveries of the former can be used for the administration, education, hygiene, well-being and development of Africans'.[3]

Hence, there came into being a style of African studies which was at the behest of the colonial system and was subsequently responsible for the type of ethnographic scrutiny to which Africans and their societies and cultures came to be subjected.

The Institute, which was to become the International African Institute, more commonly known by its initials IAI, publishes *Africa*, a quarterly journal, the first number of which appeared in January 1928, as well as African monographs and documents containing papers, written in African languages on religion, customs, myths, legends, historical and other

3. V. Foutchantse, 1967, p. 143.

traditions and social institutions, and 'tales, proverbs and riddles', all of which are translated into a European language.

Right from the time the Institute was first established, it applied itself to transcribing African languages in Roman characters and to developing a reference alphabet, the 'International African Alphabet', which is still known as the 'IAI alphabet' and which was to serve as a basis for the transcription of some sixty African languages.

In April 1929, it established a prize 'to assist and encourage the natives, with the aim of getting them to produce, in their own languages, works that will last and of which they can be proud'. This practice continued until 1950, when the Institute decided that the original aim had been achieved, since both the West African and East African Literature Bureaux were by then in a position to meet the need for works of 'vernacular literature'.

In point of fact, in 1942, the Council of American Churches on African Affairs, with the agreement of the IAI, had recommended that priority be given to Christian literature in African languages. Moreover, in 1950, the Institute established the Margaret Wrong Prize, after the name of the secretary of the International Committee for Christian Literature in Africa, 'who played a leading role in the spiritual and cultural development of Africa in the last twenty years of her life' and who died in Uganda on 11 April 1948.

Henceforward, works written in African languages or in Arabic could not be awarded the prize unless they had already been published in Afrikaans, French, English or Portuguese. The new prize was accordingly expected to encourage literature 'in European languages'.

This development clearly points to the colonialist design forming the backdrop to the undertaking. The IAI had been created to bring together isolated scholars engaged in African studies and to co-ordinate activities that were primarily geared to colonialist action, and were meant to prepare for the far-reaching changes ahead and to manage the 'development of Africans' within Western civilization. It was not a philanthropic institution dedicated to scientific research on Africa for Africa's sake. The 'African school textbook' project set up by the IAI laid down the following guidelines:

> Designed to introduce students to Western civilization and thought, they [the textbooks] will deal above all with subjects having a bearing on European life, but they will also show how Africa and its inhabitants can be the subject of serious studies, especially as they pertain to history, geography, natural history, social life and religion. It is becoming increasingly necessary to provide educated Africans with well-produced books in European languages, since their influence is expected to be decisive for the training of future chiefs.[4]

4. See V. Foutchantse, 1967, p. 143.

It is important, however, to highlight the work done by scholars and missionaries who, either at the IAI's urging or out of conscientiousness, produced European-language reference books, such as dictionaries and grammars, or educational works of a high scientific standard which provided an insight into the languages and cultures of Africa. Colonial administrators, missionaries, and specialists of all kinds, such as social anthropologists, geographers, naturalists, musicologists, educators and military officers, some of them humanists and some enlightened amateurs of both sexes, often disregarded or defied the prohibitions and instructions of the colonial administrations and engaged in the collection and the transcription, in the 'IAI alphabet' or in a script of their choosing, of historical, scientific and literary works belonging to the African cultural heritage, which they then translated into European languages. Their work was published in the journals of the period, such as the *Bulletin du Comité d'études historiques et scientifiques de l'AOF* (later to become the *Bulletin de l'Institut français de l'Afrique noire*), and, when replaced in its context, can still be useful today. It is through their action and that of their 'informers' and other African collaborators that a whole living corpus of newspapers and literature in the Yoruba, Igbo, Ewe, Hausa, Akan (Twi and Fanti), Duala and Kiswahili languages came into being in Roman script (usually the 'IAI alphabet'), especially in Nigeria, Ghana, Togo, Cameroon and Tanzania.

The shaping of a new language and cultural policy: 1960–82

Even so, as long as colonialism lasted, though some important steps were taken by private institutions and men of goodwill, there was no permanent effort to promote African languages and cultures.

A time of hesitation and trial and error

The accession of many African countries to independence in 1960 could have provided an opportunity for a critical and lucid assessment of the colonial experience, the definition of outstanding problems, and the laying-down of principles and guidelines for a fresh departure as far as national languages, cultures and education were concerned. Unfortunately, with very few exceptions, the former practices of the colonial powers were merely taken over wholesale, often without the slightest alteration. Indeed, many of the new nations attached so little importance to the cultural sphere that they allowed it to slip to the bottom of their priorities, virtually relying on the generosity of foreign countries and international organizations for its survival.

It was only little by little, acting at the instigation and prompting of

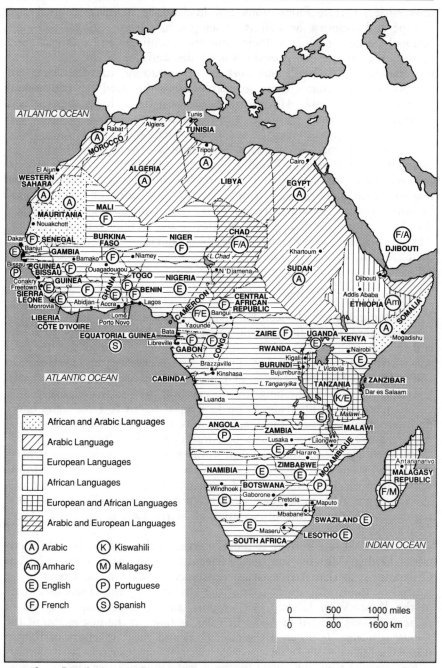

FIG. 18.1 *Distribution of official languages in Africa (Source: adapted from* The World Almanac and Book of Facts, *World Almanac of Books and Facts, New York, 1991,* © Pharos Books, 1990*)*

universities, private foundations and institutions in many countries of Europe and America, as well as under pressure from regional and subregional learned societies at their congresses, seminars and symposia, and in response to the energetically-voiced demands of youth and student movements and women's and workers' organizations, that the leaders of the post-colonial states came to acknowledge the need for educational programmes that took African languages as a basis. Even then, it was necessary to proceed with the utmost caution so as not to upset the former colonial powers and the acculturated national administrators, who regarded the 'vernacular languages' as worthless. Even political leaders as clearsighted as President Kwame Nkrumah of Ghana were reluctant to promote what they felt to be a vast number of 'backward' languages, for fear that such a policy might jeopardize the new states' efforts at nation-building by dividing the Africans to no useful purpose at a time when they ought to be united. Those political leaders could not yet visualize Africans speaking and making themselves understood in languages other than English, French or Arabic!

The break with the past

For all these reasons, African languages were first looked upon as having a geographical, social and cultural scope confined to rural areas, to adults and to oral tradition. Yet the issues at stake were immense; the question was whether the peoples of Africa would have access not only to education and culture but to the exercise of political and economic power as well. Eventually, however, the poignant observation that 'in Africa, every time an old man dies, a library goes up in flames' began to have some effect on international decision-makers, who were moved to allocate substantial resources to research on African oral traditions and cultures.

Between 1962 and 1964, a large number of African-language departments and study and research centres were created in the newly founded universities of the continent, and high-quality journals and periodicals specializing in African languages and linguistics came into being and grew rapidly, especially in the universities of Sierra Leone, Tanzania, Addis Ababa and Ibadan.

During the same period, at the Congress of the Association of Orientalists held in Moscow in 1960, Africanist studies were separated from Orientalism, so that Africa assumed a place of its own, no longer being treated by the Europeans as part of the Orient or by the Orientals as part of the West. With UNESCO's support, the International Congress of Africanists was created in Accra in 1960, notably at the instigation of the *Société africaine de culture* (Alioune Diop) and the University of Ibadan (Onwuka Dike).

Encouraged from the outset by the world-famous American and Soviet scholars, Melville Herskovits and Ivan Posteshkin, this new institution contributed to promoting African studies and to 'arousing, among Africans, a profound awareness of their own cultures'.

In 1962, in the context of its activities under the World Programme for Combating Illiteracy, UNESCO decided in favour of adult education in African languages and promised assistance for that purpose to the countries of the region. This decision marked the first step in the recognition of those languages and their introduction into the modern sector of the education system of the African countries.

Needs and realities

Thus, African languages acquired their proper status as fully-fledged languages and the disparaging terms such as 'dialects', 'tribal languages', 'vernacular languages' and so on, which had formerly been used indiscriminately to label them, gradually disappeared from the vocabulary of the specialists and only emerged from time to time in the unguarded writings or provocative pronouncements of a handful of irresponsible individuals.

It was then found that many of the purportedly scholarly studies and academic papers available on African languages had been produced by amateurs or autodidacts who had no proper grounding in linguistics, had used a rudimentary descriptive approach for immediate practical purposes, had aligned philology, phonetics and grammar too closely on European-language models and had indulged in obscure comparisons based on *a priori* judgements. What is more, although the studies were undertaken well after the emergence of modern linguistic theories, few of them had made use of the discoveries of Saussure and the structuralists.

It was therefore necessary to start all over again with the assistance of consultants, foreign counterparts, researchers and teachers. African university teachers and scholars had to be alerted to linguistic problems and arrangements had to be made for them to be awarded training fellowships in the United States, Western Europe and the Soviet Union.

UNESCO's action

Once the general guidelines and basic options had been laid down by the countries concerned, UNESCO's assistance made it possible, by consulting specialists and holding regional and sub-regional meetings of experts, to identify the methodological and technical difficulties and to point to solutions, as well as to draw up operational programmes for a set of countries and languages and to train and equip national professionals to supervise the implementation of such programmes.[5] Table 18.1, from a UNESCO publication, demonstrates the complexity of the task.

5. A detailed review of UNESCO's action can be found in A. I. Sow, 1977.

Little by little, UNESCO's activities became more systematically organized and made it possible to achieve decisive results in collecting oral traditions and promoting the languages conveying those traditions.

Among the main contributions made by UNESCO, mention must be made of the adoption, in 1964, of the Project for the Drafting of a *General History of Africa*; the organization, in 1966, of the Linguistic Conference in Bamako, which laid down the standardized transcription of a number of vehicular languages in West Africa; the definition of a Co-ordinated Regional Research Plan on Oral Traditions in 1968; assistance with the publication of literary and initiatory texts of considerable cultural significance, such as the *Kaidara* in 1968; the preparation, adoption and implementation of the Ten-Year Plan for the Systematic Study of Oral Tradition and the Promotion of African Languages as vehicles of culture and instruments of lifelong education, in 1972; support for the establishment, fitting-out and operation not only of the Aḥmed Baba Centre in Timbuktu (for Arabic and *Ajami* manuscripts of the Sahel and the Western Sudan), but also of the sub-regional centres for research on oral tradition and African languages: CELHTO (*Centre d'études linguistiques et historiques par tradition orale*) in Niamey for West Africa, CERDOTOLA (*Centre régional de documentation sur les traditions orales et les langues africaines*) in Yaoundé for Central Africa, and EACROTANAL (Eastern African Centre for Research on Oral Traditions and African National Languages) in Zanzibar for East and Central Africa.

Each of these institutions, created with international assistance under the Ten-Year Plan, co-ordinates research activities for the sub-region and publishes academic papers both in the African languages of the sub-region and on the subject of those languages. Some of the centres – for instance, the one in Niamey, even publishes a journal: the *Cahiers du CELHTO* – have established bi-lingual African/European-language collections of major historical, literary and philosophical documents.

By organizing regular meetings of experts, UNESCO also encourages personal contacts and the sharing of ideas between African scholars and their counterparts working on African languages, cultures and studies elsewhere in the world.[6]

UNESCO has also taken steps to arrange for the translation of the *General History of Africa* into some of the vehicular languages of the region, such as Arabic, Kiswahili, Hausa and Fulfulde and, at the start of the 1980s, began preparations for the publication of general and cultural dictionaries of Kiswahili, Yoruba, Fulfulde and other languages.

---

6. Among others, the meeting in Bamako in 1979 on the use of African regional or sub-regional languages, and that in Conakry in 1981 on the definition of a strategy for the promotion of African languages.

TABLE 18.1 Distribution of main national languages in Africa, by country

The table shows the linguistic situation and language policy in 46 independent African States, with the exception of Algeria, Egypt, Libya, Morocco and Tunisia where Arabic is the official language. There are eleven columns which, reading from left to right, indicate the following:

a   Excluding Algeria, Egypt, Libya, Morocco and Tunisia where Arabic is the official language.
b   Expressed in millions (m) or as part of a million.
c   The approximate number of African languages used in the country.
d   The dominant languages, including the foreign languages inherited from the colonial era.
e   The approximate number of speakers (native and other), expressed in millions or as a percentage (%).
f   The geographical area of the dominant languages within the country under consideration.
g   Other countries where the language is spoken, whether or not with the same status.
h   The official status of the language as defined by law or regulation: N = National language; O = Official language.
i   The uses of the language in the country:
    A = used in administration (local or national), including government, law, military and police forces, political speeches, etc.;
    a = used in literacy work;
    E = used in teaching:
        o = in experimental classes;
        1 = at primary-school level;
        2 = at secondary-school level;
        3 = at higher-education and university level;
        m = as a subject;
    P = used in the press;
    R = used on the radio;
    T = used on television;
    L = existence of literary works in the language.
j   The level of development of research as demonstrated by the existence of works in the language (scientific description, school textbooks, etc.):
    1 = insufficient and unsatisfactory level of research;
    2 = insufficient and partially satisfactory level of research;
    3 = satisfactory but limited level of research;
    4 = satisfactory level of research in terms of quality and quantity.
k   Public and private institutions within the country which are concerned with research in the dominant language(s).

Country[a]	Population (m)[b]	Number of languages[c]	Dominant languages[d]	Speakers (m)[e]	Geographical area[f]	Other countries where spoken[g]	Status[h]	Use[i]	Development of research[j]	Research bodies[k]
ANGOLA	7	11	Umbundu	1.5	Centre		N	RTL	2	National Institute of Languages:
			Kimbundu	1	N. + Centre		N	RTL	2	African languages; Centre
			Kikongo	0.5	N.	Congo, Zaire	N	RTL	2	d'investigation pédagogique (CIP),
			Lunda-Kioko	0.4	W.	Zaire, Zambia	N	RTL	1	Ministry of Education: Portuguese
			Ngangela	0.35	S.-E.		N	RTL	1	language
			Nyaneka-Humbe	0.2	S.-W.		N	RTL	1	
			Portuguese	–	Whole country		O	$AaE_{1,2,3}$ PRTL	3	
BENIN	3.5	52	Bariba	0.35	N.-E.	Nigeria	N	a RT	2	National Linguistic Commission;
			Fon	0.5	S. + Centre		N	a RT	2	Literacy and Rural Press
			Yoruba	0.35	S.-E. + Centre	Nigeria, Togo	N	a RT	4	Directorate; Department of
			Yom	–	N.-W.		N	a R	1	Linguistic Studies and Oral
			Ditammarie	–	N.-W.		N	a R	2	Tradition (National University of
			French	–	Whole country		O	$A E_{1,2,3}$ PRTL	2	Benin)

Country[a]	Population (m)[b]	Number of languages[c]	Dominant languages[d]	Speakers (m)[e]	Geographical area[f]	Other countries where spoken[g]	Status[h]	Use[i]		Development of research[j]	Research bodies[k]
BOTSWANA	1	±9	Setswana	90%		RSA, Namibia, Bophutatswana	NO	$AaE_{1,2m}$	PR L	3	National Language Committee; National Institute for Research, University of Botswana
			English	–	Whole country		NO	$AaE_{1,2,3m}$	PR L	4	
BURKINA FASO	7	60	Moore	48%	Centre (all parts)	Côte d'Ivoire, Ghana	N	$aE_{0,3m}$	PRTL	3	Direction générale de la recherche scientifique et technologique (DGRST)
			Juula (Dyula)	–	W. (all parts)	Mali, Niger, Côte d'Ivoire, Guinea, Senegal	N	$aE_{0,3m}$	PRTL	3	Institut national pour l'alphabétisation et la formation des adultes (INAFA); Commission nationale des langues voltaïques (CNLV)
			Fulfulde	10.4%	N.	Niger, Mali, Guinea, Senegal, Mauritania	N	aE_0	PRTL	3	SIL; IRAP
			Dagari-Lobi	7%	S.–W.	Ghana	N	a	R L	2	Ouagadougou University; DEPFD
			Bobo-bwamu	6.7%	W.	Mali	N	a	R L	2	
			Senufo	5.5%	S.–W.	Côte d'Ivoire, Mali, Niger	N	a	R	1	
			Gurunsi	5.3%	Centre + S.	Ghana	N	a	PR L	2	
			Bisa	4.7%	S.	–	N	a	R L	1	
			Gulmancema	4.5%	E.	Benin, Togo, Niger	N	a	PR L	2	
			French	7.5%	Whole country		N	$AaE_{1,2,3}$	PRTL	4	
BURUNDI	4.2	1	Kirundi	4.2	Whole country	Rwanda, Tanzania, Uganda, Zaire	NO	$AaE_{1,2m,3m}$	PR L	3	ALLR; ARFA; COO; CEPK; DLLA; CCB

Country[a]	Population (m)[b]	Number of languages[c]	Dominant languages[d]	Speakers (m)[e]	Geographical area[f]	Other countries where spoken[g]	Status[h]	Use[i]		Development of research[j]	Research bodies[k]
BURUNDI			Kiswahili	10%		Tanzania, Kenya, Uganda, Zaire, etc.		E_{3m}	R		
			French		Whole country		O	$A\,E_{1,2,3}$	PR L	4	
CAMEROON	8	237	Arabic (Choa)		Extreme N.	Chad			R	1	CREA; Department of African Languages and Literature (Faculty of Arts); SIL; CERDOTOLA
			Bamum		W.	-		a	R L	2	
			Basa		Centre + coast			a	PR L	3	
			Beti-Fang		Centre + S.	Equatorial Guinea, Gabon, Congo		a	PR L	3	
										3	
			Duala		Coast	-		a_o	R L	3	
			Ejagham		N.–W.	Nigeria		a_o	R L	3	
			Fe'Fe'		W.	-		aE_{01}	L	2	
			Fulfulde		Extreme N., N + Adamawa	Senegal, Sudan		a	R L	3	
			Gbaya		E.	CAF			R L	3	
			Ghomala		W.			a	R L	3	
			Hausa		Extreme N, N.	Nigeria, Niger		—		4	
			Lamnso		N.–W.			a_o	R L	2	
			Mafa		Extreme N.			a		2	
			Medumba		W.			a	R L	2	
			Mungaka		W.			a	R L	2	
			Meka		E.			a	R L	1	
			Ngyemboong		W.				R L	2	
			Vute		Centre			a	R L	3	
			Yemba		W.			a	R L	3	
			Pidgin English	20%	Coast, W., S.–W., N.–W.			—			
			English				O	$AaE_{1,2,3}$	PR L		
			French				O	$AaE_{1,2,3}$	PR L		

535

Country[a]	Population (m)[b]	Number of languages[c]	Dominant languages[d]	Speakers (m)[e]	Geographical area[f]	Other countries where spoken[g]	Status[h]	Use[i]	Development of research[j]	Research bodies[k]
CAPE VERDE	0.3	2	Portuguese Creole		Whole country	São Tomé,	–	AaE[1,2,3] PR L	2	
			Portuguese		Whole country	Guinea Bissau				
CENTRAL AFRICAN REPUBLIC (CAF)	2	44	Sango	2	Whole country	Chad	O	AaE[o] PRT	4	LA, IREM, INEF, CERDOTOLA
			French		Whole country		N	A E[1,2m,3m] PRTL	2	
CHAD	5.5	250	Sara	19%	S.	CAF		a R	2	INSH, INSE, SIL, University CEL (Ch. Lwanga College), Direction de la culture, de l'alphabétisation et de la promotion des langues nationales (DCAPLN)
			Arabic	60%	Whole country	Sudan, Niger, etc.	NO	AaE[1,2,3] PR L	4	
			Gorane (Daza)		Centre, N.	Niger, Libya		R		
			Maba	12%	E.	Sudan		R	1	
			French		Whole country		O	AaE[1,2,3] PR L	1	
			Fulfulde		S.-W.	Cameroon, Niger, etc.		R		
			Massa		S.-W.	Cameroon		a R		
			Kanembu		W., N.	Nigeria, Niger		a R		
			Tuburi		S.-W.	Cameroon		a R	1	
			Moundang		S.-W.	Cameroon		a R	1	
			Zaghawa		N.-E.	Sudan		R		
			Tama		E.	Sudan		R		
			Mimi		E.					
			Bidiye		Centre-E.					
			Dadjo		E. + Centre					
			Bulala		Centre, E., W.	Sudan				
			Bagirmi		S.-W. + S.					
			Kotoko		S.-W.					
			Migama		Centre, E.	Cameroon				
COMOROS	0.34	3	Arabic	–	Whole country	Somalia, Sudan, etc.	O	AaE[1,2,3] PR L	3	
			Kiswahili	–		Tanzania, Kenya, etc.	N	a	3	

Country[a]	Population (m)[b]	Number of languages[c]	Dominant languages[d]	Speakers (m)[e]	Geographical area[f]	Other countries where spoken[g]	Status[h]	Use[i]	Development of research[j]	Research bodies[k]
COMOROS			French	–	Whole country		O	AaE[1,2,3] PR L	4	
CONGO	1.4	15	Kikongo	75%	S.	Angola, Zaire	N	RTL	3	INRAP, INSSED, Department of Linguistics and Oral Literature
			Lingala	–	N.	Zaire	N	RT	3	
			French	–	Whole country		O	AaE[1,2,3] PRTL	4	
CÔTE D'IVOIRE	7.3	60	Baule	1.8	Centre	Ghana, Togo		RT	2	ILA, IES, ILENA, IHAAA, CERAV, GRIO, SIL
			Juula (Dyula)	1.5	N.-W.	Mali, Guinea, Burkina Faso		RT	2	
			Bete	0.9	Centre-W.			RT	2	
			Senufo	0.8	N.-E.			RT	1	
			Yakouba (dan)	0.35	W.			RT	1	
			French		Whole country		O	A E[1,2,3] PRTL	4	
DJIBOUTI	0.25	3	Afar	31%			O	RT	–	
			Arabic	5.4%		Sudan, Somalia, etc.		RT	3	
			Somali	36%	Whole country	Somalia	O	RT	–	
			French	–	Whole country			PRTL	4	
EQUATORIAL GUINEA	0.3	?	Spanish	–	Whole country		O	A E[1,2] PRL	4	
ETHIOPIA	30	70	Amharic	60–65%	Whole country		N	AaE[1,2m,3m] PRTL	3	Ethiopian Languages Academy; Institute of Language Studies; Addis Ababa University; Curriculum Development Division, Ministry of Education
			Oromo	27%		Kenya	a	PR	–	
			Tigrinya	14%			a	PR	1	
			English	–			E[1m,2,3]	PRTL	4	
GABON	1	42	Fang	35%	N.-W.	Cameroon	O	AaE[1,2,3] PRTL	2	ORSTOM, IRSH
			Myene	–	W.				1	
			French	–	Whole country				4	

Country[a]	Population (m)[b]	Number of languages[c]	Dominant languages[d]	Speakers (m)[e]	Geographical area[f]	Other countries where spoken[g]	Status[h]	Use[i]	Development of research[j]	Research bodies[k]
GAMBIA	0.6	?	Mandinka (Malinke)	42%		Côte d'Ivoire, Senegal, Mali		a_{OI} R	3	
			Pulaar (Fulfulde)	18%		Guinea, Guinea-Bissau, Senegal, Mali, etc.		a_{OI} R	3	
			Wolof	16%		Senegal, Mauritania		a_{OI} R	3	
			Joola (Dyola)	9.5%		Senegal, Guinea-Bissau		R	–	
			Soninke	8.7%		Mali		R	2	
			English		Whole country		O	$AaE_{1,2,3}$ PR L	4	
GHANA	11	46	Akan	6	Centre–S.	Côte d'Ivoire	N	$aE_{1,2m,3m}$ PRTL	4	Bureau of Ghana Languages, Curriculum Research and
			Ewe	2	S.–E.	Togo, Benin	N	$aE_{1,2m,3m}$ RTL	3	Development Division, School of
			Ga	1	Accra region		N	$aE_{1,2m,3m}$ RTL	3	Ghana Languages, University of
			Dangme	1.5	S.–E.		N	$aE_{1,2m,3m}$ L	2	Ghana, University of Cape-Coast,
			Dagare	0.3	N.–W.	Burkina Faso	N	$aE_{1,2m,3m}$ L	1	Ghana Institute of Linguistics
			Gonja	0.02–3	N.–Centre		N	$aE_{1,2m,3m}$ L	1	
			Kasem	–	N.		N	$aE_{1,2m,3m}$ L	2	
			Dagbani	0.35	N.–E.		N	$aE_{1,2m,3m}$ RTL	1	
			Nzema	–	S.–W.	Côte d'Ivoire	N	$aE_{1,2m,3m}$ R L	2	
			Hausa	–	N.	Niger, Nigeria, etc.	N	R L	3	
			English	–	Whole country		O	$A\,E_{1,2,3}$ PRTL	4	
GUINEA	6.6	21	Pulaar	2.4	Middle Guinea	Mali, Senegal, Cameroon, Niger, etc.	N	$AaE_{1,2m,3m}$ PRTL	2	Languages Academy, SNA, IPN, Chair of Linguistics
			Maninka	1.7	Upper Guinea (E)	Mali, Gambia, Burkina Faso	N	$AaE_{1,2m,3m}$ PRTL	2	

Country[a]	Population (m)[b]	Number of languages[c]	Dominant languages[d]	Speakers (m)[e]	Geographical area[f]	Other countries where spoken[g]	Status[h]	Use[i]	Development of research[j]	Research bodies[k]
GUINEA			Soso	1.3	Lower Guinea (W)	Sierra Leone	N	$AaE_{1,2m,3m}$ PRTL	2	
			Kisi	—		Sierra Leone	N	$aE_{1,2m,3m}$ R	2	
			Kpelle	—		Liberia	N	$aE_{1,2m,3m}$ R	2	
			Loma	—			N	$aE_{1,2m,3m}$ R	2	
			Konyagi	—			N	$aE_{1,2m,3m}$ R	2	
			Basari	—			N	$aE_{1,2m,3m}$ R	2	
			French	—	Whole country		O	$A\,E_{1,2,3}$ PRTL	4	
GUINEA-BISSAU	0.8	?	Balata	30%						
			Pulaar (Fulfulde)	21%		Guinea, Senegal, etc.					
			Manjaku	14%							
			Mande	12%		Guinea, Senegal, etc.					
			Crioulo	—			—	R		
			Portuguese		Whole country		O	$A\,E$ PR L PRTL	4	
KENYA	14	40	Gikuyu	20%				aE_1 R	4	University of Nairobi
			Dholuo (Luo)	14%		Uganda		aE_1 R		
			Luluya	13%				aE_1 R		
			Kikamba	11%				aE_1 R		
			Kalenjin	11%				aE_1 R		
			Ekegusi	6.5%				aE_1 R		
			Kimeru	5.0%				aE_1 R		
			Kiswahili	65%	Whole country	Tanzania, Uganda, Zaire, Mozambique, Malawi, Comoros, Somalia, etc.	N	$aE_{1m,2m,3m}$ PRTL	4	

Country[a]	Population (m)[b]	Number of languages[c]	Dominant languages[d]	Speakers (m)[e]	Geographical area[f]	Other countries where spoken[g]	Status[h]	Use[i]	Development of research[j]	Research bodies[k]
KENYA			English	16%	Whole country		O	A E 1,2,3 PRTL	4	
LESOTHO	1.3		Sesotho	99%	Whole country	Botswana, RSA	O	AaE 1,2m,3m PR L	3	
			English		Whole country		O	A E 1,2,3 PR L	4	
LIBERIA	1.8	25	Kpelle (Guerzé)	23%		Guinea		PRT	1	
			Grebo (Kru)	22%				RT		
			Baso (Bassa)	16%				PRT		
			Loma	6.6%				RT		
			Gio	6.1%				RT		
			Mano	4.6%				RT		
			Gola	4.7%				RT		
			English	40%	Whole country		O	A E 1,2,3 PRTL	4	
MADAGASCAR	3	1	Malagasy	3	Whole country		O	AaE 1,2m,3m PRTL	4	Institut de linguistique appliquée (ILA), Département de langue et littérature malgache, Académie malgache
			French		Whole country		O	A E 1m,2,3 PRTL	4	
MALAWI	5.6		Chichewa (Chinyanja)	86%	Whole country	Mozambique, Zambia, Zimbabwe	N	AaE 1m,2m,3m PR	3	
			Ilomwe	15%						
			Ciyao	19%		Tanzania, Mozambique				
			Citumbuka	9%						
			Chisena	–	(common)					
			Chitonga	–	(common)					
			English	6%	Whole country		O	A E 1,2,3 PR L	4	

Country[a]	Population (m)[b]	Number of languages[c]	Dominant languages[d]	Speakers (m)[e]	Geographical area[f]	Other countries where spoken[g]	Status[h]	Use[i]	Development of research[j]	Research bodies[k]
MALI	6	12	Bamana (Mande)	80%	S. + Centre	Senegal, Côte d'Ivoire, Guinea, Guinea-Bissau, Burkina Faso	N	$aE_{o,m}$* PRTL	3	DNAFLA
			Fulfulde	12%	W. + Centre	West African countries	N	$aE_{o,m}$* PR L	3	ISH
			Soninke	11%	W.	Gambia	N	a R	2	
			Senufo	9.2%	S.	Côte d'Ivoire, Burkina Faso	N	R	2	
			Songhay	6.4%	E.	Niger, Benin, Burkina Faso	N	$aE_{o,m}$* R	1	
			Tamashek	–	N., E.	Niger, Algeria, Libya	N	$aE_{o,m}$* R	1	
			French		Whole country		O	$A\,E_{1,2,3}$ PRTL	4	

*N.B. Bamanan, Fulfulde, Songhay and Tamashek are both taught as subjects and used for teaching in experimental classes.

Country[a]	Population (m)[b]	Number of languages[c]	Dominant languages[d]	Speakers (m)[e]	Geographical area[f]	Other countries where spoken[g]	Status[h]	Use[i]	Development of research[j]	Research bodies[k]
MAURITANIA	1.8	7	Hassaniya (Arabic)	80%	N.	Arab countries	NO	$AaE_{1,2,3}$ PRTL	4	Institut pédagogique national (IPN); Institut de langues nationales (ILN); Institut mauritanien de recherche scientifique (IMRS); National University, Ecole normale supérieure (ENS)
			Wolof	3%	S.–W.	Gambia, Senegal	N	aE_o R	3	
			Fulfulde (Pular)	7%	Centre–S., S.–E.	Mali, Senegal, etc.	N	aE_o R	3	
			Soninke	6%	S., S.–E.	Mali, Côte d'Ivoire, Burkina Faso, Senegal	N	aE_o R	3	
			French		Whole country		O	$A\,E_{1,2,3}$ PRTL	4	
MAURITIUS	0.9		Creole	94%	Whole country	Reunion, Seychelles		PRT	2	

Country[a]	Population (m)[b]	Number of languages[c]	Dominant languages[d]	Speakers (m)[e]	Geographical area[f]	Other countries where spoken[g]	Status[h]	Use[i]	Development of research[j]	Research bodies[k]
MAURITIUS			Hindi	50%			N	$E_{1m,2m,3m}$ PRT		
			Tamil	3.5%				E_{1m} PR	1	
			Telugu	2.1%				E_{1m} R	1	
			French	24%			N	$E_{1m,2m,3m}$ PRTL	4	
			English	2.8%	Whole country		O	$A E_{1,2,3}$ PRTL	4	
MOZAMBIQUE	9.4		Imakwa (Ilomwe)	38%		Malawi		R		
			Shitsonga	24%		Zimbabwe, RSA		R		
			Cisena (Cipodzo)	10%				R		
			Shona	10%		Zimbabwe Tanzania, Kenya, etc.		R		
			Kiswahili	6.4%				R		
			Chichewa	3.2%		Malawi, Zambia		R		
			Shichopi	4.5%				R		
			Ciyao	2.2%				R		
			Cimakonde	1.3%				R		
			Portuguese		Whole country		O	$A E_{1,2,3}$ PR L	4	
NIGER	5.2	8	Hausa	1.8	Centre–S.	Nigeria. Chad, etc.	N	$aE_{0,3m}$ PRTL	3	CELHTO
			Songhay (Zarma)	0.9	W.	Mali, Benin	N	$aE_{0,3m}$ PRTL	2	
			Fulfulde (Pulaar)	0.6	Whole country	Mali, Senegal, etc.	N	$aE_{0,3m}$ PRTL	3	
			Tamashek (Touareg)	0.5	N.	Mali, Algeria, etc.	N	$aE_{0,3m}$ PRTL	1	
			Kanuri	0.3	E.	Nigeria, Cameroon, Chad	N	$aE_{0,3m}$ PRTL	1	
			French	10%	Whole country		O	$AaE_{1,2,3}$ PRTL	4	

Country[a]	Population (m)[b]	Number of languages[c]	Dominant languages[d]	Speakers (m)[e]	Geographical area[f]	Other countries where spoken[g]	Status[h]	Use[i]	Development of research[j]	Research bodies[k]
NIGERIA	80	394?	Hausa	32%	N.	Niger, Ghana, Chad, Cameroon, etc.	NO	$AaE_{1,2m,3m}$ PRTL	4	Ahmadu Bello University, Zaria, University of Sokoto, University of Maiduguri (+Kanuri; Fulfulde), University of Ibadan, University of Ife, Bayero University, Kano (+Fulfulde, Kanuri); National Education Research Council, Lagos; various academic associations
			Yoruba	25%	W.	Benin, Togo	NO	$AaE_{1,2m,3m}$ PRTL	4	Yoruba Association, Ibadan
			Igbo	22%	E.		NO	$AaE_{1,2m,3m}$ PRTL	4	University of Ife, Lagos
			Fulfulde (Ful, Fula)	8.6%		Cameroon, Niger, Guinea, etc.	N	$aE_{1,3m}$ PR L	3	(see list above)
			Efik/Ibibio	5.3%			N	$aE_{1,2m,3m}$ PRTL	2	
			Kanuri	4.1%		Niger, Chad	N	$aE_{1,3m}$ PRTL	3	(see list above)
			Tiv	2.5%			N	$aE_{1,3m}$ RT	2	
			Ijo	2.0%			N	$aE_{1,3m}$ RT	2	
			Edo	1.7%			N	$aE_{1,3m}$ PRT	2	
			Nupe	1.2%			N	$aE_{1,3m}$ RT	1	
			Igala	1.0%			N	$aE_{1,3m}$ RT	1	
			Idoma	0.9%			N	$aE_{1,3m}$ RT	1	
			English	15%	Whole country		O	$A\ E_{1,2,3}$ PRTL	4	
REPUBLIC OF SOUTH AFRICA (RSA)	31	10	Xhosa		S.	Lesotho, Zimbabwe	N	E_1 PR		
			Zulu		E.	Botswana, Mozambique, Swaziland	N	E_1 PR		
			Sotho		Centre + S.	Lesotho	N	E_1 PR		
			Afrikaans				N	$A\ E_{1,2,3}$ PRTL	4	
			English		Whole country		O	$A\ E_{1,2,3}$ PRTL	4	

Country[a]	Population (m)[b]	Number of languages[c]	Dominant languages[d]	Speakers (m)[e]	Geographical area[f]	Other countries where spoken[g]	Status[h]	Use[i]	Development of research[j]	Research bodies[k]
RWANDA	5.3	1	Kinyarwanda	100%	Whole country	Burundi, Tanzania, Uganda, Zaire	NO	AaE$_{1,2m,3m}$ PR L	4	INRS, MINEPRISEC (Bureau pédagogique), UNR
			Kiswahili		Towns	Burundi, Tanzania, Uganda, Zaire		E$_{2,3m}$ R	1	
			French		Whole country		O	A E$_{1m,2,3}$ PR L	4	
SAO TOME AND PRINCIPE	0.08		Creole		Whole country					
			Portuguese		Whole country		O	A E$_{1,2}$ PR L	4	
SENEGAL	5.9	19	Wolof	80%	Whole country	Gambia, Mauritania	N	aE$_{0,1}$ RTL	3	IFAN, CLAD, Faculty of Arts, University
			Fulfulde (Pulaar)	21%	N.-E., S.	Guinea, Mali, Gambia, Burkina Faso, Niger	N	aE$_{0,1}$ RTL	2	
			Sereer	13%	Centre, Centre–W.	Gambia	N	aE$_{0,1}$ RTL	2	
			Joola (Dyola)	7%	S.	Gambia	N	a R L	1	
			Mande (Mandinka, Malinke)	6%	S., E.	Guinea-Bissau, Mali, Gambia	N	a R L	1	
			Soninke	2%	E., S.	Mali, Gambia, Mauritania, Guinea	N	a RTL	1	
			French	15%	Urban centres		O	AaE$_{1,2,3}$ PRTL	4	

Country[a]	Population (m)[b]	Number of languages[c]	Dominant languages[d]	Speakers (m)[e]	Geographical area[f]	Other countries where spoken[g]	Status[h]	Use[i]	Development of research[j]	Research bodies[k]
SEYCHELLES	0.06		Creole	100%	Whole country		O/N	PR L		
			French	15%			O/N	A E_{1m,2m} PR L	4	
			English	35%	Whole country		O/N	A E_{1,2} PR L	4	
SIERRA LEONE	3.1	18	Mende	31%		Guinea, Liberia	N	AaE_{1,3m} PR		
			Temne	30%		Guinea, Liberia	N	AaE_{1,3m} PR		
			Limba	8.4%			N	R		
			Kono	4.8%			N	a R		
			Fulfulde	3.1%		Guinea, Niger, etc.	N	R		
			Loko	3.0%			N	R		
			Kisi	2.2%		Guinea	N	R		
			Krio	1.9%				R		
			English		Whole country		O	AaE_{1,2,3} PRT	4	
SOMALIA	5.2		Somali	98%	Whole country	Ethiopia, Kenya, Djibouti	NO	AaE_{1,2,3} PRTL	4	Somali Academy of Sciences and Arts; Somali National University; Somali Language Department; Ministry of Education, Curriculum Development Unit, National Adult Education Centre
			Kiswahili	0.6%		Tanzania, Kenya, etc.			4	
			Arabic	75%	Whole country	Sudan, UAE, etc.	O	A E_{1m,2m,3m} PR	4	
			Italian	10%				E_3 P		
			English	15%				E_{2m,3} P		
SUDAN	17.8		Arabic	50%	Whole country	UAE, Somalia, etc.	NO	AaE_{1,2,3} PRTL	4	
			Dinka	10%				E_{1,3m} R		
			Nuer	4.5%				R		
			Zande	2.1%		Zaire		E_1 R		

Country[a]	Population (m)[b]	Number of languages[c]	Dominant languages[d]	Speakers (m)[e]	Geographical area[f]	Other countries where spoken[g]	Status[h]	Use[i]	Development of research[j]	Research bodies[k]
SUDAN			Moru	1.0%				E_1		
			English		Whole country			$E_{1m,2,3}$ PR L	4	
SWAZILAND	0.53		Siswati	91%			N	$aE_{1m,2m}$ PRT	3	
			English		Whole country		O	$A E_{1,2,3}$ PRTL	4	
TANZANIA	18	150	Kiswahili	90%	Whole country	Kenya, Uganda, Zaire, Burundi, Rwanda, Mozambique, Malawi, Somalia, Zambia, Comoros	NO	$AaE_{1,2,3}$ PRTL	4	Department of Kiswahili and Literature, Institute of Kiswahili Research, National Kiswahili Council, Institute of Kiswahili and Foreign Languages, EACROTANAL
TOGO	2.3	50	English	20%	Whole country		O	$A E_{1m,2,3}$ PRTL	4	
			Ewe	22%	S.	Benin, Ghana	N	$AaE_{1,2m}$ PRTL	4	Académie ewe, INRS, CERK (Centre d'études et de recherches de la Kara), INSE, IPN, Département de linguistiques, Université du Bénin
			Kabye	13%	Centre		N	$AaE_{1,2m}$ PRT	3	
			French	35%	Whole country		O	$A E_{1,2,3}$ PRTL	4	
UGANDA	12.4		Luganda	39%			N	$AaE_{1,2m}$ PR	3	
			Ateso (+Karimojong)	10%			N	$AaE_{1,2m}$ PR		
			Runyankore-Rukiga	15%			N	$AaE_{1,2m}$ PR		
			Rutooro	6.2%			N	$AaE_{1,2m}$ R		
			Lwo (Acholi + Lango)	10%			N	$AaE_{1,2m}$ PR		

Country[a]	Population (m)[b]	Number of languages[c]	Dominant languages[d]	Speakers (m)[e]	Geographical area[f]	Other countries where spoken[g]	Status[h]	Use[i]	Development of research[j]	Research bodies[k]
UGANDA			Lugbara	3%			N	$AaE_{1,2m}$ PR		
			Kiswahili	35%		Tanzania, Kenya, etc.	N	$A\,E_{1m,2m}$ PR L	4	
			English	21%	Whole country			$A\,E_{1m,2,3}$ PRTL		
ZAIRE	30	220	Kiswahili	39%	E., N., S.–E.	Tanzania, Kenya, etc.	N	$A\,E_{1,2,3m}$ PRTL	3	DLLA, CELTA, IRS, BUZATRA, ISP, Centre nat., IPN, etc.
			Lingala	25%	N., N.–W.	Congo, CAF	N	$A\,E_{1,2,3m}$ PRTL	3	
			Ciluba	22%	Centre–S.		N	$A\,E_{1,2,3m}$ PRTL	3	
			Kikongo	14%	W., S.–W.	Congo, Angola	N	$A\,E_{1,2,3m}$ PRTL	3	
			French		Whole country		O	$A\,E_{1,2,3m}$ PRTL	4	
			Cinyanja (Chichewa)	42%		Malawi, Mozambique	N	$AaE_{1m,2m}$ PR	3	
			Citonga	23%			N	$AaE_{1m,2m}$ PR		
			Silozi	17%			N	$AaE_{1m,2m}$ PR		
			Luvale	8%			N	$AaE_{1m,2m}$ PR		
			Kikaonde	7%			N	$AaE_{1m,2m}$ PR		
			Lunda	5%		Angola	N	$AaE_{1m,2m}$ PR		
			English	26%	Whole country		O	$A\,E_{1,2,3}$ PRTL	4	
ZAMBIA	5.1	40	Icibemba	56%		Zaire	N	$AaE_{1m,2m}$ PR	3	
			Cinyanja (Chichewa)	42%		Malawi, Mozambique	N	$AaE_{1m,2m}$ PR	3	
			Citonga	23%			N	$AaE_{1m,2m}$ PR		
			Silozi	17%			N	$AaE_{1m,2m}$ PR		
			Luvale	8%			N	$AaE_{1m,2m}$ PR		
			Kikaonde	7%			N	$AaE_{1m,2m}$ PR		

Country[a]	Population (m)[b]	Number of languages[c]	Dominant languages[d]	Speakers (m)[e]	Geographical area[f]	Other countries where spoken[g]	Status[h]	Use[i]		Development of research[j]	Research bodies[k]
ZAMBIA			Lunda	5%		Zaire Angola	N	$AaE_{1m,2m}$	PR		
			English	26%	Whole country		O	$A\,E_{1,2,3}$	PRTL	4	
ZIMBABWE	7.5	8+	Shona			Mozambique	N	aE_1	RTL	3	University of Zimbabwe
			Ndebele				N	aE_1	RTL	3	
			English		Whole country		O	$A\,E_{1,2,3}$	PRTL	4	

Source: UNESCO (1985) *The Definition of a Strategy for the Promotion of African Languages,* meeting of experts held in Conakry, Guinea, 21–25 September 1981, document CLT/85/WS/72 (Paris: UNESCO).

African studies outside Africa

One of the main results of decolonization will certainly be the significant growth of African studies outside Africa, not only in the universities of the former colonial powers where they have taken on a fresh lease of life, but also and above all in many countries in Western and Northern Europe, the Americas and Asia.

Under the irresistible impetus of the African-American communities of North, Central and South America, and as a result of the enormous interest shown in 'African affairs', many universities in the United States, the Caribbean and Brazil have set up centres for African studies and have introduced courses on such subjects as Africa past and present, its languages and literature and its different cultures.

Arabic, Kiswahili, Yoruba and Hausa studies, to mention only a few, have expanded significantly in North America. Indeed, it was a profoundly moving experience for the peasants of present-day Africa to welcome young American travellers, or Peace-Corps volunteers, or Japanese or European researchers who could speak to them in Fulfulde, Kiswahili, Yoruba, Wolof, Hausa or other languages, as if they had always been living in the neighbouring village!

The French *Agence de coopération culturelle et technique* (ACCT), which was originally created for the purpose of defending and developing the language and culture of France, has funded significant research and other work on African languages and literature. It has commissioned and published bi-lingual editions of works aimed at promoting these languages and spreading knowledge of them throughout the world.

The enthusiasm for Africa and its languages and cultures was such that it inspired African students and intellectuals to take up the call and incited African countries to show greater interest, provide more substantial resources and encourage advanced teaching and research.

What does the future hold in store?

All in all, the accession of the peoples of Africa to 'international sovereignty' opened a wide variety of horizons and prospects for them. However, the assistance their countries received from all quarters did not always help to stiffen their resistance to foreign cultural domination. The divisions and the burdensome legacy of their recent past as colonized peoples, the hesitations and lack of experience of their leaders, the watering-down of decisions at the executive level, the dilapidation and wastage of their resources and of their domestic efforts were all factors that scarcely made it possible for them to take an overall view of the situation or to spell out the issues and evolve a strategy and operational programme likely to guide their steps more surely on the path to the unity and freedom they sought.

A critical appraisal and the application of the relevant findings of certain regional or worldwide meetings – such as the Intergovernmental Conference on Cultural Policies in Africa held in Accra in 1975, or the World Conference on Cultural Policies held in Mexico City in 1982, or the regional meetings of experts which UNESCO organizes periodically in African capitals on cultures or languages and language policies – would have made it possible to reverse the trend by providing African leaders with the all-embracing and untroubled view of things which they still lack.

Unfortunately, these conclusions do not appear to have been assimilated and used to shed light on the cultural practices, or indeed the cultural policies, of any country in Africa.

The year 2000: important challenges as from 1982

In the countries of present-day Africa, there appears to be very little concern for the acquisition of written and oral fluency in African languages and the progress accomplished by linguistic research, with international assistance, is all too often disregarded.

However, unless priority is given to the development of those languages, there can be no prospect of Africa and its peoples achieving endogenous economic development and social and cultural advancement within a time-span that is humanly reasonable or acceptable. On the threshold of the third millennium, time is more than ever working against the African languages.

From oral tradition to oral communication

We are still at a stage where tape-recorders continue to be used to take down African languages and where makeshift devices are being tacked onto traditional typewriters in an attempt to transcribe them. However, it is already high time to have assimilated and gone beyond the outmoded stages represented by the mini-cassette, the long-playing gramophone record and the electric typewriter, in order to catch up with those who have taken the lead in using video-discs and word-processors.

African languages came late to the appointment with the Gutenberg galaxy and it is an acknowledged fact that they have by no means made up for the delay or still settled their score with writing.

However, the world's other languages, which are often saturated with writing, are now taking giant strides towards oral communication and the visual image. The goal to be achieved bears no relation whatsoever to the unsophisticated orality which impregnates communication in the African languages, where the human voice can only be relayed from time to time by the talking drum. On the contrary, it is a new type of oral communication, arising out of writing and industry, a technocrat's oral discourse in which video has a decisive role to play.

Perform or perish

The population experts estimate that if the current growth rates are maintained, Africa will have 850 million inhabitants by the year 2000, representing 14 per cent of the world's population at that time, compared with 10.6 per cent at the end of the 1980s. Of those Africans, 297.5 million will be under 15 years of age. What languages will they be speaking in a continent where the pace of urban growth is being stepped up? Like the cultures they epitomize and convey, African languages are currently undergoing constant changes, some of which can be ascribed to the all-pervasive domination of the foreign languages of worldwide communication that are used in all the spheres of the everyday life of the nation. Although the world linguistic scene is now tending to over-simplification in favour of that handful of universal languages, the portents are that African languages, like other minority languages, will resist and will continue to exist.

However, if African languages are to survive, they will have to evolve, and that implies that governments will have to have a clear vision of their goals and needs; they will have to draw up coherent operational pro-grammes and allocate substantial human, technical and financial resources to implementing them. This means that it will be more than ever necessary to go beyond the stage of improvisation and hesitation, expediency and the makeshift, in order eventually to evolve a genuine language policy.

Terminology committees will endeavour to draw up an inventory of the scientific and technological information accumulated by mankind as a whole, so as to integrate it systematically into African languages. Other research units will rapidly create and foster a whole range of specialized and popular press organs serving those languages.

There can be no doubt that, by the end of the present century, the technological revolution we are now witnessing will dictate the formation of major geo-political and socio-cultural units, in which speed will abolish distance and free the farthest corners of the earth from isolation through advanced technology and increasingly high-performance communications systems. In this breakneck race towards universality, there will no longer be any room for amateurs and Africa will be compelled, merely in order to retain sovereignty over the space it occupies, to ensure that computers and satellites can speak its languages.

Are we asking too much of our run-down neo-colonized economies? It is quite clear that the break-up of the old territorial units of the pre-colonial and colonial era has given rise, in present-day Africa, to states that are incapable of coping by themselves and are often condemned to beg for alms on the international scene.

551

As it approaches the threshold of the third millenium, Africa is faced with a host of strategic cultural and language issues. Year in and year out, its languages have hitherto largely defended themselves with a measure of success against the grave dangers to which they were exposed under colonial occupation. However, the problem will no longer be merely one of safeguarding knowledge when that knowledge itself has been undermined by its own conditions of preservation and by the manner in which it is handed down.

Unless Africa is to allow itself to be taken over and eventually be overwhelmed by cleverly packaged and widely disseminated values that are artificial or superficial, it will have to make its presence and performance felt in the new electronic age. If the ancestral knowledge of Africans is compiled, analysed, updated and communicated both in writing and by image and sound from the end of this second millenium onwards, it will be possible for future generations to refresh themselves at this source and to maintain the close ties with the past that are essential to them.

The development of modern literature since 1935

Ali A. MAZRUI

in collaboration with the late

Mario de ANDRADE,

M'hamed ALAOUI ABDALAOUI,

Daniel P. KUNENE *and* Jan **VANSINA**

The period since the 1930s is precisely the era which has witnessed the most extensive flowering of written literature in Africa.[1] As formal education and literacy expanded, and African access to university education increased significantly, a reservoir of literate Africans was created from which new writers finally emerged. And an expanding pool of potential *readers* of and *listeners* to African literature came into being. Although the short story, the essay and the biography as literary genres were by no means insignificant, the most basic forms of creative literature in this period of African history were, first, poetry and rhetoric; secondly, drama and the theatre; and, thirdly, the novel. Perhaps the easiest to accommodate with indigenous tradition were rhetoric and poetry. Africa had had poets, orators and composers of songs almost since the beginning of language itself. The interplay between indigenous poetic and oratorical traditions and the new forms of the Western world was in many ways the least painful area of culture contact in literature.

But if poetry was the most indigenous form of literature on the continent, the novel was the most alien. Even in the Western world the novel was primarily a product of the nineteenth century and of the industrial revolution. Of course *story-telling* as such was *primordial* in both the West and Africa. Hence the transition to short stories was not so difficult. *Griots* in West Africa go back at least a millennium. Complexity of material was not a problem. After all, very long and complex epics were told in Africa. But the novel as an art-form which fuses a single story with characterization, plot and narrative went beyond the conventions of the *griot*. Of all the literary forms which burst their way into Africa during European colonial rule, the novel was in many ways the most purely European.

This chapter discusses the main themes expressed in literature as they relate to the general history of Africa without attempting to give a

---

1. This chapter is greatly indebted to earlier work by A. A. Mazrui, especially A. A. Mazrui, 1975a, and A. A. Mazrui and M. Bakari, 1986a and 1986b.

PLATE 19.1 *A* griot, *or traditional African story-teller*

complete overview of all aspects of literature. Changes of a formal or stylistic nature are not discussed, the history of literary circles, organizations and journals is not pursued, the complex filiation of influences and innovations cascading over their generations must be left aside.

Before a discussion of the main themes of African literature can be opened, a few words must first be said about the economic and technical constraints which have impeded and still hamper the production of literary works. The scarcity of presses, the absence of substantial publishing houses in most parts of the continent and the cost of books are major obstacles. Moreover, too few of the writers' countrymen and women can read European languages and even fewer can afford to buy books. The writer in African languages paradoxically faces similar problems. More readers of diverse walks of life can enjoy the texts, but their appeal is now limited by the language itself. This is not a problem for Arabic, but it is the tragedy of much writing in sub-Saharan African languages.

The new *oral* artists, and such composers still exist, are bypassed in literary surveys because they are contemporary, yet expressing themselves in a mode associated with archaism. Moreover, they reach only those who listen to them. Thus even today African oral authors still suffer from the lack of a diversified African audience, and this in turn affects the authors. Since they can rarely take part in dialogue, they are condemned to soliloquy. Too often they write for a handful of peers, or for localized audiences. A high proportion of authors and narrators in the oral tradition are *women* with great verbal skills and virtuosity, in both verse and story-telling. Grace Ogot's early writings had links with a much older Luo tradition of oral narrative.

On poetry and politics

We shall return to the novel later, but let us first examine that most indigenous literary form – poetry. One of the most important aspects of African poetry in this period was the link with *political* experience. Several factors went towards forging this linkage. One factor was the phenomenon of cultural nationalism itself. Connected with this was the use of proverbs in traditional discourse. Yet another factor in the African poetic experience in this period was the impact of the Bible and the Ḳur'ān as sources of poetic inspiration. But underlying all these was the role of *emotion* as a basic element in both poetry and certain forms of political appeal.

Among the peoples of Africa perhaps none has had a body of poetry more closely linked to *nationalism* than the Somali. John Drysdale was once startled by how Somali nationalism was fostered by 'the national appeal of the Somali poetry'. And Colin Legum soon discovered that because of the longing for Somali reunification, Somali poetry was often 'strongly tinged with ideas of "amputation" and "the dismemberment" of the Somali nation'.[2] Poetry by Somali women is less politicized, but by no means divorced from patriotism.

A different kind of cultural nationalism erupted among Africans in Paris in the 1930s. Partly inspired by surrealism as a rebellion against the tyranny of language and bourgeois art, Francophone Africans in Paris initiated a rebellion against the colonization of the African mind, but in a European frame of reference.[3] The French imperial policy of cultural assimilation provoked the African response of *negritude*. It turned out to be a pan-African experience of unique significance. African and Caribbean writers forged an alliance of poetry to lament their own dislocation from ancestry and affirm the validity of tradition and African authenticity. The alliance between Aimé Césaire of Martinique and Léopold Sédar Senghor was a particularly important foundation of the literary movement of negritude. Indeed, Aimé Césaire invented the word 'negritude', and then embarked on what Nietzsche would have called a 'transvaluation of values'. Aimé Césaire applauded and said 'Hooray' to the following:

2. J. Drysdale, 1964, p. 15; and C. Legum, 1963, p. 505.
3. W. Soyinka, 1985, p. 564.

PLATE 19.2 *Above left: Aimé Césaire, French writer born in Martinique; above right: Léopold Sédar Senghor of Senegal, member of the Académie française*

Those who have invented neither powder nor the compass,
Those who have tamed neither gas nor electricity,
Those who have explored neither the seas nor the skies . . .
My negritude is not a rock, its deafness hurled against the
    clamour of the day,
My negritude is not a thing of dead water on the dead eye
    of the earth;
My negritude is neither a tower nor a cathedral:
It plunges into the red flesh of the earth.[4]

Writers like Jean-Joseph Rabearivelo (Malagasy), Tchicaya U Tam'si (Congo) and Yambo Ouologuem (Mali) joined the literary African forces against European cultural imperialism and in favour of African cultural vindication.

The forces of poetry and of politics were joined. In the earlier years of this period it was not clear whether we were witnessing poets with an interest in politics or politicians with an interest in poetry. It has been pointed out often enough that Léopold Senghor of Senegal was a poet, Keita Fodeba of Guinea a producer of ballets, Bernard Dadié of the Côte d'Ivoire a novelist and Cofi Gadeau a playwright, before they held political office in their respective countries. In those early years it was difficult to

4. This rendering in English is from S. W. Allen's translation of J.-P. Sartre, 1963, pp. 41–3.

draw a line between the artist and the activist, between the poet and the politician.[5]

In the fusion between art and agitation, certain African magazines played a decisive role for a while. These included *Présence Africaine* (Paris), *Black Orpheus* (Ibadan) and *Transition* (Kampala and Accra).[6]

Are *oratory and rhetoric* a branch of literature? They definitely can be – especially in societies of the oral tradition. Let us turn to a special kind of fusion between oratory and poetry.

Foreign art and African activism

Oratory and rhetoric definitely are flourishing branches of African literature. No one who ever heard Patrice Lumumba's impassioned pleas can ever doubt this. No one swayed by al-Nasser's rhetoric will ever forget it. But, alas, a record of most such performances has not survived.

Until independence, the African activist who used art for political oratory did not limit himself to indigenous art. The African politician who used poetry for political rhetoric did not limit himself to indigenous poetry either. Just as the frontier between art and activism was blurred, so was the frontier between the indigenous and the imported. Africa conscripted European languages and literature for the cause of African liberation and rhetoric.

Intimately linked is Africa's love for *the sound of words*. One of the first warnings which young Nnamdi Azikiwe pronounced on his return to Nigeria from the US was a warning against what he called 'the by-products of an imitative complex'. He urged his countrymen to go 'beyond the veneer of knowledge', and he emphasized that 'ability to quote Shakespeare or Byron or Chaucer does not indicate original scholarship'.[7]

Chinua Achebe, Nigeria's leading novelist, points at his countrymen's love for the sound of big words in a speech he allocates to the president of Omuafia Progressive Union in the novel *No Longer at Ease*. And in a play by Wole Soyinka, Nigeria's leading playwright and Nobel-Prize winner, a teacher assails the custom of paying 'bride price' with a series of long high-sounding English words – 'and only stopped because he had only the Shorter Companion Dictionary – the longer edition which he had ordered hadn't arrived'.[8]

The literary critic Donatus Nwoga refers to certain characters in Nigeria's market literature – and the satire of high-sounding words:

5. For the Francophone phenomenon, consult T. Hodgkin and R. Schachter, 1960, p. 387.
6. See especially P. Benson, 1986.
7. From a speech given in November 1934 in Lagos. See N. Azikiwe, 1961, p. 23.
8. See W. Soyinka, 1963.

557

PLATE 19.3   *Wole Soyinka of Nigeria, receiving the Nobel Prize for Literature, December 1986*

In *Veronica, My Daughter*, Chief Jombo, feeling that Veronica, his daughter, and Pauline, his wife, were trying to browbeat him with their superior knowledge of the English language, sent for Bomber Billy, reputed for the bomb words he could throw . . . This concatenation of bombasts would be greatly effective on stage in Nigeria where big words do make an impact.[9]

In addition to the sound of words, foreign literature was attractive as a source of wit – 'to point a moral or adorn a tale'. European literature was made subject to the laws of conversation of indigenous African languages. Conversational wit in many African languages postulates a ready command of diverse proverbs. As a Yoruba proverb has put it: 'A wise man who knows proverbs reconciles difficulties'.[10] Proverbs are also the staple of oratory.

9. D. Nwoga, 1965, pp. 28–9.
10. See Introduction in C. Leslau and W. Leslau, 1962.

558

The indigenous love of proverbs was transferred to quotations from foreign literature. Donatus Nwoga tells us about an Igbo dictum that to make a *speech* without using proverbs is like trying to climb a palm tree without a climbing rope. Nwoga then goes on to make a connection between traditional proverbs and Shakespearean quotations in contemporary Africa. He says:

> I suggest that the tendency towards supporting one's statements with proverbs might have carried over into this market literature in the form of using quotations. In *Veronica, My Daughter*, between pages 20 and 23, there are quotations from Richard Whateley, William Shakespeare, G. A. Gallock, Rudyard Kipling, Benjamin Harrison, William Ernest Henley and Henry Longfellow; and before the end of the story there are further quotations from Johann Wolfgang Von Goethe and some unknown poet . . .'[11]

But quotations were important not only for *conversation* but also for *political anti-colonial oratory*. Africa's new activists were often straining to be literary.

European colonial powers in Africa in the first half of the twentieth century – though sensitive to 'sedition' and 'subversion' – underestimated the political implications of those poetically expressed ideas. The late Chief Obafemi Awolowo once confessed in his autobiography: 'Some of the mighty lines of Shakespeare must have influenced my outlook on life'.[12] In Uganda, young Apollo Obote adopted a new first name, Milton, out of admiration for the author of the British classical poem, *Paradise Lost*. And in the Gold Coast in 1934, young Kwame Nkrumah was applying to the Dean of Lincoln University in the US for admission. In his application, Nkrumah quoted from Tennyson's *In Memoriam*:

> So many worlds, so much to do,
> So little done, such things to be.

In his autobiography more than 20 years later, Nkrumah confirmed that this verse 'was to me then, and is it still is today, an inspiration and a spur. It fired within me a determination to equip myself for the service of my country'.[13]

Significant also was the longest and 'in some respects the most important speech' that mature Premier Nkrumah made before independence. The speech was made on 12 November 1956. He was asking the National Assembly to approve his government's Revised Constitutional Proposals

11. D. Nwoga, 1965, p. 31.

12. 'Shakespeare is my favourite. I have read all his plays, and have re-read some of them – like *Julius Caesar, Hamlet, The Tempest, Anthony and Cleopatra* and *Henry V* – more than three times. Some of the mighty lines of Shakespeare must have influenced my outlook on life.' See O. Awolowo, 1960, p. 70.

13. K. Nkrumah, 1957, p. v.

for the Gold Coast's independence. Nkrumah opened his speech with a reference to Edmund Burke's remark: 'We are on a conspicuous stage and the world marks our demeanour'. Nkrumah asserted: 'Never has this been truer than today. How we conduct ourselves when we become independent will affect not only Ghana but the whole of Africa'.[14]

Kwame Nkrumah concluded his speech with Wordsworth's immortal lines about the French Revolution of 1789. Nkrumah said: 'I hope that someday, somewhere, we also may be able to say with William Wordsworth:

> *Bliss was it in that dawn to be alive,*
> *But to be young was very heaven!*[15]

We might therefore conclude that either directly, or by kindling a new interest in local styles of argumentation, European literature generally is part of the genesis of the linkage between art and activism in Africa. Just as African nationalists used European languages for new purposes of political struggle, so also for a while they used European literature for the same nationalistic goals. European poetry afforded quotations for use in those early days of the newly aggressive African intellectualism. Foreign literature inspired a paradoxical form of cultural nationalism among the new wave of African freedom-fighters. It afforded a new discourse by proverbs. It often merged with the Bible or the Ḳur'ān, or with Christian and Islamic hymns, to provide additional stimuli to Africa's sensibilities. Both European literature and European languages provided the basis of some of the emerging oratory of this period of African history. If oratory and rhetoric are a branch of literature, this phase was a striking mixture of foreign poetry and African rhetoric.

Tom Mboya of Kenya once recited Rudyard Kipling's poem *If* in its entirety before a huge crowd. It was the eve of an election in Nairobi. The crowd was waiting to hear Mboya's last pre-election speech. Mboya burst into foreign poetry:

> If you can keep your head when all about you
> Are losing theirs and blaming it on you,
> If you can meet with Triumph and Disaster
> And treat those two impostors just the same,
> If you can talk with crowds and keep your virtue
> or walk with kings – nor lose the common touch,
> If you can fill the unforgiving minute
> With sixty seconds worth of distance run,
> Yours is the Earth and everything that's in it,
> And – which is more, you'll be a Man, my son.[16]

14. K. Nkrumah, 1961, p. 71.
15. *ibid.*, p. 84; the italics are Nkrumah's.
16. R. Kipling, 1903.

There in Nairobi was this immortal son of Kenya, worn out by the exertions of campaigning, nervous about the election the next day, confronting an eager audience of fellow black people listening to his words of wisdom. Mboya was later to communicate to posterity the following paragraph:

> I read out to the great crowd the whole of Rudyard Kipling's poem, *If*. When facing the challenge of nation-building nobody can claim to have played a manly part if he (or she) has not ' . . . filled the unforgiving minute with sixty seconds' worth of distance run'.[17]

Again two branches of literature were interacting – poetry and rhetoric. The poetry was foreign and imperial, the oratory and rhetoric were deeply African.

Kipling, the poet of 'The White Man's Burden', had become the poet of 'The Black Man's Ambition'. On the one hand, European literature was colonizing the African mind. On the other hand, when Rudyard Kipling's poetry was mobilized in the service of Africa, it was a case of Rudyard Kipling being *decolonized*. It was Kipling himself who said in 1923: 'Words are, of course, the most powerful drug used by mankind'.[18]

But it is in the nature of nationalism in Africa, as elsewhere, to be economical and sparing in its acknowledgement to foreign inspiration – be that inspiration poetic or ideological, Shakespearean or Leninist. If it be asked why nationalism should be so inhibited in acknowledging its debt, the reply might best be given by Zimbabwe's veteran politician, Ndabaningi Sithole. His answer rests on the premise that nationalism has a strong elemental force of sheer ambition – and his answer is directly Shakespearean. Why are the imperial literary origins of modern African nationalism not acknowledged by the nationalists? Ndabaningi Sithole quotes:

> But 'tis a common proof,
> That lowliness is young ambition's ladder,
> Whereto the climber upward turns his face;
> But when he once attains the upmost round,
> He then unto the ladder turns his back,
> Looks in the clouds, scorning the base degrees
> By which he did ascend.[19]

The African orator had arrived at the rich mines of European literature. The orator saw, conquered – and took. And then climbed upwards.

17. T. Mboya, 1963b, p. 114.
18. In a speech on 14 February 1923: see *The Times*, 16 February 1923.
19. W. Shakespeare, *Julius Caesar*, II, 1; quoted by N. Sithole, 1959, p. 57. See also J. S. Coleman, 1963, pp. 114–15.

The muse of liberation

But not all African activists used borrowed foreign poetry for nationalistic African purposes. Some of the new activists and liberation fighters were themselves poets or other kinds of creative writers. Some created workshops or cultural organizations to promote wider literary creativity. Among these must be counted Agostinho Neto, later destined to be the founder-president of independent Angola.

In the winter of 1948–9, a number of militant 'exiles' got together in Lisbon. The group was small – consisting of Amilcar Cabral (1924–73), Vasco Cabral, Marcelino dos Santos, Mario de Andrade and Agostinho Neto (1922–79). The intellectuals were reading poetry and discussing literature when Neto interrupted to say:

> Today I received a letter from my friend Viriato da Cruz – perhaps you have heard of him. He is one of our poets. He says they have organized a cultural center [in Luanda] and named it 'Let's Discover Angola'. He also writes that they're going to do studies on African history and popular art, write stories and poems, and use the profits from the sale of publications to help talented and needy writers. I think we could also do this here in Lisbon. There are many people here who can write poetry and short stories, not only about student life, but also about our native countries – Angola, Mozambique, and the islands of Cape Verde and São Tomé.[20]

In the 1950s, Neto, Cabral and Mario de Andrade secretly established a Centre for African Studies (*Centro de Estudos Africanos*) with a broad agenda for promoting the study of colonized black people, including the study and promotion of creative African literature. A literary wing of the enterprise was the *Casa dos Estudantes do Imperio*. In 1951 two works on creative literature were issued – *Linha do Horizonte* ('The Horizon Line') by Aguinaldo Fonseca (Cape Verde) and the anthology *Poesia em Moçambique* edited by Orlando de Albuquerque and Victor Everisto. Among the most notable of the 25 writers from Mozambique represented in the volume were Orlando Mendes, Noemia de Sousa and Fonsesca Amaral.

Art and activism once again interacted. The Salazar regime in Lisbon, reacting to the militant anti-imperialism of post-war Africa, suppressed the *Casa dos Estudantes do Imperio* from 1952 to 1957. After its revival in 1957 it still clashed periodically with the authorities until it was closed down completely in 1965.

The word 'African' was once forbidden when referring to the 'overseas Portuguese provinces'. When referring to the spread of African traditions, colonial writers had to resort to the jargon of 'the spreading of overseas

20. O. Ignatiev, 1975, p. 15; English translation from M. Ferreira, 1986, pp. 398–9.

cultural values'. Ideas of negritude in Lusophone Africa therefore came like a breath of fresh air. Some of the poetry exploded in wild physical abandon:

> And I lift up into the equinox of my land
> the ruby of the most beautiful Ronga song;
> And on the rare whiteness of the loins of dawn
> the caress of my beautiful savage fingers
> Is like the tacit harmony of spears in the rut of the race,
> Beautiful as the phallus of another man,
> Erect within the nervous womb of the African night.[21]

Craveirinha – perhaps Mozambique's most prominent non-white poet – was arrested in 1964 when war broke out in his land. But the imperial order could not silence either him or Agostinho Neto – even if the poetry had to be published far from Portugal's reach. Both Craveirinha's and Neto's poems appeared in Italy in 1966, for example. Activism and art continued to be dramatically fused.[22]

A more complex relationship between art and activism, between poetry and politics, lay in the mind of Léopold Sédar Senghor. On the one hand, Senghor sought to rescue African culture from the contemptuous arrogance of Europe. On the other hand, Senghor fell in love with the country which colonized his own. In Senghor's own words:

> *Lord,* among the white nations, set France
>   at the right hand of the Father.
> *O,* I know she too is Europe, that she
>   has stolen my children like a
>   brigand to fatten her cornfields
>   and cottonfields, for the negro is dung.
> *She* too has brought death and
>   guns into my blue villages,
>   has set my people one against
>   the other, like dogs fighting over a bone . . .
> *Yes,* Lord, forgive France who hates her
>   occupiers and yet lays so
>   heavy an occupation upon me . . .
> *For,* I have a great weakness for France.[23]

We do have in Léopold Senghor a perfect illustration of the fusion between poetic rebellion and political collaboration, the quest for African authenticity combined with the imperial legacy of Africa's cultural

---

21. J. Craveirinha, 1964, p. 15; the English rendering is from A. S. Gerard, 1986, pp. 407–8.
22. See C. Wauthier, 1966.
23. L. S. Senghor, 1965, pp. 135–6.

dependency. Meanwhile a Namibian *guerilero* still asks in a series of rhetorical questions that roll one into the other, and are left for the reader to answer:

> Shall we meet again at home
> To talk and sing again
> To walk and sit again
> In our homes?
>
> Shall we meet at home?
> What a meeting it shall be!
> Shall we meet again in the
>   land of our love?
> In the land of our dear hope?
>
> Shall we meet again at home
> And end the longing for home
> And send the wronging home
> And from sorrow ever be free?[24]

In the case of people like Neto and Senghor, it is impossible to be sure whether we are studying political animals who became literary or literary creatures who became political. But with people like the younger Nkrumah and his Tennyson, or Awolowo and his Shakespeare, or Obote and his Milton, we are more sure that we are examining political animals who drew from literature. Even as president of Tanzania after independence, Julius K. Nyerere was, as we indicated elsewhere in this volume, sufficiently literary to embark on the task of translating into Kiswahili two of Shakespeare's plays – *The Merchant of Venice* and *Julius Caesar*.

But while politicians like Mboya and Awolowo in the latter years of colonialism and early years of independence were indeed tempted to go literary, writers throughout this period since 1935 have often been tempted to be political. Earlier African activists often touched base with art; latter-day artists have increasingly touched base with activism. It is to this latter category of politicized writers (as distinct from literary politicians) that we must now turn.

Authenticity: seven themes of conflict

Our discussion of the history of literature in Africa could not entirely be separated from more general thematic issues, but in this section we shall examine more closely some of the central areas of literary focus during that period.

A number of inter-related conflicts of values manifested themselves in African writings. One was the conflict between the African past and the

24. C. O'Brien Winter, 1977, p. 223.

African present. Quite often, themes of this kind betrayed a deep nostalgia, an idealization of what once was, or might have been.

Related to this is the conflict between tradition and modernity. That is not quite the same as the first conflict, since the dialectic between tradition and modernity can be taking place in the same historical period. It certainly continues to unfold in the Africa of today.

The third dialectic, again intimately related but by no means identical, is the conflict between the indigenous and the foreign. Indigenous traditions may struggle for supremacy with imported foreign traditions. A debate was also under way as to whether there could be a distinctly African approach to modernization which did not at the same time involve Westernization.

The fourth dialectic in the literature of this period, and indeed of the future, is the apparent conflict between the individual and society, between private rights and public duty.

The fifth dialectic which did not really gather momentum in Africa until the 1960s was the grand dilemma between socialism and capitalism, between the pursuit of equity and the quest for affluence.

The sixth, and intimately related dialectic, concerns the apparent dilemma between development and self-reliance, between rapid economic change with foreign help on one side and slower but autonomous progress on the other.

The seventh dialectic is the even more fundamental one between Africanity and humanity, between the rights of Africans as members of a particular race or inhabitants of a particular continent and the duties of Africans as members of the human race.

The first theme of nostalgia for the past has points in common with the whole movement of negritude in parts of French-speaking Africa. There is an idealization of ancestry, and sometimes an obsession with dance and rhythm as aspects of ancestral culture. A striking example is *Le regard du roi* by Camara Laye. Jomo Kenyatta, though Anglophone, belonged to this mood not only as a writer but also as president of Kenya. Literally to his last day of life he was a patron of traditional dancers, spending many hours in the course of his presidency watching dancers from different cultural backgrounds, and sometimes participating with them. This obsession with dance was a musical and artistic manifestation of cultural nostalgia. In Kenyatta's view: 'It is the culture which he inherits that gives a man his human dignity.'[25]

Kenyatta's ethnic compatriot, Joe Mutiga, addresses the fig tree in a similar mood:

---

25. J. Kenyatta, 1938; for this section on authenticity, the author is greatly indebted to previous collaboration with M. Bakari of the University of Nairobi.

Holy huge trees, you tax my memory:
Over you boys awaiting circumcision
Proudly threw '*ndorothi*' to show ability
To shoulder social responsibility,
While all dance in heartful joy,
Bearing proudly the tribal decorum:
. . . . .

A memory of olden days
When the Agikuyu were a tribe,
Though now but part of a nation . . .
. . . the beauty of old is gone.[26]

A longing for the past in Africa is interwoven with values of tradition as against modernity. Some of the writers and poets of this period were all too aware that dancing for rain was a less efficient way of increasing productivity than learning how to use a tractor. But the more romantic of the poets still longed for those rhythms of rural incantation, the music of supplication rather than the voice of an exhaust pipe.

Joseph Waiguru, another Makerere graduate, wrote a kind of ode to the 'Round Mud Hut' – a poem which was broadcast on the BBC African Service and on the old Radio Uganda. In the poem he sees the mud hut as a shared refuge for humans and their animals; for adults and their children. But the round mud hut is under siege – the forces of modernized accommodation, separating parents from children in their different rooms, humans from their animals in stables, segregating the inhabitants of the otherwise shared earth.

The round warm hut
Proud to the last
Of her noble sons
And daughters
Stands besieged.

Of late stones,
In tripartite agreement
Guarded a fire
And then a pot,
A large hot pot
Which nurtured
Black, black children

. . .

The bleating sheep
And the horned goat,

26. J. Mutiga, 1965, p. 132; see also I. N. Shariff, 1988.

Calves cud-chewing
At the end penned,
Share the warmth
Of the round mud hut.

All this and much more.
Slowly and slowly disappears:
Slowly and slowly iron appears
Lays a siege on the roof
And takes prisoner of the gourd.
The plate, the cup, the lamp,
What's this but a change
To the new oblong house?
The round mud hut is no more.[27]

But modernity in Africa is not only contrasted with tradition; it is also substantially identified with Westernization. That is why the second dialectic between modernity and tradition is so intimately linked with the third dialectic between the indigenous and the foreign. The very situation of those African writers using European languages was a dramatization of the basic tension between what was native and what was alien. Three forces were at work in facilitating this alien penetration of African societies. One was precisely Western-style education, whose pinnacle was universities like Dakar, Ibadan and Makerere. The second medium of penetration was Western Christianity, importing new paradigms of both ethics and explanation. The third medium of penetration was technology, especially those aspects which were of relevance to economic change and material production.

The writers of this period were much more conscious of the implications of Western education and Western Christianity than they seemed to be of the implications of Western technology and science. On the educational front, there was some recognition that these new processes of instruction and socialization created forms of cultural dependency. New Africans were in the process of being manufactured – somewhat less African than their parents were. Jonathan Kariara writing in English and at a Western-style university institution, wondered if he were being encased in clay, stifled by an alien structure.

I lay the other night and dreamt
That we were all being glazed
With a white clay of foreign education,
And it was stifling, stifling the sleeping blackman
Inside there.

. . . . .

27. J. Waiguru, in D. Cook, 1965, p. 132; see also I. N. Shariff, 1988.

> Will it be the pearl in the oyster shell,
> Or mere rottenness?[28]

As for the impact of Christianity, this has also been treated extensively in African literature. The best-known example certainly is Mongo Beti's *Le pauvre Christ de Bomba*. Ngugi's novels are at times obsessed with this clash, a perfectly understandable preoccupation for a writer who is a Kikuyu who grew up in the course of the Mau Mau emergency. The impact of Christianity was at many levels – it affected conceptions of knowledge, methods of rearing children, rituals of initiation and rites of passage, concepts of right and wrong, and paradigms of explaining natural phenomena, as well as the broader interpretation of metaphysical and supernatural concern. Western Christianity was thus a fundamental factor in the broader Westernization of Africa.

Okot p'Bitek drew attention to the tendency among Africans even to recreate their own gods in the image of the Christian God. As Okot p'Bitek put it:

> When students of African religions describe African deities as eternal, omnipresent, omnipotent, omniscient, etc., they intimate that African deities have identical attributes with those of the Christian God. In other words, they suggest that Africans hellenized their deities, but before coming into contact with Greek metaphysical thinking. . . . African peoples may describe their deities as 'strong', but not 'omnipotent'; 'wise', not 'omniscient'; 'old', not 'eternal', 'great', not 'omnipresent'. Like Danquah, Mbiti, Idowu, Busia, Abraham, Kenyatta, Senghor and the missionaries, modern Western Christian anthropologists are intellectual smugglers. They are busy introducing Greek metaphysical conceptions into African religious thought. The African deities of the books, clothed with the attributes of the Christian God, are, in the main, creations of the students of the religions. They are all beyond recognition to the ordinary African in the countryside.[29]

Okot p'Bitek later became Uganda's most eloquent rebel against Western cultural imperialism. His poem, *Song of Lawino*, is one of the strongest statements on cultural authenticity to have emerged out of Africa.

As for the dialectic between the individual and society, this too was linked to some extent with the impact of Christianity and the Protestant idea of personal accountability before God.

Individualism in Africa was also fostered by the ideas of private property which came with Western capitalism. In *East African Childhood*, Joseph A. Lijembe refers to his discovery of the principle of property after he left home and went to a Western-style school:

28. J. Kariara, in D. Cook, 1965, p. 100.
29. O. p'Bitek, 1971, pp. 80 and 88.

At home I had not been given a chance to care for and look after a bit of property that I could really call 'mine'. At school I found I possessed a set of articles, which, for a period, were mine. I had to begin afresh learning how to respect not only my things, but those that belonged to my class-mates and the school as a whole . . .[30]

The third major promoter of individualism was the new liberal ethos which came with Western political ideologies. The special premium which liberalism gave to individualism helped to transform the political horizons of African writers, as well as other African intellectuals. As Jonathan Kariara said of one of his short-story characters: 'He had inherited two things from the white man, a new religion and the desire to decide for himself'.[31]

In politics, Western liberalism helped to inspire demands for 'one man, one vote' and liberal forms of self-determination. In literature, individualism produced the new writers. After all, traditional oral literature was in some sense a literature without authors, a collective and cumulative heritage without individual attribution. But the new novels and poems, the new plays and short stories were works by specific artists, bearing their names or their pen-names. The very birth of written literature in European languages constituted an important departure from the collective traditions of an orally transmitted heritage. With the new trend came personalized copyright, royalties for individual authors and rules against plagiarism.

In addition, some of the art-forms which the writers were exploring themselves required a capacity on the part of the writer to create believable individual characters. As we indicated earlier, the short story in Africa has its antecedents in folk tales; modern verse can be a continuation of ancestral poetry, but the novel as normally understood is clearly a foreign art-form now being developed for African purposes. And the history of the novel is intimately connected with the rise of individualism in the West. Molly Mazrui, in her Makerere thesis on the individual and society in some African fiction, takes us back to that first English novel, *Robinson Crusoe*. She then quotes a critic who said of that book: '. . . the terms of the problem of the novel and of modern thought alike were established when the old order of moral and social relationships was shipwrecked, with Robinson Crusoe, by the rising tide of individualism'.[32]

Molly Mazrui related this observation to African societies, and argued that those societies had to some extent been shipwrecked by colonialism. Individualism in many areas of life was rapidly becoming a new order.

30. J. A. Lijembe, 1967, pp. 25–6.
31. J. Kariara, in D. Cook, 1965, p. 95.
32. I. Watt, 1969, p. 96.

Many African novelists, including Achebe and Ngugi, have explored what caused the shipwreck and tried to understand whether it was avoidable or not. They have shown us the anguish and conflict both for the individual and for his community as fluidity of values and rapidly changing standards have become the order of the day. . . . There are many reasons why this growth of individualism in Africa may be lamented, but among its more positive aspects must be counted the birth of the African novel.[33]

The fifth dialectic affecting African writers concerned the dilemma between capitalism and socialism. The initial African enthusiasm for at least socialist rhetoric was connected with the degree to which capitalism had been an ally of imperialism. Since socialism was opposed to capitalism, and African nationalism was opposed to imperialism, nationalistic ideas in Africa found a comradeship-in-arms with socialistic ideas from elsewhere.

Opposition to exploitation, whether it was by domestic capitalists or external imperialists, was just beginning to inspire African intellectuals on the eve of independence. Its major expression came a little later with the likes of Ousmane Sembene, Ayikwei Armah, Chinua Achebe or Wole Soyinka and first of all Franz Fanon.

In 1988 – a mere two years after Laureate Wole Soyinka's achievement – the Nobel Prize for Literature was once again in Africa. This time the recipient of the prize was Nagib Mahfuz, Egypt's greatest contemporary novelist, deeply concerned about exploitation. In the Dickensian tradition, much of Mahfuz's early and middle work focused on the life of the urban poor. Mahfuz demonstrated a remarkable sensitivity to the nuances and colour of life in the urban slums – especially in his most famous work, *The Valley of al-Midakk̲k̲.*

The impact of the Western world on North Africa is widely discussed in the literature of the Maghreb. Arabic and the French language compete as media of literary expression in Algeria, Tunisia and Morocco. A number of literary reviews have helped promote new radical talent. In Tunisia the journal *Al-Fik̲r* ('Thought') played a particularly historic literary role, sometimes politicized. North Africa is also leading the way in the literature of women's liberation.

'Westernization' as a theme in the modern Egyptian novel has included Tawfīk̲ al-Ḥakim's *The Bird from the East* and the novella by Yaḥyā Ḥak̲k̲i, *The Lamp of Ūmm Has̲h̲im.* A profound cultural ambivalence is at the core.

Ideological ambivalence has also been recurrent when writers have confronted exploitation. In North Africa the tension has sometimes been between Islam and secular radicalism. All over the continent the principle of social equality has often mesmerized novelists, poets and playwrights.

33. M. Mazrui, 1972, p. 407.

PLATE 19.4 *Nagib Mahfuz of Egypt, winner of the Nobel Prize for Literature, October 1988*

Ngugi wa Thiong'o, for one, later evolved into a neo-Marxist, combining more fully his rebellion against imperialism with a disgust for domestic African capitalists. But that itself was a transition from the preoccupation of colonized Africans before independence in their quest for indigenous authenticity to a new dedication concerned with social transformation and the pursuit of greater equity.

Deeply related to this transition from colonial obsessions to independent commitments is the sixth dialectic we mentioned – the dialectic between the attractions of rapid economic development as against the disciplines of self-reliance and even self-denial. This dialectic as a literary concern was most elaborately explored in Tanzania, especially in the later period of the Arusha Declaration and the pursuit of *ujamaa*. Significantly, much of the literary debate and discussion concerning self-reliance in Tanzania is to be found more in Kiswahili literature than in English writings. Poetry in Tanzania in this period is partly a transition from the disciplined rhyme of Shaaban Robert to the experimentalist blank verse of Euphrase Kezilahabi.

Cultural self-reliance is itself caught up in the very vigour of Kiswahili literature in Tanzania. To use a language more widely understood in society was itself a tribute to *ujamaa* and the ideal of real authenticity.

571

The new political literature on dependency in Africa certainly belongs to this general school of emphasis, and has affinities with the literature of *dependencia* of Latin America. The thrust of the discussion is that Africa may have attained some level of political independence, but the struggle for economic autonomy and cultural authenticity has only just begun. The economies of Africa are still penetrated by foreign capital, and members of the new black bourgeoisie are mainly allies of external foreign interests. The cultural penetration includes the prevalence of a consumer culture, the persistence of a colonial educational structure, the infiltration of African societies by alien information media and electronic services, and the survival of language policies which serve the interests of the élite and ruling classes and are inadequately sensitive to the needs of the masses. The continuing domination of élite culture in Africa by foreign languages becomes symptomatic of this deep-seated cultural dependency.

Female literary rebels against neo-colonialism have included Molara Ogundipe-Leslie of Nigeria, Abena Busia of Ghana, and Christine Obbo of Uganda. One of the ironies of their predicament is that these particular

PLATE 19.5 *Molara Ogundipe-Leslie of Nigeria: academic professor, poet, writer on literature, essayist and critic*

women are among the most Westernized of their generation.

Political writers in Anglophone Africa who are concerned with economic dependency include Adebayo Adedeji of Nigeria, Isa Shivji of Tanzania, Dan Nabudere of Uganda and Atieno-Odhiambo of Kenya. Political writers concerned with cultural dependence include Chinweizu of Nigeria, the late Okot p'Bitek of Uganda, Ali A. Mazrui of Kenya and Julius K. Nyerere of Tanzania. Much of the writing in this area is either academic or polemical: only a little has so far taken the form of poetry or fiction. But the basic dilemma between dependent development on one side and self-reliant stagnation on the other is in any case the latest incarnation of such older dilemmas as the one between tradition and modernity, and between the indigenous and the foreign. What the writers of the earlier decades of this century grappled with in terms of the tensions of modernization and freedom are now being explored in terms of the tensions of development and dependency.

But finally we have the most fundamental dialectic of them all – the dialectic between African distinctiveness and the idea of universalism, between the uniqueness of the African person and the catholicism of humanity. Our writers in the days before independence did indeed often use the language of humanity, but more often to demand rights for Africans.

Chinua Achebe has referred to 'the black writer's burden'. Achebe points out that in colonial Africa it was the African writer's job to attack colonial injustice. In independent Africa, according to Achebe, the writer must still accept the duty to challenge injustice wherever he sees it, even if it is injustice committed by Africans against Africans:

> . . . we must never agree to bargain away the right to be treated like full members of the human family. We must seek the freedom to express thought and feeling, even against ourselves, without the anxiety that what we might say might be taken as evidence against our race.[34]

In a way, political independence has been a contributory factor towards expanding the moral horizons of African intellectuals generally. To experience tyranny by Africans against Africans after experiencing the domination of Africans by white people is to learn about the universalism of rights and duties, and sin and redemption. The radicalization of writers like Kofi Awonoor and Lewis Nkosi has been part of this adventure into new categorical imperatives. Some writers have gone beyond demanding rights for Africans, or for black people – they have transcended even pan-Africanism as a specialized solidarity, and have instead sought to identify with the oppressed generally. Writers have indeed gone political – just as politicians had once gone literary. Journalists of this universalist

34. C. Achebe, 1966, pp. 138–9.

573

persuasion include Muḥammad Sid-Aḥmed of *Al-Ahram* in Cairo.

This seventh theme of conflict, between the parochial and the universal, between Africanity and humanity, is perhaps the most central issue of authenticity. The tension between the past and the present, tradition and modernity, are ultimately agonies of epochs across time. The tensions between the indigenous and the foreign are concerned with a dialectic across space. The confrontation between socialism and capitalism is a confrontation across values. The dilemma between rapid development and stagnant self-reliance is also about values, but taking the form of priorities in policy. But in the final analysis, it is the dialectic between the individual and society, on one side, and between society and universalism on the other, that lies at the heart of art itself. How the human person relates to the immediate social group and how that social group relates to humanity itself together constitute the ultimate universe of aesthetic exploration. Senghor has called it 'the Civilization of the Universal'.

The African writers we have examined in this essay are decidedly part of that exploration. Caught up in the agonies of multiple estrangement – political, educational, linguistic, aesthetic and technical – the African writers are engaged in setting the pace in the struggle to recover their memory, in the quest for ultimate renewal.

On literature and war

Although African literature after independence has paid considerable attention to the military, it has paid relatively little attention to war itself. And in discussing soldiers, African writers have been more preoccupied with military villains than with military heroes. An adversarial relationship has developed between writers and soldiers, except for liberation fighters in Northern and in Southern Africa. A whole generation of Algerian writers was inspired by armed struggle. And yet even liberation poets like Dennis Brutus of South Africa are ambivalent about 'boots, bayonets and knuckles'.

Two questions arise. Why is there so little written literature of military heroism in post-colonial Africa? Why is there so much literature about military villainy?

The dearth of a written literature of heroism is not due to a dearth of heroes. Many brave men and women have died for their respective causes in African wars since independence. But the nature of those wars has tended to make praise-songs of heroes politically sensitive. After all, apart from Egypt, most wars experienced by independent African countries have been *civil* wars, often secessionist.

Chinua Achebe – who became Biafra's ambassador-at-large while the civil war lasted – has written things about the conflict. But his status in post-war Nigeria has inevitably discouraged too obvious a glorification of

PLATE 19.6   *André Brink of South Africa, anti-apartheid writer*

Biafra and its heroes. The Federal side would not want to reactivate old wounds among the Igbo (Ibo) either.

The Ugandan military prophetess of the late 1980s, Alice Lakwena, was an Acholi equivalent of Joan of Arc. But praise-songs in her honour were unlikely since Yoweri Museveni's government regarded her as a 'tribal rebel'.

Another reason for the absence of military heroism in African literature may simply be that there has been a low level of combat involvement by the élite in many of Africa's wars since independence. Poets and writers are more likely to be inspired by the sacrifices of fellow intellectuals than by the death of unknown peasants. The death of Christopher Okigbo in the Nigerian civil war inspired a greater literary response than the death of half a million anonymous young Igbo. Ali Mazrui wrote his only novel, *The Trial of Christopher Okigbo*, in response to that death of a fellow intellectual.

In Nigeria itself, so few Igbo élite or Federal intellectuals were aroused enough to bear arms on behalf of either Biafra or Federal Nigeria. Intellectuals took sides in the war, and sometimes assumed non-combat roles in support of their side. But few intellectuals joined their respective

575

armies or volunteered to go to the front line. In the words of John De St. Jorre in his impressive book, *The Nigerian Civil War*:

> . . . the proportion of actual casualties among the élite, compared with the masses is minute and must constitute something of a record in the history of warfare. With a few courageous exceptions, the Nigerian and Biafran intellectuals, unlike their counterparts, say, in the First World War or Spanish civil war, did not believe in picking up a rifle to defend the cause. The Nigerian war produced its 'Wilfred Owen' (the Biafran poet, Christopher Okigbo, who died in action in Nsukka early in the fighting), but we have yet to see the Nigerian or Biafran equivalent of a Robert Graves, a George Orwell, or a Norman Mailer emerge.[35]

The shortage of African heroic military literature may also be due to the fact that a war against a foreign power is the most likely conflict to generate the type of patriotic fervour which celebrates heroes. Yet Africa – especially south of the Sahara – has been short of foreign military adversaries since independence.

The October war of 1973 between Egypt and Israel was regarded as heroic by Egyptians and generated poetry and songs in Egypt. Morocco's war to retain Western Sahara has also been widely seen at home as patriotic – and has similarly inspired song and poetry. The Western Sahara (recognized by the Organization of African Unity as the Saḥrāwi Arab Democratic Republic) has in turn generated heroic literature of its own about its own conflict with Morocco, while the wars in the Horn of Africa also gave birth to anguished poetry.

For Chad, Libya was a hostile foreign power. Chad's struggle against Libyan hegemony helped to nourish oral poetry and heroic songs. In 1987, Chad struck into the Libyan heartland for the first time: Libyan patriotism was wounded in a new way. It was only a matter of time before Libyan counter-moves in defence of *al-waṭān* (ancestral land) would provoke its own pool of heroic literature.

What had already inspired such songs and poetry was the American bombing of Tripoli and Benghazi in April 1986. The heroism of 'David versus Goliath' had been re-enacted on Arab soil.

South of the Sahara, the image of the warrior is used more widely in indigenous languages – but often as a metaphor for non-military forms of combat. Tanzania's Swahili poet, Kezilahabi, proclaims 'Had I been a warrior I would have bathed in blood and water' (*Kichwa na Mwili*, 1974). But it is metaphorical.

If there is such a shortage of literal African military heroes in literature, why is there a greater abundance of African military villains? Why has there developed an adversarial relationship between African writers and

35. J. De St. Jorre, 1972, pp. 374–5.

African soldiers? A major reason is that since independence, soldiers have been more inclined to be involved in politics than in war. And yet soldiers and writers have conflicting visions of the political process. Perhaps the adversarial relationship has been between writers and *rulers* – be those rulers military or civilian.

Muḥammad Hayḳal, former editor of *Al-Ahram* in Egypt, is one political writer who rose to great influence under al-Nasser – only to end up behind bars under Anwar al-Sadat. Yet Hayḳal's impact on Arab journalism has remained immense.

Wole Soyinka's angriest and perhaps most irrational book is *The Man Died*. It is a strong indictment not only of tyranny but also of the military, *per se*. It is a statement of the torment of detention to which Soyinka was subjected by General Gowon's regime. Soyinka's contempt for the soldiers is palpable in the book. On the other hand, Kenya's Ngugi wa Thiong'o was imprisoned by a *civilian* regime. His own post-detention statement was almost as angry as Soyinka's.

Somalia's leading novelist, Nuruddin Farah, has written a trilogy of novels against military tyranny in his home country. Although coming from a family of poets in the Somali language, Farah abandoned his mother-tongue as a medium for his literary work. The reasons he has given are the constraints of repression in Somalia. If he wrote in the Somali language he would not be read at all. Under Siad Barre, Farah's books were banned in the main market of the language – Somalia itself.

In his plays, Farah has also often returned to the theme of tyranny. *Yusuf and His Brothers* is indeed a story of heroism – pitched against the callous obscenities of repression. The play has been successfully staged in Nigeria.

On balance, it continues to be one of the anomalies of post-colonial literature that war has not been an inspiration for 'powerful poetic emotions, recollected in tranquillity'. It is also a post-colonial anomaly that African soldiers are more recognized in the literature as villains than as heroes. This includes Chinua Achebe's 1987 novel, *Anthills of the Savannah*, his first since the Nigerian civil war. Soldiers in their post-colonial roles have aroused among writers more hostility than hero-worship – for better or for worse.

Conclusion: literature and the triple heritage

Like other branches of culture, African literature has been subject to the wider influences of Africa's triple heritage. The heritage consists of the three legacies of indigenous values, Islamic influences and the impact of Western culture. The different branches of literature have responded differently to the three legacies.

While African fiction has been greatly enriched by contact with the West, indigenous African poetry in inland West Africa and along the shores of the Indian Ocean has been more enriched by contact with Islam. Even in the religiously controversial area of song, the Zanzibari woman singer, Siti bint Saad, was a fusion of Islam and Africanity.

The Somali have developed, as we indicated earlier, an exceptional culture of oral and even instant poetry. Their greatest modern national hero – Sayed Muḥammad 'Abdallāh Ḥassan – was (in British terms) a fusion of William Shakespeare and Winston Churchill. The exceptionally *sane* Mullah was both saviour of the nation and hero of the language. Of course the Sayed lived prior to the period of this volume, but his influence on contemporary Somali poetry is still so great that the Sayed has to be regarded as one of the persistent forces of modern Somali literature at least to the end of the twentieth century.

In Tanzania, many of the writers are not Muslims. And yet the Swahili poetic traditions within which they have operated have been partly a product of contact between Islam and African culture. Much of the imagery is rooted in words of Arabic derivation. Quite often there is one Bantu word and an Arabic synonym, a bonus for the Swahili poet. Two words for a concept, one Bantu, the other borrowed from Arabic:

> *Mapenzi* and *mahaba* (love);
> *pwaa* and *bahari* (the sea);
> *nchi* and *ardhi* (the land);
> *mnyama* and *hayawani* (animal);
> *Mtu* and *Binaadamu* (human being);
> *Ngoja* and *Subiri* (wait).

And when the poet is stuck for a new concept, the two traditional sources have been the Bantu and Islamic legacies.

Nor is the outlet for poetry limited to literary magazines and scholarly journals. Tanzanian newspapers have space not only for 'Letters to the Editor' but also for 'Poems to the Editor'. Readers send to the editor poems and verses on subjects which range from traditional medicine to a new piece of legislation, from matrimonial problems to the rate of inflation. It is again worth nothing that the debating poets of Tanzania have included highly eloquent women.

In such a literary national atmosphere it was not surprising that the head of state should try his hand at completing the triple heritage by translating Shakespeare into Kiswahili. The translations themselves generated a debate in Tanzania of a purely literary kind. Was blank verse admissible in Swahili poetry? Shakespeare had indeed written the plays in blank verse. That was perfectly compatible with the rules of poetic composition and the use of meters in the English language. Julius Nyerere had translated Shakespeare's plays also into blank verse. What was admissible in the English language was surely not necessarily admissible in Kiswahili. The debate shifted in Tanzania from the issue of translating foreign plays to the more basic indigenous issue of the nature of Swahili poetry itself.

On the issue of African languages and literature Islam has played a more paradoxical role. On the one hand, Islam appears to be linguistically intolerant. Formal prayer has to be in the Arabic language. The *Muezzin* calls believers to prayer in Arabic. The Ḳur'ān in its sacred role has to be read in Arabic.

At first sight this appears to be linguistically less tolerant than Christian behaviour. Even Catholicism has scaled down the role of Latin in worship and ritual. On the other hand, Jesus spoke Aramaic. The Bible (a work of immense influence in African literature) is a book in translation anyhow – so why not one more additional translation into an *African* language this time? If the Bible is already in English, why not also in Lunyoro-Lutoro? It has already been translated into over 100 African languages.

It is as if the Christian God was a god in exile. Christianity is a religion which failed at home and triumphed abroad. Its centre was not among the Jews and other Semites but among Caucasians – not in the Middle East but in the West. It was therefore easy to accept the word of God in translation.

But Islam triumphed among those to whom it was first revealed – and in the language in which it was revealed, Arabic. To insist on *Arabic* as the language of worship is to insist on authenticity. It is also to insist on the original poetry of the Ḳur'ān. Hausa poetry has felt that Ḳur'ānic impact.

But has the insistence on Arabic for formal worship helped or hindered both African languages in contact with Islam, and African poetry in contact with Islam?

In Muslim Africa south of the Sahara before European colonialism, Arabic was not the official language of the state but was the official language of the 'Church', or the Mosque.

On the whole, the effect was to enrich languages like Kiswahili. Other languages influenced by Arabic include Wolof, Somali, Tigrinya and Tigre.

What about African poetry and its response to Africa's triple heritage? How has African literature been affected by the imported legacies of the West and Islam? There has been a school of thought in the West which has denied Africans a capacity for art at all. Let us look at this challenge more closely.

Thomas Jefferson of America went to the extent of denying blacks a capacity for art or poetry. In Jefferson's *Notes on the State of Virginia* (Paris, 1784) there occurs the following astonishing observation:

> . . . never yet could I find that a black man had uttered a thought above the level of plain narration; never saw even an elementary trait

579

of painting or sculpture. In music they are more generally gifted than the whites with accurate ears for tune and time, and they have been found capable of imagining a small catch. Whether they will be equal to the composition of a more extensive run of melody, or of complicated harmony, is yet to be proved.

Jefferson then goes on to make an interesting statement. Pain is often a mother of poetry – anguish a stimulant to the muse. In Jefferson's words:

> Misery is often the parent of the most affecting touches in poetry. Among the blacks is misery enough, God knows, but no poetry. Love is the peculiar oestrum of the poet. Their love is ardent, but it kindles the senses only, not the imagination. Religion, indeed, has produced a Phyllis Wheatley; but it could not produce a poet. The compositions published under her name are below the dignity of criticism.

While Hegel and Hugh Trevor-Roper denied Africans a capacity for history, Thomas Jefferson had earlier denied Africans a capacity for art. Yet both forms of prejudice have been contradicted many times by the relentless march of historical and social research.

As for Thomas Jefferson's belief that blacks were a people without poetry, black Ethiopians were *writing* poetry before Jefferson's ancestors in the British Isles were taught the Latin alphabet by the Romans. And so entrenched is the poetic tradition among the Kiswahili-speaking peoples of East Africa today that the newspapers receive not only 'Letters to the Editor' but also 'Poems to the Editor' almost every day, as we indicated.

The most powerful genre of literature in Africa continues to be poetry – both oral and written, in both indigenous and foreign languages. Some of the poetry is a celebration of uniqueness; some is a cry of anguish. Considering his tragic fate as a casualty of the Nigerian civil war, few lines in African literature are as poignant and *prophetic* as the following ones by Christopher Okigbo:

> When you have finished
> And done up my stitches
> Wake me near the altar –
> And this poem will be finished.

Léopold Senghor fuses Africanity with femininity. If Eve was the mother of the human species, and Africa was the mother of Eve, where does Africa end and womanhood begin? Senghor answers thus:

> Naked woman, black woman,
> Clad in your colour that is life,
> In your form that is beauty!
> I have grown up in your shade,
> the sweetness of your hands bound my eyes.

And now in the heart of summer and noon,
I discover you, promised earth,
from the tower of your sun-scorched neck
And your beauty smites me to the full
of my heart like the flash of an eagle.
Naked woman, dark woman . . .

But there is more than sadness and joy in African literature – more than tragedy and comedy. To paraphrase and supplement a Sierra Leonean poet–diplomat, Davidson Abioseh Nicol:

'You are not a country, Africa
You are a concept . . . '
You are not a concept, Africa,
You are a glimpse of the infinite.

Arts and society since 1935

20

Jan VANSINA

Everywhere in Africa today we witness an astonishing creative outburst of the arts, bewildering in their diversity and welling up in all social strata. Many of the new trends in the arts date from the latter half of the colonial period. Indeed, some pioneers are still active today. After all, only two generations have elapsed since 1935. In this short interval of time, however, the pursuit of the arts has been so rich and diverse that this chapter can do no more than set out the major lines of development.[1]

At the outset, a few general social and cultural features affecting all of the arts must be enumerated, as they provided a matrix for all of them. These include the waxing, but uneven, impact of Europe, the growth of the cities, the increasingly sharp social stratifications resulting in the formation of new classes, the industrial division of time which created leisure time, a time for the practice and the enjoyment of the arts, the prestige attached to technicity and technical training, the changing place and role of the artist in society from artisan to cultural diviner, the changing attitudes towards works of art and their uses, the alteration of values in general and especially the shifts in religious values. Focuses for artistic production have multiplied, providing new patronage. These include not only centres of government, churches and temples or mosques, but also bars, dance halls, military institutions, schools and museums. Older centres such as palaces, masquerades, shrines, religious festivals and initiation schools still exist, but have been waning. The phenomenon of fashion has gained in intensity and its impulses originate in fewer centres now, usually major cities such as Cairo, Tunis, Algiers, Fez, Nairobi, Lagos, Dakar, Kinshasa, Luanda or Soweto. This reflects typical patterns of increased conspicuous consumption[2] and the pull of élites as

---

1. The two general bibliographies are L. J. P. Gaskin, 1965, and D. Coulet-Western, 1975. The earlier work by T. Heyse, 1950, is still useful. Journals reporting on the arts are *African Arts*, *Présence africaine*, *Afrique littéraire et artistique* and *West Africa*. The acquisition lists of the National Museum of African Art (Washington) provide another source of current bibliography. More restricted bibliographies or general works are listed under each section.

2. T. Veblen, 1899, 1981 edn, pp. 185–7 and in general pp. 66–101.

582

reference groups for millions of others. The mere listing of such features shows us how intimately the development of the arts has been tied to the general, social, intellectual and effective history of the period and the recurring imprint of these features over every art form, over every artistic expression, soon ceases to surprise the student of the arts.

Our itinerary starts from a consideration of the visual arts and the arts of the body, to consider the performing arts: music, some forms of dance, followed by the arts of the spectacle: pageantry, ballet, theatre, cinema and television. We conclude with a few remarks about the role of the African arts in the context of the world.

The visual arts

After 1935 the visual arts easily fall into four broad categories, namely, traditional,[3] tourist, urban popular and academic – as characterized by the subject matter, styles, patronage, goals and locus of production. They differ from each other mainly as follows. Traditional art, often sculpture but also wall-painting,[4] figurative or geometric, was practised in the countryside – which, as late as 1980, still encompassed some two-thirds of all the inhabitants of Africa – and in a few of the older cities. The objects made, except for mural decor, had practical uses. Among the users, institutions such as initiation ceremonies for boys or girls, funerals, next-to-village palaver houses, courts and some Christian churches,[5] as well as some palaces of former rulers, stand out. Tourist art was aimed at foreign patrons. Its subject matter accordingly favoured exotic and anecdotal themes. The style was figurative, simplified and its canons were half-Europeanized. Urban popular art was still inchoate in 1930. It consisted mainly of paintings to decorate the walls of houses in town. Arising c.1930 in Central Africa, and much earlier in North Africa, it was figurative. Portraits, historical, anecdotal and decorative subjects were favourites. Another variety of popular art is expressed in sign-paintings for shops, vehicles, cinemas, and so on. The artists, like traditional artists or producers of tourist art, see themselves as able craftsmen. Academic art was practised by artists trained in Western principles of painting and sculpture, using European techniques. Their patrons were governments, churches or the international art market. Their subject matter was often immediately similar to the repertoire in international use. Artists formally

3. The term 'traditional', although consecrated by usage is an unhappy one. Traditional arts constantly changed and some traditional arts of 1935 did not even exist in 1900 or in 1880. Still, for lack of consensus about any alternative terminology, I will use 'traditional' in this text.

4. Traditional wall-painting in many parts of Central and East Africa developed after new styles of housing became common from the 1890s onwards.

5. On Christian art, see J. F. Thiel and H. Helf, 1984; Anon., 1982; and *Etudes des religions africaines*, 1982, vol. 16, nos 31–2.

TABLE 20.1   *The social categories of the visual arts today*

Category	Type of work[b]	Goal	Patron	Urban/Rural	Artist's role
Traditional	Non-standardized copies Careful finish	For use	Local public Local private	Rural	Artisan
Tourist	Standardized Shoddy finish Forgeries of traditional art	Souvenir	Expatriate Tourist	Urban sales	Artisan
Popular[a]	Standardized Shoddy finish	Display	Local public (e.g. church) Local private	Urban	Artisan
Academic[a]	Uniform work Careful finish	Display	Government Expatriate	Urban	Inspired artist

[a] Developed mostly after 1935.
[b] Excluding thematic content and style.

trained in official academies assumed roles associated with international art while those who were trained in workshops have assumed fewer of these roles.

The categories are not absolutely exclusive. Traditional items could appeal to tourists, as happened with painting on glass in Senegal[6] where the consequent rise in prices shut out local customers from the market. Conversely tourist items could appeal to members of the local élites, who could afford going prices. Some academic art was produced by artists who had been trained as traditional artists (Lamidi Fakeye)[7] or as producers of tourist art (Felix Idubor),[8] while academic artists reverted to tourist or popular art (school of Lubumbashi, some Oshogbo artists). Yet, on the whole, the extent to which these trends remained separate strands over the two generations discussed here is the more remarkable.[9]

Before we discuss each of these separately, architecture must be at least mentioned. South of the Sahara very little modern architecture has been left to African architects, even though a handful of schools (Kinshasa, Luanda, Maputo) trained potential architects. Traditional architects were still found in Northern Africa, but not elsewhere as housing became more and more standardized and built by the users, while after *c.*1920 almost no traditional public buildings of a lasting character were realized. Hence the categories of art discussed do not apply to architecture, which in contrast to all the other arts is limited to expatriate activities, even if some of their efforts aim at reproducing features of traditional architecture.[10] Local innovative architecture of a popular kind is limited to the building of places of worship.[11]

Table 20.1 summarizes the salient points of the various categories.

6. H. Schissel, 1985.

7. T. Ogunwale, 1971. Apprenticed to Bamindele in the late 1940s, he later executed major commissions for Catholic churches in south-western Nigeria.

8. Anon., 1968; Y. A. Grillo and J. Highet, 1968. Idubor began as a tourist carver in Lagos in the late 1940s.

9. The major handbooks for the visual arts south of the Sahara are: Badi Banga Ne-Mwine, 1977; U. Beier, 1968; M. W. Mount, 1973; E. Berman, 1983 (only this edition); E. J. De Jager, 1973; S. El Mansury, 1984; R. Italiaander, 1937; J. Kennedy, 1985; E. Micaud, 1968; G. I. P. Okoro, 1984; F. Willett, 1971. U. Eckardt and G. Sievernich, 1979, is perhaps the most useful for the popular arts, which tend to be neglected elsewhere.

10. M. A. Fassassi, 1978. The CICIBA headquarters at Libreville is based on an interpretation of Bamileke architecture, but conceived and built by European architects. The St. Michael church in the same city is supposed to remind the worshiper of a Fang temple. Its many columns carved by a local sculptor on Biblical themes but in the spirit of carved columns of Gabon and Cameroon are the real modern African art here, not the building itself.

11. Among colonial churches, we find the most innovative colonial sculpture itself as well as replicas of all European styles of religious architecture. Independent churches, especially the smaller ones, have achieved some striking architectural innovations such as the Harrist church at Gregbo (P. Curtin *et al.*, 1978, p. 443), or Fang rural churches and *bwiti* temples on the road from Libreville to Cocobeach (Gabon).

Traditional arts

Although its demise had been heralded well before 1935,[12] traditional art still lives and develops today. Most Africans are still rural and still crave artistic expression. In the generations before 1936 traditional arts had not only undergone internal developments of style and the gradual adoption of imported materials (cloth, paints), tools (saws, files) and some techniques, but lively novel traditions had sprung up here and there such as figurative work on calabashes (Zaire, Kenya)[13] or in ceramics (Zaire).[14] Often substantial innovations meant sales to European residents. Thus full-length Fang funerary figures or Dan female statues are now seen as timeless traditional art. Yet they developed only after 1885 in response to local European interest. These innovations soon found a niche of use in the cultures that created them, distinguishing such works from early tourist art.

Nevertheless, the variety and output of these arts had shrunk by 1935, due to competition from cheap manufactured imports and to a loss of buying power as well as a loss of status by the traditional élites. As the depression struck in 1930, however, and imports became more expensive relative to income, the dynamics of substitution were reversed for all products, even metal wares. This situation lasted until the close of the Second World War. Then, however, the process reversed again. After 1960 even ceramics, which had held their own against enamelled ware, were being abandoned as the age of plastic dawned. Local textiles became relatively so expensive that they survived only as tourist items or as the costly materials for new national costumes.

Already by 1935, the outcry that traditional arts were dying out had led to official action in favour of handicrafts – as in Tunisia, Ghana and Zaire.[15] Government intervention, to be sure, led more often than not to the development of tourist art since the customers for the products were no longer local rural people, but it did preserve or at least retard the loss of technical know-how.

Sculpture and painting on traditional themes in a traditional setting continued their stylistic developments after 1935. Religious painting in

12. For example, see F. Willett, 1971, p. 239; and W. Gillon, 1984, pp. 347–8, citing the end of the Second World War as the end of traditional art. Most recent books on modern art tend to date the supposed demise from *c.*1960 and independence; K. Fosu, 1986.

13. J. Van den Bossche, 1955; S. Kay, 1978. Calabash carving in Lower Zaire dates at least to *c.*1885.

14. Zande and Mangbetu figurative pottery after *c.*1895, dying out by 1940. For Lower Zaire, Z. Volavka, 1977; and J. MacGaffey, 1975.

15. The *Commission pour les arts et métiers indigènes du Congo belge* dates from 1935, Tunisian schools from 1935, Ghana before 1929.

Ethiopia is an outstanding example[16] and so are buildings and carvings for traditional palaces in south-western Nigeria or the creation of *mbari* houses in south-eastern Nigeria.[17] As the dynamics of traditional art during this period have attracted little research, we cannot describe how these arts developed thematically and stylistically, apart from changes fuelled by a tourist market. In Kuba art during these years the range of media for carving increased (for example, ebony, ivory), but the repertoire of style formulae decreased in sophistication (for example, rhythms of repeated decor). Yet some new themes were developed and at least one royal statue stood in a direct line of development within the earlier series.[18] Fewer of the available models (shapes, decoration) were used and choices of clichés waxed and waned with fashions responding in part only to local European tastes. Masks in coastal West Africa increased in complexity and fancifulness as religious purpose was turning to carnival. Sometimes greater stylization and assuredness of proportion and rhythm replaced earlier preciosity (for example, Senufo), sometimes the reverse evolution occurred (Baule). Very little change took place between *c.*1930 and 1982 in some items such as icons and masks for the Kuba boys' initiation. And yet in the Genya initiations (Kisangani, Zaire) modernization of icons was continually occurring, despite the fact that the initiation never became a tourist show.[19] On the whole, one dare neither generalize about the evolution of traditional art, nor continue to proclaim its imminent demise.

In North Africa independence brought an emphasis on traditional architecture and on the renovation of ancient monuments. One thinks of the mausoleum for Mohamed V of Morocco or the stone-cutting revival in Tunisia and of restorations everywhere. New work includes such buildings as the new opera-house in Cairo with its specific Mamluk reminiscences.[20] Elsewhere such a return to the roots of regional traditions did not occur. But it is enough to contrast the utterly forlorn situation of the traditional arts in Lebowa (Republic of South Africa) to that of such arts elsewhere to realize how well and truly alive these arts still are in most of Africa.[21]

Tourist art

By 1935 tourist art was still a small business, because apart from Egypt there were few tourists. In Egypt, fake Pharaonic items and all sorts of

16. U. Eckardt and G. Sievernich, 1979, pp. 56–67.
17. H. Cole, 1982.
18. J. Cornet, 1975, p. 53, and 1974.
19. A. Droogers, 1980.
20. Anon., 1985.
21. P. Davison, 1984.

kitsch, exotic and romantic, produced in Suez, Port Said, Alexandria and Cairo was selling well. Elsewhere along the coasts selling souvenirs to sailors was also a traditional activity. Other items were produced in small numbers for European residents (ashtrays, bookstands, salad bowls) or as souvenirs to take home. But in the 1930s the foundations for the main genres and productions of later times were being laid. Where traditional carvings were liked, shoddy copies were now churned out, while rarer works were being imitated or even forged. For instance, the Foumban (Cameroon) brasses in the Ife style, using a Nigerian stamp as a model, began to be manufactured in the 1940s. An artist such as Osei Bonsu provided both for the needs of the establishment at Kumasi and made copies of well-known works for sale.[22] Secondly, existing genres developed further. Kuba statues for the tourist market in the 1930s derived from the royal statues, from charm figures and from figures for chiefs (*mwaan*). Thirdly, European representations, whether Christian or secular, were imitated. Experimentation showed what sold best. The role of missions has been paramount here, not only because missions encouraged the production of works for churches, but also because vocational schools soon produced imitations of textiles, mats, ceramics and woodwork for sale. Well before 1936 the tourist-art style of Buta Catholic Mission, with its emphasis on ebony and ivory and its carvings of elephants and genre scenes, was flourishing and profitable. By 1950, half a dozen such schools in the Belgian Congo alone were producing a variety of goods from furniture to knick-knacks.

Tourist art is bought as a souvenir. The message to be conveyed therefore had to be familiar to the foreigner even though it was supposed to be exotic. Therefore, tourist art was figurative, conformed approximately to European canons of proportion, used ebony and ivory and represented exotic wildlife or anecdotal themes (daily life in the village, dances) or the equivalent of costume dolls[23] such as Maasai warriors, Mangbetu with elongated heads or 'typical' busts such as those from the workshop of Massengo in Brazzaville (from the 1950s onwards). Two-dimensional decorative patterns had to be simple, deadeningly regular, imitating machine work as much as possible and colours should please European eyes. Then there were the practical requirements. In the age of travel by sea, massive wooden furniture such as Zanzibari chests or Benin chairs were liked. But after 1945 the age of travel by air and of mass tourism required small and light items. Crudely carved camel-saddle stools and little tables easily dismantled became favourites, whilst North African poufs, however garish, always did well, as did the new Maghrebi

---

22. D. H. Ross, 1984.

23. Costume dolls were produced in South Africa from *c*.1815 to at least the 1860s, but then fell out of favour. Elsewhere this form of souvenir never seems to have caught on.

PLATE 20.1 *Artisans working in brass at Foumban, Cameroon*

figurative carpets, labelled 'Berber' or Kabyle. Such, then, were the requirements of tourist art. Moreover, it had to be cheap and easily made. Hence its shoddy character. Higher-quality goods for export such as the carpets of Fez or the fine Kuba textiles suffered from the impact of a mass market.[24]

In the first phase, before c.1950, schools and craft shops, later co-operatives, fuelled production while professional traders with a retinue of artists were still rare.[25] Markets were near major hotels at ports and capitals. After 1950 tourist art became airport art. Tourists arrived in ever-increasing numbers, and the demand was met by co-operatives, entrepreneurs and a network of organized hawkers, the so-called 'Sénégalais' of West and Central Africa. Forgery of classical works became much more common as an appreciation of traditional art spread among

24. B. Jules-Rosette, 1984, is the basic study; see P. Ben Amos, 1977, on meaning and form; and C. Geary, 1983, pp. 74–6 and 86–7, on the decline of quality comparing traditional work at Foumban (Cameroon) with tourist copies.

25. Still, M. H. Lelong, 1946, vol. 1, p. 200, claims to have seen a sizeable factory in the Gulf of Guinea well before 1940.

PLATE 20.2 *'Tourist art' or 'airport art'*

the middle classes of the world. In general, the whole of Africa now produced works on the lines long-familiar in Egypt.

And yet all tourist art is not the same. Let us look at the Kamba and Makonde productions in Kenya and Tanzania to show two very different dynamics at work. During the First World War, Mutisya Munge was a carrier.[26] Until then he had carved the occasional ceremonial stick for a local Kamba elder. Now he derived new models and ideas from the Zaramo near Dar es Salaam, who had already been selling items to German residents, speculating on ethnographica, before 1914. Munge

26. W. Elkan, 1958.

took up full-scale carving and found a market for Christmas presents from Europeans now streaming into the highlands of Kenya. He and others imitating him hawked their wares. After 1945 business boomed as large numbers of British soldiers were stationed in Kenya. The next big market was American. Demand now required thousands of objects. An official co-operative failed, but orders were met and the curio business became a cottage industry. By 1955 Mutisya Munge attempted to set up shop in London. By 1960 'African and Akamba Handicrafts' there employed five agents and by 1970 imports into the USA totalled a quarter of a million pieces from Kenya, Tanzania and Zambia.[27] Phalanxes of Maasai warriors and coy antelopes invade the West every year.

In contrast, Makonde carvers never copied objects until very recently.[28] Mainly as a result of the guerrilla war of liberation, they moved from Mozambique to Mtwara, later to Dar es Salaam. Over one hundred carvers worked near Dar from *c.*1964 onwards and sold their works through dealers. One of them created a new icon, the representation of a spirit being (*shaitani*), which allowed for fantastic creations. At the same time, though, conventional Christian and anecdotal genres were also produced. Europeans have not denied the label 'art' to such works, especially the *shaitani*, because of the sculptural virtuosity of every piece, reminiscent of recent European sculpture. Moreover each piece is unique, made for display, and the carvers expressly label them as products of innovative creativity: art for art's sake.

The contrast between Kamba and Makonde carving is extreme, but typical for the full range of tourist art. The same contrasts can be seen for instance at Foumban (Cameroon) where some metal work, often in new media such as aluminium, is an expression of deeply-held values, while other items are but shoddy copies of traditional icons. Hackwork may be the rule but some artists create genuine works of art, expressing major metaphors in a careful form.

Such situations help us to understand the production of small paintings of rural life, often fishing scenes, which by the 1930s had begun to be sold to tourists. They were for sale to foreigners, yet expressed the nostalgia of the new urban immigrants for the simple rural life. They were folk art, whether produced in innumerable copies or not. A fair proportion of such works were bought by local people and became popular art. Continuities with earlier traditions of painting or drawing can often be traced, including antecedents for the abstract works on sale after the mid-1960s. Some artists have claimed that they expressed a creative urge in producing these, while attributing their practice of making innumerable copies to economic need.[29]

27. M. W. Mount, 1973, p. 55 and p. 217, fn. 32.
28. S. J. Ntiro, 1982, is much more reliable than A. J. Stout, 1966. See also S. Littlefield-Kasfir, 1980; and E. Herold, 1983.
29. S. Creuz, 1951; B. Jules-Rosette, 1984, pp. 30–56.

PLATE 20.3   *Makonde art*

Tourist art can be of considerable interest to the historian, especially because it embodies genuine communication directed not merely to the foreign tourist, but to a local public, even if that public is not the buyer of the product.

Popular art

South of the Sahara, urban popular art dating from after independence is the best-known.[30] But some popular art is much earlier in date and the

30. See U. Eckardt and G. Sievernich, 1979, for the best introduction to popular art.

limit between traditional and popular is blurred in rural areas – as, for example, on cemeteries with cement sculpture (Côte d'Ivoire, Akan, Cross River, Kongo),[31] or the murals of Ndebele villages in Transvaal.[32] Cement replaced mud but also stone and wood. The sculptures often represent modernity (planes, cars), new religious emblems (crosses, sexed angels) and portraits (in Kongo continuation of the wood and stone tradition). In some cases there are breaks. Ndebele murals were a total innovation *c.*1945 and Nubian murals developed only *c.*1925,[33] to die out with the creation of Lake Nasser in 1964. A certain Aḥmad Batul, probably from Ballana, invented the new murals. Hitherto murals had been the work of women. He was the first man to make them. He drew his inspiration from older geometric motifs, and from simple figurative scenes on imports. One painter even used the pictures on the lids of tin cans for inspiration. The large figurative advertisements done on the walls of establishments in the western oases of Egypt were similar to such murals. Murals were also found in parts of Central and East Africa. They were favoured by missions in Uganda to replace body-painting, of which they disapproved. Other rural products of popular art have been mostly shrines and churches, mentioned above.

In the cities, one finds some churches, some murals on interior walls in houses or bars, sign-paintings and advertisements.[34] Yoruba townhouses sported cement lions and other architectural sculpture from the 1930s to 1950s.[35] A unique form of popular visual art was the ensemble of sculpture, painting and appliqué flags for the *asafo* associations of Fante (Ghana) towns.[36]

But the most characteristic popular urban art came to be painting on canvas. This sometimes derives from the murals which in parts of West and all of Central Africa were pre-colonial or early colonial, or from body art. Figurative themes soon incorporated products of the modern age and historical scenes (foundation of administrative posts, battles). Similar graphic art developed also on calabashes, on some pottery and sometimes, as appliqué, on cloth, as well as in the shape of bas-relief on ivory or wood. Popular painting has deep roots in African traditions.

The earliest painters such as Ibrayima Njoya in Cameroon (*c.*1920), A. Onabolu in Nigeria (1920s), or A. Lubaki (*c.*1926) and others in Zaire, were inspired by such works. Lubaki was a carver on ivory before he

31. K. Nicklin and J. Salmons, 1977; D. R. Roseyear, 1984; S. Dornowitz and R. Mandirola, 1984; P. S. Breidenbach and D. H. Ross, 1978; M. Gilbert, 1981; R. F. Thompson and J. Cornet, 1981.

32. S. Priebatsch and N. Knight, 1979; E. A. Schneider, 1985; C. A. M. Vogel, 1985; T. Matthews, 1979.

33. M. Wenzel, 1972; H. Jaritz, 1973; and B. Jewsiewicki, 1986.

34. U. Beier, 1971; and O. Pritchett, 1979.

35. U. Beier, 1960.

36. G. N. Preston, 1975.

began to paint.[37] But only in the 1930s do we see the appearance, all along the Atlantic coasts, of nostalgic painting, depicting beaches, palm trees, villagers and urban genre scenes.[38] An art for sale to tourists, yes, but also for urbanites. In 1960 one could still see a camel and his escort under starry Saharan nights on the wall of a Mauritanian house in Dakar, or a monumental elephant on the wall of a watchmaker's house in Bujumbura (Burundi).[39] Similar scenes on canvas were beginning to be bought by urban dwellers, along with portraits of famous people (*marabouts* in Senegal), or self-portraits (Zaire).

A striking innovation in the themes portrayed occurred in the 1950s, first in Kinshasa, then, after independence, in Lubumbashi, and in Nigeria after the civil war, and still later in Ghana. Historical subjects became favourites. By 1960 the exotic image of Mamy Wata (or *mamba muntu*), the siren temptress, the symbol of magic and alienation, had also spread from Ghana to Shaba. A new complex of themes coalesced around 1960 in the bleak industrial landscape of Lubumbashi. Scenes from the traumatic past and the tribulation of the present directly expressed the historical consciousness of the inhabitants. Gone are nostalgic scenes of a return to the unproblematic village life. The perception of urban identities predominated now. Portrait painting evolved so that its subjects were now shown as tragic figures rent by historical contradiction. These anonymous works[40] met with great success and spread quickly to Kinshasa and Kisangani, a little later to Dar es Salaam[41] and to Lusaka. This genre will not disappear fast. Its models are various chromolithographs, including advertisements and illustrations in magazines. European perspectives and European canons for the rendering of figures are used, even if modelling and shading are not. This strongly contrasts with the local historiographical themes rendered.[42]

Popular religious art survived in Ethiopia with the production of standardized icons, historical scenes or magic scrolls. Portraits and scenes

37. M. W. Mount, 1973, pp. 161–5; O. Dapo, 1973; Badi Banga ne-Mwine, 1977; G. D. Perier, 1930.

38. G. D. Perier, 1950–2.

39. G. Sandrart, 1953, ill. on p. 7 (Bujumbura), in this case a nostalgic reminder of an animal then almost extinct in the area; J. Beinart, 1968 (Maputo, Johannesburg).

40. Signatures at first were often not the names of the painters but those of the customers. The cult of the master-painter's signature spread only among European collectors.

41. The Tingatinga school of Dar es Salaam was inspired by Zairian artists, but the themes are still on the whole the older type of nostalgic genre. J. A. R. Wembah-Rashid, 1972; and M. Teisen, 1968.

42. Contributions by Y. L. Mundara and Badi-Banga ne-Mwine, 1982, pp. 145–64; J. Fabian, 1978; I. Szombati-Fabian and J. Fabian, 1976; I. M. G. Quimby and S. T. Swank, 1980, pp. 247–92; B. Jules-Rosette, 1984, pp. 142–73 (Lubumbashi styles in Lusaka); B. Jewsiewicki, 1986; J. Salmons, 1977; U. Beier, 1976; T. Fiofori, 1986a.

are stereotyped, but from time to time a novel composition appears –
such as St Yarid accompanied by birds, for he is the saint who introduced
sacred music into the country. Elsewhere in northern Africa religiously-
inspired works were more limited, as befits Islam. Among these, images
of the Ka'ba at Mecca were the most common.[43]

With the growth of the cities and the stabilization of the immigrant
population, urban popular art and the themes mentioned steadily increase
in importance and significance. Such works attract the social historian
especially because they directly portray the perception of the changing
times among the urban masses.

Academic arts

By 1913 the practice of visual arts in the European tradition, mainly
architecture and painting, had been implanted in Egypt with the foundation of an *Ecole des Beaux-arts* in Cairo. Since then, and even before,
Egyptian painters and architects participated in all the movements of
European art as did the occasional sculptor, from the romanticists of the
late nineteenth century to the surrealists, abstract artists, and pop artists
of recent decades. Yet Egyptian painting is readily recognizable in most
instances because many of its themes and some of its forms intentionally
hark back to older Islamic or even Pharaonic traditions.[44] Elsewhere
though, only an isolated African artist here and there had made it to
Paris or London and was being trained there. In 1935 a small number of
painters returned to Tunis and started the so-called Tunisian school, a
school whose themes were often to be denounced as folkloric. Yet this
was part of the cultural revival of the country.[45] In Morocco a similar
development occurred a little later,[46] while in Algeria, local artists were
much more stifled and limited to traditional arts and crafts. Outside
Egypt, schools of fine arts appeared much later, the earliest being perhaps
the department at the University College of Makerere (1937). In the
generation between 1935 and 1960 three major trends developed on the
continent. European artists set up workshops, some of which were
transformed later into regular schools. Some local artists continued to be
trained in Europe (Paris, London, Germany) and some were trained in
local academic institutions. These trends are now discussed in turn,
starting with the earliest one: the independent artists trained abroad.

The first Africans from south of the Sahara to study art in Europe
arrived there from the later 1930s onwards, the earliest one being perhaps
Ghana's Oku Ampofo who arrived in Great Britain to study medicine

43. G. Fisseha and W. Raunig, 1985; D. Hecht, 1979.
44. S. El Mansury, 1984; G. Boctor, 1969.
45. E. Micaud, 1968.
46. D. Desanti and J. Decock, 1969.

and then art in 1932. Among the pioneers were also Iba Ndiaye (Senegal) in Paris by 1948, Gerard Sekoto (South Africa) in Paris by 1947, Afewerk Tekle (Ethiopia) in London by 1948, Kofi Antubam, a graduate of Achimota College of 1936 (Ghana) in London by 1946, Ben Enwonwu (Nigeria) in London by 1944 and Viteix (Angola) in Portugal in the 1950s.[47] This generation was to influence subsequent developments especially with regard to the role and the goals of artist, but also by example, excepting only Sekoto who practically lived in exile. The drive of many academic artists is perhaps best rendered by Iba Ndiaye:

> In fact the African graphic artists themselves must find the answers to the question: how to remain African or to become African again – while willing to be resolutely modern and attempting to explain oneself in a universal visual language. It does not suffice in order to achieve this, to proclaim one's Africanness, to state that one holds to African values. It is in the practice of painting, carving, engraving . . . that such artists will shape their singularity.[48]

The quote captures the dilemma of the academic artist. They wanted to be technicians, 'up-to-date', equals of others on the international scene and yet they refused alienation. They strove to retain a link to their specificity. The tension is visible in their works, perhaps most in those of Enwonwu who at times changes styles from international to 'modern Benin' even in a single work. It is least visible in Sekoto's dramatic expressionism, and in that of other South African graphic artists, because the concerns of the industrial society from which they sprang were so similar to those that fuelled expressionism or the *Neue Sachlichkeit* in Europe.

Ampofo, Enwonwu and Antubam were practising artists well before 1940, Sekoto from 1938 onwards. They and the others who were in Europe in the later 1940s were the spokesmen for African art at the first gatherings of artists in Paris (1956) and Rome (1959). Their successors and disciples soon merged, however, with artists trained in local schools and none founded a truly independent artistic trend as such. But their goals, standard and practice set the patterns for the artists of the generations after 1960.

The first developments after the Second World War concerned European painters, usually surrealists, who believed that techniques could be transmitted without affecting the mode of expression of the pupils at all. They would create the 'natural art' that was in the mind. By 1944 a French painter established a school in Lubumbashi, another one opened

47. In general, see M. W. Mount, 1973, pp. 160–86 and *passim*; D. Mestre, 1981, pp. 3–5 and 28–30.
48. I. Ndiaye, 1984, p. 8. For a similar quote by Kofi Antubam dating from 1961, see M. W. Mount, 1973, p. 5.

PLATE 20.4   *Above: Iba Ndiaye of Senegal, with one of his paintings; below: Kofi Antubam of Ghana, with one of his sculptures*

597

PLATE 20.5   *Viteix of Angola, with one of his paintings*

598

the school of Potopoto (Brazzaville) in 1951, and in 1961 renewed the experience in Dakar. Similar schools arose in Maputo (1960), Harare (1961), Rorke's Drift, South Africa (1963), and Oshogbo, Nigeria (1961). An artist missionary forerunner at Cyrene (Bulawayo, Zimbabwe) kept a workshop from 1939 to 1953 that was later taken over by his pupil Sam Songo, but left no enduring legacy.

Despite the declarations of the founders, it is evident that they deeply influenced the styles of their pupils. The schools of Lubumbashi, Potopoto and Dakar produced very decorative works in ochre or garish colour, reflecting colonial notions of popular art as it should be. Several styles per school were common, but they all partook of similar characteristics. As the output was brought by Europeans the border between art for art's sake and art as souvenir has waned. At the same time popular themes have renewed some of this art. At Potopoto themes from the village, Mboshi headpieces or sticklike persons in the supposedly rock-art style have waned. Crowd scenes and sometimes anguished landscapes have taken their place.[49]

Developments in Mozambique, Harare and especially Nigeria have been quite different. The first Mozambican painter, Valente Malangatana, influenced by the revolutionary school of Mexican wall-painting, has produced an art whose forms and themes were totally different. Tragic scenery, records of brutality, anguish and goals dominate; a thematic repertory shared by most black South African artists but not elsewhere. His social concerns and his preference for wall-painting have remained hallmarks of art in Maputo.[50] In Harare sculpture was favoured over painting. It was very close to German expressionism (especially Barlach) and has not evolved very much since 1961.[51]

The Oshogbo workshop certainly has been the most successful of all these ventures. It produced a spectacular variety of styles and artists still very active today, still working for the expatriate market or for public sponsors at home. Fantastic themes in local surrealist, yet decorative styles, sometimes in mixed media, especially beadwork, dominate. Most artists are painters. Very few are sculptors, which is surprising because Yoruba tradition is so heavily sculptural. But only legends and myths have been taken from the Yoruba tradition, the forms and styles of its visual arts being eschewed completely. This may well be an effect of the founder's creed: 'Art should be sincere'. In practice this meant that it should not continue in the existing line of traditional art.[52] The vitality

49. J. P. Lebeuf, 1956; d'Arschot, Comte, 1951, pp. 37–45; G. D. Perier, 1950–2; M. W. Mount, 1973, pp. 74–94.

50. M. W. Mount, 1973, pp. 160–1 and appendix; B. Schneider, 1972.

51. U. Eckardt and G. Sievernich, 1979, pp. 72–5 and introduction; M. W. Mount, 1973, pp. 117–23; F. McEwen, 1972.

52. U. Beier, 1968, pp. 89–164; M. W. Mount, 1973, pp. 147–58; J. Kennedy, 1985; G. I. P. Okoro, 1984; J. Buraimoh, 1971.

of Oshogbo artists and the favour they have found abroad is remarkable. It often obscures the fact, however, that Oshogbo only forms a fraction of contemporary Nigerian art, even Nigerian academic art. The chronology of the expansion of academic institutions teaching the arts parallels that of the workshops initiated by artists. The early ventures in Uganda and Nigeria – such as Makerere College (1927) were followed by academies in Kinshasa (1943) and Khartoum (1945), after which most countries followed suit in the 1950s and early 1960s. In every country painters and sculptors began to be trained, even while others still went to Europe to study either to complement local training or completely bypassing the local institutions. Artists were supported by official commissions and by sales to expatriates who also owned the galleries where they were shown. In this sense they tend to be alienated from their own societies, even from most of the élite. This situation changed only very slowly. Nigeria had to wait until 1962 to have its first locally-managed gallery and until the late 1970s before some of its artworks were being bought by local individuals for high prices.[53] And elsewhere south of the Sahara the situation was less brilliant.

Independent governments used art for prestige, yet artists have rarely been asked to create propaganda nor has censorship been a problem. Some governments have supported quasi-official artists such as Kofi Antubam in Ghana, Afewerk Tekle in Imperial Ethiopia, Ben Enwonwu in Nigeria or Liyolo in Zaire. In these cases their themes and styles have adapted to ensure easy communication with a wider public. There are signs that some change is in the offing. Propaganda is becoming more important. Socialist realism may well become official doctrine in some countries. Artistic freedom continues today, maybe because of the lack of resonance most academic art has in African societies, even among the élites. It is also striking how little relevance many themes have for contemporary realities beyond the celebration of cultural nationalism. The exceptions here are the artists of South Africa and Mozambique whose nightmarish portrayal of anxiety and anguish closely correspond to precise social settings.

For the most part academic art squarely belongs to the mainstream of international art. Among its tendencies, surrealism and abstract art have had much less following than expressionism. The new African expressionism recalls that of the European continent, especially Germany before 1932. Modern British art, which was important in the academic institutions of former British colonies, has steadily been losing ground. The other major trend has been neo-traditional – that is, the re-use of traditional items for inspiration, sometimes canons of style, sometimes themes in works. This tendency favours the emergence of regional (if not quite national) styles, as for instance in the Côte d'Ivoire as opposed to Ghana.

53. M. Crowder, 1978.

In parts of northern Africa the insistence on line has remained and leads to neo-calligraphy, a sparing use of figurative elements, if they are used at all, and a consequent tendency towards abstract art. Sudanese and Moroccan artists, as well as some northern Nigerian works, have often gone in this direction. Where traditional arts are still quite vigorous a contrary trend also flowed. Thus in Ethiopia abstract or starkly engineered graphics or paintings are seen as liberation from tradition.

Such major trends are not haphazard. The neo-traditional one corresponds to negritude and related movements before and after independence. The expressionist styles share deep formal links with older African art, especially sculpture, since European expressionism and the styles derived there from it had absorbed the deepest fundamental African influences relating to volume, stylization and even canons of proportion ('systematic distortion'). Abstract art had its African roots in geometric decoration or in the Islamic arts. Only surrealism was totally new. Even here its resonances echoed collective fantasies about gods and spirits or built on the rich symbolic clichés of African oral arts and ritual. At the same time all these trends underwent a strong impact of international fashions, accompanied by international concepts concerning the role of the artist and an extreme stress on individuality, the primacy of mood and emotion, the absolute values of artistic freedom, creativity *per se* and the work of art as legitimated by creativity whatever its form or content. The impact of critics has been minimal. There are few or no trained critics,[54] and critics often do not transcend the lavish praise that usually greets the exhibitions of academic artists.

Academic art exists alongside popular, tourist and often traditional streams of art which influence each other constantly. Cases are known of tourist artists developing into academic artists (Felix Idubor) and of academic artists becoming popular (some Lubumbashi artists) and tourist artists. Such interaction is bound to intensify in time. This may yet lead to the emergence of regional or national styles in painting and sculpture as soon as local markets for art predominate over expatriate sales.

The arts of the body

The body, its adornment and its garb proclaims the self as well as various group identities (status or ethnicity) and a sense of the occasion (work, festivity, mourning, and so on). Hence a history of the body arts is directly relevant to the historian for whom it may be one of the more sensitive indicators of social change and cultural influence.[55]

54. M. Crowder, 1978, pp. 142–5.
55. Such an historical study is only just beginning. See J. Eicher, 1970 and 1985; M. Pokornowski *et al.*, 1985; R. P. Dozy, 1969, for costume; A. Fisher, 1984, for jewellery. Textiles have been well studied. Overviews in J. Picton and J. Mack, 1979; and R. Sieber, 1972. Most studies, however, are not historical or do not relate to art and the body.

Traditional Africa had known an infinite variety of personal adornment by scarification, tattooing, body-painting, hairstyles and operations such as circumcision or excision which altered the body temporarily or permanently. Jewellery and costume complemented the appearance. Differences by gender, age, marital status and social position were thus expressed. The monotheistic religions had strong views about modesty and their adherents dressed accordingly. Ethnicity was also reflected, often by scarification, or by standard costume such as those of Tunisia or Morocco. Even headgear or hairstyles (veil, *tarbush*, turban, hairstyles for women in Angola, Gabon, Zaire) could be signs of ethnic, class or religious affiliation. Additional adornment (jewellery, festive paint or clothing) testified to individual standing and to the degree of competition or solidarity on occasions of public display. Fashions were set by élite groups, acting as examples to be imitated by others,[56] for 'traditional' body art was not static. Thus fashions at the Kuba court in the early years of this century or in Rwanda are well known. For a decade or so, young Kuba Brummels affected tall hats. In Rwanda the upper-class masculine rage was for haircuts leaving curved tufts imitating the styles worn by upper-class unmarried girls. The fashion began around 1900 and had died out by 1945.[57] The same men donned togas of flowery textiles from the closing years of the nineteenth century onwards until the 1950s, when European dress made them outmoded.

By 1935 the colonial situation had long made an impact and proposed the exclusion of most arts of the body in the name of civilization to such an extent that scholarly studies of body-painting or scarification are rare and of late date.[58] Tattoos and scarifications were deemed to be barbaric. So was nudity, especially if it was painted.[59] Much adornment was also discouraged in the name of thrift, good working habits or comfort. European gibes at heavy brass collars or anklets are a stereotype of the early colonial period. Proper clothing was incessantly promoted and not just by missionaries. South of the Sahara, missions had proposed patterns for a decent female dress, all variants of late nineteenth-century working-class garb or of the so-called Mother Hubbard dress (long skirt and sleeved blouse).[60] Europeans introduced various styles of administrative garb: shirt and shorts; bush jackets, military uniforms and servant uniforms. Business suits were rarely seen, except in the cities among the

56. T. Veblen, 1981 edn, pp. 115–87.

57. R. Kandt, 1905, opp. p. 80, and A. Frederick 1910, for Rwanda fashion as it developed between *c.* 1900 and 1909.

58. Works such as H. Brandt, 1956 (*Gerewol*, festive adornment of Bororo Fulani in Niger) are still descriptive. J. C. Farris, 1982, is a scholarly study.

59. E. C. Burt, 1984, pp. 60–3 and p. 80, documenting the mission-inspired transfer of this art to wall-painting at Christmas time among the Luo.

60. They were just as concerned with 'proper' underwear, to the point that some missions actually sold such garments as late as the 1950s.

European élite there, which explained their appeal first to the cream of the Europeanized African élite and then to other urban or rural men. In northern and western Africa, as well as on the east coast, varieties of Islamic dress persisted. The West African stuck to his *boubou* in the Sahel or to Yoruba-type costume on the coast, the Moroccan to his *burnous*, the Sudanese to his *jallaba* and the Swahili to his *kanzu* and *kofia*.

By the 1930s,[61] Africa can be divided into three main regions from the point of view of dress and the divisions remain important until now. In eastern and southern Africa, European business suits began to replace imitations of military uniforms as prestige dress. The fashion spread from the Tanzanian coast inland as far as Malawi and Zambia with the Beni dance association,[62] in Kenya, Uganda and Ruanda-Urundi from Nairobi and in southern Africa from its main cities, the styles in Angola and Mozambique being quite different. Shorts, shirts or bush jackets were becoming common as working clothes, although urbanites all preferred trousers to shorts and the combination loincloth and jacket was still common in rural areas. Women's wrappers gave way gradually to the standard mission dresses and came to be associated in urban areas with loose morals. Indeed, in Namibia dresses were accepted to the point that a Central-European, nineteenth-century costume became something like an ethnic dress among the Nama and Herero. African fashions for men were maintained as military costumes expressing ethnicity only among Zulu and Nguni.[63] Another innovation was the flowing white or red garb of prophets and pastors of African independent churches, complete with crook and/or staff. Biblical illustrations probably were their model. Among pastoralists in East Africa, especially in Kenya and in the southern Sudan, traditional body art and absence or scantiness of male clothing still survives. Indeed, as new media for adornment became available more spectacular variants of body art developed in Kenya.

In coastal western and equatorial Africa, European models for women's clothing were rejected. The wrapper remained the classy dress. Whether locally made or imported, its patterns had to conform to local taste and the textile industry in Europe continued to heed the preferences of its African customers.[64] Fashions in patterns were set in the major cities by courtesans (often dressed for free by importers) and African élite women. Male festive costume on the West African coast remained unaffected by European dress, but suits were adopted by professionals, scholars and clerks. At the same time in equatorial Africa, they came to be upper-

61. The following remains especially tentative, as I found not even one article sketching the main evolution of clothing in colonial and post-colonial times.
62. T. Ranger, 1975; J. Mitchell, 1956.
63. J. A. Barnes, 1952; M. Read, 1936.
64. C. B. Steiner, 1985, pp. 91–110 is basic. See also J. Fourneau and L. Kravetz, 1954.

class wear, although much less so in Western Zaire than in French colonies. Meanwhile the *boubou* held its ground in the Sahel and actually expanded to the south. In short, European fashions found much less favour here than in East and South Africa.

On the whole, northern Africa clung to its own costumes and body adornment (painting with henna). Women adopted European dresses in the main cities, but wore them under the *haik*, just as Moroccan business suits might be worn under a *burnous* or even a *jallaba* and with slippers. European working clothes, however, were adopted by men and in Egypt suits had long been the usual clothing for the middle and upper classes. The symbolic value of clothing is well illustrated by the quarrel over the *tarbush* in Egypt. Just after 1935 radicals were denouncing these hats as demeaning, an emblem of servility, and the playwright Tawfik al-Ḥakim wore a basque *béret* in defiance. The élite, however, stoutly defended the *tarbush*. Still today that headgear is gone. Only conservative businessmen still sport it.

Nationalism after 1945 found its expression in costume.[65] Nationalists decried nudity and skin adornment even more than Europeans. They developed national costumes, often quite consciously as in Sierra Leone where the Kabah cloth with embroidered yoke became a national female dress by consensus. Only the pattern of the yoke differentiated it from earlier imported dress in Freetown.[66] Nkrumah set the style for national dress in 1957 and the West African élites followed. Yoruba festive garments, *boubou* styles of Kano or Bamako[67] became expressions of nationalism. As a result, local weaving, embroidery and dyeing revived, especially when the new élites became wealthy enough to use dress as an indicator of relative status.[68] European hairstyles and beauty aids for women were anathema to nationalists – and to many rural men. They were replaced by national hairstyles.[69] In Zaire, Mobutu imposed the *abacos* by decree, outlawing the business suit and especially the wearing of neckties.[70] *Abacos* (*'A bas le costume'* – down with the suit!) were an expression of authenticity, symbolizing equality, virility, simplicity. They were at the outset inspired by Maoist dress. In time, however, the *abacos* reflected local status by the quality of the cloth and of the cut, as class differentiation in Kinshasa kept growing after 1970.

Wrappers spread again in Equatorial and Central Africa, styles and

65. The general relationships between nationalism and clothing have been well set out by P. Bogatyrev, 1971. See also A. Mazrui, 1970 (neither nudity nor European dress).

66. B. Wass, 1979.

67. J. Perani, 1979.

68. A. Perry, 1984 (some costumes worth thousands of pounds); E. De Negri, 1968; F. Smith and J. Eicher, 1982.

69. Anon., 1964. Yet by the 1980s urban women had once again turned to beauty aids and foreign hairstyles.

70. F. S. B. Kazadi, 1978.

patterns becoming more ornate and also fostering the revival of costly local textiles. But in eastern and southern Africa upper-class women resisted its re-introduction in the city. European-style fashions developed in Nairobi far more than in Dakar.[71] For men about town, business suits triumphed, although not completely in Tanzania. Nationalism was on the whole less expressed in clothing than in other ways. Elsewhere European fashions were not totally excluded either. Fads such as high platform shoes in Nigeria (*c.*1975) or Zazou outfits in the Côte d'Ivoire (*c.*1965) swept the urban landscape from time to time.

In North Africa the major development has been an attempted return to the woman's veil in urban Egypt[72] as a sign of commitment to fundamentalism. In Libya and Tunisia there has been a renaissance of a national costume derived from older rural <u>shaykh's</u> robes.

Textiles and costumes also entered the tourist trade. The man's shirt with embroidered neckline, hem and pocket became a favourite among expatriates all over the continent as well as among African-Americans and sympathizers in the USA. Figurative decoration on cloth or costume, mainly for export, developed in the Côte d'Ivoire (Senufo) whilst Lesotho began to produce tourist blankets, Botswana printed fabrics and Mali rugs.[73]

Thus patterns of dress and adornment proposed by Europeans were accepted only selectively during this period while the desire to stress national identity and later social status also left their mark on the history of costume. Concurrently, however, clothing and body adornment were still genuine expressions of aesthetic urges. If we could tell even a rudimentary history of styles in jewellery or headscarfs, the search for new expressions of beauty for its own sake would be evident. But so far even the rudiments of such a history are lacking.

Music and dance

Vocal music was the queen of popular art during the whole period, in the countryside as well as in town, for the record industry and the radio ensured its diffusion to the masses. Some singers acquired immense popularity matched only by that of major political leaders. Some contributed to the drive for independence by mobilizing people, disseminating programmes and extolling leaders. It is not surprising that governments, after independence, continued to use music as an instrument of propaganda and tried to stifle music critics. This situation affected the lyrics, but left the musical developments themselves largely untouched.[74]

71. F. Court and M. M'Wangi, 1976.
72. J. A. Williams, 1979. Several recent Egyptian films deal with this topic.
73. M. Hartland-Rowe, 1985; E. Dudley, 1986.
74. C. H. Cutter, 1968, is an example of the use of music and *griots* to launch the directives of the party, to praise its leaders and to extol the success of their policies.

The musical traditions of Africa have shown remarkable continuity despite outside pressures from the West. The potential for blending was high because of the similarities between Western and African music south of the Sahara, including the use of diatonic scales and harmony as well as the practice of accompanying the voice with percussion instruments and with stringed instruments. European models were diffused mainly through the missions and the radio.[75] Despite this, old and new African music still share common stylistic features, including a common approach to linear rhythms, a common concept of 'beat' and energy flow, use of common rhythmic motifs, cross rhythms, types of melodic progression, polyphonic parallelism and vocal techniques. But in their use of scales, harmony, form and instrumentation, old and new African music diverge.[76]

European instrumental music has had no impact. Today still, a taste for European music is seen as the sign of the most profound alienation. While some European instruments have been adopted for the accompaniment of vocal music, there are no African instrumentalists of note performing classical music. Composers, with one or two exceptions, create church music – that is, music for voices, rather than orchestral works.[77]

The history of music in recent generations must distinguish two different developments, one tied to the countryside and to sacred music, the other to the city bars and dance-halls, where the new urban music was created.

Rural music and sacred music

Although by 1935 African rural traditions were still largely intact, influences via records, radio, the spread of Islam and Christianity, and military band music were already strong, and in the last three cases old. But many of these influences are so subtle as to be really clear only to musicologists.[78] The great variety of existing songs ranged from lullabies to dirges, from work songs to protest songs, from praise poetry to satire. Many songs for accompanying dances continued to flourish, although some categories such as work songs began to wane. Purely religious music associated with specific rituals had been rare in classical African religion. But where it

75. A. Merriam, 1981, pp. 100–5.
76. L. J. P. Gaskin, 1965b; B. A. Aning, 1967; A. Merriam, 1970; and H. Tracey, 1973, are bibliographies. P. R. Kirby, 1964; G. Kubik, 1966; J. H. Kwabena Nketia, 1965, 1975 and 1978; and H. Tracey, 1961, are the general studies available for Africa south of the Sahara. In addition *West Africa* often carries articles about modern music and has a rubric 'Records' authored by 'Concobility Jane'.
77. E. Akin, 1965 (p. 61 on rejection of Western orchestral music) and 1970; and N. L. Korley, 1986 (on the transformation of Ghana's national symphonic orchestra).
78. J. H. Kwabena Nketia, 1978.

occurred the music underwent the fate of the ritual. Protest songs flourished in the colonial period and sometimes later. Their music reflected the old and the new. Typical is the situation of the Rwenzururu protest songs (Uganda). Some used music associated with the older beer parties, others hymn tunes or school songs.[79] The form reflected not the message, but the generation and age of the singers. Influences from European hit records were stronger in the 1940s and 1950s than later. In the 1950s the Mangbetu (Zaire) liked the French singer Tino Rossi[80] and in 1966 the Rwenzururu songs included the tune of *Alpenrosen*, an old sentimental Central European ditty. But rural songs also innovated. In some areas the old historical genre of epic song was used to compose new historical songs. Thus a blind Lulua troubadour recently composed a song interpreting the recent history of Kasai (Zaire) in terms of traditional chiefs and their protector spirits.[81]

Sacred music gained in importance where Islam was spreading or as the result of church activity.[82] Well before 1935, hymns were favourites, even if their scales and harmonics were unconsciously adapted to local norms. Chorales in schools were founded and by the 1950s troupes on the pattern of the *Wiener Saengerknaben* appeared in Central, East and South Africa.[83] Catholics began to experiment with 'African masses' from the 1930s onwards.[84] Masses were composed by Africans, often seminarians or priests, from 1939 onwards, a vogue reaching its peak before the Vatican Council II of 1964 and its pronouncements on liturgical language and practice.[85] Later this movement abated, even though the creation of sacred music remains strong as it keeps pace with the religious revival and the increased pace of conversion evident for the whole continent after 1980. However, hymns are now less favourite tunes for many than the new urban popular music, which affects the rural areas everywhere.

North African urban music

In 1871 Verdi's *Aida* was premiered in the new opera-house of Cairo. This is symptomatic for Egypt, the only country in Africa which came to terms with European instrumental music. Northern Africa had its own rich and long tradition of instrumental music, still associated, however,

79. P. Cooke and M. Doornbos, 1982.
80. A. Scohy, 1955, p. 113.
81. T. K. Biaya, 1984.
82. H. Weman, 1960.
83. See G. Haezon, 1960, for an example from 1954 onwards, in Shaba.
84. P. Jans, 1960. J. H. Kwabena Nketia, 1957, cites Ephraim Amu, and his 1933 collection of *Twenty-five African Songs* (hymns) in African style and with African accompaniment, as the father of African composers of sacred music.
85. T. Tshibangu, 1960.

with vocal performance. In the first part of our century, however, Sayyed Darwish developed a stable new musical style blending European and Oriental traditions. By 1929 a Higher Institute for Arabic Music was founded in which instrumental music found a place along with vocal music. The new style was such a great success that a group of musicians in Algeria and in Tunisia found it necessary in 1934 to found the *Rachidiyya*, a group devoted to fight its influence and to revive the old traditions of the *ma'lūf* orchestra and its *nuba* partitions. *Ma'lūf* became a symbol for independence in these countries and in Libya. But the lead of Egypt was followed in borrowing European instruments such as the cello, the saxophone and the accordion, the concept of a large musical ensemble and even some melodies and rhythms from Europe. In Morocco the traditional urban music had never been threatened and continued to flourish, a direct descendant of the learned Arabic music from the heyday of Islam. Its treasures include the *'arubi* quatrains of the women of Fez,[86] the sacred songs of the brotherhoods, or again the *ḥaḍḍarat* sung in chorus by women on various occasions such as marriages or circumcisions, but above all the *melḥūn*, or *griha*. The *melḥūn* is poetry. *Ḳasīḍa* poems are sung, and created according to highly complex rules. The Moroccan music remained much more traditional than others. Its musical modes continue to be adapted to the temper of the message or to be sung.[87]

Just as in Africa south of the Sahara, however, the voice remained central and only vocal artists became truly stars with a retinue of fans, and enormous popular appeal. Some enjoyed local fame such as Saliha, the great singer of Badawi *ona* in Tunisia, while others saw their fame spread all over the Arabic-speaking world. The most famous singer of this century has been Umm Khulthum, who took her name from pre-Islamic Arab poetry and had already begun her career by 1932.[88] She incarnated in the al-Nasser years the drive to return to the early greatness of Islam. In the later 1960s she developed a new style which also found its aficionados. But she has been only the first in rank among many. It is worth underlining that in North Africa no clear distinction can be made between popular and élite urban music. Neither the use of vernacular Arabic as opposed to the literary language, nor the specific genres are reliable indicators. This again corresponds to the situations south of the Sahara, where the popular song has become the élite music as well, whatever the other divisions between the social classes.

---

86. M. El Fasi, 1967. Arabic texts published in Fez, 1971.
87. The notes on Morocco are based on a contribution by His late Excellency M. El Fasi.
88. A. Elnaccash, 1968.

PLATE 20.6   *The Fez Orchestra of Morocco, an orchestra of Arabo–Andalus music*

Urban music south of the Sahara[89]

Urban music began as an accompaniment to dances in the new towns and as bar music performed by organized troupes. In the early 1930s the presentation of ethnic dances, such as the *agbaya* of Brazzaville and Kinshasa, perhaps related to the *agbadza* of Ghana and Togo.[90] Dances in European costumes, where the groups were still defined by ethnic origin and competed with each other, were also common. The complex history of one such tradition is that of the Beni ('Band') movement, originally linked to agonistic festivals in Lamu (Kenya) and influenced by German military bands. Beni spread throughout Tanzania and then to Southern and Central Africa,[91] where it was still a favourite on the Copper Belt in 1951.[92] In the Witwatersrand one of its functional equivalents was the performance of Zulu regimental dances, but with new music.[93] Competitive dancing and singing were also quite common in the West African coastal centres.

89. This section is based on a contribution by Kazadi wa Mukuna. See also Kazadi wa Mukuna, 1980.

90. E. W. Smith, 1962. Given the links between colonial Léopoldville and Accra from the 1880s onwards the similarity in name may not be fortuitous.

91. T. Ranger, 1975.

92. J. Mitchell, 1956.

93. H. Tracey, 1952.

PLATE 20.7   *The Egyptian singer Umm K̲h̲ulṯhum, during a recital in Paris in 1967*

Around 1940, a major musical style of a different nature appeared: the *rumba* of Zaire. It followed the earlier but slower development of *highlife* in Ghana which has its origins in a kind of parade during which players and dancers moved slowly along a street from one end to the other, and which was fully developed at least by 1930. Brass dominated in its instrumentation and it developed two forms, a fast-tempo variant and a slow tempo, the 'blues'. *Highlife* came to be associated with the ballroom and a Western style of dancing. As a result of this and of the use of European instruments it tends to Western harmonic usage, even though its treatment of beat rhythm and melody was Ghanaian.[94] Accra before

94. J. H. Kwabena Nketia, 1957.

1940 was the epicentre of a musical tradition embodied in large orchestras such as the Excelsior or the Accra rhythmic opera which spread all along the west coast. *Highlife* reached its peak in the 1950s, falling gradually out of favour in the 1960s both in Nigeria and in Sierra Leone, where a more Latin American type of music, inspired also by Zairian music, took over. *Highlife* had absorbed many elements of jazz, especially in the common woodwind and brass orchestras. It also had Afro-calypso and reggae facets, based on the guitar and with Caribbean inspiration.[95]

The guitar came to West Africa *c.*1935 and was first used in Nigeria along with drums, later accordion and rattles as well, as accompaniment to the styles of music called first *juju* and later *miliki*. Zairian music influenced these strongly until *c.*1968 and the rise of Afrobeat, a synthesis of *highlife* and African-American soul music. This style developed a further variant, Syncro (1976). Afrobeat is associated especially with the star singer Amikulapo Kuti Fela, who sees himself as the spokesman for the working class. In the 1970s he established a commune that was broken up in 1977. Still he persisted in his protest songs despite further harassment.[96]

The Zairian tradition took shape under the inspiration of the performances in Kinshasa of Cuban ensembles visiting there just before the Second World War. During the war, strong new influences came with American and European soldiers. With the *maringa*, a dance appeared in which the couple was the performing unit, even if they still danced separately most of the time and used local instruments, but soon also the guitar. Hitherto the use of imported instruments had failed[97] but now performers learned from European musicians who worked with them in urban bars. The guitar was first adopted in southern Zaire, where stringed instruments were traditional. It rapidly ousted the hitherto ubiquitous *likembe* (*mbira*, also *sanza*)[98] which no longer could express the complex harmonic needs of the new music. By 1946 the guitar had reached Kinshasa. This event combined with the fashion for Afro-Cuban music, the rejection of colonial models such as the polka, waltz or march, and the beginnings of a record industry[99] to give birth to a major new tradition.

The record companies backed the first singers who were a success. The diffusion of the records over the radio and through sales established the rumba style. With the creation of African jazz (1953), the still existing O.K. jazz (1956) and the gradual development of lyrics in Lingala rather than in Spanish, which had allowed only for rudimentary messages,

95. E. W. Smith, 1962; E. S. Kinney, 1970; N. W. Hooker, 1970.

96. V. Tunji, 1976; J. Labinjoh, 1982; J. Miller, 1985; C. Moore, 1982; and J. Howe, 1986.

97. N. Nlolo, 1983; M. Lonoh, n.d.; Kanza Matongo, 1972; and S. Bemba, 1984.

98. W. Soyinka, 1985.

99. Philips, Ngoma, Loningisa.

Zairian music took off. Despite its titles, jazz was of minor importance in Kinshasa, especially after *c.*1955, but remained more central in Lubumbashi, where songs in Kiswahili and Tshiluba flourished until a few years after independence, at which time the Kinshasa example and Lingala lyrics became universal. Although this correlates with the political triumph of Kinshasa over Lubumbashi (end of the Shaba secession in 1963, Second Republic in 1965), the use of the electric guitar and the spread of the transistor radio after 1960 also contributed to the success of the Kinshasa ensembles.[100]

Even though fashions in dance and variants of style followed each other almost year after year and, until 1960, were influenced by European fads such as the cha-cha-cha and the twist, the lyric tradition continued basically uninterrupted. More important than the fads were the development of lyrics into sophisticated songs or complex ballads, often carrying a strong social commentary, and the renewed influences from traditional dances. The rumba kept its basic structure – namely, an introduction, preceded by a brief instrumental prelude presenting the main motif; the development of the song and its refrains by a duo or trio; and instrumental improvisation in which the rhythmic and melodic development occur.

Meanwhile, the number of ensembles increased from 19 in 1960 to well over 200 by 1984, well supported by organizations such as the Union of Musicians (1965). Nothing comparable to these developments had occurred in neighbouring areas, so that Zairian music swept the scene not only in Central Africa, but in part also on the east coast and as far south as Zimbabwe, even though the Lingala lyrics were not widely understood. In Kinshasa, however, the themes changed. Early couplets on unsuccessful love or nostalgic verses about the simple rural life were supplemented even before 1960 by political songs celebrating independence, the country and its heroes. After 1960 social commentary grew in importance and in time became bitter and outspoken.[101] The lyrics there have much to do with the fame of great stars such as Luambo (Franco). Censure began in 1967, but dampened such trends only slightly, until Luambo's arrest and subsequent release in 1979. Less controversial lyrics appeared and protest songs gradually moved to Cameroon (the *Makossa*) and Gabon.[102] By the mid-1970s, and even more after 1979, styles changed in Kinshasa and came to reflect new social realities. Melodic line became more banale, lyrics less elaborate. At times the song is reduced to a heartfelt outcry (*cri du coeur*) accompanied by a brutal, frantic and

100. J. Fabian, 1978, pp. 315–21 for music in Lubumbashi.
101. For example, 'The dialogue of Adam and God' by Luambo. See O. Debhonvapi, 1984.
102. O. Debhonvapi, 1984, p. 130; B. Ephson, 1984; Anon., 1984; H. Kala-Lobe, 1982; C. Monga, 1983.

more acrobatic style of dancing, much more spectacular than before and more trance-like as well.[103]

The third major development in music took place in southern Africa. In the 1920s, the *marabi* originated in the clandestine urban bars of the African townships. It was influenced by Nguni polyphony with the development of complex rhythms, explosive yells and unusual harmonies (open fifths). The influence of North American jazz became predominant and in the 1940s the *marabi* developed into the *kwela*, first in Malawi and then by the 1950s in South Africa itself. The accompaniment was dominated now by a long tin flute, the penny-whistle, and rhythms became even more complex, accompanied by a steady beat.[104] The resulting type of song, requiring virtuosity beyond the usual, has become well known through the records of Miriam Makeba.[105] Jazz also influenced Kenyan urban music directly. In East African cities as well as in South Africa there has been more influence from expatriate or local white tastes linked to the fashions in Europe and the United States, than elsewhere on the continent.[106]

Dance

Africa Dances, affirmed G. Gorer in 1935 about West Africa:

> They dance for joy and they dance for grief; they dance for love and they dance for hate; they dance to bring prosperity and they dance to avert calamity; they dance for religion and they dance to pass the time.[107]

He worried needlessly about the future. Such a rich heritage does not quickly fade, all the more so in that European dance, social or artistic, never was a challenge. Social dancing was borrowed, but very little of its music and few of its steps were. Meanwhile rural dance fashions persisted and continued to develop. Such was the dynamic of this art, that even after 1900, a new complex theatrical ballet tradition, the *bobongo*, could develop in a part of Zaire, despite the colonial situation.[108] Migrants brought their dances to town where they flourished often in competitive settings with other ethnic or regional groups. Among the novelties introduced was the adaptation of military drill and of gymnastics to dance. It occurred in Beni before 1914, but also elsewhere, as among the Ewondo

---

103. N. Nkashama, 1979; G. Ewens, 1987. This is the *soukous* music.
104. M. Andersson, 1981; K. Cuper, 1958; D. Rycroft, 1959.
105. J. Gwanga and E. J. Miller, 1971.
106. G. Kubik, 1981; J. Low, n.d.; S. H. Martin, 1982.
107. G. Gorer, 1945 edn, p. 191.
108. Iyandza-Lopoloko, 1961.

of Yaoundé where by 1970 a woman's drill dance to the tune of a police whistle was hallowed as 'traditional'.[109]

Dances did not draw much colonial attention until the 1950s, except in the form of condemnation, or as an attraction for feastdays and for visiting luminaries. By then, the rural troupes that were often solicited in such circumstances began to refuse to dance, except for pay. Already by the early 1930s, a group of Dogon dancers had been sent to Paris. Out of such beginnings, professional dance troupes were born.[110] Another wellspring for the creation of the modern ballet was Fodeba Keita's concern to integrate dance into the theatre. He created his *ballets africains* by the mid-1950s. By then folkloric dance programmes in halls or the open air were becoming common elsewhere as well.[111] Yet another dynamic, nationalism, was at work now. Folk dances became so much a must for nationalists, that in Egypt, where there was no rural dancing tradition, the genre had to be invented. This was also the only African country to found an Institute for (European-style) Ballet in 1958. Elsewhere all other countries turned to their choreographic heritage to organize troupes soon after their independence. Schools of drama at universities also started from the local heritage.

These developments changed the nature of dancing in the following ways. Traditional dances in non-traditional settings meant a new relationship to the audience, now impersonal and based on payment of an entrance fee. Spectacular elements in dance were stressed, but the overall patterns of movements were simplified and shortened. The limits of space (stage) and of time radically altered the ground plan and overall organization of the dance, as well as the attitude of the dancers toward their own performance. Moreover, costumes and movements were tailored to meet urban standards of decency and new dance themes were introduced.[112] Also, programmes were composed to stress variety and hence dances from different peoples and of different nature were amalgamated. On the *Changwe Yetu* programme of 1958, war dances jostled funeral dances from another area, competitive displays of skill, satirical initiation dances, spectacular gymnastic sword dances with enthronement dances for chiefs. New pantomime drill-like dances also evolved in the cities. Since then greater artistic unity has been introduced. The dance is made to correspond to a moment in the development of an operatic (Nigeria) or theatrical plot and becomes ancillary to the theatre, or a progression of dances is

109. See J. Mitchell, 1956, for an example; and P. Harper, 1969, p. 166, for urban ethnic dance and school dances.

110. As among the Mangbetu. A. Scohy, 1955, p. 113; P. J. Imperato, 1971.

111. F. Keita, 1957. By 1958 Zaire sent its first theatrical troupe *Changwe Yetu* to the World Exhibition in Brussels. It was also organized by a theatrical producer.

112. P. Harper, 1969. For Nigeria she adds the influence of television (started in 1959) and film (after 1970) in their requirements of dance. See also R. Berger, 1967.

PLATE 20.8   *Fodeba Keita's* ballets africains

presented so as to create a structure of moods, to provide a pseudo-plot of tensions to be resolved and a succession of displays leading to the spectacular grand finale. A wholly new choreography results.

Meanwhile, social dancing in the cities changes only in minor ways as fads come and go, rural dances persist, ethnic dancing competitions are channelled in the form of 'festivals', while the urban style of social dancing daily gains ground in the countryside. Today, dance remains a well-loved activity, the art practiced by most people and, with music, the most popular of all the arts.

Pageantry and theatre

Pageantry and theatre are a single art – despite the constraints imposed by the settings of the stage or the studio contrasted to their absence during public festivities, and despite even the degree of professionalism found among actors of the theatre.

Pageantry

Parades, pantomimes, even staged dialogue by masked dancers, had been very common in pre-colonial Africa, often in sacred or ceremonial contexts. Many of these traditions have survived. The continuity sometimes is astonishing as between the ceremonial Akan processions sketched by Bowdich in 1817 and modern Akan practice, even though most such happenings have been updated,[113] inspired by new situations as well as by European practices, as in military pageants or in official ceremony. Complex masquerades are still common on the west coast especially, be they the Lantern Festival traditions of Sierra Leone or the Gambia,[114] the Fanti *asafo* displays,[115] the glitter of Akan courts, the myriad masquerades of Nigeria[116] or the carnival of Luanda. Celebrations for the Prophet's birthday in North Africa and public feasts in East African coastal towns have kept, indeed even developed, their entertainment activities. In rural areas, initiation rituals for boys, often conceived of as dramatic happenings, were still common in 1935 – or around 1950 when V. Turner studied those of the Ndembu (Zambia). In remoter areas and even in some cities[117] they have continued until today.[118] Among the most spectacular older productions were those of the Tsogho (Gabon) to whom spectacle and induced trances were crucial means to communicate with the supernatural. Their *bwiti* has declined since the 1930s, but meanwhile the ritual had spread to northern Gabon where it became part of dramatic new rituals.[119] The flair for the dramatic remains alive everywhere.

Traditional theatre in the more narrow sense of acting out a story in front of an audience of spectators was less widespread. Still from Mali to the Cross River or at various places in the basin of the River

---

113. H. Cole, 1975.

114. J. W. Nunley, 1985; and J. Bettelheim, 1985.

115. G. N. Preston, 1975.

116. See special issues of *African Arts*, vol. 6, no. 4, 1973 and vol. 11, no. 3, 1978; also N. Nzewunwa, 1982; and many descriptions in *Nigeria Magazine*.

117. See A. Droogers, 1980, who shows how the new urban elements have been fused into the dramatization.

118. Kuba initiations studied in 1982 by W. Binkley are surprisingly like similar activities in 1953.

119. J. Fernandez, 1982, pp. 436–93.

Congo/Zaire some peoples organized such spectacles.[120] Colonial authorities frowned on such performances, preferring their own parades, national-holiday ceremonials and *Te Deum*s, at least until the touristic value of such happenings began to be realized after the Second World War. Even so a few African elements slunk on occasion into European ceremonial, such as the skits performed during parades of the *Force Publique* from the Belgian Congo. These derived from mimes during dances in the equatorial zone.[121] They showed the evils of the Zanzibari slave trade. After independence these easily turned into the evils of colonialism.[122]

After independence some leaders began to use older pageantry to develop enthusiasm at political meetings. *Animation* is performances staged on public occasions to elicit the enthusiasm of the spectators for the specific political proposals made at the meeting, or in support of the regime in general. Political slogans often are launched in this fashion. As far as is known, the practice first developed in Guinea before 1965, the examples being the former *griots*, and then *animation* was transplanted to Zaire in 1967–70, where the military skits, older dance formations and even Western majorettes all became sources of inspiration.

Theatre

Theatre proper or the acting out of a plot on a stage, often following the conventions of the Italian stage, with a text learned by rote and usually in a European language, clearly is an urban innovation.[123] The form first developed in missions and schools, often as a one-act play, and served didactic purposes or as an aid to conversion.[124] Biblical or moral subjects, often quite satirical, were common. For it was not forgotten that theatre must entertain as well as teach. The development of theatre took very different pathways in areas under French, Belgian or Portuguese control, where the French tragedy was the model, and areas under British control – at least in West Africa – where the school was not the only avenue to the theatre. Moreover, the situation in North Africa was significantly different.

120. See B. Traoré, 1958; Y. Ogunbiyi, 1962; M. A. Alarinjo, 1981; J. C. Messenger, 1962 and 1971; A. De Rop, 1959; J. Cornet, 1982, pp. 272–8 (masked *itul* play); but J. Leloup, 1983, argues that these are not ancestral to modern theatre in Africa.
121. G. Hulstaert, 1953.
122. H. Deschamps, 1971, p. 560.
123. A recent bibliography can be found in *Recherche, Pédagogie et Culture*, vol. 61, 1983, pp. 101–5. Basic surveys are W. Soyinka, 1985; B. Traoré, 1958; Y. Ogunbiyi, 1962; P. Parícsy, 1971; Anon., 1971; R. Mshengu-Kavanagh, 1979 and 1981; M. Schipper, 1982.
124. For the text (the plot mainly, dialogue was free) of a 1934 schoolplay, see R. Bonneau, 1972. Also G. Hulstaert, 1953; and B. Lindfors, 1980.

In Egypt the theatre had been flourishing in the late nineteenth century. Even European opera, an art form as ethnocentric as the Noh theatre in Japan, had found favour here, since the days of Khedive Ismāʿīl. By the 1930s, most of the theatres used colloquial Arabic. Many light comedies, even farce and morality plays were produced although Tawfīḳ al-Ḥakim and others also produced dramatic plays stressing universal human dilemmas. By the mid-1950s and in the era of al-Nasser plays became more socially topical, realistic, but also symbolic. They were heavily influenced by the cinema which was, in turn, influenced by them. By 1964, nine or ten theatres in Cairo played classical or modern Arab plays, comedies and Egyptian operettas. Both realistic plays such as those of Yūsuf Idrīs and symbolic plays carrying revolutionary messages, such as Nuʿman Ashur's works on egalitarianism, were liked by the public.[125] Since then less use has been made of the theatre to indoctrinate the public but, as in the cinema, the melodramatic, comical, realistic and symbolic trends have continued.

Libya, Tunisia and Algeria shared the tradition of a puppet shadow theatre, *Karaguz*, ultimately derived from Turkey. But this had no influence during colonial times. The theatre was frowned upon by the *ʿulamāʾ* on moral grounds. Plays were performed mainly in French and Italian for expatriate communities, and for a fraction of the élite public. Moreover, censorship was stringent. Before the independence of Tunisia and Morocco the main activity there consisted in translating European plays into classical or colloquial Arabic, although a handful of plays with didactic topics (mis-spent youth, drugs, the black market) were produced in Tunisia. By the later 1960s the urban public in the Maghreb as a whole became less apathetic. The number of troupes began to grow. Radio and television productions required scripts. And so the modern theatre developed mostly one-act plays, usually satire or melodrama, except in Algeria where propaganda plays, often concerned with the war of liberation, were common.[126]

In the French-speaking areas of West Africa an academic theatre did develop in the 1950s. The playwrights were often pupils of the William Ponty school of Dakar which had required pupils to write plays about their research in 'folklore' from 1933 to 1960. Anti-colonial critique, the tensions between the older generation and its views of the world as against those held by the newer generation, and a tendency towards satire were the hallmarks of such productions, although some historical subjects also appeared. Most plays retained the existing rules for the European theatre,

125. *Encyclopaedia Britannica, Macropedia*, vol. 9, p. 981; P. Mansfield, 1965, pp. 124–5; P. J. Vatikiotis, 1980, pp. 455–6.

126. A. Roth, 1961; H. Djaziri, 1968; H. D. Nelson, 1978, p. 141. The use by trades unions in Morocco of the theatre (troupe Hammamet) to spread their cause was not successful.

except, at William Ponty, that only the skeleton of a text was produced leaving much room for improvisation in dialogue. But as later playwrights wrote longer plays this feature was eliminated. A few such as Cheick N'Dao in *L'exil d'Albouri* (1969) introduced poetry, song and dance aiming for total theatre. Most eschewed such innovations. B. Dadié of the Côte d'Ivoire is typical. He continued to write in the same form in the 1970s which he had adopted in his early play *Assemien Débylé*, which was played in Paris in 1937.[127] Zairian playwrights followed in this tradition although their theatre only developed after 1955, inspired by travelling troupes and school plays.[128]

After independence the usual repertoire was enriched by propaganda plays, which were accepted only in so far as they carried comical elements.[129] The main problem with the theatre was in fact its lack of appeal. This was due in part to language problems although some authors wrote in African languages or more usually translated their work into the local urban language. But even such works were not received with enthusiasm by the multitudes. The conventions of form, the laws of the theatre (including the unity of space and time) were just too foreign to the experience of the public.

And yet, as early as 1947, Fodeba Keita[130] had attempted to break away from them. Dance and choral singing accompanied the action and interpreted it as it was spoken by the leading actor, an adaptation of both Mande (Malinke) and classical Greek procedure. But he was not followed and the form did not develop into a more flesh-and-blood theatre. It did however become quite successful as a framework for the numerous ballet companies that followed the pattern of his *ballets africains*. Dance and spectacle took over at the expense of the richness and complexity of the plot. Moreover, such *ballets* came to be aimed more at overseas audiences than at a local public and can be seen as tourist art.[131] And so both the theatre and the ballet found themselves alienated from the culture of their public, which renders the continuing concern about negritude in the repertory all the more poignant.

Meanwhile, theatre had developed quite differently in the former British colonies of West Africa. By the 1920s, *vaudeville* theatre in English and the local languages was thriving in Ghana, followed in the 1930s by a European-inspired theatre but in the vernacular, the first success of which was a play by F. K. Fiawoo written in Ewe.[132] Both traditions

127. B. Traoré, 1969; W. Zimmer, 1985.
128. See *Jeune Afrique* (Elisabethville) issues for 1958; Y. L. Mundara, 1972; M. du Ma-Ngo, 1980; and Kadima-Nzuji, 1981.
129. N. S. Hopkins, 1971.
130. F. Keita, 1957; P. Parícsy, 1971, pp. 54–6.
131. See UNESCO, 1982c, for examples of government perception of dance troupes as tourist activities – for example, the statements by the government of Zambia.
132. In response to a competition organized by the International African Institute.

continued,[133] although the academic tradition enjoyed less success than the *vaudeville*. The academic trend continued, however, both in the vernacular and in English where there was a market for didactic plays in schools. Both trends were to develop dramatically.

The first was developed by H. Ogunde. In 1944 he created a musical play for the Church of the Lords in Lagos, using Yoruba, organizing the plot around music and dance and leaving the script to be ad-libbed. With this the West African operatic tradition began. Ogunde wedded the traditional spectacle to dialogue, staging and other elements of the *vaudeville* tradition. His ventures met with such success that the income allowed him to lay the institutional and business foundations for the theatre in Nigeria.[134]

On the academic side, W. Soyinka appeared. Trained from 1955 onwards in London and back in Nigeria by 1959 he created the first true academic plays. He was at home in the European techniques and could overcome them to incorporate Yoruba dramatic elements. His example was followed from 1960 onwards by other talented writers such as J. P. Clark.[135]

Meanwhile in Ghana E. T. Sutherland, writing in Fante, developed the academic theatre from 1958 onwards and in 1961 created a new form, first labelled musical, later opera. It was a pantomime for dancers, accompanied by chorus and soloists. These developed the plot in Fante while a commentator gave an English rendering.[136] But the opera really found its African expression with Duro Ladipo who created his first work in 1961 as well at the Oshbogo art centre. From 1962 to 1964 he produced a cycle about historical kings of Ọyọ. These became the mode for the Yoruba opera, combining a highly literate language in Yoruba with social satire and metaphysical reflection. The form was a spectacular fusion between the academic tradition and the popular genre of Ogunde, who assisted him in its development.[137]

Since the 1960s form and content have not altered very much. Inspiration is largely drawn from oral traditions, but is used to bear on contemporary situations, often to express discontent, sometimes as satire. Some major playwrights such as Soyinka in time turned from satire to despair. In turn Femi Osofisan, the best-known author of the youngest generation in Nigeria, turns to more radical political prescriptive plays. But while berating Soyinka he and others still closely follow his language, play structuring and even repertoire of topics.[138]

133. J. Collins, 1985; K. N. Biame, 1968.
134. E. Clark and H. Ogunde, 1979.
135. O. Ogunba, 1966; O. Ogunba and A. Irele, 1978; Y. Ogunbiyi, 1981; M. Etherton, 1982; A. Ricard, 1975.
136. K. Muhindi, 1985; S. Acquaye, 1971; O. Chinyere, 1980.
137. U. Beier, 1970 and 1973.
138. C. Dunton, 1984.

As a result of these developments, theatre in both its popular and academic forms has found fertile ground in Ghana and especially Nigeria. In this it differs completely from the alienated francophone tradition. But it also differs from drama elsewhere in English-speaking Africa.

In East Africa the theatre was slower to develop. Its epicentre was the University College of Makerere. The first playwright began writing one-act plays in somewhat hesitant English by the early 1960s. Given the disinterest of the public for plays in English, experimentation with local languages began early on in Kiswahili and Kiganda first, later also in Luo and Kikuyu. The one-act format was transcended only by Ngugi in 1966. Censorship has been ferocious at times in Uganda, but is a real problem in other countries as well. Elsewhere the acceptance of the European theatrical conventions in their entirety, especially at Makerere in the 1960s, has retarded public acceptance of the theatre.[139]

Apartheid in South Africa may be the main reason why the development of the theatre for African audiences has lagged so much behind the development of African literature, which had already produced a masterpiece such as Mofolo's *Shaka* before 1935. Mphalele's work was drama to be read more than to be performed. African theatre broke through with the production of *King Kong* in 1959. Its success allowed the group at Witwatersrand University that produced it to expand and to offer teaching in music and in the theatre to Africans. Meanwhile, however, more popular plays were beginning to be produced by Gibson Kente. This township art was performed in community halls and aimed at entertainment from 1958 onwards to the late 1960s. Yet another strand in the development of the theatre was school plays in African languages. In the 1970s the People's Experimental Theatre and other groups began to produce political action plays written by Credo Mutwa and others. Despite censorship and arrests this form of drama flourished until the Soweto riots. The repression led to the production of plays for which no written text existed, so that they could not be censored. Until recently[140] the political situation has prevented the development of any other theatrical repertoire apart from political issues. Plays in all of the African languages are now common and offer a wider range of content.[141]

European theatre has not easily been accepted in Africa, because of its convention, literary character, absence of audience participation and emphasis on didactic messages rather than entertainment, in addition to the barriers created by the use of foreign languages. In its classical form

139. M. M. Mahood, 1966; R. Serumaga and J. Johnson, 1970; and L. A. Mbughuni, 1976.

140. M. Hommel, 1962; special issue of *Theatre Quarterly*, vol. 7, 1977–8; M. Mabogoane, 1983.

141. In general, A. Fuchs, 1985; M. M. Mahood, 1966, pp. 25–6; and R. Mshengu-Kavanagh, 1981.

it has only been accepted by a fraction of the élites and by governments who see it as a prestige product of national pride. But where the theatre broke its conventions, admitted popular tastes, used local languages, especially in dialogue, allowed at least for some audience participation and became less highbrow, it generally became popular. At one extreme, plays became mere musical comedy with the slightest of content. But the experience, especially of Nigerian theatre and opera, has shown that popular productions can reach a high level of dramatic and literary quality.

Cinema and television

Radio, cinema and television are media whose character approximates most to that of the older performances of oral tradition. Radio, however, lacked the visual impact and was therefore a less powerful medium than cinema or television which involve both sound and sight. Cinema in turn was on the whole less close to the mainstream of African oral tradition than television using video techniques, because the latter preserve much more spontaneity than the former. Of the three, cinema was the earliest as foreign films were shown from *c.*1905 onwards in Egypt and from the 1920s south of the Sahara, both in a few urban theatres and also in the form of travelling shows in rural areas. From the outset, films were very well received – even if the foreign films shown were scarcely under-standable by the public. The situation led to the production of a substantial number of films, always didactic, even if they were feature films, aimed at an African public, but shot by foreigners. Censorship of films shown also developed.[142] Radio began for the most part in the 1930s, but became the mass medium *par excellence* only from 1960 onwards when cheap transistor radios run on batteries flooded the continent. This industry firmly remained in government hands and played its first major role in moulding public opinion in the years leading up to independence. Television started with transmissions at Ibadan in 1959, followed by Cairo in 1960. The medium spread more slowly because the costs of investment in the infrastructure were substantial and sets were expensive. Still, by 1985 almost all African countries had set up TV networks and were striving to achieve coverage over the whole of their territory. We discuss the cinema first, television later.

Cinema

The earliest film shot by an African may well be *Ghézal, the Girl of Carthage* (1924), a Tunisian production, soon followed by Egypt's *Leila* (1926) and *Zainab* (1926). These were inspired by theatrical models but theatrical conventions were soon breached and then abandoned. Misr

---

142. F. Ramirez and C. Rolot, 1985.

Studios opened in 1934 and the industry there took off, soon producing several films per year. This stands in sharp contrast to the colonies. Political considerations explain the reluctance of colonial governments to allow Africans to make films. But financial considerations also account for delay and explain why in many countries national film directors appeared only in the 1970s.

Film production is a business. It requires substantial initial inputs of capital for production, for the creation of a network of distribution, and for the building or the adaptation of theatres. Returns on the investment have to wait for box-office receipts and capital for further production costs consists of what remains after theatre operators and distribution firms have taken their profits. So far, only Egypt has succeeded in setting up an efficient self-sustaining industry. The alternative is for the state initially to finance its film industry, and then attempt to put it on sound financial bases afterwards. A small industry in Nigeria and in Morocco succeeded in this, while Senegal was able after 1969 to set up its distribution network and build theatres, and is now on the way to become self-sustaining. A more common pattern was found in Algeria, Tunisia, Mali and Burkina Faso, where the governments have sponsored propaganda and educational films, but not feature films. Still, this brought expertise to the country as well as some facilities for production, and in these countries the first film-makers have used these bases. But after 1970 the presence of television studios has been much more important in this regard. Television tended to promote the creation of films by providing facilities and an outlet. Of late, however, with the prominence of video rather than film, it has tended to depress film production.[143]

Most governments were reluctant to invest heavily in the industry because, contrary to popular belief, film is not a mass medium. It is not comparable to radio or television, which therefore have had absolute priority in all countries. When Upper Volta (now Burkina Faso) broke the hold of the foreign distributors in 1969, there were only ten cinemas in the country. Gabon in 1986 had only eight. Senegal today, with the best infrastructure in tropical Africa, has 80 cinemas and 13 million viewers a year. This begins to be mass exposure. One of the greatest successes of any film was Cheick-Oumar Sissoko's *Nyamaton* shown at the Ouagadougou film festival in July 1986. It attracted 35 000 viewers over two weeks; yet compared to the millions of television viewers per day such an audience is not massive.[144]

Still, even if films are not a mass medium, they are potent enough to provoke a constant struggle of competing cultural interests. India, Egypt,

143. P. Haffner, 1978; G. Hennebelle, 1972; G. Hennebelle and C. Ruelle, 1978; J. Binet *et al.*, 1983; P. S. Vieyra, 1968, 1975 and 1983. Vieyra also reports regularly in *Présence africaine* especially about film festivals such as those of Ouagadougou or Carthage.
144. M. Diawara, 1986 and 1987; P. Michaud, 1986.

623

France, Great Britain and the United States all vie for a share of the market and national policies must defend their markets as well as map out cultural policies of their own. Thus two French distribution companies had a stranglehold on the whole French-speaking market in western Africa until 1969, when Upper Volta broke through, and even today most of the area is still dominated by French companies.[145] The public's choice is responsible for the large share of Indian and Egyptian films shown in tropical Africa. The remaining fifth of the market is the battle-ground for Western countries. France and the United States are the main protagonists. At first African governments merely attempted to play them off against each other, but accepted co-production by which film technology was transferred. In the 1980s, however, it became common to turn to other foreign partners, especially Cuba and Latin American countries.[146]

Given such conditions, censorship is to be expected and governments hold strong views on the subject of films. Only 'good African films' are to be promoted and film should be used 'as a pleasant and elegant way of developing among African peoples certain desirable attitudes for improving welfare, hygiene, education, discipline, work . . . '.[147]

All the above considerations must be kept in mind when film is discussed as a form of art, for they both limit and deeply affect the vision of the film-maker. As we turn to this topic one must limit the discussion to the major centres of production only. There are well over 250 film producers now in Africa living and working in well over 40 different countries.

The first Egyptian cinema was romantic and appealed to the urban middle class. Ever since the opening of Misr Studios directors specialized in musicals and melodrama strongly influenced by the theatre. This tendency continues until today. But by 1939 neo-realist films appeared. The Second World War made cinema a very lucrative business. Production soared by 300 per cent, but the content was shoddy and escapist. Thus the life of night clubs became the subject of many of them. In the 1950s war films, mysteries, folkloric films, and renewed verist cinema revolving around individual psychological drama appeared, while some of N. Mahfuz's novels were also filmed. In 1952 most of the industry was nationalized but that did not alter its programming very much. Melodrama and farce maintained their dominance. After all, by then the Egyptian film industry occupied the twelfth place in the world and dominated the Middle East as well as North Africa. Most of the 50 or 60 films produced per year in the 1960s belong to the genres mentioned. But populist realism did develop, current issues such as the debate about the status of

145. M. Diawara, 1986.
146. M. Shirazi, 1987.
147. Anon., 1987.

women became topics for films, and adaptations of famous literary works were created. Critics often decry Egyptian films for their superficiality and facile plotting, but the public likes them. Per year the industry produces as many films as tropical Africa has over the last quarter of a century. Among them one finds all the genres of contemporary film. Regularly, works of high technical quality expressing original thought and sentiment appear in the flood of mediocre production.[148]

In the Maghreb[149] modest centres appeared in Algiers and in Morocco. The Algerian government decided from the start to subsidize the production of propaganda films about the war of independence and about state socialism, although it has not prevented criticism of its bureaucracies appearing in some recent productions. The few Tunisian films (1966 and later) tend to fall into the same mould. Morocco produced films in the commercially successful genres along with some intellectual films. The most remarkable movies are reminiscent of Buñuel and use symbol to captivate rather than plot or action.

French-speaking West Africans began to experiment with film by the mid-1950s, first in Paris, later in Dakar.[150] The first full-length feature film was *La Noire de . . .* by Ousmane Sembene (1966). Sembene[151] has dominated the French-speaking African film scene ever since, at least until very recently, and was also the only film director who found adequate financing for his art. Trained in the verist Russian tradition, his film used images to show social problems and support dialogue about profound truths and fundamental ideologies. With this he started an intellectualist tradition. All his films deal with the clash between colonial or European ways of life and African realities – his negritude component – with tensions between social classes – his Marxist components – and with praise for pre-colonial heroes – his nationalist component. The latter strand is expected to culminate in his six-part *Samory*, an epic for television.

Despite the dearth of financial support, almost two hundred film directors have appeared in French-speaking Africa. Much of their production was didactic and intellectualist, and the public rejected most of their films. But some producers such as Souleymane Cissé or Cheick-Oumar Sissoko transcended the Sembene legacy. The lyrical quality of Cissé brought him fame while Sissoko's recent *Nyamaton* about the lives of poor and rich schoolchildren enjoyed a huge appeal. It is half documentary, half fiction. It does not propose solutions and the emphasis

---

148. A. Elnaccash, 1968; G. Hennebelle, 1972, pp. 13–81; P. Mansfield, 1965, pp. 125–6. By 1972, Egypt had produced some 1400 films compared to 50 over 20 years for Africa south of the Sahara (G. Hennebelle, 1972, p. 77).

149. M. Berrah *et al.*, 1981; G. Hennebelle, 1972, pp. 105–94.

150. P. S. Vieyra's film *Afrique-sur-Seine* is commonly held to be the first one, but this is disputed. Cf. V. Bachy, 1983, in J. Binet *et al.*, p. 24.

151. F. Pfaff, 1984; O. Okore, 1984; M. B. Cham, 1984; R. A. Portimer, 1972.

lies on action and image rather than on intellectual debate carried by dialogue. The public loved to see a mirror image of its familiar society and all the more so as the language used was Bamana.[152] Sissoko followed a recent trend by abandoning French in favour of local languages. The Cameroonian detective story is a recent and entirely different genre. Although it is at the antipode of Cissé or Sissoko, it too broke with the Sembene legacy, albeit by yielding to public taste.

In Nigeria, television developed well before the cinema did, and provided a technical infrastructure. At first the film industry followed the Yoruba theatrical tradition and used its financial infrastructure. Feature films appeared only after 1972, the year in which a play by W. Soyinka was filmed. The first film director was trained in the French tradition, but Ogunde taught him to develop a popular, yet artistic film in the musical tradition. Nigeria has produced about one feature film a year since 1975 even though the cinema is not subsidized. Of late the industry has suffered from the stranglehold video production has acquired over television.[153]

Films using scenarios composed by Africans in South Africa date from 1975. They compete with films made for a white audience as well as with films made by government for its 'Bantu', and they face censorship. The first was a Zulu film, *Ikati elimnyama*, 'The Black Cat'. At least one later feature film has been entirely directed by an African. More important is the production of clandestine documentaries and film dossiers documenting *apartheid*. But obviously the African film is not flourishing.[154]

The general public clearly has received films much better than it has the theatre. But the success of African films compared to imported films, especially Indian and Egyptian products, points to the fact that many African film-makers have forgotten how to entertain. If Egypt is so successful, it is because of the numbers of comedies and melodramas (the soap operas of television) which it churns out year after year. African film directors aim to teach, to educate the public conscience. Their concerns are political (social class, neo-colonialism, dependency), moral (alienation and the evils of modernity as opposed to tradition), didactic (the roles of good, simple, rural women as opposed to bad, complex, urban women; the evils of drugs), personal (identity problems) or militantly cultural (traditional health care against Western medicine).[155] The public wants stories – be they romantic, historical, dramatic or comical. It craves mystery films, adventure, glamour and heroic action. And only now are some directors coming to grips with such demands.

152. M. Diawara, 1987.
153. A. Opubor and O. Nwuneli, 1979; A. Ricard, 1982; M. B. Cham, 1982; T. Fiofori, 1986b.
154. M. Pheto, 1981; T. Keya, 1981.
155. See the analysis of F. Boughedir, 1983, pp. 48–57.

Television

Television came to Cameroon and Burundi in 1984. They were among the last countries to adopt the new and costly medium. T. M. Azonga describes what the new medium meant to Cameroonians. They could now actually watch their idols, be they musicians, sportsmen or public leaders. They discovered their own country, viewing landscapes, cities and rural scenes which they had not even known about. They saw the world open before them as they learned about *apartheid* and saw its brutality in action or followed the horrors of the Iran–Iraq war. They entered into august halls of power such as the National Assembly and they saw current affairs and the stakes at hand as news developed.[156] No wonder that television soon outdid the radio's popularity, or that viewers were ready to spend much on access to it. By 1986, 50 000 sets had already been sold, many cheap black-and-white South Korean sets, but even more expensive colour sets. Nor is Cameroon alone in this. By 1986 one person in twelve owned a set in neighbouring Gabon, and in Nigeria one-fifth of the population (20 million people) watched television daily.[157] No doubt figures for other countries are comparable.

Such a success could leave no government unconcerned. And governments had learned about this power from Nigerian television which began in 1959,[158] from Cairo (1960), and from the introduction of the medium in European countries. For government, television was to be its voice, as the radio had been, but also its image. In many parts of the continent citizens distrusted the radio because on occasion news was misrepresented or suppressed and people knew about it. But television allowed governments to *show* events or situations and by that fact alone was many times more convincing than radio or other media could be. Governments wanted to create public opinion or mould it to their goals, to educate the public, to define the content of national consciousness, to create a sense of shared morality and to build a national culture. Moreover, many countries also attempted to influence the populations of neighbouring countries beyond their borders. The history of the expansion of television stations and networks in Nigeria shows clearly how intimately the medium is linked to competition in politics.[159]

One understands why governments were willing to spend very large amounts of money on infrastructure for television. Even governments such as that of Burundi, which well into 1983 resisted the wish to introduce the medium on grounds of cost, were forced to give in. Whatever the cost, television has become an essential appurtenance of sovereignty.

156. T. M. Azonga, 1986.
157. T. Fiofori, 1986b; P. Michaud, 1986.
158. O. Ikime, 1979; S. Olusola, 1979.
159. T. Fiofori, 1986b.

And the wealthier the country the more ambitious its networks. Not only has Gabon just expanded its two colour channels so that the transmissions cover the whole of that vast and underpopulated country, it is also building its own satellite, so that by 1990 it can beam its views as well as the results of its studies in Bantu civilization to much of Central Africa. It thus competes with Zaire which also aims to own its satellite.[160]

But television requires a vast number of programmes. One hundred hours a week means the equivalent of 60 feature films. Programming involved news and current affairs for at least one hour a day, children's programmes, documentaries (often related to development and recently much concerned with the rural world educational programmes), action dramas (often as serials), and comedies (often slap-stick), not forgetting sports programmes and coverage of public ceremony. The demand exceeds any other for the services of actors and programme-makers, even with the use of video. In fact, the demand cannot be met and operating costs would run too high if all programmes were original. Therefore stations built up stocks of old films and other materials and leased rights to foreign serials, thus reintroducing what has become the single most important source of cultural alienation. As governments strove to define and unify national culture, they also were obliged to introduce competing images of culture.

Is television an original art? It produced a wholly new genre: the serial, which stands to the film as an epic to a short story. Serials in Nigeria were at first vignettes around the same setting and the same principal characters, as in the series 'The Village Headmaster' which ran for almost a generation. But of late six or more hours of television can be used to develop a grand theme, such as the history of the first caliphs or the saga of Samory. All the genres of cinema too can be transformed, from the documentary with its new emphasis on 'snapshots' and in many cases the exotic at home, to children's cartoons. But many programmes cannot be structured enough to qualify as art. However absorbing they may be, soccer matches are not art and films where critics are in dialogue with cabinet ministers (popular in Gabon and Cameroon) can be given an orderly form but not an artistic one. For to be art the material must express metaphor in an apposite form. Still, several television genres can be art and exhibit many of the structural features known from oral (epic or other) tradition. But the medium is too new to assess its contribution to the performing arts. The overwhelming pressure to provide both escape and to meet immediate goals, coupled to very tight production schedules, make it quite difficult for masterpieces to emerge.

160. P. Michaud, 1986. The contracts for the House of the Radio in Kinshasa and for the relay of networks there are among the biggest development projects the country has undertaken since 1970.

The arts of Africa in world context

African sculpture revolutionized European art from 1905 onwards, especially in sculpture. By 1935 Cubism and German expressionism were outmoded but the basic influence of African art persisted and up to this day continues to dominate sculpture, as the work of Zadkine, Moore, Archipenko and others shows. In this way, the principles of classical African art have become part of the international repertoire of forms.[161] Such impulses often returned to Africa. Thus a popular artist in Benin (Nigeria) copied a work by Benson Osawe, in turn inspired by Modigliani, himself endebted to Lega mask forms from eastern Zaire.[162] The impact of expressionism on African artists trained in Europe derives from the impact of African art on expressionism. Thus Gerard Sekoto, for instance, echoes classical forms through the prism of German expressionist painting.

African music also had made its greatest contributions well before 1935 with its input in the creation of jazz and Afro–Latin music. As in the case of the visual arts, this explains why these movements in turn could contribute so much to modern African music.

During the high colonial period, after 1920, the African artistic heritage had little impact, barring only Le Corbusier's inspiration from the architecture of the Mzāb (southern Algeria). Arrogant colonialism only saw Africans as pupils to be taught, not as teachers. After independence, however, African arts once more began to influence the world. The international public was exposed first to more exhibits of African classical art, to the new music and to theatrical or ballet productions. Slowly these are recognized as original contributions to the world heritage and musicians in particular enjoy a growing international public, while at least one film, *Le mandat* by O. Sembene, had a genuine popular success in Europe. If classical art is now highly rated, modern visual art is only beginning to be known to an international public. So far, it has exerted little influence on the international scene.

The full recognition even of African classical art still remains incomplete. Despite many temporary exhibitions from Paris to Tokyo, Prague to New York, African classical art is still segregated from the repositories of what the public views as 'fine art'. Only the Metropolitan Museum of New York displays classical African sculpture as a permanent feature, but still as 'primitive art'. Nonetheless, the growing appreciation of the classical arts has boosted the market in art works. This market existed by 1900 but grew by leaps and bounds after 1945 and again after 1960. Unfortunately, this has been accompanied by the usual problems of

---

161. M. Leiris and J. Delange, 1967, pp. 117–61; D. Ola, 1980; F. Willett, 1971; S. Barron, 1983, for the magnitude of the African impact; and C. Einstein, 1915, for its manifesto.

162. P. Ben Amos, 1977, pp. 135–7 and fig. 9.10.

PLATE 20.9 *African art and Cubism: left, royal seat carved in wood: The King and his Court, Kana, Dahomey; right, 'The Prophet', a sculpture by Ossip Zadkine, 1914*

smuggling, illegal excavation, an industry of forgeries and further substantial losses of significant works of art as they are exported to other
continents.[163] Classical art has not entered the Louvre yet, but it has
reached the great auction houses. Meanwhile, modern artists, musicians,
playwrights and film producers struggle to be recognized. By the 1980s,
as shown by W. Soyinka's Nobel Prize and the 1987 award of a gold
medal at the film festival of Cannes, these struggles are producing results.

Conclusion

The half-century since 1935 does not contain two generations of artists
but three: the precursors, the pioneers of the contemporary arts and the
followers. The die was cast between 1945 and 1965. During these years,
earlier experiments coalesced into a new tradition from which later artists
did not depart. 1960 is not a crucial date in the arts. The new arts are a
product of the great age of nationalist expectation, not of political
independence. In a massive outburst, the arts reflected nationalism and
in the next generation produced scores upon scores of artists in all media,
in all genres, in all arts, still developing the insights the pioneers had
conceived.

On the whole, the new arts are not derived from European traditions,
even though they developed at the peak of European cultural influence
which spans the same years, and perhaps continues to be stronger now
than before 1945, and despite the adoption of European techniques or
instruments. In the final analysis the continuity with earlier times is more
striking. Continuities are evident for the rural arts, obvious for the popular
arts, and underlie much tourist art. A clear break is only evident in the
theatre in so far as it conforms to Italian convention, and in the cinema
which, apart from Egypt, is not yet a popular art. Intellectualist cinema
and academic theatre do not appeal even to most of the élites, which also
refuse European-inspired visual arts and eschew European classical music.
The academic arts, derived from Europe, are still foreign to collective
African sensibilities. The artists who practise them feel it and much of
their stance concerning Africanness, alienation and negritude derives from
this feeling of not belonging. On the whole, then, the new arts in Africa
are a synthesis in which a selective small portion of the European heritage
has been combined with a large African legacy.

Recently, D. Niven remarked on the close links between academic
artists and political leadership.[164] This is one facet of a wider truth: the
arts have faithfully mirrored the changing history of African societies,

163. *Arts d'Afrique noire* devotes much space to reports of sales and prices attained on
the international market. For tourist art, see the contributions of D. Crowley to *African
Arts*.
164. D. Niven, 1985.

with their tensions within and without. Urban arts became dominant as urban folk did. As social classes took shape and the gaps between them became rifts, each class found its own artistic expression. The tensions between highbrow cinema, theatre, visual arts, even costume, and the lowbrow varieties are evident everywhere. Only in music is the rift not glaring because there are almost no academic musicians. Whether academic artists agree or not with the élite, they speak their language and are recognized by them. Popular artists, on the whole, are not. African societies, once again, are the masters of their own destinies and they find the dreams and metaphors, the arts, which express their complex aspirations. The arts are new, because they mirror a new Africa.

Trends in philosophy and science in Africa

Ali A. MAZRUI *and* J. F. Ade AJAYI

in collaboration with

A. Adu BOAHEN *and* **Tshishiku**
TSHIBANGU

This chapter is dedicated to the memory of Cheikh Anta Diop

Introduction[1]

What does political subordination do to philosophy and science in a given society? The whole of Africa has been under varying degrees of foreign domination throughout the entire period since 1935, even when nominal political independence has been achieved. One central question for this chapter to consider, therefore, is the impact of this subordinate condition upon Africa's pool of knowledge and expertise. Was colonialism a new stimulus for scientific advances and technological change? Was Africa's formal philosophy enriched by colonialism? Was African philosophy actually *born* out of Africa's interaction with the Western world? Or did colonialism have an inhibiting effect on both philosophy and science?

We propose to demonstrate that partly because of colonialism, the contribution of African *scientists* to the total pool of human knowledge has been comparatively modest in the period since 1935. But we also hope to show that science has always been too important to be measured purely in terms of the activities of scientists. Just as history is not made by historians but by society, so science is not developed only by scientists but by the wider community. We hope to demonstrate how African society became one of the pillars of *Western* science and technology, precisely by being colonized. While colonialism made it difficult for science and technology to develop *within* Africa itself, the same colonial condition became a transmission belt for Africa's material contribution to science and technology in the Western world.

But African realities are not simply a derivative of colonialism. A more powerful force in Africa than the colonial experience is African culture itself. A survey of the trends in science and technology in Africa must

1. The authors of this chapter acknowledge with gratitude the stimulation and research help provided by Marcien Towa, Malu wa Kalenga and C. Wondji.

PLATE 21.1   *Cheikh Anta Diop, Senegalese philosopher and physicist, in his laboratory at IFAN, Dakar, Senegal*

therefore recognize the salience of values and traditions in both African philosophy and African science.

This chapter will address Africa's experience in philosophy and science, and examine knowledge as an empirical phenomenon. Partly because of that, when we discuss science, there will be a lot of philosophy; and when we discuss philosophy, there will be a lot of science. But both philosophy and science will be viewed – to borrow Marxist vocabulary in a new way – as part of the superstructure. The base or substructure will be culture itself.

This chapter addresses science and philosophy in Africa since 1935. But there is a sense in which philosophy and science defy the boundaries of both geographical space and historical time. The discussion of science and philosophy could not be kept strictly within the geographical boundaries of Africa and the historical limits of the period since 1935. The price for dealing with such universals as science and philosophy is the inevitable tendency to break out of the confines of space and time.

And yet even on this issue culture will help to restrain universalism. This chapter will be geographically comparative from time to time, looking at other societies in order to understand Africa better. We have come neither to bury the Caesars of African science nor to praise them. We

634

are trying to *understand* the empire of African science and philosophy in their *cultural* context, with all their strengths and limitations.

> *We* feel,
> Therefore *we* think,
> Therefore *we* are.

But in order to comprehend the *uniqueness* of Africa, we have para-doxically to compare it with other civilizations. What is distinctively African cannot be fully grasped without exploring what is universally human. It is not just the mirror which tells us what we are; it is also the traffic with the rest of humankind.

Traditional science

Recognition and some appreciation are only just beginning to be accorded the body of knowledge and expertise that sustained pre-colonial societies in agriculture, health, crafts and industries. In the colonial period such knowledge and expertise were not dignified with the name of science, but were damned as superstitious and pre-scientific. Western education and Christianity, sometimes even colonial laws and deliberate policies, were used to subvert the basis of such traditional knowledge. Those educated in Western-type schools were taught to despise and reject traditional knowledge, though nevertheless it continued under varying circumstances to be transmitted orally among the masses. Today, it is found that in spite of the impact of Western medicine, agriculture, science and technology, traditional knowledge and expertise in agriculture, healing practices and beliefs have retained a firm hold on the life of a majority of Africans.

Two features of traditional science should be noted. First, the role of individual thinkers and inventors was subordinated to that of society in nurturing knowledge and expertise within the culture. The loss of autonomy and sovereignty during the colonial period was therefore bound to have a profound effect on the further development and nurturing of such knowledge. Secondly, traditional societies made no distinction between knowledge acquired by reason, experimentation, imagination or faith. There was no dichotomy between science and religion, science and philosophy, or science and art. Scientific knowledge was not reduced only to the quantitative and the mechanistic. Thus, Western science could not begin to appreciate method or value in traditional science in Africa until the stage of relativity when Western science began to shift emphasis from discrete entities to the complexities in nature and the universe, and Western paradigms of progress and development began to be questioned.[2]

During the colonial period, African peasants were forced to produce raw material for European industries under conditions dictated by Western

2. R. Schram, 1981, pp. 391–9. See also A. O. Anya, 1987, pp. 141–60.

agricultural science developed largely in the temperate zone. Agricultural practices developed in Africa over the centuries to preserve soil fertility under tropical conditions were discouraged: they were forced to adopt monoculture instead of intercropping, and intensive agriculture with fertilizers instead of allowing cultivation to rotate and some land to remain fallow. Now that African soils, exhausted by these methods of producing cash crops, have deteriorated to the point where it is difficult to get them to produce enough food to sustain the increasing populations, scientists are beginning to draw attention to the rationality and wisdom of many traditional tropical agricultural practices:

> The destruction of forest cover made necessary . . . for large scale agriculture facilitates the degradation of the soil since the special nutrient cycling mechanism is upset leading to the degradation of the soil and consequent low agricultural productivity. In addition, the tilling of such soils facilitates oxidation of organic matter, accelerates the leaching of the little nutrients available, and disturbs the fragile ecological balance of the flora and the fauna with associated micro-organisms. As a result of the destruction of soil structure, the application of fertilizer under such conditions is a waste as the predominantly lateritic soils lack colloids which can absorb the applied fertilizer for subsequent release to plants. The high levels of iron and aluminum in such soil further neutralises the use of fertilizer as a strategy for higher agricultural productivity.[3]

As might have been expected, many African peoples both north and south of the Sahara had specialists with detailed knowledge of the weather and soil properties. They picked the location of settlements and farming areas carefully, and some societies had fertility cults to regulate agricultural practices through annual festivals and ritual observations. People like the Hausa, the Berber and the Igbo promoted good husbandry through competition and the conferment of titles on the most successful. Traditional skills in agronomy and soil conservation can still be seen in many places in Africa practising hill-top terraced agriculture undisturbed by colonial agricultural science.

Many African peoples had detailed knowledge of the varieties of tropical plants and trees in their neighbourhood. Even shrubs in the Sahara were carefully studied by the Berber and Arab nomads and cultivators. Elsewhere there were elaborate classifications of plants into families and sub-groups according to cultural and ritual properties which do not tally with modern botanical classification but were so detailed and complex that modern botanists have a lot to learn from the basis of comparison and classification. Knowledge of the pharmaceutical properties utilized in

3. A. O. Anya, 1986, pp. 11–12. See also P. Richards, 1985.

healing systems is now beginning to be investigated by Western-trained pharmacologists.[4]

From the Cape to Cairo there were detailed and elaborate studies of human and animal behaviour. These were classified into complex patterns from which traditional philosophers tried to draw analogies between human and animal behaviour. From such close observations, deductions were drawn about the essential nature and properties of different things. The intention of such analysis was often to discover the 'true' name of the thing, for it was only by knowing the true name and utilizing it in incantations that the thing could be controlled.[5]

Similarly, elaborate schemes of relationships in the spirit world were drawn up, deducting the behaviours of gods and spirit beings (*jinnis* in Muslim Africa) from the patterns of human and animal behaviour, and sometimes using the imagined patterns of the spirit world as models for human society. The consensus, based upon detailed observation and analysis, was sometimes processed into myths of creation, encoding beliefs about human nature and social psychology. Egyptians sometimes mixed pharaonic and Islamic ideas. But the example of the Dogon of Mali is the best documented in sub-Saharan Africa because they were studied by the devoted interpreters, Marcel Griaule and Germaine Dieterlen, who said:

> Within and beyond this totality of beliefs appears a logical scheme of symbols expressing a system of thought which cannot be described simply as myth. For this conceptual structure, when studied, reveals an internal coherence, a secret wisdom, and an apprehension of ultimate realities equal to that which we Europeans conceive ourselves to have attained.[6]

There were complex theories of numbers, observations of the stars and other natural phenomena which were used to produce some ordering of social, natural and metaphysical phenomena. From such ordering, diviners sought to predict the trend of events and advise clients what might be expected and how to prevent the intervention of evil forces. Egypt is the most complex. But *Ifa*, the Yoruba divination system, is probably the best documented elsewhere in Africa. A computer scientist has recently drawn attention to the similarity of the number structure in *Ifa* (multiples of four), and that of the computer system based on eight.

Among cultivators, there were specialist groups, particularly hunters as individuals and guilds, who acquired and classified knowledge of tropical animals in cultural terms. Some of this knowledge was applied

4. M. Last and G. L. Chavunduka, 1986. See also C. Wilcocks, 1962; and J. B. London, 1976.
5. Boubou Hama, 1981, pp. 170–2.
6. M. Griaule and G. Dieterlen, 1954, in D. Forde, 1954, p. 83. See also C. H. Long, 1985, pp. 369–70.

in healing systems largely on the basis of analogy: that bits of an animal prepared with herbs of known therapeutic value can pass on their characteristics to heal a person suffering from lack of those characteristics for which the animal was best known. Pastoralists such as the Fulbe and the Maasai, and some Somali, acquired extensive knowledge of their animals and their biological needs, and detailed knowledge of the animal world generally. From this many developed impressive veterinary knowledge and expertise, including noteworthy techniques of animal surgery. Some of this knowledge has been extended to surgical treatments of humans, and it is now believed that modern medicine has something to learn from such traditional surgical practices as used in therapeutic coagulation skin treatment and traditional methods of bone-setting. This last art – though more developed among some pastoralists – is a widespread skill in African medical practice. Broken legs and sprained ankles are treated much faster among traditional healers than in modern hospitals. The reputation of some African bone-setters spread so widely that medical researchers in distant lands like the Federal Republic of Germany, Scotland and Poland started focusing special investigative attention on African techniques. Such specialized African expertise has also been sought in the Middle East, sometimes through the intermediary of Arab Africa.

Traditional healing systems included some knowledge of the relationships between disease and micro-organisms and bacteria, which is at the core of Western scientific medicine. The Yoruba, ahead of even medieval Egypt, displayed a prior understanding of the relationship between diseases and what Western science called 'bacteria'. Yoruba medical culture was already predicated on a concept of 'worms' and 'insects' which were so small as to be invisible. These germs and worms had a beneficial as well as detrimental role in the body. Some of them attacked the body as a result of wrong food, excessive eating, or improper physical exertions and abuse of the body. Other 'insects' fought disease and sought to protect the healthy equilibrium of the body.

The germ and worm theory of disease was more widespread in Africa than many people realized. Evidence of a comparable paradigm has been found among the Tonga of South Africa. But the traditional healers proceeded on the assumption that health embraced more than controlling the injurious effects of bacteria on the physical plane and that the social and spiritual relationships of the patient also needed to be investigated and normalized. This holistic approach to healing is beginning to be appreciated and utilized by Western medicine, not least in the treatment of psychiatric disorders. The work of T. O. Lambo, the Nigerian psychiatrist, at the Aro Hospital of Mental Diseases in Nigeria is world-famous. He demonstrated the utility of involving local communities in the treatment of the mentally ill. He later became the Deputy Director-General of the World Health Organization (WHO).

Indeed, the rationality of this linkage between physical, social and spiritual well-being is beginning to be appreciated. For one thing, in the face of epidemics such as the Acquired Immune Deficiency Syndrome (AIDS) and other scourges for which a scientific solution is yet to be found, it offers the comfort of faith healing in spite of some unease on the part of Church authorities such as greeted the work of Bishop Emmanuel Milingo of Zambia. For another, it heightens a concern for the inter-dependence of man and the natural environment which is precisely what the advanced technologies of the Western world are beginning to wake up to. This appreciation should lead to a better understanding of traditional thought which, in the ordering of knowledge, accepted no dichotomies between the biological and the social, or the social and the metaphysical. This should ultimately end the prejudicial classification of traditional thought as pre-scientific. The emphasis on the holistic approach should, however, not obscure the purely scientific knowledge that was involved in the agricultural and healing systems, from Marrakesh to Maputo.

Indeed, African science and technology in the pre-colonial period were adequate to sustain life, especially in the areas of health care, agriculture, veterinary medicine and industrial processes such as food preservation, metallurgy, fermentation, the making of dyes, soaps, cosmetics and other toiletries. How then has Africa become so backward scientifically and technologically?

The disruption of Africa's technology

Africa's present scientific and technological backwardness is the outcome of the Western impact on the continent, especially since the establishment of colonialism. As this phenomenon has already been dealt with in Volume VII of the series, we will confine ourselves here to the scientific and technological issues. In the first place, with the establishment of colonial rule, the Europeans made it clear that they intended to use their advantage to dominate and exploit Africa and increase not only the technological but also the economic gap. They certainly showed no anxiety to reduce their advantage of superiority of science and technology which they enjoyed over Africa by any precipitous plans for the scientific and technological development of Africa. Rather, instead of stimulating and developing existing scientific and technological practices, they set out to discredit and discourage them, while secretly poaching some of these ideas and developing them within Western science. For example, principles of inoculation, metallurgy, fermentation and any of the other skills that could be used to compete with Western manufacturers were decried, made illegal and persecuted in other ways.

The most powerful factor that they used in inhibiting Africa's scientific and technological advancement was the school. First of all, formal schooling in colonial Africa was linked to the promotion of religion rather than the dissemination of science. So many of the schools were in fact Christian missionary schools. In its classes Mary Magdalen was far better known than Marie Curie, and the Law of Moses was more familiar than the Laws of Relativity. Young Africans like Kwame Nkrumah and Joseph Kasavubu were far more likely to dream of becoming priests one day than to dream of becoming physicists. The Bible was not of course a manual of technology. And yet in the first few decades of the twentieth century the Bible provided many of the aspirations and ideals of the emerging African intelligentsia.

Next to the missionary factor in inhibiting the scientification of Africa in this period was the more general literary orientation of education in French and British colonial schools. Western literary figures loomed larger as role models to colonial school children than did towering Western scientists. Obafemi Awolowo was inspired by Shakespeare himself, Kwame Nkrumah by Alfred Tennyson, Apollo Obote by John Milton (even adopting 'Milton' for his own middle name). In the biographies of the first generation of African leaders in the second half of the twentieth century one looks in vain for statesmen who had been significantly inspired by Copernicus, Galileo, Isaac Newton, Charles Darwin, Thomas Edison, Graham Bell, Henry Ford or Albert Einstein.[7]

The third colonial factor which inhibited the scientification of Africa in much of the twentieth century was indeed amnesia. Few African children outside Ethiopia knew anything about the sunken churches of Lalibela as an engineering achievement. Few children outside Southern Africa knew anything at all about the ruins of Great Zimbabwe – and very often those structures were in any case credited either to outright foreigners or to such ambiguous categories as 'Hamites'. Colonial curricula refused to acknowledge ancient Egypt as an African civilization, let alone a black one. Algerians were taught that their country was a backward extension of France. Nobody in a colonial school even raised the hypothesis that centuries before Columbus non-Europeans – perhaps even Africans – might have crossed the Atlantic to the Americas. Nobody referred to the evidence of Negroid sculptured figures in Mexico (*cabeza colossal*), pre-Columbian in origin and perhaps even pre-Christ.[8]

The scientification of twentieth-century Africa was slowed down partly because Africans were made to forget that they themselves had once been scientific achievers. Even Egyptians, who invented civilization, were taught to forget their role. This collective technological amnesia helped to create

7. For more relevant role models, consult J. A. Rogers, 1972; see also S. F. Mason, 1962.

8. The huge stone heads with Negroid physiognomy are now on display in Mexico City. The first head was discovered in 1869 by J. M. Melgar; archaeologists from the Smithsonian Institution later found further gigantic Negroid stone heads.

collective scientific impotence. It also fostered a deep-seated technological inferiority complex in large numbers of the new generation of colonized Africans. Inferiority complex and Africa's dependency complex were two sides of the same colonial coin.[9]

In addition to the missionary factor (the Bible as a priority), the literary factor (European languages and literature as blueprints) and the factor of amnesia (wiping Africa's technological slate clean), the colonial order also inhibited the march of science by its policy of 'pacification', especially in the first half of the twentieth century. Colonial policies based on 'pacification' and 'law and order' in themselves distrusted the more enterprising of the colonial subjects. Under such conditions, innovators were perceived as 'upstarts', debaters were 'agitators', self-confidence was 'cheek'.

Finally, the control of the economies and the obstacles placed in the way of industrialization in Africa also inhibited the spread of Western science and technology. Take textiles, for example. Africans in Egypt, Sudan, Uganda, northern Nigeria and elsewhere were made to grow cotton for export. Traditional dyes and design patterns in different parts of Africa were studied in Europe, and cheap textiles imitating those designs and dyes were imported into Africa, forcing hand-woven fabrics off the popular market to become occasional luxury items for ceremonial and ritual events. Similarly, imported household utensils, building materials, jewellery, toiletries and many food and drink items began to displace local manufactures. This was in addition to new demands created during the colonial period, such as school and hospital equipment, paper and other manufactured goods which had to be imported.[10]

Even communities that had lived by mining and metallurgy were prevented from working the mines except as unskilled labour. Mining areas were granted out as concessions to trans-national companies able to operate capital-intensive deep mines, and the Africans became illegal operators in the mines on their own land. The companies restricted the employment of Africans to unskilled or at best semi-skilled labour involving little or no transfer of science and technology. It should be particularly emphasized that it was in this very period when Africa's innovation was being deliberately sabotaged that Europe continued to keep ahead in the development of rockets, atomic and nuclear physics, communications, computers, electronics and high technology.

Law-and-order colonialism was basically a substitute for development colonialism. Belgian colonialism in Zaire was only marginally better than Portuguese colonialism in Angola.

It was in the 1940s that the British at long last tried to go beyond law-and-order colonialism into what they called 'colonial development and

9. Consult I. Van Sertima, 1986, and 1985; also C. Singer, 1959.

10. See, for example, P. Kilby, 1969; P. Pugh and J. F. A. Ajayi, 1990. For the impact of capital on the peoples of the Jos Plateau, see B. Freund, 1981.

welfare'. They even set up a fund by that name: the Colonial Development and Welfare Fund. Although developmental colonialism was to a large extent a contradiction in terms, even that contradiction was definitely an improvement on the arrogance of law-and-order colonialism.

It was this phase of developmental colonialism which allowed room for some expansion of education, especially at the tertiary level, partly by the award of scholarships for Africans to study in Europe, and even more by the establishment of degree-granting institutions, initially as outposts or colleges of metropolitan universities, at Ibadan, Legon, Makerere, Dakar and Lovanium in addition to older centres like Fourah Bay and Fort Hare. Their curriculum and staffing were controlled by the metropolitan universities who granted their degrees. They maintained high standards and initiated scientific research in areas of competence of the pioneering professors who came mostly from Europe. Some of the areas of strength included tropical human and veterinary medicine, especially parasitology and virology, epidemiological and biochemical investigations and establishing hospital baseline; in physics, ionosphere; in chemistry, natural products; in biology, ecology and mycology. Before the interference of politics and underfunding brought deterioration, the quality of some of the research won international acclaim. The principal areas of focus were extensions and supplementary to the research based in the metropolitan institutions.[11] Nevertheless, they did not include vital areas such as genetics and biotechnology, information science or computer technology. Instead, the university colleges were for the teaching of science rather than for advanced scientific research. Such dependent education inhibited indigenization. It developed individuals not within their culture and society but outside them. It kept the educated élite separate from the mass of society and thus stifled their creativity. From countries like Egypt the technological brain-drain to the Western world started early because of this alienation.

Institutions for scientific research and training required for the exploitation of African resources were based and developed in the European countries. Between the two world wars, stations for collecting data and specimens of flora and fauna, crafts and other local 'curiosities' were established as outposts of metropolitan museums, botanical and zoological gardens, and agriculture and forestry research institutions where basic research and possible applications were conducted. Generally, while the British expected each colony or regional group of colonies to initiate and fund the work of such stations, research organizations in France sponsored them, while the Belgians and Portuguese expected concessionaire companies to be the scientific and financial sponsors.[12]

In that inter-war period, the story of many of the stations, especially

11. For example, see J. F. A. Ajayi and T. N. Tamuno, 1973; and K. King, 1984.
12. J. W. Froje, 1989, pp. 19–22.

during the years of depression, was one of neglect, understaffing and underfunding. The French Pasteur Institute managed to achieve notable research in North Africa in tropical medicine, resulting in two Nobel Prizes, one to Alphonse Laverane in 1907 for his work on malaria, done mostly in Algiers, and the other to Henri Nicolle in 1928 for his research on typhus conducted principally in Tunis. The IFAN (*Institut français d' Afrique Noire*; French Institute of Black Africa), an interdisciplinary research institute established in Dakar in 1936 with branches in each French West African colony, was also relatively successful in stimulating research, and was later to be the centre for much of Cheikh Anta Diop's work. The Belgians also set up in 1947 the important IRSAC (*Institut pour la recherche scientifique d'Afrique Centrale*; Institute for Scientific Research in Central Africa) to serve all Belgian dependencies in Africa. The aims of the IRSAC, with its headquarters in Brussels, were defined as follows in the Decree which established the Institute on 1 July 1947: 'The purpose of the institution shall be to sponsor, promote, perform and coordinate the study of human sciences and of nature, more particularly in the Belgian Congo and in Rwanda-Urundi' (Article 2). A centre for agronomic research had already been established in the Belgian Congo in 1933 and was destined to acquire great international prestige: the *Institut national d'études agronomiques au Congo* (Congo National Institute for Agronomic Studies). Its main centre was located in the heart of the equatorial forest at Yangambi in the Eastern province of Congo, now known as Upper Zaire.

In most of Africa, the commonest colonial establishments were not science laboratories or research institutes but either workshops for maintenance of the railways, telegraphs, radio stations and survey equipment or experimental stations to improve the yield and processing of cash crops for export. The best of these were to be found in areas of European settlement such as Algeria, Kenya, Rhodesia and South Africa where settler-farmers exerted pressure on local administrations for the provision of research facilities to serve their exclusive interests. It was also in such areas, particularly the mining areas, that the potential for industrialization first emerged. In South Africa, the rich diamond and gold deposits attracted large capital investments, and settlers to manage the investments and supervise mining technology. Prosperity in the mining areas, autonomy won by the settler communities after the South African War and the shortage of imported manufactured goods during the First World War – all these set off the manufacturing sector of the South African economy. This led to an expansion of the universities and research institutes and strengthened the base of Western science and technology in South Africa as an exclusive preserve of the whites.[13]

Thus, the impact of Western science and technology on Africa during

13. A. C. Brown, 1988.

the colonial period was to strengthen underdevelopment. It was exhibited to impress and overawe Africans, shaking their confidence in traditional knowledge and expertise while keeping Western science and technology beyond reach. A few Africans managed to get to Europe to train as medical doctors but, because of discrimination in the colonial service, they usually had to operate as self-employed general practitioners, with no opportunities for research. Very few African students opted for engineering or advanced science as there was no scope for them to practise outside the restricted colonial service. More usually, Africans trained as pastors, teachers, administrators and lawyers.[14] Thus, we cannot expect to find a research scientist among the first generation of African top leaders, though one was trained in pharmacy (Algeria's Ferhat Abbas) and three of them were medical doctors (Félix Houphouët-Boigny, Agostinho Neto and Kamuzu Banda). The mass of people, impressed as they were by the marvels of European science, continued to live as best as they could by the traditional agricultural and healing systems, crafts and industries, while trying to buy predominantly literary Western education for their children. Yet traditional knowledge continued to exert its cultural force even on the Western-educated élite, and many a university graduate found occasion to consult traditional diviners and healers.

Developments since independence

In the second half of the twentieth century, when most African countries became independent, advanced scientific research in Africa took place in four types of institution. The first category were universities whose establishment was given a tremendous push following the initial nationalist enthusiasm of the 1950s and 1960s. These have produced the most widespread centres of advanced scientific research in their departments of science, engineering, agriculture and medicine. Countries like Nigeria, Ghana and Côte d'Ivoire have been able to sustain a high level of university expansion, and a few specialist universities devoted to science and technology of agriculture, but not yet medicine, have emerged.

The University of East Africa while it lasted (1963–70) was perhaps the most ambitious pan-African academic experiment. Medical and agricultural teaching and research were supposed to be a specialization of Makerere College in Uganda; engineering (teaching and research) was entrusted to the University College, Nairobi. The University College, Dar es Salaam, initially specialized in law, and later expanded into agricultural and economic research. Almost all the organs of the University of East Africa were initially intended to serve not merely the particular country in which they were located but the East African community as

14. For even more relevant role models, see J. A. Rogers, 1972; see also S. F. Mason, 1962.

a whole (Kenya, Tanzania and Uganda). The level of research into medical problems at Mulago Hospital and the Makerere Faculty of Medicine was so high in the 1960s that there were periodic rumours about a possible Nobel Prize for Medicine. Unfortunately no such prize materialized before the University of East Africa itself collapsed into its three national constituent parts. Later on Makerere University as a national institution was further damaged by the political turmoil into which Uganda was thrown after Idi Amīn captured political power in 1971.

The second category of institution is national research centres and institutions, both private and public-funded. Kenya and Nigeria have such institutes in disease control, forestry and agriculture; Zaire and Ghana in nuclear physics; Nigeria in oceanography. Nigeria, Zimbabwe and Zaire have paid considerable attention to traditional herbal medicine as an area of modern research. The Kenya Medical Research Institute under the leadership of Dr Davy Koech entered the 1990s at the forefront of research against Acquired Immune Deficiency Syndrome (AIDS). In February 1990, the Research Institute even claimed to have developed an anti-AIDS treatment drug which it called KEMRON.[15]

In 1966, IRSAC, referred to earlier, was restructured and reorganized as the ONRD (*Office national pour la recherche et le développement*; National Office for Research and Development). A few years later, it was given the new name of *Institut de recherche scientifique* (Scientific Research Institute); today, it operates a number of centres throughout Zaire, each specifically dedicated to research in a branch of natural science, the human sciences and primate studies, and also in various branches of technology. There are also national academies of science to encourage and reward excellence.

The third category of research institution in Africa is that of regional pan-African organizations and structures. Some of these have been concerned with climatic and ecological studies specific to the particular areas of Africa, such as the Sahel; others have co-operated on such regional concerns as the movement of locusts.

A special kind of pan-African scholarly or scientific organization is the professional association or academy of specialists. Cheikh Anta Diop even attempted to pan-Africanize research beyond the borders of Africa – encompassing the black world as a whole. That was the purpose of the World Black Researchers Association which was formed in 1976, and of which Diop became president. As Diop himself put it in his presidential statement:

15. For a detailed report of the work of the Kenya Medical Research Institute against AIDS, see the special issue of *The Weekly Review* (Nairobi), 9 February 1990. It should be noted that although the Kenya Institute's research work against AIDS has been admired and encouraged, its claims about the anti-AIDS drug KEMRON are widely regarded by scientists as having been 'premature'.

The association will englobe all the scientific disciplines, both the natural and social sciences. . . . In both domains scholars and scientists of the black world will be asked to direct their efforts toward solving the most vital scientific and sociological problems presently confronting the black world. This will further solidify the cultural ties binding all black populations of the globe.[16]

The final category of institutions which conduct or promote African scientific and technological research is that of international and intercontinental research organizations which go beyond the pan-African scientific fraternity. Thomas Odhiambo heads a major international community of scholars (ICIPE – International Centre of Insect Physiology and Ecology) devoted to an understanding of the world of insects. This is quite apart from Odhiambo's leadership of the African Academy of Sciences – a pan-African instrument of scholarship and academic excellence with its headquarters in Nairobi. The Academy issues a scientific magazine of its own entitled *Discovery and Innovation*, co-sponsored by the Third World Academy of Sciences.[17] The United Nations University Institute for Natural Resources in Africa (INRA) located in Yamoussoukro (Côte d'Ivoire) is yet to take off.

Nigeria plays host to the International Institute of Tropical Agriculture (IITA) with a focus on improving varieties of African food crops as distinct from cash crops. African scientists like Bede Okigbo have been prominent on its staff and the Institute has had significant success, for example in developing disease-resistant cassava varieties.[18] Cheikh Anta Diop's radiocarbon laboratory at IFAN in Dakar included national, pan-African as well as intercontinental scopes at different times. The laboratory came into being in 1966, committed to the study of low-energy radioactivity and carbon-14 dating.[19]

In the 1970s, the OAU, UNESCO and the ECA have jointly also been paying some attention to the development of science and technology in Africa. The First Conference of Ministers of African Member States responsible for the application of science and technology to development was held in Dakar (Senegal) in January 1974; this conference was organized by UNESCO in association with the OAU and the UN Economic Commission for Africa, and resulted in the adoption of recommendations for policies on science and technology.

A regional meeting for Africa was held in Cairo (Egypt) in 1978, in

16. See I. Van Sertima, 1989, p. 11.

17. In June 1986 the African Academy of Sciences co-sponsored a unique international event in Nairobi – the first conference of the Network of African Scientific Organizations – which signalled new areas of co-operation among scholars and scientists of both Africa and the rest of the world.

18. A summary of the disease-resistant cassava varieties is given in World Bank, 1989b, pp. 95–6.

19. See I. Van Sertima, 1989.

preparation for the UN Conference on Science and Technology for Development (UNCSTD), which took place in Vienna (Austria) in August 1979. Its main aim was to find ways and means of bridging the economic gulf between the Third World and the industrialized countries. This matter – which was broached, but dealt with only superficially in Vienna – was to be examined in more detail at a series of specific conferences held in each of the regions concerned.

At the sixteenth ordinary session of the Assembly of Heads of State and Government of the OAU, held in Monrovia (Liberia) in July 1979, the Monrovia Declaration of Commitment was adopted, in which the heads of state and government of the OAU expressed their will to put science and technology in the service of development by reinforcing the autonomous capacity of their countries in this field. The Assembly of Heads of State and Government of the OAU, Second Extraordinary Session, held in Lagos (Nigeria) on 28–29 April 1980 also adopted the *Lagos Plan of Action*. Chapter V of the plan in particular is devoted to science and technology and calls attention to the role of science and technology in integrated rural development.

A symposium on African science and culture as the bases of development was organized by the OAU in co-operation with UNESCO in Libreville (Gabon) from 23 to 27 January 1981; one resolution adopted at this symposium called upon the OAU to organize a meeting of scientists in Africa. Four years later, the twenty-first ordinary session of the Assembly of Heads of State and Government of the OAU, held in Addis Ababa (Ethiopia) on 18–20 July 1985 adopted Africa's Priority Programme for Economic Recovery, 1986–1990. Paragraph 34 of the programme states: 'Experience indicates that no country has attained any breakthrough in its economic development without the development of a minimum science and technology base'. At this same session, the heads of state and government of the OAU adopted resolution AHG.Res. 146 (XXI) calling on UNESCO to draw up a Programme of Assistance to Africa in the fields of scientific research and research/development, aimed primarily at developing the scientific and technical potential of African countries in the fields of geology, microbiology, agriculture, food, health, surface and underground waters.

Finally, the Second Conference of Ministers Responsible for the Application of Science and Technology to Development in Africa (Arusha, United Republic of Tanzania, 6–15 July, 1987) adopted a special Programme of Assistance to Africa in the Fields of Scientific and Technological Research and of Research and Development. The highly-realistic Special Programme sets out an objective analysis of the economic, social and cultural situation in Africa. Reference is first made here to the main obstacles, including those resulting from mental attitudes and education, which inhibit or handicap efforts to bring about economic and social development. The programme goes on to indicate the general conditions

647

for scientific development at national and regional levels, while also taking account of the environment which may or may not be propitious for scientific and technological research. Finally, research priorities are proposed, together with the procedures and strategies to be followed for the promotion of science and technology at three levels: national, sub-regional and regional.[20]

Inter-African agencies with non-governmental status, but still enjoying the support and encouragement of the OAU and the African states, have also proliferated in recent years. These include the *Institut africain d'études prospectives* (INADEP; the African Forecasting Institute), the Institute for Black Peoples (IBP) and the Pan-African Union for Science and Technology (PUST).

INADEP was established in Kinshasa in 1989 in response to a request put forward by African scientists and senior officials at a major symposium held in Kinshasa (Zaire) in 1985 on the subject of Africa and its future. A Centre for Egyptological Studies (CECAD), dedicated to the memory of Cheikh Anta Diop, has been attached to this institute.

The Institute for Black Peoples (IBP), was established in Ouagadougou (Burkina Faso) in 1990 with the aim of promoting the widest possible scientific knowledge of the black world. The Pan-African Union for Science and Technology (PUST) was set up on 30 June 1987 with its headquarters in Brazzaville, Congo, and is the most important of them all. At its Second Congress, PUST proposed a number of research sectors as being of priority interest for the development of Africa and the well-being of its population. Particular emphasis was placed on:

- traditional medicine and the study of medicinal plants;
- agriculture and self-sufficiency in foodstuffs;
- new and renewable energy sources;
- rational use of mineral resources;
- rational use of marine resources;
- progress towards industrialization;
- bio-technologies;
- catastrophes and natural disasters;
- peaceful applications of nuclear research (in agriculture, medicine and the economy).

Wide-ranging and detailed studies were recommended in the following areas: scientific education, scientific and technological planning at the regional level in every country, ways and means of disseminating scientific knowledge in Africa (cf. Second Congress of African Scientists, Accra, Ghana PUST, 1989). PUST in association with the American Association for the Advancement of Science has also published the *Directory of*

20. CASTAFRICA Special Programme of Assistance to Africa in the fields of Scientific and Technological Research and of Research and Development, 1987.

Scientific and Engineering Societies in Africa which gives an idea of the scale of the scientific and technological research movement in Africa.

Perhaps the most global of all the major organizations committed to science in Africa is the United Nations Environmental Programme (UNEP), with its headquarters in Nairobi. It has been encouraging and promoting ecological and climatic research not just in Africa but throughout the world. Two of its most passionate crusades of the 1980s concerned the issues of global warming and the question of ozone depletion to which we shall return later.

Post-colonial Africa is trying to recover from the stultifying impact of colonial rule upon its capacity for scientific research and technological innovation. The pace of recovery has been slow – though by no means insignificant. Some outstanding individual scientists have emerged in practically every field, but in no field – and in no country outside South Africa and to a lesser extent Egypt – has a critical mass capable of self-sustaining growth been realized. Many African scientists survive either because they work in foreign-assisted agencies or have links with research institutions abroad. Some achieve their best work in laboratories abroad on projects they do not control. Others get results that are not fed into industries because the industries are locked into technologies pre-determined from abroad. African scientists work against all odds in terms of the shortage of funds, equipment, uncertain supply of water and electricity, computer facilities and other means of communicating with colleagues and against a background of chronic political instability. They further exemplify the view that science is not developed by scientists alone but by society as a whole. Thus, the most significant trend in science in Africa is the evolving science policy of African states and the growing network of research institutions which are capable of being developed to create the necessary critical mass. The centres which hold promise, however constrained, do include national universities, national research centers, pan-African organizations, pan-African professional associations and intercontinental research institutions and scholarly communities.

Africa's contribution to Europe's industrialization

It has been pointed out already that it was in the colonial and post-colonial period that Europe further widened the gap between her and Africa. The question to be considered now is how Africa has contributed to this development since independence. It is quite clear from the available evidence that Africa's impact on Western technological change in the second half of the twentieth century, as in previous centuries, has been greater and more profound than the impact of the West on industrialization, science and technology in Africa. Indeed, the balance of indebtedness is in the reverse direction.

649

Western industry and technology still rely greatly on a wide range of strategic minerals from Africa. The great proportion of minerals extracted from Africa is for Western industry – very little is for Africa's own technological needs. The Third World generally produces a third of the key minerals of the world economy, but the developing countries use only one-twentieth of those minerals. Africa's share of consumption is small even by Third-World standards, but Africa's share of reserves and of production is impressive.

In the period covered by this volume, Africa has sometimes had up to 90 per cent of the world's cobalt reserves, the bulk of this being in Zaire. Africa has had at times over 80 per cent of the world's reserves of chrome, more than 50 per cent of the reserves of gold, nearly half of the planet's reserves of platinum and nearly all of the so-called 'non-communist' reserve of industrial diamonds. These are some of the strategic industrial minerals.

Then there are the exchange minerals – of which the most important is gold, often relevant for funding research as well as trade. Most of the African reserves are in Southern Africa, but there was considerable gold in other parts of the continent as well. For parts of the period since 1935, gold has provided some of the support of the international monetary system. A disrupted gold market could from time to time endanger the world's system of exchange.

Thirdly, there are Africa's fuel minerals – of high technological relevance. The continent in this period has had up to a third of the world's reserves of uranium. Africa's share of natural gas is expanding, especially in the North African countries. And of course Africa is well represented in the Organization of Petroleum Exporting Countries (OPEC) by Nigeria, Algeria, Libya and Gabon. It should also be noted that Zaire is the chief source of the world's radium – located in the uranium ores of the Shinkolobwe–Kasolo area.

Less clearly technological are Africa's gems and precious metals. The bulk of the world's gem diamonds still come from Africa. Africa in this period since 1935 had up to 80 per cent of the world's tantalum. Africa's share of the world's silver is small, but Africa's precious stones are diverse, ranging from sapphires to topaz, from malachite to opals, from rubies to tanzanite. Sometimes this wealth has indeed not only catered for the consumption patterns of others but has also helped their productive capacity.

Africa's metallic deposits also include substantial amounts of manganese, iron ore, copper, vanadium (a rare element to toughen steel), bauxite (the chief aluminium ore), lead and zinc. There is no doubt about the technological relevance of these. Many a Western factory in this period would have ground to a standstill without Africa's metallic inputs.

Then there are Africa's non-metallic deposits. Large deposits of phosphates stretch from Morocco to Senegal. Other phosphate deposits occur in the Great Lakes area. In Madagascar, Africa possesses the largest-known accumulation of flake-graphite deposits in the world. And the People's Republic of the Congo has had potash deposits in this period which were regarded as among the largest in the world.

There is no doubt that in the period since 1935 the biggest beneficiary of all this mineral wealth has been the West and its factories and laboratories. In the 1970s the United States was importing nearly half its manganese from Africa. A major reason why the West was bailing out Mobutu Sese Seko so often in those years was the importance of Zaire's cobalt for Western technology and industry. It was said at the time that the West would go to war to keep Zaire within the Western orbit. Niger's uranium mining was designed and developed in the 1970s specifically for the French nuclear programme. Iron ore from Swaziland went directly into Nippon steel.

In addition to being the main consumer of Africa's mineral wealth, the West was the main manager of that wealth. A few Western firms controlled the processing, manufacturing and marketing of Africa's resources. Anglo-American, Debeers, Roan Selection Trust, the old *Union Minière*, were only a few of the names that shaped this phase of Africa's contribution to Western technological development. This was quite apart from the oil giants – Shell, British Petroleum (BP), Gulf, Exxon, Mobil, Chevron, Texaco and smaller independents. Even the smaller ones often had a capital value which was greater than the gross national product of the majority of African states.

Of the two major areas of African production (agriculture and mining), mining was both the more capital-intensive and the more skill-intensive. It needed a lot of money to initiate and needed a lot of technological skill to operate and maintain. In the absence of an adequate Western transfer of technical and managerial skills to Africans, and against the background of Western trans-national corporations dominating the field, mining in Africa remained a preserve of Westerners even when African governments ostensibly put it under state ownership. Reliance on Western expertise and Western marketing often perpetuated the Eurocentric orientation of African mining.

When Africa's contribution to industrialism in the West was mainly through the export of labour (the slave trade), the Americas rather than Europe directly were the main importers of the slave labour. In this latest phase of mineral contribution to Western technology and industrialism since 1935, it was Europe that was the main importer. However, in both phases, the economic interconnection between European economies and those of the Americas made African resources fundamental to almost all sectors of the West's technological civilization. In the final analysis, Africa's contribution to science and technology in this period goes far beyond the work of individual African scientists. Discoveries and inventions are not made by lone researchers out of a social vacuum. Africa's biggest contribution in this field in the period since 1935 has been through the impact of Africa's labour and resources upon the factories and laboratories of the world. African minerals were the aphrodisiac of Western technological potency.

Isaac Newton was not a modest or humble man. In a self-deprecating moment he once conceded that he had seen as far as he had as a scientist because he had been 'standing on the shoulders of giants'. He was acknowledging his debt to previous towering scientists. It is also true that every major achievement in the history of science and technology has been made not simply by standing on the shoulders of previous scientific giants but more often by being carried on the backs of the less-advantaged classes. The pyramids were not simply the achievements of Egyptian engineering: they were also the triumph of Egyptian labour. Ferdinand de Lesseps used to be honoured with a statue on the bank of the Suez Canal as the innovator who promoted and sponsored the great waterway. The statue was angrily pulled down after al-Nasser nationalized the Suez Canal Company in 1956. The statue had honoured the single French planner who championed the canal and forgot the hundreds of thousands of Egyptians who built it, and literally *perished* in doing so. Who was the true builder of the Suez Canal – de Lesseps; or Egyptian labour, toil and economic martyrdom?

Great engineers may or may not have stood on the shoulders of previous engineering giants. What is certain is that they have almost always been carried on the backs of some wider society. In the modern phase of Western science and technology, it was not just the backs of Western workers which sustained the West's technological lead. It was also the resources and labour of Africans and Asians under European domination.

Bertrand Russell once said that civilization was born out of the pursuit of luxury. The frontiers of Western science and technology have been pushed forward partly in pursuit of capitalist luxury. The people of Africa were among those who have *financed* Western science and technology for over three hundred years. Africans have subsidized Western science from the slave plantations of the New World to the mines of Kimberley.

However, by 1958, it was Eastern Europe which launched the space age, with Sputnik. Was space travel the ultimate luxury? Yuri Gagarin before long became the first man in space. The first black man to go into space had to wait until the United States caught up in the space-race. Africa was participating in the new age partly through its resources, partly through its black *diaspora* in the United States, partly through space observation centres like the one in Kenya, and increasingly through the small but historically-significant body of African astronomers. Civilization was seeking a new frontier of creative luxury – and Africa was part of the effort.

Between global warming and nuclear winter

But simultaneously with the world's increasing fascination with other planets was a new global anxiety about the safety of Planet Earth itself. This anxiety has reached new levels precisely in the period since 1935. Originally African culture was – in its values – far more protective of the environment than Western science had increasingly become. At least for a while Western technology was 'bad news' for Planet Earth. The reckless destruction of vegetation, the pollution of lakes and rivers with acid rain and other hazards, the slow poisoning of the atmosphere – were all ways in which Western technology had declared war on the human habitat. Africa, as well as the rest of the world, was endangered.

To make matters worse, Africa's more environmentalist values were under attack. Traditional African culture had started from the premise that the whole universe, and not merely 'man', had been created in the image of God. And so many African societies made some trees sacred, some hills holy, some animals totemic siblings, some forests the abode of ancestors. African cultures made no sharp distinction between the human race and other species. While some monkeys were sacred, some humans were evil.

Such philosophies were inherently protective of the environment – sharing sacredness with it. But many colonized Africans permitted their values to be prostituted by the new commercialization and consumerism which came with Western capitalism and colonialism. Hence the African environment suffered both from the activities of outsiders and from the greed of those who might deservedly be called ecological traitors. Particularly poignant were the depletion of Africa's rain forests and the endangering of many African species of animals. Reckless Western technology and consumerism sometimes triumphed over African environmentalist values – and the human race was increasingly the poorer for it. Deforestation is still contributing to the warming up of the climate. When combined with carbon-dioxide and other 'greenhouse gases', the climate of the world as we know it is increasingly at risk.

As a partial redress, the United Nations decided to base its global Environmental Programme (UNEP) in Africa (Nairobi) – the first United Nations specialized agency to have its headquarters in the Third World. Africa was struggling to recover its moral leadership in the protection of Planet Earth against the dangers of the new technology and the insensitivities of the industrial age. After initial neglect, UNEP by the late 1980s was beginning to be taken more seriously. While other UN agencies were tightening their belts, UNEP was expecting its budget to be doubled.

When, in March 1989, the world began to confront more firmly the threat to the ozone layer and new commitments were called for, Africa's participation at the London conference was led by Daniel Arap Moi, the president of Kenya himself. It was a fitting role for the head of state of the host country to the UNEP. The 1989 London meeting was also addressed by Prime Minister Margaret Thatcher. A follow-up meeting in Helsinki in May 1989 on the ozone layer made further progress in seeking to phase out the dangerous anti-ozone chemicals (chloro-fluorocarbons – CFCs) by the end of the twentieth century. The head of UNEP, Mustafa Tolba, was one of the organizational leaders at Helsinki. He applauded the progress which had been made to protect the ozone layer since the earlier meetings on the subject in Montreal and London. UNEP planned more meetings on the defence of the ozone layer in the 1990s.

It is one of the ironies of imperial history that the dangers of artificial refrigeration have at last caught up with the human race in relation to the ozone layer. Now that Africa is learning this new technology at home, and countries like Algeria are manufacturing their own refrigerators, the urgent consequences for the ozone layer have become more manifest. The chloro-fluorocarbon gases (CFCs) emitted by refrigeration and air-conditioning are among the most hazardous to the ozone layer. Africa and the rest of the Third World are being called upon to *unlearn* these new skills – immediately after acquiring them. The techniques of creating artificial winter conditions by refrigeration in precisely those countries without a natural winter would now expose the human species to more sunlight and ultra-violet rays than is safe for the human skin.

Other technologies newly learnt by Africa and other developing regions have also been contributing to the rising levels of gases like carbon monoxide. Those levels were already made dangerous by the factories and consumer patterns of the industrialized world. Those richer countries of the world can now switch technologies even at this late hour and still help to save the climate of this planet. The developing countries will find it harder and doubly expensive to have to unlearn those new technologies – unless global funds are made available to ease the transition. Soon after the conference in Helsinki on the ozone layer in May 1989, UNEP sponsored a meeting in Nairobi on the greenhouse effect. Problems of funding and the costs of de-industrialization loomed large. What was at stake ultimately was something which endangered all species – the endangered climate of Planet Earth. The future of *winter* on earth was indeed on the line.

However, there is another danger facing Planet Earth whose conse-quences could be almost exactly the opposite of the demise of winter. This is the danger of there being nothing else but winter – the devastating risk of *nuclear winter*. The human race has entered the nuclear age in this period since 1935. The implications of this stage of science and technology have still not been fully understood. However, by the 1980s the horrendous risk of plunging the world into an endless winter had at last been grasped in large sections of the scientific community world-wide. Nuclear war could mean not the end of winter but its ultimate triumph. Such a war could keep *out* the sun from human habitation rather than increase its presence. A new dark age could descend upon Planet Earth – but in the most literal sense of the term 'dark': even the white man would have stopped calling Africa 'the dark continent'. The world itself would be one large, ominous dark mass of water, territory and endless fog.

In 1960 Kwame Nkrumah sensed the danger of this new science, but was ambivalent about how Africa should respond to it. Other chapters show how Nkrumah was decidedly outraged by France's use of the Sahara desert for nuclear tests. Ghana encouraged and helped organize an international march of protest against the Sahara tests – although the protestors' movement across borders was blocked. Nkrumah froze French assets in Ghana.

But Kwame Nkrumah lived at a time when it was still believed that a distinction could realistically be made between 'safe' nuclear knowledge for peaceful purposes and 'dangerous' nuclear technology for war.[21] Working on this assumption, Nkrumah inaugurated a nuclear research programme in his own country. He declared that Africa had to enter the nuclear age and learn its new science and technology. He also asserted that the socialist option in Africa had to be firmly married to the scientific spirit. To Nkrumah, socialism was one *philosophy* which had to be simultaneously a *science*. In Nkrumah's words: 'Socialism without science is void'.[22]

Ghana's attempted entry into the atomic age came after Zaire's. The Belgians had established a nuclear research reactor in the late 1950s in what was then the Congo. When Zaire became independent the research continued – and the scientific personnel was increasingly Africanized. In spite of all the vicissitudes that wider Zairean society has gone through in the last 30 years, nuclear research still continues in Kinshasa.

President Shehu Shagari in Nigeria (1979–83) also encouraged his own country to start pursuing the nuclear option. Unlike Zaire and Ghana, Shagari's regime defended the nuclear option partly for military reasons. According to Shagari, there was still a link between racism and the nuclear threat. In Nkrumah's day, the nuclear threat was in the north (in the Sahara) while the racist threat was in the south (in South Africa). But by President Shagari's time, both threats were now perceived in the south. *Apartheid* had acquired a nuclear capability. Shagari saw Nigeria's pursuit of nuclear technology partly as a response to the nuclearization of South Africa from the 1970s onwards.

And yet as the century comes to a close the chances are that the first black nuclear country could well be black-ruled South Africa. When the Republic is finally liberated, much of the industrial infrastructure will probably remain. It is more than possible that enough of the nuclear

21. K. Nkrumah, 1961, p. 213.
22. See *Ghana Today*, vol. 8, no. 21, 1964, p.1.

reactors will also remain, ready to resume work after the war of liberation. Much of the white population may also remain, or after a temporary departure return to live in that beautiful land.

Perhaps the very fact that the nuclear club acquires a black member early in the twenty-first century may cause enough consternation in the northern hemisphere to motivate all Northerners to search more effectively for truly universal nuclear disarmament. Many Westerners believe that nuclear weapons are not for Africans and children under 16. Perhaps this particular form of racist consternation could be put to good use when black-ruled South Africa joins the nuclear club. A frightened humanity could at last be genuinely converted to global nuclear disarmament, and the threat of the nuclear winter could at last be truly averted.

The social and human sciences

As for the impact of Africa on the social and human sciences, this has taken two main forms. One kind of impact does lie in the uniqueness of the African continent itself, and the attraction it has held for scholars and scientists from all over the world. The other kind of African impact has come from the contributions of African researchers and social scientists, pushing forward the frontiers of both knowledge and theory.

The scientific attractiveness of Africa included the fascination of its cultures for social and cultural anthropologists, the mysteries of its fossils for archaeologists and palaeontologists, and the challenges of the oral tradition for historians. By studying Africa, the world has learnt about itself – and the human species has learnt about its own nature and its own origins.

But it is not merely Africa as an object of study which has pushed forward the frontiers of the social and human sciences. It has also been Africans themselves as scientists and researchers. Both forms of African impact on the corpus of human knowledge have been particularly extensive in the period since 1935.

In a sense the social and human sciences lie somewhere between the physical sciences on the one side and philosophy on the other. Much of the social theorizing which is going on among sociologists, economists, political scientists and others provides a bridge between the concerns of the natural scientists and the preoccupations of philosophers. This chapter addresses the social sciences partly in terms of that role as a bridge between science and philosophy.

Africa has provided the basic ground for some of the major theorizing on economic growth in less industrialized societies in the twentieth century. The African *diaspora* has been particularly visible in liberal economic theory – with special reference to Sir Arthur Lewis from St Lucia, in the British West Indies, who won the Nobel Prize for economic science in 1979 (shared with Theodore W. Shultz, an American). Lewis's

656

achievement was in studies on economic development – with special reference to his theory linking North–South terms of trade with comparative levels of labour productivity in industrialized and less industrialized countries.

William Arthur Lewis served as adviser to governments both in Africa and the Caribbean, including Kwame Nkrumah's government in Ghana. Lewis's most influential books were *The Theory of Economic Growth* (1955), *Development Planning* (1966) and *Growth and Fluctuations, 1870–1913* (1978). William Arthur Lewis was knighted in 1963.

In radical economic theory, Samir Amin of Egypt led the way in the 1970s, exploring the nature of unequal economic exchange in a world in which capitalism had become global. Samir Amin's work was often a remarkable fusion of theoretical refinement with hard empirical data from such countries as Côte d'Ivoire.[23]

Nigeria's Adebayo Adedeji occupied a middle ground between liberal and radical economic theory. As Executive Secretary of the United Nations' Economic Commission for Africa (ECA), Adedeji in the 1970s and 1980s challenged the conventional economic wisdom of the World Bank and the International Monetary Fund (IMF) on the causes of persistent underdevelopment in Africa. Adedeji and the ECA emphasized the global constraints on Africa's development; the World Bank and the IMF often focused on Africa's 'mismanagement' and 'errors in policy'. Jointly with the Organization of African Unity, the ECA provided the basic economic analysis for the historic *Lagos Plan of Action*, which was adopted in 1980 by African heads of state. The *Lagos Plan* provided an alternative explanatory paradigm to the Elliot Berg Report of the World Bank of 1979. Paradigms of economic development were in conflict once again.[24]

In political science, Africa provided the challenges of nation-building, state-formation, political dependency, political development and political decay. International theories of all these issues in the post-colonial period have been deeply influenced by the ups and downs of African experience. One-party theories, civil–military relations, and philosophies of indigenous socialism have all been dramatically stimulated by African political realities.

Observers have sometimes assumed that Africa's theorists of dependency have simply followed the lead of Latin America's *dependencia* theorists of the 1970s. It is worth remembering that Kwame Nkrumah published his book *Neo-Colonialism: The Last Stage of Imperialism* before he was overthrown in 1966. And Ali A. Mazrui developed his ideas about 'Neo-Dependency and Africa's Fragmentation' in his D.Phil. thesis for

23. S. Amin, 1974a, 1974b, 1976, 1977.
24. A. Adedeji, 1976a, 1981, 1989; ECA, 1976, 1989a, 1989b, 1990; Organization of African Unity, 1981; World Bank, 1989b, 1990; UN, 1990.

Oxford University in the 1960s and published them in his subsequent book, *Towards a Pax Africana* (1967)[25]

Africa has been the pre-eminent laboratory of the study of languages. With one-tenth of the population of the world, Africa has about a quarter of its languages – apart from being the birthplace of human language itself. The range of languages in twentieth-century Africa has been from tonal languages like Yoruba to click languages like Xhosa, from Semitic languages like Amharic and Arabic to southern Bantu like Sindebele and Chichewa.[26]

In the period since 1935, external scholars who have had the most influence on the classification of African languages have included M. Guthrie of Britain and J. H. Greenberg of the USA. Their work has depended on whole 'armies' of African experts of African languages. Inevitably scholars like Guthrie and Greenberg have had to stand on the shoulders of African linguists themselves.[27]

Estimates of the number of indigenous languages spoken in Africa have ranged from hundreds to thousands – partly depending upon where a dialect is supposed to end and another distinct language supposed to begin.

> Even though Africa has perhaps the largest number of languages per capita of any area in the world, it is possible to group these languages into language families. Linguists base their typologies either on word similarities (e.g. Greenberg 1966...) or in historical relatedness (e.g. Guthrie 1948). The Greenberg typology is perhaps the most widely accepted...[28]

Once again, Africa's own uniqueness and complexity have continued to fascinate some of the best scholarly minds of the twentieth century – both within Africa itself and abroad. The birthplace of human language itself continues to constitute a rich diversity of verbal wealth.

A majority of Africans are probably multi-lingual. This makes the region also attractive for the study of socio-linguistics more generally. Africa is also a laboratory for the study of language policy and national integration. Scholars like Pathé Diagne of Senegal and Muhamad Hassan Abdulaziz of Kenya have been among the contributors to the unfolding scholarly discourse on these issues.[29]

Social and cultural anthropology developed as a discipline partly under the stimulation of the study of African societies. Western anthropologists

25. See K. Nkrumah, 1966; and A. A. Mazrui, 1967.

26. Papua New Guinea is widely regarded as having the widest diversity of languages per square mile in the world – but most of those are languages with only a few hundred speakers each.

27. J. H. Greenberg, 1966; M. Guthrie, 1948.

28. D. G. Morrison with R. C. Mitchell and J. N. Paden, 1989, p. 46.

29. See Chapter 18, above.

early in the century were often paternalistic towards the 'tribes' they were studying, but in the period since 1935 African scholars were beginning to correct Western condescension. Jomo Kenyatta's *Facing Mount Kenya* was published in 1938, and constituted an important milestone in the re-Africanization of ethnology. On African campuses the name 'anthropology' has not yet recovered from its previous reputation as 'the science of studying primitive societies'. Many African universities prefer the term 'sociology' to cover the study of both industrial and pre-industrial societies. But the frontiers of this entire area of social science have been extended by the challenges posed by African social realities.

Africa's oral tradition also provoked the science of historiography into looking for ways of benefiting from the unwritten transmission of evidence. Perhaps no region of the world has done more to diversify historical methodology than Africa. Precisely because many African cultures had previously been unwritten, their study demanded the scrutiny of alternative forms of documentation. Oral tradition, linguistic evidence, new archaeological techniques all reached higher levels of sophistication under Africa's challenge.

Indeed, well before the period of this volume, Egyptology had become a distinct science in its own right. No country in the world except Egypt has ever forced science to invent an entirely distinct discipline for the study of that country's past.[30]

Earlier volumes of this *General History of Africa* have dealt with the African origins of the human species. But it was especially in the period since 1935 that palaeontology and palaeo-anthropology have had their most impressive achievements in East Africa. Research work since 1935 in Tanzania, Kenya, Ethiopia and elsewhere has taken humankind much further back towards understanding the species' origins than has ever been possible before. The name of the Leakeys in Kenya has become a household word internationally. But behind that high-profile name lies a whole army of palaeontologists, archaeologists and palaeo-anthropologists, handling a delicate range of evidence about the origins of the only species which studies its own past.

The social study of *other* species has also gone further in Africa than in almost any other region in the world. Certainly the observation and study of gorillas, chimpanzees and baboons – nearest relatives to humans – has been undertaken with exceptional sensitivity and with remarkable results in places like Rwanda and Zaire. Gorillas and baboons have been studied as 'households' and 'societies'. The techniques used by scientists have sometimes come close to being 'participant observation'. By under-

---

30. The UNESCO *General History of Africa*, vol. I, is devoted to paradigms and methodologies of African historiography. The International Scientific Committee of this UNESCO Series includes among its members significant methodological innovators in the oral tradition, linguistic historiography and archaeology.

standing monkeys better, do we learn more about human beings? Once again Africa has provided the material for teaching the human race about itself. Such Western women scholars as Jane Goodall have provided impressive scientific partnership in the study of these wild relatives of *Homo sapiens*.

The period since 1935 has also witnessed new challenges to European theories about who crossed the Atlantic first. Was it Christopher Columbus – or were there African navigators before him?

The challenge to the Columbus paradigm has come from both Africa and the African diaspora. Ivan Van Sertima had led the latest diaspora challenge to the Columbus paradigm. Born in Guyana, South America, Van Sertima made his scholarly impact in the United States. His 1977 book, *They Came Before Columbus: The African Presence in Ancient America*, went into more than ten reprints. Van Sertima's pre-Columbian navigators were conceived heavily though not exclusively in terms of the Nile valley and the Mediterranean. His evidence was varied, beginning with the 'Africoid' pre-Christ stone sculptures found in Mexico with striking 'Negro' features.[31]

The African continent's direct challenge to the Columbus paradigm in this period (as distinct from the diaspora challenge) places the pre-Columbian African navigators more firmly from West Africa rather than from the Nile valley and the Mediterranean. The Senegalese scholar Pathé Diagne initiated a project in the 1980s to research jointly with Cornell University the role of Bakari II in crossing the Atlantic, ostensibly before the year 1312. (Columbus's achievement across the Atlantic is normally dated as having been in 1492.) Was the project romance or history? Pathé Diagne's partnership with Cornell had ups and downs, but they each remained separately committed to research into whether Africans were pioneers in trans-Atlantic crossing. Pathé Diagne's thesis was that the expeditions of Mansa Bakari II (an African Muslim) and Christopher Columbus were inter-related.

> Both Bakary II and Christopher Columbus learned from the African navigators of Senegambia and the Gulf of Guinea about (1) trans-oceanic traffic and trade (2) the existence of a corridor fed by North Equatorial winds and (3) the existence of a current that was easy to navigate during the summer and fall and that led to the rich Maya, Olmeque, Aztec and Inca Kingdoms and civilizations. Neither Bakary II nor Christopher Columbus were ready to share this geopolitical secret with [rivals] . . . (Project Outline, Cornell, 1990).

But we must not over-emphasize the distinction between diaspora pre-Columbian theories, focusing on navigators from the Nile valley, and

31. Consult I. Van Sertima, 1984b, which includes some photographs of the 'Africoid' sculptures. See also I. Van Sertima, 1977.

African pre-Columbian theories, focusing on West African navigators. In 1962 the official organ of the National Association for the Advancement of Colored People (NAACP) in the United States published an article by Harold G. Lawrence entitled 'African Explorers of the New World'. In the article, Lawrence referred to Abubakari II of Mali as having employed Arab navigators and equipped them with a whole armada of ships and African sailors to venture westward.

> We can now positively state that the Mandigoes of the Mali and Songay Empires, and possibly other Africans, crossed the Atlantic to carry on trade with the Western Hemisphere Indians and further succeeded in establishing colonies throughout the Americas. . . . Abubakari II (1305–1307) did not believe that it was impossible to conquer the limits of the neighbouring ocean.[32]

Is this history or a case of African romantic gloriana? Is it the history of African navigation before Columbus; or is it part of the history of black nationalism in the twentieth century? The case for a pre-Columbian African crossing of the Atlantic is far from complete, and may never be fully proven. But alternative explanations of the pre-Christ Negroid stone heads in Mexico have not been convincingly forthcoming either. The historical period since 1935 has witnessed the beginnings of a major Afrocentric and Islamic challenge to the Columbus paradigm of 'discovery'. And the challenge has been coming from both African and diaspora historians.[33]

While history and the social sciences have often grappled with the origins of things, philosophy and religion have sometimes confronted the distinction between the finite and the infinite, between what has an end and what is endless, between what has a beginning and what may not. It is to these complexities of philosophy and doctrine that we must now turn.

Between origins and 'the end of time'

What impact have all these historical and scientific developments had on philosophy in this period of African history? Whether Columbus or Bakari 'discovered' a 'new world', how has the prospect of *the end of the world* influenced philosophical thought in Africa – with or without a nuclear winter?

On the whole, the idea of 'the end of the world' has been much more important in Muslim Africa than outside it. Islam has a concept of *Qiyama*, the Day of Universal Death preceding the Day of Judgement.

32. H. G. Lawrence, 1962, pp. 2–4. Lawrence was Chairman of the Research and Education Committee of the Detroit branch of the Association for the Study of Negro Life and History.

33. See I. Van Sertima, 1984a, especially pp. 221–46; and I. Van Sertima, 1977.

Islam also has a concept of *Akhir al-Zaman*, meaning the end of time.

In reality Christianity has analogues of these Islamic concepts, but for some reason these particular Christian equivalents have had far less of an impact on Africa than have their Islamic counterparts. One reason may be the greater degree of fatalism that Islam has sometimes generated in Africa – a distortion of the concept of *Inschā' Allāh* (if God wills).

Mahdist movements in Africa have sometimes been accompanied by a notion of 'the end of time' – the *Mahdī* being a saviour not long before the Day of Judgement. Islam in Nigeria and Sudan has had a particularly strong Mahdist tendency, but the idea of *Akhir al-Zaman* (the end of time) is much more widespread than Mahdism in Muslim Africa. The self-destructiveness of the new Western science and technology has been used as evidence of a cataclysmic and inevitable doom.

Indigenous African religion is more concerned with the beginning of time than with its end. Ancestry is more important than conclusion. Every African culture is inspired by two basic myths – the myth of origin and the myth of collective purpose. The myth of origin includes the beginning of society – an African Genesis. The myth of collective purpose gives the society its sense of uniqueness and its mission in history.

African myths of origin often equate the beginnings of a particular society (the Baganda, for example) with the origins of the human species as a whole. For the secular observer, it could be argued that the Jews did the same when they turned the first mythological Jews (Adam and Eve) into the first human beings. But the Jews covered themselves by later having Abraham as the father of the Jewish nation.

What is clear is that the Semitic myth of origin (Genesis according to the Bible and the Ḳur'ān) had increasingly challenged indigenous African myths of ancestry like that of Kintu as the first Muganda or Mumbi as the first Kikuyu. Originally the first Muganda or the first Kikuyu were also the first humans. But Adam and Eve have cut African originals down to size just at the time when Western science has begun to concede that Africa was where the human species *scientifically* began after all. African myths of origin are being discredited by Western religion just at the time when Western science is demonstrating that the Garden of Eden must have been in Africa after all. What the myth of Lucifer is demolishing, the science of Leakey is re-constructing. Kintu and Mumbi are dead; long live Kintu and Mumbi! Religion and science are once again in a dialectical relationship in Africa.[34]

African religious myths sometimes even suggest that God has a beginning – but not an end. This is not unlike some scientific theories about the origins of the universe. The 'Big Bang' theory of the origins of the universe does postulate a momentous start – but not necessarily the end

34. See V. Hamilton, 1988, on comparative myths of origin; the book has illustrations which cover non-African as well as African myths.

of the universe. What is initiated does not necessarily terminate; what is born need not die.

In his book *The Mind of Africa*, the Ghanaian philosopher, William E. Abraham, addressed the concepts of 'eternity' and 'infinity' in comparable terms. Could something be 'eternal' in the sense of having no terminal moment and yet still have a specific point of commencement? Was God such a concept of infinity and eternity – self-created but never-ending? Was the Akan concept of God so envisioned?[35]

The Christian concept of the birth of Jesus is more ambivalent. Jesus was *born*. But could he ever *die* even during those three momentous days at Easter? If he died and was resurrected, is the death of the son of God ever possible again?

Many myths of ethnic origin in Africa include the origins of death itself. A myth from Sierra Leone relates that death once lived with God, and kept on pleading to God to let it go. But God had promised Man that although death had been allowed to come into the world, Man would not die. There were two things which God had to reconcile: liberating death and letting it go where it pleased, on the one side, and saving Man, on the other. God decided to send Man new skins which would protect him from the elements and save him from death. But the messenger with the skins was waylaid by a snake who stole the skins. Was the snake, in fact, death in disguise? Man discovered too late that the skins of protection against death had been stolen in transit.

Of course, such a story was articulated well before Sierra Leoneans knew anything about the Earth's ozone layer. But the new ecological anxiety in the scientific world is that death may be coming to Man through damage to the human skin. Ultra-violet rays of the sun coming through the depleted ozone layer are already playing havoc with marine creatures in Antarctica and the southern seas. The whale is facing a new danger from these rays. An international conference in Tasmania, Australia, held in mid-May 1989, heard reports about the possible aggravation of such human diseases as herpes and AIDS as a result of these ultra-violet rays penetrating the new ozone hole.

Sierra Leoneans may be justified in regarding their own myth of origin as prophetic. Man will now need extra layers of skin which God had intended him to have as protection against death. Man still blames the snake who waylaid the messenger with the skins:

> From that day onwards, Man has always borne a grudge against the Snake, and has always tried to kill him whenever he sees him. The Snake, for his part, has always avoided Man and has always lived alone. And because he still has the skins that God provided, he can always shed his own skin.[36]

35. For one interpretation of Akan philosohpy, see W. E. Abraham, 1962.
36. See M. Carey, 1970, pp. 18–19.

This Sierra Leonean myth echoes the Semitic myth of the fall of Adam through the special use of a snake or serpent. Satan, like death in the African myth, had once lived with God and then wanted to break out into liberty. What the Sierra Leonean myth had done was to fuse the concept of Satan with the concept of death into a single being. In the biblical Genesis, on the other hand, Satan was *instrumental* in creating death for human kind.

But the biblical Genesis also called upon Man to 'fill the good earth and subdue it'. Man was made master of the world and all its creatures. Modern science and technology did enable man to 'subdue' the earth and all its creatures. Therefore, man can no longer blame snakes and serpents for his misfortunes. As God's Vizier, Man is now almost Master of the Universe. But is man become master of himself as yet? Or is the 'end of time' drawing near?

> At my back I always hear
> Time's winged chariot hurrying near
> And yonder before us lie
> Deserts of vast eternity.[37]

The themes of eternity and the infinite have been part of African philosophy almost from 'the *beginning* of time' – and have continued into the post-colonial period. Two African writers exchanged poetic exclamations in a television programme in 1986:

> A: You are not a country, Africa,
>   You are a concept! . . .
>
> B: You are not a country, Africa,
>   You are a glimpse of the Infinite![38]

But while such 'eternal' themes in African philosophy and literature are, by definition, not specific to any particular period of history, the years since 1935 have exhibited their own special characteristics. Inevitably there has been both continuity and change in Africa's philosophical experience. And both science and culture have cast their shadow on the African philosophical mind at work. Let us now look more particularly at the special philosophical tendencies of these years.

Three currents of philosophy

African philosophy since 1935 can be grouped under different categories or currents. For this chapter, the most promising classifications may be cultural, ideological, and critical. Each of these schools of philosophy has

37. A. Marvell, 1981.
38. D. A. Nicol and A. A. Mazrui, 1986.

distinct characteristics – though it is worth bearing in mind that these classifications are for analytical convenience only and do allow for a good deal of overlap.

The cultural school of philosophy is rooted primarily in indigenous traditions. It is what is sometimes called 'ethno-philosophy', but we prefer the term 'cultural' mainly because it is more accurate in this instance. The fact that much of indigenous philosophy is ethnic-specific (such as the philosophy of the Lugbara) is only one attribute of that body of thought. Cultural philosophy also tends by and large to be collectivist, and transmitted mainly through the oral tradition. But the collectivism should not be exaggerated. There were individual innovators also. This corpus of African thought is sociological – encompassing the way of life of a people, the rules governing it, and the cumulative wisdom of the ancestors across generations, but sometimes guided by exceptional individuals.

If in the West philosophy begins with thought and empirical science begins with touch, cultural philosophy in Africa makes no sharp distinction between thought and touch. As we mentioned earlier, the completed syllogism of one aspect of African cultural philosophy is as follows:

> We *feel*
> Therefore we *think*,
> Therefore we *are*!

In time-scale the cultural current of philosophy in Africa includes pre-colonial, colonial and post-colonial phases. It is, almost by definition, the oldest and most durable of Africa's philosophical traditions.

But for our purposes in this chapter we distinguish between *culture* and *ideology*. Here we use the narrow sense of ideology as a policy-oriented body of ideas, mainly designed to govern political action and define political goals. Of course, culture does include ideology – and the cultural current of philosophy in our sense subsumes political goals and action. But culture is a whole way of life and not merely the arena of political relations. The cultural school of African philosophy includes such concerns as relations between man and nature, between the living and the dead, between husband and wife, as well as between rulers and subjects in those African societies which did traditionally have distinct rulers.

The ideological current of African thought is even more narrowly political. It tends to be mainly colonial and post-colonial – and ranges from Kwame Nkrumah's *Consciencism* to Franz Fanon's *The Wretched of the Earth*. There was very little of this kind of philosophizing in the pre-colonial period. Ideological thought in this particular sense is primarily a child of colonialism and its aftermath.

Cultural philosophy is, in the first instance, conceived in *indigenous*

665

languages. Ideological philosophy in black Africa is disproportionately in *European languages*.

Cultural philosophy is, as we indicated, mainly collectivist and cumulative. The tradition is not usually in terms of great individual thinkers. There are very few African Platos, African Lockes and Rousseaus, or African Hegels. The current of cultural philosophy is normally the flow of collective wisdom, cumulative across generations.

Ideological philosophy in colonial and post-colonial Africa raises the individual afresh as the fountain of ideas. African philosophy begins to be studied in terms of the ideas of individuals like Amilcar Cabral and Gamāl 'Abd al-Nasser rather than the philosophies of cultural units like the Zulu or the Berbers.

If cultural philosophy is ethnic-specific in the sense we mentioned (for example, Yoruba philosophy), ideological philosophy tends to be Africa-specific, in the sense of generalizing about Africa as a whole or the black experience world-wide. In other words, while the fountain of ideological philosophy is *narrower* than the fountain of cultural philosophy (the individual thinker instead of collective wisdom), the subject-matter of ideological philosophy is often *wider* (being concerned with Africa as a whole or black people generally rather than a particular ethnic group).

A particular thinker like Agostinho Neto was a narrower fountain of ideas than the Ovambo people as a source of collective cultural wisdom. But Neto was concerned about the black genius in international capitalist conditions – and knew more about Africa and the world than the ancestors of the Ovambo did.

The ultimate value of cultural philosophy is probably identity. All the other elements reinforce the self-awareness and identity of, say, the Wolof as a people. On the other hand, the ultimate value of ideological philosophy has tended to be *liberation*. Some thinkers have linked liberation to pan-Africanism, others to black genius. Of course, other values also come into play. But because of the nature of the colonial impact in this particular period of African history, the political focus of so much of Africa's ideological preoccupation has centred on liberation.

Although we must not confuse this with populism, cultural philosophy to some scholars is basically a philosophy of the masses. It consists of ideas which are essentially often intelligible to ordinary people. The philosophy is expressed in languages which are meaningful to the average citizen – indigenous African languages. Although there are exceptions, like the thought of Ogotommeli of the Dogon, cultural philosophy is basically about a familiar way of life, intellectually accessible to the man or woman in the village.

On the other hand, ideological philosophy in our sense is basically élitist, even when it seeks to identify with the masses. Amilcar Cabral identified with the most ordinary of Africans, and Fanon elevated even the lumpen proletariat to a level of dignity and respectability unimagined by the more sceptical Karl Marx. And yet neither Marx nor Fanon – nor, indeed, Cabral – is intelligible to the ordinary villager in Burkina Faso or among the Karimojong of Uganda. The ideas of Marx and Fanon constitute a conversation among the urbanized and Westernized African élite.

A central problem with Africa's ideological thought continues to be the language in which it is expressed. While empirical science elsewhere begins with the five senses (touch, sight, smell, hearing and feeling), linguistic philosophy is often concerned with the five *tenses* (was, is, will be, ought and eternal).

In Africa, more important than the philosophy of language is the language of philosophy. Colonial and post-colonial ideologies are disproportionately in European languages. The formal study of philosophy at African universities is done in foreign imperial languages – English, French, Portuguese, and so on. Most of the towering modern African thinkers – from Edward Blyden to P. J. Hountondji have conducted their primary discourse in European languages. The main exceptions are in Arabic-speaking Africa.

As for those African thinkers inspired by external ideologies, it is a socio-linguistic impossibility for an African to be a sophisticated Marxist without being substantially Westernized. This is because access to Marxist literature is still overwhelmingly in European languages. An African learns his or her first European language not simply as a skill but in a massive educational process of acculturation. By the time the African is competent enough in a European language to understand Marxist literature, that African is substantially Westernized.

It is this bondage of language which had made so much of ideological philosophy in Africa hopelessly élitist even when it is doctrinally opposed to élitism. Much of the philosophy of people like Eduardo Mondlane was committed to liberation and morally concerned about ordinary African people. But most of such ideological philosophy had inadvertently erected for itself a linguistic barrier to keep the ordinary people out. It is not an iron curtain. It is a curtain of the impenetrable verb. The people cannot understand the language – not because it is a technical idiom but because it is a *foreign* tongue. That is one of the most fundamental of the differences between the cultural current of African philosophy (transmitted *orally* in *indigenous* languages) and the ideological current (transmitted in *writing*, using *European* languages).

Arab Africa has been less dependent on European languages. Arabic has filled the gap. Gamāl 'Abd al-Nasser's *Philosophy of the Revolution* was originally in Arabic. On the other hand, in Arab Africa both cultural and ideological philosophy have often been inseparable from religion. Issues of mosque and magistrate, church and state, have come to the fore. The tension between secularism and religious thought was sometimes at its sharpest in Egypt. It was in 1928 that Ḥassan al-Bannā established

667

the Muslim Brotherhood – with considerable consequences for the entire period of this volume.

> In its sixty years, the Brotherhood has managed to politicise Islam as no other indigenous popular movement has ever done in Egypt. . . . In its most violent phase (1945–65) the Brotherhood was implicated in assassinations of its political opponents in both royal and revolutionary Egypt.[39]

Gamāl 'Abd al-Nasser broke the power of the Brotherhood in Egypt for a while. Later on internal divisions weakened it in the concluding years of the twentieth century. But the Muslim Brotherhood has remained one of the most activist schools of Islamic ideology throughout much of Arab Africa. Other streams of Islamic thought in Egypt have included Ṣūfism and the established authority of the *'ulamā'* of Al-Azhar.

Ideological philosophy in Morocco during this period included issues of whether or not there was a Muslim equivalent of the divine right of kings. Particularly dramatic was the famous *fatwā* (legal opinion) by Shaykh al-Islam Moulay al-Arbi 'Alaoui given in December 1963. He ruled that the legitimacy of the monarch depended on whether he ascended to the throne through *shurā* (consultation) and with the approval of the *Umma* (community of believers). The *fatwā* was a direct challenge to the principle of hereditary succession and the credentials of King Hassan II of Morocco. Debates about the nature of royal legitimacy have continued ever since.[40]

In Libya the monarch was overthrown in September 1969. When Muammar Kadhaffi launched his 'cultural revolution' in 1973, he attempted to abolish the distinction between ideology and culture. He developed Libya's philosophy of 'The Third Universal Theory' consisting of Arabo-Islamic unity, Arabo-Islamic socialism and Libyan popular democracy. The Libyan opposition to Kadhaffi's cultural revolution included liberal and socialist Libyans, sections of the Sanusi Muslims, sections of *Ikhwan* and, for a while, a dynamic and charismatic Tripoline preacher, Shaykh al-Bishti, who later disappeared under ominous and mysterious circumstances.

Tunisia took the debate about modernity and tradition in North African thought to new levels. In a way, Tunisia was continuing a controversy which was unleashed on modern Islam in an earlier generation by the Egyptian Muḥammad 'Abduh and his mentor, Jamāl al-Din al-Afghāni. And yet, ironically, Tunisia's Habib Bourguiba did not take his cue from 'Abduh and Afghāni. Bourguiba took his inspiration from Jean-Jacques Rousseau, Victor Hugo and Lamartine. Bourguiba's ambition was to recreate Tunisia in the image of the French revolution. By seeking to

39. S. E. Ibrahim, 1988, p. 640. See also E. Davis, 1987, pp. 145–68.
40. J. Benomar, 1988, pp. 550–1. See also M. W. Suleiman, 1989, pp. 16–27.

reduce the role of Islam in Tunisian society, Bourguiba unleashed a considerable philosophical and literary upsurge on the competing claims of modernity and tradition, Westernism and Islam. Once again cultural and ideological philosophy converged in an African society.[41]

The third school of African philosophy after cultural and ideological is the critical school. Like the ideological current, the critical school is also a colonial and post-colonial response. Both schools also use primarily European languages and have been profoundly influenced by Western intellectual traditions.

But while the ideological school is self-consciously political, the critical school is more narrowly academic. While the ideological school is pre-occupied with liberation, the critical school aspires to be morally agnostic or value-free. While the ideological school is often nationalist, the critical school aspires to be strictly rationalist.

The critical school of African philosophy does have a concept of 'liberation' – but what is to be liberated is *philosophy* itself rather than Africa. A rescue operation is ostensibly needed to emancipate philosophy in Africa from both ethnology (as in our concept of cultural philosophy) and ideology (as we have defined it).

The central thesis of the critical school is basically as follows:

> Philosophy only exists where there is a personal commitment by philosopher(s) to rational discourse, the only truth or value is that elaborated or revealed in the crucible of the debate between consciences and confrontation with the Real. . . . [Philosophy must cease to be] the handmaiden of Religion or Politics and become a faithful but demanding collaborator with them.[42]

To some extent, the critical school aspires to bring philosophy back to the fold of the scientific spirit. The 'confrontation with the Real' is basically a beckoning to the measurements of rationalism. Paradoxically, critical philosophy is also an invitation to some degree of empiricism – the criteria of touch in a special sense of realism.

African critical philosophers in this sense have included F. Crahay, B. F. Eboussi, P. J. Hountondji, K. Anthony Appiah, M. Towa and S. Adotevi. Their ambition is, in a sense, to make African philosophy more scientific, more disciplined, and more rigorous. They have declared war against what Hountondji (in alliance with the structuralists) calls the 'unthought'.

And yet there is a whole school of thought in this period of African history which takes pride in what might be called 'the Unscience'. We have already referred to Aimé Césaire's salute to:

41. For an early evaluation, see C. H. Moore, 1965. See also M. Boulby, 1988, pp. 590–93; and M. Madhi, 1990.

42. E. P. Elungu, 1984, pp. 40–1. This chapter is indebted to Marcien Towa and Malu wa Kalenga for bibliographical guidance.

> . . . Those who have invented neither powder nor the compass
> Those who have tamed neither gas nor electricity
> Those who have explored neither the seas nor the skies . . .[43]

Western thought has a whole sub-field called the 'philosophy of science'. What the African agenda had included is what might be called the philosophy of unscience. It is to this cluster of African philosophical values that we must now turn.

The philosophy of unscience

We have already mentioned how Europe's industrial revolution had pushed its science far ahead of its technology – and accelerated the pace of social and industrial change. With its spectacular technological successes, Europe then embarked on its mission of conquering the world.

Europe's massive cultural arrogance affected the African personality and sometimes distorted the priorities of African philosophy. Westernized Africans especially suffered acute cultural schizophrenia. One school of African thought chose to emphasize that Africa before the arrival of the Europeans had its own complex civilizations of the kind that Europeans regarded as valid and important – civilizations which produced great kings, impressive empires and elaborate technological skills. This particular school of African thought looked to ancient Egypt as an African civilization, and stressed Egypt's contributions to the later miracle of ancient Greece. Cheikh Anta Diop's scholarly commitment to demonstrate that the civilization of ancient Egypt was not only African but *black* had produced an influential school of thought not only within Africa but also in the African *diaspora* in the Americas.

We may call this school of African philosophy romantic gloriana. It seeks to emphasize the glorious moments in Africa's history, defined in part by European criteria of impressive performance, including performance in creating material monuments.

In contrast to the philosophy of romantic gloriana is what might be called romantic primitivism. This is what the philosophy of the unscience is all about. The emphasis here is not on achievements of grandeur, but on accomplishments of simplicity; not on Africa's historical monumentalism, but on the virtues of the village; not on Africa's castle-builders, but on Africa's cattle-herders.

> My negritude is neither a tower nor a cathedral;
> It plunges into the deep red flesh of the soil.[44]

43. A. Césaire, 1969.
44. *ibid.* See also A. A. Mazrui, 1986, pp. 72–6.

As Jean-Paul Sartre pointed out, this revelling in not having invented either powder or the compass, in not having built either towers or cathedrals, is a proud claim to 'non-technicalness'. In our terms the *unscience* is glorified. In Sartre's terms: 'That which might appear to be a deficiency becomes a positive source of richness'.[45]

Romantic gloriana as a philosophic disposition seeks to emphasize Africa's role in the history of science and technological achievements. But Léopold Senghor prefers to trace Africa's genius to intuition, to the wisdom of settled experience, to the instincts which are educated by history. The human instinct is a better guide to behaviour than the more precise computer.

Romantic gloriana tends to have a sense of awe towards literate civilizations. Nkrumah's cultural policy as president of Ghana sometimes tried to claim an African origin to almost every achievement in the history of science and culture before the computer. Postcards with paintings of African originators and inventors were widely distributed by Ghana at the time. Tyro, an African secretary to Cicero, was credited with the invention of shorthand in the year 63 before the Christian era. Another postcard stressed the Egyptian origins of paper. Ancient Ghana was credited with the origins of legislation and formal law. Other postcards showed Africans teaching mathematics to the Greeks or leading the way in chemistry, medicine and other sciences. Nkrumah's cultural policy sometimes carried romantic gloriana to extravagant lengths.

In its more restrained form, romantic gloriana is a branch of idealized African historiography. It tends to accept European values while rejecting European 'facts' about Africa. The gloriana tendency betrays a readiness to accept the Western assumption that respectable societies are not 'tribal' and are endowed with relatively centralized political systems, with kings or imperial structures, with monuments in bricks and mortar, and are ultimately based on the organizing principle of statehood. To the gloriana philosophical tendency, it is an insult to call the Karimojong or the Barabeg 'stateless societies'. There is once again an acceptance of Western criteria of political respectability (states are the 'in-thing') but a rejection of Western *information* about Africa. A 'yes' is given to Western values but a resounding 'no' to alleged Western 'facts' about Africa.

In contrast, the philosophy of the unscience rejects Western values but accepts Western information or 'facts'. It rejects Western criteria of respectable civilizations – towers, cathedrals and statehood – and accepts Western descriptions of Africa as a land without advanced science or technology. However, romantic primitivism takes pride in the unscience – while the West despises it.

45. J.-P. Sartre, 1963, pp. 41–3. This part of the analysis is also greatly indebted to A. A. Mazrui, 1986.

Towards cross-cultural philosophy

It is these considerations which link up the philosophy of unscience with Rousseau's tradition of 'the Noble Savage', on the one hand, and with Mahatma Gandhi's ideas about civilization, on the other.

An interviewer once asked India's Mahatma Gandhi: 'What do you think of Western civilization?' The Mahatma is reported to have replied, 'I did not know that they had any!' It was presumably the West's 'moral sensibilities' which Mahatma Gandhi was questioning.

Like Mahatma Gandhi, Africa's philosophers of unscience have not been impressed by the West's technological achievements. Those African thinkers have identified stronger moral sensibilities among the less technically-preoccupied rural peoples of the African continent itself. Rousseau's ideas about the corrosive and corrupting influences of industrial culture and Gandhi's techniques of handloom village textiles provide powerful comparisons with this primitivist tendency in modern African thought. The convergence of negritude, Gandhism and Rousseau's 'Noble Savage' is one area of cross-cultural philosophy.

Although both the primitivist and the gloriana schools are interpretations of traditional Africa, they are different from the 'cultural current' of African philosophy as we have defined it before. Romantic primitivism and romantic gloriana both belong to a cross-cultural tendency in African philosophy.

What should be borne in mind is that our three original general currents of African philosophy – cultural, ideological and critical – have not been rigidly demarcated. African Islamic thought and African Christian thought have often cut across both culture and ideology in our sense. The legacies of Jamāl al-Din al-Afghāni and his Egyptian disciple, Muḥammad 'Abduh, have continued into the second half of the twentieth century – grappling with the cross-cultural tensions between modern science and ancient sacred truth.

Secular cross-culturalism includes the impact of Marxism–Leninism on indigenous ideas of collectivism. African thinkers like Senghor and Nyerere insisted that African socialism owed nothing to class struggle. The question has often been raised whether the concept of 'class' was African at all. Why did most African languages lack a word for 'class'?

Also cross-cultural are those African versions of modernism in Islamic thought referred to earlier. These, too, have produced their own heroes and martyrs. Among the most original of Africa's Islamic thinkers in the second half of the twentieth century was the Sudanese theologian, Mahmoud Muhammad Taha. His concept of the Dual Message of Islam was more cross-temporal than cross-cultural. Taha engaged in an intellectual effort to reconcile the ethos of the twentieth century with the spirit of the ancient era of the Prophet Muḥammad. Mahmoud Taha argued cross-temporally and with a freshness that one message of the

Prophet was intended only for his followers in his own day (the Arabs of the seventh century of the Christian era) and the second message of Islam was intended for all time. The secret of true piety, according to Taha, was not only to recognize this cross-temporal duality of the Islamic message but also to be able to distinguish between what was historically specific to the seventh century and what was truly eternal. Mahmoud Muhammad Taha paid the supreme price for his cross-temporal intellectual innovations. The regime of Gaffar Nimeiri in the Sudan executed him for apostasy and heresy in 1985.[46]

Christian thinkers in Africa have done more than merely interpret their own Gospel. They have often taken the lead in re-interpreting cross-culturally the indigenous civilization of Africa as well. An impressive breakthrough in Christian interpretation of African indigenous thought came with Father Tempels's seminal book, *Bantu Philosophy*. It was a look at traditional thought viewed from the outside. The perspective was sympathetic but basically Euro-Christian. Tempels was succeeded by a whole school of Christian interpreters of the ancestral heritage of Africa.[47]

Afro-Christian interpreters of indigenous philosophy since the seminal work of Tempels have included J. Kinyongo of Zaire, A. Kagame of Rwanda, W. E. Abraham of Ghana and John Mbiti of Kenya. Sometimes the basic Christianity of these writers has distorted their Africanity – and portrayed the indigenous heritage in Christo-centric terms. Some of these writers wanted their Western readers to believe that traditional African beliefs were almost Christian – as if the African ancestors anticipated Jesus Christ and the Sermon on the Mount.

The late Ugandan anthropologist and poet, Okot p'Bitek, complained about this dual tendency among sympathetic Westernized writers to Christianize and Hellenize the indigenous heritage of Africa. Okot p'Bitek was blowing the whistle against this new cultural 'Trojan horse' which was penetrating Africa's traditional legacies.[48]

In spite of these dangers of Christo-centrism and Euro-centrism, there is little doubt that the efforts of Christianized Africans to interpret the legacy of the black ancestors had made much of that cultural heritage more intellectually accessible to the rest of the world. Books like John Mbiti's *African Religions and Philosophy* have been translated into languages which have ranged from Japanese to Finnish. It is one of the ironies of history that John Mbiti has seldom been translated into African languages. We are back to the problem of the language of philosophy in

46. See M. M. Taha, 1987.
47. R. P. Tempels, 1949. African political philosophy is discussed in W. O. Oyugi and A. Gilonga, 1987.
48. See O. p'Bitek, 1971; consult also A. Kagame, 1956; J. Mbiti, 1969; J. Kinyongo, 1974, pp. 205–11; and W. E. Abraham, 1962.

Africa – so different from the British preoccupation with the philosophy of language.

In cross-cultural terms, Julius Nyerere is the most enterprising of African political philosophers. He has philosophized extensively in both English and Kiswahili. He has tried to tear down the language barriers between ancestral cultural philosophy and the new ideological tendency of the post-colonial era. Nyerere is superbly eloquent in both English and Kiswahili. He has allowed the two languages to enrich each other as their ideas have passed through his intellect.

His concept of *ujamaa* as a basis of African socialism was itself a brilliant cross-cultural transition. *Ujamaa* traditionally implied *ethnic* solidarity. But Nyerere transformed it from a dangerous principle of ethnic nepotism into more than a mere equivalent of the European word 'socialism'. In practice his socialist policies did not work – as much for global reasons as for domestic. But in intellectual terms Nyerere is a more original thinker than Kwame Nkrumah – and linguistically much more innovative. Nkrumah tried to update Lenin – from Lenin's *Imperialism: The Highest Stage of Capitalism* to Nkrumah's *Neo-Colonialism: the Last Stage of Imperialism.* Nyerere translated Shakespeare into Kiswahili instead – both *Julius Caesar* and *The Merchant of Venice.* Nkrumah's exercise in Leninism was a less impressive cross-cultural achievement than Nyerere's translation of Shakespeare into an African language. Yet both these African thinkers will remain among the towering figures of the twentieth century in politics and thought.[49]

Conclusion

This chapter has started from the premise that Africa's contribution to science and technology is not to be measured merely by the activities of African scientists and engineers. The region's impact includes the role of African labour and material resources in global technological change. The continent's strategic minerals have equipped the factories and activated the laboratories of the Western world not only in the period since 1935 but for generations before that.[50]

Colonial rule itself was not a fertile soil for indigenous science and technology. Colonial schools managed to produce two African Nobel Prize-winners for literature (Soyinka and Mahfuz), two African Nobel Prizes for peace (Luthuli and Tutu), one diaspora Nobel Prize for economics (Arthur Lewis) – but not a single African Nobel Prize-winner for any branch of the natural sciences. Colonial schools were quite

49. K. Nkrumah, 1966; J. Nyerere, 1963a and 1969.
50. For older civilizational interaction, consult J. G. Jackson, 1970.

competent laboratories for the humanities but not effective workshops for science and technology.[51]

On the other hand, a Zairean mineral like cobalt could keep the jet engines of the Western world running when there were hardly any alternative sources of the commodity available outside Africa. It is in this sense that Western colonialism in Africa fuelled technological change in the West – while inhibiting it in the economic bosom of Africa itself. The West attempted to castrate African technology – while African minerals served as the aphrodisiac ('the *Afrodisiac*') for Western technological virility.

War is sometimes the mother of invention. After all, the Second World War played midwife to the birth of the nuclear age – often encouraged by otherwise humanitarian scientists like Albert Einstein. It was probably Einstein's advice to President Franklin Roosevelt which tipped the scale in favour of the Manhattan atomic project in the middle of the war.

Africa's wars of liberation sometimes gave birth to impressive examples of intermediate technology. The Mau Mau war in the 1950s yielded intriguing rudimentary firearms manufactured in the bush.

However, the most impressive innovative war in Africa in this period technologically was not a war of liberation but a post-colonial civil war. The Biafran side in the Nigerian civil war revealed great skills of technological improvisation. Biafra produced memorable examples of intermediate armoured vehicles and quasi-tanks. Unfortunately, the technological prowess which war had produced between 1967 and 1970 was promptly killed by the oil bonanza in Nigeria from 1973 onwards. Prosperity destroyed innovation.

In the field of philosophy colonialism helped to foster the ideological and critical schools, both of which were deeply Westernized and were often expressed in European languages. By far the most indigenously authentic branch of philosophy has been the cultural school – deeply rooted as it is in native perspectives and ways of thought. Indeed, cultural philosophy in Africa in the post-colonial era is both oral and written, both sacred and secular – and has its origins in indigenous African languages and concepts.[52]

Underlying all these trends has been that basic question which we posed at the very beginning of this chapter. What has political subordination meant for Africa's role in science and philosophy? In the field of science and technology the costs and benefits are difficult to compute. On the whole, it has not been African scientists who have had the biggest impact on global science and technology. It has been African workers and mineral resources – benefiting industries abroad.

51. There have indeed been black inventors and discoverers at levels 'below' the Nobel category. See, for example, J. A. Rogers, 1972.
52. See UNESCO, 1985–6.

In philosophy, on the other hand, colonialism may have started a process which will eventually be enriching. There is surely room for the study of secular ideologies in the Africa of the twenty-first century – and the colonial legacy has already initiated that particular endeavour. Our interest today in Fanon, Cabral, Nkrumah, Senghor and Gamāl 'Abd al-Nasser is part and parcel of that process.

The critical school is already preoccupied with such special concepts as 'post-modernism' and deconstruction and such carefully defined social predicaments as post-coloniality. Thinkers like Kwame Anthony Appiah and Nkiru Nzegwu are part of the vanguard of these new intellectual horizons.

The twenty-first century will surely also celebrate such critical African philosophy – formal, disciplined, rigorous, sometimes obscure, occasionally profound. Names of critical philosophers which may survive into the twenty-first century are likely to include V. Y. Mudimbe, W. E. Abraham, O. Bodurin Kwasi Wiredu, H. Odera, P. Hountondji and a number of others. All these were products of colonialism and yet transcended it.

As for trans-cultural schools of philosophy, these include the works of such African Christian thinkers as A. Kagame and John Mbiti and such African Islamic thinkers as Mahmoud Muhammad Taha and Abdallah Saleh Farsy. These thinkers, too, bore the stamp of colonized Africa – but their reach often exceeded their grasp.[53]

Are Africans an *historical* people? It is a matter of astonishment that right into the second half of the twentieth century, Africans have had to establish their credentials as a people with a recorded past and a past worth recording. It was as late as the 1960s that the Regius Professor of Modern History at Oxford University – Hugh Trevor-Roper – proclaimed his infamous dogma:

> Maybe in the future there will be African history. But at the moment there is none. There is only the history of the European in Africa . . . The rest is darkness – and darkness is not a subject of history.[54]

Are Africans a *philosophical* people? Perhaps the wonder is even greater on this issue – for Africans themselves are divided about the answer to the question. The critical current in African philosophy comes close to saying something like the following:

> Maybe at present there is some African philosophy. But in the past there was none. There was only philosophizing about Africa by

53. Consult, among others, L. Brown and M. Crowder, 1964. See also C. Wauthier, 1966; and O. Otite, 1978. Also useful is not only V. Y. Mudimbe's brilliant book, but also his bibliography, 1988.

54. This often-quoted statement was made in a broadcast on British television in 1968. It was in the opening lecture of the series on *The Rise of Christian Europe*, by Hugh Trevor-Roper, printed in *The Listener*, 28 November 1963, p. 871.

676

Europeans . . . The rest was ethnology and ethnology is not a subject of philosophy.

Are Africans a *scientific* people? Again Africans themselves are divided on that issue. Negritudists salute those who invented neither the compass nor the computer – while Cheikh Anta Diop came close in tracing all meaningful science to the African intellect at work.

A future Aimé Césaire and a future Davidson Abioseh Nicol may one day collaborate as poets and proclaim to the world:

> Hooray for those who pursued no science!
> Hooray for those who refused to philosophize!
> You are not a *concept* Africa,
> You are a mere country!

In fact, the age of consensus is ending in Africa. That is what all the intellectual noise is about. A restless continent is finding new issues to disagree about and new doctrines for debate. Some old paradigms are dying – some new paradigms are in the crucible of formation. Perhaps that is what both science and philosophy are all about.

When two elephants fight, it is the grass which suffers – especially if each elephant has a *scientist* to advise it.

And when two elephants make love, it is still the grass which suffers – especially when each elephant has a *philosopher* to advise it.

> (*Ancient African proverb,*
> *revised in the light of experience since 1935.*
> *A paradigm shift.*)

Education and social change

Aklilu HABTE *and* **Teshome WAGAW**

in collaboration with

J. F. Ade AJAYI

Introduction

Education is the mechanism by which a society generates the knowledge necessary for its survival and sustenance and transmits this from one generation to another, largely through processes of instructions to the young. It could be informal in the home, at the workplace or in the playground. More usually, it is formalized and is conducted in places and contexts specially set apart for the guidance of the young and the edification of older people. The young are trained to acquire knowledge, skills and aptitudes necessary both for preserving and defending the basic institutions and values of society, as well as for adapting these to meet changing circumstances and new challenges.[1]

In pre-colonial Africa, as we have seen in earlier volumes, there were different systems of education performing these tasks in different parts of the continent. Notably, there were three main patterns: the indigenous, the Islamic, and what may be called the Afro-Christian, that is the early Christian traditions that survived in Ethiopia and among the Copts of Egypt.[2] Within both the Islamic and Afro-Christian traditions, society had great respect for literacy and learning: they helped to unlock the mysteries of the Holy Ḳur'ān (Koran) and the Holy Scriptures, and they also tended to be confined largely to rulers and priests, the two most highly respected groups in society. Otherwise, the cultures remained predominantly oral. The effort of European and American missionaries in the nineteenth century to spread Christianity in Africa stimulated Western education. It expanded the scope of literacy not only in European languages, but also in several African languages, many of them being written for the first time in newly-devised schemes of orthography in Roman letters, thus in many cases superseding earlier attempts to write some of the languages in the Arabic script.

1. P. C. Lloyd, 1972, pp. 160 ff. The authors also gratefully acknowledge the contribution of Mary Achatz, School of Education, University of Michigan, Ann Arbor, USA.

2. A. A. Mazrui and T. G. Wagaw, 1985; J. F. A. Ajayi, 1985

678

The spread of literacy in African languages had the greatest potential for social change in the number of people that could learn to read and write African languages and make the transition from a predominantly oral to an increasingly literate culture. During the colonial period, however, this potentiality was played down, and the importance of the much smaller group of people able to read and write the European languages was highlighted instead. It was the knowledge of the European languages that provided access to jobs as messengers, clerks, artisans and even occasionally professionals. The degree of competence in Western education and European languages became the new index of status and, often, this also corresponded with the income level and social influence of the relevant jobs.[3]

Thus, by 1935, Western education had superseded all pre-colonial systems of education in relative importance. Within Western education, it was education in European languages that counted for more than education in Arabic and other African languages. Western education had become a factor of class formation, tending to separate the Western-educated élite from the masses often denigrated as 'illiterate' or 'unlettered', and this was in spite of the great artistry of the oral cultures in the use and manipulation of words, especially because of the tonality of the languages when spoken. For the colonial regimes, Western education became a powerful weapon of acculturation, moulding the minds of the Western-educated élite to desire particular aspects of European culture such as European clothes, food, laws, patterns of government and imported European goods. Through Western education, reinforced by colonial laws of marriage, inheritance and land tenure, as well as Christian teachings on monogamy, the educated élite were being wooed away from the communal pattern of traditional African societies towards a new model of individualism, the nuclear family, private property and accumulation. The educated élite were beginning to know less about and show little appreciation for African history, religious ideas, clothes, cuisine, art, music and life-styles generally, which were retreating to some extent from the large urban centres but continued to dominate life in the rural areas.

Yet, as we have seen in other chapters of this volume, it was this same Western-educated élite, somewhat alienated as they were from the masses, who were in a position to lead the struggle against colonialism, aggregating the grievances of the masses of farmers in the rural areas as well as those of the trades unions, market women and the unemployed in the urban areas. The colonialists had in fact exaggerated the degree of alienation and the educated élite proved this again and again whenever those of them aspiring to political leadership were challenged to demonstrate their popularity and ability to win and retain the support of the masses. The level of Western education in the official European languages was an

3. M. Bray *et al.*, 1986, ch. 4, pp. 58–78.

essential part of their ability to command the confidence of the masses. In particular, Western education enabled the nationalist leaders to transcend the bounds of ethnicity set by the African languages and attempt to speak for all the multilingual, multi-national people within the boundaries of the colonial territories. This was the major advantage they had, for example, over the traditional rulers who were their major rivals in the bid for the succession to the colonialists, but were usually able to operate only within their own particular ethnic groups. Hence the view expressed by Awolowo in 1947 that the educated élite, though an insignificant minority, were the ones who had the political awareness and '. . . this articulate minority are destined to rule . . .'[4] The level of Western education, often combined with travel or a study period abroad, had also developed in several of the leaders of the educated élite a pan-African perspective which linked them with other leaders in Africa, and this perspective was another important factor in the nationalist struggle.

Thus, the nationalist leaders valued their educational background, and they saw in education their greatest weapon of nation-building and social transformation in the search both for mental decolonization and for economic development. Some scholars may be inclined to argue about the effectiveness of education as an instrument of social change: 'It is not the consciousness of people that determines their existence but . . . their social existence that determines their consciousness', according to Karl Marx.[5] The nationalist leaders, however, shared no such hesitation. In colonial Africa, the type and level of education determined not merely the consciousness of people, but also very much their place in society and their life-style. The nationalist leaders saw in the colonialist insistence on vocational training and adaptation to suit the African situation merely a device to suit the exploitative goals of the colonial regimes, and a weapon of control calculated to delay the process of decolonization. It was this insistence, taken to a logical conclusion, that produced the monstrosity of 'Bantu education' in South Africa. The educated élite saw in Western education which emphasized intellectual attainments the possibility of Africans acquiring the knowledge and insights necessary to 'modernize' African societies, the qualification for jobs in the colonial services, and the training of the African bureaucracy that would replace the colonial officials.[6]

The demand for improved educational facilities was, therefore, high on the agenda of every nationalist movement in Africa. The emphasis was on the expansion of elementary education, the provision of improved secondary schools and teacher-training colleges, and the establishment of African universities. The political leaders were also generally aware that

4. In *The Path to Nigerian Freedom*, cited by B. Davidson, 1978, p. 197.
5. K. Marx, 1859, trans. by N. I. Stone, 1904, p. 11.
6. E. Ashby and M. Anderson, 1966, especially pp. 236–47.

PLATE 22.1 *Physics lesson at the Athénée Royal of Léopoldville, Belgian Congo (now Kinshasa, Zaire)*

if education was to serve as the instrument for mental decolonization and economic development, the system inherited from the colonial regimes needed not merely to be expanded and consolidated but also to be reformed and adapted to the needs of post-colonial African societies. Thus, the history of education throughout Africa in the contemporary period revolves round the dual theme of expansion and reform. While the agenda for expansion was clear, the programme for reform was more complex and less easy to achieve than had been expected in the euphoria of the immediate post-colonial period.

Continuing relevance of the pre-colonial systems

One reason why the Western-educated élite were not completely alienated from the masses was that, in spite of the missionary schools and other pressures of the colonial system, the pre-colonial traditions of education continued to function largely through the influence both of the home and of religion. The influence of the home could not be completely obliterated by later schooling considering that during the first five years of life the African child was very close to the mother and she usually taught the child her own language along with the basic values of her culture. Even

681

where the mother herself had received some foreign education and religious ideas, her roots in the culture might have been weakened, but never wholly severed.[7] Secondly, the religious needs of the community, especially in the Islamic and Afro-Christian areas, demanded the continuation of the traditional system of education.

There was of course no colonial system to disrupt the traditional education within the family and the Church in Ethiopia. The Orthodox Church continued to organize and support a wide range of educational establishments which have remained the core of Ethiopian cultural, spiritual, literary, artistic and scientific life.[8] At the elementary level, there was the *Nebab Bet* (School of Reading), to which the few ruling families and others who had aspirations sent their children, largely to become monks or priests. Most of the pupils were male and only some of those who graduated from there went on to the *Quedasse Bet* (School of Holy Mass) and the *Quine Bet* (School of Poetry). Institutions of higher education were collectively referred to as *Metshafit Bet* (School of the Holy Books or Scriptures), and only a select few ever completed the rigorous study in theology and philosophy. The whole process lasted some 28 years, and involved much arduous work and personal deprivation. However, those who achieved this exalted intellectual state enjoyed the envy of their colleagues, the respect of the Christian communities, and the esteem of the rulers. Usually they had by then become of advanced age. Most of them did not attempt to start a family, but devoted the rest of their lives to meditation and scholarly pursuits as monks.

Similarly, the religious needs of the Muslim communities ensured the continuance of Islamic education not only within the family but also in a wide range of formal and informal educational and religious establishments.[9] Because the message of the Ḳur'ān has to be comprehended in the original Arabic in which it was revealed, most Muslim parents wanted their children, particularly the males, to attend Ḳur'ānic schools, on a full-time or part-time basis, to learn the Ḳur'ān by heart and pick up the rudiments of Arabic grammar and syntax during their most impressionable years. Further education was available in the *'ilm* (formal school establishments) or *madrasas* (classes conducted by *mu'allimūn* (scholars) around the mosque). Subjects studied included *tafsīr* (commentaries on the Ḳur'ān), *ḥadīth* (sayings of the Prophet, especially on issues of personal conduct such as marriage, divorce and inheritance) and *fiḳh* (studies of Islamic law or *sharī'a*).

In spite of occasional periods of hostility and confrontation, the colonial regimes did not oppose the spread of Islamic education in its elementary forms at the local level. They tended, however, to discourage higher

---

7. J. F. A. Ajayi, 1985, pp. 15–16; A. A. Mazrui and T. G. Wagaw, 1985, pp. 39–44.
8. T. G. Wagaw, 1979, ch. 1.
9. A. A. Mazrui and T. G. Wagaw, 1985, pp. 48–53; M. Bray *et al.*, 1986, ch. 5.

PLATE 22.2 *Ḳurʾānic school in Lagos, Nigeria*

education, especially when it involved international contacts with anti-colonial traditions in places such as al-Azhar in Cairo. The colonial regimes tried to monitor those who went on pilgrimages, preferring to select and if possible sponsor only the more conservative scholars. This could not deter the most ambitious scholars continuing the tradition of travelling round to sit at the feet of the most reputed scholars, mastering their works and profiting from the contents of their libraries. In this way

683

some local centres of higher education emerged, such as the Mosque of Riyadha in Lamu on the East African coast which attracted students from over a wide region.

The greater problem came from the threat posed to Islam by Western education, sponsored largely by Christian missionaries as a weapon of evangelization. For this reason, there developed between Western education and traditional Islamic education not merely a gap but an actual state of hostility. In a few places the colonial regimes barred Christian missionaries from Muslim areas and tried to sponsor secular Western education through the local administrations, but this achieved little in bridging the gap or lessening the hostility. A few Muslim organizations were more successful in this when they sponsored Western education within the context of Islam, teaching the Ḳur'ān and Arabic, as well as reading and writing in English, and basic arithmetic in Western-style schools. For the most part, however, Islamic and Western education remained unreconciled and this became a factor of uneven development as Western education continued to supersede Islamic education as the gateway to jobs within the modernizing sector of society and as an index of status during the colonial period.

Indigenous education within the oral cultures also continued largely outside the purview of the Western schools.[10] Contrary to the misconception developed in the colonial period, this system of education went beyond socialization within the extended family, age-grade organizations, and institutions of puberty rites such as the Poro and Bundo of the West Atlantic region. At the elementary level, the child was taught in the informal setting of the family through word play, conundrums and similar exercises, to master the mother tongue. He was taught to count and, through sessions of story-telling, to appreciate his culture, values, world-view and historical background. Through forms of apprenticeship, usually to his father, mother or other relation, the child learnt various crafts and trades. In this process he was made to learn also about the environment, plants and animals, hunting or fishing skills, some manufacturing processes, housekeeping for girls and agriculture for boys, house construction, art, music, dancing, religion and so on. The informality of the processes should not blind us to the deliberate manner in which the education of the child was undertaken, or the extent to which society relied for its survival and sustenance on the individual human factor of ingenuity and innovation and took steps to foster them.

Higher education was reserved largely for the training of rulers and priests. The rulers, especially in the centralized state systems, learnt in depth the history of the community, the legal basis of the claims to their land and other essential properties, the laws and customs, the duties and responsibilities of the ruler, and so on. The pre-coronation period con-

10. M. Bray *et al.*, 1986, ch. 6; N. K. Dzobo, 1975.

tinued the process, emphasizing attitudes and behaviour patterns expected of the ruler, while the coronation rites themselves aimed to transform the ruler from a man to a king pertaining to the nature of a god. The priest went through a rigorous training lasting several years and covering many fields. He had to master religious philosophy and the meaning of various sacred chants, myths, praise verses of various divinities, etc. He was also required to recognize the symptoms of different ailments and know the herbal and ritual cures – for the priest was not only the diviner who communicated between the client and the divinities, he also practised as a healer and, in the more arid areas, as a rain-maker with control over the forces of nature. He had to master, with varying degrees of perfection, the classification and properties of plants and animals, as one versed not only in biology and pharmacology, but also in botanical and zoological semantics and philosophy. Some of the processes of divination also involved intricate mathematical knowledge which modern studies are just beginning to appreciate.[11]

Because of the contempt that those with Western education developed for the indigenous system of education, the spread of Western education has contributed little to the knowledge of agriculture, health sciences, crafts and traditional manufacturing processes that continue to sustain life in the rural areas. Many people, even in the rural areas, have rejected the traditional religion that was the motive force of the indigenous system of education, and identified with Islam and Christianity; but the traditional values did not cease to be important or relevant for them. The world view, the basic aesthetic values and explanations of good and evil, sickness or health, continued to derive from the traditional culture. As Africanized forms of Christianity spread in the rural areas, much of the ethos of this traditional culture, particularly about the nature of illness and the promotion of health, was incorporated. With the increasing recognition of the continuing relevance of traditional agriculture and health sciences, there is a revival of traditional religion, and growing appreciation of the achievements and continued importance of the indigenous system of education.

Expansion and reform

African leaders at independence realized the need for expanding and reforming the colonial system of education. In the words of Sékou Touré of Guinea, 'We must Africanize our education and get rid of the negative features of misconceptions inherited from an educational system designed to serve colonial purposes'.[12] All were agreed on the need for expansion. Apart from a few, like the president of Malawi advocating an unabashed

11. J. F. A. Ajayi, 1987.
12. In A. Sékou Touré, 1963, cited in L. G. Cowan *et al.*, 1965, p. 129.

685

copying of the English public school and the virtues of education based on the study of Latin and Greek, most African leaders agreed on the need for Africanization and rooting education in African cultures. Perhaps no other leader has attempted to formulate and expatiate on a philosophy of African education as clearly as Julius Nyerere of Tanzania, himself a former teacher and generally referred to as *Mwalimu* (teacher). In his *Education for Self-reliance*,[13] in which he emphasized the role of education to achieve his goal of African socialism as outlined in the Arusha Declaration, he advocated four major reforms:

(1) to integrate Western education into the life of the family and community;
(2) to end the élitism of colonial education through a programme of universal primary education that integrates Western and traditional systems of education;
(3) to bridge the gap between the educated élite and the masses through better appreciation in the educated of the accumulated knowledge and wisdom that existed within traditional societies; and
(4) to inculcate the spirit of work and service to the community in the process of education.

Although expansion and reform went on side by side, the initial emphasis was on expansion. At the Addis Ababa Conference in May 1961, convened by UNESCO, representatives of some 35 African independent or soon-to-be-independent countries met to review their systems of education and plan for their immediate and long-term development.[14] The resulting Addis Ababa Plan for African Education set specific targets for expanding enrolments and necessary financial support. Due to the absence or inadequacies of economic development plans, workforce surveys, reliable and comprehensive statistics, and because of the serious underestimation of the demographic phenomena, the Addis Ababa targets can be said, from hindsight, to have reflected more the hopes and aspirations of the participants than the economic realities of Africa. Nevertheless, the conference provided bases for further debate and clarification of the role and pace of educational development in relation to available resources and the needs in other sectors of national life.

The Addis Ababa Plan recognized the dismally inadequate provisions made up to that time for the development of human resources both in terms of quality and numbers. It noted that only 40 per cent of all primary-school-age children were enrolled in any kind of school and that an even smaller percentage of older children were enrolled. Equally important, it noted the questionable quality of the education provided. The conference participants stressed that, given the African conditions of the period:

13. J. Nyerere, 1967c, pp. 10–15.
14. UNESCO, 1961a, pp. 1–127; and UNESCO, 1961b.

the present content of education . . . is not in line with either existing African conditions, the postulate of political independence, the dominant features of an essentially technological age, or the imperatives of balanced economic development involving rapid industrialization. . . . It is based on non-African background, allowing no room for the African child's intelligence, powers of observation and creative imagination to develop freely and help him find his bearings in the world. African educational authorities should revise and reform the content of education in the areas of the curricula, textbooks, and methods, so as to take account of the African environment, child development, cultural heritage, and the demands of technological progress and economic development, especially industrialization . . .[15]

In terms of quantitative goals, the conference plan called for enrolments to expand from the 1960 ratio of 40:3:0.5 (40 per cent of the elementary, 3 per cent of the secondary and one-half of one per cent of the tertiary age group enrolled) to 100:30:20 by 1980. The goal was to make primary education universal, compulsory and free. Of those completing primary education, 30 per cent would proceed to the secondary stage, and 20 per cent of those completing the secondary stage would proceed to the tertiary level, mostly at institutions within Africa. Wastage in primary education would not exceed 20 per cent, and the average number of pupils per teacher would be 35. Increasingly, African teachers would be recruited and trained. In addition, adult education would be provided in the schools, at work-places, and in places of worship. To this end, national governments were called upon to increase their financial support from the prevailing 3–4 per cent of GNP to 4–6 per cent between 1970 and 1980. The African states were also encouraged to enlist the support of the international community in their educational efforts.

Since 1961, periodic conferences of ministers of education addressing the issues of education in Africa have been held: in Narobi 1968, Lagos 1976 and Harare 1982, besides the Tananarive Conference of 1962, specifically on higher education. Each one has built upon the experience of its predecessors – rectifying, refining, gaining knowledge and insight, expanding the visions and aspirations of the African people and their governments, and forming them into a system of co-ordinated, planned educational development. It is now possible to assess the educational development of Africa in relation to these plans and determine the extent to which it has been responsive and relevant to the socio-economic and cultural requirements of the communities as well as the progress made toward universalization of primary and adult education.

Numerically, the rate of growth in enrolment has been impressive. The continent has achieved the highest overall growth rate of any region in

15. UNESCO, 1961a, p. 23; see also UNESCO, 1961b.

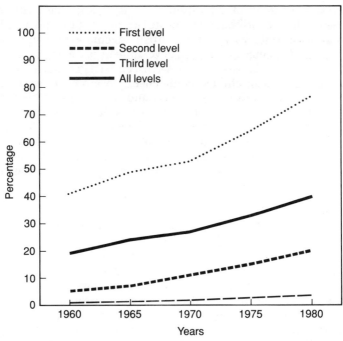

FIG 22.1 *School enrolment in Africa, 1960–80; adjusted gross enrolment ratios by level (Source: based on data obtained from UNESCO in 1982)*

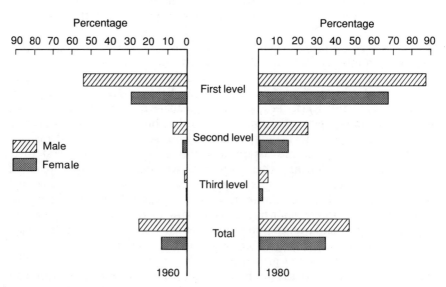

FIG 22.2 *School enrolment in Africa, 1960 and 1980; adjusted gross enrolment ratios by level and sex (Source: based on data obtained from UNESCO in 1982)*

688

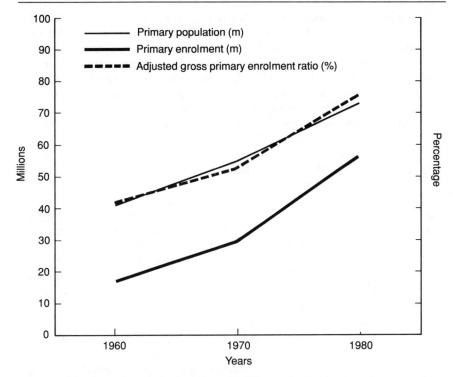

FIG 22.3   *Trends in primary-school enrolment in Africa, 1960–80, showing primary population and primary enrolment in millions, together with the adjusted gross primary enrolment ratio (percentage) (Source: based on data obtained from UNESCO in 1982)*

the world, as well as the most rapid increase in literacy. In several places programmes of universal primary education were embarked upon, and in some free education even up to secondary and tertiary levels. Few leaders championed the cause of universal and free education as consistently as Kwame Nkrumah of Ghana and Obafemi Awolowo of Nigeria. However, even in Ghana and Nigeria, severe economic and demographic pressures have led to a backing away from the effort to make elementary education universal. Resistance to the social effects of Western education – such as encouraging late marriage in girls and rural to urban migration of children – have continued, particularly in Muslim areas. Thus, in spite of the massive expansions, the 1961 targets for primary-school enrolment were not realized, and there has recently been a decline.[16]

Figures 22.1–22.3 depict the pattern of enrolment of all levels of the schooling system for the 1960–80 period. From 1961 to 1980, enrolment

16. See documents made available to the Harare Conference by UNECA, OAU and UNESCO, especially 1982, Documents ED/82/MINEDAF/4 and ED/82/MINEDAF/2 and the World Bank, 1988.

at the primary level increased by 6.2 per cent per annum, exceeding the 5.6 per cent projected in the Addis Ababa Plan. However, mainly because the data used to make projections in 1961 were incomplete, universal primary enrolment had not been achieved by the majority of African countries. About 13 states out of 51 had come close to universal enrolment. For the region as a whole, 62 per cent of primary-school-age children were enrolled by 1980. There were, of course, wide variations in achievement depending on the countries and the base from which their enrolments grew. In 1960, some countries had enrolments as low as 3 or 4 per cent for the 6–11 age group, while some others had a ratio as high as 75 per cent. In 1980, the lowest enrolment was 13 per cent while some 15 countries had attained more than 75 per cent. To achieve this measure of success, the African states embarked upon massive programmes of primary-school construction and teacher training, often with a high degree of community involvement. These efforts, however, were not sufficient to ameliorate the severe shortage of qualified teachers.[17]

Growth rates at the secondary level are even more impressive though uneven. The overall enrolment ratio achieved at the secondary level in 1980 was 20 per cent for the corresponding age groups with variations between countries ranging from 2.1 per cent to 82.3 per cent. In the past seven years some newly-independent states have increased their secondary enrolments five-fold. Female enrolment has lagged behind that of males at all levels.

Another measure of Africa's commitment to development through education can be found in the patterns of resource allocation in the region. For the years 1970 and 1978, public expenditure on education in Africa were US$2377 and US$11 144 billion respectively. When compared to the industrialized nations and other developing regions, Africa's investment in education was significantly low. However, in terms of expenditure as a percentage of GNP, Africa was competitive. For instance, Africa invested 3.8 and 4.8 per cent of GNP in education in 1970 and 1980, respectively, a higher percentage than in the developing countries of the world taken as a whole, where 3.3 per cent was recorded in 1970 and 4.1 per cent in 1980. For the industrially developed regions, the figures were 5.7 and 5.9 per cent respectively.

By 1980, education claimed 25–35 per cent of current government expenditure in Africa. In terms of per capita student-year costs for the late 1970s, it was US$22, US$133 and US$986 for primary, secondary and tertiary education respectively. This represents a commitment that is higher than any other developed or developing region in the world.[18]

In most African countries, education still claims more resources than

17. See UNESCO, UNECA and OAU, 1982, Document ED/82/MINEDAF/2.
18. T. G. Wagaw, forthcoming, ch. 10; also UNESCO, UNECA and OAU, 1982, Document ED/82/MINEDAF/REF.5.

any other function of government except general administration. The question is whether, given the limited fiscal resources of most countries of the region, current levels of investment in education will be sustainable. The answer is probably no, in which case nations may have to resort to new and unconventional methods of financing such as manipulating incentive and salary structures, introducing multiple shifts, utilizing facilities and personnel on a year-round basis (including nights), and increasing the use of long-distance education and the electronic media.

The pressure to keep up the pace of expansion was perhaps the most important factor undermining the efforts to achieve at the same time structural changes in the inherited colonial systems of education. There was no time to halt, make fundamental changes, retrain the staff and create new orientations. Usually, the constant rhetoric emphasizing the need for educational reform produced no more than cosmetic changes while the existing system reproduced itself in responding to increased demand and increased allocation of resources. Yet strenuous efforts were made at the successive pan-African conferences of ministers of education and even more within individual countries[19] to evolve national policies of education that would implement more or less the reforms outlined by President Nyerere – to integrate the traditional forms of education with Western education in a new national system of education; to use education to promote a national ethos, ideology and philosophy, and fundamental principles of a new cohesive, egalitarian society embracing a concept of social justice; to make education less élitist, oriented more to the community than to the individual interests of the educated; to evolve a pattern of education more relevant to the practical and immediate needs of society, emphasizing not only culture but also science, technology and vocational training so that the products would be more readily employable and thus reduce unemployment and underemployment, and so on.

Educational reform is a long, complex and continuous exercise, and the immediate post-independence era probably exaggerated how quickly fundamental reforms could be achieved. Economic recession and political instability have compounded the problems. This is not to deny that some significant changes have been achieved. The dominance of Western education by European and American Christian missionaries has been weakened, if not everywhere superseded by the secular state taking over control. Education has remained the most powerful factor of social mobility and in most places access has been widened if not completely democratized, though various élite and professional groups are able to establish or retain some advantages for their children, through pre-school nursery education and better command of the official European languages. The continued dominance of the European languages thus remains one

19. See, for example, U. Bude, 1980; Federal Republic of Nigeria, Federal Ministry of Education, 1981; and K. King, 1976.

of the basic pillars inhibiting fundamental reform of the colonial systems of education. The African languages that have the advantage of facilitating social integration at the local level and the key to a more thorough-going educational reform have had to play only marginal roles while European languages continue to be promoted as providing politically the most acceptable *lingua franca*. Nowhere is this factor of expansion of facilities and limitation of reform better illustrated than in the field of higher education.

Tertiary education

Institutions of higher learning are the nerve centre of African modernization. They also represent the highest expression of a society's search for continued renewal, enlightenment, growth and fulfilment. Among other things, institutions of higher learning train, certify and otherwise equip some of the sharpest minds for leadership roles in government, business and the professions. The number of people thus equipped and certified is very small but their power and influence in society are disproportionately very high. It is not surprising that these centres of higher learning are looked upon with hope, admiration, awe, fear or suspicion by young and old, and especially by politicians.

Higher education is not new to the African continent. The University of Sankore in Timbuktu flourished in the sixteenth century as a centre for scholarship and learning in law, philosophy and theology. Another institution of similar importance is al-Azhar University in Cairo, which has been in existence for over one thousand years. This institution became well known for the study of Islamic religion and law and still continues to function even as it expands and modernizes its scope by embracing other branches of study. In Ethiopia, as we have seen, scholarship was also nurtured and supported. There were centres of higher studies scattered throughout the highlands where specialists in common law as well as some of the high-level state functionaries were trained. In Sierra Leone, the Church Missionary Society of London founded the Fourah Bay College in 1927 as a centre for religious studies. In the aftermath of the Second World War, the institution formed the basis for a new state university.

There were other centres of higher education in other areas of the continent, including some established by the colonial powers, where instruction in law and the humanities as well as some vocational training were provided. For the most part, however, the 80 or more colleges and universities now operating in Africa came into being after political independence was attained, beginning in the late 1950s. Besides universities, there are different professional schools, advanced teacher-training colleges, polytechnics and colleges of technology.

One year after the 1961 conference in Addis Ababa, a second conference convened in Tananarive, Madagascar, to deal specifically with the development of higher education in Africa for the ensuing 20 years.[20] In spite of the fact that even rudimentary demographic data were still unavailable, the conference tried to determine how many institutions of higher learning were needed and what roles they should play in the development of the region. At the outset, the conference sought to delineate the goals and purposes of higher education. The mission of higher learning, according to the conference participants, was to define and confirm the wishes and aspirations of the respective societies it served. While maintaining international standards of academic excellence, African higher education must provide the African peoples their rightful place in the world and cement their unity forever. To this end, institutions of higher education must consider themselves the cultural centres of the communities in which they exist and the guardians and supporters of artistic, literary and musical heritages. They should carry out research in these heritages and make the fruits of their research available through concerts, galleries, museums, libraries and archives. African universities, like all universities, were expected to advance the frontiers of knowledge through teaching and research as well as through consultancy and service to the larger community.

The universities were established on models drawn either from Western Europe or North America. However, they derived their inspiration from African challenges. In most cases, the political leadership of the respective countries became involved in the development of higher education. Often heads of state or government served as chancellors of the institutions. President Julius Nyerere of Tanzania urged the African university to remain truthful to world standards of objectivity and the pursuit of truth without at the same time becoming isolated from the community. He challenged the University of East Africa to take an active part 'in the social revolution we are engineering' without at the same time becoming a centre of opposition to the legally constituted government. Above all, the university must maintain 'the spirit of truth; it must be as objective and scientific as possible, and must fight prejudices of all kinds, at all times, and at all places . . . the University must think and force us to think in terms of humanity – not any sectoral interests'.[21] The leaders of Ghana, Nigeria, Ethiopia, Côte d'Ivoire and Guinea, among others, reiterated similar hopes that the institutions would stand firm in the search for truth, objectivity, humanity and enlightenment even as they promised to discharge their responsibilities with a spirit of loyal dedication to their immediate society.

Two decades after the Tananarive Conference, analysis reveals that the

20. UNESCO, 1963.
21. Quoted in L. G. Cowan *et al.*, 1965, pp. 309–13; see also pp. 317–21 for extracts from speeches by Kwame Nkrumah of Ghana.

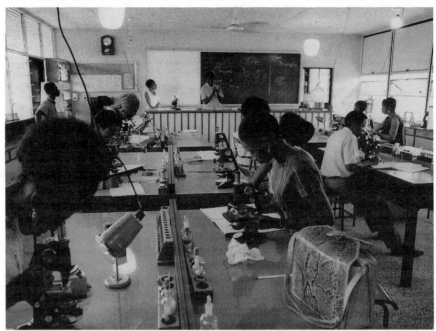

PLATE 22.3 *Above: biology laboratory in a College of Education, University of Lagos, Nigeria, 1968; below: the Kenya Polytechnic and Technical Institution, 1968*

progress of African higher education has been uneven. Overall enrolment grew from 140 000 in 1960 to 1 169 000 in 1980, a more than eight-fold increase. In 1980, 3 per cent of the college-age population were enrolled in universities, exceeding the projected 2 per cent. Indeed, enrolment in higher education continues to grow at a faster rate than enrolment at any other educational level despite the fact that governments have attempted to limit enrolment due to its high cost. This phenomenon illustrates the political realities of education.

African institutions of higher learning are very expensive. The cost of a college student per year has been estimated at $927–1045 for Africa. For the most part, these costs are borne by the national treasuries. The students contribute very little, if anything, to the cost of higher education. University teachers are among the most highly-paid members of the community. Expatriate staff, still common in many institutions, are even more expensive in their salaries, transportation and various allowances. This places an onerous burden on the limited national resources of the respective countries.

Nevertheless, since higher education is perceived as the ticket to the good life – power, money, prestige and influence – young people and their parents continue to demand adequate places in the universities. No matter how reluctant they may be, politicians must respond. As a result, enrolment in higher education continues to expand – sometimes at the expense of the lower levels of education.

A number of additional problems remain unresolved at the tertiary level. It was the hope of African policy-makers that more university students would enroll in the science and technology fields than in the humanities and social sciences. Due to a number of complex social and cultural factors, as well as a lack of adequate facilities and qualified teachers at the lower levels of the school system, this is not happening. The result is skewed. It leaves the critical need for people with specific technical skills unfulfilled, while it maintains a surplus of trained workforce in certain other areas. Some recommendations that have been put forward to reduce this distortion are to strengthen instruction in the lower grades, to provide incentives that encourage people to pursue careers in science and technology, and to provide informed guidance regarding national priorities at all levels.[22]

Another problem is the under-representation of female students in institutions of higher learning. In spite of rhetoric to the contrary, few females attend such institutions, more of them drop out before completing their studies, and those who graduate tend to concentrate in disciplines such as the social sciences and the humanities that are not considered national priorities.

22. See T. G. Wagaw, forthcoming; also A. Habte, 1969; T. M. Yesufu, 1973; and J. F. A. Ajayi, 1987.

As for overall quality, the institutions of higher learning have produced skilled people for the civil service, the military and business, which has in turn diminished Africa's reliance on expatriates. Nevertheless, expatriates still head the large commercial and industrial establishments in most African countries.

African higher education is also constantly challenged to be relevant and responsive to the myriad needs of developing societies. Africa is predominantly rural. The skills needed in farm management, agricultural engineering, home economics, repair and maintenance of farm equipment, animal husbandry, public health and extension education are in short supply. Many strongly believe that universities and colleges should provide, above all else, an adequate number of trained persons capable of addressing and satisfying these needs.

Conducting research, developing appropriate technology, and facilitating its deployment for the solution of development problems are additional critical functions that institutions of higher education are called upon to provide. The discovery, promotion and expansion of the artistic, literary and historical legacies of Africa are also responsibilities that rest on the shoulders of these institutions.

Language issues are still on the agenda. The vast majority of the African people utilize their own respective languages in business and social intercourse. Yet, in most societies, the languages of government, business and education remain the international languages – French, English or Portuguese. These languages are alien in that they are not rooted in African soil and do not draw their continued vitality from the material and cultural essence of Africans. As vectors of values, self-identity and pride, the indigenous languages must be not only researched, codified and taught, but also used as languages of instruction at all levels and as keys to the knowledge and wisdom accumulated by African societies over the centuries. More than ever before, the universities are looked to for leadership in meeting these important needs.

The expansion and revitalization of the entire educational system is an ever-present challenge. The institutions of higher learning are called upon to lead efforts to delineate and articulate educational goals, the direction of the curricula, the improvement of learning and teaching materials, the training of teachers, and the study of human learning and development. To the extent that they consciously and loyally accept their full educational responsibilities, they will come to merit the informed appreciation and the support of their societies, both material and moral. If they do not do this adequately, they deserve to be ignored.

An equally important development in higher education has been the redefinition of the concept of education. This redefinition has been followed by modifications in the philosophies and policies of education. However different the aims and purposes of education may be from one state to the next, many of them seem to have moved towards adopting more or less the following views and policies.

The first is the democratization and relevance of education. Education is more and more viewed in terms of the type of person it hopes to develop. This new person is seen as deeply rooted in the African environment without being isolated from wider human cultures and experience; conscious of his or her political, civic and family responsibilities; and ready to play a dynamic role in the economic, social and cultural development of Africa. In addition to its powerful role in the evolution of democracy, education is increasingly viewed as an instrument for individual as well as societal enlightenment and self-fulfilment.

In contrast to the 1960s when the mission assigned to education was primarily economic, African educators are now taking a more comprehensive view of the nature of the individual child and the developmental aims of education. Since 1960, many African countries have concluded that education should concern itself with all aspects of individual development: physical, intellectual, athletic, social, moral and spiritual. Also, education is now considered the best means for the rediscovery, expansion and promotion of indigenous cultures and indigenous development.[23]

Some policy-makers and educators fear that there is now too much emphasis placed on individual development independent of the larger societal institutions such as the family, and the religious and political institutions. Others think that, while such reservations may have some merit, for the time being the educational system is better organized to provide the controlled environments necessary to produce enough well-educated people to accelerate social development. To this end, they argue, education, as broadly conceived, should be provided with all the support that it needs.

As the institutions move toward increased relevance to and engagement with social needs, staff and students may come into direct conflict with established political authorities. The students and their mentors, the professoriate, may come to detect and analyse discrepancies in administration, incompetence, injustice or violations of basic human rights, and greed in the political establishment. As members of the aspiring intelligentsia, students and academicians often express and at times act on such concerns, and the political leadership usually responds with some physical action which, if successful, threatens the well-being of the institutions. When this happens, the university as well as the larger society suffers. This type of disharmonious interaction between colleges and universities on the one hand and the political leadership on the other, constitutes one of the ominous dangers that threaten the continued vitality

23. For a further analysis of the evolution of policies and aims of education, see UNESCO, UNECA and OAU, 1982, Document ED/82/MINEDAF/3, pp. 9–11; and Document ED/82/MINEDAF/1, pp. 3–20.

of institutions of higher learning. Prudence, patience and a desire to understand and engage in informed dialogue may help ameliorate this problem and thereby free the institutions to discharge their critical responsibilities to Africa and humanity.

Conclusion

African societies like many others had their indigenous systems of education for the transmission of values, skills and attitudes to the oncoming generation. Over time, the indigenous systems were joined by the Islamic and Christian types. A relative newcomer was the European model, religious as well as secular. The dominance assumed by this model during the colonial era has survived the departure of the Europeans. For the last three decades the independent African states have made concerted efforts to extend such education to as large a number of people as resources permitted without succeeding in modifying much of its alien character.

Although progress has been made in educating a significant number of people, not only for political and social consciousness but to build and operate the political, cultural, economic and industrial institutions, the efforts have not accomplished the desired goals relative to the quality and numbers of graduates. African education thus has very far to go. Millions of young people and adults have received no education (Table 22.1). Education is not equally accessible to all segments of society. Females are under-represented at all levels. Rural areas fare worse than urban areas. For a variety of reasons some ethnic or linguistic groups are inadequately served. Too often the curricula and methods of instruction remain bookish and lack relevance to the local realities and problems confronting Africa. Qualified classroom teachers are in short supply. Adequately furnished school facilities, libraries and equipment are either non-existent or inadequate. The list of problems is long and compounded by the fact that the material and human resources in most African nations are limited and already over-extended.

The urgent needs of African states include the consolidation of their independence, the expansion of their economies, and the revival and promotion of their authentic cultures. As an agent of development and social change, the educational systems in Africa are called upon to do more than pass on values and knowledge to the younger generations. They must transform the thinking and attitudes of both individuals and groups in ways that facilitate the creation of conscious citizens, productive and dynamic workers, and the movement of African societies towards achieving goals of progress, justice and liberty.[24] Given the budgetary

24. See UNESCO, 1976, pp. 49–50.

constraints mentioned earlier, imaginative approaches and the creative use of scarce resources must be applied to education at all levels.

Modern authentic education should be designed and implemented in the context of permanent, life-long education, available to all and aimed at developing aptitudes and behaviours in individuals which make them active agents of their own futures and contributors to social evolution.

The adoption of this authentic, modern, development-oriented education requires the complete restructuring of the curricula, the teaching methods, and the preparation of teachers. It calls for, as early as possible, the development of curricula whose scientific and technical nature would be evident from the creative interaction of education with its physical and social environments.

As part of this restructuring, higher education must be redefined and assume a new role. Research and training at the three levels of education must be based upon economic and social realities in such a way that education will be better able to respond to development requirements. Imitation of imported conventions and models will not do. Creating new approaches, modifying the old and incorporating and making them work for Africa are all essential to the task. This authentic, endogenous development of education should be able to assimilate and adapt the most successful foreign experiments while, at the same time, subjecting the results of the innovations undertaken or borrowed to critical analysis and reflections *vis-à-vis* the realities mandated by African conditions.[25] Some interesting experiments are being carried out today in this regard. The most fundamental ones observed are: the transition from élitist education to mass education; and the linking of the school with the life of the community and the strengthening of cultural and national unity. Approaches such as these, coupled with ongoing experimentation and research, are expected eventually to yield achievement of the sought-after goals.

TABLE 22.1 *Illiteracy in Africa: estimates and projections of illiteracy by country, population aged 15+ (M = males, F = females)*

The following table presents, for those countries for which the necessary statistics were available, the estimates and projections of illiteracy rates by country in 1985, 1990 and 2000, prepared by UNESCO. The reader should keep in mind the conditional nature of these projections.

For countries providing the relevant information, the total rate of illiteracy was derived from an analysis of the rates by demographic generation. Following the rate of a cohort from one census to another gives a relatively stable curve: adjusting this statistical curve permits the estimation and projection of the illiteracy rates in a satisfying manner.

25. *ibid.*, pp. 22–47.

For some countries, with insufficient statistical information, an estimation of the global illiteracy rate (15 years and over) was made, without taking into account the generation rates. In this way, by using all the available data for all countries, a preliminary analysis was made to decide the most significant correlation between illiteracy and several socio-economic and educational variables. One multiple regression was finally decided upon with 3 explanatory variables: infant mortality, fertility rate and enrolment ratio in primary education. Following this procedure a certain number of rates were estimated, but due to the uncertainty of some of them, not all are included in this table.

Large decreases in the illiteracy rates are expected not only in those countries where enrolment has rapidly increased, but also in countries where important literacy campaigns have been carried out or are currently underway. These campaigns can completely change the illiteracy rates of certain cohorts, but due to insufficient information the impact of the more recent campaigns has not been reflected in these projections. Consequently, it was considered preferable not to present estimates for certain countries such as Ethiopia and the United Republic of Tanzania which have recently carried out important literacy campaigns.

| Country | Illiterate population (in thousands) | | | Illiteracy rates (percentages) | | | | | | | | |
| | 1985 | 1990 | 2000 | 1985 | | | 1990 | | | 2000 | | |
				Total	M	F	Total	M	F	Total	M	F
Algeria	6 062	6 004	5 578	51.4	37.3	64.9	42.6	30.2	54.5	28.1	19.3	36.7
Angola	3 117	3 221	3 395	64.3	50.4	77.4	58.3	44.4	71.5	46.6	33.6	59.1
Benin*	1 754	1 904	2 251	81.3	74.0	88.3	76.6	68.3	84.4	65.8	56.3	74.8
Botswana*	168	175	189	30.0	18.5	39.6	26.4	16.3	34.9	19.9	12.4	26.5
Burkina Faso*	3 791	4 137	4 813	85.5	77.0	93.8	81.8	72.1	91.1	72.3	60.9	83.3
Burundi*	1 508	1 482	1 386	57.9	46.6	68.2	50.0	39.1	60.2	34.6	25.4	43.3
Cameroon	2 911	2 912	2 858	52.0	38.9	64.4	45.9	33.7	57.4	34.0	24.3	43.4
Central African Republic*	1 014	1 028	1 062	68.5	55.0	80.7	62.3	48.2	75.1	49.9	36.5	62.4
Chad*	2 230	2 280	2 354	77.0	66.0	87.5	70.2	57.8	82.1	56.6	43.3	69.4
Congo	473	485	502	48.3	34.0	61.8	43.4	30.0	56.1	34.1	23.0	44.8
Côte d'Ivoire	2 687	2 941	3 397	51.3	37.5	65.7	46.2	33.1	59.8	36.5	25.1	48.2
Egypt	15 686	16 492	18 535	55.4	40.4	70.5	51.6	37.1	66.2	43.3	30.4	56.4
Equatorial Guinea*	127	127	128	55.1	40.6	68.8	49.8	35.9	63.0	39.5	27.4	51.1
Gabon	284	311	297	43.9	30.1	56.9	39.3	26.5	51.5	30.7	20.3	40.7
Gambia*	336	350	368	79.7	69.6	89.5	72.8	61.0	84.0	58.7	45.5	71.3

Country	Illiterate population (in thousands)			Illiteracy rates (percentages)								
	1985	1990	2000	1985 Total	M	F	1990 Total	M	F	2000 Total	M	F
Ghana	3 316	3 258	2 974	47.2	36.3	57.8	39.7	30.0	49.0	26.4	19.5	33.2
Guinea*	2 879	2 947	3 060	83.2	74.5	91.6	76.0	65.1	86.6	61.5	48.5	73.9
Guinea-Bissau*	368	367	370	69.8	56.6	81.9	63.5	49.8	76.0	50.9	37.6	63.4
Kenya	3 473	3 728	4 360	35.0	22.9	46.8	31.0	20.2	41.5	23.8	15.4	32.0
Liberia	811	839	862	67.7	57.3	78.6	60.5	50.2	71.2	45.3	36.1	54.7
Libyan Arab Jamahiriya	883	890	848	43.5	29.9	59.7	36.2	24.6	49.6	24.0	16.0	32.9
Madagascar	1 309	1 305	1 303	23.1	14.2	31.6	19.8	12.3	27.1	14.5	9.0	19.7
Mali*	3 357	3 398	3 235	77.3	69.0	84.6	68.0	59.2	76.1	48.0	40.1	55.4
Mauritania*	715	740	785	72.5	60.2	84.2	66.0	52.9	78.6	53.1	39.7	65.9
Morocco	7 454	7 526	7 303	58.3	45.7	70.5	50.5	38.7	62.0	36.5	27.0	45.7
Mozambique*	5 593	5 880	6 377	72.4	60.6	83.6	67.1	54.9	78.7	55.4	43.4	66.9
Niger*	2 558	2 683	2 945	78.5	67.9	88.7	71.6	59.6	83.2	57.7	44.5	70.6
Nigeria	28 224	28 723	28 448	57.3	45.2	68.9	49.3	37.7	60.5	34.4	24.9	43.6
Rwanda*	1 701	1 838	2 149	54.6	40.7	67.9	49.8	36.1	62.9	40.9	28.5	52.8
Senegal	2 433	2 525	2 672	67.9	54.6	80.7	61.7	48.1	74.9	49.5	36.3	62.2
Sierra Leone*	1 783	1 830	1 909	86.7	79.2	93.8	79.3	69.3	88.7	64.2	51.5	76.2
Somalia*	2 877	3 003	3 235	83.1	73.3	91.2	75.9	63.9	86.0	61.3	47.9	73.5
Sudan*	9 040	10 061	12 541	75.6	60.7	90.3	72.9	57.3	88.3	66.9	50.4	83.3
Togo*	1 015	1 070	1 173	62.1	48.6	74.9	56.7	43.6	69.3	45.6	33.9	56.8
Tunisia	1 858	1 762	1 497	42.4	32.2	52.7	34.7	25.8	43.7	22.5	16.0	29.1
Uganda*	4 600	4 908	5 545	57.2	42.9	71.0	51.7	37.8	65.1	41.1	28.8	53.0
Zaire	5 641	5 466	4 919	34.1	20.6	46.8	28.2	16.4	39.3	18.3	10.1	26.3
Zambia	1 172	1 170	1 127	32.6	23.3	41.3	27.2	19.2	34.7	18.2	12.6	23.6
Zimbabwe	1 683	1 776	1 900	37.7	30.2	45.0	33.1	26.3	39.7	25.4	20.0	30.6

*Countries belonging to the group of least developed countries

Source: UNESCO (1990) *Compendium of Statistics on Illiteracy*, No. 31, Division of Statistics on Education, Office of Statistics (Paris: UNESCO).

SECTION VI

Pan-Africanism: liberation and integration since 1935

Africa and its diaspora since 1935

23

Joseph E. HARRIS

in collaboration with

Slimane ZEGHIDOUR

In the twentieth century and especially after World War I, it was the American Negro who spoke forcefully for African Negro rights during the making of the Treaty of Versailles and the formation of the League of Nations at a time when we were not in a position to speak for ourselves.[1]

We must never forget that they [diaspora blacks] are part of us. These sons and daughters of Africa were taken away from our shores, and . . . they have not forgotten their ancestral links . . . Long before many of us were even conscious of our own degradation, these men fought for African national and racial equality . . . Now that we in Africa are marching towards the complete emancipation of this continent, our independent status will help in no small measure their efforts to attain full human rights and dignity as citizens of their country.[2]

The greatest service you could render your country would be to influence thousands of Black people in the U.S.A. and the West Indies and let them come and help us develop Ethiopia.[3]

The quotations above clearly show that the historically dynamic relationship between continental Africa and its diaspora, which were discussed in the previous volumes, continued after 1935. That relationship survived the slave trade to Asia, Europe, the Americas and elsewhere, and was sustained in host countries abroad by psychological and social experiences which led to protests, revolts and the development of international efforts to liberate themselves and to assure freedom and equality for Africans and their descendants abroad. While the type, demography and severity of slavery, as well as the ratio of slaves to master, greatly influenced the socialization process and thus helped to shape the diaspora African's perspective of Africa, so too did the colonial experience of continental Africans mould their views of African people overseas. In both situations

1. A. Diop, 1958.
2. K. Nkrumah, 1958a.
3. M. Bayen, 1939.

Europeans, Americans and Asians derogated blackness and discouraged the establishment of an international black network. But the idea of a 'redemption' of Africa to provide freedom for blacks and to demonstrate their ability to govern and contribute to world civilization emerged as a powerful force in the diaspora and led to the development of a number of international black movements for freedom. As was clearly brought out in Chapter 29 of Volume VII, the peak of that emergence of African and diaspora efforts occurred in the pan-African movement between 1900 and 1935, with the greatest activities during the 1920s, thanks to the efforts of Marcus Garvey, W. E. B. DuBois and others in Europe and the United States, and those of African students, especially in France and England. What, then, happened in the field of the diaspora from 1935 onwards?

In the first place, the migration of Africans into Europe, Asia and the New World continued after 1935 though there was a significant change in the motivating factors, volume and direction. The fundamental cause of the diaspora during the centuries to about the end of the nineteenth century was, of course, the slave trade across the Mediterranean Sea, the Indian and above all the Atlantic Oceans. (See Volumes III and VII.) From the beginning of this century – particularly from 1935 until the 1960s – the colonial system became the principal motivating factor. An increasing number of Africans seeking freedom from economic and political oppression migrated to European capitals. This was particularly true of the French North African and the Belgian colonies and especially of Algeria, from which thousands of people migrated to France during the period under review. During the Algerian war of independence, for example, there were about 450 000 Algerians in France and very few of them returned home.[4] Another important push factor was the need for higher education in particular which was the direct outcome of the neglect of higher education by nearly all the colonial powers. Thus the number of African students going to Europe and the United States increased greatly between 1935 and 1960 and quite a substantial number of them never returned home. During this period the migration of Africans to South America, the Caribbean and India virtually ended, an overwhelming majority of them heading towards Europe and the United States compared with the previous two centuries. Although no figures are available, it can be confidently asserted that the number of Africans involved was rather small, confined as it was mainly to students.

After the independence revolution, that is, from the 1960s onwards, the diaspora continued although again its nature and motivation as well as its direction changed. It became more and more the migration not of students but rather of technical and highly qualified professionals such as doctors, engineers, businessmen, musicians, artists, university lecturers

4. For an excellent account of Algerian migrations to Europe, see C. R. Ageron, 1979.

and professors. During this period, the direction also resumed its world-wide aspect of the pre-twentieth-century era, for Africans moved not only to Europe and America but also into the Middle East, the socialist countries, Canada, Australia and the South Pacific. There are African lecturers and professors lecturing at the University of Papua New Guinea! This is a phenomenon which has now become known as the 'brain drain' and it assumed really alarming proportions in the 1960s and 1970s but seems fortunately to be on the decline now. During this period, African physicians, dentists, scientists, engineers, teachers and so forth become familiar figures abroad. While Africa needed their expertise, they became positive evidence that Africa had arrived, intellectually, culturally and politically.

Another very recent feature of the diaspora is the gender drain which involves the migration of literate and even semi-literate, qualified and unqualified, African women out of Africa, especially from the west coast, to Europe – particularly to France, Germany and the United Kingdom – and to the Americas in search of jobs (especially nursing) and of fortune (which has involved them in activities related to smuggling and drug-trafficking). Then there is the third feature of the modern diaspora, the male equivalent of the female phenomenon, an increasing infiltration into European capitals of Africans, semi-educated, unskilled and untrained, in search again of fortune through all sorts of ways, fair or foul, ranging from dish-washing and manual labour to smuggling and drug-trafficking.

The final new category of the recent diaspora consists of those who leave their countries to settle abroad either permanently or temporarily mainly for political reasons. Some of them are victims of civil wars in their own countries. Others are victims of inter-border disputes between two independent African countries; others are unsuccessful plotters and organizers of *coup d'Etat* against ruling governments; while finally, others are those who are expelled from their own countries by their own governments for one reason or the other, such as spying for other countries. This did occur, for instance, in 1986 in Ghana when eight Ghanaians accused of spying for the United States were deprived of their Ghanaian citizenship and repatriated in exchange for one Ghanaian security agent operating in the United States!

As can be easily deduced from the above, the main reasons for the continuing and changing nature of the diaspora are the increasingly deteriorating socio-economic and political conditions since the independence revolution (discussed in other chapters of this volume) and the consequent need to emigrate to seek new employment, job satisfaction, quick fortune or even adventure.

The Africans in the diaspora since 1935

What have the Africans in the diaspora been doing in their new homes in the area of pan-Africanism since the 1930s? As we have seen, all those pan-Africanist activities in the Americas as well as in Europe virtually disappeared after the Pan-African Congress of 1927 in New York. Two events of the late 1930s – Italy's aggression against Ethiopia (1935–41) and the rise of fascism in Europe – greatly stimulated pan-Africanism and pan-Africanist activities, especially in Europe and the Americas, culminating first in the Manchester Pan-African Congress in 1945 and partly in the independence revolution and the overthrow of the colonial system in the 1950s and 1960s. These two events dramatized not only the dependent relationship of Africa to Europe but also the ineffectiveness and lack of determination of the powers individually or under the auspices of the League of Nations to assure freedom and justice.

In England, C. L. R. James and others founded the International African Friends of Ethiopia (IAFE) in 1936. Largely through lectures, petitions and demonstrations the IAFE won support for Ethiopia. However, a broader-based more militant organization, the International African Service Bureau (IASB), was formed in 1937 and became more effective in wedding local issues to the Ethiopian crisis. The IASB was designed to serve blacks in Britain educationally, economically and politically. Through its paper, *International African Opinion*, the organization had wide appeal and sought co-operation with groups in the United States.[5]

In the midst of these developments in England was George Thomas Nathaniel Griffith, a Guyanese better known as Ras Makonnen. Having studied in and made a number of black friends in the United States, Makonnen became a major, frequently low-profile force among blacks in Britain. After having worked and saved money, he opened several restaurants and clubs in Manchester where he promoted causes of concern for workers and blacks. His several businesses included the Ethiopian Teashop, Cosmopolitan, Forum Club, Belle Etoile and others where future black leaders of Africa and the Caribbean debated issues of the day. Moreover, a number of black students supported themselves as university students by working in Makonnen's businesses.[6]

With the help of his fellow compatriot, Dr Peter Milliard, the Kenyan Jomo Kenyatta, and George Padmore, Makonnen established the Pan-African Publishing Company which published the *Pan-Africa* monthly periodical. The Economist was his bookstore.[7] This institutional base paved the way for the most successful meeting of black nationalists prior

5. V. P. Thompson, 1969, p. 32.
6. K. King, 1971, pp. 135–8.
7. *ibid.*, p. 145.

to the era of independence. More specifically, that core of leadership was joined by the South African Peter Abrahams, Sierra Leonean Wallace-Johnson, C. L. R. James and later Kwame Nkrumah, to form in 1944 the Pan-African Federation which organized the momentous Fifth Pan-African Congress which was convened in Manchester in 1945.

In the United States, under the leadership of William Leo Hansberry, blacks from Africa and the diaspora in 1934 organized the Ethiopian Research Council (ERC) to disseminate information about Ethiopia and to help forge an international black network to work on behalf of Africa-related causes. The organizers – William Leo Hansberry, Ralph Bunche and William Steen of the United States; Hosea Nyabongo of Uganda and Malaku Bayen of Ethiopia – recognized that Ethiopia had great appeal among African peoples and that historically the consciousness of the Ethiopian heritage had inspired a redemptive ideology which continued as a recurring force of identity and solidarity in Africa and the diaspora.[8]

Although the ERC was essentially a small group of professors and students associated with Howard University, it established functional relations with committed individuals in several United States' cities, Ethiopia, England, France, Italy and the Caribbean. The significance of the organization stems from its role as a clearing-house for information on Ethiopia and a facilitator/co-ordinator of activities on behalf of Ethiopia.

When Italy invaded Ethiopia many African-Americans expressed eagerness to join the Ethiopian military, but the United States proclaimed neutrality and prevented Americans from participating in the war. In spite of that official position, two African-American pilots, Hubert Julian and John Robinson, encouraged by the ERC, did go to Ethiopia to fight. Robinson became the emperor's private pilot and aviation adviser. Known as the Brown Condor, Robinson flew several missions for Ethiopia and his plane was shot down on one occasion.[9]

More significant than military participation was the diaspora's moral and material contributions. Blacks in colonial Africa as well as the diaspora organized public demonstrations and wrote editorials and articles supportive of the Ethiopian cause. A number of pro-Ethiopian organizations emerged in the United States. One notable example was the Friends of Ethiopia (FOA) organized by Willis Huggins, an African-American teacher who had visited Europe and elicited endorsements from Ethiopia's ambassadors in London and France. Within a year, the FOA had branches in 106 cities and 19 states. Joint fund-raising plans were made with the International African Friends of Ethiopia in London.[10]

8. Ethiopian Research Council, 1935; J. E. Harris, 1974, ch. 1.

9. J. Cheeks, 1936; and J. Cheeks, unpublished MS on his experiences in Ethiopia with Robinson.

10. W. N. Huggins and J. G. Jackson, 1937, pp. 90–1, n.d., and 1935.

Another notable example of support came from the Medical Committee for the Defense of Ethiopia, a group of black doctors from the Caribbean and the United States practising in New York. They sent at least one, and possibly two, shiploads of medical supplies to the embattled Ethiopians. Other groups in the United States, Jamaica, Trinidad, Panama, Barbados, St Lucia, and elsewhere distributed pro-Ethiopian pamphlets, held mass meetings and expressed their pro-Ethiopian sentiments. Not surprisingly, pro-Ethiopian sentiment was especially vocal among the Rastafarians who earlier had deified Emperor Haile Selassie and adopted his previous title, Ras Tafari.[11]

Diaspora support continued even after the emperor was forced into exile. Fund-raising continued and in at least one case African-Americans engaged in private diplomacy. A delegation was dispatched to London and persuaded the emperor, over US State Department objections, to send an emissary to rally support for Ethiopia. Thus in 1936, Malaku Bayen, a 1935 Howard University Medical School graduate and a founder of ERC, arrived in New York as the emperor's emissary to the American hemisphere. Bayen and his African-American wife were well received by African-Americans and some whites. A number of large fund-raising rallies was held. But the greatest result of Bayen's presence in the United States was the Organization of the Ethiopian World Federation (EWF) in 1937. Bayen publicly stated that 'We are out to create a United States of Africa'. He also held that the EWF would instil black pride in the black world. By 1940 Bayen was praising Marcus Garvey and crediting the UNIA with having laid the foundation for the EWF.[12]

Like Garvey, the Bayens initiated an official publication, *The Voice of Ethiopia*, 'a paper for the Vast Universal Black Commonwealth and Friends of Ethiopia Everywhere'. *The Voice* played a central role in the redefinition of African people. It opposed the use of the term 'Negro' as an 'insulting tool' to divide black people. 'We are no more West Indian and American Black people, but true Ethiopians'; 'Black America, Ethiopia is yours'. The term 'black' gained popularity: 'Black Men Let Us Get Together'; 'No Black Man Shall Shed His Blood for Europe Until Ethiopia Is Free'. These and other slogans were popularized by *The Voice*.[13]

The Voice featured articles by George Padmore, Nnamdi Azikiwe, W. E. B. DuBois, J. A. Rogers, Akiki Nyabongo and others. Quizzes on black history appeared regularly in *The Voice* along with pieces on such black personalities as Toussaint L'Ouverture of Haiti, Menelik of Ethiopia,

11. US Archives, Diplomatic Branch, 884, 142/19, Photo/Article, Enclosure; see also L. Barrett, 1977.

12. *Voice of Ethiopia*, 19 March 1938, 6 May 1939, June 1939, 8 July 1939, 3 February 1940, 24 May 1940.

13. *ibid.*, 19 March 1938, 29 April 1939, 24 June 1939, 15 July 1939, and 29 July 1939.

James Aggrey of the Gold Coast, Richard Wright of the United States, and many others.

Because branches of the EWF were established throughout the United States and the Caribbean, one can get an idea of the scope of its impact. On 23 July 1939, an estimated 800 Jamaicans witnessed the unveiling of an EWF charter, and Amy Garvey gave the main address. In November 1939, a charter was unveiled in Havana, Cuba, and in Tela, Spanish Honduras. Several speakers on these occasions praised Garvey's work.[14]

A regular section on 'News of the Black Commonwealth' gives an indication of the influence of *The Voice* and the organization. News and letters appeared from Egypt, Ethiopia, Sudan, Panama, Jamaica, Honduras, Venezuela, Nigeria and elsewhere. Reports of *The Voice's* articles appeared in *The Comet* (Nigeria), *The Boston Chronicle* (United States), *The Panama Tribune* (Panama), *The Union Messenger* (St Kitts) and *The People* (Trinidad). Contributions to the Ethiopian cause were acknowledged from British Guyana; Bocas del Toro and Gamboa, Panama; San Andres Island, Colombia; Westmoreland, Jamaica; Maracaibo and Longunillas, Venezuela.

When Haile Selassie regained the throne in 1941 he supported the establishment of the first Ethiopian co-educational school which was founded by Mignon Ford, a Barbadian who had emigrated from the United States in 1930. The physicians, pilots, teachers and other African-American emigrés of that period had returned to the United States. But in 1943, William Leo Hansberry arranged for several African-Americans to go to Ethiopia where they served as teachers and journalists. Others from Barbados, Guyana, Puerto Rico and the United States went as pilots and mechanics.[15]

Italy's invasion of Ethiopia also inspired the organization in 1937 of the International Committee on Africa which in 1941 became the Council on African Affairs.[16] The founder was Max Yergan, an African-American who had worked for about 20 years in Eastern and Southern Africa as secretary for the YMCA. He was no doubt influenced by his contacts with the African National Congress and Industrial Commercial Workers Union in South Africa. Long committed to 'helping Africa', Yergan convinced a number of blacks and liberal whites to join him in founding the Council. Paul Robeson, the noted concert singer, William Alphaeus Hunton, also an ex-YMCA worker, and Yergan were the principal leaders of the organization while wealthy white liberals provided financial support.

14. *ibid.*, 19 August 1939, 5 November 1939, 11 November 1939, and 9 December 1939.
15. US Archives, 884, 01A/72, Employment of American Citizens by the Ethiopian Government, 13 March 1944.
16. H. Lynch, 1978.

PLATE 23.1 *Some outstanding personalities of the African diaspora, famous for their fight for blacks' rights: above left, George Padmore; above right, Paul Robeson and W. E. B. DuBois; below left, Marcus Garvey; below right, Max Yergan*

Yergan, Hunton and Robeson subscribed to Marxism and had good connections with the American Communist Party, although they do not seem to have been members at the time. Still, their ideological persuasion made the Council the object of public attack. At that time, however, the general political line was a 'united front against fascism' which included co-operation with the communists. Many intellectuals, trades-unionists and others co-operated with communists to achieve particular goals, and blacks were no exception.

The Council's objectives were the promotion of the political liberation of Africans and the advancement of their social and economic status through the dissemination of relevant and current information, facilitation of training for Africans in Europe and America, and arrangement of mutual exchange of visits and co-operation among African people. One example of the latter was a public meeting between D. T. T. Jabavu and A. B. Xuma, American-educated South Africans who were leaders of the All-African National Convention (AANC) organized in 1935 to promote the rights of black South Africans.

After 1941 the Council became a more active advocate for Africa and decolonization generally. Branches were organized in several United States' cities and included Rosebery T. Bokwe, a South African medical doctor who was also a member of the African National Congress (ANC). Letters and petitions were sent to United States' and European governments and international bodies, and encouragement was given to African labour and nationalist groups. One indication of the Council's influence may be seen by the banning of its publication *New Africa* in Kenya, South Africa and the Belgian Congo.

As a precursor of a specifically African lobby in the United States, several Council members met in 1944 with officials of the recently-established Africa Division of the US State Department and recommended a pro-African policy. Indeed, the use of a few black experts on Africa seemed to have been a result. At the initial UN Conference which convened in San Francisco in 1945, Yergan and Eslanda Robeson called for the promotion of economic, political and social welfare of Africans. The Council specifically urged that the mandates and all African territories of Spain, Portugal and Italy, except Eritrea, be placed under UN trusteeship and that South Africa not become a member of the trusteeship council.

After the Second World War, the Council increasingly became anti-American in its statements. This resulted partly from the Cold War developments that pitted East against West, but also because of the accelerating freedom movements in Africa and the diaspora. The Council showed particular concern for South Africa, not only because of Yergan's experiences there but also because of the increasing repression of blacks, especially from the late 1940s. Famine in South Africa exacerbated the situation. However, the Council established the Committee for South African Famine Relief which sent money and food to alleviate the condition of hunger.

South Africa's incorporation of South-West Africa became a source of vigorous protest. The Council published editorials and pamphlets on the issue. One such pamphlet was written by I. B. Tabata, who first published the piece under the aegis of the ANC in 1945. Hunton wrote pieces about famine and political repression in South Africa; he also sent periodic reports of UN proceedings to African nationalists in Africa, Europe and the United States.

The board of the Council became all black in 1949. Paul Robeson was chosen as chairman, W. E. B. DuBois as vice-chairman, and Hunton as executive secretary. The growing radicalism of the Council became clear and brought greater harassment from the US government; but the Council continued its fight for African issues until its demise in 1955. It had thus paved the way for a more extensive and effective African-American lobby on African and black world issues for the future.

The Fifth Pan-African Congress

The several organizations and meetings in Europe, Africa and the United States to co-ordinate actions on behalf of Africans and their descendants abroad culminated in the convening of the Fifth Pan-African Congress in Manchester, England, in 1945. This Congress will be discussed in detail in Chapter 25. Suffice it to point out here that it was this Congress under the chairmanship of DuBois that really launched pan-Africanism as a liberation movement in Africa rather than in Europe and the Americas. Essentially, the Congress represented a synthesis of DuBois' intellectualism and Garvey's pragmatism, and signalled to the world that the primary struggle for liberation had transferred to Africa and its leaders. Moreover, whereas Blacks in the United States and the English-speaking Caribbean had been the most outspoken and effective leaders in pan-Africanism up to 1945, in the 1950s the movement for equality within the United States became the major locus of activity while Barbados, Jamaica, and Trinidad and Tobago attempted to make their Federation function.

Links to Africa, however, continued. Back in 1947 Alioune Diop, a Senegalese in Paris, founded *Présence africaine*, a widely-read journal devoted to African culture. In 1957 Diop issued a call for a world conference of Black writers. Out of that conference emerged the *Société africaine de culture* (SAC) which led to its US branch, the American Society of African Culture (AMSAC) headed by John A. Davis. AMSAC published the *African Forum*. Both the SAC and AMSAC collaborated in a number of conferences, exhibits and publications, thereby strengthening pan-African links.

By the mid-1960s, Malcolm X, Minister of the Nation of Islam ('Black Muslims'), had emerged as a very popular figure among African-Americans generally, but especially the young. He urged a study of the African roots and self-determination among Blacks. In 1964 he organized the Organization of African-American Unity which he hoped would unite African-Americans in their national struggle and co-operate with the OAU as well. His assassination in February 1965 cut short his efforts. But his *Autobiography* by Alex Haley and *The Wretched of the Earth* by

PLATE 23.2   *Malcolm X, a passionate figure in the fight for Black rights*

the Martinican, Franz Fanon, became virtual handbooks for emerging young leaders of the 'Black Power' movement, including Stokely Carmichael, Walter Rodney and others.

By the late 1960s, young African-Americans in the United States became the vanguard of a resurgent international African consciousness. Not only did they demonstrate their pride in life-styles derivative of Africa – wearing dashikis, decorative beads and bracelets, natural hair-styles, and assuming African names – they demanded Black studies (studies of Africa and the diaspora) in their schools and colleges. Thus a proliferation of publications appeared to support the introduction and expansion of Black studies, African-American studies, pan-African studies, African studies and so forth at many black and white American colleges and universities. Continental and diaspora Africans headed and taught in those programmes.

The Black-studies movement owed some of its success to the withdrawal of a number of African and diaspora scholars from the United States African Studies Association meeting in Canada in 1969.[17] That breakaway

17. I. S. Reid, 1976.

group, the African Heritage Studies Association (AHSA), began to hold its own conferences, sponsor publications and generally encourage the reinterpretation of black peoples' history from a black perspective. It promoted the dissemination in all schools of materials on the African heritage, and it encouraged international collaboration among black intellectuals. The high point of the AHSA occurred at its annual meeting in 1970 when over 2000 delegates from Africa and the diaspora met at Howard University.

There was also in the United States official black concentration on African and diaspora issues. Beginning in 1969 black congressmen began informal meetings under the chairmanship of Charles Diggs. The group formally organized in 1971 as the Congressional Black Caucus. In addition to monitoring and recommending policies for African-American concerns, the Caucus did the same for African and Caribbean issues. Several Caucus members have travelled widely throughout Africa and the Caribbean, criticized United States' policies there and initiated legislation supportive of those areas. This group of black congressmen has on several occasions been able to mobilize support within and outside Congress and has thus become a significant force for freedom and equality in the United States and abroad.

Since 1969 blacks in the United States have formed many cultural, political and developmental organizations with a principal interest in Africans and links with the diaspora: African-American Scholars Council, American Negro Leadership Conference on Africa, African Liberation Day Coordinating Committee, Africare, Congress of African People, and others. And once again, those organizations – along with similar developments in Africa – facilitated communication among African peoples and led to the convening of the Sixth Pan-African Congress in Dar es Salaam in 1974.

Professor St Clair Drake, pan-Africanist theorist and practitioner, has observed that the First Festival of Negro Arts in Dakar, Senegal, in 1966 signalled that cultural pan-Africanism would provide a broader base of identification and co-operation among African people than political pan-Africanism. For those observers less clairvoyant than Drake, the Sixth Pan-African Congress of 1974 certainly revealed the limited political influence of diaspora Blacks in continental forums. Diaspora delegates to the Congress witnessed the downgrading of race by a resolution which criticized 'skin-colour politics'. United States' African-Americans were also criticized for not pursuing an alliance with white workers.[18]

Drake again is helpful in analysing the problem. He has distinguished between racial pan-Africanism, which dominated the early pan-Africanists, and continental pan-Africanism, which appeals to those whose priority is continental unity. The latter not only includes North Africa; it also

18. St C. Drake and R. B. Laporte, 1982.

encourages non-blacks from countries like Brazil and Cuba – with large, possibly majority, communities of African ancestry – to represent and to speak for blacks who frequently are denied opportunities to represent themselves because of political, economic or educational inequity. Racial pan-Africanists adamantly denounce this situation.

Pan-Africanism is in fact undergoing a transformation. Continental Africans are primarily preoccupied with issues affecting national unity and development; problems common across the continent and which therefore encourage continental unity as a priority. The kind of resources African countries require for development, the magnitude of that need and the structures that are available to facilitate communication to acquire the necessary resources, all favour country-to-country relations and major funding from international agencies and super powers. Black-led countries outside Africa have similar regional-based priorities which require substantial funding. And diaspora Blacks without control over their governments have limited opportunities to render the vital support needed in Africa or elsewhere in the black world, unless they develop strong non-governmental structures with links abroad.

The United States is the only country capable of substantial assistance and which has a large and influential population of African ancestry sensitive to black world issues. But that population is a minority and neither makes nor implements foreign policy. Moreover, they and other diaspora Africans generally accept their national identity. Consequently, the early pan-African idea of a mass return to Africa is not an appealing proposition to them or to Africans, whose people are already underemployed and underserviced in the social sector. Consequently, more realistic considerations of how diaspora Africans can apply pressure at home and extend economic and political assistance are issues that dominate contemporary black debates.

Given the fact of continental over racial unity in Africa, ideological differences and the reality of citizenship in Africa and the diaspora, what is the future of the African–diaspora connection? Both retain a strong psychological and social identity which reinforces international networks and can exert pressure on national governments to support policies and programmes in the interest of African peoples. This is the philosophy which sustains TransAfrica, the African-American lobby for Africa and the Caribbean. That organization, which publishes *TransAfrica Forum*, is well respected by the Organization of African Unity and other world bodies. Indeed, TransAfrica is a product of earlier African-American lobbies and now has the expertise, black world constituency and support for its efforts.

Other examples of the TransAfrican approach may be seen in the following conferences: FESTAC-77, the World Black and African Festival of Arts and Culture in Lagos, Nigeria, which led to the establishment of the Centre for Black and African Arts and Civilization in Lagos to

717

promote communication in Africa and the diaspora through international forums, exhibitions and publications; the Congress of Black Culture in the Americas which convened in Colombia (1977), Panama (1980), Brazil (1982) and produced several publications; the Festival of the African Diaspora in Brazil (1979), Haiti (1980), Suriname (1982), Senegal (1983) and Barbados (1985); UNESCO's Meetings of Experts on the Diaspora in Haiti (1978), Barbados (1980), Benin (1983) and Brazil (1985) and which have produced several publications; the First and Second African Diaspora Studies Institutes at Howard University (1979) and the University of Nairobi, Kenya (1981), which resulted in a book and a newsletter in English, French, Portuguese and Spanish; the World Conferences on Orisha Tradition and Culture at the University of Ife, Nigeria (1981), and Bahia, Brazil (1983); the African/Afro-American Connection: From Dependency to Self-Reliance in Monrovia, Liberia (1983) which produced 'The Liberia Declaration' calling for co-operation among African peoples and the pooling of their resources.[19] Other conferences with equally important goals and results have no doubt met.

The proliferation of diaspora organizations and conferences has already strengthened the means of communication among African peoples, elevated their level of pride and action, stimulated many research projects and publications and thus expanded the pool of expertise and knowledge of African peoples. However, several descendant African groups remain too unknown because of limited research and publications.

Expanding horizons of African consciousness.

It is significant to note that the African diaspora is virtually global and that several of the lesser-known communities of African descent strongly affirm their African identity. In South America, generally, the official line is that descendant Africans have been or are being assimilated into the Hispanic and Lusophonic cultures, racial identity in most census reports was discontinued decades ago, and racial issues are difficult to identify. Nevertheless, African-South Americans not only reflect their Africanity in literature and song, they have also organized to challenge racism and co-ordinate self-help, educational and cultural programmes.[20]

Although the African presence in Argentina, Bolivia, Chile, Paraguay and Uruguay has been virtually eclipsed, the small number of blacks in Peru has a theatre group, *Expression Negra Peruna*, and an institute, the

19. The *African Diaspora Studies Newsletter*, vol. 1, no. 1, was published in 1948 in English, French, Spanish and Portuguese; see also *Carib*, 1981.

20. L. Rout, 1976, is an excellent book on this subject; important current sources include *Palenque*, the official publication of the *Centro Cultural Afro-Ecuatoriano*; the *Boletin Informativo*, the regular official publication of the *Instituto de Investigaciones Afro-Peruana*, Lima, Peru; *Centro De Estudos E Investigaciones*, 1977; and J. M. R. Guedez, 1985.

Instituto de Investigaciones Afro-Peruana. In Ecuador, where estimates of the black population range up to 10 or 15 per cent, with a few districts reportedly over 50 per cent, the *Centro de Estudios Afro-Ecuatorianos* has active branches in several cities and villages. In 1983 the *Centro* hosted a Pan-American Conference on Black Women. In Venezuela, with a black population of nearly 30 per cent, there is the Section Africa Y Afro-America at the *Instituto Autonomo Biblioteca Nacional.* Colombia's black population is estimated between 30 and 40 per cent, making it the largest African-Hispanic community of African descent. The dominant African-Colombian organizations are: the Colombian Folklore Research Foundation, the Centre for Research on Black Culture and the Black Cultural Movement. The former organized a national colloquium on African-Colombian bibliography in 1983; the latter publishes a monthly, *Presentia Negra.*[21]

In the case of Brazil, which shares the tradition of historically projecting a post-slavery assimilationist policy, there is unmistakable evidence of a sizeable, possibly 50 per cent, African-Brazilian population which would make African-Brazilians the largest diaspora community, and it has had a significant cultural impact on the non-African descendants. Still, except for the voluntary emigration of thousands of African-Brazilians to the Gold Coast, Togo, Dahomey and Nigeria during the nineteenth century, black Brazilians seem to have had very little success in establishing or sustaining links with continental Africa or the diaspora until relatively recently.

The newspaper, *Afro-Brazil,* is published in Salvadore, Bahia, where the largest African-Brazilian community lives. Also in Salvadore is the *Centro de Estudos Afro-Orientais* which houses the *Museo Afro-Brasileiro.* In the federal capital, Brasilia, a core of researchers at Pro Memoria concentrates on the African-Brazilian heritage.

The *Centro de Estudos Afro-Asiaticos* of the Candido Mendes Universidade in Rio de Janeiro sponsors lectures and publications on African-Brazilian subjects. Also in Rio is the *Instituto De Pesquisas e Estudos Afro-Brasileiros* (IPEAFRO) headed by Abdias Nascimento, a federal deputy of African descent. IPEAFRO publishes the journal, *Afrodiaspora.*[22]

The *Movimento Negro Unificado Contra a Discriminacao Racial* annually sponsors the National Day of Black Consciousness on 20 November, the day when Zumbi do Palmares, the African founder of the Palmares Quilombo, was killed by the Portuguese in 1695. A monument to commemorate Zumbi has been approved by the Brazilian government.

---

21. *Presentia Negra* is the regular official publication of the *Centro para la investigación de la cultura negra, Bogota, Colombia.*

22. *Afrodiaspora: Revisto Quadrimestal Do Mundo Negro* (Rio de Janeiro), edited by A. D. Nascimento; and *Estudos Afro-Asiaticos,* published by the *Centro de Estudos Afro-Asiáticos,* Rio de Janiero, are both regular publications.

Branches of *Movimento Negro* exist in the United States and elsewhere.[23]

The Central American countries share the Hispanic tradition. Some of them also have two types of descendant Africans, native and immigrant. The former are citizens by birth; the latter are descendants of immigrant workers from neighbouring English-speaking countries. A major conflict has thus stemmed from governmental policies of Hispanization. This is especially evident in Costa Rica where nineteenth-century mercenary soldiers and later workers for railroad construction and banana plantations arrived from Jamaica, Trinidad, and other Caribbean islands.[24]

Panama has a similar problem, but unlike Costa Rica, it has a large if not majority black population of native and immigrant groups. The latter were largely Barbadian, Jamaican, Trinidadian and some from the United States, and were used by the United States to construct and fortify the Panama Canal. The United Fruit Company also imported Blacks as plantation workers. Those American employers established their customary segregation practices which further aggravated relations. There are, however, Black consciousness groups of both black populations.

Blacks in Mexico comprise a very small minority, possibly no more than 1 per cent. The new African Studies Centre, however, is actively promoting interest in African culture and pan-Africanism. In Cuba, where the African population has been estimated at between 30 and 40 per cent, unlike other Spanish-speaking Blacks, African-Cubans have been vocal participants in Cuban politics for most of this century. However, although Nicolas Guillen founded the *negrismo* school of Cuban poetry which drew on African roots, the government emphasizes the theme of nationalism over diverse identities. But the African influence remains strong in music, literature, religion and life-styles, all of which probably have been reinforced by the participation of African-Cubans in the military and related activities in Ethiopia and Angola.[25]

Although Asia historically received many slaves, a small number of free merchants and others from Africa, there are virtually no studies of those developments or their contemporary impact. Serious studies remain to be conducted on the African dimension of the world from Turkey through the Middle East, South and East Asia, and the islands of the Indian and Pacific Oceans.

Some of the descendant Africans in India continue to practise traditional ceremonies, sing and dance to African music; and some can still speak in Kiswahili. These factors are indications that they, Siddis or Habshis, are conscious of their African ancestry. In fact, in 1973 a delegation of these

23. Zumbi, African-Brazilian Cultural Association, New York; the New York branch publishes a newsletter on the history and culture of African-Brazilians.

24. St C. Drake and R. B. Laporte, 1982; C. Melendez and Q. Duncan, 1981.

25. R. F. Thompson, 1983, is an excellent study of African influence on art and philosophy in Cuba, Haiti and other parts of the Americas, including the United States.

African-Indians visited Kenya, Uganda and Tanzania to become more aware of continental issues and to explore areas of possible co-operation.[26] Whatever effect that mission had, it did serve to inform continental Africans about African-Asians and it may well have stimulated greater interest in the African presence abroad.

The number of diaspora Africans in Europe has also greatly increased. In 1983 there were approximately 1 572 164 North Africans in France (866 595 Algerians, 492 669 Moroccans and 212 909 Tunisians). This population continues to cause tensions not only within France but between that country and the North African countries. Increasing numbers of those North Africans are becoming naturalized, in spite of opposition from elements of the French society; and the North African countries themselves oppose naturalization, being more interested in attracting a return migration. As the process of naturalization continues, relations between France and its southern neighbours in Africa will probably remain sensitive, but over the long term those descendants may well be a bridge to harmonious relations.[27] Equally great was the increase of blacks in Britain – mainly from the West Indies, America and Africa – and the interaction between them and the British people. Today, the annual festival of the West Indian communities in London has become a permanent cultural feature while Black music, dancing, food and art are having a growing impact on British culture.

In spite of the serious gaps in our knowledge about them, diaspora Africans have clearly had a significant history which has had major repercussions on other parts of the world. They have contributed inestimable labour to the agricultural, industrial and technical development of the world. Several of their religions, especially in Brazil and Cuba, retain African characteristics and have non-African adherents and symbols. Their languages have influenced many Romance and other languages and continue to be evident in Europe, the Americas and India, for example. Their art influenced Picasso and others, while their music and dance continue to syncopate the world's population.

Diaspora scientists – George Washington Carver in agriculture, Charles Drew in blood plasma, and Hildrus Poindexter in tropical medicine, and many others – have used their genius to promote human-kind. Their scholars have provided insights into the complexity of the social order. And their age-old tradition of struggle against oppression in Africa and the diaspora has made them familiar figures in the vanguard of human-rights movements as Nobel Laureates Ralph Bunche, Albert Luthuli, Martin Luther King, Jr, and Archbishop Desmond Tutu demonstrated.

26. See J. E. Harris, 1971, and in the *East African Standard*, 14 July 1982.
27. On this subject, see *La Nouvelle génération de l'immigration maghrébine, essai d'analyse sociologique*, 1982; *Esprit*, 1985; and *Les Temps Modernes*, 1985.

PLATE 23.3 *Notting Hill Carnival, the annual street festival of West Indian communities in London.*

The challenge

While many continental Africans, including several heads of state, civil and foreign servants, academics and business persons, maintain close contacts with African-Americans, such connections do not have the structural design necessary for effective and continuous interactions. Quite apart from the personal dimensions involved, ideological differences, distance and communications problems, pressing national issues, and financial constraints have all militated against the establishment of inter-national structures for black collaboration.

Moreover, African heads of state and government must consider the possible adverse effects their involvement in an international Black network may have on their diplomatic and economic affairs with the super-powers. Not all such leaders are of the mould of Kwame Nkrumah's pan-Africanism; nor are many of them as bold as Julius Nyerere who as President of Tanzania insisted in 1977 on making his major address in the United States on the campus of Howard University where many more blacks had access to him. And too few continental governments would match Nigeria's public stance of regarding itself as a guardian and spokesman for African people worldwide. And although the OAU coupled its congratulations to the United States for its space achievements in 1962 with an admonition over racial discrimination against African-Americans, and has welcomed TransAfrica's Director Randall Robinson into its confidence on a number of occasions, that body has been generally quiescent on the matter of promoting international networks of African peoples.

Yet, most African countries are only about a generation old and have had to confront a myriad of problems in an age where split-second decisions could mean life or death, success or failure. And most of those leaders were educated in a colonial ambiance and received the reins of government from colonial mentors who sought guarantees against even suggestions of race-consciousness or retribution for past exploitation of African peoples. But with a new generation of leaders in Africa and the diaspora, and a greater appreciation of the heritage and historical social condition they share, it is likely that renewed efforts to forge lasting structural links between Africa and its diaspora will be undertaken.

Not only will the twenty-first century then witness the convergence of a strong African political economy with access to its diaspora pool of knowledge and expertise, it will probably mark the inclusion of all the far-flung communities of African ancestry into a meaningful pan-African orbit.

Pan-Africanism and regional integration

S. K. B. ASANTE

in collaboration with

David CHANAIWA

The early history of pan-Africanism, which has been defined as 'a political and cultural phenomenon which regards Africa, Africans and African descendants abroad as a unit, and aims at the regeneration and unification of Africa and the promotion of a feeling of solidarity among the people of the African world',[1] has been dealt with in Volume VII of this history while other aspects of it were discussed in Chapter 23 of this volume. There are, however, two other aspects of that phenomenon since 1935 which have not been dealt with, namely, pan-Africanism as an integrative force and pan-Africanism as a movement of liberation. The former forms the theme of this chapter and the latter, that of the following chapter. As an integrative force which aims at achieving political, cultural and economic unity or co-operation in Africa, the history of pan-Africanism falls into three distinct phases: the colonial phase from 1935 to 1957; the independence phase from 1957 to the 1960s, which has been described as the heyday of pan-Africanism as a movement of liberation; and the third phase since the 1970s. During this last phase, pan-Africanism as an integrative force received a great deal of impetus following the dramatic changes in the world economy and the serious repercussions which these have had on the economies of Africa.

Though pan-Africanism as a movement of integration was vigorously pursued in the 1920s, as seen in the activities of the Congress of British West Africa, which included the formation of a British West African University, a West African Press Union and a British West African Co-operative Association, and those of student societies such as the West African Students Union (WASU), it lost its attraction in the 1930s and 1940s, the heyday of colonialism in Africa. It was revived in the 1940s to some extent, thanks to the activities of Nkrumah and Padmore in London and the Senegalese Alioune Diop. As early as 1942, Nkrumah insisted that all the West African colonies 'must first unite and become a national entity, absolutely free from the encumbrances of foreign rule, before they can assume the aspect of international cooperation on a grand

---

1. P. O. Esedebe, 1980, p. 14.

scale.'² Also, in 1947 was born *Présence africaine*, a cultural movement that took up the main ideas of the apostles of pan-Africanism and the first Pan-African Congress. Some black and European intellectuals came together around the Senegalese Alioune Diop, and they were responsible for the publication of some basic books such as *Nations nègres et culture*, by Cheikh Anta Diop. The general thinking of the militants of *Présence africaine* tended to show that the flowering of black culture was unthinkable in a situation of political dependence, and that black people needed to be united by solidarity in the struggle. They therefore had to mark themselves off from the other, the colonizer, and assert themselves. Invited to write the preface to Father Temple's *Bantu Philosophy*, Alioune Diop acknowledged that 'This is prescribed reading for blacks, for their growing awareness and their urge to understand their relationship to Europe'.

Pan-Africanism and continental integration

In spite of the integrationist efforts in the 1930s and 1940s, not much had been achieved by 1957. It was from that date, signified by the gaining of independence by Ghana under the dynamic leadership of Kwame Nkrumah, that pan-Africanism as a movement of integration was attempted with any purposiveness and dynamism. The aim during the period was not only to achieve political, cultural and economic integration but to do so at regional, continental and extra-regional (that is Africa and the European Economic Community) levels.

There is no doubt that the pace-setter of this period was Kwame Nkrumah. His first move in that direction was the formation of the Ghana–Guinea Union in 1958 and of the Ghana–Guinea–Mali Union as the first step toward the 'Union of African States'. The second was the Conference of Independent African States which he organized in Accra in April 1958 only about a year after Ghana's independence. This conference was attended by all the then-independent states of Africa, namely, Egypt, Ethiopia, Ghana, Liberia, Libya, Morocco, Sudan and Tunisia. This was followed as we shall see in the next chapter by the historic All-Africa Peoples Conference held in 1958, again in Accra; the Sanniquelli Meeting of Guinea and Liberia in July 1959; the Second Conference of Independent African States in Monrovia in August 1959; and the third in Addis Ababa in 1960. All these conferences advocated, among other things, the establishment of a broad continental common market. The first 1958 conference, for example, called for the removal of customs and other restrictions on trade among African states and the conclusion of multi-lateral payments agreements with a view to enhancing economic exchanges and the consequent establishment of a common market. To push this economic aspect the Economic Commission for

2. K. Nkrumah, 1962, p. 33.

725

Africa was set up in 1958; its activities since then have been fully discussed in Chapter 14.

All these conferences also vigorously advocated the political integration or the political unity of Africa. Nkrumah was the greatest advocate here and he pushed his ideas of African unity and a pan-African common market with uncompromising vigour and fanaticism. To him, both were the indispensable precondition for the speediest and fullest development not only of the totality of the continent, but also of the independent countries linked together in the union. He advocated the 'high politics' of continental political unity while expressing reservations about regionalism. He cautioned against such regional federations, lest regional loyalties give rise to power politics or 'enable the imperialists and neo-colonialists to fish in such troubled waters'.[3]

This linkage of the political unity movement with that of a continental common market made those African leaders who were opposed to the former give less than serious attention to the latter. For even though other African governments might accept Nkrumah's analysis, they would not necessarily choose to accept a far-reaching political solution. The threat of neo-colonialism might not have seemed to them to warrant such drastic steps as the derogation of sovereignty to an overall political authority. The Addis Ababa Conference in 1960 was of great significance since it was there that the divisions and differences among African states over the way to African unity came into the open.

The attainment of independence by a very large number of African states between 1960 and 1964 – the number of independent African states rose from 9 to 26 in 1960, including all the former French colonies, Nigeria, Zaire and Somalia, and to 33 by 1964 – very much complicated the attainment of the integrative aspect of pan-Africanism. The new African leaders became divided horizontally into pro-East and pro-West blocks and vertically into revolutionaries, progressives, reactionaries, capitalists, socialists, traditionalists and middle-of-the-roaders. Moreover, as will be seen in the next chapter, the overriding aim of pan-African conferences during the 1960s was to intensify the political struggle for independence for those countries still under colonial rule. Consequently, economic development, although of vital importance, did not constitute the principal policy objective. Moreover, the newly-independent leaders became preoccupied with immediate territorial problems of the unification of ethnic and regional groups, the consolidation of their own parties and power over the masses and against opposition leaders, the fight against poverty, disease and ignorance, as well as the defence and security of their nations against the Cold War and internal *coup d'État*. These internal priorities, tensions and conflicts made it rather difficult for some leaders of independent states to engage in pan-Africanist affairs outside their own

3. K. Nkrumah, 1963, p. 215.

PLATE 24.1   *President G. 'Abd al-Nasser of Egypt with President M. Kadhaffi of Libya and General M. Fawsi, the Egyptian war minister, on a military inspection in the United Arab Republic, 24 June 1970*

borders, or to implement pan-Africanist resolutions within their states.

Under the circumstances, African leaders began to divide into opposing camps, particularly over the future of the integrationist aspect of the pan-African movement. In 1961, Ghana, Guinea, Egypt, Mali, Morocco, Libya and the Algerian government-in-exile formed the Casablanca Group, while the remaining former French colonies plus Nigeria, Ethiopia, Liberia and Sierra Leone formed the Monrovia Group. Generally, the Casablanca Group favoured a strong political union along the lines of Nkrumah's United States of Africa. The group consisted of the militant pan-Africanist, socialist and non-aligned leaders of Africa, who believed in centralized continental economic planning and development, in a continental defence and security system, and in cultural restoration.

The Monrovia Group favoured a loose confederation of independent sovereign African states that would promote voluntary participation and co-operation in cultural exchanges and economic interaction. The group was particularly adamant about respect for the sovereignty and territorial integrity of each state. It was suspicious of the personal ambitions of some of the peers in the Casablanca Group, and of any interference in the internal affairs of their states.

Nevertheless, as will be seen in the next chapter, both groups maintained the historical commitment to the total liberation of the remaining colonies and to the policy of non-alignment. Through the relentless efforts of the Casablanca Group, especially Nkrumah, Sékou Touré and Modibo Keita, and with the support of Emperor Haile Selassie of Ethiopia, a Summit Conference of Independent African States was convened in Addis Ababa in 1963, to resolve the factionalism, unite the leaders and form a common pan-African structure. After many proposals and counter-proposals, many committee meetings and bilateral negotiations, 30 African heads of independent states and governments signed the Charter of African Unity which established the Organization of African Unity (OAU) on 25 May 1963.

The details of the OAU – its aims, structure and activities since its formation – are provided in the following chapter. Suffice it to state here that while its formation indicates a partial success for the integrationist aspect of pan-Africanism, it fell far short of the expectations of the old and radical pan-Africanists led by Nkrumah, and at practically each meeting of the OAU until his overthrow in 1966, Nkrumah in very long, detailed and moving speeches fanatically and doggedly campaigned for the conversion of the OAU into a continental union government or a fully-pledged United States of Africa – but without success.

With the formation of the OAU and its concentration on the liberation aspects of pan-Africanism to be discussed below, and with the concentration of many independent states on internal developments and on strengthening their ties with their former colonial rulers, and, above all, with the overthrow of Nkrumah, the continental integration aspect of pan-Africanism lost its momentum throughout the second half of the 1960s. It was rather replaced by movements for the formation of regional and inter-state groupings. According to Adebayo Adedeji, executive secretary of the Economic Commission for Africa (ECA), there were by 1977 over 20 inter-governmental multi-sectoral economic co-operation organizations in Africa and about one hundred single multi-national organizations that are meant to promote technical and economic co-operation in Africa.[4] Many of these were established in the 1960s, which were the halcyon years of African integration. But the decade was also characterized by the decline of several regional groupings. By the early 1970s, if not earlier, it was clear that African integration efforts were in serious trouble.

For example, the two initiatives among the French-speaking West African countries, resulting in the successive establishment of the West African Customs Union (UDAO – *Union douanière de l'Afrique de l'Ouest*)

4. A Adedeji, 1977, p. 10.

in June 1959 and of the Customs Union of West African States (UDEAO – *Union douanière et économique de l'Afrique de l'Ouest*) in June 1966, both failed. The Economic Community of West Africa (CEAO – *Communauté économique de l'Afrique de l'Ouest*), formed in 1973, is the latest of the experiments at regional integration by the majority of the states created out of the former federation of French West Africa (AOF – *Afrique-Occidentale française*). Nor did the Customs and Economic Union of Central Africa (UDEAC – *Union douanière et économique de l'Afrique centrale*), set up in January 1966, fare any better; restrictions on the opening of markets and non-compliance with its rules have sapped it of most of its energy as an integrative system. Similarly, the Council of the Entente States (*Conseil de l'Entente*) founded in 1959 through the initiative of President Houphouët-Boigny of Côte d'Ivoire seems to be diminishing in importance due to the increasing attention being focused on the larger and dynamic grouping, the CEAO. The short-lived (1968–71) Organization of Senegal River States (OERS – *Organisation des états riverains du Sénégal*) was succeeded in 1972 by the Organization for the

PLATE 24.2 *From left to right: President H. Maga of Dahomey, President F. Houphouët-Boigny of Côte d'Ivoire, President H. Diori of Niger and President M. Yameogo of Upper Volta: the four heads of state of the* Conseil de l'Entente, *after a meeting at the Elysée Palace, Paris, April 1961*

729

Development of the Senegal River (OMVS – *Organisation pour la mise en valeur du fleuve Sénégal*), which has still not been able to establish a workable machinery for co-operation. Also, the co-operation agreements of the nine-member Maghreb Permanent Consultative Committee, formed in November 1965, have never been ratified.

In Anglophone Africa, however (apart from East Africa, which attained independence as an economic community), no regional economies were established during the early years of independence. Whereas the Francophone West African countries consistently strove to maintain pre-independence joint institutions and to establish new ones, their anglophone counterparts, mainly at the insistence of Ghana, disbanded the few joint institutions – the British West African Currency Board, the West African Court of Appeal, the West African Cocoa Research Institute and the West African Airways Corporation – which the British had established, thus advancing the 'balkanization' of that part of Africa.

More worrying was the East African Community, arguably the most sophisticated regional co-operative arrangement in the Third World at the time, which experienced such acute tensions in the 1960s that by the end of the decade the level of economic integration had declined. The significance of East African integration can best be grasped by reflecting that at independence, external trade, fiscal and monetary policy, transport and communications infrastructures, and university education were all regional rather than national. Subsequently, these links and services were systematically dismantled and all the high hopes that Kenya, Uganda and Tanzania would eventually evolve into full federation under one government evaporated. By June 1977 the whole structure of the East African Community, once regarded as a model for African regional co-operation, had collapsed.

Undeniably, economic integration schemes launched optimistically in the 1960s were largely moribund by the end of the decade. Thus, despite the rhetoric of pan-African solidarity and the paraphernalia of elaborate decision-making structures, paradoxically, the period witnessed decline rather than progress in the field of effective regional integration in Africa. No solid foundations for regional groupings were laid, in spite of the countless expressions of fidelity to the principles of pan-Africanism. The question then arises, why so little progress and such faltering steps? Was it because African states failed to see the advantages of regional economic integration and collective self-reliance? Or, were there some undercurrents which rocked the very foundation of co-operation?

The problems and constraints of African regional integration during the early years of independence were many and seemingly intractable. They stemmed from internal as well as external and historical factors. One of these factors was the growth and impact of national consciousness on regional integration. Colonialism not only left behind a patchwork of many sovereign states, but the states spawned by this process were

730

PLATE 24.3   *From left to right: President J. Nyerere of Tanzania, President A. M. Obote of Uganda and President J. Kenyatta of Kenya, signing the East African Co-operation Treaty in Kampala, June 1967*

themselves artificial entities. They were, as yet, by no means nations; rather, they represented the shells of territorial independence in which the kernel of national identity had been planted by the independence movements. The major task of the new governments was to provide the soil in which the seed could grow. Anxious to encourage national integration, the new leaders were compelled to look inward and to rank as their first priority the political, economic and social developments of their own polities. The immediate concern, then, was to build viable nation states based on their own traditions and customs, and on the promises which had been held out to the masses. To the extent that national consolidation received high priority, co-operation with other African countries would have to be secondary. Since meaningful co-operation necessarily implied long-term commitment, there was an understandable reluctance to take decisions which restrained national sovereignty in certain key areas, including development-plan formulation. While this did not rule out joint endeavours in some forms of regional integration, it did suggest the existence of very real limits on the extent to which African states were willing to part with or to pool their sovereignty.

Throughout, African states did not display much willingness to sacrifice perceived national interests on the regional altar. They entered into

731

agreement to liberate trade or allocate industries on a regional basis only when these integrative objectives were not in conflict with considerations of national security, prestige, or economic advantage. This tendency was aggravated, among other things, by the different economic groupings within Africa of the pre-Lomé Convention era: the 18 French-speaking associated states with the European Economic Community (EEC) under the Yaoundé system; the Commonwealth non-associates and Commonwealth associates like Nigeria under a special trade agreement with the EEC signed in January 1966 (but never implemented); and the three East African states of Kenya, Uganda and Tanzania under the September 1969 Arusha Agreement.

From a political-economy perspective, too, a variety of factors can be said to have complicated the functioning of schemes for economic co-operation.[5] One such factor was the economic and political heterogeneity of the continent. Countries that followed vastly different development paths would not make good partners in economic co-operation schemes. Indeed, political and ideological cleavages threatened even existing and otherwise viable co-operative arrangements such as the defunct East African Community. Added to all these critical constraints and issues is what Timothy Shaw has termed the intractable problems of politicization of organizations, both of which led to institutional tension and decay.[6] Besides the classic case of the East African Community, was the bewildering frequency of changes in organizations and memberships in Francophone Africa which was partly the result of regional inequalities.

Because of such intractable difficulties, the establishment of regional groupings in Africa's first decade of recaptured independence was often no more than a declaration of intent and an indication of continental alignments. Neither Nkrumah's enthusiasm for the noble pan-African ideal of political unity and economic continentalism nor Julius Nyerere's preferred incremental regionalism leading eventually towards pan-Africanism went beyond the stage of theoretical discussions. Ironically, despite this disillusioning record, the fervour with which integration has been proposed as a response to the problems of Africa has increased tremendously in recent years. As suggested below, this is due to the development crisis in Africa and, especially, to the intensification of this appalling condition by Africa's overdependence on the Western-dominated international economy. For a while in the 1960s pan-Africanism as a movement of liberation weakened Africa's political ties with Europe. Simultaneously, the period witnessed a reinforcement of Africa's economic and cultural dependence upon Europe and the developed world generally. Thus, economic neo-colonialism and dependency waxed as political colonialism waned. It will be instructive to outline briefly what is now termed the

5. T. M. Shaw, 1975b, pp. 29–38.
6. T. M. Shaw, 1975a, pp. 667–8.

'African continental crisis' in order to appreciate the extent of the current renewed enthusiasm for pan-Africanism as an integrative quest.

Pan-Africanism, regionalism and economic development

Since the 1970s, there has been indeed a renewed enthusiasm for pan-Africanism as an integrative force at the regional level. What was the nature of this new interest and how can it be explained? Both questions have been discussed in Chapter 14 and here we will concentrate on the integrative aspects. The main reason, as Adedeji has emphasized in Chapter 14, has been the disappointing African economic performance of the last 25 years. For despite efforts to stimulate industrial growth, to foster agricultural production and to initiate other development programmes to bring about more fundamental changes in the economic situation inherited at independence, today's reality is that the transformation of the continent which was expected to follow closely on the heels of political independence still remains only a hope. There has been no marked improvement in many African economies since 1960. Africa harbours 16 out of 25 countries classified by the United Nations in 1971 as 'the least-developed' countries. And of the 32 countries identified by the 1974 Sixth Special Session of the United Nations General Assembly as 'most seriously affected' by the 'current economic crisis', 20 are in Africa.

The hopes of African leaders earlier in the 1960s – that a combination of trade with aid from the industrialized nations would provide the necessary resources to satisfy national aspirations for autonomous, self-sustaining development – failed to materialize. The record of the 1960s was therefore most disappointing. Neither the trade nor the aid policies practised by the industrialized nations appeared capable of accelerating economic expansion. Africa thus emerged from the First United Nations Development Decade (1960–70) as the region registering the lowest rate of growth among developing countries – 2 per cent as against Southern Asia (4.1 per cent), East Asia (5.6 per cent), Latin America (4.5 per cent) and the Middle East (7.2 per cent). Initial indications from the Second United Nations Development Decade (1970–80) are that the situation has changed little, if at all. Thus despite its vast natural resources, Africa is unable to point to any significant growth rate or satisfactory index of well-being in the last 25 years.[7]

In spite of exports, many African countries showed throughout the 1970s a pattern of sluggish economic growth, low levels of productivity, a circumscribed and fractured industrial base, high dependence on a vulnerably narrow spectrum of primary export commodities, low levels of life expectancy, and widening deficits on the aggregate current accounts of the balance of payments. Real per capita income declined while the

---

7. Organization of African Unity, 1981, para. 10.

rate of inflation approximately doubled, reaching an average annual rate of over 20 per cent during 1977–9. The combined current-account deficit of the balance of payments rose from about $4 billion in 1974 to close to $10 billion annually in 1978–9.[8] Above all, between 1970 and 1979 external indebtedness of sub-Saharan Africa rose from $6 billion to $32 billion and debt service (for the oil-importing countries) increased from 6 to 12 per cent of export earnings in the same period.[9] Thus, if Africa's inheritance from colonialism in 1960 was 'inauspicious', to borrow Timothy Shaw's description, by 1980 it has become even less promising.

More worrying, Africa provides a fertile ground for what has come to be known as neo-colonialism and dependency which has greatly contributed to the continent's problems. By the end of the 1970s, Africa's dependency on the economies of the industrialized Western countries had become greater than it had ever been. Most African countries had become even more heavily dependent on foreign interest, foreign investments, foreign technology, foreign expertise, foreign theories of development and economic growth and, above all, on exports of raw materials and agricultural primary commodities to the rich, industrialized West.

In the world economy, Africa has always been in a subordinate position, characterized by asymmetrical and unequal economic relationships with the industrialized Western world. Even if one does not accept dependency theory as an accurate description of African economic systems and relations, it is beyond question that the continent's position in the international economic order has been one of inequality. This disturbing condition has been aggravated by the impact of the global-crises syndrome symbolized by the collapse of the Bretton Woods Agreement, the oil-shocks of the Organization of Petroleum Exporting Countries (OPEC), the energy crunch, and the continuing stagflation of the mid-1970s onwards, which has revealed as never before the extreme vulnerability of almost all African countries to external forces. Confronted with this implacable reality, African leaders have been forced into a sobering reassessment of what their options are: what is the correct path towards economic development?

Given the imminence of catastrophe and collapse, innovative responses are imperative. For if the deterioration in economic performance is to be halted and reversed, then new directions of policy are required. Africa's hopes, then, lie in a fundamental redirection of national and regional development strategies. The OPEC success has crystallized the concepts of strength through collective action and solidarity. Such action is seen as vital to the salvation of Africa's economic problems. African states therefore strongly feel that they have to foster mutual co-operation to impart strength to their national endeavours to fortify their independence –

8. J. B. Zulu and S. M. Nsouli, 1984, p. 5.
9. World Bank, 1981, p. 3.

for although each individual country might be weak, President Nyerere counselled:

> Together, or even in groups, we are much less weak. We have the capability to help each other in many ways, each gaining in the process. As a combined group we can meet the wealthy nations on very different terms, for though they may not need any one of us for their economic health, they cannot cut themselves off from all of us.[10]

By the mid-1970s, therefore, Africa was faced with a choice between: continuing to support an inherited structure of dependence, and therefore subordination of its own development to special interests in the Western international economic system; or beginning to break away from this structure, in part through regional economic integration.

It was in response to this crucial challenge to the disillusioning performance of most African economies, coupled with the failure of the series of North–South Dialogues to realize the objective of a new international economic order (NIEO), that the *Lagos Plan of Action* (LPA) was conceived and born. The *Lagos Plan*, which has been discussed in detail in Chapter 14, is a major document formulated around the concepts of self-reliance and self-sustaining development and economic growth. Its main theme is Africa's reduction of its dependence on external strategy, as declared by the continent's leaders:

> We view, with disquiet, the over-dependence of the economy of our continent . . . This phenomenon had made African economies highly susceptible to external developments and with detrimental effects on the interests of the continent.[11]

As a counter-strategy to this phenomenon of over-dependence, African states 'resolved to adopt a far-reaching regional approach based primarily on collective self-reliance'. Regionalism, which is discussed in virtually every chapter of the *Lagos Plan*, therefore constitutes an integral condition for implementation. Without regional integration the LPA collapses as a concept and strategy.

It is against this background that pan-Africanism as an integrative quest is now seen to be an important element in reducing dependence and in helping to improve the bargaining position of African countries, thus contributing to their development potential through the broader strategy for promoting a NIEO. Apart from the more orthodox benefits promised by regional groupings in the shape of expanded trade and investment, economic integration is being vigorously advocated as a means of reducing external vulnerability. This has become increasingly urgent

10. J. Nyerere, 1970b, p. 12.
11. Organization of African Unity, 1981, para. 14.

mainly because the dependent relationship does not appear to be lessening; indeed, given the soaring foreign debts of many African states, it is increasing. Hopefully, regional economic integration would break this dependent relationship by helping each member nation to export manufactured goods and eventually capital goods to their neighbours. The underlying premise here is the desire by African states and leaders to determine as far as possible their own economic policies based on their national aspirations, natural resources and political ideologies outside the influence of developed countries. Thus the problems and prospects of recently-created regional groupings in the area of dependency reduction merit special attention.

The new regional schemes and the question of dependency

For many years now, the re-emergence of a rash of regional integration schemes in Africa as more or less explicit challenges to the external domination of the continent inherited from the colonial era has been in evidence. Among the most ambitious and dynamic is the Economic Community of West African States (ECOWAS for the English-speaking and CEDEAO for the French-speaking), which brings together 16 countries covering an area of 6m sq km stretching from Mauritania in the north-west to Nigeria in the south-east, and a total population of about 150 million. Established in Lagos, in May 1975, ECOWAS is the first serious attempt at economic co-operation and integration in the West African sub-region, cutting across divisions of language, history and existing affiliations and institutions. Of its member states, five are officially Anglophone, eight Francophone, two Lusophone and one Arabic.[12]

Besides ECOWAS, the two newest initiatives are in Southern Africa. The first is the Southern African Development Coordination Conference (SADDC), which was formally inaugurated in April 1980 by the signing of the Lusaka Declaration on Economic Liberation by the five Front-Line States (FLS) – Angola, Botswana, Mozambique, Tanzania and Zambia – joined by Lesotho, Malawi, Swaziland and Zimbabwe. Originally conceived as the economic counterpart to the FLS, which, since 1974, have been most closely involved in assisting and, to some extent, directing – militarily, politically and diplomatically – the liberation struggle in the then Rhodesia, Namibia and South Africa, the nine SADCC countries cover an area of 5m sq km, and have a total population of some 60 million. The second initiative is the Preferential Trade Area for Eastern and Southern African States (PTA), which was concluded in Lusaka in December 1981 by nine out of the potential 18 states. The PTA was finally launched in Harare in July 1984. Despite its name, the PTA does not confine itself to trade alone. The treaty is much more than an elaborate

12. For a full-scale study of ECOWAS, see S. K. B. Asante, 1985.

definition of trading relationships. It addresses itself to virtually every sector relating to the promotion of regional economic integration. Like ECOWAS, the PTA is the brainchild of Adebayo Adedeji, the executive secretary of the ECA. But whereas the PTA was an example of painstaking development from below, the SADCC, like ECOWAS, was much more an act of deliberate political will, carrying the personal authorization of its presidents and prime ministers. Just as the six French-speaking CEAO members are signatories to the ECOWAS treaty, so are all the SADCC member states potential members of the PTA. And like ECOWAS and CEAO, although the purposes and programmes of SADCC and the PTA are substantially similar, and steadily converging, distinct differences are apparent in the origins of the two organizations, their institutional structures, financial patrons, ideologies and strategies.

Another manifestation of the current concern with regional co-operation in Africa was the creation in December 1981 of the Senegambian Confederation which joins Gambia and Senegal towards an economic and monetary union. This is the culmination of many years of efforts to create closer economic co-operation between these two countries. The latest initiative is the treaty signed in Libreville, Gabon, in October 1983 to establish the Economic Community of Central African States (ECCAS), comprising the present members of UDEAC and those of the Economic Community of the Great Lakes. This is intended to be the Central African equivalent of ECOWAS.

The basic objective of these new regional integration schemes is the same – to reduce the dependence of their respective member states on the external forces which speak to influence the economic policies and directions of African countries; and to co-ordinate the development programmes in the different sectors and subsectors as a means of accelerating the rate of economic growth and development. ECOWAS, for example, has as its central objective the promotion of co-operation and development in virtually all fields of economic activity for the purpose of 'reducing gradually the Community's economic dependence on the outside world'. The lessening of a high degree of external dependence is seen as a precondition for achieving basic structural development goals. Similarly, the SADCC came about as the result of a common desire among its nine members to reduce and eventually to eliminate economic dependence upon South Africa. The emphasis in the SADCC on reducing dependence is focused 'especially', but not exclusively, on Pretoria. As President Machel of Mozambique stressed in his opening address at SADCC 2 in Maputo in 1980: 'The effects of colonial domination are still present in our countries . . . the mentality of dependence, the fatalist spirit'.[13] On the other hand, the PTA, with its broader membership, makes no direct attempt to address the issues of reducing dependence on

13. A. Kgarebe, 1981, p. 23.

South Africa. Instead it advocates a positive approach to the problem, contending that, to the extent that it succeeds in promoting intra-regional trade and development, the present dangerous dependence on South Africa will decrease. Viewed within the context of a NIEO, all these new regional initiatives must also be regarded as integral parts of a wider desire of the poor nations of Africa to eliminate, or at least to reduce, the inequalities inherent in the present international economic system.

To what extent are these new regional schemes effectively equipped in terms of resources and power to confront the disturbing problems posed by the question of dependency and neo-colonialism? Or to what extent can they create conditions that will make self-sustained, autonomous development possible? In the African setting, such developments can only come about through the transformation of productive structures. Can ECOWAS, the SADCC or the PTA contribute to this type of change? It must be stressed even *ad nauseam* that regional integration can hardly be successful while regional partners remain incorporated into the international system. Put differently, regional self-reliance is incompatible with global and trans-national integration. What, then, have the new regional initiatives achieved so far, in only a few years of existence, in the area of dependency reduction? What is the future of regional economic integration schemes in Africa?

Many development theorists now acknowledge that regional-change processes are neither autonomous nor self-generated, but rather they are responsive to a context of global interdependence and interaction. For, as Philippe Schmitter has argued, 'no matter what their original intentions, it should prove difficult to isolate regional deliberations from their context of global economic and political dependence'.[14] The actions of external actors, or what Schmitter has termed 'external penetration', have had a profound effect on the direction of integrative undertaking. The analyses by Steven Langdon and Lynn Mytelka of the Customs and Economic Union of Central Africa (UDEAC)[15] and by Peter Robson of the West African Economic Community (CEAO)[16] provide excellent case-studies of the way in which trans-national corporations (TNCs) and other external interests have not only derived benefits from African regional integration to the disadvantage of the partner states; they have also made these countries unable to take full advantage of the economic co-operation institutions to introduce changes in production and industrial structures as a means of encouraging intra-African trade and thereby reducing dependence on external forces.

Given this background, it is easy to envisage the kind of problems likely to confront the new regional integration schemes in the area of

14. P. C. Schmitter, 1972, p. 8.
15. S. Langdon and L. K. Mytelka, 1979, pp. 179–80.
16. P. Robson, 1983, p. 41.

external penetration. There is, for example, the problem of extricating the member states of ECOWAS, the SADCC, the PTA or CEEAC from existing dependency relationships with the external powers by using national and regional institutions to bring about greater control over resources. Given the complexity of this problem, the question which arises is: how adequate are the provisions made in the treaties of these new regional initiatives to confront the issues posed by dependency relationships?

Evidence tends to suggest that none of the new regional schemes has adequate provisions for attacking the all-engaging issue of dependency reduction. For example, although the ECOWAS protocol on the rules of origin anticipated the problems posed by external linkages, it does not effectively confront the issues of foreign ownership and participation. For a long time to come, most industrial enterprises in West Africa will continue to have foreign majority ownership. Of significance here is the fact that although Article 32 of the ECOWAS treaty specifically calls upon the ECOWAS Council of Ministers to take effective steps towards gradual dependency reduction, there is no institution or machinery in ECOWAS which is empowered to enter into negotiation with external actors on behalf of the Community.[17] Neither has the ECOWAS treaty any provisions for a common regime on foreign investment and divestment, nor has any institution been established to control the importation of technology, as evidenced in the case of the Andean Common Market in Latin America. Thus, the redefinition of ECOWAS's economic relationship with the outside world, which is crucial if the reduction of dependence is the goal, is largely ignored by the ECOWAS treaty.

Although SADCC countries have identified transport and communications as the first priority sector for reducing dependence on South Africa, and have consequently established the Southern African Transport and Communications Commission (SATCC) for this purpose, implementation of this laudable scheme entirely depends, paradoxically, on the availability of foreign sources of aid and investment. For an organization dedicated to self-reliance and the reduction of economic dependence on any single or group of states, the ingenuity and effort that have gone into cultivating beneficial relations with sympathetic international partners, principally in the West, may appear contradictory. The SADCC has had to recognize that its priorities are not necessarily the same as those of the interested parties from whom it seeks development assistance. As a result, the SADCC had, in the past, advanced projects on the basis of their appeal to prospective donors, rather than because they were the projects considered most beneficial for the region. Thus, anxious as SADCC members are to escape from the South African frying-pan, they seem to land in the fire of other Western donors, which constitutes a new form

17. J. P. Renninger, 1982, p. 170.

of dependency. Besides, the SADCC's concentration on the rehabilitation of transport systems inherited from colonialism may perpetuate and reinforce 'neo-colonial' patterns of trade and production and hinder intra-SADCC trade.

Regionalism *versus* extra-regional pan-Africanism

The complex problems confronting new regional initiatives within the context of dependency have been seriously compounded by the emergence of a new type of pan-Africanism at the extra-regional level in the shape of the Lomé Convention between the European Economic Community (EEC) and Africa. For – from a stance of structural change, in particular – the new Lomé 'regime' was and is in no sense a road-to-Damascus conversion for either Europe or Africa. The continuity from the age-old colonial patterns of dependency is as evident as any change. It is the EEC's brand of neo-colonialism to consolidate and maintain the *status quo* of the old order – the traditional post-1884 Berlin Conference and post-colonial dependency structures. While the Berlin Conference established the undisputed sway of colonialism in Africa, the Treaty of Rome, which gave birth to the EEC, marked the advent of neo-colonialism and dependency in Africa. Hence the stalwart pan-Africanist Kwame Nkrumah was quick to denounce the EEC as a new system of 'collective colonialism which will be stronger and more dangerous than the old evils we are striving to liquidate'. For the Lomé Agreement is not a progressive document which constitutes an inching toward a more balanced and beneficial interdependent relationship between Europe and Africa; rather, it is a shift in the nature of imperialism. Hence, despite the variety of EEC assistance, through Lomé I and Lomé II, to the new African regional groupings, it can hardly be disputed that the new relationship between Europe and Africa has greatly reinforced the latter's collective dependence on the former through trade relations, industrial co-operation, economic development through EEC-financed aid, and consultation through a range of institutions.

In many respects, therefore, this new pan-Africanism at the extra-regional level, exemplified by the Lomé Conventions, is essentially incompatible not only with the fundamental objectives of the *Lagos Plan*, but it is also certainly out of step with the perceptions, development strategies and basic objectives of pan-Africanism at the regional level. As noted above, the new African regional groupings, particularly ECOWAS, the SADCC and the PTA, have adopted the strategy of self-reliant development aimed at reducing their dependency on the former colonial powers and the international economic system generally (and in the case of the SADCC and the PTA, South Africa as well). On the other hand, Lomé represents a vertical Euro-African orientation, while the new regional schemes reflect an interest in horizontal South–South links.[18] Thus, structurally, this new level of pan-Africanism charts no new path for Africa, breaks no new ground, and offers no new perspectives. Rather, it accepts the validity of the existing approach to African development and tends towards further capitalist penetration of African economies. Briefly stated, therefore, although greater economic self-reliance is a necessity for regional economic integration schemes in Africa, since it enables them to escape from or at least reduce dependency on the industrial centres and so facilitates their development, the successful implementation of this strategy within the Lomé framework remains problematic.

Pan-Africanism and regionalism: an overview and conclusion

For better or for worse, Africa is coming of age. The golden epoch of high hopes for pan-Africanism as a movement of political decolonization has passed. In its place has emerged a new era of pan-Africanism as an instrument of regional integration and economic decolonization. The types of regionalism which emerged from the mid-1970s onwards are closely related to the broader question of collective self-reliance and Africa's historical incorporation within the world system. Undoubtedly, the continued integration of Africa within the international system has seriously affected the progress of regionalism in the continent. For today, much regional economic co-operation serves not the interests of Africa but rather those of foreign aid agencies, consultants and trans-national corporations.[19] As noted in the case of the SADCC, the UDEAC and CEAO, for example, the major beneficiaries of African regional integration have been centres of foreign investment, aid and technology. There is thus a major problem in Africa because economic co-operation, which is the backbone of collective self-reliance, cannot be effectively implemented as an instrument for regional development so long as the participating countries have no effective control over the resources flowing into joint projects, or sovereignty over the key sectors of the economy.

And what is more, African élites or foreign collaborationist groups, who have a close identity of interests with certain trans-national or external forces, are likely to resist any efforts towards a high level of integration, involving reduction of dependence, or any radical change that may lead to a restructuring of their political economies and external linkages away from inherited, external orientation. Thus the structural integration of the African economies, as well as the dominant group of social and political forces in the continent, into the international capitalist order has constituted a major constraint on the ability of African countries,

18. S. K. B. Asante, 1984, pp. 171–95.
19. A. Jalloh, 1976, p. 49.

even if they are willing, *radically* to change this structure of dependence.

Besides, given the entrenchment of neo-colonialism in Africa, and the extent of diversification in markets and sources of investment and technology among different former colonial powers, any abrupt severance of Africa's intimate linkage with the industrialized nations is likely to inflict unacceptable pain upon the continent's fragile economies. African countries, therefore, may opt to be part of the system while simultaneously seeking the kind of terms which would enable them to exercise greater control over the industrialized world. Thus it would be necessary for African regional integration schemes to adopt a pragmatic and flexible approach towards the question of dependency and the neo-colonial mesh.

In this regard, African regional groupings may have to diversify their external economic relations – trading partners and sources of technology and capital. This approach has the potential for strengthening the bargaining position of the governments of African states by enabling them to play off one developed economy against another. The importance of such diversification of external economic links cannot be overemphasized; Mazrui has recently driven it home:

> . . . there are occasions when freedom begins with the multiplication of one's masters. If one is owned and controlled by only one power, freedom is often particularly restrictive. But if an African society cultivates the skills to have more than one hegemonic power competing for it, this has possibilities for liberation. To be dependent on two giants, especially when the giants have rivalries between them, is sometimes an opportunity to play one against the other – and maximize one's own options.[20]

Another option available to African regional groupings for transcending dependency is to develop preferential economic links with the regional integration schemes in Asia and Latin America. In more concrete terms, this type of 'horizontal integration' implies the promotion of economic co-operation among developing countries, 'the new imperative of development of the 1980s' to quote Elvin Laszlo. A vast realm is open for joint action in the fields of economic and technical co-operation. Such joint action can be crucial in enabling developing countries to defend the prices of their exports of raw materials and to enhance their sovereignty over their natural resources. It can also encourage the growth of indigenous capacities in science and technology, facilitate the marketing of their products, help to increase their industrial capacity and, above all, strengthen their decision-making power in multi-lateral institutions.

Then, too, African countries and leaders should be willing to introduce fundamental policy and institutional changes. These should include a redefinition of development objectives at national and regional levels to

20. A. A. Mazrui, 1980a, p. 82.

recognize fully regional integration as an effective approach to the issues of dependency and underdevelopment. But a regional development strategy cannot be fully realized unless countries develop a common policy towards the problem of foreign investment and technology dependence through regional regulation and planning. This should be backed by an important policy directive designed to build a joint industrial research and development institute which would also look into the appropriateness of foreign technology, its purchase, acquisition or adaptation for use in joint development projects.

Finally, whatever strategy is adopted for transcending dependency, priority should be given to internal policy reforms. This calls for self-discipline and sacrifice. We in Africa must accept the discipline, restraint and austerity that are required for establishing what may be termed a new domestic order if we ever hope to transform our relationship with the industrialized nations from one of permanent dependence to one of beneficial interdependence which can generate within African society itself the engine necessary for sustained economic growth. As the distinguished African historian, Ade Ajayi, has remarked recently in a 'mood of cautious optimism':

> The vision of a new society in Africa will need to be developed *in* Africa, born out of the African historical experience and the sense of continuity of African history. The African is not yet master of his own fate, but neither is he completely at the mercy of fate.[21]

21. J. F. A. Ajayi, 1982, p. 8.

Pan-Africanism and liberation

25

Edem KODJO *and* David CHANAIWA

If pan-Africanism as a movement of integration witnessed some successes in the late 1950s and early 1960s, experienced fluctuating fortunes and failures from about the mid-1960s onwards, and from the mid-1970s received a great deal of impetus, pan-Africanism as a movement of liberation rather attained the peak of its achievements during the first decade of African independence – the heyday of pan-Africanism as a movement of liberation. However, from the late 1960s onwards, it became more of a broken reed, having survived only up to the attainment of independence. Following independence, the unifying spirit of pan-Africanism, the fight against the colonial powers, was no longer strong in some African states, despite the protracted Southern Africa conflict, that unfinished business of independent Africa.

Though pan-Africanism originated in the New World in the eighteenth and nineteenth centuries as an integral part of the black liberation struggle against white domination and exploitation, and though the earliest manifestation of pan-Africanism and liberation were in the forms of African-American religious separatism which later spread to Africa, pan-Africanism as a movement of liberation in Africa itself dates, as has been pointed out in Chapter 23, from the fascist Italian invasion of Ethiopia in 1935 and above all from the Pan-African Congress at Manchester in October 1945. For the first time in the history of the pan-African movement, African delegates predominated at the Manchester Congress and the focus of the discussions was the liberation of colonized Africa. The congress was organized by a Special International Conference Secretariat consisting of Dr Peter Milliard of British Guiana as chairman, R. T. Makonnen of the West Indies as treasurer, Kwame Nkrumah of Ghana and George Padmore of Trinidad as joint secretaries, Peter Abrahams of South Africa as publicity secretary and Jomo Kenyatta of Kenya as assistant-secretary. Altogether, there were over 200 participants, mostly from British colonies in Africa, among whom were some future presidents of independent states. DuBois, the veteran pan-Africanist, as the permanent chairman of all the sessions.

744

PLATE 25.1 *The Pan-African Congress at Manchester, England, November 1945. From left to right on the platform: Peter Milliard, Mrs Amy Jacques Garvey, the Mayor of Manchester and I. T. A. Wallace Johnson*

The tone of the discussions and, especially, the resolutions that were passed, were considerably more militant and radical than those of past congresses. Among the demands in the Declaration to Colonial Powers were:

(1) total emancipation and independence for Africans and other subject races from domination by European powers claiming sovereignty and trusteeship over them;

(2) the immediate abolition of all racial and other discriminatory laws;

(3) freedom of speech, press, association and assembly;

(4) abolition of forced labour, and the introduction of equal pay for equal work;

(5) the right of every man and woman over the age of 21 to vote and be elected; and

(6) medical, welfare and educational services to be made available to all citizens.

745

The call for economic integration has already been discussed in Chapter 14. The delegates also demanded for Africa freedom from 'foreign imperialist control, whether political or economic'. More importantly, for the first time Africans clearly warned that, if Europeans still intended to rule Africa by force, Africans would use force, in the effort to achieve freedom.

Simultaneously, the delegates made another declaration to the African peoples, which emphasized that the struggle for political independence was only the first stage and the means towards complete economic, cultural and psychological emancipation. They called upon the urban and rural masses, and upon intellectuals and professionals of Africa to unite, organize and persevere for total independence.

By the end of the Fifth Congress, pan-Africanism finally had been turned into a mass ideology of Africa, by Africans and for Africans. It had grown from a reformist, protest ideology for the peoples of African descent in the New World into a nationalist ideology for the continental liberation of Africa. The global pan-Africanism of DuBois, the militant self-determination and self-reliance of Garvey, and the cultural restoration of Césaire had then become integral elements of African nationalism. Several of the delegates, such as Nkrumah and Kenyatta, soon left London for Africa and led their peoples into independence. The constitutions of all nationalist movements included pan-Africanist clauses.

Pan-Africanism and the liberation of Africa, 1945–60

In the history of pan-Africanism as a movement of liberation, the period from 1950 to 1965 can be called the age of Kwame Nkrumah. By words, action and example, Nkrumah mobilized African leaders of both liberation movements and independent states for pan-Africanist causes. In conformity with his declaration, on the night of Ghana's independence, that the independence of Ghana was meaningless unless it was linked with the total liberation of the African continent, he organized a number of pan-African congresses immediately after Ghana's independence which have been discussed in the previous chapter. As it was pointed out, the first of these conferences was the First Conference of Independent African States, held in Accra, the capital of his newly-independent state of Ghana, in April 1958, which was attended by Egypt, Ethiopia, Ghana, Liberia, Libya, Morocco, Sudan and Tunisia, as well as by many of the former delegates of the Fifth Pan-African Congress. The agenda and resolutions of the conference centred on the relations among the independent African states, on assistance to the liberation movements throughout Africa, on the relation between independent Africa and the United Nations, and on the ways and means of protecting Africa from the divisiveness of the East–West Cold War. The conference established the major themes of post-independence pan-Africanism and arguably laid the basis for the

Organization of African Unity (OAU), namely the primacy of political independence, assistance to liberation movements, a united front at the United Nations and non-alignment.

The Second Conference of Independent African States took place in Monrovia in August 1959. It adopted four resolutions; one condemned France for its nuclear tests in the Sahara; another called for a political truce in the Cameroons; another for a negotiated peace in Algeria; and the fourth proclaimed the right of the colonial territories to self-determination. The third conference was held in Addis Ababa in 1960.

During the same period, Nkrumah and his pan-Africanist compatriots were convening conferences for leaders of both independent states and liberation movements to share ideas and strategies on the struggle for independence. The First All-African People's Conference was held in Accra in December 1958, and was attended by 250 delegates and several observers. The agenda consisted of anti-colonialism, anti-imperialism, anti-racialism, African unity and non-alignment. The delegates discussed pertinent issues such as colonial boundaries, the role of chiefs and separatist religious leaders, and regional groupings. More importantly, African politicians and trades-unionists from French-, English-, Arabic- and Portuguese-speaking states and colonies had the opportunity to establish long-lasting ideological and personal relationships, such as the one between Nkrumah and Patrice Lumumba of the then Belgian Congo. The Second All-African Peoples' Conference was held in Tunis in 1960. This was attended by 73 African delegations, and the proceedings concluded with the adoption of a series of resolutions mainly concerned with decolonization. The third was in Cairo in 1961.

PLATE 25.2   *The First All-African People's Conference in Accra, Ghana, December 1958: the opening speech*

747

There were two regional pan-Africanist organizations established mainly for the purpose of waging co-ordinated liberation struggles. One was the Pan-African Freedom Movement for Eastern, Central and Southern Africa, consisting of Ethiopia, Kenya, Somalia, Tanganyika, Uganda, Zanzibar and the nationalist movements of Central and Southern Africa, which was commonly known as PAFMECSA (1958–63). The other was *Rassemblement démocratique africain* (RDA) a trans-territorial alliance established after the Bamako Congress by nationalist leaders in former French colonies which sought to go beyond the limited self-government envisaged by the *Loi Cadre* of 1946. Then came the de Gaulle referendum of 1958 which sought to establish a Franco-African Community.[1] Through the RDA, Africans had a pan-Africanist forum to discuss the advantages and disadvantages of the community and to register their opinions with the French government. But in the de Gaulle referendum of 1958, only Sékou Touré of Guinea voted against the Community in favour of total independence, and joined Nkrumah in the Union of African States.

The OAU and liberation

If the birth of so many new African states between 1960 and 1964 complicated pan-Africanism as a movement of integration, it definitely assisted and accelerated it as a movement of liberation. While the new African leaders could not agree on the nature of the political integration that should occur in Africa, they were virtually unanimous on the urgency of the total liquidation of colonialism from Africa, and both the Monrovia and Casablanca groups maintained the historical commitment to the total liberation of the remaining colonies and to the policy of non-alignment. Indeed, it was this universal commitment to the cause of liberation that was partly if not mainly responsible for the success of the moves that brought the two groups together to form the OAU at the epoch-making meeting in Addis Ababa in May 1963. How then was OAU created and structured, and what role did it play in the cause of pan-Africanism?

As was pointed out in the last chapter, largely through the efforts of Kwame Nkrumah, Sékou Touré and Modibo Keita, on the one hand, and the Emperor of Ethiopia on the other, and also because of the attainment of independence by Algeria in 1962 which perceptibly reduced tension between the Casablanca and Monrovia groups, an agreement to form a single organization was reached and their foreign ministers met from 15 to 21 May 1963 to draw up the draft agenda for the heads of state discussion.

On 23 May 1963, the Conference of Heads of State and Government opened. Thirty states were represented: Algeria, Burundi, Cameroon, Central African Republic, Chad, Congo–Brazzaville, Congo–Léopoldville,

1. For more details, see J. de Benoist, 1980.

Dahomey, Ethiopia, Gabon, Ghana, Guinea, Côte d'Ivoire, Liberia, Libya, Madagascar, Mali, Mauritania, Niger, Nigeria, Rwanda, Senegal, Sierra Leone, Somalia, Sudan, Tanganyika, Tunisia, Uganda, the United Arab Republic and Upper Volta.[2] On 25 May the heads of state and government signed the Charter of African Unity.

In the preamble they recited the considerations on which their action was based: the peoples' right to self-determination; ideals of freedom, justice and equality; a common desire for union and mutual assistance; the preservation of national independence and sovereignty; and devotion to the Charter of the United Nations and the Universal Declaration of Human Rights. Article I sets up the Organization of African Unity; Article II defines its objectives; Article III states the principles needed to achieve them; Articles IV, V and VI deal with the members; and Articles VII–XVIII describe the institutions of the Organization. Interpretation of the Charter is contained in Article XXVII.

The Charter of African Unity embodies another aspect of pan-Africanism, namely pan-Africanism as a political ethic. Thus it states principles such as:

(1) sovereign equality as between all member states;
(2) non-interference in the internal affairs of states;
(3) respect for the sovereignty and territorial integrity of every state and its inalienable right to an independent existence;
(4) the peaceful settlement of disputes by negotiation, mediation, conciliation or arbitration;
(5) unreserved condemnation of political assassination, and of subversive activities on the part of neighbouring states or any other states;
(6) unreserved dedication to the total liberation of the African territories which are not yet independent; and
(7) affirmation of a policy of non-alignment with regard to all blocs.

This pan-Africanist ethic offered member states a set of principles calculated to strengthen their aspirations towards African unity and solidarity. Thus pan-Africanism, regarded initially as 'a movement of ideas and emotions', had managed to crystallize the feelings, strengths and aspirations of the peoples of Africa and embody them in the Charter of African Unity.

Until 1982 the Charter of African Unity underwent only minor modifications. Thus the number of specialized commissions was reduced from five to three. It was also decided to do away with permanent membership of the Commission for Mediation, Conciliation and Arbitration. In 1979, as part of the structural reform, the term 'administrative'

2. In view of the circumstances of President Sylvanus Olympio's assassination, Togo was not admitted to the conference. Morocco refused the invitation. These two states were later to sign the Charter.

was deleted from the title of the secretary-general. At the same time the sixteenth session of the Conference of Heads of State and Government set up a committee to revise the Charter in the light of the changes and new situations in Africa. The point was that after some years it became necessary to remodel the Charter so as better to reflect the struggles of the twenty-first century and the priority to be given to development in all its forms, including culture, based on respect for human rights and the basic freedoms of peoples.

The headquarters of the Secretariat-General is at Addis Ababa in Ethiopia. In 1963 the first secretariat, which was temporary in nature, was placed under the direction of Dr Tesfaye Gebre Egzy. In 1964 the Conference of Heads of State and Government elected the Guinean Diallo Telli to the post of secretary-general. In 1968 he was re-elected. In 1972 he was succeeded by the Cameroonian Nzo Ekangaki. In 1974 the latter was succeeded by his compatriot William Eteki Mboumoua. In 1978 it was the turn of the Togolese Edem Kodjo to take over as head of the Secretariat-General; in 1983, it was the turn of Peter Onu from Nigeria; in 1985, Ide Oumarou from Niger; and in 1989, Salim Ahmed Salim from Tanzania. The secretary-general is aided by assistant secretaries-general, four to begin with and five from 1979 onwards. They each represent one of the sub-regions of the continent. They run the technical departments, and with the secretary-general make up the 'political Cabinet'. The role of secretary-general has been variously interpreted. For some he is no more than a glorified clerk. Others would have liked to give him a political and co-ordinating role. President Omar Bongo, then acting chairman of the OAU, told *Jeune Afrique* in July 1978: 'the structures of the OAU have become largely archaic, precisely because they limit the Secretary-General to mere administrative duties'.

A standing order lays down the functions of the secretary-general, the assistants and the other members of staff, and the methods of recruitment. On the tenth anniversary of the OAU, the Council of Ministers set up a committee to revise the structures of the Organization and the rules that govern its working. Its conclusions were adopted by the Khartoum summit in 1978 and gradually implemented in keeping with budgetary resources.

The supreme authority of the OAU is the Conference of Heads of State and Government. It meets once a year in ordinary session, and at each session it elects a bureau headed by a chairman. Over the years the latter has become *de facto* chairman of the OAU.[3]

The second institution of the OAU is the Council of Ministers. It holds two ordinary sessions a year. One, at the beginning of the year,

3. This post is not mentioned in the Charter, but has come into being over the years. One head of state, Omar Bongo, has said of the acting chairman: 'In fact everything happens unknown to him. Nobody listens to him. Nobody reports to him'.

750

deals mainly with administrative and financial questions. The Council prepares the meetings of heads of state, and follows up the implementation of the decisions they adopt.

The OAU on decolonization and liberation

One of the most enduring and most effective pan-Africanist activities of the OAU has been its concerted assistance to national-liberation movements in colonized Africa. At the Summit Conference in Addis Ababa in May 1963, the independent states adopted a strong resolution on decolonization, in which they unanimously acknowledged 'the duty of all African Independent States to support dependent peoples in Africa in their struggle for freedom and independence'. They also agreed on the 'imperious and urgent necessity of co-ordinating and intensifying their efforts to accelerate the unconditional attainment of national independence by all African territories still under foreign domination'.[4]

After listening to representatives of national-liberation movements from East, Central and Southern Africa, speaking on settler colonialism and on the possible courses of action, the heads of state resolved:

(1) that the continuation of colonial rule was a flagrant violation of the inalienable rights of the legitimate inhabitants of the territories concerned and a menace to the peace of the continent;

(2) that Britain should observe the provision of United Nations Resolution 1515 on independence and should not grant independence to the white minority of Southern Rhodesia (Zimbabwe);

(3) that, if Britain granted the independence, OAU members would lend their effective moral and practical support to any legitimate measures which the African nationalist leaders may devise, and also take measures against any state according recognition to the white-minority government;

(4) that Namibia was an African territory under the UN mandate, whose inhabitants were entitled to self-determination and independence, and that South Africa's presence was an act of aggression; and

(5) that the Portuguese were conducting genocide in Africa, and that their Western allies had to choose between their friendship for the African peoples and their support of colonial oppression and exploitation.

The heads of state also adopted a programme of action on decolonization. They sent an African delegation consisting of the foreign ministers of Liberia, Tunisia, Madagascar and Sierra Leone to speak at

4. The first OAU Resolutions, Agenda Item I: Decolonization, Final Version, 25 May 1963.

the meetings of the UN Security Council which was examining the report of the United Nations Committee of Twenty-four on the genocide in Portuguese colonies. They agreed to the breaking-off of diplomatic and consular relations between all African states and the governments of Portugal and South Africa, and to the boycotting of trade with the two countries by prohibiting the import of goods from those two countries, closing African ports and airports to their ships and planes, and forbidding the planes of those two countries to fly over African states.

More significantly, they established the African Liberation Committee consisting of Algeria, Ethiopia, Guinea, Nigeria, Senegal, Egypt, Tanzania, Uganda and Zaire, to be headquartered in Dar es Salaam and be responsible for co-ordinating the assistance from African states and for managing the Special Fund. The Special Fund was to be raised from voluntary annual contributions by OAU members to supply the necessary practical and financial aid to the various national-liberation movements.

Member states also agreed to receive and sponsor nationalists from liberation movements for military, educational and vocational training, and to allow the transit of all material aid and volunteers. They were to use their offices to unite the liberation movements so as to strengthen the effectiveness of the struggle. They also declared 25 May as African Liberation Day on which to organize popular demonstrations and raise funds over and above the state contributions for the Special Fund.

At the same Summit Conference in Addis Ababa, the members adopted a special resolution on *apartheid* and racial discrimination in South Africa. They not only resolved to break diplomatic and trade relations with South Africa, but also to:

(1) intensify the fight for Namibian independence before the International Court of Justice;
(2) support the UN Special Committee Against Apartheid;
(3) fight for economic sanctions against South Africa; and
(4) grant scholarships, educational facilities and possibilities of employment in African government services to refugees from South Africa.

In addition, the members condemned racial discrimination in all its forms in Africa and the world. They expressed the deep concern aroused in all African peoples and governments over racial discrimination against peoples of African descent living outside Africa, particularly in the United States.

Through the African Liberation Committee, the OAU achieved considerable success on decolonization. The vast majority of the independent states maintained the diplomatic and trade boycott of Portugal and South Africa. Even the few who failed did so not because of their lack of commitment to liberation and decolonization, but because of their economic dependency and military vulnerability stemming from their historical

PLATE 25.3 *Above left: Dulcie September, representative of the ANC (African National Congress) in France, assassinated in Paris in March 1988; above right; Steve Biko of South Africa, leader of the Black Consciousness Movement, assassinated in September 1977; below left: Nelson Mandela of South Africa, leader of the ANC, before he was sentenced to life imprisonment (photographed in the early 1960s); below right: Chief Albert Luthuli of South Africa, first president of the ANC, 1952–60*

and colonialist ties with South Africa. Such states were forced to support the liberation movements covertly while professing neutrality. This ambiguity was due to economic necessity that even the leaders of the liberation movement themselves were able to understand and appreciate.

Internationally, the OAU was able to mobilize world-wide condemnation of colonialism and *apartheid*, as well as moral and practical support for the liberation movements. They secured United Nations recognition for the legitimacy of the liberation struggle. Under Resolution 2555, the General Assembly requested all its specialized agencies to give material aid and assistance to liberation movements. Partly through the OAU's pressure, the United Nations did not recognize the Unilateral Declaration of Independence (UDI) and the white-minority government of Ian Smith of Southern Rhodesia, and it established the Commission for Namibia to replace the illegal South African colonial administration. The UN, UNESCO and the International Labour Organization (ILO) established anti-*apartheid* committees. From 28 January to 4 February 1972 the Security Council met for the first time in Africa, in Addis Ababa, seat of the OAU. The acting president of the OAU was several times instructed by his colleagues to draw the colonial situation to the attention of the United Nations General Assembly. Thus, in 1969, Ahmadou Ahidjo (Cameroon) presented to the Assembly the manifesto on Southern Africa known as the Lusaka Manifesto.[5]

But that was not enough. In 1970 the OAU set out to direct its diplomacy towards the NATO countries, the Scandinavian countries, Switzerland and Japan, with the object of explaining Africans' anxieties to them, appealing for their solidarity and showing them the threat that such a situation posed to Africa and world peace. But above all the OAU sought to dissuade them from going on supporting and arming colonialist regimes. The stubbornness of the Pretoria regime, its increasing recourse to violence and repression and its illegal occupation of Namibia led the United Nations, in co-operation with the OAU, to hold an international conference on sanctions against South Africa in Paris from 20 to 27 May 1981. At the request of the OAU and the Non-Aligned Movement, the conference called for an early meeting of the Security Council with a view to adopting global mandatory sanctions against the racialist regime in South Africa for its *apartheid* policy. Sanctions were later refused by the Security Council; but the OAU had taken the opportunity of the Paris Conference to reaffirm before the international community that as regards Namibia the United Nations had a direct responsibility by virtue

5. This manifesto was drawn up by the fifth summit of states of East and Central Africa meeting in Lusaka (Zambia), 14–16 April 1969. It was attended by Burundi, Ethiopia, Uganda, Sudan, Tanzania, Zambia, the Central African Republic, Chad, Congo–Brazzaville, Congo–Léopoldville, Kenya, Malawi, Rwanda and Somalia.

of Resolution 2448 of 1967, and that SWAPO was the only genuine representative of the people of Namibia.[6]

In the course of time, the OAU was able to exert considerable influence on the liberation movements. Its official recognition of a liberation movement and of its leadership often became the decisive factor in international circles. It conferred legitimacy and acceptability to FRELIMO in Mozambique, to the *Movimento Popular de Libertaçao de Angola* (MPLA) in Angola, to the Patriotic Front in Zimbabwe, to SWAPO in Namibia, and to the African National Congress and the Pan-African Congress in South Africa.[7] OAU pressure led to the formation of FRELIMO by the Mozambique African National Union (MANU) and *União democratica nacional de Moçambique* (UDENAMO), and of the Patriotic Front by the Zimbabwe African National Union (ZANU) of Robert Mugabe and the Zimbabwe African Peoples Union (ZAPU) of Joshua Nkomo. Denial of diplomatic recognition by the OAU led to the international boycott of bantustans in South Africa, of the Smith–Muzorewa government in Zimbabwe and of the Turnhalle Alliance in Namibia. Leaders like Moïse Tshombe of Zaire and Jonas Savimbi of Angola, who were denounced by the OAU for their non-pan-Africanist, pro-West interests, became outcasts in the black world.

Simultaneously, the creation of the OAU and, especially the African Liberation Committee, had the positive effect of boosting the morale, hope, commitment and pace of the liberation struggle. With OAU support on the international scene, most liberation leaders and their followers felt that it was only a matter of time before they achieved their total independence. Their feelings often were reinforced by OAU manifestos, such as the *Lusaka Manifesto* of April 1969 on Southern Africa and the *Arusha Action Plan* of February 1981, on Namibia. There were no concrete, practical results during the years between 1963 and 1973, which were spent primarily on the organization of the African Liberation Committee and the national-liberation movements; on statements of principles and manifestos; and on military training. The armed struggle itself still was in its primary stage.

The most fruitful period was the following decade from 1973 to 1980 with respect to the Portuguese colonies of Guinea-Bissau, Angola, Mozambique, Sao Tome and Principe, as well as the Comoros, the Seychelles and Zimbabwe. The Liberation Committee's work in these

6. The Paris Conference was attended by 122 governments, 15 specialized bodies and inter-governmental organizations, 37 international non-governmental organizations, 53 national anti-*apartheid* organizations and a large number of political personalities. It was chaired by Salim Ahmed Salim, Foreign Minister of Tanzania, and it adopted two declarations, one about sanctions against South Africa and the other about Namibia.

7. For details about the origins, ideologies, activities and leaderships of these liberation movements in Central and Southern Africa, see Chapter 10 above.

areas greatly enabled the nationalists to carry on the war which led to the gradual liberation of large areas of the Portuguese colonies and the reorganization of the administration and the economy. In Guinea-Bissau, as discussed in Chapter 7 above, the PAIGC's campaign was decisive, and succeeded in overcoming the Portuguese grip on the country in 1973. FRELIMO and the MPLA did the same in Mozambique and Angola in 1975 respectively. Faced with these successes the colonialists resorted to barbarous methods – such as the political assassination of the PAIGC leader, Amilcar Cabral, and the leader of FRELIMO, Eduardo Mondlane. In addition to the armed struggle, the nationalists embarked on civic training and the organization of the liberated areas. Thus in Guinea-Bissau, popular assemblies were elected, schools and hospitals set up and new economic arrangements brought into play. The Comoros, Seychelles and Zimbabwe also became independent in 1980. The only remaining vestige of European colonialism was settler colonialism in South Africa and Namibia, but victory in Namibia was only a matter of time.

Outside Africa, the OAU has also paid particular attention to the situation in the Middle East and Palestine. Thus it has expressed its solidarity with Egypt and with the Arab countries whose territory has been occupied since June 1967.

To make this solidarity effective it resorted to two methods:

(1) appealing to its member states to use all their influence to get Israel to implement Security Council Resolution 242; and

(2) entrusting specific missions to certain heads of state. Thus the eighth ordinary session of the OAU summit of June 1971, by resolution AHG/Res. 66 (VIII), instructed the acting chairman to approach the United Nations about the renewal of hostilities because of the expiry of the cease-fire; while a commission of ten heads of state was instructed to consult with the Israeli and Egyptian governments.

Another of the OAU's concerns has been the settlement of disputes between its member states. The Bandung Declaration of 1955, to which the African nationalist leaders and the pan-Africanists subscribed, called for the settlement of all international disputes by peaceful means in accordance with the United Nations Charter.

The principle of peaceful settlement also figured in the various declarations adopted by the first conference of independent African states, in one of the resolutions of the Monrovia Conference of May 1961, and in the Charter of the OAU.

Article XIX of the Charter stipulates that:

Member States undertake to settle their disputes by peaceful means, and to this end decide to establish a commission of mediation, conciliation and arbitration whose composition and conditions of service shall be defined by a separate protocol to be approved by the

Assembly of Heads of State and Government. Said protocol shall be regarded as forming an integral part of the present Charter.

Many of these disputes arose from frontier problems inherited from colonialism. Thus in 1962 Algeria and Morocco clashed with one another, and so over the years did Uganda and Tanzania, Gabon and Equatorial Guinea, Cameroon and Nigeria, Zaire and Angola, Dahomey and Niger, Chad and the Sudan, and Guinea and the Côte d'Ivoire. The dispute between Ethiopia and Somalia over the Ogaden has lasted some time, as have those between Libya and Chad over the Aouzou strip, and between Kenya and Somalia.[8]

In 1979 the OAU had to deal with a matter of a special kind: the fact that the various political and military factions confronting each other in Chad decided on the insistence of their neighbours to refer the matter to the OAU. The latter referred the question to a committee of heads of state, which managed to compel 11 Chadian factions to come together in a transitional government of national unity (GUNT) under the leadership of Goukouni Oueddei. This alliance was short lived, and faced with a recrudescence of the civil war, the OAU in 1981 dispatched an inter-African peace-keeping force to the area. This step has been variously judged. It was the first of its kind, and despite its defects it played an appreciable role by saving many human lives.

The OAU rounded off its political and liberation activities by concerning itself with human rights and the self-determination of peoples. The reasons for such a concern go back a long way in time. Thus pan-Africanism, in seeking to rehabilitate the Africans was aiming to wipe out both the after-effects of the slavery from which the Africans of the *diaspora* were suffering and also the misdeeds of colonialism in Africa.

The African Conference on the Rule of Law was held in Lagos in 1961 to discuss the various aspects of human rights. The report of the three working parties acknowledged that the law needed to be used to safeguard and foster the wishes of the African people and the political rights of individuals. Social, economic, educational and cultural conditions therefore needed to be established such as would allow individuals to regain their dignity and achieve their legitimate aspirations in all countries, whether independent or not.

The Monrovia Conference of August 1959 adopted a resolution on racial discrimination which called upon the members of the international community:

(1) to associate themselves with the resolutions of the United Nations and with the declarations and resolutions of the Bandung and Accra conferences condemning racialism and segregation; and

(2) to combat them.

---

8. In 1963 Somalia expressed reservations about the principle of the inviolability of borders inherited from colonialism.

757

It is also worth noting that Dr Nnamdi Azikiwe of Nigeria stressed in 1961, in his book *The Future of Pan-Africanism*, the need to draw up a Human-Rights Convention applicable in the context of a pan-African organization. This was not achieved until 16 years after the setting-up of the OAU, when on President Léopold Sédar Senghor's motion, the Conference of Heads of State and Government, meeting in Monrovia, Liberia, from 17 to 20 July 1979, stated that 'considering that economic and social development is a human right; taking note of Resolution 24 (XXIV) of the Human Rights Commission on regional arrangements for the promotion and protection of human rights' it:

(1) Reaffirms the need for better international co-operation, respect for fundamental human and peoples' rights, and in particular the right to development;

(2) Calls on the Secretary-General of the OAU to:

(a) draw the attention of member states to certain international conventions whose ratification would help to strengthen Africa's struggle against certain scourges, especially apartheid and racial discrimination, trade imbalance and mercenarism;

(b) organize as soon as possible, in an African capital, a restricted meeting of highly qualified experts to prepare a preliminary draft of an 'African Charter on Human and Peoples' Rights' providing, *inter alia*, for the establishment of bodies to promote and protect human and peoples' rights [Decision 115 (XVI)].

From 28 November to 8 December 1979, African legal experts met in Dakar to draw up a preliminary draft of a charter reflecting the African conception of human rights. It would after all be a big mistake actually to claim to build a new African society without recognizing and fostering the prime mover and accelerator of such a development: man. While Africa has always contributed in the United Nations and elsewhere to the gradual development of human rights, the time had come for it to set up a precise legal framework within its own borders such as would meet perforce the basic needs of the peoples sharing its territory. After the experts, the Conference of Ministers of Justice meeting in Banjul, Gambia, in June 1980 and January 1981 next considered the preliminary draft, and it was adopted in July 1981 at the summit of heads of state in Nairobi. Both sessions of the Conference of Ministers of Justice were opened by the president of the Gambia, Sir Dawda K. Jawara, who did not fail to stress the importance of what was at stake:

A truly African Charter should reflect those of our traditions that are worth preserving, and also our values and the legitimate aspirations of our peoples, so as to round off the worldwide international campaign to reinforce respect for human rights. We do not see the individual as a being existing in a vacuum with unlimited freedom. In our view

758

he lives in a society and in continual interaction with his fellow men. Thus in addition to his rights he has his own responsibilities to fulfil towards his family and his community. We should, however, avoid the danger of extending the individual's responsibilities to the point of obliterating the individual in the interest of the group.

The African Charter of Human Rights and the Rights of Peoples, after a long preamble, comprises 67 articles divided into three parts. The first part deals with the rights and responsibilities of men and peoples, and the second with protective measures; the third covers miscellaneous provisions.

In adopting this Charter the African states obviously intended not only to strike a blow for progress and the 'duty to be free' in Africa but also to have at their command an additional weapon to repel the horrible monster of *apartheid* and colonialism.

Socio-cultural development work

In the national-liberation struggle being carried out in Africa the assertion of cultural identity has been an important feature. Culture is liberating and supportive for the emancipation movement of the colonial peoples, and so the OAU cannot neglect this factor in its work.

In 1965 it set up a Department of Scientific and Cultural Affairs within the Secretariat-General. From 27 October to 6 November 1975, in co-operation with UNESCO, it held the Intergovernmental Conference on cultural policies in Africa in Accra, Ghana. In July 1976, the thirteenth ordinary session of the Conference of Heads of State and Government adopted the African Cultural Charter, which formed a complement to the political charter of 1963.

The cultural renaissance of Africa showed itself with the holding in Algiers of the first Pan-African Festival, which gave rise to some grand artistic events from 21 July to 1 August 1969. The second festival took place in Lagos and Kaduna, Nigeria from 15 January to 12 February 1977.

A series of meetings under OAU auspices led to a clearer picture of cultural activity and its place in development. At the Algiers Pan-African Festival a symposium discussed 'African culture, its role in the liberation struggle, the consolidation of African unity and the economic and social development of Africa', and drew up the African cultural manifesto. The second festival in 1977 tackled the topic 'Black civilization and education'. In January 1981 a symposium on 'Science and culture as a foundation for African development' met in Libreville, Gabon.

Cultural co-operation bodies made their appearance over the years: centres for linguistic and historical studies through oral tradition were set up, and in 1980 an Inter-African Cultural Fund was instituted.

The relationships the OAU formed with UNESCO and ALECSO gave its activities an international dimension. Education, science and technology

759

also figure in the work of OAU. In co-operation with UNESCO it held the Conference of Ministers of Education in 1964 and 1982. In Addis Ababa in 1982 with the ECA, the UNDP, UNESCO and the Association of African Universities, it held the first Conference of Rectors and Vice-Chancellors of African Universities about the *Lagos Plan of Action*. For scientific questions the OAU has an Executive Secretariat in Lagos and an African Scientific Commission. In 1982 the OAU took two steps in this field: it instituted the African Scientific Renaissance Prizes, and it held the first Congress of Scientists in Africa.

In the field of social affairs, several meetings have been held with international and inter-African bodies about the situation of young people, women and the disabled.[9] Moreover, since 1967 the Secretariat-General of the OAU has looked after the Conference of African Ministers of Labour: this is a standing body of the OAU, and is responsible for evolving a common labour policy and facilitating the necessary co-operation between member states.

OAU action also led to the setting up in 1972 of the All-African Trades Union Organization, which is based in Accra, Ghana.

Afro-Arab co-operation

This deserves a special place in the work of the OAU. Historic relationships have of course long existed between the Arab world and Africa. Centuries of contact have resulted in cultural and economic co-operation between them. But it must be admitted that it remained ill-developed.

Pan-Africanism and pan-Arabism

Pan-Africanism and pan-Arabism were originally distinct movements in North Africa. Pan-Arabism looked eastwards to the Arabian peninsula and the Fertile Crescent. On the other hand, pan-Africanism south of the Sahara looked westwards to the black presence in the Americas. Pan-Arabism included cultural solidarity partly based on *religious* pride (the heritage of Islam). Pan-Africanism included cultural solidarity partly based on *racial* pride (the heritage of the black people). Pan-Arabism stressed the concept of a single 'Arab nation'. Pan-Africanism was evolving a concept of a unified 'African personality'.

Both movements had a profound ambivalence about Western Europe. They were both attracted and repelled by European culture and civilization. Pan-Arabism looked back to ancient Arab empires of the Umayyads and of the Abbasids – and noted how Arabs had civilized Europe in the Middle Ages. Pan-Africanism looked back to the ancient

9. The Conference of African Women, the Pan-African Youth Movement and the Supreme Council for Sport in Africa work closely with the OAU, and have observer status at it.

empires of Mali, Songhay and Ghana – and noted how ancient Egypt had civilized ancient Greece. Arab nostalgia for Islam's glorious past inspired poets and playwrights into a literary renaissance. African nostalgia for ancestral profundity provoked literary movements like negritude.[10]

It was mainly after the Second World War that pan-Africanism and pan-Arabism began to merge. Perhaps inevitably Sudan (Khartoum) was among the first to manifest elements of fusion between the two movements. An ancient kind of ambivalence affected many northern Sudanese. Were they Arabs or Africans? Poets and other writers grappled with this dilemma. A. M. Fayturi later captured it as he portrayed Africa lying unconscious in a coma, but he meant the Africa *within himself* which was in a coma. Fayturi struggled to shake the sleeping Africa *within* his own soul:

> Africa Oh Africa
> Wake up from your dark self . . .
> Many times has the earth rotated,
> And many times have the burning planets rolled
> The rebel has built what he destroyed,
> And the worshipper debased what he once adored
> But you are still as you have always been,
> A rejected skull, a (mere) skull.[11]

The partial merger of pan-Africanism and pan-Arabism entered a new phase with the Egyptian revolution of 1952. This phase went beyond the simple fact that Muhammad Naguib, who briefly succeeded King Farouk as Egypt's head of state, had black African blood in his veins. It went beyond the additional biological fact that Anwar Sadat – another Egyptian activist of the 1952 revolution and destined to lead Egypt for more than a decade later – also had black African ancestry through his mother. What was even more significant was the shift in Egypt's political orientation. Gamāl 'Abd al-Nasser, who succeeded Naguib as Egypt's leader, saw the country as the centre of three concentric circles – the Arab world, the Muslim world, and Africa. He reminded his compatriots that they could not remain indifferent to the 'sanguinary struggle' going on south of the Sahara against imperialism and racism. Perhaps influenced by the doctrine of Suez and the Nile in nineteenth-century thought, or by the historic role of Egypt as the mother of civilization, al-Nasser described his country as the very gateway into Africa. In spite of his exaggeration of the centrality of Egypt in the destiny of Africa, al-Nasser's little book, *The Philosophy of the Revolution*, constituted an important step forward in the process of linkage between pan-Africanism and pan-Arabism.[12]

10. Consult UNESCO, 1979.
11. This translation is from M. Abdul-Hai, 1976, pp. 43–4.
12. G. A. Nasser, 1954; see also, K. Osia, 1983.

An alliance was developing between the nationalist movements of Africa and the Arab world. Cairo became for a while the capital of radical nationalism of both regions. Dissidents and activists from all over Africa and the Middle East converged on Cairo, plotted change and conspired for revolution. The United Arab Republic under al-Nasser subsidized many of their activities.

Cairo Radio became the first international voice of revolution broadcast on the African continent. It broadcast not only in English, Arabic and French, but also in Kiswahili. Other languages were later added. Egypt also offered scholarships to Africans, as well as to Arabs, to study at Egyptian institutions. Colonial governments in African territories became alarmed by the radicalizing role which al-Nasser's United Arab Republic was playing in sub-Saharan Africa as a whole. This only encouraged Cairo into greater nationalist militancy.

Al-Nasser's radical credentials had been enhanced by the Suez crisis of 1956 and his successful nationalization of the Suez Canal. The nationalization had been a declaration of Africa's right to her own resources in the face of external hostility. The tripartite invasion of Egypt by Britain, France and Israel gave al-Nasser the stature of a martyr when he suffered military defeat, followed by the stature of a hero when the aggressors were forced to withdraw ignominiously under international pressure.

The next stage in the partial fusion of pan-Africanism and pan-Arabism came with the later stages of the Algerian war of independence. The war broke out in 1954 but its pan-African implications did not mature until after Ghana's independence in 1957. For a while the Algerian war divided the African continent rather than uniting it. This was because many Francophone countries were torn between their belief in anti-colonialism and their friendship towards France. Paris claimed for a long time that Algeria was part of France – and conservative opinion in Francophone Africa tended for a while to give France the benefit of the doubt. This split Africa into the Casablanca (pro-Algerian government-in-exile) and Monrovia (more conservative) groups.

What was significant about this split was that it was *not* neatly between pro-Algerian *Arabs* and pro-French *blacks*. The pro-Algerian Casablanca Group included Africa's greatest pan-Africanist – Kwame Nkrumah. The non-Arab members of the Casablanca alliance included also Guinea and Mali, as well as Ghana. This was yet another stage in the historic linkage between pan-Africanism and pan-Arabism. In the Casablanca declaration, Nkrumah for the first time joined the Arabs in denouncing Israel as a 'tool of neo-colonialism' and a surrogate of the West.

Pan-African splits were moderated not only after Algeria became independent in 1962 but also when the Organization of African Unity was formed in 1963. The OAU became Afro-Arab in composition, inspired by the mystique of a continent in which the Sahara was regarded as a bridge rather than a divide. In some respects the OAU became the most important and most ambitious Afro-Arab experiment in history. It was also another stage of linkage between pan-Africanism and pan-Arabism.

The fifth stage of linkage came with the June war of 1967 between the Arabs and Israel. Israel's conquest of Sinai was regarded as an aggression against a member of the Organization of African Unity and therefore a territorial occupation of Africa by Israeli forces. The Arab–Israeli conflict was now territorially Africanized. For nearly two decades after that, pan-Africanism and pan-Arabism were more deeply interlinked. Israeli co-operation with the racist regime in South Africa provided additional vindication for Afro-Arab solidarity. By the time of the Arab–Israeli October war of 1973 there was sufficient solidarity between Africa and the Arabs to result in an almost unanimous African break of diplomatic relations with Israel. The politics of the Middle East were now truly interlinked with the politics of Africa.

Did the rise of the Organization of Petroleum Exporting Countries (OPEC) also become one of the foundations of Afro-Arab solidarity? This is a more ambiguous area of analysis. It is true that the rise of OPEC transformed Nigeria into a pivotal state in relations between the Arabs and black Africa. For about a decade from the mid-1970s to the mid-1980s, Nigeria was a link in the chain which tied pan-Arabism with pan-Africanism – partly through the politics of oil and partly through the politics of Islam. Indeed, President Ibrahim Babangida in 1986 even took the political risk of making Nigeria a full member of the Organization of the Islamic Conference (OIC) – to the indignation of his Christian compatriots.

But while the politics of both OIC and OPEC do often provide important areas of linkage between pan-Africanism and pan-Arabism, piety and petroleum are sometimes *divisive* rather than unifying. Almost half the membership of the Organization of the Islamic Conference (total membership of nearly 50 countries) are also members of the Organization of African Unity. The proportion from Africa is higher than the African proportion in the membership of OPEC. All three organizations – the OIC, OAU and OPEC – have helped to link pan-Africanism with pan-Arabism. But religion and oil prices are often ambiguous in their impact on human relations and international diplomacy.

The agenda of Afro-Arab co-operation

On the other hand, Afro-Arab participation in the Group of 77 and North–South negotiations has created a wider alliance with the rest of the Third World. This wider agenda has, in the last few years, acquired a new dimension. Awareness of a close-knit, united Third World came into being at Bandung in 1955, and grew stronger at the summit of non-aligned countries in Algiers in 1973. The similarity between racialism in

South Africa and Zionism in Palestine and the occupied territories brought their victims, the Arab and African peoples, closer together.

The economic crisis and its effects on the development of the Third World prompted their governments to take up a common position in opposition to the deterioration of the world situation and the policies of the industrialized countries. This proved all the more necessary in that the fair increase in the oil price made the Arab countries which export this raw material a major force on international financial and monetary markets. This new situation injected a new purpose, a new basis and a new philosophy into Afro-Arab co-operation. By successive stages, relationships between Africa and the Arab world were to acquire a hitherto unknown dimension:

(1) The extraordinary session of the OAU Council of Ministers, 19–21 November 1973, set up a committee of seven members to make contact with the Arab League states and consider ways of drawing up a policy of co-operation between the African states and the Arab world.

(2) The Arab Heads of State meeting in Algiers, 26–28 November 1973, decided to set up the Arab Bank for Economic Development in Africa (BADEA – *Banque arabe pour le développement économique de l'Afrique*), in order to:
   (a) play a part in financing the economic development of African states;
   (b) encourage the participation of Arab capital in the development of Africa; and
   (c) provide the necessary technical assistance for the development of Africa.

(3) At their meeting in Cairo on 23 January 1974 the Arab oil ministers decided, in accordance with the recommendations of the Economic Council of the Arab League, to set up a Special Fund for Aid to Africa (SFAA). Its initial capital was $200 million, and it was intended in the first phase to provide emergency aid to African countries on favourable terms.

(4) Meeting from 25 to 28 March 1974 in Tunis, the Council of the Arab League approved in principle the setting up of the Arab Fund for Technical Assistance to Africa; and on 10 July in Cairo, the African and Arab inter-ministerial committee approved the draft declaration and programme of action on Afro-Arab co-operation.

(5) This document was first submitted to the Arab and African foreign ministers at their meeting in Dakar, 19–22 April 1976, then to meetings in Lusaka, 24–6 January 1977, and in Cairo, 3–6 March 1977. A summit meeting in Cairo, 7–9 March 1977, was attended by 60 member states of the Arab League and the OAU. In a declaration on Arab–African economic and financial co-operation they decided to adopt a comprehensive programme

of long-term economic, technical and financial co-operation in the fields of:
(a) trade;
(b) agriculture and stockbreeding;
(b) mining and industry;
(d) energy and hydraulic resources;
(e) transport, communications and telecommunications;
(f) financial co-operation;
(g) culture, education and social affairs; and
(h) science and technology.
To improve the co-ordination of action and to help in the implementation of the declaration, the two parties:
(a) set up a standing Afro-Arab ministerial committee;
(b) gave each other observer status at meetings of their respective organizations;
(c) appointed representatives at each other's secretariat; and
(d) invited African and Arab institutions in the same field to work closely together.

Let us take stock of the first few years of Afro-Arab co-operation. There is certainly a political will to act, and substantial means. But very early on the working of the institutions was paralysed by political conflicts in the Arab world, and both sides were irritated by administrative delays – so much so that the head of state of Niger, President Seyni Kountche, when welcoming the third session of the standing committee for Arab–African co-operation to Niamey in June 1978, recommended 'getting away from the continual deliberate shilly-shallying favoured by other forms of co-operation, more concerned to perpetuate their control than to work for the real economic and social advancement of our states'.

Capital transfers from the Arab states to African countries increased considerably from 1973 to 1980. Thus for 1974 official development aid by the OPEC countries to Third-World countries amounted to the equivalent of $2.5 billion, or 1.74 per cent of their GNP. Total transfers from OPEC members to the Third World were $5 billion in 1974 and $9 billion in 1975 – an increase of 66 per cent. But that was still not enough. As the president of BADEA wrote, 'the smallness of these transfers to Africa is even more alarming when we realize Africa's real needs for development capital'. The 'crisis' of declining oil prices in the 1980s (the 'oil glut') hurt the oil producers and reduced Arab aid.

But in the minds of its promoters, Afro-Arab co-operation is not a matter merely of some financial transfers or private investments. It must translate into action the shared aspirations and the mutual understanding of peoples and civilizations. Hence the importance of reconciling the *Lagos Plan of Action* adopted by the OAU with the *Amman Strategy* advocated by the Arab League; this would pave the way for shared development programmes. The OAU–Arab League plan to set up an

Afro-Arab Cultural Fund and an Afro-Arab Cultural Institute also promised to give a fillip to cultural exchanges and cultural development.

Conclusion

It can be seen from the discussion that one of the underlying themes of pan-Africanism was the liberation of black peoples in general and Africans in particular. While the chapter in this volume on regional integration may suggest more divisions, clashes of personalities and failures than unity and success, this chapter on pan-Africanism and liberation indicates considerable unity of purpose and action by people of African ancestry throughout the world and by the OAU in particular. In spite of the initial lack of unity among the liberation movements, national economic self-interests and vulnerability among some of the independent states, and massive economic, military and diplomatic support given to the colonial regimes by Western powers, the OAU and liberation movements were able to wage a common pan-Africanist struggle and win against European colonialism and imperialism. All independent African states participated in the struggle in one form or another, in spite of the apparent multi-dimensional national self-interests. Anti-colonialism, anti-racialism and non-alignment became the strongest bonds of pan-Africanist unity among independent states and among liberation movements. Pan-Africanist ideology and liberation struggle also permeated the masses of Africa to the extent that they were prepared to bear the economic expenses and human sacrifices of liberating their fellow Africans.

However, in the light of the vastly changing economic conditions and especially of the deteriorating economic order in Africa, the contours of pan-Africanism have now been extended to include the Middle East, and the Third World in general. The future will surely include the successful conclusion of the struggle in South Africa, as in Namibia; a more genuine economic and cultural independence for Africa; and the realization of that long-cherished but elusive dream of radical pan-Africanists – a continental government for Africa.

SECTION VII

Independent Africa in world affairs

Africa and the capitalist countries

CHINWEIZU

Three evils in modern history have coloured Africa's relationship with the capitalist world – the slave trade, imperialism and racism. Was the link between capitalism and the three evils inevitable? Or can capitalism be divorced from those ominous forces?

In a previous period of Africa's relationship with the capitalist world, it was certainly demonstrated that mature capitalism could comfortably survive the abolition of the slave trade. Indeed, the leading capitalist power of the nineteenth century (England) became also the leading abolitionist power.

Two of the most basic questions for the second half of the *twentieth* century have been, first, whether capitalism could comfortably survive the process of *decolonization*; and, secondly, whether capitalism could at last also divorce itself from *racism* once and for all. As the slave trade eventually proved unnecessary for the health of international capitalism, in its more advanced stage, can imperialism and racism be said to be similarly dispensable for international capitalism?

What the years from 1945 to 1980 demonstrated was the capitalist world's reluctant readiness to accept the *political* decolonization of Africa. What the rest of the twentieth century may also demonstrate is the capitalist world's readiness to accept the end of *apartheid* and institutionalized racism in Southern Africa – under the pressure of African liberation-fighters.

Are we therefore to conclude that capitalism is at last on the verge of shedding off all the three evils which had previously coloured its relationship with Africa – the slave trade, imperialism and racism?

There is a catch in the story. Political decolonization and formal independence in Africa have not meant the end of imperialism. They have only meant a change in the *guise* of imperialism. Political decolonization has not been accompanied by economic decolonization. And protectorate status under single European countries sometimes gives way to protectorate status under such Western collective powers as the North Atlantic Treaty Organization and the European Community. This chapter is about some of these new guises of capitalist power in Africa.

769

Upon attaining independence[1] four related ambitions determined what changes the new African states sought in their relations with the rest of the capitalist world.[2] Their élites wanted to modernize their societies and thereby gain international respect for their people. To that end, they wanted to complete the political decolonization of Africa and to end the humiliations of racism; they wanted economic development to make their countries powerful, affluent and respected members of the industrial world; and they wanted economic decolonization to free them from Western economic control. Western reactions to these aims were determined by whether their implications conflicted with or served the overriding Western interest in preserving their world dominance through the minimum necessary reforms. Where the implications went beyond or against such reforms, the West opposed them; otherwise, the West supported them.

Modernization was understood, by Africa and the West alike, as a process which would turn African societies into black replicas of twentieth-century societies. The capitalist industrial societies were the generally preferred model; the socialist industrial societies, though the preferred model for a minority of the African élite, were repugnant to the majority of the African leadership as well as to the West. Consequently, considerable Afro-Western co-operation went into fostering Western-style democracy in state affairs; into establishing Western-style schools and universities to help transplant the Western intellectual tradition into Africa; into propagating the capitalist ideology among Africans, especially the liberal version which was dominant at the time; and into creating roads, tele-communications and other technical infrastructures which would facilitate Western-style economic activity in Africa.

For the West and the African states alike, the economic aim of modernization was the rapid attainment by Africans of the contemporary Western style and level of consumerism. But whereas Africans wanted to create their own industries to supply the products they craved, the West preferred that Africans should continue to depend on the West for them. Consequently, the two sides meant rather different things by economic development.

African states saw the cornerstone of economic development as the creation of their own industrial base. The West, in contrast, limited its concept of African economic development to merely reforming Africa's productive capacity in ways that would make Africa a reliable supplier of agricultural and mineral inputs to the factories of the West, and to

1. 1960 is generally taken as the year of African independence. It was the year in which the largest number of African countries gained independence.
2. Relations between Africa and the rest of the capitalist world were, in essence, Afro-Western relations, with the West in the trilateral sense of Western Europe, North America and Japan.

developing African appetites so that Africa would become a more lucrative market for Western goods.

On economic decolonization, the African states and the West were in sharp conflict. The African states wanted to wrest control of their economies from a West which was determined to retain that control. For the West, losing control would mean giving up what a century of conquest and colonization had achieved for them, and what political decolonization had aimed to preserve. For the African states, however, not to wrest away that control would be to defeat the economic aim of their struggle for political independence.

On political decolonization itself, if their conflict seemed any less sharp than that over economic decolonization, it was only because Western economic hegemony over Africa was consistent with a variety of political arrangements: white-minority domination – as in the Republic of South Africa and the then Rhodesia; classical colonialism – as in the then unliberated colonies of Portugal; or neo-colonialism, that is, indirect political control through economic domination – as in the newly independent African states themselves. Because of these options, Western opposition to the African aims of destroying racism and ending foreign political rule over every square inch of the continent was not as implacable as its opposition to economic decolonization. Nonetheless, the Western powers were reluctant to give up any existing form of political control for another which they considered less congenial. Thus, they could publicly agree that the political decolonization of Africa and the ending of racist *apartheid* were desirable, yet hinder these objectives through delaying tactics and ambivalences which Africans found most maddening.

The details of the drama resulting from these conflicts and coincidences of interests and perceptions were shaped to no small degree by the system of multilateral institutions which the West had set up for managing the capitalist system following the disasters of the Second World War. The UN (and especially such of its agencies as UNCTAD), the EEC, the World Bank and the International Monetary Fund (IMF) would be principal actors and venues in the ensuing drama.

Multilateralism and the Atlantic Charter

In the early phases of the Second World War, it became clear to the leaders of the anti-Axis alliance that intense economic rivalries between capitalist powers must be defused if they were not to cause yet another global war. They therefore set about outlining arrangements which they hoped would enable them to manage the peace after the Second World War. The Atlantic Charter, enunciated in 1941 by US President Franklin Roosevelt and British Prime Minister Winston Churchill became their inspiration. France was under Nazi occupation. The cornerstone of the Atlantic Charter was the principle of multilateralism on which the top

771

political, economic and defence institutions of the post-war capitalist world would be organized.

The Bretton Woods agreement of 1945 created under American leadership three primary economic institutions, namely the IMF, the World Bank and the GATT. The IMF, which went into operation in 1947, was given the job of smoothing out difficulties posed by balance-of-payments surpluses and deficits from international trade. The World Bank (officially named The International Bank for Reconstruction and Development), which went into operation in 1946, was given the task of encouraging capital investment for the reconstruction and development of its member countries. To the General Agreement on Tariffs and Trade (GATT), which began operation in 1948, fell the task of promoting multilateral trade through minimizing trade barriers, reducing import tariffs and quotas, and discouraging preferential trade agreements between countries.

On the political and military sides, the Atlantic Charter inspired two organizations. First was the United Nations Organization (the UN) which came into being in 1945 with its headquarters in the USA. It thereafter served as a political forum for discussing world affairs, and its various specialized agencies provided technical assistance for managing aspects of world affairs. In 1948, the North Atlantic Treaty Organization (NATO) was given responsibility for the collective defence of the European and North American powers of the capitalist world. Again the United States was 'the first among equals'.

Later on, two other multilateral economic organizations were created which had consequences for independent Africa. The European Economic Community (EEC) was created by the Treaty of Rome in 1957, and came into being in 1958 under French leadership. It was designed to foster common external policies for its members in the areas of commerce, agriculture and transport. In 1961, a club of the leading capitalist powers, the Organization for Economic Cooperation and Development (OECD), came into being to expand world multilateral trade, among other things.

These institutions (the UN, IMF, World Bank, GATT, EEC, OECD, NATO) were the apex of a structure of rules, laws, customs and organizations which together determined the workings of the capitalist world into which African states emerged from colonialism. And without much questioning or understanding of the true purposes of these institutions, or of the system of structures over which they presided, African states were co-opted into them. They were persuaded to join the UN and its agencies; to join the IMF, the World Bank, and the GATT; and to develop subordinating relations with the EEC, NATO and the OECD. They were obliged, by various open and secret sections of the instruments transferring formal political power to them at independence, to retain whatever economic, diplomatic and cultural agreements they had been made parties to by the departing colonial administrations. Furthermore, African states were prevailed upon to join such organizations as the

PLATE 26.1   *The Sixteenth Franco-African Summit at La Baule, France, June, 1990*

(British) Commonwealth and the French Community which their former colonizers created as instruments for their continuing political hegemony. Many African states (especially former French colonies) also signed defence pacts with their departing masters, many of which permitted the ex-colonizers (especially France) to station troops in the African countries, and to intervene militarily, if need be, in the internal affairs of the new African regimes. Thus, the African states not only subordinated themselves to the apex institutions, but also tied themselves by a thousand cables to the inner working structures of the capitalist world system. And in effect, with independence, Africa changed from being a patchwork of exclusive and competing imperial territories, each lorded over by one European power or another, and became, in essence, a *NATO protectorate*.

Within the NATO umbrella, ultimate responsibility for each ex-colony remained with its former colonial master. Whenever there was civil strife within an ex-colony (as in the civil wars in Nigeria and Chad), the NATO countries usually followed the course advised by its ex-colonial master. But if an ex-colony was felt to be under serious threat from 'external communist subversion' (as with Lumumba's Congo), the USA, as the leader of NATO, would take a direct hand in the matter.

Political decolonization and East–West rivalry, 1960–84

The campaign to complete the political decolonization of Africa eventually weakened the NATO protectorship into an OECD hegemony. This happened for two principal reasons. First, as African states diversified their economic contacts with the rest of the world, the capitalist countries with strong economic ties to Africa came to include non-NATO members of the OECD like Switzerland, Ireland, Sweden and Japan. Secondly, by giving material support to African decolonization movements, the Soviet bloc gained steady influence in Africa, thus partially eroding the NATO protectorship. Beginning with the largely rhetorical friendship of radical African regimes in Ghana, Guinea and Congo-Brazzaville in the 1960s, the Soviet bloc had, by the mid-1970s, established firm footholds in Ethiopia, Angola and Mozambique, which proclaimed themselves pro-Soviet socialist or Marxist states.

PLATE 26.2 *Installation of a printing press at CICIBA, Libreville, Gabon, by technicians from the Mitsubishi Corporation of Japan*

Western fears of Soviet bloc influence in Africa seriously affected Afro-Western relations. Its impact was like the pressure of a hostile column appearing at a siege, raising uncertain hopes of escape among the besieged, and spreading alarm among the besiegers. Soviet actions and intentions thus became a crucial element in the calculations of both sides in all aspects of their relations.

It became a preoccupation of the West to keep Soviet bloc influence out of Africa. African nationalism was, however, far from averse to obtaining Soviet bloc help in its campaign to end Rhodesian settler-colonialism in Zimbabwe; Portuguese colonialism in Angola, Guinea-Bissau and Mozambique; South African rule in Namibia; and *apartheid* and white-settler rule in South Africa.

In the independent African states, NATO protectorship was preserved by various means: propaganda campaigns to foster a pro-Western and anti-Soviet political and cultural climate; political chaperonage of African regimes by Western embassies; covert political interventions; and, when all else failed, open military interventions to prop up tottering pro-Western regimes or to topple pro-Soviet regimes where they managed to emerge. The flashpoints of these activities were the numerous 'anti-communist' military interventions in Africa by Western or Western-sponsored forces. These included the UN operation in the Congo (Zaire), from 1960 to 1964, first to oust Patrice Lumumba, whom the West saw as pro-Soviet and communist, and then to install a pro-Western leadership; British interventions in Kenya and Tanganyika (1964) to suppress mutinies against pro-Western regimes; the anti-Nkrumah coup in Ghana (1966) to topple an increasingly anti-Western leader; the Shaba Operations (1977 and 1978–9) to protect the Mobutu regime from its Zairian foes; numerous French interventions to preserve pro-French regimes (as in the Côte d'Ivoire, 1964 and 1968) or to replace those no longer acceptable to France, such as the coup against Emperor Bokassa (1979); and numerous mercenary expeditions to topple 'left-leaning' African governments, as in Guinea (1970) and the Seychelles (1979 and 1982). These means were largely successful in preserving a pro-Western *status quo* in the affected countries.

The West had far less success in preventing pro-Soviet regimes from emerging from the remnants of the old colonies. There, African nationalism, with decisive Soviet-bloc support, inflicted defeats upon the West.

Despite an overall Western self-interest in extending political de-colonization to the remaining colonies, a fear, engendered particularly by the Congo experience, of pro-Soviet Africans coming to power in the wake of Europeans, made the West throw its weight behind the surviving colonialisms of Portugal, Rhodesia and South Africa. Consequently, against the NATO-backed determination of impoverished Portugal to hang on to its colonies, and of the Rhodesians to hang on to Zimbabwe, prolonged armed struggles had to be waged. Considerable Soviet-bloc military and diplomatic assistance helped to make the victorious national-ists pro-Soviet and even Marxist.

In Ethiopia, the Marxist wing of the military revolution against the feudal monarchy won the competition for power which followed the overthrow of Emperor Haile Selassie. The Marxists' victory was despite

775

considerable Western efforts (especially American) to install their pro-Western friends in power.

With these triumphs of Marxist African nationalists, NATO's protectorship over Africa was seriously breached by 1975. With its worst fears of pro-Soviet states emerging in Africa thus fulfilled, the West under US leadership saw less reason to push black majority rule and the ending of *apartheid* upon the white-settler minority ruling South Africa. It therefore also sought to entrench South African rule in Namibia. Thus, despite major African victories against Portuguese and Rhodesian colonialism, the African campaign of political decolonization was still not concluded by the mid-1980s. Namibia was still fighting for its independence; and despite mounting international pressure, the end of *apartheid* and of white-minority rule in South Africa were not yet in sight.

At the end of 1984, it could be said that whereas NATO lost its protectorship over those of its old colonies which it still had by 1970, it successfully defended its protectorship over the neo-colonies to which it had given political independence by 1970. All this vindicated the overall post-war Western strategy of granting political independence to colonies in order to be able to keep them within the Western economic orbit.

However, in 1974, the dominant theme of the Afro-Western drama had shifted from the political to the economic sphere.

Economic development and decolonization, 1960–73

Determined to preserve Africa as an economic protectorate, and fearing Soviet bloc inroads if African aspirations went unmet, the West was prepared to foster a certain amount of Africanization of the African economy, and to sponsor that limited type of development which the colonial powers had begun after the Second World War. But the demands of African nationalism went far beyond what the West under US leadership would countenance. Consequently, the first quarter-century of African political independence witnessed a steady escalation of African pressure for development and decolonization, and Western efforts to limit both.

In the accepted recipe for development, investment funds and aid grants, producer goods and technical expertise would be imported and, together with internally mobilized savings, be used to establish import substitution and raw materials processing industries. Economic infrastructure (roads, dams, railways, telecommunications, and so on) would be built to feed industries with their needs and to distribute their output. Social-welfare infrastructure (schools, hospitals, and so on) would upgrade local manpower for employment. Agriculture and mining would yield exports to pay for consumer goods, as well as supply part of the funds for industrialization. This strategy of reliance on domestic savings, foreign aid, foreign investment, foreign technology and experts, and foreign trade to upgrade local labour, local infrastructure and local raw materials was expected to produce a GDP growth rate high enough to close the gap between Western and African standards of living.

There were divergences between Africa's socialists and capitalists on the internal social arrangements through which this development strategy would be implemented. For the socialist roaders (those who believed in the socialist road to development), implementation would be through social and economic arrangements predicted on the collective ownership of the means of production. In practice, collective ownership was to mean state ownership. Marxists among the socialist roaders insisted that society and its collectivized means of production must be managed by a dictatorship of the proletariat. Other African socialists would not go that far. For them, a state run by a coalition of representatives of all classes would do. As some put it, there were no classes in Africa, therefore there was no question of leadership or dictatorship by some class. For the capitalist roaders (those who believed in the capitalist road to development), the strategy would be implemented through social and economic arrangements predicated on the capitalist principle of both state and private ownership of the means of production. They thus opted for the mixed economy, with state and private enterprise mixed in varying proportions.

The West naturally favoured the African capitalist roaders. It regarded the non-Marxist African socialists with various degrees of distrust, and African Marxists as dupes and agents of the Soviet bloc whose access to power must be blocked.

However, even before the 1960s were over, it was clear that something was profoundly wrong with the basic development recipe. By the early 1970s, there was no sign of any African country (whether capitalist, African socialist or Marxist) 'catching up' with the West. The general complaint around the world was that the rich nations were growing richer while the poor, including Africa, were getting poorer.

Prior to the OPEC oil-price hikes, only a minority of Africans actively linked economic development with the decolonizing of their external economic relations. Decolonization was generally seen as no more than Africanization, in the sense of putting more Africans into the economic structures inherited from colonial times. Only a minority of radical nationalists pressed for the nationalization of foreign enterprises and changes in the terms of Afro-Western economic relations. And only an even smaller minority of socialist roaders saw development as requiring changes in the local social and economic relations created under colonialism, together with a radical delinking of African economies from the capitalist world economy.

The West for its part preferred Africanization of the colonial economic institutions, and at the slowest possible pace. It opposed for a while nationalization and even partial expropriation, and set its face against changes in the economic linkages between Africa and the West.

777

France under Charles de Gaulle demonstrated quite early that Africa's attempts at delinking would be severely punished by a complete severance. Guinea, for instance, was forcibly cut off when France angrily conceded political independence to her in 1958, and unilaterally 'delinked' their economic relations. And in keeping with the NATO code, the other capitalist powers shunned Guinea. Her forced isolation from the advanced capitalist world lasted until 1963 – when she first restored relations with France – and forced her to rely heavily on the Soviet bloc. In contrast, Tanzania in 1967, and Angola at independence in 1975, opted for socialist development but carefully continued with as much linkage to the West as they 'needed'. For instance, Angola's oil continued to be extracted through joint ventures with Western companies.

There was a similar diversity among the capitalist roaders. Some (like the Côte d'Ivoire, Malawi, Kenya and Zaire) were closely chaperoned by the West in their economic affairs. Others, like Nigeria, preferred to travel the capitalist road under less supervision and control. Ghana was a rather peculiar case. While Nkrumah loudly espoused the socialist path, very little was done in his day to sever old colonial ties, and even less to alter the underlying capitalist reality of the Ghanaian society and economy. After Nkrumah's overthrow in 1966, the socialist rhetoric was dropped and Ghana stayed on the capitalist road to development.

The socialist roaders were more aggressive about the nationalization of foreign assets than were the capitalist roaders. The latter generally preferred indigenization, a method whereby the state and individual Africans took shares in foreign companies, and Africans were absorbed into the management echelons for apprenticeship. With time and experience, Africans were expected to assume control of the economic institutions needed for development.

Expropriation, whether by nationalization or indigenization, did not go without responses from the West. Western governments in the 1960s threatened crippling reprisals against those who nationalized their assets. France especially was tough with her former colonies. Where such threats did not deter nationalization, they demanded heavy compensation. Western hostility to indigenization was less intense, though France was again more sensitive. But even an American firm like Citibank left Nigeria rather than compulsorily sell part of its share to the Nigerian government in the mid-1970s.

The long-term French response to partial or total expropriation was a shift from equity participation to greater use of loans and supplier credits. This was followed by other Western powers. There was also a shift from parent-company direct control of African subsidiaries to management participation, technical assistance and training arrangements, production sharing and supply contracts. French investors began to rely on investment guarantee and insurance schemes provided by their home governments to cover non-commercial risks like war, revolution and expropriation.

Other European powers followed suit. Such schemes were applicable for investments in countries with whom their home governments had Investment Protection Agreements (IPAs) which provided for fair and prompt compensation in cases of expropriation. African countries which were eager to secure foreign investment found themselves entering into IPAs with Western countries. As early as 1960, France entered into such agreements with Senegal, Madagascar, the Central African Republic, Congo-Brazzaville, Chad and Gabon.

Italy, Switzerland, Germany, the Netherlands, Belgium, Denmark and France established bilateral IPAs, and conventions containing investment-protection clauses, with no less than 20 African countries by 1981. And by that year, 39 African countries had signed and ratified a multilateral Convention on the Settlement of Investment Disputes set up between the OECD and developing countries.

By such devices, the West often under both French and American leadership contained the momentum of expropriation, and made it safe for Western companies to keep investing in Africa. For African countries, to the extent that expropriation had occurred, its limits as a possible avenue for furthering development were soon evident. Neither partial nor total African ownership of companies operating in Africa improved the prices Africans got for their exports, the quantities they could sell, or the prices they had to pay for imports. They discovered that the power over these lay with the handful of Western companies which dominated world trade in each commodity.

Even by the early 1960s, Nkrumah (who had had a head start over most African leaders in tackling the problems of development, since his country gained independence as early as 1957), was denouncing the hidden powers of Western oligopolies and charging that they were obstacles to economic progress in Africa.[3] For the constraints on African development to be removed, the hold of these companies on the international market had to be broken by concerted governmental action. When Nkrumah raised these issues, most African leaders either ignored or pooh-poohed it all. Francophone African governments were often hostile. But by the mid-1970s, capitalist and socialist roaders alike had begun to come around to Nkrumah's insights. Realizing that their development plans would remain impotent so long as they were not co-ordinated with the decolonizing of their economic relations with the West, African leaders (even Francophone ones) found cause to join a gathering Third-World movement to alter the international economic order. And the final impetus which pushed them into the campaign for a New International Economic Order (NIEO) was the OPEC oil-price hikes.

3. K. Nkrumah, 1966.

The OPEC watershed

OPEC's success in unilaterally quadrupling oil prices between 1973 and 1974 changed the perception of what was possible in the international economic sense. Suddenly, producers of primary commodities realized that they had the means to take their resources and destinies into their own hands. That marked a watershed; after it, the pursuit of development and decolonization would be conducted in a different spirit.

OPEC's impact on African-Western relations was on various levels. In spite of Washington's 'restraining influence' on OPEC's most powerful member, Saudi Arabia, the oil cartel caused an acute balance-of-payments crisis for the non-oil producers, a crisis which turned economic management into something of a nightmare. But it simultaneously raised hopes for eventually resolving the crisis through spectacular increases for export earnings if the OPEC achievement for oil was repeated for other commodities. Washington was openly hostile to OPEC. Paris was more cautious. London stood to gain by high oil prices.

At the level of general consciousness, OPEC gave instant and public validity to the thesis that structural and market impediments existed which constrained development. In particular, it showed that if the commodity-pricing constraint were overcome, there could be a gush of funds to finance development and even the high consumerism which development was supposed eventually to produce. As all could see, capital funds were no longer a constraint on development in OPEC countries.

OPEC also showed that the pricing and other constraints could be overcome by producer-cartels and concerted political attacks on the structures of external economic relations. Given this visible possibility, at the propaganda and international diplomacy level, OPEC's success turned a hitherto mostly academic debate about development strategy into a public debate, and galvanized isolated calls for decolonization of international economic relations into a global chorus. The dream of changing the structure of relations to the advantage of Third-World countries energized the campaign for a New International Economic Order (NIEO) to replace that constructed under the Atlantic Charter. For Africans in particular, the OPEC example strengthened the resolve to win better terms for their side in the ongoing negotiation of economic arrangements between the ACP and the EEC countries. France's Trojan horse into OPEC was Gabon – but until the late 1980s France also assiduously cultivated the Arab members of OPEC.

And as African economies plunged from stagnation into decline and crisis, partly as a result of the jump in oil prices, pressure was maintained both for searching for effective development strategies and for the changing of external economic linkages. We shall now examine the subsequent campaign to decolonize Africa's external economic relations, and the debate on development and dependency which accompanied that campaign.

The economic decolonization campaign, 1974–84

African states pursued economic decolonization through two principal outlets: the general Third-World campaign for a New International Economic Order, and the negotiations for the Lomé Convention between the African–Caribbean–Pacific countries (ACP) and the EEC. The focus of these efforts were external economic relations; they ignored whatever contributions internal social relations within African countries might have contributed to the lack of development.

From about the mid-1960s, a campaign to reform the structures of global economic relations had been initiated by the Group of 77 at the United Nations, partly under inspiration from some Latin American economists. Emboldened by the success of OPEC, the campaign quickly gathered momentum and high visibility, and loudly articulated Third-World economic grievances against the West.

In 1974, the Group of 77 pushed through at the UN a Declaration on the Establishment of a New International Economic Order, together with a Programme of Action for it. They also had passed a Charter of Economic Rights and Duties of State. This Charter had two significant aspects. It asserted that nations had sovereignty over their natural resources, and over foreign properties and trans-national corporations in their territories, and had the right to nationalize, and to regulate compensation for, foreign goods and properties. This was in contrast to existing international law which recognized a duty, upon nationalization, to pay compensation as determined by international law. Secondly, it obliged the developed countries to redress the inequalities in the international economic structure by reorganizing the decision-making structures of the IMF, the World Bank and other international financial organizations, and by increasing net transfers of resources to developing countries, and giving them access to science and technology in accordance with their development needs and objectives.

Washington, Paris and London heard these 'alarm bells' with anxiety. The issues on which the NIEO campaign concentrated were the wide fluctuations in prices of raw materials which resulted in erratic earnings for their exporters; the deteriorating terms of trade which steadily lowered the prices of raw materials relative to those of manufactures; lack of Third-World access to Western technology for industrialization; restricted access to Western markets for such Third-World manufacturers as there were; and insufficient capital inflows from foreign trade, foreign aid and foreign investment to finance Third-World development. To remedy the situation, they proposed reforms in the monetary system, in technology transfer and industrialization mechanisms, and in international trade.

In order to make development funds more abundantly available to Third-World countries, they demanded changes in the voting structure

781

of the IMF to make it favour developing countries; substantial increases in the capitalization of the World Bank, so that it could increase loans at concessional rates to the poorest countries; refinancing and rescheduling of some Third-World debts, an interest-payment moratorium on some, and outright cancellation of others; and a minimum foreign-aid target of 0.7 per cent of GNP for donor countries by 1980.

On technology and industrialization, they sought changes in the rules so as to make it easier and cheaper for Third-World countries to acquire Western technology. They proposed reductions in the cost of patents, licences, trademarks and technical experts. Since technology transfer occurred mainly through the multi-national companies, they sought legally binding codes for regulating multi-nationals operating in the Third World. They pressed for a redistribution of world industry, and urged the developed countries to help them reach 25 per cent of world industrial output by the year 2000. To help stimulate this, they proposed that their manufactures be granted preferential access to Western markets.

On international trade, the Third World located the source of its woes in the structure of the world market. Control over the marketing of their crops and minerals, they found, was in the hands of Western trading organizations. The various commodity exchanges were located in the West and managed by them, and each was dominated by a few major companies. For instance, three multi-nationals controlled the world market in bananas; nearly 90 per cent of the leaf-tobacco export trade was controlled by six corporations; fifteen large companies controlled the international trade in cotton; six companies controlled the trade in cocoa and cocoa products; three companies controlled world trade in grains; while four companies controlled the market in bauxite, alumina and aluminium.

From the example of OPEC, Third-World governments concluded that they needed producer-cartels to wrest control of markets from the Western oligopolies. Where such cartels were not feasible, they sought to dilute Western control through International Commodities Agreements (ICAs) whose mechanisms, by manipulating prices and supplies, would stabilize and gradually expand Third-World export earnings. To preserve the purchasing power of their exports, they proposed an indexation of the prices of primary commodities to those of manufactured goods.

These ideas were brought together, and emerged from UNCTAD IV in Nairobi in 1976, as a proposal for an Integrated Programme for Commodities (IPC). It involved the extension of the few existing ICAs to cover 18 commodities and commodity groups; the setting up of a Common Fund to finance buffer stocks for stabilizing prices within agreed ranges; and the creation of Compensatory Finance Facilities for offsetting shortfalls in export earnings. This system of agreements, funds and facilities was targeted to be operational by the end of 1978.

The West did not care for reforms which would eliminate or weaken its control of the world economy. On the other hand, it did not want a proliferation of OPEC-style cartels for other commodities, nor a general climate of economic hostility and confrontation. And mindful of its long-term interest in securing stable supplies of primary commodities at the lowest possible prices, the West entered into negotiations, not with the aim of giving in to the demands, but rather to defuse Third-World pressure, wreck the movement for NIEO, and bring whatever arrangements they had to concede under the control of the IMF, the World Bank and other Western-dominated institutions. As might be expected, the negotiations did not achieve much.

By 1980, a UN publication, *Development Forum*,[4] acknowledged that there had been little change in the rules and structures governing industry and technology transfer. By 1984, ICAs existed for only five export commodities from the Third World: sugar, cocoa, coffee, tin and natural rubber. And only one of these, the International Natural Rubber Agreement, was created after UNCTAD IV. These ICAs did not work well, and were beset with operational difficulties ranging from insufficient funds for buffer stocks, quota quarrels among producers, and non-participation by key producers and consumers.

Similarly, the Compensatory Finance Facilities failed to take off. The initial UNCTAD proposal for a $44 billion fund had, by 1983, been whittled down to a proposal for a fund of $10 billion, with a paid-up capital of only $1 billion. At that level, it would, if established, be able to compensate for no more than 10 per cent of the estimated shortfall in export earnings.

The idea of indexing the prices of primary commodities to the prices of manufactures died on the vine. And any hopes for the IPC package died when the Ad-Hoc Intergovernmental Committee for the IPC held its last session in 1980.

These resounding failures notwithstanding, in February 1980, the Group of 77 advocated a revised set of targets. They wanted a 7.5 per cent annual growth rate for the Third-World GDP during the 1980s. They wanted the Third World's share of the world market in manufactures to reach 20 per cent by 1990, and 30 per cent by 2000; its share of food and agricultural exports to reach 35 per cent by 1990 and 50 per cent by 2000; and the transfer of at least $300 billion to the Third-World countries during the 1980s.

African preoccupations within the general Third-World NIEO campaign were determined by the peculiarities of the African economy. Because Africa was primarily a supplier of raw materials, its emphasis naturally centred on the stabilization of its export earnings and on indexation. And since Europe remained Africa's principal trading partner, despite spectacular increases in African trade with the USA and Japan, African efforts focused on negotiations with the EEC.

4. *Development Forum*, September 1980, p. 13.

On the eve of African independence, when the EEC was being formed, France insisted on bringing into the organization her special relations with her soon-to-be-independent colonies. Provisions were therefore made for associate membership for countries which had special relations with specific members of the EEC. The Yaoundé Conventions of 1963 and 1969 expanded these special relations into a multilateral one between the EEC countries and the 18 associated African ex-colonies of France, Belgium and Italy. This saved the African associates from the difficulties of making separate deals with the separate members of the EEC; and it joined the EEC members for the mutually far more beneficial exploitation of the markets and resources of an enlarged African collection of states.

In 1975, the Yaoundé Convention was replaced by the first Lomé Convention between nine EEC countries and 46 ACP countries. By 1979, when Lomé II was signed, the number of ACP countries had risen to 58. And by 1984, when Lomé III was being negotiated, there were 10 EEC countries and 64 ACP countries, of which 43 were African. Thus, the EEC–ACP relationship, which began with Franco-African relations at its core, evolved into one with Euro-African relations at its core.

Through these conventions, the African countries sought to guarantee their earnings from their traditional markets in Europe. By the trading rules of the Lomé Conventions, as much as 95 per cent of ACP industrial exports, such as they were, could enter the EEC duty free. Lomé I included a mechanism, STABEX, for stabilizing the prices of 34 commodities and insuring the ACP countries against shortfalls in their export earnings from these commodities. Lomé II increased the STABEX list to 44 commodities, and established a sister scheme, SYSMIN (popularly known as MINEX) for six minerals, namely copper, phosphates, bauxite/alumina, manganese, tin and iron ore. While MINEX did not compensate for shortfalls in mineral export earnings, it provided for low-interest loans from the European Development Bank to assist mining projects whose operations were constrained by sharp loss of revenue due to price drops.

The EEC countries, for their part, sought to ensure a reliable flow of cheap primary products to their factories and, by excluding competitors, to retain their African markets for consumer and capital goods. The Lomé rules therefore precluded ACP countries from forming such cartels as could, by selectively pressuring the EEC countries, weaken the EEC's competitive position with respect to the rest of the industrial world. Similarly, the Lomé Convention gave preferential rights to EEC multi-nationals active in the ACP countries, as against their American and Japanese rivals; but it did not give in to ACP demands to regulate and supervise the multi-nationals active in their countries.

On their other desires, the ACP countries were unsuccessful. For instance, the European Development Fund could give aid for investments in housing, water supply, health, energy and raw materials, but not for industries whose products could compete with European manufactures in European markets. Furthermore, there was no provision for ACP representation on the European Development Fund.

The ACP countries had many reservations about Lomé II, which helped to prolong negotiations for Lomé III. But by coming into existence and by being operated at all, the Lomé Conventions were very much an advance on the futile negotiations for an NIEO.

Imperialism triumphant

Outside the bustling diplomatic, propaganda and academic circuits of Lomé and other issues of the 1974–85 era, how were African-Western relations working out on the ground? Did the efforts to decolonize these relations accomplish much? How much development was achieved?

All in all, the efforts at economic decolonization were unsuccessful, leaving intact the order set up under the Atlantic Charter. The NIEO campaign and the Lomé Convention had no significant impact on the dependent mode of Africa's insertion into the capitalist world system. If anything, the colonial economic relations and forces waxed stronger. African countries still belonged to the UN, the World Bank, the IMF, and so on; and the character of these institutions as Western instruments of domination had not changed, nor was there any significant enhancement of African and Third-World influence in them, except in the department of rhetoric.

There were no reforms of the monetary and trading systems to tilt their operations in the Third World's favour. Despite their fervent denunciations of the IMF, African countries were still constrained to do business with it on its own terms. Similarly, Western oligopolies continued to control the marketing of Africa's exports. Efforts to circumvent them failed. For example, in 1981, Zaire began independently to market its diamonds, but gave up in 1983 and returned to the DeBeers Central Selling Organization.

There were no significant changes in the inherited colonial pattern of Africa's foreign trade, even as it increased from $4.9 billion in 1960 to $89.6 billion in 1980. Western Europe continued as Africa's principal trading partner; African trade with the Soviet bloc stagnated and declined; intra-African trade also stagnated. Consumer imports formed the largest import item, accounting for between 35 and 45 per cent.[5] Thus, in terms of the content and direction of its trade, Africa remained a supplier of primary materials to the West and a market for Western manufactures.

The figures for 1981 illustrate the consistent pattern in the post-colonial period under review. Out of a total African trade with the rest of the world worth $106 billion, the OECD accounted for $71 billion; of this, the EEC accounted for $43 billion, the USA for $13 billion, and Japan

5. ECA, 1983.

for \$7 billion. African trade with non-African developing countries accounted for \$16 billion; trade with the Soviet bloc accounted for a mere \$1.3 billion; and other unspecified and special categories of trade accounted for \$18 billion. Intra-African trade accounted for an additional, but puny, \$6.7 billion, bringing total African international trade to a grand total of \$113 billion.[6]

Internally, African economies retained their colonial character, especially since little effort had been made to change that. Their world market orientation continued to determine investment in agriculture and mining; and production in the industrial enclaves was determined by the exigencies of the international economy. There was hardly any development based on comprehensive resource inventories and on the organization of the domestic market to promote internal sectoral linkages. Consequently, African economies continued to produce what the West, through the world market, demanded from them rather than what the citizens within these economies needed.

Protected by the various IPAs, the multi-nationals continued to dominate production and distribution in Africa. For instance, the archetypical EEC multi-national operating in Africa, Britain's Lonhro, was still making most of its profits from its diverse African operations. In 1982, \$1.2 billion – that is, one quarter of its worldwide gross earnings of \$4.7 billion – came from Africa; but this yielded profits of \$120 million, about 50 per cent of Lonhro's total profits for the year, making Africa by far its most lucrative theatre of operation. And the scope of its African operations was vast. Most of its 800 subsidiaries were in Africa: in Malawi, Zimbabwe, Kenya, Zambia, Nigeria, Ghana, Mauritius, Uganda, Swaziland and South Africa. Lonhro owned newspapers, tea estates, hotels, ranches, sugar growing and processing establishments; it manufactured ploughs, textiles, beer, paints, confectionery, cosmetics and coaches; it distributed and retailed motor vehicles, oilseeds, records, tapes, mining machinery and spare parts, and also leased aircraft; it mined coal, copper, gold and platinum; and it operated construction and civil engineering works. In fact, Lonhro was Africa's single largest food producer, ranching and farming over 1.5 billion acres.[7]

And contrary to what the anti-multi-national propaganda of African governments might lead one to expect, multi-nationals were actually sought after and welcomed. For instance, Lonhro was officially welcomed back into Tanzania in 1983, five years after it was thrown out for meddling in the Zimbabwean war of independence. It was paid compensation for the assets of its 18 subsidiaries which Tanzania had nationalized, asked to reinvest the money, and invited to revive operations which had deteriorated under nationalized management.

6. Based on the IMF, 1982. Numbers rounded off.
7. *South* (London), July and September 1983; *Euromoney*, December 1983.

Lonhro's extensive operations and its return to Tanzania illustrate the general welcome, however grudging, accorded the much-denounced multinationals. By the early 1980s, even the African Marxist states were turning from Marx to the mixed economy, and were seeking closer economic ties with the once-abhored West and its multi-nationals. Guinea and Congo-Brazzaville, which had taken the socialist road in the 1960s, were making political reconciliations with the West, and seeking trade, aid and investment from the capitalist world. And within a decade of their self-proclamation as Marxist states, Ethiopia, Angola and Mozambique were turning away from the Soviet model of development and relinking with the West.

For example, Mozambique, a hardline Marxist state, began courting the West in earnest in 1982. Severe drought, shortage of management and technical expertise, and lack of foreign capital from the Soviet bloc had helped to create a crisis in its economy. Per capita GNP fell from $208 in 1981 to less than $155 in 1983. In response to the crisis, Mozambique began to shift from a totally planned economy towards a limited free market in labour and some goods. It applied to join the World Bank and the IMF, and became the sixty-fifth ACP country at the end of 1984. Furthermore, it went into joint ventures with US, Japanese and Spanish companies, and offered parts of its state farms to Lonhro.[8]

Thus, rather than drifting away from the West, Africa remained tied to the capitalist world system in the traditional colonial manner, and by the very structures it had sought to change or escape. Slavery had ended; old-style territorial empires had ended: but neo-colonialism and economic imperialism remained triumphant.

The persistence of Africa's dependency and underdevelopment

Despite an almost complete success at political decolonization, Africa failed at economic development and economic decolonization, and consequently failed at that modernization upon which it counted for world respect.

The version of modernity achieved was tacky and moribund. Like scattered drops of rain on dusty ground, artefacts of modernity dotted the African landscape – a few airports and seaports, slum towns with a smattering of modern amenities, a few factories, some ribbons of modern roads, and so on; but the spirit of modernity was not quite there, since the GDP growth which produced these artefacts had neither internal coherence nor self-sustaining engines within Africa.

Not only had Africa failed to create a robust modernity; worse still, it had lost even its traditional ability to feed itself. By 1984, it was the only

8. *South*, December 1984.

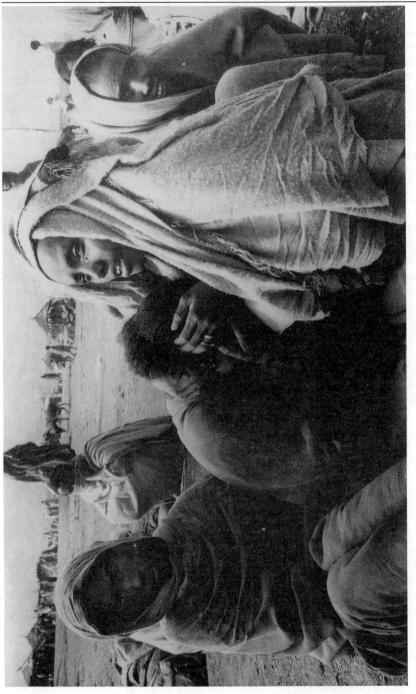

PLATE 26.3   *Famine in Ethiopia: newly arrived refugees at the Korem Centre, 1985*

continent that was unable to feed itself. Famine raged or threatened across wide swathes of Africa. Its dominant image was one of chronic incompetence symbolized by the emaciated refugee with a begging bowl glued to his palm. As African leaders clamoured for relief aid, and as millions starved and died, Africa became an object of world charity, pity and thinly disguised contempt. After a quarter of a century of effort, Africa had neither attained modernity nor gained the respect of the world.

It was an African habit, in the period under review, to blame all its woes on the West, particularly on the West's refusal to alter the inequitable relations it had set up under colonialism. But that attitude was the highest expression of African irresponsibility. After all, neither the relationships in question nor Africa's condition of underdevelopment were immutable. Within the range of what is possible, people can, and often do, change their situations.

But was it possible, in the world conditions between 1960 and 1984, for any poor underdeveloped country to develop? Yes, indeed! Development was possible, both without delinking from or altering the fundamental structures of Western capitalist dominance (as shown by Singapore, Taiwan, Hong Kong, South Korea and other Third-World NICs – New Industrial Countries), and with delinking from the capitalist system (as with China after 1949). So, why did Africa fail? Why did not even one African country become an NIC?

Some liked to claim that lack of financial capital prevented them; some claimed that they had no resources, or that they did not have sufficient population for a large internal market to sustain development. However acceptable such claims might be for the poorest of Africa's tiniest states – but really, how big was Singapore or Taiwan, and how many resources did they have? – there were others for whom these excuses certainly would not hold. Surely, with its oil billions, with its 100 million population able to provide a large internal market, with its large pool of administrative and technical manpower, with its large areas and its mineral and agricultural potential, Nigeria had the ingredients and the opportunity to develop in the first quarter-century of its independence? The reasons for its failure might cast light on why all of Africa failed.

Nigeria's enormous capital funds, derived from oil rents, were neither accumulated nor invested in enlarging the country's productive forces. Most of it was dissipated abroad. Nigeria's inability to accumulate and properly invest its enormous oil income was largely due to the origins, ideology and aspirations of its governing class. The dominant section of the élite were mandarins, largely originating from the non-producer sections of the colonial *petite-bourgeoisie*. Even those who originated from the producer sections had been turned into mandarins by their long, academic preparation for bureaucratic careers. As a result, they were, on the whole, inexperienced in production, averse to its rigours and risks, and even superciliously hostile to material production. On the other hand, they had enormous appetites for material consumption. Forgetting that hunting is not the carcass on the plate, they conceived development planning as the making of shopping lists of modern artefacts to be imported and consumed. They craved the best that the industrial world could offer, and were therefore preoccupied with the distribution for consumption of whatever income was available from an economy which remained colonial in character.

Their phrase for it was 'sharing the national cake'. Few leaders spared a thought for the need to plant more grain and build bigger ovens for baking the national cake. If the cake increased, as it was doing, through mining rents for which they did not have to exert themselves, all the merrier. But if it did not, if the size of the rent dropped, all energies would go into the desperate scramble for what was left. Preoccupied with getting and spending their rent on the most modern consumer goods, they were ill disposed to capital accumulation for productive investment.

In contrast, the bourgeoisie of the Western core were habitual accumulators of capital, highly experienced at it, and with highly developed productive organizations as well as vast sums of already accumulated capital which they could deploy for further accumulation. Thus was the stage set for a most unequal contest for accumulation between a seasoned and powerful bourgeoisie in the centre and an inexperienced mandarinate in the periphery.

Half-hearted efforts by some sections of the Nigerian élite proved inadequate to stop the drain from the country's still-colonial open veins. Exchange controls, currency over-valuation, complicated import duties and tariffs, rather than stemming outflows of funds, only promoted corruption among those sections of the mandarinate whose task it was to administer these barriers to capital flight. Industrialization by import-substitution factories and the semi-processing of agricultural products did not produce the expected savings in foreign exchange, since the factories had to be imported, and then maintained with imported parts and expertise. Through tax holidays, repatriation of dividends, transfer-pricing by multi-nationals, debt servicing, massive consumer imports, and corruption of the mandarinate who preferred to loot the national treasury and bank the proceeds abroad, the net flow of capital funds was out of Nigeria to the West. All in all, efforts at capital accumulation and investment in Nigeria were like a tug-of-war between a crawling baby and a seasoned giant.

Central to Nigeria's failure was the view of development as primarily the development of consumption. It was quite agreeable to the West, but Nigerians voluntarily adopted it, and lived by it. Their principal complaint was that enough could not be extracted from the local and international economy to satisfy their growing appetites. Rather than nudge them into developing their domestic production, that insufficiency sent them in search of foreign debt with which to finance an increased consumption of imports. Because of their high-consumption and low-production strategy of development, the modernity they attained was the mere Westernization of taste without a Nigerian productive capacity to service that taste. In other words, they implemented the Western notion of African development rather than that which Africans had set out to implement.

The wilful refusal by African élites to concentrate on the productive heart of development was influenced by the welfarist preoccupations of the social-democratic movements of the West. Such movements as the Fabian socialism of the British Labour Party and the London School of Economics were preoccupied with distribution to the utter neglect of production – which was understandable, since they were operating in societies where the production problem had been solved in the nineteenth century or earlier. But distributive welfarism was certainly inappropriate to Africa's underproductive economies. Yet it was adopted as their outlook by the founding generation of African leaders. Why? Most of them had grown up in the social-democratic atmosphere of Western universities, and had received considerable support from Western social-democratic movements during their struggle for political independence, so that was part of the atmosphere in which their world outlook had been formed.

It must be stressed that responsibility for the negative impact of Western socialist movements on African development lay squarely on the African élite who adopted what was inappropriate to their circumstances. One question remains to be addressed. When distributive welfarism produced not welfare, but poorfare societies in the peripheral and underproductive economies of Africa, why did the African leadership not abandon it and take up the cardinal task of organizing production? After all, they did not have the excuse of the Cargo Cults of Melanesia, whose members knew only of modern goods brought to their shores by ships and planes but were unaware of the factories in which the goods were produced. This widely-travelled and Western-educated African leadership could not claim ignorance of the need for and the ways of industrial production. Why then were they averse to giving production pride of place in their approach to development? This failure, it should be noted, was characteristic of all tendencies – capitalist, African socialist and Marxist alike.

There happened to be in the African élite a deep mandarin disinclination for the rigours of production. As many Nigerian businessmen put it during their oil boom, '*Why make when you can buy?*'. Those Africans who had no mineral rents for buying, and who therefore clamoured for aid instead, might as well have said: 'Why make when you can beg or borrow?'. Their mandarin disinclination to production, their commitment to distributive welfarism, and their cargo-cult view of development as the satisfying of growing appetites by growing imports constituted the main strands of a dependency mentality which prevented Africa from achieving the development it professed to be striving after.

But why did the dependency mentality persist despite its being an obstacle to the declared goal? Throughout the period under review, mining rents and aid largesse from the capitalist world system were not so lacking as to compel the African élite to produce instead of buying, begging or borrowing. Therefore, whatever little inclination some may have had for production did not have to be exercised. And for so long as the existing arrangements could satisfy the expectations of the populace by paying for modest imports of modern goods, and could sustain the hopes of the majority of the population that more goodies would soon be available for everybody, the élites felt no pressure to change their ways and submit to those rigours of capital accumulation and investment in productive forces which make for autonomous development. However slowly the GDP was growing, especially with respect to the aspiration to 'catch up', the meagre gains were still enough for the African leadership not to want to change the colonial style of African-Western relationship. The most they found politically profitable was to complain and agitate for bigger crumbs from the West's table; and when they failed to get more, as in the NIEO campaign, they would loudly rail against the West for its hardness of heart, and so gain credit among their followers as champions of African progress.

Thus, addicted to a not-too-onerous dependency, they had no irresistable urge to exploit their opportunities for development within the capitalist world system (as the Third-World NICs were doing); nor were they desperate enough to cut loose from the system and strike out on their own (as China did); nor did they have the political motive of survival in the face of foreign aggression to prompt them into industrial production (as had happened with Japan and the Soviet Union).

Thus, whereas the structural roots of Africa's failure to decolonize economically or to develop lay in inherited dependency relations, the African inability to organize and change those relations by concentrating on the enlargement of their productive forces ultimately resulted from the dependency mentality with which the African leadership was thoroughly suffused.

But when all is said and done, there is one struggle which Africans are likely to win sooner rather than later – the struggle against *apartheid* and institutionalized racism. We are back to the third evil which has historically accompanied Africa's relationship with the capitalist world. Along with the slave trade and imperialism, capitalism has always been linked to racism as well. Capital's marriage to the slave trade turned out to be resilient and multi-faceted. What about capital's marriage to racism? It is to this third historic link in a polygamous system that we should now return.

Toward deracializing capitalism

A central theme of this part of the chapter is that the alliance between old-style racism and capitalism in South Africa may be on the verge of breaking up. But while the break-up of the alliance may wound *apartheid* mortally, capitalism in South Africa may still remain intact when the struggle is all over.

If one were asked to choose the most impressive African happening of the mid-1980s, one would be tempted to choose the anger of young South Africans demonstrating against *apartheid* – and their readiness to risk their lives day after day in indignant demonstrations against the forces of repression.

If what the world was witnessing in South Africa in the 1980s and early 1990s was a revolution in its infancy, how quickly was the world to expect the maturation of the revolution? How near was victory?

The optimists saw similarities with either the Ethiopian revolution of 1974 or the Iranian revolution of 1979 – both of which began with demonstrations in the streets, and built up to a climax. Pre-revolutionary Iran and Ethiopia were each an alliance of domestic feudalism and international capitalism. In a sense, those two regimes of Iran and Ethiopia had lasted thousands of years – and yet they were overthrown in a few months of demonstrations. The alliance between domestic feudalism and international capitalism collapsed speedily.

As compared with the Shah and Haile Selassie, *apartheid* was destined to last a few years longer. It was going to be overthrown neither by street demonstrations nor by external African armies. *Apartheid* could only fall as a result of *organized struggle from within*.

External African armies were organized but were not from within. Street demonstrations were from within but were not yet a case of organized struggle.

African states could support and nourish and *arm* the internal liberation-fighters. Demonstrations could make the townships ungovernable. But without internal guerrilla fighters and saboteurs, the struggle could not triumph.

But could Western economic sanctions bring about the fundamental change? We should distinguish between *expressive* sanctions or boycott and *instrumental* sanctions or boycott. Expressive boycott is a moral judgement, but instrumental boycott is intended to be a political tool. Western sanctions will not in themselves lead to 'One man, one vote'. Expressive boycotts will boost up the morale of the oppressed. Western instrumental boycotts will help liberalize the regime – but they will fall short of 'One man, one vote'. Armed struggle from within still has to be the core of revolution.

But if *apartheid* will not be saved by White defiance and *apartheid* armaments, will it be saved by its alliance with capitalism? Actually, that

793

alliance is under severe stress now. When racism begins to interfere too much with the laws of supply and demand, capitalism begins to feel betrayed. Alternatively, when economic racism becomes inefficient, capitalism feels uneasy.

It happened in the days of the slave trade. Capitalism once prospered on slavery. And then as technology became more efficient, slave labour made less sense than wage labour. And so England – the leading slaving power of the eighteenth century – became the leading abolitionist power of the nineteenth.

Similarly, an alliance between capitalism and *apartheid* has made good, if selfish, economic sense until recently. Why is that alliance now under stress? The following reasons are at the core of the explanation. First, black purchasing power is now ready to expand dramatically if the system were economically more equitable. Western capital would like to tap black purchasing power. Secondly, black skills have reached new levels and could make the production forces more efficient. Western capitalism would like to exploit black skills. Thirdly, a better educational and training system for blacks could rapidly transform South Africa into black Australia – rich and highly industrialized. Western capitalism could retain a stake. Fourthly, opposition to *apartheid* is creating instability which is unhealthy for capitalism. Western investors would prefer stability. Moreover, instability creates uncertainty about the future – capitalist investment is a form of calculated planning which needs some degree of predictability. This is quite apart from the fact that escalating repression in South Africa alienates important sections of public opinion in the Western world – and these outraged groups begin to put pressure on business firms and chain stores. Among the latest chain stores in the mid-1980s in Britain to join in boycotting South African goods was Littlewoods. Many Western institutions have pulled out of South Africa, including Barclays Bank, once notoriously tainted by the brush of *apartheid*. Other capitalist departures from South Africa include IBM, Coca-Cola and, to some extent, General Motors.

Prolonged struggle against racism could therefore become a struggle against capitalism itself – as the activists get radicalized (as in Angola, Mozambique and, to some extent, Zimbabwe). Sooner or later capitalism has to cut its losses – and break its bond with *apartheid*.

But what is the future of capitalism in South Africa once *apartheid* is defeated? For better or worse, victory against *apartheid* will not necessarily mean victory against capitalism. First, let us remember that there is a degree of capitalist development which, when reached, makes capitalism virtually irreversible. Karl Marx thought that capitalism was a stage of development lower than socialism. When capitalist development reaches its peak, it will result in a socialist revolution. So according to Marx himself, socialism should first arrive at the most advanced capitalist countries. Strictly speaking, Britain and the USA should have gone socialist before Ethiopia and Mozambique.

Later Marxists amended the theory to say that the capitalist chain breaks at its weakest link – Ethiopia and China and Mozambique were such weak links. But what about the *strong* links? When will they ever break? When will the USA ever have a communist revolution? One possible answer is that there is a stage of capitalist development beyond which a communist revolution is impossible – unless imposed from without. The USA, France, and most other Western European countries may have reached such a stage.

But what would make a communist revolution impossible in the USA or France? There is first the fact that Marx's prediction of increasing enlargement of the proletariat has not happened, especially in the USA. What has happened is the increasing enlargement of the bourgeoisie. Secondly, Marx's prediction of increasing misery has not happened except among racial minorities. The white workers have not got poorer, but richer. And the very poorest are not workers at all (lumpen militariat at best). What this means is that American, British and French workers have a lot more to lose than their 'chains' – they have cars, TV sets and boats to lose. So why upset the capitalist system?

Nor must we forget that class consciousness in the West has not prevailed over national consciousness. On the contrary, anti-communism is linked to working-class American patriotism. Marx under-estimated capitalism's ability to co-opt, convert and corrupt others in its own support. Prosperous capitalism can do just that. Capitalism can win powerful allies among the disadvantaged themselves.

But has South Africa reached the stage of irreversible capitalism – the stage which most Western countries have reached? The chances are that it has *not*. And therefore under black rule South Africa stands an even chance of either continuing as a capitalist system (but without racism) or better embarking on a socialist path of development.

Factors in South Africa in favour of capitalism after black majority rule

After liberation from *apartheid*, black South Africa could become a sub-imperial power in Southern Africa ('Power corrupts, absolute power corrupts absolutely'). The new black leaders would have to guard against temptation. Black South Africans are the most oppressed Blacks of the twentieth century, but will probably become the most powerful Blacks of the twenty-first century. They may not want to rock the capitalist boat.

Links between mineral wealth and international capitalism (mutual need) may tempt black rulers to retain capitalism as the more profitable systemic option. Links between *gold* and the international monetary system may also tempt black South African rulers to refrain from rocking the capitalist boat. Familiarity does not always breed contempt. It sometimes breeds contentment.

Factors in favour of socialism in South Africa after black majority rule

Radicalization through prolonged struggle could turn black South Africa socialist. Moreover, class polarization as an off-shoot of racial polarization could help to socialize post-*apartheid* South Africa. Indeed, even the high degree of urbanization in South Africa is an asset for modern socialism. An enlarged black proletariat alongside arrested embourgeoisement should help the cause of building socialism. The white man's prophecy that every black nationalist is a Marxist could at last fulfil itself.

To summarize, the marriage between *apartheid* and Western capitalism may be coming to an end. Institutionalized racism may have become a liability rather than an asset to global capitalism operating in South Africa. International capital may be on the verge of ditching *apartheid* – not in the interest of justice, but in the interest of *interest* and profit. The end of *apartheid* in South Africa will not necessarily mean the end of the twin hegemony of Washington and Brussels in Africa's economic affairs.

Conclusion

In this chapter we began by drawing attention to the three traditional evils which historically have coloured the relationship between Africa and the capitalist world – the evils of the slave trade, imperialism and racism. We know from the historical record that mature capitalism could indeed get rid of the slave trade, and still move from strength to strength.[9] What we still do not know yet is whether advanced capitalism can dissociate itself from either imperialism or racism – and still retain its vigour as a coherent *system*.

In this chapter we have noted that political decolonization in Africa did not damage mortally the vigour of Western capitalism – since it was not accompanied by economic decolonization. The record shows that international capitalism no longer needs territorial empires with imperial banners in order to feed on other societies. Capitalism can be parasitic without flying the flag.

From Africa's perspective, international capitalism has always been *bicentric*. During the colonial period the twin centres were primarily London and Paris. But in the post-colonial period covered in this volume London has declined as a major factor in Africa, Washington has risen, and Paris has retained its hegemony in a new guise. The twin focus of

9. Chinweizu, 1975.

Africa's relationship with Western capitalism has shifted from the hegemony of 'London and Paris' to the pre-eminence of 'Washington and Paris'. However, there are signs in the last years of the twentieth century that the European Community as a whole will inherit the mantle of France in Africa. If the trend continues, the twin focus of Africa's relationship with Western capitalism will in time become Washington and Brussels.

If Africa's struggle against formal territorial occupation has been successful, and the continent's struggle against economic exploitation has barely started, what about Africa's crusade against *apartheid* and institutionalized racism?

The last crucial battles concern the liberation of South Africa. There are signs that Western capitalism will in time accommodate itself to the termination of *apartheid* and overt racism in Southern Africa. Indeed, *apartheid* (like slavery in the nineteenth century) may have begun to be a drag on the systemic vigour of capitalism. But the genius of capitalism is partly its capacity to invent new forms of control. The slave trade ended – and so have old-style territorial European empires in Africa. Western capitalism has survived those changes. And now overt *apartheid* and institutionalized racism may at last be buried in the battlefields of Southern Africa. Western capitalism will also survive that shock.

What is certain is that the Emperor of Capital will find a new magic equation of power. It is as if capitalism had a secret formula of self-reincarnation. When Africa celebrates the end of *apartheid* – as she once celebrated the end of the trans-Atlantic slave trade or even the end of colonialism – she would be well advised to be on the alert against the next incarnation of capitalism in the post-*apartheid* era.

Africa and the socialist countries

Iba Der THIAM *and* James MULIRA

in collaboration with
Christophe WONDJI

Africa's relations with the socialist countries go back to the period when, shortly after the Bolshevik revolution of 1917, Lenin pledged the support of the newly-formed Soviet state to all colonized peoples. Since then all socialist countries – the USSR and its allies together with the People's Republic of China – have extended various forms of aid to African states, both before and after their independence. The socialist countries' foreign policy, like that of other powers, is apparently governed by two guiding principles which always go hand in hand: an ideological one, according to which the Soviet bloc and the People's Republic of China have a duty to support countries of Marxist–Leninist persuasion; and a strategic one, according to which they defend their national interests. The communists must accordingly support liberation struggles in order to hasten the colonial revolution, which is an integral part of the world revolution.

The increasing importance of Africa in world affairs has led the socialist countries to develop their relations with the countries of that continent. The resulting interaction has affected the course of events in the African countries in many ways.

Broadly speaking, the socialist countries' policy in Africa may be divided into four periods:

(1) from 1917 to 1945 their influence was essentially indirect and relied on the European communist parties and radical pan-African leaders in Africa, the West Indies and the USA;
(2) from 1945 to 1960, encouraged by the weakened position of the colonial powers and the rise of nationalism following the Second World War, the socialist countries directly or indirectly supported national-liberation movements and newly-independent African states;
(3) from 1960 to 1975 there was a decline in the direct involvement of the socialist countries, particularly the USSR, in favour of essentially diplomatic activity;
(4) from 1975, after the end of the Vietnam War, the socialist states increased their influence, for instance in Angola and the Horn of Africa.

798

The Soviet Union and Africa: relations between Africa and the socialist countries since 1935

Writing at a time when colonialism was not yet well developed and very little was known about Africa in Europe, Karl Marx and Friedrich Engels scarcely referred to Africa in their works. Lenin, however, frequently discussed African affairs in his books on imperialism and the national and colonial question.[1] Thus, for him, Africa, on account of its particular political and socio-economic situation, was capable of arriving at the Soviet system and achieving communism without passing through the stage of capitalism.[2] Africa's anti-colonialist movements were encouraged to combat the colonizers so as to widen the anti-imperialist front. The Comintern consequently sought to enter into mutual consultation with the early nationalist organizations, such as the National Congress of British West Africa (NCBWA), the Kikuyu Central Association or the African National Congress (ANC), even though, in its view, the leadership of these movements was in the hands not of the working class, which in any case was rather small in Africa in the 1930s, but of the progressive national bourgeoisie. Some organizations linked to the Comintern played a particularly active role. These included the Red International Labour Union (RILU), the United Front From Below (UFFB) and the International Trade Union Committee of Negro Workers (ITUC-NW).[3] Among the first Africans to collaborate with some of these movements was Jomo Kenyatta, who had visited the USSR in 1929, 1932 and 1934.[4] He was a correspondent of the ITUC-NW.

African democrats and the international communist movement

The Comintern found it difficult in most cases to enter into contact with the African nationalists in the 1920s and 1930s, and so the Kremlin used African-Americans and West Indian pan-Africanists as well as communist parties in metropolitan countries to spread socialist ideas. There, a West Indian, Sylvester Williams, influenced M. Garvey, who was to play an important role among the early African nationalists, while an African-American, W. E. B. DuBois, and a West Indian, G. Padmore, influenced many African socialists including Kwame Nkrumah.[5]

1. V. I. Lenin, 1966; 1965, vol. 31, p. 150; and 1920 (published in translation in 1950), pp. 360–2.
2. V. I. Lenin, 1965, pp. 153–4.
3. Report of Joe, 100, 20, 1930, SLUT, MOMU Box 3, file 373, sub-file 51:3, cited by T. Wilson, 1974; F. Meli, n.d.
4. J. M. Brown, 1972, p. 268.
5. I. Geiss, 1974; and A. Langley, 1973.

The French Communist Party, in view of its importance in French political life, had a significant role to play in the French colonial empire. In October 1921, the Executive Committee of the Third International called on the Politburo of the French Communist Party to set up speedily a Communist Colonial Council to encourage anti-colonial activities in Africa and elsewhere.

The strategy of the French Communist Party was to develop active, sustained anti-militarist propaganda directed at ex-servicemen and war casualties and at the metropolitan assembly points for colonial troops. There were also precise directives laying down the activities to be promoted in Cameroon, Togo, French Equatorial Africa, Madagascar and French West Africa. This was the background to the exhaustive survey of the geographical, demographic, ethnic, economic, political and social situation conducted in all the colonies. The object of this survey was to enable the leadership of the French Communist Party 'to draw up a tactical plan of action and to examine the practical tasks that it [the leadership of the party] will need to pursue to induce the native masses to support the communist effort and at the same time to take up arms against capitalism and imperialism'.[6]

In November 1922, in an article entitled, 'An awakening race', *Izvestia* reported that 'black delegates took part in the Fourth Congress of the Communist International'. The newspaper added that 'this apparently insignificant fact seems to us to be the beginning of one of the most important movements in history, and destined to play a considerable role in the overall struggle against world imperialism'.[7]

The Africans' participation in the international communist movement steadily increased. Anti-colonialist groups were formed, such as the League against Imperialism and for National Independence, which was sponsored by the French Communist Party and whose members included Africans like Chadli Ben Mustapha (Tunisia), Gumede (South Africa), Tiemoko Garang Kouyate and Lamine Senghor (West Africa).

Thus two years before the world economic crisis of 1929, the ideological and strategic foundations of the anti-colonial movement had been laid. The Soviet Union and its allied parties played a crucial role in the political and ideological training of the cadres of the movement. In 1930 the Stalin School was founded in Moscow to train Marxist cadres. The repercussions of the economic crisis that was shaking the world made the anti-colonial movement's task easier. However, the rise of fascism in Europe temporarily caused the colonial question to assume minor importance among concerns of the communist parties, to the disappointment of some pan-Africanists like G. Padmore who considered this shift to be harmful to the African cause.[8]

6. Archives of the Republic of Senegal, 1923.
7. Archives of the Republic of Senegal, 1922.
8. G. Padmore, 1935, p. 3020.

After the war, European communist parties continued to play a relatively important role in French-speaking Africa, but less so in English-speaking Africa where the British Communist Party, unlike its French counterpart, had not established strong roots. The British party was much smaller in any case.

A few radical Africans who were studying in Great Britain came into contact with leaders of communist parties who exercised some influence on their political ideas. The Africans included Jomo Kenyatta of Kenya, K. Nkrumah of Ghana, F. Macauly of Nigeria, F. F. Small of Gambia, and I. K. Musazi of Uganda. Some of them, like S. Mulumba of the Bataka Party in Uganda, sought, through the Communist Party of Great Britain, to obtain the Soviet Union's assistance in achieving the political independence of East Africa.[9]

Marxism gained a stronger and more lasting foothold in other parts of Africa. The *Fédération des étudiants d'Afrique noire en France* (FEANF) included in its rank, and especially among its cadres, a majority of Marxists, like Osende Afana of Cameroon, author of an important work on the economy of West Africa. Through the communist study groups, founded during the Second World War or soon after, and the General Confederation of Labour, many trades-union cadres became receptive to Marxism and to techniques for organizing the masses. In Portuguese-speaking Africa, Marxist intellectuals trained in Portugal through their links with the Communist Party, like Agostinho Neto and Amilcar Cabral, founded the MPLA in Angola and the PAIGC in Guinea and Cape Verde.

However, at the climax of the independence movements, in the late 1950s and early 1960s, the position of communism in Africa was ambiguous. On the one hand, there were very few parties openly claiming allegiance to Marxism: where they existed, particularly in South Africa, Algeria, Egypt, Senegal and Sudan, their influence was limited by a multitude of factors, such as the weakness of the working class, the obstacle represented by traditional ideologies and the resistance of religions. But on the other hand, the socialist countries, and especially the USSR, enjoyed considerable prestige.

The Soviet Union, Eastern Europe and decolonization in Africa

It was not until after the Second World War, from which the colonial powers emerged weakened, that the socialist world began taking a close interest in Africa. The period between 1945 and 1960 was marked by a strong upsurge of anti-colonialism. The socialist world was willing to give support to the African anti-colonialist movements in order to weaken their common enemy: international imperialism.[10]

9. J. Mulira, 1974, p. 44.
10. Byakov *et al.*, 1981, p. 143.

Nevertheless, colonial Africa continued to present a theoretical problem for socialist thinkers. Who in Africa could be regarded as the driving force of the revolution and the power capable of unseating imperialism? The academician E. M. Zhukov in 1947 condemned the role of the African bourgeoisie in the liberation struggle.[11] But another Soviet professor, the Africanist I. I. Potekhin, stated in 1950 that 'In most countries of tropical and southern Africa the leading role in the national liberation movement falls to the bourgeoisie and to the national intelligentsia',[12] thus acknowledging the absence of a communist party of any significance and the weakness of the working class in the African colonies.

In fact, from 1950 until the African countries gained independence, the policy of the socialist countries and China seemed to be based more on the latter point of view than on the former. No doubt the socialist world was unstinting in its support for the African workers' unions, but the socialist countries also made contact with anti-colonialist movements through movements organized under their own auspices, such as the World Peace Movement, the Afro-Asian People's Solidarity Organization and the International Union of Students, to mention a few. They also relied on local communist parties where they existed.

After determining the channels through which, as we have seen, they might work with the anti-colonialist movements, the socialist countries embarked upon a programme of active support for the permanent decolonization of Africa in the form of material and diplomatic assistance. This was offered on the Marxist–Leninist principle that the socialist world has the duty to help those who aspire for decolonization. The CPP in Ghana was among the first to benefit from the support of the USSR, followed by the Mau Mau movement, Jomo Kenyatta and his party (KANU), the National Council of Nigeria and the Cameroons (NCNC), the Uganda National Congress, the PAI and the UPC in Cameroon, the Independence Congress Party in Madagascar, the FLN in Algeria and liberation movements of the same type, such as FRELIMO in Mozambique, the MPLA in Angola, and ZAPU and ZANU in Zimbabwe. More recently the ANC in South Africa and SWAPO in Namibia have received similar support.

The draft resolution submitted by the Soviet Union to the United Nations General Assembly at the Fifteenth Session in 1960, which called on all the colonial powers to grant independence to their colonies, and its resolution adopted in 1961 on the implementation of the decolonization process, were the basis of all the Soviet bloc's subsequent policy in regard

11. E. M. Zhukov, 1947.

12. See *Soviet Ethnography*, no. 1, 1950; V. I. Popov *et al.*, 1975, pp. 21–4; V. I. Lenin, 1965, vol. 28, p. 125; *Pravda*, 17 March 1957, p. 1; *Tass*, 1 February and 3 February 1960; and D. Skvirsky, 1967, pp. 194–7.

to its participation in the decolonization of Africa.[13] Approved by the Twenty-first Congress of the CPSU, which solemnly affirmed its support for independence movements,[14] confirmed by the Twenty-third to Twenty-seventh Congresses, these initiatives gained the Soviet Union the friend-ship of the Africans and represented a major diplomatic victory over the Western colonial powers. Since then the socialist world has willingly given assistance to most African nationalists, anxious to secure their political independence, and sees itself today as the guardian of African inde-pendence, a view that most of them agree with. Oginga Odinga, a Kenyan politician, once said 'The USSR uses its prestige to help oppressed nations that want to free themselves from all forms of neocolonialism. . . and is always with us in times of struggle. We will never forget this'.[15]

In the phase of the struggle for independence this assistance was received by the nationalist parties of such different countries as Algeria, Egypt, Ghana, Guinea, Mali, Sudan, Tunisia, Kenya, Uganda, Tanganyika and Somali. In Southern Africa, where the fight against colonialism lasted much longer, the support of the USSR and Eastern Europe proved even more decisive for the ZAPU movement in Zimbabwe, FRELIMO in Mozambique, and the MPLA in Angola. In their struggle against the *apartheid* regime, the ANC in South Africa and SWAPO in Namibia have received political, diplomatic, financial and military aid from the European socialist states.[16]

Once they had gained their independence, several states sought the co-operation of the USSR and the European peoples' democracies, either in a bid to escape neo-colonialism, which the father of Ghana's emancipation, Kwame Nkrumah, denounced as 'the last stage of imperialism',[17] or to counterbalance the unilateral influence of the capitalist states. From 1957, the date of Ghana's independence, to 1985, the USSR signed agreements with some 37 African countries. One of the most interesting aspects of this co-operation concerned education and research, in the form of the training of African cadres in the USSR and locally in Africa itself, the sending of Soviet teachers and researchers to African universities and research centres and the establishment of scientific links between Soviet and African institutions: approximately 30 000 Africans received their higher and specialized secondary education in the USSR.[18] Co-operative links with other member states of the ACMS, albeit less wide-ranging, are based on the same principles.[19]

13. D. Skvirsky, 1967, pp. 196–215.
14. *Current Soviet Policies III*, 1960, p. 20.
15. *Radio Moscow*, 16 October 1960; *Pravda*, 16 October 1960, p. 3.
16. H. Donalson and L. Nogee, 1981.
17. K. Nkrumah, 1966.
18. Communication from A. Letnev, Africa Institute, Moscow, 9 September 1987. Cf. A. A. Gromyko, 1984.
19. The ACMS Countries and Africa: Trade and Cooperation, 1980; V. Lopatov, 1987.

The People's Republic of China and the decolonization of Africa

For ideological and national reasons, the Third-World countries have pride of place in the foreign policy objectives of Beijing, and there is no better illustration of this than China's relations with Africa, whose importance to Beijing is based on three considerations.

First, Africa's efforts to achieve emancipation represent an important stage in the world revolutionary struggle of the proletariat against capitalism: socialist China therefore has a duty to support those efforts; secondly, the national interest of China demanded that it should be present in Africa where until recently its two rivals, the USA and the USSR, were already competing and where it might find support, at least at the diplomatic level, that would help it to achieve its foreign policy objectives; lastly, China believes that it has been through a semi-colonial experience similar to that of Africa and hence is in a very good position to understand the problems of colonialism and to help the continent through its process of decolonization.[20]

Several facts testify to the importance attached by China to Africa: the pledge made at the International Trade Conference held in Beijing in the mid-1950s, to assist the African countries struggling for independence;[21] the support given to the Mau Mau movement which the Chinese regarded as a force against imperialism;[22] Prime Minister Zhou En Lai's tour of Africa in late 1963 and early 1964, during which he made his famous assertion, 'Africa is ripe for revolution'; the condemnation of the 'unilateral declaration of independence' by the whites of Rhodesia (11 November 1965); the support extended to nationalist movements in the Portuguese colonies, in Zimbabwe, in South Africa and in South-West Africa; and its consistent condemnation of the *apartheid* regime and its provision of aid to the opponents of that system, particularly the Pan-African Congress.

China's first major contribution to the decolonization of Africa was the costly Tanzania–Zambia railway, the TAZARA, which it agreed to build when all the rich and technologically more advanced countries had refused. China's purpose in undertaking this $450 million project was, according to Chinese sources, to '. . . assist Zambia and Tanzania in their struggle against colonialism and aggression from the racist Southern Rhodesia, South Africa and Portugal'.[23]

The TAZARA was a useful project for land-locked Zambia whose communication links with the outside world had been cut by the racist

20. G. T. Yu, 1975, p. 67; see also Premier Zhou En Lai's speech at the banquet given by President Nkrumah, *ibid.*, p. 89.
21. *New China News Agency*, No. 447, cited by B. Larkin, 1971.
22. *Peking Review*, 15 August 1960, p. 16.
23. *Peking Review*, 17 July 1970, p. 16.

PLATE 27.1 *Chairman Mao Zedong of China meeting with President K. D. Kaunda of Zambia in Beijing, China, February 1974*

regime of Rhodesia because of President Kaunda's continual criticism of it and because of his support for ZANU and ZAPU guerrillas. The importance of the project for anti-racist and anti-colonialist movements in Africa was also demonstrated by the fears it aroused in racist South Africa, which backed the minority regime in Southern Rhodesia. The South African prime minister uneasily commented: 'the Chinese have established a bridgehead in Tanzania and the possibility that through the construction of the TAZARA railway they will infiltrate further into the heart of Africa and establish themselves on a permanent basis in Tanzania and Zambia.'[24]

China often offered military aid to several pro-Chinese guerrilla movements in South Africa such as the Pan-African Congress of South Africa[25] and especially the ZANU guerrillas, who were trained and equipped by Chinese experts in various camps in Tanzania and Mozambique[26] and who, with the massive support of the Chinese, led Zimbabwe to political

24. *Star* (South Africa), 15 May 1971; *Africa Research Bulletin*, May 1971, p. 2098c.
25. *African Communist*, 2nd quarter 1967, p. 17.
26. D. Martin and P. Johnson, 1981, pp. 11–12; *Tanzania Standard* (Dar es Salaam), 10 December 1977; *Africa Research Bulletin*, December 1977.

805

independence. China cites this victory as an example of its successful action in the cause of liberation struggles in Africa,[27] echoed by the prime minister of Zimbabwe who, in paying tribute to China's role in the emancipation of his country, stated that 'China had been the ideological and military inspiration of Zimbabwe's nationalist movement'.[28]

Several African statesmen, including Nyerere, Gowon and Kaunda, have expressed similar views and paid tribute to the role played by China in the overall decolonization process in Africa.[29] Today, anti-colonialist and anti-racist movements can continue to count on China's support, as was emphasized by the Chinese prime minister during his visit to Africa in 1980.[30]

The impact of the Vietnam War on Africa

The Vietnam War has had political, psychological, economic and military repercussions in Africa.

That war, like the wars waged by the African liberation movements, was the product of imperialism and colonialism and one of the consequences of superpower rivalry over a Third-World country. The North Vietnamese, supported by the communists, were engaged in guerrilla warfare in the south (backed by the USA) in a bid to unify the country. The USA sent to the south several hundred thousand well-equipped men against the poorly-equipped North Vietnamese, supported by the Soviet bloc and China. The Africans regarded this deployment of American force against North Vietnam as an act of neo-colonialist aggression against a vulnerable brother country and believed that the same fate might well befall any Third-World nation seeking to oppose the interests of the superpowers.[31]

In view of the Western powers' constant collaboration with the *apartheid* regime of South Africa, many Africans felt that the Vietnamese were fighting the same enemy as themselves. Their sense of solidarity was also based on the African states' and Vietnam's common membership of the Non-Aligned Movement whose security and integrity were threatened by the aggression perpetrated against Vietnam. Finally, receiving the assistance of China and the USSR (North Vietnam's two main allies) for its efforts to vanquish colonialism once and for all in the Portuguese colonies and in Southern Africa, many African leaders felt obliged in their turn to support the Vietnamese.

North Vietnam's victory over the United States had a considerable

27. *New China News Agency*, 30 June 1980; *Africa Research Bulletin*, July 1980, p. 5730.
28. *Africa Research Bulletin*, May 1981, p. 6059.
29. See, for example, *Times of Zambia*, 22 February 1974; *New Nigerian*, 18 September 1974; *Africa Research Bulletin*, March 1974, p. 3185.
30. *New China News Agency*, 30 June 1980.
31. A. A. Mazrui, 1972, p. 124.

impact on Africa. To most African nationalists, it was the victory of David over Goliath. It also destroyed the myth that military might was the only key to victory and provided confirmation that the resolve, abnegation and commitment of a people fighting for its just cause were infinitely more important. It consequently served to boost the confidence of the peoples of Zimbabwe, Namibia, Angola and Mozambique, instilling in them the conviction that, through their determination, they would overcome the military might of imperialist, colonialist and racist regimes. Since the end of that war, African nationalists have been introduced by China and Vietnam to the Vietnamese techniques of guerrilla warfare, which have greatly helped some states, like Zimbabwe, to attain independence.

The other consequence of the Vietnam war was that China and the USSR were too absorbed in that conflict to be able to give their full support to Africa in its efforts to achieve decolonization. The United States was also too involved in the conflict to concern itself with what was happening in Africa. However, once the war was over, while the United States was led by the 'Vietnam war syndrome' to pursue a prudent policy in Africa, the USSR and China increased their influence and their audience in the continent, particularly in the former Portuguese colonies, Zimbabwe, Zambia, Tanzania and the Horn of Africa.

Finally, after the end of the Vietnam War, the two superpowers shifted their interests to the African continent where the Western and Soviet blocs continued to vie with one another, for instance in Angola and the Horn of Africa. To sum up, the victory of the North Vietnamese seemed to boost the credibility of the socialist countries, especially the USSR and China, as defenders of the interests of small Third-World states against the Western superpowers.

Africa's relations with the socialist countries

True though it is that the economic and political systems of present-day Africa have indigenous precedents, they can be analysed only in the context of a long period of development, leading at first to its gradual involvement in worldwide exchanges and later, around the mid-nineteenth century, to its becoming more directly incorporated into this network, and then finally, in the early twentieth century, to its subordination to the economic and political needs and objectives of the major Western powers.[32]

The course of events in Africa confirmed the Soviet theoreticians in their belief that national liberation movements were allies in the fight against imperialism. The Bandung Conference saw the emergence of a third, intermediate force between the capitalist and socialist world systems,

32. P. C. W. Gutkind and I. Wallerstein, 1976, vol. 1, p. 7. See also I. Wallerstein, 1976a.

and one that was henceforth to be reckoned with. In Egypt, the Western attempts at destabilization and particularly the French and British expedition to Suez in 1956, led al-Nasser to accept arms from Moscow. The USSR and its allies regarded the independence of Morocco, Tunisia, Sudan, Ghana and Guinea, and the struggle of the Algerian FLN, as severe blows inflicted on colonialism and imperialism by non-communist movements and, in the eyes of Moscow, the possibility was not to be ruled out that they would subsequently become more radical. Thus the Soviet press commented that, like Fidel Castro in Cuba, the Africans Sékou Touré, Kwame Nkrumah and even Modibo Keita could transcend the interests of their class, the national *petite-bourgeoisie*, and embark on a 'non-capitalist path of development', capable of leading to socialism.

Soviet theoreticians thus came to define a non-capitalist path of development for the African countries which possessed a real revolutionary potential. This path is that taken by the 'national democracies'. A state which is 'genuinely independent, anti-imperialist, anti-colonialist, anti-dictatorial, democratic and progressive in its domestic and social policy constitutes a national democracy.'[33] In short, Soviet theoreticians considered that there was an identity of interests between the socialist world, the African liberation movements and the international workers' movement struggling against imperialism.

Thus it was that in the 1960s those African states that seemed to be moving towards the socialist path received international socialist assistance, starting with Egypt, Ghana, Guinea and Mali.

But in fact most of the independent African states retained the colonial institutions and modelled their constitutions on those of their former colonizers. They also, at least for the first few years, retained a sizeable expatriate staff, nearly always from the former colonial power, in key sectors such as the civil service, the police and the army. Even in countries like Ghana under Nkrumah, which leaned towards the socialist world, a not inconsiderable number of Western staff remained in their positions until 1961. They stayed on even longer in other former colonies like Kenya, Nigeria, Senegal and Côte d'Ivoire. These expatriate staff, who generally held key positions in governmental bodies, were bound to influence the political and economic policies of independent African states, and most likely in favour of the former Western colonial powers.

In the economic field the former colonies have found it difficult to break off their economic and trade links with the former colonial powers which, along with other Western powers, control the major world financial institutions including the World Bank, the currencies used in the African

---

33. According to the definition given by the Soviet theoretician B. Ponomarev in 1960 and the concept brilliantly analysed by the French historian J. Chesneaux, 1964, pp. 3–19.

states, the prices of raw materials and the quotas for the main exports of the African states.

In the cultural sphere, the national language of most of the former colonies remains that of the colonizers whose education systems they have copied, at the same time retaining most Western cultural values, in respect of dress and eating habits, for instance.[34] This lasting heritage is due to the fact that the colonies were long under the cultural domination of the colonial powers and that the West engages in effective propaganda for this purpose in the former colonies.

Under these circumstances the socialist countries have always found it difficult to eradicate or indeed at times to reduce the African states' dependence on the Western capitalist powers, and this factor, added to the repression of communist militants by the governments in power, explains why communist parties have found it so hard to become established in the continent. Even more disappointing to the socialist world is the fact that those African states and leaders that had initially showed interest in the socialist road to development have in one way or another reverted to dependence on the capitalist world. In Egypt for instance, al-Nasser pursued a policy of repression against the Egyptian Communist Party and under al-Sadat, Egyptian–Soviet relations reached a new low. Elsewhere in black Africa, the socialist world suffered other setbacks. In Guinea the relations established in 1959 soon deteriorated. Ambassador Daniel Solod was expelled from Conakry in 1961 and, despite Anastase Mikoyan's visit to the Guinean capital in January 1962, the dialogue between the Soviet Union and Guinea never again became as harmonious as it had been in the beginning. Guinea gradually re-entered the Western sphere of influence.

In Ghana the socialist world hoped that Nkrumah, the theoretician of African socialism, would espouse the ideas of scientific socialism and improve Ghana's relations with the socialist world. But despite the aid it had received from the Soviet bloc, the Accra regime had to wait for a time before recognizing East Germany for fear of offending the Federal Republic which had undertaken to provide it with massive economic aid.[35] And finally the *coup d'État* that overthrew Nkrumah on 24 February 1966 and established a pro-Western regime abruptly put an end to the influence of the Soviet bloc. The successive regimes in Accra have never really re-established the cordial relations existing between the socialist world and Ghana under Nkrumah. In Mali the socialist world's influence never recovered from Modibo Keita's disappearance from the political scene after the *coup d'État* of 18 November 1968.

In pro-Western Nigeria, the influence of the Soviet bloc made itself felt only during the civil war. The Eastern countries were then providing

34. A. Okolo, 1983, pp. 252–4.
35. W. S. Thompson, 1969, cited by R. Legvold, 1970, p. 25.

that country with military aid. After the civil war, however, Nigeria again became dependent on the Western bloc although it had been refused military aid by it. The USSR had complained at the beginning of the civil war that Lagos had rejected its offer of assistance.[36]

In East and Central Africa the same thing happened as in West and North Africa. Kenya, which at independence was on good terms with the socialist world,[37] became during the latter half of the 1960s one of the most pro-Western African states. This period was also marked by anti-communist hysteria in the country, ending with the expulsion of alleged communists from KANU, the ruling party.[38] Western political and economic influence, which dates from the colonial period, has continued to make itself felt through substantial Western investments, and Kenyans with radical views have always been viewed as communists and therefore dangerous to civil peace and national development.

Uganda, Zambia and Zimbabwe are also dependent on the West, though to a lesser degree. Obote's attempt to launch a socialist programme in the late 1960s divided his party and caused a split in the country between 'communists' and democrats. President Julius Nyerere also attempted, in 1967, to set Tanzania on the path of self-reliant development along socialist lines in order to reduce its dependence on foreign powers. Despite these sincere efforts, Tanzania is still dependent on the Western countries, as Nyerere has himself acknowledged: 'Our country is still economically dependent on economic and political decisions taken by other people without our participation or consent.'[39] Admittedly, Chinese aid to Tanzania has increased in recent years, but this has in no way affected that country's dependence on the Western powers. Even socialist Somalia, the Somali Democratic Republic before 1977 and socialist Ethiopia after the revolution continued to depend essentially on the Western capitalist countries economically and culturally, if not in the military field, where the socialist world has taken the place of the West, especially in Ethiopia, since 1978. To sum up, the political, economic and social influence of the Western powers in the former colonies is so well entrenched and structured in such a way that most of the newly independent African states find it difficult to break away from it without being severely penalized by the international capitalist system. Moreover, the socialist countries do not have the same close and long-established historical relations with them, and their economic system is not so well established

36. *International Affairs*, 1963, p. 79; and *African Communist*, 1965, no. 2, p. 41.
37. O. Odinga, 1969.
38. '"Kenya will not go communist" says Kenya's Prime Minister', *East African Standard* (Nairobi), 1 March 1965, p. 5.
39. Speech by J. Nyerere, reported in *Daily News* (Tanzania), 25 March 1977; *Africa Diary*, 11–17 June 1977, p. 8525.

throughout the world nor as subtly organized as the Western capitalist system.

The one area in which the socialist world has exercised an appreciable influence is that of ideology. The socialist ideology with its mobilizing appeal and unifying effect was adopted by a number of African leaders, both progressive and reactionary, as a means of setting to rights societies traditionally beset by ethnic and religious conflict. African nationalists have also used this ideology to denounce Western colonialism and alert the West to African needs.[40]

Socialism has also been adopted by a number of African leaders because as one of them, J. Nyerere, has pointed out, it fits in well with the African way of life. Africans do not need to be taught socialism as it is already rooted in their traditional society.[41] The Tanzanian leader explained that he had not been converted to socialism through reading Marxist writings, but that the main motivating factors had been his parents' influence and his peasant background.[42] Several African leaders seem to have opted for socialism for reasons of both economic and political pragmatism. It seems likely that Nkrumah to some extent adopted the socialist ideology in order to obtain from the socialist world the political and material support that the Western bloc, apparently hostile and unwilling to compromise, was not prepared to grant him. It should be noted, however, that Nkrumah transformed his tactical stance into a theoretical and strategic choice as from 1968.[43] Siad Barre would appear to have made this choice for similar reasons and because it served his irredentist policy towards neighbouring countries, Kenya and Ethiopia. When socialist aid ceased, he demonstrated the peripheral nature of his socialism as follows: 'I am a nationalist first, a Moslem second and a socialist third.'[44] Sékou Touré had to adopt socialism as his country could not have survived otherwise after the total cessation of Western aid. Colonel Mengistu seems to have opted for the socialist model of development partly as a means of unifying Ethiopia after the pro-Western emperor had been overthrown. The socialist world unhesitatingly extended support to the Derg: it has always been ready to assist African regimes showing leanings towards socialism.[45]

From the early 1960s a fruitful dialogue started up between the representatives of scientific socialism and African socialism that greatly contributed to a mutual understanding of their points of view. Despite criticism on both sides and despite certain recognized differences of

40. A. A. Mazrui, 1980b, pp. 44–6.
41. *ibid.*; see also *Africa Report* (New York), 1962.
42. P. Enahoro, 1983, pp. 98–122.
43. See S. Ikoku, 1971.
44. D. Lamb, n.d.
45. *Pravda*, 14 September 1974.

opinion, the participants in the dialogue[46] shared the same fundamental views, namely anti-imperialism, anti-racism, aspiration to social progress, and willingness to go on developing friendly relations between the forces of national liberation and world socialism. Having analysed the underlying causes, both internal and external, of the regimes inclining towards socialism in the building of the new society, Soviet researchers adopted a more realistic attitude. Without underestimating the revolutionary potential of the liberated peoples, they began to concern themselves more with the study of the huge difficulties standing in the way of those who have issued a challenge to centuries of underdevelopment and the pervasive presence of neo-colonialism.

Africa and the socialist world in economic interaction

> State what you need and we shall help you . . . in the form of loans, technical aid . . . we do not seek to get an advantage . . . we do not need profits . . . we do not ask you to participate in blocs . . . we are ready to help you as a brother helps a brother.[47]

This statement reflects the theory of the Soviet bloc's economic policy towards Africa.

The socialist countries and Africa have engaged in extensive economic, technical and trade co-operation since 1960. The socialist leaders have, since Lenin, always considered it their duty as internationalists to offer economic and technical assistance to colonized or independent African states in order to enable them to achieve self-reliance, further arguing that socialist aid, unlike that of the capitalist donors, is selfless and has no strings attached.[48]

Whereas one of the aims of the Western countries is economic domination so as to secure supplies of raw materials and outlets for manufactured goods, the prime objective of the Soviet bloc's African policy was not to tie countries within its sphere of influence to an economic zone of which it is the centre. The fact is that the USSR's known mineral reserves are ample for its needs, at least in the medium term, and the industry of the socialist bloc does not seem for the time being to need any outlets outside its domestic markets, which are far from saturated. But the Soviet bloc was concerned to help African countries take command of their own raw materials to prevent their being dominated by Europe and the USA. The socialist world nevertheless depends on Africa for some commodities such as fish and certain rare minerals.[49] At the time

46. For details, see I. I. Potekhin, 1963, pp. 71–5; *Colloque Soviéto–Congolais*, 1988.
47. Statement by A. A. Arzumanyan, head of the Soviet delegation to the Afro-Asian Peoples' Solidarity Conference in Cairo: A. A. Arzumanyan, 1958, pp. 185–6.
48. V. Rymalov, 1959b.
49. See P. Biarnès, 1980; and P. Decraene, 1982.

of *détente*, the aid of the Soviet bloc was presented as a peaceful way of competing with the capitalist countries: 'The socialist nations compete with the Western powers not in the arms race but in extending aid to underdeveloped countries'.[50] Hence, the following definition of the Aswan Dam: 'The Aswan site is an arena in which socialism and capitalism compete, and the outcome of this competition is to the undoubted advantage of socialism'.[51] Since the 1960s, however, the economists and leaders of the socialist world have tended to emphasize the mutual advantages of economic exchanges between Africa and the socialist world.[52]

The following are some of the features of the socialist countries' aid to Africa: lower interest rates than those charged by most Western donors, ranging from about 2.5 to 3 per cent yearly, with a grace period of usually one year and an average repayment period of 12 years, and the aid provided in the form of loans. The projects financed by means of this aid become, on their completion, the property of the recipients. The aim, according to Ivan Chernyshev, the official in charge of the USSR's economic relations with foreign countries in the late 1970s, was to offer easy terms to Africa.[53]

The Soviet bloc's economic co-operation with Africa developed considerably during the 1960s and 1970s owing to the growing importance of the continent for the global objectives of the socialist world. For example, trade between the USSR and Africa increased fivefold between 1960 and 1975 and the number of African states trading with the Soviet Union alone rose from six to 36 between 1960 and 1976.[54]

The choice of a recipient and the amount of aid are governed by the following considerations: the strategic importance of the receiving country; its potential until recently for reducing the influence of the United States and China; its support for Marxist–Leninist ideology; and its value as a source of raw materials and as a commercial outlet.[55] This has been more or less confirmed by Soviet commentators in the following terms:

> The provision of credits by our country is not based on any political, military or economic conditions that are unacceptable to a developing country. However, *it would be unjustifiable to reach the conclusion that the Soviet Union is indifferent as to whom and on what conditions to grant credits. This would ignore the demands of reality.*[56]

For these reasons, Egypt received massive aid up to 1975 and Ghana under Nkrumah received the second-largest volume of aid in black Africa

50. V. Rymalov, 1959a.
51. I. Belyanev, 1962; E. M'Bokolo, 1980.
52. A. A. Gromyko, 1967.
53. *Ethiopian Herald* (Addis Ababa), April 1977.
54. *Novosti*, April 1977; *Africa Research Bulletin*, 15 April–14 May 1977, p. 4281.
55. P. D. Dean and J. A. Vasquez, 1976, pp. 7–28.
56. V. Romanova and I. Tsriklis, 1978. Italics added for emphasis.

PLATE 27.2 *A. Mikoyan, minister of foreign affairs of the USSR, arrives in Ghana where he is welcomed by President K. Nkrumah, January 1962*

from the USSR despite its small population and size when compared with huge pro-Western Nigeria. Under the Soviet bloc's aid programme several projects were launched in Ghana, particularly in the mining and agricultural sectors. Several Ghanaians were also trained under the programme. Where trade was concerned, Ghana exported cocoa to the socialist countries in exchange for manufactured goods.

The socialist countries found it difficult to establish economic and trade ties with pro-Western Nigeria until after the civil war when their relations improved, but Nigeria remained among the countries receiving the least aid from the Soviet bloc. Socialist technical assistance to Nigeria, particularly in key areas like the oil and steel industries, increased after 1970 and played an essential role by enabling several thousand Nigerians to acquire skills needed for the country's development.[57] As regards trade, Nigeria has exported to the socialist world such products as cocoa beans,

57. *Africa Diary*, 28 May–3 June 1973, p. 6487; and *Africa Diary*, 6–12 November 1982, pp. 1198–9.

receiving in return cement, drugs and machinery.[58] In the military field, the Soviet bloc countries played a leading role in Nigeria, especially during the civil war when the federal government received substantial Soviet military assistance which contributed to the Lagos regime's victory, as was confirmed by General Gowon.[59] It continued to receive considerable military aid from the USSR, in the form of equipment and training. It is estimated that from 1974 to 1978 Nigeria purchased from the Soviet Union $80 million worth of arms, more than from any other country, and that this represented 40 per cent of its arms imports for that period. Several other West African states have received similar economic aid from the socialist countries and, albeit to a lesser degree, military assistance.

Among the countries of former British East and Central Africa, Kenya has received the most economic aid from the Soviet Union, despite its pro-Western positions. The $48 million it thus obtained was probably intended to put an end to the anti-communist phobia in evidence there during the 1960s. Because of this anti-communist feeling, a large part of the aid granted to Kenya by the socialist countries remained unused,[60] and some projects that it had served to finance, like the Lumumba Institute, were even interrupted, while Soviet military aid was rejected.[61] Some of these projects survived, including a 500-bed hospital in Kisumu, equipped and partly run by Soviet doctors.[62]

In the 1960s Uganda received Soviet credit of $16 million, extended to Milton Obote's African socialist regime, to finance such major projects as the building of a spinning mill, the first of its kind in East Africa, and the first mechanized-agriculture college in East Africa, which is in operation and partly run by Soviet instructors.[63]

As regards trade, Uganda has exported coffee, cotton and copper to the Soviet bloc countries in exchange for machinery and drugs. In the military field, the Soviet bloc, especially the USSR, provided massive military assistance. It is estimated that in 1978 Moscow covered 92 per cent of its arms requirements.

Tanzania, which spearheads the fight against colonialism and racism in South Africa, has received economic assistance from the socialist world. By 1976 it had received $40 million from the Soviet Union, supplemented by $13 million from the East European countries. Trade between Tanzania and the socialist world has been more modest. Tanzania has exported mainly tobacco and cotton to the Soviet bloc countries, in exchange in

58. *West Africa Pilot*, 1971.

59. *Daily Times* (Lagos), June 1974; and *Radio Moscow*, 28 May 1974.

60. C. Stevens, 1976, p. 2, quoting T. Mboya, the former Kenyan Minister of Economic Planning.

61. *Daily Nation* (Nairobi), 30 April 1965, p. 1; Kenya, *House of Representatives Debate*, 3 March 1967, cols 741–2.

62. C. Stevens, 1976, p. 259.

63. J. Mulira, 1983, p. 51.

particular for tools and vehicles.[64] Because of Tanzania's anti-colonialist stand, the socialist countries have provided it with a relatively large amount of military aid to help it to protect itself against the racist regime of South Africa.

In the case of Zambia, the Soviet bloc's aid remained minimal until 1976. After that date, however, the USSR granted that country $100 million worth of military aid to help it defend itself against racist South Africa. This aid was highly appreciated by President Kaunda, who commented on it in the following terms: 'The USSR has always been Zambia's ally'.[65]

In Central and South Africa, as has already been said, the socialist countries supplied both economic and military assistance to the national liberation movements of Mozambique, Angola and Zimbabwe, thereby enabling them to achieve independence. The $2 billion granted to Angola by the USSR under the Soviet–Angolan co-operation agreement of 1982 was the largest credit it had ever accorded to an African state. It was meant to finance various development schemes.[66] The leaders of the ANC and SWAPO guerrilla movements have expressed their profound gratitude for the economic and military aid they received from the Soviet bloc.[67]

Owing mainly to its strategic and ideological importance, Somalia was in 1977 one of the main beneficiaries of Soviet aid in Africa, receiving a total of $154 million, and received the largest volume of military assistance, worth $181 million, making the Somalian army one of the best equipped in black Africa.

Being just as important strategically and ideologically, Ethiopia also received massive economic aid, representing $100 million in 1974. This aid served to finance various development schemes including refineries.[68] After the revolution, co-operation between socialist Ethiopia and the socialist countries developed considerably. In 1979, for instance, those countries received over 3500 Ethiopian students, the highest number from any single African state.[69] In 1978 trade increased 15-fold. In the military field, the Soviet Union's commitments to Ethiopia during the Ogaden war represented $1 billion worth of arms and, in addition, 1500 Soviet military advisers were in Ethiopia during that period and an estimated 20 000 Cuban soldiers. In 1981 Soviet military aid to Addis Ababa

64. *Daily News* (Tanzania), 25 March 1977; *News Agency*, 27 March 1977.
65. *Times of Zambia*, 1977.
66. *Radio Lisbon*, in *Africa Research Bulletin*, 14 January–14 February 1982, p. 6324; and *Tass*, July 1978.
67. *Radio Moscow*, quoting a guerrilla source; see also *Voice of Kenya TV*, 3 March 1986, 21.30 hrs News.
68. *New China News Agency*, 5 July 1981; *Africa Research Bulletin*, 1–31 July 1979, p. 6122.
69. *Africa Research Bulletin*, 1–31 July 1979, p. 5355.

amounted to about $1.5 billion.[70] Ethiopia thus became indisputably the leading recipient of Soviet military aid in the continent with the exception of Egypt in the early 1970s. This situation enabled Ethiopia to build up a formidable defence capability against its enemy, Somalia, and in its own internal struggles against separatist forces and domestic foes.

China's economic aid policy towards developing countries is slightly different in some respects from that adopted by the other socialist countries and, according to Chinese officials, is based on the following principles: the aid provided must be to the mutual advantage of the donor and the recipient, whose independence is to be respected; it is granted free of charge and is intended to ensure that the recipient becomes self-reliant; it is invested in projects that rapidly become cost-effective; the quality of the products supplied is guaranteed; local technicians must be trained to carry through the projects implemented with Chinese aid; and the Chinese experts must enjoy the same advantages as the local experts.[71] China has endeavoured to comply strictly with these principles in its economic co-operation with Africa.

Generally speaking, China has been more ready to offer its aid to countries with socialist leanings following a policy of self-reliance, such as Tanzania. But, for pragmatic reasons, it has also offered aid to some pro-Western countries hostile to the Soviet Union like Zaire or Ethiopia before 1974. The purpose of Chinese aid to Africa appears to have been to eliminate or at least reduce American and Soviet influence in the continent, or to gain African support in certain international forums like the United Nations, the Non-aligned Movement and the Afro-Asian Peoples' Solidarity Organization, and lastly to help Africa to eradicate imperialism and achieve economic self-reliance. On the other hand, Beijing has sought to obtain the support of the African continent in its continual struggle towards international revolution. China, in so far as it claims to lead the Third-World countries, has the duty to be generous in assisting its weakest members, and particularly the African countries.

China's apparent generosity to Africa may be illustrated by the fact that from 1956 to 1977 it offered the continent aid representing $1.4 billion and 50 per cent of total Chinese aid to all non-socialist countries.

The main recipients of Chinese aid in West Africa have been Ghana, Sierra Leone, Gambia and Nigeria and, in the Horn of Africa, Somalia and Ethiopia. In the first group of countries, it has been used for agricultural projects and the building of bridges and, in the second, for road construction and the setting up of textile mills respectively.[72]

Uganda received financial and technical aid from China that was used

70. *Africa Research Bulletin*, 1–31 March 1981, pp. 6002–3; *Tass*, 8–10 May 1977.

71. See W. Partke, 1975, pp. 9–12; and A. Lawrence, 1965, pp. 173–4.

72. See *New China News Agency*, 13 February 1973; *West Africa* (London), 20 February 1978; *New China News Agency*, 15 February 1978; and W. Partke, 1975, p. 113.

for a successful rice-growing project.[73] Kenya received a loan of $16.8 million and a donation of $3.1 million. It was also granted $40 million to build a modern stadium.[74] One of the projects carried out in Kenya with Chinese aid concerned the bamboo industry. Zimbabwe, whose prime minister was energetically supported by China during the guerrilla war, became one of the main recipients of Chinese aid to Africa, receiving a total of some $82 million for various major development projects.[75]

However, the foremost recipient of Chinese aid to Africa is Tanzania, which presents certain particularly interesting features for China. These include the ruling party's indefatigable fight against racism. To the anti-colonialist stand of TANU and later the CCM (*Chama Cha Mapinduzi*) and their support for liberation movements should be added Tanzania's behaviour on the international scene (forcing the United States for instance to close down its satellite-tracking station on the island of Zanzibar) and its socialist policy of self-reliance, which is based on the same philosophy as that followed by China.[76] In short, Tanzania is seen by China as 'a glorious banner against old and new imperialism'.[77] And Tanzania has extended a favourable reception to China because it has regarded China as a defender of colonized and oppressed peoples.[78] This well-disposed attitude towards each other led the two countries into a sort of natural alliance.

By 1977 China had committed $362 million of aid to Tanzania out of a total of $2.5 billion to the entire continent of Africa. This made Tanzania by far the leading recipient of Chinese aid to Africa. By 1971 China had moved into first place among the donor countries, its bilateral aid exceeding the total amount of aid received by Tanzania from all other donors, including the contributions of the rich countries. A substantial proportion of this aid was used to finance the TAZARA project which cost Tanzania and Zambia a total of $456.3 million, shared equally by the two countries. The rest went into various major development projects, particularly in agriculture, communication, health services and education.[79]

China's trade policy is largely based on the financing of aid through trade. For example, 60 per cent of the credit granted for TAZARA took the form of deliveries of products for sale on the Tanzanian and Zambian markets.[80] Tanzania exported tobacco, copra and sisal, in exchange for industrial products and drugs. Despite these excellent relations between

73. *Radio Kampala*, 1 May 1965; and *New China News Agency*, no. 22, 1973.

74. *Standard of Kenya*, 17 September 1980.

75. *New China News Agency*, 18 September 1981; and *Africa Research Bulletin*, 15 December 1982–14 January 1983.

76. *Xinhua News Bulletin*, 1968, pp. 5–6 and 15.

77. *New China News Agency*, 5 June 1965.

78. J. K. Nyerere, 1967d; see also G. T. Yu, 1975, p. 7.

79. G. T. Yu, 1975, p. 80.

80. *Tanzania Standard* (Dar es Salaam), 26, 1976.

PLATE 27.3   *The Chinese-built 'Green Uhuru Railway', Tanzania–Zambia: the laying of the track across the Tanzania–Zambia border, September 1973, in the presence of Chinese officials and Presidents J. Nyerere of Tanzania and K. Kaunda of Zambia*

the two countries, the Western countries continued to be Tanzania's main trading partners: from 1970 to 1977, 63 per cent of its exports went to Western countries and 49 per cent of its imports came from them.[81]

The decision to build a railway linking Tanzania to Zambia was taken, as has been noted, after the minority white regimes of Rhodesia and South Africa had threatened to cut all the lines of communication with

81. United Republic of Tanzania, 1977, p. 40.

819

land-locked Zambia. The importance of TAZARA for that country and for all anti-colonialist and anti-racist movements was obvious. It was spelled out by the Tanzanian prime minister in the following terms:

> TAZARA is a project of special status in Africa and in the world of aid given by one country to another in a pure spirit of goodwill and mutual benefit. The status of TAZARA is a victory for co-operation between Third-World countries.[82]

This 1278 miles-long railway was built by 15 000 Chinese and 30 000 African workers, who completed it in 1975, ahead of schedule. The loan, which was interest-free, was to be paid back over a period of 30 years starting in 1983 in freely convertible currencies or in the form of goods acceptable to China.[83] These were indisputably among the best terms that a recipient could ever have hoped to obtain from a foreign donor. Even when the operation of the railway showed a deficit amounting in 1983 to $100 million, owing to pilfering and poor hauling power, China agreed to grant additional aid to purchase new locomotives from West Germany and rescheduled the repayments, with the result that in November 1983 the railway achieved a profit for the first time.[84]

In the military field, Tanzania, because of its special relationship with China, received during the period 1967–76 assistance estimated at $75 million, representing the largest share (51 per cent) of Chinese aid to Africa. China also provided other African states with military assistance, in particular Mozambique, Cameroon and Zambia.

In short, the socialist world as a whole – both the Soviet bloc and China – has granted economic, technical and military aid in various forms to most African states, and this aid, by enabling them to have recourse to donors other than Western ones alone, has reduced their dependence on the former colonizers and has allowed African societies to carry through a large number of projects relating to development (education, industry and agriculture) and to defence.

International rivalry in Africa's relations with the socialist world

Africa's political, economic and military relations with the socialist world greatly helped to fan the intense rivalry that used to exist between the two superpowers and the People's Republic of China. On many occasions Africa has, either deliberately or inadvertently, provided that rivalry with ideal situations in which to reveal itself. For instance, the inherent ethnic and regional discord in most African states, which has given rise to

82. *Peking Review*, no. 38, 22 September 1978.
83. G. T. Yu, 1975, p. 127.
84. *Africa Now*, 1983; *Africa*, 1984, pp. 18–19.

instability, has been exploited by rival powers. The Angolan crisis, the civil war in Nigeria and the Ogaden conflict are cases in point. Africa's mineral resources – bauxite, diamonds, oil, and so on – its rich markets and the strategic position of its sea ports and airports have made it one of the regions of the globe most coveted by the superpowers.

Politically, the African states that have opted for a non-capitalist course of development have met with the condemnation of the capitalist Western powers, which have supported or installed regimes favourable to themselves. The pro-Western government of Kenya, for instance, has received the support of the West against apparently pro-socialist parties like the Kenya People's Union. Ghana under Nkrumah was deprived of the aid of most Western countries because of his strongly pro-socialist stand; in the Horn of Africa, the regimes supported by the socialist camp have always been challenged by the pro-Western ones and vice versa. The socialist world for its part has tried to help and support pro-socialist regimes in power, as in Guinea, Mali, Angola and Ethiopia. The superpowers view communist and Western infiltration in Africa in the context of worldwide, East–West global rivalry and make no secret of the fact that it fills them with alarm. As Ali Mazrui has noted:

> a revolutionary ideology – Marxism – with a powerful advocate – USSR – became something of which the Western powers were increasingly fearful . . . the ideological and political competition for control of the world between USSR and the Western world gathered momentum . . . [85]

In its efforts to gain political influence in the continent, China has come up against the Western powers and the USSR alike, already competing for the same aim. Owing to its ideological differences with the USSR, China, although socialist too, criticized certain aspects of Soviet policy in Africa and regarded the USSR as simply one of the European powers exercising domination over the African continent.[86] The USSR for its part accused China of invoking racist arguments to discredit its African policy.[87]

Many regions in Africa have suffered form international rivalry, but it has been felt most acutely in Angola and the Horn of Africa. Mozambique has suffered a lot from the South-African-backed Mozambique National Resistance – but there have been no Cuban troops to defend FRELIMO.

A noteworthy feature of the policy followed by Angola is that the nationalist movements there have been supported from the beginning by the superpowers and that this state of affairs continued after the country gained independence. The Soviet bloc, including Cuba, always supported

85. A. A. Mazrui, 1977, pp. 179–80.
86. *New China News Agency*, 27 December 1967 and 3 July 1977.
87. G. V. Astafyev and A. M. Dubinsky, 1974, pp. 112–14.

the MPLA, while the Western bloc, particularly the United States, has given its support to the FNLA and UNITA. The competition between the two blocs in Angola was clearly based on ideological and strategic interests.

PLATE 27.4   *Cuban troops in Angola*

The former US Secretary of State, Henry Kissinger, placed the Soviet bloc's intervention in Angola in the context of USA–USSR rivalry throughout the world and blamed the Kremlin for having both initiated and escalated the crisis there.[88] He justified US intervention on the grounds that its purpose was to normalize the situation. The Western powers consequently undertook to provide the FNLA and UNITA

88. R. Lemarchand, 1981, p. 83.

822

guerrillas with aid equal to that received by the MPLA from the USSR. The Soviets and Cubans for their part justified their support for Angola and their presence in the country on the grounds that the Angolan people had requested their protection against imperialist aggression.[89] Since then other countries have allowed themselves to become involved in the Angolan crisis, such as China, to some extent, and South Africa, which has intervened directly in the civil war on the side of UNITA on the pretext of defending Namibia against SWAPO guerrillas operating from Angolan territory and preventing Marxism from making inroads in the region.

The MPLA, which subscribes to the Marxist ideology, readily accepted the aid offered by the socialist world, while UNITA, a pro-Western guerrilla group, received the support of the West and South Africa to oppose the power of the MPLA. But apart from these ideological motivations, the deposits of uranium and oil in Angola are not unconnected with the interest taken in that country by foreign powers. The United States, which had major economic interests in Zaire, Namibia and South Africa, saw the USSR's bid to play a role in Angola as a threat to its economic interests in the region. Finally, at the strategic level, Angola is in a very advantageous position in many respects. Its coast and harbours on the Atlantic Ocean are of great interest to maritime powers in both the NATO and Warsaw Pact groups of countries.[90]

The strategic consequences have until recently been a central concern to the superpowers owing to the intensification of the arms race, calling for new air and seaport facilities for their naval and air forces. The Horn of Africa offers one of the best examples in the continent of the crystallization of international rivalry around strategic requirements. The point is that it is strategically important for the socialist camp and the capitalist camp alike because of its position at the junction of Asia and Africa, its excellent harbour facilities in the Gulf of Aden and the Indian Ocean and, above all, its proximity to vital sea routes linking the oil-producing countries to America and Europe, through which 70 per cent of oil and other raw materials are imported by Western Europe.[91]

The presence in the Indian Ocean of large US naval forces that could be used to attack the USSR led the Kremlin to seek sea and airport facilities in the Horn of Africa for its own enlarged naval force in the Indian Ocean. More than 60 per cent of its ships visiting the area were thus said to have been based in the ports of the Horn of Africa and the Gulf of Aden.[92] Alarmed by the presence in Kagnew, Ethiopia, of American communication and surveillance facilities, the USSR increased

89. *New Times*, 1 February 1976, p. 1.
90. B. Handler, 1970.
91. *Christian Science Monitor*, 23 March 1978.
92. C. Crocker, 1976, p. 652.

its economic and military aid to Somalia in exchange for authorization to use the important port of Berbera, close to the strategic strait of Bab el-Mandeb through which all ships pass from the Red Sea. The power controlling that part of the Red Sea would be in a position to dictate changes and to exert influence in the Horn of Africa and in the Middle East. Increasing concern was therefore felt by the United States and its allies at the accentuation of the USSR's presence in the Indian Ocean and its ports.[93]

The rivalry of the superpowers which sought to establish their influence in the Horn of Africa in order to gain control of it was no doubt partly responsible for the outbreak of the Ogaden war in 1977. The fact is that the massive military aid granted to Ethiopia and Somalia by both Warsaw Pact and NATO countries encouraged the two neighbouring states to settle their differences on the battlefield. The USSR and its allies accused the United States of supporting the irredentist ambitions of Somalia against Ethiopia in exchange for the bases made available to it in Berbera and Mombasa for its Rapid Deployment Force (RDF), established not long before to threaten Soviet and African interests.[94] The United States in turn accused the Soviet Union and Cuba of being responsible for the crisis in the region, warning the USSR that if this situation continued, USA–USSR relations would be affected, with particular reference to the Strategic Arms Limitation Talks (SALT).[95]

Various African statesmen at the OAU summit meeting held in Khartoum in 1978, in particular Obasanjo of Nigeria, regretted this international rivalry in the continent, and his remarks were echoed by Sékou Touré and Nyerere.[96]

This constant rivalry between the superpowers cannot but be detrimental to the development of Africa.

Non-aligned Africa and Eastern Europe: socialist countries and the Non-Aligned Movement

It is often taken for granted that socialist countries are part of the so-called 'Eastern bloc' only. This is not always the case. Socialist countries have also been part of the Non-Aligned Movement. Indeed, among the founding fathers of the movement was Yugoslavia under Marshal Tito. Tito, Nehru, al-Nasser and Nkrumah became the architects and the vanguard of a strategy which was sometimes called 'positive neutralism',

93. S. Turner, 1977, p. 346.
94. *Radio Moscow*, 17 December 1982, in *Africa Research Bulletin*, 1–31 December 1982, p. 6688.
95. *Africa Research Bulletin*, 1–31 December 1978, p. 4775.
96. *African Currents* (London), Autumn 1978/Winter 1979, pp. 8–23.

and which became one of the cornerstones of the foreign policy of every liberated African country.

In fact, Yugoslavia was the country which first made non-alignment a universal movement – instead of its being just another name for Afro-Asian solidarity. The Bandung Conference in 1955 was an important stage in forging political alliances between Asian and African states, although the conference was held two years before Ghana's independence. If the Non-Aligned Movement had been forged only by Nehru (India), al-Nasser (Egypt) and Nkrumah (Ghana), it would have been perceived primarily as a movement of the non-white races of Africa and Asia. It was the white man, Tito, who prepared the way for such subsequent non-coloured members of the movement as Cyprus and some of the Latin-American countries. By the time of the 1979 Havana Conference, the non-aligned movement consisted of 95 members drawn from four continents of the world.

In 1986, the Non-Aligned Conference was held in Harare – its first venue south of the Sahara. Robert Mugabe, himself a socialist and whose ZANU liberation movement had achieved military victory against Ian Smith with the help of the socialist world, became chairman of the international force which had once been led by Tito, Nehru, Nkrumah and al-Nasser.

There was a time when a non-aligned stance with both West and East Germany was almost impossible. The Federal Republic's Hallstein Doctrine forced African countries to choose between the two Germanies. When Zanzibar (recognizing East Germany), united with Tanganyika (recognizing West Germany), a real diplomatic problem arose. Julius Nyerere as president of the new United Republic of Tanzania tried to solve it by letting East Germany have a consulate in Zanzibar while West Germany had an embassy in Dar es Salaam. When the Federal Republic protested against even this compromise, Nyerere's action contributed to a fundamental re-evaluation of the Hallstein Doctrine, at least as applied to the Third World. (The doctrine was designed to force all third countries apart from the USSR to choose between the two Germanies in the establishment of diplomatic relations.) In time, the Federal Republic relented, beginning with the conciliatory policies of Willie Brandt towards the Eastern alliance as a whole. Africa was subsequently spared the dilemma of choosing between the two Germanies – though the dilemma of choosing between the People's Republic of China and Taiwan got more complicated rather than less over the years.

The smaller East European countries helped Africa's non-alignment in a different way. Some African countries wanted to balance their *cultural* relations between East and West. Poland became a useful recruiting ground for African colleges and universities. Many departments in African institutions of higher learning included Polish visiting professors and researchers. Czechoslovakia and Hungary were also important for African

825

higher education, especially in terms of scholarships for African students to study in those countries. Eastern Europe could not of course outweigh the influence of Western Europe in Africa. But progress towards cultural balance was helped by the scientific, scholarly and cultural relations between Africa and the Marxist side of the European heritage.

There was non-alignment even in the choice of medical facilities when Africans suffered from terminal diseases. Three historic African figures looked to different sides of the Cold War for medical attention in their last terminal illnesses. Kwame Nkrumah looked to Romania in his last struggle against skin cancer – and died there in 1972. Franz Fanon looked to the United States in his last crusade against leukemia – and died there. Nkrumah's old comrade-in-arms, Sékou Touré, also looked to the United States when death confronted him. He died in Cleveland, Ohio. Disease and death do not respect ideological boundaries – and science, in its universalism, is the best form of non-alignment.

Conclusion

If the 1960s were the decade of greatest change in Africa, the 1980s were the decade of greatest change in the socialist world. The most basic change in Africa in the 1960s was decolonization – as more than half of the continent achieved sovereignty in that decade. The most basic change in the socialist world in the 1980s was liberalization – bearing the names *glasnost* and *perestroika* in the Soviet Union, but bearing other names all the way from Beijing to Budapest.

There is no doubt that Africa's decolonization in the 1960s was of direct relevance to Africa's relations with the socialist world. After all, formal African independence enabled one African country after another to establish diplomatic relations with socialist states. But if Africa's decolonization in the 1960s transformed its relations with the Marxist world, did the Marxist world's liberalization in the 1980s change its own relations with Africa?

In the case of the USSR, liberalization under Mikhail Gorbachev in the late 1980s affected foreign policy as well as domestic politics. The new Soviet posture sought to avoid confrontations with the West, to cut down the arsenals of war, to reduce Soviet hegemonic control over Eastern Europe and to defuse regional conflicts. There is no doubt that the Soviet Union exerted its influence on both Cuba and Angola to get them to agree to the linkage between the withdrawal of Cuban troops from Angola and the independence of Namibia. The 1988 accords between Angola, Cuba and the Republic of South Africa were not only a product of the efforts of the US assistant secretary of state, Chester Crocker. The accords in Southern Africa were also a by-product of the impact of *perestroika* on Soviet foreign policy. On the Namibian side, the accords were also an achievement for the United Nations after many years of persistent UN pressure on South Africa and the international community on behalf of the Namibian people.

The new *rapprochement* between the Soviet bloc and the Western alliance in the 1980s had risks as well as benefits. Some of the foreign aid which was coming from both sides to Africa was partly motivated by ideological and strategic rivalry between the two power blocs. If the rivalry between them declined, would there be less motivation to give the same level of aid? Of course, peace between the two superpowers was good news for everybody – but would there be less generosity towards the Third World as a result?

Another risk inherent in the *rapprochement* between the West and the Marxist world concerned future Soviet support for the liberation struggle in the Republic of South Africa itself. If the new Soviet international posture made it eager to defuse regional conflicts, would the Soviet alliance be less supportive of *armed* struggle in the Third World as a whole? If Soviet pressure was being put on the Vietnamese to reach accommodation in Cambodia and on the Palestine Liberation Organization to make concessions to Israel, and if agonizing pressure had been put on the Soviet Union itself to withdraw from Afghanistan, would there be increasing socialist pressure on the African National Congress also to make more and more concessions to the *apartheid* regime in Pretoria? Would this new mood of *rapprochement* in the Marxist world make it increasingly difficult for the ANC and the PAC to pursue the option of armed struggle for the liberation of South Africa?

Indeed, in May 1989, President Gorbachev paid an official visit to the People's Republic of China – the first Soviet leader to do so in 30 years. The reduction in the Sino-Soviet regional conflict could also have consequences for Africa – not all of them for the better. The rivalry between the two communist giants had in the past influenced their policies on military and economic aid to Africa. China's support for certain countries and movements in Africa had quite often been stimulated by competition with the Soviet Union – including China's support for Robert Mugabe and ZANU during the anti-colonial struggle. (The Soviet Union had supported Joshua Nkomo and ZAPU.) Now that there was declining rivalry between the USSR and the People's Republic of China after Gorbachev's visit in 1989, would Beijing's priorities in the Third World be re-ordered? Would Beijing's limited resources be used more exclusively for Asian neighbours? Would Africa become less important in China's foreign policy?

As the decade of the 1980s was coming to an end, these were some of the questions which were being posed by the forces of history. The answers to those questions were still not clear. The 1960s had released the new currents of post-colonial diplomacy – and transformed Africa's relations with the socialist world. Will the forces of liberalization in the socialist world in the 1980s and 1990s produce a second phase of

827

transformation? As Karl Marx would have said, what is history if not a gigantic contradiction unfolding itself in dialectical stages? If the thesis was once armed struggle in the South, and the antithesis is now *rapprochement* in the North, the synthesis lies hidden in the womb of future history.

Africa and the developing regions

28

Locksley EDMONDSON

Introduction

Among the most significant phenomena of the middle to late twentieth century must be included the rise of the developing nations, also characterized as the 'Third World' or sometimes the 'South'. While any of these labels are considered satisfactory, the term 'Third World' is the preferred one in this chapter if only because it connotes a more self-conscious identity, and remains the most frequently used self-assigned designation, among the nations and peoples of Africa, Asia, Latin America and the Caribbean.[1]

A contemporary historical perspective on this phenomenon of a rising Third-World identity becomes the more justifiable when we consider that in the 1940s the 'Third World' as such was unknown; that in the 1950s there existed neither a 'Non-Aligned Movement' nor a 'Group of 77;' or that in the 1960s the specific phrase 'New International Economic Order' was not yet in existence. As far as Africa was concerned, its relations with Asia, Latin America and the Caribbean were, prior to the 1960s, largely controlled or mediated by relevant Western colonial powers.

It is thus important to be reminded that 'One cannot grasp the reality of the Third World if the analysis is limited to contemporary data' since 'the Third World is a historical phenomenon that is part and parcel of the process of emergence of the present world order' whose 'genesis' was at least 'some two centuries ago'.[2] This broader historical perspective, while not within this chapter's scope, must always be borne in mind, the

1. The Non-Aligned Movement, formally launched in 1961, is the Third World's main political expression (see Table 28.4 below); the larger Group of 77 is the Third World's main economic bargaining unit (see Table 28.5 below). Defining the Third World in terms of the self-conscious identification of independent states with one or both of these groups, this would include all African states, except South Africa; most states located in the Asia–Middle East–Pacific region (including Cyprus, a member of both groups; excluding China, Israel, Japan, Turkey, Australia and New Zealand); all Latin American and Caribbean states; and a handful of European states, namely Yugoslavia and Malta (members of both groups) and Romania (which has joined the Group of 77).

2. I. Sabri-Abdalla, 1980, p. 32.

829

more so that the post-Second World War 'decline of the colonial frontier', in the authoritative words of Professor Hans Morgenthau, has come to represent 'one of the great turning points in the history of the world'.[3]

The reason, as Morgenthau saw it, was that this decolonization process was inextricably linked to the decline of Europe which, on the foundations of the colonial system, had been able to establish its undisputed dominance in and over the modern international system. To extend this line of argument, a significant international systemic consequence of decolonization was that it brought in its train a situation wherein the overwhelming majority of the world's peoples, hitherto subordinated politically, were now better able to establish formal bilateral and multilateral ties among themselves and with others while, in the process, challenging certain traditional assumptions of international intercourse and seeking a restructuring of relevant procedures and foundations.

The purpose of this chapter is to explore from an African perspective how, and to some extent why, this challenge from the Third World arose and evolved in the post-Second World War period (especially since the 1950s) through to around 1980. It seeks to identify broad trends and processes in an evolutionary perspective, which shed light on the widening and deepening of Africa's links with the rest of the Third World and which highlight Africa's presence and impact in the initiation and extension of Third-World collaborative processes.

Africa's Third-World condition and significance

Broaching, at this stage, some objective political, economic, racial and cultural characteristics of the African condition, past and present, will better help to establish Africa's situational and behavioural significance within the Third-World arena. This significance derives from the typical Third-World traumas which Africa's presence represents, often in exaggerated form, as well as from the accompanying impetus from Africa to mobilize the Third-World challenge against the international *status quo*.

Two political considerations immediately spring to mind. The first is that the momentum towards Africa's decolonization which moved to a new and heightened stage with Ghana's attainment of independence in 1957 – the first such experience in sub-Saharan Africa – coincided in time with (and indeed catalysed) the take-off stage of the Third-World movement beyond the foundations laid at the Asian–African Conference held in Bandung, Indonesia, in April 1955 (hereafter called the Bandung Conference) (Table 28.3 below). Secondly, the proliferation of African state actors in the aftermath of the decolonization process established a commanding African numerical presence in Third-World and other international institutions, which helped to ascribe a global salience to

3. H. J. Morgenthau, 1973, p. 351.

TABLE 28.1 *Regional composition of the United Nations, 1945–80*

Year	Africa[a]	Asia[b]	Caribbean[c]	Latin-America	North America	Europe[d]	Oceania[e]	Total
1945	4	9	3	17	2	14	2	51
1950	4	16	3	17	2	16	2	60
1955	5	21	3	17	2	26	2	76
1959[f]	10	23	3	17	2	26	2	82
1965	37	28	5	17	2	27	2	118
1970	42	30	7	17	2	27	2	127
1975	47	37	10	17	2	29	2	144
1980	51	40	13	17	2	29	2	154

[a] The four founding members were Egypt, Ethiopia, Liberia and South Africa.

[b] Including the Middle East and islands in the Pacific; also including Cyprus and Turkey.

[c] The islands in the Caribbean archipelago plus the independent mainland political 'extensions' of Guyana and Suriname.

[d] The entry of nine already independent European countries in 1955 was the result of a package deal resolving East–West controversies about the qualifications of Germany's Second World War allies as well as certain new post-war East-European communist regimes. West and East Germany were admitted separately in 1973.

[e] Australia and New Zealand.

[f] In 1958 the United Arab Republic was established by a union of Egypt and Syria – both original members of the UN – and continued as a single member state, which is reflected in this 1959 column's total membership of 82 but not in the regional breakdown which counts them separately under Africa and Asia respectively. In 1961 Syria resumed its separate membership.

Africa-related concerns within a Third-World framework.

The latter is well illustrated in Table 28.1, portraying the regional composition of the United Nations from 1945 to 1980. African-ruled states which in 1945 accounted for three (or less than 6 per cent) of the 51 founding members of the United Nations, by 1980 had risen to 50 (or 32.5 per cent) of the 154-member body.[4]

Patterns of membership or participation in certain other international organizations are similarly revealing. For example, African representation at the First Non-Aligned Summit Conference in 1961 was already prominent with 11 (or 44 per cent) of the 25 fully-fledged participants; by the time of the Sixth Non-Aligned Summit in 1979, Africa's 50 delegations comprised 54 per cent of the 92 full members in attendance (Table 28.4 below). African representation in the Group of 77 has remained fairly constant at approximately 41 per cent, beginning with 32 of the 77 founding members in 1964 and by 1980 accounting for 50 of the Group's 122 members (Table 28.5 below).

But beyond such quantitative indices of Africa's commanding Third-World presence, lie some important qualitative aspects of the African

4. White-ruled South Africa, a founding member of the United Nations, is excluded from this computation of the presence of African-ruled states in the UN.

TABLE 28.2   *Location of the LDCs (least developed countries), 1981*

Africa		Asia	Caribbean	Total
Benin	Guinea	Afghanistan	Haiti	
Botswana	Guinea-Bissau	Bangladesh		
Burundi	Lesotho	Bhutan		
Cape Verde	Malawi	Laos		
Central African	Mali	Maldives		
Republic	Niger	Nepal		
Chad	Rwanda	Samoa		
Comoros	Somalia	Yemen Arab		
Ethiopia	Sudan	Republic		
Gambia	Uganda	Yemen (People's		
	Upper Volta	Democratic		
	Tanzania	Republic)		
Total	21	9	1	31

Source: H. Lopes and H. C. Tri, 1981. These authors point out that the criteria adopted by the United Nations General Assembly in November 1971 for defining the LDCs were: 'a very low level of per capita income – barely $200 per person and per year in 1979 – as against an average of $700 in the developing countries taken as a whole and $8000 in market-economy industrialized countries; a gross domestic product (GDP) in which the industrial's sector's contribution is 10 per cent or less – against 19 per cent in the developing countries as a whole; a literacy rate of 20 per cent or less.' The original list of 25 LDCs rose to 31 by the turn of the 1980s.

condition. The international economic arena is the first place to begin since it is here where the Third World's concerns are largely focused and it is here where post-colonial Africa mirrors most clearly persisting Third-World traumas, dilemmas and predicaments.

A case in point, as documented in Table 28.2, is that easily the largest number of LDCs (least developed countries) are to be found on the African continent.[5] What is more, in the words of the OAU (Organization of African Unity), 'The effect of unfulfilled promises of global development strategies has been more sharply felt in Africa than in other countries of the world'.[6]

Such was the language of the opening paragraph of the Preamble to the now-historic *Lagos Plan of Action for the Economic Development of*

5. These LDCs – the preferred usage in this chapter – are sometimes labelled LLDCs by certain writers who would thus assign the LDC classification to the rest of the Third World.

6. Organization of African Unity, 1981, para. 1.

Africa, 1980–2000, adopted by the OAU in 1980. Submitting 'that Africa's underdevelopment is not inevitable', and that such a condition was indeed 'a paradox when one bears in mind the immense human and natural resources of the continent', the OAU proceeded to identify the causes as largely residing in the structure of international exploitation:

> Thus Africa, despite all efforts made by its leaders, remains the least developed continent. It has 20 to 21 least developed countries of the world. Africa is susceptible to the disastrous effects of natural and endemic diseases of the cruelest type and is victim of settler exploitation arising from colonialism, racism and apartheid. Indeed, Africa was directly exploited during the colonial period and for the past two decades this exploitation has been carried out through neo-colonialist external forces which seek to influence the economic policies and directions of African States.[7]

In this statement on the African economic condition are embedded certain political and associated racial and cultural humiliations visited on Africa during the colonial period, with residues even today, as in *apartheid* South Africa. This is another important qualitative dimension of Africa's situation within the Third-World setting.

It is not insignificant that in his closing address at the Bandung Conference, India's prime minister, Jawaharlal Nehru – by then recognized as one of the most influential leaders in the emerging Third-World movement – saw fit to emphasize Africa's exceptional political and racial burdens which he counselled his fellow Asians to place prominently on their agenda of concern:

> We have passed resolutions about conditions in this or that country. But I think there is nothing more terrible than the infinite tragedy of Africa in the past few hundred years. Everything else pales into insignificance when I think of the infinite tragedy of Africa ever since the days when millions of Africans were carried away as galley slaves to America and elsewhere, half of them dying in the galleys. We must accept responsibility for it, all of us, even though we ourselves were not directly involved. But unfortunately, in a different sense, even now the tragedy of Africa is greater than that of any other continent, whether it is racial or political. It is up to Asia to help Africa to the best of her ability because we are sister continents.[8]

The race-sensitive underpinnings of the early phases of the Afro-Asian movement – which were to provide the foundation for a wider Third-World movement – were largely a consequence of the African situation. The continuing presence and arrogance of racist South Africa has projected this racial dimension as a Third-World movement priority, not only in

7. *ibid.*, paras 5–6.
8. J. Nehru, 1964, p. 19.

833

terms of what *apartheid* represents objectively to a largely non-white Third World but also because, through African diplomatic persistence, the issue became lodged in the forefront of Third-World movement concern.[9]

While the Bandung Conference of 1955 is the most appropriate starting point for this examination of Africa's relations with the developing regions, certain pre-Bandung factors and forces conditioning the subsequent emergence of the Third-World movement should be recognized, since these bear centrally on Africa's location and role in the international system of at least the past century.

Reaching further back into history, the late-nineteenth-century partition of Africa is critically important as an explanation and measure of the eventual consideration of Western-world dominance which simultaneously resulted in what Lenin aptly characterized as 'the partition of the world'. Thus the creation of the Third World – in the objective sense of its structured subordination, in contradistinction to its subjective recognition as a self-conscious transformative force – is directly an outgrowth of the dominant political, economic, cultural and racial forces whose late-nineteenth-century ascendancy was best underlined in Africa's formal subjugation which completed the processes of wider Third-World subordination.

In that historical situation it is not surprising that long before the 'Third World' came to be recognized as such, its eventual rise and challenge were anticipated in certain pan-African circles, as was the case at the First Pan-African Conference of 1900, held in London, which in its 'Address to the Nations of the World' had this to say:

> In any case, the modern world must remember that in this age when the ends of the world are being brought so near together the millions of black men in Africa, America and the Islands of the Sea, not to speak of the brown and yellow myriads elsewhere, are bound to have a great influence upon the world in the future, by reason of sheer numbers and physical contact.[10]

So, too, a decade before the Bandung Conference, we find the Fifth Pan-African Congress of 1945, held in Manchester, England, not only anticipating the rise of the Third-World movement but also formulating anti-colonial and post-colonial liberationist ideologies of a kind which

9. M. El-Khawas, 1971.
10. This 'Address' is reprinted in full in V. P. Thompson, 1969, pp. 319–21. At this First Pan-African Conference, where the word 'Pan-African' was first formally used, the approximately 30 participants from Africa and the African *diaspora*, while addressing black-world conditions generally, were especially concerned about recently consolidating patterns of European colonial and racial domination on the African continent, especially in Southern Africa.

subsequently came to underpin the Third-World challenge.[11] This was evident in its 'Declaration to the Colonial Peoples of *the World*', authored by Kwame Nkrumah, the congress's joint political secretary, inciting colonized workers, farmers, intellectuals and professionals everywhere to defeat imperialism and, in its concluding message, urging that 'Colonial and Subject Peoples of *the World* – Unite'.[12]

Even more expressive of such pan-African notions of wider Third-World solidarity was this resolution of the 1945 congress – as summarized by George Padmore, its other joint political secretary – couched in language which came to be characteristic of the formative years of the Non-Aligned Movement over a decade later:

> Congress also expressed the hope that before long, the peoples of Asia and Africa would have broken their centuries-old chains of colonialism. Then, as free nations, they would stand united to consolidate and safeguard their liberties and independence from the restoration of Western imperialism as well as the danger of Communism.[13]

Such were the situational and ideological antecedents of post-colonial Africa's contribution to developing Third-World thought and practice in the pre-Bandung era. In reviewing this latter period it is, of course, hazardous to generalize, as we must, about the foreign policies and international-relations orientations of independent Africa's numerous political entities. But this problem is partially mitigated because of certain factors arising within the context of the developments being addressed in this chapter.

For one thing, the rise within the United Nations of an African caucusing group in the late 1950s and the establishment of the Organization of African Unity (OAU) in 1963 were symptoms as well as facilitators of Africa's search for common positions on matters affecting the continent as a whole. This process has not always proceeded smoothly, as testified by numerous cleavages and divisions which have arisen within the OAU, at times posing serious threats to its survival. But less fundamental intra-African cleavages have been manifested on Third-

11. Convened in Manchester, England, in October 1945, this Fifth Pan-African Congress, unlike its predecessors in the inter-war years which sought amelioration of colonial conditions, explicitly proclaimed the goal of the liquidation of colonialism. Prominent African participants included Kwame Nkrumah and Jomo Kenyatta, who later were to lead their countries, Ghana and Kenya respectively, to independence. See G. Padmore, 1963, for the official account of the Congress's proceedings.

12. K. Nkrumah, 1962, pp. 44–5; G. Padmore, 1963, pp. 6–7. Emphases supplied by the present writer to draw attention to the striking fact that the Declaration's language is couched throughout in universal colonial terms, including no specific mention of Africa anywhere in its text.

13. G. Padmore, 1956, pp. 168–9.

World-related issues *per se*, involving Africa's interests as a developing region alongside those of the remaining Third-World countries.

This suggestion is corroborated in Nweke's comprehensive study, *The Harmonization of African Foreign Policies, 1955–1975*, which concludes that while, on the one hand, 'the larger the involvement of the great powers in African conflicts, the lower the level of harmonization among African states', on the other hand 'it can be said that harmonization tends to be highest when African states join the rest of the Third World in negotiating with the great or industrial powers'.[14]

Despite some inevitable intra-African differences over ideologies, policies and priorities pertinent to Third-World causes, these in the final analysis have been outweighed by commonalities in their perception of relevant fundamental problems and needs, thus allowing the holistic view of African interests and behaviour which informs the present analysis. A remarkable degree of African solidarity on the basics of the Third-World situation and challenge has indeed proved to be a crucial underpinning of the Third-World movement.

As is being implied, certain objective realities of the African condition, past and present, are so poignant with wider Third-World challenges as to constitute one distinctive dimension of analysis. But this also constitutes a point of departure for the next stage of identifying the subjective feelings and aspirations to which such objective realities have given rise, inspiring independent Africa to seek to extend its ties to other Third-World regions and to play its part in organizing the Third-World assault on the international *status quo*.

Africa's ties with other Third-World regions

Afro-Asianism, as the very term implies, is the logical starting point of any exploration of Africa's ties with other Third-World areas. But subsumed under this broad Afro-Asian setting is the special case of Africa's relations with the Arab world, a focus which will be seen to be deserving of attention in its own right. Finally, as shall be demonstrated, the context and content of expanding interactions between Africa and the Latin American/Caribbean regions have been significant manifestations of a maturing sense of Third-World identity broadened beyond its Afro-Asian foundations.

Afro-Asianism as Third-World foundation: from the spirit of Bandung to Third-World solidarity

As illustrated in the title of Rupert Emerson's comprehensive 1962 study, the post-First World War and especially post-Second World War

14. G. A. Nweke, 1980, pp. 263 and 265.

phenomenon of the movement away 'From Empire to Nation' is largely the story of 'the rise to self-assertion of Asian and African peoples', with all the parallels and reciprocities in their respective and cumulative struggles for self-determination.[15]

This developing mutuality of interests between the colonized of Africa and Asia, which as documented by David Kimche had been manifest from time to time in the inter-war years,[16] was to mature significantly in the aftermath of the Second World War, eventually transcending the colonial experience to lay the post-colonial foundations of the Third-World movement. The impact of the Afro-Asian decolonization processes on a burgeoning commonality of interests between these two regions can be viewed at five levels.

First, the proximity of both anti-colonial struggles in terms of timing, and some critical colonial actors (notably Britain and France) present in both settings, necessarily sensitized Africans and Asians to parallels and commonalities in their colonial experience. Thus are explained, for example, the 'fraternal greetings' and pledges of solidarity communicated by the Fifth Pan-African Congress of 1945 to 'the toiling masses of India' and to 'the struggling peoples of Indonesia and Viet Nam'[17] as well as that congress's generalized hope for continuing anti-colonial and post-colonial Afro-Asian solidarity which we cited previously.

Secondly, contributing to such awareness of the bonds between the colonized of Africa and Asia was the presence in parts of eastern and southern Africa – not to mention Africa's island communities in the Indian Ocean – of significant concentrations of peoples of Asian descent experiencing alongside Africans the impositions of European domination. This is best illustrated in the experience of the historically persistent phenomenon of racism in South Africa which inspired over the years a range of parallel or convergent African and Asian challenges arising within or beyond the African continent.

For example, it was in South Africa, where he lived from 1893 to 1914, that Mahatma Gandhi initially developed his political technique of civil disobedience – *Satyragraha* – applying and refining it throughout a prolonged seven-year struggle by South Africa's Indian community against racism (1906–13), before taking it back to India eventually to undermine the colonial system. The government of India's 1946 complaint before the first session of the United Nations General Assembly, protesting against certain racist policies of the South African government being then targeted at the Indian community there, can thus be viewed as another milestone in this chain of converging experiences of oppression and struggle among Asians and Africans in South Africa.

15. R. Emerson, 1962.
16. D. Kimche, 1973, ch. 1, pp. 1–16.
17. G. Padmore, 1963, p. 67.

This was indeed explicitly recognized in the Fifth Pan-African Congress's 1945 resolution to the United Nations, applauding the anticipated protest by the government of India and demanding 'justice and social equality for the Indian community in South Africa' who 'suffer discrimination in a similar manner' to Africans. The Bandung Conference participants were similarly motivated a decade later in extending their 'warm sympathy and support for the courageous stand taken by the victims of racial discrimination, especially by the peoples of African and Indian and Pakistani origin in South Africa'.

Thirdly, as symbolized in the title of D. A. Low's essay, 'The Asian mirror to tropical Africa's independence', the earlier mobilization and successes of Asian anti-colonial struggles came to have a powerful effect in Africa, concretely because 'the imperial groups in tropical Africa were loosened by the immediately preceding upheavals in Asia',[18] and inspirationally in boosting African nationalist assertiveness.

Fourthly, in the process or as a result of their anti-colonial liberation struggles, organizational linkages were at times forged between these African and Asian enemies of empire. An early case in point was the 1927 conference in Brussels, convened by the League Against Imperialism and Colonialism, in which many Asian and African nationalists (including India's Jawaharlal Nehru, Vietnam's Ho Chi Minh and Senegal's Lamine Senghor) were involved. Significantly, Indonesian President Sukarno in his opening address at the 1955 Bandung Conference, alluded to this 1927 Brussels conference as a precursor of sorts,[19] a notion extended more recently in Kimche's unqualified assertion that the Brussels meeting was 'the father of Afro-Asian solidarity, the forerunner of the conference at Bandung'.[20]

Fifthly, common Afro-Asian sensitivities to colonial domination did not cease on the attainment of political independence. Not only did the newly independent countries collaborate to terminate remaining vestiges of colonialism elsewhere in their regions, but they also organized to protect, project and enhance their newly acquired freedom.

The formation of the Asian–African (later renamed Afro-Asian) group within the United Nations in 1950, the Bandung Conference of 1955, and the launching of the Afro-Asian Peoples' Solidarity Organization in 1957, were the major Afro-Asian precursors and foundations of the wider Third-World movement initiated in the early 1960s. Of these, the Bandung

18. D. A. Low, 1982, p. 28.

19. Sukarno, while admitting that the 1927 Brussels conference (which many Bandung delegates had attended) had given 'new strength in their fight for independence', proceeded to draw important distinctions between that earlier meeting (held 'in a foreign country' and 'convened by necessity'), and the Bandung Conference ('assembled . . . by choice' by 'free, sovereign and independent' ex-colonies 'in our own house'). See text of Sukarno's speech in R. Abdulgani, 1981, pp. 169–80.

20. D. Kimche, 1973, p. 5.

TABLE 28.3   *Countries participating in the Asian–African Conference, Bandung, Indonesia, 18–24 April 1955*

Asian countries (23)[a]			African countries (6)[b]
Afghanistan	Iraq	Syria	Egypt
Burma*	Japan	Thailand	Ethiopia
Cambodia	Jordan	Turkey	Gold Coast
Ceylon*	Laos	Vietnam (North)	Liberia
China (People's	Lebanon	Vietnam (South)	Libya
Republic)	Nepal	Yemen	Sudan
Indonesia*	Pakistan*		
Iran	Philippines		
	Saudi Arabia		

*Sponsoring countries.

[a] After deliberating on whether the remaining independent states in Asia (Israel, Mongolia, North Korea, South Korea) should be invited, the five sponsors agreed on a case-by-case basis not to do so because of various political complications their attendance might pose. Once consideration was given to inviting the People's Republic of China, this set to rest any thought of inviting Taiwan.

[b] African representation included two non-independent but internally self-governing countries, the Gold Coast (which became independent as Ghana in 1957) and the Sudan (which attained independence in 1956). The Central African Federation (then comprising the two Rhodesias and Nyasaland) although under white-minority rule, was invited, but it declined. South Africa was not invited.

Conference is the most appropriate starting point of analysis.[21]

As indicated in Table 28.3, the Asian–African Conference convened in Bandung, Indonesia, in April 1955, under the sponsorship of five Asian states (Burma – now Myanmar, Ceylon – now Sri Lanka, India, Indonesia, Pakistan), involved the participation of 29 countries, 6 African and 23 Asian. Its declared purposes, as stated in a December 1954 communiqué issued by the sponsoring countries, were:

1. to promote goodwill and co-operation among the nations of Asia and Africa, to explore and advance their mutual as well as common interests and to establish and further friendliness and neighbourly relations;
2. to consider social, economic and cultural problems and relations of the countries represented;
3. to consider problems of special interest to Asian and African

21. See G. H. Jansen, 1966, and P. Queuille, 1965, generally on Afro-Asian relations leading up to Bandung. Specifically on the immediate origins of and proceedings at the Bandung Conference, see R. Abdulgani, 1981; A. Appadorai, 1956; G. M. Kahin, 1956; D. Kimche, 1973, chs 3–4, pp. 29–79.

peoples, for example, problems affecting national sovereignty and of racialism and colonialism; and

4. to view the position of Asia and Africa and their peoples in the world of today and the contribution they can make to the promotion of world peace and co-operation.

The Asian presence at Bandung was unquestionably dominant, in terms of sponsors, location and range of participants. The low level of African representation was due simply to the fact that at that time only a handful of African countries were politically independent. Indeed, the qualifications for participation at Bandung were stretched to include two African colonies – the Sudan and the Gold Coast (now Ghana) – then on the verge of acquiring independence, a concession without which Africa's presence would have been significantly reduced from six to four. But some accounts of the conference have by other means accomplished an even greater reduction of African representation at Bandung by misleadingly identifying only three 'African' participants (Ethiopia, Gold Coast, Liberia) while classifying the other three (Egypt, Libya and Sudan) separately as part of an exclusive nine-member 'Arab' contingent.[22]

In at least two respects Africa's presence and impact at Bandung was less insignificant than its minimal representation would suggest. First there was the 'decisive contribution' made by Egypt's Gamāl 'Abd al-Nasser in the drafting committees, leading one analyst to label him as 'the hero of Bandung'.[23] What is more, al-Nasser's Bandung exposure and performance paved the way for his rapid emergence as one of the most prominent architects and leaders of the burgeoning Third-World movement.

Secondly, Africa's impact on the Bandung proceedings was registered in the importance assigned to human rights and self-determination issues on that continent, especially as these bore on institutionalized racism. For example, in the conference's final communiqué, colonial developments in Algeria, Morocco and Tunisia were addressed on two separate occasions; racial discrimination in Africa generally was cited as a prime example of the suppression under colonialism of the national cultures of dependent

22. This misleading portrayal of Africa's representation at Bandung appears, for example, in R. Abdulgani, 1981, p. 39; G. H. Jansen, 1966, p. 223; D. Kimche, 1973, pp. 238 and 248 (note 1), who eventually qualifies his initial suggestion of three African participants to read 'three African states south of the Sahara'. This is, of course, a matter of interest and concern to African historiography, which for a long time suffered from a reluctance to include North Africa within a holistic African continental framework of analysis.

23. G. H. Jansen, 1966, p. 223. See also R. Abdulgani, 1981, pp. 48 and 160–1 on al-Nasser's crucial role, as chairman of the session on peaceful coexistence, in resolving serious differences and proposing compromise wording on this, the conference's 'thorniest issue' – considered elsewhere by India's Prime Minister Nehru as 'the most important declaration of the Conference' (J. Nehru, 1964, p. 21).

peoples; and racial discrimination in South Africa was highlighted as a special case of the denial of human rights.

In addition to resolutions on 'cultural co-operation', 'human rights' and 'self-determination', and the 'problems of dependent peoples', from which the foregoing illustrations are drawn, the communiqué contained other substantive resolutions on 'economic co-operation' and 'the promotion of world peace and co-operation', with the latter subject also constituting a separate declaration. This assessment captures well the conference's accomplishments and legacies:

> Bandung was in essence a celebration of the wave of independence that swept across Asia and was then cresting in Africa. The very act of bringing together the first generation of nationalist leaders created an unprecedented sentiment of Third World change and potential. Bandung thus became the symbol of a goal . . . [and] pointed to the two principles that have remained the foundation of Third World solidarity, decolonization and economic development.[24]

As the most important organized expression of Afro-Asianism, the Bandung spirit in the immediate aftermath helped to boost other parallel ventures (such as the Afro-Asian caucus in the United Nations) and to inspire the initiation of others (such as the Afro-Asian Peoples' Solidarity Organization).

The Asian–African group which first emerged in the United Nations General Assembly in December 1950, during the Korean crisis, had continued to meet thereafter on an informal basis. It was in the aftermath of the Bandung Conference and the Suez crisis of 1956 – when Britain, France and Israel temporarily occupied the Suez Canal, recently nationalized by President al-Nasser – that the group acquired sufficient cohesion and permanence to be more formally recognized as a caucusing group. After 1960 there was a shift in nomenclature from Asian–African group to Afro-Asian group, 'indicative of the increased African influence' in this caucus.[25]

As can be seen in Table 28.1, this increased African influence was manifested in a remarkable expansion of African membership in the United Nations after 1959, the year 1960 being the critical turning point when, with the admission of 16 newly independent states, African representation came to surpass that of Asia (as well as Latin America) for the first time.

The impact of the Afro-Asian group on a range of United Nations' issues and processes through the 1950s and 1960s has been extensively analysed by D. N. Sharma.[26] Especially relevant to our present purposes is

24. R. A. Mortimer, 1980, p. 9.
25. D. Kay, 1970, p. 26.
26. D. N. Sharma, 1969.

the impact it had during these first two decades of its existence in bringing United Nations concern, influence and pressure to bear on two matters of fundamental concern to African states, namely, the general issue of decolonization – which is the subject of Y. El-Ayouty's comprehensive study[27] – and the specific problems of racism *cum* colonialism in Southern Africa.[28]

The adoption by the UN General Assembly in December 1960 of the historic 'Declaration on the Granting of Independence to Colonial Countries and Peoples'[29] sponsored by 43 Afro-Asian states, signalled dramatically the arrival of this newly reorganized and expanded Afro-Asian group in the United Nations system. Proclaiming 'the necessity of bringing to a speedy and unconditional end colonialism in all its forms and manifestations', the Declaration – in language reminiscent of the anti-colonial censures by the Fifth Pan-African Congress of 1945, the Bandung Conference of 1955 and the First Conference of Independent African States of 1958[30] – condemned colonialism as 'a denial of fundamental human rights' and 'an impediment to the promotion of world peace and cooperation', and stipulated that 'immediate steps' be taken 'to transfer all powers to the peoples' living under colonialism'.

It was no mere happenstance that the Declaration's adoption coincided with the admission of 16 new African member states in the United Nations almost three months earlier, which thus significantly boosted the Afro-Asian presence and impact in that organization. What is more, the Declaration's timing was most appropriate in view of the fact that by 1960 colonialism, while largely eradicated from Asia, was still in place in many parts of Africa.

A follow-up resolution by the UN General Assembly a year later, establishing a Special Committee to oversee the implementation of the 1960 Declaration,[31] was a further consequence of Afro-Asian resolve to

27. Y. El-Ayouty, 1971. See also D. Kay, 1970, ch. 6, pp. 146–80; D. N. Sharma, 1969, ch. 6, pp. 196–256.

28. M. El-Khawas, 1971; D. Kay, 1970, pp. 54–80; D. N. Sharma, 1969, ch. 7, pp. 257–303.

29. UN General Assembly Resolution 1514 (XV) of 14 December 1960, adopted by a vote of 89 in favour, none against and 9 abstentions (Australia, Belgium, France, Dominican Republic, Portugal, Spain, South Africa, United Kingdom, United States).

30. The Fifth Pan-African Congress's 'Declaration to Colonial Peoples of the World' insisted that 'All colonies must be free from imperialist control'; the Bandung Conference's communiqué asserted that 'Colonialism in all its manifestations is an evil which should be speedily brought to an end'; the First Conference of Independent African States (comprising Ethiopia, Ghana, Liberia, Libya, Morocco, Sudan, Tunisia and the United Arab Republic), meeting in Accra, in the year following Ghana's independence, condemned colonialism as a 'threat . . . to world peace' and called for 'rapid steps', including a 'definite date' in each instance, for the termination of colonial rule.

31. UN General Assembly Resolution 1654 (XVI) of 27 November 1961, adopted by a vote of 97 in favour, none against, 4 abstentions (France, South Africa, Spain, United Kingdom) and 1 not participating (Portugal).

dictate the ideology and institutionalize the direction of UN anti-colonial commitment and activity thereafter.

Similarly, the problems of racism *cum* colonialism in Southern Africa by the turn of the 1960s assumed a heightened salience in UN processes, thanks to the intensification of Afro-Asian pressure. The time was now appropriate to build on and expand earlier Afro-Asian initiatives, dating back to the first session of the UN General Assembly in 1946.

The question of South Africa's racial policies was first placed on the UN agenda in 1946, two years before the formal inauguration of *apartheid* with the 1948 electoral victory of the National Party, the instrument of Afrikaaner nationalism. This was in the form of a complaint by the government of India – which although not attaining its political independence until 1947 had been admitted as a founding member of the UN in 1945 – protesting against the South African government's recent enactment of discriminatory legislation targeted specifically against South Africans of Indian origin. Joined by Pakistan in 1947 (following Pakistan's separate independence and UN membership), both Asian states continued thereafter to keep this question before the United Nations. In a parallel development in 1952, 13 Afro-Asian member states (Afghanistan, Burma, Egypt, India, Indonesia, Iran, Iraq, Lebanon, Pakistan, the Philippines, Saudi Arabia, Syria and Yemen) placed on the General Assembly's agenda the wider question of racial conflicts arising from the policies of the *apartheid* regime, then in its fourth year in power.

Despite the preliminary reservations or outright opposition of certain Western powers in bringing such matters of presumed 'domestic jurisdiction' before the United Nations, the stage was set for a mounting condemnation of *apartheid* through the 1950s and for the two parallel Afro-Asian challenges to merge within the more comprehensive UN assault on *apartheid* launched in the early 1960s.

Complementing other burgeoning Afro-Asian and wider Third-World initiatives on Southern African regional problems in general, the Afro-Asian caucusing group while functioning at the peak of its visibility and influence in the 1960s was instrumental in catalysing some significant United Nations' institutional developments.

A case in point was the UN Security Council's implementation in 1963 of a voluntary embargo against the supply of arms to the government of South Africa (later strengthened to become mandatory in 1977). Also, there was the example of the Security Council's imposition of selective mandatory sanctions (1966) and later comprehensive sanctions (1968) against the minority racist regime in Rhodesia which had unilaterally declared its independence from the United Kingdom in 1965, precipitating a 15-year struggle culminating in the establishment of independent Zimbabwe under African rule in 1980.

A third instance of the Afro-Asian caucus's impact was in mobilizing

843

the UN General Assembly in 1966 to terminate the League of Nations Mandate over South-West Africa – following South Africa's prolonged betrayal of that responsibility – and in 1968 to rename that country as Namibia, which set the stage for the Security Council to declare in 1970, and for the International Court of Justice to ratify in 1971, that South Africa's occupation of Namibia was illegal and should be terminated. Finally, not the least significant of such illustrative developments was the establishment by the General Assembly in 1962 of the Special Committee Against Apartheid for the purpose of keeping South Africa's racial policies under constant review.

Another important institutional expression of Afro-Asianism catalysed by the experience of Bandung was the Afro-Asian Peoples Solidarity Organization (AAPSO), established in Cairo in 1957.[32] Strongly supported by the Soviet Union and the People's Republic of China, the AAPSO was composed of a variety of complementary group interests – at least at the outset – from the Afro-Asian world as well as from the socialist block countries.

Radical Afro-Asian nationalism superseded international socialism as AAPSO's driving force, due in large measure to the fact that 'Nasser was careful to keep the organizational controls in Egyptian hands'.[33] Additionally, as suggested in the choice of sites for its four plenary conferences (in Egypt, 1957; Guinea, 1960; Tanzania, 1963; Ghana, 1965), 'radical African states gave the greatest backing to AAPSO'.[34]

An important aspect of the organization's role is that it not only served to enhance al-Nasser's Afro-Asian leadership credentials, but it also provided yet another base for him to emerge as a major architect of a wider Third-World movement. Another significant feature was that AAPSO represented a non-governmental organizational parallel to the efforts being pursued by Afro-Asian states to build a measure of solidarity, serving in the process to broaden and popularize the ethos of Afro-Asianism in these formative years. Thus, in addition to providing a meeting place for a variety of political groups and movements not necessarily affiliated to ruling establishments, numerous conferences were organized by AAPSO between 1956 and 1965 involving Afro-Asian professionals and specialists in a range of endeavours such as medicine, law, journalism, creative writing, economics, social welfare, rural development, women and youth affairs.

AAPSO began to decline by the mid-1960s – surviving as a shadow of its former self through the 1970s – due in part to the destabilizing impact of Sino-Soviet rivalries on its internal processes. But its longer-run legacies have remained; first, in helping in a critical formative period to

32. The most detailed studies of AAPSO are D. Kimche, 1968; and 1973, chs 7–10, pp. 126–213.
33. R. A. Mortimer, 1980, p. 10.
34. *ibid.*, p. 11.

advance the Afro-Asian foundations for a wider Third-World movement; and, secondly, in directly contributing to that transition by giving birth to the parallel Afro-Asian–Latin American Peoples' Solidarity Organization (better known as the Tri-Continental Solidarity Organization) founded under AAPSO's auspices in Havana, Cuba, in 1966.

An important ingredient of emergent Afro-Asianism, deserving of recognition in its own right, was India's special relationship with Africa, which has indeed been alluded to a number of times in our previous analysis.[35] This was rooted initially in the catalytic impact of the Indian independence movement on African nationalism and the inspiration furnished organizationally by the Indian National Congress and individually by Mahatma Gandhi and Jawaharlal Nehru in their anti-colonial struggles.

Nehru proceeded to have an even greater impact on the cementing of mutual interests and ties in the post-colonial period. This was partly a function of his own profound sensitivity to Africa's political and racial burdens – 'the infinite tragedy of Africa' as he put it at the Bandung Conference, thus re-echoing a theme he had broached almost a decade earlier when, at the Asian Relations Conference in New Delhi in 1947, he spoke of 'our suffering brethren in Africa' and of Asia's 'special responsibility' to assist the African freedom-struggle.

At more concrete levels, Nehru was instrumental in the shaping of institutional arenas for a consolidation and projection of India's and Africa's mutual interests – whether in the Afro-Asian movement of the 1950s which he spearheaded, or in the Third-World movement of the early 1960s for which he was a catalyst, or in the former British Commonwealth which he helped significantly to transform into a new multi-racial Commonwealth.

As noted previously, the presence in parts of Africa of significant communities of Indian descent has catered to this sense of a special relationship. We have already illustrated how, in the case of South Africa, this served to strengthen the bonds of solidarity between India and Africa in their mutual interest in the elimination of *apartheid*, in which connection it is of significance that India was the first country in the world to break off diplomatic and economic relations with South Africa in the early 1950s. And while in parts of East Africa friction has at times surfaced in the domestic relations between Africans and Asians,[36] this has not seemed

---

35. On India's special relationship with Africa, see Indian National Congress, 1976; Indian Council for Africa, 1967; A. A. Mazrui, 1977, ch. 6, pp. 114–29; J. Nehru, 1964; R. L. Park, 1965; R. R. Ramchandani, 1980; M. J. Zins, 1983.

36. See R. R. Ramchandani, 1980, pp. 171–94, in which Ramchandani's own essay, 'Indians in East Africa: past experiences and future prospects,' convincingly argues that occasional friction between Africans and Asians in East Africa is embedded in the socio-economic and socio-racial inheritances and structures which arose essentially from warped colonial patterns of development.

sufficient to affect adversely those countries' relations with India.

If this special relationship seemed to have weakened somewhat after the mid-1960s, it was due not to any inherent problems but to wider transformations in the international system. Part of the reason seemed to lie in the decline of India's influence in the Third World, especially after Nehru's death in 1964. But as Ali Mazrui has observed, it 'has not been so much a case of the decline of India in absolute terms, but simply a restoration of balance in her stature in the Third World' relative to the 'exceptional level of diplomatic and political influence' attained under Nehru.[37]

Conversely, the more that there came to be a diversification and spread of critical Third-World centres of influence, including some on the African continent itself, this automatically modified the earlier pre-eminence of the Indian–African connection. This should not, however, blind us to the fact that while since the mid-1960s such relations seemed not to be as politically and diplomatically salient as previously, there was in fact a widening of links in other less dramatic forms, including increasing economic and technical co-operation and expanded cultural and educational exchanges.

In any event, the publication, as late as 1976, of a 132-page book by the Indian National Congress, *India and the African Liberation Struggle*, charting from Mahatma Gandhi to (then prime minister) Indira Gandhi a chain of continuity in Indian political concern and involvement in African liberation, suggested that the notion of this special relationship continued to have a powerful ideological hold.

A common tendency among analysts of the post-Second World War phenomenon of Afro-Asianism has been to characterize the period after the mid-1960s as one of 'the decline of the Afro-Asian movement',[38] or of 'the demise of Afro-Asianism'[39] or one in which 'Afro-Asianism is now officially dead'.[40]

The unsuccessful effort – aborted in 1965 – to convene a second Afro-Asian conference, along the lines of Bandung,[41] is usually cited as a primary cause as well as consequence of that decline or demise. Another contributory factor and result was an eroding influence of AAPSO by the late 1960s, as previously discussed. Additionally, during the 1970s the Afro-Asian caucusing group in the United Nations effectively ceased to operate.

One of the factors underlying the débâcle of the projected Bandung II was that it had in effect been superseded by the Non-Aligned Movement

37. A. A. Mazrui, 1977, p. 120.
38. D. Kimche, 1973, ch. 14, pp. 250–62.
39. R. A. Mortimer, 1980, pp. 18–22.
40. P. Willetts, 1978, p. 15.
41. R. A. Mortimer, 1980, pp. 20–2; F. B. Weinstein, 1965.

which had held its first two summit conferences between 1961 and 1964 (see Table 28.4), as well as by the Group of 77 established in 1964 (see Table 28.5). Such transitional developments explain this May 1965 reaction by Senegal's President Léopold Senghor, when asked about the feasibility of a second Afro-Asian conference, then still being actively mooted by others: 'For my part, I think Afro-Asianism has been super-seded, for this form of solidarity should be extended to Latin America in particular and to the *tiers monde* in general.'[42]

The launching of the Tri-Continental Solidarity Organization under AAPSO's sponsorship in Havana in 1966 was yet another measure of Afro-Asianism reaching beyond its specific geographical confines to forge a wider sense of Third-World identity. Also, given the increasing mob-ilization of Group of 77 and Non-Aligned Movement pressures directly within the UN system during the 1970s,[43] bearing especially on the search for a new international economic order, the most salient of Third-World concerns, it is not surprising that in time the Afro-Asian caucusing group became superfluous.

Thus the apparent failure of Afro-Asianism to survive as a movement was in effect a function of its success in serving as the critical catalyst and foundation for a wider Third-World coalition, as has indeed been admitted by some of those analysts pinpointing the former's decline. It is thus more appropriate to speak not of the demise but rather of the transformation of Afro-Asianism.

Africa and the Arab world: contours in a special relationship

From 7 to 9 March 1977, there met in Cairo 'the first conference of the Heads of States and Governments of the OAU and the Arab League' in which – in the official words of the conference's proceedings – 59 'African and Arab countries' met for the purpose of consolidating 'African–Arab' (at times alternatively labelled 'Arab–African') co-operation.[44]

The significance to the present analysis of this officially-styled 'Arab–African' summit is threefold. For one thing, as the first meeting of its kind, it was symptomatic of the attainment during the 1970s of a new and hitherto unsurpassed widening and deepening of political and economic ties between the African and Arab worlds. Secondly, such developments bore significantly on a heightening sense of Third-World solidarity characteristic of the 1970s, while serving as a reminder of the impact on that process of the spirit of Afro-Asianism which has always

42. L. Senghor, quoted in *Africa Diary*, 19–25 June 1965, p. 2386.
43. K. P. Sauvant, 1981, p. 112, Table 12, documents statistically the increasing frequency of meetings of both groups within the UN system between 1965 and 1979.
44. C. Legum, 1977.

been underpinned critically by the African world–Arab world nexus.

The third reason has to do with definitions and terminology which need to be clarified at the outset. Since a number of states are simultaneously African and Arab, this has given rise to a situation not of distinctly separate or mutually exclusive regional definition but of one characterized by considerable overlap and fusion of the two. This phenomenon indeed lies at the core of a special relationship between the African and Arab worlds, such terminological differentiations – as were similarly employed by the 1977 'Arab–African' summit – being thus understood in the light of the foregoing caveats.

PLATE 28.1   *The Arab League and the Organization of African Unity Conference, Cairo,* *1977*

Portraying the range of factors encompassing that special relationship were these sentiments expressed by the 1977 summit participants who were profoundly

> aware of our numerous links and interests, of the geographical, historical and cultural factors, of the desire to develop co-operation in the political, economic and social spheres, and of the requirements of our joint struggle against all kinds of domination and exploitation.

If changing national, regional and global circumstances from the 1950s onwards proved more conducive than previously to a search for cementing meaningful political, economic and social ties for mutual advancement and development, the predisposing factors of geographical contiguity, long-standing historical relationships of over 12 centuries and widespread demographic and cultural fusions gave a particular sense of urgency to that mission.

For example, at least 60 (with some estimates running as high as 80) per cent of the world's Arab population resides on the African continent. It is estimated that one-third of Africa's peoples are Muslim, comprising overwhelming majorities not only in North Africa but also in nine sub-Saharan countries (Comoros, Djibouti, Gambia, Guinea, Mali, Mauritania, Niger, Senegal, Somalia), while accounting for a plurality in another two (Chad and Nigeria) and representing a substantial minority of at least 25 per cent in another seven (Burkina Faso – previously Upper Volta, Cameroon, Ethiopia, Guinea-Bissau, Côte d'Ivoire, Sierra Leone, Tanzania). Additionally, such cultural fusion is manifested in the linguistic field since Arabic, Kiswahili and Hausa, 'the most important non-European languages in the African continent . . . have been deeply influenced by Islam'.[45]

Such demographic *cum* cultural ties have assumed significance in the structure of certain international organizations. The League of Arab States – popularly known as the Arab League – had only one African state (Egypt) among its eight founding members in 1945; by 1980, nine of the League's 22 members were from Africa, including three non-Arab but predominantly Islamic countries (Djibouti, Mauritania and Somalia). Conversely, the 50-member OAU in 1980 included nine Arab League states. The Organization of the Islamic Conference (OIC), the highest Islamic intergovernmental body, founded in 1971, had exactly one half of its 1980 membership of 42 drawn from the African continent.

The contours of this special relationship between the African and Arab worlds have been sufficiently mapped out in various studies[46] to make it possible to present the essential outlines. To start with the 1950s, this was a time when there began to emerge a burgeoning compatibility of political interests, primarily on the questions of anti-colonialism and non-alignment.

The heightened decolonization struggles in North Africa in the early post-war years, which for the most part preceded sub-Saharan equivalents, proved inherently crucial to these maturing ties. Over time these were further extended as African decolonization assumed continent-wide proportions, the more so with the prolonged and brutal colonial conflict in Algeria – an issue first brought before the United Nations by Saudi Arabia in 1955 – and the intractability of the colonial and racist regimes in Southern Africa.

45. A. A. Mazrui, 1977, p. 130.
46. Z. Cervenka, 1977, ch. 9, pp. 156–75; E. C. Chibwe, 1977; V. T. Le Vine and T. W. Luke, 1979; A. A. Mazrui, 1975c, and 1977, ch. 7, pp. 130–55; G. Nicolas, 1978; and G. A. Nweke, 1980, ch. 10, pp. 214–34.

With the establishment of the state of Israel in 1948, accomplished through the displacement of Palestinians, notions of non-alignment increasingly proved appealing to the Arab world, feeling that its interests were being sacrificed on the altar of great-power politics.[47] Even among the more conservative and Western-oriented Arab states in the Middle East, the emerging logic of international relations in that region dictated that they assume some ideological distance from both West and East. In the longer run, the rationale of non-alignment came to constitute a basis for the enhancement of parallel or convergent interests between the Arab and African worlds, both fearful of their sovereignty being jeopardized by external interests.

Of critical significance to these maturing ties was the role of Egypt – renamed the United Arab Republic, 1958–70[48] – especially after the 1952 revolution which overthrew the monarchy, culminating in al-Nasser's full assumption of power in 1954. Pre-1952 Egypt had begun to play a modest role in building bridges between Africa and the wider Arab–Asian worlds, for example in being the only African state participating – along with 11 Asian states – in the founding in 1950 of the *ad hoc* Asian–African group in the United Nations. But under al-Nasser there was a distinctive transformation in the tempo of Egyptian activism, which came to embrace and entwine the three circles – the 'Arab circle', the 'African circle' and 'the circle of our brethren-in-Islam' – which al-Nasser's 1954 publication, *Philosophy of Revolution*, identified as being central to Egypt's identity. Al-Nasser's increasingly important impact simultaneously on the politics of pan-African and pan-Arab liberation by the later 1950s equipped him thoroughly with the motivation and image to emerge to exceptional prominence as a founder of the Non-Aligned Movement, the Third World's political foundation.[49]

Beginning with Ghana's attainment of independence in 1957, the retreat of colonialism in sub-Saharan Africa paved the way for a more concerted intra-African concern with building meaningful pan-African ties across the Sahara – a priority recognized by al-Nasser and Nkrumah alike – which naturally spilled over into wider notions of African and Arab world solidarity.

With the creation of the OAU in 1963 there was now in existence an African regional organization paralleling, and in many respects comp-lementing, the Arab League. In addition to some overlapping membership,

47. F. A. Sayegh, 1964.

48. The 1958 union of Egypt and Syria assuming the name United Arab Republic disintegrated in 1961 with Syria's withdrawal, but the name continued to be used officially until 1971 when it was changed to Arab Republic of Egypt. The name Egypt is being used throughout this chapter unless it proves necessary in *ad hoc* cases to refer to 'United Arab Republic' instead.

49. On Egypt's Africa-related foreign policy in the al-Nasser era (1952–70), see T. Y. Ismael, 1971; and A. B. Sawant, 1981.

both bodies shared a common bond in being 'the first [regional] organizations created and directed by the poor nations, for the poor nations of the world'. The Arab League as the 'nucleus of the Afro-Asian group' in the United Nations during the 1950s now came to be reinforced by the OAU when the former 'began to lose its youthful dynamism'.[50]

But the most salient political issue in Arab League politics, the issue of Israel's presence and performance, was effectively insulated from OAU politics in the earlier years despite the hopes of the Arab League members of the OAU that both organizations would forge a common stand. The reason was that many of sub-Saharan Africa's newly independent states had close economic and sometimes military ties with Israel which had been active in its diplomatic efforts to build such links. Also the majority feeling prevailed that the Middle East crisis, not being strictly an African issue, did not properly fall within the OAU's purview.

However, there began to be a detectable shift in the OAU's position after the Six-Day war in 1967 which had led to Israel's occupation of Arab territory including Egypt's Sinai peninsula. A steadily emerging build-up in African condemnation of Israel's policies entered another stage at the eighth OAU summit in 1971 when it was maintained for the first time that 'the continued Israeli occupation constitutes a serious threat to the regional peace of Africa'. Simultaneously, the OAU established a committee to mediate the conflict (primarily between Egypt and Israel), but its eventual failure, attributed by its chairman Léopold Senghor to Israeli intransigence,[51] served to intensify support for the Arab cause.

In an extraordinary turn of events in October 1973, 17 sub-Saharan states severed their diplomatic relations with Israel followed by another four in November, with the result that by the end of 1973 only four member states of the OAU – Malawi, Lesotho, Swaziland and Mauritius – continued to maintain diplomatic ties with Israel.

These late 1973 developments can be evaluated in a clearer perspective when it is recalled that prior to 1967 all OAU member states excepting those belonging to the Arab League had diplomatic relations with Israel; that in the immediate aftermath of the Six-Day war only one other African state (Guinea) terminated its diplomatic ties; and that this situation remained unchanged over the better part of the next five years until a distinctly shifting African diplomatic mood became manifest over the 18-month period prior to October 1983 during which another seven states severed relations with Israel.

Three major developments in 1973 set the stage for the October diplomatic turnabout. Two of these, very much interrelated in the burgeoning contexts of African–Arab–Third-World solidarity, were first the convening of the tenth anniversary OAU summit in Addis Ababa in

50. B. Boutros-Ghali, 1975, p. 60.
51. Y. El-Ayouty, 1975a.

May and, secondly, the fourth Non-Aligned Summit Conference held in Algiers in September, which were important forums for the harmonization of Arab–African–Third-World diplomatic strategies.

An exceptionally influential role in both settings was played by Algeria's President Boumedienne. It was he who spearheaded Arab diplomacy within the OAU, establishing convincing parallels between the liberation struggles in the Middle East and Southern Africa – a position which was facilitated by Israel's increasingly close military and economic ties with *apartheid* South Africa, a significant source of the developing alienation of interests between Africa and Israel. Additionally, as chairman of the Fourth Non-Aligned Summit he could bring his prestige and influence to bear on a heightening coalescence of pan-African, pan-Arab and Third-World interests.

The third immediate development contributing to the October 1973 diplomatic ruptures was the October 1973 War (6–24 October) between Egypt and Syria on the one hand and Israel on the other. The point of no return was reached when Israel pushed further than ever before into Egyptian territory, occupying for the first time lands west of the Suez Canal, directly and unarguably on continental African soil.

Some analysts contend that African capitulation to the Arab 'oil weapon' was a major factor leading to Israel's diplomatic isolation,[52] but such a view is ahistorical and, indeed, cynical. It is true that at the height of the October 1973 War a drastic increase in the price of oil was announced by OPEC (Organization of Petroleum Exporting Countries) and that OAPEC (Organization of Arab Petroleum Exporting Countries) banned the export of crude oil to any country siding with Israel. But to see these as root causes of African states' diplomatic behaviour toward Israel in late 1973 is to 'distort the sequence of events' since 'much of Africa had already sided with the Arabs on the Palestine question' well before the oil factor came into play.[53]

This latter view is supported elsewhere in the conclusion that there is 'no evidence either that the Arabs ever mentioned the possibility of using the 'oil weapon' against African countries or that African countries threw their support behind the Arabs with financial benefit in mind.[54] The reasons lay instead in an emerging spirit of political solidarity on mutual interests between the African and Arab worlds which entered a new stage after 1967, developing with even greater intensity in the 1970s.

With the political coalition in place by 1973 and in view of the dramatic projection of Arab–Islamic oil power in the international economic arena, the question of forging viable and mutually beneficial economic ties

52. V. T. Le Vine and T. W. Luke, 1979, pp. 9–18.
53. A. A. Mazrui, 1975c, p. 736.
54. Z. Cervenka, 1977, p. 162.

inevitably emerged as a major challenge to African and Arab world relationships.

A dramatic start was the November 1973 decision by the Arab League, meeting in Algiers, to impose an oil embargo against colonialist Portugal, white-ruled Rhodesia and *apartheid* South Africa.[55] It was then also agreed to establish these three major institutions to promote economic co-operation: the Arab Bank for Economic Development in Africa, specifically intended for the benefit of African countries not belonging to the Arab League; the Special Arab Fund for Africa, designed to provide emergency financial assistance to non-Arab African countries for oil imports and development of oil resources; and the Fund for Arab–African Technical Assistance – including both Arab and African countries – for the purpose of promoting economic and technical co-operation.[56] The increasing importance of economic factors in these expanding relationships was further manifested in evolving perceptions of the responsibilities OPEC ought to assume in promoting Third-World development in general and African development in particular.[57]

These consolidating patterns of political and economic relationships during the 1970s came to be culturally reinforced by the Islamic revival, the political potency of which led, for example, to the establishment in 1971 of the intergovernmental Organization of the Islamic Conference (OIC), sited in Saudi Arabia.[58] Such then was the evolving situation conducive to the convening of the first Arab–African Summit Conference of 1977.

These manifestations of solidarity did not, of course, mean the eradication of certain important differences in political outlook and priorities. For example, the Arab League constantly failed in its efforts to obtain OAU support for the expulsion of Israel from the United Nations. And in the greatest of ironies, Egypt, which during the 1950s and 1960s had been the cornerstone of these developing links, had by 1979 become a political pariah in the Arab world – because of Anwar Sadat's signing of a peace treaty with Israel – and a source of friction in the relationship.

Thus while Egypt was immediately suspended from membership in the Arab League – its headquarters being simultaneously moved from Cairo to Tunis – as well as in the OIC, the OAU although pressured refused to take similar steps and continued to welcome Egypt's participation. Also at the Sixth Non-Aligned Summit Conference in 1979, sub-Saharan states were instrumental in working out a compromise to

55. G. A. Nweke, 1980, ch. 11, pp. 235–50.
56. These three institutions are discussed in E. C. Chibwe, 1976; W. R. Johnson, 1983; A. Sylvester, 1981; and J. Vignes, 1976–7.
57. M. J. Williams, 1976.
58. O. H. Kokole, 1984; A. Oded, 1986.

prevent Egypt's suspension from the movement, which the other Arab states were seeking.

But the most challenging issue around the turn of the 1980s was whether the promises and hopes of economic co-operation and solidarity could withstand the rising structure of oil prices and the widening patterns of international economic recession. The fact that such concerns were being aired was indeed a measure of how far African and Arab world relationships had matured since the 1950s, arriving at a stage of unparalleled initiatives and aspirations in the 1970s, and in the process profoundly influencing the thrust of the challenge from the Third World.

Latin American and Caribbean ties: a maturing sense of Third-World identity

As underscored in certain UNESCO-sponsored publications or symposia,[59] Africa's racial and cultural presence throughout Latin America and the Caribbean is a permanent reminder of the deepseated historical contacts between the African continent and these African *diasporas*, of the traumatic conditions of the trans-Atlantic slave trade under which these *diasporas* were created, and of the racial/cultural ties which have underpinned a sense of trans-continental pan-African identity.

This has been especially true of the Caribbean where the African demographic and cultural presence is far more concentrated and pronounced than in the remaining Latin American area, which is characterized by marked national variations – from Brazil, with a significant African presence, to Argentina, where it hardly exists.

Within the Caribbean – here defined as 'the islands in the area together with Belize and "the Guyanas" (Guyana, Suriname, Cayenne)'[60] – are to be found most national communities having black majorities with the rest containing substantial black minorities. Considering further that slavery *cum* colonialism came to have a more total impact on the shaping of Caribbean societies than elsewhere, there is the inevitability of a racial frame of reference in Caribbean nation-building and foreign-policy processes, necessarily leading back to Africa.[61] This is one reason why in a study of this nature it is inappropriate to treat the Latin American geographical region as one undifferentiated whole.

The historical record is replete with numerous instances of persistent interactions, often involving organized collaboration, between Africa and the Caribbean in advancing the ethos of trans-continental pan-Africanism,

---

59. M. M. Fraginals, 1984; UNESCO, 1980.

60. This was the definition adopted by the UNESCO Working Group for the Preparation of a General History of the Caribbean, meeting in Paris, 14–18 December 1981, contained in 'Final Report' (CC-81/CONF. 610/4, UNESCO, Paris, 7 April 1982).

61. L. Edmondson, 1974; L. Edmondson and P. Phillips, 1979.

most of which have been discussed in several chapters in Volume VII as well as in this volume. In the early twentieth-century experience, for example, there was the launching, beginning in 1900, of a Pan-African Conference/Congress series involving blacks from the African continent and the *diaspora*; the phenomenon of Garveyism which transcended its Caribbean roots to become a major force in the development of African nationalism, as was attested to by Kwame Nkrumah and Jomo Kenyatta among others; the joint founding by Senegal's Léopold Senghor and Martinique's Aimé Césaire of the cultural pan-African doctine of *negritude* in the 1930s; and the joint organization of the Fifth Pan-African Congress of 1945 by Ghana's Kwame Nkrumah and Trinidad's George Padmore.

Such interactions preceded – with a handful of exceptions – the rise of sovereign independent states in both Africa and the Caribbean and were thus necessarily dominated by non-governmental interests. By contrast, the post-colonial period of the 1960s and 1970s was one in which newer opportunities were present for expanding the range of collaborative pan-African endeavours, now including governments as well.

The First World Festival of Negro Arts held in Senegal in 1966, the Sixth Pan-African Congress hosted by Tanzania in 1974, and the Second World Black and African Festival of Arts and Culture (FESTAC) in Nigeria in 1977, were notable examples of activities in which African–Caribbean links were being advanced within the broader context of transcontinental pan-Africanism.

From time to time African leaders explicitly acknowledged the significance of racial ties with the Caribbean as a basis for furthering their mutual interests. 'I would broadly say that wherever there is African blood there is a basis for greater unity', Ethiopian Emperor Haile Selassie declared while addressing the Jamaican parliament in 1966. Four years earlier, Kwame Nkrumah appealed directly to West Indian heads of government to work at maintaining the then disintegrating West Indies Federation, in these terms:

> My excuse for making this appeal is the sincere conviction I hold that success in the establishment of a powerful West Indies nation would substantially assist the efforts we are making to redeem Africa's reputation in world affairs and to re-establish the personality of the African and people of African descent everywhere.

But another African president, although himself a committed pan-Africanist, warned of the possibilities of a race-conscious pan-Africanism undermining the search for a wider sense of Third-World solidarity. This was Julius Nyerere's concern which – significantly in his capacity as host – he expressed to the Sixth Pan-African Congress of 1974:

> Pan-Africanism would be doing a great disservice to human liberation if it caused Africa and the Caribbean to try to isolate themselves

from the rest of the Third World; or if it provoked other parts of the Third World into isolating Africa and the Caribbean.

However, the developing consolidating pattern of pan-African ties between Africa and the Caribbean through the 1970s, especially focused on Southern African issues, suggested to the contrary that their Third-World liberationist commitments were thereby collectively enhanced.

Africa's relations with the Caribbean cannot of course be pinned down on the basis of race alone. Another important cementing factor was that most African and Caribbean states were colonies until recently, an experience which sharpened their common sensitivities to establishing their national and international political identities.

These considerations thus came to influence African and Caribbean collaboration within the Non-Aligned Movement – which the newly-independent Caribbean states had a relatively greater propensity to join than the longer-independent Latin American states – and within the Commonwealth – where the predominantly African presence was complemented by the Anglophone states of the Caribbean.

Within these two forums, as within the UN system which enhanced their institutional opportunities for collaboration, Southern African issues and inequities in the international economic system became the two major focuses of common concern and endeavour. The salience of the latter was further underscored with the establishment in 1975 of the ACP Group (African–Caribbean–Pacific Group of States), designed to protect and advance their economic positions collectively in negotiations with the European Economic Community.[62]

Mutual international economic interests came to constitute an even more predominant force – relative to racial, cultural and political factors – in relations between Africa and the wider Latin American region beyond the Caribbean. With good reason, it was observed in the mid-1960s that, in some fundamental areas, Africa and Latin America still remained 'giant strangers'.[63] However, it was also apparent that a 'Latin American–African Partnership', in the words of another analyst,[64] had been steadily emerging since the 1950s, preliminarily on some shared sensitivities regarding decolonization and the maintenance of national sovereignty, and ultimately over a mutual concern with economic development which came to dominate their common agendas of the 1960s and 1970s.

Despite divergent levels of economic development between both continents, at times resulting in varying economic priorities, it was being confidently asserted by the late 1960s that in UN debates on socio-economic issues 'the Africans have formed a steadfast alliance with the Latin Americans who have in the economic and social fields subordinated

62. K. Hall and B. W. Blake, 1979.
63. A. Segal, 1966.
64. P. Saenz, 1969.

PLATE 28.2   *Fidel Castro of Cuba and the Group of 77 in Havana, Cuba, 21 April 1987*

the principle of hemispheric solidarity with the United States to the principle of solidarity among the "have not" countries'.[65]

Illustrative of widespread Latin American sensitivity to economic underdevelopment linked to perceptions of their neo-colonial domination was the pioneering role of Latin American scholars in advancing dependency theory as a framework for analysing and explaining the region's economic underdevelopment, an approach which soon came to acquire wider Third-World intellectual currency as well as practical political significance.[66]

Another example was the leading role of Latin American states in the establishment in 1964 of UNCTAD (United Nations Conference on Trade and Development) and in the accompanying mobilization of the Group of 77,[67] to the extent of producing UNCTAD's first secretary-general, the Argentinian economist Raul Prebisch, credited with inspiring the school of dependency theorists as well as the development of negotiating strategies for the establishment of a new international economic

65. *ibid*, p. 326.
66. H. C. F. Mansilla, 1984.
67. See Table 28.5 below on the Group of 77 within UNCTAD, whose role as the major forum for Third-World economic diplomacy is discussed later in this chapter.

order (NIEO). Similarly, the formulation of the Charter of Economic Rights and Duties of States, adopted by the United Nations General Assembly in 1974 as a major plank of the NIEO being demanded by the Third-World coalition, originated from a proposal by Mexican President Luis Echeverria.

Such dovetailing and institutionalization of Latin American and African international economic interests within an expanding framework of Third-World solidarity was – with the distinctive exception of Cuba (simultaneously sharing a Latin American and Caribbean identity) and the partial exception of Brazil – not as readily apparent in other political arenas, thus leading to the view that 'The relationship of Latin American societies to African and Asian nations is of a fundamentally ambivalent nature'.[68] A case in point, as documented in Table 28.4 below, was a general pattern of Latin American reluctance through the 1960s and 1970s to become fully-fledged participants in the Non-Aligned Movement.

At least four reasons may be advanced to explain such behaviour. First, the fact that all Latin American (unlike most Caribbean) states acquired their political independence in the nineteenth century, mostly by the 1820s, served to detach them somewhat from the heightened post-war forces of Afro-Asian nationalism which underpinned the creation of the Non-Aligned Movement. Related to this was a second factor, namely that Spain was an insignificant colonial power in the Afro-Asian world which minimized the prospect of the dominant Hispanic politico-cultural identity of Latin America naturally reaching out to Afro-Asia.

Thirdly, the reluctance of Latin American states to enter the Non-Aligned Movement – especially in the earlier years when the movement's agenda was not as dominated by economic development issues as it later came to be – was also due to the fact that they were already part of an inter-hemispheric security system, the Organization of American States, whose founding in 1948 preceded by 13 years the launching of the Non-Aligned Movement. Fourthly, in Latin American (as opposed to Caribbean) nations, even in those with distinctive Afro-Asian demographic and cultural formations, Afro-Asian constituencies have not proved significant in influencing directly respective domestic, much less foreign policy, decision-making processes.

Brazil has offered a partial exception to some of these generalizations, insufficient however to have predisposed it to join the Non-Aligned Movement in which it opted for Observer status from the very outset in 1961. Despite that, there was since the mid-1950s a steadily expanding Brazilian foreign-policy interest in the Afro-Asian world.[69] The African dimension was much the more significant underpinning of that development, due to historically, demographically and culturally significant ties

68. H. C. F. Mansilla, 1984, p. 341.
69. W. A. Selcher, 1974.

between Brazil and Africa,[70] which became all the more salient in view of Brazil's unique New-World presence as a Lusophone fragment seeking to establish a sense of special identity with Lusophone Africa.[71]

Significant political complications arose in the latter quest during the final stages of Portuguese colonialism in Africa, from the 1960s to the mid-1970s, at a time when increasing colonialist intransigence in the face of the heightening African liberation struggles led to an erosion of international diplomatic support for Portugal. Characteristic of an ambivalent position on that issue was the fact that in 1973–4, a year or two before Portugal was forced to withdraw from Africa, 'Brazil was the only Latin American State to vote consistently in the UN with Portugal, although often abstaining on South Africa votes and siding with the African bloc on Rhodesian and Namibian votes'.[72]

With Portugal's retreat, it became easier after the mid-1970s for Brazil to pursue more confidently a previously articulated interest in widening its political, economic and cultural ties beyond Lusophone Africa, even while attaching a special consideration to the Lusophone connection.[73] By the turn of the 1980s, one of its more distinctive and potentially significant manifestations was a maturing economic and political relationship being forged between Nigeria and Brazil, two rising regional powers and demographically the largest countries on their respective continents.[74]

Revolutionary Cuba, by contrast, at no stage exhibited any ambivalence whatsoever about the centrality of the African and wider Third-World connection. Compared with other Latin American and Caribbean states – or for that matter with any states from Asia or the Middle East – Cuba's political links with Africa since the 1959 revolution were unrivalled in terms of range and consistency, as attested to in the volume of literature on that subject.[75] It was thus appropriately concluded that 'Afro-Latinism as a form of solidarity between Africa and Latin America has been strengthened mainly through the Cuban connection'.[76]

The seeds of this relationship were rooted in the conditions and immediate aftermath of the 1959 Cuban revolution. Coinciding in time with the heightening Afro-Asian and burgeoning Third-World challenges to the international *status quo*, revolutionary Cuba from the outset was

70. R. Pélissier, 1982; J. H. Rodrigues, 1982.

71. W. A. Selcher, 1974.

72. A. Segal, 1974, p. A107.

73. A. Dzidzienyo and J. M. Turner, 1981; T. Forrest, 1982; H. Hoffman, 1982; and A. C. Peixoto, 1983.

74. Nigerian Institute of International Affairs, c. 1981–4; U. J. Ogwu, 1982.

75. For example, see S. Y. Abdi, 1978, pp. 17–24; *Cuba Review*, 1978, pp. 1–50; A. M. Kapcia, 1979, pp. 142–59; W. M. LeoGrande, 1980; A. A. Mazrui, 1981, pp. 329–45; C. Mesa-Lago and J. S. Belkin, 1982; E. Mestri, 1980; A. Segal, 1983b, pp. 123–47; and N. P. Valdes, 1980, pp. 49–79.

76. A. A. Mazrui, 1981, p. 343.

induced to seek to maximize its shared affinities with such forces, a posture which was further reinforced by subsequent moves, primarily through United States instigation, to isolate Cuba from Western hemispheric international institutional processes.[77]

As seen by one analyst, Cuban involvement in Africa during 1959–79 proceeded through four distinct phases.[78] The first, 1959–74, was characterized by 'loose, informal, and limited ties, often with an emphasis on contacts with African nationalist movements rather than independent governments'. The second period, 1975–6, was one in which 18 000–24 000 Cuban combat troops were introduced in Angola at the request of the MPLA (Popular Movement for the Liberation of Angola), which not only helped to secure the position of the MPLA over its rivals contending for control of the government in the light of colonial Portugal's recent withdrawal, but more significantly succeeded in neutralizing invading South African troops supporting the anti-MPLA forces.

The third period of Cuban involvement, 1977–8, was focused on the Horn of Africa where some 20 000 combat troops assisted the government of Ethiopia in defeating Somalia's military incursion into the Somali-populated Ogaden region of Ethiopia. The fourth period, beginning in 1979, was seen as one of 'consolidation and stabilization' offering promises of a reduction of Cuba's military presence and an expansion of its civilian and technical assistance programmes.

Cuba's massive military adventures in Angola and the Horn of Africa, while not without their African critics, eventually came to be seen as less controversial, given that the OAU viewed Somalia as the aggressor in the Horn and that *apartheid* South Africa's designs over Angola had been thwarted. But these episodes tended to overshadow other aspects of Cuba's deepening ties with Africa.

At the peak of its military presence in 1978, in addition to approximately 19 000 combat troops in Angola and 16 000–17 000 in Ethiopia, Cuba also had between 2455 and 2755 military advisers in another 11 African states.[79] By 1980, between 8500 and 12 200 Cuban civilian advisers – some 70 per cent of whom were based in Angola – were serving in 12 African countries,[80] providing technical assistance in such areas as health care, agronomy, education and engineering. By 1977, Cuba had diplomatic relations with 25 African states, 12 of which had ambassadors accredited in Havana.

---

77. For example, since 1962 Cuba has been suspended from the Organization of American States; in 1964 the OAS imposed sanctions. Also during 1964–75 Cuba was excluded from the deliberations of the Latin American Group within UNCTAD, which delayed its ability to join the Group of 77 before 1971 when its membership was sponsored by the African and Asian Groups and was not opposed by the Latin American Group.

78. A. Segal, 1983b, pp. 130–3.

79. W. M. LeoGrande, 1980, p. 66.

80. *ibid.*, p. 69.

The seemingly asymmetrical nature of Cuba's role in Africa, which has led one observer to lament this case of 'microdependency',[81] is perhaps better viewed as one of reciprocity, given the mutual interests of the actors involved in consolidating their ties within an ideological framework of burgeoning Third-World solidarity. Cuba's consistent commitment to advancing its Third-World identity was a significant motivation as well as a consequence of the African connection. Not only was Cuba the only Latin American/Caribbean founding member of the Non-Aligned Movement in 1961, but until joined by some other recently independent Anglophone Caribbean states in the late 1960s it was the movement's only such full member. Its role in the launching of the Tri-Continental Solidarity Organization in 1966 was another notable Third-World-focused initiative. And the selection of Cuba to chair the Non-Aligned Movement from 1979 to 1982 was the most revealing testimony of all to its political credentials among the dominant Afro-Asian interests in that major Third-World forum.

While deciding on Havana as the site of the Sixth Non-Aligned Summit scheduled for 1979, the Fifth Summit of 1976, meeting in Sri Lanka, formally congratulated Cuba for keeping militaristic South Africa at bay in Angola. As manifested in Cuba's decisive assault against an expansionist *apartheid* regime, in Brazil's ambivalent posture during the period of Portuguese colonialism, and in the firm diplomatic support among the newly independent Caribbean states for Southern African liberation struggles, the challenges associated with colonialism and racism in Southern Africa came to have significant bearing on the patterns of political relations being forged between Africa and the Latin American/Caribbean region.

African states increasingly sought to mobilize Latin American/Caribbean support for Southern African liberation causes, which explains the concern which began to develop in the late 1970s when an expansionist South Africa, in need of allies, began to court actively certain potentially receptive Latin American states to build strategic and economic ties.[82] The fact that such options were being broached on both sides was a clear reminder that there still remained a measure of political ambivalence in certain critical areas of Latin America's relations with Africa, standing in marked contrast to the solidarity attained with respect to international economic matters.

However, the entry for the first time during the 1970s of non-aligned organizational activities in the Latin American/Caribbean region – notably the Third Conference of Ministers of the Non-Aligned Movement in Georgetown, Guyana, in 1972 and the Sixth Summit in Havana in 1979 –

81. A. A. Mazrui, 1981.
82. D. Fig, 1984, pp. 239–55; E. Kannyo, 1982, pp. 52–59; North American Congress on Latin America, 1982.

mainly spearheaded by Caribbean actors, together with a slowly but steadily rising Latin American representation in the movement, seemed suggestive of an emerging potential for securing Latin America's political ties with Africa on a firmer foundation.

Africa within the Third-World movement

The expansion of independent Africa's political, economic and cultural ties with other Third-World regions, while varying in scope and intensity, collectively served to give shape and direction to a self-conscious Third-World movement challenging the international *status quo* and intent on transforming traditional international mores and structures historically implicated in the subordination of the Third World.

To comprehend Africa's role in that wider process it is profitable to focus first on the Non-Aligned Movement which emerged as the Third World's most potent organized political expression, and secondly on the new international economic order (NIEO) which in the 1970s came to represent the capstone of the Third World's economic challenge.

Africa and the Non-Aligned Movement

While its philosophical origins are often dated back to the Bandung Conference of 1955, the first Non-Aligned Summit was convened in 1961 in Belgrade among certain Afro-Asian states, Cuba and Yugoslavia. Professing an attitude of independence from Cold-War alliances and from East–West military blocs, the Non-Aligned Movement soon came to transcend its initial emphasis on international strategic issues arising in the context of East–West rivalries to become a proactive voice for Third-World political, racial and economic liberation.[83]

As indicated in Table 28.4, the Non-Aligned Movement experienced a growth in participation from 25 at the First Summit Conference in 1961, to 92 at the Sixth Summit in 1979, with Africa contributing the largest regional representation beginning with the Second Summit in 1964. Africa's numerical dominance in the movement arose less because that continent is comprised of the largest number of states than as a result of a conscious political decision by the OAU at its founding in 1963 to embrace non-alignment as a collective imperative. The explicit enunciation in the OAU's Charter of an 'affirmation of a policy of non-alignment with regard to all blocs', thus resulted in Africa being the only continent fully identified with the Non-Aligned Movement.

Consequent on the OAU's decision, the influx of African membership

83. R. Jaipal, 1983; O. Jankowitsch and K. Sauvant, 1980, pp. 41–77; G. H. Jansen, 1966; R. A. Mortimer,1980, pp. 6–42 and 74–94; P. Willets, 1978; G. Williams, 1981, pp. 46–65.

TABLE 28.4 *Record of participation in Non-Aligned Summit Conferences, 1961–79*

| Summit | Date | Location | African[b] | Asian[c] | Full membership in attendance[a] | | | Total[g] |
					Caribbean[d]	Latin American[e]	European[f]	
1st	1961	Belgrade	11	12	1	0	1	25
2nd	1964	Cairo	29	16	1	0	1	47
3rd	1970	Lusaka	32	16	4	0	1	53
4th	1973	Algiers	40	26	4	3	2	75
5th	1976	Colombo	47	29	4	3	2	85
6th	1979	Havana	50	29	6	5	2	92

[a] Full membership – as distinct from officially recognized Observers or Guests which are excluded from this Table – has at times been extended to provisional governments and liberation movements, mostly from Africa (see Note (b) below), the only other such cases being the admission of the Provisional Revolutionary Government of South Vietnam at the 1973 Summit and of the Palestine Liberation Organization since 1976.

[b] 1961 membership included colonial Algeria, represented by a provisional government until its independence in 1962. 1964 membership included colonial Angola, then represented by a provisional government, the Angolan Revolutionary Government in Exile (GRAE) led by Holden Roberto of the National Front for the Liberation of Angola (FNLA). When subsequently GRAE/FNLA ceased to be recognized by the Organization of African Unity, Angola's full membership was suspended until its acquisition of independence in 1975. 1979 membership included two African liberation movements, the South West African People's Organization (SWAPO) and the Patriotic Front (of Zimbabwe).

[c] Including Cyprus, a founding member which, while considered 'European' in certain respects, has come to be identified more regularly as part of the Afro-Asian coalition.

[d] Cuba (1961); Guyana, Jamaica, Trinidad and Tobago (1970); Grenada, Suriname (1979).

[e] Argentina, Peru, Chile (1973); Panama (1976); Bolivia, Nicaragua (1979). Following Salvador Allende's overthrow after the 1973 Summit, Chile's participation ceased.

[f] Yugoslavia (1961); Malta (1973).

[g] These totals are, in some instances, slightly lower than the full membership of the Non-Aligned Movement at that given time, due to occasional absences or exclusions of some members from certain summit conferences. For example, while the full 1979 membership was 95, the attendance at the 6th Summit was 92 as a result of the absences of Chad and Saudi Arabia and the exclusion of the two rival Kampuchean delegations.

into the Non-Aligned Movement, while on the one hand making the movement more ideologically diffuse and hence less cohesive than previously, on the other hand served more positively to strengthen it in many ways. First, with this expanded organizational infrastructure, its legitimacy as the Third World's major political voice could be better established. Secondly, this widening of ideological credentials for membership thereafter helped to minimize the type of controversies which had affected the First Summit as to which states were or were not ideologically acceptable for non-aligned membership. Thirdly, the African influx guaranteed that thereafter the movement would become even more active on a wider range of North–South issues, given the acute sensitivity of Africans to the fused challenges of political, economic and racial liberation on a continent in the throes of decolonization and early nationhood.

Besides strengthening the membership base of the Non-Aligned Movement, Africa also contributed some of the movement's most outstanding leaders. The first such example was Egypt's Gamāl 'Abd al-Nasser, who along with President Tito of Yugoslavia and Prime Minister Nehru of India were the real architects of non-alignment,[84] it being not accidental that the Preparatory Meeting for the First Summit (1961) and the Second Summit Conference (1964) were both held in Cairo. Ghana's Kwame Nkrumah, who was also a founding member of the movement when launched officially in 1961, played an exceptionally important role in helping to establish newly independent Africa's commitment to non-alignment which within Ghana's first year of independence had emerged as a cornerstone of its foreign policy and of its pan-African outlook.[85]

From the late 1960s through to the 1970s, other African leaders contributed decisively to the expansion and transformation of the vision of non-alignment. Zambia's Kenneth Kaunda, for example, in hosting the Third Summit of 1970, helped to insert the commitments of the non-aligned more uncompromisingly on the requirements of Southern African liberation and, as well, chaired the movement during a critical period of programmatic transition toward economic liberation objectives. Tanzania's Julius Nyerere at the same time emerged as one of the most important ideological catalysts for the movement's transforming focus,[86] even while Algeria's Houari Boumedienne, who succeeded Kaunda as chairman, became a most effective mobilizer of the movement's newly established mission in search of a new international economic order.

The choice of African sites for the Second, Third and Fourth Non-Aligned Summit Conferences – Cairo in 1964, Lusaka in 1970 and Algiers in 1973 – as well as Egypt's hosting of the 1961 Preparatory Meeting preceding the First Summit Conference in Belgrade, was symptomatic of

---

84. G. A. Nasser, *c.* 1966, provides glimpses of his evolving thoughts on non-alignment.
85. K. Nkrumah, 1958b, pp. 45–53.
86. J. K. Nyerere, 1970c.

PLATE 28.3   *From left to right: J. B. Tito of Yugoslavia, A. Ben Bella of Algeria, A. M. Obote of Uganda and H. Bourguiba of Tunisia at the Second Non-Aligned Conference in Cairo, 5–10 October 1964*

PLATE 28.4   *The Fourth Summit Conference of Non-Aligned Countries, Algiers, September 1973*

865

Africa's critical contributions to the movement's early development and eventual consolidation. For this was the crucial first decade of the movement's emergence, then of its institutionalization, and finally of its programmatic transformation.

Throughout the first two decades of the Non-Aligned Movement's existence, African developments and concerns bore profoundly on its purpose and direction. This was apparent from the outset, since a major 'factor in bringing the Non-Aligned together was the importance attached to African issues in 1960',[87] such as the violence of the *apartheid* South African state exhibited in the Sharpeville massacre in March of that year, the heightening ferocity of the Algerian war of independence and the breakdown of civil order in the ex-Belgian Congo (now Zaire).

Subsequently, the movement's much more sharpened anti-imperialist thrust which had become manifest by the early 1970s, coupled with its programmatic transformation assigning priority to the search for a New International Economic Order, were largely a product of Africa's objective political and socio-economic condition within the international system and of the subjective reaction of Africans to that state of affairs.

In search of a New International Economic Order (NIEO)

The Non-Aligned Movement's programmatic transition by the 1970s did not suddenly materialize, representing instead a rising Third-World concern from the 1950s with the structure of international economic relations. Thus while the NIEO as such made its first formal appearance in the early 1970s, it can also be seen as a longer-run process of Third-World mobilization for international economic change.[88]

The expression 'New International Economic Order' first formally appeared in the September 1973 Economic Declaration of the Fourth Non-Aligned Summit Conference in Algiers. It was soon after launched as the basis for the April 1974 formal discussions on raw materials and development for which the Sixth Special Session of the United Nations General Assembly was convened, and at which the Declaration and Action Programme on the Establishment of a New International Economic Order was adopted.[89] The NIEO was further formalized in December 1974 with the UN General Assembly's adoption of the Charter of Economic Rights and Duties of States.[90]

87. P. Willetts, 1978, p. 11.
88. R. A. Mortimer, 1980, and G. Williams, 1981, contain useful overviews of the development of the NIEO process.
89. UN General Assembly Resolutions 3201 (S–VI) and 3202 (S–VI) of 1 May 1974.
90. UN General Assembly Resolution 3281 (XXIX) of 12 December 1974, adopted by a vote of 120 to 6, with 10 abstentions. Voting against were Belgium, Denmark, the Federal Republic of Germany, Luxembourg, the United Kingdom and the United States.

A Seventh Special Session of the General Assembly convened in September 1975 on development and co-operation took the NIEO deliberations a stage further, as also did the initiation of the North–South dialogue in the shape of the Conference on International Economic Cooperation (which became known as the North–South Conference) between eight developed and 19 underdeveloped nations lasting from 1975 to 1977. By the late 1970s the promises as well as the frustrations of implementing the NIEO agenda gave rise to a growing Third-World recognition of a need to institutionalize South–South economic relationships on a firmer footing.

The essence of the NIEO was a search by the South (Third World) for a fundamental restructuring of the world economy, mainly in the areas of international trade, economic aid, foreign investment, technology transfer and international monetary reform. This represented the capstone and harmonization of a variety of Third-World pressures for international economic change over the previous two decades.

For example, the communiqué from the Bandung Conference of 1955 included a section exclusively devoted to 'economic co-operation'. Motivated by the formation of the European Economic Community, the First Economic Conference for Afro-Asian countries was convened in Cairo in 1958, followed by a Second Afro-Asian Economic Conference, again in Cairo, in 1960, both meetings attracting 10–11 African delegations of the 38 present on each occasion. A 1962 Conference on the Problems of Developing Countries produced the Cairo Declaration of 1962 signed by 36 mostly Afro-Asian countries – only four being from Latin America – pledging themselves to co-operate to strengthen the economic and social activities of the United Nations.

A major milestone in this evolving Third-World challenge to the traditional international economic order was the establishment of UNCTAD (United Nations Conference on Trade and Development) in 1964 as a permanent organ of the United Nations General Assembly. Formed because of the Third World's dissatisfaction with the existing international trading system, represented by the General Agreement on Tariffs and Trade which had been created exclusively by the Western world, UNCTAD's full conferences held every three to four years provided a forum where Third-World collective interests were aired and co-ordinated, from UNCTAD I in 1964 to UNCTAD V in 1979.

One of UNCTAD'S main legacies was in providing a base for the formation of the Group of 77, the Third World's main economic mobilizing and bargaining unit,[91] which, as documented in Table 28.5, expanded its original membership base of 77 to encompass by 1980 a full complement of Third-World participants numbering 122. Among the most lasting contributions of the Group of 77 was the formulation of the

91. K. P. Sauvant, 1980.

TABLE 28.5 *Composition of the Group of 77*, 1964–80*

Year	Africa[a]	Asia[b]	Caribbean[c]	Latin America[d]	Europe[e]	Total
1964	32	23	4	17	1	77
1980	50	39	13	17	3	122

*Formed in 1964 by the then 77 developing countries participating in the first UNCTAD session, for the purpose of presenting a common bargaining front in international trade and related economic negotiations.

[a] All independent states in Africa, excepting South Africa, are in the Group.

[b] Almost all states (including Cyprus) in Asia–the Pacific–Oceania are in the Group, significant exceptions being Australia, China, Israel, Japan, New Zealand and Turkey.

[c] All independent Caribbean states are members.

[d] All Latin American states are members.

[e] Yugoslavia was a founding member, Romania and Malta subsequently joined.

'Algiers Charter' in 1967, developed at its First Ministerial Conference as a joint bargaining strategy for UNCTAD II. The Algiers Charter came to be regarded as 'the Third World's first comprehensive platform on development', as 'a major achievement in Third World organizing', and as a significant precursor 'of the demands that would be reiterated with greater force in the mid-1970s'.[92]

Paralleling such Group-of-77 initiatives was a distinctive shift in the focus of the Non-Aligned Movement by the late 1960s to embrace international economic concerns as a movement priority. Thus for the first time at the Third Summit Conference in Luska in 1970 two separate declarations were adopted, one on political, the other on economic issues. The 1972 Conference of Ministers of the Non-Aligned Movement, meeting in Georgetown, Guyana, took matters a step further by developing an 'Action Programme for Economic Co-operation' while a year later, at the 1973 Algiers Summit Conference, the NIEO was for the first time articulated as such. The Non-Aligned Movement thus came to play a critical 'initiating role' in the formulation of the NIEO.[93]

In this developing context, the dramatic actions by the OPEC states in 1973 to increase the volume of their oil revenues while seeking more control over these resources is best seen as another complementary Third-World strategy to redress traditional international economic imbalances. It is not without significance that Boumedienne was simultaneously a leading force behind the OPEC and wider NIEO challenges. Also, despite the economic hardships visited on the Third-World states without oil resources, a measure of mutual empathy developed as the OPEC model seemed to commend itself as a way in which the formation of commodity

92. R. A. Mortimer, 1980, p. 28.
93. O. Jankowitsch and K. Sauvant, 1980.

producer organizations might assist in the establishment of their economic sovereignty.[94]

What the NIEO thus came to represent was a convergence of previous institutional initiatives from all parts of the Third World. If Latin Americans were the most significant force behind the establishment of UNCTAD, Africans were mainly responsible for consolidating and transforming the role of the Non-Aligned Movement along such paths, while the Arab–Islamic world primarily gave the impetus for enjoining producer associations in the Third-World economic challenge.

But at all these levels, as well as others, Africa's presence and impact was critical. 'Perhaps more than any other event', it has been argued, the impact of African decolonization on the structure of the United Nations 'changed the focus of the international community towards the problems of the LDCs'.[95] The special recognition assigned in NIEO declarations to the problems of the LDCs (see Table 28.2 above) and to landlocked countries, both of which abound in Africa, further illustrate the impact of the African condition.

Africa's important role in the establishment of the ACP Group (Africa–Caribbean–Pacific Group of States) as a permanent negotiating force with the European Economic Community in 1975 was another reminder of that continent's impact on the course of international economic change.[96] So too were the exceptional roles played by Egypt in the late 1950s to early 1960s, and more so by Algeria a decade later,[97] in mobilizing the Third-World economic challenge. And by the late 1970s, Julius Nyerere stood out as one of the Third World's leading consciences, confident in the belief in the necessity and possibility of meaningful Third-World self-reliance within institutionalized frameworks of South–South co-operation.[98]

Africa and the continuing Third-World challenge

As the world entered the 1980s, there was a distinct decline in the euphoria which attended the heightened Third-World challenge of the 1970s. An increasing economic malaise in Africa, highlighted especially in drought- and famine-stricken areas, was coming to be an often cited symptom of a wider Third-World malaise. Third-World countries being burdened by an unceasing international recession and an increasing

94. K. P. Sauvant, 1980, pp. 31–5, contains data on the range and membership of such 'producers' associations' as of 1978.

95. G. Williams, 1981, p. 4.

96. K. Hall and B. W. Blake, 1979; J. Ravenhill, 1985; R. Yakemtchouk, 1977.

97. R. A. Mortimer, 1980, emphasizes Algeria's critical role under Boumedienne at various stages of his analysis, especially in Chapter 3, pp. 24–42.

98. J. K. Nyerere, 1979a.

indebtedness were becoming more vulnerable. The North–South dialogue began to grind to a halt.

In such conditions it is easy for Third-World and especially African sympathizers to adopt a pessimistic outlook. This is where an historical perspective may serve as a tempering measure, not to blind the observer to the difficulties ahead but also to issue a reminder of the past obstacles hurdled or challenged.

As this chapter is being completed in the 1980s it is fitting to conclude with two historical reminders, which also serve to take us back to where this essay began. The year 1985 was the hundredth anniversary of the Congress of Berlin where the partition of Africa was agreed on; it was also the thirtieth anniversary of the Bandung Conference which was the first major Afro-Asian co-ordinated challenge to the kind of system represented by the Congress of Berlin. Viewed from those two perspectives, Africa's relations with the developing regions and Africa's role in the Third-World movement have made many notable strides.

Africa and the United Nations since 1945

Edmond Kwam KOUASSI

The United Nations (UN) as we know it today is the child of two major historical forces of the twentieth century – the Second World War and the process of post-war decolonization.[1] The Second World War had heightened the urgency for establishing a global body which was dedicated to the maintenance of peace. Decolonization had transformed the composition of that global body and tilted the balance of opinion within its more representative institutions.

The world conflict and the process of decolonization were themselves interlinked, and Africa was of course an integral part of both global episodes. The horrors and destruction of the Second World War prepared international opinion for another experiment in global peace-making – a more representative body than the League of Nations, and hopefully a more effective one. The brutalities of aggression and war crimes, the obscenities and inhumanities of genocide against the Jews and others, the sheer scale of destruction of life and property – all these factors made the international community ready for another global experiment.

But it was not just the war which shaped the new world body. As we shall see, it was also the era of decolonization. Many countries formerly under colonial domination achieved independence during the first 25 years of the existence of the United Nations so that the number of member nations of the Organization rose from 51 to 157 in 1980. In this connection the changes affecting Africa are undoubtedly the most striking. Thus Africa gradually emerged from a state of servitude and subjection, and especially from 1960, honestly and earnestly began to achieve its status as a continent of sovereign nations eager to balance its relations with the rest of the world.

Africa was also very poorly represented at the United Nations in 1945, one might say symbolically represented by four theoretically independent but practically dependent states. These were Ethiopia, Liberia, Egypt and

1. 'Decolonization' is defined here as the termination of colonial rule, the dismantling of colonial institutions and the elimination of colonial styles and values. While the initiative for colonization is normally taken by the imperial power, the initiative for *decolonization* usually comes from the colonized and their struggle for liberation.

871

South Africa. Nor was Africa represented at all in the equitable geo-graphical distribution of non-permanent seats on the Security Council as required by Article 23, paragraph 1, of the United Nations Charter. The agreement which operated within the organization from 1946 onwards distributed the non-permanent seats between the various regions of the world as follows: two for Latin America, one for Western Europe, one for Eastern Europe, one for the Near East and one for the Commonwealth. Africa was left out of account, and it was only much later, on 17 December 1963, that Resolution 1991 (XVIII) of the General Assembly did it justice by allocating five of the ten non-permanent seats on the Security Council to Africa and Asia.

So long as Africa remained in a state of dependence (as was the case from 1945 to 1960), the United Nations considered that it had a mission of emancipation and a responsibility of liberation towards it. From then on the UN links and contacts with Africa were unilateral and in some respects paternalistic relationships, inasmuch as they stemmed from actions planned and decided by external foreign protagonists, naturally inclined to confuse Africa's interests with those of the international community or even with their own.

But in retrospect we can now identify more clearly the wider pattern of relationships. Since its formation in San Francisco in 1945 the United Nations has played three main roles (a number of conflicting roles) in relation to Africa: the UN as a collective imperial power which it inherited from the League of Nations; secondly, as an ally of liberation; and thirdly, as a partner in development. It is these roles which this chapter will examine, and our technique here will, whenever possible, be that of examining case-studies of those three roles of the United Nations.

Because the world body's imperial role ('absentee landlord') was so benevolent, it is not easy to disentangle it from the world body's role as an ally of liberation. Unlike other imperial powers, the United Nations was keen to speed up the pace of decolonization. The UN therefore often clashed with those very colonial powers that were administering the trusteeships on its behalf. Where the world body's role as a collective imperialist ended and its role as an ally of liberation began was not always easy to ascertain. The special cases of Namibia and the Ewe people illustrated some of the dilemmas. Let us examine the latter case in historical detail.

The UN as benevolent imperialist

On 10 April 1947, while the United Nations Trusteeship Council was holding its first session, its chairman received a telegram from Accra (Gold Coast, now Ghana) which read as follows:

872

All Ewe Conference comprising Ewe of French Togoland, British Togoland, Gold Coast, greetings. We deplore and protest against partition of Eweland. Request unification of Eweland under single administration to be chosen by people themselves by plebiscite.

The Ewe affair was beginning. From its first meeting in 1947 until the independence of French Togo in 1960 the Trusteeship Council did not hold a single session without this question being dealt with directly or indirectly.

For the Trusteeship Council it was the main topic for which it drew up its doctrine and part of its method of working. For the General Assembly of the United Nations it was the avenue through which many governments began to tackle the problems of colonial politics and then engaged in a campaign for decolonization.

The Ewe habitat extends continuously over almost the whole of the south of present-day Togo and the south-east of present-day Ghana, and sporadically in the south of the People's Republic of Benin and Nigeria.

During the partition of Africa after the Berlin Conference of 1884–5 most Ewe peoples were in German Togoland, with some scattered in the Gold Coast and Nigeria. When German Togoland was partitioned into English and French zones on 1 October 1920 (Fig. 29.1) the Ewe were still more divided; but there was little agitation for their reunification until the Second World War. In 1943 a press campaign began in the Gold Coast (Ghana) demanding the annexation of Togoland under a French mandate; and in 1944 a pan-Ewe movement, the 'All Ewe Conference', was set up. On the French side the *Comité de l'unité togolaise* (CUT), the Committee for Togolese Unity, until then a purely cultural association, transformed itself so as to carry out similar propaganda, and appointed as its secretary-general Mr Sylvanus Olympio, then an official with the United Africa Company (a subsidiary of the Unilever group), later to become Togo's first president. These were the bodies that were to approach the United Nations in 1947.

The Ewe affair came before the Trusteeship Council again at its November 1947 session. Mr Sylvanus Olympio put the Ewe point of view to the Council, and criticized the Franco-British memorandum whose solutions he regarded as inadequate.

During the first debate it was noteworthy that the Council paid great attention to the petitioners, who were allowed to express their point of view to it by word of mouth. Whereas in the Mandates Committee of the League of Nations, dominated by the colonial powers, the latter enjoyed complete confidence, in the Trusteeship Council, in which they were a minority, the atmosphere was slightly anti-colonialist. If the voting was not more critical of the British and French it was partly because the solidarity between London and Paris impressed the Council.

873

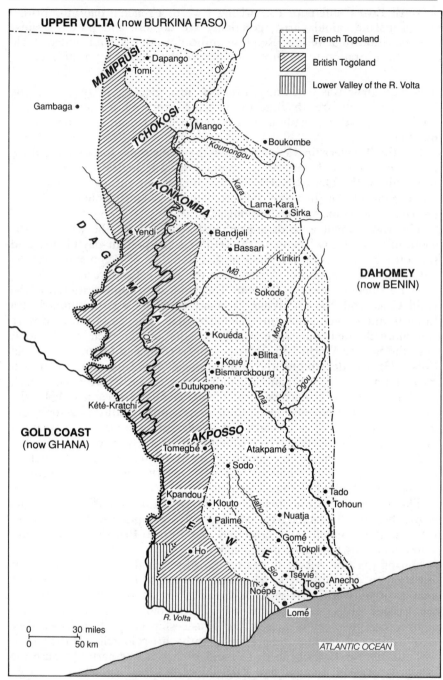

UPPER VOLTA (now BURKINA FASO)

French Togoland

British Togoland

Lower Valley of the R. Volta

MAMPRUSI

• Dapango

• Tomi

Oti

• Gambaga

TCHOKOSI

• Mango

• Boukombe

Koumongou

KONKOMBA

Kara

Lama-Kara •

• Sirka

D A G O M B A

• Yendi

• Bandjeli

• Bassari

• Kirikiri

Mô

• Sokode

DAHOMEY
(now BENIN)

Oti

Mono

• Kouéda

• Koué • Blitta

• Bismarckbourg

Ana

Ogou

• Dutukpene

Kété-Kratchi

AKPOSSO

GOLD COAST
(now GHANA)

Tomegbé •

Atakpamé •

• Sodo

• Tado

Kpandou •

• Klouto

• Tohoun

E

• Palimé

• Nuatja

Haho

W

• Gomé

E

• Ho

Tokpli •

Sio

• Tsévié

Anecho

Noépé •

Togo

Lomé

R. Volta

0   30 miles

0   50 km

ATLANTIC OCEAN

FIG. 29.1 *Togoland in 1919 – Franco–British Declaration, London, 10 July 1919 (after*
E. K. Kouassi)

In late December 1949–early January 1950, a UN visiting mission went to the area and reviewed the main points of the Ewe problem. It concluded that the problem was not merely an economic one:

> Many Togolese on both sides of the border adopt a firm political position, and only mention the border difficulties as one argument among others; *they proclaim that unification is an essential step on the road to self-government or independence.*

In other words they considered that self-government or independence, which according to the Charter are the basic objectives of the trusteeship system, must be achieved in the framework of a Togolese state with borders more or less corresponding to those of the former German Togoland and that the maintenance of the existing dual administration was incompatible with the fulfilment of their hopes.

During 1950 the administering authorities suggested enlarging the Consultative Committee to include elected, not appointed, members to represent public opinion. It also became clear that on the British side the northern peoples were asking to become part of the Gold Coast, whereas on the French side they were asking for the *status quo*. In this situation, the problem being strictly confined to the Ewe, it seemed out of the question to reconstitute ex-German Togoland.

The elections to the 'enlarged' Consultative Committee took place in the autumn of 1950. They occurred without any particular difficulty in British Togoland. In French Togoland, on the other hand, the CUT, sensing that victory would be denied because of the electoral system adopted, withdrew all its candidates four days before the elections. The seats reserved for it were given to its opponent, the *Parti togolais du progrès* (PTP), the Togolese Progressive Party. Out of a total of 47 members elected, eight (British Togoland) were in favour of becoming part of the Gold Coast, 15 in favour of Ewe unification, and 24 in favour of the *status quo*. The Committee met in November, but with six British Ewe delegates boycotting it and the CUT representatives replaced by those of the PTP, it could only come down on the side of the administering authorities. Hence the majority declared itself against Ewe unification.

The Fourth Committee of the United Nations General Assembly, which was then beginning its session, received petitions blaming the French government for the way the elections were carried out and also for the arbitrary arrests. Several delegates criticized the attitude of the French government, which had to have an inquiry set up into the propriety of the electoral procedure. For the first time at the United Nations, an administering power was the subject of harsh criticism from members not belonging to the communist bloc. At the eighth session of the Trusteeship Council (February–March 1951) the British and French found themselves on the defensive, although they had conscientiously prepared the ground in Washington and New York. The prevailing

875

impression was that the administering powers were using delaying tactics, and that firm measures should be taken to put a stop to this: the Americans and Iraqis suggested the holding of fresh elections, at any rate in the south. In the end the Council urged the administering authorities to find a solution to the problem through the enlarged Committee.

At the ninth session of the Trusteeship Council in May 1951, Britain and France seemed to lack the imagination to submit a plan that would satisfy the Council. The British were mainly concerned with the aftermath of internal self-government in the Gold Coast, while the French were envisaging sweeping reforms in West Africa: so on both sides it was thought better not to change the situation in the Togolands. Inasmuch as these reforms represented not a solution to the Ewe problem but merely a way of improving the lot of the Ewe, they were criticized by the representatives of various political bodies that gave evidence to the Council, and also by the Dutch, the Dominicans and the Argentines, who found them insufficiently constructive.

The British and French suggested the setting up of a new 'Joint Council for Togolese Affairs', whose objective would be 'to provide a meeting-place for the representatives of the peoples of the two Togos at which views could be exchanged about the development of these territories, and the measures taken co-ordinated and followed up so as to ensure their progress in all fields'. In November the affair came before the seventh session of the General Assembly. This idea was again put forward, and was criticized by 'the Ewe nationalists'.

The Fourth Committee recommended that the administering authorities should consult the parties and groups before setting up the Joint Council, and also enlarge its scope so as to enable it to consider all Ewe problems and unification. It also asked the Trusteeship Council to organize a visit to carry out a thorough examination of the problem and make recommendations. Thus the higher authority (the Fourth Committee of the General Assembly) showed itself more severe towards the administering authorities than the lower authorities (the Council). At this point the Ewe affair ceased to be a separate issue and became merely part of a triple problem, the other two being: the union of British Togoland with the Gold Coast, and self-government for the latter; and the closer integration of French Togoland with the French Union, and at the same time the beginning of internal self-government. What had initially been an ethnic and cultural problem had now become territorial and political.

The special mission of the Trusteeship Council stayed in the area for August and September 1951, toured the territories for five weeks, and received 2896 petitions. Its report summed up the situation. A majority of the population favoured independence, but attached conditions: for the British Togolese, to become Ghanaians; and for the French Togolese, to join the French Union which in practice multiplied the demands for unification.

876

On the recommendation of the Visiting Committee, the Trusteeship Council in November 1955 adopted the principle of a referendum to ascertain the wishes of the people. In British Togoland the referendum produced 93 000 votes in favour of annexation to the Gold Coast and 67 000 against; but in the south – that is, in Ewe country proper – the majority was against annexation. The Trusteeship Council recommended the annexation of British Togoland to the Gold Coast and the abrogation of the trusteeship agreement on independence day. Ghana, resulting from the union of the former Gold Coast and southern British Togoland, became a member of the United Nations in 1957.

On the French side, the independence of the Gold Coast brought with it self-government for Togo. In 1956 the self-governing Republic of Togo was proclaimed, and a referendum was held in October. There were 331 000 votes for adopting a new system and 22 000 for maintaining the trusteeship system.

Having, in the words of the Charter, achieved 'its capability to govern itself', Togo could free itself from the trusteeship agreements. But the Trusteeship Council refused to abrogate its agreements, asking for the Togolese legislative assembly to be re-elected by universal suffrage and for the elections to be supervised by a United Nations commissioner with a team of observers. Eventually the trusteeship agreements were abrogated on 27 April 1960, the day on which Togo was declared independent.

Thus the Ewe affair came to an end, 13 years after it had begun: Ghana was independent; Togo was independent; and the Ewe were still divided. The United Nations had terminated one more responsibility as a collective imperial power.

The Congo: collective imperialism in transition

If there is a country the history of whose decolonization is closely bound up with the work of the United Nations, it is surely the former Belgian colony of the Congo, now Zaire (Fig. 29.2).

The pre-conditions of Africa's development are: first, national integrity; and, secondly, basic political stability. Without these, sustained development is but an elusive mirage. The boundaries of the political community have to be intact (national integrity) and the foundations of political authority have to be relatively durable (basic political stability). The greatest challenge faced by the United Nations as a partner in Africa's development came precisely with the independence of the former Belgian Congo – now Zaire. Both the national integrity (boundaries) and the political stability (authority) of the newly-independent state were put into question; and the United Nations was caught in between. But the question still remains: was the Congo mission of the UN a new kind of collective imperialism by the world organization? Or was it a case of the UN as Africa's genuine partner? The United States was initially more supportive

877

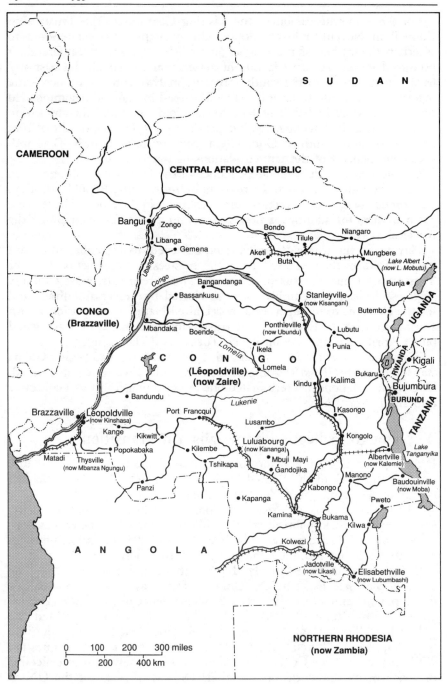

FIG. 29.2   *The Congo–Léopoldville (now Zaire) (after E. K. Kouassi)*

of the Congo's national integrity (preventing the Congo's disintegration) than of its basic political stability (supporting the duly elected government of Patrice Lumumba as prime minister). The vacillation of both the UN's secretary-general and the United States finally resulted in the assassination of Patrice Lumumba. Stability was purchased at the cost of political legitimacy. And the background to this saga did indeed go back almost to Independence Day in what was then Léopoldville, the capital of the newly 'liberated' Belgian Congo. It is to this saga that we must now turn as a special case-study of the United Nations as a partner in Africa's development, an ally in Africa's liberation and, paradoxically, as a collective imperial power in a new guise at the same time.

Two of the leading actors of the 1960–1 drama of the Congo lost their lives during this dubious combat: Lumumba was assassinated and Hammarskjöld died in a still unexplained aeroplane 'accident'.[2]

From 15 July 1960, when the first UN peace-keeping troops arrived in the Congolese capital, Léopoldville, to 14 January 1963, when the government of Katanga at last agreed to end its secession, none of the vicissitudes of the history of the Congo can be analysed without reference to the UN attitude. The latter had to respond to the appeal made to it by the first Congolese central government. The crisis included the following:

(1) the Congo's state of unpreparedness for the independence formally granted by Belgium;
(2) the virtual absence of trained technical, political and military personnel; and
(3) the arrogance of the representatives of the former colonial power.

In a daily order dated 5 July 1960, the Belgian General Jansens, commander of the Congolese gendarmerie, bluntly told his men: 'Independence is all right for civilians. For soldiers there is only discipline. Before 30 June you had white officers . . . Nothing has changed'.

For the Congolese soldiers who had been present at the independence celebrations and had heard Lumumba's speech in the presence of the King of the Belgians, this was a flagrant provocation to African history: for them something had changed. Mutiny broke out in the 'Léopold II' camps on the outskirts of the capital; and at Thysville, 200 kilometres away, the garrisons called for the Africanization of senior ranks in the gendarmerie. This revolt, brought about by the attitude of the Belgian officers, was the starting-point of the whole affair. During the night of 5 July Lumumba tried to restore calm in the mutinous camps; on the 6th he dismissed Jansens and appointed his uncle Lundula and his former secretary Mobutu as commanders of the gendarmerie. He promoted

2. C. Roire, 1967.

all the Congolese non-commissioned officers. But the military disorder intensified.

Some Europeans were ill-treated, others threatened, by this mutiny of their former servants. This affair of the gendarmerie gave the Belgians an excuse to reinforce their contingents which had remained in the country. Several battalions of parachutists were sent to Léopoldville, Luluabourg and Elisabethville to protect Belgian nationals. In the capital of Katanga province it was a matter not only of regaining control of the gendarmerie but also of making a success of secession. Three days after the arrival of Belgian reinforcements – that is, on 11 July – Tshombe appeared on the scene and proclaimed the 'independence' of the province.

In reply, the central government asked Mr Timberlake, the American ambassador, for 3000 American troops to be sent to the Congo, and Lumumba and Kasavubu cabled the UN secretary-general, then in Geneva, asking for UN military assistance. The Léopoldville government wanted intervention by the United Nations in order to put an end to that of Belgium and in this it enjoyed the support of the Asian and socialist countries as well as the more radical African states which later formed the Casablanca group. A majority of the Security Council, meeting on 13 July, and the Secretary-General, at the suggestion of one of the key figures in this whole period, the Tunisian Mongi Slim, decided to send a United Nations' force to the Congo to restore order.

So the die was cast that day, 14 July 1960: the Mongi Slim resolution (supported by the United States, whereas the British and French stayed completely loyal to Brussels in not wanting any internationalization) simply 'appealed to the Belgian Government to withdraw its troops', and provided for UN military assistance to the Congolese government until 'the National Security forces' were 'able, in the opinion of that government, fully to perform their duties'. This was a long way from the request of Lumumba and Kasavubu. In their second telegram to Hammarskjöld, they said: 'assistance sought aims not restore internal situation in Congo but rather protect national territory against act aggression by troops from metropolitan Belgium'.

On the evening of 15 July the first UN troops, 300 Tunisians and 80 Ghanaians, arrived in Léopoldville under the command of the Swedish General Van Horn. The UN force was deployed in the next few days; and when Lumumba went to the United States at the end of July the peace-keeping force numbered 11 155. The biggest contingents, which were also to play a decisive political role in the next few weeks, were those of Morocco (2465 men), Ghana (2412) and Tunisia (2151). But the presence of the UN troops solved neither of the problems which in the eyes of the Congolese government justified their presence and deployment in the country's territory: the secession of Katanga was being consolidated, and the Belgian troops were still there.

A further meeting of the Security Council took place on 21 and 22

July, producing a further resolution. The Security Council decided to abide by its initial interpretation of the role of the UN force: the maintenance of order. Hammarskjöld's hesitant attitude during this period was partly justified by the emergence into the open of dissensions within the Congolese government. While Lumumba, with his unitarist, centralist views, was demanding the end of the secession of Katanga, if necessary by the use of force, President Kasavubu continued to favour a federal solution; at the beginning of August he telegraphed to the Security Council in this sense. This federal option implicitly suggested that it was still possible to negotiate with Tshombe.

The ambiguity and confusion grew. Thus when the Security Council met for the third time on 8 and 9 August 1960, it was to hear the secretary-general asking to have his powers defined. He wanted to know whether the UN force should proceed to occupy Katanga province by every available means. This clear question was to receive another vague reply from the Security Council: the third Mongi Slim resolution certainly acknowledged that it was 'absolutely necessary' for the UN troops to enter Katanga, but it also said in the next paragraph that the UN force 'will not take part in any internal conflict, will not intervene in such a conflict in any way, and will not be used to influence its outcome'.

In these circumstances, Hammarskjöld had to make some crucial decisions alone. On 10 August, when nobody, not even Belgium, had recognized the independence of Katanga, Hammarskjöld telegraphed to Tshombe to ask for a 'frank exchange of views' about 'the arrangements for deploying United Nations troops in Katanga'. On 12 August he landed at Elisabethville with the French-Moroccan General Kettani and 300 Swedish UN troops: and in two days of talks Tshombe got him to agree to eight of the ten conditions he attached to the entry of UN troops in Katanga. Among them were the undertaking by the UN not to interfere in Katanga's internal or administrative affairs; not to permit the use of means of transport, aircraft or other, to allow elements sent by the Léopoldville government or emissaries of the latter to be introduced into Katanga; and not to meddle in the legal system or administration of Katanga, until the Congolese constitution was finally drawn up and approved by Katanga: the *status quo* would be maintained on the basis of the Katanga constitution. By accepting those terms, the secretary-general agreed to the principle of 'coexistence' between the UN force and Katanga, and implicitly undertook not to help the Congolese central government to regain control of the secessionist province. In trusting Tshombe, and through him the Belgians, the secretary-general made a serious mistake. Not only did the compromise not begin to solve the problem of Katanga's secession, it actually precipitated the start of the conflict between Hammarskjöld and Lumumba which was only to end with the death of the Congolese prime minister. The UN role was getting imperialistic.

On 14 August 1960, Lumumba protested against the Hammarskjöld agreement, and submitted to the United Nations five very precise demands which were completely at odds with the Elisabethville compromise. The Congolese prime minister asked the international organization:

(1) to give Congolese soldiers and police the task of guarding the Congo's aerodromes;

(2) to send African troops immediately to Katanga;

(3) to put aircraft at the disposal of the Congolese central government to transport its troops anywhere in the country;

(4) to proceed at once to seize all the weapons distributed by the Belgians in Katanga and hand these weapons over to the central government; and

(5) at once to withdraw all non-African troops from Katanga.

The crisis deepened and the neo-imperialist tendencies on the part of the officials and troops of the United Nations became obvious when on 5 September, after a meeting with two Belgian envoys, Messrs Denis and Van Bilsen, President Kasavubu decided to dismiss Lumumba, which he announced over the radio at 8.15 p.m. The conflict between the two men had been latent ever since the time of the struggle for independence. Kasavubu naturally chose to make an open break at a time when Lumumba seemed to have lost much of his international weight: only the communist countries, plus the United Arab Republic and Indonesia, supported him fully in his disagreement with Hammarskjöld. The prime minister certainly tried to reply: less than an hour after his rival, he went to the radio station and made a speech in which he said that 'there is no head of state any more'.

On martyrdom and reform

Here we come to one of the most disturbing episodes in the activities of the UN representatives. In the early afternoon of 6 September, Andrew Cordier, a close colleague of Dag Hammarskjöld, commandeered the Ghanaian contingent under the command of Colonel Ankrah to guard the radio-station building, and sent a note to Lumumba forbidding him in future to speak to his fellow-citizens. At the same time Kettani's Moroccan contingent of UN troops surrounded the prime minister's villa. Collective imperialism was using African troops to prevent Lumumba from maintaining the Western independence and territorial integrity of the Congo.

While Lumumba asked in vain to be found a seat on a plane bound for New York, where he wanted to go himself to state his government's position at the UN, Kasavubu, whom the UN then regarded as the only indisputable legitimate authority, went to Manhattan with no difficulty.

PLATE 29.1   *Above left: Dag Hammarskjöld (left), secretary-general of the United Nations, and Joseph Kasavubu (seated right, in profile), president of Congo, meet in Léopoldville on 29 July 1960; above right: M. Tshombe, prime minister of the secessionist province of Katanga (now Shaba), Elisabethville (now Lubumbashi), August 1960; below left: P. Lumumba, prime minister of the Republic of Congo, July 1960; below right: Colonel J. D. Mobutu, chief of staff of the Congo Army, September 1960*

At the conclusion of the discussions, both in the chamber and in the corridors, which lasted from 7 to 22 November, Kasavubu was acknowledged as the only Congolese qualified to appoint a delegation to represent his country.

When Kasavubu returned to Léopoldville in great triumph on the evening of 27 November, Lumumba was finally beaten. The head of the only Congolese central government to have been legally invested by the parliament was thus neutralized. His only hope then was Antoine Gizenga, who on 13 November had replaced Finant at the head of the Stanleyville provincial government. In trying to escape from Léopoldville in December

883

1960 to the Eastern province, he was captured by Mobutu's troops and later sent to Katanga where he was shot in the presence of Tshombe and his ministers on 17 January 1961. It was this anti-Lumumba stance on the part of the United Nations, until the official announcement of Lumumba's death by Munongo on 13 February, that most sickened world public opinion at the time.

Lumumba was not to die in vain. His death at last enabled the Security Council to emerge from the alleged 'neutrality' to which it had confined itself since the beginning of the crisis. The emotion aroused by Lumumba's murder was to compel the United Nations to give its secretary-general somewhat more precise instructions for actions than in the past.

In the tumult aroused by Lumumba's death, the Afro-Asian countries, which had long swung to and fro between the two blocs but were now genuinely indignant, managed to put through a resolution which was to give fresh impetus to UN activities. The text of 21 February, adopted when news had just been received, again through Dayal, of the massacre of six Lumumbist leaders by Kalondji in Kasai, instructed the UN troops to avert the danger of civil war and resort to force 'if necessary, as a last resort' in order to restore peace. The resolution, which also called for steps to be taken to evacuate the mercenaries and 'all Belgian military and paramilitary personnel and political advisers', referred explicitly to the unity and territorial integrity of the Congo. Hammarskjöld could thus, if he wished, put down the Katangan secession and the Belgian intervention by force. However, Kasavubu, whose authority the United Nations had recognized, denied the latter's right to intervene. But on 17 April Kasavubu yielded to the arguments of the secretary-general's two new special envoys, Gardiner from Ghana and Nwokedi from Niger: he agreed to co-operate with the United Nations in return for two promises (which were in fact kept) – the recall of the Indian Dayal and financial assistance for the Léopoldville authorities.

The result of this agreement was the Coquilhatville Conference of all the anti-Lumumbist provinces. Kasavubu said that he acknowledged the validity of the UN resolutions and wished to convene the Congolese parliament. When Tshombe indicated his disagreement soldiers loyal to Kasavubu arrested the Katangan leader; he was to remain under house-arrest at Léopoldville until he agreed to the proposed meeting of parliament. It was briefly supposed that the solution of the Congo's problems was in sight. But this hope was dashed by Tshombe's *volte-face* on his return to Elizabethville. The Congolese parliament met on 27 July; and with an absolute majority of Lumumbists, it elected a government of national unity headed by Adoula. But the problem remained intact: the Congolese army pursued its independent policy, and above all Tshombe and his protectors consolidated their secession. The total number of mercenaries and 'advisers' in Katanga at that time was estimated at 1500.

Yet, right up to the end, the UN officials in the Congo thought that they could fulfil their mission without using force.

On an order signed by Kasavubu, Indian and Swedish troops from 28 August 1961 onwards tried to arrest the mercenaries and 'evacuate' them. The UN troops did occupy the aerodrome and more strategic points of Elisabethville without firing a shot, and took 273 'non-Africans' prisoner, including 237 Belgians. Up to 13 September everything went very well. But when the Indian UN troops, with the agreement of the local UN representative, O'Brien, tried to go on to serious business – the disarming of the mercenaries of Falques and Lasimone – heavy fighting broke out. Everywhere, both at Katima and Jadotville, the UN troops were isolated and surrounded.

This 13 September offensive, which started under bad conditions without having been prepared, still less explicitly approved, by senior officials of the United Nations, was a failure for Hammarskjöld. Through the intermediary of the British, who were much in evidence and very active during this period, Mr Hammarskjöld sought and obtained from Tshombe the promise of a cease-fire and discussions. This was not to be. On 17 September, just after midnight, the aeroplane taking Hammarskjöld to Ndola in Northern Rhodesia (now Zambia) made a sharp turn over the aerodrome and crashed 12 kilometres away. Hammarskjöld's death, like Lumumba's, was not in vain, for it led to the firm decision to put down the secession of Katanga by every possible means, as is evident from the resolution of 21 November 1961 sponsored by U Thant, the new secretary-general. This resolution referred explicitly to the use of force by the UN Congo contingent if necessary to put down the mercenaries and end the secession. The UN force was now given some of the equipment it lacked; in particular the Americans provided jet aircraft. The aim of the military operation launched by the UN troops on 18 December was exclusively political; to get Tshombe to negotiate. Thus, when the centre of Elisabethville had been occupied, those who had most strongly supported the UN initiative, namely the Americans, exerted themselves to bring it to an end by making Tshombe agree to negotiate with Léopoldville. When these negotiations were frustrated by Tshombe's vacillations and evasions, the UN with the full backing of the United States launched a decisive offensive. Briskly carried out in the first days of January 1963, this ended in the declaration of submission by the Katanga ministers. By the time his last bastion at Kolwezi fell on 21 January, Tshombe was already done for: a week before, the *Union minière* had announced that from now on it was ready to pay its mining royalties to the central government. The mercenaries for their part opted to seek temporary refuge in Angola. Tshombe, after trying to stay on the political stage for a few more months, left for Europe on 15 June 1963.

He was not to return to the Congo until a year later, on 26 June 1964, four days before the departure of the UN troops, who despite all the

885

vacillations of their superiors had finally managed to put down the secession. Had the UN really finished its job in the military field? If its mandate had really been to establish peace in the Congo, the UN force would no doubt have stayed there much longer: 1964 was, after all, the year of the most terrible war the country had known since independence. The 'rebellion' spread, but the United Nations did not intervene.

During the last months of their stay, the 5350 UN troops who had stayed did little more than stand surety for the legitimacy of Adoula's central government. Nobody suggested keeping a UN military presence in the Congo at dawn on 30 June 1964.

Did the UN fulfil its mission in the Congo? Would the Congo have emerged from chaos sooner if the international organization had acted more quickly and forcefully against the Katangan secession and its supporters in certain European countries? Did the United Nations ensure success for the interests of the whole international community, or for those of only one camp? These questions, which only history will perhaps answer, cannot alter the facts: the intervention of the United Nations, called for by Patrice Lumumba, was necessary; the 'cold war' was not imported into the Congo by the international organization, it settled there because that country was both one of the richest in Africa (because of its mineral deposits) and also one of the most vulnerable (because Belgian colonialism had been neglectful). What would have happened to the Congo without the United Nations? With the UN it at least survived.

In the Congo the UN had indeed played out three of its roles in Africa. At times the UN was a collective imperial power – and its sins of both omission and commission cost Patrice Lumumba his life. The UN in the Congo was also Africa's partner in development – trying to safeguard the preconditions of national integrity and political stability for the fragile Congo. But the UN was also an ally of Africa's liberation as it tried to prevent new forms of re-colonization of the Congo by Belgians and others.

In this last role as ally in Africa's liberation the UN was maintaining its new tradition of fostering decolonization – a tradition which had received its earlier supreme test on the issue of French claims over Algeria. Let us now turn to this issue of decolonization in Algeria and elsewhere.

The UN as ally in liberation

In terms of the UN as a friend of the decolonization and liberation of Africa, the problem of Algeria was the most difficult in the 1950s. Few imperial powers have been as resistant to the loss of a colony as France was to the loss of Algeria. And yet France was a permanent member of the Security Council (with its veto) and an ally of the United States in the North Atlantic Treaty Organization (NATO) from 1948 onwards. Under those circumstances, what chance did the world body have of

886

supporting the movement for liberating Algeria? Let us study the progression of this case of Algeria in greater detail.

It is common knowledge that the UN work in helping to bring into being the new independent African states hastened the process of their decolonization. This is true for both North Africa and black Africa.

On 16 October 1952 the General Assembly decided to put on its agenda the problems posed by the maintenance of the French role in Tunisia and Morocco. France argued in vain that the United Nations had no jurisdiction, pleading the famous Article 2, paragraph 7, of the Charter which precludes the UN from intervening in the internal affairs of member states. Mr Robert Schumann could not convince the Assembly that the affairs of these protectorates were a matter solely for France, and a first resolution about them was adopted in December 1952.

The Assembly was able to exert even stronger and more vigilant pressures in the development of the Algerian crisis, which had degenerated into open warfare after 1954. The French government thought it was on firmer legal ground about non-intervention in Algeria. But (and we quote Mr Ben Bella's speech to the General Assembly on 9 October 1962, after the unanimous vote admitting his country to the United Nations),

> for seven years the Algerian question came up regularly at every session of the Assembly. The debates to which it gave rise marked out the changing course of the conflict, and delegations were in a position to appreciate the dimensions of this conflict and to become familiar with its circumstances

The case of Algeria (Fig. 29.3) is thus particularly indicative of the role played by the United Nations in decolonization. Many French government initiatives on Algeria at home seemed to coincide with the way the affair went in the General Assembly. For example, the 1957 parliamentary debates in France and the adoption of more liberal laws for Algeria were designed to counterbalance the effect on international opinion of France's intensification of the war.

In September 1955 at the Tenth General Assembly, the Afro-Asian countries made their first attempt to get the United Nations to consider the Algerian problem as a potential threat to world peace. A. Pinay, the French minister of foreign affairs, reverted to the argument based on Article 2, paragraph 7: Algeria had for 125 years been legally part of France, so that this was definitely a case in which this provision of the Charter should apply. But despite manoeuvres smacking of 'diplomatic canvassing' there were on 30 September 1955, 28 votes for putting the item on the agenda, 27 against and 5 abstentions. This was when France 'slammed the door', for some time adopting a policy of staying away and letting it be understood that it might even leave the Organization. So the Assembly was led to go back on its decision: on 25 November 1955, the Algeria problem was removed from the agenda, and France resumed its

887

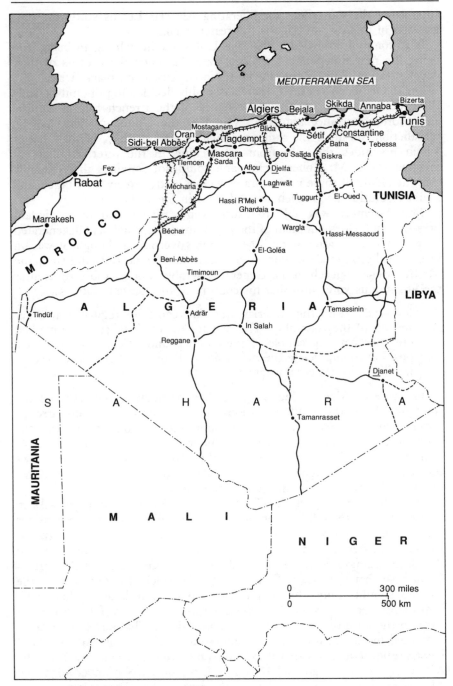

FIG. 29.3   *Algeria (after E. K. Kouassi)*

seat. It was only a postponement: the representative of the *Front de libération nationale* – FLN (National Liberation Front), with the Afro-Asian Group, soon got a special subcommittee of the group set up to deal with the matter (it was chaired by U Thant, then the delegate of Burma).

In June 1956 the Security Council received a request for it to meet, following an approach by the Arab states based on Articles 34 and 35 of the Charter (under which any member state may bring to the attention of the Security Council any 'dispute or situation . . . likely to endanger the maintenance of international peace and security'). This also failed. The Afro-Asian Group, arguing that France (which was accused of waging a war of extermination) had violated the Universal Declaration of Human Rights, therefore renewed its request for the matter to be put on the agenda of the November 1956 General Assembly, and secured it without a debate. The Latin American compromise resolution was adopted in February 1957, after the Afro-Asian draft was rejected in the Political Committee. The new resolution – designed not to offend French susceptibilities too much – did not even mention the Algerian people's right to self-determination but merely expressed the hope that 'in a spirit of co-operation, a peaceful democratic and just solution will be found, through appropriate means, in conformity with the principles of the Charter of the United Nations'.

Nevertheless, this vote was a success for the FLN inasmuch as it indirectly asserted the jurisdiction of the United Nations. The course of events at the September 1957 session was the same: inclusion on the agenda without a debate and without opposition from France, which (while maintaining its legal argument of domestic jurisdiction) hoped to take advantage of the debates to 'answer the accusations and slanders' levelled at it and not let its opponents monopolize the rostrum.

The Algerian issue was symbolic of a new anti-colonial mood in the world body. In 1958 the African Group was formed – strongly anti-imperialist. Ghana (where the leaders of the *Union des populations du Cameroun*, the UPC, were living) and Guinea supported a draft resolution calling for the lifting of the ban on the UPC and the holding of fresh elections in Cameroon under the control of the United Nations. India and most of the Asian states supported the French proposal aimed at giving Cameroon its independence without new elections. This was adopted. Pressures were also exerted by the African states in support of the Algerian FLN, and this led to a hostile atmosphere towards France at every session. Moreover the anti-*apartheid* campaign carried out by the small African Group during the year 1958–9 led the United States to vote for the resolutions condemning South Africa instead of abstaining.

1960 was Africa's year. It was also the year in which the United Nations Secretariat became aware of a certain overall responsibility towards the blank continent. Thus in January 1960 Dag Hammarskjöld, the secretary-general, went on a big six-weeks' tour of Africa, where he met most of Africa's future heads of state. Hammarskjöld was aware from then on of an enormous task to be accomplished; and this 'mood' was accompanied during that year, 1960, by a remarkable publicity campaign by the press.

An event of exceptional gravity also occurred in 1960. This was the Sharpeville shootings in South Africa, which on 25 March led to a call for a meeting of the Security Council and the adoption of the famous 1 April resolution calling on South Africa to abandon *apartheid*. This was regarded as a victory for the African Group, and was certainly not unconnected with Pretoria's decision to permit a visit by the secretary-general of the United Nations in July.

At the end of 1960 the African delegations to the General Assembly scored another notable success by securing the adoption, after a Soviet motion had been rejected, of a resolution against colonialism in Africa by 90 votes to nil, with nine abstentions. The UN became a fuller ally in Africa's struggle for liberation.

Despite their internal difficulties, the African states were playing a significant role in the glass palace at Manhattan.

Yet 1961 was to be a particularly gloomy year at the United Nations. As has been pointed out in earlier chapters, the African delegations were split between the Casablanca Group (Ghana, Guinea, Mali, Morocco, United Arab Republic and the provisional government of the Republic of Algeria) and the Brazzaville Group, comprising nearly all the other states of what had been French Africa.

1961 began with the Angola affair (riots in Luanda in February, an insurrection in March), which came up at the UN three times in March and April and ended in a vote by the Security Council (nine votes for, with two abstentions) calling on the Portuguese government to stop its repressive activity. The year continued with the Franco-Tunisian conflict at Bizerta, which ended at the extraordinary session in August in the resolution calling on France to withdraw its troops from the whole of Tunisian territory. This resolution, which was adopted by 66 votes, with 30 abstentions, received 8 votes from the Brazzaville Group.

On the problem of decolonization, the end of 1961 saw several proposals for the setting of a deadline for the independence of the African colonies. 1962, suggested by the Soviet Union, was rejected as too soon; while 1970, put forward by Nigeria and Liberia, seemed too late to many delegations. In the end it was decided not to set a deadline but a resolution was adopted setting up a Special Committee of the United Nations for the countries which were still colonized. This Committee, comprising representatives of Asian and African countries, the colonial powers, the United States and the Soviet Union, and known as the Committee of Seventeen, was in fact set up in January 1962.

From 1963 onwards the situation improved markedly, thanks in particular to the ending of the Algerian war and of the period of anarchy in the Congo. As we have seen, the Organization of African Unity (OAU) was also created, ushering in a new and different era in the development of the relationship between Africa and the United Nations. With the setting up of the OAU in May 1963, Africa could henceforth look to an organization for receptiveness, dialogue, negotiation and consultation with the outside world.

As a result the UN relations with Africa underwent profound quantitative and also qualitative changes. On the one hand the continent's coefficient of representation in the Organization rose from a tenth in 1945 to about a third in 1963 (this ratio remained constant until 1980). On the other hand, the African states came to realize both that the balance of power had changed in their favour and also that some of their interests were quite specific. They made precise demands, and their basic objective was to make their diplomatic and, indeed, their political influence proportional to their numerical strength.

The confluence of the basic philosophy of the United Nations, which had been built up during the Second World War by the victors, and the demands of the African states which for various reasons were heterogeneous, gave rise to complex, ambiguous and sometimes difficult relationships with Africa.

As it turned out, alliance in liberation between the UN and Africa was easier than partnership in development. Some of the most difficult differences in approach towards development were between UN institutions and the orientation of the Organization of African Unity. It is to some of these divergences that we must now turn.

The UN as partner in development

Africa's relations with the United Nations in the economic field are conducted partly through the Organization of African Unity and the United Nations Economic Commission for Africa; their formation and aspects of their activities have been discussed in the earlier chapters. Here, we will confine ourselves to the relations between the two at both institutional and normative levels.

In April 1958 the United Nations set up a United Nations Economic Commission for Africa (ECA), its function being to speed up the economic and social development of the African continent, to carry out studies, and to keep the United Nations Economic and Social Council, which set it up and supervises it, informed of the situation in the region.

But the OAU, when it was set up in 1963, from the outset asserted its competence for co-ordinating, strengthening and harmonizing co-operation between African peoples in all fields, including those of the ECA. Thus, Article XX of the Charter of Addis Ababa authorized the Assembly of Heads of State to set up five specialized commissions, including an Economic and Social Commission whose task was to promote economic co-operation in Africa.

At its first session in Niamey in December 1964, this Economic and Social Commission, which was established by the Assembly of Heads of State and Government in July 1964, enunciated the principles that were to govern the OAU's relations with the ECA. Having defined itself as the supreme planning and executive body, it confined the role of the ECA to technical and consultative questions: in other words, the ECA was to carry out studies and surveys which would serve as a basis for decisions by the OAU.

This attempt to subordinate a UN organ to the OAU was clearly stated by the OAU's first administrative secretary-general in 1966, when he told the representatives of the member states that the principles governing the relationship between the OAU and the ECA applied also to the relationship between the OAU and the other United Nations specialized agencies.[3] As against the OAU's determination to exercise control over the activities of the ECA, the latter's Executive Secretariat quoted its organization's statute: they pointed out that an organ of the United Nations Department of Economic and Social Affairs, which was answerable to the United Nations Economic and Social Council and whose policies were defined and financed by the United Nations, could not agree to submit to a policy defined by African states within the OAU. The OAU could only be complementary to the ECA and ready to support the latter's undertakings in the economic and social field; its recommendations, even though welcomed by the Economic and Social Council, could not be binding on the United Nations General Assembly.

The collision between these two different, not to say opposing, ideas about the ECA created dissension among the member states of the OAU which, together with financial problems, led to the suspension of the OAU's economic and social activities.

It was in these circumstances that the agreement between the United Nations and the OAU about co-operation between the latter and the ECA was signed on 15 November 1965. But this agreement, which 'can be summarized as a declaration of intent by both sides to co-operate',[4] further sanctioned a compromise between the two divergent views of the ECA and OAU in that it did not solve the real problem of the distribution of work between them. It amounted to no more than consultative procedures on minor practical and administrative questions. Hence James Magee wrote of this agreement that it merely allows each of the two organizations to take cognizance of the other's programme of work.[5]

3. See OAU documents CM/101/Rev.1, p. 8.
4. A. Mamadou, 1971.
5. J. Magee, 1970.

Neither side having changed its position, difficulties continued to exist in the evolution of the relationship between the OAU and the ECA. In 1968, on the ECA's tenth anniversary, the United Nations secretary-general, U Thant, restated the world organization's point of view as follows: the ECA, he said, is 'the window on Africa which allows the United Nations to see the economic and social problems of this continent from an African point of view, to see them in the context of the entire international economic structure'.[6]

On that occasion the secretary-general of the OAU spoke of the need for co-operation between the ECA and the OAU, whose activities should be complementary 'in order to make better use both of the technical and technological capabilities of the ECA and also of the political characteristics and sovereign decisions of the top bodies of the OAU'. The primacy of the OAU was again reasserted in the resolutions of September 1967 and February 1969.[7] Co-operation between the OAU and the ECA has thus far been a failure.

There were two main reasons for the failure, aggravated by personal rivalry: first the OAU's narrowly African view and, secondly, the two organizations' differing perceptions of African problems. The OAU having been set up by African governments which are supposed to exercise control over it, its credentials were established and its legitimacy acknowledged and asserted *vis-à-vis* the ECA, which was regarded as being an outward-looking organization and insufficiently African both as regards staff recruitment and policy formulation.

The prime grievance voiced about the ECA was that the planning and executive posts were held by non-Africans, which to some extent implied that the ECA's economic policy towards Africa was dictated from New York and not decided in Addis Ababa. The ECA perceived African problems through strictly economic criteria: the development of Africa presupposes the immediate economic integration of the continent and the creation of an African Common Market, since the multiplicity of customs barriers is an obstacle to its development.

The OAU, on the other hand, remained more sensitive to the human aspect of development; it could not disregard the linguistic, religious, cultural and ideological obstacles of all the potential conflicts that too sudden integration would cause. A step-by-step approach – that is, first a free-trade area rather than an integrated economic community – seemed to it the wise course.

This twofold approach to the economic realities of Africa, which was not conducive to harmonious co-operation, was often complicated by the contrasting temperaments and ambitions of the officials of the OAU and the ECA. The ups and downs of the relationship between the Ghanaian

6. UN document E/4651 E/CN 14/453, vol. 1, p. 297.
7. OAU document CM/Res 219 (xii) and Annex I, CM/ctee C/RPT, Rev. 1.

Robert Gardiner at the head of the ECA and the Guinean Diallo Telli of the OAU were mirrored in the tensions and difficulties in the development of the relationship between the Nigerian Adedeji Adebayo of the ECA and the Togolese Edem Kodjo of the OAU.[8]

Thus despite inter-secretariat contacts and joint meetings and conferences, relations between the two organizations were characterized rather by rivalry in the economic and social field.

It was not until 1980 that both agreed on a new development strategy contained in the *Lagos Plan of Action* adopted in April 1980. The African states fundamentally disagreed with the economic guidelines suggested in the 'Berg Report' on *Accelerated development in sub-Saharan Africa: An Agenda for Action* published by the World Bank in 1981. While the *Lagos Plan of Action* aimed at inward-looking development based on reducing dependence on the outside world and on food self-sufficiency at national and continental levels, the World Bank report encouraged the African economy to be outward-looking and lay emphasis on expanding African cash-crop exports.[9]

Towards a 'New International Economic Order'

As has been conclusively demonstrated in Chapter 25, it was Africa that opened the debate on the concept of a New International Economic Order (NIEO) in 1979. In fact the first version of the NIEO as it appears from the resolutions of May 1974 is only a somewhat rearranged version of demands made by Third-World countries since UNCTAD (United Nations Conference on Trade and Development) was set up. This being so, the work and role of the Joint ECA–OAU Committee on Trade and Development to prepare common African positions particularly stand out.

The Joint Committee has a twofold responsibility: first, to consider all Africa's short-term problems in the field of trade and development, and also their financing; and, secondly, to see how best these problems can be efficiently considered and presented at meetings of the Council of the United Nations Conference on Trade and Development. This Joint ECA–OAU Committee thus has a problem of economic checking to solve on the continental level and a strategic political stance to adopt in relation to major international negotiations in the commercial, monetary and customs field. Accordingly the joint meetings of the ECA and the OAU 'are aimed at ensuring complete co-operation between the Organization of African Unity and the Economic Commission for Africa in their efforts to harmonize the positions of African countries in the deliberations and negotiations that take place within UNCTAD, pursuant to Resolution

8. See S. Gharbi, 1981.

9. A. d'Almeida, 1983; E. K. Apkevon, 1983; E. K. Kouassi, 1983; UNESCO, 1983; Organization of African Unity, 1981.

135 (VIII) of the ECA and Resolution 158 (IX) of the OAU'.[10]

To carry out its duties the Committee generally holds two sessions a year, one at the beginning of January or in March and another one, the more important and more regular one, in August to prepare for the annual meeting of the Council of the United Nations Conference on Trade and Development.

The regularity and permanence of this Committee can be judged from the continual care which, starting from the third session, the recommendations of all the previous meetings of the Committee take to fix in advance the place and date of the next meeting.[11] This Joint Committee seems to function to the satisfaction of both organizations; and it was mainly due to its work, together with the efforts of the African Group at UNCTAD, that a common African position on the continent's economic problems was adopted and submitted to the second and third conferences of UNCTAD.

UN technical assistance to Africa is channelled through the United Nations Development Programme (UNDP), which was set up by the United Nations General Assembly in 1965. Fifteen organizations of the UN system (ILO, FAO, UNESCO, WHO, IBRD, UNCTAD, and so on) participate in the execution of UNDP projects.

Until 1971 project-financing applications were submitted by governments on a project-by-project basis. Since that date, every beneficiary country has drawn up a list of requests corresponding to its priority needs for UNDP assistance for a period of three to five years. In every case the developing countries meet 50 per cent of the financing of projects carried out with the help of the UNDP. Hence many African leaders complain about the high cost of the assistance provided by the UNDP. In Liberia in 1966, for example, the technical assistance provided by the World Bank for the road-building programme meant that the Liberian government paid the emoluments of the contractors for technical services, not to mention the interest on the long-term loans granted by the Bank.

Now the procedure operated by the UNDP for granting and apportioning this assistance rules out any action by the OAU at any stage in the execution of UN programmes. Thus multilateral technical assistance for Africa is an area organized exclusively by the United Nations.

Furthermore, the UNDP's resources come mainly from the Western world, which does not necessarily treat all African countries the same: so

10. See UN, ECA document E/CN/14/449, E/CN/14/WP 1/15; OAU/TRANS/14 of 18 January 1969.

11. Cf. the Committee's recommendations at its 3rd session in: E/CW/14/449, E/CN/14/WP 1/15, OAU/TRANS/14 of 18 January 1969, p. 9; the recommendations of the 4th session in: E/CN/14/459, E/CN/14/WP 1/14 Res.3, OAU/TRANS/23/Res.3 of 23 August 1969, Annex 1, p. 5; the recommendations of the 5th session in: E/CN/14/490, E/CN/14/WP 1/31, OAU/TRANS/30 of 24 August 1970, p. 16.

that according to the OAU aid is distributed unfairly, often according to preferences dictated by political leanings or ideologies.

Hence the OAU would like to see the Pan-African Organization acting as the natural means of co-ordinating and distributing assistance and multilateral aid.

The UN agencies for their part seem to be afraid that the OAU, which is not a homogeneous body, cannot play this disinterested and impartial role of co-ordinating and distributing international assistance. They are also disinclined to finance OAU activities connected with national liberation movements in Africa.

There is thus mutual suspicion between the OAU and the organizations of the UN family in the field of multilateral aid to Africa.

Relations between the OAU and the United Nations over economic co-operation problems are thus characterized by two factors: an unfriendly continental relationship, and the UN 'reserved sector'. But in their approaches to the wider concerns of North–South relations, there is more consensus. Africa, the United Nations and its specialized agencies are more in accord at the global level than they are when the focus is more narrowly African.

International co-operation on human resources

We must distinguish between co-operation over supposedly 'harmless' technical matters and political co-operation, which might offend the susceptibilities associated with the sovereignty of states. Technical co-operation takes place primarily between Africa and the UN specialized agencies, but also between the OAU and other UN agencies working to promote the well-being of African peoples. Let us take Africa and the International Labour Organization (ILO), for example. Until the early 1960s, Africa and the ILO had little in the way of direct relations, since these were the preserve of the colonial powers. The 29 founder-members in 1919 included only Liberia, followed by Ethiopia (1922), Egypt and the Union of South Africa (1939), Libya (1952) and Ghana (1957). Nevertheless, the International Labour Organization did manage to set up a special committee during the colonial period, the Committee of Experts on Manpower, to advise on the best way of protecting workers in colonial countries; it distinguished itself in the struggle against forced labour in Africa.

Most African countries joined the ILO between 1960 and 1964, at the same time as the latter established relations with African employers' and workers' organizations. The prime objective for Africa was to create the conditions and institutions needed to translate into reality the economic and social ideals expressed in the norms the new states had accepted.

It was in the context of these problems that the first African regional conference held in Lagos, Nigeria, in 1960 drew the ILO's attention to the need for technical assistance in industrial, commercial and agricultural training, and also in the training of management staff. The fundamental importance attached to employment and training was reaffirmed in 1964, when a special committee on women's work emphasized the need to tackle the following problems:

(1) the employment and condition of women in a rapidly changing Africa;
(2) the need to use female labour; and
(3) the need to give women and girls better means of professional training.

Aware of these problems, the ILO increased its presence in Africa by setting up a Regional Office at Addis Ababa, and made perceptible changes in its programme. Thus the sudden surge of technical assistance was to a large extent a reply to requests emanating from African states themselves. Africa gradually began to receive an increasing share of the technical co-operation resources available to the ILO from its regular budget, the United Nations Development Programme (UNDP) and many bilateral and multilateral sources.

Because of the seriousness of the twin problems of unemployment and acute shortage of skilled labour, the ILO took it as its basic task to help Africa develop its human resources. With this object, in 1963 it founded its International Centre for Professional and Technical Training at Turin, Italy, with the aim of training those who would in future train others. Since this centre was set up, many Africans have gone there on scholarships, thus ensuring a continuing 'nursery' of African specialists. To emphasize the importance of research the ILO in 1961 set up the International Institute for Labour Studies, whose main task was to study the social problems of economic development. For a very long time it was headed by an African, Professor Albert Tevoedjre.

Furthermore, through the Conference of African Ministers of Labour the OAU works on questions of interest to the ILO which are due to be debated at the next session of the international conference. The ILO had to reform its programme and structure to take account of the emergence of new states on the international scene, and concentrate on questions such as manpower development; professional and technical training; the decentralization of the International Labour Organization (ILO) and the recruitment of African officials; the election of the president of the international conference, and standing orders; the development of sub-regional offices and correspondents in Africa. The ILO conference also considered the appointment of African candidates to the governing body and the African Consultative Committee; the composition of African delegations to the international conference; the contribution of African states to the endowment fund of the International Institute for Labour Studies; and the problem of unifying the trade union movement in Africa.

897

This last problem, being bound up with the role of trades unions in the development of African states, is still being studied by the OAU. Similar activities are to be observed in the relationship between the OAU and UNESCO.

As for co-operation between Africa and UNESCO, it was in November 1960, at its sixteenth session, that the UNESCO General Conference admitted a large number of African states as members. The conference adopted a resolution under which it decided to convene a Conference of African States in 1961 with a view 'to establishing an inventory of educational needs and programme to meet those in the coming years'. It then drew up a document entitled *Outline plan for African educational development* which was approved by the UNESCO Executive Board at its fifty-second session. It was decided to set up a central planning group on school buildings in Khartoum and a textbook production centre in Yaoundé, and lastly to make 50 teachers available for some African states.

With this encouragement, the African states got UNESCO to hold another meeting in Antananarivo from 3 to 12 September 1962 devoted to higher education in Africa, including such topics as choice of syllabuses, adaptation to African realities and needs, training of staff specializing in public administration and development techniques, and so on. With this momentum the African ministers of education decided to institute a Conference of Ministers of Education of African Countries to follow up the implementation of the programmes drawn up at UNESCO.

PLATE 29.2   *Amadou-Mahtar M'Bow of Senegal, director-general of UNESCO, 1974–87*

898

When the OAU was set up in 1963 it had to define its relationship with UN bodies: and this fell to the Conference of African Ministers of Education at its first session from 17 to 24 March 1964 in Abidjan. The OAU set up an Educational and Cultural Committee to complement UNESCO's efforts. Arrangements for regional and international co-operation were the subject of an agreement signed on 10 July 1968 between the OAU and UNESCO. From then on healthy co-operation developed between the two organizations. It showed itself in the first Pan-African Cultural Festival, in the organization of Conferences of African Ministers of Education, in the Conference for the Application of Science and Technology to Africa held in Dakar from 22 to 31 January 1974, in the solution of the problem of African refugees, and so on. UNESCO's fourth director-general was an African, Mr Amadou-Mahtar M'Bow, who completed his second term of office at the head of the organization.

In all these fields the work of the OAU and UNESCO have been harmonized.

The OAU also co-operates with the other UN agencies. This takes place against a wider institutional background than the above-mentioned bilateral relations. The most favoured field is rural and agricultural development in Africa. An Inter-agency Regional Committee brings together the activities of the OAU and the main UN agencies and co-ordinates the work of the ECA and other voluntary organizations in executing their programme for integrated rural development in Africa. In this connection the role of the United Nations Development Programme (UNDP) is predominant: it finances projects, and supplies seeds, fertilizers, insecticides, pesticides and fungicides.

In the context of this co-operation, the organizations concerned have drawn up plans for the regional organization of rice cultivation in West Africa, a project for which the initiative was taken by the OAU.

Similar relations operate as regards the problems of youth, employment, technical training and literacy.

Other types of relationship also develop on the joint committees between the OAU, the Food and Agriculture Organization (FAO) and the World Health Organization (WHO) on food and nutrition in Africa, campaigns against rinderpest and trypanosomiasis, the setting up of phytosanitary centres, and so on.

There is equally fruitful co-operation between the intergovernmental agencies for the resettlement and education of refugees (the UNO, UNDP, UNHCR, ECA, UNESCO, OAU) which belong to the working group of the OAU Bureau for African Refugees. Co-operation here is especially crucial because of the importance of its subject. Of all the continents, Africa has the largest number of refugees, with a total of 3.5 million by 1979. Nowadays, half of the world's 10 million refugees live in Africa, which justifies the intensity of the co-operation with the United Nations

High Commissioner for Refugees (UNHCR) to cope with the enormous problems and difficulties caused by their presence.

Thus in 1967 the OAU, the UNHCR and the ECA took the initiative of holding a conference in Addis Ababa to analyse and assess the situation of refugees in Africa, revise current policies and strategies, and where necessary formulate new ones adapted to the ever-growing problems. Following this conference the Heads of State and Government of the OAU in 1969 adopted the *Convention governing the specific aspects of refugee problems in Africa,* which came into effect in 1974.

A second pan-African conference on the situation and rights of refugees in Africa was organized by the OAU, the UNHCR and the ECA from 7 to 17 May 1979 at Arusha, Tanzania. This conference had three objectives:

(1) to keep all the bodies concerned (governments, governmental organizations, voluntary agencies and refugee relief agencies) adequately informed of the worsening of refugee problems in Africa and of possible solutions;

(2) to examine and assess the current situation and problems of refugees in Africa; and

(3) to study and assess national laws concerning refugees and suggest improvements.

The UNHCR has since continued to attach particular importance to the implementation of the recommendations of this conference. Activities carried out in 1983 include a research project by three experts in 21 African countries on the impact of study fellowships in Africa, and a seminar on the situation of refugees in West Africa.

One result of this meeting was the holding in Geneva in April 1981 of the first International Conference for Assistance to Refugees in Africa (ICARA I). It achieved its objective, namely to draw attention to African refugees and mobilize resources for the current programme on their behalf.

On 18 December 1982 the United Nations General Assembly, drawing the lessons of this experiment, adopted Resolution 37/197, which in paragraph 5 asks the secretary-general, in close co-operation with the Organization of African Unity and the United Nations High Commissioner for Refugees, to convene a second International Conference for Assistance to Refugees in Africa (ICARA II). During the preparatory work for ICARA II the importance of identifying lasting solutions to the problems of refugees in Africa was emphasized.

One of the aims of Resolution 37/197 is to complement the work of the UNHCR by submitting to ICARA II relief programmes more concerned with development and taking account of the repercussions of the presence of refugees on national economies. The United Nations Trust Fund for South Africa put $300 000 at the UNHCR's disposal for refugee relief in South Africa during the period 1 July 1982–30 June 1983; while in 1982 the UNHCR committed $134.7 million for the financing of relief activities in Africa.[12]

In another field, that of the protection of the habitat and the environment, the General Assembly in 1974 set up the United Nations Habitat and Human Settlements Foundation, because of the serious nature of housing problems and allied problems of human settlements. In 1978 a United Nations Centre for Human Settlements (Habitat) was set up within the UN system to act as a liaison centre for activities related to these human settlements; it is housed at Nairobi (Kenya), as is the United Nations Environment Programme (UNEP), set up by the General Assembly following a recommendation by the United Nations Conference on the Human Environment held in Stockholm in June 1972.

In May 1982 the Executive Board of UNEP held a special sort of meeting at Nairobi to mark the tenth anniversary of the Stockholm conference. The Nairobi Declaration, which was adopted by consensus, provides in particular that

> the human environment would greatly benefit from an international atmosphere of peace and security, free from the threats of any war, especially nuclear war, and the waste of intellectual and natural resources on armaments, as well as from *apartheid*, racial segregation and all forms of discrimination, colonial and other forms of oppression and foreign domination.

Such is the picture of the co-operation which has been developing between Africa and the organs of the UN system in the technical and social fields. The partnership in development between Africa and the world body continues to be a many-faceted process.

Conclusion

We have examined Africa's relationship with the United Nations in this chapter from the point of view of three areas of interaction.

In its role as an absentee imperial landlord, the world organization served as a supervisory body over the administration of the former German colonies of Tanganyika, Ruanda-Urundi, Togoland, Cameroons and South-West Africa (former mandates of the League of Nations). In reality, the Republic of South Africa – which was the administering authority of South-West Africa under the League – did not recognize the United Nations as a successor to the League and therefore refused to be accountable to the UN about the 'dependent territory'. As we indicated, it took a number of battles both within the United Nations and at the

---

12. United Nations High Commission for Refugees, 1982–3.

PLATE 29.3   *S. Nujoma, first president of Namibia, and J. Perez de Cuellar, secretary-general of the United Nations, at the Independence Day ceremony of Namibia, 21 March 1990*

International Court of Justice at the Hague before the UN's jurisdiction over South-West Africa (later re-named Namibia by the liberation fighters) could at last be definitively confirmed, notwithstanding South Africa's continuing dissent.

On balance, the UN's insistence on continuing jurisdiction in Namibia was motivated by a desire to free the country from South Africa's control. It has been a case of the UN insisting on being a collective imperial power over Namibia in order to serve as Namibia's ally in liberation – a UN desire to 'reconquer' Namibia in order to free it.

Apart from Namibia, the UN's role as a collective imperial power basically ended with the independence of the prize trusteeship of Tanganyika in 1961. The other trusteeships had gained independence earlier.

The world body's role as an ally of liberation went beyond speeding up the independence of its own trusteeships. Especially after India's independence in 1947, and India's admission to the UN, voices against imperialism and colonialism in the chambers of the world organization gathered strength. In 1960 more than 15 African countries joined the UN in a single year. Before long, resolutions were being passed in the General Assembly condemning imperialism, colonialism, racism and eventually Zionism as moral offences against a new international code of justice.

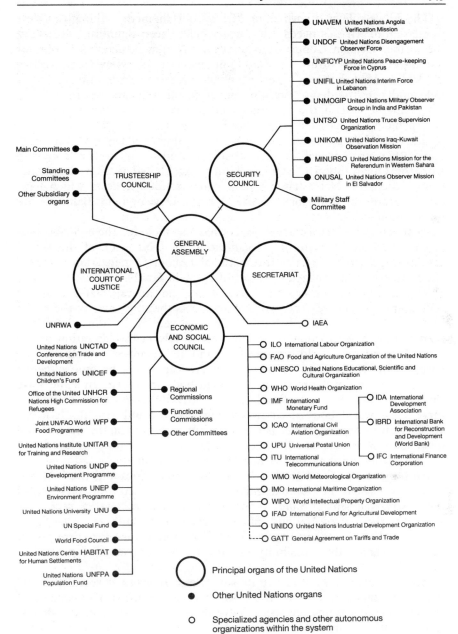

UNAVEM United Nations Angola Verification Mission

UNDOF United Nations Disengagement Observer Force

UNFICYP United Nations Peace-keeping Force in Cyprus

UNIFIL United Nations Interim Force in Lebanon

UNMOGIP United Nations Military Observer Group in India and Pakistan

UNTSO United Nations Truce Supervision Organization

UNIKOM United Nations Iraq-Kuwait Observation Mission

MINURSO United Nations Mission for the Referendum in Western Sahara

ONUSAL United Nations Observer Mission in El Salvador

Military Staff Committee

Main Committees

Standing Committees

Other Subsidiary organs

TRUSTEESHIP COUNCIL

SECURITY COUNCIL

GENERAL ASSEMBLY

INTERNATIONAL COURT OF JUSTICE

SECRETARIAT

UNRWA

ECONOMIC AND SOCIAL COUNCIL

IAEA

United Nations UNCTAD Conference on Trade and Development

United Nations UNICEF Children's Fund

Office of the United UNHCR Nations High Commission for Refugees

Joint UN/FAO World WFP Food Programme

United Nations Institute UNITAR for Training and Research

United Nations UNDP Development Programme

United Nations UNEP Environment Programme

United Nations University UNU

UN Special Fund

World Food Council

United Nations Centre HABITAT for Human Settlements

United Nations UNFPA Population Fund

Regional Commissions

Functional Commissions

Other Committees

ILO International Labour Organization

FAO Food and Agriculture Organization of the United Nations

UNESCO United Nations Educational, Scientific and Cultural Organization

WHO World Health Organization

IMF International Monetary Fund

ICAO International Civil Aviation Organization

UPU Universal Postal Union

ITU International Telecommunications Union

WMO World Meteorological Organization

IMO International Maritime Organization

WIPO World Intellectual Property Organization

IFAD International Fund for Agricultural Development

UNIDO United Nations Industrial Development Organization

GATT General Agreement on Tariffs and Trade

IDA International Development Association

IBRD International Bank for Reconstruction and Development (World Bank)

IFC International Finance Corporation

Principal organs of the United Nations

Other United Nations organs

Specialized agencies and other autonomous organizations within the system

FIG. 29.4 *The United Nations System (Source: United Nations)*

903

The UN's role as a partner in Africa's development – though modest in relation to Africa's needs – has nevertheless been significant. Rescuing the former Belgian Congo from territorial disintegration was important not only for the future of Zaire but also for all other fragile states in Africa. Had Katanga's secession succeeded so early after Africa's independence, the demonstration impact on other separatist groups elsewhere in the rest of the continent could have put severe stress on the very principle of national cohesion all over Africa.

But the UN's partnership in Africa's development has over the years taken other forms as well. In spite of stresses and strains in its relationship with the Organization of African Unity, the United Nations Economic Commission for Africa has played a major role on matters which have ranged from the functions of the African Development Bank to the formulation and promotion of the *Lagos Plan of Action*.

Partnership in Africa's development has also included the contributions of the Food and Agriculture Organization, of UNESCO, of the World Health Organization, of the International Labour Organization and of a variety of other specialized agencies of the UN family.

The question for the future is whether the African states can stay united enough to repay the two primary debts that they owe to the world body. Just as the United Nations once served as an ally in Africa's liberation, can Africa now be counted as an ally in the liberation of the UN? Just as the world organization and its agencies continue to be partners in Africa's development, will African states become effective partners in the development of the world body in return? In some ways the United Nations is as fragile as the African states it has sought to serve. The world body itself needs development and growth. It needs stability and integrity. It needs to expand its own 'per capita income' and make its own 'structural adjustments'. But, like Africa, it needs to achieve all this without risking the trauma of 'recolonization'.

An opportunity for a further linkage between Africa and the UN was sadly lost when the United States virtually 'vetoed' the election of Tanzania's statesman, Salim Ahmed Salim, to the post of secretary-general of the United Nations. The Reagan administration regarded Salim Ahmed Salim as a 'dangerous radical'. Washington therefore firmly shut the door against this possibility of the first African secretary-general of the UN.

But the future may yet have its surprises.* It may yet reveal that the historic partnership between the world body and some of its poorest and weakest member states can still achieve the miracle of their joint redemption in world affairs in the years ahead.

* Mr Boutros Boutros-Ghali (Egypt) was elected Secretary-General of the United Nations in December 1991.

Towards the year 2000

Ali A. MAZRUI

This volume has sought to delineate the special characteristics of the phase of African history since 1935, period by period. The years from 1935 to 1945 emerge as the decade of global conflict – beginning with Italy's invasion of Ethiopia in October 1935 and culminating in Japan's surrender in August 1945. The 15 years from 1945 to 1960 witnessed, as we have shown, the intensification of the anti-colonial struggle – resulting finally in the independence of 16 African countries in the single year of 1960. As for the period after independence, this has witnessed the attempts at the consolidation of freedom, the building of nations, the institutionalization of order and the struggle for development. Let us take each of these themes of this volume in turn.

A world aflame

If in 1935 Italy was heir to one of Europe's most ancient empires (classical Rome), Ethiopia was a continuation of one of Africa's oldest civilizations. The conflict between Italy and Ethiopia in the 1930s seemed to symbolize a clash of antiquities between Europe and Africa – two vehicles of ancient culture in collision.

But there was of course an uglier side to the Italian invasion of Ethiopia as well. It was a case of modern European imperialism having a last fling at contemporary Africa. Ethiopia – which had for so long been an oasis of African sovereignty in splendid isolation within a colonized continent – was at last over-run by European territorial greed.

This volume has discussed the long-term impact of the Second World War on Africa – ranging from facilitating the struggle for liberation to the incorporation of Africa more firmly into the Western capitalist orbit.[1] Two months after declaring war on Germany, the British government declared its readiness to buy all West African cocoa. The exploitation of African economies to meet European consumption patterns entered a new phase under the stimulus of war.

1. For other surveys, see also R. Oliver and M. Crowder, 1981; P. Duignan and L.H. Gann, 1973 and 1975 and G.S.P. Freeman-Grenville, 1973.

But the Second World War did not merely change Africa's destiny; it also fundamentally altered Europe's own future. Out of the global conflict was born a new division of Europe into communist and capitalist camps. By a strange twist of fate, the continental partition of Europe was symbolized by the division of *Berlin* – the very city where Africa's own partition had been plotted some six decades earlier. An African nemesis had exacted the ultimate revenge. The city which had pronounced the curse of the scramble for Africa in 1885 was also the city which had suffered the curse of the partition of Europe from 1945 onwards. Just as the fragmentation of Africa seemed irreversible for the foreseeable future, so did the division of Europe following the Second World War, in spite of Mikhail Gorbachev's vision of the 1980s. For once the ancestors of Africa had triumphed in their sacred revenge – but leaving two unhappy continents licking the wounds of partition.

What must never be forgotten is Africa's involvement in the global conflict which preceded those events and changed the face of both post-war Europe and post-war Africa. Fifty-five thousand Ugandans served in the King's African Rifles, for example. Some of the 87 000 Tanganyikans who gave service in the war participated in the 1942 invasion of Madagascar against Vichy and in favour of de Gaulle. Many African soldiers were involved in the war against Japan in Burma. As far back as 1939 the Nigerian Regiment had raised 15 battalions. And thousands of North African soldiers gave their lives for several years in the fluctuating fortunes between Rommel, Montgomery, Eisenhower and other high-profile combatants north of the Sahara.

But in the final analysis, the most poignant phase of the war for Africa took place quite early in the global conflict. Italy, the new pretender to the legacy of classical Rome, was among the first to be defeated. The resistance within Ethiopia had refused to be extinguished. Grenades were thrown at the Italian-appointed Viceroy in Addis Ababa; Abuna Abraham was blinded by poison gas as the Italians moved towards making him the head of the Ethiopian Church.

The Ethiopian resistance held down 56 Italian battalions. On 20 January 1941, Emperor Haile Selassie crossed from Sudan into Ethiopia on foot. On 7 March 1941, the British and imperial forces massively penetrated the country with the Ethiopian emperor's permission. The British, with African soldiers, took Addis Ababa in April 1941. The emperor resumed administration at the end of January 1942.

And so the battle of the Titans between heir to Caesar and heir to the Queen of Sheba ended in the ignominy of Caesar's dreams. The world had become too complicated. Competitive imperialism between rival European powers had aided the fortunes of the besieged descendant of Sheba. The heir to Caesar was isolated by some of his own former provincials. On 18 April 1945, Benito Mussolini was executed by fellow Europeans. 'How are the mighty fallen!'

The crusade against colonialism

The second sub-period of this volume concerns the years 1945 to 1960 – characterized by the intensification of the nationalist struggle against colonialism. There were three basic constituencies for this struggle. One constituency was internal to each colony – an attempt to mobilize the oppressed masses against racism and foreign rule within the particular society. The second constituency was within the governing imperial power – an attempt to enlist the progressive forces within the controlling hegemonic state. In a sense this was a strategy of dividing the enemy – creating discord within the imperial metropole.

The third constituency was the globe itself – the international community at large. How could world opinion be enlisted on the side of the forces of decolonization?

Mobilizing the masses in the colonies themselves was the most critical of the strategies. But even before the outbreak of the Second World War, North African nationalists like Bourguiba had indeed started the mobilization of their own domestic constituency. The *Parti populaire algérien* (PPA) was formed by Messali Ḥādj in 1936. And in Spanish Morocco, 'Abd al-Khalik Tares had founded the Islaḥ Party in the same year. Also in 1936 Egyptian nationalism had at last succeeded in forcing the British to lift the military occupation of Egypt with the exception of the Suez Canal Zone. But the Egyptian crusade against the residual British military presence in the Canal Zone continued to be waged even before the ink was dry on the new Anglo-Egyptian Treaty of 1936. In January 1944, the independence of Morocco was first demanded by the Nationalist Party. Aḥmed Balafredj was arrested – and riots broke out in Rabat and Fez in March. In Algeria also in 1944 Ferhāt 'Abbās founded the AML (*Amis du manifeste et de la liberté*). The movement rapidly gained half-a-million members.

Elsewhere in Africa the stirring of nationalism and domestic mobilization were also evident, taking a variety of forms. From 1933 to 1946, the French had been forced to send into exile Léon Mba from Cameroon for 'sedition'. In 1940, the Tonsi movement started in Angola as the 'Tawa cult', in cultural rebellion against alien values. In September 1946, Jomo Kenyatta returned to Kenya after 15 years abroad. He set himself the agenda of political mobilization at home.

It was not long before political associations and parties were mushrooming all over the African continent – ranging from the *Union des populations du Cameroun* (UPC) to the Convention People's Party (CPP) in Ghana, from the *Rassemblement démocratique africain* (RDA) in the French empire to the Tanganyika African National Union (TANU). Resistance to colonialism was getting institutionalized and better organized. Political mobilization at home was truly under way.

But however fundamental the domestic constituency was, it was also important to seek allies in the colonialist countries themselves. At the very minimum this could be a case of 'splitting the enemy' – turning Frenchman against Frenchman, Briton against Briton. If colonialism had operated on the basis of 'divide and conquer', anti-colonialism could adopt the counter-strategy of 'divide and liberate'. The RDA's original links with the French Communist Party could strategically be justified on those grounds if no other.

The French colonial policy of political association and integration was particularly well-suited for anti-colonial activities within metropolitan France itself. After all, the French colonies in Africa were directly represented on legislative institutions in Paris itself – a form of colonial representation which had no equivalent in the British style of colonial administration. It was in November 1945 that Léopold Senghor and Lamine Gueye (Senegal), Félix Houphouët-Boigny (Côte d'Ivoire), Apithy Sourou Migan (Dahomey), Fily Dabo Cissoko (French Sudan) and Yacine Diallo (Guinea) were elected to represent French West Africa in the French Constituent Assembly. A few weeks earlier Prince Alexandre Douala-Manga Bell and Dr L. P. Anjoulet had been elected as Cameroon's first deputies. It would have been inconceivable for Jomo Kenyatta, Obafemi Awolowo or Nnamdi Azikiwe to be elected to sit in the House of Commons in London. Instead of being directly represented in metropolitan institutions, African patriots in British colonies tried to influence British opinion less directly through native Britons of liberal or left-wing persuasion. British members of parliament like Fenner Brockway and Barbara Castle became regular channels through which African nationalists conveyed their grievances to the House of Commons. And British newspapers like the *Daily Worker*, the *New Statesman* and the *Manchester Guardian* helped to wage the anti-colonial struggle within the imperial power itself.

Algerians, on the other hand, were gaining the level of access to metropolitan France which was increasingly conceded to other French dependencies. On the eve of the end of the Second World War, a French ordinance gave Algerian Muslims 15 deputies in the National Assembly and seven senators in the Council of the Republic. This concession was made in March 1944 in anticipation of the liberation of metropolitan France. By August 1946 it was possible for Ferhāt 'Abbās, leader of the *Union démocratique du manifeste algérien*, to lay before the National Constituent Assembly in Paris a draft law for an Algerian republic federated to France. And yet about ten years later Ferhāt 'Abbās was the political head of the Algerian government-in-exile – in rebellion against French rule in Algeria.

Ferhāt 'Abbās's latter role brings us back to the third constituency of the anti-colonial struggle – the constituency of the international community at large. 'Abbās became the main international spokesman of the *Front de libération nationale* – FLN (National Liberation Front) of Algeria. Abbas travelled from one foreign capital to another to champion the Algerian cause and solicit support for it.

The United Nations (UN) also became an important ally and a good battleground for the African nationalists. But the most basic parts of the international community were inevitably one's own neighbours. For Algeria this meant fellow-African countries, especially the rest of the Maghreb and Egypt in the first instance. But Algeria also tried to win over the rest of Africa. One such determined effort was made at the 1958 All-Africa Peoples Conference in Accra.

But the African continent was not merely a recipient of external influences. It was also helping to change the agenda of global reform. Gamāl 'Abd al-Nasser's nationalization of the Suez Canal in 1956 was one of the most important African initiatives of the twentieth century. Only five years previously (1951) Iran under Muḥammad Mosadeq had nationalized its oil resources. The Central Intelligence Agency of the United States was soon to neutralize Mosadeq and reinstate the more pro-Western authority of the Pahlavi dynasty of the Shah. This seemed at first to have sealed the fate of any Third-World country wanting to nationalize and control its own resource.

The doors of Third-World initiatives in controlling their own resources were reopened by Gamāl 'Abd al-Nasser in July 1956. The resource this time was not oil – as in Mosadeq's Iran – but an Egyptian canal built by Egyptian labour at considerable human cost. Many thousands of Egyptian lives had been lost in its construction about a hundred years before al-Nasser at last nationalized the waterway. Unlike Mosadeq, al-Nasser got away with his courageous bid. After Suez, the nationalization and socialization of African resources became increasingly a safe political option for African governments to consider.

Suez and its aftermath constituted the great divide between the Soviet Union as an imperialistic threat to Africa and the Soviet Union as an ally in the struggle for independence. The USSR provided Egypt with pilots for the Suez Canal when the Western pilots were withdrawn in the escalating crisis after al-Nasser's nationalization. The Soviet Union under-took the even bigger commitment of helping Egypt construct the Aswān Dam from which Britain, the United States and the World Bank had reneged on their commitment. From then on, the Soviet Union seemed to have abandoned all territorial appetite for Africa, and the record showed a readiness to support African liberation struggles. Suez was the turning point. Al-Nasser's remarkable moves were Africa's ultimate cultivation of the international community – at least until the more recent phase of the global struggle against *apartheid*.

These then were the phases of the anti-colonial struggle – first, the mobilization of the domestic populace; secondly, the penetration of the metropolitan imperialist circles in an attempt to 'divide and liberate', and thirdly, the cultivation and conversion of the international community, beginning with a determined pan-African enlisting of one's own neigh-bours. We referred in an earlier chapter to Kwame Nkrumah's imperative: '*Seek ye first the political kingdom, and all things will be added unto you*'. After the acquisition of the political kingdom, *quo vadis* Africa? It is to this theme that we must once again return.

Earlier chapters have paid special attention to the transition from the African struggle for independence to the striving for nation-building. The other chapters discussed the efforts to give greater cultural coherence to Africa's *nationhood* and to render greater legitimacy and authority to Africa's *statehood*. This struggle has continued to consolidate freedom, ensure territorial integrity and facilitate development and progress.

But where do we go from here? The two most important revolutions awaiting Africa are, first, a *gender revolution in roles* and, secondly, a *scientific revolution in skills*. These two revolutions in *gender* and *science* are closely intertwined. Let us look more closely at this special dialectic.

A fundamental change in relations between the genders had indeed been occurring partly because of Africa's interaction with other cultures in this period. Islam and Western colonialism came with alternative paradigms of relationships between the sexes. Both the family and African society at large are caught up in these tensions of cultural change. It is this question of gender in African society since 1935 that we now address.

Gender roles in transition

Africa since 1935 has witnessed significant changes in the roles and functions of men and women in Africa. In many traditional cultures there has been a belief that God made woman the custodian of *fire*, *water*, and *earth*. God himself took charge of the fourth element of the universe – the omnipresent *air*.

Custody of fire entailed responsibility for making energy available. And the greatest source of energy in rural Africa is firewood. The African woman became disproportionately responsible for finding and carrying huge bundles of firewood, though quite often it was men who chopped down the big trees initially.

Custody of water involved a liquid which was a symbol of both survival and cleanliness. The African woman became responsible for ensuring that this critical substance was available for the family. She has trekked long distances to fetch water. But where a well needed to be dug, it was often the man who did the digging.

The custody of earth has been part of a doctrine of *dual fertility*. Woman ensures the *survival* of this generation by maintaining a central role in cultivation – and preserving the fertility of the soil. Woman ensures the *arrival* of the next generation by her role as mother – the fertility of the womb. Dual fertility becomes an aspect of the triple custodial role of

African womanhood, though always in partnership with the African man.[2]

What has happened to this doctrine of triple custody in the period since 1935? Different elements of the colonial experience affected the roles of men and women in Africa in different ways.

Among the factors which increased the woman's role on the land was wage labour for the men. According to Margaret Jean Hay, wage labour for men took some time before it began to affect women's role on the land. Hay's own work was among Luo women in Kenya:

> By 1930 a large number of men had left Kowe at least once for outside employment . . . More than half of this group stayed away for periods of fifteen years or more . . . This growing export of labour from the province might be thought to have increased the burden of agricultural work for women . . . As early as 1910, administrators lamented the fact that Nyanza was becoming the labour pool of the entire colony . . . Yet the short-term migrants of the 1920s were usually unmarried youths, who played a relatively minor role in the local economy beyond occasional herding and the conquest of cattle in war. Furthermore, the short-term labour migrants could and often did arrange to be away during the slack periods in the agricultural cycle . . . Thus labour migration in the period before 1930 actually removed little labour from the local economy and did not significantly alter the sexual division of labour.[3]

But Margaret Hay goes on to demonstrate how the Great Depression and the Second World War changed the situation as migrant labour and conscription of males took away a bigger and bigger proportion of men from the land. This was compounded by the growth of mining industries like the gold mining at Kowe from 1934 onwards:

> The long-term absence of men had an impact on the sexual division of labour, with women and children assuming a greater share of agricultural work than ever before . . . The thirties represent a transition with regard to the sexual division of labour, and it was clearly the women who bore the burden of the transition in rural areas.[4]

Women in this period, from the 1930s onwards, became more deeply involved as 'custodians of earth'. In Southern Africa the migrations of

2. I am indebted to the late Okot p'Bitek, the Ugandan anthropologist and poet, for stimulation and information about myths of womanhood in northern Uganda. Okot and I also discussed similarities and differences between African concepts of matter and the ideas of Empedocles, the Greek philosopher of the fifth century before the Christian era. Consult also O. p'Bitek, 1971.

3. M. J. Hay, 1976, pp. 98–9. For a feminist perspective, consult also M. R. Cutrufelli, 1983.

4. M. J. Hay, 1976, p. 105.

men to the mines became even more dramatic. By the 1950s a remarkable bifurcation was taking place in some South African societies – a division between a male proletariat (industrial working class) and a female peasantry. South Africa's regulations against families joining their husbands on the mines exacerbated this tendency towards *gender-apartheid*, the segregation of the sexes. Many women in the frontline states had to fulfil their triple custodial role of fire, water and earth in greater isolation than ever.

The wars of liberation in Southern Africa from the 1960s took their own toll on family stability and traditional gender division of labour. Some of the fighters did have their wives with them. Indeed, liberation armies like ZANLA and ZIPRA in Zimbabwe and FREMLIMO in Mozambique included a few female fighters. But on the whole, the impact of the wars was disruptive of family life and of the traditional gender division of labour.

After independence there were counter-revolutionary wars among some of the frontline states. The most artificial of the post-colonial wars was that of Mozambique initiated by the so-called Mozambique National Resistance (MNR of RENAMO).

Again, there have been implications for relations between the genders. In addition to the usual disruptive consequences of war for the family, the MNR, by the mid-1980s, had inflicted enough damage on the infrastructure in Mozambique that many migrant workers never got home to their families in between their contracts with the South African mines.

It is not completely clear how this situation has affected the doctrine of 'dual fertility' in relation to the role of the African woman. One possibility is that the extra long absences of the husbands have reduced fertility rates in some communities in Mozambique. The other scenario is that the pattern of migrant labour in Southern Africa generally has initiated a tendency towards *de facto* polyandry. The woman who is left behind acquires over time a *de facto* extra husband.[5]

If the more widespread pattern is that of declining fertility as a result of extra long absences of husbands, the principle of 'dual fertility' has reduced the social functions of the fertility of the womb and increased the woman's involvement in matters pertaining to the fertility of the soil.

On the other hand, if the more significant tendency in mining communities in Southern Africa is towards *de facto* polyandry, a whole new nexus of social relationships may be in the making in Southern Africa.[6]

Other changes in Africa during this period which affected relationships between men and women included the impact of new technologies on gender roles. Cultivation with the hoe still left the African woman

5. There is no doubt that such arrangements occur in Mozambique. What is not clear is how widespread *de facto* polyandry is becoming in Southern Africa.
6. I am indebted to the field research and interviews in Southern Africa which accompanied the BBC/WETA television project; see A. A. Mazrui, 1986.

centrally involved in agriculture but mechanization of agriculture in Africa has tended to marginalize women. Their role as 'custodians of earth' is threatened by male prerogatives in new and more advanced technologies.

Another threat to the central role of the African woman in the economy in this period has come from the nature of Western education. It is true that the Westernized African woman is usually more mobile and with more freedom for her own interests than is her more traditional sister. But a translation from custodian of fire, water and earth to keeper of the typewriter is definitely a form of marginalization for African womanhood. Typing is less fundamental for survival than cultivation. The Westernized African woman in the second half of the twentieth century has tended to be more free but less important for African economies than the traditional woman in rural areas.

The third threat to the role of the African woman in this period came with the internationalization of African economies. When economic activity in Africa was more localized, women had a decisive role in local markets and as traders. But the colonial and post-colonial tendencies towards enlargement of economic scale have increasingly pushed women to the side in international decision-making. It is true that Nigerian women especially have refused to be completely marginalized, even in international trade. But on the whole, the Africans who deal with international markets and sit on the boards of trans-national corporations are overwhelmingly men. At the meetings of the Organization of Petroleum Exporting Countries – where Muslims predominate – there are additional inhibitions about having even Nigeria represented by a female delegate.

But what is the future avenue which is likely to change the balance between men and women in public life in Africa? The reasons why women are politically subordinate are not to be sought in economic differentiation. Women in Africa are economically very active; women in Saudi Arabia are economically neutralized. And yet in both types of society women are politically subordinate. And so economic differences are not the real explanation of the political subjection of womanhood.

What is indeed universal is not the economic role of women but their military role. All over Africa (and indeed all over the world) women are militarily marginalized. What will one day change the political balance between men and women is when the military machine becomes bi-gender. The Somali army has started recruiting women. The Algerian air force has started recruiting women pilots. Both Muslim societies in Africa are beginning to give a military role to women. But the future needs more than tokenism in gender roles. In this continent of coups we may have to wait for the day when the announcement of a coup in West Africa declares as follows: 'Brigadier-General *Janet* Adebiyi has captured power in a military takeover in Lagos'.[7]

7. This issue is discussed in similar terms in A. A. Mazrui, 1990.

Pan-Africanism: a confederation of genders

Pan-Africanism has traditionally been viewed as relations between Africans across territorial boundaries. But pan-Africanism should be re-defined to include relations between Africans across the divide of *gender*. It is not enough to transcend the divisions of nationality and the territorial legacy of the scramble for Africa. There is a need to transcend an even older political divide between Africans – the *political* gap between men and women in the realm of public affairs.

In Nkrumah's terms, pan-Africanism was defined as readiness to share power in a territorial federation. But there is a bigger imperative to share power in a *confederation of genders*.

Traditional Africa before European colonization knew great occasions of power-sharing between genders. The eras of Hatshepsut of Egypt (fifteenth century before the Christian era), Nzinga of Angola (about 1581–1663), Yaa Asantewa of Ashanti (about 1830–1921) and Nehanda of Zimbabwe (about 1863–98) are among the highlights of pan-Africanism in this special sense of power-sharing across genders. Some of these eras have already been treated in earlier volumes of this UNESCO series.

Has the colonial impact helped or harmed the tradition of power-sharing across genders in Africa? We have indicated that the record in gender-relations has been mixed. Colonial rule and cultural Westernization have marginalized women in some of their roles – while raising them in others. Pan-Africanism as a case of gender relations has both suffered and gained from the impact of the West upon Africa.

Because the period since 1935 has witnessed the fuller incorporation of Africa into the global system, the outside world has, by definition, impinged more deeply into the ordinary lives of African men and women than ever before. A number of social contradictions have occurred. In relation to the role of women, Africa's internationalization has both diminished them economically and started their upliftment in diplomacy.

We have indicated that in this period since 1935 localized economies in Africa have provided a much bigger role for women than have economies which have gone international. We have mentioned that historically African women were often in charge of marketing surplus agricultural produce, as well as being active participants in the processes of rural production. When both production and marketing went increasingly international in colonial and post-colonial Africa, the share of women in controlling the economic processes began, as we noted, to decline. As we indicated, the Africans who sat on the boards of directors of trans-national corporations were overwhelmingly men. There seems to be little doubt that economic internationalization in colonial and post-colonial Africa has so far been a marginalizing experience for women. Economic pan-Africanism across genders has suffered in this period.

914

On the other hand, diplomacy as a career after independence opened up new pan-African opportunities for highly educated African women in the post-colonial era. In September 1969, Angie E. Brooks of Liberia was (as indicated in Chapter 1) nominated to serve as president of the United Nations General Assembly – only the second woman ever to serve in that capacity. (The first was Madame Pandit of India, a member of the Nehru family.) In New York, Angie Brooks became the most senior African diplomat. Pan-Africanism across gender benefited.[8]

PLATE 30.1 *Left: Angie Brooks of Liberia, who served as president of the United Nations General Assembly in 1969–70; right: Princess Elizabeth Bagaya of Uganda, minister of foreign affairs, addressing the United Nations General Assembly, September 1974*

Ambassador Brooks had blazed other diplomatic trails before – including her services as the first woman and the first African to preside over the United Nations Trusteeship Council. When she ascended to the presidency of the General Assembly itself in 1969, Ms Brooks affirmed: 'I am proud of my continent, my country and my sex'. The most authoritative voice in the General Assembly was for a while the voice of an African woman.

Uganda's Elizabeth Bagaya (former Princess of Toro) served as Idi

8. For stimulation on this theme, I am indebted to a conversation with Delores Mortimer, senior specialist managing international education exchange programmes at the US Information Agency (USIA) in Washington, DC, currently on leave working at the University of Michigan.

Amīn's roving ambassador and later as foreign minister in the 1970s. But Princess Elizabeth was too independent to last in such a capacity under such a volatile military regime. Indeed, she was too independent to last as Uganda's ambassador to the United States in the late 1980s under President Yoweri Museveni. She refused to be 'precipitately' transferred to Paris – and preferred to resign instead. Nevertheless, Elizabeth Bagaya Nyabongo was for a while one of the true voices of both territorial and gender pan-Africanism.

Uganda has had other women in prominent diplomatic roles from Bonn (Ambassador Bernadette Olowo) to Ottawa (High-Commissioner Anna Amailuk). In the late 1980s these included Freda Blick as ambassador to France. Also in France, as ambassador of Ghana, was Theresa Strictner-Scott. Representing Africa abroad was a case of externalized pan-Africanism in this diplomatic sense. Some of these women diplomats also represented one African country in another. Ambassador Amailuk, for example, once represented Uganda in Ghana.

Quasi-diplomatic roles involving less formal international activity have also opened up for African women. Angie Brooks served as president of the International Federation of Women Lawyers and was decorated by a number of foreign governments including Brazil, the Federal Republic of Germany, Yugoslavia, Cameroon and the People's Republic of China.

Kenyan women who have served in quasi-diplomatic roles over the years have included Margaret Kenyatta, Grace Ogot and others. The Kenyan Foreign Service has also included high-ranking women officials and diplomats – often serving both Africa and their own country.

At the time of Zambia's independence in 1964, the country's most highly publicized woman was not a diplomat at all: she was Alice Lenshina, the prophetess who led the Lumpa Church (see Chapter 17 of this volume). Alice's defiance of Zambia's government and ruling party precipitated serious civil conflict. But whichever side one preferred to take in the confrontation between Alice Lenshina and Zambia's newly independent government under Kenneth Kaunda, the phenomenon of Alice was one more indication that Africa could still produce highly committed female leaders, capable of inspiring their followers to great feats of courage and sacrifice.

Other women in Zambia since then have assumed quasi-diplomatic roles from time to time – including Dr Mutumba Bull both as a political figure and as a scholar. Such women have served both their country and the continent.

Certain spouses of African leaders in this period developed a high diplomatic and political visibility of their own. In the 1980s, Mrs Sally Mugabe became active in a number of humanitarian and international causes – especially the special cause of the welfare of the children of Africa as a whole. Mrs Mugabe went into an active diplomatic alliance with the United Nations Children's Fund (UNICEF) – and hosted pan-

African meetings in Harare to promote the cause of Africa's children. (The nearest American analogy to Mrs Mugabe was the late Mrs Eleanor Roosevelt in her diplomatic and humanitarian work, both before and after her husband's death.)

Another African presidential spouse who was diplomatically active for a while was Mrs Jehan Anwar al-Sadat of Egypt. Among conservative Muslim men in the Middle East, Mrs al-Sadat's public posture and visibility were often a liability rather than an asset. But to many women in the Arab world, Mrs al-Sadat became, at least for a while, a role model. She was forced into relative oblivion after the assassination of her husband in 1981.

PLATE 30.2 *Left: Jehan al-Sadat of Egypt, an advocate of the promotion of women's rights; right: Winnie Mandela of South Africa, a leader in the anti-*apartheid *struggle, Johannesburg, October 1985*

In Southern Africa as a whole in this period, pan-Africanism has been at its most tumultuous both politically and in gender relations. In the Republic of South Africa the most spectacular spouse of any race in the 1980s was Winnie Mandela. Although she had neither a direct diplomatic role nor an official political office in the struggle against *apartheid*, Winnie Mandela became the most famous African woman of the 1980s. She found herself in the middle of a variety of historical and pan-African processes in her part of the continent. It was not just the politics of race which affected her. It was also the politics of gender and of age-grades.

917

In Southern Africa as a whole, bridges needed to be built not only between races, but also between genders and across generations. Relations between men and women had been disrupted by repression, by wars of liberation and by labour migration. And relations between the African youth and the older generations continued to be strained by the anger and radicalization generated by *apartheid.*

In the middle of these three sets of pan-African relations – gender, race and generation – came the crisis of Winnie Mandela late in the 1980s. As a woman whose husband (Nelson Mandela) had been in prison for more than a quarter of a century, Winnie Mandela had symbolized the strain of political struggle upon gender relations. As a woman who attempted to organize young activists for social roles, Winnie Mandela had been one of the bridge-builders across generations.

But in 1988 and 1989 things went seriously wrong for Mrs Mandela – partly because of the activities of those very young people that she had tried to organize. The woman who had been a martyr to *apartheid* since her husband was sentenced to life-imprisonment in 1964, the woman who had herself suffered banning and restriction in a black ghetto for long periods of time, had now become a subject of denunciation and derision in some of the circles which once acclaimed her as 'mother of the nation'.

But her very status had been part of the wider saga concerning gender-relations in Southern Africa. Repression and war have often created 'widows of the revolution' – widows of martyrs to the liberation struggle. There have also been 'cage widows' – wives of husbands put away in detention for life. Winnie Mandela had become the most internationally illustrious of the so-called 'cage widows'.

Behind it all were some hard sociological trends. For the black youth in Southern Africa, new forms of initiation into warriorhood had emerged. Many a teenager had been enlisted into the liberation armies. And in urban centres the new warriorhood sometimes took the form of confronting armed security forces in the streets of Soweto. Winnie Mandela's experiment of a youthful soccer team with additional responsibilities of guarding her could have been a pilot scheme worth emulating. But it became an experiment which had gone wrong. Her soccer team degenerated into a gang fighting other young people. Youthful gang warfare caught up with Winnie Mandela's dreams.

Southern Africa had also created special kinds of divergence between *gender* and *class.* In South Africa's mining communities, men had not been allowed to live with their wives. As we indicated, gender *apartheid* had been added to racial *apartheid.* We have noted that women had often remained on the land as subsistence farmers – while their men travelled thousands of miles for wages. The result was, as we indicated, the creation of a migrant male proletariat and a sedentary female peasantry. As a wife separated from her own husband by an unjust system, Winnie Mandela became a role model for the rural peasant women as well.

In the struggle to build bridges across races, South Africa in this period produced two black Nobel laureates for peace – Albert Luthuli and Desmond Tutu. But there were no Nobel Prizes to be won in the struggle to build bridges between genders or bridges across generations. 'Peace' in terms of the Nobel Prize was not yet defined by the yardstick of either fighting sexism or moderating generational conflict. Winnie Mandela was too controversial in the 1980s to stand a chance of becoming the first black female to win the Nobel Prize even if her efforts across genders and generations had succeeded. However, since Mrs Mandela's political career was far from over, the final estimate of her pan-African contribution could only be computed by history itself in the fullness of time.

Also in the womb of time was whether a woman secretary-general of the Organization of African Unity would come *before* or *after* the first woman president of an African country.[9]

Colonial education: liberating but not developmental

What may come sooner to Africa than such a gender revolution is the second major shift we have referred to – a more general transformation of Africa's level of *expertise*. While the continent may indeed be awaiting both a sexual revolution and a scientific one, prospects for the latter may be more imminent than for the former.

A major point to bear in mind is that the skills which came to Africa with colonial rule happened to have one over-riding historical ambiguity. The skills turned out to be useful for *liberation* but basically useless for *development*. Colonially imported skills were essentially those of *communication* – and expertise in these new forms of literary and oral communication did help the cause of decolonization. What colonialism failed to transfer effectively were skills of *production*. It is in that sense that the colonial heritage of education and training fell short of promoting real development in African 'territories', as we have shown in the relevant chapters.

The impact of the Great Depression and the Second World War on Europe helped, as we have indicated, to make capitalism more accountable and eventually to make imperialism more responsible. It was mainly after the Second World War that the imperial powers began to pay special attention to colonial education and training in Africa. New skills of communication were being forged. It was in 1948 that the University College of the Gold Coast was established – and Ibadan opened its doors to its first pupils as a University College. In February of the following year (1949) the University of Lovanium was established by decree in the Belgian Congo, though it was not until 1954 that the first 30 Africans were admitted to a pre-university course, of whom only 11 were declared to have passed.

9. See A. A. Mazrui, 1990.

In Uganda, Makerere became a University College late in 1949. As for research institutions which were emerging, these included the Institute of Tropical Ophthalmology which was set up in Bamako, French Sudan, in 1953 and ORANO (*Organisation pour la recherche sur l'alimentation et la nutrition en Afrique*) was set up in Dakar. Research organizations of this kind did have developmental implications and were not merely based on skills of communication. But the study of nutrition or ophthalmology is not the same thing as the study of techniques of *production*. In any case, these research institutions were only a small fraction of the thrust of colonial education. The main thrust was still in the direction of literary and verbal skills.

Some of those techniques of communication were used by African patriots within the constituency of the imperial metropole, and even to communicate with the international community at large. As earlier chapters indicated, the concept of *négritude* was born among black patriots in France – especially Aimé Césaire and Léopold Senghor. The negritude movement began at the beginning of the period covered in this volume. The nearest Anglophone equivalent to negritude as a movement of cultural validation in this early period was, as was shown earlier, Jomo Kenyatta's book, *Facing Mount Kenya*, which was also a declaration of cultural vindication, and was first published in 1938. Both negritude and *Facing Mount Kenya* were important aspects of Africa's new skills of communication – addressed both to the metropole and to the world at large. In such instances, these skills were being used as part of the crusade of liberation. In 1947 Alioune Diop founded *Présence africaine* in Paris – another weapon of communication in the struggle for Africa's vindication.

On balance, these colonially-transmitted skills of literature and oratory in European language did indeed serve the cause of Africa's political liberation well. It was not by accident that anti-colonial movements were disproportionately led by Westernized and semi-Westernized African patriots. The founding fathers of the new African nations were in a large measure products of either missionary schools within Africa or Western colleges abroad – or, quite often, both. These included the founder-presidents of Ghana (Nkrumah), Senegal (Senghor), Tanzania (Nyerere), Nigeria (Azikiwe), Côte d'Ivoire (Houphouët-Boigny), Malawi (Banda), Kenya (Kenyatta), and many others. The evidence is overwhelming that although Westernized African patriots were only a small minority of the total population of the continent, they were the vanguard of the struggle for political independence. As we indicated in the political chapters of this volume, these Western-educated Africans eventually overshadowed the traditional rulers – and inherited the reins of power from the departing colonialists. It is in this sense that the skills of communication transferred to Africa during the colonial period helped the cause of Africa's political independence.

What the colonial powers did *not* transfer were genuine skills of production. To that extent colonial education – though greatly valuable for the phase of Africa's political liberation – has been unequal to the task of Africa's development. Agricultural techniques in Africa continue to be mainly rudimentary, factories have to import almost every nut and bolt, dams are often in disrepair, equipment grinds to a standstill because of lack of spare parts. Africa's industrial capacity to use its own minerals is pathetic. Even our capacity to *dig* for these minerals without foreign equipment, expertise and organization, is astonishingly modest. The continent still produces from its mines what it is unable to use; and imports for use what it is unable to produce.

PLATE 30.3 *Triga nuclear reactor, Zaire, 1965*

The conclusion is irresistible. While colonial rule did create its own grave-diggers by educating a political élite, colonialism did not create an economic vanguard for Africa's development. The mission of Africa's emancipation was well served by colonial education; but the mission of Africa's development can never be fulfilled through the colonial legacy alone. Skills of communication must now be combined with skills of production and development.

On governance and development

Africa entered its new era of independence with an even wider *skill gap* than production gap; a chasm between its new post-colonial institutions and the ability to control them effectively.

There was first the lop-sided capitalism which African countries had inherited from the colonial era. The continent had received Western consumption patterns without Western productive techniques, Western tastes without Western performance, urbanization without industrialization, capitalist greed without capitalist discipline. To paraphrase a Western poet (Alexander Pope):

> A little capitalism is a dangerous thing;
> Drink deep, or taste not the Western Spring.

Africa did not drink from the spring of capitalism as deeply as Southeast Asia had done, nor was Africa allowed not to taste capitalism at all. The result in Africa became a tragedy of greed without the atonement of efficiency.

Then there were the political institutions which post-colonial Africa had inherited. Africa's own indigenous structures of governance had been either abolished or undermined by colonial rulers. And the idea of a standing African army was inaugurated with weapons produced by a technology far in advance of the level attained *locally*. Africa emerged into independence with skills of destruction much greater than its skills of production. And yet both sets of skills were still heavily reliant on external models and foreign suppliers. This played havoc with civil–military relations in Africa, and the whole legacy of coups and counter-coups. Because of the skill gap, militarization in Africa has not fed into civilian industrialization. There has been no symbiotic relationship between defence and development. Apart from Egypt and the Republic of South Africa, almost no African country has a major 'defence industry' at all. Most African armies not only import every tank and every rocket; they also import every sten gun, every cartridge; sometimes even the uniforms of African armies are imported.

Militarization without industrialization has destabilized both economic and political systems. The marriage between politics and the military has been one problem; the divorce between defence and development has been another. There is a devastating skill gap in all these areas – political, economic and technological underdevelopment.

Among the casualties of this situation are human rights in Africa. The failure of Western liberal institutions in most of Africa is due not only to their foreignness but also to Africa's weak capacity for organizing either disciplined political parties, or efficient corporate power or effective trade unions. After all, Western democracy was *imposed* on Japan, as well as on Africa. Americans imposed it on Japan over a period of less than a decade; Africans had a longer period of colonial tutelage. And yet Western institutions prospered in alien Japanese soil, but have had difficulty surviving in alien African soil. The skill gap in *organization* may well be part of the explanation, as well as the less developed capitalist base in Africa as compared with Japan.

The relationship between the skills of governance and prospects for economic development since independence have been affected by the following inter-related factors:

(1) How big the government is (SIZE);
(2) How much the government does (ROLE);
(3) How well the government does it (EFFECTIVENESS);
(4) How representative and equitable the government is (LEGITIMACY).

The first consideration of 'bigness' has included the size of not only the civil service proper but also the parastatals. The second consideration of role has related to the role of the state in the economy and the nature of the government's functions. The third consideration has concerned competence, effectiveness and degree of rationality in governmental behaviour. The fourth conditioning factor is about democracy and representativeness – or lack of them.

It is important to remember that, in Africa, representativeness in the post-colonial era is often measured *ethnically* rather than electorally. Ethnic arithmetic often helps to reassure different groups whether or not they are truly part of the machinery and among the beneficiaries. A government is deemed to be more or less representative by the extent to which it reflects the ethnic composition of the wider society. In Nigeria this principle of representativeness since the civil war is often referred to as 'the federal character' of the nation.

The dynamic of ethnic representativeness has had a propensity to enlarge governmental and bureaucratic institutions. The civil service and the parastatals have often become 'bloated' in response to the delicate balance of ethnic arithmetic.

On the other hand, insensitivity to the need for ethnic balance in post-colonial Africa can sometimes be destabilizing. The absence of ethnic representativeness in a country like Nigeria or Uganda has often been a bigger political risk than the absence of electoral representativeness at the ballot box. Ethnic arithmetic has often been a more compelling imperative than the ballot in the liberal sense.

As for the criterion of performance of the government, one central dilemma in post-colonial Africa concerns the relationship between economic liberalization and political liberalization. There are certain countries in Africa where political pluralism has tended to be economically destabilizing. Nigeria under President Shehu Shagari (1979–83) was politically open and competitive, but economically the country was sheer economic anarchy. Ghana under Limann and Sudan under Sadiq al-Mahdī were also politically open but economically devastated societies.

923

(Southern Sudan was neither politically free nor economically protected. It was devastated both politically and economically.)

In such African countries there has been a genuine moral dilemma. Political pluralism has carried a high risk of economic decay. In the final analysis it has sometimes been an agonizing choice between *either* political freedom *or* economic development – but not both together. In such a situation what was the duty of donors and international institutions? Has there been a genuine risk that institutions like the World Bank and the International Monetary Fund would actually *prefer* military regimes like those of Ibrāhim Babangida and Jerry Rawlings to democratically elected regimes like those of Shagari, Limann and al-Mahdī?

Is there a risk in the 1990s that external bodies would encourage economic liberalization while discouraging political liberalization? Could the latter encouragement of military regimes occur implicitly – sometimes almost unconsciously?

As for the role of corruption in governance after independence, this sometimes has taken the form of *privatization of the state*. Ethnic privatization has occurred when ethnic representativeness was abandoned – and one particular ethnic group monopolized or disproportionately controlled the state. The Nubi in Idi Amīn's Uganda was one case in point.

Dynastic privatization occurred when the resources and symbols of the state were monopolized by an individual and his more immediate family. Bokassa in the Central African Empire literally attempted to create a dynasty.

Anarchic privatization has occurred when the wealth and power of the state are dissipated in a free-for-all scramble for advantage. Nigeria under Shehu Shagari became a case of anarchic privatization, especially from 1981 onwards.

In the *political* domain, Africa's worst evils since independence are the danger of tyranny on one side and the risk of anarchy on the other. Tyranny is too much government, anarchy is too little government. The tyrannical tendency is often a centralization of violence. The anarchic tendency is basically a decentralization of violence – often neighbour against neighbour.

In the *economic* domain, Africa's worst evils are the risk of economic dependency on one side and the peril of economic decay on the other. Dependency is a truncated capacity for self-reliance. Decay is a truncated capacity for development.

The crisis of governance in Africa concerns the relationship between the political evils of tyranny and anarchy on one side and the economic evils of dependency and decay on the other. What is the way out? Among the most important skills which need to be developed from the 1990s onwards are precisely those which will ameliorate this central crisis of governance.

Africans do not have to imitate Western liberal institutions in order to reconcile stability with equity. But the people of the continent do need to develop enough skills and organization to fight and defend their rights even against their own governments. Rulers everywhere tend to become arbitrary unless there is organized counterforce to check their excesses. The skill gap in Africa is part and parcel of such rampant violation of human rights in the continent. Yoweri Museveni's army in Uganda in the 1980s constituted the first successful attempt by civilians to organize militarily against an undemocratic African regime. But the problems remained enormous. Both stability and equity were still in doubt.

On population and the environment

African problems in the coming decades will extend beyond the quest for political order and viable economies. The very *ecology* of Africa is endangered; deforestation and desertification are rendering large parts of Africa desolate. Part of the problem is a weak planning capability in the continent as a whole. Although the majority of African governments favour national development plans, most of those plans are honoured more in the breach than in the observance. Forests are depleted without much of an effort at reforestation. The tropical rain forest in the Côte d'Ivoire has been devastated by French and Lebanese economic interests in collusion with the local establishment. Little attention is paid to the ecological damage or to the need for compensatory reforestation. Senegal – after considerable environmental damage – has initiated a modest attempt at growing new trees. Skills of planning still lag behind ecological protection.

The skill gap extends to the use of firewood as the most prevalent form of energy in rural Africa. Wood is also the most ancient form of domesticated energy. But rural Africa has to learn how to use this energy economically. Relatively simple alterations in methods of cooking and in the efficiency of using fire could drastically cut down the consumption of firewood. And this in turn could reduce, or even arrest, the pace of deforestation and desertification in parts of the continent.

Then there is the problem of relating livestock to available pasture in those societies where cattle, goats or camels have high cultural value. Governments have found it hard to persuade pastoralists that large numbers of cattle, goats or camels have a potentially detrimental effect on the ecology and on the future availability of grass. *Surplus cattle* and *deficit skill* have all too often become a deadly combination.

What about the morally dubious concept of 'surplus *people*' in a continent of deficit skill? A limited capacity for planning has also affected the issue of population growth in the continent. Is Africa producing more people than it can feed? Although the 1980s gave mixed signals about the relationship between food production and population growth in Africa, the risk of less food production per capita did persist. One solution was

925

PLATE 30.4 *Desertification of the Sahel*

PLATE 30.5 *Deforestation of Africa*

to improve the level of food production; the other was to decrease the rate of population growth. Both solutions required skills. On food production the relevant chapters in this book have dealt with that issue. What about population growth?

By the 1980s there were more babies being born in Africa than anywhere else in the world. The rate of population growth in black Africa became the highest in the entire history of the human race – and it was still gathering momentum (Table 30.1). The rate of growth was 2.5 per cent per year in 1960–70, 2.7 per cent in 1970–80, 3.1 per cent in 1980–86, and by 1989 it was estimated at 3.2 per cent. Countries like Kenya exceeded a growth rate of 4 per cent per year.

Africa's love of children was at once its glory and its unfolding tragedy. In the 1980s, research indicated that African families desired to be even larger than they already were. On average the African woman wanted six or more children. In 1988 the Kenyan woman aspired to be the mother of eight children. The desired family size in Africa as a whole ranged from five in Ghana to nine in Mauritania.

One major reason behind love of children was Africa's concept of *immortality*. Immortality in Africa was not simply a matter of going to heaven. It was also leaving one's blood still flowing in the veins of the living. In modern terms, no one was deemed to be really dead for as long as his or her genes were still part of the living. William Wordsworth[10] was coming close to Africa's philosophy when he said:

> Oh joy! That in our embers
> Is something that doth live;
> That Nature yet remembers
> What was so fugitive.

Because of high infant mortality, African parents in the 1980s had six children in order to be sure that they had at least four. To make allowances for the death of babies was itself a form of family planning. In many African villages death was a more familiar visitor than the doctor.

What Africa therefore needed most was not birth control, but *death control* – not how to have fewer children, but how to ensure that more babies survived. Normally, death control at first increases population growth. But after a while it is supposed to reassure parents sufficiently to make them take the risk of having fewer babies. And yet by the end of the 1980s this demographic transition had still not occurred in Africa.

Three types of conflict affected children in Africa. There was conflict between human beings (especially racial and ethnic confrontations). Secondly, there was conflict between population growth and the environment (a kind of ecological warfare). And, thirdly, there was the struggle against

10. W. Wordsworth, *Ode on Intimations of Immortality*.

poverty and ignorance (the campaign for social upliftment and for the satisfaction of at least the basic human needs).

The racial and ethnic confrontations in both civil wars and wars of liberation produce *children of war* – often deprived of at least one parent, often displaced from their village or location. Children in refugee camps are a classic illustration of such deprivation.

The struggle between population growth and the elements of nature was a more primordial engagement. Sometimes nature teased Africa in a very cruel way – drought this year, flood the next, and all very destructive. Parents and children were caught up in those upheavals of the environment.

The third struggle for Africa's children was against poverty and ignorance. Sometimes simple solutions of rehydration for children, or salt replacement, could save a million lives in Africa. Immunization campaigns of the kind undertaken by UNICEF (the United Nations' Children's Fund) and the World Health Organization (WHO) in the 1980s kept death at bay in some villages. Lessons in nutrition were also life-saving.

The three kinds of conflict were often interlinked. To fight *ignorance* about soil erosion was basically to struggle *for* soil conservation and environmental protection. Racial and ethnic confrontations had consequences for both poverty, on one side, and ecology, on the other.

What was the role of skilled Africans in all this struggle? What was the role of artists, educators and intellectuals? Their role was indeed partly educational and partly mobilizational. They had a role to play in educating both the public and policy-makers. They also had a role to play in generating commitment and enthusiasm for policies which could protect children in all three types of stressful situations and conflicts.

But the mobilizer needed first to be mobilized – the educator needed first to be educated. The artists, teachers and intellectuals needed to be exposed much more to problems of children of war, problems of ecological catastrophe and of social deprivation, than they have ordinarily tended to be.

From the mid-1980s, UNICEF started trying to enlist artists, intellectuals and other skilled Africans in a crusade to save the children of Africa.

But how was Africa to ensure a dramatic fall in infant mortality? UNICEF demonstrated that some of the methods required relatively modest skills. And yet even those modest skills had not yet been utilized. Millions of babies in both colonial and post-colonial Africa died from diarrhoea. Simple methods of re-hydration and salt-replacement could have saved most of those babies. Skilled outsiders are beginning to make small packets of 'salt-and-water' available to mothers in rural Africa. Good drinking water is another important prerequisite in this respect, and African governments and international agencies should address themselves to its provision.

928

In addition, *immunization* against the other baby-killers of Africa could make a considerable difference to life-chances. Baby-killers like dyptheria, whooping cough, measles and typhoid could be rapidly arrested with large-scale immunization. Countries like Burkina Faso have embarked on such programmes.

But in the period covered by this volume there was one disease where the skill gap affected Westerners and Africans alike. The disease which Westerners had called AIDS (Acquired Immune Deficiency Syndrome) was probably the most important disease to have hit the human race in this particular period of global history.

The disease pre-eminently belonged to the last quarter of the twentieth century, especially from the 1980s onwards. In the first place it defied all laws of international class struggle and distribution of wealth. The majority of the first casualties were either Americans in such prominent cities as New York and San Francisco or Africans in some of the poorest sectors of the continent. The skill gap was in both the West and Africa.

For once in this period of history the West was as ignorant medically as Africa. Rich and poor were afflicted alike. Westerners and Africans shared a moment of medical bewilderment.

But let us not permit this brief moment of shared ignorance disguise the distance between those who walk on the moon and those who strive to reach the village. The skill issue is fundamental not just for policy-making within each African country. As indicated earlier, it is basic to the entire North–South divide, to the stratification of the world into developed and underdeveloped countries. That is the ultimate burden of this period of human history.

Conclusion

The years covered in this volume (1935 to the present day) constitute the great connecting period between the age of colonialism and the new era of independence. We have divided this short period in Africa's history into, first, the decade of global conflict (1935–45); secondly, the decade and a half of intensified struggle against colonialism (1945–60); and thirdly, the glittering but uncertain dawn of independence and its quest for development, especially from 1960 onwards. Problems have proliferated.

But historians confront their greatest challenge when they not only study the past but also use their knowledge to try and understand the present and identify the likely trends of the future. The period covered in this volume coincides with the greatest technological revolutions in human history – from space exploration to the impact of the computer on earth. While Africa has been marching towards independence, others have walked on the moon.

TABLE 30.1 *Africa: total population and annual rate of change 1950–2025, medium variant*

	Population (thousands)							
	1950	*1955*	*1960*	*1965*	*1970*	*1975*	*1980*	*1985*
AFRICA	221 984	247 954	279 316	317 056	361 768	413 298	477 232	552 884
EASTERN AFRICA	64 984	72 774	82 326	94 165	108 228	123 675	144 172	167 815
British Indian Ocean Terr.	2	2	2	2	2	2	2	2
Burundi	2 456	2 691	2 948	3 224	3 522	3 680	4 132	4 731
Comoros	173	194	215	240	274	320	392	463
Djibouti	60	69	80	114	168	243	304	354
Ethiopia	19 573	21 680	24 191	27 150	30 623	34 309	38 750	43 083
Kenya	6 265	7 189	8 332	9 749	11 498	13 741	16 632	20 096
Madagascar	4 230	4 718	5 309	6 016	6 742	7 595	8 785	10 237
Malawi	2 881	3 169	3 529	3 975	4 518	5 244	6 183	7 340
Mauritius[a]	493	571	660	753	826	892	966	1 020
Mozambique	6 198	6 744	7 461	8 338	9 395	10 498	12 095	13 711
Réunion	257	293	339	393	441	484	508	547
Rwanda	2 120	2 391	2 742	3 183	3 728	4 384	5 163	6 102
Seychelles	34	38	42	47	53	59	63	65
Somalia	2 423	2 657	2 935	3 267	3 668	4 156	5 345	6 370
Uganda	4 762	5 556	6 562	8 047	9 806	11 183	13 120	15 647
United Republic of Tanzania	7 886	8 803	10 026	11 586	13 513	15 900	18 867	22 748
Zambia	2 440	2 753	3 141	3 614	4 189	4 841	5 738	7 006
Zimbabwe	2 730	3 257	3 812	4 466	5 260	6 143	7 126	8 292
MIDDLE AFRICA	26 316	28 792	31 811	35 343	39 599	45 243	52 183	60 209
Angola	4 131	4 437	4 816	5 180	5 588	6 520	7 723	8 754
Cameroon	4 467	4 843	5 297	5 874	6 610	7 520	8 653	10 051
Central African Republic	1 314	1 414	1 534	1 677	1 849	2 057	2 320	2 646
Chad	2 658	2 838	3 064	3 334	3 652	4 030	4 477	5 018
Congo	808	889	988	1 111	1 263	1 447	1 669	1 939
Equatorial Guinea	226	238	252	270	291	225	217	312
Gabon	469	477	486	495	504	637	806	985
Sao Tome and Principe	60	62	64	68	73	81	94	107
Zaire	12 184	13 595	15 310	17 335	19 769	22 726	26 225	30 398
NORTHERN AFRICA	51 798	57 994	65 115	73 297	83 158	93 799	107 240	123 348
Algeria	8 753	9 715	10 800	11 923	13 746	16 018	18 740	21 788
Egypt	20 330	22 990	25 922	29 389	33 053	36 289	40 875	46 511
Libyan Arab Jamahiriya	1 029	1 126	1 349	1 623	1 986	2 446	3 043	3 786

[a] Including Agalesa, Rodrigues and St Brandon

TABLE 30.1 (cont.)

	1990	1995	2000	2005	2010	2015	2020	2025
	\multicolumn{8}{c}{*Population (thousands)*}

	1990	1995	2000	2005	2010	2015	2020	2025
AFRICA	642 111	746 819	866 585	1 001 349	1 148 474	1 301 371	1 452 067	1 596 855
EASTERN AFRICA	196 873	232 243	273 594	321 148	374 399	431 034	487 868	542 536
British Indian Ocean Terr.	2	2	2	2	2	2	2	2
Burundi	5 472	6 362	7 358	8 469	9 657	10 841	11 950	12 976
Comoros	550	658	789	945	1 123	1 315	1 510	1 697
Djibouti	409	474	552	644	748	862	979	1 094
Ethiopia	49 240	57 140	66 364	76 961	88 889	101 753	114 313	126 618
Kenya	24 031	28 978	35 060	42 389	50 905	60 071	69 799	79 113
Madagascar	12 004	14 113	16 627	19 529	22 827	26 476	30 272	34 014
Malawi	8 754	10 494	12 458	14 654	17 104	19 701	22 278	24 730
Mauritius[a]	1 082	1 142	1 201	1 258	1 309	1 354	1 391	1 419
Mozambique	15 656	17 922	20 493	23 365	26 456	29 592	32 593	35 416
Réunion	598	647	692	735	777	817	855	889
Rwanda	7 237	8 602	10 200	11 973	13 791	15 511	17 196	18 847
Seychelles	69	72	75	78	80	82	83	84
Somalia	7 497	8 441	9 736	11 312	13 114	15 035	16 905	18 701
Uganda	18 794	22 666	26 958	31 730	36 982	42 561	48 101	53 144
United Rep. of Tanzania	27 318	32 971	39 639	47 460	56 333	65 845	75 485	84 917
Zambia	8 452	10 222	12 267	14 632	17 328	20 264	23 286	26 260
Zimbabwe	9 709	11 340	13 123	15 012	16 974	18 951	20 870	22 616
MIDDLE AFRICA	70 054	81 933	95 981	112 344	130 958	151 395	172 266	192 342
Angola	10 020	11 531	13 295	15 317	17 561	20 004	22 438	24 731
Cameroon	11 833	14 037	16 701	19 897	23 665	27 893	32 264	36 547
Central African Republic	3 039	3 511	4 074	4 740	5 497	6 325	7 154	7 947
Chad	5 678	6 447	7 337	8 352	9 491	10 728	12 013	13 245
Congo	2 271	2 678	3 167	3 746	4 406	5 130	5 860	6 568
Equatorial Guinea	352	400	455	519	592	671	752	828
Gabon	1 172	1 382	1 612	1 827	2 052	2 309	2 594	2 875
Sao Tome and Principe	121	135	151	167	184	201	219	235
Zaire	35 568	41 813	49 190	57 780	67 509	78 135	88 972	99 366
NORTHERN AFRICA	140 553	159 245	178 949	199 330	219 580	238 925	256 728	274 390
Algeria	24 960	28 704	32 904	37 286	41 510	45 279	48 484	51 950
Egypt	52 426	58 388	64 210	70 099	75 746	81 050	85 768	90 355
Libyan Arab Jamahiriya	4 545	5 446	6 500	7 695	8 976	10 276	11 567	12 841

TABLE 30.1 (cont.)

	Population (thousands)							
	1950	*1955*	*1960*	*1965*	*1970*	*1975*	*1980*	*1985*
NORTHERN AFRICA (cont.)								
Morocco	8 953	10 132	11 626	13 323	15 310	17 305	19 382	22 025
Sudan	9 190	10 150	11 165	12 359	13 859	16 012	18 681	21 822
Tunisia	3 530	3 860	4 221	4 630	5 127	5 611	6 384	7 261
Western Sahara	14	21	32	50	76	117	135	155
SOUTHERN AFRICA	15 736	17 639	19 892	22 623	25 581	28 866	32 379	36 372
Botswana	389	433	481	549	623	755	902	1 083
Lesotho	734	794	870	963	1 064	1 187	1 339	1 538
Namibia	666	736	817	910	1 016	1 141	1 306	1 518
South Africa	13 683	15 385	17 396	19 832	22 458	25 301	28 270	31 569
Swaziland	264	291	326	370	419	482	563	664
WESTERN AFRICA	63 150	70 754	80 173	91 628	105 202	121 715	141 258	165 141
Benin	2 046	2 111	2 237	2 430	2 693	3 033	3 459	3 985
Burkina Faso	3 654	4 012	4 452	4 961	5 550	6 202	6 957	7 877
Cape Verde	146	169	196	229	267	278	289	324
Côte d'Ivoire	2 775	3 221	3 799	4 527	5 515	6 755	8 194	9 933
Gambia	294	313	352	404	464	548	641	745
Ghana	4 900	5 759	6 774	7 828	8 612	9 831	10 736	12 839
Guinea	2 550	2 826	3 136	3 488	3 900	4 149	4 461	4 987
Guinea-Bissau	505	522	542	524	525	627	795	873
Liberia	824	914	1 039	1 195	1 385	1 609	1 876	2 199
Mali	3 520	3 911	4 375	4 922	5 484	6 169	6 863	7 915
Mauritania	825	901	991	1 096	1 221	1 371	1 551	1 766
Niger	2 400	2 689	3 028	3 660	4 165	4 771	5 586	6 608
Nigeria	32 935	37 094	42 305	48 676	56 581	66 346	78 430	92 016
St Helena[b]	5	5	5	5	5	5	5	6
Senegal	2 500	2 811	3 187	3 626	4 158	4 806	5 538	6 375
Sierra Leone	1 944	2 081	2 241	2 429	2 656	2 931	3 263	3 665
Togo	1 329	1 414	1 514	1 627	2 020	2 285	2 615	3 028

[b] Including Ascensión and Tristan de Cunha

Source: United Nations (1990) *World Population Prospects*, ST/ESA/SER. A/120.

TABLE 30.1 (cont.)

	Population (thousands)							
	1990	*1995*	*2000*	*2005*	*2010*	*2015*	*2020*	*2025*
NORTHERN AFRICA (cont.)								
Morocco	25 061	28 301	31 559	34 648	37 586	40 408	43 022	45 647
Sudan	25 203	29 128	33 625	38 647	44 017	49 416	54 627	59 605
Tunisia	8 180	9 076	9 924	10 702	11 464	12 188	12 925	13 630
Western Sahara	178	202	228	254	280	308	335	362
SOUTHERN AFRICA	40 928	45 972	51 416	57 168	63 108	69 074	74 821	80 133
Botswana	1 304	1 549	1 822	2 124	2 451	2 779	3 095	3 397
Lesotho	1 774	2 053	2 370	2 731	3 138	3 579	4 013	4 427
Namibia	1 781	2 079	2 437	2 847	3 303	3 776	4 245	4 698
South Africa	35 282	39 348	43 666	48 139	52 662	57 150	61 446	65 363
Swaziland	788	943	1 121	1 326	1 554	1 790	2 023	2 249
WESTERN AFRICA	193 702	227 426	266 645	311 360	360 430	410 942	460 383	507 455
Benin	4 630	5 421	6 369	7 486	8 745	10 065	11 369	12 587
Burkina Faso	8 996	10 396	12 092	14 080	16 349	18 822	21 327	23 710
Cape Verde	370	438	515	595	676	757	841	922
Côte d'Ivoire	11 997	14 535	17 600	21 218	25 503	30 069	34 776	39 334
Gambia	861	984	1 119	1 271	1 434	1 593	1 736	1 864
Ghana	15 028	17 608	20 564	23 845	26 931	29 884	32 708	35 442
Guinea	5 755	6 700	7 830	9 162	10 667	12 252	13 820	15 273
Guinea-Bissau	964	1 073	1 197	1 338	1 491	1 649	1 791	1 918
Liberia	2 575	3 032	3 575	4 207	4 921	5 689	6 477	7 245
Mali	9 214	10 799	12 685	14 885	17 350	19 918	22 439	24 774
Mauritania	2 024	2 335	2 702	3 129	3 612	4 129	4 642	5 119
Niger	7 731	9 104	10 752	12 694	14 884	17 167	19 406	21 482
Nigeria	108 542	127 694	149 621	174 307	201 266	228 753	255 393	280 890
St Helena[b]	7	8	10	11	13	15	17	19
Senegal	7 327	8 423	9 716	11 172	12 730	14 269	15 685	16 988
Sierra Leone	4 151	4 740	5 437	6 250	7 172	8 161	9 139	10 045
Togo	3 531	4 138	4 861	5 711	6 687	7 750	8 821	9 842

We have noted in this volume (and in previous ones) Africa's participation in the history of science. But colonialism interrupted, rather than facilitated, Africa's own technological evolution. As Walter Rodney put it, Europe *'underdeveloped* Africa'.[11] At best, the skills which Europe transferred to Africa were literary and verbal – skills more of communication rather than of production and development.

But Africa managed to make good use even of those limited skills. We have shown how the Western-educated élites exploited the new techniques to mobilize the people at home, to divide public opinion in the metropole, and to cultivate the wider international community on to the side of Africa's aspirations. The struggle continues to improve governance, safeguard the environment, achieve development and protect Africa's children. But many stresses have persisted.

Two transformations are particularly necessary if Africa's predicament is to be changed fundamentally – a social shift in relations between men and women and a paradigm shift in relations between people and their environment. Gender relations are the oldest foundations of tradition. Science is the newest basis of modernity.

Africa has to find a meeting point between the two – between a revolution in human relations (men and women) and a revolution in human performance (skill and value). This particular period of African history since 1935 may turn out to have been a fitting preparation for this dual African transformation.

11. W. Rodney, 1981.

Members of the International Scientific Committee for the Drafting of a General History of Africa

The dates cited below refer to dates of membership.

Professor J. F. Ade Ajayi
(Nigeria) from 1971
Editor Volume VI

Professor F. A. Albuquerque Mourão
(Brazil), from 1975

Professor D. Birmingham
(UK), from 1985

Professor A. Adu Boahen
(Ghana), from 1971
Editor Volume VII

The late H. E. Boubou Hama
(Niger), 1971–8 (resigned in 1978);
deceased 1982

Dr (Mrs) Mutumba M. Bull
(Zambia), from 1971

Professor D. Chanaiwa
(Zimbabwe) from 1975

Professor P. D. Curtin
(USA), from 1975

Professor J. Devisse
(France), from 1971

Professor M. Difuila
(Angola), from 1978

The late Professor Cheikh Anta Diop
(Senegal), 1971–86, deceased 1986

Professor H. Djait
(Tunisia), from 1975

The late H. E. M. El Fasi
(Morocco), from 1971; deceased 1991
Editor Volume III

Professor J. D. Fage
(UK), 1971–81 (resigned)

The late Professor J. L. Franco
(Cuba), from 1971; deceased 1989

The late Mr M. H. I. Galaal
(Somalia), 1971–81; deceased 1981

Professor Dr V. L. Grottanelli
(Italy), from 1971

The late Professor E. Haberland
(Federal Republic of Germany), from 1971;
deceased 1992

Dr Aklilu Habte
(Ethiopia), from 1971

The late H. E. A. Hampaté Bà
(Mali) 1971–8 (resigned); deceased 1991

Dr I. S. El-Hareir
(Libya), from 1978

The late Dr. I. Hrbek
(Czech Republic), from 1971; deceased 1993
Assistant Editor Volume III

Dr (Mrs) A. Jones
(Liberia), from 1971

The late Abbé Alexis Kagame
(Rwanda), 1971–81; deceased 1981

Professor I. N. Kimambo
(Tanzania) from 1971

Professor J. Ki-Zerbo
(Burkina Faso), from 1971
Editor Volume I

Mr. D. Laya
(Niger), from 1979

Dr A. Letnev
(USSR), from 1971

Dr G. Mokhtar
(Egypt), from 1971
Editor Volume II

Professor P. Mutibwa
(Uganda), from 1975

935

Professor D. T. Niane
(Senegal), from 1971
Editor Volume IV

Professor L. D. Ngcongco
(Botswana), from 1971

Professor T. Obenga
(People's Republic of the Congo),
from 1975

Professor Bethwell A. Ogot
(Kenya), from 1971
Editor Volume V

Professor C. Ravoajanahary
(Madagascar), from 1971

The late Professor W. Rodney
(Guyana), 1979–80; deceased 1980

The late Professor M. Shibeika
(Sudan), 1971–80; deceased 1980

Professor Y. A. Talib
(Singapore), from 1975

The late Professor A. Teixeira da Mota
(Portugal), 1978–82; deceased 1982

Mgr T. Tshibangu
(Zaire), from 1971

Professor J. Vansina
(Belgium), from 1971

The late Rt Hon. Dr E. Williams
(Trinidad and Tobago), 1976–8;
resigned 1978; deceased 1980

Professor Ali A. Mazrui
(Kenya)
Editor Volume VIII, not a
member of the Committee

Professor C. Wondji
Côte d'Ivoire
Assistant Editor Volume VIII, not
a member of the Committee

*Secretariat of the International
Scientific Committee*
Division of International Cultural
Co-operation, Preservation and Enrichment
of Cultural Identities
1, rue Miollis, 75015 Paris

Biographies of authors

CHAPTER 1   Ali A. Mazrui (Kenya): specialist in political science and international studies; author of numerous works and articles on the contemporary history of Africa; Director, Institute of Global Cultural Studies, State University of New York at Binghamton; Albert Schweitzer Professor at State University of New York, Binghamton; Albert Luthuli Professor At Large, University of Jos, Nigeria; Andrew D. White Professor At Large at Cornell University, Ithaca, New York.

CHAPTER 2   T. Chenntouf (Algeria): specialist in the history of Algeria and the Maghreb; author of numerous works on the subject; Director of the Section of Historical Research on Algeria, Western Africa and the Mediterranean, University of Oran.

CHAPTER 3   M. Diop (Senegal): specialist in the contemporary socio–political history of West Africa; author of various publications on the subject; former researcher at the Institut des sciences humaines of Bamako, Mali; chemist and political leader.

D. Birmingham (UK): specialist in the contemporary history of Portuguese-speaking Africa and Central Africa; author of numerous works on Angola and Central Africa; former Chairman of African Studies, University of London; presently Professor of Modern History, University of Canterbury.

I. Hrbek (Czech Republic): specialist in Arabic, African and Islamic history as well as in the Arabic sources of the history of Africa; author of numerous works and articles in these fields; Researcher at the Oriental Institute, Prague, and scientific consultant to the Czechoslovak Academy of Sciences.

A. Margarido (Portugal): specialist in the history of Portuguese-speaking Africa; author of numerous works on Angola, Mozambique, Guinea-Bissau; lecturing at the Ecole des hautes études en sciences sociales (EHESS), Paris, and Professor at the Autonomous University of Lisbon.

D. T. Niane (Senegal): specialist of the Mande world; author of a number of works on West Africa at the time of the Great Empires from the eleventh to the sixteenth century; former Director of the Fondation L. S. Senghor.

CHAPTER 4   M. Crowder (UK): specialist in West African history; author of numerous works and articles on West African history; held professorships at various universities; deceased.

CHAPTER 5   Ali A. Mazrui (Kenya)

CHAPTER 6   I. Hrbek (Czech Republic)

CHAPTER 7   J. Suret-Canale (France): 'agrégé de l'Université', 'docteur d'Etat'; specialist in pre-colonial and colonial history of West Africa and particularly of Guinea; author of numerous works on West and Central Africa; Honorary Senior Lecturer, University of Paris VII.

A. Adu Boahen (Ghana): specialist in West African colonial history; author of numerous articles and works on African history; former Professor and Head of the Department of History, University of Ghana; retired.

CHAPTER 8   E. M'Bokolo (Zaire): specialist in the history of black Africa; author of numerous works and articles on the subject; Senior Researcher at the Ecole des hautes études en sciences sociales (EHESS), lecturer at the Institut d'études politiques (IEP), Paris; producer at Radio France Internationale.

CHAPTER 9   M. Twaddle (UK): specialist in the history of East Africa; author of numerous works and articles on the subject; Professor of History, Institute of Commonwealth Studies, London.

L. Rabearimanana (Madagascar): specialist in the history of Madagascar in the nineteenth and twentieth centuries; author of numerous works on the subject; Professor of History, University of Antananarivo.

I. N. Kimambo (Tanzania): specialist in the history of Tanzania; author of numerous works on the subject; Professor of History, University of Dar es Salaam.

CHAPTER 10   D. Chanaiwa (Zimbabwe): specialist in the history of Southern Africa (nineteenth and twentieth centuries); author of numerous works on the subject and particularly on Zimbabwe; former Professor of History, California State University; presently works at the Employers Confederation of Zimbabwe, Harare.

CHAPTER 11   C. Coquery-Vidrovitch (France): specialist in the socio-economic history of Africa; author of numerous works and articles on the subject; Professor of History, University of Paris VII; Director of the 'Third World, Africa' section associated with the Centre national de la recherche scientifique (CNRS), Paris.

CHAPTER 12   M. Owusu (Ghana): specialist in African socio-political and economic transformation; author of numerous works on the subject; Professor of Anthropology and Research Scientist, Center for Research on Economic Development, The University of Michigan, Ann Arbor.

CHAPTER 13   P. Kipré (Côte d'Ivoire): specialist in the history of West Africa and particularly of Côte d'Ivoire; author of numerous works on the subject; Professor of History, Ecole normale supérieure, Abidjan.

CHAPTER 14   A. Adedeji (Nigeria): economist specializing in development economics; author of numerous works and articles on Africa's and Nigeria's develop-

938

ment problems; former Under Secretary-General of the United Nations Organization and Executive Secretary of the Economic Commission for Africa, Addis Ababa; presently Executive Director of the African Centre for Development and Strategic Studies, Ijebu-Ode, Nigeria.

CHAPTER 15   J. I. Elaigwu (Nigeria): specialist in the political development of Africa; author of numerous works on the subject and particularly on Nigeria; Visiting Professor, State University of New York at Binghamton, USA; presently Professor of Political Science, University of Jos, Nigeria.

Ali A. Mazrui (Kenya)

CHAPTER 16   J. Ki-Zerbo (Burkina Faso): specialist in the methodology of African history; author of numerous works and articles dealing with black Africa and its history; Professor of History, University of Dakar.

Ali A. Mazrui (Kenya)

C. Wondji (Côte d'Ivoire): 'Agrégé d'histoire' (Sorbonne); specialist in the modern and contemporary history of Africa; author of numerous works on African cultures and the history of Côte d'Ivoire; formerly Head of the Department of History, Faculté des lettres de l'Université nationale de Côte d'Ivoire, Abidjan, and Deputy Director of the Institut d'art et d'archéologie, University of Abidjan; presently Counsellor at the Permanent Delegation of Côte d'Ivoire at UNESCO, Paris.

A. Adu Boahen (Ghana)

CHAPTER 17   T. Tshibangu (Zaire): theologian, specialist in oral traditions in Central Africa and in the history of religions in Africa; author of works on these subjects; President of the Conseil national d'administration des Universités du Zaire.

J. F. Ade Ajayi (Nigeria): specialist in nineteenth-century West African history; author of numerous works and articles on African history; former Vice-Chancellor, University of Lagos; presently, Professor Emeritus, History Department, University of Ibadan.

L. Sanneh (Gambia): specialist in the history of religions of Africa; author of numerous articles on the religious traditions of Africa. D. Willis James Professor of Missions and World Christianity, Professor of History, Fellow of Trumbull College, Yale University, New Haven, Connecticut, USA.

CHAPTER 18   A. I. Sow (France): specialist in African linguistics; author of numerous works on African languages and cultures; Professor, Institut national des langues et civilisations orientales, Paris.

M. H. Abdulaziz (Kenya): specialist in African linguistics and socio-linguistics; author of numerous works on these subjects; Professor of Linguistics, University of Nairobi.

CHAPTER 19   Ali A. Mazrui (Kenya)

M. de Andrade (Angola): sociologist, poet, writer, political leader; author of numerous publications on Angola's liberation; deceased.

M. Alaoui Abdalaoui (Morocco): specialist in French-language Maghreb literature; author of articles and works on the subject and on the reciprocal views formed between the Arab Orient and the West; Professor, Institut universitaire de la recherche scientifique, University of Rabat; literary critic, journalist.

D. P. Kunene (South Africa): specialist in oral and written literature of Southern Africa; author of articles and works on the subject; Professor, Department of African Languages and Literature, University of Wisconsin.

J. Vansina (Belgium): specialist in African history; author of numerous works and articles on the pre-colonial history of Africa; Professor of History and Anthropology, University of Wisconsin.

CHAPTER 20   J. Vansina (Belgium)

CHAPTER 21   Ali A. Mazrui (Kenya)

J. F. Ade Ajayi (Nigeria)

A. Adu Boahen (Ghana)

T. Tshibangu (Zaire)

CHAPTER 22   Aklilu Habte (Ethiopia): specialist in primary education, secondary and higher education, educational statistics and the philosophy of education; author of numerous works and articles on education in Africa and more particularly in Ethiopia; former President of Haile Selassie I University, Addis Ababa, Minister of Culture, Sports and Youth Affairs in Ethiopia, Director of Education and Training and Special Adviser on Human Resources at the World Bank; currently Special Adviser on Education to the Executive Director of UNICEF, New York.

Teshome Wagaw (USA): specialist in education; authors of numerous works on education in Africa, and more particularly in Ethiopia; Professor and Research Scientist, The University of Michigan.

CHAPTER 23   J. E. Harris (USA): specialist in African and African diaspora history; author of numerous works and articles on those subjects; Professor of History at Howard University, Washington DC.

S. Zeghidour (Algeria): writer and researcher; specialist in Arab immigration in Latin America; author of works and articles on the subject; writer and journalist.

CHAPTER 24   S. K. B. Asante (Ghana): specialist on pan-Africanism, nationalist movements and regionalism in Africa; author of numerous works and articles on these subjects; former Professor and African Area Studies Consultant,

940

University of Florida, Gainesville, Florida; Senior Regional Adviser, Economic Commission for Africa, Addis Ababa.

D. Chanaiwa (Zimbabwe)

CHAPTER 25   D. Chanaiwa (Zimbabwe)

E. Kodjo (Togo): specialist in economics and development; author of numerous works and articles on international relations with special emphasis on Africa; former Minister of Foreign Affairs, Finance and Economics of Togo; former Secretary-General of the Organization of African Unity; founder of the Institut panafricain de relations internationales; currently, Associate-Professor, Department of Political Science, University of Paris I Panthéon-Sorbonne.

CHAPTER 26   Chinweizu (Nigeria): writer, poet, historian, environmentalist; author of numerous works and articles on African literature, culture, education, economic development and environmental affairs.

CHAPTER 27   Iba Der Thiam (Senegal): 'agrégé de l'Université'; 'docteur d'Etat', Sorbonne; specialist in modern and contemporary history of Africa (political history) and in the history of trade unionism in West Africa; author of numerous works on these subjects; former Minister of Education of Senegal; Professor of History, Cheikh Anta Diop University, Dakar.

J. Mulira (Uganda): specialist in the history of Eastern Europe and on the impact of the socialist countries' policies towards the development of Africa; author of numerous works and articles on these subjects; Chairman, Department of History and Government, University of Nairobi.

C. Wondji (Côte d'Ivoire)

CHAPTER 28   L. Edmondson (Jamaica): Caribbean specialist in the history of Africa's relations with the African diaspora; author of numerous works on the role of race and class in international relations; Professor, Africana Studies and Research Center, Cornell University, Ithaca, New York.

CHAPTER 29   E. K. Kouassi (Togo): specialist in political science and international relations; author of numerous works on inter-African relations, and more particularly on relations between the United Nations Organization and the Organization of African Unity and on International African Organizations; Professor of Law, Political Science and International Relations, Faculty of Law, University of Benin, Lomé.

CHAPTER 30   Ali A. Mazrui (Kenya)

Bibliography

The publishers wish to point out that while every effort has been made to ensure that the details in this Bibliography are correct, some errors may occur as a result of the complexity and the international nature of the work.

Abbreviations
ARSOM   Académie royale des sciences d'outre-mer, Brussels

CEA   Cahiers d'études africaines, Paris: Mouton
CEDAF   Centre d'études et de la documentation africaines
CNRS   Centre national de la recherche scientifique, Paris
CRDTO   Centre de recherche et de documentation pour la tradition orale, Niamey
CRISP   Centre de recherche et d'information socio-politiques, Brussels
CUP   Cambridge University Press

EALB   East African Literature Bureau, Nairobi
EAPH   East African Publishing House, Nairobi

HUP   Harvard University Press

IAI   International African Institute, London
IFAN   Institut français (later fondamental) de l'Afrique noire, Dakar
IUP   Ibadan University Press

JAH   Journal of African History, Cambridge: CUP

NEA   Nouvelles éditions africaines, Dakar

ORSTOM   Office de la recherche scientifique et technique d'outre-mer, Paris
OUP   Oxford University Press

PUF   Presses universitaires de France, Paris
PUP   Princeton University Press

UCP   University of California Press

YUP   Yale University Press

Bibliography

Abalogu, U. N., Asiwaju, G. and Amadi-Tshiwala, R. (eds) (1981) *Oral Poetry in Nigeria* (Lagos: Nigeria Magazine).
Abba, I. A. (1985) 'Changing patterns of local authority and the evolution of the District Head system in Gombe Emirate, *c.*1830–1960' (PhD thesis, Bayero University, Kano).
'Abbās, F. (1962) *La Nuit Coloniale* (Paris: René Julliard).
'Abd al-Raḥmān, M. (1969) *Imperialism and Nationalism in the Sudan: A Study in Constitutional and Political Development, 1899–1956* (Oxford: Clarendon Press).
Abdel-Malek, A. (1962) *Egypte, société militaire* (Paris: Editions du Seuil).
Abdel-Malek, A. (1966) 'Problématique du socialisme dans le monde arabe', *L'homme et la société*, 2, pp. 125–48.
Abdel-Malek, A. (1969) *Idéologie et renaissance nationale: L'Egypte moderne* (Paris: Editions du Seuil).
Abdel-Malek, A. (ed.) (1980) *La pensée politique arabe contemporaine* (3rd edn, 1st edn 1970; Paris: Editions du Seuil).

Abdi, S. Y. (1978) 'Cuba's role in Africa: revolutionary or reactionary?', *Horn of Africa* (Summit, NJ), 1, 4, pp. 17–24.

Abdulgani, R. (1981) *The Bandung Connection: The Asia–Africa Conference in Bandung in 1955* (Singapore: Gunung Agung).

Abdul-Hai, M. (1976) *Conflict and Identity: The Cultural Poetics of Contemporary Sudanese Poetry* (Khartoum: Institute of African and Asian Studies, University of Khartoum, African Seminar Series No. 26).

Abdurraham, M. and Canham, P. (1978) *The Ink of the Scholar: The Islamic Tradition of Education in Nigeria* (London: Macmillan).

Abercrombie, K. C. (1961) 'The transition from subsistence to market agriculture in Africa south of the Sahara', *Monthly Bulletin of Agricultural Economics and Statistics*, 10, 2, pp. 1–52.

Abraham, W. E. (1962) *The Mind of Africa* (Chicago: UCP).

Abun-Nasr, J. M. (1979) 'Islam et socialisme en Afrique', in *La contribution du Christianisme et de l'Islam à la formation d'Etats indépendants en Afrique au sud du Sahara*, Texts and Documents of the Symposium on Africa, Bonn–Bad Godesberg, 2–4 May 1979, (Tübingen), pp. 120–30.

Académie royale des sciences d'outre-mer (1983) *Le Congo belge durant la Seconde Guerre mondiale: recueil d'études*, Introduction by J. Stengers (Brussels: ARSOM).

Accelerated Development in Sub-Saharan Africa (AD) (1983) *An Agenda for Action* (Washington, DC: World Bank).

Achebe, C. (1966) 'The black writer's burden', *Third Quarterly* (English edn), 31, 39.

Acquaye, S. (1971) 'Modern folk opera in Ghana', *African Arts*, 4, 2, pp. 60–6.

Addo, N. O. (1974) 'Attitudes and opinions of cocoa farmers to matters related to work and employment', *Ghana Journal of Sociology*, 7, 2 (January), pp. 37–58.

Adedeji, A. (1976a) *Africa, the Third World and the Search for a New Economic Order*, Turkeyen Third World Lectures, Georgetown University, November (Washington, DC).

Adedeji, A. (1976b) *ECA, Revised Framework of Principles for the Implementation of the New International Order in Africa, 25 June* (Addis Ababa: ECA).

Adedeji, A. (1977) 'The need for concrete action', in African Association for Public Administration and Management (ed.) *Regional Cooperation in Africa: Problems and Prospects* (Addis Ababa).

Adedeji, A. (1978) 'Africa's development crisis', in R. Synge (ed.), pp. 24–8.

Adedeji, A. (ed.) (1981) *The Indigenization of African Economics* (London: Hutchinson).

Adedeji, A. (1983) '*The evolution of the Monrovia Strategy and the Lagos Plan of Action: a regional approach to economic decolonization*', a lecture delivered under the Nigerian Institute of Social and Economic Research (NISER). Distinguished Lecture Series at Trenchard Hall, University of Ibadan, 24 March 1983.

Adedeji, A. (1984) *Statement at the formal opening of the 7th meeting of the Conference of African Ministers of Industry, 26–28 March 1984* (Mimeograph; Addis Ababa: ECA).

Adedeji, A. (1989a) *Towards a Dynamic African Economy* (London: Frank Cass).

Adedeji, A. (1989b) *ECA, African Alternative Framework to Structural Adjustment Programmes for Socio-Economic Recovery and Transformation*, AAFF-SAP (Addis Ababa: ECA).

Adedeji, A. (1989c) *Beyond Recovery – ECA's Revised Perspectives of Africa's Development from 1990–2008* (Addis Ababa: ECA).

Adedeji, A. (1990) *African Chapter for Popular Participation in Development* (Addis Ababa: ECA).

Ady, P. H. (1965) *Oxford Regional Economic Atlas: Africa* (Oxford: Clarendon Press).

Ady, P. H. (1983) 'Africa: a statistical profile', *Africa Report*, 28, 5 (September–October), pp. 58–61.

Africa (1984) 'The train with the good news', 149, January, pp. 18–19.

African Communist (1965) 'Nigeria after the elections', No. 21 (April–June).

African Currents (1978/79) Autumn/Winter (London), pp. 8–23.

African Diaspora Studies Newsletter (1948) 1, 1 (Fall/Winter, October).

Africa Now (1983) 'Obstacles in the Freedom Railway: Tanzania–Zambia Railway', 31, November.

Ageron, C. R. (1979) *Histoire de l'Algérie contemporaine. Vol. 1: 1830–1973; Vol. 2: 1871–1954* (Paris: PUF).

Agwani, M. S. (1969) *Communism in the Arab East* (London and New York: Asia Publishing House).

Ajayi, J. F. A. (1968) 'The continuity of African institutions under colonialism', in T. O. Ranger (ed.), pp. 189–201.

Ajayi, J. F. A. (1982) 'Expectations of independence', *Daedalus*, 3, 2 (Spring).

Ajayi, J. F. A. (1985) 'The educational process and historiography in contemporary Africa', in *The Educational Process and Historiography in Africa*, General History of Africa, Studies and Documents, No. 9 (Paris: UNESCO), pp. 11–21.

Ajayi, J. F. A. (1987) 'The American factor in the development of higher education in Africa', James Coleman Memorial Lecture, UCLA, Los Angeles.

Ajayi, J. F. A. and Tamuno, T. N. (1973) *The University of Ibadan 1948–1973: A History of the First Twenty-five Years* (Ibadan: IUP).

Akin, E. (1965) 'Preface to a study of Nigerian music', *Ibadan Journal*, 21, pp. 53–62.

Akin, E. (1970) 'Traditional elements as the basis of new African art music', *African Urban Notes*, 5, 4, pp. 52–6.

Alarinjo, M. A. (1981) 'The travelling Yoruba theatre', in Y. Ogurbiyi (ed.) *Drama and Theatre in Nigeria: A Critical Source Book* (London).

Alexandre, P. (1967) *Langues et langage en Afrique noire* (Paris: Payot; English edn 1972).

al-Fāsī, A. (1954) *The Independence Movement in Arab North Africa* (Washington: American Council of Learned Societies).

Ali, T. and O'Brien, J. (1984) 'Labour, community and protest in Sudanese agriculture', in J. Barker (ed.), pp. 205–38.

Allan, W. (1965) *The African Husbandsman* (Edinburgh: Oliver and Boyd).

Almond, G. and Powell, B. (1966) *Comparative Politics: A Developmental Approach* (Boston: Little, Brown).

Aluko, S. A. (1975) 'Rural economic development', in M. Owusu (ed.) *Colonialism and Change* (The Hague: Mouton), pp. 231–54.

Amadou, A. (1971) *Réflexion sur le rôle et les fonctions de la CEA*. Unofficial publication of the ECA (UN).

Amiji, H. M. (1984) 'Religion in Afro-Arab relations', in *Historical and Socio-cultural Relations between Black Africa and the Arab World from 1935 to the Present*, General History of Africa, Studies and Documents, No. 7) (Paris: UNESCO), pp. 101–29.

Amin, S. (1965) *L'économie du Maghreb* (Paris: Editions de Minuit).

Amin, S. (1970a) *Le Maghreb moderne* (Paris: Editions de Minuit).

Amin, S. (1970b) *The Maghreb in the Modern World* (Hardmondsworth: Penguin Books).

Amin, S. (1974a) *Accumulation on a World Scale: A Critique of the Theory of Underdevelopment, Volumes 1 and 2*; trans. by B. Pearce (New York and London: Monthly Review Press).

Amin, S. (1974b) *Neo-Colonialism in West Africa* (New York: Monthly Review Press).

Amin, S. (1976) *Unequal Development*, trans. by B. Pearce (New York and London: Monthly Review Press).

Amin, S. (1977) *Imperialism and Unequal Development* (New York: Monthly Review Press).

Amin, S. (1982) *Dynamics of Global Crisis* (New York: Monthly Review Press).

Amoda M. (1978) *Reflections on the FESTAC Colloquium* (Lagos: Nigeria Magazine).

Amselle, E. M. (1985) *La découverte*.

Anderson, D. and Throup, D. (1985) 'Africans and agricultural production in colonial Kenya: the myth of the war as a watershed', *JAH*, 26, 4, pp. 327–45.

Andersson, M. (1981) *Music in the Mix: The Story of South African Popular Music* (Johannesburg).

Aning, B. A. (1967) *An Annotated Bibliography of Music and Dance in English-speaking Africa* (Legon).

Annuaire politique de l'AEF (various dates) (Brazzaville: Imprimerie du Gouvernement).

Anonymous (1960) *Congo 1960* (Brussels: Centre de recherche et d'information socio-politiques).

Anonymous (1962) *Congo 1959: Documents belges et africains* (Brussels: Centre de recherche et d'information socio-politiques).

Anonymous (1964) 'National fashions of Africa', *Ebony*, 1, 6, pp. 32–138.

Anonymous (1968) 'Felix Idubor: A sculptor from Benin', *African Arts* (Los Angeles), 2, 1, pp. 30–2.

Anonymous (1971) *Le théâtre négro-africain: Actes du colloque d'Abidjan 1970* (Paris: Présence africaine).

Anonymous (1982) *Art religieux africain* (Kinshasa: Centre d'études des religions africaines).

Anonymous (1984) 'Akendengué in Town', *West Africa*, 3487, 16 June, pp. 1264–6.

Anonymous (1985) 'The new Cairo Opera House', *Prism*, 11, pp. 2–3.

Anonymous (1987) 'Sankara on African cinema', *West Africa*, 3630, 6 April, p. 687.

Ansprenger, F. (1961) *Politik im Schwartzen Afrika* (Köln and Opladen: Westdeutscher Verlag).

Anstey, R. (1977) *King Leopold's Legacy* (London: OUP).

Anthonio, Q. B. O. (1973) 'Problems of marketing agricultural produce with special reference to foodstuffs in Nigeria', in I. M. Ofori (ed.), pp. 251–62.

Anya, A. O. (1986) *Scientific Research and Public Policy* (Lagos: Nigerian Institute of International Affairs, Lecture Series No. 38).

Anya, A. O. (1987) 'Traditions, the pursuit of the intellectual life and Nigeria's future', *Nsukka Journal of the Humanities*, 1, June, pp. 141–60.

Apkevon, K. (1983) *L'Afrique face au Plan d'action de Lagos et au rapport de la Banque mondiale* (Lomé: ESACJ-UB).

Appadorai, A. (1956) *The Bandung Conference* (New Delhi: Indian Council of World Affairs).

Applebaum, R. (1970) *Theories of Social Change* (Chicago: Markham Publishing Co.).

Apthorpe, R. (1972) *Rural Cooperatives and Planned Change in Africa: An Analytical Overview; Rural Institutions and Planned Change. Vol. V* (Geneva: United Nations Research Institute for Social Development).

Arar, A. (1980) 'The role of rainfed agriculture in the Near East region: summary of present situation, potential and constraints', in *Rainfed Agriculture in the Near East and North Africa* (FAO: Rome).

Archer, R. 'The revolt of 1947–8 in Madagascar' (MA thesis, University of London).

Archives de Kouroussa (Guinea) (1942) *Rapport politique du 25 août 1942.*

Archives of the Republic of Senegal (1922) 'Une race qui se réveille', article signed Stieckloff, published in *Izvestia*, 259, 16 November, Série 21G 126 (108).

Archives of the Republic of Senegal (1923) *Enquête du Comité d'études coloniales*, Série 21G 132 (108).

Armstrong, R. G. (1964) *The Study of West African Languages* (Ibadan: IUP).

Arnold, G. (1979) *Aid in Africa* (London: Kegan Paul).

Arrighi, G. (1970) 'The political economy of Rhodesia', in I. L. Markovitz (ed.), pp. 393–426.

Arrighi, G. and Saul, J. S. (1973) *Essays on the Political Economy of Africa* (New York and London: Monthly Review Press).

Arzumanyan, A. A. (1958) 'Statement: Report on promotion of economic cooperation', in *Afro-Asian Peoples' Solidarity Conference, Cairo, 26 December 1957–1 January 1958* (Moscow: Moscow Foreign Language Publishing House).

Asante, S. K. B. (1977) *Pan-African Protest and the Italo-Ethiopian Crisis 1934–1941* (London: Longman).

Asante, S. K. B. (1984) 'ECOWAS, the EEC and the Lomé Convention', in D. Mazzeo (ed.), *African Regional Organizations* (Cambridge: CUP), pp. 171–95.

Asante, S. K. B. (1985) *The Political Economy of Regionalism in Africa: A Decade of the Economic Community of West African States (ECOWAS)* (New York: Praeger).

Asante, S. K. B. (1986) *Pan-African Protest: West Africa and the Italo-Ethiopian Crisis 1934–1941* (Harlow: Longman).

Ashby, Sir E. and Anderson, M. (1966) *Universities: British, Indian, African – A Study in the Ecology of Higher Education* (Cambridge, MA: HUP).

Ashford, D. E. (1961) *Political Change in Morocco* (Princeton: PUP).

As-Sibaci, M. (n.d.) *Istiakiyat al-Islam* [Islamic Socialism] (Cairo).

Astafyev, G. V. and Dubinsky, A. M. (eds) (1974) *From Anti-Imperialism to Anti-Socialism: The Evolution of Peking's Foreign Policy* (Moscow: Progress Publishers).

Astrow, A. (1983) *Zimbabwe: A Revolution that Lost Its Way?* (London: Zed Press).

Aujoulat, P. (1958) *Aujourd'hui l'Afrique* (Paris and Tournai: Cantermain).

Austin, D. (1964) *Politics in Ghana 1946–1960* (Oxford: OUP).

Austin, D. (1980) 'The transfer of power: how and why', in W. H. M. Jones and G. Fischer (eds), *Decolonization and After: the British and French Experience* (London: Frank Cass), pp. 3–35.

Austin, D. (1987) 'The emergence of capitalist relations in South Asante cocoa-farming, c.1916–1933', *JAH*, 28, 2, pp. 259–79.

Awolowo, O. (1960) *Awo: The Autobiography of Chief Obafemi Awolowo* (Cambridge: CUP).

Ayache, A. (1956) *Le Maroc: bilan d'une colonisation* (Paris: Editions sociales).

Ayari, C. (1983) 'African economies: what strategy for Africa's development', *Africa Report*, 28, 3 (September–October), pp. 8–11.

Ayres, R. L. (1983) *The World Bank and World Poverty: Banking on the Poor* (Cambridge: MIT Press).

Azikiwe, N. (1961) *Zik: A Selection from the Speeches of Nnamdi Azikiwe* (Cambridge: CUP).

Azonga, T. M. (1986) 'TV steals the show', *West Africa*, 11 August, pp. 1674–5.

Bachy, V. (1983) 'Panoramique sur les cinémas sud-sahariens', in J. Binet, F. Boughedir and V. Bachy (eds), *Cinémas noirs d'Afrique* (Paris), pp. 23–43.

Badara, D., El Hadjdj (1979) 'Le Centre de Bopp à Dakar, Sénégal: modèle d'une collaboration chrétienne–islamique', in *La contribution du Christianisme et de l'Islam à la formation d'Etats indépendants en Afrique au sud du Sahara*, Texts and Documents of the Symposium on Africa, Bonn–Bad Godesberg, 2–4 May, 1979 (Tübingen).

Badi Banga ne-Mwine (1977) *Contribution à l'étude historique de l'art plastique zairois moderne* (Kinshasa).

Baeta, C. G. (1962) *Prophetism in Ghana* (London: SCM Press).

Bairoch, P. (1977) *The Economic Development of The Third World Since 1900* (Berkeley and Los Angeles: UCP).

Bakhtri, N. (1980) 'Introduction of medic/wheat rotation in the North African and Near East countries', in *Rainfed Agriculture in the Near East and North Africa* (FAO: Rome).

Balandier, G. (1963) *Sociologie actuelle de l'Afrique noire: Dynamique Sociale en Afrique centrale* (2nd edn, Paris: PUF).

Balans, J. L., Coulon, C. and Ricard, A. (eds) (1972) *Problèmes et perspectives de l'éducation dans un Etat du Tiers-Monde: le cas du Sénégal* (Institut d'études politiques de Bordeaux).

Bamgbose, A. (1976) *Mother Tongue Education: the African Experience* (London: Hodder and Stoughton; Paris: UNESCO Press).

Baran, P. A. (1968) *The Political Economy of Growth* (New York: Modern Reader Paperbacks).

Barker, J. (ed.) (1984) *The Politics of Agriculture in Tropical Africa* (Beverly Hills and London: Sage).

Barneet, D. and Harvey, R. (1972) *The Revolution in Angola: MPLA, Life, Histories and Documents* (New York: Bobbs-Merrill).

Barnes, J. A. (1952) 'History in a changing society', in *Human Problems in British Central Africa, Vol. 11* (London: OUP), pp. 1–9.

Barongo, Y. R. (ed.) (1983) *Political Science in Africa* (London: Zed Press).

Barrett, D. B. (1982) *World Christian Encyclopedia* (London: OUP).

Barrett, L. (1977) *The Rastafarians* (London: Heinemann).

Barron, S. (1983) *German Expressionist Sculpture* (Los Angeles).

Bassett, C. (1987) *Canadian International Development Agency (CIDA)*, Address to Canadian African Studies Association, University of Alberta, Edmonton, Alberta, 7–10 May.

Bates, R. H. (1981) *Markets and States in Tropical Africa: The Political Basis of Agricultural Policies* (Berkeley, Los Angeles and London: UCP).

Bates, R. S. and Lofchie, M. F. (eds.) (1980) *Agricultural Development in Africa: Issues of Public Policy* (New York: Praeger).

Bauer, P. T. (1981) *Equality, the Third World and Economic Delusion* (Cambridge, MA: HUP).

Bayart, J. F. (1979) *L'Etat au Cameroun* (Paris: Presses de la Fondation nationale de sciences politiques).

Bayen, M. (1939) 'The march of blackmen' (New York).

Beckford, G. L. (1972) *Persistent Poverty: Under-Development in Plantation Economies of the Third World* (New York: OUP).

Beier, U. (1960) *Art in Nigeria* (Cambridge: CUP).

Beier, U. (1968) *Contemporary Art in Africa* (London: Pall Mall Press).

Beier, U. (1970) 'Yoruba opera: the magic spell of Duro Lapido', *Gangan*, 3, pp. 14–23.

Beier, U. (1971) 'Signwriters art in Nigeria', *African Arts*, 4, 3, pp. 22–7.

Beier, U. (1973) *Yoruba Theatre* (London).

Beier, U. (1976) 'Middle art: the paintings of war', *African Arts*, 9, 2, pp. 20–3.

Beinart, J. (1968) 'Wall painting: popular art in two African Communities,' *African Arts*, 2, 3, pp 26–9.

Belal, A. (1972) *Renaissance du monde arabe* (Paris: Duclot).

Belaouane Gherari, R. (1984) 'L'Afrique dans les relations Sud/Sud', *Le mois en Afrique* (Paris), 225–226 (October–November), pp. 104–19.

Bellonce, G. (1978) 'A la recherche de nouvelles formules éducatives pour le Tiers-Monde: l'éducateur de base au Mali', 44, pp. 77–96.

Beltran Y Ropzide, R. (1902) *La Guinea Española* (Barcelona).

Belyanev, I. (1962) *Peuples d'Asie et d'Afrique*.

Bemba, S. (1984) 'Cinquante ans de musique du Congo-Zaïre 1920–1970: de Paul Kamba à Tabu-Ley', *Présence africaine* (Paris).

Benachenou, A. (1978) *Formation du sous-developpement en Algérie: Essai sur les limites du développement du capitalisme en Algérie, 1830–1962* (Algiers).

Ben Amos, P. (1977) 'Pidgin language and tourist art', *Anthropology of Visual Communication*, 4, 2, pp. 128–39.

Ben Bella, A. (1965) Contribution to *Le Monde*, 23 January.

Bender, G. J. (1978) *Angola under the Portuguese: The Myth and the Reality* (London: Heinemann).

Bennett, G. and Rosberg, C. (1961) *The Kenyatta Election 1960–1961* (Oxford: OUP).

Benomar, J. (1988) 'The monarchy, the Islamist Movement and religious discourse in Morocco', *Third World Quarterly*, 10, 2 (April).

Benot, Y. (1969) *Idéologies des Indépendances Africaines* (Paris: Maspéro).

Ben Ṣalah, A. (1980) Contributions to A. Abdel-Malek (ed.).

Benson, P. (1986) *Black Orpheus: Transition and Modern Cultural Awakening in Africa* (Berkeley and Los Angeles: UCP).

Berg, E. (1980) *Non-alignement et Nouvel Ordre Mondial* (Paris: PUF).

Berger, M. (1962) *The Arab World Today* (New York: Doubleday).

Berger, R. (1967) 'African and European dance', *Nigerian Magazine*, 92, pp. 87–92.

Berman, E. (1983) *Art and Artists of South Africa* (Cape Town: Balkema; 1st edn 1974).

Bernal, M. (1987) *Black Athena: The Afro-Asiatic Roots of Classical Civilization, Vol. I* (New Brunswick, NJ: Rutgers University Press).

Bernard-Duquenet, N. (1976a) 'Le Front populaire au Sénégal' (PhD thesis, University of Paris VII, Paris).

Bernard-Duquenet, N. (1976b) 'Le Front populaire et le problème des prestations en AOF', *CEA*, 16, 61–2, pp. 159–72.

Bernstein, S. (1978) 'Problems of African agriculture: food and export crop production in the seventies', in R. Synge (ed.) *Africa Guide* (Chicago: Rand McNally and Co.), pp. 57–63.

Bernstein, S. (1981) 'Concepts for the analysis of contemporary peasantries', in R. E. Galli (ed.).

Berque, J. (1960) *Les Arabes d'hier à demain* (Paris: Seuil).

Berque, J. (1964) *The Arabs: Their History and Future* (London: Faber and Faber).

Berque, J. (1968) *L'Egypte: impérialisme et révolution* (Paris: Gallimard).

Berrah, M., *et al.* (1981) *Cinémas du Maghreb* (Cinéma Action 14) (Paris).

Beshir, M. O. (1968) *The Southern Sudan: Background to Conflict* (London: Hurst).

Bessis, J. (1981) *La Méditerranée fasciste: L'Italie mussolinienne et la Tunisie* (Paris: Karthala).

Bessis, J. (1982) *La Méditerranée fasciste* (Paris: Publications of the Sorbonne).

Bettelheim, J. (1985) 'The Lantern Festival in Senegambia', *African Arts*, 18, 2, pp. 50–3.

Betts, R. F. (1985) 'Methods and institutions of European domination', in A. A. Boahen (ed.), *Africa under Colonial Domination, 1880–1935, General History of Africa, vol. VII* (London: Heinemann; Berkeley: UCP; Paris: UNESCO), pp. 312–31.

Bézy, F., Peemans, J. P. and Wautelet, J. M. (1981) *Accumulation et sous-développement au Zaire 1960–1980* (Louvain-la-Neuve: Presses universitaires de Louvain).

Biame, K. N. (1968) 'Comic play in Ghana', *African Arts*, 1, 4, pp. 30–4.

Biarnès, P. (1980) *L'Afrique aux Africains* (Paris: A. Colin).

Biaya, T. K. (1984) 'De l'aube des temps jusqu'alors: l'histoire contemporaine des Luluwa par Nyunyi wa Luimba', in B. Jewsiewicki (ed.), pp. 23–34.

Bienen, H. (1974) *Kenya: The Politics of Participation and Control* (Princeton, NJ: PUP).

Biko, B. S. (ed.) (1972) *Black Viewpoint* (Durban: Black Community Programmes).

Binder, L., Coleman, J. S., Lapalombara, J., Pye, L. W., Verba, S. and Weiner, M. (1971) *Crises and Sequences in Political Development* (Princeton: PUP).

Binet, J., Boughedir, F. and Bachy, V. (eds) (1983) *Cinémas noirs d'Afrique*, Cinéma Action 26 (Paris).

Birnie, H. and Ansre, G. (1969) *The Study of Ghanaian Languages* (Accra: Institute of African Studies and University of Ghana, Legon).

Blair, T. L. (1970) *The Land to Those Who Work It: Algeria's Experiment in Workers' Management* (Garden City: Doubleday and Co., Inc.).

Bloch-Lainé, F. and Bouvier, J. (1986) *La France restaurée, 1944–1954* (Paris: Fayard).

Bloch-Lemoine, M. (1978) 'Développement et transformation de l'éducation en Côte d'Ivoire', *Revue française d'études politiques africaines*, 150, 1, pp. 79–94.

Blundell, Sir, M. (1964) *So Rough a Wind* (London: Weidenfeld and Nicolson).

Boahen, A. A. (ed.) (1985) *Africa under Colonial Domination, 1880–1935*, UNESCO General History of Africa, vol. VII (Paris: UNESCO; London: Heinemann; Berkeley: UCP).

Boahen, A. A. (1986) *Topics in West African History* (2nd edn, Harlow: Longman).

Bochkargov, Y. (1966) 'The outlook in Africa', *New Times* (Moscow), 22 January.

Boctor, G. (1969) 'La peinture en Egypte moderne', *African Arts*, 3, 1, pp. 28–33 and 86–7.

Boeke, J. H. (1953) *Economics and Economic Policy as Exemplified by Indonesia* (New York: Institute of Pacific Relations).

Boganda, B. *Ecrits et discours* (3 vols, Bangui: J. D. Penel).

Bogatyrev, P. (1971) *The Functions of Folk Costume in Moravian Slovakia* (The Hague; original: *Matica Slovenska*, 1937).

Bohannan, P. and Dalton, G. (1965) *Markets in Africa: Eight Subsistence Economies in Transition* (Garden City: Doubleday and Co., Inc.).

Boiteau, P. (1982) *Contribution à l'histoire de la nation malgache* (Antananarivo: Editions Sociales and MCAR).

Boletín Informativo (Lima, Peru: Instituto de Investigaciones Afro-Peruana).

Bomole, N. (1970) 'Le Congo et l'Enseignement Programmé', *Cahiers Congolais*, 2, June-July, pp. 72–88.

Bonneau, R. (ed.) (1972) 'Les prétendants rivaux', *Afrique Littéraire et Artistique*, 26, pp. 83–8.

Bonner, P. L. (ed.) (1974) *Working Papers in Southern African Studies* (London: Frank Cass).

Boserup, E. (1985) 'Economic and development interrelationships in sub-Saharan Africa', *Population and Development Review*, 11, 3 (September), pp. 383–99.

Boubou Hama (1981) 'The living tradition', in J. Ki-Zerbo (ed.), pp. 62–72.

Boudhiba, A. (1975) *La sexualité en Islam* (Paris; English edn 1985, London: Routledge and Kegan).

Boughedir, F. (1983) 'Les grandes tendances du cinéma en Afrique noire', *Cinémas noirs d'Afrique* (Paris), 26, pp. 48–57.

Boulby, M. (1988) 'The Islamic challenge: Tunisia since independence', *Third World Quarterly*, 10, 2 (April), pp. 590–614.

Bourguiba, H. (1954) *La Tunisie et la France: vingt-cinq ans de lutte pour une coopération libre* (Paris: Julliard).

Boutros-Ghali, B. (1969) 'L'OUA et la coopération économique', *Revue egyptienne de droit international*, 25, April, pp. 171–85.

Boutros-Ghali, B. (1975) 'The League of Arab States and the Organization of African Unity', in Y. El-Ayouty (ed.), pp. 47–61.

Bowman, L. (1973) *Politics in Rhodesia* (Cambridge, MA: HUP).

Bown, L. and Crowder, M. (1964) *The Proceedings of the First International Congress of Africanists* (London: Longmans, Greens and International Congress of Africanists).

Bozzoli, B. (ed.) (1979) *Labour, Townships and Protest* (Johannesburg: Raven Press).

Brandt, H. (1956) *Nomades du soleil* (Lausanne: La guilde du livre).

Brandt, W. (1980) *North–South: A Program for Survival; The Report of the Independent Commission on International Development Issues Under the Chairmanship of Willy Brandt* (Cambridge, MA: MIT Press).

Bray, M., Clarke, P. B. and Stephens, O. (1986) *Education and Society in Africa* (London: Edward Arnold).

Breidenbach, P. S. and Ross, D. H. (1978) 'The Holy Place: Twelve Apostles Healing Gardens', *African Arts*, 11, 4, pp. 28–35, 95.

Brenner, L. (1984) *West African Sufi* (London: Hurst).

Brett, E. A. (1973) *Colonialism and Underdevelopment in East Africa: The Politics of Economic Change 1919–1939* (New York: Nok Publishers, Ltd).

Brett, E. A. and Belshaw, D. G. R. (eds) (1973) *Politics and Agriculture* (London: Frank Cass).

Brevie, J. (1930) *Discours d'ouverture au Conseil de Gouvernement de l'AOF.*

Brokensha, D. (1966) *Social Change in Larteh* (London: OUP).

Brokensha, D. and Hodge, P. (1969) *Community Development: An Interpretation* (San Francisco: Chandler Publishing Co.).

Brookes, E. H. (1968) *Apartheid: A Documentary Study of Modern South Africa* (London: Routledge and Kegan Paul).

Brown, A. C. (1988) *A History of Scientific Endeavour in South Africa: A Collection of Essays Published on the Occasion of the Centenary of the Royal Society of South Africa* (Capetown: RSSA).

Brown, B. (1983) 'The impact of male labour migration on women in Botswana', *African Affairs*, 82, 328 (July), pp. 367–88.

Brown, G. N. and Hiskett, G. (1975) *Conflict and Harmony in Education in Tropical Africa* (London: George Allen and Unwin Ltd).

Brown, J. M. (1972) *Kenyatta* (London: George Allen and Unwin Ltd).

Brown, P. (1970) 'Patterns of authority in West Africa', in I. L. Markovitz (ed.).

Brutents, K. (1967) 'Africa's revolution, gains and problems', *International Affairs* (Moscow), January.

Bude, U. (ed.) (1980) *Education for Kagisano in Botswana* (Bonn: DAAD).

Buijtenhuijs, R. (1982) *Contributions to Mau Mau Historiography* (Leiden: African Studies Centre).

Buraimoh, J. (1971) 'Painting with beads', *African Arts*, 5, 1, pp. 16–19.

Burt, E. C. (1984) 'Mural painting in western Kenya', *African Arts*, 16, 3, pp. 60–3 and 80.

Busia, K. A. (1969) 'Social attitudes to agriculture', in C. Legum and J. Drysdale (eds), *Africa Contemporary Record: Annual Survey and Documents 1968–1969* (London: Africa Research Limited).

Bustin, E. (1975) *Lunda under Colonial Rule: The Politics of Ethnicity* (Cambridge, MA: HUP).

Byakov *et al.* (eds) (1981) *The Priorities of Soviet Foreign Policy Today* (Moscow: Progress Publishers).

Cabral, A. (1975) *Unité et lutte: oeuvres d'Amilcar Cabral* (Paris: F. Maspero).

Cadoux, C. (1969) *La République malgache* (Paris: Berger–Levrault).

Caetano, M. (1954) *Os nativos na economia africana* (Coimbra).

Cahen, M. (1983, 1984) 'Corporatisme et colonialisme – approche du cas mozambicain, 1933–1979', *CEA*, 92, XXIII-4, pp. 383–417, and 93, XXIV-1, pp. 5–24.

Callaway, H. (1975) 'Indigenous education in Yoruba society', in G. N. Brown and G. Hiskett (eds), pp. 26–39.

Camara, C. (1973) 'Une ville précoloniale au Nigeria: Ondo', *CEA*, 13, 51.

Cameron, D. (1934) *The Principles of Native Administration and their Application* (Lagos: Government Printer).

Cameroon, J. (1970) *The Development of Education in East Africa* (New York: Teachers College Press).

Campion-Vincent, V. (1970) 'Système d'enseignement et mobilité sociale au Sénégal', *Revue Française de Sociologie*, 11, April–June.

Capet, M. (1958) *Traite d'économie tropicale* (Paris: Pichon and Durand-Auzias).

Cardoso, P. M. (1984) *Folclore caboverdeano* (2nd edn, Lisbon: Porto).

Carey, M. (1970) *Myths and Legends of Africa* (Melbourne and London: Sun Books, Hamlyn Publishing Group).

Carlsson, J. (ed.) (1982) *South–South Relations in a Changing World Order* (Uppsala: Scandinavian Institute of African Studies).

Carnoy, M. (1974) *Education as Cultural Imperialism* (New York: McKay).

Carsow, M. (1935) *Quelques aspects du commerce impérial de la France* (Paris: Geuthner).

Carter, G. (1959) *The Politics of Inequality* (New York: Praeger).

Carter, G. (ed.) (1966) *National Unity and Regionalism in Eight African States* (Ithaca: Cornell University Press).

Cary, J. (1944) *The Case for African Freedom* (London: Secker and Warburg).

CASTAFRICA (Conference of Ministers for Science and Technology in Africa) (1987) *Special Programme of Assistance to Africa in the fields of Scientific and Technological Research and of Research and Development* (Paris: UNESCO).

Castagno, A. A. (1966) 'Somali Republic', in J. Coleman and C. G. Rosberg (eds), pp. 512–60.

948

Castro, F. (1983) *The World Economic and Social Crisis: Its Impact on the Underdeveloped Countries, Its Sombre Prospects and the Need to Struggle if We Are to Survive. Report to the Seventh Summit Conference of Non-Aligned Countries* (Havana: Publishing Office of the Council of State).

Centro Cultural Afro–Ecuatoriano, *Palenque* (Quito, Ecuador).

Centro De Estudos E Investigaciones (1977) *Los Dioses Como Los Vemos* (Caracas, Venezuela).

Centro para la Investigación de la Cultura Negra, *Presencia Negra* (Bogota, Colombia).

Cervenka, Z. (1977) *The Unfinished Quest for Unity: Africa and the OAU* (New York: Africana Publishing Co.).

Césaire, A. (1969) *Return to My Native Land*, trans. by J. Berger and A. Bostock (London: Penguin).

Chagnoux, H. and Haribu, A. (1980) *Les Comores* (Paris: PUF).

Cham, M. B. (1982) 'Film production in West Africa, 1979–1981', *Presence africaine*, **124**, 4, pp. 168–89.

Cham, M. B. (1984) 'Art and ideology in the work of Sembene Ousmane and Haile Gerima', *Présence africaine*, **129**, 1, pp. 79–91.

Chambers, R. (1969) *Settlement Schemes in Tropical Africa* (London: Routledge and Kegan Paul).

Chanaiwa, D. (1976a) *Profiles of Self-Determination: African Responses to European Colonialism in Southern Africa, 1952–Present* (Northridge, CA: California State University Foundation).

Chanaiwa, D. (1976b) 'The premiership of Garfield Todd: racial partnership versus colonial interests', *Journal of Southern African Affairs*, **1**, 1 (December), pp. 83–94.

Chanaiwa, D. (1980) 'African humanism in Southern Africa: the utopian, traditionalist, and colonialist worlds of mission-educated élites', in A. G. Mugomba and M. Nyaggah (eds), pp. 9–40.

Chandos, Lord (1964) *The Memoirs of Lord Chandos* (London: Bodley Head).

Charnay, J. P. (1966) 'Courants réformistes de la pensée musulmane contemporaine', in J. A. Adonis and Y. Osman (eds) *Normes et Valeurs dans L'Islam Contemporain* (Paris: Payot).

Cheeks, J. (1936) 'Wings over Ethiopia', *New Masses*, 7 July.

Cheeks, J. Unpublished manuscript on his experiences in Ethiopia with Robinson.

Chenntouf, T. (1969) *L'Assemblée algérienne 1947–1956* (Paris: Faculté des lettres et des sciences humaines de Paris).

Chesneaux, J. (1964) 'Qu'est-ce que la démocratie nationale?', *La Pensée*, 118 (December), pp. 3–19.

Chibwe, E. C. (1976) *Arab Dollars for Africa* (London: Croom Helm).

Chibwe, E. C. (1977) *Afro-Arab Relations in the New World Order* (London: Julian Friedmann).

Chikwendu, E. (1983) 'The African peasantry: neglected by African political science', in Y. R. Barongo (ed.), pp. 37–48.

Chinweizu (1975) *The West and the Rest of Us* (New York: Vintage Books).

Chinyere, O. (1980) 'Parallelism versus influence in African literature: the case of Efua Sutherland's Edufa', *Kiabara*, **3**, 1 (Rains), pp. 113–31.

Chrétien, J. P. (1972) 'L'enseignement au Burundi', *Revue française d'études politiques africaines*, **76**, April, pp. 61–80.

CIAF (1972) *Deuxième conférence internationale des africanistes* (Paris: Présence Africaine).

CIAO (1945) *Première conférence internationale des africanistes de l'ouest, Dakar* (2 vols; vol. 1, Paris: Adrien–Maisonneuve, 1950; vol. 2, Paris: Adrien–Maisonneuve, 1951).

CIDA (1984) *CIDA's Year in Review 1982–1983: Canadians in the Third World* (Ottawa: CIDA).

Clark, E. and Ogunde, H. (1979) *The Making of Nigerian Theatre* (Oxford: OUP).

Clayton, A. (1976) *Counter-insurgency in Kenya, 1952–1960* (Nairobi: Trans-Africa Publishers).

Clayton, A. (1981) *The Zanzibar Revolution and its Aftermath* (London: C. Hurst).

Clayton, E. S. (1964) *Agrarian Development in Peasant Economies: Some Lessons from Kenya* (Oxford: Pergamon).

Cliffe, L. (1976) 'Rural political economy of Africa', in P. C. W. Gutkind and I. Wallerstein (eds), pp. 112–31.

Cliffe, L. and Cunningham, G. (1973) 'Ideology, organization and settlement experience in Tanzania', in E. A. Brett and D. G. R. Belshaw (eds).

Clute, R. E. (1982) 'The role of agriculture in African development', *African Studies Review*, **25**, 4 (December), pp. 1–21.

Cohen, R. (1979) 'Albert Nzula', in B. Bozzoli (ed.), pp. 325–40.

Cole, H (1975) 'Art festival in Ghana', *African Arts*, 8, 3 (special issue), pp. 12–24.

Cole, H. (1982) *Mbari: Art and Life among the Owerri Igbo* (Bloomington: Indiana University Press).

Coleman, J. S. (1963) *Nigeria: Background to Nationalism* (Berkeley and Los Angeles: UCP).

Coleman, J. S. and Rosberg, C. G. (1970) *Political Parties and National Integration in Tropical Africa* (Berkeley: UCP).

Collectif (1966) *L'Afrique au XXe siècle (1900–1965)* (Paris: Sirey).

Collins, J. (1985) *Comic Opera in Ghana* (London).

Collins, P. (1983) 'The state and industrial capitalism in West Africa', *Development and Change*, **14**, 3 (July), pp. 403–29.

Colloque international de Dakar sur le développement industriel africain (1972) (Dakar: NEA).

949

Colloque Soviéto-Congolais (1988) 'Théorie et pratique de la période de transition dans les pays libérés', matériaux du 6ème colloque soviéto-congolais, 30 janvier–3 février 1987 (Moscow).

Colombe, M. (1951) *L'évolution de l'Egypte, 1924–1950* (Paris: GP Maisonneuve).

Commissariat général au plan (1954 and 1955) *Rapport annuel sur l'exécution du plan de modernisation et d'équipement de l'Union française (Métropole et Outre-Mer)* (2 vols).

Commonwealth Economic Committee (1961) *Annual Report – Industrial Fibres* (London: CEC).

Confemen (1986) *Promotion et intégration des langues nationales dans les systèmes éducatifs – Bilan et inventaire* (Paris: Champion).

Conference on African Education (1953) *African Education: A Study of Educational Policy and Practice in British Tropical Africa* (Oxford: Charles Batey).

Constable, D. (1974) 'Bilingualism in the United Republic of Cameroon: proficiency and distribution', *Comparative Education*, 10, 3 (October), pp. 233–346.

Constantine, S. (1984) *The Making of British Colonial Development Policy 1914–1940* (London: Frank Cass).

Constantine, S. (1985) 'The making of an imperial slum: Nyasaland and its railways, 1895–1935', *JAH*, 16.

Cook, D. (ed.) (1965) *Origin East Africa: A Makerere Anthology* (London and Ibadan: Heinemann).

Cooke, P. and Doornbos, M. (1982) 'Rwenzururu protest songs', *Africa*, **52**, 1, pp. 50–1.

Cooper, F. (1980) *From Slaves to Squatters* (New Haven: YUP).

Cooper, F. (1981) 'Africa and the world economy', *African Studies Review*, 17, 2/3 (June/September), pp. 1–86.

Coquery-Vidrovitch, C. (1975) 'L'impact des intérêts coloniaux: SCOA et CFAO dans l'ouest africain, 1910–1965', *JAH*, 16, 4, pp. 595–621.

Coquery-Vidrovitch, C. (1976a) 'L'impérialisme français en Afrique noire: idéologie impériale et politique d'équipement, 1924–1975', *Relations internationales*, 7, pp. 261–82.

Coquery-Vidrovitch, C. (1976b) 'L'Afrique et la crise de 1930 (1924–1938)', *Revue française d'histoire d'outre-mer*, special issue, 63, 232–233, pp. 386–424.

Coquery-Vidrovitch, C. (1978) 'Industrie et dépendance: Les retards de l'industrialisation dans l'Empire français dans la première moitié du 20e siècle' (Unpublished, University of Paris VII).

Coquery-Vidrovitch, C. (1979) 'Vichy et l'industrialisation aux colonies', *Revue d'histoire de la Deuxième Guerre mondiale*, **114**, pp. 69–94.

Coquery-Vidrovitch, C. (1982) 'Le financement de la mise en valeur coloniale: Méthode et premiers résultats', in *Etudes d'histoire africaine; hommage á Henri Brunschwig* (Paris: EHESS), pp. 237–52.

Coquery-Vidrovitch, C. (1984) *Entreprises et entrepreneurs en Afrique – XIXe et XXe siècles* (2 vols; Paris: Karthala).

Coquery-Vidrovitch, C. (1985) *Processus d'urbanisation en Afrique XIXe–XXe siècles*, Proceedings of the International Symposium held at the University of Paris VII (in French, 2 vols; Paris: L'Harmattan).

Coquery-Vidrovitch, C. (1986) 'Les problèmes mondiaux vus d'Afrique noire ou les relations Sud–Nord', *Estudios de Economia*, V, 3, pp. 347–67.

Coquery-Vidrovitch, C. (1988a) *Afrique noire: permanences et ruptures* (Paris: Payot).

Coquery-Vidrovitch, C. (1988b) 'The transfer of economic power in French-speaking Africa: from "colonial exclusivity" to North–South relations', in P. Gifford and W. R. Louis (eds), pp. 105–34.

Coquery-Vidrovitch, C. (1988c) *Africa: Endurance and Change South of the Sahara* (Berkeley: UCP).

Corbett, E. M. (1972) *The French Presence in Black Africa* (Washington: Orpheus Press).

Cornet, J. (1974) 'Cultures en Zaïre et en Afrique', *African Arts*, **4**, pp. 125–36.

Cornet, J. (1975) 'Critique d'authenticité et art nègre', *African Arts*, **9**, 1, p. 53.

Cornet, J. (1982) *Art royal kuba* (Milan).

Cornell University (1990) *Du centenaire de la découverte du Nouveau Monde par Bakari II en 1312 et Christopher Columbus en 1492 (An Outline of a Project)*.

Coser, L. (1956) *The Functions of Social Conflict* (New York: The Free Press).

Cosgrove-Twitchett, C. (1978) *Europe and Africa: from Association to Partnership* (Farnborough: Saxon House)

Côte d'Ivoire, Government of (1967) *Perspectives décennales de développement économique, social et culturel, 1960–1970* (Abidjan: Ministère du Plan).

Côte d'Ivoire, Government of (1976) *La Côte d'Ivoire en chiffres* (Dakar: Société africaine d'édition).

Coulet-Western, D. (1975) *A Bibliography of the Arts of Africa* (Waltham, MA).

Courrière, Y. (1968–72) *La Guerre d'Algérie* (Paris: Fayard).

Court, F. and M'Wangi, M. (1976) 'Maridadi fabrics', *African Arts*, **10**, 1, pp. 38–41 and 99.

Cowan, L. G., O'Connell, J. and Scanlon, D. (eds) (1965) *Education and Nation Building* (New York: Frederick Praeger).

Cowen, M. (1981) 'Commodity production in Kenya's Central Province', in J. Heyer *et al.* (eds), pp. 121–43.

Cowen, M. (1984) 'Early years of the Colonial Development Corporation: British state enterprise overseas during late colonialism', *African Affairs*, **83**, 330, pp. 63–77.

Craveirinha, J. (1964) *Chifugo* (Lisbon: Casa dos Estudantes do Imperio).

Creuz, S. (1951) 'Le drame de l'éducation esthétique', *Les arts plastiques: l'art au Congo belge* (Brussels), 5th series, 1 (June–July), pp. 46–53.

Crocker, C. (1976) 'The African dimension of the Indian Ocean policy', *Orbis*, **20**, 3 (Fall), pp. 637–69.

Crowder, M. (1970) 'The white chiefs of tropical Africa', in L. H. Gann and P. Duignan (eds) *Colonialism in Africa, II: The History and Politics of Colonialism 1914–1960* (Cambridge: CUP), pp. 320–50.

Crowder, M. (1978) 'The contemporary Nigerian artist: his patrons, his audience, his critics', *Présence africaine*, **105/106**, 1/2, pp. 130–45.

Crowder, M. (1980) *West Africa under Colonial Rule* (London: Hutchinson; 1st edn, 1968).

Crowder, M. (ed.) (1984) *The Cambridge History of Africa, Vol. 8: From c.1940 to c.1975* (Cambridge: CUP).

Crowder, M. (1985a) 'Professor Macmillan goes on safari: the British government observer team and the crisis over the Seretse Khama marriage', in S. Marks and H. Macmillan (eds) *Africa and Empire: W. M. Macmillan Historian and Social Critic* (London: ICS), pp. 254–78.

Crowder, M. (1985b) 'World War II and Africa', *JAH*, **26**, 4, pp. 287–9.

Crowder, M. and Osuntokun, J. (1986) 'The First World War and West Africa', in J. F. A. Ajayi and M. Crowder (eds) *History of West Africa, Vol. II* (Harlow: Longman), pp. 546–78.

Cuba in Africa (1978) Special double issue of *Cuba Review* (New York), **8**, 3–4, pp. 1–50.

Cunha, A.-G. and Donnelly, J. (1983) 'Defusing Africa's debt', *Africa Report*, **28**, 5 (September–October), pp. 17–22.

Cunha da Silva, J. M. (1955) *O trabaiho indigena* (Lisbon: Agencia Geral do Ultramar, Divisão de Publicaçãoes e Biblioteca).

Cuper, K. (1958) 'Kwela: how it all began', *Melody Maker*, **33**, 7 June, p. 1283.

Current Soviet Policies III: The Record of the Extraordinary 21st Communist Party Congress (1960) (New York: Columbia University Press, No. 7).

Curry, R. L. (1971) 'Agricultural land development in Liberia', *The Journal of International Law and Economics*, **6**, 1 (June), pp. 125–37.

Curtin, P., Feierman, S., Thompson, L. and Vansina, J. (eds) (1978) *African History* (Boston: Little and Brown; London: Longman).

Cutrufelli, M. R. (1983) *Women of Africa: Roots of Oppression* (London: Zed Press).

Cutter, C. H. (1968) 'The politics of music in Mali', *African Arts*, **1**, 3, pp. 38–9 and 74–7.

Dakin, J., Tiffen, B. and Widdowson, H. G. (1968) *Language in Education* (London: OUP).

Dalby, D. (1970) *Language and History in Africa* (London: Frank Cass and Co. Ltd).

d'Almeida, A. (1983) *La problématique du développement en Afrique à travers le 'Rapport Berg' et le Plan d'Action de Lagos* (Lomé: ENA).

Daoud, Z. (1981) 'Agrarian capitalism and the Moroccan crisis', *Merip Reports*, **99**, September, pp. 27–33.

Dapo, O. (1973) 'Aina Onabolu', *Nigeria Magazine*, **79**, December, pp. 295–8.

d'Arschot, Comte (1951) 'Commencements de la peinture', *Les arts plastiques: l'art au Congo belge* (Brussels: Editions des Arts Plastiques, No. 1, June–July), pp. 37–46.

Dauber, R. and Cain, M. L. (eds) (1980) *Women and Technological Change in Developing Countries: AAAS Selected Symposium 53* (Boulder, CO: Westview Press).

Davidson, B. (1969) *The Africans: An Entry to Cultural History* (London and Harlow: Longman).

Davidson, B. (1972) *L'Angola au coeur des tempêtes* (Paris: Maspero).

Davidson, B. (1978) *Africa in Modern History* (Guildford: Allen Lane).

Davidson, B. (1980) 'The movement of national liberation', *Tarikh*, **6**, 4.

Davidson, B., Slovo, J. and Wilkinson, A. R. (1976) *Southern Africa: The New Politics of Revolution* (Harmondsworth: Pelican).

Davis, E. (1987) 'Religion against the state: a political economy of religious radicalism in Egypt and Israel', in R. T. Antoun and M. E. Hegland (eds) *Religious Resurgence: Contemporary Cases in Islam, Christianity and Judaism* (Syracuse: Syracuse University Press), pp. 145–68.

Davis, J., Campbell, T. M. and Wrong, M. (1946) *Africa Advancing: A Study of Rural Education and Agriculture in West Africa and the Belgian Congo* (New York: Foreign Missions Conference of North America).

Davison, P. (1984) 'Lobedu material culture: a comparative study of the 1930s and the 1970s', *Annals of the South African Museum*, **94**, 3, pp. 41–201.

de Almeida, P. R. (1979) *Historia de colonialismo portugués em Africa: cronologia* (Lisbon: Editorial estampa).

de Andrade, M. and Ollivier, M. (1971) *La guerre en Angola: étude socio-économique* (Paris: Maspero).

de Benoist, J. (1980) *La Balkanisation de l'Afrique Occidentale française* (Dakar: NEA).

de Bernis, G. D. (1975) 'L'Algérie à la recherche de son indépendance: nationalisation et industrialisation', in J. D. Esseks (ed.), pp. 19–62.

de Castro, A. (1978) *O sistema colonial portuges em Africa* (Lisbon: Editorial Caminho).

de Gaulle, C. (1968) in *Africa Research Bulletin* (London), **9**, 5, p. 1186.

Dean Jr, P. D. and Vasquez, J. A. (1976) 'From politics to issue politics: bipolarity and multipolarity in the light of the new paradigm', *Western Political Quarterly*, **29**, 1 (March), pp. 7–28.

De Gennaro, B. M. (1981) 'Ujamaa: the aggrandizement of the state', in R. E. Galli (ed.), pp. 111–55.

De Haes, R. (1982) *Les Sectes: une interpellation* (Kinshasa).

De Jager, E. J. (1973) *Contemporary African Art in South Africa* (Cape Town: C. Struik).

De Negri, E. (1968) 'Itsekiri costume', *Nigeria Magazine*, 97, pp. 101–10.

De Rop, A. (1959) *Théâtre nkundo* (Léopoldville: Editions de l'Université).

De Rosny, E. (1983) 'Les églises indépendantes africaines: fonction sociale et originalité culturelle', *Etudes*, 1 January, pp. 93–107.

De St Jorre, J. (1972) *The Nigerian Civil War* (London: Hodder and Stoughton).

De Wilde, J. C. (1967) *Experiences with Agricultural Development in Tropical Africa* (2 vols; Baltimore: The Johns Hopkins Press).

Debhonvapi, O. (1984) 'Société zaïroise dans le miroir de la chanson populaire', in B. Jewsiewicki (ed.).

Decraene, P. (1982) *Vieille Afrique, jeunes nations* (Paris: PUF).

DeGraft-Johnson, J. C. (1958) *African Experiment: Cooperative Agriculture and Banking in British West Africa* (London: Watts).

Delavignette, R. (1947) *Les vrais chefs de l'empire* (Paris: Gallimard).

Demunter, P. (1975) *Masses rurales et luttes politiques au Zaïre: Le processus de politisation des masses rurales au bas-Zaïre* (Paris: Anthropos).

Derman, W. (1984) 'USAID in Sahel: development and poverty', in J. Barker (ed.), pp. 77–99.

Desanti, D. and Decock, J. (1969) 'Farid Belkahia: artiste et animateur', *African Arts*, 2, 3, pp. 26–9.

Deschamps, H. (1971) *Histoire générale de l'Afrique, Vol. 2* (Paris: PUF).

Despois, J. (1935) *La colonisation italienne en Libye: problèmes et méthodes* (Paris: Larose).

Devèze, M. (1948) *La France d'outre-mer* (Paris: Librairie Hachette).

De Vore, R. M. (ed.) (1977) *The Arab-Israeli Historical Conflict: An Historical Political, Social and Military Bibliography* (Oxford: OUP).

Dharam, G. and Radwan, S. (1983) *Agrarian Policies and Rural Poverty in Africa* (Washington, DC: International Labor Office).

Dia, M. (1975) *Islam, sociétés africaines et culture industrielle* (Dakar: NEA).

Dia El Hadji, B. (1979) 'Le Centre de Bopp à Dakar, Sénégal: modèle d'une collaboration chrétienne-islamique', in *La contribution du Christianisme et de l'Islam à la formation d'états indépendants en Afrique au Sud du Sahara*, Texts and Documents of the Symposium on Africa, Bonn–Bad Godesberg, 2–4, May 1979 (Tübingen).

Diallo, C. A. (1972) 'Contribution à une étude de l'enseignement privé coranique au Sénégal', *Revue Française d'Etudes Politiques Africaines*, 76, April, pp. 34–48.

Diawara, M. (1986) 'Who is in control?', *West Africa*, 17 February, pp. 348–9.

Diawara, M. (1987) 'Images of children', *West Africa*, 23 March, pp. 558–9.

Dickens, C. (1975) *Great Expectations* (London: OUP).

Diop, A. (1958) 'Our Amsac brothers', in *Africa seen by American Negro Scholars* (Dijon: Présence africaine; New York, 1963).

Diop, C. A. (1957) 'Le continent noir, son histoire et sa culture', *Défense de la Paix*, July–August, p. 58.

Diop, C. A. (1974) *The African Origin of Civilization: Myth and Reality*, ed. and trans. by M. Cook (Chicago: Lawrence Hill Books).

Diop, C. A. (1981) *Civilisation ou barbarie: Anthropologie sans complaisance* (Paris: Présence Africaine).

Diop, M. (1975) 'Etude sur le salariat (Haut-Sénégal – Niger, Soudan, Mali, 1884–1969)', *Etudes maliennes* (Bamako), 14, June.

Djaziri, H. (1968) 'La situation du théâtre en Tunisie', *African Arts*, 1, 3, pp. 40–1 and 92–3.

Documentation française (1947) *Notes documentaires et études, No. 558*, February (Paris: Services français d'information).

Dodge, B. (1965) 'The significance of religion in Arab nationalism', in J. H. Proctor (ed.), pp. 94–120.

Donalson, H. and Nogee, L. (1981) *Soviet Foreign Policy since World War II* (New York: Pergamon).

Doresse, J. (1970) *Histoire de l'Ethiopie* (Paris: PUF).

Dornowitz, S. and Mandirola, R. (1984) 'Grave monuments in the Ivory Coast', *African Arts*, 17, 4, pp. 46–52.

Dorward, D. (1986) 'British West Africa and Liberia', in *The Cambridge History of Africa, Vol. III* (Cambridge: CUP).

Dozy, R. P. (1969) *Dictionnaire détaillé des noms de vêtements chez les Arabes* (2nd edn, Beirut; first edn 1845).

Drachler, J. (ed.) (1969) *African Heritage: An Anthology of Black African Personality and Culture* (London: Collier-Macmillan Ltd).

Drake, St C. (1982) 'Diaspora studies and pan-Africanism', in J. E. Harris (ed.), pp. 341–402.

Dresch, J. (1946) 'Les trusts en Afrique noire', *Servir la France*.

Droogers, A. (1980) *The Dangerous Journey: Symbolic Aspects of Boys' Initiation among the Wagenia of Kisangani, Zaire* (The Hague: Mouton).

Drysdale, J. (1964) *The Somali Dispute* (New York: Praeger).

Dubresson, A. (1979) *L'espace Dakar–Rufisque* (Paris: ORSTOM).

Dudley, E. (1986) 'Mali's rug makers', *West Africa*, 3579, 7 April, pp. 728–9.

Duffy, J. (1962) *Portugal's African Territories: Present Realities* (New York: Carnegie Endowment for International Peace).

Duggan, W. R. (1973) *A Socio-Economic Profile of South Africa* (New York: Praeger).

Duignan, P. and Gann, L. H. (eds) (1973 and 1975) *Colonialism in Africa: 1870–1960, Vols III and IV* (Cambridge: CUP).

Dummett, R. (1985) 'Africa's strategic minerals during the Second World War', *JAH*, 26.

Dumont, F. (1975) *La pensée religieuse d'Amadou Bamba, fondateur du mouridisme sénégalais* (Dakar-Abidjan: NEA).

Dumont, R. (1966) *False Start in Africa* (New York: Praeger).

Duncan, J. S. R. (1957) *The Sudan's Path to Independence* (Edinburgh and London: W. Blackwood).

Dunton, C. (1984) Review of Femi Osofisan's 'Morountodun and Other Plays', *West Africa*, 3484, 28 May, pp. 1122–4.

Durand, H. (1957) *Essai sur la conjoncture de l'Afrique noire* (Paris: Dalloz).

Durand, J. D. (1967) 'World population estimates, 1750–2000', in *Proceedings of the World Population Conference* (United Nations).

Durieux, A. (1955) *Essai sur le statut des indigènes portugais de la Guinée, de l'Angola et du Mozambique* (Brussels: Académie Royale des Sciences Coloniales).

Dutoit, D. (1981) *Capital and Labour in South Africa: Class Struggle in the 1970s* (London: Kegan Paul).

Du Vivier de Streel (1933) *L'AEF et la crise* (Brussels).

Dzidzienyo, A. and Turner, J. M. (1981) 'African–Brazilian relations: a reconsideration', in W. A. Selcher (ed.), pp. 201–18.

Dzobo, N. K. (1975) 'Values in indigenous education', in G. N. Brown and M. Hiskett (eds), pp. 76–91.

ECA (Economic Commission for Africa) (1976) *Revised Framework of Principles for the Implementation of the New International Economic Order in Africa, 1976–1981–1985* (E/CN.14/ECO/90/Rev.3), 25 June 1976 (Addis Ababa).

ECA (Economic Commission for Africa) (1981) *Lagos Plan of Action for the Economic Development of Africa 1980–2000* (Geneva: International Institute for Labour Studies).

ECA (Economic Commission for Africa) (1983) *ECA and Africa's Development 1983–2008: A Preliminary Perspective Study* (Addis Ababa).

ECA (Economic Commission for Africa) (1989a) *African Alternative Framework to Structural Adjustment Programmes for Socio-Economic Recovery and Transformation*, AAFF-SAP (Addis Ababa).

ECA (Economic Commission for Africa) (1989b) *Beyond Recovery – ECA's Revised Perspectives of Africa's Development from 1990–2008* (Addis Ababa).

ECA (Economic Commission for Africa) (1990) *African Chapter for Popular Participation in Development* (Addis Ababa).

Echenberg, M. (1978) 'Tragedy at Thiaroye: the Senegalese soldiers' uprising of 1944', in *African Labour History* (Beverly Hills: Sage), pp. 109–28.

Eckardt, U. and Sievernich, G. (eds) (1979) *Moderne Kunst aus Afrika* (Berlin: Catalogue Festspiele).

Economic Development Institute (1989) *Successful Development in Africa: Case Studies of Projects, Programs and Politics*, Analytical Case Study No. 1 (Washington, DC: The World Bank).

Edmondson, L. (1974) 'Caribbean nation-building and the internationalization of race', in W. Bell and W. E. Freeman (eds) *Ethnicity and Nation-Building: Comparative, International and Historical Perspectives* (Beverly Hills, CA: Sage Publications), pp. 73–86.

Edmondson, L. and Phillips, P. (1979) 'The Commonwealth Caribbean and Africa: aspects of third world racial interactions, linkages and challenges', in B. Ince (ed.), *Contemporary International Relations of the Caribbean* (St. Augustine, Trinidad: Institute of International Relations), pp. 33–55.

Eicher, J. (1970 and 1985) *African Dress: A Select and Annotated Bibliography of Sub-Saharan Countries* (2 vols: vol. 1, 1970; vol. 2, 1985; East Lansing, MI).

Einstein, C. (1915) *Negerplastik* (Munich : Kurt Wolff Verlag).

Eisenstadt, S. N. and Rokkan, S. (eds) (1973) *Building States and Nations* (2 vols; Beverly Hills: Sage).

Elaigwu, J. I. (1979) 'The military and state-building: Federal–State relations in Nigeria's "military-federalism"', in A. B. Akinyemi, P. Cole and W. Ofonagoro (eds), *Readings in Federalism* (Lagos: Nigerian Institute of International Affairs), pp. 155–82.

Elaigwu, J. I. (1981) 'Military intervention in politics: an African perspective', *Genève–Afrique: Journal of Swiss Society of African Society*, 19, 1, pp. 17–38.

El-Ayouty, Y. (1971) *The United Nations and Decolonization: The Role of Afro–Asia* (The Hague: Martinus Nijhoff).

El-Ayouty, Y. (1975a) 'The OAU and the Arab–Israeli conflict: a case of mediation that failed', in Y. El-Ayouty (ed.), pp. 189–212.

El-Ayouty, Y. (ed.) (1975b) *The Organization of African Unity after Ten Years: Comparative Perspectives* (New York: Praeger).

El Fasi, M. (1967) *Chants anciens des femmes de Fès* (Paris: Editions Seghers).

El-Hareir, I. S. (1985) 'North Africa and the Second World War', in UNESCO (1985b), pp. 27–36.

Elkan, W. (1958) 'The East African trade in woodcarving', *Africa*, 28, 4, pp. 314–23.

El-Khawas, M. (1971) 'The Third World stance on apartheid: the UN record', *Journal of Modern African Studies*, 9, 3 (October), pp. 443–52.

El Mansury, S. (1984) 'Modern trends in Egyptian arts', *Prism*, 6, pp. 83–7.

Elnaccash, A. (1968) 'Egyptian cinema: a historical outline', *African Arts*, 2, 1, pp. 52–5 and 70–1.

Elungu, E. P. (1984) *Eveil philosophique africain* (Paris: L'Harmattan).

Emerson, R. (1962) *From Empire to Nation: The Rise to Self-Assertion of Asian and African Peoples* (Cambridge, MA: HUP).

Enahoro, P. (1983) 'Interview with J. Nyerere', *Africa Now*, 32, December, pp. 98–122.

Encyclopaedia Britannica, Macropedia, vol. 9, p. 981.

Engels, F. (1849) in *Northern Star* (English Chartist newspaper), XI, 22 January.

Ephson, B. (1984) 'Kukurantumi: road to Accra', *West Africa*, 3488, 24 June, pp. 1303–4.

Esedebe, P. O. (1971) 'The independence movement in Sierra Leone', *Tarikh*, 4, 1.

Esedebe, P. O. (1980) 'The growth of the pan-African movement', *Tarikh*, 6, 3.

Esprit (1985) *Français-Immigrés*, June (Paris).

Esseks, J. D. (1975) *L'Afrique de l'indépendance politique á l'indépendance économique* (Paris: Maspero).

Estudos Afro–Asiáticos (Centro de Estudos Afro–Asiáticos).

Etherton, M. (1982) *The Development of African Drama* (London: Hutchinson).

Ethiopian Herald (Addis Ababa), April 1977.

Ethiopian Research Council (1935) *Memorandum* (Mimeograph, 27 April, Washington, DC: ERC).

Ettinger, S. (date unknown) 'South Africa's weight restrictions on cattle exports from Bechuanaland, 1924–41', *Botswana Notes and Records*.

Evans-Pritchard, E. E. (1949) *The Sanusi of Cyrenaica* (Oxford: Clarendon Press).

Ewens, G. (1987) 'The Zaiko cult', *West Africa*, 3621, 2 February, pp. 202–4.

Eybers, G. W. (1918) *Select Constitutional Documents Illustrating South African History, 1795–1910* (London: Routledge).

Eyongetah, T. and Brain, R. (1974) *A History of the Cameroon* (London: Longman).

Fabian, J. (1978) 'Popular culture in Africa: findings and conjectures', *Africa*, 48, 4, pp. 315–34.

Fabubmi, L. A. (1960) *The Sudan in the Anglo-Egyptian Relations* (London: Longmans).

Fanon, F. (1963) *The Wretched of the Earth*, trans. by C. Farrington (New York: Grove Press Inc.; reprinted 1983, London: Penguin).

Fanon, F. (1967a) *Toward the African Revolution: Political Essays*, trans. by H. Chevalier (New York: Monthly Review Press).

Fanon, F. (1967b) *Black Skin; White Masks*, trans. by C. L. Markmann (New York: Grove Press Inc.; 1970 edn, London: Paladin).

Fanon, F. (1968) *Sociology of Revolution* (Paris: Maspero).

FAO (1955) *Production Yearbook* (Rome: FAO).

FAO (1956) *Production Yearbook* (Rome: FAO).

FAO (1957) *Production Yearbook* (Rome: FAO).

FAO (1958) *Production Yearbook* (Rome: FAO).

FAO (1961a) *Production Yearbook* (Rome: FAO).

FAO (1961b) *State of Food and Agriculture* (Rome: FAO).

FAO (1977) *State of Natural Resources and the Human Environment for Food and Agriculture* (Rome: FAO).

FAO (1982a) *World Development Report* (Rome: FAO).

FAO (1982b) *Production Yearbook* (Rome: FAO).

FAO (1983) *Public Expenditure on Agriculture* (Computer printouts, 13 December, Rome).

Farris, J. C. (1982) *Nuba Personal Art* (Toronto; 1972 edn, London: Duckworth).

Fashole-Luke, E., Gray, R., Hastings, A. and Tasie, G. (eds) (1978) *Christianity in Independent Africa* (London: Rex Collings).

Fassassi, M. A. (1978) *L'architecture en Afrique noire* (Paris: Maspero).

Favoureu, L. (1970) *L'île Maurice* (Paris: Berger-Levrault).

Faye, C. F. (1973) *L'opinion publique dakaroise 1940–1944* (Dakar: University of Dakar, Faculté des lettres et sciences humaines, memoir).

Federal Republic of Nigeria (1972) Nigerian Enterprises Promotion Decree No. 4 (Lagos).

Federal Republic of Nigeria, Ministry of Education (1981) *National Policy on Education* (Lagos).

954

Feit, E. (1967) *African Opposition in South Africa: The Failure of Passive Resistance* (Stanford, CA: Hoover Institution Press).

Fernandez, J. (1982) *Bwiti: An Ethnography of the Religious Imagination in Africa* (Princeton: PUP).

Fernea, R. A. (ed.) (1973) *Nubians in Egypt: A Peaceful People* (Austin: University of Texas Press).

Ferreira, E. S. (1974) *Portuguese Colonialism in Africa: The End of an Era* (Paris).

Ferreira, M. (1986) 'Portuguese Africa: the new militancy', in A. Gérard (ed.), vol. I.

Fetter, B. (1973) 'L'Union minière du Haut-Katanga, 1920–1940: la naissance d'une sous-culture totalitaire', *Les Cahiers du CEDAF* (Brussels), 6, pp. 1–40.

Fetter, B. (1976) *The Creation of Elisabethville 1910–1940* (Stanford: Hoover Colonial Studies).

Fieldhouse, D. K. (1986) *Black Africa 1945–1980: Economic Decolonization and Arrested Development* (London and Boston: Allen and Unrich).

Fig, D. (1984) 'South African interests in Latin America', in South African Research Service (ed.) *South Africa Review II* (Johannesburg: Raven Press), pp. 239–55.

Fiofori, T. (1986a) 'History through art', *West Africa*, 7 July, p. 1426.

Fiofori, T. (1986b) 'Hope for better nights', *West Africa*, 17 November, pp. 2404–5.

Fisher, A. (1984) *Africa Adorned* (London: Collins).

Fisseha, G. and Raunig, W. (1985) *Mensch und Geschichte in Aethiopiens Volksmalerei* (Innsbruck).

Flint, J. (1983) 'The failure of planned decolonization in British Africa', *African Affairs*, 82, 328 (July), pp. 389–411.

Flobert, T. (1976) 'Histoire et actualité du Mouvement mahorais', *Revue française d'études politiques africaines*, 121 (January), pp. 70–90.

Foltz, W. J. (1973) 'Political boundaries and political competition in tropical Africa', in S. N. Eisenstadt and S. Rokkan (eds).

Fondation Louis de Brouckerie/Institut Emile Vandervelde (n.d.) 'Le programme colonial en 1937', in *Congo: Positions socialistes, 1885–1960*.

Forde, D. (ed.) (1954) *African Worlds: Studies in the Cosmological Ideas and Social Values of African Peoples* (London: OUP/IAI; reprinted 1960).

Forrest, T. (1982) 'Brazil and Africa: geopolitics, trade and technology in the South Atlantic', *African Affairs* (London), 81, January, pp. 3–20.

Fortes, M. and Evans-Pritchard, E. E. (eds) (1940) *African Political Systems* (London: OUP).

Foster, M. (1961) *Masters of Political Thought, Vol. I* (London: George G. Harrap).

Foster, P. (1965) *Education and Social Change in Ghana* (London: Routledge and Kegan Paul).

Fosu, K. (1986) *Twentieth-Century Art of Africa* (Zaria).

Fouquet, J. (1958) 'La traite des arachides dans le pays de Kaolack et ses conséquences économiques, sociales et juridiques', *Etudes sénégalaises* (Dakar and St Louis du Sénégal: IFAN), 8, pp. 9–163.

Fourneau, J. and Kravetz L. (1954) 'Le pagne sur la Côte de Guinée et au Congo du XVe siècle à nos jours', *Bulletin de l'Institut d'études centrafricaines*, 7–8, pp. 5–22.

Foutchantse, V. (1967) 'Promouvoir une littérature africaine', *Présence africaine*, 67, 3, pp. 124–56.

Fox, L. K. (ed.) (1967) *East African Childhood* (London: OUP).

Fraginals, M. M. (1984) *Africa En America Latina*, trans. by L. Blum (Paris: UNESCO).

Frank, A. G. (1980) *Crisis In the World Economy* (New York and London: Holmes and Meier Publishers).

Frankel, S. H. (1938) *Capital Investment in Africa: Its Causes and Effects* (London: OUP).

Frederick, A., Duke of Mecklenburg (1910) *In the Heart of Africa* (London).

Freeman, L. (1984) 'CIDA and agriculture in East and Central Africa', in J. Barker (ed.).

Freeman-Grenville, G. S. P. (1973) *Chronology of African History* (London: OUP).

Freund, B. (1981) *Capital and Labour in the Nigerian Tin Mines* (Harlow: Longman).

Frobenius, L. (1933) *Histoire de la civilisation africaine*, trans. by H. Back and D. Ermont (Paris: Gallimard).

Froje, J. W. (1989) *Science and Technology in Africa* (London: Longman).

Frost, R. (1978) *Race Against Time: Human Relations and Politics in Kenya before Independence* (Nairobi: Transafrica).

Fuchs, A. (1985) 'Le théâtre en situation', *Littératures d'Afrique Australe, l'Apartheid*, special issue of *l'Afrique littéraire et artistique*, 75, pp. 93–115.

Furedi, F. (1974) 'The social composition of the Mau-Mau movement in the White Highlands', *Journal of Peasant Studies*, 1, 4, pp. 486–505.

Furley, O. W. and Watson, T. (1978) *A History of Education in East Africa* (New York: NOK Publishers).

Fyle, C. M. (1981) *The History of Sierra Leone* (London: Evans Brothers).

Gabriel, C. (1978) *Angola: Le tournant africain?* (Paris: Editions La Brèche).

Gahama, J. (1983) *Le Burundi sous administration belge* (Paris: Karthala–CRA).

Galal, S. (1977) *Pertes de sol dans la vallée du Nil in Uniterra* (Nairobi).

Galbraith, J. K. (1979) *Nature of Mass Poverty* (Cambridge, MA: HUP).

Galissot, R. (1964) *Le patronat européen au Maroc 1931–1942* (Rabat: Editions techniques nord-africaines).

Galli, R. E. (1981) *The Political Economy of Rural Development: Peasants, International Capital and the State* (Albany: State University of New York Press).

Galtung, J. (1976) 'The Lomé Convention and neo-capitalism', *The African Review*, **6**, 1, pp. 33–43.

Galvao, H. and Salvagem, C. (1950–53) *O imperio colonial portugues* (4 vols, Lisbon: Empressa Nacional de Publicidade).

Gann, L. H. (1968) *Burden of Empire: An Appraisal of Western Colonialism in Africa South of the Sahara* (London: Pall Mall Press).

Garcia, L. (1971) 'l'organisation de l'instruction publique au Dahomey, 1894–1920', *CEA*, **11**, pp. 59–100.

Gardet, L. (1977) *Encyclopédie Universalis*, Corpus 10 (Paris: Encyclopaedia Universalis).

Garrett, R. M. (1984) *Education and Development* (New York: St Martin's Press).

Gaskin, L. J. P. (1965a) *A Bibliography of African Art* (London: IAI).

Gaskin, L. J. P. (1965b) *A Select Bibliography of Music in Africa* (London).

Gatta Gali Ngothe (1985) *Tchad, guerre civile et désagrégation de l'Etat* (Paris: Présence africaine).

Gauze, R. (1973) *The Politics of Congo-Brazzaville* (Stanford: Hoover Institution Press).

Gavin, R. J. and Oyemakinde, W. (1980) 'Economic development in Nigeria since 1800', in O. Ikime (ed.).

Geary, C. (1983) *Les choses du palais* (Wiesbaden: Franz Steiner, Studien zur Kulturkunde 60).

Geertz, C. (1963) *Old Societies and New States* (Glencoe: The Free Press).

Geiss, I. (1974) *The Pan-African Movement* (London: Methuen).

Gellar, S. (1972) *State-Building and Nation-Building in West Africa* (Bloomington: International Development Centre, Indiana University).

Gerard, A. S. (ed.) (1986) *European Language-Writing in Sub-Saharan Africa, Vols 1 and 2* (Budapest: Akadémiai Kiadó).

Gerard-Libois, J. (1964) *Sécession au Katanga* (Brussels: CRISP).

Gerhart, G. M. (1979) *Black Power in South Africa: The Evolution of an Ideology* (Los Angeles: UCP).

Gertzel, C. (1976) 'Kingdom, districts and the unitary state: Uganda 1945–1962', in D. A. Low and A. Smith (eds), pp. 65–106.

Gertzel, C., Goldschmidt, M. and Rothchild, D. (eds) (1972) *Government and Politics in Kenya* (Nairobi: EAPH).

Ghana, Government of (1964) *Ghana Seven-Year Development Plan, 1963, 1963/64–1969/70* (Accra).

Ghana Today (1964) **VIII**, 21 (16 December).

Gharbi, S. (1981) 'OUA/CEA: deux demi-soeurs rivales', *Jeune Afrique*, 1072, 22 July, pp. 28–30.

Gibson, R. (1972) *African Liberation Movements: Contemporary Struggles Against White Minority Rule* (London: OUP).

Gifford, P. (1982) 'Misconceived dominion: the creation and disintegration of federation in British Central Africa', in P. Gifford and W. R. Louis (eds.).

Gifford, P and Louis, W. R. (eds) (1982) *The Transfer of Power in Africa: Decolonization 1940–1960* (New Haven: YUP).

Gifford, P. and Louis, W. R. (eds) (1988) *The Transfer of Power in Africa, 1956–1980* (New Haven: YUP).

Gilbert, M. (1981) 'Ewe funerary sculpture', *African Arts*, **14**, 4, pp. 44–7 and 88.

Gilbert, O. P. (1947) *L'empire du silence: Congo 1946* (Brussels: La Renaissance du Livre).

Gilkes, P. (1975) *The Dying Lion: Feudalism and Modernization in Ethiopia* (London: Julian Friedman).

Gillon, W. (1984) *A Short History of African Art* (Harmondsworth: Viking).

Glaze, A. (1972) 'Senufo graphic arts', *Bashiru*, **4**, pp. 37–46.

Glélé, M. (1981) *Religion, culture et politique en Afrique noire* (Paris: Economica).

Goldsworthy, D. (1971) *Colonial Issues in British Politics, 1945–1961* (Oxford: Clarendon Press).

Gonidec, P. F. (1983) 'Esquisse d'une typologie des régimes politiques africains', in *Les pouvoirs africains, Revue Pouvoirs No. 25*, pp. 63–79.

Goodrich, L. M. (1970) 'Foreword', in D. A. Kay, *The New Nations and the United Nations, 1960–1967* (New York and London: Columbia University Press, Columbia University Studies and International Organization Series, No. 8), p. vii.

Goody, J. (1973) 'Uniqueness in the cultural conditions for political development in Black Africa', in S. N. Eisenstadt and S. Rokkan (eds), vol. 2.

Gordon, G. C. (1966) *The Passing of French Algeria* (Oxford: OUP).

Gorer, G. (1945) *Africa Dances* (2nd edn, London: Lehmann).

Gran, G. (1983) 'From the official future to a participatory future: re-thinking development policy and practice in rural Zambia', *Africa Today*, **30**, 4, pp. 5–22.

Grange, D. (1974) 'Structure et techniques d'une propagande: les émissions de Radio-Bari', *Relations Internationales*, **2**, November, pp. 165–85.

Grange, D. (1976) 'La propagande de Radio-Bari 1937–1939', *Relations Internationales*, **5**, Spring, pp. 65–103.

Green, R. H. (1977) *Toward Socialism and Self-Reliance: Tanzania Striving for Sustained Transition Projected* (Uppsala: Scandinavian Institute of African Studies).

Green, R. H., Kiljunen, M. and Kiljunen, K. (eds) (1981) *Namibia: The Last Colony* (London: Longman).

Green, R. J. and Seidman, A. (1968) *Unity or Poverty: The Economics of Pan-Africanism* (Baltimore: Penguin Books).

Greenberg, J. H. (1966) *The Languages of Africa* (Bloomington, IN: Indiana University Research Center in Anthropology, Folklore and Linguistics, Publication No. 25).

Greenfield, R. (1965) *Ethiopia: A New Political History* (London: Weidenfeld and Nicolson).

Griaule, M. and Dieterlen, G. (1954) 'The Dogon of the French Sudan', in D. Forde (ed.), pp. 83–110.

Griffin, K. (1974) *The Political Economy of Agrarian Change: An Essay on the Green Revolution* (London: Macmillan).

Griffin, K. (1979) 'Underdevelopment in theory', in C. K. Wilber (ed.), pp. 23–33.

Griffiths, I. L. L. (1989) *An Atlas of African Affairs* (New York: Chapman and Hall Inc.; London: Routledge; first edn 1984 published by Methuen and Co; revised edn 1985, published by Methuen and Co. in association with Methuen, Inc.)

Grigg, D. (1970) *The Harsh Lands: A Study in Agricultural Development* (London: Macmillan; New York: St Martin's Press).

Grillo, Y. A. and Highet, J. (1968) 'Appreciations of Idubor', *African Arts*, **2**, 1, pp. 33–5.

Gromyko, A. A. (1967) 'Soviet foreign policy in Africa', *International Affairs*, September.

Gromyko, A. A. (ed.) (1984) *The October Revolution and Africa* (Moscow: Progress Publishers).

Grove, A. T. (1974) 'Desertification in the African environment', *African Affairs*, **73**, 291 (April), pp. 137–52.

Guedez, J. M. R. (1985) *Bibliografia Afrovenezolana* (Caracas, Venezuela).

Guegan, D. (1983) *Enseignement et mathématiques en langues africaines* (Paris: ACCT).

Guérin du Marteray, C. (1977) 'Une colonie pendant la guerre ou les origines d'une révolte: Madagascar 1939–1947' (Unpublished thesis, Nice).

Gugler, J. and Flanagan, W. G. (1978) *Urbanization and Social Change in West Africa* (London: CUP).

Guralnik, D. B. (ed.) (1970) *Webster's New World Dictionary, Vol. II* (New York: The World Publishing Company).

Guthrie, M. (1948) *The Classification of Bantu Languages* (London: OUP).

Gutkind, P. C. W. and Wallerstein, I. (eds) (1976) *The Political Economy of Contemporary Africa, Vol. I* (Beverly Hills and London: Sage).

Gwanga, J. and Miller, E. J. (1971) *The World of African Song: Miriam Makeba* (Chicago).

Habte, A. (1969) *A Look Forward: A Special Report from the President* (Addis Ababa: Haile Selassie I University Press).

Hadjor, K. (1987) *On the Brink: Nuclear Proliferation and the Third World* (London: Third World Communications).

Haezen, G. (1960) 'De troubadours van Koning Boudewijn', *Band*, **19**, 2–3, pp. 61–5.

Haffner, P. (1978) *Essai sur le fondement du cinéma africain* (Abidjan-Dakar: NEA).

Hafkin, N. J. and Bay, E. G. (eds) (1976) *Women in Africa: Studies in Social and Economic Change* (Stanford, CA: Stanford University Press).

Hailey, Lord Malcolm (1936) 'Nationalism in Africa', *Journal of the Royal African Society*, **XXVI**, 143 (April), pp. 134–49.

Hailey, Lord Malcolm (1938) *An African Survey: A Study in Problems arising in Africa South of the Sahara* (London: OUP).

Hailey, Lord Malcolm (1951) *Native Administration in the British African Territories* (London: HMSO).

Hailey, Lord Malcolm (1957) *An African Survey: A Study of Problems arising in Africa south of the Sahara* (London: OUP).

Haim, S. G. (1962) *Arab Nationalism: An Anthology* (Berkeley and Los Angeles: UCP).

Halfani, M. S. and Barker, J. (1984) 'Agribusiness and agrarian change', in J. Barker (ed.), pp. 35–65.

Hall, K. and Blake, B. W. (1979) 'The emergence of the African, Caribbean and Pacific group of states: an aspect of African and Caribbean cooperation', *African Studies Review* (Los Angeles), **22**, 2 (September), pp. 111–23.

Hamilton, V. (1988) *In the Beginning* (New York and London: Harcourt Brace Jovanovich).

Hampaté Bà, A. (1972) Communication on *Les religions traditionnelles comme source de valeurs de civilisation*, in Présence Africaine.

Handler, B. (1970) 'South Africa Atlantic Pact rumored', *Washington Post*, 17 February.

Hanna, S. A. and Gardner, G. H. (1969) *Arab Socialism: A Documentary Survey* (Leiden: Brill).

Hanson, J. W. (1973) *Imagination and Hallucination in African Education* (East Lansing: Michigan State University).

Haq, K. (ed.) (1980) *Dialogue for a New Order* (New York: Pergamon Press).

Hargreaves, J. P. (1979) *The End of Colonial Rule in West Africa: Essays in Contemporary Africa* (London: Macmillan).

Hargreaves, J. P. (1985) Review of *The Cambridge History of Africa*, vol. VIII, in *JAH*, **26**.

Harper, P. (1969) 'Dance in Nigeria', *Présence Africaine*, **70**, 2, pp. 163–71.

957

Harris, J. E. (1971) *The African Presence in Asia: Consequences of the East African Slave Trade* (Evanston, Ill: Northwestern Illinois University Press).

Harris, J. E. (1974) *Pillars in Ethiopian History: William Leo Hansberry African History Note-Book* (Washington: Howard University Press).

Harris, J. E. (1982a) Article in *East African Standard* (Nairobi, Kenya), 14 July.

Harris, J. E. (ed.) (1982b) *Global Dimensions of the African Diaspora* (Washington, D.C.: Howard University Press).

Harrison-Church, R. S., Clarke, J. I., Clarke, P. J. H. and Henderson, H. J. R. (1971) *Africa and its Islands* (3rd edn; London: Longman).

Hartland Rowe, M. (1985) 'The textile prints of the Phutadikobo Museum', *African Arts*, 18, 3, pp. 84–6.

Hastings, A. (1979) *A History of African Christianity* (Cambridge: CUP).

Hay, M. J. (1976) 'Luo women and economic change during the colonial period', in N. J. Hafkin and E. G. Bay (eds), pp. 87–111.

Hazoumé, P. and Lomani-Tshibamba, P. (n.d.) *Les précurseurs*; *Archives sonores de la littérature noire* (Paris: Radio France Internationale and CLEF).

Hecht, D. (1979) 'Malerei in Aethiopien', in U. Eckardt and G. Sievernich (eds).

Helleiner, G. K. (1966) *Peasant Agriculture, Government, and Economic Growth in Nigeria* (Homewood: Richard D. Irwin, Inc.).

Helleiner, G. K. (1972) 'Beyond growth rates and plan volumes – planning for Africa in the 1970s', *Journal of Modern African Studies*, 10, 3, pp. 333–55.

Hennebelle, G. (1972) *Les cinémas africains* (Paris: Societé africaine d'édition).

Hennebelle, G. and Ruelle, C. (1978) *Dictionnaire des cinéastes d'Afrique noire* (Paris).

Herold, E. (1983) 'On some problems of the modern art of the Makonde people', *Annals of the Nápstrek Museum* (Prague), pp. 91–109.

Herskovits, M. J. (1963) *The Human Factor in Changing Africa* (London: Routledge and Kegan Paul).

Herzog, J. (1979) 'La politique extérieure des dirigeants somalis', *Revue française d'histoire politique africaine*, 165–166.

Heseltine, N. (1971) *Madagascar* (London: Pall Mall Press).

Heyer, J., Maitha, J. K. and Senga, W. M. (eds) (1976) *Agricultural Development in Kenya: An Economic Assessment* (Nairobi: OUP).

Heyer, J., Roberts, P. and Williams, G. (eds) (1981) *Rural Development in Tropical Africa* (New York: St Martin's Press and London: Macmillan).

Heyse, T. (1950) *Bibliographie du Congo belge et du Ruanda Urundi (1939–49): beaux arts, urbanisme, arts indigènes, cinéma* (Brussels: Cahiers belges et congolais, No. 11).

Hill, C. R. (1964) *Bantustans: The Fragmentation of South Africa* (London: OUP).

Hill, P. (1970) *Studies in Rural Capitalism in West Africa* (Cambridge: CUP).

Hinderink, J. and Sterkenburg, J. J. (1983) 'Agricultural policy and production in Africa: the aims, the methods, and the means', *The Journal of Modern African Studies*, 21, 1 (March), pp. 1–23.

Hiskett, M. (1974) 'Traditional Islamic and modern Western education in tropical Africa: the problems of integration', *World Development*, 2, pp. 41–3.

Hodgkin, T. and Schachter, R. (1960) 'French-speaking West Africa in transition', *International Conciliation*, 528.

Hodgkin, T. (1961) *African Political Parties: An Introductory Guide* (Harmondsworth: Penguin Books).

Hoffher, K. (1939) *La politique commerciale de la France* (Paris).

Hoffman, H. (1982) 'Towards Africa? Brazil and the South–South trade', in J. Carlsson (ed.), pp. 55–77.

Hogendorn, J. S. and Scott, K. M. (1981) 'The East African groundnut scheme: lessons of a large-scale agricultural failure', *African Economic History*, 10, pp. 81–115.

Holbrook, W. P. (1985) 'British propaganda and the mobilisation of the Gold Coast war effort, 1939–1945', *JAH*, 26, 4, pp. 347–61.

Holt, P. M. (1961) *A Modern History of the Sudan* (London: Weidenfeld and Nicolson; 2nd edn 1967).

Homburger, L. (1941) *Les langues africaines et les peuples qui les parlent* (Paris: Payot).

Hommel, M. (1962) 'South African theatre', *The New African*, 1, 11, pp. 13–14.

Hooker, N. W. (1970) 'Popular musicians in Freetown', *African Urban Notes*, 5, 4, pp. 11–17.

Hopkins, A. G. (1973) *An Economic History of West Africa* (London: Longman).

Hopkins, N. S. (1971) 'Persuasion and satire in the Malian theatre', *Africa*, 42, 3, pp. 217–28.

Houbert, J. (1980) 'Reunion: Part I, French decolonization in the Mascareignes and Reunion'; 'Part II, The politics of departmentalization', *Journal of Commonwealth and Comparative Politics*, 18, 2, pp. 145–72, and 18, 3, pp. 325–48.

Houghton, D. H. (1971) 'Economic development, 1865–1965', in M. Wilson and L. Thompson (eds), vol. 2.

Houis, M. (1971) *Anthropologie linguistique de l'Afrique noire* (Paris: PUF).

Houis, M. and Bole-Richard, R. (1977) *Intégration des langues africaines dans une politique d'enseignement* (Paris: UNESCO and ACCT).

958

Houis, M., Rodegem, F., Dieu, M. and Polak, L. (1980) *Eléments de recherche sur les langues africaines* (Paris: ACCT).

Howe, J. (1986) 'Fela rampant', *West Africa*, 3593, 14 July, p. 1475.

Huggins, W. N. and Jackson, J. G. (n.d.) *The Friends of Ethiopia* (pamphlet; New York).

Huggins, W. N. and Jackson, J. G. (1935) *The Afro-American* (Baltimore), 27 July.

Huggins, W. N. and Jackson, J. G. (1937) *An Introduction to African Civilization* (New York: Negro Universities Press).

Hulstaert, G. (1953) 'Theatre Nkundo', *Aequatoria*, **16**, 4, pp. 142–6.

Hunter, G. (1964) *The New Societies of Tropical Africa: A Selective Study* (New York: Praeger).

Huntington, S. (1968) *Political Order in Changing Societies* (New Haven: YUP).

Ḥusaynī, I. M. (1952) *Al-Ikhwān al-Muslimīn* (Beirut: Dar al-Beirut).

Hyde, G. D. M. (1978) *Education in Modern Egypt: Ideals and Realities* (London: Routledge and Kegan Paul).

Hyden, G. (1983) *No Short Cuts to Progress* (Berkeley: UCP).

Ibrahim, S. E. (1988) 'Egypt's Islamic activism in the 1980s', *Third World Quarterly*, **10**, 2 (April).

Ignatiev, O. (1975) *Amilcar Cabral, fiho de Africa* (Lisbon: Seara Nova).

Ike, V. C. (1976) *University Development in Africa: The Nigerian Experience* (Ibadan: OUP).

Ikime, O. (ed.) (1979) *Twentieth Anniversary History of W.N.T.V.* [Western Nigerian Television] (Ibadan: Heinemann).

Ikime, O. (1980) *Groundwork of Nigerian History* (Ibadan: Heinemann).

Ikoku, S. (1971) *Le Ghana de Nkrumah* (Paris: Maspero).

Iliffe, J. (1979) *A Modern History of Tanganyika* (Cambridge: CUP).

ILO (1931) *Report on the International Conference of 1930* (Geneva: ILO).

ILO (1962) *Report of the Commission – Concerning the Observance by the Government of Portugal of the Abolition of Forced Labour Convention 1957 (No. 105)* (Geneva: ILO).

ILO (1985) *Technology and Rural Women: Conceptual and Empirical Issues* (London: George Allen and Unwin).

Imbakom Qale-Wold (1970) *Traditional Ethiopian Church Education* (New York: Columbia University Teachers College Press).

Imperato, P. J. (1971) 'Contemporary adapted dances of the Dogon', *African Arts*, **5**, 1, pp. 28–33 and 68.

Indian Council for Africa (1967) *India and Africa: Perspectives of Cooperation* (New Delhi: Indian Council of Africa).

Indian National Congress (1976) *India and the African Liberation Struggle* (New Delhi: Indian National Congress).

Inkeles, A. and Holsinger D. H. (1974) *Education and Individual Modernity in Developing Countries* (Leiden, The Netherlands: E. J. Brill).

International Affairs (Moscow) (1963) 'The choice before Nigeria'.

International Institute for Labour Studies for OAU (1981) *Lagos Plan of Action for the Economic Development of Africa 1980–2000* (Geneva: IILS).

International Monetary Fund (1982) *Directory of Trade Statistics* (Washington, DC: IMF).

Ismael, T. Y. (1971) *The U. A. R. in Africa: Egypt's Policy under Nasser* (Evanston, Ill: Northwestern University Press).

Issawi, C. (1963) *Egypt in Revolution: An Economic Analysis* (London and New York: OUP).

Issawi, C. (1982) *An Economic History of the Middle East and North Africa* (London: CUP).

Italiaander, R. (1937) *Neue Kunst in Afrika* (Mannheim: Bibliographisches Institut AG).

Iyandza-Lopoloko (1961) *Bobongo: Danse renommée des Ekonda* (Tervuren: Musée royal de l'Afrique centrale, Archives d'ethnographie, No. 4).

Jabavu, D. D. T. (1920) *The Black Problem: Papers and Addresses on Various Native Problems* (Lovedale, South Africa: Lovedale Press).

Jackson, J. G. (1970) *Introduction to African Civilizations* (Secaucus, NY: The Citadel Press).

Jaipal, R. (1983) *Non-Alignment: Origins, Growth and Potential for World Peace* (New Delhi: Allied Publishers).

Jalloh, A. (1976) 'Regional integration in Africa: lessons from the past and prospects for the future', *Africa Development*, **2**, 2, pp. 44–58.

Jankowitsch, O. and Sauvant, K. (1980) 'The initiating role of the non-alignment countries', in K. Sauvant (ed.) *Changing Priorities on the International Agenda: The New International Economic Order* (Oxford: Pergamon Press), pp. 41–78.

Jans, P. (1960) 'Godsdienstige muziek voor inlanders in de apostolisch Vicariaat ban Coquilhatstad', *Band*, **19**, 2–3, pp. 66–82.

Jansen, G. H. (1966) *Non-Alignment and the Afro-Asian States* (New York: Praeger).

Japhet, K. and Japhet, S. (1967) *The Meru Land Case* (Nairobi: EAPH).

Jaritz, H. (1973) 'Notes on Nubian architecture and architectural drawings', in R. A. Fernea (ed.), pp. 49–60.

Jewsiewicki, B. (1976) 'La contestation sociale et la naissance du prolétariat au Zaïre au cours de la première moitié du XXe siècle', *Revue canadienne des études africaines* (Montreal), **10**, 1, pp. 47–71.

Jewsiewicki, B. (1977) 'Unequal development: capitalism and the Katanga economy, 1914–40', in R. Palmer and N. Parsons (eds), pp. 317–45.

Jewsiewicki, B. (ed.) (1984) *Etats indépendants du Congo, Congo belge, Republique démocratique du Congo, République du Zaïre* (Quebec).

Jewsiewicki, B (1986) 'Collective memory and the stakes of power: A reading of popular Zairian historical discourses', *History in Africa*, **13**, pp. 195–223.

Johnson, W. R. (1983) 'The role of the Arab Bank for Economic Development in Africa', *Journal of Modern African Studies*, **21**, 4 (December), pp. 625–44.

Jorgensen, J. J. (1981) *Uganda: A Modern History* (London: Croom Helm).

Joseph, R. A. (1974) 'Settlers, strikers and "sans travail": the Douala riots of 1945', *JAH*, **15**, 4, pp. 669–87.

Joseph, R. A. (1977) *Radical Nationalism in Cameroon: Social Origins of the U.P.C. Rebellion* (Oxford: Clarendon Press).

Journal of African History (1985) 'World War II and Africa', **26**, 4.

Jules-Rosette, B. (1984) *The Messages of Tourist Arts: An African Semiotic System in Comparative Perspective* (New York and London: Plenum Press).

Julien, C. A. (ed.) (1977) *Les Africains* (Paris: Jeune Afrique).

Julien, C. A. (1978) *Le Maroc face aux impérialismes 1415–1956* (Paris: Editions Jeune-Afrique).

Kaba, L. (1974) *The Wahabiyya: Islamic Reform and Politics in French West Africa* (Evanston, Ill: Northwestern University Press).

Kadalie, C. (1971) *My Life and the ICU* (London: Frank Cass).

Kaddache, M. (n.d.) *Histoire du nationalisme algérien* (2 vols, Algiers: SNED).

Kaddache, M. (1970) *La vie politique en Algérie de 1919 à 1939* (Algiers: SNED).

Kadhaffi, M. (1980) Texts in A. Abdel Malek (ed.).

Kadhaffi, M. (1981)*The Green Book* (trans. from the Arabic, 3 vols; Spain: Cromo).

Kadima-Njuzi (1981) 'La littérature au Zaïre: C. Le théâtre', *Zaïre-Afrique*, **153**, pp. 161–9.

Kagame, A. (1956) *La philosophie bantou-rwandaise de l'être* (Brussels: Académie royale des sciences coloniales).

Kahin, G. M. (1956) *The Asian–African Conference, Bandung, Indonesia, April 1955* (Ithaca, NY: Cornell University Press).

Kaké, I. B. and M'Bokolo, E. (1979) *Résistance et messianismes: L'Afrique centrale au XIXe et au XXe siècles* (Paris: Afrique Biblio Club).

Kala-Lobe, H. (1982) 'Music in Cameroun', *West Africa*, 3405, 8 November, pp. 2881–2.

Kalck, P. (1959) *Réalités oubanguiennes* (Paris: Berger-Levrault).

Kalck, P. (1973) *Histoire centrafricaine des origines à nos jours* (Lille: Service de reproductions, University of Lille).

Kalck, P. (1974) *Histoire de la République centrafricaine* (Paris: Berger-Levrault).

Kalck, P. (1977) 'Boganda, tribun et visionnaire de l'Afrique centrale', in C. A. Julien (ed.), vol. 3, pp. 105–37.

Kamarck, A. M. (1972) *The Economics of African Development* (rev. edn, New York: Praeger).

Kandt, R. (1905) *Caput Nili* (Berlin).

Kane, C. A. (1962) *L'aventure ambiguë?* (Paris: René Juillard).

Kane, C. A. (1972) *Ambiguous Adventure*, trans. by C. Woods (London: Heinemann).

Kannyo, E. (1982) 'The Latin balancing act', *Africa Report*, **27**, 4 (July–August), pp. 52–9.

Kannyo, E. (1984) 'The Banjul Charter on human and peoples' rights: genesis and political background', in C. E. Welch Jr. and R. I. Meltzer (eds), pp. 128–76.

Kanogo, T. (1987) *Squatters and the Roots of Mau Mau* (London: James Currey).

Kanza Matongo, (1972) *Mustique zairoise moderne (situation actuelle et perspective d'avenir)* (Kinshasa).

Kapcia, A. M. (1979) 'Cuba's African involvement: a new perspective', *Survey* (London), **24**, 2 (Spring), pp. 142–59.

Karabel, J. and Halsey, A. H. (1972) *Power and Ideology in Education* (New York: OUP).

Kariara, J. (1965) 'The Dream of Africa', in D. Cook (ed.).

Karis, T. and Carter, G. M. (1977) *From Protest to Challenge: A Documentary History of African Politics in South Africa 1882–1964*, Vols 1–4 (Stanford, CA: Hoover Institution Press).

Karugire, S. (1980) *A Political History of Uganda* (Nairobi: Heinemann).

Kassab, A. (1976) *Histoire de la Tunisie: l'époque contemporaine* (Tunis: STD).

Kaunda, K. and Morris, C. (1960) *Black Government: A Discussion between Colin Morris and Kenneth Kaunda* (Lusaka: United Society for Christian Literature).

Kay, D. (1970) *The New Nations in the United Nations, 1960–1967* (New York: Columbia University Press).

Kay, G. (1965) *Changing Patterns of Settlement and Land Use in Eastern Province of Northern Rhodesia* (Hull: University of Hull, Occasional Papers in Geography, No. 2).

Kay, S. (1978) 'Peter Nzuki: calabash carver of Kenya', *African Arts*, **12**, 1, pp. 40–1 and 108.

Kazadi, F. S. B. (1978) 'Mobutu, MPR and the politics of survival', *Africa Report*, **23**, 1 (January), pp. 11–16.

Kazadi wa Mukuna (1980) *Readings in African Urban Music* (East Lansing: African Urban Studies No. 6).

Keatley, P. (1963) *The Politics of Partnership* (London: Penguin Books).

Keesing's Contemporary Archives: Record of World Events (Bristol) (1986) **32**, 11 (November).

Keita, F. (1957) 'La danse africaine et la scène', *Présence africaine*, **14–15**, pp. 202–9. Trans. 'African dance and the stage', *World Theatre*, **7**, 3, pp. 164–78.

Keita, M. (1977) in L. Sylla (ed.).

Kennedy, J. (1985) *New Forms in a Landscape: African Artists in a Generation of Change* (Washington).

Kenya, Republic of (1972) 'Official Report, House of Representatives, First Parliament, Second Session, Vol. II, part II, 14 August 1964, Cols. 1707–10', in C. Gertzel *et al.* (eds).

Kenya, Republic of (1979–83) *Planning for Progress: Our Fourth Development Plan: A Short Version of the Development Plan, 1979–1983* (Nairobi: The Government Printer).

Kenya Historical Review (1977) **5**, 2, special issue on the Mau Mau.

Kenyatta, J. (1938) *Facing Mount Kenya* (London: Secker and Warburg; reprinted 1939; also London: Heinemann, 1979).

Keya, T. (1981) *The South African Film Industry* (2nd edn, Johannesburg).

Kgarebe, A. (1981) *SADCC 2-Maputo: The Proceedings of the Second Southern African Development Coordination Conference held in Maputo, People's Republic of Mozambique on 17/18 November 1980* (SADCC Liaison Committee).

Khadduri, M. (1963) *Modern Libya: A Study in Political Development* (Baltimore: Johns Hopkins University Press).

Khadduri, M. (1970) *Political Trends in the Arab World: The Role of Ideas and Ideals in Politics* (Baltimore: Johns Hopkins University Press).

Khalidi, I. R. (1956) *Constitutional Development in Libya* (Beirut: Khayat).

Kiggundu, I. (1984) *A Planned Approach to a Common Market in Developing Countries* (Nairobi: Coign Publications).

Kilby, P. (1969) *Industrialization in an Open Economy: Nigeria 1945–1966* (Cambridge: CUP).

Kilby, P. (1975) 'Manufacturing in colonial Africa', in P. Duignan and L. H. Gann (eds), vol. 4.

Killingray, D. and Rathbone, R. (eds) (1986) *Africa and the Second World War* (London: Macmillan Press).

Kimble, G. H. T. (1960) *Tropical Africa: Vol. 1, Land and Livelihood* (New York: The Twentieth Century Fund).

Kimche, D. (1968) 'Black Africa and the Afro–Asian Peoples Solidarity Movement', *Asian and African Studies* (Jerusalem), **4**, pp. 107–36.

Kimche, D. (1973) *The Afro–Asian Movement: Ideology and Foreign Policy in the Third World* (Jerusalem: Israel University Press).

King, K. (ed.) (1971) *Pan-Africanism and Education* (London: OUP).

King, K. (ed.) (1976) *Education and the Community in Africa* (Edinburgh: University of Edinburgh, Centre for African Studies).

King, K. (1984) *Education, Science and Technology Research in Eastern Africa: A Discussion* (Edinburgh: University of Edinburgh, Centre for African Studies, Occasional Paper No. 3).

Kinney, E. S. (1970) 'Urban West African music and dance', *African Urban Notes*, **5**, 4, pp. 3–10.

Kinyongo, J. (1974) 'Philosophie en Afrique: une existence', *African Philosophical Journal*, 3–4, pp. 205–11.

Kipling, R. (1903) *If*.

Kipré, P. (1985) *Villes de Côte d'Ivoire, 1893–1940* (2 vols, Dakar: NEA).

Kirby, P. R. (1964) 'The changing faces of African music south of the Equator', in *Essays on Music and History in Africa and Asia; Part 2: Africa* (London).

Kitching, G. (1980) *Class and Economic Change in Kenya: The Making of an African Petite Bourgeoisie, 1905–1970* (New Haven: YUP).

Kiyaga-Mulindwa, D. (1984) 'The Bechuanaland Protectorate and the Second World War', *Journal of Imperial and Commonwealth History*, **12**, 3, pp. 33–53.

Ki-Zerbo, J. (1972) *Histoire de l'Afrique noire* (Paris: Hatier).

Ki-Zerbo, J. (ed.) (1981) *Methodology and African Prehistory*, UNESCO General History of Africa, Vol. I (Paris: UNESCO; London: Heinemann; Berkeley, CA: University of California Press).

Klein, M. (1968) *Islam and Imperialism in Senegal* (Stanford and Edinburgh).

Klein, M. A. (1980) *Peasants in Africa: Historical and Contemporary Perspectives* (Beverly Hills and London: Sage).

Kokole, O. H. (1981) 'Stabex anatomised', *Third World Quarterly*, **3**, 3 (July), pp. 441–60.

Kokole, O. H. (1984) 'The Islamic factor in African–Arab relations', *Third World Quarterly*, **6**, 3 (July), pp. 687–702.

Kom, D. (1971) *Le Cameroun: Essai d'analyse économique et politique* (Paris: Editions sociales).

Korley, N. L. (1986) 'A pan-African orchestra', *West Africa*, 3574, 3 March, pp. 465–7.

Kothari, R. (1973) 'The confrontation of theories with national realities: report on an international conference', in S. N. Eisenstadt and S. Rokkan (eds).

Kouassi, E. K. (1983) 'Le rôle de l'Afrique dans le dévelopment du droit international en Afrique', in UNESCO (1983).

Kouassi, E. K. (1987) *Le rôle de l'Afrique dans le développement du droit international* (Paris: Berger-Levrault).
Kubik, G. (1966) 'La situation de la musique et des arts appliqués en Afrique', *Afrika*, 7, 2, pp. 11–13.
Kubik, G. (1981) 'Neo-traditional popular music in East Africa since 1945', in I. R. Middleton and D. Horn (eds), vol. 1.
Kum'aN' Dumbe III, A. (1980) *Hitler voulait l'Afrique* (Paris: L'Harmattan).
Kuper, H. (1978) *Sobhuza II, Ngwenyama and King of Swaziland* (London: Duckworth).
Kuper, L. and Smith, M. G. (eds) (1971) *Pluralism in Africa* (Los Angeles: UCP).
Kwabena Nketia, J. H. (1957) 'Modern trends in Ghana music', *African Music*, 1, 4, pp. 13–17.
Kwabena Nketia, J. H. (1965) *Ghana: Music, Dance and Drama* (Accra).
Kwabena Nketia, J. H. (1967) 'The language problem and the African personality', *Présence africaine*, 67, 3, pp. 157–72.
Kwabena Nketia, J. H. (1975) *The Music of Africa* (London: Gollancz).
Kwabena Nketia, J. H. (1978) 'Tradition and innovation in African music', *Jamaica Journal*, 11, 3, pp. 3–9.
Kyle, K. (1964a) 'Gideon's Voice', *The Spectator* (London), 7 February.
Kyle, K. (1964b) 'How it happened', *The Spectator* (London), 14 February.

La-Anyane, S. (1970 and 1971) 'Some barriers to rural and agricultural progress in West Africa', *Ghana Journal of Sociology*, 6, 2, and 7, 1, pp. 3–13.
Labinjoh, J. (1982) 'Fela Anikulapo-Kuti: protest music and social processes in Nigeria', *Journal of Black Studies*, 13, 1, pp. 119–35.
Labouret, H. (1937) *Le Cameroun* (Paris: Hartmann).
Labouret, H. (1941) *Paysans d'Afrique occidentale* (Paris: Gallimard).
Lacheraf, M. (1963) *L'Algérie, nation et société* (Paris: Maspero).
La Conférence africaine française (1944) (Brazzaville: Editions du Baobab).
Lacouture, J. and Lacouture, S. (1962) *L'Egypte en mouvement* (Paris: Editions du Seuil).
Lacroix, J.-L. (1966) *Industrialisation au Congo: la transformation des structures économiques* (Paris, La Haye: Mouton) © Mouton de Gruyter, a Division of Walter de Gruyter and Co.
Lamb, D. (n.d.) 'Russia in Somalia: they helped to develop', *Los Angeles Times*.
Langdon, S. (1986) 'Industrial dependence and export manufacturing in Kenya', in J. Ravenhill (ed.), pp. 181–213.
Langdon, S. and Mytelka, L. K. (1979) 'Africa in the changing world economy', in C. Legum, L. Mytelka, I. W. Zartman and S. Langdon (eds) *Africa in the 1980s: A Continent in Crisis* (New York: McGraw-Hill), pp. 128–213.
Lange, O. (1985) *Ifa and Computer Science* (Inaugural lecture, University of Ibadan).
Langley, A. (1973) *Pan-Africanism and Nationalism in West Africa 1900–1945* (Oxford: Clarendon Press).
Langley, J. A. (1975) *Pan-Africanism and Nationalism in West Africa 1900–1945: A Study in Ideology and Social Classes* (London: OUP).
La nouvelle génération de l'immigration maghrébine: essai d'analyse sociologique (1982) (Paris).
Laporte, R. B. 'A lesser-known chapter of the African *diaspora*: West Indians in Costa Rica, Central America', in J. E. Harris (ed.) (1982b), pp. 219–39.
Larkin, B. (1971) *China and Africa, 1949–1970* (Berkeley: UCP).
Laroui, A. (1967) *L'idéologie arabe contemporaine* (Paris: Maspero).
Last, M. and Chavunduka, G. L. (1986) *The Professionalization of Traditional Medicine* (Manchester: Manchester University Press, IAI International Seminar).
Lawrence, A. (1965) *Chinese Foreign Relations since 1949* (London and Boston: Routledge and Kegan Paul).
Lawrence, H. G. (1962) 'African explorers of the New World', *The Crisis* (Organ of NAACP, USA), June–July, pp. 2–4.
Laya, D. (ed.) (1972) *La tradition orale: méthodologie et sources de l'histoire africaine* (Niamey: CRDTO).
Lebeuf, J. P. (1956) 'L'école des peintres de Poto-Poto', *Africa*, 26, 1, pp. 277–80.
Le Cacheux, P. (n.d.) Report on 'Les prospectives de l'avenir industriel des colonies', SOM, Aff. Eco.
Lederer, A. (1983) 'Les transports au Congo pendant la Seconde Guerre mondiale', in Académie Royale des Sciences d'Outre-Mer, pp. 131–213.
Leferink, J. R. (1985) 'Les églises indépendantes du Ghana', *Pro Mundi Vita* (Brussels), 32, 1.
Lefort, R. (1983) *Ethiopia: A Heretical Revolution?* (London: Zed Press).
Legum, C. (1963) 'Somali liberation songs', *The Journal of Modern African Studies*, 1, 4 (December), pp. 503–19.
Legum, C. (1977) 'The Afro-Arab Summit 1977', in C. Legum (ed.) *Africa Contemporary Record: Annual Survey and Documents, 1976–77, Vol. 6* (London: Rex Collins), A96–A107.
Legvold, R. (1970) *Soviet Policy Towards West Africa* (Harvard, MA: HUP).
Leiris, M. and Delange, J. (1967) *Afrique noire: la création plastique* (Paris: Gallimard).
Lelong, M. H. (1946) *Mes frères au Congo* (Algiers).

Leloup, J. (1983) 'La naissance du théâtre en Afrique: théâtre traditionnel ou pré-théâtre?', *Recherche, pédagogie et culture*, **61**, pp. 89–100.

Lemarchand, R. (1970) *Rwanda and Burundi* (London: Pall Mall Press).

Lemarchand, R. (ed.) (1981) *American Policy in Southern Africa* (Washington, DC: University of America Press).

Lempert, L. O. (1968) *A History of Africa, 1918–1967* (USSR Academy of Sciences, Institute of Africa) (Moscow: Nauka).

Lengyel, E. (1957) *Egypt's Role in World Affairs* (Washington: Public Affairs Press).

Lenin, V. I. (1950) 'Preliminary draft of the theses on the national and colonial question', 5 June 1920, *Sochinenia*; excerpts trans. by A. Rubinstein, *The Foreign Policy of the Soviet Union* (New York: Random House), pp. 360–3.

Lenin, V. I. (1965) *Collected Works* (4th edn, Moscow: Progress Publishers).

Lenin, V. I. (1966) *Imperialism, The Highest State of Capitalism: A Popular Outline* (13th edn, Moscow: Progress Publishers).

Leo, C. (1981) 'Who benefited from the million-acre scheme? Toward a class analysis of Kenya's transition to independence', *Canadian Journal of African Studies*, **15**, 2, pp. 201–23.

LeoGrande, W. M. (1980) *Cuba's Policy in Africa, 1959–1980* (Berkeley: Institute of International Studies, University of California).

Léon, P. (1978) *Histoire économique et sociale du monde. Tome 5: Guerres et crises 1914–1947* and *Tome VI: Le second XXE siècle: 1947 à nos jours* (Paris: A. Colin).

Le Plan d'action de Lagos pour le développement économique de l'Afrique (1985): Contribution africaine au Nouvel Ordre Economique International, in *Mélanges Gonidec* (Paris : LGDJ).

Leslau, C. and Leslau, W. (eds) (1962) *African Proverbs* (New York: Peter Pauper Press).

Les Temps Modernes (1985) *L'immigration maghrébine* (Paris: Denoël).

Le Tourneau, R. (1962) *Evolution politique de l'Afrique du Nord musulmane 1920–1961* (Paris: A. Colin).

Levine, B. (ed.) (1983) *The New Cuban Presence in the Caribbean* (Boulder, CO: Westview Press).

Le Vine, V. (1975) *Political Corruption: The Ghana Case* (Stanford: Hoover Institution Press).

Le Vine, V. T. and Luke, T. W. (1979) *The Arab–African Connection: Political and Economic Realities* (Boulder, CO: Westview Press).

Lewis, A. (1953) *Industrialization in the Gold Coast* (Accra: Government Printer).

Lewis, I. M. (1965) *The Modern History of Somaliland: From Nation to State* (London: Longman; 2nd edn 1980).

Lewis, L. J. (1954) *Educational Policy and Practice in British Tropical Africa* (London: Thomas Nelson and Sons Ltd).

Lewis, W. A. (1969) *Some Aspects of Economic Development: The Aggrey–Fraser–Guggisberg Memorial Lectures 1968* (Accra-Tema: The Ghana Publishing Corporation).

Leys, C. (1975) *Underdevelopment in Kenya: The Political Economy of Neo-Colonialism 1964–1971* (Berkeley and Los Angeles: UCP).

Liauzu, C. (1978) *Salariat et mouvements ouvriers en Tunisie: crises et mutations de 1931 à 1939* (Paris: CNRS).

Libérons l'Afrique (1958) MLN Manifesto.

Libyan Oil (1972) *Libyan Oil 1954–1971* (Tripoli: Ministry of Petroleum).

Liebenow, J. G. (1969) *Liberia; the Evolution of Privelege* (Ithaca and London: Cornell University Press)

Lijembe, J. A. (1967) 'The valley between', in L. K. Fox (ed.) *East African Childhood* (London: OUP), pp. 1–45.

Lindfors, B. (1980) 'Nigerian high school plays: 1950–1972', *Kiabàrà*, **3**, 1 (Rains), pp. 47–88.

Ling, D. L. (1967) *Tunisia: From Protectorate to Republic* (Bloomington: Indiana University Press).

Liniger-Goumaz, M. (1979a) *Historical Dictionary of Equatorial Guinea* (Methuen, NJ and London).

Liniger-Goumaz, M. (1979b) *La Guinée Equatoriale: un pays méconnu* (Paris: L'Harmattan).

Litalien, R. (1975) *Madagascar 1956–60* (Paris).

Little, P. D. (1983) 'The livestock–grain connection in Northern Kenya: an analysis of pastoral economics and semi-arid land development', *Rural Africana*, 15/16 (Winter–Spring), pp. 91–109.

Littlefield Kasfir, S. (1980) 'Patronage and Makonde carvers', *African Arts*, **13**, 3, pp. 67–90 and 91–2.

Lloyd, P. C. (1967) *Africa in Social Change: Changing Traditional Societies in the Modern World* (Harmondsworth: Penguin Books).

Lloyd, P. C. (1971) *Classes, Crises and Coups: Themes in the Sociology of Developing Countries* (London: Paladin).

Lloyd, P. C. (1972) *Africa in Social Change: Changing Traditional Societies in the Modern World* (New York: Penguin Books).

Lloyd, P. C. (1974) *Power and Independence: Urban Africans' Perception of Social Inequality* (London: Routledge and Kegan Paul).

Lofchie, M. F. (1965) *Zanzibar: Background to Revolution* (Princeton: PUP).

Lofchie, M. F. (1967) 'Was Okello's revolution a conspiracy?', *Transition* (Kampala), **33**, 7 (ii), pp. 36–45.

Lofchie, M. F. and Commins, S. K. (1982) 'Food deficits and agricultural policies in tropical Africa', *The Journal of Modern African Studies*, **20**, 1 (March), pp. 1–25.

Lomani-Tshibamba, P. (1948) *Ngando* (Léopoldville: Ethiopian Books).

London, J. B. (ed.) (1976) *Social Anthropology and Medicine* (London and New York: Academic Press).

Londres, A. (1929) *Terre d'ébène* (Paris: Albin Michel).

Long, C. H. (1985) 'Religious doctrines and dogmas, Creation', in *Encyclopaedia Britannica*, vol. 17, pp. 369–70.

Long, F. (ed.) (1980) *The Political Economy of EEC Relations with African, Caribbean and Pacific States: Contribution to the Understanding of the Lomé Convention on North–South Relations* (Oxford: Pergamon Press).

Lonoh, M. (n.d.) *Essai de commentaire de la musique congolaise moderne* (Boulogne).

Lonsdale, J. (1982) 'A state of agrarian unrest: colonial Kenya', paper presented to Past and Present Society conference on Agrarian Unrest in British and French Africa, British India and French Indo-China (July).

Lopatov, V. (1987) *The Soviet Union and Africa* (Moscow: Progress Publishers).

Lopes, H. and Tri, H. C. (1981) 'The poverty trap: the plight of the least developed countries', *UNESCO Courier* (Paris), 34, 9 (October), pp. 5–9.

Loudon, J. B. (1976) *Social Anthropology and Medicine* (London and New York: Academic Press).

Love, K. (1969) *Suez: The Twice-fought War; A History* (1st edn, New York: McGraw-Hill).

Low, D. A. (1971) *Buganda in Modern History* (London: Weidenfeld and Nicolson).

Low, D. A. (1982) 'The Asian mirror to tropical Africa's independence', in P. Gifford and W. R. Louis (eds), pp. 1–29.

Low, D. A. and Lonsdale, J. M. (1976) 'Towards the new order 1945–1963', in D. A. Low and A. Smith (eds).

Low, D. A. and Smith, A. (eds) (1976) *History of East Africa, Vol. 3* (Oxford: Clarendon Press).

Low, J. (n.d.) 'A history of Kenya guitar music, 1945–1980', *African Music*, 6, 2, pp. 17–36.

Loxley, J. (1984) 'The World Bank and the model of accumulation', in J. Barker (ed.), pp. 65–76.

Lugard, Lord (1922) *The Dual Mandate in Tropical Africa* (London: Blackwood and Sons).

Luthuli, A. (1962) *Let My People Go: An Autobiography* (London: Collins; also London: Fount Paperbacks, 1987).

Ly, Abdoulaye (1957) *Mercenaires noirs* (Paris: Présence africaine).

Lynch, H. (1978) *Black American Radicals and the Liberation of Africa* (New York: Cornell University Africana Studies and Research Center).

Mabika, K. (1959) *Baluba et Lulua: Une ethnie à la recherche d'un nouvel équilibre* (Brussels: Editions de Remarques congolaises).

Mabika, K. (1965) *Le remise en question: base de la décolonisation mentale* (Kinshasa).

Mabogoane, M. (1983) In *The Star*, 24 June, p. 24.

Mabogunje, A. L. (1972) *Regional Mobility and Resource Development in West Africa* (Montreal and London: McGill-Queen's University Press).

Mabogunje, A. L. (1973) 'Manufacturing and the geography of development in tropical Africa', *Economic Geography*, 49, 1, pp. 1–21.

Macdonald, R. J. (1975) *From Nyasaland to Malawi* (Nairobi: EAPH).

MacGaffey, J. (1975) 'Two Kongo potters', *African Arts*, 11, 1, pp. 29–31 and 92.

Macleod, I. (1964) 'Blundell's Kenya', *The Spectator* (London), 20 March, p. 366.

Macmillan, W. M. (1938) *Africa Emergent* (London: Faber and Faber).

Macmillan, W. M. (1941) *Democratise the Empire* (London: Kegan Paul and Co.).

Macmillan, W. M. (1963) *Bantu, Boer and Briton: The Making of the South African Native Problem* (Oxford: Clarendon Press).

Macmillan, W. M. (1970) *The African Voice in Southern Rhodesia 1898–1930* (London: Heinemann).

Madagascar, Government of (1964) *Plan quinquennal 1964–1968* (Tananarive).

Madeley, J. (1982) *Diego Garcia: A Contrast to the Falklands* (London: Minority Rights Group).

Madhi, M. (1990) 'Orientalism and the study of African philosophy', *Journal of Islamic Studies*, 1, 1, pp. 73–98.

Magee, J. (1970) 'ECA and the paradox of African unity', *International Conciliation* (New York), November.

Maguire, A. (1970) 'The emergence of the Tanganyika African National Union in the Lake Province', in R. I. Rotberg and A. A. Mazrui (eds) *Protest and Power in Black Africa* (New York: OUP), pp. 639–71.

Mahmoud, H. (1970) *La Lutte des classes en Egypte de 1945 à 1968* (Paris: Maspero).

Mahmoud, H. (1973) *Class Conflict in Egypt, 1945–1971* (New York: Monthly Review Press).

Mahood, M. M. (1966) 'Le théâtre dans les jeunes états africains', *Presence africaine*, 60, 4, pp. 16–33.

Makombo, M. (1977) 'Le Congo belge: 1940–1960: De l'émergence des "évolués" à l'indépendance' (PhD thesis, Ecole des hautes études en sciences sociales, Paris).

Mali, Government of (n.d.) *Rapport sur le plan quinquennal de développement économique et social de la République du Mali 1961–1965* (Bamako).

Mamadou, A. (1971) *Réflexion sur le rôle et les fonctions de la CEA* (Unofficial publication of the ECA, UN).

Mamdani, M. (1976) *Politics and Class Formation in Uganda* (Nairobi: Heinemann).

Mandela, N. (1965) *No Easy Walk to Freedom: Articles, Speeches and Trial Addresses of Nelson Mandela* (London: Heinemann).

Manghezi, A. (1976) *Class, Elite and Community in African Development* (Uppsala: The Scandinavian Institute of African Studies).

Ma-Ngo, M. du (1980) 'L'action théâtrale au Zaïre hier et aujourd'hui', *Ethiopiques*, **24**, 1, pp. 49–56.
'Manifeste des Bahutu: note sur l'aspect social du problème racial indigène au Ruanda' (1960) in *Ruanda Politique, 1958–1960* (Brussels: CRISP).
Mansfield, P. (1965) *Nasser's Egypt* (Harmondsworth: Penguin).
Mansilla, H. C. F. (1984) 'Latin America within the Third World: the search for a new identity, the acceptance of old contents', *The Korean Journal of International Studies* (Seoul), **15**, 4 (Autumn), pp. 341–59.
Manthia, D. (1986a) 'Who is in control?', *West Africa*, 3572, 17 February, pp. 348–9.
Manthia, D. (1986b) 'Images of children', *West Africa*, 3599, 25 August, pp. 1780–1.
Marcum, J. (1969) *The Angolan Revolution; Vol. I: The Anatomy of an Explosion (1950–1962)* (Cambridge, MA: MIT Press).
Marcum, J. (1978) *The Angolan Revolution; Vol. II: Exile Politics and Guerrilla Warfare (1962–1976)* (Cambridge, MA: MIT Press).
Marcus, H. G. (1972) *The Modern History of Ethiopia* (Stanford: Stanford University Press).
Markovitz, I. L. (ed.) (1970) *African Politics and Society* (New York: The Free Press).
Markovitz, I. L. (1977) *Power and Class in Africa* (Englewood Cliff, NJ: Prentice Hall).
Marlowe, J. (1954) *Anglo-Egyptian relations, 1800–1953* (London: Cresset Press).
Marseille, J. (1984) *Empire colonial et capitalisme français: histoire d'un divorce* (Paris: Albin Michel).
Martin, D. and Johnson, P. (eds) (1981) *The Struggle for Zimbabwe* (London and Boston: Faber and Faber).
Martin, S. H. (1982) 'Music in urban East Africa: five genres in Dar es Salaam', *Journal of African Studies*, **9**, 3, pp. 155–63
Martyshin, O. V. (1978) 'The ideology of contemporary African nationalism', in *Theories of Non-Marxist Socialism in African and Arab Countries* (Prague: Oriental Institute).
Marvell, A. (1981) 'To His Coy Mistress', *Miscellaneous Poems of Andrew Marvell, Esq.* (London: Robert Boelter).
Marx, K. (1859) *A Contribution to the Critique of Political Economy*, trans. by N. I. Stone, 1904 (Chicago: Charles H. Kerr).
Marx, K. and Engels, F. (1955) *Oeuvres choisies, Vol. I* (Moscow: Editions du Progrès).
Mason, S. F. (1962) *A History of the Sciences* (New York: Collier Books).
Mass, J. (1970) 'Educational change in precolonial societies: the cases of Buganda and Ashanti', *Comparative Education Review*, 14 June, pp. 174–85.
Massignon, L. (1962) *Parole donnée* (Paris: Julliard).
Matthews, T. (1979) 'A Xhosa mural', *African Arts*, **12**, 3, pp. 48–51.
Matthews, Z. K. (1961) *African Awakening and the Universities* (Cape Town: University of Cape Town).
Mazrui, A. A. (1967) *Towards a Pax Africana* (Chicago: Chicago University Press; London: Weidenfeld and Nicolson).
Mazrui, A. A. (1969a) 'Violent contiguity and the politics of retribalization in Africa', *International Affairs*, **23**, 1.
Mazrui, A. A. (1969b) *Violence and Thought: Essays on Social Tensions in Africa* (London and Harlow: Longman).
Mazrui, A. A. (1970) 'The robes of rebellion', *Encounter*, **34**, 2, pp. 19–30.
Mazrui, A. A. (1972) *Africa's International Relations* (London: Heinemann).
Mazrui, A. A. (1975a) *The Political Sociology of the English Language* (The Hague: Mouton).
Mazrui, A. A. (1975b) 'The resurrection of the warrior tradition in African political culture', *Journal of Modern African Studies*, **13**, 3, pp. 67–84.
Mazrui, A. A. (1975c) 'Black Africa and the Arabs', *Foreign Affairs*, **53**, 4 (July), pp. 725–42.
Mazrui, A. A. (1975d) 'The African university as a multinational corporation: problems of penetration and dependency', *Harvard Education Review*, **45**, 2, pp. 191–210.
Mazrui, A. A. (1977) *Africa's International Relations: The Diplomacy of Dependency and Change* (Boulder, CO: Westview Press).
Mazrui, A. A. (1978) *Political Values and the Educated Class in Africa* (Berkeley: UCP).
Mazrui, A. A. (1980a) *The African Condition: The Reith Lectures* (London: Heinemann).
Mazrui, A. A. (1980b) 'Marxist theories, socialist policies and African realities', *Problems of Communism*, **29**, September–October, pp. 44–6.
Mazrui, A. A. (1981) 'Microdependency: the Cuban factor in Southern Africa', *India Quarterly* (New Delhi), **37**, 3 (July–September), pp. 329–45.
Mazrui, A. A. (1986) *The Africans: A Triple Heritage* (New York: Little Brown; London: BBC Publications).
Mazrui, A. A. (1990) *Cultural Forces in World Politics* (London: James Currey Publishers).
Mazrui, A. A. and Bakari, M. (1986a) 'English Eastern Africa (the early phase)', in A. S. Gérard (ed.), vol. 2, pp. 803–86.
Mazrui, A. A. and Bakari, M. (1986b) 'The triple heritage in East African literature', in A. S. Gérard (ed.), vol. 2, pp. 1045–60.
Mazrui, A. A. and Tidy, M. (1984) *Nationalism and New States in Africa* (London: Heinemann).
Mazrui, A. A. and Wagaw, T. G. (1985) 'Towards decolonizing modernity: education and culture conflict in

Eastern Africa', in *The Educational Process and Historiography in Africa*, General History of Africa, Studies and Documents, No. 9 (Paris: UNESCO).

Mazrui, M. (1972) 'Aspects of the relationship between the individual and society in some African fiction, with special reference to the works of Achebe and Ngugi' (MA thesis, Makerere, Kampala).

Mbiti, J. (1962) 'La contribution protestante à l'expression culturelle de la personnalité africaine', in *Colloque sur les religions* (Paris: UNESCO, SAC).

Mbiti, J. (1969) *African Religions and Philosophy* (London and Nairobi: Heinemann).

M'Bokolo, E. (1978) 'Ethnicité, régionalisme et nationalisme au Shaba', *Le Monde Diplomatique*, July.

M'Bokolo, E. (1980) *Le continent convoité: L'Afrique au XXe siècle* (Paris and Montreal: Editions Etudes Vivantes, Coll. Axes Sciences Humaines).

M'Bokolo, E. (1981a) *La formation de la bourgeoisie zaïroise (1945–1980): éléments pour une recherche* (Paris: Centre d'études africaines, EHESS).

M'Bokolo, E. (1981b) 'Forces sociales et idéologies dans la décolonisation de l'AEF', *JAH*, 22, pp. 393–407.

M'Bokolo, E. (1982) 'French colonial policy in Equatorial Africa in the 1940s and 1950s', in P. Gifford and W. R. Louis (eds), pp. 173–211.

Mboya, T. (1963a) A letter of reply (African Socialism), *Transition*, 3, 11, p. 6.

Mboya, T. (1963b) *Freedom and After* (London: André Deutsch).

Mbughuni, L. A. (1976) 'Old and new drama from East Africa', *African Literature Today*, 8, pp. 85–98.

McCarthy, J. (1977) *Guinea-Bissau and Cape Verde Islands: A Comprehensive Bibliography* (New York and London: Garland Publishing).

McEwen, F. (1972) 'Shona art today', *African Arts*, 5, 4, pp. 8–11.

Melendez, C. and Duncan, Q. (1981) *El Negro En Costa Rica* (San José).

Meli, F. (n.d.) 'Le Komintern et l'Afrique' (MA thesis).

Mérat, L. (1936) 'Note sur l'économie aux colonies', Overseas Section, National Archives, Aff. Pol. 2529.

Merlier, M. (1962) *Le Congo, de la colonisation belge á l'indépendance* (Paris: Maspero).

Merriam, A. (1970) *African Music on LP: An Annotated Discography* (Evanston: North Western University Press).

Merriam, A. (1981) *African Music in Perspective* (New York: Garland).

Mesa-Lago, C. and Belkin, J. S. (eds) (1982) *Cuba in Africa* (Pittsburgh: Center for Latin American Studies, University of Pittsburgh).

Messenger, J. C. (1962) 'Anang art, drama and social control', *African Studies Bulletin*, 5, 2, pp. 29–35.

Messenger, J. C. (1971) 'Ibibio drama', *Africa*, 41, 3, pp. 208–22.

Mestre, D. (1981) 'Vi Teix: Tonalidades diurnas de memorias nocturnas', *Lavra e officina* (Luanda), 3–5, pp. 28–30.

Mestri, E. (1980) *Les Cubains et l'Afrique* (Paris: Karthala).

Meyer, J. W. and Hannan, T. (1979) *National Development and the World System: Educational, Economic and Political Change, 1950–1970* (Chicago: University of Chicago Press).

Mhina, G. A. (1971) 'The place of Kiswahili in the field of translation', *Présence africaine*, 78, 2nd quarter, pp. 200–12.

Micaud, E. (1968) 'Three decades of Tunisian art', *African Arts*, 1, 3, pp. 46–55 and 78–84.

Michaud, P. (1986) 'Dynamic television', *West Africa*, 3590, 23 June, pp. 1308–10.

Middleton, I. R. and Horn, D. (eds) (1981) *Popular Music* (Cambridge: CUP).

Miège, J. L. (1966) *Le Maroc* (1st edn 1950, 7th edn 1986; Paris: PUF).

Miège, J. L. (1968) *L'impérialisme colonial italien de 1870 à nos jours* (Paris: SEDES).

Migrant Labour in Africa South of the Sahara (1961) Sixth Inter-African Labour Conference, Abidjan.

Miller, J. (1985) 'Rocking all the way to jail', *Newsweek*, 15 July, p. 67.

Milon, R. (1962) *Marxisme, communisme et socialisme africains* (Paris).

Minister for the Colonies (undated note) Marius Moutet, Archives nationales de France, Section Outre-mer, Aff. Polit. PA 28/1.

Ministry of Cooperation (n.d.) *Synthèse de la situation économique de l'ex-AOF durant la période 1948–1958* (7 vols, Mimeograph).

Ministry of Overseas (1954) *Deuxième plan de modernisation et d'équipement: rapport général* (April, Mimeograph).

Minter, W. (1972) *Portuguese Africa and the West* (New York: Monthly Review Press).

Mitchell, J. (1956) *The Kalela Dance* (Manchester: Manchester University Press, Rhodes Livingstone Institute Papers, No. 27).

Mitchell, Sir P. (1939) *Native Administration* (Entebbe: Government Printer).

Mitchell, R. P. (1969) *The Society of Muslim Brothers* (London: OUP).

Mlambo, E. (1972) *Rhodesia: The Struggle for a Birthright* (London: C. Hurst and Co.).

Monga, C. (1983) 'La parole est au Cameroun', *Jeune Afrique*, 1186, 25 May, p. 202.

Mongo Beti (1972) *Main basse sur le Cameroun: autopsie d'une décolonisation* (Paris: Maspero).

Monroe, E. (1963) *Britain's Moment in the Middle East, 1914–1956* (Baltimore: Johns Hopkins Press).

Montagu, A. (1974) *Culture and Human Development* (Englewood Cliffs, NJ: Prentice-Hall Inc.).

Monteil, V. (1964) *L'Islam noir, une religion à la conquête de l'Afrique*, ch. 6: 'La marche des femmes', pp. 149–82 (reprinted 1980; Paris: Editions du Seuil).

Moodie, T. D. (1975) *The Rise of Afrikanerdom, Power, Apartheid and the Afrikaner Civil Religion* (Los Angeles: UCP).

Moore, C. (1982) *Fela: This Bitch of a Life* (London: Allison and Busby).

Moore, C. H. (1965) *Tunisia since Independence* (Berkeley: UCP).

Morgan, D. J. (1980) *The Official History of Colonial Development (1924–1970)* (4 vols, London: Macmillan).

Morgenthau, H. J. (1973) *Politics Among Nations: The Struggle for Power and Peace* (5th edn, New York: A. A. Knopf).

Morrell, M. (1971) *Reaction and Counter-Action: A Brief Review of Non-White Political Movements in South Africa* (London: Frank Cass; Johannesburg: South African Institute of Race Relations).

Morris, M. (1976) 'The development of capitalism in South African agriculture', *Economy and Society*, **5**, 3, pp. 292–344.

Morris Jones, W. H. and Fischer, G. (eds) (1980) *Decolonization and After: The British and French Experience* (London: Frank Cass).

Morrison, D. G., Mitchell, R. C. and Paden, J. N. (1989) *Understanding Black Africa: Data Analysis of Social Change and Nation Building* (New York: Paragon House Irvington Publishers).

Mortimer, R. A. (1980) *The Third World Coalition in International Politics* (New York: Praeger).

Mosley, L. (1964) *Haile Selassie: The Conquering Lion* (London: Weidenfeld and Nicolson).

Moumouni, A. (1964) *L'éducation en Afrique* (Paris: Maspero).

Mount, M. W. (1973) *African Art: The Years since 1920* (Bloomington, IN).

Mourre, M. (ed.) (1978) 'Boumédienne', in *Dictionnaire encyclopédique d'histoire, Vol. I* (Paris: Bordas).

Mrima, B. F. and Mattoke, W. (1980) *Mapambano ya Ukombozi Zanzibar* (Dar es Salaam: Tanzania Publishing House).

Mshengu-Kavanagh, R. (1979) 'After Soweto: people's theatre and the political struggle in South Africa', *Theatre Quarterly*, **9**, 33, pp. 31–9.

Mshengu-Kavanagh, R. (1981) *South African People's Plays* (London: Heinemann).

Mudimbe, V. Y. (1985) 'African ginosis', *African Studies Review*, 2–3, pp. 149–233.

Mudimbe, V. Y. (1988) *The Invention of Africa: Gnosis, Philosophy and the Order of Knowledge* (Bloomington, IN: Indiana University Press).

Mugomba, A. G. and Nyaggah, M. (eds) (1980) *Independence without Freedom: The Political Economy of Colonial Education in Southern Africa* (Santa Barbara, CA: ABC–Clio Press).

Muhindi, K. (1985) 'L'apport de Efua Theodora Sutherland à la dramaturgie contemporaine', *Présence Africaine*, 133/134, 1/2, pp. 75–85.

Mulago, V. (1980) *La religion traditionelle des Bantu et leur vision du monde* (Kinshasa: Faculté de théologie catholique).

Mulira, J. (1974) 'The role of Soviet bloc countries in the political, economic and social development of Uganda, 1945–1970' (PhD thesis, University of Princeton).

Mulira, J. (1981) 'Soviet bloc: trade, economic, technical and military involvement in independent Africa: the case of Uganda, 1962–1979', *Genève Afrique*, UR **19**, 1, pp. 39–80.

Mulira, J. (1983) 'Soviet policy in Africa: from Lenin to Andropov – an Afrocentric interpretation', *Genève-Afrique*, UR **21**, 2, pp. 69–87.

Mundara, Y. L. (1972) 'Les problèmes du théâtre au Zaïre', *Dambi, revue zaïroise des lettres et des arts*, **3**, 5, pp. 3–5.

Mundara, Y. L. and Badi-Banga ne-Mwine (1982) *Sura Dji, visages et racines du Zaïre* (Paris).

Murdock, G. P. (1959) *Africa, Its Peoples and Their Culture History* (New York: McGraw-Hill Book Company).

Mutiga, J. (1965) 'To the ceremonial Muguma (fig tree)', in D. Cook (ed.).

Mutiiso, G. C. and Rohio, S. W. (eds) (1975) *Readings in African Political Thought* (London: Heinemann).

Nabudere, D. W. (1977) *Imperialism and Revolution in Uganda* (Dar es Salaam: Tanzanian Publishing House; 1980 edn, London: Onyx Press).

Naguib, M. (1955) *Egypt's Destiny: An Autobiographical Account of the Egyptian Revolution* (London: Gollancz).

Nasser, G. 'Abd al- (1954) *La philosophie de la révolution* (Cairo: Ministry of National Orientation; English edn 1959, Buffalo: Smith, Keynes and Marshall).

Nasser, G. 'Abd al- (c.1966) *On Non-Alignment* (Cairo: Ministry of National Guidance).

National Museum of African Art Library Acquisition Lists.

Ndiaye I. (1984) 'Art et société' (unpublished manuscript).

Ndiokwere, N. I. (1981) *Prophecy and Revolution* (London).

Ndogo Bidyogo, D. (1977) *Historia y tragedia de Guinea Ecuatorial* (Madrid).

Nduka, O. (1964) *Western Education and the Nigerian Cultural Background* (Ibadan: OUP).

Nehru, J. (1964) *Nehru and Africa: Extracts from Jawaharlal Nehru's Speeches on Africa, 1946–1963* (New Delhi: Indian Council for Africa).

Nelson, H. D. (1978) *Morocco: A Country Study* (Washington: US Government Printing Office).

New China News Agency (1967) 'Tempestuous storm over African continent', 27 December.

New China News Agency (1977) 'Soviet claims, stretching to African continent', 3 July.

New Times (Novoye Vremya) (1976) 'The peoples of Angola are not alone', 1 February, No. 2 (Moscow).

Ngindu Mushete, A. (1978) 'Authenticity and christianity in Zaire', in E. Fashole-Luke *et al.* (eds), pp. 228–42.

Nicklin, K. and Salmons, J. (1977) 'S. J. Akpan of Nigeria', *African Arts*, 11, 1, pp. 30–4.

Nicol, D. A. (1969) 'The meaning of Africa', in J. Drachler (ed.), pp. 119–22.

Nicol, D. A. and Mazrui, A. A. (1986) 'Programme 8: A clash of cultures', in A. A. Mazrui (ed.).

Nicolas, G. (1978) 'L'expansion de l'influence arabe en Afrique subsaharienne', *L'Afrique et l'Asie modernes* (Paris), 117, pp. 23–46.

Nigeria, Federal Republic of (1972) 'Nigerian Enterprises Promotion Decree No. 4, 1972'.

Nigerian Institute of International Affairs (*c.*1981–84) *Nigerian–Brazilian Dialogue on Foreign Policy: A Report of a Nigerian–Brazilian Dialogue, July 29–August 1, 1980, Sao Paulo, Brazil* (Lagos: Nigerian Institute of International Relations).

Nisbet, R. A. (1969) *Social Change and History: Aspects of the Western Theory of Development* (New York: OUP).

Niven, D. (1985) 'Africa and the arts', *African Affairs*, 84, 335, pp. 183–93.

Nkashama, N. (1979) 'Ivresse et vertige: les nouvelles danses des jeunes au Zaïre', *Afrique littéraire et artistique*, 51, pp. 94–103.

Nkenda-Mpasi, P. (1971) 'Réflexions sur la problématique de la langue d'enseignement au Congo', *Revue congolaise des sciences humaines*, 2, January, pp. 35–58.

Nkrumah, K. (1957) *Ghana: The Autobiography of Kwame Nkrumah* (Edinburgh: Thomas Nelson and Sons Ltd; 3rd edn 1976, New York: International Publishers).

Nkrumah, K. (1958a) 'All African Peoples Congress' (Accra).

Nkrumah, K. (1958b) 'African prospects', *Foreign Affairs*, 37, 1 (October), pp. 45–53.

Nkrumah, K. (1961) *I Speak of Freedom: A Statement of African Ideology* (London: Heinemann; New York: Frederick A. Praeger).

Nkrumah, K. (1962) *Towards Colonial Freedom* (London: Heinemann; 1st edn 1945).

Nkrumah, K. (1963) *Africa Must Unite* (New York: Praeger; London: Heinemann).

Nkrumah, K. (1964) *Consciencism* (London: Heinemann).

Nkrumah, K. (1966) *Neo-Colonialism: The Last Stage of Imperialism* (London: Panaf Books; New York: International Publishers; Heinemann 1968; Canton, Ohio: International Publishing, 1966; New York: State Mutual Books, 1981).

Nkrumah, K. (1969) 'African socialism revisited', in Y. Benot (ed.).

Nkrumah, K. (1970) *Class Struggle in Africa* (New York: International Publishers).

Nlolo, N. (1983) 'Influence du jazz dans la musique zaïroise moderne', in UNESCO, *Cultures africaines*, Documents de la réunion d'experts sur le apports culturels des noirs de la Diaspora à l'Afrique (Cotonou), pp. 250–9.

Norman, J. (1963a) *Edward Gibbon Wakefield: A Political Reappraisal* (Fairfield, CT: New Frontiers and Fairfield University).

Norman, J. (1963b) *Labour and Politics in Libya and Arab Africa* (New York: Bookman).

North American Congress on Latin America (1982) 'Transatlantic ties (between Latin America and South Africa)', *NACLA Report on the Americas*, 16, 3 (May–June), pp. 16–25 and 41–2.

Nouaille-Degorce, B. (1982) *La politique française de coopération avec les Etats africains et malgaches au sud du Sahara, 1958–1978* (Bordeaux: CEAN).

Nouschi, A. (1962) *La naissance du nationalisme algérien 1919–1954* (Paris: Editions de Minuit).

November, A. (1965) *L'évolution du mouvement syndical en Afrique occidentale* (Paris: Mouton).

Ntiro, S. J. (1982) *Modern Creative Makonde Sculpture* (Dar es Salaam) (Mimeograph).

Nunley, J. W. (1985) 'The Lantern Festival in Sierra Leone', *African Arts*, 18, 2, pp. 45–9.

Nuseibeh, H. Z. (1956) *The Ideas of Arab Nationalism* (Ithaca: Cornell University Press).

Nutting, A. (1967) *No end to a Lesson: The Story of Suez* (London: Gollancz).

Nweke, G. A. (1980) *The Harmonization of African Foreign Policies, 1955–1975: The Political Economy of African Diplomacy* (Boston: African Studies Center, Boston University).

Nwoga D. (1965) 'Onitsha market literature', *Transition*, 4, 19, pp. 26–34.

Nye, J. S., Jr (1966) *Pan-Africanism and East African Integration* (Cambridge, MA: HUP).

Nyerere, J. K. (1960) 'Africa's place in the world', in *Symposium on Africa* (Wellesley College, MA).

Nyerere, J. K. (1962) *Democracy and the Party System* (Dar es Salaam: Tanganyika Standard).

Nyerere, J. K. (1963a) *Julius Caesar* (Nairobi and London: OUP).

Nyerere, J. K. (1963b) 'Les fondements du socialisme africain', *Présence africaine*, 47, 19, pp. 8–19.

Nyerere, J. K. (1967a) *Uhuru na Umoja* (London: OUP).
Nyerere, J. K. (1967b) *Socialism and Rural Development* (Dar es Salaam: Government Printer).
Nyerere, J. K. (1967c) *Education for Self-reliance* (Dar es Salaam: Ministry of Information and Tourism).
Nyerere, J. K. (1967d) 'Tanzanian policy on foreign affairs', address to TANU National Congress, 16 October 1967 (Dar es Salaam).
Nyerere, J. K. (1968a) *Essays on Socialism* (Dar es Salaam: OUP).
Nyerere, J. K. (1968b) *Ujamaa: Essays on Socialism* (London: OUP).
Nyerere, J. K. (1968c) *Freedom and Socialism* (London: OUP).
Nyerere, J. K. (1969) *Mabepari wa Vanisi* (Dar es Salaam: OUP).
Nyerere, J. K. (1970a) *Socialisme, démocratie et unité africaine* (Paris: Présence Africaine).
Nyerere, J. K. (1970b) *Non-alignment in the 1970s* (Dar es Salaam: Government Printer).
Nyerere, J. K. (1970c) 'Developing tasks of non-alignment', in J. K. Nyerere, *Freedom and Development: A Selection from Writings and Speeches, 1968–1973* (London: OUP), pp. 159–71.
Nyerere, J. K. (1972) *Decentralization* (Dar es Salaam: Government Printer).
Nyerere, J. K. (1977) 'The Arusha Declaration, ten years', *Daily News* (Tanzania); *International Herald, Africa Diary*, 11–17 June, p. 8525.
Nyerere, J. K. (1979a) 'South–South dialogue: a brief report', *Third World Quarterly*, 1, 2 (April), pp. 117–22.
Nyerere, J. K. (1979b) Address by his Excellency Mwalimu Julius K. Nyerere, President of the United Republic of Tanzania to the Fourth Ministerial Meeting of the Group of 77, Arusha, 12–16 February 1979, text reprinted in K. P. Sauvant, *The Group of 77* (New York: Oceana, 1981).
Nzewunwa, N. (1982) *The Masquerade in Nigerian History and Culture* (Port Harcourt: University of Port Harcourt Press).

Oberlé, P. (1971) *Afars et Somalis: les dossiers de Djibouti* (Paris: Présence Africaine).
O'Brien, D. C. (1971) *The Mourides of Senegal* (Oxford: Clarendon Press).
O'Brien, J. (1981) 'Sudan: an Arab breadbasket?', *Merip Reports*, **99**, September.
O'Brien Winter, C. (1977) *Namibia* (Grand Rapids, MI).
Ocitti, J. P. (1973) *African Indigenous Education as Practised by the Acholi of Uganda* (Nairobi: Kenya Literature Bureau).
Oded, A. (1986) 'The Islamic factor in Afro-Arab relations', *Middle East Review* (New York), 18, 3 (Spring), pp. 15–23.
Odinga, O. (1969) 'Defence of socialism', official report, *Kenya Legislative Council 76*, 54th session (9 December), cols 881–2.
Oduho, J. and Deng, W. (1963) *The Problem of the Southern Sudan* (London: OUP).
OECD (1981) 'La nutrition et l'agriculture, résultats intermédiaires du projet de recherche', INTER FUTURS, OCDE, March 1978, cited in UNEP, *Environment and Development in Africa, Vol. 2* (Oxford: Pergamon Press).
Ofori, I. M. (ed.) (1973) *Factors of Agricultural Growth in West Africa* (Legon: Institute of Statistical, Social and Economic Research).
Ogot, B. A. (1977) 'Politics, culture and music in colonial Kenya: a study of Mau–Mau hymns 1951–1956', *Kenya Historical Review*, **5**, 2, pp. 275–86.
Ogunba, O. (1966) 'Le théâtre au Nigéria', *Présence africaine*, **58**, 2, pp. 67–90.
Ogunba, O. and Irele, A. (1978) *Theatre in Africa* (Ibadan: IUP).
Ogunbiyi, Y. (1981) *Drama and Theatre in Nigéria: A Critical Source Book* (Lagos: Nigeria Magazine).
Ogunwale, T. (1971) 'Lamidi Fakeye: Nigerian traditional sculptor', *African Arts*, **4**, 3, pp. 66–7.
Ogwu, U. J. (1982) 'Nigeria and Brazil: a model for the emerging South–South relations?', in J. Carlsson (ed.), pp. 102–27.
Okeke, U. E. (1985) 'Independence and the economy', *African Technical Review* (now *African Review of Business and Technology*) September.
Okello, J. (1967) *Revolution in Zanzibar* (Nairobi: EAPH).
Okolo, A. (1983) 'Dependency in Africa: stages of African political economy', *Alternatives: Journal of World Policy*, **9**, 2 (June), pp. 252–4.
Okonjo, C. (1971) 'Africa: a decade of independence (an economic assessment)', in *Présence Africaine*, Special Number, pp. 119–36.
Okore, O. (1984) 'The film world of Ousmane Sembene' (PhD thesis, Columbia University).
Okoro, G. I. P. (1984) 'African contemporary art in Nigeria' (PhD thesis, School of Education, Columbia University, NY).
Okumu, T. M. (1962) *Angola in Ferment: The Background and Prospects of Angolan Nationalism* (Boston: Beacon Press).
Ola, O. (1980) 'De-Africanization and Europeanization: the non-acknowledgement of African influence on modern art', *Kiabara*, **3**, 1 (Rains), pp. 93–112.

Olatunbosun, D. (1967) *Nigerian Farm Settlements and School Leavers' Farms* (East Lansing and Ibadan: CSNRD, No. 9).

Oliver, R. and Crowder, M. (eds) (1981) *The Cambridge Encyclopaedia of Africa* (Cambridge and New York: CUP).

Ollawa, P. E. (1983) 'Focus on the political economy of development: a theoretical reconsideration of some unresolved issues', *African Studies Review*, **26**, 1 (March), pp. 125–55.

Olusola, S. (1979) *Some Notes on 20 Years of Television in Nigeria* (Yaba: Ariya Productions).

O'Meara, D. (1974) 'The 1946 African mineworkers' strike in the political economy of South Africa', in P. L. Bonner (ed.), pp. 179–235.

Omo-Fadaka, J. (1978) 'Drought and famine', in R. Synge (ed.).

Onoh, J. K. (1982) *Money and Banking in Africa* (London: Longman).

Opubor, A. and Nwuneli, O. (1979) *The Development and Growth of the Film Industry in Nigeria* (Lagos).

Organization of African Unity (OAU) (1981) *Lagos Plan of Action for the Economic Development of Africa 1980–2000* (Geneva: International Institute for Labour Studies; Addis Ababa).

Organization of African Unity, Memorandum on the responsibilities and role of the OAU in the economic and social field, Cm/Res 219 (XV) and Annex 1.

Osia, K. (1983) *Israel, South Africa and Black Africa: A Study of the Primacy of Politics of Expediency* (New York: University Press of America).

Otite, O. (1978) *Themes in African Social and Political Thought* (Enugu, Nigeria: Fourth Dimension).

Owusu, M. (1972) 'The search for solvency: background to the fall of Ghana's Second Republic, 1969–1972', *Africa Today*, **19**, 1, pp. 52–61.

Owusu, M. (1975) 'Economic nationalism, pan-Africanism and the military: the National Redemption Council of Ghana', *Africa Today*, **22**, 1 (January–March), pp. 31–53.

Oyugi, W. O. and Gilonga, A. (eds) (1987) *Democratic Theory and Practice in Africa* (London: Heinemann).

Padmore, G. *La vie et les luttes des travailleurs nègres* (Paris: Petite Bibliothèque de l'Internationale Syndicale Rouge).

Padmore, G. (1935) 'An open letter to Earl Browder', The CPUUSA *Crisis*, **32**, October, p. 3020.

Padmore, G. (1956) *Pan-Africanism or Communism? The Coming Struggle for Africa* (London: Dennis Dobson).

Padmore, G. (1963) *History of the Pan-African Congress* (2nd edn, London: Hammersmith Bookshop Ltd; 1st edn 1947).

Palmer, R. (1977) *Land and Racial Discrimination in Rhodesia* (London: Heinemann).

Palmer, R. (1986) 'Working conditions and workers responses on Nyasaland tea estates, 1930–1935', *JAH*, **27**, 1, pp. 105–26.

Palmer, R. and Parsons, N. (eds) (1977) *The Roots of Rural Poverty in Central and Southern Africa* (London: Heinemann).

Pankhurst, L. E. S. and Pankhurst, R. K. (1953) *Ethiopia and Eritrea: The Last Phase of the Reunion Struggle* (Woodword: Green).

Pankhurst, R. K. (1955) *Ethiopia: A Cultural History* (London).

Pankhurst, R. K. (1981) 'Decolonization of Ethiopia, 1945–1955', in UNESCO (1981b), pp. 119–33.

Parícsy, P. (1971) Histoire du théâtre en Afrique occidentale', in P. Parícsy (ed.) *Etudes sur la littérature africaine contemporaine* (Budapest: Centre pour la recherche de l'Afro-Asie de l'Académie des Sciences de Hongrie), pp. 51–71.

Park, R. L. (1965) 'Indian–African relations', *Asian Survey* (Berkeley, CA), **5**, 7 (July), pp. 350–8.

Parsons, N. (1985) 'Seretse Khama and the Bangwato succession crisis, 1948–1953', paper presented at the 28th Meeting of the African Studies Association, New Orleans, USA, 23–6 November 1985.

Partke, W. (1975) *Chinese Economic Aid* (London: C. Hurst and Co.).

Payer, C. (1982) *The World Bank: A Critical Analysis* (New York and London: Monthly Review Press).

p'Bitek, O. (1971) *African Religions in Western Scholarship* (Nairobi: EALB)

Peace, A. (1979) 'Industrial protest in Nigeria', in R. Cohen *et al.* (eds) *Peasants and Proletariat* (New York: Monthly Review Press).

Pearce, R. D. (1982) *The Turning Point in Africa: British Colonial Policy 1938–48* (London: Frank Cass).

Pearce, R. D. (1984) 'The Colonial Office and planned decolonization in Africa', *African Affairs*, **83**, 330, pp. 77–93.

Peel, J. D. Y. (1983) *Ijeshas and Nigerians: the Incorporation of a Yoruba Kingdom, 1890s–1970s* (Cambridge: CUP).

Peil, M. (1977) *Consensus and Conflict in African Societies* (London: Longman).

Peil, M. and Sada, P. O. *African Urban Society* (Chichester: John Wiley and Sons).

Peixoto, A. C. (1983) 'Le Brésil et l'Afrique: solidarités culturelles et stratégies commerciales', *Politique africaine* (Paris), **10**, 10 June, pp. 25–38.

Pélissier, R. (1978) *La colonie du Minotaure: nationalismes et révoltes en Angola (1926–1961)* (Montamets-Orgeval: Editions Pélissier).

Pélissier, R. (1979) *Le naufrage des caravelles: études sur la fin de l'empire portugais (1961–1975)* (Montamets-Orgeval: Editions Pélissier).

Pélissier, R. (1982) 'Aspects de l'africanisme brésilien', *Les Mois en Afrique* (Paris), 200, pp. 56–76.

Perani, J. (1979) 'Nupe costume crafts', *African Arts*, 12, 3, pp. 53–7.

Perham, M. (1967, 1970) *Colonial Sequence* (2 vols, London: Methuen).

Perier, G. D. (1930) *Nègreries et curiosités congolaises* (Brussels: L'Eglantine).

Perier, G. D. (1950–52) 'Artisanat et arts populaires', in *Encyclopédie du Congo belge, Vol. 3* (Brussels: Editions Bieleveld), pp. 799–814.

Perry, A. (1984) 'The art of hand weaving', *West Africa*, 3496, 20 August, pp. 1682–3.

Person, Y. (1979) 'Le Front populaire au Sénégal (May 1936–October 1938)', *Mouvement social* (Paris), 107, pp. 77–101.

Pfaff, F. (1984) *The Cinema of Ousmane Sembene: A Pioneer of African Film* (Westport: Greenwood Press).

Pfeifer, K. (1981) 'Algeria's agrarian transformation', *Merip Reports*, 99 (September), pp. 7–14.

Pheto, M. (1981) 'Black film makers', *Index on Censorship*, 10, 4.

Pichon, P. (1945) *La question de la Libye dans le règlement de la paix* (Paris: Peyronne).

Picton, J. and Mack, J. (1979) *African Textiles: Looms, Weaving and Design* (London: British Museum Publications).

Plateau Students Association (1974) 'Our stand for a Plateau State', letter to His Excellency General Yakubu Gowon, HFMG, dated 13 June 1974 (Unpublished mimeographed letter).

Pokornowski, M. *et al.* (1985) *Africa in Dress II: A Select and Annotated Bibliography* (East Lansing).

Politika Frantsii v. Azii i v Afrike (1965) (Moscow: Nauka).

Ponsionen, J. A. (1971) *Education and Political Values* (Nairobi: EAPH).

Popov, V. I. *et al.* (1975) *Studies of Soviet Foreign Policy* (Moscow: Progress Publishers).

Portimer, R. A. (1972) 'Ousmane Sembene and the cinema of decolonization', *African Arts*, 5, 3, pp. 26–31 and 62.

Post, K. (1964) *The New States of West Africa* (Harmondsworth: Penguin).

Post, K. (1977) 'Peasantization in West Africa', in P. Gutkind and P. Waterman (eds) *African Social Studies: A Radical Reader* (New York and London: Monthly Review Press), pp. 241–51.

Potekhin, I. V. (1963) 'Reply to my opponents on African Socialism', *International Affairs* (Moscow), January, pp. 71–5.

Pratt, R. C. (1976) *The Critical Phase in Tanganyika 1945–1968: Nyerere and the emergence of a Socialist Strategy* (Cambridge: CUP).

Présence Africaine (1961) *Colloque sur les religions, Abidjan, April 5–12* (Paris: Présence africaine).

Présence Africaine (1972) *African Religions as a Source of Civilization Values, Cotonou Symposium, 16–22 August 1970* (Paris: Présence Africaine).

Preston, G. N. (1975) 'Perseus and Medusa in Africa: military art in Fanteland (1834–1972)', *African Arts*, 8, 3, pp. 36–41 and 68–71.

Priebatsch, S. and Knight, N. (1979) 'Ndebele figurative art', *African Arts*, 12, 2, p. 32.

Pritchett, O. (1979) 'Nigerian truck art', *African Arts*, 12, 2, pp. 27–31.

Proctor, J. H. (ed.) (1965) *Islam and International Relations* (New York: Praeger).

Proshin, N. I. (1975) *Istoriya Livii* [History of Libya] (Moscow: Nauka).

Pugh, P. and Ajayi, J. F. A. (1990) *Cementing a Partnership: The Story of WAPCO (West Africa Portland Cement Company) 1960–90* (Cambridge: Cambridge Business Publishing).

Pye, L. (1962) *Aspects of Political Development* (Boston: Little, Brown).

Queuille, P. (1965) *Histoire de l'Afro-Asiatisme jusqu'à Bandoung* (Paris: Payot).

Quimby, I. M. G. and Swank, S. T. (1980) *Perspective on American Folk Art* (New York: Norton).

Qubain, F. (1960) *Inside the Arab Mind: A Bibliographical Survey of Literature in Arabic on Arab Nationalism and Unity; With an annotated list of English-language books and articles* (Arlington, VA: Middle East Research Associates).

Rabearimanana, L. (1980a) *La presse d'opinion à Madagascar de 1947 à 1956* (Antananarivo: Librairie Mixte).

Rabearimanana, L. (1980b) 'Presse d'opinion et luttes politiques à Madagascar de 1946 à 1956', *Revue française d'histoire d'outre-mer*, 67, 246–7, pp. 99–122.

Rabemananjara, R. W. (1952) *Histoire de la nation malgache* (Paris: Lachaud).

Radwan, S. (1981) *Capital Formation in Egyptian Industry and Agriculture 1882–1967* (London: Ithaca Press; 1st edn, 1974).

Ramchandani, R. R. (ed.) (1980) *India and Africa* (New Delhi: Radiant Publishers).

Ramirez, F. and Rolot, C. (1985) *Histoire du cinéma colonial au Zaïre, au Rwanda et au Burundi* (Tervuren: Musée royal de l'Afrique centrale).

Raneiro, R. (1982) 'La colonisation démographique en Libye: un essai d'analyse', *Mondes et culture*, 42, 3, pp. 485–99.

Ranger, T. O. (1975) *Dance and Society in Eastern Africa* (London: Heinemann).

Ranger, T. O. (1983) *Peasant Consciousness and Guerrilla War in Zimbabwe* (London: James Currey).

Ranger, T. O. (1968a) 'Connexions of "primary resistance" movements and modern mass nationalism in East and Central Africa', Part 1: *JAH*, 9, 3, pp. 437–53; Part 2: *JAH*, 9, 4, pp. 631–41.

Ranger, T. O. (1968b) *Emerging Themes of African History* (Nairobi: EAPH).

Ranger, T. O. (1986) 'Religious movements and politics in Africa', *African Studies Review*, 29, 2, pp. 1–70.

Ranger, T. O. and Weller, J. (eds) (1975) *Themes in the Christian History of Central Africa* (Berkeley: UCP).

Raunig, W. (1985) *Catalogue of Exhibition on Ethiopian Art* (Munich: Munich Museum).

Ravenhill, J. (1985) *Collective Clientelism: The Lomé Conventions and North–South Relations* (New York: Columbia University Press).

Ravenhill, J. (ed.) (1986) *Africa in Economic Crisis* (Basingstoke: Macmillan; New York: Columbia University Press).

Raymond, A. (1955) *La Tunisie* (Paris: PUF).

Read, M. (1936) 'Tradition and prestige among the Ngoni', *Africa*, 9, 4, pp. 453–84.

Read, M. (1955) *Education and Social Change in Tropical Areas* (London: Thomas Nelson and Sons Ltd).

Reader, D. H. (1964) 'A survey of categories of economic activities among the peoples of Africa', *Africa*, 34, 1 (January), pp. 28–45.

Recherche, pédagogie et culture (1983) 61, pp. 101–5.

Reid, I. (1976) 'Black Americans and Africa', in M. M. Smythe (ed.) *The Black American Reference Book* (New York: Prentice Hall), pp. 648–84.

Rejai, M. and Enloe, C. (1969) 'Nation-states and state-nations', *International Studies Quarterly*, 13, 2 (June).

Renninger, J. P. (1982) 'The future of economic cooperation schemes in Africa, with special reference to ECOWAS', in T. M. Shaw (ed.) *Alternative Futures for Africa* (Boulder, CO: Westview Press), pp. 153–79.

Report of the Advisory Commission (1960) Cmd 1148 (London: HMSO).

Report of the HCR's relief activities in 1982–1983. Document a/ac.96/620 (United Nations).

Report of the Nyasaland Commission of Inquiry (1959) Cmd 814 (London: HMSO).

Revue française d'histoire d'outre-mer (1976) Special issue: C. Coquery-Vidrovitch (ed.), 'L'Afrique et la crise de 1930 (1924–1938)', 63, 232–3.

Ricard, A. (1975) 'Le théâtre populaire de l'Afrique de l'Ouest', *Revue d'histoire du théâtre*, 1, pp. 1–104.

Ricard, A. (1982) 'Le cinéma populaire nigérian', *Recherche, pédagogie et culture*, 58, 4, pp. 65–9.

Richards, A. (1982) *Egypt's Agricultural Development 1800–1980: Technical and Social Change* (Boulder, CO: Westview Press).

Richards, P. (1983) 'Ecological change and the politics of African land use', *African Studies Review*, 26, 2 (June), pp. 1–72.

Richards, P. (1985) *Indigenous Agricultural Revolution: Ecology and Food Production in West Africa* (London: Hutchinson).

Robert, M. (1976) *La Réunion: Combats pour l'autonomie* (Paris: L'Harmattan).

Roberts, R. (1974) *French Development Assistance: A Study in Policy and Administration* (London: Sage).

Robinson, R. (1980) 'Sir Andrew Cohen and the transfer of power in tropical Africa, 1940–1957', in W. H. M. Jones and G. Fischer (eds) *Decolonization and After: The British and French Experience* (London: Frank Cass), pp. 50–72.

Robson, P. (1983) *Integration, Development and Equity: Economic Integration in West Africa* (London: George Allen and Unwin).

Rodinson, M. (1968a) *Israël et le refus arabe: 75 ans d'histoire* (Paris: Editions du Seuil).

Rodinson, M. (1968b) *Israël and the Arabs* (Harmondsworth: Penguin).

Rodney, W. (1972, 1981) *How Europe Underdeveloped Africa* (Dar es Salaam: Tanzania Publishing House; Washington, DC: Howard University Press).

Rodrigues, J. H. (1982) *Brasil e Africa: Outro Horizonte* (extended 3rd edn; Rio de Janeiro: Editora Novo Fronteira).

Roesch, O. (1984) 'Peasants and collective agriculture in Mozambique', in J. Barker (ed.), pp. 291–317.

Roger, T. O. and Weller, J. (1975) *Themes in the Christian History of Central Africa* (Berkeley and Los Angeles: UCP).

Rogers, J. A. (1972) *World's Greatest Men of Colour, Vols 1 and 2* (New York: Collier Books).

Rohrbach, J. (1940) *Das Neue deutsche Kolonialreich in Afrika*, DWI, A.26/44, 29 August 1940 (Berlin).

Roire, C. (1967) 'Le Congo et l'ONU', *Revue française de politique africaine*, 21.

Rokkan, S. (1973) 'Centre-formation, nation-building and cultural diversity: Report on a UNESCO programme', in S. N. Eisenstadt and S. Rokkan (eds), vol. 1, pp. 13–38, Building States and Nations, vol II (Beverly Hills: Sage).

Romanova, V. and Tsriklis, I. (1978) 'Ekonomitcheske Syvazi SSR razvivayouchtochimcia Stranami', *Ekonomitcheskie Naouki*, 3.

Romero, R. H. (1986) 'Enjeux sahariens dans les plans de guerre de l'axe durant la 2ème guerre mondiale', in *Proceedings of the Euro-African Symposium on L'histoire du Sahara et des relations sahariennes entre le Maghreb et l'Ouest africain du Moyen-Age à la fin de l'époque coloniale* (Bergamo), pp. 213–18.

Rondot, P. (1958) *L'Islam et les musulmans d'aujourd'hui* (2 vols; Paris: Editions de l'Orante).

Rood, L. L. (1976) 'Nationalization and indigenization of Africa', *Journal of Modern African Studies*, **14**, 3, pp. 427–47.

Rosberg, C. G. and Nottingham, J. (1966) *The Myth of 'Mau Mau': Nationalism in Kenya* (Nairobi: EAPH).

Roseyear, D. R. (1984) 'Cross River tombstones', *African Arts*, **18**, 1, pp. 44–7 and 94.

Ross, A. (1977) 'The Capricorn Africa Society and European reactions to African nationalism in Tanganyika, 1949–60', *African Affairs*, **76**, pp. 519–35.

Ross, A. (1981) 'Multiracialism and European politics in Tanganyika, 1945–61' (PhD thesis, University of London).

Ross, D. H. (1984) 'The Art of Osei Bonsu', *African Arts*, **17**, 2, pp. 28–40 and 90.

Rotberg R. I. (1966) *The Rise of Nationalism in Central Africa: The Making of Malawi and Zambia 1873–1964* (Cambridge, MA: HUP).

Roth, A. (1961) *Le théâtre algérien de langue dialectale 1926–1954* (Paris: Maspero).

Rothchild, D. and Rogin, M. (1966) 'Uganda', in G. Carter (ed.), pp. 337–440.

Rouissi, M. (1977) *Population et société au Maghreb* (Tunis: Ceres-Production).

Rout, L. (1976) *The African Experience in Spanish America* (Cambridge: CUP).

Royal Institute of International Affairs (1937) *The Colonial Problem: A Report by a Study Group of Members of the Royal Institute of International Affairs* (London: OUP).

Ruanda Politique, 1958–1960 (1960) (Brussels: CRISP).

Rubin, L. and Weinstein, B. (1974) *Introduction to African Politics: A Continental Approach* (New York: Praeger).

Rweyemanu, J. F. (1973) *Underdevelopment and Industrialization in Tanzania* (Nairobi: OUP).

Rweyemanu, J. F. (1978) 'Africa and the New International Economic Order', in R. Synge (ed.), pp. 36–43.

Rweyemanu, A. M. and Hyden, G. (eds) (1975) *A Decade of Public Administration in Africa* (Nairobi: EALB).

Rymalov, V. (1959a) in *Temps nouveaux*.

Rymalov, V. (1959b) 'Soviet assistance to the underdeveloped countries', *International Affairs*, **9**, September.

Rycroft, D. (1959) 'African music in Johannesburg: African and non-African features', *International Folk Music Council*, **11**, pp. 25–30.

Saadallah, A. K. (1981) *La monté du nationalisme en Algérie* (Algiers: ENAL).

Sabri-Abdalla, I. (1980) 'Heterogeneity and differentation: the end for the Third World', in K. Haq (ed.).

SAC (1967) 'Table-ronde sur les langues africaines', *Présence africaine*, **67**, 3rd quarter, pp. 53–123.

SAC (1971) 'Table-ronde sur le swahili comme langue de culture, d'enseignement et grand véhiculaire interafricain', *Présence africaine*, **78**, 2nd quarter, pp. 49–117.

Sadat, A. al- (1957) *Revolt on the Nile* (London: Wingate).

Sadie, J. (1960) 'The social anthropology of economic underdevelopment', *Economic Journal*, **70**, 278, pp. 294–303.

Saenz, P. (1969) 'A Latin American–African partnership', *Journal of Inter-American Studies* (Coral Gables, FL), **11**, 2 (April), pp. 317–27.

Saint-Véran, R. (1977a) *A Djibouti avec les Afars et les Issas* (Paris).

Saint-Véran, R. (1977b) *Djibouti, Pawn of the Horn of Africa: An Abridged Translation*, by V. Thompson and R. Adloff (Methuen, NJ: Scarecrow Press).

Salmons, J. (1977) 'Mammy Wata', *African Arts*, **10**, 3, pp. 8–15 and 87–8.

Samoff, J. (1981) 'Crises and socialism in Tanzania', *The Journal of Modern African Studies*, **19**, 2, pp. 279–306.

Sandrart, G. (1953) *Ruanda Urundi* (Brussels: Dessart).

Sanneh, L. (1986) *Islam, Christianity and Social Change in Africa: The Evolution of Research between 1960 and 1985* (unpublished).

Santerre, R. (1977) 'Aspects conflictuels de deux systèmes d'enseignement au Nord-Cameroun', *Canadian Journal of African Studies*, **5**, Spring, pp. 157–69.

Sarraut, A. (1931) *Grandeur et servitude coloniales* (Paris: Edition du Sagittaire).

Sartre, J. P. (1963) 'Introduction to African poetry', in *Black Orpheus*, trans. S. W. Allen (Paris: Présence africaine).

Sastre, R. (1962) 'Contribution de l'Eglise catholique à l'expression culturelle de la personnalité africaine', in *Colloque sur les religions* (UNESCO and SAC: Paris).

Sauvant, K. P. (1980) 'The origins of the NIEO discussions', in K. Sauvant (ed.) *Changing Priorities on the International Agenda: The New International Economic Order* (New York: Pergamon Press), pp. 7–40.

Sauvant, K. P. (1981) *The Group of 77: Evolution, Structure, Organization* (New York: Oceana Publications).

Sawant, A. B. (1981) *Egypt's Africa Policy* (New Delhi: National Publishing House).

Sayegh, F. A. (ed.) (1964) *The Dynamics of Neutralism in the Arab World: A Symposium* (San Francisco: Chandler).

Scanlon, D. G. (1964) *Traditions of African Education* (New York: Columbia University Teachers College Press).

Schipper, M. (1982) *Theatre and Society in Africa* (Johannesburg: Raven Press).

Schissel, H. (1985) 'Through a glass colourfully', *West Africa*, 3547, 19 August, pp. 1698–9.

Schmitt, M. (1942) 'Leisting und Potential der Afrikanischen Wirtschaft', *DKD*, 9110, pp. 91–8.

Schmitter, P. C. (1972) *Autonomy or Dependence as Regional Integration Outcomes: Central America* (Berkeley: Institute of International Studies, University of California, Research Series No. 17).

Schneider, B. (1972) 'Malangatana of Mozambique', *African Arts*, **5**, 2, pp. 40–5.

Schneider, E. A. (1985) 'Ndebele mural art', *African Arts*, **18**, 3, pp. 60–7.

Schoepf, B. G. (1984) 'Man and biosphere in Zaire', in J. Barker (ed.), pp. 269–91.

Schram, R. (1981) 'Traditional medicine and modern medicine', in R. Oliver and M. Crowder (eds), pp. 391–2 and 392–6.

Scohy, A. (1955) *L'Uele secret* (Brussels: Office international de la librairie).

Sebag, P. (1951) *La Tunisie: essai de monographie* (Paris: Editions sociales).

Segal, A. (1966) 'Giant strangers: Africa and Latin America', *Africa Report* (Washington, DC), **11**, 4, pp. 48–53.

Segal, A. (1983a) 'Latin America's year in Africa', in C. Legum (ed.) *Africa Contemporary Record: Annual Survey and Documents, 1973–1974, Vol. 6* (London: Rex Collings, 1st edn, 1974), A107–A111.

Segal, A. (1983b) 'Cuba and Africa: military and technical assistance', in B. Levine (ed.), pp. 123–47.

Seidman, A. (1972) *An Economics Textbook for Africa* (London: Methuen).

Sékou Touré, A. (1963) *Guinean Revolution and Social Progress*.

Sékou Touré, A. (1977) '*L'Afrique et la révolution, Vol XIII*', in L. Sylla (ed.).

Selcher, W. A. (1974) *The Afro-Asian Dimensions of Brazilian Foreign Policy, 1956–1972* (Gainesville: University Press of Florida).

Selcher, W. A. (ed.) (1981) *Brazil in the International System: The Rise of a Middle Power* (Boulder, CO: Westview Press).

Senegal, Archives of the Republic of (1922) 'An awakening race', article signed Steikloff published in *Izvestia* 259 (16/11/22) in Série 21G 126 (108).

Senegal, Archives of the Republic of (1923a) Circular from the Minister of the Colonies to the Governor-General of French West Africa, No. 30 of 13 January, in Série 21G 132 (108).

Senegal, Archives of the Republic of (1923b) *Enquête du Comité d'études coloniales* in Série 21G 132 (108).

Senghor, L. S. (1964) *Négritude et humanisme* (Paris: Editions du Seuil).

Senghor, L. S. (1965) 'Prayer for peace', in J. Reed and C. Wake (eds and trans.) *Senghor: Prose and Poetry* (London: OUP).

Senghor, L. S. (1971) *Liberté II: nation et voie africaine du socialisme* (Paris: Editions du Seuil).

Serapiao, L. B. and El-Khawas, M. A. (1979) *Mozambique in the Twentieth Century: From Colonialism to Independence* (Washington, DC: University Press of America).

Serfontein, J. H. P. (1979) *Brotherhood of Power: An Exposé of the Secret Afrikaner Broederbond* (London: Rex Collings).

Serumaga, R. and Johnson, J. (1970) 'Uganda's experimental theatre', *African Arts*, **3**, 3, pp. 52–5.

Shaath, N. A. (1975) 'African manpower needs and the role of technical assistance', in A. M. Rweyemanu and G. Hyden (eds), pp. 97–109.

Shamrai, I. V. (1968) 'The problems of realizing economic co-operation between socialist and developing countries', *Narodvi Azii i Afriki*, **4**, pp. 3–15.

Shamuyarira, N. M. (1965) *Crisis in Rhodesia* (London: Deutsch).

Shariff, I. N. (1988) *Tungo Zetu* (Trenton, NJ: The Red Sea Press).

Sharma, D. N. (1969) *Afro-Asian Group in the United Nations* (Allahabad: Chaitanya Publishing House).

Shaw, T. M. (1975a) 'Regional co-operation and conflict in Africa', *International Journal*, **30**, 4 (Autumn), pp. 667–8.

Shaw, T. M. (1975b) 'The political economy of African international relations', *Issue*, **5**, 4 (Winter), pp. 29–38.

Shenton, R. (1986) *The Development of Capitalism in Northern Nigeria* (London: James Currey).

Sheriff, A. and Ferguson, E. (eds) (1991) *Zanzibar under Colonial Rule* (London: James Currey).

Shirazi, M. (1987) 'Film festival host', *West Africa*, 3628, 23 March, pp. 558–9.

Shivji, I. G. (1976) *Class Struggles in Tanzania* (New York and London: Monthly Review Press).

Sieber, R. (1972) *African Textiles and Decorative Arts* (New York: Museum of Modern Art).

Sik, E. (1966) *Histoire de l'Afrique noire, Vol. II* (Budapest: Akademiai Kiado).

Silva, L. A. (1982) *L'immigration cap-verdienne* (Paris: Mémoire de DEA, Centre de recherches africaines, University of Paris I).

Singer, C. (1959) *A Short History of Scientific Ideas* (Oxford: Clarendon Press).

Sithole, N. (1959) *African Nationalism* (London: OUP).

Skvirsky, D. (1967) *Milestones of Soviet Foreign Policy 1917–1967* (Moscow: Progress Publishers).

Smelser, N. J. (1968) *Essays in Sociological Explanation* (Englewood Cliffs, NJ: Prentice Hall).

Smith, A. (1976) 'The end of the Arab Sultanate: Zanzibar 1945–1964', in D. A. Low and A. Smith (eds).

Smith, E. W. (1962) 'Popular music in West Africa', *African Music*, 3, 1, pp. 11–17.

Smith, F. and Eicher, J. (eds) (1982) *African Arts*, 15, 3.

Smith, M. G. (1971) 'Institutional and political conditions of pluralism', in L. Kuper and M. G. Smith (eds), pp. 27–67.

Smith, P. G. (1970) *Theories of Value and Problems of Education* (Urbana: University of Illinois Press).

Smollan, R. (1987) *Black Advancement in the South African Economy* (London: Macmillan).

Smyth, R. (1984) 'War propaganda during the Second World War in Northern Rhodesia', *African Affairs*, 83, July, pp. 345–58.

Smyth, R. (1985) 'Britain's African colonies and British propaganda during the Second World War', *Journal of Imperial and Commonwealth History*, 14, 1, pp. 65–83.

Solodnikov, V. (1976) 'Elimination of colonial system: an expression of the general crisis of capitalism', *International Affairs*, August.

Soubbotine, V. (1973) 'L'Afrique occidentale et équatoriale sous la domination française', in *L'Afrique dans les études soviétiques* (Moscow: Nauka), pp. 128–51.

South Africa Research Service (ed.) (1984) *South Africa Review II* (Johannesburg: Raven Press).

Southall, A. (1979) *Small Urban Centers in Rural Development in Africa* (Madison, WI: African Studies Program, University of Wisconsin).

Soviet Ethnography (1950) 1.

Sow, A. I. (ed.) (1966) *La femme, la vache, la foi: écrivains et poètes du Fouta-Djalon* (Paris: Classiques africains, Julliard).

Sow, A. I. (1977) *Langues et politiques de langues en Afrique noire: l'expérience de l'Unesco* (Paris: Nubia).

Soyinka, W. (1963) *The Lion and the Jewel* (London: OUP).

Soyinka, W. (1985) 'The arts in Africa during the period of colonial rule', in A. A. Boahen (ed.) pp. 581–609.

Spacensky, A. (1970) *Madagascar: 50 ans de vie politique* (Paris: Nouvelles éditions latines).

Spence, C. F. (1951) *The Portuguese Colony of Mozambique: An Economic Survey* (Cape Town: Balkema).

Spence, J. E. (1964) 'British policy towards the High Commission Territories', *Journal of Modern African Studies*, 2, 2, pp. 221–46.

Spencer, J. (1985) *The Kenya Africa Union* (London: KPI).

Stamp, D. L. (1960) *Our Developing World* (London: Faber and Faber).

Stavenhagen, R. (1975) *Social Classes in Agrarian Societies* (Garden City: Anchor Press; Doubleday).

Steiner, C. B. (1985) 'Another image of Africa: toward an ethnohistory of European cloth marketed in West Africa, 1873–1960', *Ethnohistory*, 32, 2, pp. 91–110.

Stengers, J. (1983) 'Introduction', in *Le Congo belge durant la Seconde Guerre mondiale: recueil d'études* (Brussels: Académie royale des sciences d'outre-mer).

Stevens, C. (1976) *The Soviet Union and Black Africa* (London: Macmillan).

Stevens, R. P. (1967) *Lesotho, Botswana and Swaziland: The Former High Commission Territories in Southern Africa* (London: Pall Mall Press).

Stichter, S. (1982) *Migrant Labour in Kenya: Capitalism and African Response 1895–1975* (Harlow: Longman).

Still, M. H. Lelong (1946) *Mes frères du Congo* (Algiers: Editions Bacconier).

Stout, A. J. (1966) *Modern Makonde Sculpture* (Nairobi: Kibo Art Gallery Publications).

Streeten, P. (1972) *Aid to Africa: A Policy Outline for the 70s* (New York: Praeger).

Suleiman, M. W. (1989) 'Morocco in the Arab and Muslim world: attitudes of Moroccan youth', *The Maghreb Review*, 14, 1–2.

Sundkler, B. (1961) *Bantu Prophets in South Africa* (London: OUP).

Suret-Canale, J. (1961) *Afrique noire, occidentale et centrale, Vol. I: Géographie, civilisations, histoire* (Paris: Editions sociales; 3rd rev. edn, 1968).

Suret-Canale, J. (1964) *Afrique noire, occidentale et centrale, Vol. II: L'ère coloniale, 1900–1945* (Paris: Editions Sociales).

Suret-Canale, J. (1972) *Afrique noire, occidentale et centrale, Vol. III: De la colonisation aux indépendances, 1945–1960* (Paris: Editions sociales).

Suret-Canale, J. (1987) *Afrique et capitaux, Vol. II* (Paris: A L'Arbre Verdoyant).

Sykes, J. (1971) *Portugal and Africa: The People and the War* (London: Hutchinson).

Sylla, L. (ed.) (1977) *Tribalisme et parti unique en Afrique noire* (Paris: Fondation nationale des sciences politiques).

Sylvester, A. (1981) *Arabs and Africans: Co-operation for Development* (London: Bodley Head).

Synge, R. (ed.) (1978) *Africa Guide* (Chicago: Rand McNally).

Szombati-Fabian, I. and Fabian, J. (1976) 'Art, history and society', *Studies in the Anthropology of Visual Communication*, 3, 1, pp. 1–21.

Taha, M. M. (1987) *The Second Message of Islam* (Evanston: Northwestern University Press).

Tangri, R. (1975) 'From the politics of union to mass nationalism: the Nyasaland African Congress, 1944–59', in R. J. Macdonald (ed.), pp. 254–81.

Teisen, M. (1968) *Tingatinga* (Copenhagen).

Tempels, R. P. (1949) *La philosophie bantoue* (Paris: *Présence africaine*).

Tenreiro, F. (1961) *A ilha de S. Tome* (Lisbon: Sociedade de Geografia de Lisboa).

Tessler, M. A., O'Barr, W. M. and Spain, D. H. (1973) *Tradition and Identity in Changing Africa* (New York: Harper and Row).

The ACMS Countries and Africa: Trade and Cooperation (1980) (in Arabic; Moscow: Progress Publishers).

Theatre Quarterly (1977–8) 'The theatre in South Africa', special issue, **7**, 28.

The Listener (London) (1963) Opening lecture of the series on *The Rise of Christian Europe*, broadcast by Hugh Trevor-Roper, 28 November, p. 871.

Thiel, J. F. and Helf, H. (1984) *Christliche Kunst in Africa* (Berlin: D. Riemer).

Third World Quarterly (1979) 'South–South dialogue: a brief report', **1**, 2 (April), pp. 117–22.

Thoahlane, T. (ed.) (1975) *Black Renaissance: Papers from the Black Renaissance Convention* (Johannesburg: Raven Press).

Thomas, L. V. (1958–9) *Les Diola: essai d'analyse fonctionnelle sur une population de Basse-Casamance* (vol. 1: 1958; vol. 2: 1959; Dakar: IFAN).

Thompson, K. W. and Fogel, B. R. (1976–7) *Higher Education and Social Change, Vols I and II* (New York: Praeger).

Thompson, R. F. (1983) *Flash of the Spirit* (New York).

Thompson, R. F. and Cornet, J. (1981) *The Four Moments of the Sun* (Washington: National Gallery of Art).

Thompson, V. M. and Adloff, R. (1960) *The Emerging States of French Equatorial Africa* (Stanford: Stanford University Press).

Thompson, V. M. and Adloff, R. (1965) *The Malagasy Republic* (Stanford: Stanford University Press).

Thompson, V. M. and Adloff, R. (1968) *Djibouti and the Horn of Africa* (Stanford: Stanford University Press).

Thompson, V. P. (1969) *Africa and Unity: The Evolution of Pan-Africanism* (London: Longman).

Thompson, W. S. (1969) *Ghana's Foreign Policy, 1957–1966: Diplomacy, Ideology and the New State* (Princeton: PUP).

Throup, D. (1985) 'The origins of Mau Mau', *African Affairs*, **84**, 336, pp. 399–435.

Throup, D. (1987) *Economic and Social Origins of Mau Mau* (London: James Currey).

Tombalbaye, F. (1977) in L. Sylla (ed.).

Tomiche, F. J. (1974) *Syndicalisme en RAU (Egypte) 1900–1967* (Paris: Maisonneuve et Larose).

Tomiche, N. (1966) *L'Egypte moderne . . .* (Paris: PUF).

Touval, S. (1963) *Somali Nationalism* (Cambridge, MA: HUP).

Tracey, H. (1952) *African Dance of the Witwatersrand* (Johannesburg: Gold Mines).

Tracey, H. (1961) *The Evolution of African Music and its Function in the Present Day* (Johannesburg: Institute for the Study of Man in Africa).

Tracey, H. (1973) *Catalogue: The Sound of Africa Series* (Roodeport: International Library of African Music).

TransAfrica, *TransAfrica Forum*.

Transition (Kampala) (1963), **3**, 11 (November).

Traoré, A. (1983) *Cheikh Hamahoullah: homme de foi et résistant* (Paris: Maisonneuve et Larose).

Traoré, B. (1958) *Le théâtre négro-africain et ses fonctions sociales* (Paris).

Traoré, B. (1969) 'Le théâtre africain au festival culturel panafricain d'Alger', *Présence Africaine*, **72**, 4, pp. 179–89.

Trapido, S. (1970) 'Political institutions and Afrikaner social structures in the Republic of South Africa', in I. L. Markovitz (ed.), pp. 368–93.

Trevaskis, G. K. N. (1960) *Eritrea: A Colony in Transition, 1941–1952* (London: OUP).

Trimingham, S. J. (1952) *Islam in Ethiopia* (London: OUP).

Trincaz, P. X. (1984) *Colonisation et régionalisme: Ziguinchor en Casamance* (Paris: ORSTOM).

Tronchon, J. (1983) *L'insurrection malgache de 1947* (Antananarivo: Maspero and MCAR; 1st edn 1974, Paris: Maspero).

Tshibangu, T. (1960) 'Comment assumer dans l'Eglise le chant et l'art chorégraphique africains', *Band*, **19**, 2–3, pp. 66–82 and 94–105.

Tunisia, Government of (1962) *Perspectives décennales de développement 1962–71* (Tunis).

Tunji, V. (1976) 'Lagos state music and dance', *African Arts*, **9**, 2, pp. 35–9.

Turner, H. W. (1968) *Bibliography of Modern African Religious Movements*, Supplement 1, *Journal of Religions in Africa* (Leyden), **1**, pp. 173–211.

Turner, Admiral S. (1977) 'The naval balance is not a number game', *Foreign Affairs*, **55**, 2 (January), pp. 339–55.

Twaddle, M. (1978) 'Was the Democratic Party of Uganda a purely confessional party?', in E. Fashole-Luke, *et al.* (eds), pp. 255–66.

Twitchett, C. C. (1979) *Europe and Africa: From Association to Partnership* (Farnborough: Saxon House).

Twose, N. (1984) 'No pastures new', *West Africa*, 3484, 28 May, pp. 1115–16.

Uchendu, V. C. (1967) 'Some principles of haggling in peasant markets', *Economic Development and Cultural Change*, 16, 1 (October), pp. 37–51.

Uchendu, V. C. and Anthony, K. R. M. (1975) *Agricultural Change in Teso District, Uganda* (Nairobi, Kampala, Dar es Salaam).

Uganda Argus (1964) 4 April.

UNCTAD (1976) Preservation of the Purchasing Power of Developing Countries' Exports (Item 8 – Supporting Paper), UNCTAD TD/184/Supp. 2 May (Geneva and Nairobi).

UNCTAD (1980) *Handbook of International Trade and Development Statistics*, Supplement.

UNEP (1981) *Environment and Development in Africa, Vol. 2* (Oxford: Pergamon Press).

UNESCO (1961a) *Conference of African States on the Development of Education in Africa (Addis Ababa), Outline of a Plan for African Educational Development*, UNESCO ED/181 (Paris: UNESCO).

UNESCO (1961b) *Conference of African States on the Development of Education in Africa (Addis Ababa), Final Report*, UNESCO/ED/181 (Paris: UNESCO).

UNESCO (1963) *Conference on the Development of Higher Education in Africa, Tananarive* (Paris: UNESCO).

UNESCO (1975a) *Young People and African Cultural Values*, Abomey, 1974, Documents SHC/75/WS/9 (Paris: UNESCO).

UNESCO (1975b) *Intergovernmental Conference of Cultural Policies in Africa (Accra, 1975), Final Report* (Paris: UNESCO).

UNESCO (1975c) *Young People and African Cultural Values*, Abomey, 1974, Document SHC/75/WS/9 (Paris: UNESCO).

UNESCO (1976) *Conference on Education in Africa in the Light of the Lagos Conference* (Paris: UNESCO).

UNESCO (1979) *Symposium on Historical and Socio-cultural Relations between Black Africa and the Arab World from 1935 to the Present*, The General History of Africa, Studies and Documents, No. 7 (Paris: UNESCO).

UNESCO (1980) *Meeting of Experts on 'The African Cultural Presence in the Caribbean and in North and South America', Bridgetown, Barbados, 21–25 January 1980, Final Report*, Document CC-79/CONF.601, 30 May (Paris: UNESCO).

UNESCO (1981a) *African Languages* (Harmonization of African languages and African reference alphabet, Niamey, 1978), Documents CC.80/WS/60 (Paris: UNESCO).

UNESCO (1981b) *The Decolonization of Africa: Southern Africa and the Horn of Africa*, The General History of Africa, Studies and Documents, No. 5 (Paris: UNESCO).

UNESCO (1981c) *Langues africaines* (Langues africaines régionales et sous-régionales, Bamako, 1979), Documents CC.80/WS/57 (Paris: UNESCO).

UNESCO (1982) *World Conference of Cultural Policies, 26 July–6 August, Mexico City, Final Report*, CLT/MD/1 (Paris: UNESCO).

UNESCO (1983) *L'Afrique et le Nouvel Ordre Economique International; Conference on 'The Teaching of International Law in Africa', Yaoundé, Cameroon, 28 November–2 December* (Paris: UNESCO).

UNESCO (1985a) *La définition d'une stratégie relative à la promotion des langues africaines, Conakry, 1981*, Documents CLT/85/WS/72 (Paris: UNESCO).

UNESCO (1985b) *Africa and the Second World War*, The General History of Africa, Studies and Documents, No. 10 (Paris: UNESCO).

UNESCO (1985–6) 'The survival of African religious traditions in the Caribbean and in Latin America', in *African Cultures*, Document CC-86/WS/24 (Paris: UNESCO).

UNESCO (forthcoming) *The Role of African Student Movements in the Political and Social Evolution of Africa from 1900 to 1975*, The General History of Africa, Studies and Documents, No. 12 (Paris: UNESCO).

UNESCO, UNECA and OAU (1982) *Conference on Specific Aspects of Educational Development in Africa, Harare*, Documents ED/82/MINEDAF/REF/1: 'African development strategies and their implications for education'; 2: 'Development of education in Africa: a statistical review'; 3: 'Education and endogenous development in Africa: trends, problems and prospects'; 4: 'Final Draft Report'; 5: 'Specific aspects of educational development in Africa' (Paris: UNESCO).

United Nations (1959) *Economic Survey of Africa since 1950* (New York: UN).

United Nations (1970) *Statistical Yearbook* (New York: UN).

United Nations (1981) 'Patterns of urban and rural population growth', *Population Studies* (New York: UN), 68.

United Nations (1990) *Africa's Commodity Problems: Towards a Solution* (the Fraser Report) (New York: UN).

977

United Nations Economic Commission for Africa (1976) *Revised Framework of Principles for the Implementation of the New International Economic Order in Africa 1976–1981–1985*, Document E/CN.14/ECO/90/Rev. 3, 25 June (New York: UN).

United Nations Economic Commission for Africa (1979) *Development Strategy for Africa for the Third United Nations Development Decade*, ECA Resolution 332 (xiv), Document E/CN.14/INF/109/Rev. 1, adopted, July by OAU Heads of State and Government.

United Nations Economic Commission for Africa (1983) *ECA and Africa's Development 1983–2008: Preliminary Perspective Study* (Addis Ababa).

United Nations Economic Commission for Africa (1989) *African Alternative Framework to Structural Adjustment Programmes for Socio-Economic Recovery and Transformation* (Addis Ababa and New York: United Nations Economic Commission for Africa).

United Nations High Commission for Refugees (1982–83) *Report on the HCR's Relief Activities in 1982–1983*, Document A/AC, 96/620.

United Nations Secretary-General (1974) *Permanent Sovereignty over Natural Resources*, Document A/9716 (Supplement to E/5425), 20 September.

United Republic of Tanzania (n.d.) *Julius Nyerere, Socialism and Rural Development* (Dar es Salaam: Government Printer).

United Republic of Tanzania (1967a) *Arusha Declaration: Answers and Questions* (Dar es Salaam: Government Printer).

United Republic of Tanzania (1967b) *The President Explains the Arusha Declaration* (Dar es Salaam: Information Services).

United Republic of Tanzania (*c.* 1977) *United Republic of Tanzania: The Economic Survey and Annual Plan 1970–1977* (Dar es Salaam: Government Printer).

United States Archives, Diplomatic Branch, 884.142/19, photo/article, enclosure.

United States Archives (1944) 884.01A/72, 'Employment of American citizens by the Ethiopian Government', March 13.

United States Committee for Refugees (1981) *World Refugee Survey* (New York: Hudson Press).

Vacono, S. (1974) *Les étapes de la décolonisation française* (Paris: PUF).

Vail, L. (1975) 'The making of an imperial slum: Nyasaland and its railways, 1895–1935', *JAH*, **16**, 1, pp. 89–112.

Vail, L. (1977) 'Railway development and colonial underdevelopment: the Nyasaland case', in R. Palmer and N. Parsons (eds), pp. 365–95.

Vail, L. (1983) 'The state and the creation of colonial Malawi's agricultural (1983) economy', in R. Rotberg (ed.) *Imperialism, Colonialism and Hunger: East and Central Africa* (Lexington, MA: MIT), pp. 39–87.

Valdes, N. P. (1980) 'Cuba's involvement in the Horn of Africa', *Cuban Studies* (Pittsburgh), **10**, 1 (January), pp. 49–79.

Van Bilsen, A. A. J. (1977) *Vers l'indépendance du Congo et du Ruanda-Urundi: réflexions sur les devoirs et l'avenir de la Belgique en Afrique centrale* (Kinshasa: Presses universitaires du Zaïre).

Van den Berghe, P. (1968) 'Les langues européennes et les mandarins noirs', trans. by K. Mateene, *Présence africaine*, **68**, 4th quarter.

Van den Bossche, J. (1955) *Madya, graveur de calebasses* (Brussels: ARSOM).

Vanderlinden, J. *Du Congo au Zaïre, 1960–1980: Essai de Bilan* (Brussels: CRISP).

Van Donge, J. K. (1985) 'An episode from the independence struggle in Zambia: a case-study from Mwase Lundazi', *African Affairs*, **84**, 335, pp. 265–78.

Van Sertima, I. (1977) *They Came Before Columbus: The African Presence in Ancient America* (New York: Random House).

Van Sertima, I. (ed.) (1984a) *Nile Valley Civilizations*, Proceedings of the Nile Valley Conference, Atlanta, 26–30 September, special issue of *Journal of African Civilizations*, **6**, 2 (November).

Van Sertima, I. (1984b) 'Nile valley presence in America B.C.', in I. Van Sertima (ed.).

Van Sertima, I. (ed.) (1985) *Nile Valley Civilizations* (Atlanta, GA: Journal of African Civilizations).

Van Sertima, I. (ed.) (1986) *Blacks in Science: Ancient and Modern* (New Brunswick and London: Transaction Books).

Van Sertima, I. (1989) *Great African Thinkers, Vol. I: Cheikh Anta Diop* (New Brunswick: Transaction Books).

Vansina, J. (1961) *The Oral Tradition: A Study in Historical Methodology* (Chicago: Aldine Publishing Co.)

Vatikiotis, P. J. (1961) *The Egyptian Army in Politics* (Bloomington: Indiana University Press).

Vatikiotis, P. J. (1969) *The Modern History of Egypt* (London: Weidenfeld and Nicolson).

Vatikiotis, P. J. (1980) *Egypt from Muhammad Ali to Sadat* (Baltimore).

Vatin, J. C. L. (1974) *L'Algérie politique: histoire et société* (Paris: Fondation nationale des sciences politiques; A. Colin).

Veblen, T. (1899) *The Theory of the Leisure Class: An Economic Study of Institutions* (New York; new edn 1981).

Vellut, J.-L. (1983) 'Le Katanga industriel en 1944: malaises et anxiétés dans la société coloniale', in Academie royale des sciences d'outre-mer, pp. 495–525.

Vengroff, R. (1982) 'Food and dependency: P. L. 480 aid to Black Africa', *Journal of Modern African Studies*, 20, 1 (March), pp. 27–43.

Verhaegen, B. and Bethune, E. de (1965) 'Consultations électorales et élections au Congo, 1957–1959', *Cahiers économiques et sociaux*, 3, 3, pp. 247–91.

Vermeer, D. E. (1983) 'Food sufficiency and farming in the future of West Africa: resurgence of traditional agriculture?', *Journal of African Studies*, 10, 3 (Fall), pp. 74–84.

Vieyra, P. S. (1968) 'Le film africain d'expression française', *African Arts*, 1, 3, pp. 60–9.

Vieyra, P. S. (1975) *Les cinémas africains des origines à 1973* (Paris: Présence Africaine).

Vieyra, P. S. (1983) *Le cinéma au Sénégal* (Brussels: L'Harmattan).

Vignes, J. (1976–7) 'Revenus du pétrole arabe et l'aide à l'Afrique', *Jeune Afrique*, annual supplement, pp. 181–7.

Vogel, C. A. M. (1985) 'Pedi mural art', *African Arts*, 18, 3, pp. 78–83.

Voice of Ethiopia (1938) 19 March.

Voice of Ethiopia (1939) 29 April, 6 May, 24 June, 8 July, 15 July, 29 July, 19 August, 5 November, 11 November, 9 December.

Voice of Ethiopia (1940) 3 February, 24 May.

Volavka, Z. (1977) 'Voania Muba: contribution to the history of central African pottery', *African Arts*, 10, 2, pp. 59–66 and 92.

Vore, R. M. de (1976) *The Arab–Israeli Historical Conflict: A Historical, Political, Social and Military Bibliography* (Oxford and Santa Barbara: Clio Books).

Wadajo, J. (1959) 'Post-war reform in Ethiopian education', *Comparative Education Review*, 2 (February), pp. 24–8.

Wagaw, T. G. (1979) *Education in Ethiopia: Prospect and Retrospect* (Ann Arbor, MI: The University of Michigan Press).

Wagaw, T. G. (forthcoming) *Development of Higher Education and Social Transformation: An African Case.*

Wa-Githumo (1983) 'The quagmire of the urban poor in Nairobi', *Journal of East African Research and Development*, 13, pp. 126–48.

Wagret, J. M. (1963) *Histoire et sociologie politique de la République du Congo* (Paris: LGDJ).

Waiguru, J. (1965) 'The round mud hut', in D. Cook (ed.), pp. 4–10.

Wallerstein, I. (1976a) 'The three stages of African involvement in the world economy', in P. C. W. Gutkind and I. Wallerstein (eds), pp. 35–64.

Wallerstein, I. (1976b) *The Modern World System* (New York: Modern Reader).

Wallerstein, I. (1977) 'Class and status in contemporary Africa', in P. Gutkind and P. Waterman (eds) *African Social Studies: A Radical Reader* (New York and London: Monthly Review Press), pp. 277–84.

Wallerstein, I. (1983) *Historical Capitalism* (London: Verso).

Walls, A. F. (1978) 'Religion and the press in the enclave in the Nigerian Civil War', in G. R. Fashole-Luke *et al.* (eds), pp. 207–15.

Walshe, P. (1971) *The Rise of African Nationalism in South Africa: The African National Congress, 1912–1952* (Los Angeles: UCP).

Walters, R. W. (1987) *South Africa and the Bomb: Responsibility and Deterrence* (Lexington, MA: D. C. Heath Lexington Books).

Wandira, A. (1977) *The African University in Development* (Johannesburg: Zenitt Printers).

Wangwe, S. M. and Skarstein, R. (1986) *Industrial Development in Tanzania: Some Critical Issues* (Uppsala and Dar es Salaam: Scandinavian Institute of African Studies and Tanzania Publishing House).

Wanyande, P. (1987) 'Democracy and the one-party state: the African experience', in W. Oyugi and A. Gilonga (eds).

Wanyoike, E. N. (1974) *An African Pastor: The Life and Work of the Rev. Wanyoike Kamawe, 1888–1970* (Nairobi: EAPH).

Wass, B. (1979) 'The Kabah sloth', *African Arts*, 12, 3, pp. 62–5 and 96.

Waterbury, J. (1970) *The Commander of the Faithful: The Moroccan Political Elite* (New York: Columbia University Press).

Waterbury, J. (1975) *Le Commandeur des croyants* (Paris).

Waterman, P. (1983) 'The concept of the "semi-proletarianized peasantry": an empirical and theoretical note', in B. Magubane and Nzongola-Ntalaja, *Proletarianization and Class Struggle in Africa* (San Francisco: Synthex Press), pp. 172–83.

Waterston, A. (1974) 'A viable model for rural development', *Finance and Development*, 11, 4 (December), pp. 22–5.

Watt, I. (1969) *The Rise of the Novel* (Harmondsworth: Penguin Books).
Watts, M. and Shenton, R. (1984) 'State and agrarian transformation in Nigeria', in J. Barker (ed.), pp. 173–205.
Wauthier, C. (1966) *The Literature and Thought of Modern Africa: A Survey* (London: Pall Mall Press).
Weber, M. (1949) *The Theory of Social and Economic Organization* (New York: Grove Press).
Webster, J. B. and Boahen, A. A. (1980) *The Revolutionary Years: West Africa since 1800* (new edn; London: Longman).
Weekly Review (Nairobi) (1990) 9 February.
Weeks, S. (1967) *Divergence in Educational Development: The Cases of Kenya and Uganda* (New York: Columbia University Teachers College Press).
Weinstein, B. (1966) *Gabon: nation-building on the Ogooue* (Cambridge, MA: MIT Press).
Weinstein, B. (1967) 'Leon Mba: the ideology of dependence', *Genève – Afrique*, 6, 1, pp. 49–63.
Weinstein, B. (1983) *The Civic Tongue: Political Consequences of Language Choices* (New York and London: Longman).
Weinstein, F. B. (1965) 'The Second Asian–African Conference: preliminary bouts', *Asian Survey* (Berkeley, CA), 5, 7 (July), pp. 359–73.
Welch, C. E., Jr and Meltzer, R. I (eds) (1984) *Human Rights and Development in Africa* (Albany, NY: State University of New York Press).
Welch, C. E., Jr and Smith, A. K. (1974) *Military Role and Rule* (Massachusetts: Duxbury Press).
Weman, H. (1960) *African Music and the Church in Africa* (Uppsala: Svenska Institutet för Missionforskning).
Wembah-Rashid, J. A. R. (1972) 'Tingatinga of Tanzania', *African Arts*, 5, 4, pp. 20–1.
Wenzel, M. (1972) *House Decoration in Africa* (London: Duckworth).
White, J. (1981) *Central Administration in Nigeria 1914–1948* (London and Dublin: Irish Academic Press and Frank Cass).
Whiteley, W. (1974) *Swahili: The Rise of a National Language* (London: Methuen).
WHO (1976) *World Health Statistics Report – Rapport de statistiques sanitaires mondiales*, OMS, 29, 10 (Geneva).
Wicker, E. R. (1958) 'Colonial development and welfare, 1929–1957: the evolution of a policy', *Social and Economic Studies*, 7, 4, pp. 170–92.
Wilber, C. K. (1979) *The Political Economy of Development and Underdevelopment* (2nd edn, New York: Random House).
Wilcocks, C. (1962) *Aspects of Medical Investigation in Africa* (London and New York: OUP).
Wilcox, W. F. (1931) 'Increase in the population of the earth and of the continents since 1650', *International Migrations* (New York: National Bureau of Economic Research).
Willet, F. (1971) *African Art* (London: Thames and Hudson).
Willetts, P. (1978) *The Non-Aligned Movement: The Origins of a Third-World Alliance* (London: Frances Pinter Ltd).
Williame, J.-C. (1983) 'Le Congo dans la guerre: la coopération économique belgo-alliés de 1940 à 1944', in Académie royale des sciences d'outre-mer, pp. 213–53.
Williams, G. (1981) *Third World Political Organizations* (London: Macmillan).
Williams, J. A. (1979) 'A return to the veil in Egypt', *Middle East Review*, 11, 3, pp. 49–54.
Williams, M. J. (1976) 'The aid programs of the OPEC countries', *Foreign Affairs*, 54, 2 (January), pp. 308–24.
Williams, M. J. (1983) 'Toward a food strategy for Africa', *Africa Report*, 28, 5, pp. 22–7.
Wilson, J. (1963) *Education and Changing West African Culture* (New York: Columbia University Teachers College Press).
Wilson, M. and Thompson, L. (eds) (1985) *The Oxford History of South Africa, Vol. I* (London: OUP); *Vol. II*, 1971 (Oxford: Clarendon Press).
Wilson, T. (1974) *Russia and Black Africa before World War II* (Holmes and Meir).
Windstrand, C. and Amin, S. (1975) *Multinational Firms in Africa* (New York: Africana Publishing Company).
Woddis, J. (1962) *Africa: The Roots of Revolt* (New York: The Citadel Press).
Woddis, J. (1967) *An Introduction to Neocolonialism* (New York: International Publishers).
World Bank (1981) *Accelerated Development in Sub-Saharan Africa: An Agenda for Action* (Washington, DC: World Bank Publication).
World Bank (1982) *World Development Report* (New York: OUP).
World Bank (1985) *World Development Report 1985*.
World Bank (1986) *Financing Adjustment with Growth in Sub-Saharan Africa, 1986–1990*
World Bank (1988) *Education in Sub-Saharan Africa: Policies for Adjustment, Revitalization and Expansion* (2 vols: Main Text and Statistical Annex; Washington, DC).
World Bank (1989a) *Successful Development in Africa: Case Studies of Projects, Programs and Policies*, Analytical Case Study No. 1, Economic Development Institute (Washington, DC: World Bank).
World Bank (1989b) *Sub-Saharan Africa: From Crisis to Sustainable Growth*, A Long-Term Perspective Study (Washington, DC: World Bank Publication), November.

World Bank (1990) *World Development Report: World Poverty* (Washington, DC).

Xinhua News Bulletin (Dar es Salaam) (1968) 'The United Republic of Tanzania moves forward', 552, 20 June.

Yakemtchouk, R. (1977) *La Convention de Lomé: Nouvelles formes de la coopération entre la C.E.E. et les Etats d'Afrique, des Caraïbes et du Pacifique* (Brussels: ARSOM).
Yamalov, V. L. 'Soviet assistance to the underdeveloped countries', *International Affairs*, 9 (September).
Yesufu, T. M. (1973) *Creating the African University* (Ibadan: OUP).
Yglesias de la Riva, A. (1947) *Politica indigena en Guinea* (Madrid: Instituto de Estudios Africanos).
Young, C. (1965) *Politics in the Congo: Decolonization and Independence* (Princeton: PUP).
Yu, G. T. (1975) *China's African Policy: A Study of Tanzania* (New York: Praeger).

Zartman, W. (1976) 'Europe and Africa: decolonization or dependency?' *Foreign Affairs*, **54**, 1, pp. 325–44.
Zedong, M. (1966) 'Correct handling of the contradictions among the People' (27 February 1957), in *Philosophical Essays* (Beijing: Foreign Language Press).
Zhukov, E. M. (1947) 'Bourgeois nationalism is the nationalism of black intellectuals trained in the school of colonialism', *New Times (Novoye Vremya)* (Moscow).
Zimmer, W. (1985) *Répertoire du théâtre camerounais* (Paris: L'Harmattan).
Zins, M. J. (1983) 'L'Inde et l'Afrique: le Non-alignement au service des intérêts nationaux', *Politique Africaine* (Paris), 10, 10 June, pp. 39–54.
Zoctizoum, Y. (1983) *Histoire de la Centrafrique; Tome I: 1879–1959* (Paris: L'Harmattan).
Zulu, J. B. and Nsouli, S. M. (1984) 'Adjustment programs in Africa', *Finance and Development*, **21**, 1 (March), pp. 5–10.

Index